Fodor's 90
Germany

" *"When it comes to information on regional history, what to see and do, and shopping, these guides are exhaustive."*

—*USAir Magazine*

"Usable, sophisticated restaurant coverage, with an emphasis on good value."

—Andy Birsh, *Gourmet Magazine* columnist

"Valuable because of their comprehensiveness."

—*Minneapolis Star-Tribune*

"Fodor's always delivers high quality...thoughtfully presented...thorough."

—*Houston Post*

"An excellent choice for those who want everything under one cover."

—*Washington Post* "

Fodor's Travel Publications, Inc.
New York • London • Toronto • Sydney • Auckland

Fodor's Germany

Editor: Hannah Borgeson

Editorial Contributors: Robert Andrews, Robert Blake, David Lakein, Graham Lees, Anne Midgette, Mary Ellen Schultz, M. T. Schwartzman, Dinah Spritzer, Robert Tilley

Creative Director: Fabrizio La Rocca

Cartographer: David Lindroth

Cover Photograph: Owen Franken

Text Design: Between the Covers

Copyright

Special Sales

CONTENTS

ON THE ROAD WITH FODOR'S

A GOOD TRAVEL GUIDE is like a wonderful traveling companion. It's charming, it's brimming with sound recommendations and solid ideas, it pulls no punches in describing lodging and dining establishments, and it's consistently full of fascinating facts that make you view what you've traveled to see in a rich new light. In the creation of *Germany '96*, we at Fodor's have gone to great lengths to provide you with the very best of all possible traveling companions—and to make your trip the best of all possible vacations.

About Our Writers

The information in these pages is a collaboration of a number of wonderful, hard-working writers.

Robert Tilley landed in Germany more than 25 years ago (via Central Africa, South Africa, and England), intending to stay a year before settling somewhere *really* civilized. German women were responsible for his extended stay—he married one, and she's now a seasoned Fodor's researcher. Robert runs a media company in Munich and writes (mostly for English-language programs he produces for German TV) in a lakeside hideaway in the Bavarian Alps. His branch office is in a local brewery cellar.

Anne Midgette, who has been living in Munich since 1986, edited the monthly magazine *Munich Found* before becoming a freelance travel and arts writer. She has written and contributed to travel guides to Munich, Bavaria, New York, and the U.S. and is an opera and arts critic for U.S., U.K., and German publications, including *The Wall Street Journal/The Wall Street Journal Europe*. Recent assignments include reporting on music in war-torn Croatia and interviewing underground leaders of the Iranian opposition for British television. In her spare time, Anne terrorizes her neighbors by practicing to become an opera singer.

Fate, superb German language skills, an academic scholarship, and the pull of café life all conspired to land **David Lakein** in Berlin straight out of college; he had first steeped himself silly in Berlin life during a semester abroad. Pursuing writing and performance projects in the German capital for the past three years, David has also cultivated a reputation as a semiprofessional address-changer, averaging four months per locale.

We'd also like to thank Helga Brenner-Khan, of the German National Tourist Office, and the German Wine Information Bureau.

What's New

A New Design

If this is not the first Fodor's guide you've purchased, you'll immediately notice our new look. More readable and easier-to-use than ever? We think so—and we hope you do, too.

New Takes On Hannover, Tübingen, and Ulm

As a result of readers' requests, we've added three towns to this edition of the guide. Robert Tilley is responsible for the new sections about Hannover and Ulm, and Anne Midgette traveled to Tübingen to research that section.

Travel Updates

Just before your trip, you may want to order a Fodor's Worldview Travel Update. From local publications all over Germany, the lively, cosmopolitan editors at Worldview gather information on concerts, plays, opera, dance performances, gallery and museum shows, sports competitions, and other special events that coincide with your visit. See the order blank in the back of this, call 800/799–9609, or fax 800/799–9619.

And in Germany

The **450th anniversary of Martin Luther's death** is in 1996, and events commemorating the Protestant reformer's life and work are planned throughout the country, especially in Wittenberg, Eisenach, and Erfurt. A special Martin Luther route, stretching from northern Bavaria deep into Saxony, will be inaugurated in 1996.

The Deutsche Fachwerkstrassen, **new driving routes** through parts of central and eastern Germany, link some of Germany's loveliest and least-known villages containing ensembles of half-timbered houses.

There's never a dull moment along the **Rhine.** In early 1995, the river **flooded** severely for the second time in 13 months. Many businesses did all they could to pull through the first floods, leaving little or no resources for the second go-round. At press time it was too early to know which establishments, if any, will have to close.

MUSEUMS➤ The new **Bauhaus Museum,** on Weimar's Theaterplatz, traces the Bauhaus artistic movement, whose school was founded by architect Walter Gropius in Weimar in 1919.

The **Rummel collection,** one of Bavaria's finest collections of faiences, is now on display in a special museum devoted to the ceramics in the northern wing of Bayreuth's Neues Schloss.

A museum describing the life and work of Germany's great medieval poet **Wolfram von Eschenbach** (author of the epic *Parzival* on which Richard Wagner based his famous opera) opened in 1995 in the Franconian town that bears his name, Wolframs-Eschenbach.

ENTERTAINMENT➤ A huge cinema complex will open in Nürnberg in 1996. Called the **Cinecitta,** it will have two restaurants, two cafés, a beer garden, and 12 cinemas, including an open-air one.

The opening of Freiburg's new multistage complex, the **Konzerthaus,** is scheduled for summer 1996.

A theme park in Bottrup is slated to open in late 1996. The 12-acre complex, called **Warner Bros. Movie World,** is modeled on California's Universal Studios.

LODGING➤ Two German states are introducing a **star system,** awarding one to five to indicate the class of comfort and range of facilities offered by hotels. More than 300 hotels in Bavaria were "starred" by mid-1995, and hotels in Rhineland-Westphalia were expected to follow by the end of the year.

A family in Creglingen, on the Romantic Road, has opened Germany's first "**hay hotel,**" which gives travelers a unique option—the chance to sleep in a hayloft.

The **Hotel Erfurter Hof,** where wildly cheering crowds of dissatisfied East Germans once greeted West German Chancellor Brandt, shut its doors in 1995. If the capital needed for extensive renovations can be raised, it may open under a new name and management.

How to Use This Book

Organization

Up front is the **Gold Guide,** comprising two sections on gold paper that are chockfull of information about traveling within your destination and traveling in general. Both are in alphabetical order by topic. **Important Contacts A to Z** gives addresses and telephone numbers of organizations and companies that offer detailed information or publications. Here's where you'll find information about how to get to the book from wherever you are. **Smart Travel Tips A to Z,** the Gold Guide's second section, gives specific tips on how to get the most out of your travels, as well as information on how to accomplish what you need to in Germany. Chapters in the book are arranged geographically, going roughly from south to north; each chapter covers exploring, shopping, sports, dining, lodging, and arts and nightlife, and ends with a section called Essentials, which tells you how to get there and get around and gives important local addresses and telephone numbers.

At the end of the book you'll find a chronology and suggestions for pretrip reading, both fiction and nonfiction.

Stars

Stars in the margin are used to denote highly recommended sights, attractions, hotels, and restaurants.

Restaurant and Hotel Criteria and Price Categories

Restaurants and lodging places are chosen with a view to giving you the cream of the crop in each location and in each price range. In all restaurant price charts, costs are per person, excluding drinks, tip, and tax. In hotel price charts, rates are for standard double rooms, including taxes and service charges.

Hotel Facilities

Note that in general you incur charges when you use many hotel facilities. We wanted to let you know what facilities a hotel has to offer, but we don't always specify whether or not there's a charge, so when planning a vacation that entails a stay of several days, it's wise to ask what's included in the rate.

Dress Code in Restaurants

The **What to Wear** section at the beginning of some chapter dining sections tells you what's most common in that area. In general, we note dress code only when men are required to wear a jacket or a jacket and tie.

Credit Cards

The following abbreviations are used: **AE,** American Express; **DC,** Diners Club; **MC,** MasterCard; and **V,** Visa. Discover is not accepted outside the United States.

Please Write to Us

Everyone who has contributed to *Germany '96* has tried hard to make the text accurate. All prices and opening times are based on information supplied to us at press time, and the publisher cannot accept responsibility for any errors that may have occurred. The passage of time will bring changes, so it's always a good idea to call ahead and confirm information when it matters—particularly if you're making a detour to visit specific sights or attractions. When making reservations at a hotel or inn, be sure to speak up if you have a disability or are traveling with children, if you prefer a private bath or a certain type of bed, or if you have specific dietary needs or any other concerns.

Were the restaurants we recommended as described? Did our hotel picks exceed your expectations? Did you find a museum we recommended a waste of time? We would love your feedback, positive and negative. If you have complaints, we'll look into them and revise our entries when the facts warrant it. If you've happened upon a special place that we haven't included, we'll pass the information along to the writers so they can check it out. So please send us a letter or postcard (we're at 201 East 50th Street, New York, New York 10022). We'll look forward to hearing from you. And in the meantime, have a wonderful trip!

Karen Cure

Karen Cure
Editorial Director

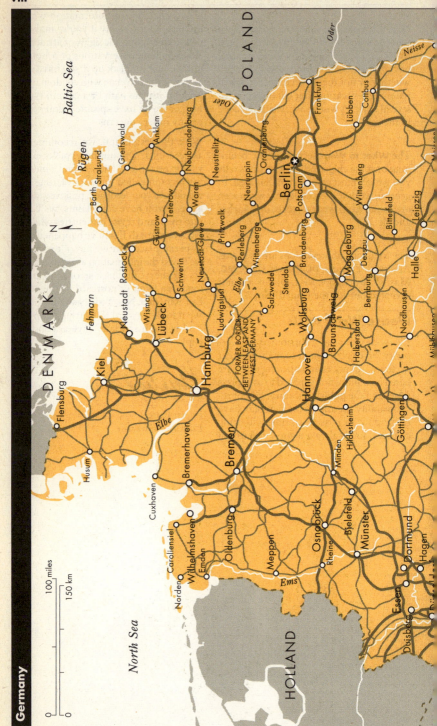

Germany

POLAND

Oder

Neisse

Baltic Sea

DENMARK

Rügen

Barth Stralsund

Greifswald

Anklam

Neubrandenburg

Neustrelitz

Oranienburg

Frankfurt

Lübben

Cottbus

Fehmarn

Neustadt

Rostock

Güstrow

Teterow

Waren

Neuruppin

Berlin

Potsdam

Wittenberg

Bitterfeld

Leipzig

Kiel

Flensburg

Schwerin

Pritzwalk

Perleberg

Wittenberge

Brandenburg

Magdeburg

Dessau

Halle

Nordhausen

Wismar

Neustadt-Glewe

Ludwigslust

Elbe

Salzwedel

Stendal

Wolfsburg

Bernburg

Lübeck

Hamburg

FORMER BORDER BETWEEN EAST AND WEST GERMANY

Wolfsburg

Braunschweig

Halberstadt

Mühlhausen

Elbe

Hannover

Hildesheim

Göttingen

Husum

Bremerhaven

Bremen

Minden

Cuxhaven

Carolinensiel

Wilhelmshaven

Emden

Oldenburg

Meppen

Osnabrück

Rheine

Bielefeld

Münster

Dortmund

Hagen

Norden

Ems

Essen

Duisberg

North Sea

HOLLAND

N

100 miles

150 km

0

0

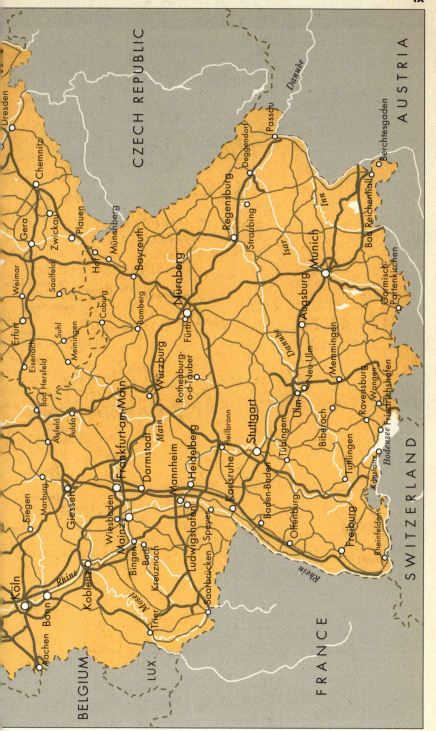

ICELAND

Reykjavík

NORTHERN
IRELAND

SCOTLAND

Edinburgh

NORWA

Bergen

*North
Sea*

Skag

DENMA

IRELAND

Belfast

*Irish
Sea*

Dublin

UNITED

KINGDOM

WALES

ENGLAND

NETHERLANDS

Hambu

*ATLANTIC
OCEAN*

Cardiff

London

The Hague

Amsterdam

Rotterdam

G E

Brussels

Bonn

BELGIUM

English Channel

Paris

LUXEMBOURG

Frankfurt

F R A N C E

Zürich

Bern

M

SWITZERLAND

Lyon

LIECHTEN

Milan

PORTUGAL

Madrid

ANDORRA

Marseille

Nice

Monte
Carlo

MONACO

Floren

Lisbon

S P A I N

Barcelona

Corsica

Seville

Granada

*Balearic
Islands*

Sardinia

Gibraltar

Mediterranean Sea

Tyrrh

MOROCCO

ALGERIA

400 miles

0

0

600 km

TUNISIA

World Time Zones

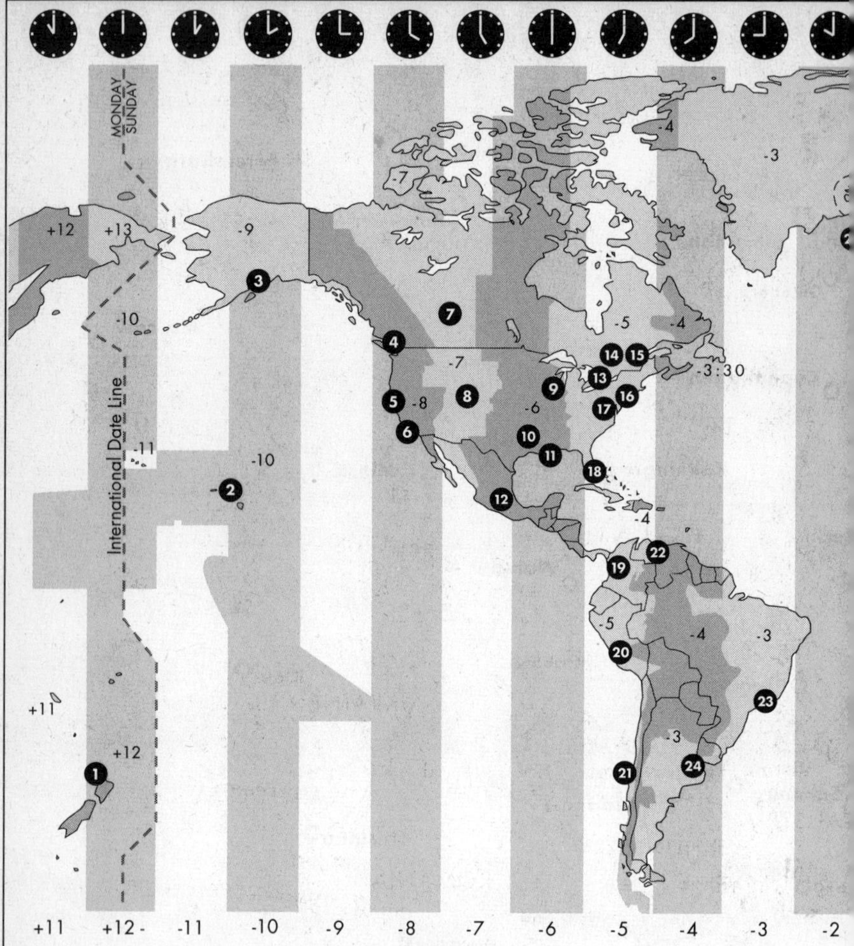

Numbers below vertical bands relate each zone to Greenwich Mean Time (0 hrs.).
Local times frequently differ from these general indications,
as indicated by light-face numbers on map.

Algiers, **29**
Anchorage, **3**
Athens, **41**
Auckland, **1**
Baghdad, **46**
Bangkok, **50**
Beijing, **54**

Berlin, **34**
Bogotá, **19**
Budapest, **37**
Buenos Aires, **24**
Caracas, **22**
Chicago, **9**
Copenhagen, **33**
Dallas, **10**

Delhi, **48**
Denver, **8**
Djakarta, **53**
Dublin, **26**
Edmonton, **7**
Hong Kong, **56**
Honolulu, **2**

Istanbul, **40**
Jerusalem, **42**
Johannesburg, **44**
Lima, **20**
Lisbon, **28**
London
(Greenwich), **27**
Los Angeles, **6**
Madrid, **38**
Manila, **57**

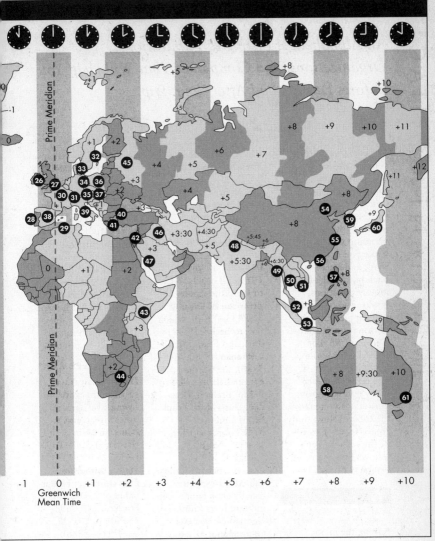

Prime Meridian

Greenwich Mean Time

-1 0 +1 +2 +3 +4 +5 +6 +7 +8 +9 +10

Mecca, **47**
Mexico City, **12**
Miami, **18**
Montréal, **15**
Moscow, **45**
Nairobi, **43**
New Orleans, **11**
New York City, **16**

Ottawa, **14**
Paris, **30**
Perth, **58**
Reykjavík, **25**
Rio de Janeiro, **23**
Rome, **39**
Saigon (Ho Chi Minh City), **51**

San Francisco, **5**
Santiago, **21**
Seoul, **59**
Shanghai, **55**
Singapore, **52**
Stockholm, **32**
Sydney, **61**
Tokyo, **60**

Toronto, **13**
Vancouver, **4**
Vienna, **35**
Warsaw, **36**
Washington, D.C., **17**
Yangon, **49**
Zürich, **31**

IMPORTANT CONTACTS A TO Z

An Alphabetical Listing of Publications, Organizations, and Companies That Will Help You Before, During, and After Your Trip

No single travel resource can give you every detail about every topic that might interest or concern you at the various stages of your journey—when you're planning your trip, while you're on the road, and after you get back home. The following organizations, books, and brochures will supplement the information in *Fodor's Germany '96*. For related information, including both basic tips on visiting Germany and background information on many of the topics below, study Smart Travel Tips A to Z, the section that follows Important Contacts A to Z.

A

AIR TRAVEL

Among the major gateways to Germany are Düsseldorf, Köln, Frankfurt, Munich, and Berlin. Flying time to Frankfurt is 7½ hours from New York, 10 hours from Chicago, and 12 hours from Los Angeles.

CARRIERS

U.S. airlines serving Germany include **Continental** (☎ 800/231–0856), which flies to Frankfurt and Munich; **Northwest Airlines** (☎ 800/447–4747), which flies to Berlin and Frankfurt; **Delta** (☎ 800/241–4141), which flies to Berlin, Frankfurt, Hamburg, Munich, and Stuttgart; **TWA** (☎ 800/892–4141), **United** (☎ 800/241–6522), and **USAir** (☎ 800/622–1015), all of which fly to Frankfurt; and **American Airlines** (☎ 800/433–7300), which flies to Berlin, Düsseldorf, and Frankfurt. **Lufthansa** (☎ 800/645–3880), the German national airline, flies to Berlin, Bremen, Dresden, Düsseldorf, Frankfurt, Hamburg, Köln/Bonn, Leipzig, Munich, Nürnberg, and Stuttgart. To fly to smaller cities from the United States, you usually get a connection in Frankfurt. Another German carrier, **LTU International Airways** (☎ 800/888–0200), flies from Los Angeles, Miami, New York, Orlando, San Francisco, and Tampa to Düsseldorf and Munich.

FROM THE U.K.

British Airways (☎ 0181/897–4000) and **Lufthansa** (☎ 0181/750–3300) are the main airlines flying from London to Germany. Between them, they serve 13 German destinations. **RFG Regional Flug** (☎ 01293/567–977), a Lufthansa subsidiary, flies daily from Gatwick to Münster. **Air UK** (☎ 0345/666–777) flies weekdays from London's third airport, Stansted, to Frankfurt and Düsseldorf. Flying time from London to Frankfurt is 1 hour and 15 minutes, from London to Munich is 1 hour and 40 minutes, from London to Berlin is 1 hour and 45 minutes.

WITHIN GERMANY

Details of air travel services are available from travel agents; otherwise, contact **Deutsche BA** in Berlin (Poststr. 4-5, D-10178 Berlin, ☎ 030/4101–2647); **Lufthansa** in Frankfurt (Am Hauptbahnhof 2, D-60065 Frankfurt, ☎ 069/25540); or **LTU** (☎ 0221/941–8888).

COMPLAINTS

To register complaints about charter and scheduled airlines, contact the U.S. Department of Transportation's **Office of Consumer Affairs** (400 7th St. NW, Washington, DC 20590, ☎ 202/366–2220 or 800/322–7873).

CONSOLIDATORS

Established consolidators selling to the public include **BET World**

Travel (841 Blossom Hill Rd., Suite 212-C, San Jose, CA 95123, ☎ 408/229–7880 or 800/747–1476), **Council Charter** (205 E. 42nd St., New York, NY 10017, ☎ 212/661–0311 or 800/800–8222), **Euram Tours** (1522 K St. NW, Suite 430, Washington DC, 20005, ☎ 800/848–6789), **TFI Tours International** (34 W. 32nd St., New York, NY 10001, ☎ 212/736–1140 or 800/745–8000), **Travac Tours and Charter** (989 6th Ave., 16th Floor, New York, NY 10018, ☎ 212/563–3303 or 800/872–8800; 2601 E. Jefferson, Orlando, FL 32803, ☎ 407/896–0014 or 800/872–8800), and **UniTravel** (Box 12485, St. Louis, MO 63132, ☎ 314/569–0900 or 800/325–2222).

PUBLICATIONS

For general information about charter carriers, ask for the Office of Consumer Affairs' brochure **"Plane Talk: Public Charter Flights."** The Department of Transportation also publishes a 58-page booklet, **"Fly Rights"** ($1.75; Consumer Information Center, Dept. 133-B, Pueblo, CO 81009).

For other tips and hints, consult the Consumers Union's monthly **"Consumer Reports Travel Letter"** ($39 a year; Box 53629, Boulder, CO 80322, ☎ 800/234–1970) and the newsletter **"Travel Smart"** ($37 a year; 40 Beechdale Rd., Dobbs Ferry, NY 10522, ☎ 800/327–3633); *The Official*

Frequent Flyer Guidebook, by Randy Petersen ($14.99 plus $3 shipping; 4715-C Town Center Dr., Colorado Springs, CO 80916, ☎ 719/597–8899 or 800/487–8893); *Airfare Secrets Exposed,* by Sharon Tyler and Matthew Wonder (Universal Information Publishing; $16.95 plus $3.75 shipping from Sandcastle Publishing, Box 3070-A, South Pasadena, CA 91031, ☎ 213/255–3616 or 800/655–0053); and *202 Tips Even the Best Business Travelers May Not Know,* by Christopher McGinnis ($10 plus $3 shipping; Irwin Professional Publishing, 1333 Burr Ridge Pkwy., Burr Ridge, IL 60521, ☎ 708/789–4000 or 800/634–3966).

B
BETTER BUSINESS BUREAU

For local contacts in the home town of a tour operator you may be considering, consult the **Council of Better Business Bureaus** (4200 Wilson Blvd., Arlington, VA 22203, ☎ 703/276–0100).

BUS TRAVEL

FROM THE U.K.
Eurolines (☎ 071/730–3499) has up to three departures a day from London's Victoria Coach Station. The buses cross the Channel on Sealink's Dover–Zeebrugge ferry service and then drive via the Netherlands and Belgium to Köln (14½ hours), Frankfurt (17½ hours), Mannheim (18¾ hours), Stuttgart/Nürn-

berg (20½ hours), and Munich (22¾ hours). **Hoverspeed** (☎ 01304/240–241) runs two buses in winter and one in summer to Berlin from Victoria Station. Travel time is 23 hours, including a three-hour stopover in Brussels.

WITHIN GERMANY

The railways, in the guise of **Deutsche Touring,** operate the German sections of the Europabus network. Contact them at Am Römerhof 17, D–60426 Frankfurt/Main, ☎ 069/79030, for details about a range of two-to seven-day package tours.

C
CAR RENTAL

Major car-rental companies in Germany include **Avis** (☎ 800/331–1084, 800/879–2847 in Canada), **Budget** (☎ 800/527–0700, 0800/181–181 in the U.K.), **Eurodollar Rent a Car** (☎ 800/800–6000), **Hertz** (☎ 800/654–3001, 800/263–0600 in Canada, 0181/679–1799 in the U.K.), and **National** (sometimes known as **Europcar InterRent** outside North America; ☎ 800/227–3876, 0181/950–5050 in the U.K.). Rates vary considerably, depending upon type of car and rental location. In Munich or Berlin, prices begin at $15 a day and $100 a week for an economy car with unlimited mileage—although they can go much higher. Not included is VAT tax, which in Germany is 15%.

RENTAL WHOLESALERS

Contact **Auto Europe** (Box 7006, Portland, ME 04112, ☎ 207/828–2525 or 800/223–5555); **Europe by Car** in New York City (write 1 Rockefeller Plaza, 10020; visit 14 W. 49th St.; or call 212/581–3040, 212/245–1713, or 800/223–1516) or Los Angeles (9000 Sunset Blvd., 90069, ☎ 800/252–9401 or 213/272–0424 in CA); or the **Kemwel Group** (106 Calvert St., Harrison, NY 10528, ☎ 914/835–5555 or 800/678–0678).

THE CHANNEL TUNNEL

For information, contact **Le Shuttle** (☎ 01345/353535 in the U.K., 800/388–3876 in the U.S.), which transports cars, or **Eurostar** (☎ 0171/922–4486 in the U.K., 800/942–4866 in the U.S.), the high-speed train service between London (Waterloo) and Paris (Gare du Nord). Eurostar tickets are available in the United Kingdom through **InterCity Europe,** the international wing of BritRail (London's Victoria Station, ☎ 0171/834–2345 or 0171/828–8092 for credit-card bookings), and in the United States through **Rail Europe** (☎ 800/942–4866) and **BritRail Travel** (1500 Broadway, New York, NY 10036, ☎ 800/677–8585).

CHILDREN AND TRAVEL

BABY-SITTING

In Munich, for a tourist-office-approved service offering sitters who speak English, call 089/229–291. Also, contact the **Munich American High School** (Cincinnatistr. 61A, D–81549 München, ☎ 089/6229–8354). The **American Women's Club of Frankfurt** (Abrams Bldg., Frankfurt, Germany, APO, NY 09757) runs a child-care center at the military base near the Abrams Building (☎ 069/553–129).

FLYING

Look into **"Flying with Baby"** ($5.95 plus $1 shipping; Third Street Press, Box 261250, Littleton, CO 80126, ☎ 303/595–5959), cowritten by a flight attendant. **"Kids and Teens in Flight,"** free from the U.S. Department of Transportation's Office of Consumer Affairs, offers tips for children flying alone. Every two years the February issue of *Family Travel Times* (*see* Know-How, *below*) details children's services on three dozen airlines.

KNOW-HOW

Family Travel Times, published 10 times a year by Travel with Your Children (TWYCH, 45 W. 18th St., New York, NY 10011, ☎ 212/206–0688; annual subscription $55), covers destinations, types of vacations, and modes of travel.

The *Family Travel Guides* catalogue ($1 postage; ☎ 510/527–5849) lists about 200 books and articles on family travel. Also check *Take Your Baby and Go! A Guide for Traveling with Babies, Toddlers and Young Children,* by Sheri Andrews, Judy Bordeaux, and Vivian Vasquez ($5.95 plus $1.50 shipping; Bear Creek Publications, 2507 Minor Ave., Seattle, WA 98102, ☎ 206/322–7604 or 800/326–6566). *Innocents Abroad: Traveling with Kids in Europe,* by Valerie Wolf Deutsch and Laura Sutherland ($15.95 plus $2 shipping; Penguin USA, 120 Woodbine St., Bergenfield, NJ 07621, ☎ 201/387–0600 or 800/253–6476), covers child- and teen-friendly activities, food, and transportation.

LOCAL INFORMATION

"Young People's Guide to Munich" is a free pamphlet available from the German National Tourist Office.

TOUR OPERATORS

If you're outdoorsy, look into programs from the **American Museum of Natural History** (79th St. and Central Park W., New York, NY 10024, ☎ 212/769–5700 or 800/462–8687).

LODGING

A likely choice for families is any one of the Schloss (castle) hotels in Germany; many have parklike grounds. U.S. representatives are **Europa Hotels and Tours** (14178 Woodinville–Duval Rd., Box 1278, Woodinville, WA 98072, ☎ 800/523–9570, reservations only) and **DER Tours** (Box 1606, Des Plaines,

IL 60017, ☎ 800/782–2424).

U.S. CITIZENS

The **U.S. Customs Service** (Box 7407, Washington, DC 20044, ☎ 202/927–6724) can answer questions on duty-free limits and publishes a helpful brochure, **"Know Before You Go."** For information on registering foreign-made articles, call 202/927–0540.

CANADIANS

Contact **Revenue Canada** (2265 St. Laurent Blvd. S, Ottawa, Ontario, K1G 4K3, ☎ 613/993–0534) for a copy of the free brochure **"I Declare/Je Déclare"** and for details on duties that exceed the standard duty-free limit.

U.K. CITIZENS

HM Customs and Excise (Dorset House, Stamford St., London SE1 9NG, ☎ 0171/202–4227) can answer questions about U.K. customs regulations and publishes **"A Guide for Travellers,"** detailing standard procedures and import rules.

D

FOR TRAVELERS WITH DISABILITIES

ORGANIZATIONS

FOR TRAVELERS WITH HEARING IMPAIRMENTS➤ Contact the **American Academy of Otolaryngology** (1 Prince St., Alexandria, VA 22314, ☎ 703/836–4444, FAX 703/683–5100, TTY 703/519–1585).

FOR TRAVELERS WITH MOBILITY IMPAIRMENTS➤ Contact the **Information Center for Individuals with Disabilities** (Fort Point Pl., 27–43 Wormwood St., Boston, MA 02210, ☎ 617/727–5540, 800/462–5015 in MA, TTY 617/345–9743); **Mobility International USA** (Box 10767, Eugene, OR 97440, ☎ and TTY 503/343–1284, FAX 503/343–6812), the U.S. branch of an international organization based in Belgium (*see below*) that has affiliates in 30 countries; **MossRehab Hospital Travel Information Service** (1200 W. Tabor Rd., Philadelphia, PA 19141, ☎ 215/456–9603, TTY 215/456–9602); the **Society for the Advancement of Travel for the Handicapped** (SATH, 347 5th Ave., Suite 610, New York, NY 10016, ☎ 212/447–7284, FAX 212/725–8253); the **Travel Industry and Disabled Exchange** (TIDE, 5435 Donna Ave., Tarzana, CA 91356, ☎ 818/344–3640, FAX 818/344–0078); and **Travelin' Talk** (Box 3534, Clarksville, TN 37043, ☎ 615/552–6670, FAX 615/552–1182).

FOR TRAVELERS WITH VISION IMPAIRMENTS➤ Contact the **American Council of the Blind** (1155 15th St. NW, Suite 720, Washington, DC 20005, ☎ 202/467–5081, FAX 202/467–5085) or the **American Foundation for the Blind** (15 W. 16th St., New York, NY 10011, ☎ 212/620–2000, TTY 212/620–2158).

IN THE U.K.

Contact the **Royal Association for Disability and Rehabilitation** (RADAR, 12 City Forum, 250 City Rd., London EC1V 8AF, ☎ 0171/250–3222) or **Mobility International** (Rue de Manchester 25, B1070 Brussels, Belgium, ☎ 00–322–410–6297), an international clearinghouse of travel information for people with disabilities.

PUBLICATIONS

Several free publications are available from the U.S. Information Center (Box 100, Pueblo, CO 81009, ☎ 719/948–3334): **"New Horizons for the Air Traveler with a Disability"** (address to Dept. 355A), describing legally mandated changes; the pocket-size **"Fly Smart"** (Dept. 575B), good on flight safety; and the Airport Operators Council's worldwide **"Access Travel: Airports"** (Dept. 575A).

The 500-page *Travelin' Talk Directory* ($35; Box 3534, Clarksville, TN 37043, ☎ 615/552–6670) lists people and organizations who help travelers with disabilities. For specialist travel agents worldwide, consult the *Directory of Travel Agencies for the Disabled* ($19.95 plus $2 shipping; Twin Peaks Press, Box 129, Vancouver, WA 98666, ☎ 206/694–2462 or 800/637–2256).

The German Railways issues a booklet dealing with its services for disabled travelers, with an English-language section. It can be obtained from **Deutsche Bahn AG** (German Railways; Güterstr. 9, D–60327 Frankfurt/Main, ☎ 069/9733–6774).

TRAVEL AGENCIES AND TOUR OPERATORS

The Americans with Disabilities Act requires that travel firms serve the needs of all travelers. However, some agencies and operators specialize in making group and individual arrangements for travelers with disabilities, among them **Access Adventures** (206 Chestnut Ridge Rd., Rochester, NY 14624, ☎ 716/889–9096), run by a former physical-rehab counselor. In addition, many general-interest operators and agencies (*see* Tour Operators, *below*) can arrange vacations for travelers with disabilities.

For Travelers with Hearing Impairments➤ One agency is **International Express** (7319-B Baltimore Ave., College Park, MD 20740, ☎ and TDD 301/699–8836, FAX 301/699–8836), which arranges group and independent trips.

For Travelers with Mobility Impairments➤ A number of operators specialize in working with travelers with mobility impairments: **Flying Wheels Travel** (143 W. Bridge St., Box 382, Owatonna, MN 55060, ☎ 507/451–5005 or

800/535–6790), a travel agency that specializes in European cruises and tours; **Hinsdale Travel Service** (201 E. Ogden Ave., Suite 100, Hinsdale, IL 60521, ☎ 708/325–1335 or 800/303–5521), a travel agency that will give you access to the services of wheelchair traveler Janice Perkins; **Nautilus Tours** (5435 Donna Ave., Tarzana, CA 91356, ☎ 818/344–3640 or 800/345–4654); and **Wheelchair Journeys** (16979 Redmond Way, Redmond, WA 98052, ☎ 206/885–2210), which can handle arrangements worldwide.

For Travelers with Developmental Disabilities➤ Contact the nonprofit **New Directions** (5276 Hollister Ave., Suite 207, Santa Barbara, CA 93111, ☎ 805/967–2841).

DISCOUNTS

Options include **Entertainment Travel Editions** (fee $28–$53, depending on destination; Box 1068, Trumbull, CT 06611, ☎ 800/445–4137), **Great American Traveler** ($49.95 annually; Box 27965, Salt Lake City, UT 84127, ☎ 800/548–2812), **Moment's Notice Discount Travel Club** ($25 annually, single or family; 163 Amsterdam Ave., Suite 137, New York, NY 10023, ☎ 212/486–0500), **Privilege Card** ($74.95 annually; 3391 Peachtree Rd. NE, Suite 110, Atlanta, GA 30326, ☎ 404/262–0222 or 800/236-9732), **Travelers Advantage** ($49

annually, single or family; CUC Travel Service, 49 Music Sq. W, Nashville, TN 37203, ☎ 800/548–1116 or 800/648–4037), and **Worldwide Discount Travel Club** ($50 annually for family, $40 single; 1674 Meridian Ave., Miami Beach, FL 33139, ☎ 305/534–2082).

DRIVING

AUTO CLUBS

There are three principal automobile clubs: **ADAC** (Allgemeiner Deutscher Automobil-Club, Am Westpark 8, D–81373 Munich; tel: 089/76760), **AvD** (Automobilclub von Deutschland, Lyonerstr. 16, D–60528 Frankfurt; ☎ 069/66060), and **DTC** (Deutscher Touring-Automobil Club, Amalienburgstr. 23, D–81247 Munich; tel: 089/811–1048).

FROM THE UNITED KINGDOM BY CAR

The following companies operate car ferries between the United Kingdom and ports in the Netherlands: **Sealink** (☎ 01233/646–801), **Eurolink Ferries** (☎ 01795/581–000), **P&O European Ferries** (☎ 0181/575–8555), **North Sea Ferries** (☎ 01482/795–141), and **Motorail** (☎ 071/409–3518).

E

ELECTRICITY

Send a self-addressed, stamped envelope to the **Franzus Company** (Customer Service, Dept. B50, Murtha Industrial Park, Box 142, Beacon Falls, CT 06403, ☎ 203/723–

6664) for a copy of the free brochure "Foreign Electricity Is No Deep Dark Secret."

GAY AND LESBIAN TRAVEL

ORGANIZATION

The **International Gay Travel Association** (Box 4974, Key West, FL 33041, ☎ 800/448–8550), a consortium of 800 businesses, can supply names of travel agents and tour operators.

PUBLICATIONS

The premier international travel magazine for gays and lesbians is **Our World** ($35 for 10 issues; 1104 N. Nova Rd., Suite 251, Daytona Beach, FL 32117, ☎ 904/441–5367). The 16-page monthly **"Out & About"** ($49 for 10 issues; ☎ 212/645–6922 or 800/929–2268) covers gay-friendly resorts, hotels, cruise lines, and airlines.

TOUR OPERATORS

For mixed gay and lesbian travel, contact **Toto Tours** (1326 W. Albion, Suite 3W, Chicago, IL 60626, ☎ 312/274–8686 or 800/565–1241) for group tours worldwide.

TRAVEL AGENCIES

The largest agencies serving gay travelers are **Advance Travel** (10700 Northwest Freeway, Suite 160, Houston, TX 77092, ☎ 713/682–2002 or 800/695–0880), **Islanders/Kennedy Travel** (183 W. 10th St., New York, NY 10014,

☎ 212/242–3222 or 800/988–1181), **Now Voyager** (4406 18th St., San Francisco, CA 94114, ☎ 415/626–1169 or 800/255–6951), and **Yellowbrick Road** (1500 W. Balmoral Ave., Chicago, IL 60640, ☎ 312/561–1800 or 800/642–2488). **Skylink Women's Travel** (746 Ashland Ave., Santa Monica, CA 90405, ☎ 310/452–0506 or 800/225-5759) works with lesbians.

HEALTH ISSUES

FINDING A DOCTOR

For members, the **International Association for Medical Assistance to Travellers** (IAMAT, 417 Center St., Lewiston, NY 14092, ☎ 716/754–4883; 40 Regal Rd., Guelph, Ontario N1K 1B5, ☎ 519/836–0102; 1287 St. Clair Ave., Toronto, Ontario M6E 1B8, ☎ 416/652–0137; 57 Voirets, 1212 Grand-Lancy, Geneva, Switzerland; membership free) publishes a worldwide directory of English-speaking physicians meeting IAMAT standards.

MEDICAL-ASSISTANCE COMPANIES

Contact **International SOS Assistance** (Box 11568, Philadelphia, PA 19116, ☎ 215/244–1500 or 800/523–8930; Box 466, Pl. Bonaventure, Montréal, Québec H5A 1C1, ☎ 514/874–7674 or 800/363–0263), **Medex Assistance Corporation** (Box 10623, Baltimore,

MD 21285, ☎ 410/296–2530 or 800/573–2029), **Near Services** (Box 1339, Calumet City, IL 60409, ☎ 708/868–6700 or 800/654–6700), and **Travel Assistance International** (1133 15th St. NW, Suite 400, Washington, DC 20005, ☎ 202/ 331–1609 or 800/ 821–2828). Because these companies also sell death-and-dismemberment, trip-cancellation, and other insurance coverage, there is some overlap with the travel-insurance policies sold by the companies listed under Insurance, *below.*

INSURANCE

Travel insurance covering baggage, health, and trip cancellation or interruptions is available from **Access America** (Box 90315, Richmond, VA 23286, ☎ 804/285–3300 or 800/284–8300), **Carefree Travel Insurance** (Box 9366, 100 Garden City Plaza, Garden City, NY 11530, ☎ 516/294–0220 or 800/323–3149), **Near Services** (Box 1339, Calumet City, IL 60409, ☎ 708/868–6700 or 800/654–6700), **Tele-Trip** (Mutual of Omaha Plaza, Box 31716, Omaha, NE 68131, ☎ 800/228–9792), **Travel Insured International** (Box 280568, East Hartford, CT 06128-0568, ☎ 203/528–7663 or 800/243–3174), **Travel Guard International** (1145 Clark St., Stevens Point, WI 54481, ☎ 715/345–0505 or 800/826–1300), and **Wallach & Company**

(107 W. Federal St., Box 480, Middleburg, VA 22117, ☎ 703/687–3166 or 800/237–6615).

IN THE U.K.

The **Association of British Insurers** (51 Gresham St., London EC2V 7HQ, ☎ 0171/600–3333; 30 Gordon St., Glasgow G1 3PU, ☎ 0141/226–3905; Scottish Provident Bldg., Donegall Sq. W, Belfast BT1 6JE, ☎ 01232/249176; and other locations) gives advice by phone and publishes the free **"Holiday Insurance,"** which sets out typical policy provisions and costs.

L
LODGING

APARTMENT AND VILLA RENTAL

Among the companies to contact are **Europa-Let** (92 N. Main St., Ashland, OR 97520, ☎ 503/482–5806 or 800/462–4486), **Hometours International** (Box 11503, Knoxville, TN 37939, ☎ 615/588–8722 or 800/367–4668), **Interhome** (124 Little Falls Rd., Fairfield, NJ 07004, ☎ 201/882–6864), **Property Rentals International** (1008 Mansfield Crossing Rd., Richmond, VA 23236, ☎ 804/378–6054 or 800/220–3332), **Rent-a-Home International** (7200 34th Ave. NW, Seattle, WA 98117, ☎ 206/789–9377 or 800/488–7368), **Vacation Home Rentals Worldwide** (235 Kensington Ave., Norwood, NJ 07648, ☎ 201/767–9393 or 800/633–3284), and **Villas**

International (605 Market St., Suite 510, San Francisco, CA 94105, ☎ 415/281–0910 or 800/221–2260).

The German Automobile Association issues listings of family holiday apartments; write **ADAC Reisen** (Am Westpark 8, D–81373 Munich).

CAMPING

For a listing of camping sites throughout Germany contact the **DCC**, or German Camping Club (Mandlstr. 28, D–80802 Munich , ☎ 089/380–1420).

CASTLE HOTELS

For a brochure listing nearly 60 castle hotels, contact **Gast im Schloss**, D 4, 9–10, Postfach 120620, D–68057 Mannheim, Germany (☎ 0621/126–620). This organization and your travel agent can also advise on a number of packages available for castle hotels, including four- to six-night tours.

FARM VACATIONS

The **DLG** (German Agricultural Association) produces an illustrated brochure listing more than 1,500 inspected and graded farms, from the Alps to the North Sea, that offer accommodations. It costs DM 7.50 (send an international reply coupon if writing from the United States) and is available from **DLG Reisedienst, Agratour** (Eschborner Landstr. 122, D–60489 Frankfurt/Main, ☎ 069/247–880) or the National Tourist Office.

HOME EXCHANGE

Principal clearinghouses include **HomeLink International/Vacation Exchange Club** ($60 annually; Box 650, Key West, FL 33041, ☎ 305/294–1448 or 800/638–3841), which gives members four annual directories, with a listing in one, plus updates; **Intervac International** ($65 annually; Box 590504, San Francisco, CA 94159, ☎ 415/435–3497), which has three annual directories; and **Loan-a-Home** ($35–$45 annually; 2 Park La., Apt. 6E, Mount Vernon, NY 10552-3443, ☎ 914/664–7640), which specializes in long-term exchanges.

HOTELS

An excellent nationwide hotel reservation service is also operated by **ADZ** (Corneliusstr. 34, D–60325 Frankfurt/Main, ☎ 069/740–767, FAX 069/751–056). The service is free of charge.

ROMANTIK HOTELS

A detailed brochure listing all Romantik Hotels and Restaurants, which costs $7.50 (including mailing), and a free mini-guide are available from **Romantik Hotels Reservations** (Box 1278, Woodinville, WA 98072, ☎ 206/486–9394; for reservations, ☎ 800/826–0015); information is also supplied by the National Tourist Office.

SPAS

A complete list of spas, giving full details of their springs and treatments, is available from the German National

Tourist Office, or from **Deutsche Bäderverband,** the German Health Resort and Spa Association (Postfach 190 147, D–53037 Bonn, ☎ 0288/262–010).

M
MONEY MATTERS

ATMS

For specific foreign **Cirrus** locations, call 800/424–7787; for foreign Plus locations, consult the **Plus** directory at your local bank.

CURRENCY EXCHANGE

If your bank doesn't exchange currency, contact **Thomas Cook Currency Services** (41 E. 42nd St., New York, NY 10017, or 511 Madison Ave., New York, NY 10022, ☎ 212/757–6915 or 800/223–7373 for locations) or **Ruesch International** (☎ 800/ 424–2923 for locations).

WIRING FUNDS

Funds can be wired via **American Express MoneyGram**sm (☎ 800/ 926–9400 from the U.S. and Canada for locations and information) or **Western Union** (☎ 800/325–6000 for agent locations or to send using MasterCard or Visa, 800/321–2923 in Canada).

P
PASSPORTS AND VISAS

U.S. CITIZENS

For fees, documentation requirements, and other information, call the **Office of Passport Services** information

line (☎ 202/647– 0518).

CANADIANS

For fees, documentation requirements, and other information, call the Ministry of Foreign Affairs and International Trade's **Passport Office** (☎ 819/994– 3500 or 800/567– 6868).

U.K. CITIZENS

For fees, documentation requirements, and to get an emergency passport, call the **London Passport Office** (☎ 0171/271– 3000).

PHONE MATTERS

The country code for Germany is 49. For local access numbers abroad, contact **AT&T** USADirect (☎ 800/ 874–4000), **MCI** Call USA (☎ 800/444– 4444), or **Sprint** Express (☎ 800/793–1153).

PHOTO HELP

The **Kodak Information Center** (☎ 800/242– 2424) answers consumer questions about film and photography.

R
RAIL TRAVEL

BAGGAGE SERVICE

From train stations throughout Germany, you can use the Deutsche Bahn *KurierGepäck* service to send your baggage to Frankfurt Airport; call 0180/332–0520 to have them pick up you baggage from your hotel. The service costs DM 28 per suitcase (with a valid ticket), and overnight delivery is guaranteed on weekdays.

DISCOUNT PASSES

The **German Rail Pass,** not available to Germans, allows you to travel the entire German rail network for 5, 10, or 15 days within a single month; cost is $260, $410, and $530 in first class, respectively, and $178, $286, and $386 in second class. A **German Twin Pass** discounts these rates for two people traveling together; cost per person is $234, $369, and $477 for first class, and $160, $257, and $331 for second class. A **Youthpass,** sold to those age 12–25 for second-class travel, costs $138–$238. All of these passes can be used on buses operated by the Deutsche Bahn, as well as on tour routes along the Romantic and Castle roads served by Deutsche Touring (*see* Bus Travel, *above*), and Rhine, Main, and Mosel river cruises operated by the Köln-Düsseldorfer (KD) Line. Passes are sold by travel agents and **DER Tours** (Box 1606, Des Plaines, IL 60017, ☎ 800/782–2424), and can now also be purchased in Germany directly from German Rail.

EurailPasses, which provide unlimited first-class rail travel during their period of validity, are also valid in Germany. If you plan to rack up the miles and cross many borders, they can be an excellent value. Standard passes are available for 15 days ($498), 21 days ($648), one month ($728), two months ($1,098), and three months ($1,398). **Eurail Saverpasses,** valid for 15 days, cost $430 per person, 21 days for $550, one month for $678 per person; you must do all your traveling with at least one companion (two companions from April through September). **Eurail Youthpasses,** which cover second-class travel, cost $578 for one month, $768 for two; you must be under 26 on the first day you travel. **Eurail Flexipasses** allow you to travel first class for 5 ($348), 10 ($560), or 15 ($740) days within any two-month period. **Eurail Youth Flexipasses,** available to those under 26 on their first travel day, allow second class travel for 5 ($255), 10, ($398), or 15 ($540) days within any two-month period. Another option is the **Europass,** featuring a minimum of 5 and a maximum of 15 days (within a two-month period) of unlimited rail travel in your choice of three to all five of the participating countries (France, Germany, Italy, Spain, and Switzerland); cost for 5 days is $280 first class, $198 second class (3 countries); for 8 days, $394 first class, $284 second class (4 countries), and for 11 days, $508 first class, $366 second class (all five countries). Each extra rail day costs $38 for first class and $28 for second class. Apply through your travel agent or **Rail Europe** (226–230 Westchester Ave., White Plains, NY 10604, ☎ 914/682–5172 or 800/848–7245; or 2087 Dundas

E, Suite 105, Mississauga, Ont. L4X 1M2, ☎ 416/602–4195), **DER Tours** (Box 1606, Des Plaines, IL 60017, ☎ 800/782–2424), or **CIT Tours Corp.** (342 Madison Ave., Suite 207, New York, NY 10173, ☎ 212/697–2100 or 800/248–8687; 310/670–4269 or 800/248–7245 in western U.S.).

FROM THE UNITED KINGDOM BY TRAIN

For information on rail travel between London and Germany, *see* The Channel Tunnel, *above.* For time tables and information about German rail services and fares, contact the **German Rail Passenger Services** (23 Oakhill Grove, Surbiton, Surrey KT6 6DU, ☎ 0181/390–8833).

S
SENIOR CITIZENS

EDUCATIONAL TRAVEL

The nonprofit **Elderhostel** (75 Federal St., 3rd Floor, Boston, MA 02110, ☎ 617/426–7788), for people 60 and older, has offered inexpensive study programs since 1975. The nearly 2,000 courses cover everything from marine science to Greek myths and cowboy poetry.

For people 50 and over and their children and grandchildren, **Interhostel** (University of New Hampshire, 6 Garrison Ave., Durham, NH 03824, ☎ 603/862–1147 or 800/733–9753) runs 10-day summer programs involving lectures, field

trips, and sightseeing. Most last two weeks and cost $2,125–$3,100, including airfare.

ORGANIZATIONS

Contact the **American Association of Retired Persons** (AARP, 601 E St. NW, Washington, DC 20049, ☎ 202/434–2277; $8 per person or couple annually). Its Purchase Privilege Program gets members discounts on lodging, car rentals, and sightseeing.

For other discounts on lodgings, car rentals, and other travel products, along with magazines and newsletters, contact the **National Council of Senior Citizens** (membership $12 annually; 1331 F St. NW, Washington, DC 20004, ☎ 202/347–8800) and **Mature Outlook** (subscription $9.95 annually; 6001 N. Clark St., Chicago, IL 60660, ☎ 312/465–6466 or 800/336–6330).

PUBLICATIONS

The 50+ Traveler's Guidebook: Where to Go, Where to Stay, What to Do, by Anita Williams and Merrimac Dillon ($12.95; St. Martin's Press, 175 5th Ave., New York, NY 10010, ☎ 212/674–5151 or 800/288–2131), offers many useful tips. **"The Mature Traveler"** ($29.95; Box 50400, Reno, NV 89513, ☎ 702/786–7419), a monthly newsletter, covers travel deals.

SPORTS

BICYCLING

Information on all aspects of cycling in Germany is available from the **Allgemeiner Deutscher Fahrrad-Club** (The German Cycle Club; Hollerallee 23, D–28209 Bremen, ☎ 0421/346–290).

FISHING

Details on fishing in Germany are available from local tourist offices or from the **Verband Deutscher Sportfischer** (Siemensstr. 11–13, D–63071 Offenbach, ☎ 069/855–006).

GOLF

For information, contact the **Deutscher Golf-Verband** (German Golf Association; Friedrichstr. 12, D–65185 Wiesbaden, ☎ 0611/990–200).

HIKING AND CLIMBING

The **Verband Deutscher Gebirgs- und Wandervereine e.V.** (Reichs-Str. 4, D–66111 Saarbrücken 3, ☎ 0681/390–070) can provide information on routes, hiking paths, overnight accommodations, and mountain huts.

For Alpine walking, contact the **Deutsche Alpenverein** (Von-Kahr-Str. 2–4, D–80997 Munich, ☎ 089/140–030). It administers more than 50 mountain huts and about 15,000 kilometers (9,500 miles) of Alpine paths. In addition, it can provide courses in mountaineering and touring suggestions for routes in both

winter and summer. Foreigners may become members.

Various mountaineering schools offer week-long courses ranging from basic techniques for beginners to advanced mountaineering. Contact **Herr Hechmeier** (Lindenstr. 16, D–87561 Oberstdorf ☎ 08322/3638) for further information.

SAILING

For details on sailing vacations and sailboat rental, contact **Deutscher Segler-Verband** (Gründgensstr. 18, D–22309 Hamburg, ☎ 040/632–0090).

WINDSURFING

For windsurfing information contact the German National Tourist Office or **VDWS** (Heimgarten 9a, D–82362 Weilheim, Oberbayern, ☎ 0881/4261).

STUDENTS

GROUPS

Major tour operators include **Contiki Holidays** (300 Plaza Alicante, Suite 900, Garden Grove, CA 92640, ☎ 714/740–0808 or 800/466–0610) and **AESU Travel** (2 Hamill Rd., Suite 248, Baltimore, MD 21210-1807, ☎ 410/323–4416 or 800/638–7640).

HOSTELING

Contact **Hostelling International–American Youth Hostels** (733 15th St. NW, Suite 840, Washington, DC 20005, ☎ 202/783–6161) in the United States, **Hostelling International–Canada** (205 Catherine St., Suite 400,

Ottawa, Ontario K2P 1C3, ☎ 613/237–7884) in Canada, and the **Youth Hostel Association of England and Wales** (Trevelyan House, 8 St. Stephen's Hill, St. Albans, Hertfordshire AL1 2DY, ☎ 01727/855215 and 01727/845047) in the United Kingdom. Membership ($25 in the U.S., C$26.75 in Canada, and £9 in the U.K.) gets you access to 5,000 hostels worldwide that charge $7–$20 nightly per person.

For listings of German youth hostels, contact the **Deutsches Jugendherbergswerk Hauptverband** (Bismarckstr. 8, D–32754 Detmold, ☎ 05231/74010).

I.D. CARDS

To get discounts on transportation and admissions, get the **International Student Identity Card** (ISIC) if you're a bona fide student or the **International Youth Card** (IYC) if you're under 26. In the United States, the ISIC and IYC cards cost $16 each and include basic travel-accident and illness coverage, plus a toll-free travel hot line. Apply through the Council on International Educational Exchange (*see* Organizations, *below*). Cards are available for $15 each in Canada from **Travel Cuts** (187 College St., Toronto, Ontario M5T 1P7, ☎ 416/979–2406 or 800/667–2887) and in the United Kingdom for £5 each at student unions and student travel companies.

ORGANIZATIONS

A major contact is the **Council on International Educational Exchange** (CIEE, 205 E. 42nd St., 16th Floor, New York, NY 10017, ☎ 212/661–1450) with locations in Boston (729 Boylston St., Boston, MA 02116, ☎ 617/266–1926), Miami (9100 S. Dadeland Blvd., Miami, FL 33156, ☎ 305/670–9261), Los Angeles (1093 Broxton Ave., Los Angeles, CA 90024, ☎ 310/208–3551), 43 college towns nationwide, and the United Kingdom (28A Poland St., London W1V 3DB, ☎ 0171/437–7767). Twice a year, it publishes *Student Travels* magazine. The CIEE's Council Travel Service is the exclusive U.S. agent for several student-discount cards.

Campus Connections (325 Chestnut St., Suite 1101, Philadelphia, PA 19106, ☎ 215/625–8585 or 800/428–3235) specializes in discounted accommodations and airfares for students. The **Educational Travel Centre** (438 N. Frances St., Madison, WI 53703, ☎ 608/256–5551) offers rail passes and low-cost airline tickets, mostly for flights departing from Chicago. For air travel contact **TMI Student Travel** (100 W. 33rd St., Suite 813, New York, NY 10001, ☎ 800/245–3672).

In Canada, also contact **Travel Cuts** (*see above*).

PUBLICATIONS

See the *Berkeley Guide to Germany and Aus-*tria ($17.95; Fodor's Travel Publications, ☎ 800/533–6478 or from bookstores).

T
TOUR OPERATORS

Among the companies selling tours and packages to Germany, the following have a proven reputation, are nationally known, and have plenty of options to choose from.

GROUP TOURS

Super-deluxe escorted tours of Germany are available from **Abercrombie & Kent** (1520 Kensington Rd., Oak Brook, IL 60521-2141, ☎ 708/954–2944 or 800/323–7308) and **Travcoa** (Box 2630, Newport Beach, CA, 92658, ☎ 714/476–2800 or 800/992–2003). For less costly but still deluxe tours, try **Tauck Tours** (11 Wilton Rd., Westport CT 06881, ☎ 203/226–6911 or 800/468–2825) or **Maupintour** (Box 807, Lawrence, KS 66044, ☎ 913/843–1211 or 800/255–4266). Another operator falling between deluxe and first-class is **Globus** (5301 South Federal Circle, Littleton, CO 80123-2980, ☎ 303/797–2800 or 800/221–0090). The leader in first-class tours to Germany is **DER Tours** (11933 Wilshire Blvd., Los angeles, CA 90025, ☎ 310/479–4140 or 800/782–2424). Other operators selling first-class and first-class superior tours are **Trafalgar Tours** (21 E. 26th St., New York, NY 10010, ☎ 212/689–8977 or 800/854–0103), **Brendan Tours** (15137 Califa St., Van Nuys, CA 91411, ☎ 818/785–9696 or 800/421–8446), and **Insight International** (745 Atlantic Ave., Boston MA, 02111, ☎ 617/482–2000 or 800/582–8380). For budget and tourist-class programs, try **Cosmos** (*see* Globus, *above*).

PACKAGES

DER Tours (*see* Group Tours, *above*) has the greatest variety of independent vacation packages. Among U.S. airlines flying to Germany, contact **American Airlines Fly AAway Vacations** (☎ 800/321–2121), **Continental Airlines' Grand Destinations** (☎ 800/634–5555), **Delta Dream Vacations** (☎ 800/872–7786), and **United Airlines' Vacation Planning Center** (☎ 800/328–6877). Other leading packagers are **CIE Tours** (108 Ridgedale ave., Box 2355, Morristown, NJ 07962-2355, ☎ 201/292–3899 or 800/243–8687), **Jet Vacations** (1775 Broadway, New York, NY 10019, ☎ 212/474–8740 or 800/538–2762), and **VE Tours** (1150 NW 72nd Ave., Suite 450, Miami, FL 33126).

THEME TRIPS

ADVENTURE➤ **All Adventure Travel** (5589 Arapahoe #208, Boulder, CO 80303, ☎ 800/537–4025) can book biking, hiking, and kayaking in Germany. Also try **Himalayan Travel** (112 Prospect St., Stamford,

CT 06901, ☎, 800/ 225–2380 or FAX 203/ 359–3669), and **Uniquely Europe** (2819 First Ave., #280, Seattle, WA 98121, ☎ 206/ 441–8682 or 800/426– 3610).

ART AND ARCHITECTURE➤ Contact the **Smithsonian Institution's Study Tours and Seminars** (1100 Jefferson Dr. SW, Room 3045, Washington, DC 20560, ☎ 202/357– 4700) for programs on Germany's artistic achievements.

BARGES/RIVER CRUISES➤ Contact **Köln-Düsseldorfer (KD) Rivers Cruises of Europe** (2500 Westchester Ave., Purchase, NY 10577, ☎ 914/ 696–3600 or 800/346– 6525, or 323 Geary, San Francisco, CA 94102, ☎ 415/392– 8817 or 800/858– 8587), or **Abercrombie & Kent** (*see* Group Tours, *above*) for itineraries throughout Germany. For a cruise on the Mosel River, contact **Etoile de Champagne** (88 Broad St., Boston, MA 02110, ☎ 800/280–1492).

BEER➤ **MIR Corp** (85 South Washington St., #210, Seattle, WA 98104, ☎ 206/624– 7289 or 800/424– 7289) and **Value Holidays** (10224 N. Port Washington Rd., Mequon, WI 53092, ☎ 414/241–6373 or 800/558–6850) lead you to Germany's famous breweries. Virtually all the general-interest operators listed above run Oktoberfest tours.

BICYCLING➤ For bike tours through Germany, contact **Backroads** (1516 5th St., Suite L101, Berkeley, CA 94710, ☎ 510/527– 1555 or 800/462– 2848), **Butterfield & Robinson** (70 Bond St., Toronto, Ontario, Canada M5B 1X3, ☎ 416/864–1354 or 800/387–1147), Euro-Bike (Box 990-P, DeKalb, IL 60115, ☎ 800/321–6060 or FAX 815/758–8851), and **Classic Adventures** (Box 153, Hamlin, NY 14464-0153, ☎ 800/ 777–8090, FAX 716/ 964–7297).

CARRIAGE TOURS➤ **Travelwide Tours** (Box 2577, Redwood City, CA 94064, ☎ 415/ 361–1222 or 800/254– 9433) will take you through Bavaria in a horse-drawn coach.

FOOD AND WINE➤ **The German Wine Academy** (c/o German Wine Information Bureau, 79 Madison Ave., New York, NY 10016, ☎ 212/213–7028) has seminars in English designed to improve your knowledge and enjoyment of German wine.

HORSEBACK RIDING➤ **FITS Equestrian** (685 Lateen Rd., Solvang, CA 93463, ☎ 805/ 688–9494 or 800/ 6566–3487) leads eight-day rides through the Black Forest.

MOTORCYCLING➤ Beach's Motorcycle Adventures (2763 W. River Parkway, Grand Island, NY 14072, ☎ 716/773–4960, FAX 716/773–5227) can take you on a guided adventure through alpine Germany.

MUSIC➤ **Dailey-Thorp Travel** (330 W. 58th St., New York, NY 10019, ☎ 212/307–1555; book through travel agents) specializes in classical-music and opera programs throughout Germany; its packages include tickets that are otherwise very hard to get. Also try **Keith Prowse Tours** (234 W. 34th St., Suite 1000, New York, NY 10036, ☎ 212/ 398–1430 or 800/669– 8687).

ORGANIZATIONS

The **National Tour Association** (546 E. Main St., Lexington, KY 40508, ☎ 606/ 226–4444 or 800/682– 8886) and **United States Tour Operators Association** (USTOA, 211 E. 51st St., Suite 12B, New York, NY 10022, ☎ 212/750–7371) can provide lists of member operators and information on booking tours.

PUBLICATIONS

Consult the brochure **"Worldwide Tour & Vacation Package Finder"** from the National Tour Operators Association (*see above*) and the Better Business Bureau's **"Tips on Travel Packages"** (publication No. 24-195, $2; 4200 Wilson Blvd., Arlington, VA 22203).

TRAVEL AGENCIES

For names of reputable agencies in your area, contact the **American Society of Travel Agents** (1101 King St., Suite 200, Alexandria, VA 22314, ☎ 703/739– 2782).

U

U.S. GOVERNMENT TRAVEL BRIEFINGS

The U.S. Department of State's Overseas Citizens Emergency Center (Room 4811, Washington, DC 20520; enclose SASE) issues **Consular Information Sheets,** which cover crime, security, political climate, and health risks as well as embassy locations, entry requirements, currency regulations, and other routine matters. For the latest information, stop in at any U.S. passport office, consulate, or embassy; call the interactive hot line (☎ 202/647–5225 or fax 202/647-3000);

or, with your PC's modem, tap into the Bureau of Consular Affairs' computer bulletin board (☎ 202/647–9225).

V

VISITOR INFORMATION

IN THE UNITED STATES

Contact the **German National Tourist Office** (122 E. 42nd St., New York, NY 10168, ☎ 212/661–7200; 11766 Wilshire Blvd., Suite 750, Los Angeles, CA 90025, ☎ 310/575–9799).

IN CANADA

The **German National Tourist Office** is at 175

Bloor Street East, North Tower, Suite 604, Toronto, Ontario M4W 3R8, ☎ 416/968–1570.

IN THE U.K.

The **German National Tourist Office** is at Nightingale House, 65 Curzon Street, London W1Y 7PE, England, ☎ 0891/600–100 (calls charged at 39p per minute cheap rate, 49p per minute other times).

WEATHER

For current conditions and forecasts, plus the local time and helpful travel tips, call the **Weather Channel Connection** (☎ 900/932–8437; 95¢ per minute) from a touch-tone phone.

SMART TRAVEL TIPS A TO Z

*Basic Information on Traveling in Germany and
Savvy Tips to Make Your Trip a Breeze*

The more you travel, the more you know about how to make trips run like clockwork. To help make your travels hassle-free, Fodor's editors have rounded up dozens of tips from our contributors and travel experts all over the world, as well as basic information on visiting Germany. For names of organizations to contact and publications that can give you more information, *see* Important Contacts A to Z, *above*.

A

AIR TRAVEL

If time is an issue, **always look for nonstop flights,** which require no change of plane and make no stops. If possible, **avoid connecting flights,** which stop at least once and can involve a change of plane, although the flight number remains the same; if the first leg is late, the second waits.

CUTTING COSTS

The Sunday travel section of most newspapers is a good source of deals.

MAJOR AIRLINES➤ The least-expensive airfares from the major airlines are priced for round-trip travel and are subject to restrictions.

You must usually **book in advance and buy the ticket within 24 hours** to get cheaper fares, and you may have to **stay over a Saturday night.** The lowest fare is subject to availability, and only a small percentage of the plane's total seats are sold at that price. It's good to **call a number of airlines—and when you are quoted a good price, book it on the spot**—the same fare on the same flight may not be available the next day. Airlines generally allow you to change your return date for a $25 to $50 fee, but most low-fare tickets are nonrefundable. However, if you don't use it, you can apply the cost toward the purchase price of a new ticket, again for a small charge.

CONSOLIDATORS➤ Consolidators, who buy tickets at reduced rates from scheduled airlines, sell them at prices below the lowest available from the airlines directly—usually without advance restrictions. Sometimes you can even get your money back if you need to return the ticket. Carefully read the fine print detailing penalties for changes and cancellations. If you doubt the reliability of a consol-idator, **confirm your reservation with the airline.**

WITHIN GERMANY

Germany's internal air network is excellent, with frequent flights linking all major cities. Services are operated by **Deutsche BA,** a British Airways subsidiary, **Lufthansa,** and **LTU.** In addition, small airlines operate services between a limited number of northern cities and the East and North Frisian islands, though many of these flights operate only in the summer.

Lufthansa also offers train service from Köln to the Frankfurt airport, acting as a supplement to existing air services. Only passengers holding air tickets may use the train. It is cheaper than normal rail travel, and luggage is automatically transferred to your plane on arrival at the airport. Service is first class. German Rail operates a similar service called "Rail and Fly" (*see* Rail Travel, *below*), and most trains that stop at Frankfurt City also stop at Frankfurt airport.

ALOFT

AIRLINE FOOD➤ If you hate airline food, **ask for special meals when booking.** These can be vegetarian, low-choles-terol, or kosher, for example; commonly prepared to order in smaller quantities than standard catered fare, they can be tastier.

JET LAG➤ To avoid this syndrome, which occurs when travel disrupts your body's natural cycles, try to maintain a normal routine. At night, **get some sleep.** By day, move about the cabin to **stretch your legs, eat light meals, and drink water—not alcohol.**

SMOKING➤ Smoking is banned on all flights within the U.S. of less than six hours' duration and on all Canadian flights; the ban also applies to domestic segments of interna-tional flights aboard U.S. and foreign carri-ers. Delta has banned smoking system-wide. On U.S. carriers flying to Germany and other destinations abroad, a seat in a no-smoking section must be pro-vided for every passen-ger who requests one, and the section must be enlarged if necessary to accommodate such passengers, as long as they have complied with the airline's dead-line for check-in and seat assignment. If smoking bothers you, **request a seat far from the smoking section.**

Foreign airlines are exempt from these rules but do provide no-smoking sections (British Airways has banned smoking); some nations have banned smoking on all domestic flights, and others may ban smoking on some

flights. Talks continue on the feasibility of broadening no-smoking policies.

B

BOAT TRIPS

EurailPasses and Ger-man Rail Passes are valid on all services of the KD German Rhine Line and on the Mosel between Trier and Koblenz. (If you use the fast hydrofoil, a supple-mentary fee is required.) Regular rail tickets are also accepted, meaning that you can **go one way by ship and return by train.** All you have to do is pay a small surcharge to KD Rhine Line and get the ticket endorsed at one of the landing-stage offices. But note that you have to buy the rail ticket first and *then* get it changed.

KD Rhine Line also offers a program of luxury cruises along the Rhine, Main, Mosel, Elbe, and Danube rivers. The cruises include four-day trips from Frankfurt to Trier (from DM 660), five-day journeys from Amsterdam to Basel in Switzerland, and seven-day holidays from Passau to Budapest (from DM 1,320). Prices include all meals. The cruises are supple-mented by trips of one day or less on the Rhine and Mosel. During the summer there are good services between Bonn and Koblenz and be-tween Koblenz and Bingen; both trips take around five hours.

The cruises, especially for the newer Elbe routes, are in great

demand, so reservations are necessary several months in advance.

BUSINESS HOURS

BANKS

Times vary from state to state and city to city, but banks are generally open weekdays from 8:30 or 9 to 2 or 3 (5 or 6 on Thursday), with a lunch break of about an hour. Branches at airports and main train stations open as early as 6:30 AM and close as late as 10:30 PM.

MUSEUMS

Most museums are open from Tuesday to Sunday 9–6. Some close for an hour or more at lunch, and some are open on Monday. Many stay open late on Thursday.

SHOPS

Most shops are open 9 or 9:15–6:30 weekdays and until 2 PM on Saturday, except for the first Saturday in the month, when the bigger stores stay open until 6 in winter and 4 in summer. Many shops also remain open on Thursday evening until 8:30.

BUS TRAVEL

Germany has good local bus services, but no proper nationwide network like Grey-hound. A large portion of services are operated by the railways (Bahn-bus) and are closely integrated with train services, while on less busy rail lines, services are run by buses in off-peak periods—normally midday and weekends. Rail tickets are valid on these services.

One of the best services is the Romantic Road bus between Würzburg (with connections to and from Frankfurt and Wiesbaden) and Füssen (with connections to and from Munich, Augsburg, and Garmisch-Parten-kirchen). This is an all-reserved-seats bus with a stewardess, offering one- or two-day tours in each direction in summer, leaving in the morning and arriving in the evening. Details and reservations are available from Deutsche Touring (*see above*) or big city tourist offices.

All towns of any size operate their own local buses. For the most part, those link up with local trams (streetcars), electric railway (S-Bahn), and subway (U-Bahn) services. Fares vary according to distance, but a ticket usually allows you to transfer freely between the various forms of transportation. Most cities issue 24-hour tickets at special rates.

C

CAMERAS, CAMCORDERS, AND COMPUTERS

LAPTOPS

Before you depart, **check your portable computer's battery,** because you may be asked at security to turn on the computer to prove that it is what it appears to be. At the airport, you may prefer to **request a manual inspection,** although security X-rays do not harm hard-disk or floppy-disk storage.

Also, **register your foreign-made laptop with U.S. Customs.** If your laptop is U.S.-made, call the consulate of the country you'll be visiting to find out whether it should be registered with local customs upon arrival. You may want to **find out about repair facilities at your destination** in case you need them.

PHOTOGRAPHY

If your camera is new or if you haven't used it for a while, **shoot and develop a few rolls of film** before you leave. Always **store film in a cool, dry place**—never in the car's glove compartment or on the shelf under the rear window.

Every pass of your film through an X-ray machine increases the risk of clouding. To protect it, carry it in a clear plastic bag and **ask for hand inspection at security.** Such requests are virtually always honored at U.S. airports and are usually accommodated abroad. Don't depend on a lead-lined bag to protect film in checked luggage—the airline may increase the radiation to see what's inside.

VIDEO

Before your trip, **test your camcorder, invest in a skylight filter to protect the lens, and charge the batteries.** (Airport security personnel may ask you to turn on the camcorder to prove that it's what it appears to be.) The batteries of most newer camcorders can be recharged with a universal or worldwide AC

adapter charger (or multivoltage converter), usable whether the voltage is 110 or 220. All that's needed is the appropriate plug.

Videotape is not damaged by X-rays, but it may be harmed by the magnetic field of a walk-through metal detector, so **ask that videotapes be hand-checked.** Videotape sold in Germany is based on the PAL standard, which is different from the one used in the United States. You will not be able to view your tapes through the local TV set or view movies bought there in your home VCR. Blank tapes bought in Germany can be used for camcorder taping, but they are pricey. Some U.S. audiovisual shops convert foreign tapes to U.S. standards; contact an electronics dealer to find the nearest.

THE CHANNEL TUNNEL

The Channel Tunnel provides the fastest route across the Channel—25 minutes from Folkestone to Calais, or 60 minutes from highway to highway. It consists of two large, 50-kilometer-long (31-mile-long) tunnels for trains, one in each direction, linked by a smaller service tunnel running between them.

Le Shuttle, a special car, bus, and truck train, operates continuously, with trains departing every 15 minutes at peak times and at least once an hour through the night. No reservations are necessary, although tickets may be purchased in advance from travel agents. Most passengers travel in their own car, staying with the vehicle throughout the "crossing," with progress updates via radio and display screens. Motorcyclists park their bikes in a separate section with its own passenger compartment, and foot passengers must book passage by coach. At press time, prices for a one-day round-trip ticket began at £107–£154 for a car and its occupants. Prices for a five-day round-trip ticket began at £115.

Eurostar operates high-speed passenger-only trains, which whisk riders between new stations in Paris (Gare du Nord) and London (Waterloo) in 3 hours and between London and Brussels (Midi) in 3¼ hours. At press time, fares were $154 for a one-way, first-class ticket and $123 for an economy fare.

The Tunnel is reached from Exit 11a of the M20/A20. Tickets for either Tunnel service can be purchased in advance (*see* Important Contacts A to Z, *above*.)

Drivers purchase tickets from toll booths, then pass through frontier control before loading onto the next available service. Unloading at Calais takes 8 minutes. At press time, promotional prices for a one-day round-trip ticket began at £49 for a small car and its occupants. Prices for a five-day round-trip ticket began

at £75. However, fares were expected to rise as demand for the tunnel increased.

CHILDREN AND TRAVEL

Almost every city in Germany has its own children's theater, and the country's puppet theaters rank among the best in the world. Many movie theaters also screen films for children, normally in the morning and afternoon. Playgrounds are around virtually every corner, and about a half dozen major theme parks around the country now entertain the younger ones. *See the* What to See and Do with Children *sections in* Chapters 3–18.

BABY-SITTING

For recommended local sitters, **check with your hotel desk.** Updated lists of well-screened baby-sitters are also available from most local tourist offices. Rates are usually about DM 25 per hour.

Many large department stores in Germany provide baby-sitting facilities or areas where children can play while their parents go shopping.

DRIVING

If you are renting a car, **arrange for a car seat when you reserve.** Sometimes they're free.

FLYING

On domestic flights, children under 2 not occupying a seat travel free, and older children currently travel on the "lowest applicable" adult fare. Some routes

are considered neither international nor domestic and have still other rules.

BAGGAGE➤ In general, the adult baggage allowance applies for children paying half or more of the adult fare. Before departure, **ask about carry-on allowances** if you are traveling with an infant. In general, those paying 10% of the adult fare are allowed one carry-on bag, not to exceed 70 pounds or 45 inches (length + width + height), and a collapsible stroller; you may be allowed less if the flight is full.

SAFETY SEATS➤ According to the FAA, it's a good idea to **use safety seats aloft.** Airline policy varies. U.S. carriers allow FAA-approved models, but airlines usually require that you buy a ticket, even if your child would otherwise ride free, because the seats must be strapped into regular passenger seats. Foreign carriers may not allow infant seats, may charge the child's rather than the infant's fare for their use, or may require you to hold your baby during takeoff and landing, thus defeating the seat's purpose.

FACILITIES➤ When making your reservation, **ask for children's meals and a freestanding bassinet** if you need them; the latter are available only to those with seats at the bulkhead, where there's enough legroom. If you don't need the bassinet, **think twice before**

requesting bulkhead seats—the only storage for in-flight necessities is in the inconveniently distant overhead bins.

LODGING

Most hotels allow children under a certain age to stay in their parents' room at no extra charge, while others charge them as extra adults; be sure to **ask about the cut-off age.**

CUSTOMS AND DUTIES

IN GERMANY

Since a single, unrestricted market took effect within the European Union (EU) early in 1993, there are no longer restrictions for citizens of the 12 member countries traveling between EU countries. For citizens of non-EU countries and anyone entering Germany from outside the Union, the following limitations apply.

On goods obtained (duty- and tax-paid) within another EU country, you are allowed (1) 800 cigarettes or 400 cigarillos or 200 cigars or 1 kg. of tobacco; (2) plus 10 liters of spirits, 20 liters of fortified wine, 90 liters of wine, and 110 liters of beer; (5) other goods to the value of DM 780.

On goods obtained anywhere outside the EU or for goods purchased in a duty-free shop within an EU country, you are allowed (1) 200 cigarettes or 100 cigarillos or 50 cigars or 250 grams of tobacco (twice that if you live outside of Europe); (2) 2 liters of still table wine plus (3) 1 liter of spirits over 22% volume or 2 liters of spirits under 22% volume (fortified and sparkling wines) or 2 more liters of table wine; (4) 60 milliliters of perfume and 250 milliliters of toilet water; (5) other goods to the value of DM 115.

Tobacco and alcohol allowances are for visitors age 17 and over. Other items intended for personal use can be imported and exported freely. There are no restrictions on the import and export of German currency.

BACK HOME

IN THE U.S.➣ You may bring home $400 worth of foreign goods duty-free if you've been out of the country for at least 48 hours and haven't already used the $400 exemption, or any part of it, in the past 30 days.

Travelers 21 or older may bring back one liter of alcohol duty-free, provided the beverage laws of the state through which they reenter the United States allow it. In addition, 100 non-Cuban cigars and 200 cigarettes are allowed, regardless of your age. Antiques and works of art more than 100 years old are duty-free.

Travelers may mail packages valued at up to $200 to themselves and up to $100 to others duty-free, with a limit of one parcel per addressee per day (and no alcohol or tobacco products or perfume valued at more than $5); outside, identify the package as being for personal use or an unsolicited gift, specifying the contents and their retail value. Mailed items do not count as part of your exemption.

IN CANADA➣ Once per calendar year, when you've been out of Canada for at least seven days, you may bring in C$300 worth of goods duty-free. If you've been away less than seven days but more than 48 hours, the duty-free exemption drops to C$100 but can be claimed any number of times (as can a C$20 duty-free exemption for absences of 24 hours or more). You cannot combine the yearly and 48-hour exemptions, use the C$300 exemption only partially (to save the balance for a later trip), or pool exemptions with family members. Goods claimed under the C$300 exemption may follow you by mail; those claimed under the lesser exemptions must accompany you.

Alcohol and tobacco products may be included in the yearly and 48-hour exemptions but not in the 24-hour exemption. If you meet the age requirements of the province through which you reenter Canada, you may bring in, duty-free, 1.14 liters (40 imperial ounces) of wine or liquor *or* 24 12-ounce cans or bottles of beer or ale. If you are 16 or older, you may bring in, duty-free, 200 cigarettes, 50 cigars or cigarillos, and 400 tobacco sticks or 400 grams of manufactured tobacco. Alcohol and tobacco must accompany you on your return.

An unlimited number of gifts valued up to C$60 each may be mailed to Canada duty-free. These do not count as part of your exemption. Label the package "Unsolicited Gift— Value under $60." Alcohol and tobacco are excluded.

IN THE U.K.➤ If your journey was wholly within EU countries, you no longer need to pass through customs when you return to the United Kingdom. If you plan to bring large quantities of alcohol or tobacco, check in advance on EU limits.

D

DINING

The choice of eating places in Germany is varied both in style and price. The most sophisticated spots—and the most expensive—are in cities. At the opposite end of the scale, almost every street of the old West Germany has its *Gaststätte,* a sort of combination diner and pub, and every village its *Gasthof,* or inn, and such places are almost as easy to find in eastern Germany. The emphasis in the Gaststätte and Gasthof is on *gutbürgerliche Küche,* or good home cooking—simple food, wholesome rather than sophisticated, at reasonable prices. These are also places where people meet in the evening

for a chat, a beer, and a game of cards. They normally serve hot meals from 11:30 AM to 9 or 10 PM; many places stop serving hot meals between 2 and 6 PM, although you can still order cold dishes. Lunch rather than dinner is the main meal in Germany, a fact reflected in the almost universal appearance of a *Tageskarte,* or suggested menu, every lunchtime. And at a cost of less than DM 20, in either a Gaststätte or Gasthof, for soup, a main course, and simple dessert (though this is not always offered), it's an excellent value. Coffee is generally available, although quality may vary, and it's perfectly acceptable to go into a Gaststätte or country pub and order just a pot of coffee outside busy lunch periods. Some, though not all, expensive restaurants also offer a table d'hôte (suggested or special) daily menu. Prices will be much higher than in a Gaststätte or Gasthof, but considerably cheaper than à la carte.

Regional specialties are given in the Dining sections of individual chapters. For names of German foods and dishes, *see the* Menu Guide *at the end of this book.*

BUDGET EATING

TIPS

BUTCHER SHOPS➤

Known as *Metzgerei,* these often have a corner that serves warm snacks. The **Vinzenz-Murr** chain in Munich

and Bavaria has particularly good-value food. Try *Warmer Leberkäs mit Kartoffelsalat,* a typical Bavarian specialty, which is a sort of baked meat loaf with sweet mustard and potato salad. In north Germany, try *Bouletten,* small hamburgers, or *Currywurst,* sausages in a piquant curry sauce.

DEPARTMENT STORES➤ For lunch, restaurants in local department stores (*Kaufhäuser*) are especially recommended for wholesome, appetizing, and inexpensive food. **Kaufhof, Karstadt, Horton,** and **Hertie** are names to note, as well as the enormous **KaDeWe** in Berlin.

FAST FOOD➤ A number of fast-food chains exist all over the country. The best are **Wienerwald, McDonald's, Pizza Hut,** and **Burger King.** There are also **Nordsee** fish bars, serving hot and cold fish dishes.

FOREIGN RESTAURANTS➤ Germany has a vast selection of moderately priced Turkish, Italian, Greek, Chinese, and Balkan restaurants. All offer good value. Italian restaurants are about the most popular of all specialty restaurants in Germany—the pizza-to-go is as much a part of the average German's diet as *Bratwurst* or a hamburger. You'll find that Chinese restaurants in particular offer special lunch menus.

PICNICS➤ Buy some wine or beer and some cold cuts and rolls (*Brötchen*) from a department store, supermarket, or deli-catessen and turn lunchtimes into picnics. You'll not only save money, but you'll also be able to enjoy Germany's beautiful scenery. Or leave out the beer and take your picnic to a beer garden, sit down at one of the long wood tables, and order a *Mass* (liter) of beer.

STAND-UP SNACK BARS➤ Often located in pedestrian zones, *Imbiss* (snack) stands can be found in almost every busy shopping street, in parking lots, train stations, and near markets. They serve *Würste* (sausages), grilled, roasted, or boiled, of every shape and size, and rolls filled with cheese, cold meat, or fish. Prices range from DM 3 to DM 6 per portion.

RATINGS

The restaurants in our listings are divided by price into four categories: $$$$, $$$, $$, and $. See Dining *in individual chapters for specific prices.* Nearly all restaurants display their menus, with prices, outside; all prices shown will include tax and service charge. Prices for wine also include tax and service charge.

FOR TRAVELERS
WITH DISABILITIES

Nearly 100 German cities and towns issue special guides for visitors with disabilities, which offer information, usually in German, about how to get around destinations and

suggestions for places to visit.

All the major hotel chains (Hilton, Sheraton, Marriott, Holiday Inn, Steigenberger, and Kempinski) have special facilities for guests with disabilities, including specially equipped and furnished rooms. Some leading privately owned hotels also cater to travelers with disabilities; local tourist offices can provide lists of these hotels and additional information.

The Deutsche Bahn (German Rail) provides a complete range of services and facilities for travelers with disabilities. All InterCity Express (ICE) and InterRegio trains and most EuroCity and InterCity trains have special areas for wheelchair users. Seat and wheelchair-space reservations are free of charge for wheelchair users. The German Red Cross and a welfare service called the Bahnhofs-Mission (Railway Station Mission) have support facilities at all major and many smaller, regional stations. They organize assistance in boarding, leaving, and changing trains and also help with reservations.

When discussing accessibility with an operator or reservationist, **ask hard questions.** Are there any stairs, inside *or* out? Are there grab bars next to the toilet *and* in the shower/tub? How wide is the doorway to the room? To the bathroom? For the most extensive facilities, **opt for newer facilities,**

which more often have been designed with access in mind. Older properties or ships must usually be retrofitted and may offer more limited facilities as a result. Be sure to **discuss your needs before booking.**

DISCOUNT CLUBS

Travel clubs offer members unsold space on airplanes, cruise ships, and package tours at as much as 50% below regular prices. Membership may include a regular bulletin or access to a toll-free hot line giving details of available trips departing from three or four days to several months in the future. Most also offer 50% discounts off hotel rack rates. Before booking with a club, **make sure the hotel or other supplier isn't offering a better deal.**

DRIVING

Entry formalities for motorists are few: All you need is proof of insurance, an international car-registration document, and a US or Canadian driver's license (an international license is helpful, but not a must). If you or your car are from an EU country, Norway, or Switzerland, all you need is your domestic license and proof of insurance. *All* foreign cars must have a country sticker.

Roads in the western part of the country are generally excellent, but many surfaces in eastern Germany, where an urgent improvement program is under way, are in poor condition.

ADAC and AvD operate tow trucks on all autobahns; they also have emergency telephones every 1½ miles/2.7 km. On minor roads, go to the nearest call box and dial 19211. Ask, in English, for "road service assistance," if you have to use the service. Help is free, but all materials must be paid for.

FROM THE UNITED KINGDOM BY CAR

It is recommended that drivers **get a green card** from their insurance companies, which extends insurance coverage to driving in Europe. Extra breakdown insurance and vehicle and personal security coverage is also advisable.

FUEL AVAILABILITY AND COSTS

Gasoline (petrol) costs are between DM 1.10 and DM 1.60 per liter. As part of antipollution efforts, most German cars now run on leadfree fuel. Some models use diesel fuel, so if you are renting a car, find out which fuel the car takes. Some older vehicles cannot take unleaded fuel. German filling stations are highly competitive and bargains are often available if you shop around, but *not* at autobahn filling stations. Self-service, or *SB-Tanken*, stations are cheapest. Pumps marked *Bleifrei* contain unleaded gas.

SCENIC ROUTES

Germany boasts many specially designated tourist roads, all covering areas of particular scenic and/or historic interest. The longest is the Deutsche Ferienstrasse, the German Holiday Road, which runs from the Baltic to the Alps, a distance of around 1,070 miles. The most famous, however, and also the oldest, is the Romantische Strasse, the Romantic Road, which runs from Würzburg in Franconia to Füssen in the Alps, covering around 355 kilometers (220 miles) and passing through some of the most historic cities and towns in Germany. (*See* Chapter 8 for full details.)

Among other notable touring routes—all with expressive and descriptive names—are the Grüne Küstenstrasse (Green Coast Road), running along the North Sea coast from Denmark to Emden; the Burgenstrasse (Castle Road), running from Mannheim to Nürnberg; the Deutsche Weinstrasse (German Wine Road), running through the heartland of the German wine country; and the Deutsche Alpenstrasse (German Alpine Road), running the length of the country's south border. In addition, there are many other equally delightful, if less well-known, routes, such as the Märchenstrasse (Fairy-tale Road), the Schwarzwälder Hochstrasse (Black Forest High Road), and the Deutsche Edelsteinstrasse (German Gem Road).

RULES OF THE ROAD

In Germany you drive on the right, and road signs give distances in kilometers. There is no speed limit on autobahns, although drivers are advised to keep below 130 kph (80 mph). Speed limits on non-autobahn country roads vary from 80 to 100 kph (50 to 60 mph). Alcohol limits on drivers are equivalent to two small beers or a quarter of a liter of wine. Note that seat belts must be worn at all times by front- *and* back-seat passengers.

H

HEALTH CONCERNS

Sanitation and health standards in Germany are as high as those anywhere in the world, and there are no serious health risks associated with travel there. No inoculations are required.

HOLIDAYS

The following national holidays are observed in Germany: January 1; January 6 (Epiphany, Bavaria and Baden-Württemberg only); April 5 (Good Friday); April 8 (Easter Monday); May 1 (Workers' Day); May 16 (Ascension); May 27 (Pentecost Monday); June 6 (Corpus Christi, south Germany only); August 15 (Assumption Day, Bavaria and Saarland only); October 3 (German Unity Day); November 1 (All Saints' Day); November 20 (Day of Prayer and

Repentance); December 24–26 (Christmas).

I
INSURANCE

Travel insurance can protect your investment, replace your luggage and its contents, or provide for medical coverage should you fall ill during your trip. Most tour operators, travel agents, and insurance agents sell specialized health-and-accident, flight, trip-cancellation, and luggage insurance as well as comprehensive policies with some or all of these features. Before you make any purchase, **review your existing health and homeowner's policies** to find out whether they cover expenses incurred while traveling.

BAGGAGE

Airline liability for your baggage is limited to $1,250 per person on domestic flights. On international flights, the airlines' liability is $9.07 per pound or $20 per kilogram for checked baggage (roughly $640 per 70-pound bag) and $400 per passenger for unchecked baggage. However, this excludes valuable items such as jewelry and cameras that are listed in your ticket's fine print. You can buy additional insurance from the airline at check-in, but first **see if your homeowner's policy covers lost luggage.**

FLIGHT

You should **think twice before buying flight insurance.** Often pur-
chased as a last-minute impulse at the airport, it pays a lump sum when a plane crashes, either to a beneficiary if the insured dies or sometimes to a surviving passenger who loses eyesight or a limb. Supplementing the airlines' coverage described in the limits-of-liability paragraphs on your ticket, it's expensive and basically unnecessary. Charging an airline ticket to a major credit card often automatically entitles you to coverage and may also include travel by bus, train, and ship.

HEALTH

If your own health insurance policy does not cover you outside the U.S., consider buying supplemental medical coverage. It can cover $1,000–$150,000 worth of medical and/or dental care required as a result of an accident or illness during a trip. These policies also may include a personal-accident, or death-and-dismemberment, provision, which pays a lump sum ranging from $15,000 to $500,000 to your beneficiaries if you die or to you if you lose one or more limbs or your eyesight, and a medical-assistance provision, which may either reimburse you for the cost of referrals, evacuation, or repatriation and other services, or may automatically enroll you as a member of a particular medical-assistance company. (*See* Health Issues *in* Important Contacts A to Z, *above.*)

FOR U.K. TRAVELERS➤ You can buy an annual travel-insurance policy valid for most vacations during the year in which it's purchased. If you go this route, make sure it covers you if you have a preexisting medical condition or are pregnant.

TRIP

Without insurance, you will lose all or most of your money if you must cancel your trip due to illness or any other reason. Especially if your airline ticket, cruise, or package tour is nonrefundable and cannot be changed, it's essential that you **buy trip-cancellation-and-interruption insurance.** When considering how much coverage you need, look for a policy that will cover the cost of your trip plus the nondiscounted price of a one-way airline ticket should you need to return home early. Read the fine print carefully, especially sections defining "family member" and "preexisting medical conditions." Also **consider default or bankruptcy insurance,** which protects you against a supplier's failure to deliver. However, such policies often do not cover default by a travel agency, tour operator, airline, or cruise line if you bought your tour and the coverage directly from the firm in question.

L
LANGUAGE

The Germans are great linguists and you'll find that English is spoken in virtually all hotels, restaurants, airports, stations, museums, and other places of interest. However, English is not always widely spoken in rural areas; this is especially true of the eastern part of Germany.

Unless you speak fluent German, you may find some of the regional dialects hard to follow, particularly in Bavaria. While most Germans can speak "High," or standard, German, some older country people are only able to speak in their dialect.

LODGING

The standard of German hotels—from sophisticated luxury spots (of which the country has more than its fair share) to the humblest country inn—is very high. Rates vary enormously, though not disproportionately so in comparison with other north European countries. You can nearly always expect courteous and polite service and clean and comfortable rooms. Larger hotels often have no-smoking rooms or even no-smoking floors, so it's always worth asking for one when you check in.

In addition to hotels proper, the country has numerous *Gasthöfe* or *Gasthäuser,* which are country inns that serve food and also have rooms; pensions, or *Fremdenheime* (guest houses); and, at the lowest end of the scale, *Fremdenzimmer,* meaning simply "rooms," normally in private houses (look for the sign reading ZIMMER FREI or ZU VERMIETEN on

a green background, meaning "to rent"; a red sign reading BESETZT means that there are no vacancies).

Lists of German hotels are available from the German National Tourist Office and all regional and local tourist offices. (Most hotels have restaurants, but those listed as *Garni* will provide breakfast only.) Tourist offices will also make bookings for you at a nominal fee, but they may have difficulty doing so after 4 PM in high season and on weekends, so don't wait until too late in the day to begin looking for your accommodations. (If you do get stuck, ask someone who looks like a native—a mail carrier, police officer, or waiter, for example—for directions to a house renting a Fremdenzimmer or a Gasthof; in rural areas especially you'll find that people are genuinely helpful).

Many major American hotel chains—Hilton, Sheraton, Holiday Inn, Radisson, Marriott, Ramada, Preferred—have hotels in the larger German cities. European chains are similarly well represented.

The hotels in our listings are divided by price into four categories: **$$$$, $$$, $$**, and **$**. *See* Lodging *in individual chapters for specific prices.* Note that there is no official grading system for hotels in Germany. Rates are by no means inflexible, and depend very much on supply and demand; you can

save money by inquiring about reductions. Many resort hotels offer substantial ones in winter, except in the Alps, where rates often rise then. Likewise, many **$$$$** and **$$$** hotels in cities cut their prices on weekends and when business is quiet. Always be careful about trying to book late in the day at peak times. During trade fairs (most commonly held in the spring and fall), rates in city hotels can rise appreciably. Breakfast is usually but not always included. Inexpensive rooms may have neither shower nor tub. **Ask about breakfast and bathing facilities** when booking. Usually you pay more for the tub. When you arrive, if you don't like the room you're offered, ask to see another.

APARTMENT AND VILLA RENTALS

If you want a home base that's roomy enough for a family and comes with cooking facilities, **consider a furnished rental.** It's generally cost-wise, too, although not always—some rentals are luxury properties, economical only when your party is large. Home-exchange directories do list rentals—often second homes owned by prospective house swappers—and some services search for a house or apartment for you (even a castle if that's your fancy) and handle the paperwork. Some send an illustrated catalogue and others send photographs of specific properties, sometimes at a charge;

up-front registration fees may apply.

Bungalows or apartments (*Ferienhäuser* or *Ferienwohnungen*), usually accommodating two to eight people, can be rented throughout Germany. Rates are low, with reductions for longer stays. There is usually an extra charge for gas and electricity, and sometimes one for water. There is also normally a charge for linens, though you may also bring your own.

CAMPING

Campsites—some 2,000 in all—are scattered across the length and breadth of Germany. The DCC, or German Camping Club (*see* Lodging *in* Important Contacts A to Z, *above*) produces an annual listing of 1,600 sites; it also details sites where trailers and mobile homes can be rented. Similarly, the German Automobile Association ADAC, *see* Driving in Important Contacts A to Z, *above*) publishes a listing of all campsites located at autobahn exits. In addition, the German National Tourist Office publishes a comprehensive and graded listing of campsites.

Sites are generally open from May to September, though about 400 are open year-round for the very rugged. Most sites get crowded during high season, however. Prices range from around DM 10 to DM 25 for a car, trailer, and two adults; less for tents. If you want to camp elsewhere, you must get permission

from the landowner beforehand; ask the police if you can't track him or her down. Drivers of mobile homes may park for one night only on roadsides and in autobahn parking-lot areas, but may not set up camping equipment there.

CASTLE HOTELS

Of comparable interest and value are Germany's castle, or *Schloss*, hotels, all privately owned and run and all long on atmosphere. A number of the simpler ones may lack some amenities, but the majority combine four-star luxury with valuable antique furnishings, four-poster beds, stone passageways, and a baronial atmosphere. Some offer full resort facilities (tennis, swimming pools, horseback riding, hunting, and fishing). Nearly all are away from cities and towns.

FARM VACATIONS

The *Urlaub auf dem Bauernhof*, or vacation down on the farm, has increased dramatically in popularity throughout Germany over the past five years, and almost every regional tourist office now produces a brochure listing farms in its area that offer bed-and-breakfasts, apartments, and entire farmhouses to rent.

HOME EXCHANGE

If you would like to find a house, an apartment, or other vacation property to exchange for your own while on vacation, **become a**

member of a home-exchange organization, which will send you its annual directories listing available exchanges and will include your own listing in at least one of them. Arrangements for the actual exchange are made by the two parties to it, not by the organization.

ROMANTIK HOTELS

Among the most delightful places to stay—and eat—in Germany are the aptly named Romantik Hotels and Restaurants. The Romantik group now has establishments throughout northern Europe (and even a few in the United States), with more than 60 in Germany. All are in atmospheric and historic buildings—a precondition of membership—and are personally run by the owners, with the emphasis on excellent food and service. Prices vary considerably, but in general represent good value, particularly the special-weekends and short-holiday rates. A three- or four-day stay, for example, with one main meal, is available at about DM 300 to DM 400 per person.

In addition, German Rail offers a special "Romantik Hotel Rail" program, which, in conjunction with a German Rail Tourist Ticket, gives nine days' unlimited travel. You don't need to plan your route in advance—only your first night's accommodation needs to be reserved before you leave. The remaining nights can be reserved as you go. The package also includes sightseeing trips, a Rhine/Mosel cruise, bicycle rentals, and the like.

SPAS

Taking the waters in Germany, whether for curing the body or merely beautifying it, has been popular since Roman times. There are more than 300 health resorts and mineral springs in the country—the word *Bad* before the name of a place usually means it's a spa—offering treatments, normally at fairly high prices. Although spas exist in eastern Germany, most are run down and not highly recommended.

There are four main groups of spas and health resorts: (1) the mineral and moorland spas, where treatments are based on natural warm-water springs; (2) those by the sea on the Baltic and North Sea coasts; (3) hydropathic spas, which use an invigorating process developed during the 19th century; and (4) climatic health resorts, which depend on their climates—usually mountainous—for their health-giving properties.

The average cost for three weeks of treatment is from DM 3,000 to DM 5,000; for four weeks, DM 3,500 to DM 6,000. This includes board and lodging, doctors' fees, treatments, and tax.

M
MAIL

POSTAL RATES

Airmail letters to the United States and Canada cost DM 3; postcards cost DM 2. All letters to the United Kingdom cost DM 1; postcards cost 80 pfennigs.

RECEIVING MAIL

You can arrange to have mail sent to you in care of any German post office; have the envelope marked "Post-lagernd." This service is free. Alternatively, have mail sent to any American Express office in Germany. There's no charge to cardholders, holders of American Express traveler's checks, or anyone who has booked a vacation with American Express. Otherwise, you pay DM 2 per collection (not per item).

MEDICAL ASSISTANCE

No one plans to get sick while traveling, but it happens, so **consider signing up with a medical assistance company.** These outfits provide referrals, emergency evacuation or repatriation, 24-hour telephone hot lines for medical consultation, dispatch of medical personnel, relay of medical records, cash for emergencies, and other personal and legal assistance.

MONEY AND EXPENSES

The unit of currency in Germany is the Deutschmark (DM),

and it's divided into 100 pfennigs (pf). There are bills of 5 (rare), 10, 20, 50, 100, 200, 500, 1000 marks and coins of 1, 2, 5, 10, and 50 pf and 1, 2, and 5 marks.

ATMS

Cirrus, Plus, and many other networks connecting automated-teller machines operate internationally. Chances are that you can **use your bank card at ATMs** to withdraw money from an account and get cash advances on a credit-card account if your card has been programmed with a personal identification number, or PIN. Before leaving home, **check frequency limits** for withdrawals and cash advances and **ask whether your card's PIN must be reprogrammed** for use in Germany. Four digits are commonly used overseas. Note that Discover is accepted only in the United States.

On cash advances you are charged interest from the day you receive the money whether from an ATM or a teller. Although transaction fees for ATM withdrawals abroad may be higher than fees for withdrawals at home, Cirrus and Plus exchange rates are excellent because they are based on wholesale rates only offered by major banks.

COSTS

Western Germany has an admirably high standard of living, and eastern Germany's prices are rapidly rising, making the country expensive for visitors, particularly those who spend time in the cities. Lots of things—gas, food, hotels, and trains, to name but a few—are more expensive than in the United States.

A way to cut your budget is to **visit less-known cities and towns and avoid summer and winter resorts.** All along the Main and Neckar rivers, for example, you will find small towns as charming as, but significantly less expensive than, the likes of Rothenburg and Heidelberg; similarly, Westphalia offers atmosphere but lower prices than the fabled towns and cities of the Rhine. Wine lovers should explore the Palatinate instead of the classical Rhine-Mosel tour. Ski enthusiasts would do well to investigate the advantages of the Harz and Eifel mountains, the Bavarian Oberpfalz, and the Bayerischer Wald in Lower (East) Bavaria.

The five new states (Saxony, Thuringia, Mecklenburg, Saxon-Anhalt, Brandenburg) of former East Germany still have a lower standard of living than does old West Germany. Outside large cities you will find such things as public transportation and dining in moderate restaurants cheaper than they are in, say, the Black Forest or the Rhineland. Prices in leading hotels and restaurants in such places as Dresden and Leipzig already match rates in Frankfurt and Munich. As the stan-

dard of living in the new states continues to rise, so will the cost of traveling in them.

EXCHANGING CURRENCY

For the most favorable rates, **change money at banks.** You won't do as well at exchange booths in airports, rail, and bus stations, or in hotels, restaurants, and stores, although you may find their hours more convenient. To avoid lines at airport exchange booths, **get a small amount of currency before you leave home.**

At press time, the mark stood strong at DM 1.32 to the U.S. dollar, DM .99 to the Canadian dollar, and DM 2.17 to the pound sterling.

TRAVELER'S CHECKS

Whether or not to buy traveler's checks depends on where you are headed; **take cash to rural areas and small towns, traveler's checks to cities.** The most widely recognized are American Express, Citicorp, Thomas Cook, and Visa, which are sold by major commercial banks for 1% to 3% of the checks' face value—it pays to **shop around.** Both American Express and Thomas Cook issue checks that can be counter-signed and used by you or your traveling companion, and they both provide checks, at no extra charge, denominated in marks. You can cash them in banks without paying a fee (which can be as much as 20%) and use them as readily as cash in many hotels,

restaurants, and shops. **Buy a few checks in small denominations** to cash toward the end of your trip so that you won't be left with excess foreign currency. Record the numbers of the checks, crossing them off as you spend them, and keep this information separate from your checks.

WIRING MONEY

You don't have to be a cardholder to send or receive funds through MoneyGram[SM] from American Express. Just go to a MoneyGram agent, located in retail and convenience stores and in American Express Travel Offices. Pay up to $1,000 with cash or a credit card, anything over that in cash. The money can be picked up within 10 minutes in the form of U.S. dollar traveler's checks or local currency at the nearest Money-Gram agent, or, abroad, the nearest American Express Travel Office (in Bonn, ☎ 0228/260–080). There's no limit, and the recipient need only present photo identification. The cost runs from 3% to 10%, depending on the amount sent, the destination, and how you pay.

You can also send money using Western Union. Money sent from the United States or Canada will be available for pickup at agent locations in 100 countries within 15 minutes. Once the money is in the system, it can be picked up at any one of 25,000 locations. Fees range

SMART TRAVEL TIPS

THE GOLD GUIDE / SMART TRAVEL TIPS

from 4% to 10%, depending on the amount you send.

P

PACKAGES AND TOURS

A package or tour to Germany can make your vacation less expensive and more convenient. Firms that sell tours and packages purchase airline seats, hotel rooms, and rental cars in bulk and pass some of the savings on to you. In addition, the best operators have local representatives to help you out at your destination.

A GOOD DEAL?

The more your package or tour includes, the better you can predict the ultimate cost of your vacation. Make sure you know exactly what is included, and **beware of hidden costs.** Are taxes, tips, and service charges included? Transfers and baggage handling? Entertainment and excursions? These can add up.

Most packages and tours are rated deluxe, first-class superior, first class, tourist, and budget. The key difference is usually accommodations. If the package or tour you are considering is priced lower than in your wildest dreams, **be skeptical.** Also, **make sure your travel agent knows the hotels** and other services. Ask about location, room size, beds, and whether there's a pool, room service, or programs for children, if you care

about these. Has your agent been there or sent others you can contact?

BUYER BEWARE

Each year consumers are stranded or lose their money when operators go out of business—even very large ones with excellent reputations. If you can't afford a loss, take the time to **check out the operator**—find out how long the company has been in business, and ask several agents about its reputation. Next, **don't book unless the firm has a consumer-protection program.** Members of the United States Tour Operators Association and the National Tour Association are required to set aside funds exclusively to cover your payments and travel arrangements in case of default. Nonmember operators may instead carry insurance; look for the details in the operator's brochure— and the name of an underwriter with a solid reputation. Note: When it comes to tour operators, **don't trust escrow accounts.** Although there are laws governing those of charter-flight operators, no governmental body prevents tour operators from raiding the till.

Next, **contact your local Better Business Bureau and the attorney general's office** in both your own state and the operator's; have any complaints been filed? Last, **pay with a major credit card.** Then you can cancel payment, provided that you can document your com-

plaint. Always **consider trip-cancellation insurance** (see Insurance, above).

BIG VS. SMALL➤ An operator that handles several hundred thousand travelers annually can use its purchasing power to give you a good price. Its high volume may also indicate financial stability. But some small companies provide more personalized service; because they tend to specialize, they may also be experts on an area.

USING AN AGENT

Travel agents are an excellent resource. In fact, large operators accept bookings only through travel agents. But it's good to **collect brochures from several agencies,** because some agents' suggestions may be skewed by promotional relationships with tour and package firms that reward them for volume sales. If you have a special interest, **find an agent with expertise in that area;** the American Society of Travel Agents can give you leads in the United States. (Don't rely solely on your agent, though; agents may be unaware of small-niche operators, and some special-interest travel companies only sell direct).

SINGLE TRAVELERS

Prices are usually quoted per person, based on two sharing a room. If traveling solo, you may be required to pay the full double occupancy rate. Some operators eliminate this surcharge if you agree to be matched up with a roommate of the same sex, even if one is not found by departure time.

What you pack depends more on the time of year than on any particular dress code. Winters can be bitterly cold; summers are warm but with days that suddenly turn cool and rainy. In summer, take a warm jacket or heavy sweater for the Bavarian Alps, where the nights can be chilly even after hot days.

For cities, pack as you would for an American city: dressy outfits for formal restaurants and nightclubs, casual clothes elsewhere. Jeans are as popular in Germany as anywhere else, and are perfectly acceptable for sightseeing and informal dining. In the evening, men will probably feel more comfortable wearing a jacket and tie in more expensive restaurants although it is almost never required. Many German women are extremely fashion-conscious and wear stylish outfits to restaurants and the theater, especially in the larger cities.

To discourage purse snatchers and pickpockets, carry a handbag with long straps that you can sling across your body, bandolier-style, and with a zippered compartment for money and other valuables.

For stays in budget hotels, take your own soap. Many provide no soap at all or only one small bar. Bring an extra pair of eyeglasses or contact lenses in your carry-on luggage, and if you have a health problem, **pack enough medication** to last the trip or have your doctor write a prescription using the drug's generic name, because brand names vary from country to country (you'll then need a prescription from a doctor in the country you're visiting). **Don't put prescription drugs or valuables in luggage to be checked,** for your bags could go astray. To avoid problems with customs officials, carry medications in original packaging. Also don't forget the addresses of offices that handle refunds of lost traveler's checks.

ELECTRICITY

To use your U.S.-purchased electric-powered equipment, **bring a converter and an adapter.** The electrical current in Germany is 220 volts, 50 cycles alternating current (AC); wall outlets take Continental-type plugs, with two round prongs.

If your appliances are dual voltage, you'll need only an adapter. Hotels sometimes have 110-volt outlets for low-wattage appliances marked "For Shavers Only" near the sink; don't use them for high-wattage appliances like blow-dryers. If your laptop computer is older, carry a converter; new laptops operate equally well on 110 and

220 volts, so you need only an adapter.

LUGGAGE

Free airline baggage allowances depend on the airline, the route, and the class of your ticket; **ask in advance.** In general, on domestic flights and on international flights between the United States and foreign destinations, you are entitled to check two bags—neither exceeding 62 inches, or 158 centimeters (length + width + height), or weighing more than 70 pounds (32 kilograms). A third piece may be brought aboard; its total dimensions are generally limited to less than 45 inches (114 centimeters), so it will fit easily under the seat in front of you or in the overhead compartment. In the United States, the Federal Aviation Administration gives airlines broad latitude to limit carry-on allowances and tailor them to different aircraft and operational conditions. Charges for excess, oversize, or overweight pieces vary.

If you are flying between two foreign destinations, note that baggage allowances may be determined not by piece but by weight—generally 88 pounds (40 kilograms) in first class, 66 pounds (30 kilograms) in business class, and 44 pounds (20 kilograms) in economy. If your flight between two cities abroad *connects* with your transatlantic or transpacific flight, the piece method still applies.

SAFEGUARDING YOUR LUGGAGE➤ Before leaving home, **itemize your bags' contents** and their worth, and label them with your name, address, and phone number. (If you use your home address, cover it so that potential thieves can't see it.) Inside your bag, **pack a copy of your itinerary.** At check-in, **make sure that your bag is correctly tagged** with the airport's three-letter destination code. If your bags arrive damaged or not at all, file a written report with the airline before leaving the airport.

PASSPORTS AND VISAS

If you don't already have one, **get a passport.** While traveling, **keep one photocopy of the data page** separate from your wallet and leave another copy with someone at home. If you lose your passport, promptly call the nearest embassy or consulate and the local police; having the data page can speed replacement.

U.S. CITIZENS

All U.S. citizens, even infants, need a valid passport to enter Germany for stays of up to three months. New and renewal application forms are available at any of the 13 U.S. Passport Agency offices and at some post offices and courthouses. Passports are usually mailed within four weeks; allow five weeks or more in spring and summer.

CANADIANS

You need a valid passport to enter Germany for stays of up to three months. Application forms are available at 28 regional passport offices as well as at post offices and travel agencies. Whether for a first or a subsequent passport, you must apply in person. Children under 16 may be included on a parent's passport but must have their own to travel alone. Passports are valid for five years and are usually mailed within two to three weeks of application.

U.K. CITIZENS

Citizens of the United Kingdom do not need a valid passport to enter Germany for stays of up to three months. Applications for new and renewal passports are available from main post offices as well as at the passport offices located in Belfast, Glasgow, Liverpool, London, Newport, and Peterborough. You may apply in person at all passport offices, or by mail to all except the London office. Children under 16 may travel on an accompanying parent's passport. All passports are valid for 10 years. Allow a month for processing.

R
RAIL TRAVEL

To save money, **look into rail passes** (*see* Important Contacts A to Z, *above*). But be aware that if you don't plan to cover many miles, you may come out ahead by buying individual tickets.

Many travelers assume that rail passes guarantee them seats on the trains they wish to ride. Not so. You need to **book seats ahead even if you are using a rail pass;** seat reservations are required on some European trains, particularly high-speed trains, and are a good idea on trains that may be crowded—particularly in summer on popular routes. You will also need a reservation if you purchase overnight sleeping accommodations.

The German railway system is being privatized, so routes and timetables may still change in some areas. The two separate rail networks of East and West Germany merged in 1994 into Deutsche Bahn (DB, or German Rail), bringing Berlin and the cities of the old German Democratic Republic much closer to the main railheads of the west. The electrification and renovation of the ancient tracks in eastern Germany also made big strides forward, allowing the extension there of the high-speed InterCity Express (ICE) service. InterCity (IC) and EuroCity services have been improved and expanded, and the regional InterRegio network now extends nationwide. All overnight InterCity services and the slower D-class trains have sleepers, with a first-class service that includes breakfast in bed.

All InterCity and Inter-City Express trains have restaurant cars, InterRegio services have bright bistro-cars, and the Hamburg–Berchtesgaden service has an on-board McDonald's as an experiment. A DM 6 surcharge is added to the ticket price on all InterCity and EuroCity journeys irrespective of distance (DM 12 return); InterCity Express fares are about 20% more expensive than normal ones. Seat reservations are free of charge. Bikes cannot be transported on Inter-City Express services, but InterCity, EuroCity, and some D-class trains have special storage facilities, and InterRegio trains even have compartments where cyclists can travel next to their bikes.

Changing trains couldn't be easier. You often only have to cross to the other side of the platform. Special train maps on platform notice boards give details of the layout of trains arriving on that track, showing where first- and second-class cars and the restaurant car are, as well as where they will stop along the length of the platform.

Rail passengers with a valid round-trip air ticket can buy a heavily discounted "Rail and Fly" ticket for DB trains connecting with 14 German airports: Berlin's Schönefeld and Tegel airports, Bremen, Dresden, Düsseldorf, Frankfurt/Main, Hamburg, Hannover, Köln-Bonn, Leipzig/Halle, Munich, Münster/Os-nabrück, Nürnberg, and Stuttgart.

Note that in high season you will frequently encounter lines at ticket offices for seat reservations. Unless you are prepared to board the train without a reserved seat, taking the chance of a seat being available, the only way to avoid these lines is to **make an advance reservation by phone.** Call the ticket office (Fahrkarten-Schalter) of the rail station from which you plan to depart. Here again, you will probably have to make several attempts before you get through to the reservations section (Reservierungen/Platzkarten), but you will then be able to collect your seat ticket from a special counter **without having to wait in line.**

FROM THE U.K. BY TRAIN

There are several ways to reach Germany from London on British Rail. Travelers coming from the United Kingdom should **take the Channel Tunnel to save time, the ferry to save money.** Fastest and most expensive is the route via the Channel Tunnel on Eurostar trains (*see* The Channel Tunnel in Important Contacts A to Z, *above*). Departures leave hourly from Waterloo and require a change of trains in Brussels. Cheapest, and slowest, are the 8–10 departures daily from Victoria using the Ramsgate-Ostend ferry, jetfoil, or SeaCat catamaran service.

TOURIST RAIL CARDS

In 1995 a more comprehensive version of the popular InterRail ticket became available. The system divides Europe into seven zones, with different InterRail tariffs within each one. Germany belongs to Zone C, along with Switzerland, Austria, and Denmark. A one-month InterRail ticket for travel within this zone and an additional zone of your choice costs DM 500, and a two-week ticket DM 420; the age limit is 26. Young travelers intending to tour only Germany can get an even better deal by buying a Euro Domino ticket, allowing travel on all German trains for 3, 5, or 10 days within one month (for DM 231, DM 257, and DM 378). No age limit is linked to other special deals, such as the Sparpreis and ICE-Super Sparpreis, which offer big savings on return journeys made on off-peak days. One tip: There is very little difference between first- and second-class compartments in the newer InterCity trains and all InterCity Express trains but there's a big difference in fares.

Holders of British Rail Senior Citizens' Rail Cards can buy an "add-on" European Senior Citizens' Rail Card that permits half-price train travel in most European countries, including Germany.

Travelers under 26 who have not invested in a rail pass should inquire

THE GOLD GUIDE / SMART TRAVEL TIPS

about discount travel fares under the Billet International Jeune (BIJ) scheme. The special one-trip tariff (also known as a twen-tickets fare) is offered by EuroTrain International, with offices in 22 European cities. You can purchase a Euro-train ticket at one of these offices or at travel-agent networks, mainline rail stations, and specialist youth-travel operators.

R
RENTING A CAR

CUTTING COSTS

To get the best deal, **book through a travel agent and shop around.** When pricing cars, **ask where the rental lot is located.** Some off-airport locations offer lower rates—even though their lots are only minutes away from the terminal via compli-mentary shuttle. You may also want to **price local car-rental compa-nies,** whose rates may be lower still, although service and maintenance standards may not be up to those of a na-tional firm. Also **ask your travel agent about a company's customer-service record.** How has it responded to late plane arrivals and vehicle mishaps? Are there often lines at the rental counter, and, if you're traveling during a holiday period, does a confirmed reservation guarantee you a car?

Always **find out what equipment is standard** at your destination before specifying what you want; **do without automatic transmission** or air-conditioning if they're optional. In Europe, manual trans-missions are standard and air-conditioning is rare and often unneces-sary.

Also in Europe, **look into wholesalers—** companies that do not own their own fleets but rent in bulk from those that do and often offer better rates than traditional car-rental operations. Prices are best during low travel periods, and rentals booked through whole-salers must be paid for before you leave the United States. If you use a wholesaler, **know whether the prices are guaranteed** in U.S. dollars or foreign currency, and if unlim-ited mileage is available; find out about required deposits, cancellation penalties, and drop-off charges; and confirm the cost of any required insurance coverage.

INSURANCE

When you drive a rented car, you are generally responsible for any damage or personal injury that you cause as well as damage to the vehicle. Before you rent, **see what coverage you already have** under the terms of your personal auto-insurance policy and credit cards. For about $14 a day, rental com-panies sell insurance, known as a collision damage waiver (CDW), that eliminates your liability for damage to the car; it's always optional and should never be automatically added to your bill.

REQUIREMENTS

In Germany your own driver's license is ac-ceptable. An Interna-tional Driver's Permit, available from the American or Canadian Automobile Associa-tion, is a good idea.

SURCHARGES

Before picking up the car in one city and leaving it in another, **ask about drop-off charges or one-way service fees,** which can be substantial. Note, too, that some rental agencies charge extra if you return the car before the time specified on your contract. To avoid a hefty refueling fee, **fill the tank just before you turn in the car.**

S
SENIOR-CITIZEN DISCOUNTS

In Germany, the num-ber of citizens over 60 is growing; this section of the population has also become more affluent and demanding and even has its own politi-cal party, the Gray Panthers. The strength of this special-interest age group has won them special privileges in Germany—such as price adjustments on the railways and re-duced admission to museums—and elderly visitors from abroad can also take advantage of these discounts. Contact the German National Tourist Board (*see* Visitor Information *in* Important Contacts A to Z, *above*).

To qualify for age-related discounts, **mention your senior-**

citizen status up front when booking hotel reservations, not when checking out, and before you're seated in restaurants, not when paying your bill. Note that discounts may be limited to certain menus, days, or hours. When renting a car, **ask about promotional car-rental discounts**—they can net lower costs than your senior-citizen discount.

STUDENTS ON THE ROAD

To save money, **look into deals available through student-oriented travel agencies.** To qualify, you'll need to have a bona fide student I.D. card. Members of international student groups also are also eligible. *See* Students *in* Important Contacts A to Z, *above.*

HOSTELING

Germany's youth hostels—*Jugendherbergen* —are probably the most efficient, up-to-date, and proportionally numerous of any country's in the world. There are more than 600 in all, many located in castles that add a touch of romance to otherwise utilitarian accommodations. Since unification, many eastern German youth hostels have closed down. An effort is being made, however, to keep as many open as possible, and renovations are currently under way to bring eastern hostels up to the standards of their western counterparts.

Apart from Bavaria, where there is an age

limit of 27, there are no restrictions on age, though those under 20 take preference when space is limited. Accommodation is available only to members of the International Youth Hostel Federation (IYHF); guest membership for non-Germans costs DM 36 annually in Germany. Accommodation charges range from about DM 15 to DM 21 for youth under 27 and DM 22 to DM 38 for adults (breakfast included). Cards are available from the American Youth Hostels Association, the Canadian Hostelling Association, and the United Kingdom's Youth Hostels Association (*see* Students *in* Important Contacts A to Z, *above*).

T
TELEPHONES

Apart from the more remote rural corners of eastern Germany, telephone links between western and eastern areas of the country have now been completely upgraded.

LOCAL CALLS

Local public phones charge a minimum 30 pfennigs per call (for six minutes). All public phones take 10 pf, DM 1, and DM 5 coins. If you're anticipating making a lot of phone calls, purchase a phone card at any German post office (also available at many exchange places). They come in denominations of DM 12 and DM 50, the latter good for DM 60 worth of calls. Most phone booths have

instructions in English as well as German.

LONG-DISTANCE

International calls can be made from public phones bearing the sign INLANDS UND AUSLANDS-GESPRÄCHE. Using DM 5 coins is best for long-distance dialing; a four-minute call to the United States costs DM 15. To avoid weighing yourself down with coins, however, **make international calls from post offices**; even those in small country towns will have a special booth for international calls. You pay the clerk at the end of your call. Never make international calls from your hotel room; rates will be at least double the regular charge.

The long-distance services of AT&T, MCI, and Sprint make calling home relatively convenient and let you avoid hotel surcharges; typically, you dial a local number abroad. Before you go, **find out the local access codes** for your destinations.

OPERATORS AND INFORMATION

The German telephone system is fully automatic, and it's unlikely that you'll have to employ the services of an operator. If you do, dial 010, or 0010 for international calls. If the operator doesn't speak English (also unlikely), you'll be passed to one who does.

TIPPING

HOTELS➤ The service charges on bills suffice for most tips in your hotel, though you should **tip bellhops and porters**; DM 2 per bag or service is ample. It's also customary to leave a small tip (a couple of marks per night) for the room cleaning staff. Whether you tip the desk clerk depends on whether he or she has given you any special service.

RESTAURANTS➤ Service charges are included in all checks (listed as *Bedienung*), as is tax (listed as *MWST*). Nonetheless, it is customary to **round out the bill to the nearest mark or to leave about 5%** (give it to the waiter or waitress as you pay the bill; don't leave it on the table).

TAXIS➤ **Round out the fare to the nearest full mark as a tip.** Only give more if you have particularly cumbersome or heavy luggage (though you will be charged 50 pfennigs for each piece of luggage anyway).

W
WHEN TO GO

The tourist season in Germany runs from May to late October, when the weather is at its best. In addition to many tourist events, this period has hundreds of folk festivals.

The winter sports season in the Bavarian Alps runs from Christmas to mid-March. Prices everywhere are generally higher during the summer, so you may find considerable advantages to visiting out of season. Most resorts offer between-season (*Zwischensaison*) and edge-of-season (*Nebensaison*) rates, and tourist offices can provide lists of hotels that offer special low-price inclusive weekly packages (*Pauschalangebote*). Many winter ski resorts lower rates for the periods between mid-January (after local school holidays) and Easter. The other advantage of out-of-season travel is fewer crowds. The disadvantages of visiting out-of-season, especially in winter, are that the weather is often cold and gloomy, and that some tourist attractions, especially in rural areas, are closed or have shorter hours. Ski resorts are the exception.

The major cities, especially Berlin, Hamburg, and Munich, are active year-round. Avoid Leipzig the first few weeks in March and September, when the trade fair commandeers all accommodations and prices soar.

CLIMATE

Germany's climate is temperate, although cold snaps can plunge the thermometer well below freezing, particularly in the Alps, the Harz region of Lower Saxony, the Black Forest, and the higher regions of northern Franconia. Summers are usually sunny and warm, though you should be prepared for a few cloudy and wet days. The south is normally always a few degrees warmer than the north. As you get nearer the Alps, however, the summers get shorter, often not beginning until the end of May. Fall is sometimes spectacular in the south—warm and soothing. The only real exception to the above is the strikingly variable weather in South Bavaria caused by the *Föhn*, an Alpine wind that gives rise to clear but very warm conditions. The Föhn can occur in all seasons. Sudden atmospheric pressure changes associated with the Föhn give some people headaches.

The following are the average daily maximum and minimum temperatures for Munich.

Climate in Germany

Jan.	35F	1C	May	64F	18C	Sept.	67F	20C
	23	– 5		45	7		48	9
Feb.	38F	3C	June	70F	21C	Oct.	56F	14C
	23	– 5		51	11		40	4
Mar.	48F	9C	July	74F	23C	Nov.	44F	7C
	30	– 1		55	13		33	0
Apr.	56F	14C	Aug.	73F	23C	Dec.	36F	2C
	38	3		54	12		26	– 4

1 Destination: Germany

WHAT IS GERMANY?

THE HONEYMOON IS OVER and a unified but still disunited Germany has entered what its residents call the *grauer Alltag,* or "gray everyday." With the fifth anniversary of the fall of the Wall passed (1994) as well as the 50th anniversary of the end of World War II (1995), 1996 is the first year in recent German memory outside the shadow cast by a date of sober remembrance. But that doesn't mean Germany is any the happier: From all sides Germany hears that it is the powerhouse of Europe, but it's not certain that it matches the image. Nor is the new Germany so self-effacing. In many areas—politics and economics most notably—Germany is flexing muscles that have been growing stronger while other nations have been accumulating flab. The Germans of the late '90s are self-confident citizens of a country they are finally proud to call their own.

But if you ask a German to define his or her country, you might get an evasive answer. Six years after unification the country still has deep divisions and unhealed wounds, and its people are constantly reminded of their condition by statistics that still reflect conditions in two halves of a country—one that Chancellor Helmut Kohl had hoped would by now be a happy whole. Inflation and unemployment are higher in the east than in the west, and wages are lower. In mid-1995, one adult in five was out of work in some moribund industrial towns of Brandenburg and Saxony near the East European border.

The monetary cost of unification, as well as the sheer human sacrifice involved, have vastly exceeded all predictions. A special tax levy meant to be a temporary source of funding for what was East Germany was reimposed at the start of 1995, rekindling resentment among west Germans who felt they had already paid enough. This was closely followed by an authoritative report in *Der Spiegel*—neither confirmed nor denied by the government—claiming that 65 billion marks raised in taxes for investment in the East had been totally wasted,

through inefficiency, sheer ignorance, or criminal misuse.

No, it wasn't a happy country that Kohl and his paper-thin coalition majority surveyed in late 1995—from a capital city tottering on uncertain foundations. By the beginning of the 21st century, Berlin is to take its place as the seat of German government from Rhineland Bonn, which assumed the role in the post-war years because it had few logistical or historical issues. As the Cold War grew ever icier and the East—West divide widened, Bonn's provisional role took on a kind of permanence. When reunited Berlin restaked its claim, the parliamentary vote in favor of moving the capital was close, and the extra-parliamentary debate about the wisdom of the move continues. Berlin, too, is having problems adjusting to its new role: In 1995, half the construction projects connected with the move still awaited official approval.

The tax burden caused by unification and the impending move weighed heavily on the Bonn government in 1995, testing the alliance between Chancellor Kohl's Christian Democrats and the liberal Free Democrats to an extent not seen since the coalition first came to power. Despite waning popularity that threatened its very existence, the small but resilient Free Democratic Party challenged the Kohl Cabinet's tax package and opened a split that could bring early elections.

An irony of history is that after celebrating the fall of the Iron Curtain and triumphantly dismantling the barbed-wire fences that separated East and West Europe for nearly four decades, Germany is putting up new border defenses at many weak frontier points to keep out unwanted "refugees." New legislation is making it much more difficult for emigrants from the Third World, Russia, and Eastern Europe to find refuge in Germany. Guard dogs might be brought back into service, too.

With such signs of political instability it was perhaps surprising that the unpleasant specter of ultra right-wing, neo-Nazi militancy lost some of its menacing form in 1995. Although the number of attacks on foreigners in Germany decreased, the number of anti-Semitic offenses nearly doubled from 1993 to 1994, and the trend was equally disturbing in 1995. Developments like these have a significance of their own in Germany, and many concerned Germans are warning against underestimating the extent of the threat from the racist Right.

Thinking twice about that trip to Germany? Don't worry—apart from beggars in Bonn subway passages, junkies in Frankfurt parks, and homeless people camping out in central Munich, a tourist could travel from the Danish border in the north to the Bavarian Alps in the south without witnessing much more than a smudge on the travel posters that trumpet Germany's attractions. It is an undeniably beautiful country, full of contrasts. But this diversity makes it difficult to find a common element that defines Germany and its people.

There has always been a perceptible north—south division, across which the Hamburger and the Bavarian view each other with a theatrical animosity that reduces the rivalry between the English and the Scots to schoolboy banter. But now the symbiosis has been disturbed by the arrival of the east German Saxon—to many west Germans a very backward species who chirps an incomprehensible language.

Like the English-Scottish rivalry, these unneighborly sentiments within Germany are rooted in a shared history scarred by internecine quarrels and further complicated by the long parallel rule of two great royal dynasties, the Hohenzollerns and the Wittelsbachs. Bavarians are proud that their line—the Wittelsbachs—is older and lasted longer than the Prussian Hohenzollerns. The fact that two latter-day Bavarian rulers were insane is smilingly dismissed as a slight deviation. Indeed, the insanity of young King Ludwig II is welcomed as *Glück im Unglück* (a common German expression meaning "fortune in misfortune"), for the eccentric ruler built a collection of castles that bankrupted the royal purse but now reap huge sums of money in tourist revenues. Similarly, Ludwig's munificent patronage of Wagner

cost the Bavarians dearly in terms of hard cash—but what an investment!

But there are other more visible differences that distinguish Bavarians from their neighbors to the north or, for that matter, the Berliner from the Rhinelander and all of them from the Saarlander or the Saxon. You've only got to join them at table and watch what they eat and particularly what and how they drink to sort out one from another.

The Berliner and Bavarian both enjoy a beer brewed from wheat—but the Bavarian watches with horror how the Berliner sweetens it with fruit juice. In the Rhineland, beer is served in small glasses that have been known to provoke threats of legal action from Bavarians believing they were getting short measure. Saarlanders claim to produce the best German beer and Bavarians the purest (brewed, despite European Union pressure to conform, according to a 16th-century purity law).

Germany produces great wines too, of course, but beer is the country's national beverage and its emblem; there are more breweries in Germany than in the rest of Europe put together. Unification gave German brewing a boost, and Germany regained its world title as number one in the per capita consumption of beer. Germans down 144 liters (254 pints) a year, far surpassing Britain (197 pints) and the United States (165 pints). Bavarians drink a staggering 200 liters (352 pints) per head.

A great German institution is the beer garden, traditionally Bavarian but now being introduced throughout Germany. Beer gardens are the center of Bavarian life in the summer, which in a good year means the long, balmy span between Easter and the first cold snap of October. This is the time to visit Bavaria, and particularly Munich, when the velvety southern German nights draw families out to the lantern-hung chestnut tree bowers of throbbing beer gardens.

But the Bavarians by no means have a monopoly on outdoor delights such as these. In bustling Frankfurt, on off-duty summer nights, the city's businessmen can be found in the cider pubs of Sachsenhausen; in Berlin, the pavement cafés are an extension of the German living room; while along the Rhine, the arrival of the first new wine after the grape harvest signals party time.

In cities like Munich it's always party season, with even Lent producing an excuse for brewing an especially strong beer (locals say it kept monks going during their 40 days' fast). The weeks preceding Lent are Carnival time (known in southern Germany as Fasching), celebrated in Germany with an abandon found scarcely anywhere else in Europe.

Behind the uninhibited fun, though, is a precision-made mechanism that is peculiarly German, a kind of "Now you will enjoy yourself" compulsion. The Carnival season begins precisely at 11 AM on the 11th day of the 11th month and ends at the stroke of midnight on Shrove Tuesday—you can't organize your fun more efficiently. Since the Germans are so good at arranging their hedonism, we can be confident they will sort out their problems, too. And that's good news for us all.

— *Robert Tilley*

WHAT'S WHERE

Munich

Chic and cosmopolitan, carefree and kitschy. As Bavaria's capital and one of Germany's biggest cites, Munich has more than its share of great museums, architectural treasures, historic sites, and world-class shops, restaurants, and hotels. The same could be said of its abundance of lederhosen and oompah bands. But it's the overall feeling of *Gemütlichkeit* that makes the city so special—an open-air market here, a park there, and beer halls everywhere. Tourists flock to Munich year-round, but festival dates—especially Fasching, or Carnival, in the winter, and Oktoberfest in the fall—draw the most.

The Bavarian Alps

This region of fir-clad mountains stretches from Munich south to the Austrian border. Quaint towns full of half-timbered houses fronted by flowers in the summer, buried by snow in the winter, pop up among the peaks, as do the creations of "Mad" King Ludwig II. Shimmering alpine lakes abound, and the whole area has sporting opportunities galore, centering on Garmisch-Partenkirchen. Long before sports were a part of the region's livelihood, however, wood-carving was quite the industry; you'll still see it in many towns, notably Oberammergau and Berchtesgaden.

The Bodensee

If you're in the area, be sure to take at least one boat trip on the Bodensee, the largest lake in the German-speaking world. Some towns are built on islands near the shore, and their incredible beauty is best surveyed from the water. Other features of the area appreciated by tourists are its climate, which allows near-tropical growth in places, and its proximity to Switzerland and Liechtenstein. Konstanz, the largest city on the lake, is German but has parts in Switzerland.

The Bavarian Forest

Low-key and understated, the Bavarian Forest is a welcome alternative to Germany's hyped-up, overcrowded tourist regions. Good-quality dining and lodging at budget prices make it even more attractive. Farming and forestry are mainstay industries, tourism is growing, and glass-blowing shouldn't be missed. Passau, a 2,000-year-old town at the confluence of three rivers, is visited for its beauty as much as its history.

The Black Forest

Cake and smoked ham aren't the only reasons to visit the Black Forest, but they are good ones. Spa and casino resorts, outdoor activities, and cuckoo clocks are other draws. The Romans were the first to take advantage of the area's healing waters, 19 centuries ago, and royalty and the cultural elite paraded about the region in the 1800s. Today, watching vacationers here is a study in contrasts; high-fashion, high-cost towns like Baden-Baden share the trees with down-home German country villages.

The Romantic Road

One of Germany's so perfectly planned tourist routes, the Romantic Road is just that, albeit in the sense of the word meaning wondrous and fanciful. *Minnesänger* Walther von der Vogelweide and medieval sculptor Tilman Riemenschneider are among the people whose legacies you'll discover as you travel the route. You'll also visit Würzburg, home to a glorious Baroque palace; the wonderfully preserved medieval town of Rothenburg-ob-der-Tauber; and Ludwig II's fantastic Neuschwanstein castle.

Franconia

A predominantly rural area, Franconia was most important politically in the days of the Holy Roman Empire. You'll want to see its beautiful and historic towns: Coburg, Bayreuth, Bamberg, Nürnberg, and Regensburg. Wagner fans especially shouldn't miss Bayreuth, where the great composer settled and built his theater. The annual festival that honors him brings other town functions to a halt every summer.

Rhineland Palatinate

This less-famous stretch of the Rhine has less spectacular scenery than along the riverbanks farther north, but it's also less crowded and less expensive. The Weinstrasse, or Wine Road, wends through part of the region, leading travelers to the tempting vintages around every turn. North of its end are Speyer, Worms, and Mainz, latter-day imperial centers, each home to a Romanesque cathedral more spectacular than the last.

Heidelberg and the Neckar Valley

This chapter's tour bounces between industrial cities and quaint university towns, Mannheim and Stuttgart among the former, Heidelberg and Tübingen among the latter, with castles, small villages, and the Neckar throughout. Along the scenic Burgenstrasse (Castle Road), each medieval town is guarded by a castle, but it is arguably Heidelberg that is most worth a stop (just ask—and beware of—its 2½ million visitors annually). This town seems to work magic for all who give it a chance; look for signs of Johann Wolfgang von Goethe, Mark Twain, Carl Maria von Weber, and Robert Schumann, for example.

Frankfurt

Because it is the air gateway to Germany—and to Europe—you'll probably at least land in Frankfurt. Many German banks are headquartered here, and the Frankfurt Börse is Germany's leading stock exchange. All this has contributed to a high rise–spiked skyline that would stun the 30 Holy Roman Emperors who were elected and crowned here. Their portraits line the banquet hall of the Römer, or city hall. Across the River Main from the heart of downtown is the residential, medieval-feeling Sachsenhausen quarter, home to many of the city's best museums.

The Rhineland

Vater Rhein, or "Father Rhine," is Germany's historic lifeline, and the region from Mainz to Koblenz (Tours 1 and 2) is its heart. Its banks are crowned by magnificent castle after castle and breathtaking, vine-terraced hills that provide the livelihood for many of the villages hugging the shores. Bigger cities, too, such as Bonn, Köln, and Koblenz, thrive along the great river. Koblenz lies at the meeting of the Rhine and its most famous tributary, the Mosel, on whose banks Germany's oldest city, Trier, was established. Other cities included in the chapter are Aachen and Düsseldorf.

The Fairy-Tale Road

If you're in search of Cinderella, Hansel and Gretel, the Pied Piper, and Rumpelstiltskin, the Fairy-Tale Road is the place to look. One of Germany's special tourist routes, it leads through parts of Germany where the brothers Grimm lived and worked. From its start in Hanau, just east of Frankfurt, to its end in Bremen, 600 kilometers (370 miles) north, it passes dozens of picturesque towns full of half-timbered houses and guarded by castles. Hannover is the site of a magnificent Baroque park.

Hamburg

The Free and Hanseatic City of Hamburg, the city's official title, is an apt description. Water—in the form of the Alster lakes and the River Elbe—is its defining feature and the secret of its success. Even before the formation of the Hanseatic League, Hamburg shipped to and from all parts of the world; this is evident in many of the city's main attractions, including the Fischmarkt, its diverse restaurants, and the red-light district (the infamous Reeperbahn). A fire in the 1800s and wartime bombings destroyed much of Hamburg's early architecture but cleared room for fantastic new creations, among them beautiful Jugendstil and Nordic Renaissance structures.

Berlin

Berlin isn't as old as many German cities, but it gets more than its share of space in the history books. It became capital of the newly unified German Empire under Bismarck in the late 1800s and hung on to that position until it was almost bombed out of existence in the struggle against Hitler and Nazism. Following the war, Berlin was artificially partitioned and later barricaded, and the division between East and West became tangible as well as symbolic; reunification was like an impossible dream come true. Through it all, Berliners displayed a remarkable resilience, a trait they continue to need as the city works to rebuild and resume its role as Germany's capital. Berlin has enough museums, notorious nightlife, shops, and restaurants to fill any itinerary, but sites related to its complex history make it worth a longer visit. Potsdam, site of Frederick the Great's equally magnificent Sanssouci palace, is a popular excursion.

The Baltic Coast

Between the former East—West border town of Lübeck and the Polish frontier, East Germany's vacation hot spot is now open for all to enjoy, even if many of its beach towns still seem trapped in the '30s. Miles of sandy coastline, peppered with chalk cliffs and charming little coves, have largely escaped the attention of developers. Evidence of the Hansa merchants and a wealth of architectural delights await inspection, from the well-preserved medieval town squares to the simple whitewashed seaside cottages with their roofs of reed thatch.

Saxony and Thuringia

This area is worth visiting for its traditional tourist sites and because it is in transition—it was bound more closely with the Soviet Union than West Germany for 45 years. Dresden's Zwinger palace complex is a cultural wonder; Leipzig, the largest eastern German city after Berlin, is an important commercial center (avoid the trade fair dates); and Weimar has many traces from its days as a cultural center in the 19th century.

PLEASURES & PASTIMES

Beer

The Germans don't just produce *a* beverage called beer, they brew more than 5,000 varieties in a range of tastes and colors. Germany has about 1,300 breweries, 40% of the world's total. The hallmark of the country's dedication to beer is the purity law, *das Reinheitsgebot,* unchanged since Duke Wilhelm IV introduced it in Bavaria in 1516. The law decrees that only malted barley, hops, yeast, and water may be used to make beer, except for specialty wheat beers.

Asking for a "beer" in most German hostelries is like going into a cheese shop and asking for cheese. Even the simplest country inn will more than likely have a choice of beers, and in many pubs there may be several different draft beers in addition to the standard selection of bottled beers. The type available varies from one part of the country to another, and in areas of south Germany, the choice can also depend on the time of year.

In north Germany, the most popular standard beers are export lagers or the paler, more pungent pilsners. The breweries of Rhine cities Köln and Düsseldorf produce "old-fashioned" beers similar to English ales. Germany's biggest breweries are in the northern city of Dortmund, which feeds the industrial Ruhr region. But Bavaria is where the majority of the country's breweries—and beer traditions—are found. Indeed, while Germany as a whole is at the head of the international beer-drinking table, the Bavarians and the Saarlanders to the southwest consume more beer per person than does any other group in the country.

Ultimately, all beer routes lead to the world's beer-drinking capital: Munich. This is where you'll find the biggest beer halls, the largest beer gardens, the most famous breweries, the biggest and most indulgent beer festival, and the widest selection of brews; even the beer glasses are bigger. It's a measure of how seriously the Germans take their beer that they see no conflict in the fact that one of the most cosmopolitan cities in the country—a place with great art galleries and museums, an opulent opera house, and chic lifestyles—is internationally recognized as the most beer-drenched city on Earth. Postcards are framed with the message "Munich, the Beer City."

Bavarians are sometimes regarded with disdain by their less-indulgent Prussian brothers to the north. But not even the widest-girthed southerners can be held wholly responsible for the staggering consumption of beer and food at the annual Oktoberfest, which starts in September. Typically, 5 million *liters* of beer, as well as 750,000 roasted chickens and 650,000 sausages, are put away by revelers. Clearly, visitors must be helping a little.

A BEER GLOSSARY➤ The alcohol content of German beers varies considerably. At the weaker end of the scale is the light Munich *Helles* (3.7% alcohol by volume); stronger brews are *Pilsner* (around 5%) and *Doppelbock* (more than 7%).

Alt: Literally, "old," referring to beer made according to an old formula.

Bock: Strong beer, which can be light or dark, sweet or dry.

Doppelbock: Stronger than *Bock,* usually dark, and not to be trifled with.

Dunkles: Dark beer, often slightly sweeter or maltier than pale (light) beers.

Export: Usually a pale (light-colored) beer of medium strength.

Feierabend: Called out when a drinking establishment is closing for the day.

Halbe: Half a *Mass,* the standard beer measure in Bavaria (*see below*).

Hefe: Yeast.

Helles: Light beer.

Klar, Kristall: Wheat beer with the yeast removed.

Kleines: A small glass of beer (in Bavaria).

Krug: An earthenware drinking vessel, often referred to as a stein.

Lager: In Germany, the term, which means "store," refers to that stage of the brewing process during which beer matures in the brewery.

Leichtbier: Beer with low alcohol and calorie content, usually pale in color.

Mass: A 1-liter (almost 2-pint) glass or earthenware mug.

Naturtrüb: A new term for unfiltered beer, implying that the yeast has not been removed.

Obergärig: Top-fermented.

O' zapftis!: "Barrel is tapped!" Cry that announces the opening of the Munich Oktoberfest.

Pils, Pilsner: A golden-colored, dry, bitter-flavored beer named after Pilsen, the Czech town where in the 19th century the style was first developed.

Polizei Stunde: Literally, "police hour"—closing time. Midnight or 1 AM in some big cities, usually earlier in small towns and villages.

Prost: German for "cheers."

Radler: Lemonade and beer mixed.

Rauchbier: Smoked beer. Usually a dark brew with a smoky flavor that comes from infusing the malted barley with beechwood smoke.

Untergärig: Bottom-fermented.

Weissbier, Weizenbier: Wheat beer. A highly carbonated, sharp and sour brew, often with floating yeast particles.

Boat Trips

River and lake trips are among the greatest delights of a vacation in Germany, especially along the Rhine, Germany's longest river. The Rhine may be viewed at a variety of modes. For those in a hurry, there is a daily hydrofoil service from Düsseldorf right through to Mainz (book in advance). For gentler souls, there is a wide range of more leisurely cruises. German cruise ships also operate on the Upper Rhine as far as Basel, Switzerland; on the Main between Frankfurt and Mainz; on the Danube to Vienna and Budapest; on the Europe Canal joining the Main and the Danube; on the Elbe and Weser and their estuaries; on the Inn and Ilz; and on the Ammersee, Chiemsee, Königsee, Bodensee, and many other smaller German lakes.

History

Germany's past is glorious at times, horrifying at others. No matter what part of the country you visit, you'll be bombarded with it. In northern Germany, the devastation of the Thirty Years' War is as visible as the riches brought by the Hanseatic League. Throughout the country are remainders from leading figures—Charlemagne's throne in Aachen, Wittelsbach castles in Bavaria, Hitler's Alpine retreat. Many concentration camps, including Dachau, outside Munich, and Sachsenhausen, outside Berlin, have been reopened as education centers and memorials to their victims. In the former East Germany, many reminders of Communism—such as statues of Marx—were obliterated, but citizens fought to retain some, and won.

Theme tours can help you focus on an area of specific interest. See, for example, the Castles of Ludwig II itinerary (*below*), or take a theme road, such as the tourist office's new Martin Luther route, to explore the country's past.

Scenery

Many of the tours in this book are designed to help you take in Germany's beauty. From the medieval brick buildings in the tiny towns on the Baltic coast to the spectacular, castle- and vine-covered hills along the Rhine, to the densely wooded forests in the south, to the crystal-clear Alpine lakes, Germany's scenery is as diverse as it is breathtaking. Whether you're in the shadow of high rises or driving past geranium-bedecked, half-timbered houses on a country road, be sure to appreciate what's around you.

Sports and Outdoor Activities

The Germans are nothing if not sports-crazy, and practically every sport, however arcane, can be arranged almost anywhere in the country. A good number of sports packages—for sailing, tennis, climbing, walking, horseback riding, to name only a few—are also available. Below, we give details of some of the more popular participant sports. Information about important sporting events is also published every month by regional and local tourist offices.

BICYCLING➤ There are no formalities governing the importation of bikes into Germany, and no duty is required. Bikes can also be carried on trains—though *not* on ICE trains—if you buy a *Fahrradkarte,* or bicycle ticket. These cost DM 8.60 per journey and can be bought at any train station. It is also possible to send your bike

to your next destination for DM 21, where it will be held for you in storage until your arrival. Full details are given in German Rail's brochure *Radler-Bahn.*

Bicycles are also available for rental at more than 370 train stations throughout the country, most of them in south Germany, from April 1 to October 31. The cost is DM 11–DM 13 per day, DM 7–DM 9 if you have a valid rail ticket.

FISHING➤ Fishing is possible at many locations in Germany, but a permit, valid for one year and costing from DM 10 to DM 20, available from local tourist offices, is required, as is a local permit to fish in a particular spot. Get this from the owner of the stretch of water in which you plan to fish.

A number of hotels offer fishing for guests, but you will normally be expected to deliver your catch—if any—to the hotel.

GOLF➤ The popularity of golf in Germany is rapidly increasing, as is the number of courses. If they are not too busy, clubs will usually allow nonmembers to play; charges will be about DM 30 during the week and up to DM 60 on weekends and on public holidays.

HIKING AND CLIMBING➤ Germany's hill and mountain regions have thousands of miles of marked hiking and mountain-walking tracks. They are administered by regional hiking clubs and, where appropriate, mountaineering groups, all of which are affiliated with the Verband Deutscher Gebirgs- und Wandervereine e.V. (*see* Sports *in* Important Contacts A to Z).

Local tourist offices and sports shops can usually supply details about mountain guides.

HORSEBACK RIDING➤ Riding schools and clubs can be found all over Germany. Rates are generally high, and most schools will insist on a minimum standard of competence before allowing novices to venture out. Alternatively, pony treks are available in many parts of the country.

SAILING➤ Sailing vacations and opportunities to rent sailboats are available throughout Germany. Most North Sea and Baltic resorts and harbors have either sailing schools or sailboats of varying types to rent. Lake sailing is equally popular, particularly on the Chiemsee in Bavaria and on the Bodensee.

SWIMMING➤ Almost all larger towns and resorts have open-air and indoor pools, the former frequently heated, the latter often with wave or whirlpool machines. In addition, practically all coastal resorts have indoor seawater pools, as well as good, if bracing, beaches. Similarly, all German spas have thermal or mineral-water indoor pools (*see* Spas *under* Lodging *in* Smart Travel Tips A to Z). Finally, Bavaria's Alpine lakes and a large number of artificial lakes elsewhere have marked-off swimming and sunbathing areas.

Note that swimming in rivers, especially the larger ones, is not recommended and in some cases is forbidden—look for the BADEN VERBOTEN signs—because of shipping, pollution, or both.

You'll probably notice that many Germans sunbathe nude. Some pools will have special days for nude bathing only, and on beaches with signs, nudity is also allowed.

TENNIS➤ In the home country of champions Steffi Graf and Boris Becker, courts are available practically everywhere, summer and winter. Local tourist offices will supply details of where to play, charges, and how to book, the latter being essential in most areas. Charges vary from DM 20 to DM 30 for outdoor courts and DM 25 to DM 35 for indoor courts.

WINDSURFING➤ This has become so popular, particularly on the Bavarian lakes, that it has been restricted on some beaches as a result of collisions between surfers and swimmers. Nonetheless, there are still many places where you can rent and use Windsurfers. Lessons, at around DM 25 per hour, are also generally available.

WINTER SPORTS➤ South Bavaria is the big winter-sports region, and Garmisch-Partenkirchen is the best-known center. There are also winter-sports resorts in the Black Forest, the Harz region, the Bavarian Forest, the Rhön Mountains, the Fichtelgebirge, the Sauerland, and the Swabian mountains. The season generally runs from the middle of December to the end of March, but at higher altitudes, such as the Zugspitze (near Garmisch), you can usually ski from as early as the end of November to as late as the middle of May. There's

no need to bring skis with you—you can rent or buy them on the spot. Look for the special winter off-season rates (*Weisse Wochen*) offered by most winter-sports resorts for cross-country and downhill skiing vacations. Prices include seven days' bed and breakfast (or half-board) plus ski lessons.

For cross-country (or *Langlauf*) skiing, which is becoming increasingly popular, there are stretches of prepared tracks (or *Loipen*) in the valleys and foothills of most winter-sports centers, as well as in the suburbs of larger towns in south Bavaria.

Ski-bobbing is on the increase. There are runs and schools at Bayrischzell, Berchtesgaden, Garmisch-Partenkirchen, Füssen, and Oberstdorf in the Alps, as well as at Altglashütten, Bernau, and Feldberg in the Black Forest. Ice rinks, many open all year, can be found everywhere.

Wine

More than 2,000 years ago, Romans saw the potential for grape growing in their newly conquered land, and vineyards have held their own in the beer-guzzling country ever since. Germany has nearly 240,000 acres of vineyards, about 87% of which are planted with white-wine grapes. Because it is so far north, the wines Germany produces are light and delicate; Riesling grapes and wines are the best known.

Wine grapes grow in 13 specified regions in the area around the Bodensee; along the Rhine and its tributaries, up to near Bonn; and east of the French border, on the slopes of the Black Forest, and on the Elbe north of Dresden. As with beer, German law governs different aspects of wine production and labeling. A stipulation of the Treaty of Versailles states that Germany (and all other European countries) may not use the name Champagne; Sekt is what German sparkling wines are called. The grape harvest takes place in October and November, but its products are celebrated by festivals year-round. The "Rivers of Wine" itinerary, *below*, and Tour 1 in Chapter 9 are good tours for connoisseurs.

FODOR'S CHOICE

Dining

★ **Aubergine, Munich,** for streamlined service, modern decor, and gourmet nouvelle cuisine. **$$$$**

★ **Bado-La Poele d'Or, Köln,** with surprisingly simple and light classical cuisine in a hushed setting. **$$$$**

★ **Colombi, Freiburg,** has two sections: one rustic, the other elegant. Both serve excellent meat dishes. **$$$$**

★ **Landhaus Scherrer, Hamburg,** for sophisticated nouvelle specialties and down-to-earth local dishes. **$$$$**

★ **Säumerhof, Grafenau,** an unexpectedly good restaurant in the middle of the Bavarian Forest. It serves original, nouvelle-inspired dishes made with ingredients found locally. **$$$$**

★ **Weinhaus Brückenkeller, Frankfurt,** where you'll find time-honored yet light German specialties in an arched cellar. **$$$**

★ **Schloss Bevern, Bevern,** a romantic and stylish restaurant where you'll dine on such traditional country dishes as roast pheasant or partridge. **$$$**

★ **Wullenwewer, Lübeck,** a particularly attractive setting for sophisticated cuisine. **$$$–$$$$**

★ **Alte Schwede, Wismar,** for traditional game and fish dishes. **$$**

★ **Bad Dürkheimer Riesenfass, Bad Dürkheim,** which serves 420 people in the biggest wine barrel in the world. **$$**

★ **Fischerhaus, Hamburg,** a busy restaurant that specializes in classic fish dishes. **$**

★ **Weinhaus Moschner, Rottach-Egern,** a dark old tavern with a menu that's heavy on sausage. The camaraderie and atmosphere are just as important as the food. **$**

★ **Zum Stachel, Würzburg,** for satisfying Franconian fare served beneath a canopy of vine leaves. **$**

Lodging

★ **Brenner's Park Hotel, Baden-Baden,** a stately mansion outfitted with luxury accommodations. **$$$$**

★ **Dom-Hotel, Köln,** old-fashioned, formal, and gracious, with a stunning location right by the cathedral. It offers Old World elegance and discreetly efficient service. **$$$$**

★ **Bristol Hotel Kempinski, Berlin,** a classic in the heart of the city. Rooms and suites are sumptuously decorated. **$$$$**

★ **Rafael, Munich,** a newer downtown hotel in an older building. Service and style are the hallmarks. **$$$$**

★ **Romantik Hotel zum Ritter St. Georg, Heidelberg,** Renaissance atmosphere by the barrel. **$$$$**

★ **Schlosshotel Bühlerhöhe, Bühl,** a castle-hotel with spectacular views over the heights of the Black Forest. **$$$$**

★ **Vier Jahreszeiten, Hamburg.** Antiques line the public rooms and embellish the stylish bedrooms; armloads of flowers stand in massive vases; rare oil paintings hang on the walls; and, of course, all rooms are individually decorated in superb taste. **$$$$**

★ **Garden Hotels Pöseldorf, Hamburg,** classy accommodations in three attractive city mansions. **$$$**

★ **Parkhotel Luisenbad, Bad Reichenhall,** the quintessential fin-de-siècle German spa hotel. Outside are pink porticoes and pillars, inside it's deep comfort and dark woods. **$$$**

★ **Pannonia Parkhotel, Meissen,** a Jugendstil villa on the banks of the Elbe with incredible suites under its eaves. **$$$**

★ **Deidesheimer Hof, Deidesheim,** a traditional old Deidesheimer house, immaculate and comfortable. **$$–$$$**

★ **Dornröschenschloss, Sababurg,** a small luxury hotel set in castle walls. **$$–$$$**

★ **Wilder Mann, Passau.** You sleep in beds of carved oak beneath chandeliers and richly stuccoed ceilings in this tastefully modernized 11th-century house. **$$–$$$**

★ **Hotel Ludwig der Bayer, Ettal,** a fine old hotel backed by mountains. **$$**

Castles and Palaces

★ **The Altes Schloss,** in Meersburg, a private residence, it watches majestically over the town and lake and only some of its rooms are open to the public.

★ **Burg Eltz,** in Mosel, is the real thing—an 800-year-old castle perched on the spine of an isolated rocky outcrop, bristling with towers and pinnacles.

★ **Burg Trifels,** in Annweiler, first constructed during the mid-12th century by the emperor Barbarossa. Today's castle is a 1937 replica.

★ **Heidelberg Schloss,** a mix of architectural styles. It has a particularly harmonious, graceful, and ornate Renaissance courtyard.

★ **Neuschwanstein,** in Füssen. The most fanciful of Ludwig II's fantasy castles, it rises out of the mountainside like nothing you've ever seen.

★ **Schloss Sanssouci,** Potsdam, Frederick the Great's magnificent summer palace and grounds.

★ **Wartburg Castle,** Eisenach, begun in 1067 and added to throughout the centuries. It hosted the German minstrels Walter von der Vogelweide and Wolfram von Eschenbach, Martin Luther, Richard Wagner, and Goethe. It's captivating inside and out.

Museums

★ **Deutsches Museum,** Munich, a monumental building full of stimulating, innovative scientific exhibits, a planetarium, and an IMAX theater.

★ **Domschatzkammer,** in Aachen, is one of the richest cathedral treasuries in Europe. Among its prizes are Charlemagne's bones, interred in a golden shrine, and his throne.

★ **The Gemäldegalerie,** Berlin, housing a broad selection of European paintings from the 13th to the 18th century.

★ **Kunsthalle,** Hamburg, the city's principal gallery. It has one of the most important art collections in Germany, with paintings from the Middle Ages to the present.

★ **Museum der Bildenden Künste,** Leipzig, an art gallery of international standard.

★ **Museum für Moderne Kunst,** Frankfurt, a distinctive triangular building with a great collection of contemporary art.

★ **Römisch-Germanisches Museum,** Köln, built around a huge Dionysus mosaic, houses stone Roman coffins and a series of memorial tablets, among other Roman-related exhibits.

★ **Wallraf-Richartz Museum and Museum Ludwig,** Köln. The former contains pictures spanning the years 1300 to 1900, with Dutch and Flemish schools particularly well represented, and the latter is devoted to 20th-century works. Together they form the Rhineland's largest art collection.

Churches

★ **Kölner Dom,** Köln, an extraordinary Gothic cathedral. Its 515-foot towers soar heavenward, and its immense interior is illuminated by light filtering through acres of stained glass.

★ **The Kaiserdom,** Aachen. Built over the course of 1,000 years, it reflects architectural styles from the Middle Ages to the 19th-century. Its commanding image is its magnificent octagonal royal chapel, rising up in two arched stories to end in the cap of the dome.

★ **Kaiserdom,** Speyer, one of the finest Romanesque cathedrals in Europe. It conveys, more than any other building in Germany, the pomp and majesty of the early Holy Roman Emperors.

★ **Mainzer Dom,** Mainz, basically finished in the 12th century; alterations to its Romanesque purity include an 18th-century Baroque spire.

★ **Münster, Freiburg.** That the cathedral took more than 300 years to build is evidenced by different architectural styles. Its 370-foot spire is delicately perforated.

★ **St. Margaretha, Osterhofen.** Frescoist and painter Cosmas Damian Asam and sculptors Egid Quirin Asam and Johann Michael Fischer decorated here in a rare partnership between 1728 and 1741.

★ **Trierer Dom,** Trier, an architectural jumble of Romanesque, Gothic, and Baroque styles, has the air of a vast antiques shop.

★ **Vierzehnheiligen,** in Franconia, built by Balthasar Neumann between 1743 and 1772. The entire building seems to be in motion—almost all the walls are curved and alive with delicate stucco.

★ **Wieskirche,** near Rottenbuch, has a simple exterior that gives little hint of the brilliantly colored stuccos, statues, and gilt and the luminous ceiling fresco inside.

★ **Wörmser Dom,** in Worms. A Romanesque masterpiece, though it was remodeled in keeping with new styles and attitudes.

Towns Where Time Stands Still

★ **Alsfeld.** Its medieval town center consists of beautifully preserved half-timbered houses that in places lean out to almost touch one another across narrow, winding cobbled streets. The Rathaus, with two pointy towers amid all the jumble, is particularly remarkable.

★ **Bad Wimpfen,** founded by the Romans, has remains of Barbarossa's imperial palace and a picture-postcard jumble of Gothic and Renaissance buildings.

★ **Bernkastel-Kues,** complete with Marktplatz, fountain, fortress, and vineyards.

★ **Hameln,** the town of Pied Piper fame, which has a street where no music is ever played.

★ **Rothenburg-ob-der-Tauber,** still enclosed by a wall, is a treasure of gingerbread architecture, fountains, and flowers against a backdrop of towers and turrets.

★ **St. Martin** Grape vines have practically taken over; they encroach on the narrow streets and link the ancient houses with curling green garlands.

★ **Wasserburg,** an auto-free island-town in the Bodensee, started as a fortress built on the site of a Roman watchtower.

Memorable Sights

★ **Baden-Baden's casino,** designed along the lines of the greatest French imperial palaces, with a series of richly decorated gaming rooms.

★ **The Brandenburger Tor and Wall remains** in Berlin give pause for reflection.

★ **The confluence of the Inn and Danube rivers at Passau** produces a special quality of light, a lovely complement to the fine old houses that line the waterfront.

★ **Munich's Oktoberfest,** a 16-day festival of beer (5 million liters of it), pretzels, rides, and oompah bands, on Munich's Theresienwiese exhibition grounds.

★ **Opera night in Bayreuth,** with a Wagner masterpiece performed in the theater he designed—an incredible thrill for Wagner fans.

★ **The Rhine in Flames fireworks,** an orgy of rockets and flares. It lights up St. Goar and St. Goarshausen and their surrounding vineyards every September.

★ **The Semper Opera House,** Dresden, built and named after a Dresden architect, and then rebuilt twice. Its lavish interior is sure to impress.

★ **The Street Dragon Festival,** in Furth im Wald in August. It sees townsfolk dressed in period costume taking part in the ritual slaying of a fire-breathing "dragon" that stalks the main street.

Unforgettable Excursions

★ **A boat ride on Bavaria's Königsee,** driven by a silent electric motor, allows you to glide serenely along the cliffs that plunge into the dark green water.

★ **A cruise on the Rhine,** a great way to appreciate this legendary river.

★ **A Hamburg harbor cruise at night** introduces you to the city like nothing else can.

★ **A round-trip ride from Freiburg on the Black Forest railway,** which will take you through Hell and other spectacular scenery.

★ **A steam-train ride from Bad Doberan to the Baltic Sea** aboard the *Molli,* the perfect way to make this 10-mile journey.

★ **A trek to the summit of the Zugspitze,** Germany's highest mountain, just 10 minutes by cable car.

★ **The depths of the country's largest salt mine,** at Berchtesgaden, once open only to select guests. Today, anyone can don miner's clothes and ride the miniature train that tours the Salzbergwerk.

★ **A torchlit sleigh ride through the Bavarian snow or a nighttime toboggan ride down an Alpine slope** gives you a different view of the mountains.

GREAT ITINERARIES

The Castles of Ludwig II

Munich tour operators offer day trips to the four famous castles of Bavaria's flamboyant King Ludwig II, but if you want to get to know them without distracting interruptions, there's no alternative but to strike out into the magnificent countryside on your own. If you're relying on public transportation, you'll have to return to Munich to visit the fourth castle, Herrenchiemsee, but arrange your itinerary so you can spend the night outside the city.

DURATION➤ 6 to 7 days

GETTING AROUND➤ **By Car:** From Munich, this is a 340-kilometer (210-mile) round-trip drive.

By Public Transportation: Füssen and the Chiemsee lake are reached by fast trains from Munich, with local buses making connections. A train service links Munich with Oberammergau, but allow two hours.

THE MAIN ROUTE➤ **Two Nights: Füssen.** You can walk to both Neuschwanstein and Hohenschwangau (Ludwig's childhood home) from Füssen or rent bikes at the station. Allow at least a full day at Neuschwanstein.

Two Nights: Ettal. Buses run from the picturesque mountain village of Ettal to Linderhof, which some consider the finest product of Ludwig's imagination. Find time to visit the Ettal monastery. Oberammergau is a 10-minute bus ride away.

Two Nights: Chiemsee. The unfinished Herrenchiemsee palace stands on Herren Island in the Chiemsee. Passenger boats offer regular service to the island (and to the smaller, equally charming Fraueninsel) from the lakeside resorts of Prien and Gstadt. A mainline train service runs from Munich to Prien, and the Munich-Salzburg Autobahn runs alongside the south shore of the Chiemsee.

Information: *See* Excursions from Munich, *in* Chapter 3; Chapter 4; and Chapter 8.

The Castle Road

Just outside the city of Heilbronn, amid rich vineyards, are the romantic ruins of the castle of the "Faithful Women." The explanation of its strange name is as romantic as the castle's setting. The German King Konrad III laid siege to the castle in 1140, and in a moment of uncharacteristic weakness allowed the women living within its walls to leave with as many of their possessions as they could carry. He is said to have lost his regal cool when the women of the castle trooped out carrying their menfolk on their backs. But he kept his word—and the men of the castle were spared. It's a marvelous yarn, typical of the stories you'll hear throughout this "castle" trail. There are about 50 castles along the 291-kilometer (180-mile) route between Mannheim and Nürnberg, a greater concentration than in any other part of Germany. Time and other circumstances (some of the castles are in private hands or serve some municipal function and can't be visited) will prevent you from looking over them all. On the other hand, some are now hotels where you'll be tempted to linger at least for a meal, perhaps to stay the night.

DURATION➤ 12 to 14 days

GETTING AROUND➤ **By Car:** It's 291 kilometers (180 miles) from Mannheim to Nürnberg. Follow the Neckar Valley road, B-27, from Mannheim to Heilbronn, then take the Burgenstrasse (the Castle Road itself) to Rothenburg-ob-der-Tauber. From Rothenburg, head for Colmberg and Hessbach, joining B-13 for the final stretch to Ansbach and Nürnberg.

By Public Transportation: Mannheim, Heidelberg, Heilbronn, and Nürnberg are all connected by regular express train services, but you'll have to rely on country bus services to reach many of the remoter castles.

THE MAIN ROUTE➤ **One Night: Mannheim.** Take part of the day to visit Mannheim's magnificent 18th-century Elector's Palace, one of the largest Baroque buildings in Europe, and the Reiss-Insel Park and its walks alongside the Rhine.

Two Nights: Heidelberg. Spend a full day exploring Heidelberg itself, then make an excursion to the Heiligenberg, into the Odenwald Forest or to the castles of Schadeck, Hornberg, Hirschorn (all of them hotels, with excellent restaurants), or to Zwingenberg and Minneburg.

Three Nights: Heilbronn. Plan excursions to the remains of the imperial palace of Bad Wimpfen and to the castles of Horneck, Guttenberg (with its aviary of birds of prey, including some fine eagles), Bad Rappenau, Ehrenberg, Weinsberg (the castle of "Faithful Women"), Neuenstein, and perhaps to the museum of bicycle and motorcycle technology at Neckarsulm.

Two Nights: Rothenburg-ob-der-Tauber. You'll want to spend at least a full day exploring Rothenburg, Europe's best-preserved medieval town. After that, make excursions along the Tauber River valley and to the castles of Langenburg, Bartenstein, and Colmberg.

Two Nights: Ansbach. Visit the margraves' palace and the 12th-century monastery church of Heilsbronn.

Two Nights: Nürnberg.

INFORMATION➤ *See* Chapters 8, 9, and 11.

Rivers of Wine

The Rhine and Mosel need no introduction, but who knows the attractions of their tributaries—the rivers Saar and Nahe? Or the remote villages scattered across the Hunsrück range of hills, which is bordered by all four rivers? A tour of the four "rivers of wine" will take you from the crowds and crush of the Rhine of picture-postcard fame to the less dramatic but much more peaceful valley of the Saar. The Hunsrück high road leads you back at your own pace to the point where the well-trodden tourist trail picks up again on the Nahe River. In little more than a week, you'll have skirted (and perhaps visited) Germany's most famous vineyards—and you should have tasted some of the country's finest wines.

DURATION➤ 10 to 12 days

GETTING AROUND➤ **By Car:** It's a 454-kilometer (280-mile) round-trip drive from Wiesbaden.

By Public Transportation: The rail journey along the Rhine between Bingen and Koblenz is Germany's most spectacular train ride. Riverboats also make the journey, and you can stop off at any point on the way. From Koblenz, the rail line hugs the contours of the Mosel River to Trier; alternatively, you can again choose to travel the river by boat. A combination of train and bus will complete the itinerary along the Saar and across the Hunsrück to the Nahe River. Bus tours are offered by travel agencies in Wiesbaden, Bingen, Koblenz, and Trier.

THE MAIN ROUTE➤ **Two Nights:** The **Rheingau** region, between Eltville and Rüdesheim. Visit the vineyards of the Rheingau (they produce Germany's finest wine) and Bingen, at the mouth of the Nahe River.

Four Nights: Along the **Rhine** between Rüdesheim and Koblenz. See the vineyards of Bacharach, Boppard, Brey, Kaub, Lorch, Oberwesel, Spay, and St. Goar, and the castles (or what remains of them) of Ehrenfels, Katz, Reichenstein, Rheinstein, Schönburg, and Sooneck.

Four Nights: Along the **Mosel** between Koblenz and Trier. Take excursions to the Deutsche Eck (where the Mosel and Rhine meet) and to the vineyards of Alken, Bernkastel-Kues, Bremm (Europe's steepest vineyard), Ediger, Kobern-Gondorf, Kröv, Nehren, Neumagen (Germany's oldest wine town, praised by the 4th-century Roman poet Ausonius in his work *Mosella*), Piesport, Traben-Trarbach, Winningen (its August wine festival is one of Germany's oldest), Zell, and to the castles of Cochem, Ehrenburg, Eltz (a medieval picture-book castle so treasured by the Germans that they've engraved its image on their DM 500 bank notes), and Thurant.

Two Nights: Trier. Explore Trier and follow the Saar River to Saarburg, Mettlach, and as far as the great "Saar Bend," a spectacular point where the river nearly doubles back on itself.

Two Nights: Idar-Oberstein. Venture into the Hunsrück hills and along the Nahe River to Bad Kreuznach. Take a day tour of the *Edelsteinstrasse* or Gem Road, a well-marked 48-kilometer (30-mile) itinerary, starting and ending in Idar Oberstein, where precious stones are still mined and polished.

INFORMATION➤ *See* Chapter 13.

Through the Black Forest

Many first-time visitors to the Black Forest literally can't see the forest for the trees. There are so many contrasting attractions that the basic, enduring beauty of the area passes them by. So in your tour of the forest, take time to stray from the tourist path and inhale the cool, mysterious air of its darker recesses. Walk or ride through its shadowy corridors or across its open upland; row a canoe and tackle the wild water of the Nagold and Wolf rivers. Then take time out to relax in any of the many spas, order a Baden wine enlivened by a dash of local mineral water, seek out the nearest restaurant that confesses to its food being influenced by the cuisine of neighboring France. And, if you have money to spare at the end of your tour, return to Baden-Baden, try your luck on the gaming tables, and celebrate your good fortune or forget ill fate at the bar of the casino's "Griffen's" nightclub.

DURATION➤ 12 to 14 days

GETTING AROUND➤ **By Car:** It's a 405-kilometer (250-mile) round-trip drive from Stuttgart.

By Public Transportation: Stuttgart, Baden-Baden, and Freiburg are all on InterCity train routes, and local trains and buses link them with most towns and spas of the Black Forest. Bus tours of the Black Forest are offered by travel agencies in Baden-Baden and Freiburg.

THE MAIN ROUTE➤ **Two Nights: Freudenstadt.** Take excursions to the Schwarzwald Museum at Lossburg, the Freilicht Museum Vogtsbauernhof near Wolfach, the Alpirsbach brewery, and the Glasswald lake near Schapbach.

One Night: Triberg area. See the Triberg waterfall and the clock museums of Triberg and Furtwangen.

Two Nights: Hinterzarten or **Titisee.** Visit the Feldberg, the Black Forest's highest mountain, and the lakes of Titisee and Schluchsee.

Two Nights: Freiburg. Explore Freiburg, the Schauinsland Mountain, the Dr. Faustus town of Staufen, and the vineyards on the slopes of the Kaiserstuhl.

One Night: Offenburg. Visit the surrounding vineyards.

Two Nights: Baden-Baden. Enjoy the sights in and around Baden-Baden and travel to the summit of nearby Merkur Mountain, to Schloss Favorite, and to Windeck Castle.

One Night: Bad Liebenzell. *See* Chapter 7.

INFORMATION➤ *See* Chapter 7.

Toward East Bavaria

There's a corner of Germany that's on the doorstep of the country's most popular tourist area and yet can seem 1,000 miles from it. It stretches east from Munich to the Austrian border, its south edge marked by the Salzburg-bound autobahn, which propels most visitors and tourists to the greater attractions of the Bavarian Alps looming in the hazy distance. It's a gentle, pastoral region of rolling farmland, forgotten villages asserting their presence with hilltop, onion-dome Baroque churches, of reed-fringed lakes and willow-bordered rivers. And what rivers! You'll meet the Inn as it meanders northward in search of the Danube, Salzburg's Salzach River, then the mighty Danube itself as it surges into Austria, and finally the Isar, ice-green and—just as the poet promised—still "rolling rapidly" from its mountain source.

DURATION➤ 7 to 8 days

GETTING AROUND➤ **By Car:** It's a 405-kilometer (250-mile) round-trip drive from Munich.

By Public Transportation: The route can be covered entirely by train, beginning with the main-line route from Munich to Wasserburg and then using local services between the remaining towns.

THE MAIN ROUTE➤ **One Night: Wasserburg.** Visit the medieval Amerang Castle (in summer, scene of chamber-music concerts) and the farmhouse museum at Amerang.

One Night: Laufen, on the Austrian border. Take excursions to the Waginger See, Germany's warmest lake, and across the Salzach River to the Austrian town of Oberndorf, where the Christmas carol "Silent Night" was composed.

One Night: Burghausen. In Altötting, see the 14th-century "Black Madonna" in an 8th-century chapel chosen by the Wittelsbachs to be the repository of silver urns containing the hearts of the Bavarian rulers.

Two Nights: Passau. Venture north into the Bavarian Forest and perhaps across the border into the Czech Republic.

One Night: Straubing. Travel to the Danube towns Deggendorf and Bogen.

INFORMATION➤ *See* Chapter 6.

FESTIVALS AND SEASONAL EVENTS

Top seasonal events in Germany include Carnival festivities throughout the country in January and February, spring festivals (nationwide), Munich's Opera Festival in July, Bayreuth's Richard Wagner Festival in August, horse racing at Baden-Baden in August, wine festivals throughout the Rhineland in August, the Oktoberfest in Munich in late September and early October, the Frankfurt Book Fair in October, and December's Christmas markets (nationwide).

WINTER

DECEMBER➤ **Christmas Markets** are held in Augsburg, Munich, Heidelberg, Hamburg, Nürnberg, Lübeck, Freiburg, Berlin, Essen, and numerous other cities and smaller towns.

Grand Slam Cup, in Munich, is the world's richest tennis tournament.

JANUARY➤ **New Year International Ski Jumping**, among other winter-sports competitions, occur at Garmisch-Partenkirchen.

Fasching season. The Rhineland is Germany's capital of Carnival events, including proclamations of Carnival princes, street fairs, parades, masked balls, and more. Some of the main Carnival cities are Koblenz and Köln, Mainz, Bonn, and Düsseldorf; although there's also plenty

of activity in Munich and in smaller cities and towns throughout southern Germany. Festivities always run through February, finishing on *Fasching Dienstag* (Shrove Tuesday or Mardi Gras).

International Green Week Agricultural Fair is held in Berlin.

Max Ophüls Film Festival, in Saarbrücken, is one of Germany's smallest but most provocative film festivals.

FEBRUARY➤ **Black Forest Ski Marathon** is a 60-kilometer (37-mile) ski race in Schonach-Hinterzarten.

Frankfurt International Fair is a major consumer goods trade fair.

International Clock, Watch, Jewelry, Gems, and Silverware Trade Fair is held in Munich.

International Filmfestspiele is a two-week film festival held in Berlin.

International Toy Fair, with models, hobbies, and handicrafts, takes place in Nürnberg.

Handel Music Festival comes to Karlsruhe.

SPRING

MARCH➤ **ITB,** one of Europe's largest international tourism fairs, takes place in Berlin.

International Easter Egg Fair takes place in Köln.

Leipzig Trade Fair attracts businesspeople from throughout Europe.

Munich Fashion Week is a popular trade fair of the latest fashions.

Spring Fairs. In such towns as Erfurt, Münster, Hamburg, Nürnberg, Stuttgart, and Augsburg, festivities ring in the spring season.

APRIL➤ **Frankfurt International Art Fair.**

Mannheim May Fair is a traditional spring fair with flower floats and parades.

Munich Ballet Days.

Stuttgart Jazz Festival.

Walpurgis Festivals. Towns in the Harz Mountains celebrate this night before May Day.

MAY➤ **Dresden Musikfestspiele** (orchestral concerts and opera), at the Semper Opera House and some of the city's palaces, starts in late May and runs into June.

Hamburg Summer is a whole season of festivals, concerts, plays, and exhibitions; events runs through October.

Folk, Jazz, Rock, and Pop Music are featured on weekends of entertainment in Köln's Rheinpark.

Four Castles Illumination presents fireworks on the heights of Neckarsteinach.

German Open Tennis Tournament takes place in Hamburg.

Hamburg Ballet Festival with the Hamburg State Opera company.

International May Festival brings a month of opera, ballet, and theater performances to Wiesbaden.

International Mime Festival, in Stuttgart, attracts some of the best in the world.

International Jazz Festival takes place in Nürnberg.

Mozart's Heritage in Dresden celebrates the composer with opera, symphony, and chamber music concerts.

Red Wine Festival is held at Assmannshausen near Rüdesheim.

Schwetzinger Festspiele (orchestral concerts, opera, and ballet) at the Schwetzingen Schloss starts in April and continues until June.

SUMMER

EARLY JUNE–AUGUST➤ **Castle Concerts** and musical events are held in Munich's Residenz and Nymphenburg Palace.

Castle Illuminations, with spectacular fireworks, are presented in Heidelberg.

Franco-German Folk Festival is held in Berlin.

Festival of the Arts, with theater and ballet performances, takes place in Weimar.

Frankfurt Craft Week.

Frankfurt Summertime Festival features outdoor activities throughout the city.

Händel Festival is celebrated in Halle.

International Theater Festival takes place in Freiburg.

Kiel Week is an international sailing regatta in Kiel.

Kuntsfest Weimar is a month-long series of concerts held in Weimar.

Mosel Wine Week celebrations take place in Cochem.

Munich Film Festival.

Music Days highlight Leipzig's cultural calendar.

Nymphenburg Summer Festival, with concerts at Nymphenburg Palace, is held in Munich.

Weilburg Castle Concerts.

Würzburg Mozart Festival is held in several Würzburg locations.

JULY➤ **Bach Festival** in Berlin pays homage to one of Germany's greatest composers.

Folk Festivals. Outdoor festivities are held in Krov, Wald-Michelbach, Waldshut-Tiengen, Würzburg, Geisenheim, Speyer, Lübeck, Karlsruhe, Düsseldorf, Oestrich-Winkel, and Paderhorn.

German-American Folk Festival is Berlin's celebration of two cultures.

International Weissenhof Tennis Tournament for the Mercedes Cup is played in Stuttgart.

Kulmbach Beer Festival.

Old Town Festival includes castle illuminations in Neckarsteinach.

Opera Festival is Munich's major operatic affair.

Theater der Welt Festival takes place in Essen.

AUGUST➤ **Bad Hersfeld Festival** of opera is performed amid monastery ruins.

BMW Golf International takes place at the Eschenried course near Munich.

Castle Festival features open-air theater presentations at the castle in Heidelberg.

Grand Baden-Baden Week highlights international horse racing at Iffezheim in Baden-Baden.

Partenkirchen Festival Week is held in Garmisch-Partenkirchen.

Rhine in Flames, Germany's oldest and largest fireworks display.

Richard Wagner Festival is a major musical event in Bayreuth.

Stuttgart European Music Festival.

Wine Festivals break out throughout the Rhineland.

AUTUMN

SEPTEMBER➤ **Berlin Festival Weeks** feature classical music concerts all month long.

Berlin International Marathon.

Bonn's International Beethoven Festival begins in mid-September and continues into October.

Eltville Summer Festival at Schloss Reinhartshausen offers fine wine and music.

Leipzig Trade Fair again draws commercial interests to that city.

Oktoberfest (late Sept.–early Oct.) in Munich attracts millions of visitors from throughout Germany, Europe, and abroad.

OCTOBER➢ **Art and Antiques Fair** happens in Munich.

Bremen Freimarkt is a centuries-old folk festival and procession in Bremen; it's the largest in northern Germany.

Frankfurt Book Fair is a famous annual literary event.

NOVEMBER➢ **Antiques Fair** is held in Berlin.

Art Cologne, held in Köln, is a festival of modern art.

St. Martin's Festival, with children's lantern proces-sions, is celebrated throughout the Rhineland and Bavaria.

Six-Day Cycle Race takes place in Munich.

Forum Vini is Munich's annual wine bash in a beer hall.

2 Munich

Chic and cosmopolitan, carefree and kitschy. As Bavaria's capital and one of Germany's biggest cites, Munich has more than its share of great museums, architectural treasures, historic sites, and world-class shops, restaurants, and hotels. The same could be said of its abundance of lederhosen and oompah bands. But it's the overall feeling of Gemütlichkeit that makes the city so special—an open-air market here, a park there, and beer halls everywhere.

MUNICH—München to the Germans—third-largest city in the Federal Republic and capital of the Free State of Bavaria, is the single most popular tourist destination for Germans. This one statistic attests to the enduring appeal of what by any standard is a supremely likable city. Munich is kitsch and class, vulgarity and elegance. It's a city of ravishing Rococo and smoky beer cellars, of soaring Gothic and sparkling shops, of pale stucco buildings and space-age factories, of millionaires and lederhosen-clad farmers.

Germany's favorite city is a place with extraordinary ambience and a vibrant lifestyle all its own, in a splendid setting within view—on a clear day—of the towering Alps.

Munich belongs to the relaxed and sunny south. Call it Germany with a southern exposure—although it may be an exaggeration to claim, as some Bavarians do, that Munich is the only Italian city north of the Alps.

Still, there's no mistaking the carefree spirit that infuses the place, and the easygoing approach to life, liberty, and the pursuit of happiness, Bavarian style. The Bavarians refer to this positively un-Teutonic joie de vivre as *Gemütlichkeit,* loosely translated as conviviality.

It may be all too easy to point to the abundance of beer that flows through the city and its numerous beer restaurants, beer cellars, and beer gardens as the most obvious manifestation of this take-life-as-it-comes attitude. Certainly it's hard not to feel something approaching awe at the realization that Munich University has a beer faculty.

What makes Munich so special? How can its secret be explained? Is it that Munich, despite a population in excess of 1.3 million, retains something of a small-town, almost villagelike atmosphere? Is it in the variety of buildings that dot its center, giving the city, on the one hand, a baroque grandeur, on the other the semblance of a toy town.

One explanation is that a flair for the fanciful is deeply rooted in the Bavarian culture. And no historical figure better personifies this tradition than Ludwig II, one of the last of the Wittelsbachs, the royal dynasty that for almost 750 years ruled over Munich and southern Germany, until the monarchy was forced to abdicate in 1918.

For while Bismarck was striving from his Berlin power base to create a modern unified Germany, "Mad" Ludwig—also nicknamed the "Dream King"—was almost bankrupting the state's treasury by building a succession of fairy-tale castles and remote summer retreats in the mountains and countryside.

Munich bills itself as *Die Weltstadt mit Herz* (the cosmopolitan city with heart), which it most assuredly is. A survey suggests that, given the choice, most Germans would prefer to live in Munich rather than where they currently reside, even though it is probably the most expensive place in reunited Germany.

This is not to suggest that all Germans subscribe to the "I Love Munich" concept. Certain buttoned-up types in Hamburg or Düsseldorf, for example, might look down their imperious noses at Munich as being just a mite crass and somewhat tacky, and the Bavarians as only a few rungs up the ladder from the barbarians. So be it.

Munich is obviously Germany's "good-time city," its image indelibly tied to a series of splashy celebrations that have spread the city's fame far and wide. Mention of Munich invariably triggers thoughts of the colorful carnival season that goes by the name *Fasching*, and the equally gaudy spectacle of the 16-day beer festival known as *Oktoberfest*. The city has become synonymous with beer, *Wurst* (sausage), and Gemütlichkeit. This triad comes close to the essence of the Munich experience.

The stock image is the cavernous beer hall (such as the world-famous Hofbräuhaus) filled with the deafening echo of a brass oompah band and rows of swaying burly Bavarians in lederhosen being served by frumpy Fraus in flaring dirndl dresses. Every day of the week, in different parts of the city, you'll find scenes like this. But there are also many Müncheners who never step inside a beer hall, who never go near the Oktoberfest. They belong to the *other* Munich—a city of charm, refinement, and sophistication, represented by two of the world's most important art galleries and a noted opera house, a city of expensive elegance, where high-fashion shops seem to compete to put the highest price tags on their wares, a city of five-star nouvelle cuisine.

Endowed with vast tracts of greenery in the form of parks, gardens, and forests; grand boulevards set with remarkable edifices; fountains and statuary; and a river spanned by graceful bridges, Munich is easily Germany's most beautiful and interesting city. If the traveler could visit only one city in Germany, this should be it. No question about it.

Add the fact that the city has changed dramatically over the past decade or so, and for the traveler who has not been here for a number of years, one might say that a whole new Munich has evolved in the interim. For, quietly and without fanfare, Munich has taken its place as the high-tech capital of Germany, developing into the number-one postindustrial-age center in the country and one of the most important cities in Europe. The concentration of electronics and computer firms—Siemens, IBM, Apple, and the like—in and around the city has turned the area into the Silicon Valley of Germany.

All this has made Munich one of Europe's wealthiest cities. And it shows. Here everything is extremely upscale and up-to-date. At times the aura of affluence may become all but overpowering. But that's what Munich is all about these days and nights: a new city superimposed on the old; conspicuous consumption on a scale we can hardly imagine as a way of life; a fresh patina of glitter along with the traditional rustic charms. Such are the dynamics and duality of this fascinating metropolis that remains a joy to explore and get to know.

EXPLORING

Tour 1: Old Town

Numbers in the margin correspond to points of interest on the Munich map.

❶ Begin your tour of the city at the **Hauptbahnhof,** the main train station and site of the city tourist office, which is located on the corner of Bayerstrasse. Pick up a detailed city map here. Cross Bahnhofplatz, the square in front of the station, and walk toward Schützenstrasse, which marks the start of Munich's pedestrian shopping mall, the Fussgängerzone, 2 kilometers (1½ miles) of traffic-free streets. Running virtually the length of Schützenstrasse is Munich's largest department store,

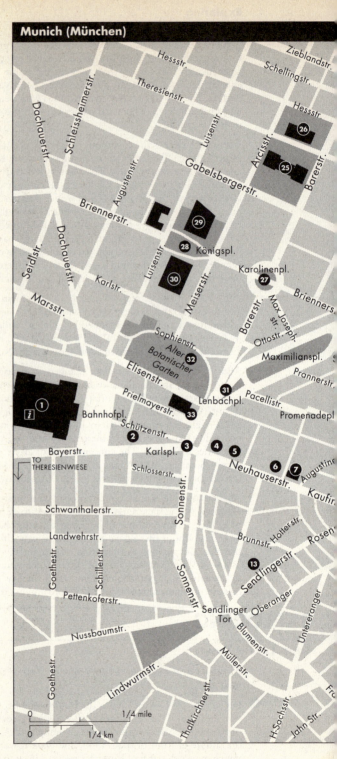

Munich (München)

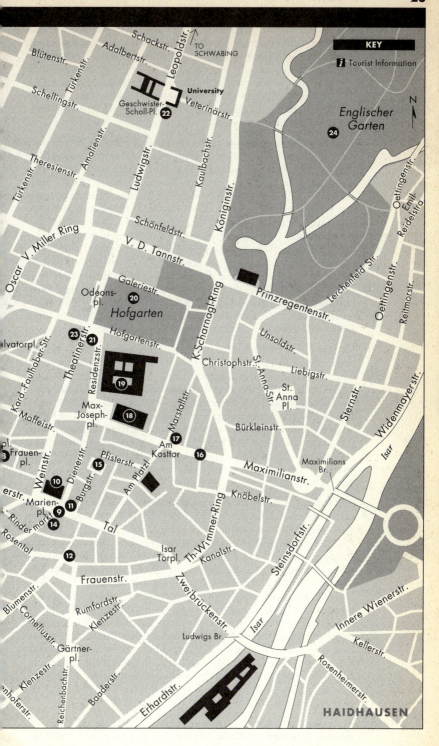

KEY

i Tourist Information

Schackstr.

Leopoldstr.

TO
SCHWABING

Blütenstr.

Adalbertstr.

Türkenstr.

Schellingstr.

University

Geschwister-
Scholl-Pl. **22**

Veterinärstr.

Amalienstr.

Theresienstr.

Türkenstr.

Ludwigstr.

Kaulbachstr.

Königinstr.

*Englischer
Garten*

24

N

Oettingenstr.

Reidelstr.
Emil

Oscar V. Miller Ring

Schönfeldstr.

V. D. Tannstr.

Prinzregentenstr.

Lerchenfeld Str.

Oettingenstr.

Reitmorstr.

Galeriestr.

Odeons-
pl.

20

Hofgarten

Unsoldstr.

Liebigstr.

Sternstr.

Salvatorpl.

23

21

Hofgartenstr.

K.-Scharnagl-Ring

Christophstr.

St.-Anna-Str.

St.
Anna
Pl.

Widenmayerstr.

Kard.-Faulhaber-Str.

Theatinerstr.

Residenzstr.

19

Marstallstr.

Bürkleinstr.

Maffeistr.

Max-
Joseph-
pl.

18

Am
Kosttor

17

16

Maximilianstr.

Maximilians
Br.

Isar

Frauen-
pl.

Weinstr.

Dienerstr.

Pfisterstr.

15

Burgstr.

Am Platzl

Knöbelstr.

10

9 **11**

Marien-
pl.

Rinder-
markt

14

Tal

Isar
Torpl.

Th.-Wimmer-Ring

Kanalstr.

Steinsdorfstr.

Rosental

12

Frauenstr.

Zweibrückenstr.

Innere Wienerstr.

Blumenstr.

Corneliusstr.

Rumfordstr.

Klenzestr.

Gärtner-
pl.

Ludwigs Br.

Isar

Rosenheimerstr.

Kellerstr.

Klenzestr.

Reichenbachstr.

Baaderstr.

Erhardtstr.

HAIDHAUSEN

② **Hertie.** At the end of the street you descend via the pedestrian underpass into another shopping empire, a vast underground complex of boutiques and cafés. **③** Above you is the busy traffic intersection, **Karlsplatz,** known locally as *Stachus*. You'll emerge at one of Munich's most popular fountains, a circle of water jets that act as a magnet on hot summer days for city shoppers and office workers seeking a cool corner. The semicircle of yellow-front buildings that back the fountain, with their high windows and delicate cast-iron balconies, give the area a southern, almost Mediterranean, air.

Ahead stands one of the city's oldest gates, the **Karlstor,** first mentioned in local records in 1302. Beyond it lies Munich's main shopping thoroughfare, Neuhauserstrasse and its extension, Kaufingerstrasse. On your left as you enter Neuhauserstrasse is another attractive Munich fountain, a jovial, late-19th-century figure of Bacchus. Neuhauserstrasse and Kaufingerstrasse are a jumble of ancient and modern buildings. This part of town was bombed almost to extinction during World War II and has been extensively rebuilt. Great efforts were made to ensure that the designs of these new buildings harmonized with the rest of the old city, though some of the newer structures are little more than functional. Still, even though this may not be one of the architectural high **④** points of the city, there are at least some redeeming features. **Haus Oberpollinger,** a department store hiding behind an imposing 19th-century facade, is one. Notice the weather vanes of old merchant ships on its high-gabled roof.

Shopping, however, is not the only attraction on these streets. Worldly department stores rub shoulders with two remarkable churches: **⑤** Michaelskirche and the Bürgersaal. Your first stop will be the **Bürgersaal,** built in 1710. Beneath its modest roof are two contrasting levels. The upper level—the church proper—consists of a richly decorated Baroque oratory. Its elaborate stucco foliage and paintings of Bavarian places of pilgrimage project a distinctly different ambience from that of the lower level, reached by descending a double staircase. This gloomy, cryptlike chamber contains the tomb of Rupert Mayer, a famous Jesuit priest renowned for his energetic and outspoken opposition to the Nazis.

A few steps farther is the restrained Renaissance facade of the 16th-**⑥** century **Michaelskirche.** It was built by Duke Wilhelm V. Seven years after the start of construction the principal tower collapsed. The duke regarded the disaster as a sign from heaven that the church wasn't big enough, so he ordered a change in the plans—this time without a tower. Completed seven years later, the Michaelskirche was the first Renaissance church of this size in southern Germany. The duke is buried in the crypt, along with 40 members of Bavaria's famous Wittelsbach family (the ruling dynasty for seven centuries), including the eccentric King Ludwig II. A severe neoclassical monument in the north transept contains the tomb of Napoléon's stepson, Eugene de Beauharnais, who married one of the daughters of Bavaria's King Maximilian I and died in Munich in 1824. You'll find the plain white stucco interior of the church and its slightly barnlike atmosphere soothingly simple after the lavish decoration of the Bürgersaal. Guided tours of the church are given every Wednesday at 2 PM. ☛ DM 5.

TIME OUT   Across the road beckons the *Jugendstil* (German) facade of the **Augustiner Gaststätte.** Within its late-19th-century interior, beer from Munich's oldest brewery is served. Even if you don't want a drink, look inside for more stunning examples of Bavarian Jugendstil.

The massive building next to Michaelskirche was once one of Munich's oldest churches, built during the late 13th century for Benedictine monks. It was secularized during the early 19th century, served as a warehouse for some years, and today houses the **Deutsches Jagd-und Fischereimuseum** (German Museum of Hunting and Fishing). Lovers of the thrill of the chase will find it a fascinating place. It also contains the world's largest collection of fishhooks. *Neuhauserstr. 2.* ☞ *DM 5 adults, DM 3 children and senior citizens.* ☺ *Tues., Wed., Fri.–Sun. 9:30–5; Mon. and Thurs. 9:30–9.*

Turn left on Augustinerstrasse and you will soon arrive in Frauenplatz, a quiet square with a shallow sunken fountain. Towering over it is **Frauenkirche** (Church of Our Lady), Munich's cathedral. It's a distinctive late-Gothic brick structure with two enormous towers. Each is more than 300 feet high, and both are capped by very un-Gothic, onion-shape domes. The towers have become the symbol of Munich's skyline, some say because they look like overflowing beer mugs. The cathedral is open again after being closed for external and internal renovations that took more than two years to complete and cost DM 26 million.

The main body of the cathedral was completed in 20 years—a record time in those days. The towers were added, almost as an afterthought, between 1524 and 1525. Jörg von Polling, the Frauenkirche's original architect, is buried within the walls of the cathedral. The building suffered severe damage during the Allied bombing of Munich and was lovingly restored from 1947 to 1957. Inside, the church combines most of von Polling's original features with a stark, clean modernity and simplicity of line, emphasized by slender white octagonal pillars that sweep up through the nave to the yellow-traced ceiling far above. As you enter the church, look on the stone floor for the dark imprint of a large footstep—the *Teufelstritt* (Devil's footprint). According to local lore, the Devil challenged von Polling to build a nave without windows. Von Polling wagered his soul and accepted the challenge, building a cathedral that is flooded with light from 66-foot-high windows that are invisible to anyone standing at the point marked by the Teufelstritt. The cathedral houses an elaborate, 15th-century black-marble memorial to Emperor Ludwig the Bavarian, guarded by four 16th-century armored knights.

A splendid view of the city is yours from an observation platform high in one of the towers. The elevator runs April–October, Monday–Saturday 10–5 (DM 4 adults, DM 2 children). But beware—you must climb 86 steps to reach the elevator! From the cathedral, follow any of the alleys heading east and you'll reach the very heart of Munich, **Marienplatz,** which is surrounded by shops, restaurants, and cafés. The square is named after the gilded statue of the Virgin Mary that has been watching over it for more than three centuries. It was erected in 1638 at the behest of elector Maximilian I as an act of thanksgiving for the survival of the city during the Thirty Years' War, the cataclysmic religious struggle that devastated vast regions of Germany. When the statue, which stands on a marble column, was taken down to be cleaned for a eucharistic world congress in 1960, workmen found a small casket in the base containing a splinter of wood that was said to have come from the cross of Christ.

Marienplatz is dominated by the 19th-century **Neues Rathaus** (New Town Hall), built between 1867 and 1908 in the fussy, urreted, neo-Gothic style so beloved by King Ludwig II. Architectural historians are divided over its merits, though its dramatic scale and lavish detailing are impressive. Perhaps the most serious criticism is that the Dutch and

Flemish style of the building seems out of place amid the Baroque and Rococo of so much of the rest of the city. The **Altes Rathaus** (Old Town Hall), a medieval building of assured charm, sits modestly, as if forgotten, in a corner of the square. Its great hall—destroyed in 1944 but now fully restored—was the work of architect Jörg von Halspach.

In 1904, a glockenspiel (a chiming clock with mechanical figures) was added to the tower of the new town hall; it plays daily at 11 AM and noon (also at 5 PM and 9 PM June–Oct.). As the chimes peal out over the square, doors flip open and brightly colored dancers and jousting knights go through their paces. They act out two events from Munich's past: a tournament held in Marienplatz in 1568 and the *Schäfflertanz* (Dance of the Coopers), which commemorated the end of the plague of 1517. When Munich was in ruins after the war, an American soldier contributed some paint to restore the battered figures, and he was rewarded with a ride on one of the jousters' horses, high above the cheering crowds. You, too, can travel up there by elevator, to an observation point near the top of one of the towers. On a clear day the view is spectacular. The fare for the ride is DM 2 for adults, DM 1 for children. The elevator is in operation April–October, Monday–Saturday 10–5.

TIME OUT   If you're visiting Munich after mid-1996, you'll be able to ride one of the newly installed glass-enclosed elevators to the sixth-floor **Hoch-Cafe,** opposite the Neues Rathaus, where the view of the glockenspiel is unbeatable. (Work on installing the lifts and renovating and enlarging the café and Press Club premises began in 1995 and was scheduled for completion by mid-1996.) The café is open daily until 10 PM and serves medium-priced light meals as well as morning coffee and afternoon tea.

If you're thinking of lunch after the glockenspiel performance, cross the square, head through the old town-hall arcade, turn right, and join the crowds doing their day's shopping at the **Viktualienmarkt,** the city's open-air food market (*Viktualien* is an old German word for food). A wide range of produce, German and international food, Bavarian beer, and French wines make the market a feast for the eyes as well as the stomach. It is also the realm of the garrulous, sturdy market women, dressed in traditional country costume, who run the stalls with dictatorial authority; one of them was reprimanded roundly by Munich's leading newspaper for rudely warning an American tourist not to touch the fruit!

On *Fasching Dienstag* (Shrove Tuesday), the last day of the carnival period before Lent, the market women soften a little as they lead dancing and singing in the market square. There's more dancing on May Day (May 1), this time round the blue-and-white maypole. Figures adorning the pole represent the traditional crafts of the city. The characters atop several small fountains scattered about the market square represent legendary Bavarian music-hall stars, singers, and comedians from the past.

In summer, take a chair at one of the tables of a lively beer garden set up beneath great chestnut trees and enjoy an alfresco lunch of Bavarian sausages and sauerkraut.

Various *Metzgereien* (butcher shops) in and around the market dispense different types of sausages and will make sandwiches either to go or to be eaten on the premises. For *Thüringer Rostbratwurstl*—a slightly spicy, long thin sausage—or *Nürnberger Bratwurstl,* head for the Schlemmermeyer Brotzeit Standl stalls.

The market even has a champagne bar where high-tone tidbits go along with the bubbly served by the glass.

From the market, follow Rosental into Sendlingerstrasse, one of the city's most interesting shopping streets, and head left toward Sendlinger Tor, a finely restored medieval brick gate. On your right as you head down Sendlingerstrasse is the remarkable 18th-century church of St.

★ ⑬ Johann Nepomuk, known as the **Asamkirche** because of the two Asam brothers, Cosmas Damian and Egid Quirin, who built it. The exterior fits so snugly into the housefronts of the street (the Asam brothers lived next door) that you might easily overlook the church as you pass; yet the raw rock foundation of the facade, with its gigantic pilasters, announces the presence of something unusual. Before you go in, have a look above the doorway at the statue of St. Nepomuk, a 14th-century Bohemian monk who drowned in the Danube; you'll see that angels are conducting him to heaven from a rocky riverbank. Inside you'll discover a prime example of true southern German, late-Baroque architecture. Red stucco and rosy marble cover the walls; there is an explosion of frescoes, statuary, and gilding. The little church overwhelms with its opulence and lavish detailing—take a look at the gilt skeletons in the little atrium—and creates a powerfully mystical atmosphere. This is a vision of paradise on earth that those who are more accustomed to the gaunt Gothic cathedrals of northern Europe may find disconcerting. It is a fine example, though, of the Bavarian taste for ornament and, possibly, overkill. Is it vulgar or a great work of architecture? You be the judge.

Return down Sendlingerstrasse toward the city center and turn right into the Rindermarkt (the former cattle market) and you'll be beneath

⑭ the soaring tower of **Peterskirche,** or Alter Peter (Old Peter), as Munich's oldest and smallest parish church is affectionately called. The church traces its origins to the 11th century and over the years has been restored in a variety of architectural styles. Today you'll find a rich Baroque interior with a magnificent late-Gothic high altar and aisle pillars decorated with exquisite 18th-century figures of the apostles. From the top of its 300-foot tower there's a fine view of the city. In clear weather it's well worth the climb—the view includes glimpses of the Alps to the south. ☛ *Tower: DM 2.50 adults, DM 1.50 children.* ☉ *Weekdays 9–6, Sat. 8:30–6, Sun. 10–6.*

From Peterskirche, reenter Marienplatz and pass in front of the Altes Rathaus once again to step into Burgstrasse. You'll soon find yourself

⑮ in the quiet, airy **Alter Hof,** the inner courtyard of the original palace of the Wittelsbach rulers of Bavaria. They held court here starting in 1253, and something of the medieval flavor of those times has survived in this quiet corner of the otherwise busy downtown area. Don't pass through without turning to admire the medieval oriel (bay window) that hides modestly on the south wall, just around the corner as you enter the courtyard.

TIME OUT After all this sightseeing, take an opportunity to rest your legs and have lunch. Turn right into Pfisterstrasse to reach the little square called Am Platzl and Munich's most famous beer hall, the **Hofbräuhaus.** *Hofbräu* means "royal brew," a term that aptly describes the golden beer that is served here in king-size liter mugs. Duke Wilhelm V founded the brewery in 1589, and although it still boasts royal patronage in its title, it's now state-owned. If the downstairs hall is too noisy for you, try the quiet restaurant upstairs.

Tour 2: Cultural Munich

16 Turn right from the Hofbräuhaus for the short walk to **Maximilianstrasse,** Munich's most elegant shopping street, named after King Maximilian II, whose statue you'll see far down on the right. The king wanted to break away from the Greek-influenced classical style of city architecture favored by his father, Ludwig I, so he ingenuously asked his cabinet whether he could be allowed to create something original. Maximilianstrasse was the result. This broad boulevard, its central stretch lined with majestic buildings (now museums and government offices), culminates on a rise beyond the Isar River in the stately outlines of the Maximilianeum, a 19th-century palace now housing the Bavarian *Landtag* (parliament). Across Maximilianstrasse as you enter from the

17 Hofbräuhaus stands another handsome city palace: the **Hotel Vier Jahreszeiten,** a historic watering hole for princes, millionaires, and the expense-account jet set.

Turn left down Maximilianstrasse, away from the Maximilianeum, and you'll enter the square called Max-Joseph-Platz, dominated by the pil-

18 lared portico of the 19th-century **Nationaltheater,** home of the Bavarian State Opera Company. The statue in the center of the square is of Bavaria's first king, Max Joseph. Along the north side of this untidily arranged square (marred by the entrance to an underground parking

★ **19** lot) is the lofty and austere south wall of the **Residenz,** the royal palace of Wittelsbach rulers for more than six centuries. It began as a small castle, to which the Wittelsbach dukes moved during the 14th century, when the Alter Hof became surrounded by the teeming tenements of an expanding Munich. In succeeding centuries the royal residence developed parallel to the importance, requirements, and interests of its occupants. As the complex expanded, it came to include the **Königsbau** (on Max-JosefPlatz) and then (clockwise) the **Alte Residenz;** the **Festsaal** (Banquet Hall); the **Altes Residenztheater** (Cuvilliés Theater); **Allerheiligenhofkirche** (All Soul's Church, now ruined); the **Residenztheater;** and the **Nationaltheater.**

Building began in 1385 with the Neuveste (New Fortress), which comprised the northeast section; it burned to the ground in 1750, but one of its finest rooms survived: the 16th-century **Antiquarium,** which was built for Duke Albrecht V's collection of antique statues (today it's used chiefly for state receptions). The throne room of King Ludwig I, the **Neuer Herkulessaal,** is now a concert hall. The accumulated treasures of the Wittelsbachs can be seen in the **Schatzkammer,** or Treasury (one rich centerpiece is a small Renaissance statue of St. George, studded with 2,291 diamonds, 209 pearls, and 406 rubies), and a representative collection of paintings and tapestries is housed in the **Residenzmuseum.** Antique coins and Egyptian works of art are located in the two other museums of this vast palace. In the center of the complex, entered through an inner courtyard where chamber-music concerts are given in summer, is a small Rococo theater, built by François Cuvilliés from 1751 to 1755. The French-born Cuvilliés was a dwarf who was admitted to the Bavarian court as a decorative "bauble." Prince Max Emanuel recognized his latent artistic ability and had him trained as an architect. The prince's eye for talent gave Germany some of its richest Rococo treasures. *Admission to Treasury and Residenzmuseum: DM 4 adults, children under 15 free.* ☻ *Tues.–Sun. 10–4:30. Admission to Staatliche Münzsammlung (coin collection): DM 3.50 adults, DM 2 children, free Sun. and holidays.* ☻ *Tues.–Sun. 10–4:30. Admission to Staatliche Sammlung Ägyptischer Kunst (Egyptian art): DM 4.50 adults, DM 2.50 children, free Sun. and holidays.* ☻ *Tues. 9–9,*

Wed.–Fri. 9–4, weekends 10–5. Admission to Cuvilliés Theater: DM 2.50 adults, children under 15 free. ☉ Mon.–Sat. 2–5, Sun. 10–5.

20 Directly north of the Residenz on Hofgartenstrasse lies the former royal garden, the **Hofgarten.** Two sides of the pretty, formal garden are bordered by arcades designed during the 19th century by the royal architect Leo von Klenze. On the east side of the garden stands the new State Chancellery, built around the ruins of the 19th-century Army Museum and incorporating the remains of a Renaissance arcade. Its most prominent feature is the large copper dome. Bombed during World War II air raids, the museum stood untouched for almost 40 years as a grim reminder of the war.

In front of the chancellery stands one of Europe's most unusual—some say most effective—war memorials. Instead of looking up at the monument you are led down to it: It is a sunken crypt covered by a massive granite block. In the crypt lies a German soldier from World War I.

TIME OUT Munich's oldest café, the **Annast,** is in the Hofgarten at the border of busy Odeonsplatz. In summer tables under the trees of the Hofgarten offer a delightful retreat from the hum of city traffic only 100 yards away.

21 You can be forgiven for any confusion about your whereabouts ("Can this really be Germany?") when you step from the Hofgarten onto Odeonsplatz. To your left is the 19th-century **Feldherrnhalle,** a local hall of fame modeled on the 14th-century Loggia dei Lanzi in Florence. In the '30s and '40s it was the site of a key Nazi shrine, marking the place where Hitler's abortive rising, or *Putsch*, took place in 1923. All who passed it had to give the Nazi salute.

22 Looking north up Ludwigstrasse, the arrow-straight avenue that ends at the Feldherrnhalle, you'll see the **Siegestor,** or victory arch, which marks the beginning of Leopoldstrasse. The Siegestor also has Italian origins: It was modeled on the Arch of Constantine in Rome. It was built to honor the achievements of the Bavarian army during the Wars of Liberation (1813–15).

23 Completing this impressively Italianate panorama is the great yellow bulk of the former royal church of St. Kajetan, the **Theatinerkirche,** an imposing Baroque building. Its lofty towers frame a restrained facade capped by a massive dome. The church owes its Italian appearance to its founder, Princess Henriette Adelaide, who commissioned it as an act of thanksgiving for the birth of her son and heir, Max Emanuel, in 1663. A native of Turin, the princess distrusted Bavarian architects and builders and thus summoned a master builder from Bologna, Agostino Barelli, to construct her church. He took as his model the Roman mother church of the newly formed Theatine order of Catholicism. Barelli worked on the building for 11 years but was dismissed before the project was completed. It was another 100 years before the Theatinerkirche was finished. Step inside to admire its austere stucco interior.

Now head north up Ludwigstrasse. The first stretch of the street was designed by court architect Leo von Klenze. In much the same way Baron Haussmann was later to demolish many of the old streets and buildings in Paris, replacing them with stately boulevards, so von Klenze swept aside the small dwellings and alleys that stood here to build his great avenue. His high-windowed and formal buildings have never quite been accepted by Müncheners, and indeed there's still a sense that Ludwigstrasse is an intruder. Most visitors either love it or hate it. Von

Klenze's buildings end just before Ludwigstrasse becomes Leopoldstrasse, and it is easy to see where he handed construction over to another leading architect, Friedrich von Gärtner. The severe neoclassical buildings that line southern Ludwigstrasse—including the Bayerische Staatsbibliothek (Bavarian State Library) and the Universität (University)—fragment into the lighter styles of Leopoldstrasse. The more delicate structures are echoed by the busy street life you'll find here in summer. Once the hub of the legendary artists' district of **Schwabing,** Leopoldstrasse still throbs with life from spring to fall, exuding the atmosphere of a Mediterranean boulevard, with cafés, wine terraces, and artists' stalls. In comparison, Ludwigstrasse is inhabited by the ghosts of the past.

At the south end of Leopoldstrasse, beyond the Siegestor, lies the great open quadrangle of the university, Geschwister-Scholl-Platz, named after brother and sister Hans and Sophie Scholl, who were executed in 1943 for leading the short-lived anti-Nazi resistance movement known as the Weisse Rose (White Rose). At its north end, Leopoldstrasse leads into Schwabing itself, once Munich's Bohemian quarter but now distinctly upscale. Explore the streets of old Schwabing around Wedekindplatz to get the feel of the place. (Those in search of the Bohemian mood that once animated Schwabing should head to Haidhausen, on the other side of the Isar.)

★ **24** Bordering the east side of Schwabing is the **Englischer Garten** (English Garden). Five kilometers (3 miles) long and 1½ kilometers (about 1 mile) wide, it's Germany's largest city park, stretching from the central avenue of Prinzregentenstrasse to the city's northern boundary. It was designed for the Bavarian prince Karl Theodor by a refugee from the American War of Independence, Count Rumford. Though Count Rumford was of English descent, it was the open, informal nature of the park—reminiscent of the rolling parklands with which the English aristocracy of the 18th century liked to surround their country homes—that determined its name. It has an appealing boating lake, four beer gardens, and a series of curious decorative and monumental constructions, including the Monopteros, a Greek temple designed by von Klenze for King Ludwig I and built on an artificial hill in the southern section of the park. In the center of one of the park's most popular beer gardens is a Chinese pagoda erected in 1789, destroyed during the war, and then reconstructed. The Chinese Tower beer garden is world-famous, but the park has prettier places for downing a beer: the Aumeister, for example, along the northern perimeter. The Aumeister's restaurant is in an early 19th-century hunting lodge.

The Englischer Garten is a paradise for joggers, cyclists, and, in winter, cross-country skiers. The Munich Cricket Club grounds are in the southern section—proof, perhaps, that even that most British of games is not invulnerable to the single-minded Germans—and spectators are welcome. The park also has specially designated areas for nude sunbathing—the Germans have a positively pagan attitude toward the sun—so don't be surprised to see naked bodies bordering the flower beds and paths.

On the southern fringe of Schwabing are Munich's two leading art galleries, the Alte Pinakothek and the Neue Pinakothek, located next to each other on Barerstrasse. They are as complementary as their buildings are contrasting. The Alte Pinakothek (old picture gallery) was built by von Klenze between 1826 and 1836 to exhibit the collection of Old Masters begun by Duke Wilhelm IV during the 16th century, while the Neue Pinakothek (new picture gallery), a low brick structure, was

opened in 1981 to house the royal collection of modern art left homeless when its former building was destroyed in the war.

★ ㉕ The **Alte Pinakothek,** among the great picture galleries of the world,
closed in 1994 for renovations that are expected to take about three
years. Meanwhile, the gallery's most famous pictures (including most
of the Dürers, Rembrandts, Rubenses, and two celebrated Murillos)
have been moved for display to the Neue Pinakothek.

㉖ Across a sculpture-studded stretch of lawn is the **Neue Pinakothek.** It's
a low brick building that combines high-tech and Italianate influences
in equal measure. From outside, the museum does not seem to measure up to the standards set by so many of Munich's other great public buildings. On the other hand, the interior offers a magnificent
environment for picture-gazing, at least partly due to the superb natural light flooding in from the skylights. The highlights of the collection are probably the Impressionist and other French 19th-century
works—Monet, Degas, and Manet are all well represented. But there's
also a substantial collection of 19th-century German and Scandinavian
paintings—misty landscapes predominate—that are only now coming
to be recognized as admirable and worthy products of their time. *Bar-
erstr. 29. ☛ DM 6 adults, DM 1 children, free Sun. and holidays.
☉ Tues. and Thurs. 9–8, Wed. and Fri. 9–5, weekends 9–5.*

Back on Barerstrasse, walk south toward the city center. Before you
㉗ stretches the circular **Karolinenplatz,** with its central obelisk; it's a memorial, unveiled in 1812, to Bavarians killed fighting Napoléon. Turn right
㉘ onto Briennerstrasse. Opening up ahead is the massive **Königsplatz,** lined
on three sides with the monumental Grecian-style buildings by von Klenze
that gave Munich the nickname "Athens on the Isar." In the '30s the
great parklike square was laid with granite slabs, which resounded with
the thud of jackboots as the Nazis commandeered the area for their
rallies. Only recently were the slabs removed; since then the square has
taken on something of the green and peaceful appearance originally
intended by Ludwig I. The two templelike buildings he had constructed
㉙ there are museums: The **Glyptothek** features a permanent exhibition
㉚ of Greek and Roman sculptures; and the **Antikensammlungen** (Antiquities Collection) has a fine group of smaller sculptures, Etruscan
art, Greek vases, gold, and glass. *Glyptothek: Königspl. 3. ☛ DM 5
adults, DM 1 children, free Sun. and holidays. ☉ Tues., Wed., and
Fri.–Sun. 10–4:30, Thurs. noon–8:30. Antiquities Collection: Königspl.
1. ☛ DM 5 adults, DM 1 children, free Sun. and holidays. ☉ Tues.
and Thurs.–Sun. 10–4:30, Wed. noon–8:30. A combined ticket to
both museums costs DM 8.*

Return to Karolinenplatz and then head south along Barerstrasse.
You'll come to Lenbachplatz, a busy square scarred by road intersections and tramlines, and lined by a series of handsome turn-of-the-century buildings. At the point where Lenbachplatz meets Maximiliansplatz
you'll see one of Munich's most impressive fountains: the monumen-
㉛ tal late-19th-century **Wittelsbacher Fountain.**

At the southwest corner of Lenbachplatz is the arched entrance to the
㉜ park that was once the city's botanical garden, the **Alter Botanischer
Garten.** A huge glass palace was built here in 1853 for Germany's first
industrial exhibition. In 1931 the immense structure burned down; six
years later the garden was redesigned as a public park. Two features
from the '30s remain: a small square exhibition hall still used for art
shows; and the 1933 Neptune Fountain, an enormous work in the heavy,
monumental style of the prewar years. At the international electricity

exhibition of 1882, the world's first high-tension electricity cable was run from the park to a Bavarian village 48 kilometers (30 miles) away.

TIME OUT Tucked away on the north edge of the Alter Botanischer Garten is one of the city's central beer gardens. It's part of the **Park Café**, which at night becomes a fashionable disco serving magnums of champagne for DM 1,500 apiece. Prices in the beer garden are more realistic.

㉝ Opposite the southern exit of the park loom the ornate contours of the 1897 law courts, the **Palace of Justice.** Just around the corner is the **Hauptbahnhof** (main railway station)—and the end of our tour.

Outside the Center

The site of Munich's annual beer festival—the infamous Oktoberfest—is only a 10-minute walk from the main train station; alternatively, take the U-4 or U-5 subway one stop. The festival site is Munich's enormous exhibition ground, the **Theresienwiese,** named after a young woman whose engagement party gave rise to the Oktoberfest. In 1810 the party celebrated the betrothal of Princess Therese von Sachsen-Hildburghausen to the Bavarian crown prince Ludwig, later Ludwig I. It was such a success, attended by nearly the entire population of Munich, that it became an annual affair. Beer was served then as now, but what began as a night out for the locals has become a 16-day international bonanza at the end of September and the start of October, attracting more than 6 million people each year (it qualifies as the "Oktoberfest" by ending on the first Sunday in October). In enormous wooden pavilions that heave and pulsate to the combined racket of brass bands, drinking songs, and thousands of dry throats demanding more, the hordes knock back around 5 million liters of beer.

Overlooking the site is a 19th-century hall of fame—one of the last works of Ludwig I—and a monumental bronze statue of the maiden **Bavaria,** more than (100 feet high). The statue is hollow, and 130 steps take you up into the braided head for a view of Munich through Bavaria's eyes.

★ The major attraction away from the downtown area is **Schloss Nymphenburg,** a glorious Baroque and Rococo palace in the northwest suburb that was a summer home to five generations of Bavarian royalty. To reach it, take the U-1 subway from the Hauptbahnhof to Rotkreuzplatz, then pick up Streetcar 12 heading for Amalienburg.

Nymphenburg is the largest palace of its kind in Germany, stretching more than a half mile from one wing to the other. The palace grew in size and scope over a period of more than 200 years, beginning as a summer residence built on land given by Prince Ferdinand Maria to his beloved wife, Henriette Adelaide, on the birth of their son and heir, Max Emanuel, in 1663. As mentioned earlier, she had the Theatinerkirche built as a personal expression of thanks for the birth. The Italian architect Agostino Barelli, brought from Bologna for that project, was instructed to build the palace. It was completed in 1675 by his successor, Enrico Zuccalli. Within that original building, now the central axis of the palace complex, is a magnificent hall, the Steinerner Saal, extending over two floors and richly decorated with stucco and swirling frescoes. In the summer, chamber-music concerts are given here. The decoration of the Steinerner Saal spills over into the surrounding royal chambers, one of which houses the famous **Schönheitsgalerie** (Gallery of Beauties). The walls are hung from floor to ceiling with portraits of women who caught the roving eye of Ludwig I, among them a butcher's daughter and an English duchess. The most famous portrait is of Lola Montez, a sultry beauty and high-class courtesan who, after a time as the mistress of Franz Liszt and later Alexandre Dumas, captivated Ludwig I to such an extent that he gave up his throne for her.

The palace is set in a fine park, laid out in formal French style, with low hedges and gravel walks, extending into woodland. Tucked away among the ancient trees are three fascinating structures built as Nymphenburg expanded and changed occupants. Don't miss the **Amalienburg** hunting lodge, a Rococo gem built by François Cuvilliés, architect of the Residenztheater. The silver-and-blue stucco of the little Amalienburg creates an atmosphere of courtly high life that makes it clear that the pleasures of the chase here did not always take place out-of-doors. In the lavishly appointed kennels you'll see that even the dogs lived in luxury. For royal tea parties, another building, the **Pagodenburg**, was constructed. It has an elegant French exterior that disguises a suitably Oriental interior in which exotic teas from India and China were served. Swimming parties were held in the **Badenburg**, Europe's first post-Roman heated pool.

Nymphenburg contains so much of interest that a day hardly provides enough time for it all. Don't leave without visiting the former royal stables, the **Marstallmuseum**, or Museum of Royal Carriages. It houses a fleet of vehicles, including an elaborately decorated sleigh in which King Ludwig II once glided through the Bavarian twilight, postilion torches lighting the way. On the floor above are fine examples of Nymphenburg porcelain, produced here between 1747 and the 1920s. *Admission to the entire Schloss Nymphenburg complex: DM 6 adults, DM 4 children under 15 (ask for a Gesamtkarte, or combined ticket). A ticket for just the palace, Schönheitsgalerie, and Marstallmuseum costs DM 2.50 adults, DM 2 children under 15. ☉ Apr.–Sept., daily 9–12:30 and 1:30–5; Oct.–Mar., daily 10–12:30 and 1:30–4. All except Amalienburg and gardens closed Mon. (Munich's botanical garden with its interesting tree collection and tropical greenhouses is adjacent to the palace grounds.)*

Beyond Nymphenburg, on the northwest edge of Munich, lies medieval **Schloss Blutenburg**, now the home of an international collection of children's books—500,000, in more than 100 languages. Alongside this library are collections of original manuscripts, illustrations, and posters. The castle chapel, built in 1488 by Duke Sigismund, has some fine 15th-century stained glass. Take any S-bahn train to Pasing station, then Bus 73 or 76 to the castle gate. ☛ *Free.* ☉ *Weekdays 10–5.*

In 1597 Duke Wilhelm V also decided to look for a peaceful retreat outside Munich and found what he wanted at **Schloss Schleissheim**, then far beyond the city walls but now only a short ride on the suburban S-1 line (to Oberschleissheim station) and then bus number 292 (which doesn't run on weekends). A later ruler, Prince Max Emanuel, extended the palace and added a second, smaller one, the Lustheim. Separated from the main palace by a formal garden and a decorative canal, the Lustheim houses Germany's largest collection of Meissen porcelain. ☛ *Combined ticket for the palaces and the porcelain collection, DM 4 adults; DM 2.50 children under 15. ☉ Tues.–Sun. 10–12:30 and 1:30–5.*

The undulating circus-tentlike roofs that cover the stadia built for the 1972 Olympic Games are unobtrusively tucked away in what is now known as the **Olympiapark**. The roofs are made of translucent tiles that glisten in the midday sun and act as amplifiers for such visiting rock bands as the Rolling Stones. Tours of the park on a Disneyland-style train run throughout the day from March through November. Take the elevator up the (960-foot) Olympia Tower for a view of the city and the Alps; there's also a revolving restaurant near the top. *Admission to main stadium: DM 1 adults, 50 pf children. ☉ Daily 9–4:30. Combined ticket for park tour and a ride up the tower: DM 7 adults, DM 4 children. Tower open daily 9 AM–midnight. The elevator ride costs DM 5 adults, DM 2.50 children. A family ticket for 2 adults and up to 3 children costs DM 13. Restaurant open daily 11–5:30 and 6:30 PM–midnight; call 089/3067–2818 for reservations.*

What to See and Do with Children

★   Take your children to the **zoo** (Tierpark Hellabrun), which is just a 20-minute ride from downtown. There are special areas where children can touch the animals and feed them and go for pony rides. It's a hands-on sort of place.

The **Deutsches Museum** (*see* Museums and Galleries *in* Sightseeing Checklists, *below*) rates as the city's number-one museum for children. Budding scientists and young dreamers alike will be delighted by its extensive collections and its many activities that provide buttons to push and cranks to turn. It's on the Museuminsel (Museum Island) in the Isar River, a 10-minute walk from downtown.

The tower of the Gothic **Altes Rathaus** (Old Town Hall) provides a satisfyingly atmospheric setting for a little toy museum. It includes several exhibits from the United States. *Marienpl.* ☛ *DM 4 adults, DM 1 children; family ticket (2 adults plus children), DM 8. ☉ Daily 10–5:30.*

Munich has several theaters for children, and with pantomime such a strong part of the repertoire, the language problem disappears. The best of them is the **Münchner Theater für Kinder** (Dachauerstr. 46, ☎ 089/595–454 or 089/593–858). Two puppet theaters offer regular performances for children; the **Münchner Marionettentheater** (Blumenstr. 29a, ☎ 089/265–712) and **Otto Bille's Marionetten**bühne (Breiterangerstr. 15, ☎ 089/150–2168 or 089/310–1278). Munich is the winter quarters of the **Circus Krone** (Marsstr. 43, ☎ 089/558–166), which has its own permanent building. The circus performs there from Christmas until the end of March.

In summer seek out the 100-year-old **carousel** at the edge of the Englischer Garten beer garden, a beer-mug's throw from the famous Chinese Pagoda.

For young roller skaters, Munich has a roller disco, the **Roll Palast,** in the western suburb of Pasing (Stockackerstr. 5); take the suburban rail line S-5 or S-6 to Westkreuz. Roller skates can be rented. Just east of Munich in the village of Poing is **No-Name City** (Gruberstr. 60a), a mock-up Western town, with saloons, acorral, live country music, and daily duels. Take suburban line S-6 to Poing; from there it's only 200 yards. ☛ *DM 15 adults, DM 10 children. ☉ Apr.–Oct., Tues.–Sun. 9:30–6, Sat. 9:30 AM–midnight.*

Munich is Germany's leading **movie-making** center, and in the summer the studios at Geiselgasteig, on the southern outskirts of the city, open their doors to visitors. A "Filmexpress" transports you on a 1½-hour tour of the sets of *The Boat, Enemy Mine, The Neverending Story,* and other productions. Children should enjoy the stunt shows, staged three times a day on weekends and public holidays. Call 089/649–3767 or 089/6499–2304 for show times. Take Streetcar 25 to Bavariafilm-platz. ☛ *DM 12 adults, DM 8 children. Stunt shows: DM 8 adults, DM 8 children. A combined ticket for a tour of the studios and a stunt show costs DM 19 adults, DM 15 children.* ☉ *Mar.–Oct., daily 9–5. The last tour begins at 4 daily.*

Off the Beaten Track

For the cheapest sightseeing tour of the city center on wheels, board **Streetcar 19** outside the main train station (on Bahnhofpl.) and make the 15-minute journey to Max Weber Platz. Explore the streets around the square, part of the picturesque old residential area of Haidhausen, and then return by a different route on the **Streetcar 18** to Karlsplatz. On a nice day, join the **chess players** at their open-air board at Schwabing's forumlike Münchner Freiheit Platz. On a rainy day, pack your swimming things and splash around in the setting of the **Müllersches Volksbad**, Ludwigsbrücke opposite the Deutsches Museum. On a sunny day, join the locals for ice cream and a stroll along the Isar River, where the more daring sunbathe nude on pebble islands. Alternatively, walk up the hill from the Volksbad and see what art exhibition or avant-garde film (often in English) is showing at the modern, redbrick **Gasteig Culture Center.**

Also in this area is a museum-piece cemetery, the **Südfriedhof**, where you'll find many famous names but few tourists. Four hundred years ago it was a graveyard beyond the city walls for plague victims and paupers. During the 19th century it was refashioned into an upscale last resting place by the city architect von Gärtner. Royal architect Leo von Klenze designed some of the headstones, and both he and Friedrich von Gärtner are among the famous names you'll find there. The last burial here took place more than 40 years ago. The Südfriedhof is on the Thalkirchnerstrasse, a short walk from the Sendlinger-Tor-Platz U-bahn station.

Sightseeing Checklists

Many of the points of interest listed here are discussed in greater detail in Exploring, above.

Historical Buildings and Sites
Alter Hof (Old Palace). The first of the Wittelsbach royal residences in Munich, the palace now serves as local government offices.
Altes Rathaus (Old Town Hall). This was Munich's first city hall, built in 1474 and restored after wartime bomb damage.
Bavaria. This monumental statue, Munich's Statue of Liberty, overlooks the Theresienwiese, site of the Oktoberfest.
Feldherrnhalle. Modeled on Florence's Loggia dei Lanzi, this arcade dominates the south end of Odeonsplatz.
Friedensengel (Angel of Peace). This striking gilded angel crowns a marble column in a small park overlooking the Isar River. It marks one end of Prinzregentenstrasse, the broad, arrow-straight boulevard laid out by Prince Regent Luitpold at the end of the 19th century.
Königsplatz. This enormous city square, laid out by Ludwig I, is flanked on three sides by Grecian temple–style exhibition halls and a massive neoclassical arch.
Marienplatz. Invariably animated by visitors and locals alike, this substantial square rates as the historic heart of Munich.

Maximilianeum (Maximilianstr.). The Bavarian State Government meets in this lavish mid-19th-century arcaded palace built for Maximilian II as part of an ambitious city-planning scheme. Today only the terrace can be visited.

Münze (Pfisterstr. 4). Originally the royal stables, the Münze (mint) was created by court architect Wilhelm Egkl between 1563 and 1567. A stern neoclassical facade was added in 1809; the courtyard retains its Renaissance look.

Nationaltheater. The sturdy neoclassical bulk of the premier theater in Munich, home of the Bavarian State Opera Company, dominates the east side of Max-Joseph-Platz.

Neues Rathaus. The city's New Town Hall has a famed glockenspiel, the largest musical clock in Germany.

Residenz. This massive palace complex of the Wittelsbach rulers of Bavaria was remodeled numerous times over the centuries; much of it is open to the public (*see* Museums and Galleries, *below, and* Tour 2 *in* Exploring, *above*).

Schloss Blutenburg. The well-preserved walled and moated castle was the hunting retreat of Duke Albrecht III. The castle's 15th-century chapel and Baroque hall can be visited.

Schloss Nymphenburg. The summer residence of the Wittelsbachs, this is Germany's largest Baroque palace (*see* Outside the Center *in* Exploring, *above, and* Museums and Galleries *and* Parks and Gardens, *below*).

Viktualienmarkt. Munich's open-air food market is among the most colorful and diverting sights in the city.

Museums and Galleries

Alte Pinakothek. This museum (closed for renovations) usually displays one of the world's leading collections of Old Master paintings (*see* Tour 2 *in* Exploring, *above*). Its most famous works are temporarily on exhibit across the street in the Neue Pinakothek.

Bayerisches Nationalmuseum. The Bavarian National Museum contains an extensive collection of Bavarian and other German art and artifacts. The highlight for some will be the medieval and Renaissance wood carvings, with many works by the great Renaissance sculptor Tilman Riemenschneider. Fine tapestries, arms and armor, a unique collection of Christmas crèches (the Krippenschau), Bavarian arts and crafts, and folk artifacts compete for your attention. *Prinzregentenstr. 3.* ☛ *DM 5 adults, DM 1 children, free Sun. and holidays.* ⊙ *Tues.–Sun. 9:30–5.*

BMW Museum. Munich is the home of the famous car firm. Its futuristic-looking museum, adjoining the factory next to Olympiapark, contains a dazzling collection of BMWs old and new. *Petuelring 130 (U-bahn 2 or 3 to Olympiazentrum station).* ☛ *DM 4.50 adults, DM 2 children, and DM 10 family ticket.* ⊙ *Daily 9–5 (last entry 4 PM).*

Deutches Jagd- und Fischereimuseum (German Museum of Hunting and Fishing). The world's largest collection of fishhooks and 500 stuffed animals make up just part of the attraction of one of Munich's most popular museums (*see* Tour 1 *in* Exploring, *above*).

★ **Deutsches Museum** (German Museum of Science and Technology). Founded in 1903 and housed in its present monumental building since 1925, this is one of the most stimulating and innovative science museums in Europe. Nineteen kilometers (12 miles) of corridors, six floors of exhibits, and 30 departments make up the immense collections. Set aside a full day if you plan to do justice to the entire museum (*see* What to See and Do with Children, *above*). The technically most advanced planetarium in Europe was recently opened within this huge museum complex. The planetarium has up to six shows daily, including a Laser Magic display. (Admission varies from DM 10.90 to DM 24.90 adults, DM 7.90–DM 21.90 children.) The old Deutsches Museum concert hall now houses an IMAX theater—a wraparound screen six stories high, showing documentary films in which spectators feel as if they're part of the action; a space feature entitled *Blue Planet* transports you into orbit for an astronaut's view of the earth. There are up to 14 performances daily. Call 089/2112–5180 to reserve tickets at both the planetarium and the IMAX cinema. *Admission to IMAX only: DM 10.90 adults, DM 7.90 children). Museumsinsel 1.* ☛ *DM 8 adults, DM 2.50 children.* ☉ *Daily 9–5.*

Münchner Stadtmuseum (City Museum). Munich's history is illustrated by means of puppets, musical instruments, and photographs, as well as an exhibition that features old brewing artifacts. *Sankt-Jakobs-Platz 1.* ☛ *DM 5 adults, DM 2.50 children, DM 7.50 family ticket (DM 1 extra for special exhibitions); free Sun. and holidays.* ☉ *Tues.–Sun. 10–5, Wed. until 8:30.*

Neue Pinakothek. Late-18th- and 19th-century paintings, with strong French collections, make this one of the most compelling art galleries in Europe (*see* Tour 2 *in* Exploring, *above*).

Paläontologisches Museum. The 10-million-year-old skeleton of a mammoth is the centerpiece of this paleontological and geological collection. *Richard-Wagner-Str. 10.* ☛ *Free.* ☉ *Mon.–Thurs. 8–4, Fri. 8–2.*

Prähistorische Staatssammlung (State Prehistoric Collection). This is Bavaria's principal record of its prehistoric, Roman, and Celtic past. The perfectly preserved body of a young girl who was ritually sacrificed, recovered from a Bavarian peat moor, is among its more spine-chilling exhibits. Head down to the basement to see the fine Roman mosaic floor. *Lerchenfeldstr. 2.* ☛ *DM 4 adults, DM 1 children, free Sun. and holidays.* ☉ *Tues., Wed., and Fri.–Sun. 9–4, Thurs. 9–8.*

Residenzmuseum. This is the former royal palace of the Wittelsbachs, with priceless collections of state treasures (*see* Historical Buildings and Sites *and* Tour 2 *in* Exploring, *above*).

Schack-Galerie. Those with a taste for florid and romantic 19th-century German paintings will appreciate the collections of the Schack-Galerie, originally the private collection of one Count Schack. Others may find the gallery dull, filled with plodding and repetitive works by painters who now repose in well-deserved obscurity. *Prinzregentenstr. 9.* ☛ *DM 3 adults, DM 1 children, free Sun. and holidays.* ☉ *Wed.–Mon. 10–5.*

Staatliche Antikensammlungen und Glyptothek (State Collection of Antiquities and Sculpture). Ancient Greek and Roman collections are housed in two appropriately neoclassical buildings on the vast Königsplatz (*see* Tour 2 *in* Exploring, *above*).

Staatliche Graphische Sammlung (State Collection of Graphic Arts). A comprehensive collection of drawings and prints from the late-Gothic period to the present day is housed here. *Meiserstr. 10.* ☛ *Free.* ☉ *Weekdays 10–1 and 2–4:30.*

Staatliches Museum für Völkerkunde (State Museum of Ethnology). Arts and crafts from around the world are displayed in this extensive museum. There are also regular ethnological exhibits. *Maximilianstr. 42.* ☛ *DM 3.50 adults, 50 pf children, free Sun. and holidays.* ☉ *Tues.–Sun. 9:30–4:30.*

Staatliche Sammlung Ägyptischer Kunst (State Collection of Egyptian Art). This is just part of the remarkable collection housed in the Residenz, the former royal palace (*see* Historical Buildings and Sites *and* Tour 2 *in* Exploring, *above*).

Staatsgalerie Moderner Kunst (State Gallery of Modern Art). The gallery is in the west wing of the Hitler-era Haus der Kunst, a monumental pillared building at the south end of the Englischer Garten (the east wing has regular temporary exhibits). It features one of the finest collections of 20th-century paintings and sculptures in the world. *Prinzregentenstr. 1.* ☛ *DM 5 adults, DM 1 children, free Sun. and holidays.* ☉ *Tues., Wed., and Fri.–Sun. 10–5, Thurs. 10–8*

Städtische Galerie im Lenbachhaus. This internationally renowned picture collection is housed in a delightful late-19th-century Florentine-style villa, former home and studio of the artist Franz von Lenbach. It contains a rich collection of works from the Gothic period to the present, including an exciting assemblage of art from the early 20th-century *Blaue Reiter* (Blue Rider) group: Kandinsky, Klee, Jawlensky, Macke, Marc, and Münter. *Luisenstr. 33.* ☛ *DM 6 adults, DM 3 children, free Sun. and holidays.* ☉ *Tues.–Sun. 10–6.*

Villa Stuck. Like the Lenbach Gallery, this museum is the former home of one of Munich's leading turn-of-the-century artists, Franz von Stuck. His work covers the walls of the haunting rooms of the neoclassical villa, which is also used for regular art exhibits organized by the museum's newly appointed Australian director. *Prinzregentenstr. 60.* ☛ *Varies from DM 6 upward according to exhibits.* ☉ *Tues., Wed., and Fri.–Sun. 10–5, Thurs. 10–9.*

Parks and Gardens

Botanischer Garten (Botanical Garden). A collection of 14,000 plants, including orchids, cacti, cyads, alpine flowers, and rhododendrons, makes up one of the most extensive botanical gardens in Europe. The park is located at the eastern edge of the Nymphenburg Palace park. *Menzingerstr. 65.* ☛ *DM 3 adults, 50 pf children.* ☉ *Daily 9–4:30; hothouses open daily 9–noon and 1–4.*

Englischer Garten. This is the largest city park in Germany, laid out at the end of the 18th century. Lakes, gravel paths, beer gardens, a Chinese pagoda, and a series of small, eye-catching temples number among its attractions (*see* Tour 2 *in* Exploring, *above*).

Hirschgarten. A former deer park, the Hirschgarten still has wild buck and roe deer in enclosures. There are children's playgrounds and an attractive beer garden. It's located in the suburb of Nymphenburg; take any of the westbound S-bahn train lines to Laim.

Hofgarten. This is the former royal palace garden, located just to the north of the Residenz (*see* Tour 2 *in* Exploring, *above*).

Isar Valley. Munich's Isar River is no built-up waterway—north and south of the city center there are green, unspoiled banks, ideal territory for cyclists, joggers, and walkers. Nude sunbathing is allowed on the banks and islands, although the river isn't recommended for swimming.

Luitpold Park (Karl-Theodor-Str.). This is Schwabing's city park, which includes a tobogganing hill made from the rubble of World War II air raids. Try the beer brewed in the cellar of Bambergerhaus, a café-restaurant owned by Prince Luitpold.

Olympiapark. Site of the 1972 Olympic Games, this is still very much the sporting center of the city (*see* Sports and Fitness, *below, and* Outside the Center *in* Exploring, *above*).

Schloss Nymphenburg. The 500 acres of Schloss Nymphenburg's park are popular with walkers and joggers. In winter, marked trails beckon cross-country skiers (*see* Historical Buildings and Sites, Museums and Galleries, *and* Outside the Center *in* Exploring, *above*).

Tierpark Hellabrun. Animals are arranged according to their geographical origin in this city zoo, which is among the finest in the world. Cages are kept to a minimum, with preference given to enclosures wherever possible. The zoo's 170 acres include restaurants and children's areas. Take Bus 52 from Marienplatz or the U-3 subway. ☛ *DM 7 adults, DM 3 children.* ☉ *Apr.–Sept., daily 8–6; Oct.–Mar., daily 9–5.*

West Park. Laid out for the 1983 International Horticultural Exhibition, this has become one of the most popular of the city's parks. It was designed to resemble the landscape of Upper Bavaria, with gently undulating hills (popular among joggers and cross-country skiers) and lakes and valleys, the whole planted with regional and international flora. There are restaurants, cafés, beer gardens, children's play areas, an open-air theater, and a concert arena. Take U-bahn lines 3 or 6 to West Park.

Churches

Asamkirche. Built by the brothers Asam, this is the most important and lavishly decorated late-Baroque church in the city,. Don't miss it (*see* Tour 1 *in* Exploring, *above*).

Bürgersaal. The building is actually two churches in one, located in the heart of the city. The magnificently opulent Rococo upper church contrasts with the simple, cryptlike chapel below (*see* Tour 1 *in* Exploring, *above*).

Dreifaltigkeitskirche (Pacellistr.). This is the church of the Holy Trinity, built after a local woman prophesied doom for the city unless a new church was erected. It's a striking Baroque building, with heroic frescoes by Cosmas Damian Asam.

Franziskanerklosterkirche St. Anna im Lehel (St.-Anna-Str.). Though less opulently decorated than the Asamkirche, this small Franciscan monastery church, consecrated in 1737, impresses with its sense of movement and its heroic scale. It was largely rebuilt after wartime bomb damage. The ceiling fresco by Cosmas Damian Asam was removed before the war and, after restoration, now glows in all its original vivid joyfulness. The ornate altar was also designed by the Asam brothers.

Frauenkirche (Church of Our Lady). Munich's soaring, brick Gothic cathedral has two lofty towers capped by onion-shape domes—enduring symbols of the city (*see* Tour 1 *in* Exploring, *above*).

Ludwigskirche (Ludwigstr. 22). Planted halfway along the severe, neoclassical Ludwigstrasse is this curious neo-Byzantine/early Renaissance–style church. It was built at the behest of Ludwig I to provide his newly completed suburb with a parish church. Though most visitors will find the building a curiosity at best, it can be worth a stop to see the fresco of the *Last Judgment* in the choir. At 60 by 37 feet, it is one of the world's largest.

Michaelskirche. One of the most important and largest Renaissance churches in Germany, its construction began in 1583 (*see* Tour 1 *in* Exploring, *above*).

Peterskirche. Munich's oldest and smallest parish church was consecrated in 1368 on the site of four previous churches. Its tower, Alter Peter, is a local landmark (*see* Tour 1 *in* Exploring, *above*).

Salvatorkirche (Salvatorstr.). The bare brick exterior of this church points to the fact that it was almost certainly built by the same architect who

constructed the Frauenkirche. Today it's the principal Greek Ortho-
dox church in Munich.

Theatinerkirche (St. Kajetan's). The dominating, ocher-yellow facade
of the Theatinerkirche, framed by twin towers and a commanding dome,
is one of the striking pieces of architecture in the downtown area (*see*
Tour 2 *in* Exploring, *above*).

SHOPPING

Gift Ideas

Munich is a city of beer, and items related to its consumption are obvious choices for souvenirs and gifts. **Ludwig Mory** (Marienplatz 8,
☎ 089/224–542) is the most centrally located beer-mug and coaster
specialty shop, tucked away inconspicuously in the arcades of the City
Hall on Marienplatz. **Sebastian Wesely** (Petersplatz, ☎ 089/264–519)
has shelves of glistening pewter mugs and plates and ceiling-high piles
of Baroque-style, colorfully decorated candles, another Bavarian specialty.

Munich is also the home of the famous **Nymphenburg porcelain** factory. The **Nymphenburg** store (on the corner of Odeonsplatz and Briennerstrasse, ☎ 089/282–428) resembles a drawing room of the
famous Munich palace, with dove-gray soft furnishings and the delicate, expensive porcelain safely locked away in bow-fronted cabinets.
You can also buy direct from the factory, on the grounds of Schloss
Nymphenburg (Nördliches Schlossrondell 8). For Dresden and Meissen ware, go to **Kunstring Meissen** (Briennerstr. 4, ☎ 089/281–532).

Otto Kellnberger's Holzhandlung (Heiliggeiststr. 7–8, ☎ 089/226–479)
specializes in another Bavarian craft—woodwork. **Geschenk Alm**
(Heiliggeiststr. 7–8, ☎ 089/225–147) has nooks and crannies where
brushes of every kind are stowed away. Looking for that pig's bristle
brush to get to the bottom of tall champagne glasses? This is the place
to find it.

Obletter's (Karlsplatz 8, ☎ 089/231–8601; Marienplatz, ☎ 089/264–
062) has a total of five floors packed with toys, many of them handmade German playthings of great charm and indestructible quality. An
exceptionally friendly staff will help you make the right choice, to the
point of engaging you in the latest computer game. This is also the place
to find that great German market leader, the miniature train set.

Antiques

Bavarian antiques can be found in the many small shops around the
Viktualienmarkt; Westenriederstrasse is lined with antiques shops.
Also try the area north of the university; Türkenstrasse, Theresienstrasse,
and Barerstrasse are all filled with stores that sell antiques. **Seidl Antiquitäten** (Sieges-str. 21, near Münchner Freiheit, ☎ 089/349–568) is
so full of antique goods you might literally stumble over what you've
always wanted to put on that corner of the mantelpiece. **Carl Jagemann's**
(Residenzstr. 3, ☎ 089/225–493) has been in the antiques business for
more than a century despite the shop's high prices. Perhaps friendly
and knowledgeable service are the success of its secret. **Robert Müller's**
antiques shop (Westenriederstr. 4, ☎ 089/221–726) is where you'll find
German military memorabilia (spiked helmets from the First World War
sell for upwards of DM 600).

Horst Fuchs (Westenriederstr. 17, ☎ 089/223–791) has one of Munich's
best selections of antique beer mugs. His crowded shelves also hide sen-

timental embroidered pictures, kitschy souvenirs, and other amusing and inexpensive German knickknacks.

In **Antike Uhren Eder** (Prannerstr. 4, in the Hotel Bayerischer Hof building, ☎ 089/220–305), the silence is broken only by the ticking of dozens of highly valuable German antique clocks and discreet bargaining over the high prices. The nearby **Antike Uhren H. Schley** (Kardinal-Faulhaber-Str. 14a, ☎ 089/226–188) also specializes in antique clocks.

Interesting and/or cheap antiques and assorted junk from all over Eastern Europe are laid out on the tarmac of the old airport at Riem (take the S-6 S-bahn). The flea market there on Fridays and Saturdays is one of Europe's largest.

Folk Costumes

Those who feel the need to deck themselves out in lederhosen or a dirndl, or to sport a green loden coat and little pointed hat with feathers, have a wide choice in the Bavarian capital. **Loden-Frey** (Maffeistr. 7–9, ☎ 089/236–930) is the top address for traditional Bavarian wear, although its rich brass and mahogany shelves also have other fine-quality German-made clothes. **Wallach** (Residenzstr. 3, ☎ 089/220–871) is small and exclusive and sets its clothes off against amusing shop-window displays (a Bavarian forest, for instance, with real trees). The aptly named **Lederhosen Wagner** (Tal 77, ☎ 089/225–697) has been in business since 1825, and the one-story shop hasn't changed much over the years. Nor have the traditionally styled lederhosen.

Shopping Districts

Munich has an immense **central shopping area**, 2 kilometers (1½ miles) of pedestrian streets stretching from the train station to Marienplatz and north to Odeonsplatz. The two main streets here are Neuhauserstrasse and Kaufingerstrasse. This is where most of the major department stores are located (*see* Department Stores, *below*). For upscale shopping, Maximilianstrasse, Residenzstrasse, and Theatinerstrasse are unbeatable and contain a fine array of classy and tempting stores that are the equal of any in Europe. **Schwabing,** located north of the university, has several of the city's most intriguing and offbeat shopping streets—Schellingstrasse and Hohenzollernstrasse are two to try.

Malls

Two new shopping malls opened in the past three years in the main pedestrian area, near Kaufingerstrasse and Neuhauserstrasse. **Kaufinger Tor** (Kaufingerstr. 117) has several floors of boutiques and cafés packed neatly together under a high glass roof. The aptly named **Arcade** (Neuhauserstr. 5) is where the young Munich crowd finds the best designer jeans and chunky jewelry.

Department Stores

Hertie (☎ 089/55120) occupying an entire city block between the train station and Karlsplatz, is the largest and, some claim, the best department store in the city. The basement has a high-class delicatessen with champagne bar and a stand-up bistro offering a daily changing menu that puts many high-priced Munich restaurants to shame. Hertie's Schwabing branch (at the square known as Münchner-Freiheit) was recently given a top-to-bottom face-lift that left it loaded with high-gloss steel and glass. **Kaufhof** has two central Munich stores (one standing opposite Hertie on Karlsplatz 2, ☎ 089/51250, and the other at one corner of Marienplatz, ☎ 089/231–851). Both offer a wide range of goods in

42

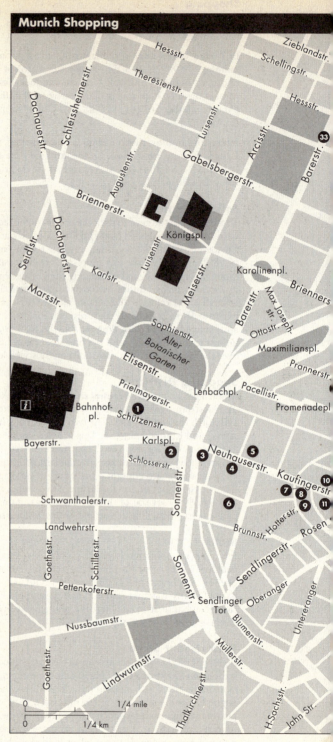

Munich Shopping

KEY

ℹ️ Tourist Information

Englischer Garten

N

Blütenstr.

Adalbertstr.

Schackstr.

Schellingstr.

Türkenstr.

Prof.-Huberpl.

Veterinärstr.

Amalienstr.

Theresienstr.

Ludwigstr.

Kaulbachstr.

Königinstr.

Oettingenstr.

Emil-Reidelstr.

Türkenstr.

Schönfeldstr.

Lerchenfeld Str.

Oettingenstr.

Reitmorstr.

Oscar v. Miller Ring

V. D. Tannstr.

Prinzregentenstr.

Galeriestr.

Odeons-pl.

Hofgarten

K.-Scharnagl-Ring

Unsoldstr.

Sternstr.

Widenmayerstr.

Isar

Salvator-pl.

Theatinerstr.

Hofgartenstr.

Christophstr.

St.-Anna-Pfarrstr.

Liebigstr.

St. Anna Pl.

Kard.-Faulhaber-Str.

Residenzstr.

Maffeistrasse

Marstallstr.

Bürkleinstr.

Max-Joseph-pl.

Am Kosttor

Maximilianstr.

Maximilians Br.

Frauen-pl.

Weinstr.

Dienerstr.

Pfisterstr.

Am Platzl

Knöbelstr.

Th.-Wimmer-Ring

Steinsdorfstr.

Marienpl.

Rindermarkt

Tal

Isar Torpl.

Kanalstr.

Rosental

Frauenstr.

Zweibrückenstr.

Innere Wienerstr.

Blumenstr.

Rumfordstr.

Klenzestr.

Ludwigs Br.

Kellerstr.

Corneliusstr.

Gärtner-pl.

Reichenbachstr.

Klenzestr.

Baaderstr.

Erhardtstr.

Rosenheimerstr.

Fraunhofer

the middle price range. If you catch an end-of-season sale you're sure of a bargain.

Karstadt (☎ 089/290–230), in the 100-year-old **Haus Pollinger,** at the start of the Kaufingerstrasse shopping mall, is another high-class department store, with a very wide range of Bavarian arts and crafts. **Ludwig Beck** (Marienpl. 11, ☎ 089/236–910) is one of the smaller department stores, but it's packed from top to bottom with highly original wares, from fine feather boas to roughly finished Bavarian pottery. It comes into its own as Christmas approaches when a series of booths, each delicately and lovingly decorated, are occupied by craftsmen turning out traditional German toys and decorations. **Hirmer** (Kaufingertrasse 22, ☎ 089/236–830) has Munich's most comprehensive collection of German-made men's clothes, with a markedly friendly and knowledgeable staff. **K & L Ruppert** (Kaufingerstr. 15, ☎ 089/231–1470) has a good, fashionable range of German-made clothes in the lower price brackets.

Food Markets

Munich's **Viktualienmarkt** is *the* place. Located just south of Marienplatz, it's home to an array of colorful stands that sell everything from cheese to sausages, flowers to wine. A visit here is more than just an excuse to buy picnic makings: It's central to an understanding of the easy-come–easy-go nature of Müncheners. If you are staying in the Schwabing area the daily market at **Elisabethplatz** is worth a visit— it's much, much smaller than the Viktualienmarkt, but the range and quality of produce is comparable.

Dallmayr (Dienerstr. 14-15, ☎ 089/21350) is an elegant gourmet food store with delights ranging from the most exotic fruits to English jams, served by efficient Munich matrons in smart blue-and-white linen costumes. The store's famous specialty is coffee, with more than 50 varieties to blend as you wish. There's also an enormous range of breads, and a temperature-controlled cigar room.

The **Zerwick Gewölbe** (Ledererstr. 3, ☎ 089/226–824) is Munich's oldest venison shop, with a a mouthwatering selection of smoked meats, including wild boar.

SPORTS AND FITNESS

The **Olympiapark,** built for the 1972 Olympics, is the largest sports and recreation center in Europe. For general information about clubs, organizations, events, etc., contact the **Haus des Sports** (Briennerstr. 50, ☎ 089/520–151) or the **Städtisches Sportamt** (Neuhauserstr. 26, ☎ 089/233–6224).

Beaches and Water Sports

There is sailing and windsurfing on Ammersee and Starnbergersee. Windsurfers should pay attention to restricted areas at bathing beaches. Information on sailing is available from **Bayrischer Segler-Verband** (Georg-Brauchle-Ring 93, ☎ 089/157–02366). Information on windsurfing is available from **Verband der Deutschen Windsurfing Schulen** (Weilheim, ☎ 0881/5267).

Golf

Munich Golf Club has two courses that admit visitors on weekdays. Visitors must be members of a club at home. Its 18-hole course is at Strasslach in the suburb of Grünwald, south of the city (☎ 08170/450). Its nine-hole course is more centrally located, at Thalkirchen, on the Isar River (☎ 089/723–1304). The greens fee is DM 75 for both courses.

Hotel Fitness Centers

Bayerischer Hof (Promenadepl. 2–6, ☎ 089/21200) has a rooftop pool, a sun terrace, a sauna, and tennis nearby.

München Sheraton (Arabellstr. 6, ☎ 089/92640) has a large indoor pool that opens onto a garden. In the room with the pool are weights and some exercise equipment.

Park Hilton International München (Am Tucherpark 7, ☎ 089/38450), facing the Englischer Garten, has marked running trails, an indoor pool, a sauna, and massage and spa facilities.

Vier Jahreszeiten Kempinski (Maximilianstr. 17, ☎ 089/230–390) is proud of its rooftop swimming pool; it also has a gym with weights and exercise equipment, sauna, massage room and solarium, and jogging maps in each room.

Hiking and Climbing

Information is available from **Deutscher Alpeinverein** (Praterinsel, ☎ 089/235–0900) and from the sporting-goods stores **Sport Scheck** (☎ 089/21660) and **Sport Schuster** (☎ 089/237–070).

Jogging

The best place to jog is the **Englischer Garten** (U-bahn stop: München-Freiheit or Universität), which is 11 kilometers (7 miles) around and has lakes and dirt and asphalt paths. You can also jog through **Olympiapark** (U-bahn stop: Olympiazentrum). A pleasant morning or evening jog can be had along the **Isar River,** or you can go for a jog in the (500-acre) park of **Schloss Nymphenburg.** For a longer jog along the Isar River, take the S-bahn to Unterföhring and pace yourself back to Münchner-Freiheit—a distance of 6.5 kilometers (4 miles).

Ice Skating

There is an indoor ice rink at the **Eissportstadion** in Olympiapark (Spiridon-Louis-Ring 3) and outdoor rinks at **Prinzregenten Stadium** (Prinzregentenstr. 80) and **Eisbahn-West** (Agnes-Bernauer Str. 241). There is outdoor skating in winter on the lake in the **Englischer Garten** and on the **Nymphenburger Canal,** where you can also curl (Eisstockschiessen) by renting equipment from little wooden huts; these also sell hot drinks. Players rent sections of machine-smoothed ice on the canal. Watch out for the *Gefahr* (danger) signs warning of thin ice. Additional information is available from **Bayerischer Eissportverband** (Betzenweg 34, ☎ 089/81820).

Rowing

Rowboats can be rented on the southern bank of the **Olympiasee** in Olympiapark and at the **Kleinhesseloher See** in the Englischer Garten.

Swimming

You can try swimming outdoors in the Isar River at Maria-Einsiedel, but be warned that because the river flows from the Alps the water is frigid even in summer. Warmer natural swimming can be found off the beaches of the lakes near Munich—for example, the **Ammersee** and **Starnbergersee.** There are pools at **Cosima Bad** (corner of Englschalkingerstr. and Cosimastr., in Bogenhausen), with man-made waves; **Dantebad** (Dantestr. 6); **Nordbad** (Schleissheimerstr. 142, in the

Schwabing district); **Michaelibad** (Heinrich-Wieland-Str. 24); **Olympia-Schwimmhalle** (Olympiapark); and **Volksbad** (Rosenheimerstr. 1).

Tennis

There are indoor and outdoor courts at **Münchnerstrasse 15,** in München-Unterfohring; at the corner of **Drygalski-Allee** and **Kistler-hofstrasse,** in München-Fürstenried; and at **Rothof Sportanlage** (Denningerstr.), behind the Arabella and Sheraton hotels. In addition, there are about 200 outdoor courts all over Munich. Many can be booked via **Sport Scheck** (☎ 089/21660), which has installations around town. Prices vary from DM 18 to DM 25 an hour, depending on the time of day. Full details on tennis in Munich are available from the **Bayerischer Tennis Verband** (Georg-Brauchle-Ring 93, ☎ 089/157–02640).

DINING

Munich rates as Germany's gourmet capital, and it has an inordinate number of high-class French restaurants, some with chef-owners who honed their skills under such Gallic masters as Paul Bocuse. For connoisseurs, wining and dining at Aubergine or the Königshof could well turn into the equivalent of a religious experience; culinary creations are accorded the status of works of art on a par with a Bach fugue or Dürer painting, with tabs worthy of a king's ransom. Epicureans are convinced that one can dine as well in Munich as in any other city on the Continent, including Paris, Brussels, and Rome, and perhaps it's true. Certainly it is in a number of the top-rated restaurants listed below.

However, for many the true glory of Munich's kitchen artistry is to be experienced in those rustically decorated, traditional eating places that serve down-home Bavarian specialties in ample portions. The city's renowned beer and wine restaurants offer superb atmosphere, low prices, and as much wholesome German food as you'll ever want. They're open at just about any hour of the day or night—you can order your roast pork at 11 AM or 11 PM.

Snacking in Munich

Munich's pre-McDonald's type of fast food derives from a centuries-old tradition. A tempting array of delectables is available at most hours of almost anytime during the day or night; knowing the various Bavarian names will help.

The generic term for Munich snacks is *Schmankerl.* And Schmankerl are served at *Brotzeit,* which literally translated is "bread time": This is a snack break, or what the English might call elevenses. According to a saying, *"Brotzeit ist die schönste Zeit"* (snack time is the best time).

In the morning in Munich, one eats *Weisswurst,* a tender minced-veal sausage, made fresh daily, steamed, and served with sweet mustard, a crisp roll or a pretzel, and *Weissbier* (wheat beer). This white sausage is not to everyone's taste, but it is certainly worth trying. Legend has it that this sausage was invented in 1857 by a butcher who had a hang-over and mixed the wrong ingredients. A plaque on a wall in Marien-platz marks the spot where the "mistake" was made. The claim is that the genuine article is available only in and around Munich, served only between midnight and noon.

Another favorite Bavarian specialty is *Leberkäs,* literally "liver cheese," although neither liver nor cheese is involved in its construction. It is a spicy meat loaf baked to a crusty turn each morning and served in succulent slabs throughout the day. A *Leberkäs Semmel*—a wedge of the meat loaf between two halves of a crispy bread roll smeared with a bittersweet mustard—is the favorite Munich on-the-hoof snack.

After that comes the repertoire of sausages indigenous to Bavaria, including types from Regensburg and Nürnberg.

More substantial repasts include *Tellerfleisch,* boiled beef with freshly grated horseradish and boiled potatoes on the side, served on wooden plates. (There is a similar dish called *Tafelspitz.*)

Among roasts, *Sauerbraten* (beef) and *Schweinsbraten* (pork) are accompanied by dumplings and red cabbage or sauerkraut.

Haxn refers to ham hocks roasted until they're crisp on the outside, juicy on the inside. They are served with sauerkraut and potato puree.

You'll also find soups, salads, fish and fowl, cutlets, game in season, casseroles, hearty stews, desserts, and what may well be the greatest variety and the highest quality of baked goods in Europe, including pretzels. In particular, seek out a *Käsestange*—a crispy long bread roll coated in baked cheese. No one need ever go hungry or thirsty in Munich.

Old Munich restaurants, called *Gaststätten,* feature what's referred to as *gutbürgerliche Küche,* loosely translated as good regional fare, and include brewery restaurants, beer halls, beer gardens, rustic cellar establishments, and *Weinstuben* (wine houses). More than a hundred such places brighten the scene.

What to Wear
Many Munich restaurants serve sophistiated cuisine, and they require that their patrons dress for the occassion. Other, usually less-expensive restaurants will serve you regardless of what you wear.

Ratings

CATEGORY	COST*
$$$$	over DM 95
$$$	DM 65–DM 95
$$	DM 45–DM 65
$	DM 30–DM 45

per person for a three-course meal, excluding drinks

$$$$
★ **Aubergine.** Professional gourmets swear by the upscale nouvelle cuisine of Eckhart Witzigmann, chef and owner of this respected restaurant. The service is appropriately polished, in keeping with the modern, streamlined decor. If you want a gastronomic experience on the grand scale, try the pigeon cutlets in lentils, or the elaborately prepared devilfish, and the semolina soufflé with pears in cinnamon. ✗ *Maximilianspl. 5,* ☎ *089/598–171. Reservations required. Jacket and tie. DC, MC, V. Closed Sun., Mon., 2 wks in Dec.*

$$$$ **Königshof.** The view here is great inside and out—ask for a panoramic window table overlooking Karlsplatz, in what is probably Munich's most exquisitely decorated restaurant. The service is of equally high standard. French nouvelle cuisine dominates. ✗ *Karlspl. 25,* ☎ *089/551–360. Reservations required. Jacket and tie. AE, DC, MC, V.*

$$$$
★ **Tantris.** Chef Hans Haas has kept this restaurant with a modernist look among the top five dining establishments in Munich places to dine, and in 1994 he was voted Germany's top chef by Germany's top critics. You, too, will be impressed by the exotic nouvelle cuisine on the menu, including such specialties as shellfish and creamed potato soup, and roasted wood pigeon with scented rice. But you may wish to ignore

48

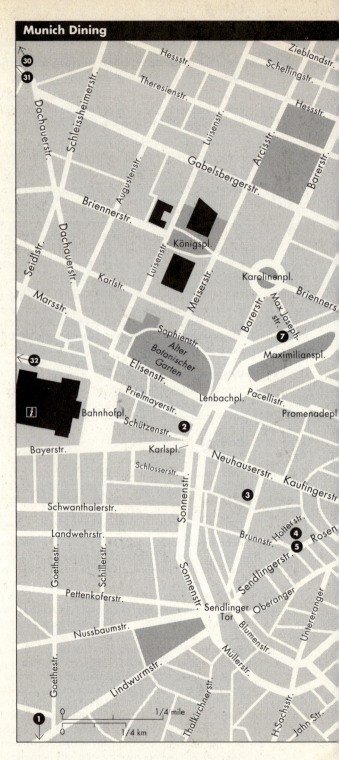

Munich Dining

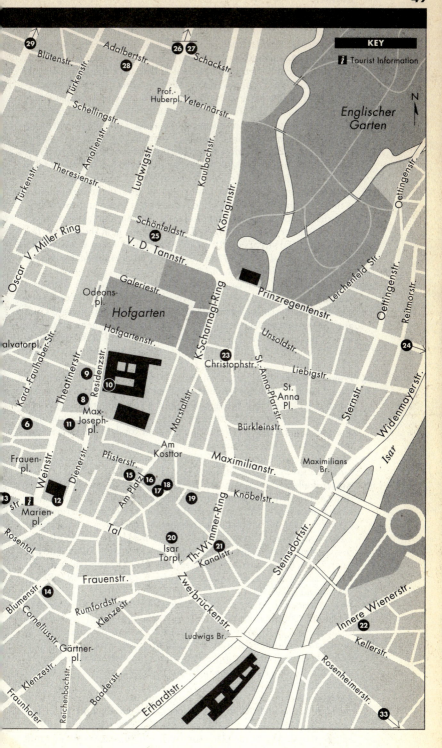

KEY

i Tourist Information

Englischer Garten

Blütenstr.

Adalbertstr.

Schackstr.

Türkenstr.

Prof.-Huberpl. Veterinärstr.

Schellingstr.

Amalienstr.

Ludwigstr.

Kaulbachstr.

Königinstr.

Oettingenstr.

Türkenstr.

Theresienstr.

Schönfeldstr.

Oscar v. Miller Ring

V. D. Tannstr.

Galeriestr.

K.-Scharnagl-Ring

Prinzregentenstr.

Lerchenfeld Str.

Oettingenstr.

Reitmorstr.

Odeons-pl.

Hofgarten

Hofgartenstr.

Unsoldstr.

alvatorpl.

Kard.-Faulhaber-Str.

Theatinerstr.

Residenzstr.

Christophstr.

St.-Anna-Pfarrsl.

Liebigstr.

Sternstr.

Widenmayerstr.

Isar

St. Anna Pl.

Max-Joseph-pl.

Marstallstr.

Bürkleinstr.

Frauen-pl.

Weinstr.

Dienerstr.

Pfisterstr.

Am Platzl

Am Kosttor

Maximilianstr.

Knöbelstr.

Maximilians Br.

Steinsdorfstr.

Str. **i**

Marien-pl.

Rosental

Tal

Th.-Wimmer-Ring

Isar Torpl.

Kanalstr.

Frauenstr.

Blumenstr.

Corneliusstr.

Rumfordstr.

Klenzestr.

Zweibrückenstr.

Ludwigs Br.

Innere Wienerstr.

Kellerstr.

Gärtner-pl.

Klenzestr.

Reichenbachstr.

Baaderstr.

Erhardtstr.

Rosenheimerstr.

Fraunhofer

the bare concrete surroundings and the garish orange and yellow decor. ✗ *Johann-Fichter-str. 7,* ☎ *0889/362–061. Reservations required. Jacket and tie. AE, DC, MC, V. Closed Sun., Dec. 25, and Whitsun.*

$$$ Hunsingers Bouillabaisse. After establishing a nationwide reputation for excellent cuisine from a restaurant in Munich's southern suburbs, Werner Hunsinger has moved into the city center. The sleek and elegant decor of this place, just off fashionable Maximilianstrasse, represents a break in style from the solid traditional look of his previous home, but the cuisine hasn't changed. The menu is full of light and imaginative dishes created from the simplest of ingredients—calves' tongue, for instance, with avocado vinaigrette, or black noodles with mussels. ✗ *Falkenturmstr. 10,* ☎ *089/297–909. Reservations advised. Jacket and tie. AE, DC, MC, V. Closed Sun. and last 3 wks in Aug.*

$$$ Käferschanke. Fresh seafood, imported daily from the south of France, is the attraction here. Try the grilled prawns in a sweet-and-sour sauce. The rustic decor, complemented by some fine antiques, is sure to delight no matter what you order. The restaurant is in the upscale Bogenhausen suburb, a 10-minute taxi ride from downtown. ✗ *Schumannstr. 1,* ☎ *089/41681. Reservations advised. Jacket and tie. AE, DC, MC. Closed Sun. and holidays.*

$$$ Le Gourmet. This old local favorite, decorated with red silk wallpaper and mahogany woodwork, is known for its creative blend of French and German dishes. Recommended here are the catfish in mustard sauce and the venison with cherries. The DM 200 gourmet menu is only for serious palates. ✗ *Hartmannstr. 8,* ☎ *089/212–0958. Reservations required. Jacket and tie. AE, DC, MC, V. Closed Sun., Mon., and Dec. 25–Jan. 1.*

$$$ Preysing Keller. Devotees of all that's best in modern German cook-
★ ing—food that's light and sophisticated but with recognizably Teutonic touches—will love the Preysing Keller. It's in a 16th-century cellar, though it has been so overrestored that there's practically no indication of its age or original character. Never mind; it's the food, the extensive wine list, and the perfect service that make this restaurant special. *Innere-Wiener-Str. 6,* ☎ *089/481–015. Reservations required. Jacket and tie. No credit cards. Closed Sun. and Dec. 23–Jan. 10.*

$$ Austernkeller. Oysters (Austern) are the specialty of this cellar restaurant, although many other varieties of seafood—all flown in daily from France—help fill its imaginative menu. The lobster thermador is expensive (DM 46) but surpasses that served elsewhere in Munich, while a richly stocked fish soup can be ordered for less than DM 10. The fussy, fishnet-hung decor is a shade too maritime, especially for downtown Munich, but the starched white linen and glittering glassware and cutlery add a note of elegance. *Stollbergstr. 11,* ☎ *298–787. Reservations advised. MC.*

$$ Bistro Terrine. The name gives the impression that this is no more than a humble, neighborhood French-style restaurant. Don't be deceived: Excellent classic French dishes are served within its appealing Art Nouveau interior. Order from the fixed-price menu to keep the check low; à la carte dishes are appreciably more expensive. *Amalienstr. 89,* ☎ *089/281–780. Reservations advised. Jacket and tie. AE, MC. Closed Mon., Sat. lunch, and Sun.*

$$ Franziskaner. Vaulted archways, cavernous rooms interspersed with intimate dining areas, bold blue frescoes, long wood tables, and a sort of spic-and-span medieval atmosphere—the look without the dirt—set the mood. This is the place for an early morning Weisswurst and a beer; Bavarians swear it will banish all trace of that morning-after feeling. The Franziskaner is located right by the State Opera. ✗ *Peruastr. 5,* ☎ *089/231–8120. No reservations. No credit cards.*

$$ Friesenstube. Even if you won't be journeying to the North Sea or the Baltic resorts, you can taste authentic cuisine from Germany's coast at this modest little restaurant. Delicious Busumer shrimp is a welcome staple; *Labskaus,* Hamburg's favorite stew, has its day on Thursday. The menu is mostly seafood all the time, although some Westphalian meat dishes do intrude. The place is small and easily recognizable by its timber-clad exterior, reminiscent of a harbor pub. But alas, this is in Munich, and it's late-working officials from nearby Bavarian government offices who are the regulars here. ✕ *Thomas-Wimmer-Ring 16,* ☎ *089/294–600. No reservations. AE, MC. Dinner only, closed Sat. AE, MC.*

$$ Glockenbach. This small, highly popular restaurant with dark-wood paneling inside serves mostly fish entrées, prepared by the acclaimed chef and owner, Karl Ederer. Book ahead to enjoy such specialties as freshwater fish ragout from the Starnberger Lake, or marinated wild hare fillets with perfumed horseradish. ✕ *Kapuzinerstr. 29,* ☎ *089/534– 043. Reservations required. MC, V. Closed Sun., Mon., Dec. 25, Jan. 1, and 2 wks in July.*

$$ Halali. The Halali is an old-style Munich restaurant—polished wood paneling and antlers on the walls—that offers new-style regional specialties, such as venison in juniper-berry sauce and marinated beef on a bean salad. Save room for the homemade vanilla ice cream. ✕ *Schönfeldstr. 22,* ☎ *089/285–909. Reservations advised. Jacket and tie. MC. Closed Sun. and holidays.*

$$ James Cafe. James is an immigrant from Kenya, but there aren't any African specialties on his restaurant's small but very fine menu. James cooks Italian, and so well that his cozy café is considered by local aficionados to be one of *the* Italian eating places in town. One of Munich's leading restaurant critics said most of the city's Italian cooks should turn "green, white, and red with shame." The menu changes daily; if pheasant is on it, then that's the dish to order. ✕ *Hochbrückenstr. 14,* ☎ *089/298–940. Reservations accepted. No credit cards. Closed Sun. lunch.*

$$ Jeeta's. The restaurant that is arguably Munich's best for Indian food is just a tiny neighborhood eatery, tucked away in a side street of upmarket Lehel. The food is pungently Punjabi, although concessions are also made to other regional influences. Don't miss the bean-curd soup. The few tables are packed close together, so this isn't the place for a quiet tête-à-tête or a large party. And reservations are a must. ✕ *Seitzstr 13 (corner of Christophstr.),* ☎ *223931. Reservations required. AE, MC.*

$$ Ratskeller. Munich's Ratskeller is one of the few city-hall cellar restaurants to offer vegetarian dishes alongside the normal array of hearty and filling traditional fare. If turnip in cheese sauce is on the menu, you won't need to be a vegetarian to appreciate it. The decor is much as you would expect, with vaulted stone ceilings and flickering candles. ✕ *Marienpl. 8,* ☎ *089/220–313. Reservations advised at lunchtime. AE, MC, V.*

$$ ★ Spatenhaus. A view of the opera house and the royal palace complements the Bavarian mood of wood-paneled and beamed Spatenhaus. The menu is international, however, with more or less everything from artichokes to *Zuppa Romana* (alcohol-soaked, fruity Italian cake-pudding). But since you're in Bavaria, why not do as the Bavarians do? Try the Bavarian Plate, an enormous mixture of local meats and sausages. ✕ *Residenzstr. 12,* ☎ *089/227–841. Reservations advised. DC, MC, V.*

$$ Spöckmeier. This rambling solidly Bavarian beer restaurant spread over three floors, including a snug *Keller* (cellar), is famous for its home-made Weisswurst. If you've just stopped in for a snack and you don't fancy the fat breakfast sausage, order coffee and pretzels or, in the afternoons, a wedge of cheesecake. The daily changing menu also offers more than two dozen hearty main-course dishes and a choice of four draft beers. The house *Eintopf* (a rich broth of noodles and pork) is a meal in itself. The Spöckmeier is only 50 yards from Marienplatz; on sunny summer days tables are set outside in the auto-free street. ✕ *Rosen-str. 9, ☎ 089/268–088. Reservations accepted. AE, DC, MC, V.*

$$ Weichandhof. This rambling old farmhouse-style restaurant is on the northwestern outskirts of town, in the leafy residential suburb of Obermenzing and near the start of the Stuttgart autobahn. If you're heading that way, a stop here is strongly recommended, but even a special trip from the city center is worthwhile. The food is excellent, with a menu based on traditional Bavarian and regional German and Austrian fare; roast suckling pig, pork knuckle, and Vienna-style boiled beef are basic staples. In summer or on warm spring and autumn evenings the vine-clad terrace beckons. In winter, tiled stoves give a warm glow to the wood-paneled dining rooms. ✕ *Betzenweg 81, ☎ 089/111–621. Reservations advised. MC. Closed weekends.*

$$ Welser Kuche. It's less a question of what you eat at this medieval-style cellar restaurant than how you eat it—with your fingers and a hunting knife, in the manner of 16th-century baronial banquets. You're welcomed by pretty "serving wenches" who tie a protective bib around your neck, proffer a hunting horn of mead, and show you to a place at one of the oak trestle tables that complete the authentic-looking surroundings. It's best to go in a group, but room will always be found for those dining alone or as couples. The full menu runs to 10 dishes, although you can settle for less and choose à la carte. ✕ *Residenzstr. 2, ☎ 089/296–565. Reservations advised. MC. Closed lunch.*

$ Altes Hackerhaus. Since 1570, beer has been brewed or served here, the birthplace of Hacher-Pschorr, a Munich brewery that is still active. Today the site is a cozy, upscale restaurant with three floors of wood-paneled rooms. In summer you can order a cheese plate and beer in the cool, flower-decorated inner courtyard; in winter you can snuggle in a corner of the Ratsstube and warm up on thick homemade potato broth, followed by schnitzel and *Bratkartoffein* (pan-fried potatoes). ✕ *Sendlinger-str. 75, ☎ 089/260–5026. Reservations accepted. No credit cards.*

$ Augustiner Keller. This 19th-century establishment is the flagship beer restaurant of one of Munich's oldest breweries, Augustiner. The decor emphasizes wood—from the refurbished parquet floors to the wood barrels from which the beer is drawn. The menu changes daily and offers a full range of Bavarian specialties, but try to order *Tellerfleisch*—cold roast beef with lashings of horseradish, served on a big wood board. Follow that with *Dampfnudeln* (suet pudding served with custard) and you won't feel hungry again for 24 hours. The communal atmosphere of the two baronial hall–like rooms makes this a better place for meeting locals than for attempting a quiet meal for two. ✕ *Arnulfstr. 52, ☎ 089/594–393. Reservations accepted. No credit cards.*

$ Baltzer. Vegetarians say they eat better at this evenings-only restaurant than fellow epicurean omnivores do in their starred temples of haute cuisine. The dishes certainly have a flair not usually associated with the stringency of vegetarian fare (eggplant, for instance, stuffed with oysters, mushrooms, and wild rice). The Baltzer team's credo, which you, too, will be sure of after eating here, is that "Plants have a myriad different tastes." ✕ *Volkartstr. 70, ☎ 089/1239–1919. No reser-*

vations. No credit cards. Closed Mon. and lunchtime; open Sun. 9 AM–midnight.

$ **Brauhaus zum Brez'n.** This hostelry is bedecked in the blue-and-white-checked colors of the Bavarian flag. The eating and drinking are spread over three floors and cater to a broad clientele—from local business lunchers to hungry night owls emerging from Schwabing's bars looking for a bite at 2 AM. Brez'n offers a big all-day menu of traditional roasts, to be washed down with a choice of three draft beers. ✕ *Leopoldstr. 72,* ☎ *089/390–092. Reservations accepted. No credit cards.*

$ **Dürnbräu.** A fountain plays outside this picturesque old Bavarian inn. Inside, the mood is crowded and noisy. Expect to share a table; your fellow diners will range from businesspeople to students. The food is resolutely traditional. Try the cream of spinach soup and the boiled beef. ✕ *Dürnbräugasse 2,* ☎ *089/222–195. Reservations accepted. AE, DC, MC, V.*

$ **Grigoris.** Traditional and off-beat Greek dishes are served in this very friendly, small Schwabing venue run by owner Grigoris and his wife, Johanna—whose recipes are available in a book on sale at the restaurant. Lamb is served daily with a changing range of sauces. Vegetarians can choose from five different dishes. ✕ *Tengstr. 31,* ☎ *089/271–5625. Reservations advised. AE, DC, V. Closed Mon.*

$ **Grüne Gans.** This small, chummy restaurant near Viktualienmarkt is popular with local entertainers, whose photographs clutter the walls. International fare with regional German influences dominates the menu, although there are a few Chinese dishes. Try the chervil cream soup, followed by calves' kidneys in tarragon sauce. ✕ *Am Einlass 5,* ☎ *089/266–228. Reservations required. MC. Closed lunch and Sat.*

$ **Haxnbauer.** This is one of Munich's more sophisticated beer restaurants. There's the usual series of interlinking rooms—some large, some small—and the usual sturdy yet pretty Bavarian decoration. But there is a much greater emphasis on the food here than in similar places. Try the *Schweineshaxn* (pork shanks) cooked over a charcoal fire. ✕ *Munzstr. 2,* ☎ *089/221–922. Reservations advised. MC, V.*

$ **Hofbräuhaus.** The sound of the constantly playing oompah band draws passersby into this father of all beer halls, in which trumpet, drum, and accordion music blends with singing and shouting drinkers to produce an ear-splitting din. This is no place for the faint-hearted, though a trip to Munich would be incomplete without a visit to the Hofbräuhaus. In 1992, Mikhail Gorbachev paid a visit. Upstairs is a more peaceful restaurant. In March, May, and September, ask for one of the special, extra-strong seasonal beers (Starkbier, Maibock, Märzen) that complement the heavy traditional Bavarian fare. ✕ *Am Platzl,* ☎ *089/221–676. No reservations. No credit cards.*

$ ★ **Hundskugel.** This is Munich's oldest tavern, dating back to 1440; history positively drips from its crooked walls. The food is surprisingly good. If *Spanferkel*—roast suckling pig—is on the menu, make a point of ordering it. This is simple Bavarian fare at its best. ✕ *Hotterstr. 18,* ☎ *089/264–272. Reservations advised. No credit cards.*

$ **Santa Fe.** Munich's surprisingly large Native American population holds regular powwows in this authentic southwestern American bar and restaurant, which is run by a German and a New Mexico native. A real totem pole sits solemnly in a place of honor, and Native American handicrafts and paintings adorn the rough-plastered adobe-esque walls. The food is convincingly New Mexican (turkey with pumpkin and maize-bread stuffing, for instance) and the portions are American-size (large). On Sundays, American breakfasts are served all day long, with cowboy-style coffee cans on the rough-wood tables. You'll find the Santa Fe in the center of Munich's lively Haidhausen district, behind the Gasteig cultural center. ✕ *Balanstr. 16,* ☎ *089/484736. No reservations. AE, MC.*

$ **Pfälzer Weinprobierstube.** A warren of stone-vaulted rooms of various sizes, wood tables, flickering candles, dirndl-clad waitresses, and a vast range of wines add up to an experience as close to everyone's image of timeless Germany as you're likely to get. The food is reliable rather than spectacular. Local specialties predominate. ✕ *Residenzstr. 1,* ☎ *089/225–628. No reservations. No credit cards.*

$ **Weinhaus Neuner.** Munich's oldest wine tavern serves good food as well as superior wines in its three varied nooks and crannies: the wood-paneled restaurant, the wine tavern (*Weinstübl*), and the small bistro. The choice of food is remarkable, from nouvelle German to old-fashioned country. Specialties include home-smoked beef and salmon. ✕ *Herzogspitalstr. 8,* ☎ *089/260–3954. Reservations advised. AE, DC, MC. Closed Sat. lunch, Sun., and holidays.*

LODGING

Make reservations well in advance, and be prepared for higher-than-average rates. Though Munich has a vast number of hotels in all price ranges, many of the most popular are full year-round; this is a major trade and convention city as well as a prime tourist destination. If you plan to visit during the *Mode Wochen* (fashion weeks) in March and September or during the Oktoberfest at the end of September, make reservations at least four months in advance.

Some of the large, very expensive ($$$$) hotels that cater to expense-account business travelers have very attractive weekend discount rates—sometimes as much as 50% below normal prices. Conversely, regular rates can go up during big trade fairs. Check well in advance either through your travel agent or directly with the hotel.

The tourist office at Rindermarkt 1, D-80331 Munich 1, has a reservations department, but note that it will not accept telephone reservations. There's also a reservations office at the airport. The best bet for finding a room if you arrive without a reservation is the tourist office in the main train station, on the south side abutting Bayerstrasse (open daily 8 AM–10 PM, no telephone bookings).

Ratings

CATEGORY	COST*
$$$$	over DM 300
$$$	DM 200–DM 300
$$	DM 140–DM 200
$	under DM 140

All prices are for two people in a double room, including tax and service charge.

$$$$ **Bayerischer Hof.** This is one of Munich's most traditional luxury hotels. It's on a ritzy shopping street, and there's a series of exclusive shops right outside the imposing marble entrance. Public rooms are decorated with antiques, fine paintings, marble, and painted wood. Old-fashioned comfort and class abound in the older rooms; some of the newer rooms are more functional. ⌂ *Promenadenpl. 2–6,* ☎ *089/21200, FAX 089/212–0906. 440 rooms with bath. 3 restaurants, outdoor pool, beauty salon, massage, sauna, nightclub, parking. AE, DC, MC, V.*

$$$$ Grand Continental. Part of the Royal Classic chain, this hotel combines super modern luxury with old-fashioned style. Bedrooms are individually furnished with antiques, and the ornately designed public rooms feature marble and sculptures. ⊡ *Max-Joseph-str. 5,* ☎ *089/551–570,* FAX *089/5199–5420. 149 rooms with bath. 2 restaurants, bar, beauty salon, parking. AE, DC, MC, V.*

$$$$ Park Hilton. The hotel is big on the outside but intimate on the inside, with as cheerful and accommodating a staff as you're likely to encounter in any European hotel, the glitziness of the lobby and reception area notwithstanding. The hotel is beside the vast Englischer Garten, away from the city center, but a downtown-bound tram stops nearby—or you can take the hotel's own courtesy minibus, which runs a return service for guests. A fast-flowing stream with a beer garden beside it runs throughout the grounds. ⊡ *Am Tucherpark 7,* ☎ *089/38450,* FAX *089/3845–1845. 477 rooms with bath. 3 restaurants, pool, massage, sauna, health club,. AE, DC, MC, V.*

$$$$ Platzl. This hotel stands in the historic heart of Munich, near the famous Hofbräuhaus beer hall and a couple of minutes' walk from Marienplatz and many other landmarks. The Aying brewery owners have done rooms in rustic Bavarian style. Adjoining the hotel is Platzl Bühne, a famous Bavarian folk theater where though you may not understand the thigh-slapping humor, you're sure to have fun. ⊡ *Sparkassenstr. 10,* ☎ *089/237-030,* FAX *089/2370–3800. 167 rooms, 2 suites, all soundproofed, with bath. Restaurant, bar, sauna, steam room, exercise room, parking. AE, DC, MC, V.*

$$$$ Rafael. ★ This elegant downtown hotel opened in 1989, in a beautifully renovated neo-Renaissance building that was a high-society ballroom during the late 19th century. Today it tries to recapture some of that bygone era with 24-hour service, including such personalized amenities as in-house butlers. Rooms are individually furnished and extravagantly decorated in addition to offering many extras, including fax machines. ⊡ *Neuturmstr. 1,* ☎ *089/290–980,* FAX *089/222–539. 67 rooms and 7 suites (up to DM 1,150 per night) with bath. Restaurant, 2 bars, pool. AE, DC, MC, V.*

$$$$ Vier Jahreszeiten Kempinski. ★ The Vier Jahreszeiten—it means the Four Seasons—has been playing host to the world's wealthy and titled for more than a century. It has an unbeatable location on Maximilianstrasse, Munich's premier shopping street, only a few minutes' walk from the heart of the city. Elegance and luxury set the tone throughout; many rooms have handsome antique pieces. The main floor's restaurant is Bistro Eck, and the Theater bar/restaurant is in the cellar. ⊡ *Maximilianstr. 17,* ☎ *089/230–390, reservations in the U.S. from Kempinski Reservation Service,* ☎ *516/794–2670,* FAX *089/2303–9693. 322 rooms with bath; 44 suites; presidential suite. 2 restaurants, piano bar, pool, massage, sauna, exercise room, car rental, parking. AE, DC, MC, V.*

$$$ Admiral. ★ Although it's in the heart of the city, close to the Isar River and Deutsches Museum, the small, privately owned Admiral enjoys a quiet side-street location and its own garden. Many of the cozily furnished and warmly decorated bedrooms have a balcony overlooking the garden. Bowls of fresh fruit are part of the friendly welcome awaiting guests. The breakfast buffet is a dream, complete with homemade jams, in-season strawberries and Italian and French delicacies. ⊡ *Kohlstr. 9,* ☎ *089/226–6414,* FAX *089/293–674. 33 rooms with bath. Bar, garage. AE, DC, MC, V.*

$$$ Arabella Airport. This first-class lodging is only five minutes from the new Franz Josef Strauss Airport, and the hotel operates a courtesy shuttle bus. Built primarily to cater to businesspeople (there are numerous

56

Munich Lodging

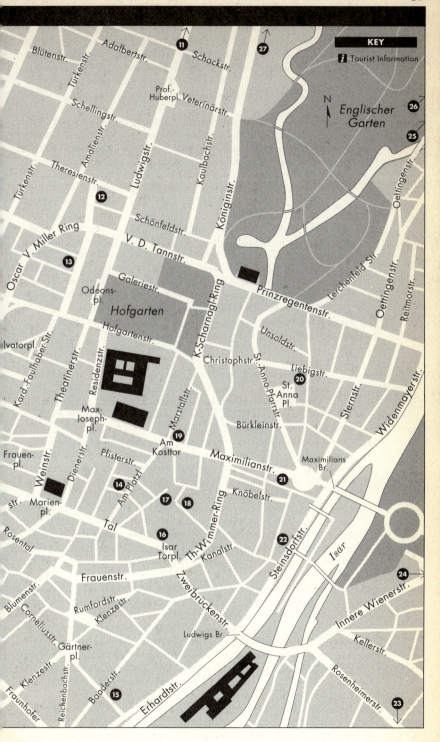

conference-room facilities), the Arabella has plenty of leisure facilities and is ideal for any traveler who has an early morning departure or a late-evening arrival flight. The three-story Bavarian rustic-style building is surrounded by greenery. Rooms are furnished in light pinewood, with Laura Ashley fabrics. ⊞ *Freisingerstr. 80, D-85445 Schwaig,* ☎ *08122/8480,* FAX *08122/848–800. 170 rooms, 7 suites with bath. 2 restaurants, bar, indoor pool, sauna, steam room, exercise room. AE, DC, MC, V.*

$$$ **Carlton.** This is a diplomats' favorite: a small, elegant, discreet hotel on a quiet side street in the best area of downtown Munich. The American and British consulates are a short walk away, and so are some of the liveliest Schwabing bars and restaurants. Art galleries, museums, and cinemas are also in the immediate area. Rooms are on the small side, but there are four apartments with cooking facilities. ⊞ *Fürstenstr. 12,* ☎ *089/282–061,* FAX *089/284–391. 49 rooms, 4 apartments with bath. AE, DC, MC, V.*

$$$ **Eden Hotel Wolff.** Chandeliers and dark-wood paneling in the public rooms underline the old-fashioned elegance of this downtown favorite. It's directly across the street from the train station and near the Theresienwiese fairgrounds. The rooms are comfortable; most are spacious. You can dine on excellent Bavarian specialties in the intimate Zirbelstube restaurant. ⊞ *Arnulfstr. 4,* ☎ *089/551–150,* FAX *089/5511–5555. 210 rooms with bath. Restaurant. AE, DC, MC, V.*

$$$ **Erzgiesserei Europe.** Its location on a dull little street in an uninteresting section of the city is this restaurant's only drawback, but even that is easily overcome—the nearby subway whisks you in five minutes to central Karlsplatz, convenient for the pedestrian shopping area and the main railway station. Rooms in this attractive hotel are particularly bright, decorated in soft pastel tones with good reproductions on the walls. The cobblestone garden café is a haven of peace. ⊞ *Erzgiessereistr. 15,* ☎ *089/126–820,* FAX *089/123–6198. 106 rooms with bath. Rrestaurant, bar, café, parking. AE, DC, MC, V.*

$$$ **Hotel Concorde.** The centrally located Concorde wants to do its bit toward relieving traffic congestion, so guests who arrive from the airport on the S-bahn can exchange their ticket at the reception desk for a welcome champagne or cocktail. With the nearest S-bahn station (Isartor) only two minutes' walk away, why not take the hotel up on its offer? Rooms were completely refurnished in 1994 and decorated in pastel tones and light woods, with modern prints on the walls. The hotel has no restaurant, but a large breakfast buffet is served in its stylish, mirrored Salon Margarita. ⊞ *Herrnstr. 38,* ☎ *089/224515,* FAX *089/2283282. 67 rooms and 4 suites with bath. Lounge. AE, DC, MC, V.*

$$$ **Schloss-Hotel Grünwald.** On the southern edge of the city, this rustic, newly renovated lodging offers quiet, eclectically designed rooms (from Bavarian farmhouse motifs to Laura Ashley) with clifftop views of the Isar River valley stretching toward the Alps. Its restaurant has an international menu of high standard and an extensive wine list. Next door is a castle with a local-history museum. Nearby is the terminus of Tram 25 , which will take you into the city. ⊞ *Zeillerstr. 1,* ☎ *089/641–9300,* FAX *089/6419–3036. 13 rooms and 3 suites with bath. Restaurant, beer garden, wine bar. AE, DC, MC. Closed Jan. 1–14.*

$$$ **Splendid.** Chandelier-hung public rooms, complete with antiques and
★ Oriental rugs, give this small hotel something of the atmosphere of a spaciously grand 19th-century inn. The service is attentive and polished. Have breakfast in the small courtyard in summer. There's no restaurant, but the bar serves snacks as well as drinks. The chic shops of the Maximilianstrasse are a five-minute stroll in one direction; an equally

brief walk in the other takes you to the Isar River. ☎ *Maximilianstr. 54,* ☎ *089/296–606,* FAX *089/291–3176. 40 rooms, 1 suite, and 5 apartments with bath. Bar. AE, DC MC, V.*

$$$ **Torbräu.** You'll sleep under the shadow of one of Munich's ancient city gates—the 14th-century Isartor—if you stay here. This snug hotel offers comfortable, Scandinavian-modern rooms and an excellent location midway between the Marienplatz and the Deutsches Museum (and around the corner from the Hofbräuhaus). The Torbräu has a moderately priced Italian restaurant, the Firenze, and a good café tucked away in a corner of the arcaded facade. ☎ *Tal 41,* ☎ *089/225–016,* FAX *089/225–019. 82 rooms and 4 suites with bath. Restaurant, café, bowling. AE, MC, V.*

$$ **Adria.** This modern, comfortable hotel is ideally located in the up-market area of Lehel, in the middle of Munich's museum quarter. Rooms are large and tastefully decorated, with old prints on the pale-pink walls, Oriental rugs on the floors, and flowers beside the large double beds. A spectacular breakfast buffet (including a glass of sparkling wine) is included in the room rate. There's no hotel restaurant, but the area is rich in good restaurants, bistros, and bars. ☎ *Liebigstr. 8a,* ☎ *089/293– 081,* FAX *089/227–015. 47 rooms with bath. AE, DC, MC, V.*

$$ **Amba.** Families get an especially good deal at the Amba, member of a hotel group that prides itself on being child-friendly. A modern, brightly furnished double room comes for as little as DM 110, and additional beds cost DM 35. The hotel is right across the street from the main railway station and has its own porter service. A hotel bus collects guests from the airport. ☎ *Arnulfstr. 20,* ☎ *089/545–140,* FAX *089/5451–4555. 86 rooms, 73 with bath. Restaurant, coffee bar, parking. AE, DC, MC, V.*

$$ **Bauer.** Head here for a good-value Bavarian-rustic inn that provides country comforts (painted wardrobes, raw light pine, lots of blue-and-white-check patterns) yet is within easy reach of the city. The family-run Bauer, 10 kilometers (6 miles) from the city center, is best for those traveling by car, although the S-bahn train line S-3 is nearby. ☎ *Münchnerstr. 6, Feldkirchen,* ☎ *089/90980,* FAX *089/909–8414. 103 rooms with bath. Restaurant, café, indoor pool, sauna. AE, DC, MC, V.*

$$ **Brack.** This modest but comfortable hotel is on a tree-lined thoroughfare just south of the center, near the Oktoberfest grounds and opposite the Poccistrasse subway station. The Brack has no restaurant, but the buffet breakfast will set you up for the day. ☎ *Lindwurmstr. 153,* ☎ *089/771–052,* FAX *089/725–0615. 50 rooms with bath. AE, DC, MC, V.*

$$ **Gästehaus am Englischen Garten.** Reserve well in advance for a room
★ at this popular converted 200-plus-year-old water mill adjoining the Englischer Garten park. The hotel, complete with ivy-clad walls and shutter-framed windows, is only a five-minute walk from the bars and shops of Schwabing. There's no restaurant, but who needs one with Schwabing's numerous eating possibilities so close? Be sure to ask for a room in the main building; the modern annex down the road is cheaper but lacks charm. In summer, breakfast is served on the terrace. ☎ *Liebergesellstr. 8,* ☎ *089/392–034,* FAX *089/391-233. 30 rooms, 27 with bath or shower. No credit cards.*

$$ **Königin Elisabeth.** A bright, modern interior, with emphasis on the color pink, lies behind the protected neoclassical facade of this Pannonia-group hotel, opened in 1990 and a 15-minute tram ride northwest of the center. Children under 12 stay free in their parents' room. ☎ *Leonrodstr. 79,* ☎ *089/126–860,* FAX *089/1268-6459. 80 rooms. Restau-*

rant, bar, beer garden, fitness center, sauna, steam room. AE, DC, MC, V.

$$ **Mayer.** If you are willing to sacrifice a convenient location for good value, head for this family-run hotel 25 minutes by suburban train from the Hauptbahnhof. The Mayer's first-class comforts and facilities cost less than half what you'd pay at similar lodgings in town. Built in the 1970s, it is furnished in Bavarian country-rustic style—lots of pine and solid green, red, and check fabrics. Chef (and hotel owner) Rainer Radach was a student of two of Germany's most respected master chefs. The Mayer is a 10-minute walk, or short taxi ride, from Germering station, on the S-5 suburban line, eight stops west of the Hauptbahnhof. ☎ *Augsburgerstr. 45, D-82110 Germering,* ☎ *089/840–1515,* FAX *089/844–094. 56 rooms with bath. Restaurant, indoor pool. AE, MC.*

$$ ★ **Tele-Hotel.** This modern, well-appointed hotel on the outskirts of Munich is handy for the television studios at Unterföhring (hence the name) and is also conveniently located on the airport S-bahn line 8, a 15-minute ride from downtown. Television people escape their drab canteen fare by popping into the hotel's Bavarian Hackerbräu restaurant, where a lunchtime menu for less than DM 30 is a hot favorite. ☎ *Bahnhofstr. 15, Unterföhring,* ☎ *089/950–146,* FAX *089/950–6652. 60 rooms with bath, 1 apartment. Restaurant, bar, bowling, parking. AE, DC, MC, V.*

$ ★ **Fürst.** On a quiet street just off Odeonsplatz on the edge of the university quarter, this very basic, clean guest house is constantly busy with families annd students traveling on a budget. Book early. ☎ *Kardinal-Döpfnerstr. 8,* ☎ *089/281–043. 19 rooms, 12 with bath. No credit cards.*

$ ★ **Hotel-Pension Beck.** American and British guests receive a particularly warm welcome from the Anglophile owner of the rambling, friendly Beck. Rooms are sometimes furnished in haphazard and garish style, but the pension has a prime location in the heart of fashionable Lehel (handy for museums and the Englischer Garten). ☎ *Thierschstr. 36,* ☎ *089/220–708 and 089/225–768,* FAX *089/220–925. 44 rooms, 4 with shower. No credit cards.*

$ **Kriemhild.** If you're traveling with children you'll appreciate this welcoming, family-run pension in the western suburb of Nymphenburg. It's a 10-minute walk from the palace itself and around the corner from the Hirschgarten park, site of one of the city's best beer gardens. The tram ride (No. 12) from downtown is 30 minutes. There's no restaurant. ☎ *20 rooms, some with bath. Guntherstr. 16,* ☎ *089/170–077,* FAX *089/177–478. Bar. MC, V.*

$ **Mariandl.** Large families are catered to at this rambling, friendly pension with huge rooms furnished in a variety of styles. Only four of the rooms have their own showers, so be specific when booking. The ground floor is taken up by a Viennese-style restaurant, with Biedermeier furnishings and a menu featuring every variety of Wiener schnitzel. The large grand piano isn't there just for decoration: Soirees in the style of the Viennese evenings once enjoyed by Schubert (portraits of the composer adorn the walls) and his friends are given here every weeknight. ☎ *Goethestr. 51,* ☎ *089/534–108 or 089/535–158. 30 rooms, 4 with shower. Restaurant. AE, DC, MC, V.*

THE ARTS AND NIGHTLIFE

The Arts

Details of concerts and theater performances are listed in "Vorschau" and "Monatsprogramm," booklets available at most hotel reception desks, newsstands, and tourist offices. Some hotels will make ticket reservations; otherwise use one of the ticket agencies in the city center, such as either of the two kiosks in the underground concourse at Marienplatz; the **Abendzeitung Schalterhalle** (Sendlingerstr. 10, ☎ 089/267–024); **Residenz Bücherstube** (concert tickets only; Residenzstr. 1, ☎ 089/220–868); or the **Max Hieber Konzertkasse** (Liebfrauenstr. 1, ☎ 089/290–080). There's also a special ticket agency for visitors with disabilities: **abr-Theaterkasse** (Neuhauser Str. 9, ☎ 089/12040).

Theater

Munich has scores of theaters and variety-show haunts, although most productions will be largely impenetrable if your German is shaky. A very active American company, the American Drama Group Europe, presents regular productions at the Theater an der Leopoldstrasse (Leopoldstr. 17, ☎ 089/343–803 for program details), while a British theater group, the Munich English Theater (MET) is at home in the Theater im Karlshof, a backyard theater with friendly bar (☎ 089/570–3034 for program details). Listed here are all the better-known theaters, as well as some of the smaller and more progressive spots. A visit to one or more will underline just why the Bavarian capital has such an enviable reputation as an artistic hot spot. Note that most theaters are closed during July and August.

Bayerisches Staatsschauspiel/Neues Residenztheater (Bavarian State Theater/New Residence Theater) (Max-Joseph-Pl. The box office is at Maximilianstr. 11, ☎ 089/2185–1920). ⊙ Weekdays 10–1 and 2–6, Saturday 10–1, and one hour before the performance.

Cuvilliés-Theater/Altes Residenztheater (Old Residence Theater) (Max-Joseph-Pl.; entrance on Residenzstr.). The box office, at Maximilianstrasse 11 (☎ 089/221–1316), is open weekdays 10–1 and 2–6, Saturday 10–1, and one hour before the performance.

Deutsches Theater (Schwanthalerstr. 13, ☎ 089/5523–4360). The box office is open weekdays noon–6, Saturday 10–1:30.

Gasteig (Rosenheimerstr. 5, ☎ 089/5481–8181). This modern cultural complex includes two theaters—the Carl-Orff Saal and the Black Box—where plays in English are occasionally performed. The box office is open weekdays 10:30–2 and 3–6, Saturday 10:30–2.

Kleine Komödie, two theaters sharing a program of light comedy and farce (Bayerischer Hof Hotel, Promenadepl., ☎ 089/292–810; Max-II-Denkmal, Maximilianstr. 27, ☎ 089/221–859). The box office at Bayerischer Hof is open Monday–Saturday 11–8, Sunday and holidays 3–8. The box office at Max-II-Denkmal is open Tuesday–Saturday 11–8, Monday 11–7, Sunday and holidays 3–8.

Marionettentheater (Blumenstr. 29A, ☎ 089/265–712). The box office is open Tuesday–Sunday 10–noon.

Münchner Kammerspiele-Schauspielhaus (Maximilianstr. 26, ☎ 089/237–21328). The box office is open weekdays 10–6, Saturday 10–1, closed Sundays and holidays.

Platzl Bühne (Am Platzl 1, ☎ 089/237–030). Daily show (except Sunday and Monday) with typical Bavarian humor, yodeling, and *Schuhplattler* (the slapping of Bavarian leather shorts in time to the oompah music).

Prinzregententheater (Prinzregentenpl. 12, ☎ 089/470–6270). The box office is at Maximilian Str. 11. ⏱Weekdays 10–1 and 2–6, Saturday 10–1, and one hour before the performance.

Theater an der Leopoldstrasse (Leopoldstr. 17, ☎ 089/343–803) features the American Drama Group Europe with English-language performances. No box office.

Concerts

Munich and music go together. Paradoxically, however, it's only since 1984 that the city has had a world-class concert hall: the Gasteig center, a lavish brick complex standing high above the Isar River, east of downtown. It's the permanent home of the Munich Philharmonic Orchestra, which regularly performs in its Philharmonic Hall. In addition to the Philharmonic, the city has three other orchestras: the Bavarian State Orchestra, based at the National Theater; the Bavarian Radio Orchestra, which gives regular Sunday concerts at the Gasteig; and the Kurt Graunke Symphony Orchestra, which performs at the Gärtnerplatz theater. The leading choral ensembles are the Munich Bach Choir, the Munich Motettenchor, and Musica Viva, the latter specializing in contemporary music. (*See above for information on where to buy tickets.*)

Bayerischer Rundfunk (Rundfunkpl. 1, ☎ 089/558–080). The box office is open weekdays 9–noon and 1–5.

Herkulessaal in der Residenz (Hofgarten, ☎ 089/2906–7263). The box office opens one hour before performances.

Hochschule für Musik (Arcisstr. 12, ☎ 089/559–101). Concerts featuring music students are given free of charge.

Olympiahalle (☎ 089/306–13577). The box office is open Monday–Saturday 11–6. For pop concerts.

Opera, Ballet, Operetta, and Musicals

Munich's Bavarian State Opera Company and its ballet ensemble perform at the **Nationaltheater** (also called the Bayerisches Staatsoper). The ticket office is at Maximilianstrasse 11 (☎ and opening times as above). The evening ticket office, at the Maximilianstrasse entrance to the theater, opens one hour before curtain time. A less ambitious but nevertheless high-quality program of opera, ballet, operetta, and musicals is presented at the romantic Jugendstil **Staatstheater am Gärtnerplatz**, Gärtnerplatz 3 (☎ 089/201-6767). The ticket office is also at Maximilianstr. 11. An evening ticket office opens at the theater one hour before performances begin.

Nightlife

Munich's nighttime attractions vary with the seasons. The year starts with the abandon of *Fasching*, the Bavarian carnival time, which begins quietly in mid-November with the crowning of the King and Queen of Fools, expands with fancy-dress balls, and ends with a great street party on *Fasching Dienstag* (Shrove Tuesday). No sooner has Lent brought the sackcloth curtain down on Fasching than the local weather office is being asked to predict when the spring sunshine will be warm enough to allow the city's 100 beer gardens to open. From then until late fall the beer garden dictates the style and pace of Munich's nightlife. When it rains, the indoor beer halls and taverns absorb the thirsty like blotting paper.

The beer gardens and most beer halls close at midnight, but there's no need to go home to bed then: Some bars and nightclubs are open until 6 AM. A word of caution about some of those bars, however: Most are run honestly and prices are only slightly higher than normal, but a few may be unscrupulous. The seedier are near the main train station. Stick to beer or wine if you can, and pay as you go. And if you feel you're being duped, call the cops—the customer is usually, if not always, right.

Clubs

Munich's club scene has fallen victim to changing tastes. Gone are the '60s-generation nightclubs combining a good restaurant, a dance combo, and high-class exotic dancers. In their place are tiny cabaret stages and even smaller strip bars. The cabarets, most of which are in Schwabing, are usually political satire, performed in dialects that are incomprehensible to non-Germans.

The Bayericher Hof's Night Club has dancing to live music and a very lively bar. American visitors will also do well in the Vier Jahreszeiten, where there's piano music until nine and then dancing on the bar's small floor.

Discos

Schwabing is discoland. There are more than a dozen in the immediate area around Schwabing's central square, the Münchner-Freiheit. One, the Skyline, is at the top of the Hertie store that towers above the busy square. Other old-time favorites in a constantly changing scene include **Peaches,** on nearby Feilitzstrasse, and **Albatros,** just up the street on Occamstrasse (which is lined with lively clubs and pubs). Schwabing's central boulevard, Leopoldstrasse, also has its share of discos: **Ba-Ba-Lu** has survived here for 30 years, updating its tape collection with every swing in musical taste. Across town, **Canterville** (Rosenheimerstr. 30) has an older clientele (well, not too old) and lots of plush and class. **Pl** (on the east side of the Haus der Kunst), **Maximilian's Nightclub** (Maximilianplatz 16), and the **Park-Café** (Sophienstr. 7) are the most fashionable discos in town, but you'll have to talk yourself past the doorman to join the chic crowds inside. **Nachtwerk** (Landsbergerstr. 185), in a converted factory, blasts out a range of sounds from punk to avant-garde nightly between 8 PM and 4 AM. Live bands also perform there regularly.

Bars and Singles

Try **Schumann's** (Maximilianstr. 36) anytime after the curtain comes down at the nearby opera house (and watch the barmen shake those cocktails; closed Sat.), but wait till after midnight before venturing into the **Alter Simpl** (Türkenstr. 57) for a sparkling crowd despite the gloomy surroundings. Back on fashionable Maximilianstrasse, **O'Reilly's Irish Cellar Pub** offers escape from the German bar scene, and it serves genuine Irish Guinness. Great Caribbean cocktails and a powerful Irish-German Black and Tan (Guinness and strong German beer) are served at the English nautical-style **Pusser's** bar (Falkenturmstrasse 9; it replaced Munich's own Harry's Bar). Stiff competition is nearby at **Havana** (Herrnstr. 3), which does its darnedest to look like a run-down Cuban dive, although the chic clientele spoils those pretensions. Making contact at the **Wunderbar** (Hochbrückenstr. 3) is made easier on Tuesday nights when telephones are installed on the tables and at the bar and the place hums like a stygian switchboard. The lively (at any time) basement bar is run by an innovative young New Yorker. Munich's gay scene is found between Sendlingertorplatz and Isartorplatz. Its most popular bars are **Together** (Rumfordstr. 2), **Nil** (Hans-Sachs-Str. 2), **Ochsengarten** (Müllerstr. 47), and **Pimpernel** (Müllerstr. 56).

Jazz

Munich likes to think it's Germany's jazz capital, and to reinforce the claim, some beer gardens have taken to replacing their brass bands with funky combos. Purists don't like it, but jazz enthusiasts are happy. The combination certainly works at **Waldwirtschaft Grosshesselohe** (Georg Kalb-Str. 3), in the southern suburb of Grosshesselohe. Sundays are set aside for jazz, and if it's a nice day the excursion is much recommended. Some city pubs also set aside Sunday midday for jazz: Try **Doktor Flotte** (Occamstr. 8). The best of the jazz clubs are the **Scala Music Bar** (Oskar-von-Miller-Ring 3); **Nachtcafé** (Maximilianpl. 5, open until 5 AM); **Schwabinger Podium** (Wagnerstr. 1); **Unterfahrt** (Kirchenstr. 96); and **Jenny's Place in the Blue Note** (Moosacherstr. 24, near the Olympiazentrum, ☎ 089/351–0520), the live-jazz venue of a vivacious English actress and singer who has a terrific voice and a warm welcome for visitors from the United States and Britain.

EXCURSIONS

The excursions covered here are by no means the only ones possible from Munich. Practically all the attractions in the Alps, for example, or those at the south end of the Romantic Road—the resort town of Garmisch-Partenkirchen and Ludwig II's palaces and castles preeminently—make ideal destinations for one- or two-day trips out of town. For full details of these and many other destinations around Munich, *see* Chapters 3 and 7.

Tour 1: Ammersee and Andechs

The Ammersee is the country cousin of the better-known, more cosmopolitan Starnbergersee, and many Bavarians (and tourists, too) like it all the more as a result. Fashionable Munich cosmopolites of centuries past thought it too distant for an excursion, not to mention too rustic for their sophisticated tastes. So the shores remained relatively free of the villas and parks that ring the Starnbergersee, and even though the upscale holiday homes of Munich's moneyed classes today claim some stretches of the eastern shore, the Ammersee still offers more open areas for bathing and boating than the bigger lake to the west. Bicyclists can circle the 19-kilometer-long (12-mile-long) lake (it's nearly 6 kilometers across at its widest point) on a path that rarely loses sight of the water. Hikers can spin out the tour for two or three days, staying overnight in any of the comfortable inns that crop up along the way. Dinghy sailors and windsurfers can zip across in minutes with the help of the Alpine winds that swoop down from the mountains. A ferry boat cruises the lake at regular intervals during summer, dropping and picking up passengers at several pier head stops. Join it at Herrsching.

Getting There

BY CAR

Take Autobahn 96—follow the signs to Lindau—and 20 kilometers (12 miles) west of Munich, take the exit for Herrsching, the lake's principal town. Herrsching is 40 kilometers (25 miles) from Munich.

Herrsching, on the east bank of the lake, is the end of the S-5 suburban line, a half-hour ride from Munich's central Marienplatz. From Herrsching station, Bus 952 runs north along the lake, and Bus 956 runs south.

Exploring

In Herrsching, head for the lake and the delightful promenade, part of which winds through the resort's park. The 100-year-old villa that sits so comfortably in the park, overlooking the lake and the Alps beyond, seems as though it might have been built by Ludwig II, such is the romantic and fanciful mixture of medieval turrets and Renaissance-style facades. It was built for the artist Ludwig Scheuermann and is now a municipal cultural center and the scene of chamber-music concerts on some summer weekends.

Five kilometers (3 miles) south of Herrsching—you can reach it on Bus 956—is one of southern Bavaria's most famous places of pilgrimage, the Benedictine monastery of **Andechs.** The crowds of pilgrims are drawn not only by the beauty of the hilltop monastery and its 15th-century pilgrimage church, decked out with glorious Rococo decoration in the mid-18th century and a repository of religious relics said to have been brought from the Holy Land 1,000 years ago, but also by the beer brewed there. The monastery makes its own cheese as well, and it's an excellent accompaniment to the rich, almost black beer. You can enjoy both at large wood tables in the monastery tavern or on the terrace outside. Archduke Otto von Hapsburg, the son of the last Austro-Hungarian emperor, who lives beside the lake, celebrated his 80th birthday in the church in 1992; a family party followed in the tavern.

Follow the lake to its southwest corner and you'll find the little town of **Diessen,** with its magnificent Baroque abbey-church. Stop in to admire its opulent stucco decoration and sumptuous gilt-and-marble altar. Visit the church in late afternoon, when the light falls sharply on its crisp gray, white, and gold facade, etching the pencil-like tower and spire against the darkening sky over the lake. Don't go without at least peeping into neighboring St. Stephen's courtyard, its cloisters smothered in wild roses.

Dining

In Herrsching, the **Gasthof zur Post** (Andechsertr. 1) is everything a Bavarian tavern should be. The weekday lunch menu is an unbeatable value, and the locally brewed dark beer is unbeatable, period. Along the lakeside promenade you'll find several idyllic terrace restaurants; the **Alba-Seehotel** is the best. For the best *tiramisù* outside Italy, stroll to the end of the promenade and call in at the **Restaurante da Mario.** In Diessen, make for the central Carl-Orff-Platz and pause to admire the rustic exterior of the **Gasthaus Unterbräu,** then venture inside for another indelible culinary impression (or, in summer, find a table outside in the leafy beer garden). The nearby **Hotel-Gasthof-Seefelder Hof** (Alexander-Koester-Weg 6) also has a delightful beer garden.

Tour 2: Dachau

The first Nazi concentration camp was built just outside this town. Dachau preserves the memory of the camp and the horrors perpetrated there with deep contrition while trying, with commendable discretion, to signal that it also has other things to offer visitors. It's an older place than nearby Munich, for example, with local records going back to the time of Charlemagne in the 9th century. And it's a handsome town, too, built on a hilltop with fine views of Munich and the Alps.

Getting There

BY CAR

Dachau is 20 kilometers (12 miles) northwest of Munich. Take the B–12 country road, or the Stuttgart autobahn to the Dachau exit.

BY TRAIN

Dachau is on the S-2 suburban railway line, a 20-minute ride from Munich's Marienplatz.

Exploring

Head to the town center and climb the hill to the **castle.** What you'll see is the one remaining wing of a palace built by the Munich architect Josef Effner for the Wittelsbach ruler Max Emanuel in 1715, a replacement for the original castle built during the 15th century. During the Napoleonic Wars at the beginning of the 19th century the palace served as a field hospital, treating French and Russian casualties from the Battle of Austerlitz (1805). The wars made a casualty, too, of the palace, and three of the four wings were demolished by order of King Max I Joseph. What's left now was once the ballroom, and, on weekends in summer, it's still used for concerts. There's a 16th-century carved ceiling, with painted panels representing characters from ancient mythology. There's also a 250-year-old Schlossbrauerei (castle brewery), which hosts the town's own beer and music festival each year during the first half of August.

Downtown you'll find the parish church of **St. Jacob,** a towering 16th-century building that dominates the adjacent square, the former haymarket.

Dachau served as a lively artists' colony during the 19th century, and the tradition lives on: There are art shops wherever you look. The **Dachauer Gemäldegalerie** in Konrad-Adenauer-Strasse is a good place to try.

To reach the **Dachau Concentration Camp Memorial** (Alte Römerstr. 75) by car, leave the center of the town along Schleissheimerstrasse and turn left into Alte Römerstrasse; the site is on the left. By public transport, take Bus 722 from the Dachau S-bahn train station to Robert-Boschstrasse and walk along Alte Römerstrasse for 100 yards or board Bus 720 and get off at Ratiborer Strasse. Photographs, contemporary documents, the few remaining cell blocks, and the grim crematorium create a somber and moving picture of the camp, where many thousands lost their lives. ☛ *Free. ⊙ Tues.–Sun. 9–5. A documentary film (in English) is shown at 11:30 and 3:30.*

Dining

The **Bräustüberl,** 50 yards from the castle, has a shady beer garden for summer lunches. In the town center, the **Helferwirt** has a secluded garden and a cozy restaurant that serves Bavarian fare. Next to the ivy-covered town hall, on Freisingerstrasse, is the solid, historic **Zieglerbräu,** once a 17th-century brewer's home and now a wood-paneled restaurant.

Tour 3: Landshut

If fortune had placed Landshut 64 kilometers (40 miles) south of Munich, in the protective folds of the Alpine foothills, instead of the same distance north, in the dull flatlands of Lower Bavaria, this delightful, historic town would have been overrun by visitors long ago. All the same, Landshut's geographical misfortune is the discerning visitor's good luck, for the town is never overcrowded, with the possible exception of the three summer weeks every four years (next in 1997), when the *Landshuter Hochzeit* is celebrated. The festival commemorates the marriage in 1475 of Prince George of Bayern-Landshut, son of the expressively named Ludwig the Rich, to Princess Hedwig, daughter of the king of Poland. The entire town is swept away in a colorful reconstruction of the event that increased its already regal importance and helped to give it the majestic air you'll still find within its ancient walls.

Getting There

BY CAR

Landshut is a 45-minute drive northwest from Munich on either Autobahn 92—follow the signs to Deggendorf—or the B-11 highway.

BY TRAIN

Landshut is on the Plattling–Regensburg–Passau line, a 40-minute ride by express train from Munich.

Exploring

A 10-minute bus ride will take you from the train station to the heart of the old town. There are parking lots right outside it, too. Landshut has two magnificent, cobbled market streets: The one in **Altstadt** (Old Town) is considered by many to be the most beautiful city street in Germany; the one in **Neustadt** (New Town) projects its own special appeal. The two streets run parallel to each other, tracing a course between the Isar River and the heights overlooking the town. A steep path from Altstadt takes you up to **Burg Trausnitz,** sitting commandingly on the heights. This castle was begun in 1204 and accommodated the Wittelsbach dukes of Bayern-Landshut until 1503. *Admission, including guided tour: DM 3 adults, children free.* ☉ *Daily 9–noon and 1–5.*

During the 16th century the Wittelsbachs moved to the **Altstadt** and into a new palace (the *Stadtresidenz*), the first Italian Renaissance building of its kind north of the Alps. The Renaissance facade of the palace forms an almost modest part of the architectural splendor and integrity of Altstadt, where even the ubiquitous McDonald's has to serve its hamburgers behind a baroque facade. ☞ *DM 2 adults, children free.* ☉ *Daily 9–noon and 1–5.*

Soaring above the street scene is the 436-foot tower and bristling spire of **St. Martin's** church, the tallest brick church tower in the world. The church contains some magnificent Gothic treasures and a 16th-century carved Madonna. Moreover, it is surely the only church anywhere in the world to contain an image of Hitler, albeit in devilish pose. The Führer and other Nazi leaders are portrayed as executioners in a 1946 stained-glass window showing the martyrdom of St. Kastulus. In the nave of the church is a clear and helpful description of its history and its treasures, an aid to English-speaking visitors that could profitably be copied by other churches and historical sites in Germany.

Dining

There are several attractive Bavarian-style restaurants in Altstadt and Neustadt, most of them with charming beer gardens. The best are **Brauereigasthof Ainmiller** (Altstadt 195), **Gasthaus Schwabl** (Neustadt

500), **Zum Hofreiter** (Neustadt 505), and the **Hotel Goldene Sonne** (Neustadt 520). The **Klausenberg Panorama-Restaurant** (Klausenberg 17) has a terrace with a fine view of the town and the surrounding countryside. For a reasonable three-course lunch, try the **Buddha** (Apothekergasse), which serves a good, fixed-price Chinese meal for around DM 15 per person. If you're looking for an authentic Bavarian dining experience, make your way to the old Episcopal town of Freising, halfway between Landshut and Munich. It's the site of the world's oldest brewery (AD 1040), the **Bayerische Staatsbrauerei Weihenstephan,** where you can select from a beer menu that lists 11 different brews. Freising is the final stop on the S-1 suburban railway line from Munich and one stop from Landshut by express train.

Lodging

Landshut has several hotels and a handful of reasonably priced, comfortable inns. The hotels are: **Hotel Kaiserhof** (Papiererstr. 2, ☎ 0871/6870, FAX 0871/687–403; **$$$**), an attractive 18th-century–style riverside building; **Romantik Hotel Fürstenhof** (Stethaimerstr. 3, ☎ 0871/82025, FAX 0871/89042; **$$$**), a tastefully modernized villa; and **Hotel Goldene Sonne** (Neustadt 520, ☎ 0871/23087, FAX 0871/24069; **$$**), a historic inn in the Old Town. North of Landshut (20 kilometers/12.4 miles) you can sleep in a 16th-century moated castle, **Schlosshotel Neufahrn** (Schlossweg 2, ☎ 08773/874, FAX 08773/1559; **$$$**).

Tour 4: Starnbergersee

The Starnbergersee was one of Europe's first pleasure grounds. Royal coaches trundled out from Munich to its wooded banks in the Baroque years of the 17th century; in 1663 Elector Ferdinand Maria threw a huge shipboard party at which 500 guests wined and dined as 100 oarsmen propelled them around the lake. Today pleasure steamers perform the same task for visitors of less than noble rank. The lake is still lined with the Baroque palaces of Bavaria's aristocracy, but their owners must now share the lakeside with public parks, beaches, and boatyards. The Starnbergersee is one of Bavaria's largest lakes—19 kilometers (12 miles) long and 5 kilometers (3 miles) across at its widest point—so there's plenty of room for swimmers, sailors, and windsurfers. On its west shore is one of Germany's finest golf courses, but it's about as difficult for the casual visitor to play a game there as it was for a Munich commoner to win an invitation to one of Prince Ferdinand's boating parties. Those on the trail of Ludwig II should note that it was on the Starnbergersee (beside the village of Berg) that the doomed monarch met his watery death under circumstances that remain a mystery.

Getting There

BY CAR

The north end of the lake, where the resort of Starnberg sits in stately beauty, is a 30-minute drive from Munich on Autobahn 95. Follow the signs to Garmisch and take the Starnberg exit. Country roads then skirt the west and east banks of the lake.

BY TRAIN

The S-6 suburban line runs from Munich's central Marienplatz to Starnberg and three other towns on the lake's west bank: Possenhofen, Feldafing, and Tutzing. The journey from Marienplatz to Starnberg takes 35 minutes. The east bank of the lake can be reached by bus from the town of Wolfratshausen, the end of the S-7 suburban line.

Exploring

From Starnberg train station, stroll along the lakeside promenade and take in the shimmering beauty of this fascinating stretch of water, with the hazy hint of mountains at its southern rim. Rent bicycles at the station and pedal around the top of the lake to Percha, where a well-marked path will lead you south 3 kilometers (2 miles) to Berg. Leave the bicycles outside the castle park and walk the kilometer (½ mile) through thick woods to the **King Ludwig II Memorial Chapel,** built near the point in the lake where the king's body was found on June 13, 1886. He had been confined in nearby Berg Castle after the Bavarian government took action against his withdrawal from reality and into expensive castle-building fantasyland. Look for the cross in the lake, which marks the point where his body was recovered. One-half kilometer (⅓ mile) across the lake is the castle of **Possenhofen,** home of Ludwig's favorite cousin, Sissi. Local lore says they used to send affectionate messages across the lake to each other. Sissi married the Austrian emperor Franz Joseph I but frequently returned to the Starnbergersee; she spent more than 20 consecutive summers in the lakeside castle (which has now been converted into luxury apartments). Just offshore is the tiny **Roseninsel** (Rose Island), where King Maximilian II built a summer villa. You can swim to its tree-fringed shores or sail across in a dinghy or on a Windsurfer (Possenhofen's boatyard is one of the lake's many rental points).

Dining

The most elegant dining in Starnberg is at the **Bajazzo** (Ostwaldstr. 16), which serves Bavarian fare with chic nouvelle touches. The **Gasthof in der Au** (Josef-Jäger-Huber-Str. 15) is an airy tavern. If you fancy a view of the lake, make for the **Seerestaurant Undosa,** where the atmosphere is always boisterous. Farther down the lake, on the outskirts of Possenhofen, is the **Forsthaus am See** (Am See 1, Pocking-Possenhofen), where you dine beneath a carved panel ceiling imported from Austria's South Tyrol. The restaurant has a lakeside beer garden and its own pier for guests who arrive by boat. From Tutzing, at the end of the S-6 suburban line, a short walk up into the hills leads to the **Forsthaus Ilka-Höhe,** a rustic lodge with a fine view of the lake and excellent Bavarian food (closed Tues. Oct.–Mar.). On the other side of the lake, near the Berg Castle grounds and the King Ludwig II Memorial Chapel, try the **Dorint Seehotel Leoni** (Assenbucherstr. 44, Berg-Leoni), where you can also rent bicycles (☎ 08151/5060), or the **Strandhotel Schloss Berg** (Seestr. 17), which has a lakeside dining terrace.

Tour 5: Wasserburg am Inn

Wasserburg floats like a faded ship of state in a benevolent, lazy loop of the Inn River, which comes within a few yards of cutting the ancient town off from the wooded slopes of the encroaching countryside. The river caresses the southern limits of the ancient town center, embraces its eastern boundary with rocky banks 200 feet high, returns westward as if looking for a way out of this geographical puzzle, and then heads north in search of its final destination, the Danube. Wasserburg sleeps on in its watery cradle, a perfectly preserved, beautifully set medieval town, once a vitally important trading post but later thankfully ignored by the industrialization that gripped Germany in the 19th century.

Getting There

BY CAR

Take the B-304 highway from Munich, which leads directly to Wasserburg. It's a 45-minute drive.

BY TRAIN

Take either the suburban line S-4 to Ebersberg and change to a local train to Wasserburg, or the Salzburg express, changing at Grafing Bahnhof to the local line. Both trips take 90 minutes.

Exploring

You're never more than 100 yards or so from the river in Wasserburg's old town center. There are two large parking lots on the north and east banks, and you're advised to use one of them; the town council is expanding the traffic-free zone. It's only a few minutes' walk from the lots to central Marienplatz. There you'll find Wasserburg's late-Gothic brick **town hall.** ☛ DM 1 adults, 50 pf children. Guided tours Tues.–Fri. at 10, 11, 2, 3, and 4; weekends at 10 and 11.

Marienplatz is also the site of the town's oldest church, the 14th-century **Frauenkirche,** which incorporates an ancient watchtower. Head up the hill to the imposing 15th-century parish church of **St. Jakob** to view its intricate Baroque pulpit, carved in 1640. Head south toward the river again; in two minutes you'll be at the walls of the castle that originally gave Wasserburg (Water Castle) its name. Take the river path back toward the town center, cross the bridge, and look back at the collection of Gothic and Renaissance buildings along the town's shore. It has a southern, almost Italian look, typical of many Inn River towns. At the end of the bridge, next to the 14th-century town gate, is one of Germany's most unusual museums, the **Erstes Imaginäres Museum,** a collection of more than 400 world-famous paintings. There isn't an original among them: Every single one is a precise copy. ☛ DM 3 adults, DM 1.50 children. ☉ May–Sept., Tues.–Sun. 11–5; Oct.–Apr., Tues.–Sun. 1–5.

Wasserburg is a convenient base for enticing walks along the banks of the Inn River and into the surrounding countryside. A half-hour walk south leads to the village of **Attel.** Another half hour into the Attel River valley and one reaches the enchanting castle-restaurant of **Schloss Hart** (☎ 08039/1774).

Dining

You'll find the most compelling atmosphere for dining in Wasserburg at the **Herrenhaus** (Herrengasse 17, ☎ 08071/2800; $$); it has a centuries-old vaulted wine cellar. For simple and traditional Bavarian fare, make for the **Gasthaus Zum Löwen** (Marienpl. 10, ☎ 08071/7400; $), a wood-paneled restaurant whose tables spill out onto the sidewalk in summer.

Lodging

For solid comfort along with antiques in some of the rooms, good, hearty food, and a beer garden, try the **Hotel Fletzinger** (Fletzingergasse 1, ☎ 08071/8010, ℻ 08071/40810; $$). Directly on Marienplatz, the ancient **Paulanerstuben** Marienpl. 9, ☎ 08071/3903; $), with its delightful Rococo facade, offers simple yet reassuring comforts.

MUNICH ESSENTIALS

Arriving and Departing

By Bus

Long-distance buses arrive at and depart from the north side of the main train station. A taxi stand is located right next to it.

By Car

From the north (Nürnberg and Frankfurt), leave the Autobahn at the Schwabing exit. From Stuttgart and the west, the Autobahn ends at Obermenzing. The Autobahns from Salzburg and the east, Garmisch and the south, and Lindau and the southwest all join the Mittlerer Ring (city beltway). When leaving any Autobahn, follow the Stadtmitte signs for downtown Munich.

By Plane

Munich's **Franz Josef Strauss (FJS) Airport**—named after the late Bavarian former state premier—opened in 1992. It is 28 kilometers (18 miles) northeast of the city center, between the small towns of Freising and Erding. One of the biggest and most modern airports in Europe, FJS took 10 years to build. It is capable of handling 14 million passengers a year and replaces the old Riem Airport, which is now a collection of discos and concert halls.

BETWEEN FJS AIRPORT AND DOWNTOWN

A fast train service links **FJS Airport** with Munich's Hauptbahnhof (the main train station). The S-8 line operates from a terminal directly beneath the airport's arrival and departure halls. Trains leave every 20 minutes, and the journey takes 38 minutes. Several intermediate stops are made, including Ostbahnhof (convenient for lodgings east of the Isar River), as well as such city-center stations as Marienplatz. A one-way ticket costs DM 12.80, DM 10 if you purchase a multiple-use "strip" ticket (*see* Getting Around, *below*). A family of up to five (two adults and three children) can make the trip for DM 20 by buying a *Tageskarte* ticket. A bus service was reintroduced in 1994, but it's slower and more expensive (DM 15) than the S-bahn link (*see* Getting Around by Public Transportation, *below*). An airport-city taxi fare costs between DM 80 and DM 100. During rush hour (7 AM–10 AM and 4 PM–7 PM), you need to allow up to one hour traveling time. If you're driving from the airport to the city, take route A–9 and follow the signs for München Stadtmitte. If you're driving to FJS from the city center, head north through Schwabing, join the A–9 Autobahn at the Frankfurter Ring intersection, and follow the signs for the airport ("Flughafen").

By Train

All long-distance rail services arrive at and depart from the main train station; trains to and from destinations in Bavaria use the adjoining Starnbergerbahnhof. The high-speed InterCity Express trains connect Munich, Frankfurt, and Hamburg on one line; Munich, Würzburg, and Hamburg on another. For information on train schedules, call 089/19419; most railroad information staff speak English. For tickets and travel information, go to the station information office or try the ABR travel agency, right by the station on Bahnhofplatz.

Getting Around

By Bicycle

Munich and its environs are easily navigated on two wheels. The city is threaded with a network of specially designated bike paths. A free map showing all bike trails is available at all city tourist offices.

You can rent bicycles at the **Englischer Garten** (corner of Königstr. and Veterinärstr., ☎ 089/397–016) for DM 5 per hour or DM 15 for the day (May–Oct., weekends in good weather); **Aktiv-Rad** (Hans-Sachs Str. 7, ☎ 089/266–506) and **A–Z Fahrräder** (Zweibrückenstr. 8, ☎ 089/223–272) hire them out for DM 70 to DM 90 per week. Bikes can also be rented at the Hauptbahnhof (Radius Touristik, opposite platform 31), and at some S-bahn and main-line stations around Munich. A list of stations that offer the service is available from the Deutsche Bahn. The cost is DM 6–DM 8 a day if you've used public transportation to reach the station; otherwise it's DM 10–DM 12, depending on the type of bike.

By Car

CAR RENTAL

Avis: Nymphenburgerstrasse 61, ☎ 089/1260–0020; Balanstrasse 74, ☎ 089/403–091.

Europcar: Hirtenstrasse 14, ☎ 089/557–145.

Hertz: Nymphenburgerstrasse 81, ☎ 089/129–5001.

Sixt-Budget: Seitzstrasse 9, ☎ 089/223–333.

By Public Transportation

Munich has an efficient and well-integrated public transportation system consisting of the **U-bahn** (subway), the **S-bahn** (suburban railway), the **Strassenbahn** (streetcars), and **buses.** Marienplatz forms the heart of the U-bahn and S-bahn network, which operates from around 5 AM to 1 AM. An all-night tram and bus service was introduced on main city routes in 1994. For a clear explanation in English of how the system works, pick up a copy of *Rendezvous mit München,* available free at all tourist offices.

Fares are uniform for the entire system. As long as you are traveling in the same direction, you can transfer from one mode of transportation to another on the same ticket. You can also interrupt your journey as often as you like, and time-punched tickets are valid for up to four hours, depending on the number of zones you travel through. Fares were expected to increase by up to 15% by early 1996, but at press time a basic **Einzelfahrkarte** (one-way ticket) cost DM 3.20 (DM 1.40 for children under 15) for a ride in the inner zone; if you plan to take a number of trips around the city, you'll save money by buying a **Mehrfahrtenkarte,** or multiple strip ticket. Red strip tickets are valid for children under 15 only. Blue strips cover adults. DM 15 buys a 12-strip ticket. Most inner-area journeys cost two strips, which must be canceled at one of the many time-punching machines at stations or on buses and trams. For a short stay, the simplest idea is the **Tageskarte** ticket, which provides unlimited travel for up to five people (maximum of two adults, plus three children under 15). It is valid weekdays from 9 AM to 4 AM the following day and at any time on weekends and public holidays. The costs are DM 10 for an inner-zone ticket and DM 20 for the entire network.

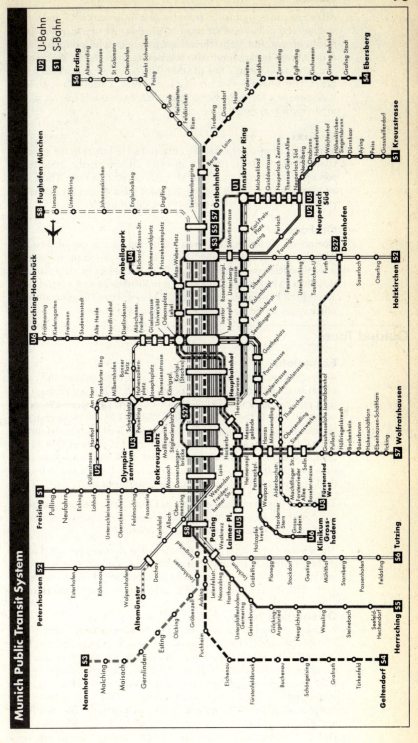

Munich Public Transit System

All tickets can be purchased from the blue dispensers at U- and S-bahn stations and at bus and streetcar stops. Bus and streetcar drivers, all tourist offices, and Mehrfahrtenkarten booths (which display a white *K* on a green background) also sell tickets. Spot checks are common and carry an automatic fine of DM 60 if you're caught without a valid ticket. One final tip: Holders of a Eurail Pass, a Youth Pass, an Inter-Rail card, or a Deutsche Bahn Tourist Card can travel free on all suburban railway trains.

By Taxi

Munich's cream-color taxis are numerous. Hail them in the street; or telephone 089/21610 (there's an extra charge for the drive to the pickup point). Rates start at DM 3.90 for the first mile. There is an additional charge of 50 pfennig for each piece of luggage. Expect to pay DM 10–DM 12 for a short trip within the city.

On Foot

Downtown Munich is only a mile square and is easily explored on foot. Almost all of the major sights in the city center are on the interlinking web of pedestrian streets that run from Karlsplatz by the main train station to Marienplatz and the Viktualienmarkt and extend north around the Frauenkirche and up to Odeonsplatz. The central tourist office issues a free map with suggested walking tours.

Guided Tours

Excursions

Bus excursions to the Alps, to Austria, to the royal palaces and castles of Bavaria, or along the Romantic Road can be booked through **ABR** (Hauptbahnhof, ☎ 089/591–315 or 089/59041). **PanoramaTours** (Arnulfstr. 8, next to the Hauptbahnhof, ☎ 089/120–4248) operates numerous trips, including the Royal Castles Tour (Schlösserfahrt) of "Mad" King Ludwig's dream palaces (cost: DM 75 adults, DM 38 children, excluding entry fees to the palaces). Bookings can also be made through all major hotels in the city. The tours depart from in front of the Hauptbahnhof outside the Hertie department store.

The Upper Bavarian Regional Tourist Office (*see* Important Addresses and Numbers, *below*) provides information and brochures for excursions and accommodations outside Munich.

The **S-bahn** can quickly take you to some of the most beautiful places in the countryside around Munich. Line S-6, for example, will whisk you lakeside to Starnberger See in a half hour; line S-4 runs to the depths of the Ebersberger Forest. You can take a bicycle on S-bahn trains.

Orientation Tours

A variety of city bus tours is offered by **Panorama Tours** (Arnulfstr. 8, ☎ 089/120–4248). The blue buses operate year-round, departing from in front of the Hertie department store on Bahnhofplatz (across from the main entrance to the train station). The Kleine Rundfahrt, a one-hour city tour, leaves daily at 10 AM and 2:30 PM, as well as 11:30 AM in midsummer. The cost is DM 15 for adults, DM 8 for children. The "Olympiatour," which lasts about 2½ hours, explores the Olympia Tower and grounds; it departs daily at 10 AM and 2:30 PM, and the cost is DM 27 (DM 14 for children). The Grosse Rundfahrt, or extended city tour, comes in two varieties; each lasts around 2½ hours and costs DM 27 (DM 14 for children). The morning tour includes visits to the

Frauenkirche and Alte Pinakothek; the afternoon tour visits Schloss Nymphenburg. They run Tuesday–Sunday, leaving at 10 and 2:30, respectively. The München bei Nacht tour provides five hours of Munich by night and includes dinner and visits to three nightspots. It departs May–October, Friday and Saturday at 7:30 PM; the cost is DM 100.

Walking and Bicycling Tours

The Munich tourist office (*see* Important Addresses and Numbers, *below*) organizes guided walking tours for groups or individuals; no advance booking is necessary. The meeting place is the **Fischbrunnen** (Fish Fountain) on Marienplatz (Mon., Tues., and Thurs. at 10 AM; cost: DM 6 per person). **City Hopper Touren** (☎ 089/272–1131) offers daily escorted bike tours March–October. Bookings must be made in advance, and starting times are negotiable.

Important Addresses and Numbers

Consulates

U.S. Consulate General, Königinstrasse 5, ☎ 089/28880. **British Consulate General**, Bürkleinstrasse 10, ☎ 089/211090. **Canadian Consulate**, Tal 29, ☎ 089/222–661.

Emergencies

Police: ☎ 089/110. **Fire department:** ☎ 089/112. **Ambulance:** ☎ 089/19222. **Medical emergencies:** ☎ 089/558–661. **Pharmacy emergency service:** ☎ 089/594–475. **Internationale Ludwigs-Apotheke** (Neuhauserstr. 11, ☎ 089/260–3021; open weekdays 8–6, Sat. 8–1) and **Europa-Apotheke** (Schützenstr. 12, near the Hauptbahnhof, ☎ 089/595–423) stock a large variety of over-the-counter medications and personal-hygiene products.

English-Language Bookstores

The **Anglia English Bookshop** (Schellingstr. 3, ☎ 089/283–642) has the largest selection of English-language books in Munich. **Wordsworth Books** (Schellingstr. 21a, ☎ 089/280–9141), the **Internationale Presse** store at the main train station, and **Hugendubel** bookshop (2nd floor, at Marienplatz, and at Karlsplatz) also sell English-language books.

Tourist Information

The **Fremdenverkehrsamt** (central tourist office) is located in the heart of the city (Rindermarkt 10, just up the street from central Marienplatz, ☎ 089/23911; open Mon.–Thurs. 8:30–4, Fri. 8;30–2). Longer hours are kept by the citytourist office at the **Hauptbahnhof** train station (at the entrance on Bayerstr., ☎ 089/239–1256; open Mon.–Sat. 8 AM–10 PM, Sun. and holidays 11–7. There is also a tourist office at Munich's airport (open Mon.–Sat. 8:30 AM–10 PM, Sun. and holidays 1–9 PM).

For information on the Bavarian mountain region south of Munich, contact the **Fremdenverkehrsverband München-Oberbayern** (Upper Bavarian Regional Tourist Office) on Sonnenstrasse 10 (☎ 089/597–347).

Munich Found, an English-language monthly, has articles and information about the city as well as a complete calendar of events. It's sold (DM 4) in kiosks downtown. An official monthly listing of upcoming events, the *Monatsprogramm,* is available at most hotels and newsstands and all tourist offices for DM 2.50. Information in English about museums and galleries can be obtained round-the-clock by dialing 089/239–162, and about castles and city sights by dialing 089/239–172.

Travel Agencies

American Express, Promenadeplatz 6, ☎ 089/21990. **ABR,** the official Bavarian travel agency, has outlets all over Munich; call 089/12040 for information.

3 The Bavarian Alps

This region of fir-clad mountains stretches from Munich south to the Austrian border. Quaint towns full of half-timbered houses fronted by flowers in the summer, buried by snow in the winter, pop up among the peaks, as do the creations of "Mad" King Ludwig II. Shimmering alpine lakes abound, and the whole area has sporting opportunities galore.

OBERBAYERN, OR UPPER BAVARIA, is Germany's favorite year-round vacationland, for visitors and Germans alike. This part of Bavaria, fanning south from Munich to the Austrian border, comes closest to what most of us think of when we see or hear the name Germany. Stock images from tourist-office posters—the fairy-tale castles you've seen in countless ads, those picturebook villages of too-good-to-be-true wood homes with brightly frescoed facades and window boxes filled with flowers in summer, sloping roofs heavy with snow in winter—are brought to life here. To complete the picture, onion-dome church spires rise out of the mist against the backdrop of the mighty Alps. Even the people sometimes appear to be actors completing a carefully staged scene.

Coming south from Munich, you will soon find yourself on a gently rolling plain leading to a lovely land of lakes fed by Alpine rivers and streams, surrounded by ancient forests. In time, the plain merges into foothills, which suddenly give way to a jagged line of Alpine peaks. In places such as Tegernsee, snowcapped mountains seem to rise straight up from the gemlike lakes.

If you continue south you will encounter cheerful villages with richly frescoed houses, some of the finest Baroque churches in Germany, and any number of minor spas where you can stay on to "take the waters" and tune up the system.

Sports possibilities are legion: downhill and cross-country skiing and ice-skating in winter; tennis, swimming, sailing, golf, and, above all, hiking in summer. Marked hiking trails lead from the glorious countryside, along rivers and lakes, through woods, and high into the Alps.

For those who enjoy driving, the Deutsche Alpenstrasse (German Alpine Road) is a spectacular journey by car. The entire route between Lindau, on the Bodensee, and Berchtesgaden adds up to about 485 kilometers (300 miles). The dramatic stretch between Garmisch-Partenkirchen and Berchtesgaden runs about 300 kilometers (185 miles) and affords wonderful views.

This tour of the Alps takes you east from Garmisch-Partenkirchen to Berchtesgaden. Oberammergau, the magnificent 18th-century abbey of Ettal, and Ludwig II's Versailles-style château at Herrenchiemsee are all covered, along with numerous villages, lakes, and other Alpine attractions. (Note that Neuschwanstein, the most famous of Ludwig's castles, is in our Romantic Road chapter. It's just outside Füssen and makes an ideal day trip from Garmisch-Partenkirchen.)

EXPLORING

Tour 1: Garmisch-Partenkirchen

Numbers in the margin correspond to points of interest on the Bavarian Alps map.

① **Garmisch-Partenkirchen,** or Garmisch, as it's more commonly known, is the undisputed Alpine capital of Bavaria, a bustling, year-round resort and spa. Once two separate communities, Garmisch and Partenkirchen fused in 1936 to accommodate the winter Olympics. Today, with a population of 27,000, the area is large enough to offer every facility expected from a major Alpine resort but small enough not to overwhelm.

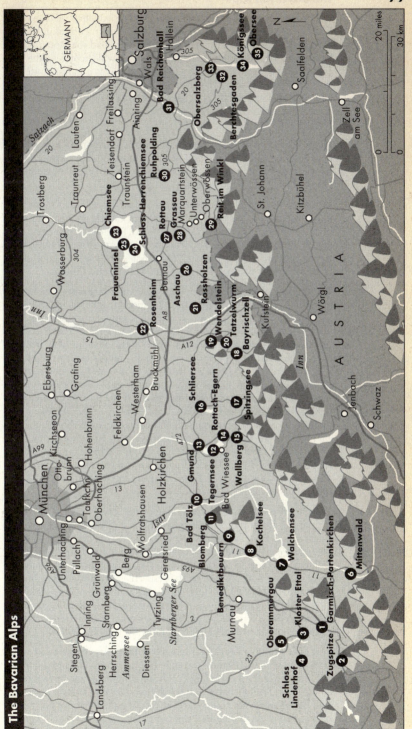

The Bavarian Alps

Although it seems essentially modern—few of its buildings predate World War I—Garmisch-Partenkirchen has a long history. Partenkirchen, the older half, was founded by the Romans. The road the Romans built between Partenkirchen and neighboring Mittenwald, a piece of the principal road between Rome and Germany that was a major route well into the 17th century, can still be followed. Much of the astounding wealth of the Fugger family in Augsburg (*see* Chapter 8) resulted from trade between the south of Germany and Venice, connected by the Roman route.

Partenkirchen was spared physical destruction but devastated economically by the Thirty Years' War. By the early 18th century, it was rejuvenated by the discovery of iron ore. Today, of course, tourism keeps Garmisch-Partenkirchen thriving.

Winter sports rank high on the agenda here. There are more than 62 miles of downhill ski runs, 40 ski lifts and cable cars, and 115 miles of cross-country ski tracks (called *Loipen*). One of the principal stops on the international winter-sports circuit, the area hosts a week of international races every January. You can usually count on good skiing from December through April, or into May on the Zugspitze.

★ ❷   The number-one attraction in Garmisch is the **Zugspitze,** the highest mountain (9,731 feet) in Germany. The hotel that stood for so long at the summit has closed—a restaurant and sunny terrace are now in its place—so don't miss the last lift down to the valley. There are two ways up the mountain: a leisurely 75-minute ride on a cog railway from the train station in the center of town or a 10-minute hoist by cable car, which begins its giddy ascent from the Eibsee, just outside town on the road to Austria. Either way, a separate cable car carries you the final 1,037 feet to just below the peak. A round-trip combination ticket allows you to mix your mode of travel up and down the mountain. Prices are lower in winter than in summer, even though they include use of all the ski lifts on the mountain. Fares were due to be increased by 1996, but at press time a round-trip ticket cost DM 56 for adults and DM 33 for children ages 4–16 (free for children under 4); family tickets cost DM 109–DM 154; one-way fare is DM 37 for train or cable car.

You can also take a cable car to one of the lesser peaks. The round-trip fare to the top of the **Alpspitze,** some 2,000 feet lower than the Zugspitze, is DM 34 for adults and DM 21 for children ages 4–16; to the top of the **Wank** and back costs DM 33 for adults and DM 24 for children (you ride in four-seat cable cars). In winter months, fares include the use of all ski lifts on the respective mountains. Both mountains can be tackled on foot, provided you're properly shod and physically fit. For details on other mountain hikes and on staying in mountain huts, contact Deutscher Alpenverein (German Alpine Association, Praterinsel 5, D–80538 Munich, ☎ 089/235–0900).

There are innumerable less arduous but hardly less spectacular walks (186 miles of marked trails) through the pine woods and upland meadows that cover the lower slopes of the mountains. If you have the time and stout walking shoes, try one of the two that lead to striking gorges. The **Höllentalklamm** route starts at the Zugspitze Mountain railway terminal in town and ends at the top of the mountain (you'll want to turn back before reaching the summit unless you have mountaineering experience). The **Partnachklamm** route is even more challenging; to do all of it, you'll have to stay overnight in one of the mountain huts along the way. It starts at the Olympic ice stadium in town and takes you through a spectacular tunneled water gorge, past a pretty little mountain lake, and far up the Zugspitze. An easier way to tackle this route is to ride part of the way up in the Eckbauer cable car that sets out from the Olympic ice stadium. There's a handy inn at the top where you can gather strength for the hour-long walk back down to the cable-car station. Horse-drawn carriages also cover the first section of the route in summer; in winter you can skim along it in a sleigh (call the local coaching society, the Lohnkutschevereinigung, ☎ 08821/53167 for information).

Garmisch-Partenkirchen isn't all skiing, skating, and hiking, however. In addition to the two Olympic stadiums in the Partenkirchen side of the city, there are some other attractions worth seeing. In Garmisch, the 18th-century parish church of St. Martin, off the Marienplatz, contains some significant stucco-work by the Wessobrunn artists Schmuzer, Schmidt, and Bader. Across the Loisach River on Pfarrerhausweg stands another, older St. Martin's, whose Gothic wall paintings include a larger-than-life-size figure of St. Christopher. Nearby, on Frühlingstrasse, are some beautiful examples of Upper Bavarian houses; at the end of Zöppritzstrasse lies the villa of composer Richard Strauss, who lived there until his death in 1949.

Not a culture-vulture? Then it might interest you to know that après-ski festivities begin as early as 4 PM, and the nightlife only picks up from there.

Excursions from Garmisch

Garmisch-Partenkirchen is an excellent center from which to tour the magnificent surrounding Alpine region. For many, a visit to the little village of Oberammergau, combined with a side trip to the monastery of Ettal and Ludwig II's jewel-like Linderhof château, is a highlight of their stay in Germany. This trip can be extended by visits to Ludwig II's most famous royal castle, Neuschwanstein, and the exquisite Rococo Wieskirche (*see* Chapter 8). Oberammergau is 20 kilometers (12 miles) north of Garmisch. To reach it, you must first pass the massive

★ ❸ walls of **Kloster Ettal**, the great monastery founded in 1330 by Holy Roman Emperor Ludwig der Bayer (Ludwig the Bavarian) for a group of knights and a community of Benedictine monks. The abbey was replaced with new buildings during the 18th century and now serves as a school. The original 10-side church was brilliantly redecorated in 1744–53, becoming one of the foremost examples of Bavarian Rococo, and is open to visitors. The church's chief treasure is its enormous dome fresco (83 feet wide), painted by Jacob Zeiller, circa 1751–52. The mass of swirling clouds and the pink-and-blue vision of heaven is typical of the Rococo fondness for elaborate and glowing illusionistic ceiling painting.

A liqueur with legendary health-giving properties, made from a centuries-old recipe, is still distilled at the monastery by the monks. It's made with more than 70 mountain herbs. You can't get the recipe, but you can buy bottles of the libation (about DM 20) from the small stall outside the monastery.

TIME OUT Across the road you'll find one of the area's best and coziest restaurants, within the traditional old **Hotel Zur Post** (Kaiser-Ludwig-Pl. 18, ☎ 08822/3596). If it's a cold day, try for a spot near the ancient tile stove and order a steaming pot of the best coffee in town; if it's lunchtime get a Bavarian garlic soup or venison stew. In the evening, candlelight glows off the pine-paneled walls and the pewter pots ranged around the ceiling skirting. There are also 24 comfortable and moderately priced guest rooms upstairs.

 Some 10 kilometers (6 miles) west from Ettal, along a narrow mountain valley road, is **Schloss Linderhof,** the only one of Ludwig II's royal residences to have been completed during the monarch's short life, and the only one in which he spent much time. It was built on the grounds of his father's hunting lodge between 1874 and 1878.

For a proper appreciation of Linderhof and the other royal castles associated with Ludwig, it helps to understand the troubled king for whom they were created.

"Mad" King Ludwig II, the haunting presence indelibly associated with Alpine Bavaria, was one of the line of dukes, electors, and kings of the Wittelsbach dynasty who ruled Bavaria from 1180 to 1918. The Wittelsbachs are credited with having fashioned the grandiose look of Munich. This art-loving family started the city's great art collections, promoted the fine arts and music (Ludwig II was a patron of Richard Wagner), and set up a building program that ran for centuries. Ludwig II concentrated on building monumental edifices for himself rather than for the people, and devoted a good part of his time and energies (along with an inordinate percentage of the royal purse) to this endeavor.

Grandest of his extravagant projects is Neuschwanstein, the monumental structure to the king's monumental ego, which came close to breaking the Wittelsbach bank. It was built over a 17-year period starting in 1869, and today, ironically, is one of Germany's top tourist attractions (*see* Chapter 8).

Towering Neuschwanstein offered highly visible proof that the eccentric king had taken leave of his senses and was bleeding the treasury dry. In 1886, the government officially relieved Ludwig of his royal duties for reasons of insanity and had him confined in the small Schloss Berg on the shore of his beloved Starnbergersee (*see* Chapter 3), where he had spent summers in his youth.

On day two of the king's stay at the Schloss, he drowned under mysterious circumstances. A cross in the lake in front of the castle marks the place where his body was recovered from the water.

Linderhof was the smallest of this ill-starred king's castles, and yet, ironically, his favorite country retreat. Set in grandiose sylvan seclusion, between a reflecting pool and the green slopes of a gentle mountain, this charming French-style Rococo confection is said to have been inspired by the Petit Trianon of Versailles. From an architectural standpoint, it could well be considered a disaster, a mishmash of conflicting styles, lavish on the outside, vulgarly overdecorated on the inside. Ludwig's bedroom is filled with brilliantly colored and gilded ornaments; the Hall of Mirrors is a shimmering dreamworld; and the dining room boasts a fine piece of 19th-century engineering—a table that rises and descends from and to the kitchens below. The formal gardens contain further touches of Ludwig's love of fantasy. There's a Moorish Pavilion—bought wholesale from the 1867 Paris Universal Exposition—and a grotto, said to have been modeled on Capri's Blue Grotto but with a rock that slides back at the touch of a button. The gilded Neptune fountain in the lake in front of the palace shoots a jet of water 105 feet into the air, higher than the roof of the building.

According to stories, while staying at Linderhof the eccentric king would dress up as Lohengrin to be rowed in a swan boat on the grotto pond; in winter he took off on midnight sleigh rides behind six plumed horses and a platoon of outriders holding flaring torches. ☛ *DM 7 adults, DM 4 children.* ☉ *Apr.–Sept., daily 9–12:15 and 12:45–5:30, Oct.–Mar., daily 10–12:15 and 12:45–4. Only the Schloss and grounds can be visited in the winter months, for a reduced admission charge of DM 5 adults, DM 2.50 children.*

★ ❺ The renowned wood-carver's village of **Oberammergau** is magnificently situated above an Alpine valley, 11 kilometers (7 miles) northeast of Linderhof. Its main streets are lined with beautifully frescoed houses, occupied for the most part by families whose men are highly skilled wood-carvers, a craft that has flourished here since the depredations of the Thirty Years' War.

However, Oberammergau is best known for its Passion Play, which started in 1634 as an offering of thanks that the Black Plague stopped just short of the village. In faithful accordance with a solemn vow, it has been presented every 10 years since 1680 (excepting 1940, and with an additional 350th-anniversary performance in 1984), so the next play year is 2000. Its 16 acts, which take 5½ hours, depict the final days of Christ, from the Last Supper through the Crucifixion and Resurrection. It is presented on a partly open-air stage against a mountain backdrop every day from late May to late September each Passion Play year.

A visit to Oberammergau when the play is on may be considered something of a mixed blessing, in view of the crowds (half a million or more visitors) and the difficulty of obtaining tickets (most are available only through package tours). The entire village is swept up by the play, with some 1,500 residents directly involved in its preparation and presentation. Men grow beards in hopes of capturing key roles; young women put off their weddings—the role of Mary went only to unmarried girls until the 1990 performances. In that year tradition was broken amid much local controversy when a 31-year-old mother of two was given the part.

If you travel to Oberammergau in a nonplay year you can still visit the theater, the Oberammergau Passionsspielhaus, and explore backstage. Tours of the huge building, with its 5,200-seat auditorium, and vast stage open to the mountain air, are given by guides who will demonstrate the remarkable acoustics by reciting Shakespearean soliloquies. *Passionstheater, Passionswiese. Admission with guided tour: DM 4 adults, DM 2 children.* ☉ *May–Oct., daily 9:30–noon and 1–4. Nov.–Apr., Tues.–Sun. 10–noon and 1:30–4. Closed Jan. 5–31. Festival information: Verkehrsbüro, Oberammergau,* ☎ *08822/1021. Closed Jan. and Mon. Apr.–Oct.*

Play year or no, you will find many wood-carvers at work here, and Oberammergau's shop windows will be crammed with their creations. From June through October, a workshop is open free to the public at the Pilatushaus (Verlegergasse); working potters and traditional painters can also be seen. You can even sign up for a weeklong course in wood carving (classes are in German), at a cost of between DM 460 and DM 650, bed and breakfast included.

Historic examples of the skill of Oberammergau craftsmen are on view at the Heimatmuseum, which also includes one of Germany's finest collections of Christmas crèches, dating from the mid-18th century. *Dorfstr. 8.* ☛ *DM 3 adults, DM 1 children.* ☉ *Mid-Apr.–mid-Oct., Tues.–Sun. 2–6; mid–Oct.–mid–Apr., Sat. 2–6.*

Many of the exteriors of Oberammergau's homes, such as the 1784 Pilatushaus on Ludwig-Thoma-Strasse, are decorated with stunning frescoes. In summer, geraniums pour from every window box, and the village explodes with color.

Oberammergau's 18th-century **St. Peter and St. Paul church** is regarded as the finest work of Rococo architect Josef Schmuzer and has striking frescoes by Matthäus Günther.

Tour 2: Along the Alps

A range of attractions line the Alps between Garmisch and Berchtesgaden to the east. Many of them lie on the Deutsche Alpenstrasse, the German Alpine Road, the most scenic of the west–east Alpine routes. All can be visited on day trips from Garmisch-Partenkirchen and/or
❻ Berchtesgaden. This tour goes first to **Mittenwald,** 20 kilometers (12 miles) southeast of Garmisch and snugly set beneath the towering peaks of the Karwendel range, which separates Bavaria from Austria.

Many regard Mittenwald as the most beautiful town in the Bavarian Alps. In the Middle Ages, it became the staging point for goods shipped up from Verona by way of the Brenner Pass and Innsbruck. From there, goods were transferred to rafts, which carried them down the Isar to Munich. As might be expected, Mittenwald grew rich on this traffic; its early prosperity is reflected in the splendidly decorated houses with ornately carved gables and brilliantly painted facades that line its main street. In the mid-17th century, however, the international trade route was moved to a different pass, and the fortunes of Mittenwald declined.

Prosperity returned in 1684, when farmer's-son-turned-master-violin-maker Matthias Klotz returned from a 20-year stay in Cremona. There he had studied with Nicolo Amati, who gave the violin its present form. Klotz brought his master's pioneering ideas back to Mittenwald and taught the art to his brothers and friends; before long, half the men in the village were making violins. With the ideal woods coming from neighboring forests, the trade flourished. Mittenwald soon became known as "The Village of a Thousand Violins," and stringed instruments—violins, violas, and cello—made in Mittenwald were shipped around the world. Klotz's craft is still carried on in Mittenwald, and the town has a fascinating museum, the **Geigenbau und Heimatmuseum,** devoted to it. *Ballenhausgasse 3,* ☎ *08823/2511.* ☞ *DM 2.50, DM 1 children.* ☉ *Weekdays 10–noon and 2–5, weekends and holidays 10–noon.*

Ask the curator of the museum to direct you to the nearest of the several violin makers who are still active—he'll be happy to demonstrate the skills handed down to him by the successors of Klotz. The museum itself is next to Mittenwald's 18th-century **St. Peter and St. Paul Church.** Check the back of the altar and you'll find Klotz's name, carved there by the violin maker himself. In front of the church is a monument to him. The church itself, with its elaborate and joyful stucco-work coiling and curling its way around the interior, is one of the most important Rococo structures in Bavaria. Note its Gothic choirloft, incorporated into the church in the 18th century. The bold frescoes on its exterior are characteristic of *Lüftlmalerei,* an art form that reached its height in Mittenwald. You can see other fine examples of it on the facades of three famous houses: the Goethehaus, the Pilgerhaus, and the Pichlerhaus.

TIME OUT   Just down the street from the museum and the church is the 17th-century **Hotel Post** (Obermarkt 9). Ask for their *Apfelkuchen* (apple cake) with coffee. The choices on the lunch menu will give you the strength for an afternoon hike in the surrounding mountains.

7
8 The road north from Mittenwald, B–11, runs between the **Walchensee** and the **Kochelsee,** two of the most popular Bavarian Alpine lakes. They are longtime favorites for summer getaways, and offer good swimming, water sports, and mountain walks (the 5,400-foot-high Benedikten-wand, east of Kochel, is a challenge for mountaineers; the 5,300-foot-high Herzogstand, above the Walchensee, is more suitable for the less adventurous—the summit can be reached by chair lift (DM 12 round-trip). On the shores of the Kochelsee is one of the most extensive swimming lidos in Bavaria, with a collection of indoor and outdoor pools, water slides, and enough other games to keep a family amused the whole day. *Trimini, Kochel,* ☎ *08851/5300.* ☛ *3-hr ticket DM 8 adults, DM 6 children; all-day family ticket DM 33.* ☉ *Daily 9–8:30, closed 1st 3 wks of Dec.*

The hero of the attractive little lakeside town of Kochel is the Schmied von Kochel or Blacksmith of Kochel. His fame stems from his role—and eventual death—in the 1705 peasants' uprising at Sendling, just outside Munich. You can see his statue in the town center.

9 Some 10 kilometers (6 miles) north of Kochel on B–11 lies the Benedik-tenwand, a mountain that takes its name from **Benediktbeuren,** a mid-8th-century monastery thought to be the oldest Benedictine institution north of the Alps. It was a flourishing cultural center in the Middle Ages; paradoxically, it also gave birth to one of the most profane musical works of those times, the *carmina burana* (also known as the Go-liardic songs). The 1937 orchestration of the work by Bavarian composer Carl Orff is regularly performed in the monastery courtyard, the place where the original piece was first heard during the 12th century. The painter of the frescoes of the 17th-century monastery church was the father of the Asam brothers, whose church-building and artistic dec-oration made them famous far beyond the borders of 18th-century Bavaria. Cosmas Damian Asam, the eldest son, was born at Benedik-tbeuren. *Monastery church open daily 8–6. Guided tours of the monastery are given July–Sept., daily at 2:30; Oct.–mid-May, week-ends 2:30; mid-May–June, Sat. and Wed. 2:30, Sun. 10:30 and 2:30.*

10 Sixteen kilometers (10 miles) northeast of Benediktbeuren on B–472 lies the old market town of **Bad Tölz.** Visit, if you can, on a Wednes-day morning—market day—when the main street is lined with stalls that stretch to the Isar River, the dividing line between the Old and New towns. The latter, dating from the mid-19th century, sprang up with the discovery of iodine-laden springs, which allowed the locals to call their town *Bad* (bath or spa) *Tölz*. You can take the waters, enjoy a full course of health treatment at a specially equipped hotel, or just splash around in Bad Tölz's large lido, the **Alpamare,** where an indoor pool is disguised as a South Sea beach, complete with surf. Its four wa-terslides include a 330-meter- (1,082-foot-) long adventure run, Ger-many's longest. Another—the "Alpa-Canyon"—has 90° drops, and only the hardiest swimmers are advised to try it. *Ludwigstr. 13.* ☛ *4-hr ticket DM 29 (weekends DM 35) adults, DM 22 (weekends DM 24) chil-dren. From 6 PM the ticket price drops by up to DM 11.* ☉ *Sun.–Thurs. 8 AM–9PM, Fri.–Sat. 8 AM–10 PM.*

Bad Tölz clings to its ancient customs and traditions more tightly than does any other Bavarian community. Folk costumes, for example, are worn regularly. The town is also famous for its painted furniture, par-ticularly farmhouse cupboards and chests. You can admire samples of painted furniture, as well as folk costumes and other historic crafts, in the **Heimatmuseum,** housed in the Altes Rathaus (Old Town Hall). *Markt-str. 48.* ☛ *DM 3 adults, DM 2 children.* ⊘ *Tues.–Wed. and Fri.–Sat. 10–noon and 2–4, Thurs. 10–noon and 2–6, Sun. 10–1.*

If you're in Bad Tölz on November 6, you'll witness one of the most colorful traditions of the Bavarian Alpine area: the Leonhardifahrt equestrian procession, which marks the feast day of St. Leonhard, the patron saint of horses. The procession ends north of the town at an 18th-century chapel on the Kalvarienberg, above the Isar River.

⑪ Drive 3 kilometers (2 miles) west of Bad Tölz along B–472 and you'll reach the base of the town's local mountain, the **Blomberg.** It's an easy walk to the top, but you can also take a chair lift, which makes the journey in 12 minutes. In winter, you can sled back to the valley on Bavaria's longest toboggan run (5 kilometers/3 miles); in summer, you can make the trip on Germany's longest dry toboggan run, which snakes 1,200 meters (3,938 feet). It's great fun for children, but it can be expensive unless you ration the number of runs. ☛ *DM 10 a ride adults, DM 6.50 children.* ⊘ *Dec.–Nov., daily 9–5; Nov.–Dec., depending on weather conditions.*

★ ⑫ About 17 kilometers (10 miles) east of Bad Tölz on B–472 is the **Tegernsee,** an Alpine lake dotted with sails in summer and ice-skaters in winter. Its wooded shores are lined with flowers in late spring; in fall, its trees provide a colorful contrast to the dark, snowcapped mountains. Elbowing each other for room on the banks of this heavenly stretch of water are expensive health clinics, hotels, and, in parklike grounds on the southeast shore, a former **Benedictine monastery.** Founded in the 8th century, this was one of the most productive cultural centers in southern Germany; the musician and poet Minnesänger Walther von der Vogelweide (1170–1230) was a welcomed guest. Not so welcome were Hungarian invaders who had laid the monastery to waste in the 10th century. Fire caused further damage in following centuries, and secularization sealed the monastery's fate at the beginning of the 19th, when Bavarian king Maximilian I bought the surviving buildings for use as a summer retreat. Maximilian showed off this corner of his kingdom to emperors Alexander of Russia and Franz-Josef of Austria during their journey to the Congress of Verona in October 1822, and you can follow their steps through the woods to one of the loveliest lookout points in Bavaria, the **Grosses Paraplui.** A plaque marks the spot where they admired the open expanse of the Tegernsee and the mountains beyond.

TIME OUT   You can follow King Max's footsteps, too, into the vaulted rooms of the neighboring **Bräustüberl,** in which busy waitresses bustle where Benedictine monks once meditated. The dark beer is very strong; the food is basic Bavarian.

In addition to the beer tavern, the property houses a church, a brewery, a restaurant, and a high school. Students here, in what was the monastery, write their exams beneath inspiring Baroque frescoes. The late-Gothic **church** was refurbished in Italian Baroque style in the 18th century. Opinions remain divided as to the success of the remodeling, which was the work of a little-known Italian architect named Antonio Riva. Whatever you think of his designs, you'll admire the frescoes by Hans Georg Asam, whose work you saw at Benediktbeuern. ⑬ The parish church of **Gmund,** at the north end of the lake, and the church ⑭ of St. Laurentius at **Rottach-Egern,** on the south shore also have Baroque influences.

Rottach-Egern is a fashionable and upscale resort. Its classy shops, chic restaurants, and expensive boutiques are as well-stocked and interesting as many in Munich, its leading hotels world-class. For a stylish visit, Bachmair's (Seestr. 47, ☎ 08022/2720), on the water's edge, is the place to stay: It has a nightclub featuring international acts. The casino at Bad Wiessee, on the west shore of the lake, can also help you spend your money (*see* The Arts and Nightlife, *below*).

⑮ The mountain slopes above Bad Wiessee offer fine views, but for the best vista of all climb the 5,700-foot **Wallberg,** at the south end of the Tegernsee. It's a hard, four-hour hike, though anyone in good shape should be able to make it since it involves no rock climbing. A cable car makes the ascent in just 15 minutes and costs DM 13 one-way, DM 22 round-trip (children DM 6 one way, DM 10 round-trip). At the summit there's a restaurant and sun terrace, and several trailheads; in winter the skiing is excellent.

⑯ From the town of Tegernsee on the eastern shore you can follow an upland footpath 9 kilometers (6 miles) east—or drive 27 kilometers (18 miles)—to the quieter, less fashionable **Schliersee.** There are fine walking and ski trails on the mountain slopes that ring the Schliersee. The difference between the two lakes is made clear in the names local people have long given them: the Tegernsee is called the Herrensee (or Master's Lake), while the Schliersee is known as the Bauernsee (or Peasant's Lake).

Like its neighbor, the Schliersee was the site of a monastery, built in the 8th century by a group of noblemen. It subsequently became a choral academy, which was eventually moved to Munich. Today only the restored 17th-century **abbey church** recalls this piece of the Schliersee's history. The church has some fine frescoes and stucco-work by Johann Baptist Zimmermann.

⑰ A spectacular 10-kilometer (6-mile) drive south from Schliersee takes you around hairpin bends to the tiny **Spitzingsee,** cradled 3,500 feet up between the Taubenstein, Rosskopf, and Stumpfling peaks. The walking in this area is breathtaking in every sense. There's skiing, too.

⑱ **Bayrischzell,** 10 kilometers (6 miles) east, is the next stop. To reach it,
⑲ you pass one of the highest mountains of the area, the 6,000-foot **Wendelstein.** At its summit is a tiny stone-and-slate-roof chapel that's much in demand as an off-beat place for wedding ceremonies. The cross above the entrance was carried up the mountain by Max Kleiber, who designed the 19th-century church. Today there are two easier ways up: by cable car (which sets out from beside the train station at Osterhofen and costs DM 27 round-trip for adults and DM 13 for children) and by historic cog railway (catch it at Brannenburg, on the north side of the mountain; round-trip DM 36 for adults and DM 19 for children).

While the steep slopes of the Wendelstein attract expert skiers, those above Bayrischzell beckon the rest. The town is in an attractive family resort area, where many a Bavarian first learn to ski. The wide-open slopes of the Sudelfeld Mountain are ideal for those who enjoy undemanding skiing; in summer and fall they offer innumerable upland walking trails.

★ ⑳ A mile or two east of Bayrischzell on the Sudelfeld Road is the **Tatzelwurm** gorge and waterfall, named for a winged dragon who supposedly inhabits these parts. Dragon or no, this can be an eerie place to drive through at dusk. From the gorge, the road drops sharply to the valley of the Inn River, leading to another busy ski resort, Oberaudorf.

The Inn River valley, an ancient trade route, carries the most important road link between Germany and Italy. The wide, green Inn gushes here, and in the parish church of St. Bartholomew at **Rossholzen,** 16 kilometers (10 miles) north of Oberaudorf, you can see memorials to the local people who have lost their lives in its chilly waters. The church has a fine late-Gothic altar.

Rossholzen is 10 kilometers (6 miles) south of **Rosenheim,** a medieval market town that has kept much of its character despite the onslaught of industrial development. The arcaded streets of low-eaved houses are characteristic of Inn valley towns.

Rosenheim, a good center from which to explore the Chiemgau region, is an area of mountainous lakes set amid rich, rolling farmland and largely forgotten by the crowds who head to the nearby Alps. The largest stretch of water in Bavaria is the more popular **Chiemsee,** which retains something of the quiet charm and strange melancholy that attracted Ludwig II in the last century. It was here on one of three islands that he built the sumptuous **Schloss Herrenchiemsee,** based on Louis XIV's great palace at Versailles. But this was the result of more than simple admiration of Versailles: Ludwig, whose name was the German equivalent of Louis, was keen to establish that he, too, possessed the absolute authority of his namesake, the Sun King. As with most of Ludwig's projects, the building was never completed, and Ludwig never stayed in its state rooms. Nonetheless, what remains is impressive—and ostentatious. Regular ferries out to the island depart from Stock, on the shore. If you want to make the journey in style, take the 100-year-old steam train—which glories in the name *Feuriger Elias,* or *Fiery Elias*— from the neighboring town of Prien to Stock. A horse-drawn carriage takes you to the palace itself. Most spectacular in the palace is the Hall of Mirrors, a dazzling gallery (modeled on that at Versailles) where candle-lit concerts are held in the summer. Also of interest are the ornate bedrooms Ludwig planned and the stately formal gardens. The south wing houses a museum containing Ludwig's christening robe and death mask, as well as other artifacts of his life. *Palace and museum* ☛ *DM 7.50 adults, DM 4 children.* ☼ *Apr.–Sept., daily 9–5; Oct.–Mar., daily 10–4. Guided tours offered May–Sept.*

The smaller **Fraueninsel** (Ladies' Island) is a charming retreat. The Benedictine convent founded here 1,200 years ago now serves as a school. One of its earliest abbesses, Irmengard, daughter of King Ludwig der Deutscher, died here in the 9th century. Her grave was discovered in 1961, the same year that early frescoes in the convent chapel were brought to light.

Just south of the Chiemsee, in a small, flat valley of the Chiemgauer Alps, is the enchanting village of **Aschau,** site of **Schloss Hohenaschau,** one of the few medieval castles in southern Germany to have been restored in the 17th century in Baroque style. The renovation gave its stately rooms a new elegance. Chamber-music concerts are presented regularly in the Rittersaal (Knights Hall) during the summer. ☎ *08052/392.* ☛ *DM 3 adults, children free.* ☼ *Apr.–Oct., Tues.–Fri. 9– 5.*

At Aschau you'll join the most scenic section of the Alpine Road, route B–305, as it heads into the mountains before ending at the Austrian border just beyond Berchtesgaden. In this stretch it passes through a string of villages—Bernau, Rottau, Grassau, Marquartstein, and Oberwössen—pretty enough to make you want to linger. Rosenheim, Bad Reichenhall, and Berchtesgaden—all with good road connections to the rest of Germany—are ideal centers from which to explore this part of the Alps.

(27) In summer, the farmhouses of **Rottau** virtually disappear behind facades of flowers, which have won the village several awards. The houses of (28) **Grassau** shrink beside the bulk of the 15th-century Church of the Ascension, worth visiting for its rich 17th-century stucco-work. The 11th-century castle above Marquartstein is in private hands and can't be visited, so press on to the villages of Unter-, Hinter-, and Oberwössen.

TIME OUT The **Hotel zur Post** at Unterwössen (Hauptstr. 51, ☎08641/8736) beckons the traveler at any time of day with strong coffee, delicious homemade pastries, and Bavarian specialties. *Closed Mon.*

(29) Eight kilometers (5 miles) farther, not much more than a snowball's throw from the Tyrolean border, lies the mountain resort of **Reit im Winkl,** famous for the clarity of its light in summer and the depth of its snowfalls in winter. The Winklmoosalm Mountain, towering above Reit im Winkl, can be reached by bus or chair lift and is a popular ski area in winter and a great place for bracing upland walks in summer and fall.

(30) The next stretch of the Alpine Road takes you past three shimmering mountain lakes—the Weitsee, the Mittersee, and the Lödensee—before dropping down to busy **Ruhpolding,** once a quiet Alpine village and now a leading resort. This is where the Bavarian tourist boom began back in the '30s. Back then, tourists were welcomed at the train station by a brass band. The welcome isn't quite so extravagant these days, but it's still warm. In the 16th century, the Bavarian rulers journeyed out to Ruhpolding to hunt, and the Renaissance-style hunting lodge of Prince Wilhelm V still stands (it's now used as the offices of the local forestry service). The hillside 18th-century **Pfarrkirche St. Georg** (parish church of St. George) is one of the finest Baroque and Rococo churches in the Bavarian Alps. In one of its side altars stands a rare 13th-century carved Madonna, the Ruhpoldinger Madonna. Note also the atmospheric crypt chapel in the quiet churchyard.

(31) East of Ruhpolding, almost surrounded by the Austrian border, lies a small corner of Bavaria that is dominated by two resorts of international fame: Bad Reichenhall and Berchtesgaden. Although Berchtesgaden is more famous, **Bad Reichenhall** is older, with saline springs that made the town rich. Europe's largest saline source was first tapped in pre-Christian times; the salt provided in the Middle Ages supported the economies of cities as far away as Munich and Passau. In the early 19th century King Ludwig I built an elaborate salt works and spa house here—the **Alte Saline** and **Quellenhaus**—in vaulted, pseudomedieval style. Their pump installations are astonishing examples of 19th-century engineering. A fascinating museum in the same building looks at the history of the salt trade, which helped build Bad Reichenhall's wealthy foundations. *Admission to the Quellenhaus and Salzmuseum: DM 4 adults, DM 2 children. ☉ Apr.–Oct., daily 10–11:30 and 2–4; Nov.–Mar., Tues. and Thurs. 2–4. The Alte Saline also houses a typical Upper Bavarian glass foundry and a showroom with articles for sale. ☞ Free. ☉ Weekdays 9–6, Sat. 9–1.*

Salt is so much a part of the town that you can practically taste it in the air. There's even a 19th-century "saline" chapel, part of the spa's facilities and built in exotic Byzantine style at the behest of Ludwig I. Many hotels base special spa treatments on the health-giving properties of the saline springs and the black mud from the surrounding waterlogged moors. The waters can also be taken in the attractive spa gardens throughout the year (open Apr.–Oct., daily 7 AM–10 PM; Nov.–Mar., daily 7–6). Bad Reichenhall's symphony orchestra performs five days a week during the summer season and four days a week in winter. Like most resorts in the area, this one also has a casino (*see* The Arts and Nightlife, *below*).

It's ironic that Bad Reichenhall, which flourishes on the riches of its underground springs, has a 12th-century basilica dedicated to **St. Zeno,** patron saint of those imperiled by floods and the dangers of the deep. Much of this ancient church was remodeled in the 16th and 17th centuries, but some of the original cloisters remain.

㉜ Berchtesgaden, 18 kilometers (11 miles) south of Bad Reichenhall, is an ancient market town set in the noblest section of the Bavarian Alps. While as a high-altitude ski station it may not have quite the charm or cachet of Garmisch-Partenkirchen, in summer it serves as one of the region's most popular (and crowded) resorts, with top-rated attractions in a heavenly setting. Members of the ruling Wittelsbach dynasty started coming here in 1810. Their ornate palace stands today and is one of the town's major attractions, along with a working salt mine and a retreat used by Hitler.

Salt—or "white gold," as it was known in medieval times—was the basis of Berchtesgaden's wealth. In the 12th century Emperor Barbarossa gave mining rights to a Benedictine abbey that had been founded here a century earlier. The abbey was secularized early in the 19th century, when it was taken over by the Wittelsbach rulers. The last royal resident, Crown Prince Rupprecht, who died here in 1955, furnished it with rare family treasures that now form the basis of a permanent collection—the **Königliches Schloss Berchtesgaden** museum. Fine Renaissance rooms provide the principal exhibition spaces for the prince's collection of sacred art, which is particularly rich in wood sculptures by such great late-Gothic artists as Tilman Riemenschneider and Veit Stoss. You can also visit the abbey's original, cavernous 13th-century dormitory and cool cloisters, which still convey something of the quiet and orderly life led by medieval monks. ☛ *DM 7 adults, DM 3 children under 16.* ☉ *Easter–Sept., Sun.–Fri. 10–1 and 2–5; Oct.–Easter, weekdays 10–1 and 2–5. No admission after 4 PM, when last tour starts.*

Wood carving in Berchtesgaden dates back to long before Oberammergau established itself as the premier wood-carving center of the Alps. Examples of Berchtesgaden wood carvings and other local crafts are on display at one of the most interesting museums of its kind in the Alps, the Heimatmuseum, in the Schloss Adelsheim. *Schroffenbergallee 6.* ☛ *DM 3 adults, DM 1 children. Entry allowed only as part of the guided tours given weekdays at 10 and 3.*

For many travelers, the pièce de résistance of a Berchtesgaden stay might well be a visit to its salt mine, the **Salzbergwerk.** In the days when the mine was owned by Berchtesgaden's princely rulers, only select guests were allowed to see how the source of the city's wealth was extracted from the earth. Today 90-minute tours of the mines are available. Dressed in traditional miner's clothing, visitors sit astride a miniature train that transports them nearly ½ mile into the mountain to an enormous chamber where the salt is mined. Rides down the wooden chutes used by the miners to get from one level to another, and a boat ride on an underground saline lake the size of a football field are included in the 1½-hour tour. *1 mi from Berchtesgaden on the B–305 Salzburg*

Rd. ☛ *DM 16 adults, DM 8 children under 11.* ☉ *May–mid-Oct., daily 8:30–5; mid-Oct.–Apr., Mon.–Sat. 12:30–3:30.*

Berchtesgaden's name is indelibly linked to that of Adolf Hitler—it was "Der Führer's" favorite mountain retreat—and many a top-level Nazi staff meeting were held here. In the summer you can take a bus up to ㉝ **Obersalzberg**, site of Hitler's luxurious mountain retreat on the north slope of the Hoher Goll. Most of the Nazi complex was destroyed in 1945, as was Hitler's chalet; only a few basement walls remain. Further along, the hairpin bends of Germany's highest road come to the base of the 6,000-foot peak on which sat the so-called Adlerhorst or ★ Eagle's Nest, the **Kehlsteinhaus.** Hitler had the road built in 1937–39. It climbs more than 2,000 feet in less than 6 kilometers (4 miles) and ends at a lot that clings to the mountain about 500 feet below the Kehlsteinhaus. A tunnel in the mountain brings you to an elevator that whisks you up to what appears to be the top of the world. There are refreshment rooms and a restaurant where you can fill up before the giddy descent to Berchtesgaden. The round-trip by bus and lift (Berchtesgaden post office to Eagle's Nest and back) costs DM 25.50 per person (there is no family ticket per se, though each family group is only required to pay fares for two children). By car you can travel only as far as the Obersalzberg bus station. The return fare from there is DM 19. The full round-trip takes one hour. ☉ *Mid-May–mid-Oct.*

Schellenberg Caves, Germany's largest ice caves, lie 10 kilometers (6 miles) north of Berchtesgaden. By car, take the B–305 to the village of Marktschellenberg, or take the bus from the Berchtesgaden post office to Marktschellenberg. Once you arrive in Markteschellenberg, you can reach the caves on foot only by walking along a clearly marked route. The walk takes more than an hour, so you'll need to be in reasonably good physical shape. A guided tour of the caves takes one hour. ☛ *DM 8.* ☉ *Mid-June–mid-Oct., daily 10–4 (guided tours every hour).*

South of Berchtesgaden is what many consider to be the most tranquil lake in the entire Alpine region, the **Königssee,** together with its much smaller sister, the **Obersee.** Both lakes lie within the Berchtesgaden National Park, 210 square kilometers (82 square miles) of wild mountain country where flora and fauna have been left to develop as nature intended. No roads penetrate the area, and even the mountain paths are difficult to follow. The park administration organizes guided tours of the area from June until September (contact the Nationale Parkverwaltung, Doktorberg 6, D–83471 Berchtesgaden, ☎ 08652/61068).

★ ㉞ One less strenuous way into the Berchtesgaden National Park is by boat. A fleet of 21 excursion boats, electrically driven so that no noise disturbs the peace, operates on the **Königssee.** Only the skipper of the boat is allowed to shatter the silence with a trumpet fanfare to demonstrate the lake's remarkable echo. The notes from the trumpet bounce back and forth from the almost vertical cliffs that plunge into the dark, green water. A cross on a rocky promontory marks the spot where a boatload of pilgrims hit the cliffs and sank more than 100 years ago. The voyagers, most of whom drowned, were on their way to the tiny, twin-towered Baroque chapel of St. Bartholomä, built in the 17th century on a peninsula where an early Gothic church once stood. The princely rulers of Berchtesgaden built a hunting lodge at the side of the chapel; a tavern and a restaurant now occupy its rooms.

㉟ The much smaller but equally beautiful **Obersee** can be reached by a 15-minute walk from the second stop on the boat tour. The lake's backdrop of jagged mountains and precipitous cliffs is broken by a waterfall, the Rothbachfall, that plunges more than 1,000 feet to the valley floor. *Boat service on the Königsee runs year-round (except when the lake freezes). Round-trips can be interrupted at St. Bartholomä and Salet, the landing stage for the Obersee. The boat trips stop only at St. Bartholomä Oct.–Apr. The round-trip to the Königsee and the Obersee lasts almost 2 hrs, without stops, and costs DM 19 adults, DM 9.50 children. The shorter trip to St. Bartholomä and back costs DM 15.50 adults, DM 8 children.*

What to See and Do with Children

If it's winter, **rent skis or a sled** from any resort sports shop and head for the slopes. Bayerischzell, Lengries, Neuhaus am Schliersee, and Oberammergau have excellent facilities for young beginners. Wishing you could take a **sleigh ride** through the snow? Call Harald Zischg at Bad Wiessee (☎ 08022/81096) or Schorsch Flossmann at Kreuth (☎ 08029/1218 or 08029/679).

If it's summer, head for any of the lakes or, if the water's not warm enough for **swimming,** try one of the numerous lidos. The best are at Garmisch, Oberammergau, Kochel, Bad Tölz, Bad Wiessee, and Penzberg. Also in summer, the Blomberg Mountain outside Bad Tölz has one of Europe's longest **dry toboggan runs.** You hurtle at great speed for nearly a mile down the mountain on a wheeled toboggan. In winter the Blomberg Mountain has Bavaria's longest toboggan run, at 5 kilometers (3 miles). At any resort in the Bavarian Alps you can rent a toboggan and take it to the nearest mountain slopes. There are special toboggan runs in most resorts, including a 2-mile run at Ramsau, just outside Berchtesgaden.

In winter, children can accompany foresters to **feed deer** at several points in the Alps. *For Berchtesgaden, ☎ 08657/988–920; Oberammergau, ☎ 08824/422; Tegernsee, ☎ 08029/1218; Schliersee, ☎ 08026/356 or 08657/1213; Ruhpolding, ☎ 08663/1227.*

A 90-year-old **steam train** (☎ 08022/3956 for timetable details), with original cars, puffs along a 16-kilometer (10-mile) stretch of private track in and out of Tegernsee at two-week intervals in summer. *Full round-trip fare: DM 8.50 adults, DM 4.50 children.*

Children interested in history will appreciate a trip into the past at the **open-air museum** at Grossweil, near the Kochelsee (just off the Munich-Garmisch Autobahn). The museum, the Freilichtmuseum an der Glentleiten (☎ 08851/1850), is a reconstructed Bavarian village that looks and functions just as it did centuries ago, complete with cobbler, blacksmith, and other craftsmen who kept the community self-sufficient. ☛ *DM 7 adults, DM 2 children.* ◷ *Apr.–Oct., Tues.–Sun. 9–6.*

For the very young there's a charming **fairy-tale park** (Märchenwald) at Wolfratshausen, about 20 kilometers (12 miles) north of Bad Tölz on the B–11. Mechanical tableaux tell 24 favorite fairy tales in German and English, and there are also gentle rides. *Märchenwald im Isartal, Kräterstr. 37–39.* ☛ *DM 9.50 per person (includes fairground rides).* ◷ *Easter–mid-Oct., daily 9–5.*

Off the Beaten Track

On weekends year-round, Bavarian Alps resorts can be uncomfortably crowded. But there are still valleys and peaks where you can find solitude. Avoid any place with a cable car or funicular railway. Travel by water whenever possible. Board a boat at **Königssee,** for instance, and glide silently among the cliffs that plunge into the lake; then leave your fellow passengers behind at one of the two stopping points and strike out into **Berchtesgaden National Park.** No roads penetrate it, and the few hiking trails are refreshingly uncrowded. The Königssee itself is crowded at the resort end, but there are other lakes in the region where you can get away from it all. Try the **Wagingersee,** Germany's warmest lake.

Looking to trace your German roots? The **Deutsches Wappenmuseum** (Jennerbahnstr. 30, Königssee, ☎ 08652/61910) has 4,000 German coats of arms, and visitors can root around in search of illustrious family trees. There are no fixed opening hours, so call to arrange an appointment.

The world's largest small-gauge model railway competes for attention with more than 200 old automobiles in the **German Automobile History Museum** (Museum für Deutsche Automobilgeschichte) at Ammerang, near the Chiemsee Lake. The two collections share 6,000 square meters (about 65,000 square feet) of exhibition space. *Wasserburger Strasse 38.* ☞ *DM 10 adults, DM 5 children.* ☉ *Tues.–Sat. 10–6.*

In the village of Hasslberg near Ruhpolding you can visit a 300-year-old **bell foundry,** now a fascinating museum of the ancient craft of the foundryman and blacksmith. ☞ *DM 4.50 adults, DM 2 children.* ☉ *Mon.–Sat. 10–noon and 2–4.*

SHOPPING

Berchtesgaden and Oberammergau have centuries-old **wood-carving** traditions. In both towns and in surrounding villages you'll find shops crammed with the work of local craftsmen. In Berchtesgaden, there's a central selling point at **Schloss Adelsheim** (Schroffenbergallee 1, ☎ 08652/4410). Berchtesgaden is also famous for its *Spanschachtel,* delicate, finely constructed wood boxes made to contain everything from pins and needles to top hats. You'll find modern versions in every souvenir shop and, if you're lucky, you might even come across a 100-year-old example in one of the town's antiques shops. In Oberammergau, you can buy wood carvings directly from craftsmen who demonstrate their skills from April through June and September through November in a "living workshop" at the **Pilatushaus** (Verlegergasse).

Some of the **flowers** and **herbs** that grow in the Bavarian Alps have healing properties, and some long-established "apothecaries" put together herbal mixtures that are redolent of the elixir of life. **Josef Mack KG** (Ludwigstr. 36, Bad Reichenhall, ☎ 08651/78280) has been in this business since 1856. **Dricoolo KG** (Ludwigstr. 27, Bad Reichenhall, ☎ 08651/78331) is another established herb vendor. In Ruhpolding there's an herb garden at **Gasthaus Jürgant** (Branderstr. 23a, ☎ 08651/1288), where visitors can pick the basic ingredients of the preparations on sale, which include a potent herbal liqueur.

It's not the kind of gift every visitor wants to take home, but just in case you'd like a violin, cello, or even a double bass from a town that has been making these instruments for centuries, the Alpine resort of Mittenwald is the place to visit. There are at least a dozen craftsmen whose work is coveted by musicians throughout the world. If you're buying or even if you're just curious, call on **Benedict Lang** (Dammkarstr. 22, ☎ 08651/8544) or **Geigenbau Leonhardt** (Mühlenweg 53a,

☎ 08651/8010). For traditional Bavarian costumes—dirndls, embroidered shirts and blouses, and lederhosen—try the **Trachtenstub'n** (Obermarkt 35, Mittenwald, ☎ 08651/3785), **Trachten Werner-Leichtl** (Dekan Karl Pl. 1, Mittenwald, ☎ 08651/8282), **Trachten Brendl** (Hauptstr. 8, Tegernsee) or any of the **Dollinger** shops throughout southern Bavaria. And if at the end of your Upper Bavarian tour you're still looking for *something*, stop at the busy market town of Miesbach (between Tegernsee and Schliersee) and climb the stairs to **Cilly's Gschirrladn** (Bavarian for china shop, Stadlplatz 10, ☎ 08025/1705). A warren of rooms is packed ceiling-high with every variety of item for the home, from embroidered tablecloths to fine German porcelain. Owner Cilly Keckowski or one of her assistants will happily pack your parcel as if it came straight from under the Christmas tree.

SPORTS AND FITNESS

Bicycling

Most local rail stations rent bikes for DM 12 a day (DM 6 if you have a valid train ticket). Many local sports shops also have bikes for rent: **Sport Eich** (Fendtgasse 5, Oberammergau, ☎ 08822/6148), **Sport Bittner** (Andreas-Fendt-Ring 1, Bischofswiesen, near Berchtesgaden, ☎ 08652/7511), **Alfred Guggenbichler** (Münchner Str. 11, Gmund, Tegernsee, ☎ 08022/7257), **"Fly and Bike"** (Schwaighofstr. 77, Tegernsee, ☎ 08022/6069), and **Radsport Papperger** (Salzstr. 9, Bad Tölz, ☎ 08041/2105) are just some. Rates are around DM 20–30 per day and up to DM 85 per week. Mountain-bike tours are arranged from Berchtesgaden. Call the **Outdoor Club** (Ludwig-Ganghoferstr. 20, ☎ 08652/5001). The Chiemsee area is a popular (and flat) area for cycling. For details of tours lasting from three hours to three days, contact Chieming Tourist Office, D–83339 Chieming, ☎ 08664/245.

Bowling

Many resort hotels have their own bowling alleys (usually for English-style skittles; rarely tenpins). The **Hotel Bayerischer Hof** in Bad Reichenhall (☎ 08651/6090) organizes skittle weeks occasionally in the quiet seasons (Apr.–June and Oct.–Nov.). Half-pension lodging rates include unlimited skittling and competitions.

Gliding

Hang-gliding is permitted from a number of peaks. Best bets are in **Berchtesgaden** (☎ 08652/2363 for advice on local conditions and equipment rental), **Lenggries** (☎ 08042/4559), **Oberammergau** (☎ 08822/520 or 08822/4470), and Tegernsee (☎ 08022/6069). For plane gliding, try the Alpine Gliding School in Unterwössen (☎ 08641/8205).

Golf

There is an American-run golf course at **Obersalzberg** (☎ 08652/2100) in Berchtesgaden. It has nine holes, set 3,300 feet up, and a distracting view of the Watzmann Range. It is open for play from May through October. A spectacular 18-hole course is located at **Bad Wiessee** (☎ 08022/8769), high above the Tegernsee. Bad Tölz has two nine-hole courses (☎ 08041/9994).

Hiking

The Bavarian Alps are veined with marked paths. You can set off from just about any resort and find a number of scenic routes to follow. Mountain guides are available for the Berchtesgaden and Bad Reichenhall areas (☎ 08652/2420 or 08651/3776 for details). Oberammergau is an ideal starting point for hiking tours into the surrounding mountains. There are a variety of paths to choose from. Each year, on August 24, visitors can take part in an organized Mountain Hiking Day (*Gebirgswandertag*) called "In King Ludwig's Footsteps" in memory of Bavaria's "Dream King." At dusk, huge bonfires are set ablaze on surrounding mountains.

Hot-Air Balloons

Hot-air balloon rides over the Alps can be booked in the **Berchtesgaden** area (☎ 08652/5001 or 08652/2530) or the Lenggries-Bad Tölz area (Ballooning Reichart, ☎ 08041/3220).

Mountain Climbing

The Zugspitze climbing school in Garmisch-Partenkirchen (☎ 08821/58999) organizes courses in rock climbing, ski touring, and deep-snow skiing, and provides guides for walking, skiing, or climbing tours of one day or longer. In the Berchtesgaden area, contact the Outdoor Club (☎ 08652/5001) for hiking, climbing, and other mountain pursuits.

Skiing

The Bavarian Alps are Germany's winter playground. All you have to do is choose your resort and everything is laid out: ski rentals, ski school, lifts, and transportation. Vacations cost as little as DM 500 per week. Contact local tourist offices for details. If you're a Nordic skier, match your speed against Bavaria's best in Oberammergau's annual King Ludwig Race, held the first weekend in February. Oberammergau also hosts events over distances of 6 kilometers (4 miles) and 15 kilometers (9 miles) every Wednesday during the winter season.

Swimming

The lakes are warm enough in summer for swimming, often topping 70°F, but Bavaria has fine resorts for year-round fun in the water. The best are in Garmisch-Partenkirchen, Oberammergau, Kochel, Penzberg, Bad Tölz, and Bad Wiessee (*see* Along the Alps *in* Exploring, *above*).

Water Sports

Sailing schools can be found everywhere on Bavaria's lakes. **Captain Glas** (☎ 08157/8100) at Possenhofen on the west shore of the Starnbergersee has one of the largest fleets and can fix you up with anything from a small sailboat to a cabin cruiser. **Windsurfing** equipment can be hired for DM 18 an hour from the boat yard at **Seeshaupt** at the south end of the lake, and for a similar fee at other lakes, especially in Urfeld, at the northern end of the Walchensee.

DINING AND LODGING

Dining

Specialties here are much the same as in the rest of Bavaria, but local dishes to try are *Forelle* (trout), *Lachsforelle* (lake trout), and *Bachsaibling* (freshwater salmon trout). If you visit Chiemsee or Walchensee, look for *Renke*, a meaty white lake fish.

WHAT TO WEAR

Because most businesses in the area serve outdoorsy types, informal dress is the norm. Exceptions are the casinos and the most expensive restaurants, which are more formal.

RATINGS

CATEGORY	COST*
$$$$	over DM 90
$$$	DM 55–DM 90
$$	DM 35–DM 55
$	under DM 35

*per person for a three-course meal, including service but not drinks

Lodging

With few exceptions, all hotels and Gasthäuser in the Bavarian Alps and lower Alpine regions are traditionally styled, featuring geranium-covered balconies—the Bavarian summer standard–pine woodwork, and steep Alpine roofs. Quality is high, even in simpler lodgings. Sophisticated Alpine resort areas is where you'll find luxury resorts; cozy—and much less expensive—inns are in the villages. Garmisch-Partenkirchen and Berchtesgaden are bountifully supplied with accommodations in all price ranges. Check out the special seven-day packages. In addition, all through the region private homes offer Germany's own version of bed-and-breakfasts, indicated by signs of *Zimmer Frei* (rooms available). These rates may be under DM 25 per person. As a general rule, the farther from the popular Alpine resorts you stay, the lower the rates will be.

CATEGORY	COST*
$$$$	over DM 200
$$$	DM 160–DM 200
$$	DM 120–DM 160
$	under DM 120

*All prices are for two people in a double room, including tax and service charge.

Bad Reichenhall

DINING AND LODGING

Parkhotel Luisenbad. If you fancy spoiling yourself in a typical German fin-de-siècle spa hotel, then this is *the* establishment—a fine porticoed and pillared building whose imposing pastel-pink facade holds the promise of spacious luxury. Inside, the promise is fulfilled. Rooms are large, furnished in deep-cushioned, dark-wood comfort, most of them with flower-smothered balconies or loggias. The elegant restaurant serves international and traditional Bavarian cuisines, while a pine-paneled tavern, Die Holzstubn'n, is the place for a glass or two of the excellent local brew. ☎ *Ludwigstr. 33,* ☎ *08651/6040,* ℻ *08651/62928. 80 rooms and 8 apartments with bath. Restaurant, bar, beer garden, indoor pool, hot tub, sauna, exercise room, recreation room, bicycles. DC, MC, V. $$$-$$$$*

LODGING

Steigenberger-Hotel Axelmannstein. Ludwig would have enjoyed the palatial air that pervades this hotel—and he would have been able to pay the price, which rivals that of top hotels in Germany's most expensive cities. If you stay here, you'll reside in luxurious comfort, in rooms ranging in style from Bavarian rustic to Laura Ashley demure. Outside is a manicured park and the town center. ☎ *Salzburgerstr. 2,* ☎ *08651/7770,* ℻ *08651/5932. 143 rooms with bath and 8 apart-*

ments. *2 restaurants, bar, indoor pool, beauty salon, sauna, spa, exercise room, tennis court, baby-sitting. AE, DC, MC, V. $$$$*

★ **Pension Hubertus.** This delightfully traditional family-run lodging stands on the banks of the tiny Thumsee Lake, 5 kilometers (3 miles) from the town center. The Hubertus's private grounds lead down to the lake, where guests can swim or boat. Rooms are Bavarian rustic in style. Ask for one with a balcony overlooking the lake. Special, full-board discounts are offered October–May. ☎ *Thumsee 5, D–83435 Bad Reichenhall 3, ☎ 08651/2252, FAX 08651/63845. 16 rooms with shower. Restaurant, exercise room, boating. AE. $*

Bad Tölz

LODGING

★ **Hotel Jodquellenhof-Alpamare.** *Jodquellen* are the iodine springs that have made Bad Tölz wealthy. You can take advantage of these revitalizing waters at this luxurious spa hotel, where the emphasis is on fitness. The imposing 19th-century building, with its own private access to the Alpamare lido, contains comfortable and stylish rooms, many of which were enlarged in 1994. ☎ *Ludwigstr. 13–15, ☎ 08041/5090, FAX 08041/509–441. 81 rooms with bath. Restaurant, outdoor pool, indoor thermal baths, sauna. AE, DC, MC, V. $$$$*

Hotel Gasthof Pension Am Wald. This modern but traditionally designed lodging is set in its own spacious grounds in the "new" half of town, a 10-minute stroll from Bad Tölz's ancient quarter. Rooms are decorated and furnished country style. ☎ *Austr. 39, ☎ 08041/9014, FAX 08041/72643. 32 rooms with bath, 2 apartments. Restaurant, indoor pool, sauna, exercise room. AE, DC, MC, V. Closed Nov. 7–Dec. 20. $$*

Bad Wiessee

DINING

★ **Freihaus Brenner.** Proprietor Josef Brenner has brought a taste of nouvelle cuisine to the Tegernsee, where his attractive restaurant commands fine views from high above the lake. Try any of his suggested dishes—they range from wild rabbit in elderberry sauce to fresh lake fish. German chancellor Kohl and French president Mitterrand ate well here during one of their regular summits. ✗ *Freihaushöhe 4, ☎ 08022/82004. Reservations advised. MC. $$*

LODGING

Seegarten. This lakeside hotel, with pinewood wall paneling and matching furniture, has cheerful rooms decorated in the bright primary colors typical of the Bavarian country farmhouse style. Ask for a room with a balcony overlooking Tegernsee Lake. The Seegarten's kitchen makes its own cakes, for which it is famous. ☎ *Adrian-Stoopstr. 4, ☎ 08022/81155, FAX 08022/85087. 33 rooms with bath. Restaurant. AE, V. $$$*

Margaritenhaus. This handsome Bavarian-style mansion has 25 individually designed and furnished apartments, all with their own kitchen facilities and either balconies or garden terraces, most with lake views. One (Apartment Mathilde) even has a modern, glassed-in fireplace for winter evenings. The lake and mountain slopes are just a short walk away. Also nearby are a number of Bavarian restaurants and taverns, and several hotels that have regular evenings of Bavarian zither music and dancing. ☎ *Adrian-Stoopstr. 32, ☎ and fax 089/224–591. 25 apartments. Laundry. No credit cards. $$*

Berchtesgaden

DINING

★ **Alpenhotel Denninglehen.** Nonsmokers will appreciate the special dining room set aside just for them in this mountain hotel's restaurant. The restaurant is 3,000 feet up in the resort area of Oberau, just outside Berchtesgaden, and its terrace offers magnificent views. ✗ *Am Priesterstein 7, Berchtesgaden-Oberau,* ☎ *08652/5085. Reservations advised. No credit cards. Closed Sat., and late Nov. until Dec. 25.* $$

Hotel Post. This is a centrally located and solidly reliable hostelry with a well-presented international menu. If fish from the nearby Königssee is offered, order it. In summer you can eat in the beer garden. ✗ *Maximilianstr. 2,* ☎ *08652/5067. Reservations advised. AE, DC, MC, V. Closed Tues.* $$

Fischer. You can pop into this farmhouse-style eatery for *Apfelstrudel* and coffee or for something more substantial from a frequently changing international and local menu. It's a short walk across the bridge from the railway station. ✗ *Königsseerstr. 51,* ☎ *08652/9550. Reservations advised July and Aug. MC. Closed Nov. 1–Dec. 18.* $

DINING AND LODGING

Geiger. With steeply eaved, Bavarian-green roofs that rival the dramatic mountain-peak backdrop, this hotel matches almost anyone's idea of how a German Alpine retreat should look. It stands alone on a mountain slope overlooking the town, with fine views and the forest firs creeping up to the rooms' flower-wreathed balconies. Antiques, thick Oriental rugs, hunting trophies, and old engravings complete the picture. You have a wide choice of dining rooms—from the paneled, Bavarian-style restaurant to the aptly named Biedermeier Salon or a cozy "farmer's tavern." ⌂ *Alpenkette, Stanggas,* ☎ *08652/965–555,* FAX *08652/965–400. 55 rooms with bath. 2 restaurants, bar, indoor and outdoor pools, massage, sauna, exercise room, recreation room. V. Closed mid-Nov.–mid-Dec.* $$$–$$$$

Hotel Watzmann. The USAAF Director of Operations in Berchtesgaden awarded the Hotel Watzmann a special certificate of appreciation for its hospitality to American servicemen. Today's American visitors, in turn, appreciate its cozy Bavarian style and good restaurant. Rooms were recently refurbished with Bavarian antique furniture. ⌂ *Franziskanerpl.,* ☎ *08652/2055,* FAX *08652/5174. 35 rooms, 16 with shower. Restaurant. AE, MC, V. Closed early Nov.–mid-Dec.* $

LODGING

Stolls Hotel Alpina. Set above the Königssee in the delightful little village of Schönau, the Alpina offers rural solitude and easy access to Berchtesgaden. Families are catered to: There are special family-size apartments, a resident doctor, and a playroom. ⌂ *Ulmenweg 14,* ☎ *08652/65090,* FAX *08652/61608. 44 rooms, 6 apartments with bath. Restaurant, indoor and outdoor pools, sauna, beauty salon. AE, DC, MC, V. Closed Nov. 4–Dec. 17.* $$–$$$

Hotel Wittelsbach. Bearing the name of Bavaria's former royal rulers, this is one of the oldest (built in 1892) and most traditional lodgings in the area. The cozy rooms have dark pinewood furnishings and deep red and green drapes and carpets. Ask for one with a balcony. ⌂ *Maximilianstr. 16,* ☎ *08652/96380,* FAX *08652/66304. 20 rooms, 3 apartments with bath. Restaurant. AE, DC, MC, V.* $$

Hotel Grünberger. The cozy rooms at this older-style residence have farmhouse-style furnishings and some original antiques. Only a few strides from the train station in the town center, the Grünberger overlooks the River Ache, beside which you can relax on a private sun-terrace. ⌕ *Hansererweg 1,* ☎ *08652/4560,* FAX *08652/62254. 65 rooms with bath. Restaurant, beer garden, indoor pool, sauna. No credit cards. Closed Nov.–mid-Dec. $$*

Hotel-Garni zum Türken. The view alone justifies making the 10-minute journey from Berchtesgaden to this hotel. Confiscated during World War II by the Nazis, it's located at the foot of the road up to Hitler's mountaintop retreat. Remains of Nazi wartime bunkers adjoin the hotel. ⌕ *Obersalzberg-Berchtesgaden,* ☎ *08652/2428,* FAX *08652/4710. 17 rooms, 12 with bath or shower. AE, DC, MC, V. Closed Nov. 1–Dec. 20. $*

Seehotel Gamsbock. Situated in the village of Ramsau, 7 kilometers (4 miles) west of Berchtesgaden, the Gamsbock stands directly on the banks of Hintersee Lake. It's ideal for anglers: The crystal-clear lake contains trout and saibling. Book one of the *olde worlde* balconied rooms overlooking the lake; each is furnished in the Bavarian rustic style, with ornately hand-painted wardrobes, pinewood beds, and dried flowers. ⌕ *Am See 75, Ramsau,* ☎ *08657/279 or 08657/439,* FAX *08657/748. 25 rooms, 20 with bath. Restaurant. No credit cards. $*

Chiemsee

DINING AND LODGING

Residenz Heinz Winkler. In 1991, award-winning chef Heinz Winkler moved his kitchen from Munich to the red-roof village of Aschau, 6 kilometers (4 miles) south of Chiemsee, where he converted a 300-year-old coaching inn into one of the country's most sought-after restaurants. Gourmets flock here to sample Heinz's expensive nouvelle-cuisine creations in elegant surroundings. Specialties include truffle soup, crab legs with basil, and carpaccio of beef fillet in cream sauce. The Residenz also offers individually designed guest rooms, with tasteful modern furnishings and Laura Ashley accessories. ⌕ *Kirchpl. 1,* ☎ *08052/17990,* FAX *08052/179–966. 32 rooms with bath. Restaurant, bar, café, sauna. AE, DC, V. $$$$*

Unterwirt zu Chieming. You can catch the boat to the islands of the Chiemsee right outside this small pension. Rooms are cozily furnished in traditional Bavarian style. The cheerful little restaurant serves hearty portions of such local fare as pork knuckle and potato dumplings. ⌕ *Hauptstr. 32,* ☎ *08664/551. 11 rooms with shower. No credit cards. Restaurant. The restaurant is closed Mon. and Tues., and the pension and restaurant are closed Nov. $*

LODGING

Seehotel Wassermann. The Wassermann stands in the village of Seebruck right by the mouth of the River Alz, which flows into the Chiemsee. The hotel was built in the 1980s, in the traditional style of Bavarian pine. Ask for a balconied room with a four-poster bed. ⌕ *Ludwig-Thomastr. 1,* ☎ *08667/8710,* FAX *08667/871–498. 42 rooms with bath. Restaurant, indoor pool, hot tub, sauna, steam room, boating, bicycles. AE, MC, V. $$–$$$*

Hotel Post. This historic family-run coaching inn offers reasonably priced lodging in the center of Seebruck. Rooms are simply furnished in pinewood. In summer guests can dine in the tree-shaded beer garden. The hotel sponsors Bavarian music evenings. ⌕ *Ludwig-Thomastr. 8,* ☎ *08667/8870,* FAX *08667/1343. 35 rooms with bath, 31 with shower. Beer garden. AE, MC, V. $*

Ettal

DINING AND LODGING

★ **Hotel Ludwig der Bayer.** Backed by mountains, this fine old hotel is run by the Benedictine order from across the road. But there's nothing monastic about it, except for the exquisite religious carvings and motifs that adorn the walls. The hotel also has its own Bavarian-style apartment houses equipped with individual kitchens, but its eateries would tempt even the most dedicated cook. Two atmospheric restaurants and a vaulted tavern serve sturdy Bavarian fare (the pork knuckle and dumplings fuels even the most energetic mountain-hiker for the day) and beer brewed at the monastery. Even the schnapps is distilled by the monks. ⊞ *Kaiser-Ludwig-Pl. 10–12,* ☎ *08822/6601,* FAX *08822/74480. 70 rooms with bath, 30 apartments with kitchen. 2 restaurants, 2 bars, indoor pool, sauna, tennis court, bowling, exercise room, paddle tennis, bicycles. MC, V. $$*

LODGING

Benediktenhof. The open beams and colorfully painted walls are part of this former farmstead's 250-year history. Bedrooms are furnished in Bavarian Baroque or peasant style, with brightly decorated cupboards and bedsteads. ⊞ *Zieglerstr. 1,* ☎ *08822/4637,* FAX *08822/7288. 16 rooms and 1 apartment with bath or shower. Restaurant. No credit cards. Closed Nov. 1–Dec. 22. $$*

Hotel-Gasthof Zur Post. This traditional Gasthof is in the center of town, but it has its own gardens. Its child-friendliness is also a plus: The restaurant has a children's menu, and there's a playground. ⊞ *Kaiser Ludwig Pl. 18,* ☎ *08822/3596,* FAX *08822/6971. 18 rooms and 4 apartments, most with bath or shower. Restaurant, playground. AE, DC, MC, V. Closed Oct. 26–Dec. 18. $*

Garmisch-Partenkirchen

DINING

Posthotel Partenkirchen. A 500-year-old vaulted cellar with a hand-painted ceiling is the setting for an elegant restaurant whose menu combines traditional Bavarian dishes with French and vegetarian specialties. ✕ *Ludwigstr. 49,* ☎ *08821/51067. Reservations advised. AE, DC, MC, V. $$$*

Reindl's. Named after the proprietor, this pine-paneled restaurant at the Partenkirchner Hof Hotel serves high-quality regional dishes, such as pork fillets in sour cream sauce. The chef's apple cakes in vanilla sauce are recommended. ✕ *Bahnhofstr. 15,* ☎ *08821/58025. Reservations advised. Jacket and tie. AE, DC, MC, V. $$$*

Riessersee. Situated on the shores of a tranquil, small, green lake a 3-kilometer (2-mile) walk from town, this café-restaurant is an ideal spot for lunch or afternoon tea (on weekends there's live zither music 3–5 PM). House specialties are fresh trout and local game. The Riessersee also has five comfortable rooms. ✕ *Riess 6,* ☎ *08821/95440,* FAX *08821/72589. Reservations not necessary. No credit cards. $*

DINING AND LODGING

Gasthof Fraundorfer. "Bavarian evenings"—lots of yodeling and folk dancing—are held six nights a week in the bustling restaurant of this friendly Alpine Gasthof. The Bavarian influence extends throughout the house, from the pinewood-clad public rooms to the farmhouse furnishings of the cozy bedrooms—some of which have romantic four-poster beds. ⊞ *Ludwigstr. 24,* ☎ *08821/71071,* FAX *08821/71073. 29 rooms with shower. Restaurant, sauna, steam room. AE, MC, V. $$*

★ **Grand Hotel Sonnenbichl.** This elegant, established lodging on the outskirts of Garmish offers panoramic views of the Wetterstein Mountains and the Zugspitze, but only from its front rooms —the rear rooms face a wall of rock. ☎ *Burgstr. 97,* ☎ *08821/7020,* FAX *08821/702–131. 90 rooms, 3 suites with bath. 3 restaurants, bar, indoor pool, hot tub, sauna, exercise room. AE, DC, MC, V. $$$$*

★ **Wittelsbach.** Dramatic mountain vistas from bedroom balconies and a spacious garden terrace make this hotel especially attractive. Public rooms are rustic, and the bedrooms are spacious with corner lounge areas. Ask for a room facing south for Zugspitze views. ☎ *Von-Brugstr. 24,* ☎ *08821/53096,* FAX *08821/57312. 60 rooms with bath or shower. Restaurant, piano bar, indoor pool, sauna. AE, DC, MC, V. $$$*

Edelweiss. Taking its name from the famous Alpine flower is just one way this small downtown hotel oozes mountain charm. The place is inlaid with warm pinewood, with Bavarian furnishings and primary colors to match. In summer, that other favorite Bavarian bloom—the geranium—adorns. There is no restaurant here, but there's a buffet breakfast. ☎ *Martinswinkelstr. 17,* ☎ *08821/2458,* FAX *09621/24122. 13 rooms with bath. No credit cards. $$*

Gasthof Drei Mohren. All the simple, homey comforts you'd expect of a 150-year-old Bavarian inn can be found here, in the historic Partenkirchen village. The rooms are painted in pastel colors, and most of them have pinewood furniture. The tavern and restaurant are spruced up with polished pine. ☎ *Ludwigstr. 65,* ☎ *08821/2075,* FAX *08821/18974. 24 rooms with bath. Restaurant, bar. No credit cards. $$*

Vier Jahreszeiten. This turn-of-the-century, four-story hotel, with red roof tiles and an attractive yellow stonework exterior, is in the center of town, only two minutes from the special Zugspitze train departure point. Its rooms offer a curious mix of Bavarian pinewood and Scandinavian modern furnishings; some have mountain views. ☎ *Bahnhofstr. 23,* ☎ *08821/58084,* FAX *08821/4486. 50 rooms, 45 with bath. Restaurant, beer garden. AE, DC, MC, V. $$–$$$*

Hotel Bergland. Comfortable, reasonably priced, and well located— what more could you ask of this small, traditional guest house? Great views of Zugspitze? Well, from some rooms. This hotel is in the village of Grainau, on the lower slopes of the Zugspitze, 2 kilometers (1 mile) outside Garmisch. Rooms are furnished in traditional Bavarian style, right down to the painted cupboards and headboards. The cozy lounge, with its open fireplace, is just the place to relax after a day in the mountains. ☎ *Alpspitzstrasse 14,* ☎ *08821/8509,* FAX *08821/82368. 9 rooms, 1 apartment all with bath. Restaurant, bar, café. AE, DC, M, V. $–$$*

Kochel

Arabella Brauneck Hotel. Arabella is a German chain known for its refinements, and its leading Bavarian Alpine hotel does not disappoint. Many of the rooms have views of the area's skiing region, the Brauneck, and lifts are a short walk from the hotel. The Isargrotte sauna-whirlpool "grotto" offers great après-ski relaxation. ☎ *Münchner Strasse 25,* ☎ *08042/5020,* FAX *08042/4224. 98 rooms, 7 apartments with bath. Restaurant, bar, hot tub, sauna, steam room. AE, DC, MC, V. $$$*

Alpenhotel Schmied von Kochel. The Schmied von Kochel (Blacksmith of Kochel) was a local folk hero, and the use of his name is one of several traditional touches that distinguish this 100-year-old Alpine-style hotel. A zither player can be heard most summer evenings in the restaurant. ☎ *Schlehdorferstr. 6,* ☎ *08851/9010,* FAX *08851/7331. 28 rooms with bath or shower. Restaurant, bar, café, hot tub, sauna. MC, V. $$–$$$*

Grauer Bär. The friendly atmosphere at this hotel has much to do with the family that has owned and managed it since 1905. Ask for one of the spacious, newly renovated rooms overlooking the pretty Kochelsee Lake, where the hotel also has its own stretch of private beach. ☎ *Mittenwalderstr. 82–86,* ☎ *08851/861,* FAX *08851/1607. 26 rooms, 4 apartments with bath. Restaurant, café. AE, DC, MC, V. $$*

Lenggries
DINING AND LODGING
Altwirt. The history of this former coaching inn stretches back to the 15th century. Its restaurant serves such regional specialties as venison with cranberry sauce and egg noodles; its rooms are neat and plain. ☎ *Marktstr. 13,* ☎ *08042/8085,* FAX *08042/5357. 22 rooms, 2 apartments with bath. Restaurant, sauna. No credit cards. $*

Mittenwald
DINING
Arnspitze. Get a table at the large picture window and soak in the view of the towering Karwendel Mountain range as you ponder the choices on a menu that combines the best Bavarian traditional ingredients with international flair. The fish pot-au-feu is Mediterranean in flavor and appearance, while the jugged hare in red wine is truly Bavarian. ✕ *Innsbrucker Str. 68,* ☎ *08823/2425. Reservations advised. Closed Tues., Wed. lunch, and Nov. AE. $$–$$$*

DINING AND LODGING
Alpenrose. Once part of a monastery and later given a beautiful baroque facade, the Alpenrose is one of the most handsome hotels in the area. Bedrooms and public rooms are decorated in typical Bavarian style, with lots of wood paneling, farmhouse cupboards and finely woven fabrics. The restaurant devotes the entire month of October to venison dishes, for which it has become renowned. ☎ *Obermarkt 1,* ☎ *08823/5055,* FAX *08823/3720. 18 rooms with bath. Restaurant, bar, indoor pool, sauna. AE, DC, MC, V. $$*

Post. Stagecoaches carrying travelers and mail across the Alps stopped here as far back as the 17th century. The hotel has changed a lot since then, but it still retains much of its historic charm. If you're eating, pause by the open fire in the cozy lounge-bar while you choose between the wine tavern or the low-beamed Poststüberl. The food in each is excellent, with the emphasis on hearty Bavarian fare. ☎ *Obermarkt 9,* ☎ *08823/1094,* FAX *08823/1096. 80 rooms with bath, 7 apartments. 2 restaurants, bar, indoor pool, sauna, bowling. No credit cards. $$–$$$*

LODGING
Hotel Rieger. A rustic Bavarian hotel of great charm, the Rieger boasts modern health/cure facilities and deep-pile comfort. *Dekan-Karl-Pl. 28,* ☎ *08823/5071,* FAX *08823/5662. 46 rooms with bath. Restaurant, indoor pool, hot tub, sauna, recreation room. AE, DC, MC, V. Closed mid-Oct.–Dec. 19. $$$*

Murnau

LODGING

Hotel Seidlpark. Formerly the Regina, this long-established hotel is now a member of the Best Western group and has been renamed after the park in which it stands. It's a good stopping-off point on the route between Munich and Garmisch-Partenkirchen, and from the balcony of your room you'll have a fine preview of the mountain vistas awaiting you on the rest of your journey. The rooms are luxurious. ⊞ *Seidlpark 2,* ☎ *08841/4940,* ℻ *08841/494–333. 60 rooms, 2 apartments with bath. Restaurant, bar, indoor pool, sauna, bowling. AE, DC, MC, V. $$$$*

Oberammergau

DINING

Ammergauer Stubn. A homey beer tavern in the Wittelsbach hotel, the Stubn offers a comprehensive menu that combines Bavarian specialties with international dishes. ✕ *Dorfstr. 21,* ☎ *08822/1011. Reservations advised. AE, DC, MC. Closed Tues. and Nov. 7–Dec. 10. $$*

Alte Post. You can enjoy carefully prepared local cuisine on the original pine tables in this 350-year-old inn. There's a special children's menu, and in summer meals are also served in the beer garden. ✕ *Dorfstr. 19,* ☎ *08822/1091. AE, MC, V. $*

DINING AND LODGING

Hotel Böld. A boldly painted facade and geranium-hung balconies make the Böld one of the handsomest buildings in central Oberammergau. It's a rambling, friendly house, owned by the Ring group, but still family-run—and as such keeps its old-fashioned Bavarian character. The restaurant prides itself on a menu that combines traditional fare with international cuisine. All rooms here are designed to accommodate people in wheelchairs. ⊞ *König-Ludwig-Str. 10,* ☎ *08822/3021,* ℻ *08822/7102. 57 rooms with bath. Restaurant, beer garden, hot tub, sauna, steam room, exercise room, paddle tennis, bicycles. $$$*

LODGING

Parkhotel Sonnenhof. Away from the sometimes crowded town center, at the modern Sonnenhof you can sun yourself on your bedroom balcony (every room has one) and soak up the Alpine view. There's a children's playroom. ⊞ *König-Ludwigstr. 12,* ☎ *08822/1071,* ℻ *08822/3047. 70 rooms with bath. Restaurant, bar, indoor pool, sauna, bowling. AE, DC, MC, V. $$$*

★ **Hotel Wolf.** Americans in particular value this attractive old hotel—about 30% of guests are from the United States. Blue shutters punctuate its white walls; the steeply gabled upper stories bloom with flowers. The hotel's Hafner Stube is a popular local haunt. ⊞ *Dorfstr. 1,* ☎ *08822/3071,* ℻ *08822/1096. 32 rooms with bath. Restaurant, café, 2 bars, outdoor pool, sauna. AE, DC, MC, V. $$–$$$*

Hotel Turmwirt. Rich wood paneling reaches from floor to ceiling in this transformed 18th-century inn, located in the shadow of Oberammergau's mountain, the Kofel. The hotel's own band presents regular Bavarian folk evenings. Rooms have corner lounge areas, and most come with balconies and sweeping mountain views. ⊞ *Ettalerstr. 2,* ☎ *08822/3091,* ℻ *08822/1437. 22 rooms with bath. Restaurant, recreation room. AE, DC, MC, V. Closed most of Jan. and Nov.–mid-Dec. $$–$$$*

Landhaus Feldmeier. This quiet country-style hotel, built in 1990, has mostly spacious rooms decorated with modern pinewood furniture. It's only a five-minute walk from the town center. ⊞ *Ettalerstr. 29,* ☎

08822/3011, FAX *08822/6631. 22 rooms with bath. Restaurant, hot tub, sauna, steam room. AE, V. $$–$$$*

Reit im Winkl

DINING

Kupferkanne. Outside, a garden surrounds the building; inside, you could be in an Alpine farmstead. The food is good country fare enhanced by some interesting Austrian specialties. Try the *Salzburger Brez'n,* a thick, creamy bread-based soup. ✕ *Weitseestr. 18,* ☎ *08640/1450. Reservations advised. No credit cards. Closed Sat. and Nov. $$*

DINING AND LODING

Landgasthof Rosi Mittermaier. Rosi Mittermaier, skiing star of the 1976 Innsbruck Olympics, runs this charming Bavarian Gasthof with her husband, Christian Neureuther, a champion skier himself. If you're here to hit the slopes, then you're in good hands—Rosi was skiing the runs here practically before she could walk. In summer, she and Christian are also on hand with advice on the trails to surrounding mountains. The Gasthof only has eight large apartments, so it's essential to book in advance. But even if you're not staying, a visit to its rustic Cafe Olympia or cozy, pine-paneled tavern-restaurant is recommended. The duck dishes are a specialty of the house, and the *Käsekuchen* here is legendary. ⌧ *Chiemseestr. 2a,* ☎ *08640/1011,* FAX *08640/1013. 8 apartments. 2 restaurants, café, sauna. AE, DC, MC, V. $$*

Rosenheim

DINING AND LODGING

Goldener Hirsch. Rooms maintain a high standard of comfort in this central and established hotel in the heart of Rosenheim. It's an ideal place from which to explore the Alpine region, and in the car-free streets around the hotel you'll find a wealth of restaurants and taverns. The hotel's restaurant has a large menu that combines local dishes (roast pork and dumplings, Bavarian sausage) with international specialties. ⌧ *Münchnerstr. 40,* ☎ *08031/21290,* FAX *08031/212–949. 23 rooms with bath. Restaurant. AE, DC, MC, V. $$*

Rottach-Egern

DINING

★ **Weinhaus Moschner.** You're pretty much expected to drink wine in this dark old tavern on the edge of fashionable, ritzy Rottach Egern. Beer, from the monastery brewery across the lake in Tegernsee, is also served, and the smiling waitresses probably won't protest if you order it. The menu sticks to local Bavarian fare (heavy on the sausage), but nobody comes here just to eat. Join the locals at a rough wood table in the log-walled tavern tap room, order a plate of smoked pork and a glass of ale or Franconian wine, and leave the fine dining until tomorrow—it's the camaraderie and atmosphere here that counts. Under-thirties will love the first-floor disco, although the charm of the lederhosen-clad locals may distract you. ✕ *Kisslinger Str. 2,* ☎ *08022/5522. No credit cards. Closed Mon.–Tues., Dec. 25, and Jan. 1. $*

DINING AND LODGING

Bachmair Weissach. This traditional hotel has been in the same family since it was constructed in 1864; its rooms are pleasantly furnished in Bavarian-farmhouse style. Ask for one overlooking the little Weissach stream. The lodging's Gourmet Restaurant, decorated with flowers, paintings, and mirrors, offers updated versions of regional dishes, such as veal steak and mushrooms with black-cherry sorbet. ⊞ *Tegernseerstr. 103,* ☎ *08022/2710,* FAX *08022/67240. 51 rooms with bath. Restaurant, bar, indoor pool, beauty salon, massage, sauna, tennis courts. AE, DC, MC, V. $$$*

Ruhpolding

DINING

Zur Post. Look for the Zur Post sign in any Bavarian town or village and you can be confident of good local fare. In business for more than 650 years, Ruhpolding's has been in the hands of the same family for 150 of those years. It is also possible to obtain lodging here; call beforehand for room reservations. ✗ *Hauptstr. 35,* ☎ *08663/1035,* FAX *08663/1483. No reservations. MC. Closed Mon. $$*

Schliersee

DINING AND LODGING

Schlierseer Hof am See. You can eat and sleep well in this modern, traditional-style, lakeside hostelry with many facilities. The restaurant concentrates on local fish (ask for *Renke,* a delicate white fish from the lake) and game (if it's being offered, try the braised venison in the rich house sauce). Rooms are fashioned with pinewood and bright check fabrics. ⊞ *Seestr. 21,* ☎ *08026/4071,* FAX *08206/4953. 43 rooms, 3 apartments. Restaurant, weinstube, outdoor pool, sauna, boating. AE, DC, MC, V. $$–$$$*

Spitzingsee

DINING AND LODGING

★ **Arabella Alpenhotel.** For an out-of-the-way break in the mountains, head for this modern motel on the banks of the small and quiet Spitzingsee Lake. Rooms are decorated with modern Scandinavian furnishings. If you can't stay overnight, come for a leisurely lunch of lake fish or a vegetarian meal. In winter the frozen lake is used for ice sports. ⊞ *Seeweg 7,* ☎ *08026/7980,* FAX *08026/798–879. 120 rooms with bath. Restaurant, indoor pool, sauna, steam room, exercise room, tennis courts, bowling alley, boating, library. AE, DC, MC, V. $$$$*

Tegernsee

DINING

Der Leeberghof. This gentrified country restaurant offers traditional Bavarian cooking with flair and panoramic views. Try chef Michael Hamburger's jellied duck with plums, or vegetable-stuffed pork and fried potato cakes. An alternative to dessert might be goat cheese and coriander bread. On warm evenings take an aperitif or an after-dinner Bavarian schnapps on the bar-terrace above the lake—the view will root you to the spot. If you really have problems leaving, the Leeberghof has six luxurious guest rooms. ✗ *Ellingerstr. 10,* ☎ *08022/3966. Reservations advised. MC. $$$*

Seehotel Zur Post. This is another lakeside hotel-restaurant, with a fine winter garden and terrace. Fresh lake fish is recommended, but the hotel also has special venison weeks that are worth a long detour to catch. ✗ *Seestr. 3,* ☎ *08022/3951. Reservations advised. DC, MC, V. Closed Jan.–Feb. 15. $$*

★ **Herzogliches Bräustuberl.** Once a monastery, then a royal retreat, the Bräustuberl is now a beer hall and brewery popular with locals. Only basic Bavarian snacks (sausages, pretzels, a deliciously marshmallow-like baked Camembert) is served in this crowded place, but hearty Bavarian meals can be ordered in the adjoining Keller. In summer, quaff it beneath the huge chestnuts and admire the lake and mountains over the rim of your glass. ✕ *Schlosspl. 1,* ☎ *08022/4516. No reservations. No credit cards. Closed Nov. $*

Urfeld

DINING AND LODGING

Post Hotel. Traditional local fare becomes memorable when sampled in this old coach inn on the banks of the Walchensee. On warm days you can dine outside and watch the Windsurfers glide by. Specialties include Bavarian lake perch pike. Moderately priced rooms are available, as are lakeside apartments in a modern annex. ☎ *8111 Urfeld,* ☎ *08851/249,* FAX *08851/5067. No credit cards. $*

Waging am See

DINING

★ **Kurhausstüberl.** The southeastern corner of Bavaria was a backwater before the Kurhausstüberl's fame spread. Award-winning chef Alfons Schubeck bases his nouvelle cuisine on solid Bavarian foundations, revealing the possibilities of a tiny lake fish that anglers usually throw back, and making soups from cress and side dishes from wild asparagus. Look out for the leg of venison, too. ✕ *Am See,* ☎ *08681/4666. Reservations required. AE, DC, MC, V. Dinner only. Closed Mon., Tues., Jan., and 2 wks of Oct. $$$$*

THE ARTS AND NIGHTLIFE

The Arts

Concerts

Every summer, **Schloss Hohenaschau,** regarded as one of the finest castles of southern Germany, hosts a series of chamber concerts in its courtyard, its chapel, and its impressive banquet hall. Contact the Kurverwaltung (D–83229 Aschau im Chiemgau, ☎ 08052/392) for program details and reservations. King Ludwig's fantastic **Schloss Neuschwanstein** is the scene every September of a short season of chamber-music concerts, presented in the richly decorated minstrels' hall. (It was here that Ludwig hoped to stage concerts of music by his lifelong hero, Richard Wagner, an ambition that, like so many of the doomed monarch's aims, remained unfulfilled.) Contact the Schlossverwaltung Neuschwanstein (D–87645 Hohenschwangau, ☎ 08362/81035) for details and tickets.

Bavarian folk music and dancing are performed on Saturday evenings during the summer in the **Bayernhalle** (Brauhausstr. 19, Garmisch-Partenkirchen). Concerts of classical and popular music are presented Saturday through Thursday, mid-May through September, in the resort park bandstand in Garmisch, and on Friday in the Partenkirchen resort park.

Bad Reichenhall's own symphony orchestra offers regular concerts throughout the year at the town's theater in the **Kurgastzentrum,** where operettas and chamber music evenings are also staged. For program details, call 08651/60651.

Theater

Both **Berchtesgaden** and **Garmisch-Partenkirchen** have entertaining *Bauerntheaters* (folklore theaters). A working knowledge of German helps if you plan a visit. Berchtesgaden's theater company (Franziskanerpl., ☎ 08652/2858) has daily performances in summer and performs Thursday through Sunday in winter (except from November to December 25). The Garmisch-Partenkirchen company (Rassensaal, Ludwigstr. 45) performs less frequently. Call 08821/55598 for program details.

Nightlife

There are **casinos** in Garmisch-Partenkirchen (☎ 08821/53099), Bad Reichenhall (☎ 08651/4091), and Bad Wiessee (☎ 08022/82028). They are state-run, and the same regulations apply to all of them. You'll need your passport to get in, and you must be respectably dressed (jacket and tie). These establishments are open daily from 3 PM to 3 AM.

In all resorts there's a surprisingly lively after-dark scene. Garmisch-Partenkirchen is famed for its après-ski revelries, but even in quiet spas such as Bad Wiessee there are clusters of discos and singles bars. Rottach-Egern, also on the shores of the Tegernsee Lake, has an international-class nightclub (in the Hotel Bachmaier am See, Seestr. 47). Farther around the lake, the Leeberghof, on the edge of Tegernsee town (Ellingerstr. 10), has a sensational terrace-bar with prices to match, inclusive of one of Bavaria's finest views.

THE BAVARIAN ALPS ESSENTIALS

Arriving and Departing

By Bus
The Alpine region is not well served by long-distance bus services. The southern section of the Europabus route, along the Romantische Strasse (Romantic Road), connects Frankfurt, Wiesbaden, Würzburg, Munich, and Augsburg with the resorts of Schongau and Füssen (*see* Chapter 8). Seat reservations, which are obligatory, can be made through **Deutsche Touring GmbH** (Am Römerhof 17. D–60486 Frankfurt/Main 90, ☎ 069/790–3240). Many travel agents—ABR in Bavaria, for instance—can also make reservations.

By Car
Three Autobahns reach deep into the Bavarian Alps: A–7 coming in from the northwest (Frankfurt, Stuttgart, Ulm) to Füssen; A–95 from Munich to Garmisch; and A–8 from Munich to Salzburg, for Berchtesgaden. All provide speedy access to the Alpine foothills, where they connect with a comprehensive network of well-paved country roads that penetrate high into the mountains. (Germany's highest road runs through Berchtesgaden at more than 5,000 feet.)

By Plane
Munich, 95 kilometers (60 miles) northwest of Garmisch-Partenkirchen, is the main airport for the Bavarian Alps. There is easy access from Munich to the Autobahns that lead to the Alps (*see* Arriving and Departing by Car, *above*). If you're staying in Berchtesgaden at the east end of the Alps, the airport at Salzburg in Austria is closer but has fewer international flights.

By Train
Garmisch-Partenkirchen and Mittenwald are on the InterCity network, which has regular direct service to all regions of the country. (Klais, just outside Garmisch, is Germany's highest InterCity train station.)

Bad Reichenhall and Berchtesgaden are linked directly to north German cities by the FD (Fern-Express) "long-distance express" service.

Getting Around

By Boat

Passenger boats operate on all the major Bavarian lakes. They're mostly excursion boats and many run only in summer. However, there's an important year-round service on the Chiemsee that links the mainland with the islands of Herreninsel and Fraueninsel. Four boats on the Starnbergersee and four on the Ammersee (including a fine old paddle steamer) make round-trips of the lake several times a day (Apr.–Oct.) leaving from Starnberg and Stegen/Inning. Eight boats operate year-round on the Tegernsee, connecting Tegernsee town, Rottach-Egern, Bad Wiessee, and Gmund, from which a regular train service runs to Munich. A fleet of 21 silent, electrically driven boats glides through the waters of the Königssee near Berchtesgaden to the most remote of Bavaria's lakes, the Obersee.

By Bus

Villages not served by train are connected by post bus. This is a fun and inexpensive way to get around, but service is slow and irregular. Larger resorts operate buses to outlying areas.

By Car

The Deutsche Alpenstrasse, not a continuous highway but a series of roads, runs from Lindau in the west to the Austrian border beyond Berchtesgaden in the east, skirting the northern edge of the Alps for most of the way before heading deep into the mountains on the final stretch between Inzell and Berchtesgaden. Another route, the so-called Blaue Route (Blue Route), follows the valleys of the Inn and Salzach rivers along the German-Austrian border above Salzburg. This off-the-beaten-track territory includes three quiet lakes: the Tachingersee, the Wagingersee, and the Abstdorfersee. They are the warmest bodies of water in Upper Bavaria, ideal for family vacations. At Wasserburg, on the Inn River, southeast of Munich, you can join the final section of the Deutsche Ferienstrasse (German Holiday Road), another combination of roads that run on to Traunstein, east of Chiemsee, and then into the Alps. The Chiemsee and four other popular lakes—Tegernsee, Schliersee, Starnbergersee and Ammersee—are within easy reach of Munich by Autobahn.

CAR RENTAL

Avis: Hindenburgstrasse 35, ☎ 08821/55066, **Garmisch-Partenkirchen;** Nymphenburgerstr. 61, ☎ 089/126–0020, **Munich.**

Europcar: St. Martin-Str. 6, ☎ 08821/50168, **Garmisch-Partenkirchen;** Hirtenstr. 14, ☎ 089/557–145, **Munich.**

Hertz: Zugspitzstrasse 81, ☎ 08821/18787, **Garmisch-Partenkirchen;** Nymphenburger-Strasse 81, ☎ 089/129–5001, **Munich.**

Sixt-Budget: Bergwerkstr. 89, ☎ 08652/66591, **Berchtesgaden;** Seitzstrasse 9, ☎ 089/223–333, **Munich.**

By Train

Most Alpine resorts are connected with Munich by regular express and slower services. Munich's S-bahn (suburban service) extends as far as two lakes, the Starnbergersee and the Ammersee, where the Alpine foothills really begin.

Guided Tours

Bus tours to King Ludwig II's castles at Neuschwanstein and Linderhof and to the Ettal monastery near Oberammergau are offered by the **ABR** travel agencies in Garmisch-Partenkirchen (☎ 08821/55125) and Oberammergau (☎ 08822/1021 or 4771). Tours to Neuschwanstein, Linderhof, Ettal, and into the neighboring Austrian Tyrol are also offered by a number of other Garmisch travel agencies: **Hans Biersack** (☎ 08821/4920), **Heinz Karrasch** (☎ 08821/2111), **Dominikus Kümmerle** (☎ 08821/4955), **Hilmar Röser** (☎ 08821/2926), and **Weiss-Blau–Reisen**(☎ 08821/3766). The Garmisch mountain railway company, the **Bayerische Zugspitzbahn** (☎ 08821/58058) offers special excursions to the top of the Zugspitze, Germany's highest mountain, by cog rail and/or cable car (*see* Tour 1 *in* Exploring, *above*). **Deutsche Bahn** (German Railways; ☎ 089/598–484 or 0821/19419) offers special excursion fares from Munich and Augsburg to the top of the Zugspitze. In Berchtesgaden, the **Schwaiger** bus company (☎ 08652/2525) offers bus tours of the area and across the Austrian border as far as Salzburg.

Important Addresses and Numbers

Visitor Information

The Bavarian regional tourist office in Munich, **FVV München Oberbayern** (Sonnenstr. 10, D–80331 Munich, ☎ 089/597–347), provides general information about Upper Bavaria and the Bavarian Alps. There are local tourist information offices in the following towns:

Bad Reichenhall: Kur-und-Verkehrsverein, im Kurgastzentrum, Wittelsbacherstr. 15, D–83435 Bad Reichenhall, ☎ 08651/3003.

Bad Tölz: Kurverwaltung, Ludwigstrasse 11, D–83646 Bad Tölz, ☎ 08041/70071.

Bayerischzell: Kuramt, Kirchplatz 2, D–83735 Bayerischzell, ☎ 08023/648.

Berchtesgaden: Kurdirektion, Königseerstrasse 2, D–83463 Berchtesgaden, ☎ 08652/9670.

Garmisch-Partenkirchen: Verkehrsamt der Kurverwaltung, Richard-Strauss-Platz 2, D–82467 Garmisch-Partenkirchen, ☎ 08821/1806.

Mittenwald: Kurverwaltung, Dammkarstrasse 3, D–82481 Mittenwald, ☎ 08823/33981.

Oberammergau: Verkehrsamt, Eugen-Papst-Strasse 9a, D–82487 Oberammergau, ☎ 08822/1021.

Prien am Chiemsee: Kurverwaltung, Alter Rathausstr. 11, D–83209 Prien, ☎ 08051/69050.

Reit im Winkl: Verkehrsamt, Rathausplatz 1, D–83242 Reit im Winkl, ☎ 08640/80020.

Rottach-Egern/Tegernsee: Kuramt, Hauptstrasse 2, D–83684 Tegernsee, ☎ 08022/180–140.

4 The Bodensee

If you're in the area, be sure to take at least one boat trip on the Bodensee, the largest lake in the German-speaking world. Some towns are built on islands near the shore, and their incredible beauty is best surveyed from the water. Other features of the area appreciated by tourists are its climate, which allows near-tropical growth in places, and its proximity to Switzerland and Liechtenstein. Konstanz, the largest city on the lake, is German but has parts in Switzerland.

THE BODENSEE (Lake Constance) is the largest lake in the German-speaking world—424 kilometers square, 339 kilometers around (163 miles square, 210 miles around)—and is bordered by Germany, Switzerland, and Austria. It's called a lake, but actually it's a vast swelling of the Rhine, gouged out by a massive glacier in the Ice Age and flooded by the river as the ice receded. The Rhine flows into its southeast corner, where Switzerland and Austria meet, and flows out at its west end.

Visitors should be grateful: These immense natural forces have created a ravishing corner of Germany, a natural summer playground, ringed with little towns and busy resorts. Gentle, vineyard-clad hills slope down to the lakeshore. To the south, the Alps are a jagged and dramatic backdrop. It's one of the warmest areas of the country, too, the result not just of its location—it's almost the southernmost region of Germany—but of the warming influence of the water, which gathers heat in the summer and releases it in the winter like a massive radiator. There are near-tropical corners of the Bodensee, where lemons, bougainvillea, and hibiscus flourish and vines grow in abundance. The lake itself practically never freezes (it has done so only once this century and twice during the last).

R&R may be the major reason for visiting the Bodensee, but it's by no means the only one. The natural attractions of the lake, not least its abundance of fresh fish and its fertile soil, were as compelling several thousand years ago as they are today, making this one of the oldest continually inhabited areas of Germany. Highlights include the medieval island town of Lindau; Friedrichshafen, birthplace of the zeppelin; the Rococo abbey church of Birnau; and the town of Konstanz on the Swiss-German border. It would be a shame, too, once you're at the Bodensee, not to take advantage of the area's proximity to Austria and Switzerland (and to little Liechtenstein). A day trip to one or more is easy to make, and formalities are few.

EXPLORING

Tour 1: Lindau and Environs

Numbers in the margin correspond to points of interest on the Bodensee map.

❶ The showpiece of the Bodensee is **Lindau,** located at the southeastern part of the lake just a mile or two from the Austrian border. Lindau is an island town, tethered to the shore by a 210-yard causeway. Stand at the water's edge in its newer, mainland section, the so-called Gartenstadt (Garden Town—referring to its abundance of flowers and shrubs), on a hazy summer's day and the walls and roofs of old Lindau seem to float on the shimmering water, an illusion intensified by the miragelike backdrop of the Alps.

Lindau was originally three islands, on one of which the Romans built a military base. Under the Romans, the islands developed first as a fishing settlement, then as a trading center along the route connecting the rich lands of Swabia to the north with Italy. (It was a role that continued for hundreds of years: The Lindauer Bote, one of the most important stagecoach services between Germany and Italy in the 18th and 19th centuries, was based here—Goethe traveled on it on his first visit to Italy in 1786.) In 1275 little Lindau was made a Free Imperial City

The Bodensee (Lake Constance)

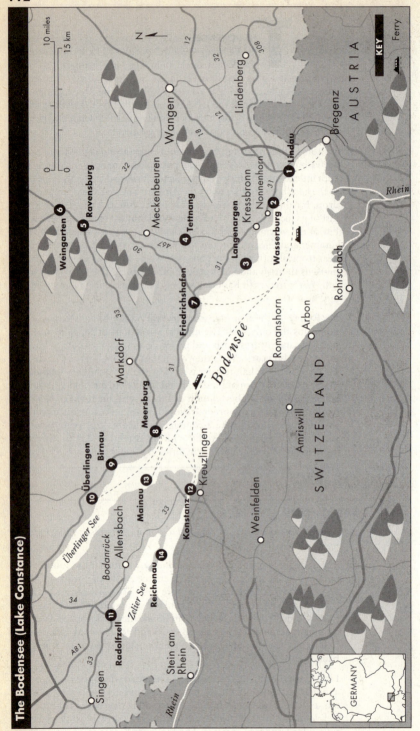

KEY

Ferry

N

10 miles
15 km

GERMANY

AUSTRIA

Bregenz

Lindau **1**

Rhein

Rohrschach

Arbon

Romanshorn

SWITZERLAND

Amriswill

Weinfelden

Kreuzlingen

Konstanz **12**

Stein am Rhein

Rhein

Radolfzell **11**

Singen

A81

34

Zeller See

Reichenau **14**

Bodanrück

Allensbach

Mainau **13**

Überlinger See

Überlingen **10**

Birnau **9**

Meersburg **8**

Markdorf

33

31

Bodensee

Friedrichshafen **7**

Weingarten **6**

Ravensburg **5**

30

467

31

Tettnang **4**

3

Wasserburg **2**

Langenargen

Kressbronn

Nonnenhorn

Meckenbeuren

Wangen

32

18

21

32

12

308

Lindenberg

33

33

within the Holy Roman Empire. As the Empire crumbled toward the end of the 18th century, battered by Napoléon's revolutionary armies, Lindau fell victim to competing political groups. It was ruled by the Austrian Empire before passing into Bavarian rule in 1805.

The proud symbol of Bavaria, a **seated lion,** is one of Lindau's striking landmarks. The lion in question, 20 feet high and carved from Bavarian marble, stares out across the lake from a massive plinth at the end of one of the harbor walls. At the end of the facing wall there's a lighthouse, the **Neuer Leuchtturm.** You can climb up to its viewing platform for a look out over the waters. On a clear day you'll see the Three Sisters, three peaks in Liechtenstein. ☞ *DM 1 adults, 50 pf children..* ⊙ *Apr.–Oct., daily 9:30–6.*

The **Alter Leuchtturm,** or old lighthouse, stands at the edge of the inner harbor on the weathered remains of the original 13th-century city walls.

From the harbor, plunge into the maze of ancient streets that make up the Altstadt (the Old Town). Eventually they all lead to the **Altes Rathaus** (Old Town Hall), the finest of Lindau's handsome historical buildings. It was constructed between 1422 and 1436 in the midst of a vineyard (that's now a busy thoroughfare) and given a Renaissance face-lift 150 years later, though the original stepped gables remain. The emperor Maximilian I held an imperial council here in 1496; a fresco on the south facade depicts a scene from this high point of local history. Part of the building served as the town prison. An ancient inscription, enjoining the townsfolk "to turn aside from evil and learn to do good," identifies it.

Face away from the town hall and walk down to the **Barfüsserkirche,** the Church of the Barefoot Pilgrims. Built from 1241 to 1270, it has for many years been Lindau's principal theater. The Gothic choir is a memorable location for concerts, especially of church music. The tourist office on Bahnhofplatz can provide details of performances.

Continue along Ludwigstrasse to Fischergasse, where you'll find a watchtower, once part of the original city walls. Pause in the little park behind it, the **Stadtgarten.** If it's early evening, you'll see the first gamblers of the night making for the neighboring casino.

Lindau's market square, Marktplatz, is just around the corner. A series of sturdily attractive old buildings line it, among them the 18th-century **Haus zum Cavazzen,** richly decorated with stucco and frescoes. Today it's the municipal art gallery and local history museum. *Am Marktpl.* ☞ *DM 3 adults, DM 1 children.* ⊙ *Apr.–Oct., Tues.–Sun. 10–noon and 2–5.*

The simple, sparely decorated Gothic Stephanskirche and the more elaborate, Baroque Marienkirche stand on Marktplatz. Both have charm—the Stephanskirche for its simplicity, the Marienkirche for its exuberance.

From Marktplatz, walk along pedestrian-only **Maximilianstrasse,** the main street of the Old Town, distinguished by half-timbered and gabled old houses.

TIME OUT The **Weinstube Frey** is a 16th-century wine tavern. Try fresh lake fish and a crisp white Bodensee wine for an excellent lunch. Smoked ham from the Black Forest is also a specialty. *Maximilianstr. 15.*

Turn right off Maximilianstrasse down cobbled Schafsgasse to reach the **Peterskirche** on Schrannenplatz. It's a solid Romanesque building, constructed in the 10th century and reputedly the oldest church in the Bodensee region. Step inside to see the frescoes by Hans Holbein the Elder (1465–1524). A number depict scenes from the life of St. Peter, the patron saint of fishermen and thus an important figure to the inhabitants of Lindau.

From Lindau, head west along the lake. The first attraction you'll reach is **Wasserburg,** 6 kilometers (4 miles) away. It's a sort of Lindau in miniature, actually situated *in* the lake, at the end of a narrow causeway. *Wasserburg* means "water castle," describing exactly what this enchanting town once was—a fortress built on the site of a Roman watchtower. The original owners, the counts of Montfort zu Tettnang, sold it to the Fugger family of Augsburg to pay off mounting debts. When, in the 18th century, the Fuggers fell on hard times, the castle passed into the hands of the Hapsburgs. In 1805 it was taken over by the Bavarian government.

The Fuggers, when they bought Wasserburg, were among the richest families in Europe. During the final days of their ownership, they were so impoverished that they couldn't even afford to pay for the upkeep of the drawbridge that connected the castle with the shore. Instead they built a causeway. Cars aren't allowed into Wasserburg these days, and one of the pleasures here is to wander undisturbed through the tangle of ancient streets. The castle itself is now the Schloss Hotel Wasserburg (Hauptstr. 5, ☎ 08382/887–588, FAX 08382/8141), a surprisingly reasonably priced accommodation.

The most unusual castle in the region stands at the water's edge in **Langenargen,** 8 kilometers (5 miles) west. **Montfort Castle**—it was named for the original owners, the counts of Montfort-Werdenberg—was a conventional enough medieval fortification until it was rebuilt in the 19th century in pseudo-Moorish style by its new owner, King Wilhelm I of Württemberg. If you can, see it from a steamer on the lake: The castle is especially memorable in the early morning or late afternoon, when the softened, watery light gives additional mystery to its outline. These days, very unromantically, the castle houses local government offices and *is not* open to the public. Its tower, however, can be climbed. ☺ *Easter–Oct., daily 9–5.* ☛ *DM 1.50. adults.*

Langenargen is worth visiting to see its Marktplatz, site of a Baroque parish church and the town museum. The museum contains a series of paintings by German painter Hans Purrmann (1880–1966), an admirer of Henri Matisse and cofounder of the Academie Matisse in Paris in 1908. The academy faltered soon after it was founded, and between 1915 and 1935 (at which point Purrmann's work was outlawed by the Nazis), he lived in Langenargen. The museum may appeal only to those with an advanced taste for lesser-known 20th-century painting. *Marktpl. 20.* ☛ *DM 3.* ☺ *Apr.–Oct., Tues.–Sun. 10–noon and 2:30–5. Closed Mon.*

Tour 2: Tettnang, Ravensburg, and Weingarten

Leave the lake now and head north 12 kilometers (8 miles) on B–467 to the little town of **Tettnang,** former ancestral home of the counts of Montfort zu Tettnang. By 1780 the dynasty had fallen on such hard times that it sold the entire town to the Hapsburgs. Twenty-five years later it passed to the Bavarian Wittelsbachs. You'll want to visit principally to see what remains of its extravagant Baroque palace, the Neues Schloss. It was built in the early 18th century, burned down in 1753, and then partially rebuilt before the family's finances ran dry. Enough remains, however, to give some idea of the Montforts' former wealth and ostentatious lifestyle. ☎ 0751/403–418. ☛ DM 1 adults, 50 pf children. ☉ Apr.–Oct., daily 10–5.

TIME OUT The last of the Montfort line, Count Anton IV, spent his declining years in a modest house in the town, now the **Gasthof Krone.** The inn has its own brewery, and you can try its excellent beer in the parlor where Count Anton dreamed of former glories. If you visit in late spring, order up one of the asparagus dishes: Tettnang is one of Germany's leading asparagus-growing centers. *Bärenpl.*

5 Thirteen kilometers (8 miles) north of Tettnang on B–467, then B–30, is **Ravensburg,** an attractive city that once competed with Augsburg and Nürnberg for economic supremacy in southern Germany. It proved an uneven contest. The Thirty Years' War finally put an end to Ravensburg's remaining hopes of economic leadership; after the war, the city was reduced to little more than a medieval backwater. The city's loss proved fortuitous only in that many of its original features have remained much as they were when built. Fourteen of the town gates and towers survive, for example, and the Altstadt (the Old Town) is among the best preserved in Germany. Leave your car at the Untertor gate and explore the city on foot—cars are banned from the Old Town. Head down Bachstrasse and you'll come to one of Ravensburg's most interesting churches, the former **Karmelitenklosterkirche,** once part of a 14th-century monastery and now a Protestant church. Ecclesiastical and commercial life were never entirely separate in medieval towns such as Ravensburg. The stairs on the west side of the chancel in the church, for example, lead to the former meeting room of the Ravensburger Gesellschaft (the Ravensburg Society), an organization of linen merchants established in 1400 to direct trade of the product that was largely responsible for the town's rapid economic growth.

The adjacent Marienplatz Square has many old buildings that recall Ravensburg's wealthy years: the late-Gothic **Rathaus,** with a picturesque Renaissance bay window; the 14th-century **Kornhaus,** once the corn exchange for the entire Upper Swabia; the 15th-century **Waaghaus,** the town's weighing station and central warehouse, incorporating a tower where the watchman had his lookout; and the colorfully frescoed **Lederhaus,** once the headquarters of the leather workers.

TIME OUT Traffic-free Marienplatz is lined with historic facades. They front a variety of inns whose signs announce a welcome to thirsty visitors, with **Am Kornhaus** (Marienplatz 8) and the **Bierkanne** (Marienplatz 48) among the friendliest. Step into either traditional interior for a taste of true Bodensee cooking. Ask for wine from any of the Bodensee vineyards or for the Ravensburg-brewed beer.

One of the city's defensive towers is visible from Marienplatz, the **Grüner Turm** (Green Tower), so called because of its green tiles; many are the 14th-century originals. Walk past the Grüner Turm and the neighboring Frauenturm to the **Liebfrauenkirche** (Church of Our Lady). It, too, is a 14th-century structure, elegantly simple on the outside but almost entirely rebuilt inside. Some of the original stained glass remains, however, as does the heavily gilded altar. Seek out the *Ravensburger Schutzmantelmadonna,* a copy of the 15th-century original that's now in Berlin's Dahlem Museum.

A short walk southeast of the Liebfrauenkirche is the massive **Obertor,** the oldest gate in the city walls. This was once one of Ravensburg's most secure defensive positions. From it you can see another of the city's towers, the **Mehlsack,** or Flour Sack tower (because of its bulk and the original whitewash exterior), 170 feet high and standing on the highest point of the city. If you can stand the 240-step climb, head up to the summit for the view south to the Bodensee and the Alps. ☛ *Free.* ☯ *Mid-Mar.–mid-Oct., 3rd Sun. of the month only, 10–noon.*

Five kilometers (3 miles) north of Ravensburg on B–30 is the pilgrimage town of **Weingarten,** which at 220 feet high and more than 300 feet long is the site of the largest Baroque church in Germany. It's the church of one of the oldest and most venerable convents in the country, founded in 1056 by the wife of Guelph II. (The Guelph dynasty ruled large areas of Upper Swabia.) Generations of Guelphs lie buried in the Weingarten basilica. The reason the majestic basilica was built is centers around the little vial it possesses, said to contain drops of Christ's blood. First mentioned by Charlemagne, the vial passed to the convent in 1094, entrusted to its safe keeping by the Guelph Queen Juditha, sister-in-law of William the Conqueror. At a stroke Weingarten became one of Germany's foremost places of pilgrimage. On the Friday after Ascension, the anniversary of the day the relic was entrusted to the convent, a huge procession of pilgrims, headed by 2,000 horsemen (many local farmers breed horses just for this procession) wends its way to the basilica. It was decorated by some of the leading German and Austrian artists of the early 18th century, with stucco by Franz Schmuzer, ceiling frescoes by Cosmas Damian Asam, and an altar— one of the most breathtakingly ornate in Europe; the towers on either side— by Donato Frisoni—are nearly 80 feet high. The organ, installed between 1737 and 1750, is among the largest in the country.

Weingarten achieved additional recognition in the '50s, when archaeologists discovered hundreds of Alemann graves from the 6th, 7th, and 8th centuries just outside the town. If you want to learn about these early Germans, visit the **Alemannenmuseum** in the Kornhaus, at one time a granary. *Karlstr. 28.* ☛ *Free.* ☯ *Wed. and weekends 3–5. Closed Feb. and Nov.*

Tour 3: Friedrichshafen and Meersburg

The road back to the lake, B–30, takes you to **Friedrichshafen,** named for its founder, King Friedrich I of Württemberg. It's a young town (1811) that was almost wiped off the map by wartime air raids on its munitions factories. Curious though it may seem in an area otherwise given over to resort towns and agriculture, Friedrichshafen played a central role in Germany's aeronautic tradition, a tradition that saw the development of the zeppelin airship before World War I and the Dornier flying boat in the '20s and '30s. In both cases, it was the broad, smooth waters of the lake that made Friedrichshafen attractive to the pioneer airmen: The zeppelins were built in enormous floating hangars on the lake; the Dorniers were tested on its calm surface. The story of the zeppelins is fascinating. If you're interested, head to the **Zeppelin–Museum Technik und Kunst,** where the whole unlikely tale is told in detail, complete with models—one 26 feet long—plans, photographs, and documents (*see also* the Dornier Museum in Meersburg, *below*). In 1995, the museum was being moved from its location at Adenauerplatz 1 to a special wing of the Hafenbahnhof (harbor railway station), where it was scheduled to reopen in July 1996. The part of the old museum relating the zeppelin story is open until the spring of 1996. ☛ *Free.* ☯ *Daily 10–noon and 2–5. Closed Feb.*

From either museum location it's a short walk along the lakeside promenade to Friedrichshafen's **Schloss Hofen,** a small palace that served as the summer residence of the kings of Württemberg until 1918. The palace was formerly a priory—its foundations date from the 11th century—and the adjoining priory church is a splendid example of local Baroque architecture. The swirling white stucco of the interior was executed by the Wessobrun Schmuzer family, whose master craftsman, Franz, was responsible for much of the finest work in the basilica of Weingarten. Franz Schmuzer also created the priory church's magnificent marble altar.

★ ❽ Your next stop, 18 kilometers (11 miles) west along the lake, is the historic old town of **Meersburg.** The most romantic way to approach Meersburg is from the lake. Seen from the water on a summer afternoon, with the sun slanting low across the water, the steeply terraced town can seem floodlit, like an elaborate stage setting. (Meersburg is well aware of its too-good-to-be-true charm—some may find the gusto with which it has embraced tourism crass, and the town can at times get unpleasantly crowded.) Assuming your visit is by ferry boat, you'll step ashore in the Unterstadt, the lower town, which clings to the lakeshore about 150 feet below the Oberstadt, or upper town. The climb between the two halves is not arduous, but there's a bus if you can't face the hike.

★ Meersburg is said to have been founded in 628 by Dagobert, king of the Franks, the man who, it's claimed, laid the first stone of the **Altes Schloss** (Old Castle), which watches majestically over the town and the lake far below. It's Germany's oldest inhabited castle, and one of the most impressive. The massive central tower, named for Dagobert, has walls 10 feet thick. In 1526, the Catholic bishop of Konstanz set himself up in the castle after Konstanz had embraced Protestantism and thrown him out. The castle remained the home of the bishops until the middle of the 18th century, when they had, as they saw it, a more suitable residence built—the Baroque Neues Schloss. Plans to tear down the Altes Schloss in the early 19th century were shelved when it was taken over by one Baron Joseph von Lassberg, a man much taken by the castle's medieval romance. He turned it into a home for like-minded poets and artists, among them his sister-in-law, Annette von Droste-Hülshoff (1797–1848), generally considered one of Germany's finest poets. Her small-scale, carefully crafted poems are drenched in impressions gained from the lake and the mountains laid out before the castle. The Altes Schloss is still private property, but much of it can be visited, including the richly furnished rooms where Annette von Droste-Hülshoff lived, as well as the imposing knights' hall, the minstrels' gallery, and the sinister dungeons. The **castle museum** contains a unique collection of medieval jousting equipment. *Schlosspl. ☞ DM 8 adults, DM 5 children (discounts for families).* ⊙ *Mar.–Oct., daily 9–6; Nov.–Feb., daily 10–5.*

The spacious and elegant **Neues Schloss** is directly across from the castle. It was built partly by Balthasar Neumann, the leading German architect of the 18th century, and partly by an Italian, Franz Anton Bagnato. Neumann's work is most obvious in the stately sweep of the grand double staircase, with its intricate grillwork and heroic statues. The other standout of the interior is the glittering Speigelsaal, the hall of mirrors, now the site of an international music festival held in the summer (*see* The Arts and Nightlife, *below*). In an unlikely combination of 18th-century grace and 20th-century technology, the top floor of the palace houses the **Dornier Museum.** It traces the history of the

German aircraft and aerospace industries. *Schlosspl.* ☞ *DM 4 adults,
DM 3 children, family ticket DM 10.* ☼ *Apr.–Oct., daily 10–1 and
2–6. Guided tours in English can be arranged in advance*
(☎ 07532/440–265).

Sun-bathed, south-facing Meersburg has been a center of the Bodensee
wine trade for centuries. You can pay your respects to the noble trade
in the **Weinbau Museum,** one of the most comprehensive wine museums in Germany. A barrel capable of holding 50,000 liters and an immense wine press dating from 1607 are highlights of the collection. The
museum has another claim to fame: It's in the house where Dr. Frank
Anton Mesmer (1734–1815), pioneer of hypnotism—"mesmerism"—
lived in the early 19th century. *Vorburggasse 11.* ☞ *DM 1 adults, children free.* ☼ *Apr.–Sept., Tues., Fri., and Sun. 2–5. Admission at other
times during tourist-office tours of the town.*

From the museum it's only a short walk to Meersburg's picturesque
market square, **Marktplatz,** surrounded by pretty, half-timbered houses,
among them the medieval Rathaus.

TIME OUT   The **Weinkeller in Truben** (Steigstr.) continues the wine theme—its front
door is one end of a huge wine barrel. Inside, wine racks stretch from
the floor to the whitewashed, vaulted ceiling. Order a bottle of local
wine and try one of the cheese-base dishes.

East of the Obertor, the town gate at the north end of the town, is an
idyllic retreat almost hidden among the vineyards, the **Fürstenhäusle,**
built in 1640 by a local vintner and later used as a holiday home by
poet Annette von Droste-Hülshoff. It's now a museum containing
many of her personal items and giving a vivid sense of Meersburg in
her time. *Stettenerstr. 9.* ☞ *DM 4 adults, DM 2.50 children, family
ticket DM 10.* ☼ *Easter.–mid-Oct., Mon.–Sat. 10–noon and 2–6,
Sun. and holidays 2–6.*

Tour 4: Birnau, Überlingen, and Radolfzell

**❾
★** If you have any interest in the Rococo, you won't want to miss **Birnau,** 10 kilometers (6 miles) along the lake. It's the site of the **Walls-
fahrtskirche** pilgrimage church, the Rococo masterpiece of architect Peter
Thumb. Built between 1746 and 1750, the church has a simple exterior, with plain gray-and-white plaster and a tapering clock tower
spire above the main entrance; the interior, by contrast, is overwhelmingly rich, full of movement, light, and color. It's hard to single
out highlights from such a profusion of ornament, but seek out the
Honigschlecker (the Honey Sucker), a gold-and-white cherub beside
the altar dedicated to St. Bernard of Clairvaux, "whose words are sweet
as honey" (it's the last altar on the right as you face the high altar).
The cherub is sucking honey from his finger, which he's just pulled out
of a beehive. If this sort of dainty punning strikes you as misplaced in
a place of worship, you'll probably find the small squares of glass set
into the pink screen that rises high above the main altar; the gilt drip-
ping from the walls; the swaying, swooning statues; and the swoop-
ing figures on the ceiling equally tasteless. If, like many, you are
entranced by the plump cherub, odds are the rest of the building will
be very much to your liking.

❿ Birnau stands 3 kilometers (2 miles) or so along the lake from **Überlingen,** the German Nice, as the tourist office likes to call it. It's midway along the north shore of the Überlingersee, a narrow branch of
the Bodensee that projects northwest out of the main body of the lake.

Überlingen is an ancient city, a Free Imperial City since the 13th century, with no fewer than seven of its original city gates and towers left, as well as substantial portions of the old city walls. (What was once the moat is now a delightfully grassy place in which to walk, with the walls of the Old Town towering over you on one side and the Stadtpark—city park—stretching away on the other.) The heart of the city is the Münsterplatz, site of the Altes Rathaus (Old Town Hall) and the

★ **Nikolausmünster** (Church of St. Nicholas), a huge church for such a small town. It was built between 1512 and 1563 on the site of at least two previous churches. The interior is all Gothic solemnity and massiveness, with a lofty stone-vaulted ceiling and high, pointed arches lining the nave. The single most remarkable feature is not Gothic at all, however, but opulently Renaissance—the massive high altar, carved from white painted wood that looks almost like ivory. Statues, curlicues, and columns jostle for space on it.

Left of the church is the intricate, late-Gothic **Town Hall** (Altes Rathaus). Go inside to see the **Ratsaal,** the council chamber, a high point of Gothic decoration. Its most striking feature amid the riot of carving is the series of figures representing the states of the Holy Roman Empire. There's a naiveté to the figures—their beautifully carved heads are all just a little too large, their legs a little too spindly—that makes them easy to love. *Münsterpl.* ☛ *Free.* ☼ *Apr.–mid-Oct., weekdays 9–noon and 2:30–5, Sat. 9–noon.*

From Überlingen you can either drive the 10 kilometers (6 miles) back to Meersburg and take the ferry over to Konstanz or continue around the end of the Überlingersee, drive across the neck of the Bodanrück Peninsula—which juts into the west end of the Bodensee to Radolfzell—and continue from there to Konstanz. If you take the latter route, it's 23 kilometers (14 miles) from Überlingen to Radolfzell, and another 16 kilometers (10 miles) to Konstanz.

⓫ It's worth the extra mileage to see **Radolfzell,** an old lakeside town that wears its history with some style (aside from the ugly high rises surrounding it). It was an Austrian outpost for much of its existence, Austrian property from 1267 to 1415 and again from 1455 to the early 19th century. There are the same half-timbered buildings and sinewy old streets that you'll find in other historic Bodensee towns, that same elegant lakeside promenade, and those same chic shops. But the tourist hype is less obtrusive—there's not the sense that Radolfzell has decided it might as well give up being a real town and turn itself over entirely to the tourist trade. There are no outstanding sights here, it's true, but it's an appealing place for a night or two. And if you must have some culture, go and see the 14th-century **Liebfrauenmünster,** a sturdy Gothic church right on the lakeshore.

Tour 5: Konstanz

⓬ And so to **Konstanz,** the largest and most famous city on the Bodensee, the only German city on the south shore (parts of the town actually *are* in Switzerland; the border runs across the southern half of Konstanz—crossing it is easy, with formalities reduced to a minimum). Because it's practically in Switzerland, Konstanz (or Kreuzlingen, as the Swiss call their part) suffered no wartime bombing—the Allies were unwilling to risk inadvertent bombing of neutral Switzerland—with the result that Konstanz is among the best-preserved major medieval towns in Germany. Its proximity to Switzerland also made this one of the tensest borders in the war. There's a famous story of a German Jew who, having crossed the border, was stopped by a Swiss policeman in

Kreuzlingen. Having no papers, the German could do little more than pretend that he was Swiss, out for a stroll and a beer. The policeman looked him up and down, and said *"Ja, Schweizerisches Bier ist gut."* ("Yes, Swiss beer is good.") Then he walked slowly away.

It's claimed that Konstanz was founded during the 3rd century by the emperor Constantine Chlorus, father of Constantine the Great. The story is probably untrue, though it's certain that there was a Roman garrison here. By the 6th century, Konstanz had become a bishopric; in 1192 it was made a Free Imperial City. But what really put Konstanz on the map was the Council of Konstanz, held between 1414 and 1417 and probably one of the most remarkable gatherings of the medieval world. Upwards of 100,000 people are said to have descended on the city during the great council. It was an assembly that was to have profound consequences, consequences that are still felt today. The council was not principally a political gathering so much as a religious one, though the point at which the politics stopped and the religion began was not always easy to identify: To enjoy either religious supremacy or political power in medieval Europe was, to a large extent, to enjoy both.

What was the council? It was convened to settle the Great Schism, the rift in the church brought about during the 14th century when the papacy moved from Rome to Avignon in the south of France. With the move, a rival pope declared himself in Rome. Whatever else it may not have done, the council did at least resolve the problem of the pope: In 1417 it elected Martin V as the true, and only, pope. What it failed to do, however, was solve the underlying problems about the nature of the church that, in part at least, had caused the schism in the first place. At stake was the primacy of the German Holy Roman Emperor in electing the pope (thus extending imperial power) and the primacy of the pope in determining church affairs (and thus in extending the power of the Holy Roman Emperor still further).

Leading the rebel camp was Jan Hus (1372–1415), a theologian from Prague in Bohemia (part of today's Czech Republic), opposed both to the political power of the Holy Roman Emperor and to the religious primacy of the pope. He was, in effect, a church reformer 100 years before his time, a man calling for a fundamental reinterpretation of Christian dogma and for the cleansing of the church's corrupt practices.

What happened at Konstanz? Hus attended the council, having been promised safe conduct by the emperor Sigismund on condition that he would not say mass or preach. The emperor, however, needed a deal with the church that would restore his role in electing the pope. The church agreed, on condition that Hus be done away with. (Sigismund, too, had much to gain from Hus's death; with Hus out of the way, he hoped to restore his control of Bohemia.) So, safe conduct notwithstanding, Hus was accused of having broken his side of the agreement—the emperor was seen to blush as the charges were read—and condemned to be burned at the stake, as indeed he duly was, in July 1415.

Neither the emperor nor the papacy gained much in the long run. Hus's death sparked violent uprisings in Bohemia that took until 1436 to suppress. Likewise, his reforming doctrines gave direct inspiration, a century later, to Martin Luther, a man whose actions caused a far greater schism—the Reformation itself, and the permanent division of the church between Catholics and Protestants. (Konstanz itself became a

Protestant city in the Reformation, a revenge of sorts for the brutal treatment of Hus.)

Hus remains a key figure in Konstanz: There's a Hussenstrasse (Hus Street); the spot where he was killed is marked by a stone slab (the Hussenstein) and, appropriately, the square it's in is now the Lutherplatz; and a statue of Hus is outside the magnificent Konzilgebäude (Council Hall)—so called because it's claimed that the council of cardinals met here to choose the new pope in 1415 (they actually met in the cathedral). The Dominican monastery where Hus was held before his execution is still here, too, doing duty as a luxurious hotel, the Steigenberger Insel-Hotel (*see* Dining and Lodging, *below*).

The **Hus Museum,** dedicated to the life of Hus and his movement, has been opened in a 16th-century house on the street named for him. The museum contains illustrations and documents tracing his life and campaigns against Rome. *Hus-str. 64.* ☛ *Free.* ⊗ *June–Sept., Tues.–Sun. 10–5; Oct.–May, Tues.–Sat. 10–noon and 2–4, Sun. 10–noon.*

But for most visitors, Konstanz, for all its vivid history, is a town to be enjoyed for its more worldly pleasures—its elegant Altstadt (Old Town), trips on the lake, walks along the promenade, the classy shops, the restaurants, the views. The heart of the city is the **Gondelhafen** (harbor) with the simple bulk of the Konzilgebäude looming behind it. Erected in 1388 as a warehouse, the building is now a concert hall. Alongside the Hus statue is one of Graf Zeppelin, born in Konstanz in 1837.

Continue up Marktstatte to the **Altes Rathaus** (Old Town Hall), built in the Renaissance and painted with boldly vivid frescoes—swags of flowers and fruits, shields, architectural details, sturdy knights wielding immense swords. Walk into the courtyard to admire its Renaissance restraint.

To see where Hus was killed, continue past the town hall along Paradiesstrasse to Lutherplatz. Alternatively, turn right down Wessenbergstrasse, the main street of the Old Town. It leads to **St. Stephanskirche,** an austere, late-Gothic church with a very un-Gothic Rococo chancel. It stands in a little square surrounded by fine half-timbered houses. Look at the **Haus zur Katz** (on the right as you walk into the square). It was the headquarters of one of the city's trade guilds in the Middle Ages; now it houses the city archives.

Walk through to the **Münster** (the cathedral), built on the site of the original Roman fortress. Building on the cathedral continued from the 10th through the 19th century, resulting in today's oddly contrasting structure. The twin-towered facade, for example, is sturdily Romanesque, blunt and heavy-looking; the elegant and airy chapels along the aisles are full-blown 15th-century Gothic; the complex nave vaulting is Renaissance; the choir is severely neoclassical. Make a point of seeing the Holy Sepulchre tomb in the Mauritius Chapel at the far end of the church behind the altar. It's a richly worked 13th-century Gothic structure, 12 feet high, still with some of its original, vivid coloring and gilding, and studded with statues of the Apostles and figures from the childhood of Jesus.

Finally, you should walk up to the Rhine, through the **Niederburg,** the oldest part of Konstanz, a tangle of old, twisting streets. Once at the river, take a look at the two city towers here, the **Rheintor**—it's the one nearer the lake—and the aptly named **Pulverturm** (Powder Tower), the former city arsenal.

There are two easy island excursions you can make from Konstanz. The first is to **Mainau,** "the island of flowers," 7 kilometers (4½ miles) north of Konstanz and easily reached by car, then (since cars aren't allowed on the island) by boat. One of the most unusual sites in Europe, Mainau is a tiny island given over to the cultivation of rare plants. Not many people visit Germany expecting to find banana plantations, let alone such exotic flora as bougainvillea and hibiscus. But on Mainau these (and hundreds of more commonplace species) flourish, nurtured by the freakishly warm and moist climate. Visit in the spring and you'll find more than a million tulips, hyacinths, and narcissus in bloom; rhododendrons and roses flower in May and June; dahlias dominate the late-summer display. The island was originally the property of the Teutonic Knights, who settled here during the 13th century. During the 19th century, Mainau passed to Grand Duke Friedrich I of Baden, a man with a passion for botany. He laid out most of the gardens and introduced many of the island's more exotic specimens. His daughter, Victoria, later queen of Sweden, gave the island to her son, Prince Wilhelm, and it has remained Swedish ever since. Today it's owned by Prince Wilhelm's son, Count Lennart Bernadotte (who lives in the castle, which is closed to the public). There is a children's zoo to help keep younger visitors amused: Its wandering groups of tiny potbelly pigs are a hit with all visitors. ☞ *DM 12 adults, DM 10 senior citizens, DM 3 children 6–16, children under 6 free.* ☉ *Mid-Mar.–mid-Oct., daily 7–7.*

There's something of the same profusion of plant life to be seen on the other island excursion from Konstanz, **Reichenau,** though in this case it's vegetables that dominate rather than flowers. In fact, Reichenau is the single most important vegetable-growing area in Germany, with fully 15% of its area covered by greenhouses and practically the entire remainder of the island growing vegetables of one kind or another. Though it seems unlikely, amid the cabbages and the cauliflowers and the lettuces and the carrots and the potatoes, there are three of the most important and—for some, anyway—beautiful **Romanesque churches** in Europe on the island. Little Reichenau, 3 miles long and 1 mile wide, connected to the Bodanrück Peninsula by just a narrow causeway, was a great monastic center of the early Middle Ages. Secure from marauding tribesmen on its fertile island, the monastic community blossomed from the 8th to the 12th century, in the process developing into a major center of learning and the arts.

There are three villages on the island—Oberzell, Mittelzell, and Unterzell. Each is the site of one of the churches, with Mittelzell the site of the monastery itself. The first church you'll reach is the **Stiftskirche St. Georg** (Collegiate Church of St. George), in Oberzell, built around 900. Cabbages grow in serried ranks up to its rough plaster walls. Small round-headed windows, a simple tower, and russet-color tiles provide the only exterior decoration. Inside, look for the wall paintings along the nave; they date from around 1000 and show the miracles of Christ. Their simple colors and unsteady outlines have an innocent, almost childlike charm. The striped backgrounds are typical of Romanesque frescoes.

The next church, begun in 816, is the largest and most important of the trio. It's the **Münster of St. Maria and St. Markus,** the monastery church itself. The monastery was founded in 725 by St. Pirmin; under the abbots Waldo (786–806) and Hatto I (806–23), it became one of the most important cultural centers of the Carolingian Empire. It reached its zenith around 1000 under the rule of Abbot Hermanus Contractus, "the miracle of the century," when 700 monks lived here. It was then probably the most important center of book illumination in Germany. Though it's larger than St. George, the church here has much the same simplicity. It's by no means crude (though it can't be called technically sophisticated), just marvelously simple, a building that's utterly at one with the fertile soil in which it stands. Visit the **Schatzkammer** to see some of the more important treasures that are still here. They include a 5th-century ivory goblet with two carefully incised scenes of Christ's miracles and some priceless stained glass that is almost 1,000 years old. ☞ *DM 1 adults, 50 pf children.* ☉ *May–Sept., daily 11–noon and 3–4. Guided tours (☎ 07534/276) possible at other times.*

The third church, the **Stiftskirche St. Peter and St. Paul,** at Niederzell, contains some Romanesque frescoes in the apse, uncovered in 1990 during restoration work.

A local-history museum in the Niederzell town hall offers interesting insights into life on the island over the centuries. ☞ *DM 2 adults, 50 pf children.* ☉ *May–Sept., Tues.–Sun. 3–5.*

What to See and Do with Children

If your children are tired of swimming and putting balls around the miniature golf courses, take them to the zoo at **Affenburg** to feed the apes. It's about 8 kilometers (5 miles) north of Überlingen, in a forest. There are 200 Barbary apes here. Your admission price includes food you can give the apes. ☞ *DM 6 adults, DM 3 children.* ☉ *Mid-Mar.–Oct., daily 9–noon and 1–6.*

There's another **zoo** halfway between Konstanz and Radolfzell. It features wild animals from all over Europe: bears, wolves, bison, and boars. It also has a petting zoo, with small goats, donkeys, and deer. *Allensbach.* ☞ *DM 4 adults, DM 2 children 4–16, children under 4 free.* ☉ *Mar.–Sept., daily 9–6; Oct.–Feb., daily 10–5.*

In Lindau there's a large **model railway** located in the Luitpold Kaserne (camp) behind the train station. *Hintere Inselstr.,* ☎ *08382/26000.* ☞ *DM 3 adults, DM 1.50 children.* ☉ *Apr.–end of Oct.; hours vary, advisable to call ahead.*

For a day trip to Switzerland with the kids, try **Conny-Land,** just south of Konstanz on the road to Zurich. It's Europe's biggest dolphin aquarium, and it also has go-carts, a minitrain, pony rides, a monorail, remote-control boats, and a petting zoo. The admission price allows unlimited use of all rides and facilities. Have lunch in the restaurant: Huge glass panels allow a look into the dolphin pool. ☞ *9 Swiss francs adults, Sfrs. 6 children.* ☉ *Daily 9–6; dolphin and sea lion shows at 1:30 and 4:30.*

In Überlingen, at the **Heimatmuseum,** a vast collection of dollhouses can be seen. ☞ *DM 2 adults, DM 1 children.* ☉ *Apr.–Oct., Tues.–Sat. 9–12:30 and 2–5, Sun. 10–3; Nov.–Mar., Tues.–Sat. 10:30–12.*

Or down the Rhine at Stein am Rhein you'll find Switzerland's largest doll collection in the **Puppenmuseum.** *Schwarzhorngasse 136.* ☞ *3 Sfrs. adults, 1.50 Sfrs children.* ☉ *Mid-Mar.–Oct., Tues.–Sun. 10–5.*

Off the Beaten Track

Head for the **Hat Museum** at Lindenberg, 16 kilometers (10 miles) northeast of Lindau in the Allgäu. It charts two centuries of hat making. (☞ *DM 1.* ☉ *Wed. 3–5:30 and Sun. 10–noon.)* Or contemplate the achievements of the crusade for world peace as documented in Europe's first **Peace Museum.** It's in Bad Schachen, just outside Lindau. *Lindenhofweg 25.* ☛ *Free.* ☉ *Mid-Apr.–mid-Oct., Tues.–Sat. 10–noon and 2:30–5, Sun. 10–noon.*

If you're in Friedrichshafen you can make a nostalgic return to school with a visit to the **School Museum;** it's in the Schnetzenhausen suburb. There are convincing reconstructions of schoolrooms from 1850, 1900, and 1930—and not a pocket calculator in sight. *Friedrichstr. 14,* ☎ *07541/32622.* ☛ *Free, but donations are appreciated.* ☉ *Mid-Mar.–mid-Nov., daily 10–5; mid-Nov.–mid-Mar., Tues.–Sun. 2–5.*

The Bodensee region produces good wines *and* some fine beers. One local brewery in Bad Schussenried, north of Friedrichshafen, recently opened Germany's first beer-mug museum, with more than 1,000 exhibits of mugs spanning five centuries. *Schussenried Bierkrugmuseum, Wilhelm-Schussen-Str. 12.* ☛ *DM 4.50 adults, DM 3.50 children.*

The small town of Bad Schussenried lies on Germany's "Baroque Road," a vacation route north of the Bodensee studded with jewels of Baroque architecture. They include the extraordinary church of Steinhausen, claimed to be the world's most beautiful parish church and so out of the ordinary that it completely dominates the tiny community of Steinhausen. Combine a visit with a call at the Weingarten pilgrimage basilica; you'll find the contrast breathtaking and well worth the small detour.

Just north of Konstanz on the Bodanrück Peninsula is the 1,000-acre **Wollmatinger Ried,** an area of moorland that's now a bird sanctuary. There are three-hour guided tours of the moor on Wednesday and Saturday, April through mid-October, at 4 PM, and two-hour tours June through mid-September on Tuesday, Thursday, and Friday at 9 AM. Most of the birds you'll see are waterbirds, naturally; there are also remains of prehistoric stilt houses. Bring sturdy, comfortable shoes and mosquito repellent (if you can). Binoculars can be rented. Contact **DBV Naturschutzzentrum Wollmatinger Ried** (FritzArnold-Str. 2e, Konstanz, ☎ 07531/78870).

SHOPPING

The Bodensee is artists' territory, and shopping here means combing the many small galleries and artists' shops in lakeside towns and resorts for watercolors, engravings, and prints. **Hans Müsken's** shop in Konstanz (Zollernstr. 3 ☎ 07531/24631) is quite reliable. **Michael Zeller,** who has two reputable shops in Lindau (Bindergasse 7 and Hintere Metzgergasse 2, ☎ 08382/93020 for both), organizes the celebrated, twice-yearly **Internationale Bodensee-Kunstauktion** (art auction); it's held in the spring and fall.

There's some fine local antiques and jewelry to hunt out, too. Two prominent craftsmen are **Christoph Rose** in Singen/Hohentwiel, just outside Radolfzell (Engestr. 1, ☎ 07731/66990), and **Michael Zobel** in Konstanz (Rosgartenstr. 4, ☎ 07531/25962).

Pottery is a craft that's practiced in many places around the lake. You can find fine examples at **Angelika Ochsenreiter's** shop in Lindau (Ludwigstr. 29, ☎ 08382/23867).

SPORTS AND FITNESS

Bicycling

Bikes can be rented from the train stations at Friedrichshafen, Konstanz, Lindau, and Überlingen for DM 12 a day (DM 6 with a valid train ticket) and from some sports shops (inquire at tourist offices). Bikes can be taken on all lake ferries. Twenty-five hotels and pensions in Friedrichshafen and the surrounding area offer discounts of up to 20% on room rates for guests arriving by bike. The Friedrichshafen tourist office (☎ 07541/30010) has details.

Radeltours, set up by a bike fan, Dieter Siever, who says he got the idea while working in the United States, organizes bike tours of the Bodensee, including accommodations en route. Tours with Dieter can be booked with Radeltours, J.A. Feuchtmayer–Str. 5, Konstanz (☎ 07531/34793) or directly in the U.S. (Radeltours USA, 455 Elm St., Dartmouth, MA 02748, ☎/FAX 508/993–4122). Konstanz-based **Velotours** has similar offerings (Mainaustr. 34, ☎ 07531/52083), and also rents out bikes at DM 20 per day, or DM 50 for three days.

Boating

There are more than 30 boat yards and sailing schools where you can rent boats; most will ask to see some kind of document (a proficiency certificate, for example, from a sailing school) to show you know how to handle a vessel under sail. Motorboats and rowboats can be rented in every resort without any such formalities. Windsurfers will also have no trouble finding boards to rent from any of the 35 rental points around the lake. Canoes can be rented from the **Huber** sports shop in Konstanz (Gottlieberstr. 32). Water-skiers are catered to on the lake, although the fun isn't inexpensive. The Bodensee is fine cruising water, too, and yachts can be chartered from the **Segelschule Ludwigshafen-Bodensee** (Sernatingerstr. 16, ☎ 07773/1235), the **Segelschule Müller KN–Wallhausen** (Wittmoosstr. 10, ☎ 07531/4780), or the **Bodensee Yachtschule** in Lindau (Christoph Eychmüller Schiffswerfte 2, ☎ 08382/5140) and Radolfzell (Zeppelinstr. 23, ☎ 07732/54390).

Bowling

Every resort has at least one hotel with a bowling alley. Konstanz has two bowling centers, each with eight alleys—the **Kegelzentrum** Oberlohn (Maybachstr. 18) and the **Kegel-und Freizeit-Center** (Markgrafenstr 27). In Lindau, head for the **Gaststaette Schützenhaus** (Kemptenerstr. 132).

Fishing

Anglers have a wide choice of fish to pursue on the Bodensee: Carp, pike, zander, whitefish, trout, and perch are the most common catches; but giant catfish are also found in the lake. You'll need a license to fish; they are available, usually for a nominal fee, through any tourist office. Information about fishing vacations can be obtained from the tourist office in the town hall (Rathaus at Moos, near Radolfzell, ☎ 07732/2544).

Golf

Lindau has two 18-hole courses at **Schloss Schönbühl.** Guests are welcome. Contact the **Golf-Club Lindau-Bad Schachen** (Kemptenerstr. 125, D–88131 Lindau, ☎ 08382/78090) and **Golfclub Bodensee,** (☎ 08389/8910 or 08389/8202) at nearby Weissensberg. Konstanz also has an 18-hole course that welcomes foreign visitors provided they are members of clubs in their own countries. Contact the **Golf-Club Konstanz** (Langenrain, ☎ 07531/5124 or 07531/4124).

Horseback Riding

There are riding stables in most Bodensee resorts, and some fine lakeside bridle paths, including a 12-mile trail from Konstanz to Radolfzell. You can rent horses from the **Reitschule Braunschweig** (Mainaustr. 78a, D–78464 Konstanz, ☎ 07531/61604); and in the Lindau area in Taufenberg at **Reitstall Baronin von Ungern-Sternberg** (☎ 08382/28771).

Swimming

The resorts of the Bodensee ensure that Germans needn't travel as far as the Mediterranean—the lake has comparable beaches and cleaner water. The beaches' boast is debatable, but the water certainly sparkles. Open-air pools and lidos abound—at last count there were 150 around the lake. Lindau's **Eichwald** lido has a lake beach a half mile long and an acre of sunbathing lawns (Eichwaldstr. 16, Reutin district). The **Jakob** lido in Konstanz has a lakeside leisure area and heated pools.

Tennis

Every resort has its tennis club, and you should have no difficulty getting a court. The biggest complexes are at **Lindau** (Tennis und Squash Insel Häsenacker 1, ☎ 08382/887–788) and **Konstanz** (Tennis-Park Helle Müller, Eichhornstr. 84a, ☎ 07531/62577).

DINING AND LODGING

Dining

Fish specialties predominate around the Bodensee. There are 35 different types of fish in the lake, with *Renke* and *Felchen* (both meaty white fish) the most highly prized. Felchen belongs to the salmon family and is best eaten *blau* (poached) in rosemary sauce or *Müllerin* (baked in almonds). Wash it down with a top-quality Meersburg white wine. If you venture north to Upper Swabia, *Pfannkuchen* and *Spätzle* are the most common specialties. Both are flour-and-egg dishes. Pfannkuchen (pancakes) are generally filled with meat, cheese, jam, or sultanas, or chopped into fine strips and scattered in a clear consommé soup known as *Flädlesuppe*. Spätzle are roughly chopped, golden-color fried egg noodles that are the usual accompaniment to the Swabian Sunday roast-beef lunch of *Rinderbraten*. One of the best-known Swabian dishes is *Maultaschen,* a kind of ravioli, usually served floating in a broth strewn with chives.

WHAT TO WEAR

The dress code in area restaurants tends to vary according to price: In the most expensive restaurants, formal dress is expected, and in the least expensive restaurants, casual clothes are the norm.

RATINGS

CATEGORY	COST*
$$$$	over DM 90
$$$	DM 55–DM 90
$$	DM 35–DM 55
$	under DM 35

*per person for a three-course meal, including tax and tip but not wine

Lodging

There's a wide range of hotels in all the towns and resorts around the lake, from venerable, wedding-cake-style fin-de-siècle palaces to more modest *Gasthöfe* (inns). If you're visiting in July and August, make reservations well in advance and expect higher-than-average prices. For lower rates and a more rural atmosphere, consider staying away from the lake in Upper Swabia or the Allgäu.

CATEGORY	COST*
$$$$	over DM 200
$$$	DM 160–DM 200
$$	DM 120–DM 160
$	under DM 120

All prices are for a standard double room for two, including tax and service charge.

Friedrichshafen

DINING AND LODGING

Ringhotel Buchhorner Hof. This traditional lakeside hotel, now part of the Ring group, has been run by the same family since it opened in 1870. Hunting trophies on the walls, leather armchairs, and Turkish rugs decorate the public areas; bedrooms are large and comfortable, and all were totally renovated in the past two years. The restaurant is plush and subdued, with delicately carved chairs and mahogany-paneled walls. It offers a choice of menus that feature such dishes as pork medallions, perch fillet, and lamb chops. *Friedrichstr. 33, ☎ 07541/2050, FAX 07541/32663. 64 rooms with bath, 1 suite, 1 apartment. Restaurant, bar, massage, sauna, exercise room, miniature golf, bicycles. AE, DC, MC, V. Closed mid-Dec.–mid-Jan. $$$–$$$$*

Ringhotel Krone Schnetzenhausen. This hotel with Bavarian modern rustic decor—not to be confused with the City-Krone—is in the district of Schnetzenhausen in quiet, semirural surroundings. It's ideal for a sporting holiday. The restaurant specializes in game dishes and fish from the nearby Bodensee. *Untere Mühlbachstr. 1, ☎ 07541/4080, FAX 07541/43601. 120 rooms with bath and balcony. Restaurant, bar, indoor and outdoor pools, hot tub, sauna, outdoor and indoor tennis courts, bowling, exercise room. AE, DC, MC, V. Closed Dec. 10–25. $$$–$$$$*

Konstanz

DINING

Zum Guten Hirten. At this late-15th-century wine tavern, whose name means the Good Shepherd, owner Diana Zoeller maintains a traditional atmosphere. This is particularly true in the Bauernstube, or country corner, which serves such Swiss specialties s *rösti*—pan-fried potatoes and onions mixed with chopped, smoked ham. Try the dish with a crisp white wine from the Bodensee vineyards. *Zollernstr. 8, ☎ 07531/27344. Reservations advised. No credit cards. Closed Sun. and holidays. $*

DINING AND LODGING

★ **Seehotel Siber.** The hotel, in a turn-of -the-century villa, is small, and its adjoining restaurant—the most elegant dining in the region—is the major attraction. The food, prepared by Bertold Siber, one of Germany's leading chefs, is classical with regional touches. Try his lobster salad or bouillabaisse with local lake fish, followed by punch sorbet with ginger-flavored doughnuts. The restaurant is divided into three rooms: One is done up like a library, with massive bookcases; the center room is airy and spacious, with a white ceiling and bold modern paintings; the third has mint-color walls and a deep-green carpet. In summer you can eat on a terrace overlooking the lake. Bedrooms 3 and 7 have balconies affording similar views. *Seestr. 25,* ☎ *07531/63044,* FAX *07531/64813. 11 rooms with bath, 1 suite. Restaurant (reservations essential; jacket and tie), café. AE, DC, MC, V. Hotel and restaurant closed in Feb. $$$$*

★ **Steigenberger Insel-Hotel.** If the Seehotel offers the best dining in town, then this Steinberger group hotel must be the best lodging, or at least the most luxurious. It's a former 13th-century monastery—the original cloisters are still here—and the place where Jan Hus was held before his execution and, much later, Graf Zeppelin was born. Bedrooms are spacious and stylish, more like those of a private home than a hotel, and many have lake views. The restaurant is very imposing, with some fine arches and superb views across the lake. The Dominikaner Stube has regional specialties, and there's the clubby, relaxed Zeppelin Bar. Gardens bright with flowers surround the hotel, keeping the bustle of Konstanz at bay. *Auf der Insel 1,* ☎ *07531/1250,* FAX *07531/26402. 100 rooms, 3 suites with bath. 2 restaurants, bar, beach, recreation room, baby-sitting. AE, DC, MC, V. $$$$*

Graf Zeppelin. A small, family-run place in the historic heart of Konstanz, the Zeppelin has an eye-catching painted facade depicting town scenes from the Middle Ages. Rooms are modest but neat and clean, and there are special family accommodations, including an enormous tower-room. Fresh fish from Lake Constance lands daily on the restaurant's menu. *St. Stephans-Pl. 15,* ☎ *07531/23780,* FAX *07531/17226. 30 rooms, 22 with shower. Restaurant, café. AE, DC, MC, V. $*

Lindau

DINING

★ **Restaurant Hoyerberg Schlössle.** A commanding view across the lake to Bregenz and the Alps combined with elegant nouvelle cuisine make this just about the best dining experience in Lindau. The specialties are fish and game, which change seasonally. There are fixed-price menus of six and eight courses; one offers lobster, noodles with white truffles and goose liver, and roast breast of squab. The decor features brick-trimmed arched windows, fresh flowers, and elegant, high-back chairs. Dine on the terrace for the terrific view. *Hoyerbergstr. 64,* ☎ *08382/25295. Reservations essential. Jacket and tie. AE, DC, MC, V. Closed mid-Jan.–Feb. and Mon. $$$$*

Gasthaus zum Sünfzen. Located in the heart of the Old Town, the Gasthaus zum Sünfzen is an appealing old inn with small leaded windows and a simple, wood-paneled interior. Entrées include venison shot on forest hunts led by landlord Hans Grättinger, as well as locally caught fish and sausages from the restaurant's own butcher shop. Try either the spinach Spätzle or the Felchen fillet. The menu changes daily and seasonally. *Maximilianstr. 1,* ☎ *08382/5865. Reservations advised. AE, DC, MC, V. Closed Feb. $*

DINING AND LODGING

Hotel Bayerischer Hof. This is *the* address in town, a stately hotel directly on the edge of the lake, bordered by gardens lush with semitropical, long-flowering plants, trees, and shrubs. Most of the luxuriously appointed rooms have views of the lake and the Swiss mountains beyond. Freshly caught pike perch from the lake is a highlight of the extensive menu in the stylish restaurant. If the hotel is full or can't provide the rooms you want, two neighboring, less expensive establishments are under the same management (the Reutemann and the Seegarten). *Seepromenade, D-8990, Lindau,* ☎ *08382/5055,*

FAX *08382/5054. 104 rooms with bath. Restaurant, bar, café, outdoor pool, massage, boating, bicycles, recreation room. DC, MC, V. $$$$*

Schachen-Schlössle. A turreted 15th-century manor house set amid peaceful gardens compensates for not being on Lindau Island, and you are still very close to the waterfront in the Bad Schachen district of the mainland town. This is a remarkably good value, with rooms decorated in authentic rustic style. Book well in advance. The restaurant serves traditional German dishes with a light French accent, and lake fish is always on the menu. *Enzisweilerstr. 1–5,* ☎ *08382/5069,* FAX *08382/3956. 16 rooms, 16 apartments with bath. [df]Restaurant, bar, indoor pool, sauna. AE, DC, MC, V. Closed Nov.–Feb. $$*

Gasthof Engel. With the claim of being the oldest inn in Lindau, the Engel can trace its pedigree back to 1390. Tucked into one of the Old Town's ancient, narrow streets, the family-run property creaks with history. Twisted oak beams are exposed inside and outside the terraced house. The bedrooms are simply furnished but comfortable. Frau Zech's changing menu features lake fish and local white wines. *Schafgasse 4,* ☎ *08382/5240. 9 rooms, most with bath. [df]Restaurant. No credit cards. Closed Nov. $*

Meersburg
DINING AND LODGING

Löwen. This centuries-old, ivy-clad tavern on Meersburg's market square is a local landmark. Its cozy restaurant serves such regional specialties as Spätzle and Maultaschen, and in season venison and asparagus find their way onto the menu. Guest rooms are cozily furnished with their own sitting-room corners. *Marktpl. 2,* ☎ *07532/43040,* FAX *07532/430–410. 21 rooms with bath. [df]Restaurant, weinstube, no-smoking rooms, bicycles. AE, DC, MC, V. $$–$$$*

LODGING

Strandhotel Wilder Mann. This 18th-century nobleman's home has its own 750-foot stretch of shoreline. Modern, deep-pile comforts are to be found in the antiques-filled guest rooms, with dark-pine furniture and tapestries predominating. The restaurant's pastries are first-rate, as is the wine cellar. *Bismarckpl. 2,* ☎ *07532/9011,* FAX *07532/9014. 29 rooms, 2 apartments with bath. [df]Restaurant, beach. AE. Closed Jan.–Feb. $$$$*

Hotel-Cafe Off. Although this small and friendly hotel fronts the lake, don't worry if you can't get a room overlooking the water—those on the side look out over vineyards. There's a bright, cheerful feel about the hotel, accentuated by the light woods and matching pastel tones of the furnishings. Rooms have broad beds and many homey touches. There's a playroom and sandpit for youngsters. *Uferpromenade 51,* ☎ *07532/333,* FAX *07532/5805. 19 rooms with bath, 2 suites. [df]Restaurant, café, bicycles. DC, MC. $$–$$$*

Zum Bären. Built in 1605, the Zum Bären will be the choice of those who value atmosphere over modern convenience. Creaking staircases and wood ceilings ensure maximum Old World charm, though colorful wallpapers, gaily painted cupboards and bright bedspreads lighten the mood. Service is excellent, the result perhaps of the fact that the hotel has been owned and run by the same family since the mid-19th century. *Marktpl. 11,* ☎ *07532/43220,* FAX *07532/432244. 17 rooms with shower. Restaurant. No credit cards. Closed Dec.–Feb. and Mon. $$*

Ravensburg

DINING AND LODGING

Romantikhotel Waldhorn. This traditional old house has been welcoming travelers on Ravensburg's central Marienplatz since 1860. It's now a member of the Romantik group, and the accent certainly is on the "romantic." For a combination of romance and comfort, book a room or apartment in the annex. Those in the main house are more basic, though they do have new furnishings and modern facilities. The highly recommended restaurant is done in a Biedermeier style; you dine beneath sturdy beams at tables covered with crisp blue linen. *Marienpl. 15,* ☎ *0751/36120,* FAX *0751/361–2100. 30 rooms with bath, 3 apartments. Restaurant, bar. AE, DC, MC, V. $$$$*

Reichenau

LODGING

Strandhotel Löchnerhaus. The steep-eaved, white-stuccoed Strand (Beach) hotel stands imposingly at the water's edge at the southern end of the island, with its own bathing beach and boat jetty. Most of the rooms, brightly furnished in light woods and floral fabrics, have lake views and some have large, sunny balconies. *An der Schiffslände 12,* ☎ *07534/8030,* FAX *07534/582. 44 rooms with bath or shower. Restaurant, beach. MC, V. $$$.*

Überlingen

DINING AND LODGING

★ **Parkhotel St. Leonard.** Located about a mile from the lake on a vineyard-covered hillside, the modern St. Leonard offers elegance and style. All rooms have balconies, but try for one with a view of the lake. Facilities include indoor and outdoor tennis courts as well as a tennis school. There are two restaurants, one sleekly contemporary and the other traditional, both in the hands of a French chef. Lake fish are a specialty, but also check to see whether local lamb in spinach is on the menu, or the homemade Maultaschen. In summer you'll dine on a canopied terrace. *Obere St. Leonardstr. 71,* ☎ *07551/808–100,* FAX *07551/808–531. 140 rooms, 5 apartments with bath. 2 restaurants, bar, indoor pool, beauty salon, sauna, tennis, exercise room, billiards, bicycles. AE, MC, V. $$$$*

LODGING

Seehof. This popular family hotel is on the lakeshore, with direct access to a beach and boat pier. Most rooms have their own balconies looking out over the lake. Fitness fanatics can book a cold-water cure within the hotel's own health facility. The restaurant regularly serves fish caught in the lake—the pike perch is particularly tasty. *Strandweg 6,* ☎ *07551/63020,* FAX *07551/68166. 35 rooms with bath. Restaurant, sauna, boating, bicycles. No credit cards. Closed Nov.–Mar. $$*

THE ARTS AND NIGHTLIFE

The Arts

Music

The region has its own orchestra, the **Bodensee Symphony Orchestra,** founded in 1932 and based in Konstanz, with a season running from October through April. Program details and bookings are available from the Konstanz tourist office (☎ 07531/284–376). **Konstanz** also has an annual summer music festival, from mid-June to mid-July, with a program of international events, including celebrated organ concerts in the cathedral. Performances are held in the picturesque Renaissance-hof (courtyard) of the town hall. For program details and bookings, contact the Konstanz tourist office. **Konstanz** and **Friedrichshafen** combine efforts to stage an annual Bodensee Festival which includes orchestral concerts and theater productions from early May to early June. The tourist offices of the two towns will provide program details. **Überlingen** also has an international music festival, with concerts every Tuesday from May through September in the lakeside Kursaal. For program details and bookings, contact the **Städtische Verwaltung** (Landungspl. 14, D–88648, Überlingen, ☎ 07551/991–122.) **Meersburg** has an annual international chamber music festival in the magnificent Hall of Mirrors (Spiegelsaal) of the Neues Schloss. The concerts are held every Saturday from June through September. The **Städtische Kur und Verkehrsverwaltung** has program details and handles bookings (Kirchstr. 4, D-88709, Meersburg, ☎ 07532/431–110). Several other castles and churches in the region are the scene of regular chamber music concerts and recitals, particularly in summer. For program details, contact the regional tourist office, the **Internationaler Bodensee-verkehrsverein** (Schützenstr. 8, 7750 Konstanz, ☎ 07531/22232).

Theater

Konstanz claims Germany's oldest active theater. Its **Stadttheater** (Konzilstr.; or the festival office, ☎ 07531/52016) has staged plays since 1609 and has its own repertory company. The local season runs from September through June. During July through August, the company moves to its summer theater in Meersburg. For program details, contact the **Stadttheater Konstanz** (Konzilstr. 11, D–78462 Konstanz, ☎ 07531/20070). For the Meersburg program, call 07532/82383. **Lindau** has a traveling theater in town October–April. Call 08382/275-402.

Nightlife

Most of the towns and resorts of the Bodensee have regular evenings of entertainment for visitors, ranging from traditional folk music and dancing to more modern fare, including jazz and pop concerts. Local tourist offices have programs. Many resort hotels also organize regular *Heimatabende* (folk-music evenings) or *Gästeabende* (guests' evenings); in some, Saturday night really is dance night.

In summer you can dance on the water—on one of the evening cruises organized by the Bodensee **Weisse Flotte** operators. The boats pick up dancers and revelers every Saturday night from May to September in Konstanz, Lindau, Meersburg, Rorschach, and Überlingen. For further details and bookings, contact the **Bodensee-Schiffsbetriebe** (Hafenstr. 6, D–78462 Konstanz, ☎ 07531/281–398).

The **disco** scene is concentrated in Konstanz. **Babalu** (Kreuzlingerstr. 15) and **Excalibur** (Hussenstr. 6) are among the best. In Meersburg try the **Diskothek-Dome** (Bregenzerstr. 103) or, for a more romantic ambience, **Barcarole,** candlelit and overlooking the lake (Fährhaus Meersburg, Fährepl.).

Konstanz and Lindau have **casinos,** called Spielbank. They are open 3 PM–3 AM daily. The Konstanz casino has a restaurant overlooking the lake. The Las Vegas of the lake is at **Bregenz,** just across the Austrian border on the southeast shore. Perhaps the secret of its success lies in the generous practice of handing visitors their entrance money back in chips. You'll need a passport to secure entrance to all three casinos.

BODENSEE ESSENTIALS

Arriving and Departing

By Car

The A–96 Autobahn runs virtually all the way from Munich to Lindau, but for a less hurried, more scenic route take the B–12 via Landsberg and Kempten. If you want to take a more scenic but slower route from Frankfurt, take the B–311 at Ulm and follow the Oberschwäbische Barockstrasse (the Upper Swabian Baroque Road) to Friedrichshafen. An alternative, no less scenic route to Lindau, at the east end of the lake, is on the Deutsche Alpenstrasse (the German Alpine Road). It runs east–west from Salzburg to Lindau, passing Garmisch-Partenkirchen and Füssen along the way.

By Train

There are InterCity trains to Lindau from Frankfurt (via Stuttgart and Ulm) and from Munich. There are also frequent and fast train services from Zurich and Basel in Switzerland.

By Plane

The closest international airport to the Bodensee is Zurich, in Switzerland, 60 kilometers (40 miles) from Konstanz. Munich Airport is 240 kilometers (150 miles) from Konstanz; Frankfurt Airport is 375 kilometers (230 miles) from Konstanz. The little airport at Friedrichshafen, on the north shore of the lake, has flights from all three airports.

Getting Around

By Boat

The **Weisse Flotte** (White Fleet) line of boats links most of the larger towns and resorts; numerous excursions are also available (*see* Guided Tours, *below*). If you plan to use the ferries extensively, buy a **Bodensee Pass**. It is valid for 15 days and allows half-price travel on all ferries, as well as many Bodensee trains, buses, and mountain cable cars (in Germany, Switzerland, and Austria). The pass costs DM 48 (adults only—children under 14 get half-price fares). Contact **Bodensee-Schiffsbetriebe** (Hafenstr. 6, D–78462 Konstanz, ☎ 07531/281–398). There are also offices in Friedrichshafen (☎ 07541/201–389) and Lindau (☎ 08382/6099).

By Bus

Railway and post buses serve most smaller communities that have no train links. Service is less than frequent, however; use local buses only if time is no object.

By Car

Lakeside roads in the Bodensee area are good, if crowded in summer; all offer scenic diversions to compensate for the occasional slow going in heavier traffic. You may want to drive around the entire lake, crossing into Switzerland and Austria; formalities at border crossing points are few. However, in addition to your passport, you'll need insurance and registration papers for your car. If you're taking a rental car, check with the rental company to make sure it imposes no restrictions on crossing these frontiers. Car ferries link Romanshorn in Switzerland on the south side of the lake with Friedrichshafen on the north side next to

Lindau, and Konstanz with Meersburg. Taking either saves substantial mileage while driving around the lake.

CAR RENTAL

Avis: Eberhardstrasse 31, **Friedrichshafen,** ☎ 07541/23030; Reichenaustr. 45, **Konstanz,** ☎ 07531/66630.

Europcar: Eugenstrasse 47, **Friedrichshafen,** ☎ 07541/23053; von-Emmerich-Strasse 3, **Konstanz,** ☎ 07531/52833.

Hertz: Friedrichshafen airport, ☎ 07541/930–700; Bregenzerstrasse 25, **Lindau,** ☎ 08382/940–000.

Sixt-Budget: Zeppelinstrasse 66, **Friedrichshafen,** ☎ 07541/33066.

By Train
Local trains encircle the Bodensee, stopping at most towns and villages.

Guided Tours

Boat Tours
The Weisse Flotte organizes numerous excursions around the lake lasting from one hour to a full day. Many cross to Austria and Switzerland; some head west along the Rhine to the Schaffhausen Falls, the largest waterfall in Europe. (*See* Getting Around by Boat, *above,* for addresses.) Information on excursions on the lake is also available from all local tourist offices and travel agencies.

City Tours
Most of the larger tourist centers have regular tours with English-speaking guides. In **Friedrichshafen** there are tours from May through September on Tuesday at 9:30, leaving from the tourist office (Friedrichstr. 18).The tours are free of charge and include visits to the Zeppelin Museum and Schlosskirche. Tours of **Konstanz** leave from the tourist office (Bahnhofpl. 13) from April through October on Monday (9:30 AM), Wednesday (4:30 PM), and Friday and Saturday (10:30 AM). **Lindau** offers tours, also starting from the tourist office (Am Hauptbahnhof), from April through October on Tuesday and Friday at 10. Meersburg tourist office (Kirchstr. 4) offers guided tours that include a visit to the wine museum; tours are held from April through October on Wednesday at 10. The **Radolfzell** tourist office (Marktpl. 2) arranges tours from May through September on Saturday at 10 for groups of 10 or more.

Excursions
Bus trips to destinations in and around the Bodensee can be booked from tour operators in all the larger towns. Typical tours include visits to cheese makers in the Allgäu, the rolling Alpine foothills east of the Bodensee; tours around the Black Forest; tours to Baroque churches and castles around the lake; and tours to the ancient town of St. Gallen across the border in Switzerland. Operators include **Reisebüro Rominger** (Marktstätte 17, ☎ 07531/26031, and Zähringerplatz 34, ☎ 07531/5503, Konstanz), **Reisebüro Lemke** (Schmiedgasse 13, Lindau, ☎ 08382/25025), **Bregenzer Autoreisen** (Rengoldhauserstr. 11, Überlingen, ☎ 07551/4044), and **Reisebüro Kast** (Münsterstr. 31–33, Überlingen, ☎ 07551/63628).

Special-Interest Tours
Flights around the Bodensee are offered by **Konair** (Flugpl., Konstanz, ☎ 07531/61110). A 20-minute flight over Konstanz and part of the

Bodensee costs DM 95 per person. A 45-minute flight over the entire lake costs DM 150. For DM 190, you can have the plane for an hour, easily time enough to fly south over parts of the Alps. Sightseeing flights also operate from the Lindau-Wildberg airstrip (☎ 08389/271).

Wine-tasting tours are also available. In Überlingen, tastings are held in the atmospheric Spitalweingut zum Heiligen Geist, Mühlbachstrasse 115, on Thursday at 7 PM; contact the tourist office or call 07551/65855. In Konstanz, wine-tasting is by appointment only at the Spitalkellerei (Brückengasse 12, ☎ 07531/288–342). In Meersburg, tastings are held Tuesday and Friday at 6 PM; contact the tourist office (☎ 07532/431–110).

Important Addresses and Numbers

Tourist Information

Information on the entire Bodensee region is available from the **Internationaler Bodensee-Verkehrsverein** (Schützenstr. 8, D–78462 Konstanz, ☎ 07531/22232). There are local tourist information offices in the following towns:

Friedrichshafen: Tourist-Information, Friedrichstrasse 18, D–88045 Friedrichshafen, ☎ 07541/30010.

Konstanz: Tourist-Information Konstanz, Bahnhofplatz 13, D–78462 Konstanz, ☎ 07531/900–377.

Langenargen Verkehrsamt, Obere Seestr. 2, D–88085 Langenargen, ☎ 07543/30292.

Lindau: am Hauptbahnhof, D–8990 Lindau, ☎ 08382/26000.

Meersburg: Kur- und Verkehrsverwaltung, Kirchstrasse 4, D–88709 Meersburg, ☎ 07532/431–110.

Radolfzell: Städtisches Verkehrsamt, Rathaus, Marktplatz 2, D–78315 Radolfzell, ☎ 07732/3800.

Ravensburg: Städtisches Verkehrsamt, Kirchstr. 16 (Weingartner Hof), D–88212 Ravensburg, ☎ 0751/82324.

Reichenau: Verkehrsbüro, Ergat 5, D-78479 Reichenau, ☎ 07534/276.

Tettnang: Verkehrsverein, Montfortplatz 1, D–88069 Tettnang, ☎ 07542/510–213.

Tuttlingen: Städtisches Verkehrsamt, Rathaus, D–78532 Tuttlingen, ☎ 07461/99203.

Überlingen: Verkehrsamt Überlingen, D–88648, Überlingen, ☎ 07551/991–122.

5 The Bavarian Forest

Low-key and understated, the Bavarian Forest is a welcome alternative to Germany's hyped-up, overcrowded tourist regions. Good-quality dining and lodging at budget prices make it even more attractive. Farming and forestry are mainstay industries, tourism is growing, and glass-blowing shouldn't be missed. Passau, a 2,000-year-old town at the confluence of three rivers, is visited for its beauty as much as its history.

FOR YEARS THIS PICTURESQUE, WOODED REGION of southeast Germany was one of the most isolated parts of Western Europe, its eastern boundary flanked by the Iron Curtain. Ancient villages of jumbled red roofs and onion-dome churches still pepper the vast forest because of this isolation, and because a tract of the Bayerischer Wald, or Bavarian Forest, is protected. Farming and forestry are the chief industries in the area, and the centuries-old craft of glassmaking still survives. The people are reserved. Even the accent here is gentler than that of southern countrymen. The region's flavor is vastly different from the stock concept of Bavaria, a world supposedly populated by men in lederhosen and funny green hats with feathers, and buxom women decked out in flowing dirndls who spend their time singing along with oompah bands and knocking back great mugs of beer.

Following the collapse of communism in Czechoslovakia and the formation of the Czech Republic, old contacts between Germans and Bohemian Czechs are rapidly being revived. The centuries-old trading route between Deggendorf and Prague—the Böhmweg—has been revived for walkers. No visit to the Bavarian Forest would be complete without at least a day trip across the border; bus trips into Bohemia are organized by every local tourist office. The Bavarian Forest has long been a secret with Germans in search of relaxing, affordable holidays at mountainside lodges or country inns, and tourism is growing as the region opens up. All those in search of peace and quiet—hikers, nature lovers, anglers, horseback riders, skiers looking for uncrowded slopes, and golfers distressed by the steep greens fees of more fashionable courses—will do well here.

EXPLORING

Tour 1: From Cham to Dreiburgenland

Numbers in the margin correspond to points of interest on the Bavarian Forest map.

❶ The gateway to the Bavarian Forest—and a key point on the Ostmarkstrasse scenic route—is the little town of **Cham.** Located on the Regen River, Cham is distinguished by intact sections of original 14th-century town walls, including a massive tower, the Straubinger Turm. It also possesses a 15th-century town hall and an even older town-wall gate, the Biertor.

❷ Heading southeast from Cham on B–85, watch on the left for the ruins of a medieval castle perched on the 2,500-foot-high **Haidstein** peak. Around the year 1200, it was home to the German poet Wolfram von Eschenbach. On the slopes is a 1,000-year-old linden tree known as Wolframslinde (Wolfram's linden tree). With a circumference of more than 50 feet, its hollow trunk could easily shelter 50 people.

As you head south on B–85 you'll pass sunny villages with trim streets and gardens and see two sinuous lakes created by the dammed Regen River. From here the Weisser (white) Regen soon becomes the Schwarzer (black) Regen.

❸ Between the village of Prackenbach and the little town of Viechtach you'll see a dramatic section of the **Pfahl,** one of Europe's most extraordinary geological phenomena. The ridge of glistening white quartz

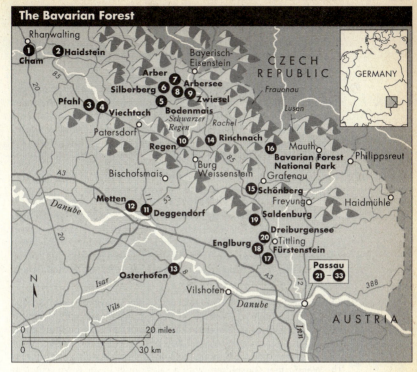

The Bavarian Forest

juts dramatically out of the ground in an arrow-straight spur that extends more than 100 kilometers (60 miles) through the Bavarian Forest. Here the quartz rises in folds to heights of 100 feet or more.

4 Stop in **Viechtach** to see its spectacularly decorated Rococo church of St. Augustin, and to visit **Gläserne Scheune,** the unique workplace of glass artist Rudolf Schmid. The roof of his barn studio is made from a mosaic of painted glass fragments. *Raubühl 3,* ☎ *09942/8147.* ☛ *DM 4 adults, DM 2 children.* ☉ *Apr.–Sept., daily 10–5; Oct., daily 10–6. Closed Nov.–Mar.*

Ten kilometers (6 miles) beyond Viechtach is Patersdorf. Turn left here
5 and head to **Bodenmais,** 14 kilometers (9 miles) northeast of Patersdorf. This health resort is tucked into a valley below the Bavarian Forest's highest mountain, the 4,800-foot-high Arber. A nearby silver mine helped Bodenmais prosper before tourism reached this isolated part of the country. The 700-year-old mine was closed in 1962, but you can still view its workings near the summit of the 3,000-foot-high
6 **Silberberg** (Silver Mountain). You can take the chair lift from the Arber Road, about 3 kilometers (2 miles) north of Bodenmais, or enjoy the easy, 25-minute walk from the road to the entrance of the mine. ☛ *DM 9 adults, DM 5 children.* ☉ *Apr.–June, daily 10–4; July–Sept., daily 9–5; Oct.–Dec., daily 10–4; Jan.–Mar., daily 1–3. Call 09924/304 for details on guided tours.*

Glass foundries have been busy in the Bavarian Forest for centuries; indeed, some Germans still call it the Glass Forest. Bodenmais's long tradition of glassmaking includes Bavaria's largest glassworks, the **Joska Waldglashütte,** which welcomes visitors at both of its foundries, at Scharebenstrasse and in the Am Moosbach industrial zone. Both foundaries are open to visitors weekdays 9–11:45 and 1–3:45, Saturdays 9–1:45; showrooms are open weekdays 9–6 and Saturdays 9–2. The **Austen Glashütte** foundry can also be visited weekdays 9:30–5:30 and Saturdays 9:30–2:30.

7 The **Arber**—the highest mountain of both the Bavarian Forest and the Bohemian Forest on the other side of the border—is 13 kilometers (8 miles) north of Bodenmais. A bus service runs from Bodenmais to the base of the mountain, where a chair lift makes the 10-minute trip to **8** the summit. A short walk from the bottom of the lift leads to the **Arbersee Lake,** surrounded by thick forest.

TIME OUT   You can quench your thirst or fortify yourself for a hike up the Arber at the friendly **Gasthof Schareben** on the shores of the lake.

From the lake, follow the signs for Zwiesel, and turn right at the junction with the B–11. Travelers who can't resist quirky sights may wish to take a detour here 6 kilometers (4 miles) to the left for the little town of **Bayerisch Eisenstein,** where the Germany-Czech Republic border visibly cuts the local train station in half (*see* Off the Beaten Track, *below*).

Otherwise, proceed to the northern end of the Bavarian Forest National **9** Park and the town of **Zwiesel.** As the region's glassmaking center, it has 18 crafts firms involved in shaping, engraving, or painting glass. The biggest company employs 1,800 people, while the smallest business is just one person. Among the companies that welcome visitors is the **Weinfurtner Glashütten,** with a sales outlet in the town center, at Stadtplatz 36 (call 09922/6806 if you want to view the foundry). The **Waldmuseum Zwiesel** offers displays dedicated to the customs and heritage of the entire forest region during the past few centuries. *Stadtpl. 29,* ☎ *0992/9640.* ☛ *DM 3 adults, DM 2.50 children.* ☼ *Mid-May–mid-Oct., weekdays 9–5, weekends 10–noon and 2–4; mid-Oct.–mid-May, weekdays 10–noon and 2–5, weekends 10–noon. Closed Nov.*

Zwiesel also produces a variety of beers and a notorious schnapps, Bärwurz. You can sample the house-brewed bitter Janka Pils or a malty dark wheat brew at the Gasthof Deutscher Rhein, a 300-year-old inn (*see* Dining and Lodging, *below*). The Bärwurz distillery (Bayerwald Bärwurzerei, Heinrich Hieke, ☎ 09922/1515) is only for the hardy and is open during regular shop hours and also, during the summer, on Sundays.

10 From Zwiesel, continue southward along the B–11 to **Regen,** a busy market town with fine 16th-century houses around its large central square. On the last weekend in July the town celebrates an event that made culinary history: the creation in the 17th century of *Pichelsteiner Eintopf* (pork and vegetable stew), a filling dish that has become a staple throughout Germany. The celebrations include sports events on the Regen River, so pack a swimsuit if you fancy joining in.

Regen has another claim to fame: an extraordinary display of Christmas crèches created by Frau Maria-Elisabeth Pscheidl, who has been making the items for more than 30 years. Today her collection is claimed to be the largest—and (according to the local tourist office) the best—of its kind in the world—even the Vatican has given it a seal of approval. Many of her creations are displayed in the **Pscheidl Bayerwald-Krippe Museum,** run by the town council in Frau Pscheidl's home. *Ludwigsbrücke 3,* ☎ *09921/2893.* ☛ *DM 2 adults, DM 1.50 children.* ☼ *Daily 1–5.*

⑪ If you continue southwest from Regen along the E–53 (23 kilometers), you'll reach **Deggendorf,** which nestles between the Danube and the forested hills that rise in tiers to the Czech border. The town was once on the banks of the Danube, but repeated flooding forced its inhabitants to move to higher ground in the 13th century. You can still see a 30-yard stretch of the protective wall built around the medieval town. Points of interest from later centuries include a 16th-century **Rathaus** (Town Hall) located in the center of the wide main street, the Marktstrasse. ☎ 0991/296–0199. ☛ *Tower DM 1.50. Tower open weekdays 10–noon and 2–4, Sat. 10–noon..*

★ At one end of the Marktstrasse stands the **Heilig Grabkirche,** which was originally built as a Gothic basilica in the 14th century. Its lofty tower—regarded as the finest Baroque church tower in southern Germany—was added 400 years later by the Munich master builder Johann Michael Fischer. ☛ *Free.* ☽ *Daily 9–sunset.*

The church stands on the edge of a remarkable tract of town planning: Deggendorf's "culture quarter," created from a section of its Old Town. Lining the leafy, traffic-free square are the city museum; a public library; a new handicrafts museum, the only one of its kind in the Bavarian Forest; and the Kapuzinerstadl, a warehouse converted into a concert hall and a large foyer that is also frequently used as a concert and theater venue. Exhibits at the **Handwerksmuseum** (Museum of Trades and Crafts) study typical regional handicrafts. The **Stadtmuseum** (City Museum) traces the history of the Danube people. ☛ *Handwerksmuseum: DM 2 adults, DM 1 children.* ☽ *Tues.–Sun. 10–4 (Thurs. 10–6).* ☛ *Stadtmuseum: DM 2 adults, DM 1 children.* ☽ *Tues.–Sun. 10–4 (Thurs. 10–6).*

★ ⑫ To see two outstanding examples of Baroque art, you can take the 7-kilometer (4-mile) trip along the Danube, heading northwest of Deggendorf, to the ancient Benedictine abbey of **Metten,** founded in the 9th century by Charlemagne. Within its white walls and quiet cloisters is one of Germany's outstanding 18th-century libraries, a collection of 160,000 books whose gilded leather spines are complemented by the heroic splendor of their surroundings: Herculean figures support the frescoed, vaulted ceiling, and allegorical paintings and fine stucco work identify different categories of books. In the monastery church is Cosmas Damian Asam's altar painting of *Lucifer Destroyed by St. Michael,* created in about 1720, its vivid coloring and swirling composition typical of the time. ☛ *Free (donations welcome). Guided tours daily at 10 and 3, except Easter.*

⑬ If you travel 15 kilometers (9 miles) south of Metten along the banks of the Danube via Hengersberg, you'll reach the village of **Osterhofen** and the church of St. Margaretha. This structure contains important work by Baroque artists, including a series of large ornate frescoes and altar paintings by Cosmas Damian Asam, and elaborate sculptures of angels and cherubs, entwined on the church pillars, by Egid Quirin Asam and Johann Michael Fischer. The three worked here in a rare partnership between 1728 and 1741. Look for Cosmas Damian's self-portrait amid the extravagant decor. ☽ *Daily 9–7, except during Sun. services. Free guided tour Thurs. at 3. (Assemble at main church door.)*

⑭ Those seeking more Baroque architecture may wish to travel to the village of **Rinchnach,** 8 kilometers (5 miles) east of Regen (*see above*). Here an 11th-century monk's lonely retreat grew under royal patronage into an important monastery. The church you see was built in the 15th century. In 1727, Johann Michael Fischer was summoned from Munich to extend and renovate it in Baroque style. Visit its expansive and lordly interior to see his masterful wrought-iron work and some typically heroic frescoes. Two early 18th-century altar paintings by Cosmas Damian Asam are also on view.

Retrace your route northward via Hengersberg, passing lovely undulating forested countryside, to the Ostmarkstrasse, or B–85 (31 kilometers), and the village of **Schönberg.** Linger in its Marktplatz (market square), where arcaded shops and houses present an almost Italian air. As you head farther south down the Inn Valley, this Italian influence—the so-called Inn Valley style—becomes more pronounced.

Some 15 kilometers (9 miles) northeast of Schönberg is Neuschönau and the main entrance to the **Bavarian Forest National Park,** a 32,000-acre stretch of protected dense forest. Bears, wolves, and lynx roamed wild in these parts until well into the 19th century. Substantial efforts have been made to reintroduce these and other animals to the park, though today the animals are restricted to large enclosures. Well-marked paths lead to points where the animals can best be seen. Bracing walks also take you through the thickly wooded terrain to the two highest peaks of the park, the 4,350-foot **Rachel** and the 4,116-foot **Lusen.** Specially marked educational trails trace the geological and botanical history of the area, and picnic spots and playgrounds abound. In winter, park wardens will lead you through the snow to where wild deer from the mountains feed. A visitor center—**The National Park-Haus**—is located at the main entrance to the park. Slide shows and English-language brochures provide introductions to the area.

Back on the Ostmarkstrasse (B–85) south of Schönberg lies the **Dreiburgenland,** (the Land of the Three Castles). The name comes from three famous castles: **Fürstenstein, Englburg,** and **Saldenburg.** The little village of Fürstenstein likes to call itself the "Pearl of the Dreiburgenland." From the walls of its castle you can get a fine view of the Danube plain to the south and the mountains of the Bavarian Forest to the north. On the shores of the **Dreiburgensee** in Tittling, you'll find the **Freilichtmuseum** (Open-Air Museum), which boasts 50 reconstructed Bavarian Forest houses. You can sit on the benches of a 17th-century schoolhouse, drink schnapps in an 18th-century tavern, or see how grain was ground in a 15th-century mill. *Museumsdorf Bayerischer Wald, by Hotel Dreiburgensee, Tittling* ☎ *08504/8482.* ☛ *DM 3.* ☉ *Daily 8–5.*

TIME OUT   After your tour of the village you'll probably be hungry and thirsty; the **Gasthaus Mühhiasl** waits at the end of the main street with a menu of hearty and inexpensive Bavarian fare and locally brewed beer. In summer the shady beer garden is the place to be.

Tour 2: Passau

Twenty kilometers (12 miles) south on the Ostmarkstrasse, at the eastern limit of lower Bavaria and the Bavarian Forest, lies the ancient city of **Passau,** a remote yet important embarkation point for the traffic that has plied its way along the Danube River for centuries, traveling between Germany, central Europe, and the Black Sea.

Passau sits on a narrow point of land where the Inn and the Danube meet, with wooded heights rising on the far sides of both rivers; the much smaller River Ilz also joins the Danube nearby. Little wonder that the 18th-century traveler Alexander von Humboldt included Passau in his list of the seven most beautifully situated cities in the world. Its fine old homes face the waterfront, and streets of varying levels rise to a hill in the center of the old city. These harmonious proportions are complemented by the typical Inn Valley houses that line the streets, joined to one another by picturesque archways. While Passau is no "Venice of the North," it does have a Mediterranean air, due in part to the many Italian architects who worked here, and a special quality of light that painters throughout the centuries have been attracted to and tried to capture in their work.

Settled more than 2,000 years ago by the Celts, then by the Romans, Passau later passed into the possession of prince-bishops, whose power once stretched into present-day Hungary. The influence they wielded over nearly six centuries has left its traces in the town's Residenz (bishop's palace), Veste Oberhaus (the bishops' summer castle), and magnificent Dom (cathedral).

For 45 years Passau was a backwater because of its location in a "lost" corner of West Germany. But recent political changes have placed the old city back in the limelight, and you will find it elegant and dignified; its grande-dame atmosphere has far more in common with the stately demeanor of Vienna or Prague than with the brash approach of some cities in the Federal Republic.

Numbers in the margin correspond to points of interest on the Passau map.

Start your tour at a city square—the Kleiner Exerzierplatz—where progress has pushed aside a more gracious past. What was once a Bene-

22 dictine monastery garden now houses a parking lot and the **Nibelung-enhalle,** a Nazi-era hall that seats 8,000. The name is taken from the *Nibelungenlied,* an epic poem about German mythology written in Passau during the 12th century. Among other things, the poem describes the love of Siegfried for Kriemhild and the overthrow of the Nibelungen—the Burgundians of France—by the German Hun tribes. Richard Wagner chose it as the theme for his immense 19th-century operatic cycle, *The Ring of the Nibelung.* Later Hitler recast the legend in an attempt to legitimize the Nazi creed. His obsession with Wagner—almost surpassing that of Ludwig II—was another example of his desire to see himself as an extension of an established Germanic tradition. The hall is still used for political rallies and was also the reception center for the first refugees who fled East Germany in late summer 1989, presaging the collapse of the Berlin Wall. From late November until just before Christmas it takes on a very a political appearance, housing Passau's glittering Christmas market, the Christkindlmarkt. There's a tourist office adjoining the hall.

Turn right from the tourist office onto busy Ludwigsplatz. Beyond it stretches the city's main shopping street, Ludwigsstrasse, part of an attractive pedestrian zone. The first street on the right leading off Lud-

23 wigstrasse is Heiliggeistgasse, the site of the 15th-century **Spitalkirche Heiliger Geist,** or Infirmary Church of the Holy Ghost. It has some fine 16th-century stained glass and an exquisite 15th-century marble relief depicting the Way of the Cross. Evidence of the influence of Passau's religious establishments—and of their central European, as opposed to purely Germanic interests—is provided by the fact that the church still possesses vineyards in neighboring Austria.

TIME OUT You can sample one of the Austrian wines produced from the church vineyards at the **Heilig Geist Stift-Schenke und Stifts-Keller,** a neigh-

Passau

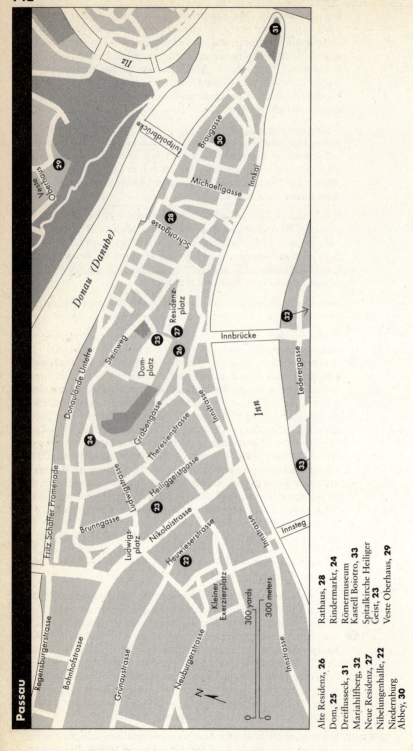

Ilz

Luitpoldbrücke

Braugasse

Oberhaus
Veste

Michaeligasse

Innkai

Schrottgasse

Donau (Danube)

Residenz-
platz

Steinweg

Donaulände Untere

Dom-
platz

Grabengasse

Innbrücke

Innstrasse

Theresienstrasse

Ledergasse

Inn

Fritz Schäffer Promenade

Ludwigstrasse

Heiliggeistgasse

Brunngasse

Nikolaistrasse

Heuwieserstrasse

Innstrasse

Innsteg

Regensburgerstrasse

Bahnhofstrasse

Ludwigs-
platz

Grünaustrasse

Kleiner
Exerzierplatz

Neuburgerstrasse

Innstrasse

N

0   300 yards

0   300 meters

Alte Residenz, **26**
Dom, **25**
Dreiflusseck, **31**
Mariahilfberg, **32**
Neue Residenz, **27**
Nibelungenhalle, **22**
Niedernburg
Abbey, **30**

Rathaus, **28**
Rindermarkt, **24**
Römermuseum
Kastell Boiotro, **33**
Spitalkirche Heiliger
Geist, **23**
Veste Oberhaus, **29**

boring tavern. The union of church and vineyard is underlined by the crucifixes that hang from the darkened beams.

㉔ Back on Ludwigstrasse, walk to **Rindermarkt,** the old cattle market. On the way you'll pass the 17th-century Baroque **Church of St. Paul** and walk through the medieval **Paulusbogen** (Paul's Arch), part of the original city walls. From Rindermarkt, turn right into narrow Luragogasse (named for one of the Italian builders who were busy in Passau in the 18th century) and continue until you reach **Domplatz,** the expansive square fronting the cathedral. The statue you see in its center is of Bavarian King Maximilian Joseph I.

㉕ Now turn your attention to the **Dom,** the cathedral. A baptismal church stood here in the 6th century. Two hundred years later, when Passau became the seat of a bishop, the first basilica was built. It was dedicated to St. Stephan and became the original mother church of St. Stephan's Cathedral in Vienna. Little was left of the medieval basilica after a fire reduced it to smoking ruins in the 17th century. What you see today is an impressive Baroque building, complete with dome and flanking towers. There's little in its marble- and stucco-encrusted interior to remind you of Germany and much that proclaims the exuberance of Rome. Beneath the octagonal dome is the largest church ★ **organ** in the world. Built between 1924 and 1928, and enlarged from 1979 to 1980, it claims no fewer than 17,388 pipes and 231 stops. Concerts (DM 4 adults, DM 2 children) are given on the monstrous instrument from May through October weekdays at noon and on Thursday at 7:30 PM (DM 6–DM 10 depending on the program).

Bordering Domplatz are a number of sturdy 17th- and 18th-century **㉖** buildings, including the **Alte Residenz,** the former bishop's palace. ★ **㉗** Today it's a courthouse. The **Neue** (New) **Residenz** is next door, though its main entrance faces Residenzplatz, one of the most gracious and quiet corners of the town. Step through the stately Baroque entrance of the palace to see the staircase, a scintillating study in marble, fresco, and stucco. The Neue Residenz also houses one of Bavaria's largest collections of religious treasures, the legacy of Passau's episcopal history. ☛ *DM 2 adults, DM 1 children.* ⊙ *May–Oct. and mid-Dec.–mid-Jan., Mon.–Sat. 10–4.*

From the Neue Residenz, turn into Schrottgasse and head toward the Danube. You'll soon find yourself staring at the bright Gothic facade **㉘** of Passau's 13th-century **Rathaus** (town hall). Originally the home of a successful merchant, it was declared the seat of city government after an uprising in 1298. Two assembly rooms contain wall paintings depicting scenes from local history and lore, including the (fictional) arrival in the city of Siegfried's fair Kriemhild. The Rathaus can be visited only on guided tours arranged by the tourist office (*see* Guided Tours *in* Bavarian Forest Essentials, *below*).

Outside the Rathaus, face the Danube, cross the bridge on your right— **㉙** the Luitpoldbrücke—and climb up to the **Veste Oberhaus,** the powerful fortress and summer castle commissioned by Bishop Ulrich II in 1219. Today the Veste Oberhaus is Passau's most important museum, containing exhibits that illustrate the 2,000-year history of the city. It ★ also commands a magnificent **view** of Passau and the three rivers that converge on it. *Museum* ☛ *DM 4 adults, DM 2 children.* ⊙ *Tues.–Sun. 9–5 (Fri. 9–7). Closed Feb. A bus takes visitors from Rathauspl. to the museum Apr.–Oct. at half-hour intervals 11:30–5.*

③⓪ Walk back across the Luitpoldbrücke and turn left into Bräugasse for the **Niedernburg Abbey.** Founded in the 8th century as a convent, it was destroyed by fire and rebuilt in the last century in a clumsy Romanesque style. Today it's a girls' school. In its church you can see the 11th-century tomb of a queen who was once abbess here—Gisela, sister of the emperor Heinrich II and widow of Hungary's first and subsequently sainted king, Stephan, who became the patron of the Passau cathedral.

③① Now head to Passau's other major river, the Inn, just a few steps away. Follow the river to the **Dreiflusseck** (Corner of the Three Rivers), where the Inn's green water, typical of a mountain river, slowly gives way to the darker hues of the Danube, and the brownish Ilz adds its small contribution to this colorful natural phenomenon. It's the end of the journey for the Inn—which flows here from the mountains of Switzerland and through Austria—and the much shorter Ilz, which rises in the Bavarian Forest; from here their waters are carried by the Danube to the Black Sea.

③② Another place to take in the meeting of the three rivers is the **Mariahilfberg,** site of a 17th-century monastery pilgrimage church. It is on the other side of the Inn, in the so-called Innstadt, or Inn City. It was here that in 1974 archaeologists uncovered the site of the Roman citadel of Boiotro, a stout fortress with five defense towers and walls more than 12 feet thick. A Roman well was also found, its water still plentiful and fresh. The pottery, lead figures, and other archaeological dis-
③③ coveries from the site are housed at the nearby **Römermuseum Kastell Boiotro.** *Lederergasse 43.* ☛ *DM 2 adults, DM 1 children.* ⊗ *Mar.–Nov., Tues.–Sun. 10–noon and 2–4 (June–Aug. from 1 PM).*

What to See and Do with Children

Passau has a fascinating toy museum, the **Spielzeugmuseum,** which includes many exhibits from the United States. There is a good collection of dolls, as well as many ancient model steam engines. *Residenzpl.* ☛ *DM 3 adults, DM 1 children, family ticket DM 5.* ⊗ *Apr.–Oct., daily 9:30–5:30; Nov.–Mar., weekends only.*

At Ortenburg, 22 kilometers (14 miles) west of Passau, there's an extensive **deer park** where children can feed the animals. ☛ *DM 4 adults, DM 2 children.* ⊗ *Daily 8–6.*

In winter youngsters can accompany wardens into the **Bavarian Forest National Park** to feed the wild deer. Contact Parkverwaltung Bayerischer Wald (Grafenau, ☎ 08552/1300).

In the hamlet of Irgenöd, just outside Ortenburg, is the biggest **aviary** in eastern Bavaria. ☛ *DM 5 adults, DM 2.50 children.* ⊗ *Apr.–Oct., 10–6.*

Beside the Grosse Arbersee Lake children can wander through the **Märchenwald** (Fairytale Wood), which features a collection of colorful model scenes from famous stories. *Entrance opposite Hotel Arberseehaus.* ⊗ *Easter–mid-Oct., daily 9–5.*

In Loifling, near Cham, the **Churpfalz Park** offers hours of fun—from a puppet theater to miniature trains and a water carousel—while parents can wander around the extensive gardens. ☛ *DM 9.50, DM 4.50 children.* ⊗ *Apr.–mid-Oct., daily 9–6.*

Off the Beaten Track

Anywhere in the Bavarian Forest is off the beaten track, but if you're looking for something more than isolated forest walks and glades, seek out two extraordinary private collections. The world's largest **snuff-box collection** is on the third floor of Weissenstein Castle near Regen. The 1,300 snuffboxes on display were collected over a period of 46 years by Regen's former mayor, Alois Reitbauer. His reward was an entry in the *Guinness Book of Records*. ☯ *Late May–mid-Sept., daily 10–noon and 1–5.*

At Rhanwalting, near Cham, you'll find one of Germany's most unusual **collections of clocks** and time-measuring machines. It's in the back room of a country inn, the Uhren Wirt (literally, Clock Inn). Landlord Gerhard Babl has spent more than 30 years building up his collection of more than 400 timepieces.

In Passau the history of central Europe's glassmaking is revealed through an exquisite display of 20,000 items at the Passau **Glasmuseum.** *Hotel Wilder Mann, Am Rathauspl.* ☛ *DM 3 adults, DM 2 children (under 11 free).* ☯ *Mar.–Sept., daily 10–5; Oct.–Feb., daily 2–4.*

An unusual reminder of the border that cuts through this forested region—and until recently divided two opposing political systems—is visible in **Bayerisch Eisenstein.** Here, at the foot of the Arber, the border runs through the middle of the sleepy town's train station. You might still see traces of Iron Curtain fortifications, though most were removed during 1990. The frontier gets confusing around the summit of Mt. Dreisessel, west of Altreichenau, and it's possible to walk in and out of a virtually forgotten corner of the Czech Republic—a feat that was possible even when the border was guarded everywhere else by heavily armed soldiers.

Dreisessel means "three armchairs," an apt description of the summit and its boulders, which are shaped like the furniture of a giant's castle. If you're driving to the Dreisessel, take B–12 to Philippsreut, just before the frontier, then follow the well-marked country road. The mountain is about 67 kilometers (40 miles) from Passau.

SHOPPING

In virtually every resort of the Bavarian Forest you'll find shops selling **glassware,** local **pottery,** and **wood carving.** In Passau, head to the Ludwigstrasse pedestrian zone. In Deggendorf, the small streets of the old quarter around the Rathaus are prime territory for shoppers.

Bavarian Forest glassware has been made in tiny workshops for the past 500 years. Today more than 100 family glassware-making firms survive. At some you can watch craftsmen blow glass shapes; nearly all have on-site exhibits and shops. The largest direct-sales outlet is the **Joska Waldglashütte** foundry (*see* Exploring, *above*) in Bodenmais. ☎ *09924/7790.* ☯ *Weekdays 9–11:45 and 1–3:45, with free tours during these times; Sat. 9–1:45.*

Glass is also for sale in Bodenmais at **Austen Glashütte.** *Bahnhofstr. 57.* ☯ *Weekdays 9:30–5:30, Sat. 9:30–2:30.*

The **Eisch** family in Frauenau, on the edge of the Bavarian Forest National Park, has been making glass since 1680 and their winged elephant trademark is internationally recognized as a mark of quality. Their glass foundry in Frauenau (Am Steg 7, ☎ 09926/1890) is open to visitors weekdays 9–3 and Saturday 9:30–noon. You can buy directly from the showroom. At the **Weinfurtner** foundry at Arnbruck, near Bodenmais, your monogram is engraved free of charge on anything you buy. (Foundry open weekdays 9–12:30 and 1–5, Sat. 9–2, Sun. 10–noon and 2–4.) Its two sale rooms, in Arnbruck and Bodenmais, are open normal shop hours.

SPORTS AND FITNESS

Bicycling

The number of bike paths and recommended car-free routes through the Bavarian Forest is increasing. The banks of the Danube from Regensburg, via Passau and into Austria beyond Linz, are popular with cyclists. Excursion boats that ply the Danube between Regensburg and Passau carry bikes, enabling you to cycle one stage of the journey and float back. Bikes can be rented at most rail stations (DM 12 per day; DM 6–DM 8 if you have a valid ticket) and at many resorts. Passau has declared itself a Radlerstadt (bicycle town); its tourist office (Rathauspl. 3, ☎ 0851/33421) publishes bike-route maps for the Old Town and eight tours of the surrounding countryside as well as detailed information on other routes and rental points in the area.

Fishing

The Weisser and Schwarzer Regen rivers are a challenge for anglers; there's also good fishing in the Danube, Inn, and Ilz rivers. Local tourist offices can supply permits.

Golf

Golfers can enjoy at least two advantages in the Bavarian Forest: lower greens fees (sometimes a fraction of what's charged in Upper Bavaria) and clubs that welcome visitors. There's a challenging course (☎ 0991/8911) at **Schaufling,** high above Deggendorf, that offers fine views of the Bavarian Forest and the Danube plain. **Furth im Wald** has a nine-hole course (☎ 09973/2089); There are 18-hole courses at **Thyrnau** (☎ 08501/1313) and **Lam** (☎ 09943/777), which is particularly welcoming to visitors. An 18-hole course recently opened at **Oberzwieselau,** near Zwiesel (☎ 09922/2367).

Hiking

The Bavarian Forest is prime hiking country, crisscrossed with trails of varied challenge. The longest, the **Pandurensteig,** runs nearly 167 kilometers (100 miles) from Waldmünchen in the northwest to Passau in the southeast, crossing the heights of the Bavarian Forest National Park. The trail can be covered in stages with the aid of a special tourist program that transfers hikers' luggage from one overnight stop to the other. Get details from **Fremdenverkehrsverband Ostbayern** (Landshuterstr. 13, D–93047 Regensburg, ☎ 0941/57186). Resorts between Deggendorf and Bayerisch Eisenstein on the Czech border have remapped the centuries-old **Böhmweg** trading route, and it can be comfortably covered in three or four days, with accommodations at village taverns en route (maps and information from the Bavarian Forest National Park authority, the Natur Park Bayerischer Wald Informationshaus, D-8372 Zwiesel, ☎ 09922/5555). Three Bavarian Forest resorts—Kellberg, Hauzenberg, and Buchelberg—have joined in a hiking-holiday scheme called **Wandern mit Tapetenwechsel** (Hiking with Change of Scene). The package consists of 14 days' hiking, bed-and-breakfast accommodations, tour assistance, and luggage transportation, all for around

DM 450. For details, contact the **Verkehrsamt Kellberg** (D–94136 Thyrnau, ☎ 08501/320) or the **Lichtenauer Pension** (☎ 08501/426).

Horseback Riding

Bridle paths crisscross the Bavarian Forest, and there's some fine open country as well. Local tourist offices have the addresses of stables. In the Regen area, the **Reitclub Kattersdorf** (☎ 09921/3397) has horses for rent and a large indoor riding area.

Skiing

Alpine skiers make for the World Cup slopes of the **Grosser Arber** (the summit is reached by chair lifts from Bayerisch-Eisenstein and from just outside Bodenmais). Other ski areas in the Bavarian Forest are not as demanding, and many resorts are ideal for family skiing vacations. St. Englmar, Frauenau, Furth im Wald, Waldmünchen, and the villages around the Brotjackelriegel, near Deggendorf, are the best. Cross-country trails are everywhere in the Bavarian Forest; a map of 22 of the finest can be obtained free of charge from the **Fremdenverkehrsverband Ostbayern** (*see* Hiking, *above*). The pretty resort of Thurmansbang has a trail that stops at all of the best bargain inns of the area. For around DM 250, Thurmansbang offers a week's bed-and-breakfast accommodations, cross-country ski instructions, and equipment rentals. Contact the **Verkehrsamt Thurmansbang** (☎ 08504/1642).

Swimming

There are multipool lidos throughout the Bavarian Forest. The best are at Deggendorf, Passau, Vilshofen, Viechtach, and Waldkirchen. In summer the forest lakes beckon swimmers, but avoid the Danube—there's a fast current, and the water is polluted.

Water Sports

Sailboats and surfboards can be rented at most lakes; the Dreiburgensee, the Rannasee, the Perlsee, and the Egingersee are four of the prettiest. The Regen and the Inn rivers are perfect for canoeing. Canoes can be rented from **Johannes Denk** (Schmiedgasse 18, Passau, ☎ 0851/31450) or through the tourist office (☎ 09461/1066) in Roding, on the banks of the Regen.

DINING AND LODGING

Dining

Food in the Bavarian Forest tends toward the wholesome and the hearty; large portions are very much the norm. Specialties include *Regensburger* (short, thick, spicy sausages, rather like the *Bratwurst* of Nürnberg). Another sausage served here is *Bauernseufzer* (farmer's sigh). Dumplings, made out of virtually anything and everything, appear on practically every menu. Try *Deggendorfer Knödel* if you fancy something really local. The Danube provides a number of excellent types of fish, particularly *Donauwaller* (Danube catfish), from Passau. This is served *blau* (boiled) or *gebacken* (breaded and fried). The town of Tirschenreuth in the north of the region is the home of the equally delicious *Karpfen* (carp). Radishes are a specialty, especially *Weichser Rettiche*, and are a good accompaniment to the many local beers. Passau alone has four breweries—at the Hacklberg brewery, one of the most photogenic in all Germany, you can sample excellent beer at the brewery's own tavern.

Neat, casual dress is appropriate at the restaurants listed below.

RATINGS

CATEGORY	COST*
$$$$	over DM 90
$$$	DM 55–DM 90
$$	DM 35–DM 55
$	under DM 35

per person for a three-course meal, including tax and tip but not drinks

Lodging

Prices here are among the lowest in Germany. Many hotels offer special 14-day packages for the price of a 10-day stay, and 10-day packages for the price of a 7-day stay. There are also numerous sports packages, with accommodations at low rates. All local tourist offices can supply lists of accommodations; most can help with reservations.

RATINGS

CATEGORY	COST*
$$$$	over DM 200
$$$	DM 160–DM 200
$$	DM 120–160
$	under DM 120

All prices are for a standard double room for two, including tax and service charge.

Bayerisch-Eisenstein

LODGING

★ **Ferienhotel Waldspitze.** The former Hotel Waldwinkel has changed hands and name, which now identifies it as a "holiday hotel." Its forest location and range of facilities certainly make it an ideal holiday base. Rooms have been enlarged and extensively renovated, with new bathrooms and heavy, Bavarian-style furniture. ☒ *Hauptstr. 4,* ☎ *09925/308,* FAX *09925/1287. 55 rooms with bath. Restaurant, café, indoor pool, table tennis, sauna, steam room, exercise room, billiards. No credit cards.* $–$$

Bodenmais

LODGING

Bodenmaiser Hof. The geranium-bedecked Hof's quality and reputation bring German visitors back year after year. Guest rooms paneled in pale pine are a cut above the average, with ample facilities. The Hof even has its own bakery and butcher shop, which ensures the freshness and quality of the food prepared for guests. ☒ *Risslochweg 4,* ☎ *09924/1841,* FAX *09924/7457. 10 rooms, 10 apartments with bath. Restaurant, café, sauna, exercise room. No credit cards.* $$

Böhmhof. Situated on the edge of town and forest, this lodging encourages relaxation and recreation. The outdoor and indoor pools allow for year-round swimming; walking and cross-country ski trails start at the front door. Rooms have modern pinewood furnishings and balconies. ☒ *Böhmhof 1,* ☎ *09924/222,* FAX *09924/1718. 26 rooms with bath. Restaurant, café, 2 pools, sauna, hot tub, recreation room. No credit cards.* $$

Cham

DINING

Bürgerstuben. The Stuben is in Cham's central Stadthalle (city hall). Tasty local dishes and an appealingly simple atmosphere add up to an authentic Bavarian experience. ✕ *Fürtherstr. 11, ☎ 09971/1707. Reservations advised on weekends. No credit cards. Closed Mon. $$*

LODGING

Randsbergerhof. A German knight lived here before this house became a hotel. It's a rambling, old building with beamed ceilings and ornate, hand-painted walls. The present owner, Fritz Wittmann, and his family sponsor public evenings of folk music and dancing. ⌂ *Randsbergerhofstr. 15, ☎ 09971/1266, FAX 09971/20299. 90 rooms with bath, 4 apartments. Restaurant, sauna, bowling, squash. AE, DC, MC, V. $$*

Gästeheim am Stadtpark. The most expensive single room in this friendly guest house costs all of DM 39 — and that includes a hearty breakfast! The basic comfort is also unbeatable. ⌂ *Tilsiterstr. 3, ☎ 09971/2253, FAX 09971/79253. 11 rooms with shower. No credit cards. $*

Deggendorf

DINING

Charivari. Richard Kerscher's flower-bedecked restaurant offers a complete change from the typical fare of the region. Classic French dishes include duck in orange sauce, but the local specialty, *Pickelsteiner Eintopf,* a fish-and-vegetable hot pot, often with salmon is worth trying. ✕ *Bahnhofstr. 26, ☎ 0991/7770. Reservations advised. AE, MC. Closed Sun., Mon., and Sat. lunch. $$$*

Ratskeller. If you eat here, beneath the vaulted ceilings of the Rathaus, you could easily find yourself sharing a table with a town councillor, perhaps even the mayor. The menu is strictly Bavarian; the beer flows freely. ✕ *Oberer Stadtpl. 1, ☎ 0991/6737. No reservations. MC. Closed Fri. $$*

Zum Grafenwirt. In winter, ask the host for a place near the fine old tile stove that sits in the dining room. Try such filling dishes as roast pork and Bavarian dumplings. In summer, watch for Danube fish on the menu. ✕ *Bahnhofstr. 7, ☎ 0991/8729. Reservations advised on weekends. AE, DC, MC, V. Closed Tues. and 1st 2 wks in June. $$*

DINING AND LODGING

Flamberg Parkhotel. This luxury hotel opened in 1991 and has rapidly established itself as one of the best in the region. A monumental mural by Elvira Bach welcomes you in the reception area, and the artistic touch is continued in the large and airy guest rooms, all of which have original paintings on the walls. The Tassilo restaurant and adjoining winter garden have an international menu with an Italian flair. In summer a shady beer garden beckons; in winter a log fire burns invitingly in the lounge. The Danube promenade and the Old Town center are both a few minutes' walk away. ⌂ *Edlmairstr. 4, ☎ 0991/6013, FAX 0991/31551. 112 rooms and 13 suites, all with bath. Restaurant, bar, beer garden, hot tub, sauna, exercise room, bicycles. AE, DC, MC, V. $$$*

LODGING

★ **Schlosshotel Egg.** The "Egg" isn't something you might eat in this castle-hotel's excellent restaurant; it comes from the name Ekke, the 12th-century owner. Today the hotel is an atmospheric and memorable place in which to lay your head, but try for a room in the castle rather than in the adjoining guest house—all are large, and some have four-poster beds. The hotel is 13 miles outside Deggendorf. ⌂ *94505 Schloss Egg-Bernried, ☎ 09905/289 or 09905/8316, FAX 09905/691. 19 rooms with bath. Restaurant. AE, DC, MC, V. $$$$*

Donauhof. This lovely 19th-century stone warehouse, painted cream and white, was made a hotel in 1988. The spotless rooms have modern Scandinavian furniture. The Wintergarden Café is a local favorite for its homemade cakes and coffee. ☎ *Hafenstr. 1,* ☎ *0991/38990,* FAX *0991/389–966. 42 rooms with bath, 3 apartments. Restaurant, weinstube, sauna. AE, MC, DC, V. $$*

Grafenau
DINING
★ **Säumerhof.** The Bavarian Forest isn't known for haute cuisine but here, in one of its prettiest resorts, is a restaurant that bears comparison with Germany's best. It's part of a small country hotel (with 10 moderately priced and homey rooms) run by the Endl family. Gebhard Endl's territory is the kitchen, where he produces original, nouvelle-inspired dishes using ingredients obtainable locally. Try the pheasant on champagne cabbage, or the roast rabbit in herb-cream sauce. ✕ *Steinberg 32,* ☎ *08552/2401. Reservations advised. AE, DC, MC, V. $$$$*

LODGING
Steigenberger-Avance Sonnenhof. If you are traveling with children, this is the hotel for you: The staff includes a *Spieltante* (playtime auntie) who keeps youngsters amused. The ultramodern hotel is set in extensive grounds, and there's lots to do—even horse-drawn sleigh rides in winter. ☎ *Sonnenstr. 12,* ☎ *08552/4480,* FAX *08552/4680. 194 rooms with bath. 2 restaurants, bar, indoor pool, beauty salon, saunas, spa, indoor and outdoor tennis courts, miniature golf, bowling, exercise room nightclub. AE, DC, MC, V. $$$$*

Bierhütte. The name means "beer hut," and it was once a royal brewery. Now a member of the select Romantik hotel group, the elegant 18th-century building has its own quiet grounds beside a lake. It has all the trappings of a regal residence, with ornate furnishings and tapestries in public rooms and bedrooms. ☎ *Bierhutte 10, Hohenau,* ☎ *08558/315,* FAX *08558/2387. 37 rooms with bath, 6 suites. Restaurant, sauna, exercise room, recreation room, library. AE, DC, MC, V. $$$–$$$$*

Haidmühle
DINING
Adalbert Stifter. Named for a popular 19th-century Bavarian Forest poet, this friendly country hotel-restaurant at the foot of the Dreisessel Mountain is at its best turning out the sort of time-honored dishes Stifter knew. Try one of the Bohemian-style roasts, for instance, served with fresh dumplings. ✕ *Frauenberg 32,* ☎ *08556/355. Reservations advised. Closed Nov.–Dec. 20. MC. $$*

Mauth
DINING AND LODGING
Barnriegel. This family-run restaurant is on the edge of the Bavarian Forest National Park and caters to those made hungry by a day's walking. Sauerbraten is one of the best dishes on the menu; local lake fish is also a specialty. The weary can stay here, too, in one of 13 inexpensive rooms. ☎ *Hauptstr. 2, Finsterau,* ☎ *08557/96020. Reservations advised. No credit cards. Closed Mon. Apr.–June. $$*

Passau
DINING
★ **Heilig-Geist-Stiftsschenke.** For atmospheric dining, this monastery turned wine cellar, dating from the 14th century, is a must. In summer

you eat beneath chestnut trees; in winter, seek out the warmth of the vaulted dining rooms. The wines are excellent and suit all seasons. ⊞ *Heiliggeistgasse 4, ☎ 0851/2607. Reservations advised. AE, DC, MC, V. Closed Wed. and Jan. 10–Feb. 10. $$*

Gasthof Andorfer. A good wheat beer is brewed and served here, and you can drink it on a lime-tree-shaded terrace overlooking the grain fields. The brewery tavern is in Passau-Ries, a couple of miles north of the city center, near the Veste Oberhaus fortress. The menu is basic, but the beer and the surroundings are what count. There are a few rooms if you fancy spending the night. ✕ *Rennweg 2, ☎ 0851/51372. No reservations. No credit cards. Closed Sat. $*

Peschl Terrasse. The beer you sip on the high sun terrace overlooking the Danube is brought fresh from the Old Town brewery below, which, along with this traditional Bavarian restaurant, has been in the same family since 1855. ✕ *Rosstränke 4, ☎ 0851/2489. No reservations. AE, DC, MC, V. Closed Mon. $*

Zum Hirschen. This is a traditional Bavarian hostelry, with blue-and-white-checkered tablecloths and a menu of solid fare, ranging from roast pork and dumplings to vanilla steamed pudding. The 400-year-old building stands beside the Niedernburg Abbey. ✕ *Im Ort 6, ☎ 0851/36238. No reservations. Closed Mon. No credit cards. $*

DINING AND LODGING

Passauer Wolf. Try for a room with a view of the Danube at this leading riverside hotel, where elegance and comfort are matched by outstanding cuisine. The restaurant attracts diners from neighboring Austria, who come for its light French touch. The accent is on fish—if freshly caught Danube pike perch is on the menu, you're in for a treat. ⊞ *Rindermarkt 6, ☎ 0851/34046, ҒAX 0851/36757. 40 rooms with bath. Restaurant, bar. AE, DC, MC, V. $$$*

LODGING

Hotel König. Though built only in 1984, the König blends successfully with the graceful Italian-style buildings alongside its elegant waterfront setting on the Danube. Rooms are large and airy; most have a fine view of the river. ⊞ *Untere Donaulände 1, ☎ 0851/3850, ҒAX 0851/385–460. 41 rooms with bath. Sauna, steam room. AE, DC, MC, V. $$$*

Hotel Weisser Hase. The White Rabbit was accommodating travelers at the beginning of the 16th century. In 1993–94 it was given a complete face-lift and overhaul courtesy of its new owners, the Ring Group. Rooms were redecorated in sleek Ring Group style, with cherry wood and mahogany veneers and soft matching colors. It stands sturdily in the town center, at the start of the pedestrian shopping zone, a short walk from all the major sights. All rooms have satellite TV. ⊞ *Ludwigstr. 23, ☎ 0851/92110, ҒAX 0851/921-1100. 108 rooms with bath. Restaurant, in-room modem lines. AE, DC, MC, V. $$$–$$$$*

★ **Wilder Mann.** Passau's most historic hotel shares prominence with the ancient city hall on the waterfront market square. You sleep beneath chandeliers and richly stuccoed ceilings in beds of carved oak in a house that dates from the 11th century (renovated in the 19th and 20th centuries and subsequently kept up to contemporary standards of comfort). Guests have ranged from the consort of the Austrian emperor Franz-Josef to the American astronaut Neil Armstrong. The swimming pool is in the 11th-century vaulted cellars. ⊞ *Am Rathauspl. 1, ☎ 0851/35071, ҒAX 0851/31712. 48 rooms with bath, 5 apartments. Restaurant, bar, café, indoor pool. AE, DC, MC, V. $$–$$$*

Rotel Inn. "Rotels" are usually hotels on wheels, an idea developed by a local entrepreneur to accommodate travel groups on tours in North Africa and Asia. Now he has built the first permanent Rotel Inn, on the banks of the Danube in central Passau. Its rooms are just as small as the cabinlike accommodation of his Rotel, but they're clean, decorated in a lively pop-art style (the entrance lobby is smothered in colorful graffiti), and amazingly cheap (DM 60 for a double). The whole building breaks with traditional styles, and its design—red, white, and blue facade and flowing roof lines—has actually been patented. For young travelers, definitely—but also fun for families. ☎ *Am Hauptbahnhof/Donauufer,* ☎ *0851/95160,* FAX *0851/951–6100. 93 rooms with bath. No credit cards. $*

Regen
LODGING

Burggasthof Weissenstein. The ruins of the neighboring medieval Weissenstein Castle loom above you as you breakfast on the sunny terrace overlooking the Old Town. Ask for a room with a view of either. The recently opened cellar tavern has dancing on weekends. ☎ *Weissenstein 32,* ☎ *09921/2259,* FAX *09921/8759. 15 rooms with bath. Restaurant. No credit cards. Closed Nov. $*

Pension Panorama. This modern, friendly hotel on the outskirts of Regen chose its name because most of its rooms enjoy fine south-facing views of the Bavarian Forest. In summer there's a spacious sun-terrace and garden to relax in. In winter a log fire blazes in the open hearth of the beamed lounge. Rooms are furnished in light veneers with bright prints on the walls. ☎ *Johannesfeldstr. 27,* ☎ *09921/2356. 17 rooms with bath. Restaurant, bar, indoor pool, paddle tennis. MC. $*

Schönberg
DINING AND LODGING

★ **Hotel Antonios Hof.** This chalet-style lodging, located on the edge of the Bavarian Forest National Park, has an exterior distinguished by ornately carved Victorian balconies. Inside, the pinewood trimmings—from the low beams of the snug tavern to the restaurant's carved pillars—help to create a warm, homey atmosphere. The rooms are equally welcoming and are decorated in the Bavarian country style with pinewood furnishings. Try the fish if you eat here; it comes directly from the hotel's own pond. ☎ *Unterer Marktpl. 12,* ☎ *08554/9700,* FAX *08554/970–100. 40 rooms with bath. Restaurant, indoor pool, sauna, bowling. AE, DC, MC, V. $$*

Tittling
LODGING

Ferienhotel Dreiburgensee. This is primarily a place for longer vacations, but it's also convenient for an overnight stop if you're touring the Bavarian Forest or visiting the nearby Dreiburgensee open-air museum. All of the hotel's rooms have balconies with views of the Dreiburgensee Lake or the surrounding forest. Some have Bavarian-style four-poster beds with painted headboards and large, fluffy goosedown covers. Children love the sturdy bunk beds in the spacious family rooms. ☎ *Am Dreiburgensee,* ☎ *08504/2092 or 08504/4040,* FAX *08504/4926. 100 rooms with bath or shower. Restaurant, café, indoor pool, sauna, exercise room, miniature golf, boating, bicycles, playground. Closed Nov.–Dec. No credit cards. $–$$*

Viechtach
DINING AND LODGING

Kur-und-Sporthotel Schmaus. This place, run by the same family for generations, is for the energetic. The kitchen turns out meals on the assumption that every guest has just finished a 25-mile hike through the forest, though the all-weather sports facilities could make you equally hungry. In summer, dine in the grill garden. Ask for a room in the older part—some of the modern rooms are somewhat plain. ⌧ *Stadtpl. 5,* ☏ *09942/1627,* ℻ *09942/6042. 42 rooms with bath. Restaurant, weinstube, pool, sauna, tennis. AE, DC, MC, V. Closed last 3 wks of Jan.* $$

Zwiesel

DINING AND LODGING

Gasthof Deutscher Rhein. Although this lodging is in the Bavarian Forest, it exudes a Bohemian atmosphere—from the crenulated facade of the 300-year-old building bearing the founder's Czech name to the specialties from the kitchen and the house brewery. You can sample traditional Bohemian game dishes and enjoy a Pilsner beer, which tastes as if it could have come from Pilsen, the famous Czech brewing town across the border. The modern rooms were recently refurbished to become the showpiece of the Ring hotel group in the Bavarian Forest. The wood-paneled Wirtsstube tavern provides visitors with a warm country-style welcome. ⌧ *Am Stadtpl. 42,* ☏ *09922/84100,* ℻ *09922/1652. 20 rooms with bath. AE, DC, MC, V. Closed 1st 3 wks of Dec.* $$

LODGING

Kurhotel Sonnenberg. Located high above Zwiesel, the Sonnenberg offers fine views of the forest and quick access to mountain walks and ski runs. It's a sporty hotel, with numerous fitness facilities and large, plushly furnished rooms, most with balcony. ⌧ *Augustinerstr. 9,* ☏ *09922/2032,* ℻ *09922/2913. 20 rooms, 1 apartment, all with bath or shower. Restaurant, indoor pool, sauna, exercise room, beauty salon. MC.* $$

Hotel zur Waldbahn. The great-grandfather of the current owner, assisted by 13 children, built the Hotel zur Waldbahn more than 100 years ago to accommodate travelers on the trains connecting Czechoslovakia with all points south. Today the emphasis is still put on making the traveler feel at home within the hotel's historic, wood-paneled walls. ⌧ *Bahnhofpl. 2,* ☏ *09922/3001. 28 rooms with bath or shower. Restaurant, hot tub, sauna, exercise room. No credit cards. Closed Nov.* $$

THE ARTS

Passau is the cultural center of Lower Bavaria. The Stiftung Wörlen Museum Moderner Kunst (Bräugasse 17, ☏ 0851/34091), a modern-art gallery, opened in Passau in 1990. The town's Europäische Wochen (European Weeks) festival—featuring everything from opera to pantomine—is now a major event on the European music calendar. The festival runs from June to early August. For program details and reservations, write the **Kartenzentrale der Europäischen Wochen Passau** (Dr. Hans Kapfinger Str. 22, Passau ☏ 0851/7966).

Passau also has a thriving theater company, the **Stadttheater,** which has its home in the beautiful little Baroque opera house of Passau's prince-bishops. Get program details and reservations from **Stadttheater** Passau (Gottfried-Schäffer-Str., ☏ 0851/929–1913). The city's cabaret company, the **Theater im Scharfrichter-Haus** (Milchgasse 2, ☏ 0851/35900) is nationally famous and hosts a German cabaret festival every fall (Oct.–Dec.). Fall is also the time for Passau's annual Kirmes (fair), followed in December by a **Christkindlmarkt** in the Nibelungenhalle (late Nov.–just before Chirstmas). Christmas markets are also held in towns throughout the Bavarian Forest—Deggendorf's is particularly spectacular.

In Deggendorf's newly completed "culture quarter," something of interest—a new Brecht production, perhaps, or a visiting jazz combo—is always going on.

At **Furth im Wald** (north of Cham), August sees Germany's oldest street **folk festival,** dating from medieval times. Dressed in period costume, townsfolk take part in the ritual slaying of a fire-breathing "dragon" that stalks the main street. Call 09973/3813 for exact dates and seat reservations.

Jazz fans head to nearby Vilshofen every June for the annual international jazz festival, staged in a special tent on the banks of the Danube. For program details and reservations, call 08541/2080. Live jazz programs are also regularly presented at Passau's Theater im Scharfrichterhaus (*see above*).

BAVARIAN FOREST ESSENTIALS

Arriving and Departing

By Car
The principal road links with the Bavarian Forest are the A–3 Autobahn from Nürnberg and the A–92 Autobahn from Munich. Nürnberg is 104 kilometers (65 miles) from Regensburg and 229 kilometers (140 miles) from Passau. Munich is 120 kilometers (75 miles) from Regensburg and 179 kilometers (110 miles) from Passau. Traffic on both roads is relatively light, even at peak periods.

By Plane
The nearest airports are at Munich and Nürnberg. Each is about 160 kilometers (100 miles) from the western edge of the Bavarian Forest.

Getting Around

By Boat
Ludwig Wurm (Donaustr. 71, D–93464 Irlach, ☎ 09424/1341) concentrates on a range of small cruise-ship services upriver between Passau and Regensburg, taking in Deggendorf, Metten, Straubing, and Walhalla, while its bigger sister company, **Wurm & Köck** (Höllgasse 26, D–94032 Passau, ☎ 0851/929–292), and the rival **Erste Donau**-Dampfschiffahrts-Gesellschaft, or **DDSG-Donaureisen** (Im Ort 14a, D–94032 Passau, ☎ 0851/33035), operate bigger ships and cruises from Passau into Austria as far as Vienna. In 1993, Wurm & Köck added the *Regina* Danubia, a 225-foot luxury day-cruise vessel, to its fleet, which travels between Passau and Austria, usually as far as Linz.

By Bus
Villages not on the railway line are well served by post bus. Passau has a municipal bus service that reaches into the hinterland.

By Car
The small country highways and side roads within this region are less traveled, making the entire area something of a paradise for those who have experienced only the high-speed mayhem of most other German roads. B–85 runs the length of the Bavarian Forest from Passau to Cham,

and its designation as a route of special scenic interest (the Ostmark-strasse) extends northward to Bayreuth.

CAR RENTAL
Budget: Stelzlhof 7 (on the Franz Josef Strauss bridge), ☎ 0851/603–839, **Passau.**

Europcar: Graflingerstr. 125, ☎ 0991/28181, **Deggendorf;** Bahnhofs-trasse 29 (west wing of main railway station), ☎ 0851/54235, **Passau.**

Hertz: Industriestrasse 12, ☎ 0851/801211, **Passau.**

By Train

Two main rail lines cross the region: One runs west–east via Nürnberg, Regensburg, Passau, and Vienna; the other runs south–north via Munich, Landshut, and Straubing. This latter route slices right through the heart of the Bavarian Forest on its way to the Czech Republic (if you fancy overnighting in Prague, this is the train route to take). Plattling, just south of Deggendorf, and Cham are the main rail junctions for the area. Passau is the principal rail gateway on the border between southeast Germany and Austria.

Guided Tours

The tourist offices at Freyung, Grafenau, and Tittling organize bus tours of the region and excursions into Czechoslovakia. The Freyung tourist office (☎ 08551/58850) has weekly half-day trips to the Bavarian National Park and to the Dreisessel Mountain for DM 8. The **Wolff Ost-Reisen** bus company in Furth im Wald (☎ 09973/5080) offers one- and two-day excursions to Prague twice a week between May and October, as well trips to the former royal spa town of Karlsbad (now Karlovy Vary) in Bohemia, as do the tourist offices of Grafenau (☎ 08552/42743) and Tittling (☎ 08504/40114). In Tittling, the **Hötl** bus company (☎ 08504/4040) has daily excursions into the Bavarian Forest in summer. The **Furth im Wald** tourist office (☎ 09973/3813) publishes a sightseeing guide to border areas of the Czech Republic, including the historic town of Domažlice.

Guided tours of **Passau** are organized from April through October by the city tourist office (☎ 0851/39190). There are two tours (at 10:30 and 2:30) on weekdays and one (at 2:30) on weekends. Tours start at King Max Joseph monument in the Domplatz (the cathedral square) and last one hour. The cost is DM 3.50 adults, DM 2 children. Tours of the **Dom** take place Monday through Saturday from May through October at 12:30 (assemble at the front right-hand aisle of the cathedral), and from November through April at noon (assemble under the cathedral organ). The tour costs DM 2.

Cruises on Passau's three rivers begin and end at the Danube jetties on Fritz-Schäffer Promenade. Forty-five-minute trips on the Danube, Inn, and Ilz are run from March through October by **Wurm & Köck** (☎ 0851/929292). The cost is DM 10 for adults and DM 5 for children. The Three Rivers trip can be combined with a cruise as far as Linz, Austria (including an overnight stay in Passau or Linz), for DM 135. Another cruise overnights in four-star hotels in Linz and Vienna and ends with a rail journey back to Passau (DM 379–DM 399). Every Friday and Saturday from May through October, a Wurm & Köck ship becomes a floating dance floor, with live bands performing on deck during evening cruises on the Danube (for DM 25). From mid-May through September, the Hungarian cruise ship *Rakoczi* invites revellers aboard every Thursday and Saturday for an evening of Hungarian music, food, and wine. The **DDSG** company (☎ 0851/33035) offers two-day cruises to Vienna, with passengers sleeping in two-bed cabins, for around DM 250 per person one-way. DDSG also offers Danube cruise connections via Budapest all the way to the Black Sea.

On the Inn River, an Austrian shipping operator, **M. Schaurecker** (A.-Stifterstr. 581, A-4780 Schärding, ☎ 0043/771–23231), runs a daily service Tuesday through Sunday, mid-March through October, between Passau and the enchanting Austrian river town of Schärding. The round-trip fare is DM 12.

Important Addresses and Numbers

Tourist Information

There are local tourist information offices in the following towns:

Bayerisch-Eisenstein: Verkehrsamt Bayerisch-Eisenstein, Schulbergstrasse, D–94252 Bayerisch-Eisenstein, ☎ 09925/327.

Bodenmais: Kur-Verkehrsamt, Bodenmais, Bahnhofstrasse 56, D–94249 Bodenmais, ☎ 09924/77835.

Cham: Verkehrsverein Cham, Propsteistrasse 46, D–93413 Cham, ☎ 09971/4933.

Deggendorf: Verkehrsverein Deggendorf, Oberer Stadtplatz 4, D–94469 Deggendorf, ☎ 0991/296–0169.

Freyung: Verkehrsamt Freyung, Rathausweg 1, D–94078 Freyung, ☎ 08551/58850.

Furth im Wald: Verkehrsverein Furth im Wald, Schlossplatz 1, D–93437 Furth im Wald, ☎ 09973/3813.

Grafenau: Verkehrsamt Grafenau, Rathausgasse 1, D–94481 Grafenau, ☎ 08552/42743.

Passau: Fremdenverkehrsverein Passau, Rathausplatz 3, D–94032 Passau, ☎ 0851/39190.

Regen: Verkehrsamt Haus des Gastes, Stadtplatz, D–94209 Regen, ☎ 09921/2929.

St. Englmar: Verkehrsamt St. Englmar, Rathausstrasse 6, D–94379 St. Englmar, ☎ 09965/221.

Straubing: Städtisches Verkehrsamt Straubing, Rathaus, Theresienplatz, D–94315 Straubing, ☎ 09421/944–307.

Tittling: Verkehrsamt Tittling, Marktplatz 10, D–94104 Tittling, ☎ 08504/40114.

Viechtach: Städtisches Kur- und Verkehrsamt, Rathaus, D–94234 Viechtach, ☎ 09942/1661.

Waldkirchen: Fremdenverkehrsamt Waldkirchen, Ringmauerstrasse 14, D–94065 Waldkirchen, ☎ 08581/20250.

Zwiesel: Kurverwaltung, Stadtplatz 27, D–94227 Zwiesel, ☎ 09922/1308 or 9623.

6 The Black Forest

Cake and smoked ham aren't the only reasons to visit the Black Forest, but they are good ones. Spa and casino resorts, outdoor activities, and cuckoo clocks are other draws. The Romans were the first to take advantage of the area's healing waters, 19 centuries ago, and royalty and the cultural elite paraded about the region in the 1800s. Today, watching vacationers here is a study in contrasts; high-fashion, high-cost towns like Baden-Baden share the trees with down-home German country villages.

THE BLACK FOREST—SCHWARZWALD IN GERMAN—is a name that conjures up images of a wild, isolated place where time passes so slowly it can be measured by the number of rings on the trunks of felled trees. And this southwest corner of Germany is indeed a rural region where dense woodland stretches away to the horizon; but it is neither inaccessible nor a backwater. The first recorded holidaymakers checked in here 19 centuries ago, when the Roman emperor Caracalla and his army rested and soothed their battle wounds in the natural-spring waters of what later became Baden-Baden.

Celebrated names have long been associated with the Black Forest. In 1770 the 15-year-old daughter of the empress Maria Theresa, traveling between Vienna and Paris with an entourage of 250 officials and servants in some 50 horse-drawn carriages, made her way along the coach road through the Höllental (Hell Valley) to spend the night at Hinterzarten, where the future Queen Marie Antoinette checked into a renowned coach inn that had been in business since 1446; now called the Park Hotel Adler, it's still number one in that prestigious resort town (*see* Dining and Lodging, *below*).

In the 19th century just about everyone who mattered in Europe gravitated to Baden-Baden: kings, queens, emperors, princes and princesses, members of Napoléon's family, and the Russian nobility, along with actors, actresses, writers, and composers. Turgenev, Dostoyevsky, and Tolstoy were among the Russian contingent. Victor Hugo was a frequent visitor. Brahms composed lilting melodies in this calm setting. Queen Victoria spent her vacations here. Today it's a favorite vacation setting for millionaires, movie stars, and the new corporate royalty.

Mark Twain could be said to have put the Black Forest on the tourist map for Americans. In his 1880 book *A Tramp Abroad* he waxed poetic on the beauties of this forest.

Today you can come here for rest and relaxation and to "take the waters," as the Romans first did, at thermal resorts large or small. The Black Forest offers a wide range of sporting activities, catering particularly to the German enthusiasm for hiking with its virtually limitless trails wending their way in and out of the woods. In winter these same trails serve as tracks for cross-country skiing on some of Europe's most ideally suited terrain for this popular sport.

The Black Forest's enviable sporting scene is blessed by dependable snow in winter and warming sun in summer. Freudenstadt, at the center of the Black Forest, claims the greatest number of annual hours of sunshine of any town in Germany. You can play tennis, swim, or bike at most resorts, and some have golf courses of international standards.

The Black Forest is Germany's southernmost wine region and home to some of the country's finest traditional food. Black Forest smoked ham and Black Forest cake are both world-famous, and that's only the beginning.

The Black Forest also happens to be the home of the cuckoo clock, despite Orson Welles's claim in *The Third Man* that all Switzerland managed to create in 500 years of peace and prosperity was this trivial timepiece. Cuckoo clocks are still made (and sold) here, as they have been since more or less time immemorial, along with hand-carved wood artifacts and exquisite examples of glassblowing (*see* Shopping, *below*).

Despite its fame and the wealth of some of its visitors, the Black Forest can be a great value. It's possible to stay at a modest, family-run country inn or farmhouse where the enormous breakfast they'll feed you will keep you going for the better part of the day—all for not much more than the price of a meal in a German city restaurant.

EXPLORING

Tour 1: Pforzheim to Freiburg

Numbers in the margin correspond to points of interest on the Black Forest map.

❶ Our tour begins at **Pforzheim**, an ancient city founded by the Romans at the meeting place of three rivers, the most important of which is the Würm. The city is just off the A–8 Autobahn, the main Munich–Karlsruhe route. Pforzheim was almost totally destroyed in World War II; it has since been rebuilt in a blocky postwar style and continues to prosper. For a sense of its former flair, visit the restored church of **St. Michael** in the center of the city. The original mixture of 13th- and 15th-century styles has been faithfully reproduced; contrast the airy Gothic choir with the church's sturdy Romanesque entrance.

Pforzheim owes its prosperity to Europe's jewelry trade, of which it is a center. To get a sense of "Gold City," explore the jewelry shops on streets around Leopoldplatz. The Reuchlinhaus, the city cultural cen-
★ ter, has a jewelry museum, the **Schmuckmuseum.** Its glittering collection of 17th- to 20th-century pieces is one of the finest in the world. *Jahnstr. 42,* ☎ *07231/392–126.* ☛ *DM 5 adults, DM 3 children.* ☉ *Tues.–Sun. 10–5.*

Pforzheim is also known as a center of the German clock-making industry. In the **Technisches Museum,** one of the country's leading museums devoted to the craft, you can see watch- and clock-makers at work; there's also a reconstructed 18th-century clock factory. *Bleichstr. 81.* ☛*Free.* ☉ *Wed. 9–noon and 3–6, and every 2nd and 4th Sun. of the month 10–noon and 2–5.*

Leave Pforzheim on the road south, B–463, which follows the twists and turns of the pretty little Nagold River. Gardening enthusiasts should follow the signs to the **Alpine Garden** (on the left as you leave the city limits). The garden, on the banks of the Würm River, stocks more than 100,000 varieties of plants, including the rarest Alpine flowers. ☉ *Mid-Apr.–Oct., daily 8–7.*

❷ Back on B–463, you'll soon reach picturesque **Bad Liebenzell,** one of the Black Forest's oldest spas. Bathhouses were built here as early as 1403. Nearly six centuries later, the same hot springs feed the more modern installations that have taken the place of the medieval originals. Apart from medicinal baths (highly recommended for the treatment of circulatory problems), there is a lido with outdoor and indoor hot-water pools. *Paracelsus Baths.* ☛ *DM 11.50 adults, DM 5 children for 3 hrs.* ☉ *Mon. 8:30–5, Tues.–Sat. 8:30–8, Sun. and holidays 8:30–7.*

The other principal pastime in and around Bad Liebenzell is walking along the Nagold River valley. Winding through the thick woods around the little town is a path that leads to the partially restored 13th-

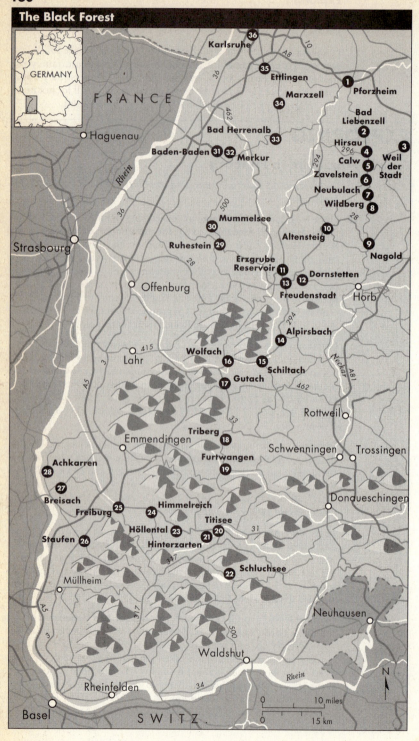

The Black Forest

GERMANY

FRANCE

Karlsruhe **36**

35 Ettlingen

Marxzell

34

Pforzheim **1**

Bad
Liebenzell **2**

Bad Herrenalb

33

Hirsau **3**

4

Baden-Baden **31** **32** Merkur

Calw **5**

Zavelstein **6**

Neubulach **7**

Wildberg **8**

Weil
der
Stadt

Mummelsee **30**

Ruhestein **29**

Altensteig **10**

Nagold **9**

Erzgrube
Reservoir **11**

Dornstetten **12**

13

Freudenstadt

Horb

Haguenau

Strasbourg

Offenburg

Alpirsbach **14**

Wolfach **16** **15** Schiltach

17 Gutach

Lahr

Neckar

Rottweil

Triberg **18**

Emmendingen

Furtwangen **19**

Schwenningen

Trossingen

Achkarren **28**

27

Breisach

Freiburg **25**

24 Himmelreich

Donaueschingen

Höllental **23**

Titisee

21 **20**

Staufen **26**

Hinterzarten

Schluchsee **22**

Müllheim

Neuhausen

Waldshut

Rheinfelden

Rhein

Basel

SWITZ.

Rhein

N

| 0 | 10 miles |
| 0 | 15 km |

century castle of **Liebenzell,** today an international youth center and youth hostel.

❸ If you have time, drive into the hills behind Bad Liebenzell to the former imperial city of **Weil der Stadt,** a small, sleepy town with only its well-preserved city walls and fortifications to remind the visitor of its onetime importance. The astronomer Johannes Kepler, born here in 1571, was the first man to track and accurately explain the orbits of the planets; the **Kepler Museum** in the town center is devoted to his discoveries. *Keplergasse 2.* ☛ *DM 1.* ☉ *Tues.–Fri. 10–noon and 2–4, Sat. 11–noon and 2–4, Sun. and holidays 11–noon and 2–5; (open only 1st and 3rd Sun. of the month Oct.–May).*

❹ **Hirsau,** 5 kilometers (3 miles) southwest on B–463, is the site of the ruins of a 9th-century monastery, now the setting for open-air theater performances in the summer.

❺ **Calw,** 3 kilometers (2 miles) farther south, is one of the Black Forest's prettiest towns. The novelist Hermann Hesse (1877–1962) was born here. Pause on the town's 15th-century bridge over the Nagold River; you might see a local tanner spreading hides on the river wall to dry, as his ancestors did for centuries. The town's market square, with its two sparkling fountains surrounded by 18th-century half-timbered houses whose sharp gables stab at the sky, is an ideal spot for relaxing, picnicking, or people-watching.

❻ On the road south again, watch for a sign to **Zavelstein,** 5 kilometers (3 miles) out of Calw. The short detour up a side valley to this tiny town is well worth taking, particularly in spring, when surrounding meadows are carpeted with wild crocuses.

❼ Back on the main road going south you'll come next to a turnoff marked **Talmühle/Seitzental.** From here, a winding road leads to **Neubulach,** a town that was home to one of the oldest and, until it closed in 1924, most productive silver mines of the Black Forest. Since then a new use has been found for the mine's extensive workings: Doctors discovered that the dust-free interior of the mine helped in the treatment of asthma patients. Today, rather incongruously, a therapy center is located in the mine. The ancient shafts can also be visited. ☛ *Guided tour of mine: DM 4 adults, DM 3 children.* ☉ *Apr.–Nov., daily 10–4:15.*

❽ Arrive in **Wildberg,** 8 kilometers (5 miles) farther south, on the third Sunday of July in an even-numbered year and you'll witness one of Germany's most picturesque contests, the **Schäferlauf,** in which Black Forest shepherds demonstrate their skill and speed in managing their flocks. Those unable to time their arrival quite so precisely will find that the appealing little fortified town nonetheless has much to command attention, including a 15th-century wooden town hall and the remains of a medieval castle.

⑨ Leaving **Nagold,** head west toward Freudenstadt on local highway B–28.
⑩ The road that skirts another jewel of the Black Forest, the ancient town
of **Altensteig,** which is on a sunny terracelike slope above the Nagold
River. A steep, marked route up the hill through the narrow, medieval
streets brings you (huffing and puffing) into a marvelous, unspoiled
old town with half-timbered houses and a city museum in the old castle.

⑪ In summer, pause at the man-made reservoir by **Erzgrube,** 12 kilometers (8 miles) away (follow signs to Erzgrube), for a swim, a picnic, or
a hike through one of the thickest parts of the Black Forest, where 200-
year-old trees tower to heights of 150 feet or more.

B–28 continues, passing the oldest town of the northern Black Forest,
⑫ **Dornstetten.** If you fancy another dip into the past, stop to see the 17th-
century town hall, flanked by equally venerable old buildings, the low
eaves of their red roofs framing magnificent half-timbered facades. The
fountain dates from the 16th century.

⑬ The road then snakes through lush farmland to **Freudenstadt,** another
war-torn city rebuilt with painstaking care. It's a young city by German standards, founded in 1599 to house workers from the nearby
silver mines and refugees from religious persecution in what is now the
Austrian province of Carinthia (*Freudenstadt* means City of Joy).
You'll find the streets still laid out in the checkerboard formation decreed by the original planners, the vast central square still waiting for
the palace that was intended to stand there. It was to have been built
for the city's founder, Prince Frederick I of Württemberg; he, unfortunately, died before work could begin. Don't miss Freudenstadt's
Protestant parish church, just off the square. Its lofty nave is L-shaped,
a rare architectural liberty in the early 17th century, when this imposing
church was built. Freudenstadt claims to have more annual hours of
sunshine than any other German resort, so you should be able to sit
in the sunbathed Renaissance arcades of the fine main square and bask
in the warmth of the rays.

TIME OUT   Sixteen kilometers (10 miles) farther south, take a break for a glass of
beer at any of the small taverns in the town of **Alpirsbach.** The unusually
soft water gives the village-brewed beer a flavor that is widely acclaimed. The brewery was once part of a monastic settlement and visitors are welcome to look around. In summer concerts are held regularly
in Alpirsbach's fine 11th-century parish church.

⑮ ⑭ South of **Alpirsbach,** stop at **Schiltach,** 10 kilometers (6 miles) along,
to admire the frescoes on the 16th-century town hall. They tell the town's
history more vividly than any local chronicle could. Look for the figure of the Devil, who was blamed for burning down the town on more
than one occasion.

★ ⑯ Leaving Schiltach, follow the B–294 highway 14 kilometers (9 miles)
to **Wolfach.** It's the site of the **Dorotheenhütte,** one of the only remaining
Black Forest factories where glass is blown using the centuries-old techniques that were once common throughout the region. ☞ *Guided
tours: DM 4 adults, DM 3 children.* ☼ *Weekdays 9–4:30, Sat. 9–2.*

Just outside Wolfach is one of the most diverting museums in the Black
Forest, the **Vogtsbauernhof Freilichtmuseum** (Open-Air Museum).
Farmhouses and other rural buildings from all parts of the region have
been transported here from their original locations and reassembled,
complete with traditional furniture, to create a living museum of Black

Forest building types through the centuries. ☎ 07831/230. ☛ *DM 5 adults, DM 3 children.* ⊙ *Apr.–Oct., daily 8:30–6.*

The road south from Wolfach follows the **Gutachtal,** a valley famous for the traditional costume, complete with pom-pom hats, worn by its women on feast days and holidays. The pom-poms' color has significance: Married women wear black pom-poms; those who are unmarried wear red. The village of **Gutach** is one of the few places in the Black Forest where you can still see traditional thatched roofs. However, escalating costs caused by a decline in thatching skills, in addition to the ever-present risk of fire, mean that there are substantially fewer thatched roofs in Gutach than there were 20 years ago.

At the head of the valley, 13 kilometers (9 miles) south, lies the town of **Triberg,** the site of Germany's highest waterfall, where the Gutach River plunges nearly 500 feet over seven huge granite steps. The pleasant 30-minute walk from the center of Triberg to the top of the spectacular falls is well signposted. ☛ *To view waterfall: DM 2.50 adults, DM 1 children (this may be waived in winter).*

Another of Triberg's attractions is its famous **Schwarzwaldmuseum,** which has exhibits related to Black Forest culture. This is cuckoo-clock country, and the museum has an impressive collection of clocks. The oldest dates from 1640; its simple wooden mechanism is said to have been carved with a bread knife. *Wallfahrtstr. 4.* ☛ *DM 4 adults, DM 2 children.* ⊙ *May–Sept., daily 9–6; Oct. and mid-Dec.–Apr., daily 10–noon and 2–5; Nov.–mid-Dec., weekends 10–noon and 2–5.*

Triberg is on a tourist route dubbed "The Cuckoo-Clock Road;" die-hard clock enthusiasts can continue on to the **Uhren,** or clock, **museum** in **Furtwangen,** 16 kilometers (10 miles) south. This is the largest clock museum in Germany, and it charts the development of Black Forest clocks, the cuckoo clock taking pride of place. Its massive centerpiece is a 25-hundredweight astronomical clock built by a local master. *Gerwigstr. 11,* ☎ *07723/920–117.* ☛ *DM 4 adults, DM 2 children.* ⊙ *Apr.–Oct., daily 9–5. Nov.–Mar., daily 10–4.*

From Furtwangen you're only 21 kilometers (13 miles) from the Black Forest's lakeland, with the **Titisee,** a rare jewel among lakes, as star attraction. Set in a mighty forest, the 1½-mile-long lake is invariably crowded in summer with boats and Windsurfers. Boats and boards can be rented at several points along the shore.

From Titisee it's 5 kilometers (3 miles) to the lovely 800-year-old town of **Hinterzarten,** the most important resort in the southern Black Forest. Some buildings date from the 12th century, among them **St. Oswald's** church, built in 1146. Hinterzarten's oldest inn, **Weisses Rossle,** has been in business since 1347. The **Park Hotel Adler,** established in 1446, has been under the same family management for 14 generations, although the original building was burned down during the Thirty Years' War and the inn where Marie Antoinette and her retinue stayed in 1770 has been considerably altered since her visit.

Hinterzarten is situated at the highest point along the Freiburg–Donaueschingen road, and from it a network of far-ranging hiking trails fan out into the surrounding forest. In winter Hinterzarten is one of Germany's most popular centers for *Langlauf* (cross-country skiing).

The largest of the Black Forest lakes, mountain-enclosed **Schluchsee,** is 25 kilometers (16 miles) from Hinterzarten. Take Highway B–317 along the lower slopes of the 4,500-foot Feldberg, the Black Forest's highest mountain, then pick up B–500. Schluchsee is a diverse resort, offering swimming, windsurfing, fishing, and, in winter, skiing. For details, contact the local tourist office (☎ 07656/7732).

From Schluchsee head toward Freiburg, the largest city in the southern Black Forest. To get there by the shortest route you'll have to brave **㉓** the curves of the winding road through **Höllental** (Hell Valley). The first stop at the end of the valley is a little village called, appropriately enough, **㉔** **Himmelreich,** or Kingdom of Heaven. The village is said to have been given its name in the 19th century by railroad engineers, who were grateful that they had finally laid a line through Hell Valley. At the entrance to Höllental is a deep gorge, the **Ravennaschlucht.** It's worth scrambling through to reach the tiny 12th-century chapel of **St. Oswald,** the oldest parish church in the Black Forest.

Back on B–31, watch for the appearance of a bronze statue of a deer high on a roadside cliff, 5 kilometers (3 miles) farther. It commemorates the local legend of a deer that amazed hunters by leaping the deep gorge at this point. Another 16 kilometers (10 miles) will bring you to Freiburg.

㉕ **Freiburg,** or Freiburg im Breisgau (as it's called to distinguish it from another Freiburg in eastern Germany) was founded in the 12th century. After extensive wartime bomb damage, skillful restoration has helped re-create the original and compelling medieval atmosphere of one of the loveliest historic towns in Germany. Freiburg has had its share of misadventures through the years. In 1632 and 1638, Protestant Swedish troops in the Thirty Years' War captured the city; in 1644 it was taken by Catholic Bavarian troops; and in 1677, 1713, and 1744 French troops captured it. Perhaps more interesting to Americans, the 16th-century geographer Martin Waldseemüller, who first put the name America on a map in 1507, was born here. Between April and October, the tourist office sponsors English walking tours on Monday and Friday–Sunday at 2:30, Wednesday and Thursday at 10:00. The two-hour tours cost DM 8 for adults, DM 2 for children.

★ Towering over the rebuilt medieval streets of the city is its most famous landmark, the **Münster,** Freiburg's cathedral. The pioneering 19th-century Swiss art historian Jacob Burckhardt described its delicately perforated 370-foot spire as the finest in Europe. The cathedral took three centuries to build, from around 1200 to 1515. You can easily trace the progress of generations of builders through the changing architectural styles, from the fat columns and solid, rounded arches of the Romanesque period to the lofty Gothic windows and airy interior of the choir, the last parts of the building to be completed. Of particular interest are the luminous 13th-century stained-glass windows; a 16th-century triptych (three-panel painting) by Hans Baldung Grien; and paintings by Holbein the Younger and Lucas Cranach the Elder. If you can summon the energy, climb the tower; the reward is a magnificent view of the city and the Black Forest beyond.

The cathedral square, or Münsterplatz, also hosts a daily market, where you can buy everything from strings of garlic to scented oils before the facade of the 16th-century market house, the **Kaufhaus.** The square is also lined with traditional taverns serving such local specialties as Black Forest ham and Swabian *Spätzle* (small, chewy noodles).

The city's other main square is **Rathaus Platz,** where Freiburg's famous **Rathaus** (Town Hall) stands, constructed from two 16th-century patrician houses joined together. Among its attractive Renaissance features is an oriel, or bay window, clinging to a corner and bearing a bas-relief of the romantic medieval legend of the Maiden and the Unicorn.

For a more intimate view of Freiburg, wander through the streets around the Münster, or follow the main shopping artery of Josephstrasse. After you pass a reconstructed city gate (this one is **Martinstor;** the other is called **Schwabentor**), follow **Fischerau** off to the left. River fishermen used to live on this little alley. You'll come to quaint shops along the bank of one of the city's larger canals, which continues past the old **Augustine cloister** to the equally picturesque areaaround **Insel** island. This canal is a larger version of the brooklets running through many streets in Freiburg's old town; tradition has it that anyone who steps into one of these *Bächle* is sure to return to Freiburg.

TIME OUT For an atmospheric taste of Old Freiburg, look into the little *Weinstube* called **Zur Trotte** on Fischerau. This establishment serves simple, local specialties (both lunch and dinner) and a variety of local wines in a traditional, rustic interior featuring a big tile oven (*Kachelofen*).

Once you've braved Hell Valley to get to Freiburg, a visit to the nearby ❷❻ town of **Staufen,** where Dr. Faustus is reputed to have made his pact with the Devil, should hold no horrors. It's 20 kilometers (12 miles) south of Freiburg via B–31. The legend of Faustus is remembered today chiefly because of Goethe's 1808 drama *Faust,* perhaps the leading single work of German literature. Goethe's Faust, fed up with life and the futility of academic studies, is driven to make a pact with the Devil, selling his soul in return for youth, action, and other Satanic favors. In fact, the original Faustus was an alchemist, an early scientist, in the 16th century. His pact was not with the Devil but with a local baron who was convinced that Faustus could make his fortune by discovering the secret of how to make gold from base metals. In his attempts Dr. Faustus died in an explosion that produced such noise and sulfurous stink that the townspeople were convinced the Devil had carried him off. You can visit the ancient inn, the **Gasthaus zum Löwen** in the town center (Hauptstr. 47), where Faustus lived and died. The frescoes on its walls tell his story in vivid detail.

Tour 2: North to Baden-Baden and Karlsruhe

Staufen is on the Wine Road, the **Weinstrasse,** another of the routes drawn up by the tourist authorities of the Black Forest. It's also the southernmost point of this Black Forest tour. From here the tour makes its way north through the southernmost vineyards of Germany, source of the prized Baden wine, to Baden-Baden.

Twenty kilometers (12 miles) northwest of Freiburg on B–31 is the town ❷❼ of **Breisach.** It stands by the Rhine River; everything you see to the west on the opposite bank is in France. Towering high above the town and the surrounding vineyards is the **Stephansmünster,** the cathedral of St. Stephen, built between 1200 and 1500 (and almost entirely rebuilt after World War II). As at Freiburg, the transition from sturdy Romanesque styles to airy and vertical Gothic styles is easy to see. North of the town rises the **Kaiserstuhl,** or Emperor's Chair, a volcanic outcrop clothed in vineyards that produce high-quality wines. Sample some in one of ❷❽ the taverns of the village of **Achkarren,** 5 kilometers (3 miles) north of Breisach; you can also visit the fine little **wine museum** in the village. ☛ *Museum: DM 2 adults, DM 1 children. Open Apr.–Oct., weekdays 2–5, weekends 11–4 by arrangement.*

As you make your way north you'll drive past numerous vineyards and wine villages. Most of these vineyards offer tastings. There's no obligation to buy, and you certainly won't be pressured into it. But praise is considered polite. You'll leave the Weinstrasse at **Lahr,** 40 kilometers (25 miles) north of the Kaiserstuhl. Here you should turn right (east) onto B–415 and head along the narrow **Shuttertal Valley** to **Zell,** 15 kilometers (10 miles) away. A winding mountain road takes you the 21 kilometers (13 miles) to the A–28 highway. Turn right to **Freudenstadt,** then left for B–500 and Baden-Baden.

㉙ You're back on the Black Forest High Road now, the Schwarzwald Hochstrasse, in the land of myth and fable. At the little village of **Ruhestein,** the side road on the left leads to the **Allerheiligen** monastery ruins. This 12th-century monastery was secularized in 1803, at which point plans were drawn up to turn it into a prison. Two days later, lightning started a fire that burned the monastery to the ground. To this day the locals claim it was divine intervention.

㉚ Five kilometers (3 miles) north of Ruhestein you'll reach another source of local myth. This is the **Mummelsee,** a small, almost circular lake that has fascinated local people and visitors alike for centuries. Because of the lake's high mineral conten there are no fish in it. According to legend, however, sprites and other spirits of the deep find it to their liking. The Romantic lyric poet Mörike (1804–1875) immortalized the lake in his ballad *The Spirits of the Mummelsee.* The lake is a popular destination in the summer; if you can, visit during the mist-laden days of spring and allow yourself to fall victim to its full mysterious appeal.

★ **㉛** From the Mummelsee it's downhill all the way to the famous and fashionable spa of **Baden-Baden,** set in a wooded valley of the northern Black Forest and sitting atop the extensive underground hot springs that gave the city its name. The Roman legions of the emperor Caracalla discovered the springs when they settled here in the 1st century and named the place Aquae. The leisure classes of the 19th century rediscovered the bubbling waters, establishing Baden-Baden as the unofficial summer residence of many of Europe's royal families, who left their imprint on the city in the palatial homes and stately villas that still grace its tree-lined avenues.

The small, neat city, so harmoniously set within the surrounding forest, has a flair and style all its own. As Germany's ultimate high-fashion resort, it basks unabashedly in leisure and pleasure. Here the splendor of the Belle Epoch lives on to a remarkable extent. Some claim that one out of five residents is a millionaire. In the evening, Baden-Baden is a soft-music-and-champagne-in-a-silver-bucket kind of place, and in the daytime it follows the horseback-riding-along-the-bridle-paths tradition. It has a crowded season of ballet performances, theater, concerts, and recitals, along with exciting horse racing and high-stakes action at its renowned casino.

Baden-Baden claims that the casino, Germany's first, is the most beautiful in the world, a boast that not even the French can challenge, for it was a Parisian, Jacques Bénazet, who persuaded the sleepy little Black Forest spa to build gambling rooms to enliven its evenings. In 1853, his son Edouard Bénazet commissioned Charles Séchan, a stage designer associated with the Paris opera house, to come up with a design along the lines of the greatest French imperial palaces. The result was a series of richly decorated gaming rooms in which even an emperor could feel at home—and did. Kaiser Wilhelm I was a regular visitor, as was his chancellor, Bismarck. Visitors as disparate as the Russian novelist Dostoyevsky, the Aga Khan, and Marlene Dietrich were all patrons.

Few people visit Baden-Baden to go sightseeing (though those who feel the urge might want to see the **Neues Schloss,** or New Castle, a 19th-century fortress that was rebuilt in the Renaissance style for the grand dukes of Baden; today it's a museum of local history). If you come here to take the waters, still have a flutter in the casino (*see* The Arts and Nightlife, *below*), and perhaps take a swim in the positively palatial **Caracalla Baths,** a vast complex with no fewer than seven pools, opened in 1985 (*see* Sports and Fitness, *below*). Above all, you'll want to stroll around this supremely elegant resort and sample the gracious atmosphere of a place that, more than almost anywhere else in Europe, retains the feeling of a more unhurried, leisured age.

TIME OUT At the start of the pedestrian shopping street, Lichtentalerstrasse, stands a Baden-Baden institution, the **Cafe König;** step inside to soak up its warmly inviting elegance. Order a pot of coffee and a wedge of Black Forest cake and listen to the hum of money and leisure from the spa crowd, who have made this quiet corner their haunt.

Leaving Baden-Baden, take the road to **Gernsbach,** a couple of miles to the east. The road skirts Baden-Baden's own mountain peak, the **32** 2,000-foot-high **Merkur,** named after a Roman monument to the god Mercury, which still stands just below the mountain summit. You can take the cable car to the summit, but it's not a trip for the faint-hearted—with an incline of more than 50%, this is one of Europe's steepest mountain lifts. *Cost round-trip: DM 5 adults, DM 3 children.* ☼ *Mid-Feb.–mid-Dec., daily 10–6.*

33 Drive the 15 kilometers (10 miles) to **Bad Herrenalb,** another popular Black Forest spa, set amid the wooded folds of the Alb River valley. Railway enthusiasts will admire the train station here; it's actually Baden-Baden's original station, built in the 19th century. It was saved from destruction during the modernization of the Baden-Baden station when it was transported and erected here.

Eight kilometers (5 miles) north on the road to Karlsruhe, the final point **34** of the tour, lies the village of **Marxzell.** A group of ancient locomotives and other old machines at the side of the road announces the presence of the **Fahrzeugmuseum,** a wonderland for the technically minded. Every kind of early engine is represented in this museum dedicated to the German automobile pioneer Karl Benz (1844–1929). Germans claim that it was he who built the first practical automobile in 1888, a claim hotly disputed by the French. *Albtalstr. 2,* ☎ *07248/6262.* ☛ *DM 5 adults, DM 3 children.* ☼ *Daily 2–5.*

35 From Marxzell, head for **Ettlingen,** a 1,200-year-old town that's now practically a suburb of its newer and much larger neighbor, **Karlsruhe.** Bordered by the Alb River, Ettlingen's ancient center is a maze of auto-free cobbled streets. Visit in summer for the annual Schlossberg theater and music festival in the beautiful **Baroque Schloss** (palace) (*see* The Arts and Nightlife, *below*). The palace was built in the mid-18th century, and its striking domed chapel—today a concert hall—was designed by Cosmas Damian Asam, a leading figure of south German Baroque. Its ornate, swirling ceiling fresco is typical of the heroic, large-scale, illusionistic decoration of the period.

36 **Karlsruhe,** founded at the beginning of the 18th century, is a young upstart compared with ancient Ettlingen. But what it lacks in years, it makes up for in industrial and administrative importance, sitting as it does, astride a vital Autobahn and railroad crossroads. It holds little of major attraction for the visitor, apart from the former palace of the Margrave Karl Wilhelm, today the **Badisches Landesmuseum,** the museum of local history. The town quite literally grew up around the palace, which was begun in 1715; 32 avenues radiate out from it, 23 leading into the extensive grounds and the remaining nine forming the grid of the old town. It's said that the margrave fell asleep under a great oak while searching for a fan lost by his wife and dreamed that his new city should be laid out in the shape of a fan. True or false, the fact is that the city is built on a fan pattern, and all the principal streets, with one exception, lead directly to the palace. The exception is the Kaiserstrasse, constructed in 1800, which runs parallel to the palace.

Despite wartime bomb damage, much of the old town retains its original and elegant 18th-century appearance thanks to faithful restoration. Walk to the **Marktplatz,** the central square, to see the austere stone pyramid that marks the margrave's tomb and the severe neoclassical **Stephanskirche,** the church of St. Stephen, modeled on the Pantheon in Rome and built around 1810. The interior, rebuilt after the war, is incongruously modern.

What to See and Do with Children

Take a slide down the **dry toboggan run** at **Poppeltal,** located on the Schwarzwald-Baderstrasse, 20 kilometers (12 miles) south of Wildbad. The narrow, twisting run descends more than a half mile through the forest.

In Baden-Baden there's a toy museum, **Spielzeugmuseum,** featuring dollhouses, some of which are 200 years old. *Gernsbacherstr. 48,* ☎ *07221/32511.* ☛ *DM 3.50 adults, DM 2 children.* ☉ *Tues.–Fri. and Sun. 3–6.*

There's a similar toy museum in Bad Herrenalb. ☉ *Tues.–Sat. 2:30–5:30, Sun. and holidays 10–noon and 2:30–5:30.*

Stargazers will love Freiburg's **planetarium.** *Friedrichstr. 51,* ☎ *0761/276–099.* ☛ *DM 3 adults, DM 2 children. Shows: Tues. at 7:30 PM, Wed. at 3 PM, and Fri. at 7:30 PM.*

Tour the disused silver mines at **Neubulach,** at Talmühle (*see* Exploring, *above*). Ride the **Black Forest Railway** through Hell Valley from Freiburg to the mountain resort of Hinterzarten; trains depart regularly from Freiburg's main station (contact the Deutsche Bahn in Freiburg at 0761/19419). **Steam trains** along the Wutach River valley depart from Blumberg, 55 kilometers (34 miles) southeast of Titisee. Another historic steam train makes occasional trips from the old station at Bad Herrenalb; for information and schedule, contact H. Heger at the Karlsruhe branch of the Ulmer Eisenbahnfreunde (☎ 07247/21230). Spend a few hours, or even the day, at the Black Forest's own Disneyland, **Europa Park,** at Ettenheim, 40 kilometers (25 miles) north of Freiburg on the Karlsruhe–Basel Autobahn. It's open from April to the third Sunday of October (☎ 07822/770). In Steinen-Hofen, 20 kilometers (12 miles) north of Rheinfelden, **Vogelpark Wiesental** has 300 species of exotic birds on display, many of them housed in a giant building with a tropical ecosystem. ☛ *DM 8 adults, DM 4 children.* ☉ *Mar. 15–Oct. 31, daily 9–6; off-season Sun. noon–5.*

Off the Beaten Track

At **Schapbach,** in the enchanting Wolf River valley, head up into the hills to **Glaswald Lake** and you should have this tree-fringed stretch of water all to yourself. Parts of the neighboring Poppel Valley are so wild that carnivorous flowers number among the rare plants that carpet the countryside. Visit the valley's **Hohloh Lake** nature reserve, near Enzklösterle, in July and August and you'll find the bug-eating *Sonnentau* in full bloom. Farther north, just off B–500 near **Hornisgrinde Mountain,** a path to the remote and romantic **Wildsee** passes through an experimental area of forest where the trees are left untended.

SHOPPING

Baden-Baden

Gaisser (Lange Strasse 22, ☎ 07221/24393), located in Baden-Baden's attractive pedestrian shopping zone, stocks glass, porcelain, and handicrafts from all over Germany, with many specialties from the Black Forest.

The region's wines, especially the dry Baden whites and delicate reds, are highly prized in Germany. Buy them directly from any vintner on the Wine Road. At Yburg, outside Baden-Baden, visit the 400-year-old **Nägelsförster Hof** wine tavern and shop (☎ 07221/35550), where you can also enjoy panoramic views of the town. It has daily wine tastings (weekdays 8–6).

Freiburg

Clock fans should check out **Zifferblatt** (Münsterplatz 2, ☎ 0761/33138), which has an extensive selection ranging from fine gold watches to the ubiquitous cuckoo clocks.

For fine handmade jewelry, look in at master goldsmith Jürgen Brandes's shop **Goldschmiede in der Oelmühle,** located in an old mill on the canal (Insel 1a, ☎ 0761/22969). Each piece is handcrafted and unique, and priced accordingly; but you can't beat the free attraction—watching jewelers and apprentices at work on new creations.

Another regional specialty is honey, which seems nowhere so attractive as at **Honig-Waetzel** (Fischerau 8, ☎ 0761/35568). The little store is perfumed with the aromas of honey and gingerbread; it also offers everything from beeswax candles to wooden cookie molds.

Freudenstadt

Black Forest smoked ham (*Schwarzwälder Schinken*) is an aromatic souvenir that's prized all over Germany. You can buy one at any butcher shop in the region, but it's more fun to visit a *Schinkenräucherei* (smokehouse), where the ham is actually cured. Hermann Wein's **Schinkenräucherei** (☎ 07443/2450), in the village of Musbach, near Freudenstadt, is one of the leading smokehouses in the area. Call ahead to find out if the staff can show you around. The Schinkenräucherei's shop is open weekdays 9–6 and Saturday 9–noon.

Furtwangen

Across from the Clock Museum, the **Uhrenkabinett Wehrle** (Lindenstrasse 2, ☎ 07223/53240) has an extensive selection of antique and modern clocks in all shapes and sizes—including, of course, plenty of cuckoo clocks.

Triberg

For anyone looking for a cuckoo clock, the clear place to start is **House of 1000 Clocks.** The shop lives up to its name: The town branches are two picturesque old houses overflowing with all manner of clocks; the main branch out of town is distinguished by a huge cuckoo clock on the roof and a special section devoted exclusively to grandfather clocks (*Standuhren*). The staff is multilingual and very friendly, and shipping goods abroad and arranging tax refunds is a matter of course. *Branches on Triberg's main street just down from the entrance to the waterfall and off the B33 toward Offenburg,* ☎ *07722/1085.* ☉ *Mon.–Sat. 9–5.*

SPORTS AND FITNESS

Bicycling

Bicycles can be rented at nearly all the train stations in the Black Forest. The cost is DM 10 a day (DM 6 if you have a railway ticket). Several regional tourist offices offer tours on which the biker's luggage is transported separately from one overnight stop to the next. Six- to 10-day tours are available for as little as DM 174 per person, including bed-and-breakfast and bike rental. Contact the **Fremdenverkehrsverband Schwarzwald** in Freiburg (for full details *see* Important Addresses and Numbers, *below*). The **Kurverwaltung** (☎ 07441/86429), in Freudenstadt, organizes bike tours of the surrounding countryside. For the superfit, Titisee-Neustadt organizes a tour through 12 of the Black Forest's mountain passes. Contact the **Kurverwaltung** (D–79822 Titisee-Neustadt, ☎ 07651/20668) for details.

Fishing

The Black Forest, with its innumerable mountain rivers and streams, is a fisherman's paradise. Fishing without a license is forbidden, and fines are automatically levied on anyone caught doing so. Licenses cost DM 8–DM 12 a day and are available from most local tourist offices, which can usually also provide maps and rental equipment. Contact the **Fremdenverkehrsverband Schwarzwald** (Bertoldstr. 45, D–79098 Freiburg, ☎ 0761/31317) for details.

Golf

There are courses at Baden-Baden, Bad Herrenalb, Badenweiler, Donaueschingen, Freiburg, and Freudenstadt. The 18-hole Baden-Baden course is considered one of Europe's finest. Contact the **Golf Club** (Fremersbergstr. 127, Baden-Baden, ☎ 07221/23579).

Horseback Riding

Farms throughout the Black Forest offer riding vacations; addresses are available from local tourist offices and the **Fremdenverkehrsverband Schwarzwald** in Freiburg. Many of the larger towns have riding clubs and stables where visitors can rent horses, including **Baden-Baden** (Gunzenbachstr. 4a, ☎ 07221/31876). The resort of **Wehr** (☎ 07762/80888) offers a 14-day stay in a bed-and-breakfast and 10 hours of riding; similar vacation packages are offered throughout the region.

Swimming

Most of the larger resorts and towns in the Black Forest have pools, either indoor or outdoor. You can also swim in any of the region's lakes, if you can stand the cold. The most lavish swimming pool in the region is the **Caracalla** complex in Baden-Baden. Enlarged and completely modernized, it has five indoor and two outdoor pools, a sauna, a solarium, and Jacuzzis, as well as thermal water-therapy treatment courses. *Römerpl. 11,* ☎ *07221/275–940.* ☛ *DM 18 for 2 hrs, DM 24 for 3 hrs.* ☉ *Daily 8 AM–10 PM.*

The **Friedrichsbad** swimming pool in Baden-Baden offers mixed nude bathing. *Römerpl. 1,* ☎ *07221/275–920.* ☛ *DM 38 (includes massage) for 3 hours; children under 18 not admitted.* ☉ *Mon.–Sat. 9 AM–10 PM, Sun. 2–10 PM.*

There's also mixed nude bathing at the Sauna Pinea in the Paracelsusbad lido complex at Bad Liebenzell. The sauna, which some consider the most beautiful in the Black Forest, has panoramic views of the surrounding wooded slopes. German swimming champions trained in the Paracelsusbad for the 1992 Barcelona Olympics. ☎ *07052/408–250.* ☛ *DM 11.50 adults for 3 hours, DM 5 for children.* ☉ *Apr.–Oct., Tues., Wed., Fri.–Sun. 7:30 AM–8 PM. Mon., Thurs. 7:30 AM–5 PM; Nov.–Mar., Tues., Wed., Fri.–Sun. 8:30 AM–8 PM, Mon., Thurs. 8:30 AM–5 PM.*

Walking

The Black Forest is ideal country for walkers. The three principal trails are well marked and cross the region from north to south, the longest stretching from Pforzheim to the Swiss city of Basel, 280 kilometers (175 miles) away. Walks vary in length from a few hours to a week; here, as in many other German regions, the tourist office has gotten together with local inns to create so-called "Hike Without Luggage" tours (*Wandern ohne Gepäck*) along the old clock-carriers route. Your bags are transported ahead by car to meet you each evening at that day's destination. Prices are reasonable: Three nights with hotel and breakfast start at DM 305. For reservations and information, contact the "Uhrenträgergemeinschaft" in Triberg (Postfach 1423, 78094 Triberg, ☎ 07722/860236, *FAX* 860290).

Winter Sports

Despite Swiss claims to the contrary, the Black Forest is the true home of downhill skiing. In 1891 a French diplomat was sighted sliding down the slopes of the **Feldberg,** the Black Forest's highest mountain, on what are thought to be the world's first downhill skis. The idea caught on among the locals, and a few months later Germany's first ski club was formed. In 1907, the world's first ski lift opened at Schollach. There are now more than 200 ski lifts in the Black Forest, but the slopes of the Feldberg are still the top ski area. Five days' skiing lessons in Hinterzarten start at DM 155; liftpasses are DM 26 a day (DM 18 for children). Accommodations can be had for about DM 180 a week. (Call the **Verkehrsamt,** Hinterzarten, ☎ 07652/120–642, for details.) Cross-country ski instruction is given in every resort, and tours of two days and more are offered by many tourist offices.

DINING AND LODGING

Dining

Restaurants in the Black Forest range from the well-upholstered luxury of Baden-Baden's chic eating spots to simple country inns. Old *Kachelöfen* (attractive yet functional large, traditional tiled heating stoves) are still in use in many area restaurants; try to sit by one if it's cold outside. Some specialties here betray the influence of neighboring France, but if you really want to go native, try *z'Nuni,* the local farmers' second breakfast, generally eaten around 9 AM. It consists of smoked bacon, called *Schwarzwaldgeräuchertes*—the most authentic is smoked over fir cones—a hunk of bread, and a glass of chilled white wine. No visitor to the Black Forest will want to pass up the chance to try *Schwarzwälder Kirschtorte*, Black Forest cherry cake. *Kirschwasser*, locally called *Chriesewässerle* (from the French *cerise*, meaning cherry), is cherry brandy, the most famous of the region's excellent *schnapps*.

RATINGS

CATEGORY	COST*
$$$$	over DM 90
$$$	DM 55–DM 90
$$	DM 35–DM 55
$	DM 25–DM 35

per person for a three-course meal, excluding drinks, service charge, and tax

Lodging

Accommodations in the Black Forest are varied and numerous, from simple rooms in farmhouses to five-star luxury. Some properties have been passed down through the generations of the same family for what seems to be an impossible amount of time. *Gasthofs* (inns), all offering as much local color as you'll ever want and low prices, abound. In summer, Schluchsee and Titisee are crowded, so make reservations well in advance. Some spa hotels close for the winter.

RATINGS

CATEGORY	COST*
$$$$	over DM 230
$$$	DM 170–DM 230
$$	DM 120–DM 170
$	under DM 120

All prices are for two people in a double room, excluding service charge.

Baden-Baden

DINING

Zum Alde Gott. The draw here is the classy combination of upscale rustic appeal with distinctive nouvelle German cooking. With only 12 tables, the mood is intimate and sophisticated. The restaurant has a spectacular location amid rolling vineyards in the suburb of Neuweier. In summer you can take a table on the broad terrace and enjoy the view as well as the local wine. Figs in beer pastry make for a memorable dessert anytime of the year. ✕ *Weinstr. 10, Neuweier,* ☎ *07223/5513. Reservations advised. AE, DC, MC, V. Closed Fri. lunch, Thurs. $$$$*
Klosterschänke. This rustic restaurant is a 10-minute drive from the center of Baden-Baden, and the food is well worth the trip, particularly on a summer evening, when you can dine outside on a tree-covered terrace. You'll probably share a rough oak table with locals; the Baden wine and locally brewed beer ensure conviviality. The menu is surprisingly imaginative, with Black Forest trout prepared in a local meunière variation. This is the best place for venison when it's in season. ✕ *Landstr. 84,* ☎ *07221/25854. No credit cards. Closed Mon. and mid-Dec.–mid-Jan. $–$$*
Gasthaus Münchner Löwenbräu. Munich's famous Löwenbräu is the only beer served at this Bavarian-style restaurant and in its tree-shaded beer garden—along with a wide selection of Baden wines. The food is simple and filling, with regional specialties predominating. ✕ *Gernsbacherstr. 9,* ☎ *07221/22311. MC, V. $*

DINING AND LODGING

★ **Romantik Hotel Der Kleine Prinz.** This is the showpiece of the whole Romantik organization. Owner Norbert Rademacher, a veteran of the New York Hilton and Waldorf Astoria, and his interior-designer wife have skillfully combined two elegant city mansions into a lodging of unique appeal, with each room decorated in a different style, from Oriental ("Star of the East") to contemporary Manhattan. A penthouse suite, with open fireplace, covers the entire floor space of one half of the hotel. Two other rooms have fireplaces, and many come with double bathtubs with Jacuzzi. In winter, take an armchair in front of a blazing log fire and wait to be called to your table in the hotel's romantic little restaurant. Chef Berthold Krieger has been in charge of the kitchen for more than a decade, and by combining nouvelle-cuisine flair with unmistakable German thoroughness, he has elevated the restaurant to a leading position in demanding Baden-Baden. ⊞ *Lichtentalerstr. 36,* ☎ *07221/3464,* ℻ *07221/38264. 24 rooms, 15 junior suites and 1 penthouse suite, all with bath. Restaurant (reservations required, jacket and tie required), bar, laundry service, parking. AE, DC, MC, V. $$$$*

Pospisil's Merkurius. A log fire on cool days adds to the warm atmosphere of this country-style restaurant and small, friendly hotel in the district of Varnhalt on the southern fringe of Baden-Baden. The dining room's menu offers classic and regional dishes with a light touch: goose-liver soufflé and imaginative preparations of wild hare and pheasant, for example. The extensive wine list features a selection of fine vintages. The restaurant borders on the expensive (menus range up to DM 125), but the four comfortable hotel rooms are very reasonably priced (DM 110–DM 130). ⊞ *Klosterbergstr. 2,* ☎ *07223/5474,* ℻ *07223/60996. Reservations required. No credit cards. Closed Mon. and Tues. lunch. $$–$$$*

LODGING

★ **Brenner's Park Hotel.** This hotel claims, with some justification, to be one of the best in the world. It's a stately mansion off Baden-Baden's leafy Lichtentaler Allee, set on spacious private grounds. Luxury abounds, and all the rooms and suites (the latter costing up to DM 2,200 a day) are sumptuously furnished and appointed. ⊞ *Schillerstr. 6,* ☎ *07221/9000,* ℻ *07221/38772. 68 rooms and 32 suites with bath. 2 restaurants, bar, indoor pool, beauty salon, fitness room, sauna, spa. AE, DC, MC, V. $$$$*

Quisisana. You could lock yourself away from the outside world for days in this elegant turn-of-the-century hotel set in its own spacious park. Most of the guest rooms, decorated in the style of an English country house, have balconies, and the hotel's spa facilities are extensive. ⊞ *Bismarck-str. 21,* ☎ *07221/369–269,* ℻ *07221/38195. 46 rooms and 9 suites with bath. 2 restaurants, bar, indoor pool, beauty salon, massage, sauna, spa. MC, V. $$$$*

Deutscher Kaiser. This centrally located, old, established hotel offers homey and individually styled rooms at comfortable prices in an otherwise expensive town. All the double rooms have balconies on a quiet street off one of the main thoroughfares. The hotel is just a few minutes' stroll from the Kurhaus. ⊞ *Merkurstr. 9,* ☎ *07221/2700,* ℻ *07221/270–270. 44 rooms and 1 apartment with bath. Restaurant (closed Sun. dinner and in winter), bar, wine and beer tavern, bicycle rental. AE, DC, MC, V. $$$*

★ **Laterne.** Dating from the late 17th century, this is one of Baden-Baden's oldest hotels, as well as one of its smallest. The public rooms, the restaurant, and some of the bedrooms have original beams and woodwork, and antique Black Forest furnishings. It's centrally located in a pedes-

trian zone. ☎ *Gernsbacherstr. 10–12,* ☎ *07221/29999,*
FAX *07221/38308. 16 rooms, 3 apartments, with bath or shower. Restaurant, café. AE, DC, MC, V. $$*

Am Markt. The Bogner family has run the place for more than three decades—a relatively short amount of time in the history of this 250-plus-year-old building. It's in the quiet, traffic-free zone and close to such major attractions as the Roman baths. ☎ *Marktpl. 17–18,* ☎ *07221/22747,* FAX *07221/391–887. 28 rooms, 14 with bath. Restaurant. AE, DC, MC, V. $*

Bad Herrenalb

LODGING

Mönchs Posthotel. Beautiful gardens surround this half-timbered, 19th-century building with an ornate turret. Two restaurants (Locanda, with Mediterranean fare, and Kloster Schänke, which serves local fare) and comfortable quarters await inside. Each room is elegantly furnished, and no two are the same. ☎ *Doblerstr. 2,* ☎ *07083/7440,* FAX *07083/74422. 35 rooms with bath. 2 restaurants, outdoor pool, beauty salon, massage. AE, DC, MC. $$$*

Bad Liebenzell

LODGING

Thermen-Hotel. This luxurious spa hotel, on the edge of Bad Liebenzell's spa park, is an old half-timbered mansion spruced up with a modern face. The Black Forest creeps to the very edge of the garden. Rooms are spacious and comfortable, and most have pergola-like balconies. ☎ *Am Kurpark,* ☎ *07052/408–300,* FAX *07052/408–305. 22 rooms with bath. Café, indoor pool, hot springs. AE, DC, V. $$$*

Baiersbronn

DINING AND LODGING

Bareiss. The mountain resort of Baiersbronn is blessed with two of Germany's leading restaurants. The most notable is the Bareiss, in the luxury hotel of the same name. Its dark-wood furniture and tapestry papered walls are warmly lit by candles and traditional lamps. Guests, some from across the border in Alsace, are lured by the light, classic cuisine and carefully selected wines (30 brands of champagne alone). The hotel itself is among the most luxurious and best-equipped in the Black Forest. Suites (DM 710 and up; DM 840 in season) have their own sauna, solarium, and whirlpool baths. ☎ *Gärtenbühlweg 14, Mitteltal,* ☎ *07442/470,* FAX *07442/47320. 51 rooms with bath, 42 apartments, 7 suites. 2 restaurants, bar, 3 swimming pools, beauty salon, sauna, bowling, exercise room, tennis, billiards, bicycles. AE, DC, MC, V. $$$$*

★ **Traube Tonbach.** Baiersbronn's second award-winning restaurant, the Schwarzwaldstube, is also part of a luxurious mountain hotel. The Traube Tonbach has two outstanding restaurants, and if the fabulous Schwarzwaldstube is full or too expensive for your pocketbook (menus range from DM 150 to DM 200), then the Köhlerstube is an acceptable alternative. In both, you dine beneath beamed ceilings at tables bright with fine silver and glassware. The hotel is a harmonious blend of old and new, each room enjoying sweeping views of the Black Forest. Guests are nearly outnumbered by a small army of extremely helpful and friendly staff. ☎ *Tonbachstr. 237, Tonbach,* ☎ *07442/4920,* FAX *07442/492–692. 134 rooms with bath, 38 apartments, 8 suites. 2 restaurants, bars, cafeteria, 3 swimming pools, beauty salon, sauna, bowling, exercise room, tennis. AE, DC, MC, V. $$$$*

Hotel Lamm. The half-timbered exterior of this 200-year-old building presents a clear picture of the traditional Black Forest hotel within. Rooms are furnished with heavy oak fittings and some fine antiques. In winter, logs flicker in the open fireplace of the lounge, a welcome sight for guests coming in from the slopes (the ski lift is nearby). In its beamed restaurant you can order fish taken from the hotel's trout pools. ☎ *Ellbacherstr. 4,* ☎ *07442/4980,* ℻ *07442/49878. Restaurant, indoor pool, sauna, billiards. AE, DC, MC, V. $$–$$$*

Bühl
DINING
★ **Wehlauer's.** This outstanding restaurant in the small Badischer Hof Hotel mixes classic French cuisine and delicate variations on regional dishes. Try the pigeon salad or halibut in horseradish sauce if they're on the menu. In summer, take a table in the shady garden at the edge of the Bühlot River. ✗ *Hauptstr. 36, 07223/23063. Reservations required. Jacket and tie. AE, DC, MC, V. Closed Jan. $$$*

DINING AND LODGING
★ **Schlosshotel Bühlerhöhe.** One of the leading luxury hotels of the entire Black Forest, this "castle hotel" stands majestically in its own extensive grounds high above Baden-Baden, with spectacular views out over the heights of the Black Forest and walking trails starting virtually at the hotel door. The more expensive of its two restaurants, Imperial, features such delicacies as lamb and artichoke roulades. ☎ *Schwarzwaldhochstr. 1,* ☎ *07226/550,* ℻ *07226/55777. 78 rooms, 12 suites with bath. 2 restaurants (closed Wed., Thurs., and Jan.–mid–Feb.), bar, indoor pool, sauna, health club, tennis courts. AE, DC, MC, V. $$$$*

LODGING
★ **Plättig.** You can enjoy views across the Rhine into France at this excellent traditional hotel. Under the same management as the neighboring Schlosshotel, but more affordable, it has such pleasantries as a summer terrace, where you can feast on homemade Black Forest cake. ☎ *Schwarzwaldhochstr. 1,* ☎ *07226/55300,* ℻ *07226/55444. 38 rooms, 10 apartments with bath. Restaurant, wine bar, indoor pool, sauna, exercise room. AE, DC, MC, V. $$$*

Cafe-Pension Jägersteig. Magnificent views of the wide Rhine Valley as far as the French Vosges Mountains are included in the reasonable room rate at this spectacularly located mountain pension, high above the town of Bühl and its surrounding vineyards. ☎ *Kappelwindeckstr. 95a,* ☎ *07223/24125,* ℻ *07223/985–998. 12 rooms with bath or shower. Restaurant. AE, MC, V. Closed mid–Jan.–mid–Feb. $$*

Calw
DINING AND LODGING
Ratsstube. Most of the original features, including 16th-century beams and brickwork, are still intact at this historic house in the center of Calw. Rooms aren't spacious, but they are brightly decorated with pastel colors and floral patterns. The restaurant offers sturdy, traditional German fare, such as marinated beef and noodles, thick soups, and Black Forest sausage. ☎ *Marktpl. 12,* ☎ *07051/1864,* ℻ *07051/70826. 13 rooms with bath. Restaurant. No credit cards. $$*

Ettlingen
DINING
Ratsstuben. Originally used to store salt, this 16th-century cellar by the fast-flowing Als River is now a good place to eat. The food is heartily

Teutonic. ✕ *Am Markt/Kirchgasse 1–3,* ☎ *07243/14754. Reservations advised. DC, MC, V. $$*

DINING AND LODGING

★ **Hotel-Restaurant Erbprinz.** This is one of the most historic hotels in Ettlingen, and it even has its own trolley-car stop. For many, the real reason for staying here is the top-rated restaurant, which offers magnificent nouvelle German specialties. In the summer, dine in the charming garden, hidden away behind the hotel's green-and-gilt fencing. ⌂ *Rheinstr. 1,* ☎ *07243/3220,* FAX *07243/16471. 41 rooms with bath or shower, 6 apartments. Restaurant. AE, DC, MC, V. $$$$*

Freiburg

DINING

Alte Weinstube zur Traube. The fruit of the vine is not the only item on the menu at this cozy, old wine tavern, which offers a rich and varied selection of classic French and Swabian dishes. *Zander* (pike) roulade with crab sauce and braised pork with lentils are especially recommended. ✕ *Schusterstr. 17,* ☎ *0761/32190. Reservations advised on weekends and in Aug. AE, MC, V. Closed Sun., Mon. lunch, and for 2 or 3 wks July–Aug. $$$*

Enoteca. The Enoteca offers its customers three dining possibilities—a bright and cheerful bistro, a smart restaurant, and, for late-night eating (until 1:30 AM), a bar. The bar menu is limited, but the bistro and restaurant call equally on a kitchen that is rapidly building a reputation for Italian dishes of skill and imagination. Try the osso buco, the rolled lamb with Gorgonzola filling, or any of the ravioli. The wine list is extensive. ✕ *Schwabentorpl.,* ☎ *0761/30751. Reservations advised for restaurant. AE, MC, V. Closed Sun. and holidays. $$–$$$*

Kühler Krug. Venison dominates the proceedings at this restaurant, which has even given its name to a distinctive saddle-of-venison dish. Those who prefer fish shouldn't despair: there's an imaginative range of freshwater varieties available. ✕ *Torpl. 1,* ☎ *0761/29103. Reservations advised. MC. Closed Thurs. and 3 wks in June. $$*

DINING AND LODGING

★ **Colombi.** Freiburg's most luxurious hotel also has the city's finest and most original restaurant in two reconstructed 18th-century Austrian farmhouse guest rooms, now luxuriously furnished and decorated with selected Black Forest antiques (including a handsome cuckoo clock, of course). In the rustic part of the restaurant, which is named after the Black Forest artist Hans Thoma, you can order such hearty local dishes as lentil soup and venison, while in its more elegant section the menu goes decidedly upmarket, combining traditional meat and fish dishes with innovative sauces. The hotel, centrally located but very quiet, received an addition in 1995. ⌂ *Am Colombi Park/Rotteckring 16,* ☎ *0761/21060,* FAX *0761/31410. 86 rooms, 42 suites with bath. Reservations required for restaurant (closed Sun.). AE, DC, MC, V. $$$$*

Zum Roten Bären. Now a showpiece of the Ring Group, this inn, which dates to 1311, has retained its individual character, with very comfortable lodging and excellent dining in a cozy warren of four restaurants and taverns. If it's a chilly evening, order a table next to the large Kachelofen, which dominates the main, beamed restaurant. A tour of the two basement floors of cellars, dating from the original 12th-century foundation of Freiburg and now well stocked with fine wines, is also recommended. ⌂ *Oberlinden 12,* ☎ *0761/36913,* FAX *0761/36916. 19 rooms with bath, 3 apartments. Restaurant, wine bar, sauna, parking. AE, DC, MC, V. $$$$*

Oberkirchs Weinstuben. The landlord of this Old Town tavern in a small (and quite expensive!) hotel personally bags some of the game that ends up in the kitchen. Fresh trout is another specialty. In summer the dark-oak dining tables spill onto a garden terrace. ☎ *Münsterpl. 22, ☎ 0761/31011. V. Closed Sun., public holidays, and Jan. 10–Feb. 2. $$–$$$*

LODGING

Park Hotel Post. The Post has been a hotel since the turn of the century, with good, old-fashioned service to prove it. The Jugendstil facade with stone balconies and central copper-dome tower has earned the building protected status. It's right next to the train station. ☎ *Eisenbahnstr. 35, ☎ 0761/385–480, FAX 0761/31680. 41 rooms with bath. AE, DC, MC, V. $$$*

Schwär's Hotel Löwen. Heinrich Schwär's "Lion Hotel" stands imposingly on the edge of town, with its back on Freiburg's golf course. Ask for a room with a south-facing balcony and soak up the sun in summer and the Black Forest view in winter. Most of the rooms are furnished in rustic Black Forest style; all are spacious. The hotel operates a minibus service into town for guests. ☎ *Kapplerstr. 120, ☎ 0761/63041, FAX 0761/60690. 62 rooms, 42 with bath or shower. Restaurant, bar, parking. AE, DC, MC, V. $$–$$$*

Rappen. In the heart of the pedestrian-only Old Town, this hotel's brightly painted farmhouse-style rooms overlook the marketplace and cathedral (and overhear the latter's bells). The rustic theme extends to the restaurant, where wine lovers will appreciate the wide choice—more than 200—of regional vintages. ☎ *Münsterpl. 13, ☎ 0761/31353, FAX 0761/382–252. 25 rooms, 13 with bath. Restaurant. AE, DC, MC, V. $$$*

Freudenstadt

DINING

★ **Ratskeller.** Ask for a table near the Kachelofen, a central feature of this atmospheric haunt on picturesque Marktplatz. Swabian dishes and venison are featured prominently on the menu, but try the homemade trout roulade with crab sauce if it's available. The fixed-price menu, starting at DM 15, is the best value. ✗ *Marktpl. 8, ☎ 07441/2693. Reservations advised. MC, V. Closed Mon. $$*

DINING AND LODGING

Bären. The sturdy old Gasthof Bären has been owned by the same family since 1878, and they strive to maintain tradition and service with a personal touch. Rooms are modern but contain such homey touches as farmhouse-style bedsteads and cupboards. The beamed restaurant is a favorite with the locals and has a menu that combines heavy German dishes (roasts and hearty sauces) and lighter international fare. The trout is caught locally. ☎ *Lange Str. 33, ☎ 07441/2729, FAX 07441/2887. 23 rooms with bath. Restaurant, parking. DC, MC, V. $$*

Lutz Posthotel. This is an old coaching inn in the heart of the town that has also been managed by the same family for a long time—since 1809. However, there's nothing old-fashioned about the rooms, which are both modern and cozy. The restaurant offers Swabian delicacies. During the summer there's a coffee terrace. ☎ *Stuttgarterstr. 5, ☎ 07441/2421, FAX 07441/84533. 40 rooms, 4 apartments with bath, some with balcony. Wine bar, library. AE, DC, MC, V. Closed Nov. $$*

Warteck. This centrally located Biedermeier-style restaurant is a feast for the eyes—flowers are everywhere, from freshly picked posies on the immaculately laid and linened tables to the nooks and crannies between the handsome, lead-paned windows. From the imaginative menu you can feast in real style, on succulent lamb in meadow herbs, venison with Swabian noodles, or veal in mushroom sauce. In season, the asparagus comes in an aromatic hazelnut vinaigrette. The Biedermeier style extends to the comfortable furnishings of the guest rooms. ⊞ *Stuttgarter Str. 14,* ☏ *07441/7418,* ₣ₐₓ *07441/2957. 13 rooms with bath. Restaurant closed Tues.; restaurant and hotel closed Nov. and 1st 3 wks after Easter. DC, V. $$*

LODGING

★ **Schwarzwaldhotel Birkenhof.** If you need to recharge tired batteries (figuratively speaking), there are few better places in which to do so than this superbly equipped hotel. Old-fashioned comfort and a woodland setting complement a wide range of sports facilities. The two restaurants offer a choice between classic French cuisine and sturdy Black Forest fare. ⊞ *Wildbaderstr. 95,* ☏ *07441/8920,* ₣ₐₓ *07441/4763. 57 rooms with bath. Restaurant, bar, café, indoor pool, sauna, bowling, squash. AE, DC, MC, V. $$$*

Gut Lauterbad. This tastefully renovated 18th-century house turned hotel is peppered with antiques, such as ornate carved wardrobes and Meissen porcelain. Nestled in its own tranquil park, complete with trout-fishing ponds, the hotel is on the edge of the forest, south of the town center. All this adds up to excellent value. ⊞ *Dietrichstr. 5,* ☏ *07741/7496,* ₣ₐₓ *07741/61968. 21 rooms with bath. Restaurant, bar, café, indoor pool, sauna, exercise room. AE, DC, MC, V. Closed Nov. 20–Dec. 18 and Jan. 10–31. $$*

Gutach im Elztal
DINING AND LODGING

★ **Romantik Hotel Stollen.** The flower-strewn balconies and low roofs of this hotel disguise a distinctive and luxurious interior. Run by the same family for 140 years, it combines understated comfort—some rooms have four-poster beds—with attentive service: You are treated as if you were staying in a family home rather than a hotel. The restaurant—complete with a roaring log fire—serves regional food with nouvelle touches. The hotel is 21 kilometers (15 miles) northeast of Freiburg. ⊞ *79261 Gutach im Elztal,* ☏ *07685/207,* ₣ₐₓ *07685/1550. 12 rooms with bath. Restaurant. AE, MC, V. Closed 2 wks in Jan.; restaurant closed Tues. $$$$*

Hinterzarten
LODGING

Park Hotel Adler. The Riesterer family has owned this historic property since 1446. It's one of Germany's finest hotels, standing on nearly 2 acres of grounds that are ringed by the Black Forest. Marie Antoinette once ate here, and the highest standards are maintained in the French restaurant and a paneled 17th-century dining room. An orchestra accompanies dinner and later moves to the bar to play for dancing. All rooms are sumptuously appointed. ⊞ *Adlerpl. 3,* ☏ *07652/1270,* ₣ₐₓ *07652/127–717. 42 rooms and 32 suites with bath. 2 restaurants, bar, indoor pool, sauna, driving range, tennis courts, paddle tennis. AE, DC, MC, V. $$$$*

★ **Sassenhof.** Traditional Black Forest styles reign supreme here, from the steep-eaved, wood exterior to the comfortable rooms, furnished with rustic pieces that are brightly painted, many of them decoratively carved. There's no restaurant, but guests are welcome to use the kitchen. ⊞ *Adlerweg 17,* ☏ *07652/1515,* ₣ₐₓ *07652/484. 16 rooms and*

6 suites with bath. Indoor pool, beauty salon, massage, sauna, bicycles. No credit cards. Closed mid-Nov.–mid-Dec. $$–$$$

Nagold
DINING
★ **Romantik Restaurant Alte Post.** This 17th-century half-timbered inn has the kind of ambience lesser establishments believe can be built in with false beams. The menu ranges from traditional Swabian dishes to classic French offerings. For best value try the local food; the veal in mushroom sauce and venison (in season) are reliable favorites. ✗ *Bahnhofsstr. 2,* ☎ *07452/4221. Reservations advised. Jacket and tie. AE, DC, MC, V. Closed Fri. lunch, 2 wks in Jan., and 2 wks in July–Aug. $$$*

LODGING
Hotel Post Gästehaus. Run by the former proprietors of the neighboring Alte Post restaurant, this hotel is part of a historic and charming old coach inn. Parts of the ivy-clad building are modern, but the same standards of comfort are offered throughout. ☎ *Bahnhofstr. 3,* ☎ *07452/4048 or 07452/4040. 24 rooms with bath. AE, DC, MC, V. $$–$$$*

Pforzheim
DINING
★ **L'Escale.** Long Pforzheim's leading restaurant, L'Escale reopened under new management in 1994, and has managed to retain its place high on the city's list. The new menu features an expanded but still combines international cuisine (with a nouvelle twist) and regional specialties. ✗ *Parkstr. 16,* ☎ *07231/32075. Reservations advised. No credit cards. Closed 3 wks in Aug. $$$*

Silberburg. Nouvelle cuisine with a Swiss touch, emphasizing poultry, fish, and fresh vegetables, is the policy of this cozy restaurant. Try the duck in one of chef Gilbert Noesser's exquisite sauces. ✗ *Dietlingerstr. 27,* ☎ *07231/41159. Reservations advised. AE, DC, MC, V. Closed Mon., Tues. afternoon, and mid–July–mid–Aug. $$$*

LODGING
Ruf. When it opened at the beginning of the century, this hotel was described by a visiting English journalist as "a house that is aware of its importance for the numerous German and foreign visitors . . . to Pforzheim." Whether or not it is still of such importance, it aims to offer the same degree of reliable comfort—the hotel is nothing fancy, but it is dependably efficient and welcoming. The excellent restaurant is decorated with wrought iron and stained glass. ☎ *Bahnhofpl. 5,* ☎ *07231/106–011,* FAX *07231/33139. 90 rooms with bath. Restaurant. AE, DC, MC, V. $$–$$$*

Schluchsee (Feldberg)
LODGING
Kur-und Sporthotel Feldberger Hof. This is the biggest and best-appointed hotel in the area. Set amid woods and meadows on the slopes above Feldberg and a pleasant walk from the Schluchsee lake, it has everything for sports-loving guests—from a large pool to ski lifts, which are right outside the hotel. ☎ *Am Seebuck,* ☎ *07676/180,* FAX *07676/1220. 140 rooms with bath. 3 restaurants, bars, café, pool, beauty salon, health club, theater. AE, DC, MC, V. $$*

Hotel Waldeck. In summer and autumn, geraniums smother the sundrenched balconies of the Waldeck, while in winter snow piles up on the slopes outside and beckons skiers. Walking trails also begin practically at the front door, and the local forest creeps up to the hotel terrace. Some rooms have traditional furnishings, and others are generic, modern-hotel style. ☎ *Feldberg Altglasshütten,* ☎ *07655/364 or 07655/374,* FAX *07655/231. 19 rooms with bath. Restaurant, bar, parking. DC, MC, V. $*

Titisee

DINING AND LODGING

Romantik Hotel Adler Post. Located in the Neustadt district of Titisee, about 5 kilometers (3 miles) from the lake, this solid old building has been owned and run by the Ketterer family for 140 years. All the rooms are comfortably and traditionally furnished. The restaurant, the Rotisserie zum Postillon, offers excellent local specialties. ☎ *Hauptstr. 16,* ☎ *07651/5066,* FAX *07651/3729. 24 rooms, with bath, 4 apartments. Restaurant, indoor pool, beauty salon, massage, sauna. AE, DC, MC, V. Closed mid–Mar.–early Apr. $$–$$$*

Triberg

DINING AND LODGING

Parkhotel Wehrle. Since 1707, this imposing mansion has been in the Wehrle family's possession; its steep-eaved, wisteria-covered facade dominates the town center between the marketplace and the municipal park. Guests should find the service impeccable. The comfortable rooms are individually furnished, with a variety of woods and such pleasant touches as fresh flowers. ☎ *Am Marktpl. 1,* ☎ *07722/86020,* FAX *07722/860–290. 52 rooms, 2 apartments, 2 suites, all with bath. Outdoor and indoor pool, sauna, exercise room, parking. AE, DC, MC, V. $$–$$$*

Römischer Kaiser. The Roman Emperor has been owned by the same family for more than 150 years, and Black Forest tradition practically oozes from its walls. Rooms are comfortably furnished in solid Black Forest style, with heavy wooden bedsteads and painted furniture. The restaurant serves German and international dishes, with a bit of a French flair. Fresh mountain trout is on the menu almost daily. ☎ *Sommeraustr. 35, Nussbach,* ☎ *07722/4418,* FAX *07722/4401. 26 rooms with bath. Restaurant, parking. AE, DC, MC, V. Restaurant closed Sun. dinner and Mon. $–$$*

THE ARTS AND NIGHTLIFE

The Arts

Music

Freiburg's new multistage complex, to be called the **Konzerthaus,** is scheduled to open in the summer of 1996; until then, the city's orchestra will continue to give concerts in the city theater. Summer is when the music scene really comes alive. The annual **Zeltmusik** (tent music) festival is a musical jamboree held in June and July, so named because many of the musical events are held in huge tents. The emphasis is on jazz, but most types of music, including classical, can be heard. Also in summer are chamber music concerts in the courtyard of the ancient Kaufhaus, opposite the Münster, and the Münster itself hosts an annual summer program of organ recitals. For program details and tickets for the above, contact **Freiburg Verkehrsamt** (Rotteckring 14, ☎ 0761/368–9090). For jazz, head for the **Jazz Haus** (Schnewlinstr. 1), which has live music nightly.

Baden-Baden also has an annual two-week summer festival, the **Musikalischer Sommer;** the **Kurhaus** (Werderstr.) hosts concerts year-round. For program details and tickets, call 07221/932–700.

Theater

There's some talk that Freiburg's opera company may move to the new Konzerthaus in 1996, but until that happens the fine little troupe continues to perform in the **City Theater** (☎ 0761/34874). Pforzheim's recently built **Stadttheater** is even smaller; its emphasis is on operetta and musicals, but there's also opera and theater (☎ 07231/392–440). By far the best opera house in the region, however, is the **Badisches Staatstheater** in Karlsruhe (☎ 0721/60202). Baden-Baden has one of Germany's most beautiful performance halls, the **Theater am Goetheplatz**, a late-Baroque jewel built in 1860–62 in the style of the Paris Opera. It opened with the world premiere of Berlioz's opera *Beatrice et Benedict*. Today the theater presents a regular program of drama, opera, and ballet. Call 07221/275–268 for program details and tickets. Performances in Freiburg's annual summer-theater festival are centered in the city's theater complex, spilling out into the streets and squares. Street theater is also featured in Karlsruhe's annual **Schlossberg** festival in August, a popular and informal carnival-like event centering on the castle.

Nightlife

Black Forest nightlife means Baden-Baden's elegant **casino,** first and foremost. There's a DM 5 admission charge; bring your passport as ID. You'll have to sign a form guaranteeing that you can meet any debts you run up (minimum stake is DM 5—maximum DM 20,000). If your tastes run to the less formal, try the city's leading disco, **Griffon's** (closed Mon. and Tues.), in the same building. For a more subdued evening, stop by at the **Oleander Bar** in Baden-Baden's top hotel, Brenner's Park Hotel (Schillerstr.), or **Le Piano** piano-bar (Sophienstr. 15).

Nightlife in Freiburg revolves around the city's wine bars and wine cellars. **Oberkirch's Weinstuben** and **Die Zwiebel,** both on Münsterplatz, are typically atmospheric; you can also look for night spots on any of the streets around the cathedral. Leading discos last year (1995) in Freiburg's constantly changing scene were **Agar** (Löwenstr. 8) and **Arena** (Schwarzwaldstr. 2).

THE BLACK FOREST ESSENTIALS

Arriving and Departing

By Car

The Rhine Valley Autobahn, A–5, runs the length of the Black Forest, connecting with the rest of the Autobahn system at Karlsruhe, north of the Black Forest.

Freiburg, the region's major city, is 410 kilometers (260 miles) from Munich and 275 kilometers (170 miles) from Frankfurt.

By Plane

The closest international airports are at Stuttgart, Strasbourg in the neighboring French Alsace, and the Swiss border city of Basel, the latter just 70 kilometers (40 miles) from Freiburg, the largest city in the Black Forest.

By Train

The main rail route through the Black Forest runs north–south, following the Rhine Valley from Karlsruhe to Basel. There are fast and frequent trains to Freiburg and Baden-Baden from most major German cities (you generally have to change at Karlsruhe).

Getting Around

By Car

Good two-lane highways crisscross the entire region, making driving here easy and fast. The region's tourist office (*see* Important Addresses and Numbers, *below*) has established a series of specially designated tourist driving routes: the High Road, the Low Road, the Spa Road, the Wine Road, and the Clock Road. Though the routes are intended primarily for drivers, most points along them can also be reached by train or bus.

CAR RENTAL

Avis: in **Baden-Baden,** Maximilianstrasse 54–56, ☎ 07221/71088; in **Freiburg,** St-Georgenerstrasse 7, ☎ 0761/19719; in **Pforzheim,** Westliche Karl-Friedrich-Strasse 141, ☎ 07231/40828.

Europcar: in **Baden-Baden,** Rheinstrasse 29, ☎ 07221/64031; in **Freiburg,** Wilhelmstrasse 1A, ☎ 0761/31066; in **Pforzheim,** Ostliche Karl-Friedrich-Strasse, ☎ 07231/13535.

Hertz: in **Baden-Baden,** Langestrasse 101, ☎ 07221/1210 or 07221/1201; in **Freiburg,** Lörracherstrasse 49, ☎ 0761/475–051.

By Train

Local lines connect most of the smaller towns. Two east–west routes— the Black Forest Railway and the Höllental Railway—are among the most spectacular in the country. Details are available from **Deutsche Bahn** (German Railways) in Freiburg (☎ 0761/19419).

Guided Tours

Bus tours of the Black Forest are available from **Freiburg** and **Baden-Baden.** The Freiburg tourist information office (*see below*) offers a number of one-day tours, in English, of the Black Forest and parts of neighboring France and Switzerland. Tours start at DM 32 for adults and DM 22 for children. In Baden-Baden, contact **Armbruster Reisen** (Jahnstrasse 1, 77830 Bühlertal, ☎ 07223/72227), which offers a range of day tours for between DM 35 and 55.

Important Addresses and Numbers

Tourist Information

Information for the entire Black Forest is available from **Fremdenverkehrsverband,** Bertoldstrasse 45, D–79098 Freiburg, ☎ 0761/31317. There are local tourist information offices in the following towns:

Baden-Baden. Kurverwaltung, Augustaplatz 8, D–76530 Baden-Baden, ☎ 07221/275–200.
Badenweiler. Kurverwaltung, Ernst-Eisenlohr-Strasse 4, D–79410 Badenweiler, ☎ 07632/72110.
Bad Herrenalb. Kurverwaltung, D–76332 Bad Herrenalb, ☎ 07083/7933.
Bad Liebenzell. Kurverwaltung, Kurhausdamm 4, D–75378 Bad Liebenzell, ☎ 07052/408–100.

Feldberg. Kurverwaltung im Ortsteil Altglashütten, Kirchgasse, 1, D–79868 Feldberg, ☎ 07655/8019.

Freiburg. Verkehrsamt, Rotteckring 14, D–79098 Freiburg im Breisgau, ☎ 0761/368–9090.

Freudenstadt. Kurverwaltung, Promenadenplatz 1, D–72250 Freudenstadt, ☎ 07441/86420.

Pforzheim. Stadtinformation, Rathaus, Marktplatz 1, D–75175 Pforzheim, ☎ 07231/39900.

Schluchsee. Kurverwaltung, Fischbacherstrasse 7, D–79859 Schluchsee, ☎ 07656/7732.

Titisee-Neustadt. Kurverwaltung, in Kurhaus, D–79822 TitiseeNeustadt, ☎ 07651/810–104.

Triberg. Kurverwaltung im Kurhaus, Luisenstrasse 10, D–78098 Triberg, ☎ 07722/8123–0231.

7 The Romantic Road

One of Germany's so perfectly planned tourist routes, the Romantic Road is just that, albeit in the sense of the word meaning wondrous and fanciful. Minnesänger Walther von der Vogelweide and medieval sculptor Tilman Riemenschneider are among the people whose legacies you'll discover as you travel the route. You'll also visit Würzburg, home to a glorious Baroque palace; the wonderfully preserved medieval town of Rothenburg-ob-der-Tauber; and Ludwig II's fantastic Neuschwanstein castle.

OF ALL THE SPECIALLY DESIGNATED TOURIST ROUTES that crisscross Germany, none rivals the aptly named Romantische Strasse, or Romantic Road. The scenery along the road (with a few exceptions) is more domestic and rural than spectacular, but the Romantic Road is memorable because of the medieval towns, villages, castles, and churches that stud its 420-kilometer (260-mile) length. Many of these are tucked away beyond low hills, their spires and towers poking up through the greenery.

Within the massive gates of formerly fortified settlements, half-timbered houses lean against one another along narrow cobbled lanes. Ancient squares are adorned with fountains and flowers, and formidable walls are punctuated by watchtowers built to keep a lookout for marauding enemies. The sights add up to a pageant of marvels of history, art, and architecture, providing an essence of Germany at its most picturesque and romantic.

The road runs south from Würzburg in the north of Bavaria to Füssen on the border with Austria. You can, of course, follow it in the opposite direction, as a number of bus tours do. Either way, among the major sights you'll see Würzburg one of Europe's most scintillating Rococo palaces, and Rothenburg-ob-der-Tauber, perhaps the best-preserved medieval town on the Continent. Ulm, a short trip off the Romantic Road, is included here because of its magnificent cathedral. Then there's the handsome Renaissance city of Augsburg. Finally, for most visitors, the highlight will be Ludwig II's captivating fantasy castle of Neuschwanstein.

The concept of the Romantic Road developed as West Germany was trying to rebuild its tourist industry in the wake of World War II. An enterprising public-relations type dreamed up the catchy title for a historic passage through several regions of southern Germany so they could be advertised as a unit. And in 1950 the Romantic Road was born, soon to evolve into one of Europe's most heavily traveled tourist trails.

The name itself refers not so much to the kind of romance of lovers as to a variation of the word meaning wonderful, fabulous, imaginative. And, of course, the Romantic Road started as a road on which the Romans traveled.

On its way the road crosses former battlefields where armies fought for control of the region. It was the most cataclysmic of these conflicts, the Thirty Years' War, that destroyed the region's economic base in the 17th century, thereby assurring the survival of the historic Romantic Road towns.

As you travel the Romantic Road, two names crop up again and again: Walther von der Vogelweide and Tilman Riemenschneider. It might be helpful to know a little about these masters of the Middle Ages.

Walther von der Vogelweide, who died in Würzburg in 1230, was the most famous of the German *Minnesänger,* poet-musicians who wrote and sang of courtly love in the age of chivalry. Knights and other nobles would hire them for their artistic services to help win the favors of fair ladies. Von der Vogelweide broke with this tradition by writing love songs to maidens of less-than-noble rank; he also accepted commissions of a political nature, producing what amounted to medieval political manifestos. His work was romantic, lyrical, witty, and filled with a sighing wistfulness and philosophical questioning.

Tilman Riemenschneider, Germany's master of late-Gothic sculpture, lived an extraordinary life. His skill with wood and stone was recognized at an early age. His success became so great that he soon presided over a major Würzburg workshop, with a team of assistants. Riemenschneider worked alone, however, on the life-size figures that dominate his sculptures. His characteristic grace and harmony of line can be identified in such features as the folds of a robe.

At the height of his career Riemenschneider was appointed city councillor; later he became mayor of Würzburg. In 1523, however, he made the fateful error of siding with the revolutionaries in the Peasants' Revolt. He was arrested and held for eight weeks in the dungeons of the Marienburg fortress above Würzburg, where he was frequently tortured. Most of his wealth was confiscated, and he returned home a broken man, with little will to continue his work. He died in 1531.

For nearly three centuries he and his sculptures were all but forgotten. Only in 1822, when ditchdiggers uncovered the site of his grave, did Riemenschneider once again come to be included among Germany's greatest artists. Today Riemenschneider is recognized as the giant of German sculpture. The richest collection of his works is in Würzburg, although other masterpieces are on view in churches and museums in other cities along the Romantic Road as well as in other parts of Germany; for example, the renowned Windsheim Altar of the Twelve Apostles is found in the Palatine Museum in Heidelberg. Two major Riemenschneider works were discovered in 1994–95 and are now on display in Würzburg (see Tour 2 in Exploring, below).

EXPLORING

Tour 1: Aschaffenburg to Würzburg

Numbers in the margin correspond to points of interest on the Romantic Road map.

① If you're approaching the Romantic Road from Frankfurt, the first town you'll reach is **Aschaffenburg,** on the Main River, gateway to Franconia (see Chapter 8) and the streams and woods of the Spessart Hills. It's a small town, which, despite being a major textile-producing center with a ring of factories encircling it, has retained its quiet, market-town atmosphere. The historic center has been carefully preserved, with much of it now an elegant pedestrian mall.

Begin your visit at **Schloss Johannisburg.** This imposing Renaissance castle, built between 1605 and 1615, was the residence of the prince-electors of Mainz, hereditary rulers of Aschaffenburg. The exterior of the doughty sandstone castle harks back to the Middle Ages. Four massive corner towers guard the inner courtyard. The interior contains the **Schloss Museum** (Castle Museum), which charts the history of the town and contains a representative collection of German glass, and the **Staatsgalerie** (City Art Gallery). A small section of the latter is devoted to Lucas Cranach the Elder (1472–1553), a leading painter of the German Renaissance, including typical enigmatic nudes and haunting landscapes. The palace grounds contain a striking copy of the temple of Castor and Pollux in Pompeii, constructed for Ludwig I of Bavaria in 1840. If you've admired the lavish neoclassical buildings Ludwig put up in Munich, this powerful structure will also impress you. ☛ *Cas-*

The Romantic Road

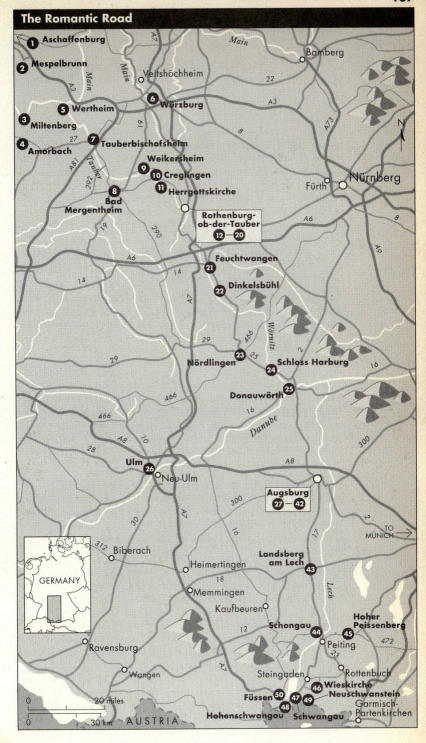

1 Aschaffenburg
2 Mespelbrunn
Bamberg
Main
22
A3
Veitshöchheim
5 Wertheim
6 Würzburg
3 Miltenberg
8
A73
7 Tauberbischofsheim
4 Amorbach
Nürnberg
Weikersheim
Fürth
9
10 Creglingen
11 Herrgottskirche
8 Bad
Mergentheim
Rothenburg-
ob-der-Tauber
12 — 20
A6
A9
21 Feuchtwangen
A6
22 Dinkelsbühl
14
Wörnitz
23 Nördlingen
25 Schloss Harburg
24
466
25 Donauwörth
16
Danube
300
Ulm
26 Neu-Ulm
A8
Augsburg
27 — 42
TO
MÜNCHEN
Biberach
GERMANY
Heimertingen
Landsberg
am Lech
43
18
Memmingen
Lech
Kaufbeuren
Hoher
Peissenberg
12
Schongau
44 45
472
Peiting
Ravensburg
23
Rottenbuch
Wangen
Steingaden
46 Wieskirche
Füssen 50 Neuschwanstein
47 49
48
Hohenschwangau Schwangau
Garmisch-
Partenkirchen
AUSTRIA
0
20 miles
0
30 km
N

tle and museums: DM 3.50 adults, DM 2.50 children. ⊘ *Apr.–Sept., Tues.–Sun. 9–noon and 1–5; Oct.–Mar., Tues.–Sun. 10–noon and 1–4.*

TIME OUT For an ideal introduction to Franconian wines and regional specialties, stop at the **Schlossweinstuben** (☎ 06021/12440; closed Mon.), a wine cellar/restaurant in the castle. From the terrace there's a fine view over the Main Valley.

To reach the center of Aschaffenburg, start on Karlsstrasse and continue along Fürstengasse, which leads to Landlingstrasse and the **Stiftskirche** (Collegiate Church) of Sts. Peter and Alexander, on a small hill. Little remains of the original Romanesque building here save the cloisters; most of what you see dates from the 16th and 17th centuries. Pause before you go in to admire the tapering green spire and the imposing, slightly out-of-kilter facade. Inside, the *Lamentation of Christ,* a gaunt and haunting painting by Matthias Grünewald (c. 1475–1528), is the most notable of a number of paintings on view. It was part of a much larger and now lost altarpiece. See how, in spite of the lessons of Italian Renaissance painting, naturalism and perspective still produce an essentially Gothic image, attenuated and otherworldly.

② Castle lovers may enjoy a 17-kilometer (10-mile) excursion southeast from Aschaffenburg on B–8 to the small, romantic castle of **Mespelbrunn.** It lies in the still sparsely populated forest area of the Spessart, a walker's paradise that used to be the hunting grounds of the archbishops of Mainz.

The castle of Mespelbrunn is surrounded by a moat and dominated by a massive round tower dating from the mid-16th century. The **Rittersaal** (Knight's Room) on the first floor displays Teutonic suits of armor, assorted weapons, and massive, dark furniture. A more delicate note is struck by the 18th-century **Chinesische Salon** (Chinese Room) upstairs. From the castle, hiking paths lead into the forested surroundings. ☛ *DM 5 adults, DM 2 children (includes a guided tour).* ⊘ *Mid-Mar.–mid-Nov., Mon.–Sat. 9–noon and 1–5, Sun. 9–5.*

From Aschaffenburg you can take the A–3 Autobahn 63 kilometers (40 miles) direct to Würzburg, the official starting point of the Romantic Road (*see below*), or first head south on Route B–469, along the banks of the Main, to Miltenberg. From Miltenberg you can take a more leisurely drive east past a succession of riverside towns on the way to Würzburg.

③ The little town of **Miltenberg** stands amid the hills and forests of the Odenwald. (If you've seen Rothenburg-ob-der-Tauber and loved it but hated the crowds, Miltenberg will provide the antidote.) For most, the Marktplatz, the steeply sloping town square, is the standout. A 16th-century fountain, bordered by geraniums, splashes in its center; tall half-timbered houses, some six stories high with crooked windows bright with yet more flowers, stand guard all around. To see more of these appealing buildings, stroll down Hauptstrasse, site of the Rathaus (Town Hall) and the 15th-century Haus zum Riesen (House of the Giant). The town takes its name from its castle, whose entrance is on the Marktplatz. You can peek into the courtyard (open in summer only) to see the standing stone in it. Though the stone's origins and meaning are obscure, most scholars agree that it's probably Roman and is connected with a fertility rite (there's no denying its phallic qualities).

TIME OUT   The **Haus zum Riesen** (Hauptstr. 99), built in 1590, is one of the oldest
inns in Germany. Stop in for a glass of beer or wine and to admire its
gnarled and ancient timbers.

4 From Miltenberg you can take a side trip to **Amorbach,** 8 kilometers
(5 miles) south on B–469. The town itself is not the attraction; rather,
it's the massive onetime Benedictine abbey church of **St. Maria** that will
claim your attention. The building is interesting chiefly as an example
of the continuity of German architectural traditions, the superimpo-
sition of one style on another. You'll see examples of works here from
the 8th through the 18th century. The facade of the church seems a
run-of-the-mill example of Baroque work, with twin domed towers flanking a lively and well-proportioned central section; in fact, it is a rare
example of the Baroque grafted directly onto a Romanesque building.
Look closely and you'll notice the characteristic round arches of the
Romanesque marching up the muscular towers. It's the onion-shape
domes at their summits and the colored stucco applied in the 18th century that make them seem Baroque. There are no such stylistic confu-
sions in the interior, however: All is Baroque power and ornamentation.
☛ *DM 4 adults, DM 3 children (includes guided tour of church and
former monastery buildings).* ☉ *Apr.–Sept., Mon.–Sat. 9–noon and 1–
6, Sun. 11–6; Mar. and Oct., Mon.–Sat. 9–noon and 1:30–5:20, Sun.
11–6; Nov.–Feb., weekdays 11 and 2:15, Sat. 11 and 2–4, Sun. 2–4.*

From Amorbach, backtrack to Miltenberg and follow B–469 70 kilometers (43 miles) to Würzburg. For most of the drive you'll be stick-
ing close to the Main River. A succession of riverside towns remind
you that this is an appealingly unspoiled region of Germany. The
5 largest town is **Wertheim,** 30 kilometers (18 miles) from Miltenberg,
located where the Main and Tauber rivers meet. It was founded in 1306
and proclaims its medieval origins through a jumble of half-timbered
houses with jutting gables. Those in the central Marktplatz are the most
attractive. The principal sight is the ruined **Kurmainzisches Schloss** (castle), built for the counts of Wertheim during the 11th century. The ruins
are romantic; the view from them over the Main Valley is memorable.
Würzburg is 40 kilometers (24 miles) from here.

Tour 2: Würzburg

6 The basically Baroque city of **Würzburg,** the pearl of the Romantic Road,
is a heady example of what happens when great genius teams up with
great wealth. Starting in the 10th century, Würzburg was ruled by the
powerful (and rich) prince-bishops who created the city with all the
glittering attributes that you see today.

Situated at the confluence of two age-old trade routes, on the banks
of the Main River as it passes through a calm valley backed by vineyard-covered hills, this glorious old city is overlooked by a fortified
castle on high ground across the river. This is Festung Marienberg, constructed between 1200 and 1600, and for 450 years residence of the
prince-bishops.

Present-day Würzburg is by no means 100% original. On March 16,
1945, seven weeks before Germany capitulated, Würzburg was all but
obliterated in an Allied saturation bombing raid. Although the bombing lasted no more than 20 minutes, 87% of Würzburg was wiped off
the map, with some 4,000 buildings destroyed and at least that many
people killed. Reconstruction, in many cases using original stones from
the bombed-out structures, has returned most of the city's famous sights
to their former splendor. Those who knew prewar Würzburg insist that

the heart of the city is now every bit as impressive as it was prior to 1945. Except for a new pedestrian zone, it remains a largely authentic restoration.

★ High on the list of compelling reasons for visiting Würzburg is the **Residenz,** the glorious Baroque palace where the line of prince-bishops lived after coming down from Festung Marienberg, their hilltop fortress. Construction started in 1719 under the brilliant direction of Balthasar Neumann, the German architectural genius of his age. Most of the interior decoration was entrusted to the Italian stuccoist Antonio Bossi and the Venetian painter Giovanni Battista Tiepolo. But the man whose spirit infuses the Residenz is pleasure-loving Prince-Bishop Johann Phillip Franz von Schönborn, who financed the venture but did not live to see the completion of what has come to be considered the most beautiful palace of Germany's Baroque era and one of Europe's most sumptuous buildings, frequently referred to as the "Palace of Palaces." This dazzling structure is a 10-minute walk from the railway station, along pedestrian-only Kaiserstrasse and then Theaterstrasse.

From the moment you enter the building, the splendor of the Residenz is evident, as the largest Baroque staircase in the country, the **Treppenhaus,** stretches away from you into the heights. Halfway to the second floor, the stairway splits and peels away at 180 degrees to the left and right.

Dominating the upper reaches of this vast space is Tiepolo's giant fresco **The Four Continents,** a gorgeous exercise in blue and pink with allegorical figures at the corners representing the four continents known at the time.

Next, make your way to the **Weissersaal** (the White Room) and then beyond to the grandest of the state rooms, the **Kaisersaal** (Throne Room). The Baroque/Rococo ideal of *Gesamtkunstwerk*—the fusion of the arts—is perfectly illustrated here. Architecture melts into stucco, stucco invades the frescoes, the frescoes extend the real space of the room into their fantasy world. Nothing is quite what it seems, and no expense was spared to make it so. Tiepolo's frescoes show the visit of the emperor Frederick Barbarossa to Würzburg during the 12th century to claim his bride. The fact that the characters all wear 16th-century Venetian dress hardly seems to matter. Few interiors anywhere use such startling opulence to similar effect. You'll find more of this expansive spirit in the **Hofkirche,** the chapel, which offers proof that the prince-bishops experienced little or no conflict between their love of ostentation and their service to God. Among the lavish marbles, rich gilding, and delicate stuccowork, note the Tiepolo altarpieces, ethereal visions of *The Fall of the Angels* and *The Assumption of the Virgin.* Finally, tour the palace garden, the **Hofgarten;** the entrance is next to the chapel. This 18th-century formal garden, with its stately gushing fountains and trim, ankle-high shrubs outlining geometric flower beds and gravel walks, is the equal of any in the country. ☛ *DM 5 adults, DM 3.50 children, including guided tour.* ☉ *Apr.–Oct.., Tues.–Sun. 9–5; Nov.–Mar., Tues.–Sun. 10–4.*

TIME OUT Sample your first Würzburg wine either in the extensive cellars of the Residenz, where you'll find a cozy **tavern,** or by making for one of two famous institutions in the immediate area. The nearest is the **Bürgerspital:** From the square fronting the Residenz, take the first street on the right, Theaterstrasse; the Bürgerspital is about halfway down the street on the right. Originally this was a medieval hospice established by wealthy burghers for Würzburg's poor and old. Ask for a tour of the wine cellar: Its barrels are the size of a Volkswagen. Just down the road, on Juliuspromenade, is another of these charitable institutions, the **Juliusspital** (Julius Hospice), established in 1576 by a Würzburg bishop.

To the left is Würzburg's attractive pedestrian shopping area, Schönbornstrasse, named after the bishop who commissioned Neumann to build the Residenz. On the left as you enter the street is another example of Neumann's work, the distinctive Baroque **Augustinerkirche** (Church of St. Augustine). The church was a 13th-century Dominican chapel; Neumann's additions date from the early 18th century. At the end of Schönbornstrasse is Würzburg's Romanesque cathedral, the **Dom,** begun in 1045. Step inside and you'll find yourself, somewhat disconcertingly, in a shimmering Rococo treasure house. This is only fitting: Prince-bishop von Schönborn is buried here, and it's hard to imagine him slumbering amid the dour weightiness of a Romanesque edifice.

Alongside the cathedral is the **Neumünster,** built above the grave of the early Irish martyr St. Kilian, who brought Christianity to Würzburg and, with two companions, was put to death here in 689. Their missionary zeal bore fruit, however, for 17 years after their death a church was consecrated in their memory. By 742, Würzburg had become a diocese; over the following centuries 39 churches flourished throughout the city. The Neumünster's former cloistered churchyard contains the grave of Walther von der Vogelweide, the most famous minstrel in German history.

Across the pedestrian zone toward the river lies Würzburg's market square, the **Markt,** with shady trees and a framework of historic old facades. At one end, flanked by a Rococo mansion, are the soaring late-Gothic windows of the 14th- to 15th-century **Marienkapelle** (St. Mary's Chapel), where architect Balthasar Neumann lies buried. Pause beneath its finely carved portal and inspect the striking figures of Adam and Eve; you shouldn't have great difficulty recognizing the style of Tilman Riemenschneider. The original statues are in Würzburg's museum, the Mainfränkische Museum, on the Marienberg, across the river; the ones in the portal are copies.

On your explorations along the edge of the pedestrian zone and market square note the exquisite "house Madonnas," small statues of the Virgin set into corner niches on the second level of many old homes. So many of these lovely representations of the city's protective patron can be seen that Würzburg is frequently referred to as "the town of Madonnas."

On the way to the **Marienburg Fortress** you'll cross the Old Main Bridge, which was already standing when Columbus sighted America. Twin rows of infinitely graceful statues of saints line the bridge. Note particularly the *Patronna* Franconiae (more commonly known as the Weeping Madonna). There's also a beautiful view of the fortress from the bridge—statues in the foreground, Marienburg and its surrounding vineyards as the focal point—which makes the perfect photograph to treasure as a souvenir of this historic city.

To reach the Marienburg you can make the fairly stiff climb on foot or take the bus from the Old Main Bridge. It runs every half hour starting at 9:45 AM.

The Marienburg was the original home of the prince-bishops, beginning in the 13th century. The oldest buildings—note especially the

Marienkirche, the core of the complex—date from around 700. In addition to the rough-hewn medieval fortifications, there are a number of fine Renaissance and Baroque apartments. The highlight of a visit to the Marienburg is the **Mainfränkisches Museum** (the Main-Franconian Museum). The rich and varied history of Würzburg is brought alive by this remarkable collection of art treasures. The standout is the gallery devoted to Würzburg-born sculptor Riemenschneider, including the originals of the great Adam and Eve statues, copies of which adorn the portal of the Marienkapelle. Two previously unknown works by Riemenschneider—a Madonna and child and a crucifixion—were discovered in 1994–95 in what German art critics hailed as a "sensational find." Both had been in private collections, where they had remained for decades without anyone suspecting they were by Riemenschneider. They were added to the Mainfränkisches Museum collection, together with two other works recently discovered in private possession and thought to be by pupils of Riemenschneider. You'll also be exposed to fine paintings by Tiepolo and Cranach the Elder, and to exhibits of porcelain, firearms, antique toys, and ancient Greek and Roman art. Wine lovers won't want to miss the old winepresses, some of which are enormous. Other exhibits chart the history of Franconian wine. ☛ *Marienburg Fortress is free.* ☉ *Apr.–Sept., Tues.–Sun. 9–noon and 1–5; Oct.–Mar., Tues.–Sun. 10–noon and 1–5.* ☛ *Mainfränkische Museum: DM 3.50 adults, DM 2 children.* ☉ *Apr.–Oct., Tues.–Sun. 10–5; Nov.–Mar., Tues.–Sun. 10–4.*

To see the original summer palace of the prince-bishops, you have to go a little north of Würzburg, to Veitshöchheim. Though it has little of the glamorous appeal of the Residenz, the sturdy Baroque building provides further evidence of the great wealth of the worldly rulers of Würzburg. ☛ *DM 3 adults, DM 2 children (including guided tour).* ☉ *Apr.–Sept., Tues.–Sun. 9–noon and 1–5.*

Tour 3: The Tauber Valley

The Romantic Road heads south from Würzburg, following the B–27 country highway, to the lovely valley of the Tauber and the small town ➐ of **Tauberbischofsheim,** 36 kilometers (22 miles) southwest. There are no major sights here. What you'll want to do is linger in its shady pedestrian mall; stroll down to the sleepy Tauber River; and visit the parish church, site of a side altar richly carved by a follower of Tilman Riemenschneider.

➑ Follow B–290 16 kilometers (10 miles) south to **Bad Mergentheim,** the premier resort of this region. Between 1525 and 1809, Bad Mergentheim was the home of the Teutonic Knights, one of the most successful of the medieval orders of chivalry. Their greatest glories came during the 15th century, when they had established themselves as one of the dominant powers of the Baltic, ruling large areas of present-day eastern Germany, Poland, and Lithuania. The following centuries saw a steady decline in the order's commercial success. In 1809, Napoléon expelled the Teutonic Knights from Bad Mergentheim. The French emperor had little time for what he considered the medieval superstition of orders such as this and felt no compunction for disbanding them as he marched east through Germany in the opening stages of his ultimately disastrous Russian campaign. The expulsion of the order seemed to sound the death knell of the little town. But in 1826 a shepherd discovered mineral springs on the north bank of the river. They proved to be the strongest sodium sulfate and bitter-salt waters in Europe, with health-giving properties that ensured the little town's future prosperity. Excavations subsequently showed that the springs had been known in the Iron and Bronze ages before becoming choked with silt. A museum tracing the history of the Teutonic Knights was recently opened in the knights' former castle—the **Deutschordensschloss**—at the eastern end of the town. *Deutschordensmuseum, Schloss 16,* ☏ *07931/52212.* ☛*DM 3 adults, DM 2 children.* ⊙ *Tues.–Sat. 2:30–5:30, Sun. 10–noon, 2:30–5:30. A guided tour, costing DM 4, is given every Sun. at 3.*

Eleven kilometers (7 miles) southeast of Bad Mergentheim stands the village of **Stuppach,** whose chapel guards one of the great Renaissance German paintings, the so-called *Stuppacher Madonna* by Matthias Grünewald (circa 1475–1528). The painting is believed to have been produced for a church in nearby Aschaffenburg; no one seems clear on how it found its way here in 1812. It was only in 1908 that experts finally recognized it as the work of Grünewald; repainting in the 17th century had turned it into a flat and unexceptional work. Grünewald was one of the leading painters of the early Renaissance in Germany. Though he was familiar with the developments in perspective and natural lighting of Italian Renaissance painting, his work remained resolutely anti-Renaissance in spirit: tortured, emotional, dark. You'll want to compare it with that of Dürer, his contemporary, if you know his work. Whereas Dürer used the lessons of Italian painting to reproduce its clarity and rationalism, Grünewald used them for expressionistic purposes to heighten his essentially Gothic imagery.

❾ B–19 leads you 12 kilometers (8 miles) to the little town of **Weikersheim,** which provides another excuse to linger on the long road south. The town is dominated by the castle of the counts of Hohenlohe. The great hall of the castle is the scene each summer of an international youth music festival, and the Rittersaal (Knight's Hall) contains life-size stucco wall sculptures of animals, reflecting the counts' love of hunting. In the cellars you can drink a glass of cool wine drawn from the huge casks that seem to prop up the building. Outside again, stroll through the enchanting gardens and enjoy the view of the Tauber and its leafy valley.

❿ Follow the Tauber Valley 20 kilometers (12 miles) farther to **Creglingen.** Here you can detour up a side valley, the Herrgottstal (Valley of the Lord). The valley has been an important place of pilgrimage since the 14th century, when a farmer had a vision of a heavenly host plowing his field. A chapel, the **Herrgottskirche** (Chapel of Our Lord), was **⓫** built by the counts of Hohenlohe. During the early 16th century, Tilman Riemenschneider was commissioned to carve an altarpiece for it. This enormous work, 33 feet high, depicts in minute detail the life and ascension of the Virgin Mary. Riemenschneider entrusted much of the background detail to the craftsmen of his Würzburg workshop, but he allowed no one but himself to attempt the life-size figures of this masterpiece. Its intricate detail and attenuated figures are a high point of late-Gothic sculpture.

Now drive the remaining 20 kilometers (12 miles) to Rothenburg-ob-der-Tauber, for most people the quintessential town of the Romantic Road.

Tour 4: Rothenburg-ob-der-Tauber

★ **⓬** **Rothenburg-ob-der-Tauber** (literally, "the red castle on the Tauber") is the kind of medieval town that even Walt Disney might have thought too good to be true, with gingerbread architecture galore and a wealth of fountains and flowers against a backdrop of towers and turrets. The reason for its survival is simple. Rothenburg was a small but thriving 17th-century town that had grown up around the ruins of two 12th-century churches that had been destroyed by an earthquake. Then it was laid low economically by the havoc of the Thirty Years' War, the cataclysmic religious struggle that all but destroyed Germany in the 17th century. The town's economic base was devastated, and it slumbered until modern tourism rediscovered it. And here it is, milking its "best-preserved-medieval-town-in-Europe" image to the full, undoubtedly something of a tourist trap, but genuine enough for all that. There really is no place quite like it. Whether Rothenburg is at its most appealing in summer, when the balconies of its ancient houses are festooned with flowers, or in winter, when snow lies on its steep gables and narrow streets, is a matter of taste. Few people are likely to find this extraordinary little survivor from another age anything short of remarkable.

Numbers in the margin correspond to points of interest on the Rothenburg-ob-der-Tauber map.

⓭ Begin your visit by walking around the **city walls,** more than a mile long. Stairs every 200 or 300 yards provide ready access. There are superb views of the tangle of pointed and tiled roofs, and of the rolling
⓮ country beyond. Then make for the **Rathaus,** the logical place to begin an exploration of Rothenburg. Half the building is Gothic, begun in 1240, the other half classical, begun in 1572. A fire in 1501 destroyed the part of the structure that is now the newer, Renaissance section, which faces the main square. Go inside to the vaults below the building to see the **Historiengewölbe,** a museum that charts Rothenburg's role in the Thirty Years' War. Great prominence is given to account of the Meistertrunk (Master Drink), an event that will follow you around Rothenburg. It came about when the Protestant town was captured by Catholic forces. During the victory celebrations, so the story goes, the conquering general was embarrassed to find himself unable to drink a great tankard of wine in one go, as his manhood demanded. He volunteered to spare the town further destruction if any of the city councillors could drain the mighty draught. The mayor, a man by the name of Nusch, took up the challenge and succeeded, and Rothenburg was preserved. The tankard itself is on display at the Reichsstadtmuseum (*see below*). As it holds 6 pints, the wonder is not so much that the conquering general was unable to knock it back but that he should have tried it in the first place. On the north side of the main square is a fine clock placed there 50 years after Nusch's feat. Today, he's surmounted by a mechanical figure that acts out the epic Master Drink daily on the hour from 11 to 3 and at 8, 9 and 10 PM. The town also holds an annual pageant celebrating the feat, with townsfolk parading the streets dressed in 17th-century garb. The festival begins in the courtroom of the town hall, where the event is said to have occurred. *Rathauspl. Rathaus tower.* ☞ *DM 1 adults, 50 pf children.* ☉ *Weekdays 9:30–12:30 and 1–5, weekends and holidays noon–3. Historiengewölbe museum (and dungeons)* ☞ *DM 2.50 adults, DM 1 children.* ☉ *Mid-Mar.–Apr., daily 10–5; May–Sept., daily 9–6; Nov.–Dec., Fri. and weekends 10–5.*

⓯ Just north of the town hall is the **Stadtpfarrkirche St. Jakob** (parish church of St. James), the repository of additional Riemenschneider works, including the famous Heiliges Blut (Holy Blood) altar. Above the altar a crystal capsule is said to contain drops of Christ's blood. The church has other items of interest, including three 14th- and 15th-century

Rothenburg-ob-der-Tauber

stained-glass windows in the choir and the famous Herlin-Altar, with its 15th-century painted panels. ☉ *Easter–Oct., daily 9–5; Nov.–Easter, daily 10–noon and 2–4.*

16 Another of Rothenburg's churches, **St. Wolfgang's,** is built into the defenses of the town. From within the town it looks like a peaceful parish church; from outside it blends into the forbidding city wall. Through an underground passage you can reach the sentry walk above and follow the wall for almost its entire length.

17
18 Two museums you won't want to miss are the **Mittelalterliches Kriminalmuseum** (Medieval Criminal Museum) and the **Puppen und Spielzeugmuseum** (Doll and Toy Museum). The former sets out to document the history of German legal processes in the Middle Ages and contains an impressive array of instruments of torture. The latter is housed in a 15th-century building near the Rathaus. There are 300 dolls, the oldest dating from 1780, the newest from 1940. *Mittelalterliches Kriminalmuseum: Burggasse 3.* ☎ *DM 5 adults, DM 2.50 children.* ☉ *Apr.–Oct., daily 9:30–6; Nov.–Mar., daily 2–4. Puppen und Spielzeugmuseum: Hofronnengasse 13.* ☎ *DM 5 adults, DM 1.50 children.* ☉ *Mar.–Dec., daily 9:30–6; Jan.–Feb., daily 11–5.*

19 The **Reichsstadtmuseum** (Imperial City Museum) turns out to be two attractions in one. It's the city museum, and it contains artifacts that illustrate Rothenburg and its history. Among them is the great tankard, or *Pokal,* of the Meistertrunk. The setting of the museum is the other attraction; it's a former convent, the oldest parts of which date from the 13th century. Tour the building to see the cloister, the kitchens, and the dormitory, then see the collections. *Hofronnengasse 13.* ☎ *DM 4* *adults, DM 2 children.* ☉ *Apr.–Oct., daily 10–5; Nov.–Mar., daily 1–4.*

㉒ Cobbled Hofronnengasse runs into the Marktplatz (Market Square), site of an ornate Renaissance fountain, the **Herterlichbrunnen.** To celebrate some momentous event—the end of a war, say, or the passing of an epidemic—the *Schäfertanz* (Shepherds' Dance) was performed around the fountain. The dance is still done, though for the benefit of tourists rather than to commemorate the end of a threat to Rothenburg. It takes place in front of the Rathaus several times a year, chiefly at Easter, in late-May, and throughout June and July.

Tour 5: Feuchtwangen, Dinkelsbühl, and Nördlingen

Numbers in the margin correspond to points of interest on the Romantic Road map.

Our next main stop on the Romantic Road is the captivating little town of Dinkelsbühl, within a ring of tower-capped ramparts and a moat. **㉑** However, if you're driving there from Rothenburg, stop first at **Feuchtwangen,** the town just before it. Its central market square, with a splashing fountain and an ideal setting of half-timbered houses, rivals even the attractions of Rothenburg and Dinkelsbühl. Summer is the time to go, when open-air theater productions are staged in the low, graceful cloisters next to the **Stiftskirche,** the collegiate church, from mid-June to the beginning of August. Inside the church is a 15th-century altar carved by Albrecht Dürer's teacher, Michael Wohlgemut. Don't miss the **Heimatmuseum** (local history museum), with its excellent collection of folk arts and crafts. *Fränkisches Museum, Museumstr. 19.* ☛ *DM 4 adults, DM 2 children.* ☉ *Daily 10–noon and 2–5. Closed Jan.–Feb.*

TIME OUT Call in for a coffee at the half-timbered house opposite the museum, the **Cafe am Kreuzgang.** It makes its own chocolates as well as delicious pastries.

★ **㉒** **Dinkelsbühl** is only 12 kilometers (8 miles) farther south. Within its mellow walls the rush of traffic seems an eternity away. There's less to see here than in Rothenburg, but the mood is much less tourist-oriented. It's thought that the town originated during the 6th century as the court of a Franconian king. Like Rothenburg, Dinkelsbühl was caught up in the Thirty Years' War, and, again like Rothenburg, it preserves a fanciful episode from those bloody times. Local lore says that when Dinkelsbühl was under siege by Swedish forces and in imminent danger of destruction, a young girl led the children of the town to the enemy commander and implored him in their name for mercy. The commander of the Swedish army, Colonel Klaus Dietrich von Sperreuth, is said to have been moved almost to tears, and he spared the town. Whether or not it's true, the story is a charming one, and it is retold every year in a pageant by the children of Dinkelsbühl during a 10-day festival in July.

Touring Dinkelsbühl is not so much a matter of taking in specific sights—museums, palaces, parks, and churches, say—as of simply wandering around the historic area, pausing to admire a facade, a shop window, or the juxtaposition of architectural styles—from Gothic through Baroque—that makes this little town memorable. The one standout sight for many is the **Stadtpfarrkirche St. Georg** on the Marktplatz. Large enough, at 235 feet long, to be a cathedral, St. Georg's is among the best examples in Bavaria of the late-Gothic style. Note especially the complex fan vaulting that spreads sinuously across the ceiling. If you can face the climb, head up the 200-foot tower for amazing views over the jumble of Dinkelsbühl's rooftops.

㉓ The cry of *So G'sell so*—"All's well"—still rings out every night across the ancient walls and turrets of **Nördlingen,** the next stop along the Romantic Road. The town employs sentries to sound out the traditional message from the 300-foot-high tower of the central parish church of St. Georg at half-hour intervals between 10 PM and midnight. The tradition goes back to an incident during the Thirty Years' War when an enemy attempt to slip into the town was detected by an alert townswoman. From the church tower—known locally as the Daniel (open 9 AM–dusk)—you'll get an unsurpassed view of the town and the surrounding countryside, including, on clear days, 99 villages. However, the climb is only for the fit: The tower has 365 steps, one for each day of the year. The ground plan of the town is two concentric circles. The inner circle of streets, whose central point is St. Georg's, marks the earliest boundary of the medieval town. A few hundred yards beyond it is the outer boundary, a wall built to accommodate the expanding town. Fortified with 11 towers and punctuated by five massive gates, it's one of the best-preserved town walls in Germany. You can stroll along it for about 2 miles of its length.

For an even more spectacular view of Nördlingen, contact the local flying club, the **Rieser Flugsportverein** (☎ 09081/4099), and take to the sky in a light aircraft. The sight of Nördlingen nestling in the trim, green Swabian (southwestern Germany) landscape is well worth the cost. You'll notice another phenomenon from the air: the basinlike formation of the **Ries,** a 24-kilometer-wide (15-mile-wide) crater. Until the beginning of this century, it was believed that the crater was the remains of an extinct volcano. In 1960, it was proven by two Americans that the Ries was caused by a meteorite at least 1 kilometer (½ mile) in diameter that hit the ground at more than 100,000 miles per hour. The impact had the destructive energy of 250,000 atomic bombs of the size that obliterated Hiroshima. It also turned the surface rock and subsoil upside down, hurling debris as far as Slovakia and wiping out virtually all plant and animal life within a radius of more than 100 miles. The compressed rock, or *suevit*, formed by the explosive impact of the meteorite was used to construct many of the town's buildings, including St. Georg's tower.

The story of the Ries crater is the subject of the **Rieskrater Museum,** which opened recently in a converted 15th-century barn. *Hintere Gerbergasse 3.* ☛ *DM 5 adults, DM 2.50 children (family ticket DM 12.50).* ☺ *Tues.–Sun. 10–noon and 1:30–4:30.*

㉔ The next stop on the Romantic Road is where the little Wörnitz River breaks through the Franconian Jura Mountains, 20 kilometers (12 miles) south. Here you'll find one of southern Germany's best-preserved medieval castles. **Schloss Harburg** was already old when it passed into the possession of the counts of Oettingen in 1295; before that time it belonged to the Hohenstaufen emperors. The ancient and noble house of Oettingen still owns the castle, and treasures collected by the family through the centuries can be seen in it. The collection includes some works by Tilman Riemenschneider, along with illuminated manuscripts dating as far back as the 8th century and an exquisite 12th-century ivory crucifix. ☛ *DM 5 adults, DM 3 children (including guided tour).* ☺ *Mid-Mar.–Sept., Tues.–Sun. 9–5. Oct., Tues.–Sun. 9:30–4:30.*

㉕ Eleven kilometers (7 miles) south, the Wörnitz River meets the Danube at the old walled town of **Donauwörth.** If you're driving, pull off into the clearly marked lot on B–25, just north of town. Below you sprawls a striking natural relief map of Donauwörth and its two rivers. The oldest part of town is on an island in the river, connected to the rest of town by a wood bridge and greeted on the north bank by the single surviving town gate, the Riederstor. North of the gate is one of the finest avenues of the Romantic Road: Reichsstrasse (Empire Street), so named because it was once a vital link in the Road of the Holy Roman Empire between Nürnberg and Augsburg. The broad street—known by the locals as the Gute Stube (front room) of their town—is lined by solid, centuries-old houses and shops that tell their own tales of Donauwörth's prosperous past. The Fuggers, a famous family of traders and bankers from Augsburg, acquired a palatial home here in the 16th century; its fine Renaissance-style facade under a steeply gabled roof stands proudly at the upper end of Reichsstrasse.

Tour 6: Ulm and Augsburg

㉖ About an hour (70 km/ 40 mi) west of the Romantic Road lies the city of **Ulm,** which has at least three claims to fame: its mighty minster, with the world's tallest church tower (528 feet); as the birthplace of Albert Einstein in 1879; and as the site of the most spectacular attempt to fly since Icarus, made by a local tailor. To get to Ulm from Donauwörth, take take the B-16 highway west, connecting with B-28. For a prettier ride, head back to Nördlingen and take the Schwäische Albstrasse (Swabian Alp Road, the B-466 highway) south to Ulm. From Nördlingen, it's about 60 km/36mi.

Ulm grew as a medieval trading city thanks to its location on the Danube, and, like so many towns in the area, declined as a result of the Thiry Years' War. It was transferred between neighboring states of Baden-Württemberg and Bavaria, becoming part of the latter in 1810. In response, Bavaria built Neu-Ulm in its territory, on the southern shore of the Danube. World War II bombing caused extensive damage, but there's been considerable restoration work. Today Ulm's Old Town presses against the river, the cobblestone alleys and stone-and-wood bridges over the Blau (a small Danube tributary) in its Fisherman's and Tanner's Quarter especially picturesque.

The famed tailor was Ludwig Berblinger. A local eccentric, he cobbled together a pair of wings and in 1811 made a big splash by trying to fly across the river. He didn't make it, but he grabbed a place in German history books. A reproduction of his flying machine hangs from the ceiling of the central hall of the **Rathaus** (Marktplatz 1). Einstein's home was a casualty of an Allied raid and never rebuilt; the **Einstein Monument,** erected in 1979, marks the site (on the eastern side of Friedrich-Ebert Strasse, opposite the main railway station). Ulm's **Münster,** the largest church in southern Germany, was unscathed by bombing. It stands over the huddled medieval gables of old Ulm, visible long before you hit the ugly suburbs encroaching on the Swabian countryside. Its single, filigreed tower challenges stout-hearted tourists to plod 143 meters (472 feet) up 768 steps, through the giddily twisting spiral stone staircase, to a spectacular observation point below the spire. The climb may be rewarded by views of the Swiss and Bavarian alps, 160 km (100 mi) to the south. The Münster was begun in the late-Gothic age (1377) and took five centuries to build, with completion in the neo-Gothic years of the late 19th century. It contains some notable treasures, including fine late-Gothic choir stalls and a Renaissance altar.

Münsterplatz. ☉ *Daily 9–5.* ☛*Tower: DM 2.50 adults, DM 1.50 children.*

Behind the Münster and closer to the river (take Kramgasse) is **Marktplatz,** bordered by handsome medieval houses with stepped gables. A colorful market is held here on Wednesday and Saturday mornings. On its southern side is **Ulmer Museum,** an excellent natural history and art museum. Exhibits illustrate centuries of development in this part of the Danube Valley, and a modern art section has works by Kandinsky, Klee, Léger, and Roy Lichtenstein. *Marktplatz 9.* ☛ *DM 5 adults, DM 3 children.* ☉ *Tues., Wed., and Fri.–Sun. 10–5, Thurs. 10–8.*

German bread is world renowned, so it's not surprising that a national museum is devoted to bread making. The **Deutsches Brotmuseum** is housed in a former salt warehouse just north of the Münster. It's by no means as crusty or dry as some might fear, with some often amusing tableaux illustrating how bread has been baked over the centuries. *Deutsches Brotmuseum. Salzstadelgasse 10.* ☛ *DM 4.50 adults, DM 3 children.* ☉ *Tues.–Sun. 10–5.*

TIME OUT If thinking about bread has made you hungry, head back towards Münsterplatz, turning left into the street called Lautenberg. Here you'll find the Barfüsser, a brewery-tavern that prepares its own delicious, Swabian variety of pretzels and brews its own beer in shining copper "Kessel" that form part of the brick-walled restaurant's decor. *Lautenberg 1,* ☎*0731/602-1110.*

Complete your visit to Ulm with a walk down to the banks of the Danube, where you'll find long sections of the old city wall and fortifications intact. Every four years the river is the scene of one of Germany's strangest festivals, the Ulmer Fischerstechen, in which teams of young men dressed in historical costume and balancing on narrow canoe-like craft try to knock each other into the river with long poles—rather like jousting, but from boats (the next one is in July, 1997). Another local tradition—daily performances of the medieval coopers' dances—comes around again in July, 1996.

㉗ **Augsburg,** 60 km (36 mi) east along A-8, is the next stop on the Romantic Road. Augsburg is Bavaria's third-largest city, after Munich and Nürnberg. It dates to 15 years before the birth of Christ, when one Drusus, son of the Roman emperor Augustus, set up a military camp here on the banks of the Lech River. The settlement that grew up around it was known as Augusta, a name Italian visitors to the city still give it. It was granted city rights in 1156, and 200 years later, the first mention of it can be found in municipal records of the Fugger family, who were to Augsburg what the de' Medicis were to Florence. On your tour of the city you will encounter traces of that extraordinary family at almost every turn.

Numbers in the margin correspond to points of interest on the Augsburg map.

Touring Augsburg is easy for the visitor because signs point the way to the city's chief sights. The signs, on practically every street corner, are integrated into three color-charted tours plotted by the tourist office, the Verkehrsverein, on Bahnhofstrasse, the street running into the city center from the main railway station, or Hauptbahnhof. The true **㉘** center of the city is **Maximilianstrasse,** once a medieval wine market and today Augsburg's main shopping street, where the high-gabled, pastel-color facades of the 16th-century merchant houses assert them-

200

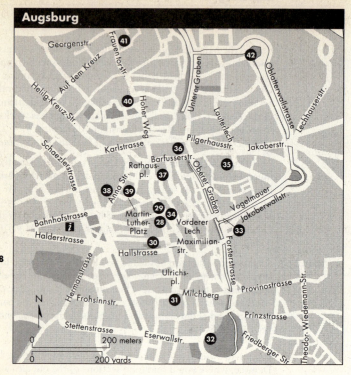

Augsburg

(29) selves against encroaching post–World War II shops. Most of the city's chief sights are on this thoroughfare or a short walk away. Two monumental and elaborate fountains punctuate the long street. At the north end, the **Mercury Fountain,** 1599, by the Dutch master Adrian de Vries (after a Florentine sculpture by Giovanni da Bologna) shows winged Mercury in his classic pose. Farther up Maximilianstrasse is another de Vries fountain: a bronze Hercules struggling to defeat the many-headed Hydra. On the right, as you walk up the slight incline of the street, stands the former home and business quarters of the Fuggers. The 16th-century building now houses a restaurant in its cellar and offices on the upper floors. In the ground-floor entrance are busts of two of Augsburg's most industrious Fuggers, Raymund and Anton, tributes from a grateful city to the wealth these merchants brought to the community. Beyond a modern glass door is a quiet courtyard with colonnades, originally reserved for the Fugger women.

Another wealthy family, the von Liebenhofens, built a rival palace only a few paces up the street. The 18th-century palace now bears the name of a baron who married into the banking family, von Schaezler. The von Liebenhofens wanted to outdo the Fuggers—but not at any price. Thus, to save money in an age when property was taxed according to the size of the street frontage, they constructed a long, narrow building running far back from Maximilianstrasse. The palace is composed of a series of interconnecting rooms that lead into a green-and-white Rococo ballroom: an extravagant, two-story hall heavily decorated with mirrors, chandeliers, and wall sconces. Marie Antoinette, on her way from Vienna to Paris to marry Louis XVI, was guest of honor at the inauguration ball in 1770.

30 Descendants of the von Liebenhofens bequeathed the palace to the city of Augsburg after the war; today its rooms contain the **Deutsche Barockgalerie** (German Baroque Gallery), a major art collection that features works of the 17th and 18th centuries. The palace adjoins the former church of a Dominican monastery. A steel door behind the banquet hall of the palace leads into another world of high-vaulted ceilings, where the Bavarian State Collection highlights an exhibition of early Swabian Old Master paintings. Among them is a Dürer portrait of one of the Fuggers. *Maximilianstr. 46.* ☛ *DM 4 adults, DM 2 children.* ☉ *May–Sept., Tues.–Fri. 10–1 and 2–5, weekends 11–1 and 2–5; Oct.–Apr., Tues.–Fri. 10–1, weekends 11–1 and 2–4.*

31 At the top of Maximilianstrasse on Ulrichsplatz, at the highest point of the city, is the former monastery church of **Sts. Ulrich and Afra,** two churches built on the site of a Roman cemetery where St. Afra was martyred in AD 304. The original, Catholic building was begun as a late-Gothic construction in 1467; a Baroque-style preaching hall was added in 1710 as the Protestant church of St. Ulrich. St. Afra is buried in the crypt, near the tomb of St. Ulrich, a 10th-century bishop credited with helping to stop a Hungarian army at the doors of Augsburg in the battle of the Lech River. The remains of a third patron of the church, St. Simpert, are preserved in one of the church's most elaborate side chapels. From the steps of the magnificent altar, look back along the high nave to the finely carved Baroque wrought-iron and wood railing that borders the entrance. As you leave, pause to look into the separate but adjacent Protestant church of St. Ulrich, the former monastery assembly hall that was taken over and reconstructed by the Lutherans after the Reformation.

32 Behind the churches are the city's ancient fortifications and its most important medieval entrance gate, the **Rotes Tor** (Red Gate), which once straddled the main trading road to Italy. From here you can follow the traces of the early city fortifications northward and back to the city **33** center, passing the Gothic **Vogeltor** (Bird Gate) astride Oberer Graben. **34** On the street called Vorderer Lech is **Holbein Haus** the rebuilt 16th-century home of Hans Holbein the Elder, one of Augsburg's most famous sons (the homes of two others, Leopold Mozart and Bertolt Brecht, are also on our route). The Holbein Haus is now a city art gallery with a regularly changing program of exhibitions. *Vorderer Lech 20.* ☉ *May–Oct., Tues., Wed., and Fri.–Sun. 10–5, Thurs. 10–8; Nov.–Apr., Tues., Wed., and Fri.–Sun. 10–4, Thurs. 10–8.*

35 At the end of Vorderer Lech you'll reach a bridge over a small stream, which leads to the tranquillity of the **Fuggerei.** This is the world's oldest social housing project, established by the Fugger family to accommodate the city's deserving poor. The 147 homes still serve the same purpose; the annual rent of "one Rheinish Guilder" (DM 1.72) hasn't changed, either. Understandably, there's quite a demand to take up residence in this peaceful, leafy estate. There are four requirements: Residents must be Augsburg citizens, Catholic, and destitute through no fault of their own, and they must pray daily for their original benefactors, the Fugger family.

TIME OUT If you make a sharp left as you leave the Fuggerei, into Jakobenstrasse, you'll find a welcoming tavern and restaurant, the **Fuggerei Stube** (Jakoberstr. 26), built into the outside walls of the ancient enclave (closed Mon. and Sun. morning).

36 On the way back to the city center, along the small street called Auf dem Rain, you'll see the **Brecht Haus,** a modest artisan's house where the renowned playwright Bertolt Brecht, author of *The Threepenny Opera*, was born. He lived here until he moved to Munich and then, during Hitler's reign, to Scandinavia and later the United States. After the war he settled in East Berlin, to direct the Berliner Ensemble. Today the house serves as a memorial center dedicated to Brecht's life and work. *Auf dem Rain 7.* ☛ *DM 2.50 adults, DM 1.50 children.* ☉ *May–Sept., Tues.–Fri. 10–1 and 2–5, weekends 11–1 and 2–5; Oct.–Apr., Tues.–Fri. 10–1, weekends 11–1 and 2–4.*

③⑦ Two left turns will take you to Rathausplatz, the center of Augsburg, dominated by the 258-foot-high **Perlachturm** (open Apr.–Sept., daily 10–6) and the adjacent massive, square **Rathaus** (Town Hall). The great building, Germany's largest city hall when it was built during the early 17th century, is one of the finest Renaissance structures north of the Alps. (The Rathaus interior can be visited between 10 and 6 on days when no official functions are taking place.)

TIME OUT   Directly opposite the Rathaus, on the western side of the great square, you'll find the **Cafe Bertele,** a convenient stop for coffee or a meal. Its downstairs café makes delicious pastries and chocolates, while the smart first-floor restaurant serves an excellent lunch.

③⑧ On Annastrasse, the pedestrian street immediately west of the Rathaus square, you'll find one of Augsburg's many historic churches, **St. Annakirche** (St. Anna Church). This former Carmelite monastery dates from the 14th century. Visitors can wander through its quiet cloisters and view the chapel used by the Fugger family until the Reformation. In 1518, Martin Luther stayed in the monastery during his meetings with Cardinal Cajetanus, the papal legate sent from Rome to persuade the reformist to renounce his heretical views. Luther refused, and the place where he publicly declared his rejection of papal pressure is marked with a plaque on Augsburg's main street, the Maximilianstrasse.

③⑨ Across the Rathaus square in front of the St. Anna Church is the city's chief museum, housed in a 16th-century merchant's mansion, the **Maximilian-Museum,** with a permanent exhibition of Augsburg arts and crafts. *Phillipine-Welser-Str. 24.* ☛ *DM 4 adults, DM 2 children.* ☉ *May–Sept., Tues.–Fri. 10–1 and 2–5, weekends 11–1 and 2–5; Oct.–Apr., Tues.–Fri. 10–1, weekends 11–1 and 2–4.*

★ ④⓪ A five-minute stroll north along Annastrasse (recommended to window shoppers) will take you to the **Dom St. Maria** (Cathedral of the Virgin Mary); its square Gothic towers will signal the way. An Episcopal church stood here during the 9th century, and a 10th-century Romanesque crypt, built in the time of Bishop Ulrich, remains from those early years. The heavy bronze doors on the south portal date from the 11th century; 11th-century windows on the south side of the nave depict the prophets Jonah, Daniel, Hosea, Moses, and David, to form the oldest cycle of stained glass in central Europe. Five important paintings by Hans Holbein the Elder adorn the altar. The cathedral's treasures were moved in 1994 from the Maximilian Museum to an Episcopal museum in the complex of ancient buildings on Domplatz. The new museum—the Domschatz Museum—was scheduled to open in 1995. Call 0821/31660 for details.

A short walk from the cathedral, still following the green route, will take you to the quiet courtyards and small raised garden of the former Episcopal residence, a series of fine 18th-century buildings in Baroque and Rococo styles that now serve as the offices of the Swabian regional government. Although less than 64 kilometers (40 miles) from the capital of Bavaria, we're now firmly in Swabia, once such a powerful dukedom under the Hohenstaufens that its territory covered virtually all of present-day Switzerland. Today Swabia has become an administrative district of Bavaria, and Augsburg has yielded the position it once held to the younger city of Munich.

㊶ A three-minute walk north along Frauentorstrasse takes you to the **Mozarthaus,** birthplace of Leopold Mozart, father of Wolfgang Amadeus Mozart and an accomplished composer and musician in his own right. A comfortable 17th-century home, it now serves as a Mozart memorial and museum, with some fascinating contemporary documents on the Mozart family. The last Augsburg family connection died just a few years ago. *Frauentorstr. 30.* ☞ *DM 2.50, DM 1.50 children.* ☉ *May–Sept., weekdays 10–1 and 2–5, weekends 11–1; Oct.–Apr. weekdays 10–1, weekends 11–1.*

㊷ Retrace your steps to the city center. If you have time and energy, you can continue your tour with a walk along the remains of the city's ancient north and east defenses. For part of the way a pleasant walk follows the moat, which was once part of the fortifications. At the **Oblatter Wall** you can rent a boat and row between the green, leafy banks—a welcome break and a fine way to say farewell to Augsburg.

Tour 7: Toward the Alps

Numbers in the margin correspond to points of interest on the Romantic Road map.

Leaving Augsburg southward on B–17—the southern stretch of the Romantic Road—you'll drive across the Lech battlefield, where the Hungarian invaders were stopped in 955. Rich Bavarian pastures extend as far as the Lech River, which follows the country road for much of **㊸** its way. About 32 kilometers (20 miles) south is the historic old town of **Landsberg am Lech,** in whose prison Adolf Hitler wrote much of *Mein Kampf.* The town was founded by the Bavarian ruler Heinrich der Löwe (Henry the Lion) during the 12th century and grew wealthy from the salt trade. You'll see impressive evidence of Landsberg's early wealth among the solid old houses packed within its turreted walls; the early 18th-century Altes Rathaus (Old Town Hall) is one of the finest of the region.

The German artist Sir Hubert von Herkomer was born in a small village just outside Landsberg. Within the town walls is an unusual monument—not to Sir Hubert (he was knighted in England in 1907) but to his mother, Josefine. It's a romantic, medieval-style tower, bristling with turrets and galleries, built by Sir Hubert. He called it his Mutterturm, or "mother tower." The young Hubert was taken by his parents to the United States and later, when they couldn't settle in America happily, to England. He died in Devon in 1914. A permanent exhibition on the life and work of this remarkable man can be seen within its rough-stone walls (open Tues.–Sun. 2–5).

Beyond Landsberg, the Bavarian Alps rise along the southern horizon, signaling the end of the Romantic Road. Some 30 kilometers (18 **㊹** miles) south is another old walled town **Schongau,** founded at about the same time as Landsberg, with virtually intact wall fortifications, together with towers and gates. In medieval and Renaissance times, the town was an important trading post on the route from Italy to Augsburg. The steeply gabled, 16th-century Ballenhaus was a warehouse before it was elevated to the rank of Rathaus (Town Hall).

If you're driving, leave the Romantic Road just beyond Schongau, at the village of **Peiting,** and take B–472 to the nearby summit of the 3,000-foot-high **Hoher Peissenberg,** the first real peak of the Alpine chain. A pilgrimage chapel was consecrated on the mountain in the 16th century; a century later a larger church was added, with a fine ceiling fresco and delicate carvings by local Bavarian masters.

After returning to Peiting, take B–23 to **Rottenbuch,** where the Augustinian order built an impressive monastery on the Ammer River during the 11th century. The Gothic basilica was redecorated in Rococo style during the 18th century. The lavish interior of cream, gold, and rose stuccowork and statuary is stunning.

★ ㊻ Rottenbuch is a worthy preparation for the next—and most glorious—example of German Rococo architecture, the **Wieskirche,** open again after four years of extensive restoration work (alarming cracks in the stucco had been caused by low-flying military aircraft). It stands in an Alpine meadow just off the Romantic Road near Steingaden, its yellow-and-white walls and steep red roof set off by the dark backdrop of the Trauchgauer Mountains. The architect Dominicus Zimmermann (former mayor of Landsberg and creator of much of that town's Rococo architecture) was commissioned in 1745 to build the church on this spot, where, six years earlier, a local woman claimed to have seen tears running down the face of a picture of Christ. Although the church was dedicated as the Pilgrimage Church of the Scourged Christ, it is now known as the Wieskirche (Church of the Meadow). Visit it on a bright day if you can, when Alpine light streaming through its high windows displays the full glory of the glittering interior. Together with the pilgrimage church of Vierzehnheiligen in north Bavaria, the Wieskirche represents the culmination of German Rococo ecclesiastical architecture. As at Vierzehnheiligen, the simple exterior gives little hint of the ravishing interior. A complex oval plan is animated by a series of brilliantly colored stuccos, statues, and gilt. A luminous ceiling fresco completes the decoration. Note the beautifully detailed choir and organ loft. Concerts are presented in the church in the summer. Contact the tourist office (☎ 08861/7216) in Schongau for details. Zimmermann, the architect of the church, is buried in the 12th-century former abbey church of Steingaden. Although his work was the antithesis of Romanesque architecture, he was laid to rest in a dour, late-Romanesque side chapel.

㊼ From Steingaden, the road runs beneath the Ammergau Range 22 kilometers (13 miles) to **Schwangau,** a lakeside resort town and an ideal center from which to explore the surrounding mountains. Schwangau is where you'll encounter the heritage of Bavaria's famous 19th-century king, Ludwig II. Ludwig spent much of his youth at Schloss Hohenschwangau; it is said that its neo-Gothic atmosphere provided the primary influences that shaped the construction of the wildly romantic Schloss Neuschwanstein, the fairy-tale castle Ludwig built across the valley after he became king. *The two castles are ½ mi from each other and about 1 mi from the center of Schwangau. Cars and buses are barred from the approach roads, but the 1-mi journey to Neuschwanstein can be made by horse-drawn carriages, which stop in the village of Hohenschwangau. A bus from the village takes a back route to the Aussichtspunkt Jugend; from there it's only a 10-min walk to the castle. The Schloss Hohenschwangau is a 15-min walk from the village.*

㊽ **Hohenschwangau Palace** was built by the knights of Schwangau during the 12th century. Later it was remodeled by Ludwig's father, the

Bavarian crown prince (and later king) Maximilian, between 1832 and 1836. It was here that the young Ludwig met the composer Richard Wagner. Their friendship shaped and deepened the future king's interest in theater, music, and German mythology—the mythology upon which Wagner drew for his "Ring" cycle of operas. Wagner saw the impressionable Ludwig principally as a potential source of financing for his extravagant operas rather than as a kindred spirit. For all his lofty idealism, the composer was hardly a man to let scruples interfere with his self-aggrandizement. ☞ *DM 8 adults, DM 5 children under 14 and senior citizens (including guided tour).* ☼ *Apr.–Sept., daily 8:30–5:30; Oct.–Mar., daily 10–4.*

★ 49 Ludwig's love of the theater and fantasy ran so deep that when he came to build **Neuschwanstein,** he employed a set designer instead of an architect. The castle soars from its mountainside like a stage creation—it should hardly come as a surprise that Walt Disney took it as the model for his castle in the movie *Sleeping Beauty* and later for the Disneyland castle itself.

The life of the proprietor of this spectacular castle reads like one of the great Gothic mysteries of the 19th century. Here was a king, a member of the Wittelsbach dynasty that had ruled Bavaria since 1180, who devoted his time and energies to creating architectural flights of fancy that came close to bankrupting the Bavarian government. Finally, in 1886, before Neuschwanstein was finished, members of the government became convinced that Ludwig had taken leave of his senses. A medical commission set out to prove that the king was insane and forced him to give up his throne. Ludwig was incarcerated in the much more modest lakeside castle of Berg on the Starnbergersee. Then, on the evening of June 13, 1886, the king and the doctor attending him disappeared. Late that night their bodies were pulled from the lake. The circumstances of their deaths remain a mystery.

The interior of Ludwig's fantasy castle is a fitting setting for this grim tale. His bedroom is tomblike, dominated by a great Gothic-style bed. The throne room is without a throne; Ludwig died before one could be installed. Corridors are outfitted as a ghostly grotto, reminiscent of Wagner's *Tannhäuser.* During the 17 years from the start of construction until his death, the king spent only 102 days in this country residence. Chamber concerts are held at the beginning of September in the gaily decorated minstrels' hall, one room at least that was completed as Ludwig conceived it. (Program details are available from the Verkehrsamt, Schwangau, ☎ 08362/81980.) There are some spectacular walks around the castle. Be sure to visit the **Marienbrücke** (Mary's Bridge), spun like a medieval maiden's hair across a deep, narrow gorge. From this vantage point there are giddy views of the castle and the great Upper Bavarian Plain beyond. ☞ *Schloss Neuschwanstein (including guided tour): DM 8 adults, DM 5 children under 14.* ☼ *Apr.–Sept., daily 8:30–5:30; Oct.–Mar., daily 10–4.*

If you plan to visit Hohenschwangau or Neuschwanstein, bear in mind that more than 1 million people pass through the two castles every year. Authorities estimate that on some summer weekends the number of people who tour Neuschwanstein is matched by the number who give up at the prospect of standing in line for up to two hours. If you visit in the summer, get there early. The best time to see either castle without waiting in a long line is a weekday in January, February, or early March. The prettiest time, however, is in the fall.

The castles are only 5 kilometers (3 miles) from the official end of the Romantic Road, the border town of **Füssen,** set at the foot of the mountains that separate Bavaria from the Austrian Tyrol. Füssen also has a notable castle, the **Hohes Schloss,** one of the best-preserved late-Gothic castles in Germany. It was built on the site of the Roman fortress that once guarded this Alpine section of the Via Claudia, the trade route from Rome to the Danube. The castle was the seat of Bavarian rulers before Emperor Heinrich VII mortgaged it and the rest of the town to the bishop of Augsburg for 400 pieces of silver. The mortgage was never redeemed, and Füssen remained the property of the Augsburg episcopate until secularization during the early 19th century. The castle was put to good use by the bishops of Augsburg as their summer Alpine residence. It has a spectacular 16th-century Rittersaal (Knights' Hall) with a fine carved ceiling, and a princes' chamber with a Gothic tiled heating oven. *Magnuspl. 10.* ☛ *DM 10 adults, children under 15 free.* ☉ *Daily 10–4.*

The presence, at least in summer, of the bishops of Augsburg ensured that Füssen received an impressive number of Baroque and Rococo churches. A Benedictine abbey was built during the 9th century at the site of the grave of St. Magnus, who spent most of his life ministering in Füssen and the surrounding countryside. A Romanesque crypt beneath the Baroque abbey church has a partially preserved 10th-century fresco, the oldest in Bavaria.

The abbey was secularized and never reclaimed by the Catholic church, and today it's Füssen's Rathaus (Town Hall). In summer, chamber concerts are held in the high-ceiling, Baroque splendor of the abbey's Fürstensaal (Princes' Hall). Program details are available from the Füssen tourist office (Augsburger Torpl. 1, ☎ 08362/7077).

Complete your tour of the Romantic Road with a stroll down a street that—like Augsburg's Maximilianstrasse—was once part of the Roman Via Claudia. Now it's Füssen's main shopping street—a cobblestone pedestrian walkway lined with high-gabled medieval houses and backed by the bulwarks of the castle and the easternmost buttresses of the Allgäu Alps. The Lech River, which has accompanied you for much of the final section of the Romantic Road, rises in those mountains and embraces the town as it rushes northward. One of several lakes in the area, the Forggensee is formed from a broadening of the river. *Pleasure boats cruise the lake June–Sept. Fares for the cruises vary (according to length) from DM 9 to DM 14 (children half price).*

What to See and Do with Children

In Würzburg, take a boat trip on the Main River (*see* Guided Tours *in* Romantic Road Essentials, *below*). In Rothenburg-ob-der-Tauber, young imaginations soar while roaming through the dungeons beneath the Rathaus and the grisly exhibits in the **Mittelalterliches Kriminalmuseum.** A rack, thumbscrews, and various other torture devices will keep parents busy answering questions. The town also has the enchanting **Puppen und Spielzeugmuseum,** with enough dolls to keep youngsters amused for hours (*see* Rothenburg-ob-der-Tauber, *above*). You might also seek out the adventure playground in the dry moat in front of the **Würzburger Tor,** where, on a fine day, you can sun yourself while the children play in the shadow of Rothenburg's ancient walls.

Aschaffenburg claims to have the largest collection of historic sports cars in the world at the **Automuseum Rosso Bianco.** *Obernauer Str. 125,*

☎ 06021/21358. ☛ *DM 10 adults, DM 6 children.* ☉ *Apr.–Oct., Tues.–Sun. 10–6; Nov.–Mar., Sun. 10–6.*

Museum 3 Dimension, the world's first museum of three-dimensional technology, opened recently in Dinkelsbühl. Exhibitions describe how the three-dimensional effect is achieved in photography, the cinema, and other art forms. Children enjoy the 3-D film run at various times during the day, as well as the 3-D art on display. *Nördlinger Tor.* ☉*Apr.–Oct., daily 10–6; Nov.–Mar., weekends 11–4.*

Augsburg has an excellent **puppet theater** (Spitalgasse 15, next to the Rotes Tor) and a zoo with more than 1,900 animals (Brehmplatz 1). ☛ *DM 6 adults, DM 3.50 children.* ☉ *Apr.–Sept., daily 8:30–6; Oct.–Mar., daily 8:30–dusk or 5 (whichever is earlier). Augsburg also has a fascinating nature museum and planetarium (Ludwigstr. 2).* ☉ *Tues., Wed., and Fri.–Sun. 9–5, Thurs. 9–8 PM.*

The **doll museum** in Landsberg is a favorite. *Hintere Salzgasse 5.* ☉ *Tues.–Sun. 2–5.*

Young cowboys will feel at home in **"Western City,"** in the village of Dasing, just outside of Augsburg. ☛ *DM 6 adults, DM 5 children.* ☉ *Palm Sunday–Nov., Tues.–Sun. 9–6.*

At Königsbrunn, just outside Augsburg, is a **lido** with five heated pools, complete with water cannons, chutes, and geysers. *Admission 2 hrs: DM 14 adults, DM 8 children.* ☉ *Daily 10:30–7:30.*

A 60-meter **water chute** is one of the top attractions at a new lido in the Marienhöhe district of Nördlingen. Young film fans will love another newly opened attraction in Nördlingen, a museum tracing the history of movies (Laterna Magica, Pfarrgasse 2). Neither attraction had a phone number at press time.

A mile (1½ km) outside Schongau, suitably set in a wood, is one of the popular **Märchenwälder** (fairy-tale forests) that dot the German landscape, complete with mechanical models of fairy-tale scenes, deer enclosures, and an old-time miniature railway. *Diessenerstr. 6.* ☛ *DM 4 adults, DM 2 children.* ☉ *Easter–Oct., daily 9–7.*

If you're in Schongau during the winter, take a **sleigh ride** into the mountains to feed the wild deer. Josef Kotz sets off daily from the Karbrücke Bridge at 2:30 (☎ 08362/8581).

Off the Beaten Track

Getting off the beaten track in one of Germany's most popular tourist areas is not as hard as you might think. Even in Rothenburg-ob-der-Tauber there are corners that the world passes by. Pull on the bell at the **Staudthof** in Herrngasse, hand over DM 1, and you'll gain admittance to the town's oldest patrician home, a 450-year-old haven of peace that's belonged to the von Staudt family for three centuries. The yew trees in the quiet courtyard have been there that long, too; some are thought to be 1,000 years old. The shutters are painted in the yellow and black of the Hapsburgs as tribute to the fact that it was the Hapsburgs who raised two members of the von Staudt family to the nobility. Linger at the low wall along Rothenburg's **Burggasse** as dusk falls on the valley below. Watch the sun set from the west defense walls of the lovely little hilltop town of **Schillingsfurst,** halfway between Feuchtwangen and Rothenburg.

For an off-the-beaten-track experience that combines overnight accommodation, book a space in the hayloft of the Stahl family's farm at Creglingen. The Stahls have opened what they describe as southern Germany's first **"hay hotel,"** where visitors bed down in freshly turned hay in the farmhouse granary. If the hay is too prickly bed linen and blankets can be borrowed. The overnight rate of DM 28 (children under 11 DM 25) includes a cold supper and breakfast (tel 07933/378 for details and reservations).

Eight km (5 mi) outside Creglingen, within the stout castle walls of Schloss Waldmannshofen, is a fascinating **fire-brigade museum,** with an impressive collection of old fire engines. ☯ *Easter–Oct., daily 10–noon and 2–4.*

One of Germany's most unusual museums, the **Fingerhutmuseum,** can be found opposite the Herrgottskirche outside Creglingen. *Fingerhut* is German for "thimble," and the museum has thousands of them, some dating from Roman times. ☯ *Apr.–Oct., daily 9–6; Nov.–Mar., daily 1–4.*

The official end of the Romantic Road trails off into the mountain valleys around Füssen, where you'll leave the beaten track far behind.

SHOPPING

Hummel porcelain figures are a perennial favorite among visitors to this area of Germany. Prices vary dramatically, so be sure to shop around. You'll find a wide selection at competitive prices at Otto Wolf (Marktpl., ☎ 09081/841–161) in Nördlingen. Hummel figures and other German porcelain and glassware can be found in Dinkelsbühl at **Weschcke and Ries** (Segringerstr. 20, ☎ 09851/9439). In Rothenburg at **Unger's** (Herrngasse 10, ☎ 09861/8904), there's a similar selection of porcelain and glassware. The **Kunstwerke Friese** (Grüner Markt, near the Rathaus, ☎ 09861/1425) stocks a selection of the beautifully crafted porcelain birds made by the Hummel manufacturers, the Goebel Porzellanfabrik, as well as porcelain and glassware by other German manufacturers.

Donauwörth is the home of the famous and well-loved Käthe-Kruse dolls. You can see them being made in the **Heimatmuseum.** *Im Ried.* ☯ *May–Sept., Tues.–Sun. 2–5.*

Locally made **pottery** is enjoying a renaissance in some of the Romantic Road towns. **Jürgen Pleilkles** (Segringerstr. 53, ☎ 09851/7596) in Dinkelsbühl is energetically trying to restore his town's former reputation for fine earthenware; he also offers courses at the potter's wheel. Local artists don't lack for inspiration in these beautiful Romantic Road towns; a large selection of their work can be found at the **Reichstadt** gallery (Segringerstr. 33, ☎ 09851/3123).

Children will love **Käthe Wohlfahrt's** shop (Herrngasse 1, ☎ 09861/4090) in Rothenburg. **Weihnachtsdorf** (Christmas Village) is a wonderland of locally made toys and decorations; even in summer there are Christmas trees hung with brightly painted wood baubles. In Rothenburg, the centuries-old onetime home of **Georg Nusch** (Burggasse)—the councillor who saved the town by accepting General Tilly's wine-drinking challenge—is a shop stacked high with local glassware and other handicrafts.

In Augsburg a good place for shopping is the **Viktoria Passage,** an arcade of diverse shops and boutiques opposite the main railway station.

The main street, broad **Maximilianstrasse,** was once the city's wine market and is now another good shopping area. The Romantic Road's true **wine** center is Würzburg. Visit any of the vineyards that rise from the Main River and choose a *Bocksbeutel*, the distinctive green, flagon-shape wine bottles of Franconia. It's claimed that the shape came about because wine-guzzling monks found it the easiest to hide under their robes. In Würzburg itself, you'll want to linger on traffic-free **Schönbornstrasse** and the adjacent marketplace. Wine and the familiar goblets in which it is served in this part of the world are sold in many of the shops here. You can buy directly from the **Bürgerspital** (Theaterstr. 19, ☎ 0931/13861), an ancient city institution. The **Juliusspital** (Juliuspromenade 19, ☎ 0931/30840), also old, sells wine from its own vineyards, as well as the glasses from which to drink it.

SPORTS AND FITNESS

Ballooning
James Seyfert-Joiner (☎ 06106/79641), an Englishman, has a fleet of hot-air balloons based near Aschaffenburg and takes visitors on flights over the Romantic Road region.

Bicycling
Bikes can be rented at all train stations on the Romantic Road. Rental is DM 12 a day (DM 6 if you have a valid rail ticket). Some tourist offices—Dinkelsbühl is one—have a limited number of bikes for rent. You'll need ID, such as a passport, as a deposit against the safe return of the bike. Cycle paths along the Main River start and end at Würzburg, where you can hire bikes at the main railway station or at the Max und Moritz sports shop (Pleicherkirchplatz 11). Tandems are rented for DM 8 an hour (DM 35 per day) by the bicycle museum Zumhaus in Feuchtwangen. Bike fans will love prowling around the museum, the first in southern Germany. ☉ *May–Sept., daily 10–5; Mar., Apr. and Oct., Sun. 1:30–4:30.*

Canoeing
The Lech River, which follows the southern stretch of the Romantic Road for much of its way, offers excellent canoeing. There's good sport, too, to be had on the Tauber and Wörnitz rivers. Contact Krezschmer's **Kanu-Laden in Donauwörth** (Alte Augsburger Str., ☎ 0906/8086).

Golf
Augsburg Golf Club (☎ 08234/5621) welcomes visiting members of overseas golf clubs. For scenery and a mild challenge, try the nine-hole course at **Schloss Colberg** (☎ 09803/615). It's 20 kilometers (12 miles) east of Rothenburg. There are also attractive nine-hole courses at Aschaffenburg (Am Heigenberg, Hösbach-Feldkahl, ☎ 06024/4666), Würzburg (Rottendorfer Str. 16, ☎ 0931/71092), and just outside Landsberg, at Schloss Igling (☎ 08248/1003).

Hang Gliding
This is a leading center of the sport. For information, contact the **Drachenflugschule Aktiv** (☎ 08362/81796) or Chris Vogel's **Drachenflugschule** (☎ 08362/5138).

Mountain Climbing and Walking

The mountains above Füssen and Schwangau beckon climbers and walkers. Contact the **Kurverwaltung Füssen,** (☎ 08362/7077) for guides, maps, and other information.

Sailing and Windsurfing

The lakes around Füssen are excellent for sailing and windsurfing. **Selbach Bootsvermietung** has several boathouses, two of which, Hopfensee and Weissensee (☎ 08362/7164), rent dinghies and Windsurfers. For boats and Windsurfers on the larger Forggensee, try the **Yachtschule Gruber und Jürgensen** (☎ 08367/471).

Skiing

Füssen, Schwangau, and surrounding villages are popular ski resorts. All have sports shops offering lessons and equipment. Instruction on the Füssen slopes is organized by the **Skischule Tegelberg-Füssen** (Schwangau, ☎ 08362/81018).

DINING AND LODGING

Dining

The best Franconian and Swabian food combines hearty regional specialties with nouvelle elements. Various forms of pasta are common. Try *Pfannkuchen* (pancakes) and *Spätzle* (small tagliatelle-like ribbons of rolled dough), the latter often served with roast beef, or *Rinderbraten,* the traditional Sunday lunchtime dish. One of the best regional dishes is *Maultaschen,* a Swabian version of ravioli, usually served floating in broth strewn with chives. Würzburg is one of the leading wine-producing areas of Germany, and beer lovers will want to try the many Franconian beers, whose brands and flavors change from one town to another.

WHAT TO WEAR

Many of the moderately priced restaurants listed below cater to tourists just passing through and don't expect fancy attire. Finer dress is usually appropriate at the more expensive restaurants.

RATINGS

CATEGORY	COST*
$$$$	over DM 90
$$$	DM 55–DM 90
$$	DM 35–DM 55
$	DM 20–DM 35

*per person for a three-course meal, including tax and excluding drinks

Lodging

With a few exceptions, the Romantic Road hotels are mostly quiet and rustic rather than slick, modern purpose-built city lodgings. You'll find high standards of comfort and cleanliness throughout the region. Make reservations as far in advance as possible if you plan to visit in the summer. Hotels in Würzburg, Rothenburg, and Füssen in particular are often full year-round. Augsburg hotels are now in great demand because of accommodation shortages in nearby Munich. Tourist information offices can sometimes help with accommodations, even in high season, especially if you arrive early in the day.

RATINGS

CATEGORY	COST*
$$$$	over DM 200
$$$	DM 160–DM 200
$$	DM 120–DM 160
$	under DM 120

All prices are for two people in a double room, excluding service charges.

Aschaffenburg

DINING AND LODGING

★ **Romantik Hotel Post.** This is the number-one choice in town for both dining and lodging. Despite extensive wartime damage, the restored Post exudes class and that inimitable German coziness. All rooms are individually furnished. Eating here can be an experience not just for the excellent local specialties but because there's an original 19th-century mail coach in the rustic-looking restaurant. ⌂ *Goldbacherstr. 19–21,* ☎ *06021/3340,* ℻ *06021/13483. 71 rooms with bath or shower. Restaurant, bar, indoor pool, sauna. DC, MC, V. $$$*

Zum Goldenen Ochsen. Located just around the corner from Schloss Johannisburg, this cozy old hotel-tavern serves hearty Franconian fare at very reasonable prices. Rooms offer a high standard of comfort, with mostly traditional Bavarian furnishings. ⌂ *Karlstr. 16,* ☎ *06021/23132,* ℻ *06021/25785. 39 rooms. Restaurant, café. AE, DC, MC, V. Closed 3 wks in Aug. and 1 wk in Jan. $$*

Augsburg

DINING

★ **Zum alten Fischertor.** This is one of the culinary high points along the Romantic Road, offering a mix of regional specialties and French haute cuisine. Try the Swabian dumplings, for instance, with cuttlefish filling. The Augsburg-style herb soup is also delicious. ✕ *Pfärrle 14,* ☎ *0821/518–662. Reservations advised. Jacket and tie. AE, DC, MC, V. Closed Sun. dinner, Mon., Aug. 1–19, and Dec. 24–30. $$$*

Die Ecke. "Ecke" means "corner," and that describes the location of this attractive and popular restaurant, tucked away behind Augsburg's very fine city hall. Die Ecke is valued for the imaginative variety of its cuisine and the scope of its wine list. In season, the venison dishes are among Bavaria's best. Fish—particularly locally caught trout (the *truit meunière* is magnificent)—is another house specialty. ✕ *Elias-Holl-Pl. 2,* ☎ *0821/510–600. Reservations required. AE, DC, MC, V. $$*

Fuggerkeller. The vaulted cellars of the former Fugger home on Augsburg's historic Maximilianstrasse are now a bright and comfortable restaurant, owned and run by the luxurious Drei Mohren Hotel above it. The midday specials are a particularly good value; try the Swabian-style stuffed cabbage rolls in a spiced meat sauce. Prices for dinner are higher. ✕ *Maximilianstr. 38,* ☎ *0821/516–260. Reservations advised. AE, DC, MC, V. Closed Sun. dinner and 1st 3 wks in Aug. $$*

★ **Welser Kuche.** You can practically hear the great oak tables groan under the eight-course menus of Swabian specialties offered here. You'll need to give a day's notice if you want the eight-course menu, however. Be sure to try Spätzle. ✕ *Maximilianstr. 83,* ☎ *0821/96110. Reservations advised.* ☽ *Evenings only. $$*

LODGING

★ **Steigenberger Drei Mohren Hotel.** Kings, princes, even Napoléon slept here; so did the British commander who defeated him at Waterloo, the duke of Wellington. The historic hotel, however, takes its name from three very early guests of less renown: three Abyssinian bishops who sought shelter in this worldly German city. ☎ *Maximilianstr. 40,* ☎ *0821/50360,* FAX *0821/157864. 100 rooms and 5 suites with bath. Restaurant, bar, beauty salon. AE, DC, MC, V. $$$$*

Hotel am Rathaus. This hotel derives its name from its unrivaled position, tucked neatly away down a quiet side street literally within the shadow of Augsburg's superb city hall. The attractive lobby, furnished with deep-seated armchairs, Tiffany lamps, and Oriental rugs, sets the style for the subdued, dark-wood decor of the comfortable rooms. *Am Hinteren Perlachberg 1,* ☎ *0821/509–000,* FAX *0821/517–746. 32 rooms, 1 apartment with bath. AE, DC, MC, V. $$$*

★ **Dom Hotel.** Just across the street from Augsburg's cathedral, this is a snug, comfortable establishment with a personal touch. Ask for one of the attic rooms, where you'll sleep under beam ceilings and wake to a rooftop view of the city. Recent additions to the hotel include a garden terrace (bordering the old city walls) and an indoor pool with sauna and solarium. ☎ *Frauentorstr. 8,* ☎ *0821/153–031,* FAX *0821/510– 126. 43 rooms with bath or shower. Indoor pool, sauna. AE, DC, MC, V. $$$*

Romantikhotel Augsburger Hof. A preservation order protects the beautiful Renaissance facade of this charming old Augsburg mansion, the interior of which was completely reconstructed to create a comfortable and up-to-date hotel. The cathedral is around the corner, the town center a five-minute stroll away. ☎ *Auf dem Kreuz 2,* ☎ *0821/314– 083,* FAX *0821/38322. 40 rooms with bath. Restaurant, sauna. AE, MC, V. $$*

Gaststätte-Hotel-Pension Jakoberhof. This sturdy, turreted city mansion has been in the Schoderer family's possession for more than 75 years. One son reigns in the kitchen while his parents attend to the everyday hotel tasks. The lodging is centrally located and only a few minutes' walk from the famous Fuggerei. Rooms are simply but cheerfully furnished. ☎ *Jakoberstr. 39–41,* ☎ *0821/510–030,* FAX *0821/150–844. 36 rooms, most with bath or shower. Restaurant, bar, beer garden. No credit cards. $–$$*

Bad Mergentheim

DINING

Kettler's Altfränkische Weinstube. You'll want to come here to try the *Nürnberger Bratwürste*—finger-size spicy sausages—and to enjoy the atmosphere of a snug 180-year-old Franconian tavern. The wine list is enormous. ✗ *Krumme Gasse 12,* ☎ *07931/7308. Reservations advised. Closed Wed. No credit cards. $*

DINING AND LODGING

★ **Victoria.** This is one of the area's finest spa hotels, combining cosmopolitan flair with rural peace and quiet. Rooms are large, luxurious, and furnished in the style of a country mansion, with king-size beds, well-cushioned armchairs, subdued lighting, and fine prints on the textile-hung walls. The lounge is scarcely less opulent, with an open fireplace and a library. The excellent restaurant, with a magnificent tile oven taking pride of place, draws a clientele from far afield. ☎ *Poststr. 2–4,* ☎ *07931/5930,* FAX *07931/593–500. 80 rooms with bath. Restaurant, bar, pub, beauty salon, sauna. AE, DC, MC, V. $$$$*

Dinkelsbühl

DINING AND LODGING

Hotel Goldene Kanne. Within its historic walls, this centrally located hotel (now a member of the budget-conscious Minotel group) offers a high standard of comfort. The rooms even have faxes—a rarity in this part of Germany. It's particularly recommended for families (seven of the rooms have children's beds), although lovers are also catered to with a special honeymoon suite. The fine restaurant offers both local and international cuisine. ☎ *Segringerstr. 8,* ☎ *09851/6011,* FAX *09851/2281. 23 rooms and 3 suites, all with bath/shower. Restaurant, café. AE, MC, V. $$*

LODGING

Deutsches Haus. This picture-postcard medieval inn with a facade of half-timbered gables and flower boxes has many rooms fitted with antique furniture. ☎ *Weinmarkt 3,* ☎ *09851/6058,* FAX *09851/7911. 14 rooms and 1 suite with bath. Restaurant, sauna. AE, DC, MC, V. Closed Dec. 24–Jan. 6. $$$*

Blauer Hecht. A brewery-tavern in the 18th century (they still brew in the backyard), this Ring hotel has been renovated and furnished with the sleek, dark-veneer and pastel-shaded contrasts favored by the group's interior designers. It's central but quiet. ☎ *Schweinemarkt 1,* ☎ *09851/811,* FAX *09851/814. 44 rooms with bath. Indoor pool, sauna, steam room. AE, DC, MC, V. Closed Jan. $$*

Donauwörth

DINING AND LODGING

Posthotel Traube. Mozart and Goethe are among the notable guests who have stayed at the Traube in the course of its 300-year history. It's one of the oldest coaching inns in the area. Part of the Ring group now, the hotel offers a high degree of comfort within its sturdy old walls. The restaurant is one of Donauwörth's best, with a wide-ranging menu with local and international cuisines. ☎ *Kapellstr. 14–16,* ☎ *0906/6096,* FAX *0906/23390. 41 rooms, 2 suites with bath. Restaurant, weinstube, sauna. AE, DC, MC, V. $$*

LODGING

★ **Parkhotel.** A recently established group brings together hotels that have one feature in common: an idyllic location. This one qualifies because of its fine site high above Donauwörth. Rooms were renovated in 1994, and most have balconies with panoramic views. ☎ *Stern-schanzenstr. 1,* ☎ *0906/6037,* FAX *0906/23283. 45 rooms with bath or shower. Weinstube, bowling. AE, DC, MC, V. $$$*

Feuchtwangen

DINING AND LODGING

★ **Romantik Hotel Greifen Post.** The solid, market-square exterior of this historic house (formerly a staging post on the medieval route between Paris and Prague) gives little hint of the luxuries within. Ask for the room with the four-poster or, if that's taken, settle for one of the other so-called "romantic" rooms. In the indoor pool you'll splash around within the original Renaissance walls of this ancient part of the house. In the hotel's fine restaurant you'll dine within walls decorated with frescoes of Feuchtwangen's past; the pictures illustrate that past guests here included a German emperor and the notorious dancer who cost a king his throne, Lola Montez. ☎ *Marktpl. 8,* ☎ *09852/6800,* FAX *09852/68068. 35 rooms, 2 apartments with bath. Restaurant, bar, indoor pool, sauna, bicycles. AE, DC, MC, V. $$*

Füssen

DINING

Gasthaus zum Schwanen. This modest, cozy establishment offers good regional cooking with no frills, at low prices. The excellent Swabian

Maultaschen are made on the premises. ⊡ *Brotmarkt 4,* ☎ *08362/6174.
No credit cards. Closed Sun. evening, Mon., and Nov. $*

DINING AND LODGING

Alpen-Schlössle. A *Schlössle* is a small castle, and although this comfortable, rustic hotel and restaurant isn't one, it is located on a mountain site, just outside Füssen, that King Ludwig might well have chosen for one of his homes. If wild duck is on the restaurant's menu, don't leave without tasting it. There are 12 cozy rooms, furnished in traditional Bavarian style. ⊡ *Alatseestr. 28,* ☎ *08362/4017,* FAX *08362/39847. Restaurant (closed Tues.) No credit cards. $$*

Hotel-Gasthof Zum Hechten. Geraniums flower for most of the year in the balcony boxes in front of the bedroom windows at this comfortable guest house, one of the town's oldest. It has been in the possession of the Pfeiffer family for several generations and is noted for its personalized service. The family's butcher shop provides the meat for the restaurant, where you'll eat at sturdy round tables within colorfully frescoed walls. ⊡ *Ritterstr. 6,* ☎ *08362/7906,* FAX *08362/39841. 35 rooms, 28 with bath or shower. Restaurant, paddle tennis, bowling, exercise room. No credit cards. $–$$*

LODGING

Hotel Sonne. *Sonne* means "sun," and this is an appropriately bright, cheerful, and modern hotel in Bavarian style with traditional furnishings. ⊡ *Reichenstr. 37,* ☎ *08362/9080,* FAX *08362/908100. 32 rooms with bath or shower. Restaurant, café, nightclub. AE, DC, MC, V. $$–$$$*

Nördlingen

DINING

Meyer's-Keller. An unassuming exterior belies the cozy, rustic interior of this restaurant, a short walk from Nördlingen's Altstadt. The menu is anything but simple Bavarian; try any of the fish dishes, all prepared with flair. ✕ *Marienhöhe 8,* ☎ *09081/4493. Reservations advised. AE, MC, V. Closed Mon. and Tues. lunch. $$$*

DINING AND LODGING

Flamberg Hotel Klösterle. Where monks of the Barfuss order once went about their frugal daily routine you can dine in a restaurant that incorporates the ancient stonework of the original monastery. Guest rooms are anything but monastic—modern and comfortably furnished with dark leather and pastel tones and bright prints on the walls. The hotel's striking white and yellow facade, with its Renaissance-look windows and steeply stepped gables, fits snugly into the Old Town center, whose jumble of roofs you can admire while relaxing in the fitness center and sauna-steam bath on the hotel's top floor. ⊡ *Am Klösterle 1,* ☎ *09081/88054,* FAX *09081/22740. 100 rooms with bath. Restaurant, weinstube, sauna, bicycles. AE, DC, MC, V. $$$*

Hotel Schützenhof. This small, comfortable hotel in traditional style, on the outskirts of town, is known for its excellent restaurant, which specializes in fresh fish from the surrounding lakes and rivers. ⊡ *Kaiserwiese 2,* ☎ *09081/3940 or 09081/3948,* FAX *09081/88815. 15 rooms with shower. Restaurant, beer garden, bowling. AE, DC, MC, V. Closed 1st 2 wks in Aug. and 2 wks in Jan. $$–$$$*

LODGING

★ **Kaiserhof-Hotel-Sonne.** The great German poet Goethe stayed here and was only one in a long line of distinguished guests headed by Emperor Friedrich III in 1487. The vaulted cellar wine-tavern is a reminder of those days. The three honeymoon suites are furnished in 18th-century style, with hand-painted four-poster beds. ⊞ *Marktpl. 3,* ☎ *09081/5067,* FAX *09081/23999. 40 rooms, all with bath or shower. Restaurant, weinstube. AE, MC, V. Closed Dec. 26–mid-Jan. $$$–$$$$*

Rothenburg-ob-der-Tauber

DINING

★ **Die Blaue Terrasse.** The view of the Tauber Valley from the windows of the Hotel Goldener Hirsch's restaurant almost rivals its nouvelle cuisine, prepared with regional touches. Snails and asparagus (in season) are perennial favorites. ✕ *Untere Schmiedgasse 16/25,* ☎ *09861/7080. Reservations advised. Jacket and tie. AE, DC, MC, V. Closed midDec.–Jan. $$$*

★ **Baumeisterhaus.** In summer you can dine in one of Rothenburg's loveliest courtyards, a half-timbered oasis of peace that's part of a magnificent Renaissance house. If the weather's cooler, move inside to the paneled dining room. The menu, changed daily, features Bavarian and Franconian specialties. ✕ *Obere Schmiedgasse 3,* ☎ *09861/94700. Reservations advised. AE, DC, MC, V. $$*

DINING AND LODGING

Reichs-Küchenmeister. Master chefs in the service of the Holy Roman Empire were the inspiration for the name of this historic old hotel-restaurant, one of the oldest trader's houses in Rothenburg. The present proprietors, Barbara and Wolfgang Niedner, carry on the tradition with energy and flair. The excellent fish come from their own tanks, the venison from hunters they know. Rooms are furnished in old German style, with oak and heavy fabrics. ⊞ *Kirchpl. 8,* ☎ *09861/2046,* FAX *09861/86965. 44 rooms and 6 apartments with bath. Restaurant, pub, hot tub, sauna. AE, DC, MC, V. $$–$$$*

LODGING

★ **Hotel Eisenhut.** It's appropriate that the prettiest small town in Germany should have one of the prettiest small hotels in the country. It stands in the center of town and is located in what were originally four separate town houses, the oldest dating from the 12th century, the newest from the 16th. Inside there are enough oil paintings, antiques, and heavy beams to make any Teutonic knight feel at home. ⊞ *Herrngasse 3,* ☎ *09861/7050,* FAX *09861/70545. 79 rooms, with bath. Restaurant, café, piano bar. AE, DC, MC, V. $$$$*

★ **Romantik Hotel Markusturm.** This hotel belongs to the Romantik group, and romantic it certainly is: a 13th-century (but fully modernized) sharp-eaved house that is practically embraced by the ancient Markus tower and gate. If you stay at the height of the season, you'll hear the night watchman making his rounds. ⊞ *Rödergasse 1,* ☎ *09861/2098,* FAX *09861/2692. 21 rooms, 5 suites with bath. Restaurant, no-smoking rooms, sauna. DC, MC, V. $$$–$$$$*

Hotel Goldener Hirsch. This lantern-hung, green-shuttered 15th-century patrician house is an inextricable part of Rothenburg's history: It was here that the Meistertrunk play was first performed. Baroque antiques are everywhere, from the lobby to the uppermost, bay-windowed bedroom. ⊞ *Untere Schmiedgasse 16–25,* ☎ *09861/7080,* FAX *09861/708100. 72 rooms, with bath or shower. AE, DC, MC, V. Closed mid-Dec.–Jan. $$$–$$$$*

Hotel-Gasthof Zum Rappen. Close to the Würzburger Tor (a town gate) and first mentioned in town records in 1603, this tavern offers a surprisingly high standard of comfort behind its stout, yellow-stuccoed, geranium-smothered facade. Guest rooms have a colorful, airy touch, with light woods and pastel-shaded and floral furnishings.

Those in the modern annex have balconies overlooking a quiet court-yard. If you ask for traditional German furnishings the Rappen will oblige. 🏠 *Würzburger Tor 6 & 10,* ☎ *09861/6071,* FAX *09861/6076. 60 rooms, 11 apartments with bath or shower. Restaurant, bar, beer garden. AE, DC, MC, V. Closed Jan. $$–$$$*

Gasthof Klingentor. This sturdy old staging post is outside the city walls but still within a 10-minute walk of Rothenburg's Old Town center. Rooms have recently been redecorated and furnished to a high standard of comfort. A well-marked cycle and hiking path starts outside the front door. 🏠 *Mergentheimer Str. 14,* ☎ *09861/3468. 22 rooms, most with bath. Restaurant. MC, V. $*

Schillingfurst

LODGING

Hotel Zapf "An der Wörnitzquelle." The River Wörnitz rises practically in the back garden of this enchanting and remarkably good-value country hotel whose name means "source of the Wörnitz." Although this inn has a striking stepped-gable Renaissance facade, most rooms are in the less lovely modern extension; they are nevertheless comfortable and well-furnished, with balconies offering views of the fortified town of Schillingfurst and the surrounding countryside. 🏠 *Dombühlerstr. 9,* ☎ *09868/5029,* FAX *09868/5464. 28 rooms with bath/shower. Restaurant, beer garden, café, sauna, paddle tennis, bicycles. AE, DC, MC, V. $*

Schongau

DINING AND LODGING

Hotel Holl. The Holl is a 10-minute stroll from the town center, but it's located on wooded slopes, with great views from most rooms—ideal for travelers seeking peace and quiet. The restaurant under the steep eaves of the Alpine-style hotel draws on local rivers and lakes to stock the menu with fresh, imaginative fish dishes. 🏠 *Altenstädter Str. 39,* ☎ *08861/4051,* FAX *08861/9843. 22 rooms with bath. Restaurant, recreation room. AE, DC, MC, V. $$*

LODGING

Hotel Rössle. Although it was built in 1987, the Rössle has a traditional atmosphere, with old copper lamps lighting up its arched entrance and setting the general tone of this comfortable, friendly hotel. The location, in the old town and right next to the old town wall, couldn't be better. 🏠 *Christophstr. 49,* ☎ *08861/2305,* FAX *08861/2648. 17 rooms with bath. Restaurant. AE, DC, MC, V. $$*

Schwangau

DINING AND LODGING

Hotel Müller. Built in 1910, this sturdy family-run hotel retains many of its Art Nouveau features despite extensive renovations over the years. It's ideally located between the Neuschwanstein and Hohenschwangau castles—some rooms have views of both. The rustic-style restaurant has a a creative menu, with Bavarian roast meats a good bet. 🏠 *Alpseestr. 16, Hohenschwangau,* ☎ *08362/81990,* FAX *08362/819–913. 42 rooms and 3 suites, with bath. Restaurant, café. AE, DC, MC, V. $$$–$$$$*

König Ludwig. This handsome Alpine hotel-restaurant, smothered in flowers in summer and in snow in deep winter, is named for the king who felt so at home in these surroundings. The wood-paneled restaurant serves Bavarian fare with an international touch, and venison is a specialty when it's in season. Rooms are cozily furnished in rustic

Bavarian style. Room rates include a substantial breakfast buffet. ⌂ *Kreuzweg 11–15,* ☎ *08362/8890,* ℻ *08362/81779 and 08362/81867. 102 rooms and 36 apartments with bath. Restaurant, pub, indoor and outdoor pool, beauty salon, massage, sauna, steam room, tennis court, bowling, bicycles. No credit cards. $$–$$$*

Ulm

DINING

Zunfthaus. The sturdy, half-timbered Zunfthaus has stood here for more than 500 years, first as a fishermen's pub and now a tavern-restaurant of great charm. Ulm fishermen used the building as their guild head-quarters, and when the nearby Danube flooded the fish swam right up to the door. Today they land on the menu. "Foreign" intruders on the menu include Bavarian white sausage, the *Weisswurst,* which even in Ulm should be eaten by midday. The local beer is an excellent accom-paniment. ✕ *Fischergasse 31,* ☎ *0731/64411. No credit cards. $$*

LODGING

Inter-City Hotel. This is one of the newest and smartest of the German Inter-City hotels you'll find at many main railway stations. Although Ulm is a busy rail junction you won't hear a thing within your sound-proofed room, and the hotel has the advantage of being located directly in the city center. Rooms have special work corners (with small desks and fax-modem outlets) for visitors who are traveling on business. ⌂ *Bahnhofplatz 1,* ☎ *0731/96550,* ℻ *0731/965–5999. 135 rooms with shower. Restaurant, bar. AE, DC, MC, V. $$$*

Landgasthof Hirsch. A tithe barn was converted 100 years ago into this country tavern, extended in recent years into a comfortable hotel. In winter a fire burns in the large fireplace of the rustic lounge, while the excellent restaurant is a draw throughout the year. The hotel is 3 kilo-meters (2 miles) from Ulm, in the Finningen district, but bus stops are nearby. *Dorfstr. 4, D-89231 Finningen,* ☎ *0731/70171,* ℻ *0731/724–131. 22 rooms with shower. Restaurant, lounge, bowling. AE, DC, MC, V. $$–$$$*

Weikersheim

LODGING

Laurentius. This traditional old hotel on Weikersheim's market square is an ideal stopover on a tour of the Romantic Road. You can avoid the crowds and the relatively high prices of nearby Rothenburg and still be within an hour's car ride of most sights on the northern part of the route. Owners Heinrich and Lony Koch, who ran the hotel for many years, recently handed it over to their son Jürgen, who contin-ues the family tradition with winning charm. Rooms are very comfortable and individually furnished, some with fine old German antiques. The vaulted ground floor has a cozy wine-tavern, a very good restaurant named, like the hotel, after the patron saint of cooks (and, slyly, after the family Koch—German for cook) and a newly opened brasserie. ⌂ *Marktpl. 5,* ☎ *07934/7007,* ℻ *07934/7077. 14 rooms with bath. Restaurant, brasserie, weinstube. DC, MC, V. $$*

Würzburg

DINING

Juliusspital Weinstuben. The wine you drink here is from the tavern's own vineyard; the food—predominantly hearty Franconian specialties—takes second billing. ✕ *Juliuspromenade 19,* ☎ *0931/54080. No credit cards. Closed Wed. $$*

★ **Ratskeller.** The vaulted cellars of Würzburg's Rathaus shelter one of the city's most popular restaurants. Beer is served, but Franconian wine is what the regulars drink. The food is staunch Franconian fare. ✕ *Beim Grafeneckart, Langgasse 1,* ☎ *0931/13021. No reservations. AE, DC, MC, V. $$*

Backofele. More than 400 years of tradition are sustained by this historic old tavern. You can dine well and inexpensively on such dishes as oxtail in Burgundy sauce and homemade *rissoles* filled pastries) in wild-mushroom sauce. ✕ *Ursulinergasse 2,* ☎ *0931/59059. Reservations advised. AE, MC, V. $*

★ **Zum Stachel.** On a warm spring or summer day, take a bench in the ancient Mediterranean-like courtyard of the Stachel, which is shaded by a canopy of vine leaves and girded by high walls of mellow, creeper-hung stone. The food is satisfying Franconian fare, from lightly baked onion cake to hearty roast pork, but the reason for stopping here is to sample the wine, which is made from grapes grown in the tavern's own vineyard. ✕ *Gressengasse 1,* ☎ *0931/52770. MC. Closed Sun. and holidays. $*

DINING AND LODGING

Wittelsbacher Höh. From most of the cozy, newly refurbished rooms under the steep eaves of this historic redbrick mansion you'll have a fine view of Würzburg and the surrounding vineyards. The restaurant's wine list embraces most of the leading local vintages, and Franconian and international dishes pack the menu. In summer take a table on the terrace and soak in the view. ⌗ *Hexenbruchweg 10,* ☎ *0931/42085,* ℻ *0931/415–458. 75 rooms with bath. Restaurant, sauna. AE, DC, MC, V. $$$*

Fränkischer Hotelgasthof zur Stadt Mainz. This traditional Franconian inn dates from the 15th century, and recipes from its 19th-century cookbook form the basis of its imaginative, fish-dominated menu. Eel from the Main River, prepared in a dill sauce, and locally caught carp and pike are specialties of the house. Homemade apple strudel is served with afternoon coffee and also finds its way onto the dinner dessert menu; the breakfast buffet is enormous. Rooms are simply but comfortably furnished. ⌗ *Semmelstr. 39,* ☎ *0931/53155,* ℻ *0931/58510. 15 rooms with bath or shower. AE, MC, V. Closed Dec. 20–Jan. 20. $$–$$$*

Hotel Greifenstein. The Greifenstein, recently modernized with care and taste, offers comfortable, individually furnished rooms in a quiet corner of the city just off the market square. The cheaper doubles are small but lack no comforts or facilities. The hotel restaurant, the Fränkische Stuben, has very good cuisine—mostly Franconian specialties. ⌗ *Häfnergasse 1,* ☎ *0931/35170,* ℻ *0931/57057. 37 rooms with bath. Restaurant. AE, DC, MC, V. $$–$$$*

LODGING

Hotel Walfisch. You'll breakfast on the banks of the Main in a dining room that commands views of the river valley and the vineyard-covered Marienberg above Würzburg. For lunch and dinner, try the hotel's cozy Walfischstube restaurant. Rooms were recently renovated and now seem far more luxurious; they're furnished in solid Franconian style with farmhouse cupboards, floral fabrics, and heavy drapes. ⌗ *Am Pleidenturm 5,* ☎ *0931/50055,* ℻ *0931/51690. 41 rooms with bath. Restaurant. AE, DC, MC, V. $$$$*

★ **Hotel Rebstock.** Centuries of hospitality are contained behind this hotel's Rococo facade. The spacious lobby, with its open fireplace and beckoning bar, sets the tone. All rooms are individually decorated. ⌗ *Neubaustr. 7,* ☎ *0931/30930,* ℻ *0931/309–3100. 52 rooms, 27* *suites with bath. Restaurant, bar, weinstube, no-smoking rooms. AE, DC, MC, V. $$$$*

Strauss. Close to the river and the pedestrian-only center, this lodging has been run by the same family for more than 100 years. The emphasis is on clean, simple comforts. The restaurant specializes in Franconian cuisine. ⌂ *Juliuspromenade 5,* ☎ *0931/30570,* FAX *0931/305–7555. 77 rooms and 2 suites with bath or shower. Restaurant. AE, DC, MC, V. Closed Dec. 20–mid-Jan. $$*

THE ARTS

Most of the towns on the Romantic Road have annual arts festivals. Local tourist information offices can supply details of programs and make ticket reservations. The leading festivals are Würzburg's Mozart Festival, held in the Residenz in June; Augsburg's Mozart Festival in September; Rothenburg's Meistertrunk drama festival in June; and Dinkelsbühl's Kinderzeche festival in July. Those in Rothenburg and Dinkelsbühl celebrate historical events when the towns were saved from conquest and destruction, and combine plays, concerts, and carnival-like attractions. Every other year—1996 is the next—Nördlingen and nearby villages host the Rieser Cultural Season.

Music

Augsburg has chamber and symphony orchestras, as well as a ballet and opera companies. Performances are given September through July in the Kongresshalle (Gögginerstr. 10, ☎ 0821/324–2348). Würzburg has a highly regarded Philharmonic orchestra, directed by Britain's Jonathan Seers. For information, call 0931/58686. Chamber-music concerts are given year-round at Oettingen Castle (☎ 09082/20000) and at Neuschwanstein Castle (☎ 08362/81051). The mighty organ of the Ulm Münster can be heard in special recitals every Sunday at 11:15 from Easter until November.

Theater

Augsburg and Würzburg both have city theater companies that offer a regular repertoire of German classics, modern drama, and comedy. Good knowledge of German is required if you plan a visit. Augsburg also has an annual open-air drama season, with the old city walls as a backdrop, in June and July; it moves to the romantic setting of the inner courtyard of the Fugger Palace in July and August (for details, call 0821/36604). Dinkelsbühl has an open-air theater season from late-June to mid-August, and Feuchtwangen has the Kreuzgangspiele, a summer theater festival that runs from mid-June until early August.

ROMANTIC ROAD ESSENTIALS

Arriving and Departing

By Bus

From April until the end of October, daily bus service covers the northern stretch of the Romantic Road, leaving Frankfurt at 8 AM and arriving in Munich at 8 PM. A second bus covers the section of the route between Dinkelsbühl and Füssen: Buses leave Dinkelsbühl daily at 4:15 PM and arrive in Füssen at 9 PM. In the other direction, also from April until the end of October, buses leave Füssen daily at 8 AM, arriving in Dinkelsbühl at 1:05 PM. Buses leave Munich daily at 9 AM and arrive at Frankfurt at 8:30 PM. All buses stop at the major sights along the road. Reservations are essential; contact **Deutsche Touring GmbH** (Am Römerhof 17, D–60486 Frankfurt/Main, ☎ 069/790–3256). Local buses cover much of the route but are infrequent and slow.

By Car

The northernmost city of the Romantic Road—and the natural starting point for a tour—is Würzburg on the Frankfurt–Nürnberg Autobahn. It's 115 kilometers (72 miles) from Frankfurt and 280 kilometers (175 miles) from Munich. Augsburg, the largest city on the Romantic Road, is 70 kilometers (44 miles) from Munich and 365 kilometers (228 miles) from Frankfurt. Full information on the Romantic Road is available from **Tourist Information Land an der Romantischen Strasse** (Kreisverkehrsamt, Crailsheimerstrasse 1, D–91522 Ansbach, ☎ 0981/4680) or from **Arbeitsgemeinschaft** Romantische Strasse (Marktplatz, D–91550 Dinkelsbühl, ☎ 09851/90271).

By Plane

The major international airports serving the Romantic Road are Frankfurt, at its north end, and Munich, at its south end. Regional airports include Nürnberg, Stuttgart, and Augsburg, home base of the private airline Interot.

By Train

Both Würzburg and Augsburg are on the InterCity and high-speed InterCity Express routes and have fast, frequent service to and from Frankfurt, Munich, Stuttgart, and Hamburg. Less frequent trains link most of the other major towns of the Romantic Road.

Getting Around

By Car

The Romantic Road is most easily traveled by car, starting from Frankfurt or Würzburg as outlined above and following the B–27 country highway south to meet roads B–290, B–19, B–292, and along the Wörnitz River on B–25.

CAR RENTAL

Avis: Klinkerberg 31, ☎ 0821/38241, **Augsburg;** Nürnberger-strasse 107, ☎ 0931/200–3939, **Würzburg.**

Europcar: Pilgerhausstrasse 24, ☎ 0821/312–033, **Augsburg;** Am Hauptbahnhof (at the main railway station), ☎ 0931/12060 **Würzburg.**

Hertz: Steinerne Furt, ☎ 0821/700–8101, **Augsburg;** Hoechbergerstrasse 10, ☎ 0931/415–221, **Würzburg.**

Sixt-Budget: Meierweg 3, ☎ 0821/412003, **Augsburg;** Rottendorfer-strasse 46, ☎ 0931/72093, **Wu(u)rzburg.**

Guided Tours

Boat Trips

Three shipping companies offer excursions on the Main River from Würzburg. The **Fränkische Personenschiffahrt** (Kranenkai 1, ☎ 0931/51722) and the **Würzburger Personenschiffahrt Kurth & Schiebe** (Am Alten Kranen, ☎ 0931/58573) operate excursions to the vineyards in and around Würzburg; wine-tasting is included in the price. Fränkische Personenschiffahrt (FPS for short) also offers cruises of up to two weeks on the Main, Neckar, and Danube rivers, and on the Main–Danube canal. **Kurth & Schiebe** and **Veitschöchheimer Person-**

enschiffahrt (Am Alten Kranen, ☏ 0931/55633) offer daily service to Veitschöchheim, site of the palace that was once the summer residence of the bishops of Augsburg. A passenger service on the most romantic section of the Main, between Lohr and Miltenberg is operated by a Wertheim line, the Wertheimer (Personenschiffahrt, ☏ 09342/1414).

Bus Tours

From April through October, the **Deutsche Touring** company (*see* Arriving and Departing by Bus, *above*) operates four tours of one to three days' duration to Rothenburg and sections of the Romantic Road. Prices vary from DM 435 (for a tour including one night in Rothenburg) to DM 1085 (with overnights in Rothenburg and Heidelberg).

City Tours

All the cities and towns on the Romantic Road offer guided tours, either on foot or by bus. Details are available from the local tourist information offices. Following is a sample of the more typical tours.

In **Würzburg,** guided tours on foot and by bus (in German) start at the tourist office at 10:30 AM Monday through Saturday, early April through October. Tours in English are given Tuesday to Saturday at 11 AM from early April through October. The German-language tour costs DM 8 adults, DM 6 children and the English-language tour DM 12 adults, DM 9 children. The latter tour includes a visit to the Residenz.

Augsburg has self-guided walking tours, with routes of varying lengths posted on color-coded signs throughout the downtown area. A daily bus tour starts out from the Rathaus at 10:30 from May through October. The cost is DM 12 adults, DM 6 children. Tours on foot set out from the Rathaus daily at 2 PM, May–October.

Rothenburg-ob-der-Tauber's night watchman, dressed in traditional garb, conducts visitors on a nightly tour of the town, leading the way with a lantern. Tours in English begin at 8 PM from April through December and cost DM 4. There is also a daytime tour at 1:30 (Apr.–Oct.), also costing DM 4. The night watchman in **Dinkelsbühl** also does a nightly round at 9 PM from April through October, and though he doesn't give official tours he is always happy to answer questions from inquisitive visitors (but don't expect a reply in fluent English). Daily guided tours of Dinkelsbühl in horse-drawn carriages (Apr.–Oct.) are a fun way to see the little town; the cost is DM 8 adults, DM 4 children.

A visit to the Münster, the old town hall, the Fischerviertel, and the Danube river bank are included in the 90-minute guided tour of **Ulm** offered by the tourist office. From May through October, there are tours at 10 and 2:30 Monday–Saturday, 11 and 2:30 Sunday and public holidays; from November to April, tours are at 10 on Saturday and 11 on Sunday. The departure point is the tourist information office at Münsterplatz; the cost is DM 7 adults, DM 3.50 children.

Train Tours

The **Deutsche Bahn** (German Railways) offers special weekend excursion rates covering travel from most German railroad stations to Würzburg and hotel accommodations for up to four nights. Details are available at any train station.

Important Addresses and Numbers

Visitor Information

A central tourist office based in Dinkelsbühl covers the entire Romantic Road: the **Touristik-Arbeitsgemeinschaft Romantische Strasse,** Marktplatz, D–91550 Dinkelsbühl, ☎ 09851/90271, FAX 09851/90279. The office produces a color brochure describing all the main towns and attractions along the Romantic Road.

Amorbach: Rathaus, D–63916, ☎ 09373/4778.

Aschaffenburg: Dalbergstrasse 6, D–63739, ☎ 06021/30426.

Augsburg: Verkehrsverein, Bahnhofstrasse 7, D–86150, ☎ 0821/502–070.

Dinkelsbühl: Tourist-Information, Marktplatz, D–91550, ☎ 09851/90240.

Donauwörth: Städtisches Verkehrsamt, Rathausgasse 1, D–86607, ☎ 0906/789–145.

Feuchtwangen: Fremdenverkehrsamt, Marktplatz 1, D–91555, ☎ 09852/90444.

Füssen: Kurverwaltung, Augsburger Torplatz 1, D–87629, ☎ 08362/7077.

Harburg: Fremdenverkehrsverein, Schlossstrasse 1, D–86655, ☎ 09003/96990.

Landsberg am Lech: Fremdenverkehrsamt, Hauptplatz 1, D–89896, ☎ 08191/128–246.

Mespelbrunn: Hauptstrasse 173, D–63875 Mespelbrunn, ☎ 06092/319.

Nördlingen: Städtisches Verkehrsamt, Marktplatz 2, D–86715, ☎ 09081/84116.

Rothenburg-ob-der-Tauber: Tourist-Information, Rathaus, Marktplatz 2, D–91541, ☎ 09861/40492.

Schongau: Verkehrsverein, Münzstr. 5, D–86956, ☎ 08861/7216.

Schwangau: Kurverwaltung, Rathaus, Münchenerstrasse 2, D–87645, ☎ 08362/81980.

Ulm: Tourist-Information, Münsterplatz (Stadthaus), D-89073 Ulm/Donau, ☎ 0731/161–2830.

Wertheim: Am Spitzen Turm, D–97877 Wertheim, ☎ 09342/1066.

Würzburg: Fremdenverkehrsamt, Am Congress-Centrum, D–97070 Würzburg, ☎ 0931/37335.

8 Franconia

A predominantly rural area, Franconia was most important politically in the days of the Holy Roman Empire. You'll want to see its beautiful and historic towns: Coburg, Bayreuth, Bamberg, Nürnberg, and Regensburg. Wagner fans especially shouldn't miss Bayreuth, where the great composer settled and built his theater. The annual festival that honors him brings other town functions to a halt every summer.

THE ANCIENT KINGDOM OF THE FRANKS is known today as Franconia or, in German, Franken. Although it's mainly rural, the castles and architecturally rich towns provide a solid reminder of the region's past importance in the Holy Roman Empire. It was only in the early 19th century, following Napoléon's conquest of what is now southern Germany, that the area was incorporated into northern Bavaria. Modern Franconia stretches from the Bohemian Forest on the Czech border in the east to the outskirts of Frankfurt in the west. But its heart—and the focal point of this tour—is an area known as the Fränkisches Schweiz (the Franconian Switzerland), bounded by Nürnberg (Nuremberg) on the south, Bamberg on the west, and the cultural center of Bayreuth on the east.

Despite its beauty and history, Franconia is not a mainstream tourist destination; many Germans simply drive straight through on their way south. But the region rates high with epicures in search of authentic German regional cuisine. It is also noted for its liquid refreshments, from both the grape and the grain. Franconian white wine, usually sold in distinctive stubby bottles called *Bocksbeutel*, is renowned as one of the dryest in Germany. And the region has the largest concentration of village breweries in the world, producing a wide range of brews, the most distinctive of which is the dark and heady smoked *Rauchbier*.

Our tour of Franconia begins at Coburg in the north and ends at Regensburg, on the Danube River, in the south. En route, it covers the historic cities of Bayreuth, Bamberg, and Nürnberg, as well as such memorable sights as the magnificent Baroque abbey of Weltenburg and the Rococo pilgrimage church of Vierzehnheiligen. The unspoiled hills and valleys of the Frankenwald (Franconian Forest) provide bucolic relief from the competing urban attractions of Franconia. (For information on Würzburg, perhaps the most celebrated of all the historic cities of Franconia and the starting point of the Romantic Road, *see* Chapter 7.)

EXPLORING

Tour 1: Coburg, Bayreuth, and Bamberg

Numbers in the margin correspond to points of interest on the Franconia map.

❶ **Coburg,** reached from Würzburg on B—19 and B—303, is a historic town on the Itz River, just a few miles from the former East German border. Whether glittering under the summer sky or frosted white with the snows of winter, Coburg is a treasure, and a surprisingly little-known one. It was founded in the 11th century and remained in the possession of the dukes of Saxe-Coburg-Gotha until 1918; the present duke still lives there. In fact, it's as the home of the remarkable Saxe-Coburgs, as they are generally known, that the town is most famous. Superficially just one among dozens of German ruling families, they established themselves as something of a royal stud farm, providing a seemingly inexhaustible supply of blue-blooded marriage partners to ruling houses the length and breadth of Europe. The most famous of these royal mates was Prince Albert. He married Queen Victoria, after which she gained special renown in Coburg: Legend has it that on a visit to her new husband's hometown, she had the first flush toilet in

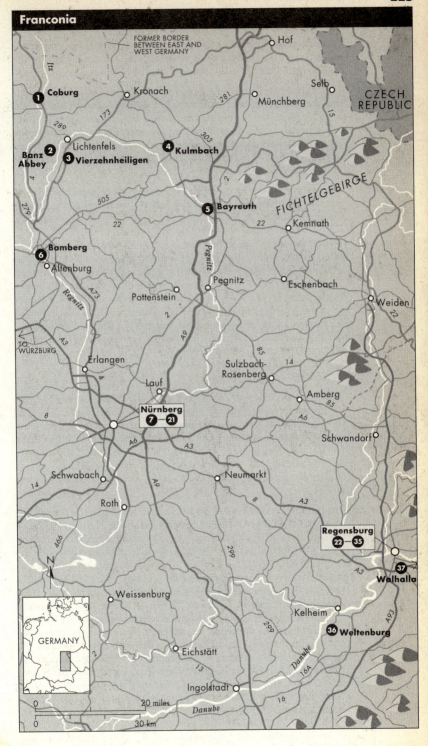

Germany installed. Whether or not that's true, Albert and Victoria were a prolific pair. Their numerous children, married off among more of Europe's kings, queens, and emperors, helped to spread the tried-and-tested Saxe-Coburg stock even farther afield. There's a statue of the high-minded consort in the Marktplatz, the main square.

The Marktplatz, ringed with gracious Renaissance and Baroque buildings, is the place to start your tour. The **Rathaus** (Town Hall), begun in 1500, is the most imposing structure. A forest of ornate gables and spires projects from its well-proportioned facade. Look at the statue of the **Bratwurstmännla** on the building; the staff he carries is claimed to be the official length against which the town's famous bratwurst sausages are measured.

TIME OUT If this sounds to you like guidebook garble, convince yourself otherwise by trying a bratwurst from one of the stands in the square that sell them Monday–Saturday.

Just off the square, on Schlossplatz, you'll find **Schloss Ehrenburg,** the ducal palace. Built in the mid-16th century, it has been greatly altered over the years, principally following a fire in the early 19th century. The then duke took the opportunity to rebuild the palace in a heavy Gothic style. It was in this dark and imposing heap that Prince Albert spent much of his childhood. The throne room; the Hall of Giants, named for the larger-than-life statues that support the stuccoed ceiling; and the Baroque-style chapel can all be visited. *Schlosspl.* ☛ *DM 3 adults, children (with parents) free. Tours Apr.–Sept., Tues.–Sun. at 10, 11, 1:30, 2:30, 3:30, and 4:30; and Oct.–Mar., Tues.–Sun. at 10, 11, 1:30, and 2:30.*

The major attraction in Coburg, however, is the **Veste Coburg** fortress, one of the largest and most impressive in the country. On your way there you'll pass through the **Hofgarten** (Palace Gardens), today the site of the **Naturkunde-museum** (Natural History Museum). This is the country's leading museum of its kind, with more than 8,000 exhibits of flora and fauna, as well as geological, ethnological, and mineralogical specimens. ☛ *DM 2 adults, DM 1 children.* ☼ *Daily 9–noon and 1–5.*

The brooding bulk of the castle lies beyond the garden on a small hill above the town. The first buildings were constructed around 1055, but with progressive rebuilding and remodeling through the centuries, today's predominantly late-Gothic/early Renaissance edifice bears little resemblance to the original rude fortress. It contains a number of museums. See the **Fürstenbau,** or Palace of the Princes, where Martin Luther was sheltered for six months in 1530. Among the main treasures are paintings by Cranach. Dürer, Rembrandt, and Cranach (again) are all represented at the **Kunstsammlungen,** the art museum in the fortress, as are many examples of German silver, porcelain, arms and armor, and furniture. Finally, there's the **Herzoginbau,** the duchess's building, a sort of 18th-century transportation museum, with carriages and ornate sleighs for speeding in style through the winter snows. *Castle open Apr.–Oct., Tues.–Sun. 9:30–5, Nov.–Mar., Tues.–Sun. 2–5.* ☛ *Kunstsammlungen and Herzoginbau: DM 4 adults, DM 2 children.* ☼ *Apr.–Oct., Tues.–Sun. 9:30–1 and 2–5; Nov.–Mar., Tues.–Sun. 2–5.* ☛ *Fürstenbau: DM 4 adults, DM 2 children.* ☼ *Apr.–Oct., Tues.–Sun. 9:30–noon and 2–4; Nov.–Mar., Tues.–Sun. 2–3:30.*

TIME OUT In the castle's own tavern you can soak up the history of centuries while sampling a Coburg beer and one of the traditional dishes from the basic but appetizing menu. The **Burgschänke** (☎ 09561/75153) is closed Mondays and January–mid-February.

From Coburg, take B—4 south for a mile or so, then turn left (south-west) onto B—289 and follow the signs to Lichtenfels, 9 kilometers (5 miles) away. Lovers of Baroque and Rococo church architecture should make a right here to see Banz Abbey and Vierzehnheiligen, probably the two most remarkable churches in Franconia. They stand on opposite sides of the Main River valley, about 5 kilometers (3 miles) southwest of Lichtenfels. The larger, though in some ways the less impressive, ❷ is **Banz Abbey,** standing high above the Main on what some call the "holy mountain of Bavaria." There had been a monastery here since 1069, but the present buildings—now a political-seminar center and "think tank"—date from the end of the 17th century. The highlight of the complex is the **Klosterkirche** (Abbey Church), the work of architect and stuccoist Johann Dientzenhofer. Its two massive onion-dome towers soar above the restrained yellow sandstone facade. Note the animated statues of saints set in niches, a typical Baroque device. Inside, the church shimmers and glows with lustrous Rococo decoration. ☉ *Apr.–Sept., daily 8:30–11:30 and 1–5:30; Oct.–Mar., Mon.–Sat. 8:30–11:30 and 1–4:30.*

★ ❸ From the terrace there's a striking view over the Main to **Vierzehnheiligen.** What you're seeing is probably the single most ornate Rococo church in Europe, although you might not know it just from looking at the exterior. There are those same onion-dome towers and the same lively curving facade, but little to suggest the almost explosive array of paintings, stucco, gilt, statuary, and rich rosy marble inside. The church was built by Balthasar Neumann (architect of the Residenz at Würzburg; *see* Chapter 7) between 1743 and 1772 to commemorate a vision of Christ and 14 saints—*Vierzehnheiligen* means "14 saints"—that appeared to a shepherd in 1445. Your first impression will be of the richness of the decoration and the brilliance of the coloring, the whole more like some fantastic pleasure palace than a place of worship. Notice the way the entire building seems to be in motion—almost all the walls are curved—and how the walls and ceiling are alive with delicate stucco. In much the same way that builders of Gothic cathedrals aimed to overwhelm through scale and verticality, Neumann wanted to startle worshipers through light, color, and movement. Anyone who has seen the gaunt Romanesque cathedrals of Protestant north Germany will have little difficulty understanding why the Reformation was never able to gain more than a toehold in Catholic southern Germany. Few buildings in Europe are more uplifting.

If it was to find the perfect liquid to lift your spirits that you came to Germany, you'll want to drive the 32 kilometers (20 miles) east from ❹ Lichtenfels along B—289 to **Kulmbach.** In a country in which the brewing and drinking of beer breaks all records, this town produces more per capita than anywhere else in Germany: 9,000 pints per man, woman, and child. A quarter of the workforce in Kulmbach earns a living directly or indirectly from beer. As if to show that the town didn't have enough breweries, a new one began production in 1994. In the same month, a brewery museum opened in the Mönchshof-Brauerei (Hofer Strasse 20). One of Kulmbach's six breweries produces the strongest beer in the world—the *Doppelbock* Kulminator 28—which takes nine months to brew and has an alcohol content of more than 11%. Tours of the Erste Kulmbacher Union brewery (EKU-str. 1,

☎ 09221/882–283), where Kulminator 28 is made, are given Monday through Thursday, but on a reservation-only basis. The tour costs DM 10, but this is more than offset: At the end of the tour you're served a beer and a snack, *and* you walk away with a gift pack of six beers, two EKU glasses, and a handsome bottle opener! A similar deal is offered by the Kulmbacher Reichelbräu brewery (Lichtenfelser Str., ☎ 09221/705–225); the DM 10 cost for a tour of a third, the Mönchshof-Bräu (Hofer Str. 20, ☎ 09221/80519 or 09221/4264), is returned as a voucher to spend in the brewery's own tavern. They're great deals, but do remember to book as far ahead as possible. Another special local brew is *Eisbock,* which is frozen as part of the brewing process to make it stronger. The locals claim it's the sparklingly clear spring water from the nearby Fichtelgebirge hills that makes their beer so special. Kulmbach celebrates its beer every year in a nine-day festival that starts on the last Saturday in July. The main festival site, a mammoth tent, is called the Festspulhaus, or, literally, "festival swallowing house," a none-too-subtle dig at nearby Bayreuth and its Festspielhaus, where Wagner's operas are performed.

TIME OUT The **Kupferpfanne** tavern-restaurant (Klostergasse 7) serves some of Kulmbach's less potent brews on draft, plus a good selection of local dishes. Buy a bottle of Kulminator 28 as a souvenir.

It would be unfair to pretend that Kulmbach is nothing but beer, beer, and more beer. The old town, for example, contains a warren of narrow streets that merit exploration. Likewise, no visitor here will want to miss the **Plassenburg,** symbol of the town and the most important Renaissance castle in the country. It's on a rise overlooking Kulmach, a 20-minute hike from the old town. The first building here, begun in the mid-12th century, was torched by marauding Bavarians who were anxious to put a stop to the ambitions of Duke Albrecht Alcibiades— a man who seems to have had few scruples when it came to self-advancement and who spent several years murdering, plundering, and pillaging his way through Franconia. His successors built today's castle starting in about 1560. Externally, there's little to suggest the graceful Renaissance interior, but as you enter the main courtyard the scene changes abruptly. The tiered space of the courtyard is covered with precisely carved figures, medallions, and other intricate ornaments, the whole comprising one of the most remarkable and delicate architectural ensembles in Europe. Inside, you may want to see the **Deutsches Zinnfigurenmuseum** (Tin Figures Museum), with more than 300,000 ministatuettes, the largest collection of its kind in the world. ☛ *DM 3 adults, DM 2 children.* ☉ *Apr.–Sept., Tues.–Sun. 10–5; Oct.–Mar., Tues.–Sun. 10–3.*

❺ Twenty-two kilometers (14 miles) south of Kulmbach on Route 303, then Route 2, is **Bayreuth,** pronounced "By-roit," though it might as well be called Wagner. This small Franconian town was where 19th-century composer and man of myth Richard Wagner finally settled after a lifetime of rootless shifting through Europe, and here he built his great theater, the Festspielhaus, as a suitable setting for his grandiose and heroic operas. The annual Wagner festival, first held in 1876, regularly brings the town to a halt as hordes of Wagner lovers descend on Bayreuth, pushing prices sky-high, filling hotels to bursting, and earning themselves much-sought-after social kudos in the process (to some, it's one of *the* places to be seen). The festival is held from late July until late August, so unless you plan to visit the town specifically for it, this is the time to stay away (*see* The Arts, *below*). Likewise, those whose tastes do not include opera and the theater will find little here to divert them. Bayreuth has no picture-postcard setting, and there is little here that is not connected in some way with music, specifically Wagner's.

As it's Wagner who brings most visitors to Bayreuth, it's only fitting to start a tour of the town with a visit to the house he built here, the only house he ever owned, in fact: **Wahnfried.** It's a simple, austere neoclassical building, constructed in 1874, just south of the town center. Today it's a museum celebrating the life of this maddening and compelling man, though, after wartime bomb damage, all that remains of the original construction is the facade. Here Wagner and his wife, Cosima, daughter of composer Franz Liszt, lived; and here they are buried. King Ludwig II of Bavaria, the young and impressionable "dream king" who provided much of the financial backing for Wagner's vaultingly ambitious works, is remembered, too; there's a bust of him in front of the entrance to the house. Though the house is something of a shrine to Wagner, even those who have little interest in the composer will find it intriguing and educational. Standout exhibits include the original scores for a number of his operas, including *Parsifal, Tristan und Isolde, Lohengrin, Der fliegende Holländer,* and *Die Götterdämmerung.* You can also see designs, many of them original, for productions of his operas, as well as his piano and huge library. At 10, noon, and 2, excerpts from his operas are played in the living room, and a video film on his life is shown at 11 and 3. *Richard-Wagner-Str. 48.* ☛ *DM 3 adults, DM 1.50 children.* ⊙ *Daily 9–5.*

From the museum, you will be close to the **Neues Schloss** (New Palace). Though Wagner is the man most closely associated with Bayreuth, it's well to remember that he would never have come here in the first place had it not been for the woman who built this glamorous 18th-century palace. She was the margravine Wilhelmina, sister of Frederick the Great of Prussia and a woman of enormous energy and decided tastes. She devoured books, wrote plays and operas (which she directed and, of course, acted in), and built, transforming much of the town and bringing it near bankruptcy. Her distinctive touch is much in evidence at the New Palace, built when a mysterious fire conveniently destroyed parts of the original palace. Anyone with a taste for the wilder flights of Rococo decoration will love it. The **Staatsgalerie** (State Art Gallery), containing a representative collection of mainly 19th-century Bavarian paintings, is also housed in the palace. *Ludwigstr. 21.* ☛ *DM 4 adults, children free.* ⊙ *Apr.–Sept., Tues.–Sun. 10–noon and 1:30–4:30; Oct.–Mar., Tues.–Sun. 10–noon and 1:30–3. English-language tours of Schloss. Times vary; call 0921/88588 for details.*

★ Wilhelmina's other great architectural legacy is the **Markgräfliches Opernhaus** (Margrave Opera House), just a step or two from the New Palace. Built between 1745 and 1748, it is a Rococo jewel, sumptuously decorated in red, gold, and blue. Apollo and the nine Muses cavort across the frescoed ceiling. It was this delicate 500-seat theater that originally drew Wagner to Bayreuth, since he felt that it might prove a suitable setting for his own operas. In fact, while it may be a perfect place to hear Mozart, it's hard to imagine a less suitable setting for Wagner's epic works. Catch a performance here if you can (*see* The Arts, *below*); otherwise, take a tour of the ravishing interior. ☛ *DM 3 adults, children free.* ⊙ *Apr.–Sept., Tues.–Sun. 9–11:30 and 1:30–4:30; Oct.–Mar., Tues.–Sun. 10–11:30 and 1:30–3.*

Now you'll want to head up to the **Festspielhaus;** it's located a mile or so north of the downtown area at the head of Bürgerreutherstrasse.

This plain, almost intimidating building is the high temple of the cult of Wagner. The building was conceived, planned, and financed by the great man specifically as a setting for his monumental operas. Today it is very much the focus of the annual Wagner festival, still master-minded by descendants of the composer. The spartan look is explained partly by Wagner's near-permanent financial crises and partly by his desire to achieve perfect acoustics. For this reason, the wood seats have no upholstering, and the walls are bare of all ornament. The stage is enormous, capable of holding the huge casts required for Wagner's largest operas. *Auf dem Grünen Hügel.* ☛ *DM 2.50 adults, DM 1.50 children. Tours are given Tues.–Sun. at 10, 10:45, 2:15, and 3. Closed afternoons during festival and Nov.*

The **Altes Schloss Eremitage** (Old Castle and Hermitage), 5 kilometers (3 miles) north of Bayreuth, makes an appealing departure from the sonorous and austere Wagnerian mood of much of the town. It's an early 18th-century palace, built as a summer palace and remodeled in 1740 by the margravine Wilhelmina. While her taste is not much in evidence in the drab exterior, the interior, alive with light and color, displays her guiding hand in every elegant line. The standout is the extraordinary **Japanese room,** filled with Asian treasures and chinoiserie furniture. The park and gardens, partly formal, partly natural, are enjoyable for idle strolling in summer. ☛ *Schloss (includes a guided tour, given every 30 min): DM 4 adults, children free.* ☉ *Apr.–Sept., Tues.–Sun. 9–11:30 and 1.30–4:30; Oct.–Mar., Tues.–Sun. 10–11:30 and 1–2:30.*

TIME OUT   Seek out Bayreuth's oldest inn, the **Braunbierhaus,** for local atmosphere, Franconian dishes, and locally brewed beer. *Kanzleistr. 15, off Maximilianstr. Closed Sun. evening.*

❻ Bamberg, the next major city on the tour, is 60 kilometers (37 miles) back to the west on B—22. Bamberg is one of the great historic cities of Germany, filled with buildings and monuments that recall its glorious days as the seat of one of the most powerful ruling families in the country. Though founded as early as the 2nd century AD, Bamberg rose to prominence only in the 11th century, under the irresistible impetus provided by its most famous son, Holy Roman Emperor Heinrich II. His imperial cathedral still dominates the historic area.

The city lies on the Regnitz River, about 80 kilometers (50 miles) north of Nürnberg. The historic center is a small island in the river; to the west is the so-called Bishops' Town, to the east the so-called ★ Burghers' Town. Connecting them is a bridge on which stands the **Altes Rathaus** (Old Town Hall), a highly colorful rickety Gothic building dressed extravagantly in Rococo. It's best seen from the adjacent bridge upstream, where it appears to be practically in danger of being swept off by the river. The preeminent pleasure of a visit is to stroll through the narrow, sinuous streets of old Bamberg, past half-timbered and gabled houses and formal 18th-century mansions. Peek into cobbled, flower-filled courtyards or take time out in a waterside café, watching the little steamers as they chug past the colorful row of fishermen's houses that make up Klein Venedig (Little Venice).

Start your tour at the **Dom,** the imperial cathedral, on Domplatz, heart of Bishops' Town. It's one of the most important of Germany's cathedrals, a building that tells not only Bamberg's story but that of much of Germany as well. The first building here was begun by Heinrich II in 1003, and it was in this partially completed cathedral that he was crowned Holy Roman Emperor in 1012. In 1237 it was mostly destroyed by fire, and the present late-Romanesque/early Gothic building was begun. From the outside, the dominant features are the massive towers at each corner. Heading into the dark interior, you'll find one of the most striking collections of monuments and art treasures of any

★ European church. The most famous is the **Bamberger Reiter** (*Bamberger Rider*), an equestrian statue, carved—no one knows by whom—around 1230 and thought to be an allegory of knightly virtue. The larger-than-life-size figure is an extraordinarily realistic work for the period, more like a Renaissance statue than a Gothic piece. Compare it with the mass of carved figures huddled in the tympana, the semicircular spaces above the doorways of the church; while these are stylized and obviously Gothic, the *Bamberg Rider* is poised and calm. In the center of the nave you'll find another great sculptural work, the massive tomb of Heinrich and his wife, Kunigunde. It's the work of Tilman Riemenschneider, Germany's greatest Renaissance sculptor. Pope Clement II is also buried in the cathedral, in an imposing tomb under the high altar; he is the only pope to be buried north of the Alps.

After you've toured the cathedral, go next door to see the **Diözesanmuseum** (Cathedral Museum). In addition to a rich collection of silver and other ecclesiastical objects, the museum contains a splinter of wood and the *heilige Nagel*, or "holy nail," both reputedly from the cross of Jesus. A more macabre exhibit is Heinrich's and Kunigunde's skulls, mounted in elaborate metal supports. The building itself was designed by Balthasar Neumann, the architect of Vierzehnheiligen Church, and constructed between 1730 and 1733. *Dompl. 5.* ☛ *DM 2 adults, 50 pf children.* ☉ *Daily 10–5. Free guided tours in English at 11 and 3.*

From the cathedral museum, visit the adjoining **Neue Residenz** (Dompl. 8). This immense Baroque palace was the home of the prince-electors. Their wealth and prestige can easily be imagined as you tour the glittering interior. Most memorable is the **Kaisersaal** (Throne Room), complete with impressive ceiling frescoes and elaborate stuccowork. You'll also be able to visit the rose garden in back of the building. ☛ *DM 3 adults, DM 2 children.* ☉ *Apr.–Sept., daily 9–noon and 1:30–5; Oct.–Mar., daily 9–noon and 1:30–4.*

The palace also houses the **Staatsbibliothek** (State Library). Among the thousands of books and illuminated manuscripts are the original prayer books belonging to Heinrich and his wife, a 5th-century manuscript by the Roman historian Livy, and handwritten manuscripts by the 16th-century painters Dürer and Cranach. ☛ *Free.* ☉ *Weekdays 9–5, Sat. 9–noon. Closed afternoons in Aug.*

End your tour of Domplatz with a visit to the **Alte Hofhaltung,** the former imperial and episcopal palace. It's a sturdy and weather-worn half-timbered Gothic building with a graceful Renaissance courtyard. Today it contains the **Historisches Museum,** with a collection of documents and maps charting Bamberg's history that will appeal most to avid history buffs and/or those who read German well. *Dompl. 7.* ☛ *DM 2 adults, DM 1 children.* ☉ *May–Oct., Tues.–Sun. 9–5.*

From Domplatz, walk down the hill to the **Altes Rathaus,** 200 or so yards away, one of the most bizarrely situated municipal buildings in Europe. It is perched on a little island in the Regnitz River, a stone bridge connecting it to the onetime rival halves of Bamberg. Half the building is Gothic, half is Renaissance; between them is an ornate Baroque gateway topped by an elegantly tapering spire. While here you'll get just about the best view of the fishermen's houses of Klein Venedig (Little Venice).

From the bridge you can walk over to the **Hoffmann-Haus** on Schiller-platz. Ernst Theodor Hoffmann, a Romantic writer, composer, and illustrator lived in this little house between 1809 and 1813. Hoffmann is probably best remembered not for one of his own works but for an opera written *about* him and his stories, by composer Jacques Offenbach, *The Tales of Hoffmann*. The house has been preserved much as it was when Hoffmann lived here—complete with the hole in the floor of his upstairs study through which he talked to his wife below. *Schillerpl. 26.* ☎ *DM 1 adults, 50 pf children.* ⊙ *May–Oct., Tues.–Fri. 4–6, weekends and public holidays 10–noon.*

TIME OUT The **Brauereiausschank Schlenkerla** (Dominikanerstr. 6, ☎ 0951/56060) is a centuries-old monastery turned beer tavern. The black furniture, wall paneling, and dresses worn by the waitresses match the beer—Rauchbier—a strong malty brew with a smoky after-taste. The unusual flavor comes from a beechwood-smoke brewing process. There are also excellent Franconian specialties at reasonable prices. Try the *Rauchschinken* (smoked ham) or the *Bierbrauervesper*—composed of smoked meat, sour-milk cheese, and black bread and butter, all served on a wood platter. *Prost!* (Closed Tues. and Jan. 6–20.)

Tour 2: Nürnberg to Regensburg

❼ **Nürnberg** (Nuremberg) is the principal city of Franconia, and second in size and significance in Bavaria only to Munich. It goes at least as far back as 1040. It's among the most historic and visitable of Germany's cities; the core of the old town, through which the Pegnitz River flows, is still surrounded by its original medieval walls. Nürnberg has always taken a leading role in German affairs. It was here, for example, that the first "diet," or meeting of rulers, of every Holy Roman Emperor was held. And it was here, too, that Hitler staged the most grandiose Nazi rallies; later, this was the site of the Allies' war trials, where top-ranking Nazis were charged with—and almost without exception convicted of—"crimes against humanity." Wartime bombing destroyed much of medieval and Renaissance Nürnberg, though faithful reconstruction has largely re-created the city's prewar atmosphere.

The city grew because of its location at the meeting point of a number of medieval trade routes. With prosperity came a great flowering of the arts and sciences. Albrecht Dürer, the first indisputable genius of the Renaissance in Germany, was born here in 1471, and he returned in 1509 to spend the rest of his life here. (His house is one of the most popular tourist shrines in the city.) Other leading Nürnberg artists of the Renaissance include woodcarver Michael Wolgemut and sculptors Adam Kraft and Peter Vischer. Earlier the minnesingers, medieval poets and musicians, chief among them Tannhäuser, had made the city a focal point in the development of German music. In the 15th and 16th centuries their traditions were continued by the Meistersingers. Both groups were celebrated much later by Wagner. Among a great host of inventions associated with Nürnberg, the most significant were the pocket watch, gun casting, the clarinet, and the geographical globe (the first of which was made before Columbus discovered the Americas).

Nürnberg is rich in special events and celebrations. By far the most famous is the Christkindlmarkt, an enormous pre-Christmas market that runs from November 27 to Christmas Eve. The highlight is the December 10 candle procession, in which thousands of children march through the city streets. There are few sights in Europe to compare with

Nürnberg

Albrecht-
Dürer-
Haus, **18**

Altes
Rathaus, **14**

Die
Kaiserburg, **17**

Frauen-
kirche, **12**

Gänsemännch-
enbrunnen, **15**

Germanisches
National-
museum, **20**

Heilig Geist-
Spital, **10**

Königstor, **8**

St. Lorenz
Kirche, **9**

St. Sebaldus
Kirche, **13**

Schöner
Brunnen, **11**

Spielzeug-
museum, **19**

Stadt-
museum, **16**

Verkehrs-
museum, **21**

the flickering of their tiny lights in the cold night air, the entire scene
played out against the backdrop of centuries-old buildings.

*Numbers in the margin correspond to points of interest on the Nürn-
berg map.*

The historic heart of Nürnberg is compact; all principal sights are within
easy walking distance. To get a sense of the city, begin your tour by
walking around all or part of the **city walls.** Finished in 1452, they come
complete with moats, sturdy gateways, and watchtowers. Year-round
floodlighting adds to their brooding romance. Stop at the **Königstor**
(Royal Gate), by the Hauptbahnhof (main train station), to see the
Handwerkerhof, a "medieval mall" with craftspeople busy pretend-
ing it's still the Middle Ages. They turn out puppets, baskets, pewter
mugs and plates, glassware, and the city's famous *Lebkuchen* (gingerbread cookies). ☉ *Mid-Mar.–Dec. 24, weekdays 10–6:30, Sat. 10–
2:30 (1st Sat. of every month until 6:30).*

TIME OUT The **Bratwurstglöcklein** (Am Königstor, ☎ 227–625), located in the
Handwerkerhof, offers some of the best bratwurst in Nürnberg.
Sauerkraut and potato salad are the traditional accompaniments. Wash
it all down with a glass of beer. *Closed Sun., holidays, and Dec. 25–
Mar. 20.*

From the Königstor, head up Königstrasse to **St. Lorenz Kirche.** Opinions are divided regarding which church is the most beautiful in the
city, but many think St. Lorenz Kirche deserves the honor. If you visit
it and St. Sebaldus Kirche (*see below*), you can make up your own mind.
St. Lorenz was begun around 1220 and completed in about 1475. It's

a sizable church; two towers flank the main entrance, which is covered with a forest of carvings. In the lofty interior, note the works by sculptors Adam Kraft and Veit Stoss: Kraft's great stone tabernacle to the left of the altar and Stoss's *Annunciation* at the east end of the nave are considered their finest works. There are many other carvings throughout the building, a fitting testimonial to the artistic richness of late-medieval Nürnberg.

From the church, walk up to the Hauptmarkt, crossing the little museum bridge over the Pegnitz River. To your right, set on graceful arcades over the river, is the **Heilig-Geist-Spital** (Holy Ghost Hospital), begun in 1381. It's worth looking into the courtyard to admire its elegant wood balconies and spacious arcades. Continue the few paces to the **Hauptmarkt** (Main Market). Like Munich's Viktualienmarkt, Nürnberg's market is more than just a place to do the shopping. Its colorful stands, piled high with produce and shaded by striped awnings, are a central part of the city. The red-armed market women, whose acid wit and earthy homespun philosophy you'll have to take on trust unless your command of German extends to an in-depth familiarity with the Nürnberg dialect, are a formidable-looking bunch, dispensing flowers, fruit, and abuse in equal measure. It's here that the Christkindlmarkt is held.

There are two principal sights in the market. One is the **Schöner Brunnen** (Beautiful Fountain). It's an elegant, 60-foot-high Gothic fountain carved around the year 1400, looking for all the world as though it should be on the summit of some lofty Gothic cathedral. Thirty figures arranged in tiers stand sentinel on it. They include prophets, saints, local noblemen, sundry electors of the Holy Roman Empire, and one or two strays, such as Julius Caesar and Alexander the Great. A gold ring is set into the railing surrounding the fountain, reputedly placed there by an apprentice carver. Stroking it is said to bring good luck. Cynics will enjoy the sight of Germans and tourists alike examining the railing for the ring and surreptitiously rubbing it.

The other major attraction is the **Frauenkirche** (Church of Our Lady), which was built, with the approval of Holy Roman Emperor Charles IV, in 1350 on the site of a synagogue that burned down in a pogrom in 1349. (The area covered by the Hauptmarkt was once the Jewish quarter of the city.) These days, most visitors are drawn not so much by the church itself as by the **Männleinlaufen,** a clock dating from 1500 that's set in its facade. It's one of those colorful mechanical marvels at which the Germans have long excelled—a perfect match between love of punctuality and ingenuity. Every day at noon the electors of the Holy Roman Empire glide out of the clock to bow to Emperor Charles IV before sliding back under cover. It's worth scheduling your morning to catch the display.

From the Hauptmarkt, continue the short distance north to the 13th-century **St. Sebaldus Kirche,** on Sebaldkircheplatz. Though the church lacks the number of art treasures boasted by rival St. Lorenz, its lofty nave and choir are among the purest examples of Gothic ecclesiastical architecture in Germany: elegant, tall, and airy. Veit Stoss carved the crucifixion group at the east end of the nave, while the elaborate bronze shrine, containing the remains of St. Sebaldus himself, was cast by Peter Vischer and his five sons around 1520.

Abutting the rear of the church is the **Altes Rathaus** (Old Town Hall), built in 1332, destroyed in World War II, and subsequently restored.

It can be visited only by prior arrangement (call the local tourist office at 0911/23360) or when special exhibitions are held there.

⓯ Facing the town hall is the bronze **Gänsemännchenbrunnen** (Gooseman's Fountain). It's an elegant work of great technical sophistication, cast in 1550.

Walk north from the Altes Rathaus along Burgstrasse. On your left you'll
⓰ pass the Fembohaus, now the **Stadtmuseum** (City Museum). A dignified, patrician dwelling completed in 1598, it's one of the finest Renaissance mansions in Nürnberg. The story of the city is told in its museum. *Burgstr. 15.* ☛ *DM 4 adults, DM 2 children.* ⊙ *Mar.–Oct., Tues. and Thurs.–Sun. 10–5, Wed. 1–9; Nov.–Feb., Tues. and Thurs.–Fri, 1–5, Wed. 1–9, weekends 10–5.*

TIME OUT In a medieval courtyard off Burgstrasse 19, under the shadow of the castle, the **Hausbrauerei Altstadthof** offers food, drink, and a working cottage industry. Reactivating brewing rights granted the tavern in the 16th century, the new owners use 19th-century equipment ordinarily confined to a museum.

At the end of Burgstrasse you'll reach Nürnberg's number-one sight,
⓱ **Die Kaiserburg** (the Imperial Castle). This immense cluster of buildings, standing just inside the city walls, was the residence of the Holy Roman Emperors. Impressive rather than beautiful, the complex comprises three separate groups of buildings. The oldest, dating from around 1050, is the **Burggrafenburg,** the Burgrave's Castle, with a craggy, ruined seven-side tower and bailiff's house. It stands in the center of the complex. To the east is the **Kaiserstallung** (Imperial Stables). These were built during the 15th century as a granary, then converted into a youth hostel after the war. (If you're backpacking, stay here if only for the view of old Nürnberg from the bedrooms and dormitories.) The real interest of this vast complex of ancient buildings, however, centers on the Imperial Castle itself, the westernmost part of the fortress. The standout feature here is the Renaissance **Doppelkappelle** (Double Chapel). The upper part, richer, larger, and more ornate than the lower chapel, was where the emperor and his family worshiped. Also visit the **Rittersaal** (Knight's Hall) and the **Kaisersaal** (Throne Room). Their heavy oak beams, painted ceilings, and sparse interiors have changed little since they were built in the 15th century. ☛ *DM 3 adults, DM 2 children.* ⊙ *Apr.–Sept., daily 9–noon and 1–5; Oct.–Mar., daily 9:30–noon and 1–4.*

Descending from the west part of the castle, walk across the cobbled
★ ⓲ square to the **Albrecht-Dürer-Haus,** opposite the Tiergärtner gate. This was the home of the great German painter from 1509 until his death in 1528. It is also just about the best-preserved late-medieval house in the city, typical of the prosperous merchants' homes that once filled Nürnberg. Admire the half-timbering of the upper stories and the tapering gable before stepping inside. Dürer was the German Leonardo, the Renaissance man incarnate, bursting with curiosity. His talent for painting was equaled by his printmaking ability; he raised the woodcut, a notoriously difficult medium, to new heights of technical sophistication, combining great skill with a haunting, immensely detailed drawing style and complex allegorical subject matter. A number of original prints adorn the walls. The house also gives a realistic sense of what life was like in early 16th-century Germany. *Albrecht-Dürer-Str. 39.* ☛ *DM 4 adults, DM 2 children and senior citizens.* ⊙ *Mar.–Oct. and Christkindlmarkt, Tues. and Thurs.–Sun. 10–5, Wed. 1–9; Nov.–Feb., Tues., Thurs., and Fri. 1–5, Wed. 1–9, weekends 10–5.*

19 The impressive **Spielzeugmuseum** (Toy Museum) is on Karlstrasse. To reach it, walk down the street that runs past Dürer's house. There are few places where homage to toys seems more appropriate. Nürnberg likes to call itself the toy capital of the world, and this museum does its best to prove why. One or two exhibits date from the Renaissance; most, however, are from the 19th century. Simple dolls vie with mechanical toys of extraordinary complexity. There's even a little Ferris wheel. *Karlstr. 13.* ☛ *DM 5 adults, DM 2.50 children.* ☉ *Tues. and Thurs.–Sun. 10–5, Wed. 10–9.*

20 A final sight in the historic area for those with an interest in German cultural achievements is the **Germanisches Nationalmuseum** (Germanic National Museum), located near the Hauptbahnhof. You could spend an entire day visiting this vast and fascinating museum. It is the largest of its kind in Germany, and about the best-arranged. The setting gets everything off to a flying start; the museum is located in what was once a Carthusian monastery, complete with cloisters and monastic outbuildings. Few aspects of German culture, from the Stone Age to the 19th century, are not covered here, and quantity and quality are evenly matched. For some visitors the highlight may be the superb collection of Renaissance German painting (with Dürer, Cranach, and Altdorfer well represented). Others may prefer the exquisite medieval ecclesiastical exhibits—manuscripts, altarpieces, statuary, stained glass, jewel-encrusted reliquaries—or the collections of arms and armor, or the scientific instruments, or the toys. Few will be disappointed. *Kartäusergasse 1.* ☛ *DM 5 adults, DM 2 children, free Sun.* ☉ *Tues. and Thurs.–Sun. 10–5, Wed. 10–9.*

21 Children love the **Verkehrsmuseum** (Transportation Museum), located just south of the National Museum outside the city walls. December 7, 1835, saw the first-ever train trip in Germany, from Nürnberg to nearby Fürth. A model of the epochal train is here at the museum, along with a series of original 19th- and early 20th-century trains and stagecoaches. Philatelists will want to check out some of the 40,000-odd stamps in the extensive exhibits on the German postage system. There's also a fascinating exhibition on a mammoth, broad-gauge rail system planned by Hitler to link the Atlantic to the Urals but overtaken by the war. *Lessingstr. 6.* ☛ *DM 5 adults, DM 2 children.* ☉ *Daily 9:30–5.*

The enormous parade ground where Hitler addressed his most monumental Nazi rallies vegetates on the eastern edge of the city. The vast site, the **Zeppelinfeld,** is big enough to accommodate four soccer fields and still leave room for a game of hockey. Nowadays it sometimes shakes to the amplified beat of pop concerts, but otherwise it is a depressing, empty stretch of wasteland where dusty grass and weeds claw an existence from slabstones that once resounded to the martial click and clack of Nazi jackboots. It's open to the public and reachable on the S-2 line (Frankenfeld station).

Numbers in the margin correspond to points of interest on the Franconia map.

22 **Regensburg,** 90 kilometers (56 miles) southeast of Nürnberg, is one of the best-preserved cities in Germany. Everything here is original, since the city suffered no major damage in World War II. It is also one of Germany's most historic cities. The mystery, then, would appear to be: Why is Regensburg not better known? Few visitors to Bavaria (or even Franconia) venture this far off the well-trod tourist trails. Even Germans are astonished that such a remarkable city should exist in comparative obscurity.

The key to Regensburg is the Danube. The city marks the northern-most navigable point of the great river, and it was this simple geographic fact that allowed Regensburg to control trade along the Danube between Germany and central Europe. The great river was a highway for more than commerce, however: It was a conduit of ideas as well. It was from Regensburg, for example, that Christianity was spread across much of central Europe during the 7th and 8th centuries. By the Middle Ages, Regensburg had become a political, economic, and intellectual center of European significance. For many centuries it was the most important city in southeast Germany, eclipsed by Munich only when Napoléon ordered the dismemberment of the Holy Roman Empire during the early years of the 19th century. That he presided over its decline from Regensburg, a Free Imperial City since the 13th century and meeting place of the Imperial Diet (parliament) since the 17th, was an irony he appreciated.

Regensburg's story begins with the Celts in around 500 BC. They called their little settlement Radasbona. In AD 179, as an original marble inscription in the Museum der Stadt Regensburg proclaims, it became a Roman military post called Castra Regina. Little remains of the Roman occupation save a fortified gate, the Porta Praetoria, in the old town. When Bavarian tribes migrated to the area during the 6th century, they occupied what remained of the Roman town and, apparently on the basis of its Latin name, called it Regensburg. Irish missionaries led by St. Boniface in 739 made the town a bishopric before heading down the Danube to convert the heathen in lands even more far-flung. Charlemagne, first of the Holy Roman Emperors, arrived at the end of the 8th century, incorporating Regensburg into his burgeoning lands. And so, in one form or another, prospering all the while and growing into a glorious medieval and, later, Renaissance city, Regensburg remained until Napoléon turned up.

Any serious tour of Regensburg—not for nothing is it known as "the city of churches"—involves visiting an unusually large number of places of worship. If your spirits wilt at the thought of inspecting them all, you should see at least the Dom (cathedral), famous for its boys' choir and the Domspatzen (Cathedral Sparrows), before moving on to the secular attractions.

Numbers in the margin correspond to points of interest on the Regensburg map.

★ ㉓ Begin your tour at the **Steinerne Brücke** (Stone Bridge). It leads south
㉔ over the Danube to the almost-too-good-to-be-true **Brückturm** (Bridge Tower): all tiny windows, weathered tiles, and pink plaster. (The brooding building with a massive roof to the left of the tower is an old salt warehouse that now serves as a restaurant where you can try your first Regensburger sausages.) The bridge is a central part of Regensburg history. Built in 1141, it was rightfully considered a miraculous piece of engineering at the time—and, as the only crossing point over the Danube for miles, effectively cemented Regensburg's control of trade in the region.

★ ㉕ From the bridge, seek out the commanding towers of the **Dom St. Peter.** The cathedral, modeled on the airy, vertical lines of French Gothic architecture, is something of a rarity this far south in Germany—it wouldn't look out of place in Köln or Bonn. Begun during the 13th century, it stands on the site of a much earlier Carolingian church. Construction dragged on for almost 600 years, and it was finally finished when Ludwig I of Bavaria, then the ruler of Regensburg, had the tow-

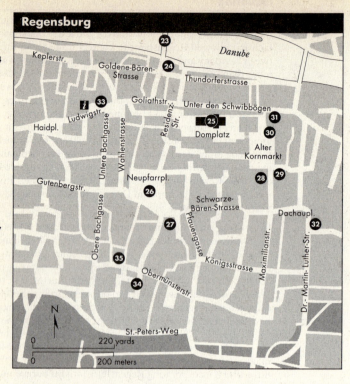

ers built. These had to be replaced during the mid-1950s after their
original soft limestone was found to be badly eroded.

Walk under the Bridge Tower to Domplatz, the cathedral square. Before heading into the building, admire its intricate and frothy facade,
embellished with delicate and skillful carving. A remarkable feature
of the cathedral is its capacity of 7,000 people, three times the population of Regensburg when construction began. Standouts of the austere interior are the glowing 14th-century stained glass in the choir and
the exquisitely detailed statues of the archangel Gabriel and the Virgin in the crossing (the meeting point of nave and choir). The **Domschatzmuseum** (Cathedral Museum) contains more valuable treasures.
The entrance is in the nave. ☞ *DM 2 adults, DM 1 children.*
⊙ *Apr.–Nov., Tues.–Sat. 10–5, Sun. noon–5; Dec.–Mar., Fri. and Sat.
10–4, Sun. noon–4; closed Nov.*

Complete your tour of the cathedral with a visit to the **cloisters,** reached
via the garden. There you'll find a small octagonal chapel, the **Aller-
heiligenkapelle** (All Saints' Chapel), a typically solid Romanesque
building, all sturdy grace and massive walls. You can barely make out
the faded remains of stylized 11th-century frescoes on its ancient walls.
The equally ancient shell of St. Stephan's church, the **Alter Dom** (Old
Cathedral), can also be visited. ☞ *DM 3 adults, DM 2 children. The
cloisters, chapel, and Alter Dom can be seen only on guided tours: mid-
May–Oct., daily at 10, 11, and 2; Nov.–Mar., weekdays at 11, Sun. at
noon; Apr.–mid-May, daily at 11 and 2. Tours last about 1 hr.*

To the south of the cathedral are the Neupfarrkirche and the church
of St. Kassian. To the east lie the Niedermünster church, the

㉖ Karmelitenkirche, and the Alte Kapelle. The **Neupfarrkirche** (at Ne-upfarrplatz), built between 1519 and 1540, is the only Protestant church in Regensburg, indeed one of a very few in Franconia. It's an imposing building, substantially less ornate than any other in the city. Some may find its restraint welcome after the exuberance of so many
㉗ of the other places of worship. **St. Kassian** is a much older building, the oldest church in the city, in fact, founded during the 8th century. Don't be fooled by its dour exterior; inside, the church has been endowed with delicate Rococo decoration.

From St. Kassian, turn right onto the pedestrians-only Schwarze-Bären-Strasse, one of the best shopping streets in the city. Turn left at the end.
㉘ This will bring you to the **Alte Kapelle,** the Old Chapel. It, too, is a Carolingian structure, erected during the 9th century. As is the case at St. Kassian, the dowdy exterior gives little hint of the joyous Rococo treasures within, extravagant concoctions of sinuous gilt stucco, rich marble, and giddy frescoes, the whole illuminated by light pouring in from the upper windows.

㉙ The adjoining **Karmelitenkirche** is Baroque from crypt to cupola. Finally, head north through the Alter Kornmarkt square to the former
㉚ parish church, the **Niedermünster,** another ancient structure (construction started in 1150) with a Baroque interior. Here in 1982 workmen discovered a Roman altar, dating from between AD 180 and 190, dedicated to the emperor Commodus. ☎ 0941/57796. ☛ *Advance booking only.*

A more obvious Roman relic is just round the corner from the church
㉛ (turn right as you leave it). This is the **Porta Praetoria,** one of the original city gates, a rough-hewn and blocky structure. Look through the grille on its east side to see a section of the original Roman street, located about 10 feet below today's street.

From the Porta Praetoria you can either backtrack through Korn-
㉜ markt to the **Museum der Stadt Regensburg** or walk west to the Fischmarkt and Altes Rathaus (Old Town Hall). For many, the museum is one of the highlights of a visit to the city, both for its unusual and beautiful setting—a former Gothic monastery—and for its wide-ranging collections, from Roman artifacts to Renaissance tapestries, all helping to tell the story of Regensburg. The most significant exhibits are the paintings by Albrecht Altdorfer (1480–1538), a native of Regensburg and, along with Cranach, Grünewald, and Dürer, one of the leading painters of the German Renaissance. His work has the same sense of slight distortion—of heightened reality—found in that of his contemporaries, in which the lessons of Italian painting are used to produce an emotional rather than a rational effect. What's really significant about Altdorfer is his interest in landscape not merely as the background of a painting but as its subject. In many of his works figures are simply incidental. Even more intriguing is that Altdorfer's obviously emotional response to landscape would not have seemed out of place during the 19th century. Far from seeing the world around him as essentially hostile, or at least alien, he was more akin to the Romantics of the 19th century in that he saw it as something intrinsically beautiful, to be admired for its own sake, whether wild or domesticated. *Dachaupl. 2–4.* ☛ *DM 4 adults, DM 2 children, DM 8 family ticket.* ☉ *Tues.–Sat. 10–4, Sun. and holidays 10–1.*

㉝ The **Altes Rathaus,** a picture-book complex of medieval buildings with half-timbering, windows large and small, and flowers in tubs, is among the best-preserved of its kind in the country, as well as one of the most historically important. It was here, in the imposing Gothic **Reichssaal** (Imperial Hall), that the "everlasting Imperial Diet" met from 1663 to 1805. This could be considered a forerunner of the German parliament, where representatives from every part of the Holy Roman Empire—plus the emperor and the prince-electors—assembled to discuss and determine the affairs of the far-reaching German lands. The hall is sumptuously appointed with tapestries, flags, and heraldic designs. Note especially the wood ceiling, built in 1408. If you have children in tow, they'll want to see the adjoining torture chamber, the **Fragstatt,** and execution room, the **Armesünderstübchen.** Medieval notions of justice can be gauged by the fact that any prisoner who withstood three days of "questioning" here without confessing was released. *Rathauspl.* ☛ *DM 5 adults, DM 2.50 children under 18, DM 10 family ticket.* ☉ *Daily 9–4. Tours in English May–Sept., Mon.–Sat. 3:15.*

TIME OUT Across the square from the Altes Rathaus, at Rathausplatz 2, is Germany's oldest coffeehouse, the **Prinzessin Cafe,** which first opened its doors to the general public in 1686. Coffee is served on the first floor and tea one floor above, in a lounge furnished like the living room of a Biedermeier mansion, with soft sofas and elaborate little side tables.

After tea (or coffee), turn left outside the café and head down Bachgasse, which will lead you to the massive **Schloss Emmeram complex.** The palace, formerly a Benedictine monastery, is bigger than Buckingham Palace. Its more than 500 rooms are a testimony to the fabulous wealth accumulated by the Thurn-und-Taxis family from running the German postal system, a monopoly they enjoyed until 1867. The former abbey cloisters are probably the architectural treasure of the palace itself, with their elegant and attenuated late-Gothic carving. As for the rest of the building, much of which was extensively rebuilt at the end of the 19th century, opinions remain divided. Some consider it the most vulgar and ponderously overdecorated specimen of its kind in Germany. Others admire its Victorian bombast and confidence. You can also visit the **Marstallmuseum** (Transport Museum) in the palace if you have a weakness for 18th- and 19th-century carriages and sleighs. ☛ *Palace and cloisters: DM 10.* ☉ *Guided tours only, Apr.–Oct., weekdays at 2 and 3:30, weekends 10, 11:15, 2, and 3:15; Nov.–Mar., weekends and holidays only, 11:15, 2, 3:15.* ☛ *Marstallmuseum: DM 6.* ☉ *Guided tours only, weekdays at 2, 2:40, and 3:15, Sun. at 10, 10:40, and 11:15. Combined ticket: DM 15. Family ticket: DM 40.*

Next to the palace there's one more church to be visited, **St. Emmeramus.** It's the work of the Asam brothers and is decorated in their customary and full-blown late-Baroque manner.

Numbers in the margin correspond to points of interest on the Franconia map.

There are two noteworthy sights in the environs of Regensburg (either of them makes a good day trip). The first is the great abbey church of St. George and St. Martin, by the banks of the Danube at **Weltenburg.** The most dramatic approach to the abbey is by boat from Kelheim, 10 kilometers (6 miles) downstream (*see* Guided Tours in Franconia Essentials, *below*). On the stunning ride, the boat winds between towering limestone cliffs that rise straight up from the tree-lined riverside. The abbey church, constructed between 1716 and 1718, is commonly regarded as the masterpiece of the brothers Cosmas Damian and Egid Quirin Asam, two leading Baroque architects and decorators of Bavaria (Cosmas Damian was the architect, Egid Quirin was the painter, sculptor, and stuccoworker). If you've seen their little church of St. John Nepomuk in Munich, you'll know what pyrotechnics to expect here, albeit on a substantially larger scale. To some, this kind of frothy confection, with painted figures whirling on the ceiling, lavish and brilliantly polished marble, highly wrought statuary, and stucco dancing rhythmic arabesques across the curving walls, is more high kitsch than high art. To others, the exuberance, drama, and sheer technical sophistication of this concentrated style may appear to be like Mozart's music in stone. Whichever view you take, it's hard not to be impressed by the bronze equestrian statue of St. George above the high altar, reaching down imperiously with his flamelike, twisted gilt sword to dispatch the winged dragon at his feet.

TIME OUT The abbey monks brew their own delicious dark beer, which you can sample on draft while sitting under ancient chestnut trees in the courtyard. Meals are also served. ☉ *Daily until 6.*

Another excursion from Regensburg you won't want to miss (especially if you have an interest in the wilder expressions of 19th-century German nationalism) is by Danube riverboat (*see* Guided Tours in Franconia Essentials, *below*) to the incongruous Greek-style Doric temple ★ ㊲ of **Walhalla,** 11 kilometers (7 miles) east of the city. To get to the temple from the river you'll have to climb 358 marble steps; this is not a tour to take if you're not in good shape. (There is, however, a parking lot near the top. To drive to it, take the Danube river valley country road (unnumbered) east from Regensburg 8 km to Donaustauf. The Walhalla is 1 km outside the village and well signposted.) Walhalla— a name resonant with Nordic mythology—was where the god Odin received the souls of dead heroes. This monumental temple on a commanding site high above the Danube was erected in 1840 for Ludwig I to honor German heroes through the ages, in the prevailing neoclassical style of the 19th century; it's actually a copy of the Parthenon in Athens. Even if you consider the building more a monument to kitsch than a tribute to the great men of Germany, you will at least be able to muse on the fact that it is a supremely well-built structure, its great, smooth-fitting stones and expanses of costly marble evidence of both the financial resources and the craftsmanship that were Ludwig's to command.

What to See and Do with Children

Nürnberg is a children's paradise, with a host of museums and a medieval castle that ignites young imaginations (and a supposedly bottomless well into which much pocket money has disappeared in search of its depth). The **Altes Rathaus** (Old City Hall) has intact medieval dungeons and a torture chamber that causes young, impressionable types to break out in a cold sweat. ☛ *DM 3 adults, DM 1.50 children.* ☉ *Apr.–Sept., weekdays 10–4, weekends and public holidays 10–1.*

One of the star attractions among the museums is the **Spielzeug Museum** (Toy Museum) (*see* Nürnburg to Regensburg, Tour 2, *above*). Nürnberg also has a **zoo;** children love its **dolphinarium,** which is worth the extra admission fee. *Am Tiergarten 30,* ☎ *0911/543–0348.* ☛ *DM 8 adults, DM 4 children. (The dolphinarium costs an extra DM 6 adults, DM 3 children. Displays daily at 11, 2, and 4.)* ☉ *Zoo and dolphinarium Apr.–Sept., daily 8–7:30; Oct. and Mar., daily 8–5:30; Nov.–Feb., daily 9–5.*

If you're in Franconia during the four weeks prior to Christmas, by all means consider taking your children to Nürnberg's **Christkindlmarkt,** the most lavish and spectacular Christmas market in Germany. The highlight is the December 10 candle procession.

Young railway fans are fascinated not only by Nürnberg's Transport Museum but by Germany's "railway village," **Neuenmarkt,** near Kulmbach. More than 20 beautifully preserved, gleaming old locomotives huff and puff here in a living railroad museum. A functioning 60-year-old restaurant car will take care of their appetites.

In Regensburg, visit the **Figurentheater,** or Puppet Theater (Dr.-Johann-Maier-Str. 3, ☎ 0941/28328). There are performances September–May, weekends at 3. And the torture chamber at the **Altes Rathaus** can unlock kids' imagination.

Children may not be too struck by the Abbey Church at Weltenburg or by Ludwig I's grandiose Walhalla, but they'll appreciate the **boat** rides to them on the Danube (*see* Guided Tours in Franconia Essentials, *below*). For trips on the Main River between Aschaffenburg and Würzburg, call 0931/91553.

Neustadt, north of Coburg, is a center of toy and doll making. The **Museum der Deutschen Spielzeugindustrie** (Museum of the German Toy Industry) shows how toys were made throughout the centuries, providing a fascinating diversion for a rainy afternoon. *Hindenburgpl. 1,* ☎ *09568/5600.* ☛ *DM 5 adults, DM 2.50 children.* ☉ *Mon.–Sun. 10–5.*

Bayreuth also has a **toy museum,** in the Boltz auction rooms. *Brandenburger Str. 36,* ☎ *0921/20616.* ☉ *During Wagner festival only, and visitors are asked to make an appointment.*

Coburg's **Naturwissenschaftliches Museum** (Natural History Museum) can provide a diverting hour or two (*see above*). Coburg also has a doll museum, **Coburger Puppenmuseum.** *Rückertstr. 2, next to Schloss Ehrenburg,* ☎ *09561/74047.* ☛ *DM 4 adults, DM 2.50 children.* ☉ *Daily 10–5.*

In Regensburg, children will welcome a break in sightseeing to spend some time in the town's **reptile zoo,** which has 200 different species. *Obertraublingerstr. 25.* ☛ *DM 5 adults, DM 3 children.* ☉ *Daily 10–6.*

Off the Beaten Track

The area between Aschaffenburg and Würzburg is wine country. Though many of the local wineries offer tours, few can beat the one at Miltenburg's **St. Kilian Kellerei** offered by wine master Bernard Lorenz. Call two days in advance to be sure of getting his services (☎ 09371/2120). In addition to giving you the full story of how the wines are made, he'll take you to the wine cellars set in the cliffs along the river, time permitting.

Few tourists visit the delightful small medieval town of **Kronach,** east of Coburg. It was here that Renaissance master painter Lucas Cranach the Elder was born at the end of the 15th century; you can visit his house at Marktplatz 1. A cluster of half-timbered buildings and a fine Renaissance town hall complete the appeal of this flower-strewn square. Outside the town, see the **Rosenberg fortress.** *Guided tours Tues.–Sun. at 11 and 2.* ☛ *DM 2.*

Fans of the British monarchy may want to visit the 550-year-old castle in which Prince Albert was born in 1819. Located in an English-style park beside the Itz River near the village of Rödental, 9 kilometers

(6 miles) north of Coburg, **Schloss Rosenau** was restored in 1990 and opened to the public. A mix of architectural styles ranging from Renaissance to neo-Gothic, the castle features furniture made especially for the Saxe-Coburg family by noted Viennese craftsmen, and other pieces from the period of Albert's youth. One room houses exhibits devoted to Victoria and Albert. ☛ *Guided tour only. Tours (in German only) Tues.–Sun., seven times daily, 10–4, Cost: DM 3, children under 16 free.*

If you feel like hiking to a Disney-style castle, visit **Altenburg,** 3 kilometers (2 miles) outside Bamberg (or take the Bus 10). It's a "medieval" castle built on the site of a much older castle during the 19th century, during the full flood of Romantic enthusiasm for the days of chivalry and courtly love. ☛ *Free. ⊘ Apr.–Oct., daily 9–5.*

For a change of pace after Franconia's castles, palaces, and churches, take a look at the **Teufelhöhle** (Devil's Cave) at Pottenstein, midway between Bayreuth and Nürnberg. It contains some spectacular stalagmites and stalactites. *⊘ Mid-Mar.–Oct., daily 8–5.*

There's another cave 5 kilometers (3 miles) outside Kelheim, at Essing near Regensburg. This is the **Schulerloch** (Schoolboy's Cave), once inhabited by Stone Age hunters and gatherers. ☎ *09441/3277 for tour details. ⊘ Easter–Oct.*

At Neustadt, 18 kilometers (11 miles) northeast of Coburg, inspect the world's only "stone beer" brewery, **Rauchenfelser Steinbier** (Am Brunn 1, ☎ 09261/52051). Entrepreneur Gerd Borges has revived a preindustrial-age method of brewing using special, heated stones. The result is a uniquely flavored brew. Call ahead to arrange a tour.

Eighteen kilometers (11 miles) northwest of Coburg, at **Rodach,** you can rest your travel-weary muscles at the therapeutic thermal baths. ☛ *DM 10.50. ⊘ Mon. and Fri.–Sun. 9–7, Tues.–Thurs. 9–9. Children under 10 must have a doctor's certificate.*

For about DM 500 per person, you can live like Bayreuth's 18th-century marquis and marchioness for a weekend. The price includes lodging, royal tours of Bayreuth and district, and a five-course "royal" banquet attended by servants in powdered wigs. For dates and details, contact the Bayreuth tourist office (☎ 0921/88588).

SHOPPING

Specialties in **Coburg** include some delicious foods (not all of which you'll be permitted to take home with you; check to see that you're not infringing customs regulations). For bratwurst, smoked ham, *Schmätzchen* (gingerbread), and *Elizenkuchen* (almond cake), try any of the **Grossman Shops** (Ketchengasse 24, ☎ 09561/90762; Rodacherstr. 10a, ☎ 09561/90767; or Wirtsgrund 24, ☎ 09561/32012). For other traditional German goods, take a look at **Franz Denk's** shop (Kirchhof 2); his stoneware is expensive but exceptional. Off the market square you'll find **Kaufmann's** (Judengasse 1a, 09561/92022). Run by a husband-and-wife team, the shop has fine hand-blown glass and homemade jewelry.

Lichtenfels, southeast of Coburg, is the place for baskets; there's even a state-run basket-weaving school here. The best selection is at **Es Körbla** (Stadtknechtgasse, ☎ 09571/7304), just off the market square.

If you've enjoyed a visit to Kulmbach's **Plassenburg museum,** the world's largest collection of tin figures, visit **Wanderer und Ramming**

(Obere Stadt 34, ☎ 09221/4679) and buy some to take home. The shop boasts more than 1,000 tin figures in all shapes and sizes. Traditional *Trachtenschmuck* silver jewelry is sold in three shops in town: **Brückner** (Langgasse 12, ☎ 09221/58108) and **Juwelier Hubschmann** (corner Holzmarkt and Langgasse, ☎ 09221/4322), and **Giorgio Canola** (Kressinsteinerstr. 11, ☎ 09221/81210).

Bayreuth's main shopping streets are Maximilianstrasse and Richard-Wagner-Strasse, where you'll find both department stores and sophisticated boutiques. The city's largest and most comprehensive store is **Hertie** (Maximilianstrasse 55, ☎ 0921/53000). The **Hofgarten Passage,** an arcade off Richard-Wagner-Strasse, has several fine shops, including Piccola Tazza, which sells puppets, and Laurenstein, which features chocolates from Germany, Belgium, and Switzerland. The **Schmuckbasar** (Maximilianstr. 55, ☎ 0921/58108), **Glasskunst Wolf** (Richard-Wagner-Str. 11, ☎ 0921/54717), and **Ursula Grüner's** beautifully laid-out shop (Sophienstr., 1, ☎ 0921/63588) all have a large selection of locally produced jewelry, glassware, and other quality handicrafts.

Bamberg's main shopping area runs along Hauptwachstrasse. Across from the tourist information center is **Pappenberg's** (☎ 0951/52949), a shop that sells communion, wedding, and baptism candles, all of which can be engraved. It also features beeswax candles, pewter, and wood carvings. An excellent place to shop for pottery is **Der Töpferladen** (Untere Brücke 1, ☎ 0951/56913), near the Altes Rathaus. The shop's selection of decorative plates, mugs, and bowls comes from more than 70 potters. If you want a small gift, try **Renate's Allerlei** (Untere Brücke 7, ☎ 0951/56964), just around the corner. It has stuffed animals, porcelain, nutcrackers, and linen tablecloths. **Zenzinger's** (Am Katzenberg 4, ☎ 0951/58188) has unusual decorative glass and a large assortment of polished-stone necklaces and crystals. **Wilhelm Pierron's Shop** (Hauptwachstr. 6, ☎ 0951/28983) has polished-stone necklaces, garnets, and the ornate silver jewelry worn with traditional costumes.

Across from the main train station in **Nürnberg** is the famous **Handwerkerhof** (Handicraft Court). It has many shops where engravers, glassblowers, silversmiths, goldsmiths, and other artisans make their wares. **Zinn Menna** (Bischof-Meiserstr. 3, ☎ 0911/227–481) claims to stock 1,000 gifts made from pewter, glass, ceramic, and porcelain. The historic area has numerous quality shops, especially on Königstrasse and Karolinenstrasse. Children will love the **Spielwaren Virnich** toy store (corner of Königstr. and Luitpoldstr., ☎ 0911/203077), or the equally well-stocked **Spielwaren Schweiger** (Färberstr. 11, ☎ 0911/241–8989). For a wide range of souvenirs, try **Elsässer** (Königstr. 45, ☎ 0911/222–277). If you don't find what you're looking for there, try **Ostermayr** (Königstr. 33–37, ☎ 0911/992–100), or turn down Karolinenstrasse, where there are three more large stores that sell souvenirs. **Schmidt's** (Zollhaustr. 30, Plobenhofstr. 6, ☎ 0911/242–204) sells the famous Nürnberg *Lebkuchen* (gingerbread cookies) year-round. During the month before Christmas, you can shop at the **Christkindlmarkt** for tree decorations, toys, polished stones, woolens, spices, and Lebkuchen.

Regensburg is famous for its crafts. **Gewürz-Eckerl** (Unter d. Schwibbögen 1, ☎ 0941/507–678) sells attractive handmade puppets, glass ornaments, and fine jewelry. If you fancy yourself in a dirndl or sporting a pair of lederhosen, try **Emess Mode** (Am Kohlenmarkt 5, ☎ 0941/560–646).

SPORTS AND FITNESS

Bicycling
Bikes can be rented at train stations for DM 12 per day (DM 6 if you have a valid rail ticket). Local tourist offices can suggest other places to rent bikes (*see* Getting Around in Franconia Essentials, *below*). In Regensburg city tours are offered by bike May–September, Tuesday and Sunday after 2 PM. The cost is DM 10 including bike rental. Call 0941/507–4410 to book.

Fishing
Various areas along the Main River have good fishing. The Miltenburg tourist office offers a seven-day fishing vacation, with reduced prices for board and lodging; call 09371/400–119 for details. The fishing around Coburg, with up to 13 different kinds of fish to catch, is good. Contact the local tourist office (☎ 09561/74180). Note that you'll need a license to fish anywhere in Germany. They can be purchase at tourist offices; the cost is DM 10 for one year. In addition, expect to pay daily charges of between DM 8 and DM 15; reduced weekly rates are also available.

Golf
Coburg has a nine-hole course (☎ 09567/1212) across from Schloss Tambach on B—303. Visitors are always welcome. There's an 18-hole course at Bayreuth-Thurnau (☎ 0921/970–704).

Hang Gliding
Hang-gliding enthusiasts can take part in a 14-day training course at Stadtsteinach in the Frankenwald. Contact the tourist office (Badstr. 5, 8652 Stadtsteinach, ☎ 09225/774).

Hiking
The vast stretches of forest and numerous nature parks in much of northern Franconia make this an ideal destination for hiking vacations, a fact that the Germans have not been slow to exploit. There are more than 25,000 miles of hiking trails, with the greatest concentration in the Altmühltal Nature Park—Germany's largest—and in the Frankenwald. There are also marked trails in the Fichtelgebirge Mountains. For maps and further guidance, contact Fremdenverkehrsverband Franken (☎0911/264–202).

Sailing and Windsurfing
There are numerous opportunities to take to the water in Nürnberg—you can even crew a raft down the River Regnitz. Contact the city tourist office (☎ 0911/23360).

DINING AND LODGING

Dining
Franconia offers a wide range of dining experiences, though *Gasthaüser,* inns offering simple but good local specialties, are definitely preponderant. Most have inexpensive lunch menus. Traditional dishes you'll want to try include *Sauerbraten* (marinated slices of beef), *Schweinshaxe* (pig's knuckle), and the ever-present *Knödeln* (dumplings). The region has hundreds of small breweries (Bamberg alone has 10; Bayreuth 7), so you should be able to get a local brew wherever you're staying.

In the Main Valley towns you should try the delightfully dry wines produced there; they are served in the familiar bulbous green bottles known as *Bocksbeutel.*

WHAT TO WEAR
Unless otherwise noted, dress is casual but neat in the less expensive restaurants. Reviews indicate which places *require* a jacket or a jacket and tie; at the more expensive ($$$ and $$$$) restaurants men may feel more appropriately dressed with a jacket and tie even if they aren't required.

RATINGS

CATEGORY	COST*
$$$$	over DM 90
$$$	DM 55–90
$$	DM 35–55
$	under DM 35

*per person for a three-course meal, including sales tax and excluding drinks and service charge

Lodging

Make reservations well in advance for hotels in all the larger towns and cities if you plan to visit anytime between June and September. If you're visiting Bayreuth during the annual Wagner festival in July and August, consider making reservations up to a year in advance. And remember, too, that during the festival prices can be double the normal rates. Standards of comfort and cleanliness are high throughout the region, whether you stay in a simple pension or in a modern, international chain hotel.

RATINGS

CATEGORY	COST*
$$$$	over DM 200
$$$	DM 160–DM 200
$$	DM 120–DM 160
$	under DM 120

*All prices are for two people in a double room.

Bamberg

DINING

★ **Würzburger Weinstuben.** For unmistakably German, Old World atmosphere and good-value local specialties, this should be your choice. A wide range of wines is available, and there's a garden for romantic summer dining. ✕ *Zinkenwörth 6,* ☎ *0951/22667. Reservations advised. AE, DC, MC, V. Closed 1st 2 wks in Sept., Tues. dinner, and Wed. $$*

Brauerei Spezial. Unpretentious Franconian fare fills the menu in this traditional beer restaurant, one of nine pubs in Bamberg that brew their own beer. The dining style is communal, with everybody sitting at gnarled and scrub-top wooden benches. Order *fränkische Klöe,* the local herb-filled version of a Bavarian dumpling, with any cut of pork. A natural accompaniment is the delicately flavored smoked house beer. Rooms are also available. ✕ *Obere Königstr. 10,* ☎ *0951/24304. No credit cards. Closed Sat. afternoon and dinner. $*

DINING AND LODGING

St. Nepomuk. Nestled alongside the River Regnitz and situated in a former mill, the St. Nepomuk is the ideal place for that special dinner for two. You'll dine amid lovingly renovated stonework. Rooms here are neat and modern; ask for one overlooking the river. ⌨ *Obere*

Mühlbrücke 9, ☎ *0951/25183,* FAX *0951/26651. 42 rooms, 5 suites with bath. Restaurant. AE, DC, MC, V. $$$$*

★ **Romantik Hotel and Restaurant Messerschmitt.** Built in 1422 and owned and run by the same family since 1832, this will be the choice of anyone who values small, one-of-a-kind hotels. The 18th-century exterior is opulent; the dark-paneled interior is tasteful and soothing. The restaurant is exceptional. Look for the chestnut soup and Franconian duck; for a culinary adventure, try the eels in dill sauce. ⊡ *Langestr. 41,* ☎ *0951/27866,* FAX *0951/26141. 24 rooms with bath. Restaurant. AE, DC, MC, V. $$$*

Gasthof Weierich. Located alongside the walls of the towering cathedral, the Weierich boasts three charmingly decorated restaurants, each offering game (in season), fish, and other Franconian specialties. Lodging is also available in three moderately priced rooms. ⊡ *Lugbank 5,* ☎ *0951/54004,* FAX *0951/55800. Restaurant (reservations advised). Closed Sun. dinner. No credit cards. $$*

LODGING

National. This old favorite stands in the new—in other words, 19th-century—part of Bamberg. The National retains its handsome turn-of-the-century facade, but inside it's elegant and modern, with rooms furnished in English country style. ⊡ *Luitpoldstr. 37,* ☎ *0951/24112,* FAX *0951/22436. 38 rooms with bath, 3 apartments. Restaurant, bar. AE, DC, MC, V. $$$*

Cafe am Dom. If you blink you'll miss it, because this tiny place is tucked away in one of Bamberg's narrow medieval streets, a favorite retreat for older women in hats who know where to find the best cakes in town. The smell of home baking greets you when you awake in one of the newly enlarged and renovated rooms above the café. One suite occupies an entire floor and has a spellbinding view across the ancient red-tile rooftops of Bamberg. ⊡ *Ringleingasse 2,* ☎ *0951/56852,* FAX *0951/59042. 3 rooms, 1 suite with bath. No credit cards. $$*

Bayreuth

DINING

★ **Schloss Hotel Thiergarten.** Just 6½ kilometers (4 miles) from Bayreuth in the Thiergarten suburb, this small, onetime hunting lodge, now beautifully converted into a hotel (*see below*) and two stunning restaurants, provides one of the most elegant dining experiences in Franconia. The intimate Kaminhalle (the name means fireplace, a reference to the lavishly ornate one here) and the Venezianischer Salon, dominated by a glittering 300-year-old Venetian chandelier, both offer regional and nouvelle specialties. ✕ *Oberthiergärtener Str. 36,* ☎ *09209/9840. Reservations required. Jacket and tie. DC, MC, V. Closed Feb. 15–Mar. 15, Sun. for dinner and Mon. $$$$*

Cuvee. Within a couple of years, owner Wolfgang Hauenstein elevated the status of this restaurant from elegant to the don't-miss category, with his mixture of nouvelle cuisine and traditional regional specialties prepared with a modern twist. The cellar includes 14 varieties of champagne. ✕ *Markgrafenallee 15,* ☎ *0921/23422. Reservations advised. Jacket and tie. AE, MC. Closed Sun. and last 2 wks in Sept. $$$*

Weihenstephan. Long wood tables, fulsome regional specialties, and beer straight from the barrel (from the oldest brewery in Germany) make this a perennial favorite with tourists and locals alike. In summer the crowded, flower-strewn terrace is the place to be. ✕ *Bahnhofstr. 5,* ☎ *0921/82288. No credit cards. Closed Fri. $$*

Brauereischänke am Markt. They make their own bratwurst (spicy grilled sausage) at this boisterous old town inn. Another local specialty is *Bier-*

rippchen, pork ribs braised in a dark beer sauce. The inn's yeasty Zwickel beer is the ideal accompaniment to a meal. On sunny summer days you'll enjoy the beer garden on the pedestrian street. ✕ *Maximilianstr. 56,* ☎ *0921/64919. AE, MC.* $

LODGING

★ **Schloss Hotel Thiergarten.** If you plan to stay in this near-regal little hotel, be sure to make reservations well in advance. Recent renovations have given the rooms a modern touch without depriving them of their plush, lived-in character. A stay here is what you imagine staying with your favorite elderly millionaire aunt would be like. (*See above* for details of the two restaurants.) ☎ ☎ *09209/9840,* FAX *09209/98429. 8 rooms with bath. 2 restaurants, bar, sauna. DC, MC, V. Closed Feb. 15 – Mar. 15.* $$$$

★ **Goldener Anker.** No question about it: If you're booking far enough in advance, this is *the* place to stay while you're in Bayreuth. The hotel is right by the Markgräfliche's Opernhaus and has been entertaining composers, singers, conductors, and players for more than 100 years, as the signed photographs in the lobby and the signatures in the guest book make clear. Rooms are small but individually decorated; many have antique pieces. The restaurant is justly popular. ☎ *Opernstr. 6,* ☎ *0921/65051,* FAX *0921/65500. 38 rooms, 1 suite, 4 apartments with bath. Restaurant. MC, V. Closed Dec. 20 – Jan. 10.* $$$

Goldener Löwe. A trusty yet stylish old inn close to the town center, the Löwe (Lion) provides a traditional Franconian welcome, especially to overseas visitors. Rooms are furnished in Franconian farmhouse style, with pinewood and floral prints. The kitchen is known for its selection of *Klössen* (regional dumplings). At the tavern bar you may meet some friendly folks and find yourself invited to join in a game of cards. ☎ *Kulmbacherstr. 30,* ☎ *0921/41046,* FAX *0921/47777. 12 rooms with bath. Restaurant (closed Sun.), beer garden. AE, DC, MC, V.* $$

Coburg

DINING

★ **Coburger-Tor Restaurant Schaller.** This hotel-restaurant provides surprisingly upscale dining in softly lit and distinctly well-upholstered quarters just south of the city center. The food is sophisticated nouvelle, with such offerings as wild-duck breasts in sherry sauce and stuffed dates with nougat sauce. ✕ *Ketschendorfer-Str. 22,* ☎ *09561/25074. Reservations required. Jacket and tie. No credit cards. Closed Sun.* $$$$

Ratskeller. An entirely different experience is offered in the stone vaults of this establishment, the sort of emphatically Teutonic place where local specialties always taste better. Try the Sauerbraten, along with a glass of crisp Franken white wine. ✕ *Markt 1,* ☎ *09561/92400. Reservations advised. No credit cards.* $$

★ **Goldenes Kreuz.** In business since 1477, this restaurant has all the rustic decor you'll ever want to accompany large portions of equally authentic Franconian food. Goose with dumplings provides a hearty experience. Nouvelle cuisine it is not. ✕ *Herrngasse 1,* ☎ *09561/90473. Reservations advised. No credit cards.* $

LODGING

★ **Blankenburg Parkhotel.** Located north of the town center, this excellent-value modern hotel encourages families with the offer of free lodging for children up to 15 sharing their parents' room. The stylish restaurant has become noted for its gourmet fare. Admission to an adjoining indoor swimming and wave pool is free to guests. ☎ *Rosen-*

auerstr. 30, ☎ *09561/75005,* FAX *09561/75674. 44 rooms and 2 suites with bath. Restaurant. AE, DC, MC, V. $$$*

Goldene Traube. Book a room overlooking the square and on summer evenings you can fall asleep to the plash of the fountain named after Queen Victoria. The hotel feels such a strong link with Britain's former queen and empress that it even named its bar after her. The recently refurbished rooms are recently refurbished and comfortable, with cable TV. Another recent addition is a sauna complex with solarium. ☎ *Am Viktoriabrunnen 2,* ☎ *09561/8760,* FAX *09561/876–222. 77 rooms with bath. Restaurant, bar, sauna, steam room, exercise room, bicycles, miniature golf. AE, MC, V. $$$*

Kulmbach
DINING AND LODGING

Romantik Posthotel. This traditional country hotel, owned and run by the same family since 1870, is an excellent base from which to explore the area as well as an ideal getaway. It has a discreetly friendly and cozy atmosphere, whether you're relaxing in the gardens, at the putting green, in the library, at the rustic restaurant—or at the whirlpool. The newly enlarged spa gets tired muscles into action after a day in the country. The hotel is in the quiet village of Wirsberg, 5 kilometers (3 miles) east of Kulmbach. ☎ *Markt 11,* ☎ *09227/2080,* FAX *09227/5860. 35 rooms, 12 suites and apartments with bath. Bar, café, hot tub, massage, sauna, steam room, exercise room, bicycles, library. AE, DC, MC, V. $$$*

Nürnberg
DINING

Entenstub'n. The name (Duck Tavern) seems inappropriate for such a regal restaurant, which looks like an 18th-century drawing room—it was once a shooting lodge for Bavarian King Ludwig III. The menu, a mix of regional and nouvelle cooking styles, matches the elegant setting, with such specialties as parfait of creamed pigeon and white fish in chives galantine. ✕ *Günthersbühlerstr. 145,* ☎ *0911/598–0413. Reservations advised. AE, MC. Closed Sun., Mon. $$$$*

★ **Goldenes Posthorn.** The authentic heart of old Nürnberg still beats in this ancient restaurant beside the cathedral, the fact that it was rebuilt after the war notwithstanding. In their day, both Dürer and the poet and Meistersinger Hans Sachs ate here. The food is nouvelle Franconian; try the venison in red wine with plums or quail stuffed with walnuts and goose liver. The wine list is extensive. ✕ *An der Sebalduskirche,* ☎ *0911/225–153. Reservations required. AE, DC, MC, V. Closed Sun. $$$$*

★ **Essigbrätlein.** Some rank this the top restaurant in the city, and even among the best in Germany. As the oldest restaurant in Nürnberg, built in 1550 and originally used as a meeting place for wine merchants, it is unquestionably one of the most atmospheric. Today its elegant period interior is *the* place to eat *Essigbrätlein* (roast loin of beef). Other dishes blend Franconian and nouvelle recipes. ✕ *Weinmarkt 3,* ☎ *0911/225–131. Reservations required. AE, DC, MC, V. Closed Sun.–Mon., 1st 10 days in Jan. $$$*

Nassauer Keller. The exposed-beam-and-plaster decor complements the resolutely traditional cooking. Try the duck and the apple strudel. The restaurant has a memorable location in the cellar of a 13th-century tower beside the church of St. Lorenz. ✕ *Karolinenstr. 2–4,* ☎ *0911/225–967. Reservations advised. AE, DC, MC. $$*

Bratwurst Haüsle. There are few better places to try Nürnberg's famous grilled sausages—roasted over an open fire and served on heavy pewter plates with horseradish and sauerkraut—than this dark, old, wood-paneled inn. The mood is noisy and cheerful. ✕ *Rathauspl. 1,* ☎ *0911/227–695. Reservations not necessary. No credit cards. Closed Sun.* $

★ **Heilig-Geist-Spital.** Heavy wood furnishings and a choice of more than 100 wines make this 650-year-old wine tavern a popular spot for visitors. The traditional cuisine includes grilled pork chops, pan-fried potatoes, and German cheeses. ✕ *Spitalgasse 16,* ☎ *0911/221–761. Reservations not necessary. AE, DC, MC, V.* $

LODGING

Maritim. If you value modern convenience over Old World charm, consider staying in this luxuriously modern hotel, opened in 1986. You won't find so much as a hint of the medieval glories of old Nürnberg here, but the service is impeccable, the spacious rooms are tastefully furnished, mostly with gleaming dark veneers and pastel-shaded fabrics, and the public areas are elegantly well-heeled. The Maritim, part of a French chain, is just south of the historic area. Breakfast costs an extra DM 22, but the range and excellence of the buffet fully warrant the expense. ☎ *Frauentorgraben 11,* ☎ *0911/23630,* FAX *0911/236–3836. 306 rooms, 10 suites with bath. 2 restaurants, bar, indoor pool, massage, sauna, exercise room. AE, DC, MC, V.* $$$$

Altea Hotel Carlton. This stylish old hotel, sturdy in a grande-dame way and part of the Altea group, is quietly efficient and offers thick-carpeted, old-fashioned luxury. The restaurant is plushly expensive and a pleasure in the summer, when you can sit out on the shaded terrace. It's on a quiet side street close to the train station. Although room rates are in the higher price bracket, they are almost halved during off-peak periods (most of April and October) and on weekends. ☎ *Eilgutstr. 13–15,* ☎ *0911/20030,* FAX *0911/200–3532. 127 rooms, 2 suites and 1 apartment with bath. Restaurant, bar, weinstube, sauna, exercise room. AE, DC, MC, V.* $$$

Burg-Hotel Grosses Haus, Burg-Hotel Kleines Haus. Two hotels, one name. Both stand under the castle's gaze in the old town a few blocks from each other, and both provide private-home comforts and facilities such as indoor pools and saunas. Their chief difference is price: The larger hotel, Grosses Haus, offers smarter rooms bedecked with Laura Ashley fabrics, and better views (it's next to Dürer's house), and subsequently is costlier than its smaller sister. It also has more facilities, including a solarium. Neither has a restaurant. ☎ *Grosses Haus: Lammsgasse 3,* ☎ *0911/204–414,* FAX *0911/223–882. 41 rooms and 5 suites with bath. Indoor pool, sauna. AE, DC, MC, V.* $$$ *Kleines Haus: Schildgasse 16,* ☎ *0911/203–040,* FAX *0911/226–503. 23 rooms with bath. AE, DC, MC, V.* $$

Flair Hotel Steichele. This skillfully converted former 19th-century wine-merchant warehouse is now part of the Flair hotel group but is still managed by the family that has been running it for three generations. It's handily situated close to the main train station, yet on a quiet street of the old walled town. The rooms, decorated in Bavarian rustic decor, are cozy rather than luxurious. ☎ *Knorrstr. 2–8,* ☎ *0911/204–377,* FAX *0911/221–914. 49 rooms, 45 with shower. Restaurant (closed Mon.), weinstube. AE, DC, MC, V.* $$$

Regensburg

DINING

Historisches Eck. A wealthy tradesman's family once owned this historic old house. Today paying customers sit at antique tables beneath the cross-vaulted ceiling that dates from the 13th century; leaded windows complete the medieval look. There's a less atmospheric dining room upstairs, so specify where you want to sit when you reserve a table. In both rooms the cuisine is identical and uniformly excellent, combining traditional fare with a light French-tinted flair—maize-fed roast chicken, for instance, with a delicate salad of *mange-tout* (snap beans). ✗ *Watmarkt. 6, ☎ 0941/58920. Reservations required. AE, MC. $$$*

Alter Simpl. Sit in one of the cozy nooks and crannies of this old inn and try one of chef Harry Flashar's fresh beef steaks, a specialty of the house. ✗ *Fischgässe 4, ☎ 0941/999–395. Reservations not necessary. No credit cards. Closed Sun. $$*

Historische Wurstküche. Succulent Regensburger sausages—the best in town—are prepared right before your eyes here on an open beechwood charcoal grill in the tiny kitchen, and if you eat them inside in the tiny dining room you'll have to squeeze past the cook. In summer they are served at trestle tables set outside on the banks of the Danube. Inside are plaques recording the levels the river reached in the various floods that have doused the restaurant's kitchen in the past 100 years. ✗ *Thundorferstr. 3. No credit cards. $*

DINING AND LODGING

Hotel-Restaurant Bischofshof am Dom. This is one of Germany's most historic hostelries, a former bishop's palace where guests can sleep in an apartment that includes part of a Roman gateway. Other chambers are only slightly less historic, and some have seen emperors and princes as guests. Recent renovations have put well-equipped bathrooms into all rooms; they're still large and comfortably furnished. In summer the central, cobbled courtyard is a delight. If your room overlooks it you'll awake to a neighboring church's carillon playing a German hymn, and you'll retire to the strains of the Bavarian national anthem. The hotel's restaurant is a gourmet mecca in these reaches of Bavaria. Yet the prices are sensible, and the beer comes from a brewery founded in 1649. ⊞ *Krauterermarkt 3, ☎ 0941/59086, ℻ 0941/53508. 54 rooms with bath. Restaurant, bar, beer garden. AE, DC, MC, V. $$$–$$$$*

Altstadthotel Arch. A beautifully renovated 18th-century house, this small family hotel in the center of the old city is convenient for visiting all the main attractions. Rooms are tastefully decorated, with furnishings leaning toward Scandinavian modern. All have cable TV. The restaurant is in a Gothic-style stone-vaulted cellar. It offers an international menu, but it's dominated by Franconian dishes, such as Sauerbraten; the Knödeln are homemade. ⊞ *Haidpl. 4, ☎ 0941/502–060, ℻ 0941/5020–6168. 62 rooms, 6 apartments with bath or shower. Restaurant, bar. AE, DC, MC, V. $$$$*

LODGING

★ **Parkhotel Maximilian.** A handsome 18th-century building in the old town, this is the most elegant and sophisticated hotel in Regensburg. Its fine facade was restored in 1992, and public rooms are memorably exotic. Bedrooms are less opulent, but all are intelligently and comfortably decorated and come with cable TV. An extensive refurbishing program was under way in 1995. If you're feeling homesick, you should eat at the American-style steak house. ⊞ *Maximilianstr. 28, ☎ 0941/568–5300, ℻ 0941/52942 (bookings can also be made in the U.S.: ☎ 800/447–7462 or 800/223–0888). 46 rooms, 6 suites with bath. 2 restaurants, bar, café, beauty salon, recreation room. AE, DC, MC, V. $$$$*

Kaiserhof am Dom. Stay here for the great view of the cathedral. The building itself oozes 18th-century charm, with exposed beams, stone walls, and rough plaster. Rooms are more modern, with pastel-color walls, cherry-wood furnishings, and new carpeting. Try to get one with a view. ⊠ *Kramgasse 10,* ☎ *0941/585–350,* FAX *0941/585–3595. 32 rooms with bath. Restaurant, café. AE, MC. Closed Dec. 23–Jan. 6.* $$

THE ARTS

Opera

Opera lovers cheerfully admit that there are few more intense operatic experiences than that offered by the annual **Wagner festival** in Bayreuth, held in July–August. If you want tickets, write to the **Festspielhaus** (Festspielhügel 2, ☎ 0921/20221) or call 0921/78780, but be warned: The waiting list is years long! You have only a slim chance of obtaining tickets unless you plan your visit a couple of years in advance. Rooms can be nearly impossible to find during the festival, too. If you don't get tickets, you can console yourself with visits to the exquisite 18th-century **Markgräfliches Opernhaus;** performances are given most nights in July and August. Check with the tourist office for details. A wide repertoire of opera is also offered at the **Landestheater** in Coburg, October through mid-July. Call 09561/92742 (from 9–1) for tickets.

Concerts

Ansbach hosts a **Bach Week** in odd-numbered years in early August. Contact **Geschäftsstelle im Rathaus** (Postfach 1741, 8800 Ansbach, ☎ 0981/51243) for tickets. Bamberg is a city of music. The **Bamberg Symphony Orchestra** gives regular concerts; those in the cathedral, normally given with the Bamberg Choir, can be memorable. Call 0951/25256 for tickets. Organ concerts are given in the cathedral at noon every Saturday, May through October. Since 1993 the orchestra has had a new, permanent home: the concert and congress hall **Synfonie an der Regnitz** (Mussstrasse 20, ☎ 0951/964–7200). You can catch opera and operetta at the **Hoffmann Theater** (Schillerpl. 5, ☎ 0951/871–431), September through July. In June and July, open-air performances are also given at the **Alte Hofhaltung.** Call 0951/25256 for tickets. Regensburg offers a range of musical experiences, though none so moving as a performance by the famous boys' choir **Domspatzen** (Cathedral Sparrows). The best-sung mass is held on Sunday at 9 AM. It can be a remarkable experience, and it's worth scheduling your visit to the city to hear the choir.

Theater

The best theaters in Franconia are in Nürnberg and Regensburg. In Nürnberg, the chief theater is the **Städtische Bühnen** (Richard Wagner-Platz 2, ☎ 0911/231–3808. For details about shows and concerts in Nürnberg, call 0911/204–295. The leading theater in Regensburg is the **Stadttheater** (Bismarckpl. 7, ☎ 0941/59156).

FRANCONIA ESSENTIALS

Arriving and Departing

By Car

Franconia is served by five main Autobahns: A—7 from Hamburg; A—3 from Köln and Frankfurt; A—81 from Stuttgart; A—6 from Heilbronn; and A—9 from Munich. Nürnberg is 167 kilometers (104 miles) from Munich and 222 kilometers (139 miles) from Frankfurt.

Regensburg is 120 kilometers (75 miles) from Munich and 332 kilometers (207 miles) from Frankfurt.

By Plane

The major international airports near Franconia are at Frankfurt and Munich; both have regular flights to and from the United States. The most important regional airports are at Nürnberg and Bayreuth. There are frequent flights between Frankfurt and Nürnberg.

By Train

Regular InterCity services connect Nürnberg and Regensburg with Frankfurt and other major German cities. Trains run hourly from Frankfurt to Munich, with stops at Würzburg and Nürnberg. The trip takes about three hours. There are also hourly trains from Munich direct to Regensburg and to Nürnberg.

Getting Around

By Bicycle

Renting bicycles is popular in Franconia, and the tourist authorities have made great efforts to attract cyclists. The scenic, wooded terrain of the Altmühltal Valley is particularly suitable for biking. The tourist board for the Altmühltal (the Fremdenverkehrsamt Naturpark Altmühltal, Notre Dame 1, D-85072 Eichsta(u)tt, ☎ 08421/6733) issues leaflets with suggested cycling tours and lists of outlets where you can rent bikes. Bicycles can also be rented from most major train stations (the cost is DM 12 per day, DM 6 if you have a rail ticket). Other tourist offices can supply details of special cycling routes in their regions.

By Boat

A total of 15 different lines operate cruises through the region from April through October. Contact the **Fremdenverkehrsverband Franken** (Am Plärrer 14, Nürnberg, ☎ 0911/264–202) and ask for details of their "Weisse Flotte" cruises. Or contact a travel agent in advance.

By Bus

The bus service between major centers in Franconia is poor; it's better to drive or ride the train. Other than the buses along the Romantic Road, the only major service is from Rothenburg-ob-der-Tauber to Nürnberg. Local buses run from most train stations to smaller towns and villages, though the service isn't frequent. Buses for the Fichtelgebirge in northern Franconia leave from Bayreuth's post office near the train station.

By Car

The most famous scenic route in Franconia is the Romantic Road (*see* Chapter 7), but almost as interesting are the east section of the Burgenstrasse, the Castle Road, which runs west to east from Heidelberg to Nürnberg; and the Bocksbeutel Strasse, the Franconian Wine Road, which follows the course of the Main River from Zeil am Main along the wine-growing slopes of the valley to Aschaffenburg.

CAR RENTAL
Avis: Markgrafenallee 6, ☎ 0921/789–550, **Bayreuth;** Schmidtstrasse 39, ☎ 069/730–111, **Frankfurt;** Allersbergerstrasse 139, ☎ 0911/49696, **Nürnberg.**

Europcar: Schlossstr. 32, ☎ 069/775–033, **Frankfurt;** Nürnberg airport, ☎ 0911/528–484, **Nürnberg;** Straubingerstrasse 8, ☎ 0941/793–011, **Regensburg;** Friendenstrasse 15, ☎ 0931/881–150, **Würzburg.**

Hertz: Gutleutstrasse 87, ☎ 069/242–52, **Frankfurt;** Nürnberg airport, ☎ 0911/527–710, **Nürnberg;** Bahnhofstrasse 22, ☎ 0941/51515, **Regensburg.**

Sixt-Budget: Frankfurt airport, ☎ 069/697–0070, **Frankfurt;** Ingolsta(u)dter Str. 21, ☎ 0911/438–710, **Nürnberg;** Im Gewerbepark A7, ☎ 0941/401–035, **Regensburg.**

By Train

If you start in Frankfurt and plan to visit the wine towns along the Main River, you can take good local trains to Aschaffenburg, Miltenberg, and other small river towns (*see* Chapter 7). Some InterCity trains stop in Bamberg, which is most speedily reached from Munich. Locals trains from Nürnberg connect with Bayreuth and areas of southern Franconia.

Guided Tours

The most popular excursions are boat trips on the Danube from Regensburg to Ludwig I's imposing Greek-style Doric temple of Walhalla, or to the monastery at Weltenburg. There are daily sailings to Walhalla from Easter through October. The round-trip costs DM 12 for adults and DM 6 for children under 14 and takes three hours. Changing boats at Kelheim will allow you to reach Weltenburg from Regensburg, or you can pick up a shorter cruise from Kelheim. The Regensburg–Kelheim boat ride takes 2½ hours. The journey from Kelheim to Weltenburg takes only 30 minutes (the fare is DM 9 adults, DM 6 children under 12). Daylong upstream cruises from Regensburg that take in Weltenburg via the Altmühltal (a scenic wooded gorge) are also possible. Regensburg boats depart from the Steinerne Brücke; for information, call 0941/55359. For information on Kelheim departures, call 09441/3402 or 09441/8290.

There are also regular trips in the summer along scenic routes following the Main River from Aschaffenburg to Würzburg and from Würzburg to Bamberg. These are worth considering if you plan to spend a lot of time in the region. For information, contact **Fränkische Personen-Schiffahrt**, Kranenkai 1, Würzburg, ☎ 0931/55356 and 0931/51722, or the Würzburg tourist office, Marktplatz, D-97070 Würzburg, ☎ 0931/37398.

For boat tours around Bamberg, contact **Fritz Kropf**, Kapuzinerstrasse 5, ☎ 0951/26679. Tours leave daily at 2:30 and 4; the cost is DM 5.50 for adults and DM 4 for children.

In Nürnberg, tours of the old town center start daily at 2:30 at the tourist information office, Hauptmarkt. The two-hour tour, which is in German, costs DM 8 (children free). Two-and-a-half-hour tours in English start at 9:30 daily, May–October, in front of the Mauthalle, Hallplatz. The cost is DM 20 adults, DM 10 children.

Important Addresses and Numbers

Tourist Information

The principal regional tourist office for Franconia is **Fremdenverkehrsverband Franken**, Am Plärrer 14, D–90443 Nürnberg,

☎ 0911/264–202. There are local tourist information offices in the following towns:

Ansbach. Rathaus, Martin-Luther-Platz 1, D–91522 Ansbach, ☎ 0981/51243.

Bamberg. Geyerswörthstrasse 3, D–96047 Bamberg, ☎ 0951/871–161.

Bayreuth. Luitpoldplatz 7–9, D–95444 Bayreuth, ☎ 0921/88588.

Coburg. Herrngasse 4, D–96450 Coburg, ☎ 09561/74180.

Ingolstadt. Hallstrasse 5, D–85049 Ingolstadt, ☎ 0841/305–417.

Kloster Banz and **Vierzehnheiligen.** Alte Darre am Stadtturm, D–96231 Staffelstein, ☎ 09573/4192.

Kronach. Marktplatz, D–96317 Kronach, ☎ 09261/97236.

Kulmbach. Stadthalle, Sutte 2, D–95311 Kulmbach, ☎ 09221/95880.

Lichtenfels. Am Marktplatz 1, D–96215 Lichtenfels, ☎ 09571/795–221.

Nürnberg. Frauentorgraben 3, D–90443 Nürnberg 70, ☎ 0911/23360.

Regensburg. Altes Rathaus, D–93047 Regensburg, ☎ 0941/507–4410.

Weissenburg. Martin-Luther-Platz 3, D–91781 Weissenburg, ☎ 09141/907–124.

Travel Agencies

American Express (Adlerstrasse 2, Nürnberg, ☎ 0911/232–397) makes travel arrangements.

9 Rhineland Palatinate

This less-famous stretch of the Rhine has less spectacular scenery than along the riverbanks farther north, but it's also less crowded and less expensive. The Weinstrasse, or Wine Road, wends through part of the region, leading travelers to the tempting vintages around every turn. North of its end are Speyer, Worms, and Mainz, latterday imperial centers, each home to a Romanesque cathedral more spectacular than the last.

FOR MOST TRAVELERS—EVEN SEASONED ONES—the Rhineland means the spectacular stretch between Bingen (where the river leaves the Rheingau region and swings north) and the ancient city of Koblenz (at the mouth of the Mosel). But there's another part of the Rhineland where vineyards climb slopes crowned by ancient castles. This is the Rhineland Palatinate (Rheinland-Pfalz in German). It lacks the spectacular grandeur of the river above Bingen, the elegance of the resorts of Boppard and Koblenz, and the cachet of the wines of the Rheingau. But for that reason the crowds are smaller, the prices lower, and the pace slower. And there are attractions here you won't find in the more popular stretch of the river farther north, including the warmest climate in Germany. The south-facing folds of the Palatinate Hills shelter communities where lemons, figs, and sweet chestnuts grow alongside vines. It's a region where few Autobahns penetrate and where most other roads lead to truly off-the-beaten-track territory. One of these roads is Germany's first specially designated Weinstrasse (Wine Road), a winding, often narrow route with temptations—vineyards and farmsteads that beckon the traveler to sample the current vintage. If you're covering the route by car, take along a nondrinker as codriver, or split the driving between you. And take your time.

Where the Wine Road ends, three of Germany's oldest cities beckon: Speyer, Worms, and Mainz. They are among the Rhineland's great imperial centers, where emperors and princes met and where the three greatest Romanesque cathedrals in Europe stand. After covering the Wine Road, this chapter explores these cities. From the most northerly, Mainz, you are poised to explore the remainder of the Rhineland. (For full details, *see* Chapter 12.)

EXPLORING

Tour 1: Along the Wine Road

Numbers in the margin correspond to points of interest on the Rhineland Palatinate map.

Although the north end of the Wine Road is a favored starting point for many visitors because of its proximity to Mainz and Frankfurt, the logical place to begin your tour is its south point, at the town in which ❶ the Wine Road itself began, **Schweigen-Rechtenbach,** on the French border. It was in this little wine village, in July 1935, that a group of vintners hit on the idea of establishing a tourist route through the vineyards of the region. To get the road off to a suitable start they put up a massive stone arch, the **Deutsches Weintor** (German Wine Gate). There's an open gallery halfway up the arch that offers a fine view of the vineyards that crowd the countryside between the Vosges Mountains over the French border and the Rhine away to the east. Some of Schweigen's best wine comes from the vineyards on the French side of the border; you can walk across the frontier—it's only 200 yards from the arch—with no formalities and compare vintages. For a further investigation of the region's wines, follow the **Weinlehrpfad,** the "wine inspection path." It begins in Schweigen and ambles for about a mile through the vineyards of the nearby Sonnenberg. It was the first of scores of such walking routes that you'll find in wine-producing areas throughout Germany. The path is well marked and easy to follow.

Rhineland Palatinate

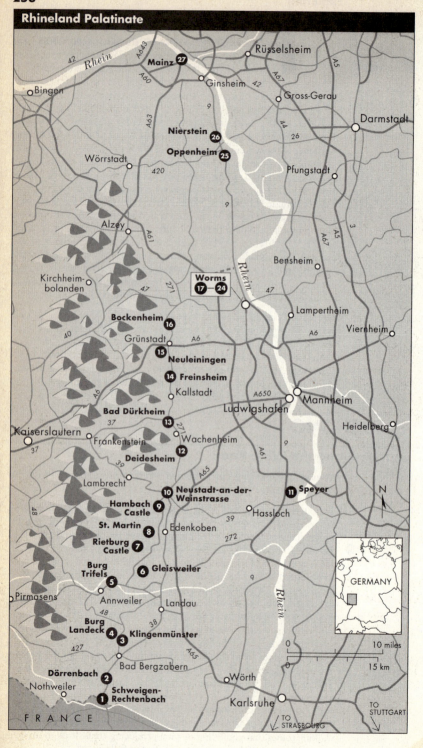

Drive north on B–38 toward Bad Bergzabern, 10 kilometers (6 miles) away. A mile before you reach the town, turn left to see the village of ★ ❷ **Dörrenbach.** It's an enchanting place, tucked snugly in a protective fold of the Palatinate Hills. The Renaissance **Rathaus** (Town Hall) has a flower-hung facade, crisscrossed with so many half-timbers that there's hardly room for the tiny-paned windows.

TIME OUT The little spa town of **Bad Bergzabern** rivals any in Germany for its wealth of half-timbered old houses. Notable among these—in age and appearance—is the distinctive Renaissance stone building of the tavern Zum Engel. Its exterior is marked by unusual bay windows at the corners of the facade; inside, there's food and wine aplenty. *Königstr. 45, ☎ 06343/4933. Closed Tues.*

❸ Drive north, following the signs to **Klingenmünster,** 8 kilometers (5 miles) away. The village has the ruins of a 7th-century Benedictine monastery, with a still-intact Baroque chapel. If castles are your thing, you should ❹ walk from the monastery to the ruins of **Burg Landeck.** The walk, through silent woods of chestnut trees, takes about half an hour. Your reward will be a magnificent view from the castle over the Rhine Valley and south as far as the Black Forest.

There's a more spectacular, and more famous, castle another 8 kilo- ★ ❺ meters (5 miles) north, outside the village of Annweiler. This is **Burg Trifels,** one of the most romantic buildings in the country, its drama only slightly spoiled by the fact that what you see today is a rather free reconstruction of the original Romanesque castle, rebuilt in 1937 (a period when a lot of Germans were keen on reestablishing what they saw as the glories of their "race"). The original castle was constructed during the mid-12th century by the emperor Barbarossa, who once wrote: "Whoever has Trifels possesses the empire." From 1126 to 1273 Burg Trifels housed the imperial crown jewels. That's what's said to have led to the legend that Burg Trifels was the site of the Holy Grail, the bowl used by Christ at the Last Supper. In the Middle Ages, the Holy Grail was the object of numerous knightly quests, the purpose of which was not so much to find the Grail as to prove one's steadfastness and Christian virtue by embarking on an impossible task. Replicas of the imperial crown jewels are on display in the castle museum. ☞ *DM 5 adults, DM 2 children under 14.* ☉ *Daily 9–5. Closed Dec.*

If you visit Burg Trifels, you'll pass the ruins of two neighboring castles as you head up the hill. These are the castles of **Scharfenberg** and **Anebos.** Their craggy, overgrown silhouettes add greatly to the romance of the visit to their neighbor.

Head back to the Wine Road and follow the signs toward **Edenkoben.** A drive of 12 kilometers (8 miles) will bring you to the little town of ❻ **Gleisweiler,** reputedly the warmest spot in Germany. A flourishing subtropical park supports the claim. Further proof of the mild climate hereabouts is supplied by the fig trees that grow in abundance on many south-facing walls. This is also just about the only area in Germany in which lemons are grown. The sun-drenched charms of the region attracted Bavaria's King Ludwig I in the middle of the 19th century. He called it "a garden of God" and compared its light to that of Italy. In the 1850s he built himself a summerhouse in the hills above the town; Edenkoben responded by putting up a statue of its royal guest in the main square. You can pay your respects to the Bavarian monarch by visiting his handsome neoclassical villa. Today it houses paintings by the German Impressionist Max Slevogt (1868–1932). The paintings have a certain dreamy charm, but many visitors will find the grandiose setting more diverting. *Villa Ludwigshöhe,* ☎ *06323/3148.* ☛ *DM 5 adults, 50 pf children (includes guided tour in German).* ☉ *Apr.–Sept., Tues.–Sun. 9–1 and 2–6; Oct.–Mar., Tues.–Sun. 9–1 and 2–5.*

7 On the opposite (north) side of the valley, facing the Villa Ludwigshöhe, are the ruins of **Rietburg Castle.** The only chair lift in the Rhineland Palatinate will whisk you up to them if you feel like checking out the terrific view.

TIME OUT The other reason for visiting Rietburg Castle is to have lunch on the terrace of the **café** here. Drink in the view as you eat.

★ **8** Back on the Wine Road, a mile or two will bring you to the village of **St. Martin.** It's known as one of the most beautiful in the area, a reputation it nurtures by encouraging the surrounding vineyards to encroach on its narrow streets. You'll find vines clinging everywhere, linking the ancient houses with curling green garlands. Visit the little 15th-century church to see the imposing Renaissance tomb of the Dalberg family. Their castle, now romantically ruined, stands guard over the village.

9 There's another castle hereabouts that you can visit, especially if your blood is stirred by tales of German nationalism and the overthrow of tyranny. It's **Hambach Castle,** standing about a half mile outside the village of Hambach, itself about 8 kilometers (5 miles) north of St. Martin. It's not the castle, built in the 11th century and largely ruined in the 17th, that's the attraction. Rather, you'll visit to honor an event that happened here in May 1832. Fired by the revolutionary turmoil that was sweeping across Europe and groaning under the repressive yoke, as they saw it, of a distant and aristocratic government, 30,000 stalwart Germans assembled at the castle demanding democracy, the overthrow of the Bavarian ruling house of Wittelsbach, and a united Germany. The symbol of their heroic demands was a flag, striped red, black, and yellow, that they flew from the castle. The old order proved rather more robust than these protodemocrats had reckoned on; the crowd was rapidly dispersed with some loss of life. The new flag was banned. It was not until 1919 that the monarchy was ousted and a united Germany became fully democratic. Fittingly, the flag flown from Hambach nearly 90 years earlier was adopted as that of the new German nation. (It was a short-lived triumph: Hitler did away with both democracy and the flag when he came to power in 1932, and it was not until 1949, with the creation of the Federal Republic of Germany, that both were restored.) The castle remains a focus of the democratic aspirations of the Germans. Exhibits chart the progress of democracy in Germany. ☎ *06321/30881* ☛ *DM 4 adults, DM 2.50 children.* ☉ *Mar.–Nov., daily 9–6:30.*

10 A mile or two north of Hambach, high rises announce the presence of the biggest town on the Wine Road and the most important wine-producing center in the region, **Neustadt-an-der-Weinstrasse.** It's a bustling town, the narrow streets of its old center still following the medieval street plan. It's wine that makes Neustadt tick, and practically every shop seems linked with the wine trade. A remarkable 5,000 acres of vineyards lie within the official town limits. If you need to get your sightseeing fix, head to central Marktplatz to see the **Stiftskirche** (Collegiate Church). It's an austere Gothic building, constructed during the 14th century for the elector of the Rhineland Palatinate. Inside, a wall divides the church in two, a striking reminder of former religious strife. The church, indeed the entire region, became Protestant in the

Reformation during the 16th century. At the beginning of the 18th century, the Catholic population of the town petitioned successfully to be allowed a share of the church. The choir (the area around the altar) was accordingly designated the Catholic half of the church, while the nave, the main body of the church, was reserved for the Protestants. To keep the squabbling communities apart, the wall was built inside the church. Is it an instance of religious tolerance or intolerance? And who got the better deal? As you wander around the church—be sure to look at the intricate 15th-century choir stalls and the little figures, monkeys, and vine leaves carved into the capitals of the nave columns—you can ponder these matters.

TIME OUT Duck into the ancient confines of the **Herberge aus der Zunftzeit,** a 14th-century tavern offering excellent local wines and specialties. Try a slice of *Zwiebelkuchen* (onion tart) and a glass of Kirchberg wine. *Mittelgasse, Closed Mon.*

⓫ If you have time, make the side trip to **Speyer,** 29 kilometers (18 miles) east of Neustadt on the west bank of the Rhine. Speyer was one of the great cities of the Holy Roman Empire, founded probably in Celtic times, taken over by the Romans, and expanded during the 11th century by the Ottonian Holy Roman emperors. Between 1294 and 1570, no fewer than 50 full diets (meetings of the rulers of the Holy Roman Empire) were convened here. The focus of your visit will be the imperial cathedral, the **Kaiserdom,** one of the largest medieval churches in Europe, certainly one of the finest Romanesque cathedrals, and a building that more than any other in Germany conveys the pomp and majesty of the early Holy Roman emperors. It was built in only 30 years, between 1030 and 1060, by the emperors Konrad II, Heinrich III, and Heinrich IV. A four-year restoration program in the 1950s returned the building to almost exactly its condition when first completed. If you have any interest in the achievements of the early Middle Ages, don't miss this building. Speyer Cathedral, thanks chiefly to the fact that later ages never saw fit to rebuild it, and partly to the intelligent restorations of the '50s, embodies all that is best in Romanesque architecture.

There's an understandable tendency to dismiss most Romanesque architecture as little more than a cruder version of Gothic, the style that followed it and that many consider to be the supreme architectural achievement of the Middle Ages. Where the Gothic is seen as delicate, soaring, and noble, the Romanesque by contrast seems lumpy and earthbound, more fortresslike than divine. It's true that even the most successful Romanesque buildings are ponderously massive, but they possess a severe confidence and potency that can be overwhelming. What's more, look carefully at the decorative details and you'll see vivid and often delicate craftsmanship.

See as much of the building from the outside as you can before you venture inside. You can walk most of the way around it, and there's a fine view of the east end from the park by the Rhine. If you've seen Köln Cathedral, the finest Gothic cathedral in Germany, you'll be struck at once by how much more massive Speyer Cathedral is in comparison. The few windows are small, as if crushed by the surrounding masonry. Notice, too, their round tops, a key characteristic of the style. The position of the space-rocket–like towers, four in all (two at either end), and the immense, smoothly sloping dome at the east end give the building a distinctive, animated profile; it has a barely suppressed energy and dynamism. Notice, too, how much of a piece it is; having been built all in one go, the church remains faithful to a single vision. Inside, the cathedral is dimly mysterious, stretching to the high altar in the distance. In contrast to Gothic cathedrals, whose walls are supported externally by flying buttresses, allowing the interior the minimum of masonry and the maximum of light, at Speyer the columns supporting the roof are massive. Their bulk naturally disguises the side aisles, drawing your eye to the altar. Look up at the roof; it's a shallow stone vault, the earliest such vaulted roof in Europe. Look, too, at the richly carved capitals of the columns, filled with naturalistic details—foliage, dogs, birds, faces.

No fewer than eight Holy Roman emperors are buried in the cathedral, including, fittingly enough, the three who built it. They lie in the crypt. This, too, should be visited to see its simple beauty, uninterrupted by anything save the barest minimum of decorative detail. The entrance is in the south aisle. *Kaiserdom.* ⊘ *Weekdays 9–5, Sat. 9–6, Sun. 1:30–5. For information about guided tours, call 06232/102–267.*

Treasures from the cathedral and the imperial tombs are kept in the city's excellent museum, the **Historisches Museum der Pfalz,** opposite the cathedral, on Domplatz. ☛ *DM 7 adults, DM 2 children.* ⊘ *Tues.–Sun. 10–6.*

Tour 2: North to Worms

⑫ Back on the Wine Road, the wine town of **Deidesheim,** 6 kilometers (4 miles) from Neustadt, is the next stop north. It was here that the bishops of Speyer, among the most powerful clerics in Germany during the Middle Ages, had their administrative headquarters. Their former palace is now mostly a ruin, its moat a green and shady park. Make sure you see the town square, Marktplatz. It's bordered on three sides by flower-smothered, half-timbered houses, the whole forming one of the most picturesque ensembles in the Rhineland Palatinate. Climb the impressive stairway to the Rathaus (Town Hall); the entrance is through a curious porch crowned by a helmetlike roof and spire. Ask to view the fine wood-paneled assembly hall where councillors and envoys of successive bishops of Speyer haggled over church finances.

TIME OUT Look for the golden lion sign of the **Deidesheimer Hof** (Marktpl.) on the right side of the three-cornered market square. Within this ancient inn is one of the best restaurants in the region; there's also the more affordable St. Urban wine tavern, where you can eat and drink in quiet comfort. Look, too, for the names Gerümpel and Goldbächel on the wine list: They are the very best the area has to offer.

Don't leave Deidesheim without strolling down the street called Feigengasse. It's named after the fig trees (*Feigen*) that grow in front of practically every house.

⑬ Eight kilometers (5 miles) and two charming wine villages (Forst and Wachenheim) farther, you'll reach another bustling little Wine Road town: **Bad Dürkheim.** Bad Dürkheim has a distinction that's hard to beat: a wine cask so big it contains a restaurant with seating for 420 (the Bad Dürkheimer Riesenfass, am Wurstmarktgelände) and a live brass band on weekends. In mid-September it's the focal point of what the locals claim is the world's biggest wine festival, a week of revelry and partying during which the wine flows freely.

On a more serious note, another Bad Dürkheim highlight is the remains of the old **Limburg Monastery** above town; this is counted as one of the most important Romanesque buildings in Germany.

The **Pfälzerwald** nature park begins just beyond Bad Dürkheim's town limits. It's Germany's largest uninterrupted area of forest and a favorite stretch for hiking. If you don't fancy a full-fledged walking tour, at least give yourself an hour or two to experience its lonely, rugged grandeur.

⓮ Head north from Bad Dürkheim a couple of miles to Kallstadt. Turn right to see **Freinsheim,** 4 kilometers (2½ miles) away. The little town is one of the best-preserved in the region, a winning combination of winding medieval streets and high-gabled, half-timbered buildings. The original medieval walls still encircle the old town; conical-roofed towers punctuate them at rhythmic intervals. A counterpoint to this toy-town charm is provided by the stately Baroque Rathaus (Town Hall), an elegantly classical building with an unusual covered staircase leading up to the imposing main entrance.

⓯ More too-good-to-be-true charm is provided by the town of **Neuleiningen,** 10 kilometers (6 miles) north of Kallstadt. Until quite recently, this was among the most backward and impoverished areas of the country. The people were called *Geesbocke,* or "billy goats," a mocking reference to the fact that these were the only animals they could afford to keep. The name lives on today in the village's most historic inn, Zum Gäsbock. Stop in to sample a glass or two of local wine or for a tasty bite to eat and to admire the Renaissance interior. The Wine Road ends ⓰ at **Bockenheim,** 10 kilometers (6 miles) north of Neuleiningen.

Tour 3: Worms to Mainz

⓱ From Bockenheim you can continue north along B–271 to Mainz and the Rheingau or make the detour to the ancient imperial city of **Worms** (pronounced "Vawrms"). Why visit Worms? First, to see the great, gaunt Romanesque cathedral; it presents a less-perfect expression of the Romanesque spirit than does Speyer Cathedral but exudes much of the same craggy magnificence. Second, because Worms, though devastated in World War II, is among the most ancient cities in Germany, founded as far back perhaps as 6,000 years ago, settled by the Romans, and later one of the major centers of the Holy Roman Empire. More than 100 diets of the empire were held here, including the one in 1521 before which Martin Luther came to plead his "heretical" case. Third, because Worms is one of the most important wine centers in Germany; anyone who has fallen under the spell of the Rhineland Palatinate's golden wines will want to sample more here. There's some industry on the outskirts of the city, but the rebuilt old town is compact and easy to explore.

It was the Romans who made Worms important, but it was a Burgundian tribe, established in Worms from the 5th century, that gave the city its most compelling legend—the *Nibelungenlied.* The story, probably written during the 12th century and considerably elaborated throughout the years, is complex and sprawling, telling of love, betrayal, greed, war, and death. It ends when the Nibelungen—the Burgundians—are defeated by Attila the Hun, their court destroyed, their treasure lost, their heroes dead. (One of the most famous incidents tells how Hagen, treacherous and scheming, hurls the court riches into the Rhine; by the Nibelungen bridge there's a bronze statue of him, caught in the act.) The *Nibelungenlied* may be legend, but the story is based on historical fact. For instance, a Queen Brunhilda is supposed to have lived here; it's known, furthermore, that a Burgundian tribe was defeated, in present-day Hungary, by Attila the Hun in 437.

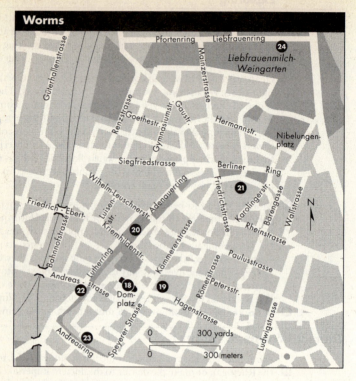

Not until Charlemagne resettled Worms almost 400 years later, making it one of the major cities of his empire, did the city prosper again. Worms wasn't just an administrative and commercial center but a great ecclesiastical city as well. The first expression of this religious importance was the original cathedral, consecrated in 1018. In 1171 a new cathedral was started. This is the one visitors come to Worms to see.

Numbers in the margin correspond to points of interest on the Worms map.

★ **18** If you've seen Speyer Cathedral, you'll quickly realize that **Worms Cathedral,** by contrast, contains many Gothic elements. In part this is simply a matter of chronology. Speyer Cathedral was completed more than 100 years before the one at Worms was even begun, long before the lighter, more vertical lines of the Gothic style were developed. But there's another reason. Once built, Speyer Cathedral was left largely untouched in later periods; at Worms, the cathedral was remodeled frequently as new styles in architecture and new values developed. Nonetheless, as you walk around the building you'll find that same muscular confidence, that same blocky massiveness characteristic of Speyer. The ground plan of the church is similar, too, with two towers at each end, a prominent apse at the east end, and short transepts (the "arms" of the church). The Gothic influence is most obvious inside, especially in the great rose window at the west end (over the main entrance). It could almost be in a French church and presents a striking contrast to the tiny, round-headed windows high up in the nave. Notice, too, how a number of the main arches in the nave are pointed, a key characteristic of the Gothic style. It wasn't only in the Gothic period that the cathedral was altered, however. As you near the main altar you'll see the lavish Baroque screen of columns supporting a gold crown that towers above the marvelous altar by the great Balthasar Neumann: an example of Baroque at its most opulent. The choir stalls, installed in 1760, are equally opposed in spirit to the body of the church. Intricately carved and gilded, they proclaim the courtly and sophisticated glamour of the Rococo. ⊘ *Apr.–Oct., daily 8–6; Nov.–Mar., daily 9–5.*

19 Outside the cathedral, cross the square to see the simple **Dreifaltigkeit Church** (Church of the Holy Trinity). Remodeling of the church during the 19th and 20th centuries produced today's austere building (the facade and tower are still joyfully Baroque). It's a Lutheran church, and therefore a reminder of the beginnings of Protestantism, which started as Martin Luther's "protest" against the excesses and corruption of the Catholic Church in that period. Luther called for reform (hence the term Reformation), and appeared in this city in 1521 before the Holy Roman Emperor and massed ranks of Catholic theologians to defend his supposedly heretical beliefs. Luther ended his impassioned plea, "Here I stand, I can do no different. God help me. Amen!" He was duly excommunicated. ⊘ *Daily 9–5. Tours of the tower: 2nd Sun. of the month at 2 and 4.*

20 While we're on the subject, walk back past the cathedral to see the **Lutherdenkmal (Luther monument)** commemorating this event. This is a 19th-century group of statues of Luther and other figures from the Reformation, set in a small park on the appropriately named street Lutherring.

Worms was also one of the most important Jewish cities in Germany, a role that came to a brutal end with the rise of the Nazis. From the ★ **21** Lutherdenkmal you can walk along Adenauerring to see the rebuilt **synagogue,** one of the oldest in the country. It was founded during the 11th century; in 1938, on Kristallnacht, it was entirely destroyed. In 1961, the synagogue was rebuilt, using as much of the original masonry as had survived. ⊘ *May–Oct., daily 10–noon and 2–5; Nov.–Apr., daily 10–noon and 2–4.*

Next to the synagogue, in a former Jewish family home, is the **Judaica Museum,** which documents the history of the Jewish community in Worms. The exhibits include artifacts from as far back as the 11th century. *Raschi-Haus, Judengasse.* ☛ *DM 2 adults, DM 1 children.* ⊘ *Tues.–Sun. 10–noon and 2–5.*

22 You can also visit the Jewish cemetery, the **Judenfriedhof,** west of Domplatz off the Lutherring. It's the oldest Jewish cemetery in Europe, with graves dating back to 1076. ☛ *Free.* ⊘ *Daily 10–noon and 2–4.*

23 To bone up on the history of the city, visit the **Städtisches Museum** (Municipal Museum). It's housed in the cloisters of a former Romanesque church; the exhibits within shed considerable light on Worms's Roman past. *Weckerlingpl.* ☛ *DM 3 adults, DM 1.50 children.* ⊘ *Tues.–Sun. 10–noon and 2–5.*

If you visit the city in late August or early September, you'll find it embroiled in its carnival, the improbably named Backfischfest, or Baked Fish Festival. The highlight is the **Fischerstechen,** a kind of waterborne jousting in which contestants spar with long poles while balancing on the wobbly decks of flat-bottom boats. The winner is crowned King of the River; the losers get a dunking. Baked fish is the culinary high-light of the festival, of course. The wine is never in short supply.

Don't leave Worms without visiting the vineyard that gave birth to Germany's most famous export wine, Liebfraumilch (Our Lady's Milk). The vineyard encircles the Gothic pilgrimage church of the **Liebfrauen** convent, the **Liebfrauenkirche,** an easy 20-minute walk north from the old town. Buy a bottle or two from the shop at the vineyard. *Church and vineyard open Apr.–Oct., daily 9–6; Nov.–Mar., daily 9–5.*

Numbers in the margin correspond to points of interest on the Rhineland Palatinate map.

Two of Germany's most famous wine towns—Oppenheim and Nierstein—lie between Worms and Mainz, the end of this tour. **Oppenheim** is 26 kilometers (16 miles) north of Worms on B–9; Nierstein is a mile or two beyond. Oppenheim is said to have been the center of Charlemagne's wine estates. Take a look at the fine market square, fussily bordered on all sides by time-honored half-timbered buildings. Then climb the steep stepped streets to the Gothic church of St. Catherine, the **Katharinenkirche.**

Nierstein is a town that lives for wine; entire streets contain shops that sell nothing but the precious liquid. Many have ornate wood or wrought-iron signs, brilliantly painted and gilded, advertising their wares.

Sixteen kilometers (10 miles) north lies the city of **Mainz,** a bustling, businesslike but friendly Rhine-side city. With its half-timbered buildings housing shops, restaurants, and wine taverns, it's a fine example of sensitive postwar reconstruction following near-total destruction by bombings. The well-planned central pedestrian zone makes touring on foot a pleasure. All streets lead to the spacious market square, filled with stalls selling produce and other articles. Watching over them is the sturdy, turreted **Dom,** the third of the Rhine's great Romanesque cathedrals. Inside you'll find that the mantle of one thousand years of history accompanies you through the aisles and chapels. The first cathedral here—dedicated to Saints Martin and Stephan—was built at the end of the 10th century. In 1002, Heinrich I, the last Saxon emperor of the Holy Roman Empire, was crowned in the still-far-from-complete building. In 1009, on the very day of its consecration, the cathedral burned to the ground. Rebuilding began almost immediately. The cathedral you see today, though substantially rebuilt at the end of World War II, was largely finished at the end of the 11th century. During the Gothic period, however, rebuilding and remodeling diluted the Romanesque purity of the original; and an imposing Baroque spire was added in the 18th century. Still, despite these additions and modifications, the building remains essentially Romanesque. At the very least, its ground plan demonstrates a clear link to the cathedrals at Speyer and Mainz. Notice the towers at each end and the spires that rise between them; one may be Baroque, but its positioning and something of its bold impact produce an effect that is nothing if not Romanesque. Inside, though pointed arches proliferate, the walls have the same grim, fortresslike massiveness of Speyer. True, there's more stained glass, but the weight of masonry is full-fledged Romanesque. (English-language tours of the cathedral and Old City are given daily, at 2 PM, July–Aug. Cost: DM 8.) Scheduled to be under renovation until some time in 1996, the **Dom und Diözesan Museum** (Cathedral Treasury and Museum) will confine itself to a single room and continue to display at least some of the cathedral's treasures. These include some marvelous Romanesque stone carvings, including an Atlas groaning and holding his lower back from the strain of supporting a heavy stone arch and a very unhappy group of damned souls, not at all pleased about having to go to hell. ☛ *Free.* ◷ *Mon.–Wed. and Fri. 10–4, Thurs. 10–5, Sat. 10–2. Closed Sun. and holidays.*

★ Opposite the east end of the cathedral on Liebfrauenplatz is one of the most popular attractions in the Rhineland, the **Gutenberg Museum,** devoted to the life and times of Mainz's most famous and influential son, Johannes Gutenberg (1390–1468). It was in Mainz, in 1456, that Gutenberg built the first machine that could print from movable type. The significance of his invention was immense, leading to an explosion in the availability of information. This wasn't actually the building in which Gutenberg worked—that's long since disappeared—but you can see fine reconstructions of his printing machine and get a sense of his original workshop. Exhibits explain the history of printing through the ages, with machines displayed below and manuscripts above. Among the latter, the unquestioned highlight is the copy of the Gutenberg Bible, one of only 47 extant, not only one of the most historically significant books in the world but one of the most beautiful. Gutenberg is so important to Mainz that he has his own festival, *Johannisnacht,* in mid-June. *Liebfrauenpl. 5.* ☛ *Free.* ◷ *Tues.–Sat. 10–6, Sun. 10–1.*

From the Gutenberg Museum, walk north along the Rhine, where a confrontation of historic styles is evident in the face-off between the **Eisenturm,** a reconstruction of one of the original city gates, on your left, and the unabashedly modern, 20th-century **Rathaus** (Town Hall), on your right. Continuing along the river, you'll come to the **Kurfürstliches Schloss** (Electoral Palace), a building oddly asymmetrical for its day (it appears to be missing a wing but was, in fact, built that way). This houses testimony to Mainz's even more ancient past: the **Römisch-Germanisches Museum.** Exhibited are artifacts, from statues to armor and jewelry, of the Roman settlement that once flourished here. ◷ *Tues.–Sun. 10–6.*

On the opposite side of town, commanding a hilltop view of the city, is the church of **St. Stephan.** It's worth making the climb up, and not only for the view. The church itself is one of the oldest single-nave Gothic buildings in this part of the Rhineland. Its main highlight, however, is far newer: Around the choir, behind the altar, are six stained-glass windows depicting scenes from the Bible, designed in the 1970s by Russian-born painter Marc Chagall. The windows' vivid blue is a beautiful complement to the austere Gothic design of the rest of the church.

Not far from here is the source of a beverage a little more upscale than the local wine: the **Kupferberg Sektkellerei,** the local producer of *Sekt* (sparkling wine). The oldest cellars here date to the days of the Romans; newer additions include the spectacular Art Deco (*Jugendstil*) Traubensaal, or "Grape Hall." The two-hour tour of the facility includes, of course, a sampling of its product. *Am Kupferbergterrasse,* ☎ *06131/5550.* ☛ *DM 15 per person.*

Mainz claims to host the wildest pre-Lent carnival in Germany. Be here in early February if you want to put that claim to the test. The city erupts in a Rhineland riot of revelry, the high point of which is the procession through the old town.

What to See and Do with Children

On the Wine Road you'll find what is claimed to be one of Europe's biggest leisure parks, the **Hassloch Holidaypark.** It's at Hassloch, on

B–39 between Neustadt and Speyer. A circus, a dolphinarium, a replica of the Lilliputians' town from the book *Gulliver's Travels*, an adventure playground, and an elaborate medieval mock-up, the "Robber Knights of Falkenstein Mountain," number among the attractions. *D–67454 Hassloch-Pfalz,* ☎ *06324/599–3900.* ☛ *DM 27.50 adults, DM 24.50 children.* ☉ *Apr.–Oct., daily 9–6.*

A swimming-pool complex with several pools and a giant water slide was recently added to the Hassloch Holidaypark. ☉ *Mon. noon–9, Tues.–Sun. 9–9.*

There's another, smaller park, the **Kurpfalz Park,** close by at Wachenheim, between Deidesheim and Bad Dürkheim. It has all the fun of the fair, plus a wildlife park. ☎ *06325/2077.* ☛ *Kurpfalz Park: DM 15 adults, DM 13 children.* ☉ *Apr.–Oct., daily 9–6.* ☛ *Wildlife park: DM 6 adults, DM 5 children.* ☉ *Year-round (Nov.–Mar. 10–4).*

Nierstein has two museums, both in the Altes Rathaus on Marktplatz, that seem to fascinate youngsters. One is the **Palaeontological Museum,** with a 265-million-year-old fly among the exhibits of fossils and dinosaur bones. ☛ *Free.* ☉ *Sun. only 10–1.*

The other, the **Schiffartmuseum** (Shipping Museum), charts in graphic form the history of shipping on the Rhine. ☛ *Free.* ☉ *Sun. only 10–noon.*

If **zoos** are your thing, there's a little one at Landau. *Hinderburgstr. 12,* ☎ *06341/13161.* ☛ *DM 5 adults, DM 2 children under 14.* ☉ *Daily 9–6.*

Neustadt has a **railway museum** that's packed with old-timers from the age of steam. From May to October, you can take the historic steam train along the 11-kilometer (7-mi) stretch from Neustadt to Elmstein (call 06325/1810 or 06325/8626 for information). *Neustadt railway station, Schillerstr. entrance,* ☎ *06321/30390.* ☛ *DM 4 adults, DM 2 children.* ☉ *Weekends and holidays 10–4.*

The animals in Mainz's **Natural History Museum** may all be stuffed and mounted, but these lifelike groups can demonstrate the relationships among various families of fauna better than any zoo. *Reichklarastr. 1,* ☎ *06131/122–646.* ☛ *DM 5 adults, DM 2.50 children.* ☉ *Tues. and Thurs. 10–8; Wed., Fri., and Sat. 10–5.*

In Mainz's **Gutenberg Museum** youngsters can play at being printers in the age when type was set by hand. *Liebfrauenplatz 5,* ☎ *06131/122–644. Printing shop open weekdays 10–5.*

There's a charming wildlife park with an adventure playground at Silz, the **Wildpark Südliche Weinstrasse.** Every second Sunday, May through October, there is a children's fest. ☛ *DM 4 adults, DM 2 children.* ☉ *Daily 8:30–dusk.*

Children can scramble up the artificial sand dunes at **Freizeitbad Moby Dick,** a water sports–oriented leisure center in Rülzheim, south of Landau. ☎ *07272/92840.* ☛ *DM 8 adults, DM 5 children.* ☉ *Mon. 1–10 PM, Tues.–Thurs. 9 AM–10 PM, weekends 9–6.*

A turn-of-the-century factory hall in Speyer houses the **Technology Museum,** a huge collection of locomotives, aircraft, old automobiles, and fire engines. A major attraction here is the 420-ton U-boat on display outside. *Geibstr. 2,* ☎ *06232/78844.* ☛ *DM 12 adults, DM 7 children. Family ticket DM 24.* ☉ *Daily 9–6.*

Off the Beaten Track

Climb through the woods above the town of **Frankenstein** on A–37, between Kaiserslautern and Mannheim, to the ruins of the medieval castle that watches over the ugly, brooding town. Whether it's the castle that helped inspire Mary Shelley, author of *Frankenstein*, no one knows, but it's easy to imagine how a romantic soul might be stirred by the ruins.

Stroll through the groves of **sweet chestnut trees** in the hills above Bad Dürkheim. The descendants of saplings planted by the Romans 2,000 years ago, the trees are among the few of their kind remaining in Germany.

The click and whir of roulette balls may not suggest an off-the-beaten-track activity, but Bad Dürkheim's little **casino** is definitely a change from the high rollers of Baden-Baden and Mainz. If you fancy a quiet flutter, try your luck here. ☛ *DM 5. Jacket and tie.* ☉ *Daily 2 PM–2 AM.*

If plants are your passion, seek out the unusual **Kakteenland Bisnaga** at Steinfeld, just north of the French border. This is cactus country, with more than 1,000 different spiny and spiky species. *Wengelspfad 1.* ☛ *Free.* ☉ *Weekdays 8–5.*

In nearby Nothweiler there's an ancient iron mine, the **St. Anna Ironworks,** that's now open to visitors. The mine is said to date from Celtic times, before the birth of Christ. ☛ *DM 4 adults, DM 1.50 children.* ☉ *Apr.–Oct., Tues.–Fri. 2–6, Sat. 1–6, Sun. 11–6.*

SHOPPING

Bad Dürkheim
Shopping in the Rhineland Palatinate means **wine.** Entire streets in many towns and villages are dominated by shops devoted to the product of the grape. Likewise, vineyards along the roadside invite you in to pass judgment on the year's vintage. Bad Dürkheim is one particularly inviting center. **Heinrich Bühler** (Hinterbergstr. 12, ☎ 06322/2102) offers wine tastings accompanied by explanations in English. You can also taste and learn with vintner **Roland Bauer** (Seebacher Str. 12, ☎ 06322/2487). Another local winegrower, **Hermann Frey** (Michelsbergstr. 5, ☎ 06322/4151), has a reasonably priced package deal on eight different kinds of wine and a plate of homemade sausages. These wine outlets are family-run affairs: Don't expect to be able to use credit cards.

Edenkoben
A center for wine consumption is the local **Winzergenossenschaft** (Vintner's Association) at Edenkoben, south of Neustadt (Weinstr. 130; open daily).

Mainz
Mainz boasts the area's oldest merchant district, **Am Brand,** a pedestrian zone that runs parallel to the marketplace toward the river. Locals did their shopping here as long ago as the late 13th century; today, the merchant tradition is still carried on with a modern area of shops, boutiques, and supermarkets. Here you'll find Mainz's largest clothing store: **Sinn** (Am Brand 41, ☎ 06131/2730), with a selection of both men's and women's clothing. Also centrally located, although not on

Am Brand itself, is another leading store, **Leininger** (Ludwigstr. 11, ☎ 06131/288820), which stocks articles for women and children only.

Such souvenirs of Mainz as distinctive local wineglasses emblazoned with the city's coat of arms are available from the **tourist office** (Bahnhofstr. 15, ☎ 06131/286–210). Another local product is Sekt (Champagne by any other name) from the local **Kupfenberg Sektkellerei.** You can buy it from the facility itself (Am Kupfenbergterrasse, ☎ 06131/5550) or at most local shops.

Mainz's famous **flea market,** the Krempelmarkt, is held along the banks of the Rhine every third Saturday of the month (except Apr. and Oct.).

Pirmasens
Located on the edge of the Palatinate forest, the Pfälzerwald, Pirmasens is Germany's shoe center; it can be worth a detour from the Wine Road to stock up on a pair or two from factory outlets. **Buchholz** (Horebstr. 38, ☎ 06331/24790) stocks men's shoes. The place for children's shoes is **Hummel** (Charlottenstr. 8, ☎ 06331/76085). Women, however, will have to content themselves with the selection in regular (nonoutlet) shoe stores, of which the town has plenty.

Wachenheim
At the foot of the castle ruins of Wachtenburg, between Deidesheim and Bad Dürkheim, the regional **Winzergenossenschaft** (Vintner's Association) is a great place to taste a wide variety of the local vintages—and, if you like, to purchase some. *Weinstrasse 2, ☎ 06322/8101; open weekdays 8–noon and 1–5, Sat. 8–noon.*

Worms
Even if you're not buying wine, you can still pick up such related souvenirs as wineglasses, bottle openers (some of them elaborately carved from local wood), or wine coolers. Worms's **tourist office** (Verkehrsverein, Neumarkt 14, ☎ 06241/25045) sells the most original wine cooler: a terra-cotta replica of a Roman model unearthed in the region by archaeologists.

SPORTS AND FITNESS

Bicycling
The vineyard-lined country roads on either side of the Wine Roadare a cyclist's dream. You can rent bikes at any of the main train stations for DM 12 a day (DM 6 if you have a valid train ticket). The tourist offices have arranged a number of bike trips where a flat fee includes meals and accommodations in some lovely hotels and restaurants (contact the Pfalz Tourist Office; *see* The Rhineland Palatinate Essentials, *below*). Many of the towns and villages along the Wine Road also have shops where you can rent a bike. In Annweiler, try the **Fahrradgeschäft Seel** (Gerbergasse 27); in Bad Dürkheim, **Robl Sport** (Bruchstr. 51); and in Neustadt, the **Firma Rottmayer** (Remigiusstr. 13).

Climbing
The sandstone cliffs of the Palatinate Forest (Pfälzerwald) are fun and relatively safe to tackle. The tourist office in **Annweiler am Trifels** (☎ 06346/2200) will tell you the best places to climb.

Golf

The Palatinate has its own golf club, the **Golf Club Pfalz e.V.,** with an 18-hole course at Geinsheim, near Neustadt an der Weinstrasse (☎ 06327/97420). Visitors who are members of a golf club back home are welcome. There's also a club at Bad Kreuznach (☎ 06708/2145).

Hiking

You can cover the entire Wine Road on foot, along a clearly marked trail that winds its way between the vineyards covering the slopes of the Palatinate forest. Contact the Wine Road tourist offices (*see* The Rhineland Palatinate Essentials, *below*) for maps and information. Local tourist offices and hotels also have a wide variety of other walking tours lasting anywhere from two days to a week, where a fixed price pays for accommodation, meals, and the transportation of your baggage from one hotel to the next. There are all kinds of perks on the various tours, down to a walking stick and a bottle of locally made schnapps to help you cover the distance; on the "gourmet walking tours," the meals are especially fine. The Palatinate Forest is Germany's largest single tract of woodland—and offers especially fine walking, notably in the Wasgau nature park at one edge of it. Contact the Pfalz Tourist Office in Neustadt (*see* The Rhineland Palatinate Essentials, *below*) or local tourist offices for a complete list of walking routes.

Horseback Riding

There is ample opportunity in this fine riding country. Recommended stables include the **Gut Hohenberg** (☎ 06346/2592) and the **Ferien und Reiterhof Münz** (☎ 06346/5272), both of which are near Annweiler am Trifels. In a nature-preserve area midway between Worms and Oppenheim is the **Gut Liebfrauenthal** in Eich, a stable (that's also a hotel and restaurant) offering a range of riding classes (☎ 06246/7578). Local tourist offices can give you more information.

Swimming

There are open-air and indoor pools in many parts of the Rhineland Palatinate. One of the largest swimming complexes in Germany is in **Wörth** (on Autobahn 65, between Landau and Karlsruhe, ☎ 07271/1310). The **Wörth Badepark** (Bad-Allee) has 10 pools, a wave machine, and two water slides, each more than 80 yards long. **Speyer's** lido (Geibstr. 4) also has a spectacular water slide. There are thermal baths at **Bad Bergzabern** and **Bad Dürkheim** (☎ 06322/66727); here you can splash around in warm pools overlooking the sun-drenched vineyards that clothe the hills around the town.

Tennis

Tennis players will be pleased to find courts in most towns and villages. Those in the Kurpark of **Bad Dürkheim** are so beautifully located that concentrating on the game becomes difficult (☎ 06322/67979). Speyer has a tennis club that accepts visitors: the **Tennisclub Weiss-Rot Speyer** (Holzstr., ☎ 06232/76423).

DINING AND LODGING

Dining

Local specialties, served in local inns, are what you'll eat in the towns and villages here. The bigger cities, such as Mainz and Worms, have more elegant establishments. Sausages are more popular in the Rhineland Palatinate than in almost any other area of the country, with the herb-flavored *Pfälzer* a favorite. *Hase im Topf,* a highly flavored rabbit pâté made with port, Madeira, brandy, and red wine, is another specialty to look for. The Rhineland Palatinate, though geographically not the largest wine-producing area in the country, nonetheless produces more wine than does any other region in Germany, and all restaurants will have a range of wines to offer.

WHAT TO WEAR

Casual clothes are the norm in all local inns. For the restaurants listed below, dress is informal unless otherwise noted.

RATINGS

CATEGORY	COST*
$$$$	over DM 90
$$$	DM 55–90
$$	DM 35–55
$	under DM 35

per person for a three-course meal, not including drinks

Lodging

Accommodations are plentiful, with those along the Wine Road mostly simple and inexpensive inns. The region has many bed-and-breakfasts; keep an eye open for signs reading *Zimmer Frei,* meaning "rooms available." If you plan to visit during any of the wine festivals in the late summer and fall, make reservations well in advance—and expect higher prices.

RATINGS

CATEGORY	COST*
$$$$	over DM 200
$$$	DM 150–DM 200
$$	DM 100–DM 150
$	under DM 100

All prices are for two people in a double room.

Annweiler

DINING

Burg-Restaurant Trifels. Eat in the shadows of Burg Trifels, where Richard the Lion-Hearted once stayed in less happy circumstances. In summer, try for a table on the terrace; the view is terrific. Palatinate specialties—including delicious dumplings—are featured on the menu. ✕ *Auf den Schlossackern,* ☎ 06346/8479. *Reservations advised. MC, V. Closed Mon. $$*

LODGING

Zum Goldenen Lamm. At this half-timbered country inn at Ramberg, 7 kilometers (4.5 miles) north of Annweiler, the Lergenmüller family carries on an old rural tradition of supplying beer, wine, and meat to the neighborhood—there's a butcher shop in the inn! ☎ *76857 Ramberg,* ☎ 06345/8286, FAX 06345/3354. *35 rooms with bath. Restaurant. No credit cards. Restaurant closed Tues. $*

Bad Dürkheim

DINING

★ **Bad Dürkheimer Riesenfass.** This must be Germany's most unusual restaurant, located in the biggest wine barrel in the world, with room for 420 people inside and an additional 230 on the terrace. The food, like the wine, is robustly local. It's touristy but fun. ✕ *Am Wurstmarktgelände,* ☎ 06322/2143. *Reservations advised. No credit cards. $$*

Restaurant-Weinstube Käsbüro. Despite the name—it means "cheese office"—this historic old tavern specializes in fish and game dishes. It's about a mile from the center of Bad Dürkheim, in Seebach, and is well worth hunting out. ✗ *Dorfpl., Seebach,* ☎ *06322/8694. Reservations advised. MC, V. Closed Wed. $$*

LODGING

Kurparkhotel. Ask for a room overlooking the little spa park; on summer evenings you'll be serenaded by the orchestra that plays on its bandstand. Rooms are large and airy, and some have views of the vineyards above the town. Temptation lurks in the lobby—the hotel has direct access to the spa's casino. ⊡ *Schlosspl. 1–4,* ☎ *06322/7970,* FAX *06322/797–158. 110 rooms, 3 suites with bath. Restaurant, bar, indoor pool, beauty salon, sauna, spa. AE, DC, MC, V. $$$–$$$$*

Garten-Hotel Heusser. The Garten Hotel-Heusser describes itself as an "oasis of peace"—and it's not much of an exaggeration. There are vineyards all around, and most rooms have fine views of the rolling Palatinate countryside. One disadvantage: This vineyard oasis is a thirsty 20-minute walk from the town center. ⊡ *Seebacherstr. 50–52,* ☎ *06322/9300,* FAX *06322/930–499. 80 rooms with bath. Restaurant, indoor pool, outdoor pool, sauna. AE, DC, MC, V. $$$*

Hotel-Restaurant Fronmühle. Located on the edge of Bad Dürkheim's spa park, this whitewashed farmhouse-style hotel has won first prize several times in a district-wide competition for hotel management. If your tastes are similar to those of the judges, you'll praise the Fronmühle's high-quality accommodations and services and the efficient management of the Kraus family. Bathrooms are a bit small for a hotel of this price category—there are no bathtubs—but large, airy rooms make up for that; they're individually decorated with dark-wood furnishings and brightly colored prints. ⊡ *Salinenstr. 15,* ☎ *06322/94090. 22 rooms with shower. Restaurant, pool, sauna. AE, DC, MC, V. $$$*

Weingut und Gastehaus in den Almen. You'll stay in the midst of vineyards, and proprietor Ernst Karst will gladly and proudly show you around his own cellars, inviting you to try his vintages. Rooms are light and airy, furnished mostly in pine; all of them have splendid views of the surrounding countryside—which you are invited to explore on the bikes that Herr Karst loans out. The hotel's lovely restaurant is 1 kilometer (½ mile) from the hotel itself. ⊡ *In den Almen 15,* ☎ *06322/2862,* FAX *06322/65965. 4 rooms with shower, 1 apartment. Restaurant, bicycles. No credit cards. Closed Nov.–Jan. $*

Deidesheim

DINING AND LODGING

★ **Deidesheimer Hof.** This is the showpiece hotel of the Deidesheim-based Hahnhof group, a country-wide chain of wine restaurants. It's a traditional old Deidesheimer house, immaculately clean and comfortable, and run with slick but friendly efficiency. German Chancellor Kohl likes to entertain official guests in the hotel's Schwarzer Hahn restaurant. It's one of the best establishments in the region, with traditional oak and pine furnishings and broad vaulted ceilings. The menu includes German-style nouvelle cuisine and hearty Palatinate dishes. Margaret Thatcher and Mikhail Gorbachev have been among the restaurant's distinguished guests. ⊡ *Am Marktpl.,* ☎ *06326/1811,* FAX *06326/7685. 18 rooms, 2 suites with bath. Restaurant, weinstube. AE, DC, MC, V. Closed Jan. and Aug. $$$–$$$$*

Haardt Hotel Zum Geissbock. The pillared front façade of this lodging stands directly on the Wine Road, in the center of Deidesheim. Front-facing rooms can be noisy, so ask for one at the back. Under the steeply pitched roof is a well-designed pool and sauna/solarium area, where you can swim and enjoy views of the neighboring countryside. The renowned Reichsrat von Buhl vineyard supplies the excellent wines served in the hotel's restaurant and basement wine-tasting tavern. ⊞ *Weinstr. 11,* ☎ *06326/7070, fax. 06326/707–112. 80 rooms with bath. Restaurant, bar, pool, sauna, bowling, paddle tennis. DC, MC, V. $$–$$$*

Hotel St. Urban. The oriel windows under the steep eaves give a complete view of Deidesheim—ask for a room with one. Even if your request isn't granted, however, the village center is just a few minutes' walk away. The hotel is well-modernized and elegantly appointed; a soothing dove gray is the predominant color used in the decor, from the walls of the restaurant to the carpeting of the comfortable rooms. ⊞ *Im oberen Grain 1,* ☎ *06326/6024,* ℻ *06326/79485. 18 rooms with bath. Restaurant, café, weinstube, sauna. AE, MC, V. $$*

Grünstadt
LODGING

Pfalzhotel Asselheim. This fine old country hotel stands on the outskirts of Grünstadt, a town near the north end of the Wine Road. Surrounded by vineyards, the Pfalzhotel is situated near the edge of the Pfälzerwald nature park. Low beams, fine wood paneling, rustic antiques, and huge tile ovens combine harmoniously in the restaurant and public areas—even the indoor swimming pool has half-timbered walls. The bedrooms aren't quite so atmospheric, but they are modern and comfortable. ⊞ *Holzweg 6, 67269 Grünstadt-Asselheim,* ☎ *06359/80030,* ℻ *06359/800–399. 33 rooms with bath or shower, 2 apartments. Restaurant, weinstube, indoor pool, sauna, bowling, paddle tennis, bicycles. AE, DC, MC, V. $$$*

Mainz
DINING

Kartäuser Hof. If the weather is warm, try for a table in the walled courtyard, a pretty sunlit area smothered in flowers in the summer. There's a warm welcome at any time of year, however, in this pleasant restaurant that often features locally caught fish. There's also an impressive wine list, dominated by local vineyards. ✕ *Kartäuser Str. 14,* ☎ *06131/222–956. Reservations advised. AE, DC, MC, V. $$*

★ **Rats- und Zunftstuben Heilig Geist.** The most atmospheric dining in Mainz is offered here. Parts of the building date from Roman times, but most of it is Gothic, with vaulted ceilings and stone floors. The menu features Bavarian specialties with nouvelle touches. ✕ *Rentengasse 2,* ☎ *06131/225–757. Reservations advised. AE, DC, MC, V. Closed Sun. dinner and Mon. $$*

Weinhaus Schreiner. Mainz's oldest wine tavern has been in the hands of the Schreiner family since the mid-18th century and has won many awards from the local Vintner's Association. The menu is shorter than the wine list, but it's full of robust Palatinate fare. It's your lucky day if marinated beef Rhineland style is available when you visit. ✕ *Rheinstr. 38,* ☎ *06131/225–720. Reservations advised. No credit cards. Closed Sun. $*

LODGING

★ **Hilton International.** A terrific location right by the Rhine, allied with the reliable standards of comfort and service expected of the chain, make the Hilton the number-one choice in Mainz. Don't come looking for too much in the way of old German atmosphere, however. The hotel has a casino and two restaurants; one serves an international menu with nouvelle cuisine, and the other has plainer, more traditional fare. ☎ *Rheinstr. 68,* ☎ *06131/2450,* FAX *06131/245–589. 419 rooms and 14 suites, all with bath. 2 restaurants, beauty salon, sauna, exercise room. AE, DC, MC, V. $$$$*

Hotel-Restaurant Am Lerchenberg. The location isn't ideal—some 6½ kilometers (4 miles) from the city center—but this family-run hotel is friendly, comfortable, and peaceful, and there's a bus stop right outside the door. This could be a very good choice, though, if you're interested in biking and hiking—open countryside is only a few steps away. ☎ *Hindemithstr. 5,* ☎ *06131/934–300,* FAX *06131/934–3099. 53 rooms with shower. Restaurant, sauna, exercise room. AE, DC, MC, V. $$$*

Ibis. If you're visiting Mainz on the weekend you can stay here for a discount of up to 50%—a very good deal. The hotel offers the sleek, though somewhat spartan, comfort and facilities that have enabled the Ibis group to keep its prices down. This one (unlike some of its German siblings) is also centrally located, with a restaurant that can be recommended. ☎ *Holzhofstr. 2,* ☎ *06131/2470,* FAX *06131/234–126. Restaurant, bar. AE, DC, MC, V. $$–$$$*

Hotel Stadt Coblenz. In the heart of town, you get what you pay for at this hotel: budget rooms (bath in the hall) at budget prices. Ask for a room facing the back to avoid the noise of street traffic, and spend the money you saved on dinner in the rustic restaurant, which serves local and German specialties. ☎ *Rheinstr. 49,* ☎ *06131/227602. Restaurant. No credit cards. $*

Neustadt-an-der-Weinstrasse

DINING

Ratsherrenstuben. Local vintners often meet in this half-timbered building; if you come here, you're likely to overhear them discussing business, and perhaps you'll pick up some advice on which wine to order from the long list available. The comprehensive menu specializes in Palatinate dishes, such as the Pfälzer butcher's plate, piled high with various meats. ✗ *Marktpl. 10–12,* ☎ *06321/2070. Reservations advised. Closed Mon. MC, V. $$*

Gerberhaus. Two floors of a half-timbered 17th-century tanner's house, next to the medieval gate leading to the old town, are occupied by this fine old Pfalz restaurant. The menu ranges from stout local fare (Pfälzer sausage and cuts of marinated pork) to more sophisticated international dishes (lamb medallions with young beans in bacon). The local wines are excellent. ✗ *Hintergasse 6,* ☎ *06321/88700. MC. Closed Mon. $$*

Weinstube Eselsburg. A consummate artist is in charge here. The tavern's jovial landlord finds time between serving creative Palatinate dishes to sketch and paint. He sings, too—the evenings can lengthen into quite a party. The tavern is in the Musbach area of Neustadt, a 10-minute drive from the town center. ✗ *Kurpfalzstr. 62, Neustadt-Mussbach,* ☎ *06321/66984. No credit cards. Closed Sun.–Tues. $*

LODGING

Hotel-Restaurant Zur Festwiese. Centrally located but quiet, this is one of the area's leading hotels. Rooms are light and airy, decorated in pastel tones and with such individual touches as dried-flower arrangements on the walls. ☎ *Festplatzstr. 6,* ☎ *06321/82081,* FAX *06321/31006. 32 rooms with bath. Restaurant, bicycles. AE, DC, MC, V. $$$*

Oppenheim

DINING AND LODGING

Rondo. "Rondo" (in the round) is exactly what this hotel is. Every room has a view, and many of them look out over the nearby Rhine. The best view of all, though, is from the hotel's roof-terrace café. Because of its circular construction, the hotel's interior is light and airy; this is complemented in guest rooms by light-wood furnishings and bright fabrics. ⊞ *Sant-Ambrogio-Ring,* ☎ *06133/70001,* ℻ *06133/2034. 35 rooms with bath. Restaurant, café, sauna, recreation room. AE, DC, MC, V. $$$*

St. Martin

DINING AND LODGING

St. Martiner Castell. An ancient vintner's house, once virtually a ruin, was transformed into a fine hotel and restaurant in the late 1980s. Many of the building's original features were retained and restored—the restaurant's gnarled beams and old wine press, for example. Guest rooms are adorned with antique furnishings and decorative pieces; most rooms have balconies that afford views of the surrounding vineyards. ⊞ *Maikammer Str. 2,* ☎ *06323/9510,* ℻ *06323/2098. 18 rooms with bath. Restaurant, weinstube, sauna. No credit cards. Closed Feb.–mid-Mar. $$–$$$.*

Speyer

DINING

★ **Wirtschaft zum Alten Engel.** Regional dishes from the Palatinate and the French Alsace region dominate the menu in this historic cellar tavern in the heart of the city. Try the mushroom gratinée. ✗ *Mühlturmstr. 1,* ☎ *06232/132–680. Reservations advised. AE, DC, MC, V. Closed lunch, Sun., and Aug. $$*

LODGING

Goldener Engel. The "Golden Angel" has been in business since 1701 and offers simple, time-honored atmosphere with appealing modern comfort. There's no restaurant, but it adjoins the Wirtschaft zum Alten Engel (*see above*). ⊞ *Mühlturmstr. 1a,* ☎ *06232/13260,* ℻ *06232/132–695. 46 rooms and 2 apartments with bath. AE, DC, MC, V. Closed Dec. 23–Jan. 10. $$–$$$*

Hotel Morgenstern. Flowers in window boxes adorn the immaculate white facade of this stately modern mansion in Speyer's Römerberg district. It was built in a combination of attractive styles, with high French windows under an imposing mansard roof, and the interior lives up to its exterior—bright and airy rooms are furnished in a combination of modern and traditional styles. ⊞ *Römerberg 1 at Berghausen,* ☎ *06232/8001,* ℻ *06232/8028. 21 rooms with bath. Restaurant, bar. AE, MC. $$*

Worms

DINING

★ **Bei Bacchus.** The name is apt: Here you'll drink some of the best wine in the region. This restaurant is perhaps a bit stuffy, but the food is quite good, with local specialties predominating. ✗ *Obermarkt 10,* ☎ *06241/6913. Reservations advised. Jacket and tie. AE, DC, MC, V. Closed Sun. $$$*

Rotisserie Dubs. Make the trek to Wolfgang Dubs's sleekly appointed restaurant to eat his excellent steak in snail sauce, a substantially more appetizing dish than it sounds. The restaurant is in the suburb of Rheindürkheim, a 10-minute ride from downtown. ✗ *Kirchstr. 6,*

☎ *06242/2023. Reservations required. Jacket and tie. MC. Closed Sat. lunch, Tues., and 2 wks in July. $$$*

DINING AND LODGING

Hotel and Restaurant Römischer Kaiser. Despite what you'd expect from a hotel with this name in this region, the ground floor here is a high-class Asian restaurant that serves Chinese, Japanese, and Korean dishes. Rooms at the hotel are sturdy and affordable, with sleek dark-wood furnishings and such individual touches as oil paintings on the walls and fresh flowers on the dressing tables. ⌑ *Römerstr. 72,* ☎ *06241/6936,* ℻ *06241/229–953. 11 rooms with bath. AE, DC, MC, V. $$–$$$*

Kriemhilde. Reliable comfort and a central location next to the cathedral are the advantages of this rustic-style hotel. Its restaurant's menu offers a wide range of German specialties, including seasonal dishes: asparagus in May, wild boar in December, and goose for St. Martin's Day, November 11. The wine list is also gratifying—to anyone, at least, who wants to sample the local vintages. ⌑ *Hofgasse 2–4,* ☎ *06241/6278,* ℻ *06241/6277. 20 rooms with bath. AE, DC, MC, V. $$–$$$.*

LODGING

Dom Hotel. Although this modern and centrally located hotel is the best in Worms, all it really provides is functional comfort. The restaurant Bei Bacchus (*see above*) compensates, however. ⌑ *Obermarkt 10,* ☎ *06241/6913,* ℻ *06241/23515. 60 rooms with bath, 2 apartments. Restaurant. AE, DC, MC, V. $$$*

Gästehaus Bech☞ The Bechtel family expanded its vineyard farmhouse into a guest house. Rooms are comfortable and have TVs and telephones. The guest house lies on the outskirts of Worms, in the village of Heppenheim, with fine views of the surrounding vineyards. ⌑ *Pfälzerwaldstr. 98,* ☎ *06241/36536,* ℻ *06241/34745. 12 rooms with bath or shower. No credit cards. $*

THE ARTS AND NIGHTLIFE

The Arts

Music

Regular organ- and chamber-music concerts are given in the three great Romanesque cathedrals of the area—in **Mainz, Speyer,** and **Worms.** Mainz also has an annual **cathedral-music festival** that lasts through the summer. Organ recitals are given in the cathedral every Saturday at noon from mid-August to mid-September. Classical-music concerts are also given regularly at the **Kurfürstliches Schloss.** Mainz's recently acquired cultural center, the **Frankfurter Hof** (Augustinerstr. 55, ☎ 06131/220–438), offers a constantly changing music program of classical, pop, folk, and jazz. You can get complete information on concerts in Mainz, as well as tickets, from the ticket office Kartenhaus (Schillerstr. 11, ☎ 06131/228–729). Speyer's concert scene received a boost from the musical events marking the town's 2,000th anniversary in 1990. Contact the local tourist office for details about current concerts.

Theater

The area's theatrical activity is concentrated in Mainz. The city's resident company, the **Theater der Landeshauptstadt Mainz,** performs regularly in the Staatstheater, Gutenbergerplatz, and at two other smaller venues. Opera and ballet productions are also staged at the Staatstheater.

Call 06131/285–1222 for program details and tickets. The Palatinate has its own repertory theater company, the **Pfalz Theater,** in Kaiserslautern (Fruchthallstr. 24, ☎ 0631/80020). In the summer it tours the region, giving performances in local theaters and in many of the area's ruined castles. Worms has a city theater, the **Städtisches Spiel und Festhaus,** where concerts and drama productions are staged. For program details and tickets, contact the box office on Rathenaustrasse or call 06241/22525. In Speyer, the city's theater is the **Stadthalle** (Obere Langgasse); contact the local tourist office, the Verkehrsamt (Maximilianstr. 11), for program details and tickets.

Nightlife

Mainz and Bad Dürkheim both have **casinos,** with adjacent bars for celebrating a lucky evening or drowning losers' sorrows. Bad Dürkheim's nightlife is otherwise crammed into Friday and Saturday nights at the Dorint Hotel's **Cotton Club** dance bar (Kurbrunnenstr. 30-32, ☎ 06322/6010). In **Mainz,** night owls congregate in the Altstadt, the old town, which is full of historic old wine and beer taverns (**Schinderhannes** is recommended). The central Marktplatz is the scene of a nightly program of open-air pop music, jazz, and street cabaret from May through September. Disco fans dance at **M Discothek** (Rheinallee 175) or **Lindenbaum** (Holzstr. 32). Worms has a square-dance club, **The Crackers,** which welcomes guests. Call 06241/23400 if you'd like to join in. The discotheques and bars of **Worms** are concentrated around Judengasse. If you tire of the wine taverns of the Wine Road, try the exotic **Bahama Club** (Landauerstr. 65) in Neustadt-an-der-Weinstrasse. Neustadt has a surprisingly upbeat nightlife; **Madison** (am Kartoffelmarkt 2) is the "in" place.

Wine Festivals

The wine festivals of the towns and villages of the Wine Road are numerous enough to take up several vacations. From late May through October, the entire area seems to be caught up in one long celebration. The most important festivals are the **Dürkheimer Wurstmarkt** (Germany's biggest wine festival), in mid-September; the **Weinlesefest,** in Neustadt-an-der-Weinstrasse (with the coronation of the local Wine Queen), in the first half of October; Schweigen-Rechtenbach's **Rebenblütenfest,** in the first week of July; Bad Bergzabern's **Böhammerfest,** in early July; Landau's **Herbstmarkt,** in mid-September; Edenkoben's **Südliches Weinstrasse Grosses Weinfest,** in late September; and the **Mainzer Weinmarkt** in Mainz's Volkspark, the last weekend of August and the first weekend of September.

THE RHINELAND PALATINATE ESSENTIALS

Arriving and Departing

By Plane

Frankfurt, which has regular flights from the United States, is the closest major international airport for the entire Rhineland. Autobahn access to Mainz, the northernmost point of the itinerary, is fast and easy. Stuttgart Airport serves the southern half of the region. Take Autobahn 8 to Karlsruhe and then drive the 36 kilometers (22 miles) to the southern point of the wine route.

Getting Around

By Bus

Buses crisscross the region, with most running to and from Mainz. Post buses connect smaller towns and villages. For information, timetables, and reservations, contact **Deutsche Touring GmBH** (Am Römerhof 17, D–60486 Frankfurt/Main, ☎ 069/79030).

By Car

Most roads in the region are narrow and winding, a far cry from the highways of much of the rest of Germany. Autobahn 6 runs northeast–southwest across much of the southern part of the region, from Saarbrücken on the French border to the Rhine, reaching it just above Mannheim. Halfway along, take 61 to 63 north to Mainz. Driving conditions are good everywhere, with all roads well surfaced.

CAR RENTALS

Avis: Schmidtstrasse 39, ☎ 069/730–111, **Frankfurt;** Wormser Landstrasse 22, ☎ 06232/32068, **Speyer;** Alzeyer Strasse 44, ☎ 06241/591–081, **Worms.**

Europcar: Schlossstrasse 32, ☎ 069/775–033, **Frankfurt;** Rheinallee 107, ☎ 06131/677–073, **Mainz.**

Hertz: Hanauer Landstrasse 106–108, ☎ 069/449–090, **Frankfurt;** Bensheimerstrasse 1, ☎ 06241/43790, **Worms.**

By Train

Mainz is the only major city in the region with regular InterCity services; there are hourly connections to and from major German cities. To reach the southern part of the region, travel through Karlsruhe and Landau. Railroad buses serve those towns not on the rail network.

Guided Tours

A number of the smaller towns and villages offer sightseeing tours in the summer, some including visits to neighboring vineyards. At Annweiler, for example, tours of the town are given on Wednesdays from May to October, beginning with a glass of wine at the Rathaus at 10 AM. Details of this and all other tours in the region are available from local tourist information offices. There are city tours of Speyer and Worms. Mainz also offers a walking tour of its old town on Saturdays, starting from the tourist office at 10 AM (cost: DM 6); in July and August, there are English-language tours of the cathedral, Gutenberg Museum, and Old City daily at 2 PM. The shipping company **Köln-Düsseldorfer DeutscheRheinsschiffarht** has daily tours from Mainz to Köln between Good Friday and October; contact 06131/286–2126. For details of Rhine River tours in the United States, contact **KD River Cruises of Europe** (2500 Westchester Ave., Purchase, NY 10577, ☎ 914/696–3600; 323 Geary St., Suite 603, San Francisco, CA 94102, ☎ 415/392–8817).

Important Addresses and Numbers

Tourist Information

The central tourist office for the Palatinate is the **Pfalz Tourist Office** (Martin-Luther-Strasse 69, 67433 Neustadt a. d. Weinstrasse, ☎ 06321/2466). Information on the Wine Road can be obtained from the **Weinstrasse Zentrale für Tourismus** (Postfach 2124, D–76829 Landau); **Fremdenverkehrsverband** (Bezirksstelle Pfalz, Hindenburgstrasse 12, D–67433 Neustadt an der Weinstrasse); and **Mittelhaardt-Deutsche Weinstrasse** (Weinstrasse 32, D–67146 Deidesheim an der Weinstrasse). There are local tourist-information offices in the following towns:

Bad Dürkheim (Verkehrsamt, Mannheimer Strasse 24, D–67098 Bad Dürkheim, ☎ 06322/935–156).

Deidesheim (Verkehrsamt Stadthalle, Bahnhofstrasse 11, D–67146 Deidesheim, ☎ 06326/5021).

Landau (Büro für Tourismus, Marktstrasse 50, D–76825 Landau, ☎ 06341/13181).

Mainz (Verkehrsverein Mainz, Bahnhofstrasse 15, D–55116 Mainz, ☎ 06131/286–210).

Neustadt an der Weinstrasse (Verkehrsamt, Exterstrasse 2, D–67433 Neustadt an der Weinstrasse, ☎ 06321/926–892).

Speyer (Verkehrsamt der Stadt Speyer, Maximilianstrasse 11, D–67346 Speyer, ☎ 06232/14392).

Worms (Verkehrsverein der Stadt Worms, Neumarkt 14, D–67547 Worms, ☎ 06241/25045).

10 Heidelberg and the Neckar Valley

This chapter's tour bounces between industrial cities and quaint university towns, Mannheim and Stuttgart among the former, Heidelberg and Tübingen among the latter, with castles, small villages, and the Neckar throughout. Along the scenic Burgenstrasse (Castle Road), each medieval town is guarded by a castle.

THE NECKAR RIVER LACKS THE DRAMATIC BEAUTY and historic resonance of the Rhine, but the attractions along its banks make for a memorable vacation. Much of the following route is on the Burgenstrasse, the Castle Road (this section of the Neckar has proportionately more castles than any comparable stretch of the Rhine), which charms every bit as much as the Romantic Road without all the tourist hype. Along the way there are opportunities aplenty to escape into quiet side valleys and visit little towns that slumber in leafy peace. Scarcely one of these towns is without its guardian castle, standing in stern splendor above medieval streets. This is a region that can delight—and sometimes surprise—even the most hardened traveler.

This chapter covers the area's most distinctive stretch; don't expect off-the-beaten-track territory. The tour begins where the Neckar empties into the Rhine, 80 kilometers (55 miles) south of Frankfurt, in Mannheim. From Mannheim, whose industrial suburbs enclose a city of surprising charm, the route runs southeast to the ancient university town of Heidelberg, for many the apotheosis of romantic Germany. With the exception of a detour south to the town of Schwetzingen (glorying in the name "Germany's asparagus capital"), the route next snakes its scenic way east, then south, between the river and the wooded slopes of the Odenwald Forest, before hitting the rolling, vine-covered countryside around Heilbronn. From there it's a 49-kilometer (30-mile) drive, partly along the Neckar, to Stuttgart; about 40 kilometers (25 miles) farther, you rejoin the Neckar at the picturesque university town of Tübingen.

EXPLORING

Tour 1: Mannheim

Numbers in the margin correspond to points of interest on the Neckar Valley map.

❶ The tour begins where the Neckar and the Rhine meet—at **Mannheim,** a major industrial center and the second-largest river port in Europe. Inside its industrial sprawl lurks an elegant old town that was carefully rebuilt after wartime bomb damage. "Old" is not as meaningful here as in other Rhine cities, however—Mannheim is unusual for having been founded only in 1606, and it's even more unusual for having been laid out on a grid pattern. It was the forward-looking Palatinate elector Friedrich IV who built the city, imposing on it the rigid street

★ plan that forms the heart of the old town, or **Quadratstadt** (literally, "squared town"). Streets running northeast–southwest—from one river to the other—are labeled A through U; those running northwest–southeast are numbered 1 through 7. The central Marktplatz is G–1 on your map; the best restaurant in town—Da Gianni—is R–7. Rationalism rules. The only exception to this system are the two main streets of the pedestrian shopping zone—Heidelbergerstrasse, which runs a parallel course to the two rivers, and Kurpfalzstrasse, which cuts through the heart of the town, leading southwest from the Neckar to the **Residenzschloss** (palace). There's a terrific view down it from the main staircase of the palace.

Though it was the elector Friedrich IV who built Mannheim, his court was at Heidelberg. In 1720, the elector Carl Philip went one stage fur-

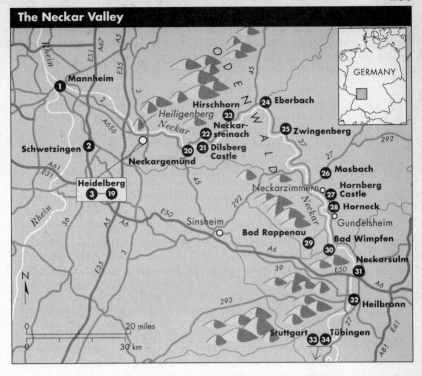

The Neckar Valley

ther, moving the court to Mannheim rather than rebuilding what remained of his castle at Heidelberg after it had been sacked by Louis XIV's French troops in 1689 and again in 1693. (What, ironically, helped prompt his decision was the desire to build a palace modeled on the absolutist, classical lines of Louis XIV's great palace at Versailles; like many 18th-century German rulers, Carl Philip eagerly seized the example provided by Louis XIV to reinforce his own absolute right to rule.) The palace was 40 years in the building, completed only in 1768. Five separate architects were employed, their combined efforts producing one of the largest buildings in Europe, a vast, relentlessly symmetrical edifice containing more than 400 rooms and 2,000 windows, and with a frontage more than a quarter-mile long. The palace was reduced to a smoking ruin in World War II, rebuilt in the '50s, and today belongs to Mannheim University. The great hall and some of the state rooms can be visited; they're impressive, but strangely lifeless now. *Kurfürstlichtes Residenzschloss,* ☎ 0621/292–2890. ☛ DM 3 adults, DM 1.50 children. ☉ Apr.–Oct., Tues.–Sun. 10–noon and 3–5; Nov.–Mar., Sat. and Sun. only 10–noon and 3–5. Tours daily Apr.–Oct.

From the palace, you can either head off to the right to visit the Städtische Kunsthalle (City Art Museum) or make a left to see the Jesuitenkirche (Jesuit Church) three blocks away at A–4. The **Jesuitenkirche** is the largest and most important Baroque church in this part of Germany, its immense, rigorously classical facade flanked by graceful dome spires (known as *Spitzhelm* for their resemblance to old-time German helmets) and topped by a massive dome. It was begun in 1733, commissioned by the elector Carl Philip to commemorate his family's return to Catholicism. The church, too, was severely bombed during the war, and most of the internal decorations were lost, including what were probably the most lavish ceiling and dome paintings in the country. But, though plainer now, the airy grandeur of the interior suggests something of its former magnificence. Pause as you go in to look at the ornate wrought-iron gates at the entrance.

The **Städtische Kunsthalle** (City Art Museum) is located at Friedrichsplatz, at the eastern fringe of the Quadratstadt, a 10-minute walk from the Jesuit Church. The building itself is a prime example of Jugendstil (Art Nouveau) architecture, constructed in 1907. Provocative and large-scale modern sculptures stand outside. Inside you'll find one of the largest and best collections of modern art in Germany. All the big names are here, from Manet (including his famous painting *The Execution of the Emperor Maximilian*) to Warhol. Regular exhibitions of major importance are also presented, giving Mannheim a reputation as one of Germany's leading fine-arts centers. *Friedrichsplatz 4.* ☛ *DM 4 adults, DM 2 children.* ☉ *Tues.–Sun. 10–5 (Thurs. noon–5).*

❷ Heidelberg is the next major stop on this tour, but detour south to **Schwetzingen** on A–6—it's only 8 kilometers (5 miles)—to see the palace there, a formal 18th-century building constructed as a summer residence by the Palatinate electors. It's a noble, rose-color building, imposing and harmonious; a highlight is the charming Rococo theater in one wing, site of a music and opera festival each May and June. Another main attraction is the extensive park, a blend of formal French and informal English styles, with neatly bordered gravel walks trailing off into the dark woodland. The 18th-century planners of this delightful park had fun adding such touches as an exotic mosque, complete with minarets and a shimmering pool (although they got a little confused and gave the building a very German Baroque portal), and the "Classical ruin," virtually de rigueur for landscape gardeners of this period. Another rare pleasure awaits you if you're in Schwetzingen in April, May, or June: The town is Germany's asparagus center, and fresh-asparagus dishes dominate the menu of every local restaurant.

Tour 2: Heidelberg

❸ And so on to **Heidelberg,** 10 kilometers (6 miles) northeast. If any city in Germany encapsulates the spirit of the country, it is Heidelberg. Scores of poets and composers—virtually the entire 19th-century German Romantic movement—have sung its praises. Goethe and Mark Twain both fell in love here: the German writer with a beautiful young woman, the American with the city itself. Sigmund Romberg set his operetta *The Student Prince* in the city; Carl Maria von Weber wrote his lushly Romantic opera *Der Freischütz (The Marksman)* here. Composer Robert Schumann was a student at the university. It was the university, the oldest in the country, that gave impetus to the artistic movement that claimed Heidelberg as its own, but the natural beauty of the city—embraced by mountains, forests, vineyards, and the Neckar River, and crowned by its ruined castle—provided the materials for their trade. The campaign they waged on behalf of the town has been astoundingly successful. Heidelberg's fame is out of all proportion to its size; more than 2½ million visitors crowd its streets every year. If you want to find the *feine Heidelberg* (fine Heidelberg) of poet Viktor von Scheffel's day, avoid visiting in summer. Late fall, when the vines turn a faded gold, or early spring, with the first green shoots of the year appearing, can be captivating. Best of all, visit in the depths of winter, when hoary river mists creep through the narrow streets of the old town and awaken the ghosts of a romantic past.

Heidelberg was the political center of the Rhineland Palatinate. At the end of the Thirty Years' War (1618–1648), the elector Carl Ludwig married his daughter to the brother of Louis XIV in hopes of bringing peace to the Rhineland. But when the elector's son died without an heir, Louis XIV used the marriage alliance as an excuse to claim Heidelberg, and, in 1689, the town was sacked and laid to waste. Four years later he sacked the town again. From its ashes arose what you see today: a Baroque town built on Gothic foundations, with narrow, twisting streets and alleyways. The new Heidelberg changed under the influence of U.S. army barracks and industrial development stretching into the suburbs, but the old heart of the city remains intact, exuding the spirit of romantic Germany.

Extending west to east through the old town is **Hauptstrasse,** an elegant pedestrian mall that runs straight as an arrow for ½ mile to the main square, **Marktplatz.** This tour will take you down Hauptstrasse, where you can explore the attractions there and on its narrow side streets before going on to the number-one sight, the castle. You can then visit the rest of the town around Marktplatz.

Numbers in the margin correspond to points of interest on the Heidelberg map.

④ As you walk down Hauptstrasse, the **university**—or part of it anyway; there are four separate university complexes in the town—enfolds you almost immediately On Brunnengasse, a lane to your left, is the anatomy wing, a former monastery taken over by the university in 1801. What had been a chapel became a dissecting laboratory; the sacristy became a morgue.

Out on Hauptstrasse again, pause in front of the **Haus zum Riesen** (the Giant's House), so called because the local worthy who built it in 1707 (using stone from the destroyed castle) put up the larger-than-life statue of himself that you see above the front door. As you continue, on your right will be the Protestant **Providence Church,** built by the elector Carl Ludwig in the mid-16th century, and the richly ornate door-
⑤ way of the **Wormser Hof,** former Heidelberg seat of the bishops of Worms. Look at its lead-paned Renaissance oriel (bay window) on the second floor: It's one of the finest in the city.

Opposite, on the left in a Baroque palace, is Heidelberg's leading mu-
⑥ seum, the **Kurpfälzisches Museum** (Electoral Palatinate Museum). Its collections chart the history of Heidelberg. Among the exhibits are two contrasting standouts. One is a replica of the jaw of Heidelberg Man, a key link in the evolutionary chain thought to date from a half-million years ago; the original was unearthed near the city in 1907. You'll need rare powers of imagination to get much of a sense of this early ancestor from just his (or her) jaw, however. The other attraction pre-
★ sents no such problems. It's the **Twelve Apostles Altarpiece,** one of the largest and finest works of early Renaissance sculptor Tilman Riemenschneider. Its exquisite detailing and technical sophistication are matched by the simple faith that radiates from the faces of the Apostles. On the top floor of the museum there's a rich range of 19th-century German paintings and drawings, many depicting Heidelberg. *Hauptstr. 97. ☞ DM 4 adults, children free (free for all Sun. and public holidays). ☉ Tues.–Sun. 10–5 (Wed. 10–9).*

TIME OUT Turn down the small street, Baumgasse, next to the museum and slip into the cool, dark interior of the **Schnitzelbank.** It's been a favorite student

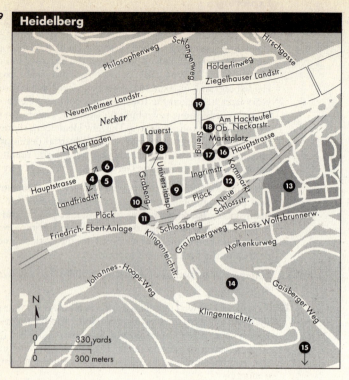

Heidelberg

haunt for more than a century, and the walls are covered with photographs of the student fraternities that have met here through the years.

7 From the museum, you're two blocks from the **Old University,** founded
in 1386 and rebuilt during the early 18th century for the elector Johann Wilhelm. Behind it, in Augustinerstrasse, is the former students'
8 prison, the **Studentenkarzer,** where, from 1712 to 1914, unruly students were incarcerated (tradition dictated that students couldn't be
thrown into the town jail). The students could be held for up to 14
days; they were left to subsist on bread and water for the first three
but thereafter were allowed to attend lectures, receive guests, and have
food brought in from the outside. A stay in the jail became as coveted
as a scar inflicted in the university's fencing clubs. There's bravado,
even poetic flair, to be deciphered in the graffiti of two centuries that
cover the walls and ceiling of the narrow cell. ☛ *DM 1.50 adults, DM
1 children.* ☉ *Apr.–Oct., Tues.–Sat. 10–noon and 2–5; Nov.–Mar.,
Tues.–Sat. 10–1.*

9 Across Universitätsplatz (University Square) is the **New University,**
built between 1930 and 1932 with funds raised in the United States
by a former American student at the university who became U.S. ambassador to Germany, J. G. Schurman. The ancient section you see incorporated in the new building is all that remains of the old city walls.
It's the **Hexenturm,** the Witches' Tower, where witches were locked up
in the Middle Ages.

Opposite the New University, on the street called Plöck, is the univer-
10 sity library, the **Universitätsbibliothek.** Its 1.5 million volumes include

the 14th-century *Manesse Codex,* a collection of medieval songs and poetry once performed in the courts of Germany by the Minnesänger. *Plöck 107–109.* ☞ *Free.* ☽ *Mon.–Sat. 10–7 Easter–Nov. 1, Sun. and holidays 11–4).*

⑪ Across from the library is the city's oldest parish church, the Gothic church of **St. Peter.** Look around in its graveyard; the graves of many leading citizens are here, some dating from more than 500 years ago. The Baroque building you see immediately east of the church was originally a Jesuit seminary, later became a lunatic asylum, and is now a students' dormitory.

⑫ From here, continue along Plöck to the **Königstuhl funicular,** which hoists visitors to the Königstuhl heights, 1,860 feet above Heidelberg, stopping at the ruined **castle** on the way. The round-trip fare to the castle ⑬ and back is DM 4.50 for adults and DM 2.90 for children; the 17-minute journey to the Königstuhl heights and back costs DM 7 for adults, DM 5 for children. The funicular leaves every 20 minutes in the morning and every 10 minutes in the afternoon. A winding road provides a slower way up to the castle; if you take it you'll be following in the footsteps of generations of earlier visitors. (You can always walk down from the castle if you want to pretend to be Mark Twain but don't fancy the hike up.)

The castle was already in ruins when Germany's 19th-century Romantics fell under its spell, drawn by the mystery of its Gothic turrets and Renaissance walls etched against the verdant background of the thick woodland above Heidelberg. The oldest parts still standing date from the 15th century, though most of the great complex was built in the Renaissance and Baroque styles of the 16th and 17th centuries, when the castle was the seat and power base of the Palatinate electors. What's most striking is the architectural variety of the building, vivid proof of changing tastes through the years. There's even an "English wing," built in 1610 by the elector Friedrich V for his teenage Scottish bride, Elizabeth Stuart; its plain square-windowed facade appears positively foreign in comparison with the more opulent styles of the rest of the castle. (The enamored Friedrich also had a charming garden laid out for his young bride; its imposing arched entryway, the Elisabethentor, was put up overnight to surprise her on her 19th birthday.) The architectural highlight, however, remains the Renaissance courtyard—harmonious, graceful, and ornate.

★ Allow at least two hours to tour the complex—and expect long lines in summer (up to 30 minutes is usual). Even if you have to wait, however, you should make a point of seeing the **Heidelberger Fass** and the fascinating **Apothekenmuseum.** The Heidelberger Fass is an enormous wine barrel in the cellars, made from 130 oak trees and capable of holding 49,000 gallons. It was used to hold wines paid as tax by winegrowers in the Palatinate. During the rule of the elector Carl Philip, the barrel was guarded by the court jester, a Tyrolean dwarf called Perkeo. Legend has it that, small or not, he could consume frighteningly large quantities of wine—he was said to have been the most prodigious drinker in Germany—and that he died when he drank a glass of water by mistake. A statue of Perkeo stands opposite the massive barrel. The Apothekenmuseum is a delight, filled with ancient carboys and other flagons and receptacles (each with a carefully painted enamel label), beautifully made scales, little drawers, shelves, a marvelous reconstruction of an 18th-century apothecary's shop, dried beetles and toads, and a mummy with a full head of hair. *Castle* ☞ *DM 4 adults, DM 2 children; for tour of castle courtyard and Fass, DM 2 adults,*

DM 1 children. ✆ *Daily 9–5. Guided tours 9–noon and 1:30–4. Apothekenmuseum* ☞ *DM 3 adults, DM 1.50 children.* ✆ *Mid–Mar.–Oct., daily 10–5; Nov.–Mar., weekends only 11–5.*

The castle is floodlit in the summer, and in June and September fireworks are shot from the terraces. In August, the castle is the setting for an open-air theater festival. Performances of *The Student Prince* figure prominently.

14 ★ 15   There are fine views of the old town from the castle terraces, but for an even better view, ride the funicular up to either of the next two stops, **Molkenkur** and, at the summit, **Königstuhl.** If the weather's clear, you can see south as far as the Black Forest and west to the Vosges Mountains of France.

TIME OUT   Both the Molkenkur and Königstuhl stops have comfortable restaurants with terraces commanding sweeping views. If you don't want a full-fledged lunch, stop in for just a cup of coffee and a pastry.

Back in town, walk toward the river from the funicular station to **Kornmarkt.** It's one of the oldest squares in Heidelberg, graced with a fine Baroque statue of the Virgin Mary. The impressive building on the corner of Mittelgasse was once Heidelberg's foremost hostelry, the Prinz Karl, where Mark Twain stayed in 1874. A few years earlier it had been used as a barracks by Bismarck's triumphant Prussian army as they swept through the Rhineland forcibly uniting Germany. The young Prince Wilhelm von Preussen, later Kaiser Wilhelm I, was among the soldiers stationed there; prudently, he brought along his own camp bed. The **16**   **Rathaus** (Town Hall), a stately Baroque building dating from 1701, faces you now. Be here at 7 PM to hear the melodious chimes that ring out from the building. The west side of the Rathaus fronts Heidelberg's market square, the Marktplatz. It was here, in the towering shadow **17**   of the 14th-century **Heiliggeistkirche** (Church of the Holy Ghost) that criminals were tortured and decapitated and witches were burned. The church itself fell victim to the plundering General Tilly, leader of the Catholic League, during the Thirty Years' War. Tilly loaded the church's greatest treasure, the *Biblioteka Palatina*, at the time the largest library in Germany, onto 500 carts and trundled it off to Rome, where he presented it to the pope. Few of the volumes found their way back to Heidelberg. At the end of the 17th century, French troops plundered the church again, destroying the family tombs of the Palatinate electors; only the 15th-century tomb of Elector Ruprecht III and his wife, Elisabeth von Hohenzollern, remain today.

★ 18   Opposite the church, on Hauptstrasse, you'll see the elaborate Renaissance facade of the **Hotel zum Ritter,** all curlicues, columns, and gables. It takes its name from the statue of a Roman knight ("Ritter") atop one of the many gables. Its French builder, Charles Bélier, had the Latin inscription *Persta Invicta Venus* added to the facade in gold letters—"Beauty, Remain Unconquerable." It was an injunction that seems to have had the desired effect: This was the only Renaissance building in the city to have been spared the attentions of the invading French in 1689 and 1693. Between 1695 and 1705, it was used as Heidelberg's town hall; later it became an inn. Today it's the most atmospheric hotel in town (*see* Dining and Lodging, *below*).

19   Skirt the cathedral, cross the former fish market, the Fischmarkt, and turn down picturesque Steingasse. Within a few steps you'll have reached the river and the romantically turreted **Alte Brücke** (Old Bridge). It's the fifth bridge to be built here since medieval times, its

predecessors having suffered various unhappy fates (one was destroyed by ice floes). The elector Carl Theodor, who built it in 1786–1788, must have been confident that it would last: He had a statue of himself put on it, the plinth decorated with Neckar nymphs (river maidens). Just to be on the safe side, he also put up a statue of the saint appointed to guard over it, St. John Nepomuk. You can walk onto the bridge from the Old Town under a portcullis spanned by two Baroque towers, each capped with a *Spitzhelm* spire. In the left (west) tower are three dank dungeons that once held common criminals. Between the towers, above the gate, were more salubrious lockups, with views of the river and the castle; these were reserved for debtors. Above the portcullis you'll see a memorial plaque that pays warm tribute to the Austrian forces who helped Heidelberg beat back a French attempt to capture the bridge in 1799. From the bridge, or from the road leading along the other bank of the river, you'll have some of the finest views of the old town and the castle above. For the best view of all, climb
★ up the steep, winding **Schlangenweg** (Snake Path) to **Philosophenweg,** a path through the woods above the river. Be here as the sun sets, turning the castle to gold, for a vision to cherish for a lifetime.

Tour 3: Along the Burgenstrasse

Numbers in the margin correspond to points of interest on the Neckar Valley map.

From Heidelberg, drive down the Neckar Valley on the Burgenstrasse, following the bank of the river through a gentle landscape of orchards and vineyards. Wooded hills crowned with castles rise above the soft-flowing water.

⑳ The first town you'll reach is **Neckargemünd,** just 12 kilometers (8 miles) upstream from Heidelberg. Once it was a bustling river town; today it's a sleepy sort of place, though it can make a good base from which to see Heidelberg if you want to avoid the summertime crowds there.

㉑ Eight kilometers (5 miles) farther, perched impregnably on a hill, is **Dilsberg Castle,** one of the few castles hereabouts to have withstood General Tilly's otherwise all-conquering forces in the Thirty Years' War. Until the students' jail in Heidelberg was built, its dungeons were used to accommodate the university's more unruly dissidents. The view from its battlements over the valley and the green expanse of the Odenwald Forest beyond is worth the climb.

㉒ Opposite Dilsberg is **Neckarsteinach,** known as the **Vierburgenstadt** (Town of the Four Castles), for the fairly obvious reason that there are four castles here. They form one large complex—the **Schadeck**—most of which dates from the 12th century. What remains is largely ruins Today it's mostly ruined, but the sections that are still intact comprise the baronial residence of an aristocratic German family.

TIME OUT As along the Rhine, a number of the castles that stand on the Neckar have been converted into hotels. The castle above the pretty little town
㉓ of **Hirschhorn,** 10 kilometers (16 miles) east of Neckarsteinach, is one such conversion (*see* Dining and Lodging, *below*). If you don't plan to stay here, a stop for lunch would certainly be worthwhile. The view is superb. If you prefer a less formal lunchtime layover, carry on to the next
㉔ village—**Eberbach**—just a few miles up the valley, and visit the **Krabbenstein.** It's a 17th-century inn, one of the oldest along the river. The walls are decorated with frescoes that illustrate trades carried on in the village since the Middle Ages.

25 Eight kilometers (5 miles) beyond Eberbach, there's another castle, this one standing above the village of **Zwingenberg,** its medieval towers thrusting through the dark woodland. Some say it's the most romantic of all the castles along the Neckar (the one at Heidelberg excepted). It's owned by the margraves of Baden and is open on a limited basis only, but if you happen along at the right time, stop in to admire the frescoed 15th-century chapel and the collection of hunting trophies. ☞ *DM 3.* ⊙ *May–Sept., Tues., Fri., and Sun. only 2–4.*

26 The little town of **Mosbach** is 16 kilometers (10 miles) up the valley. It's one of the most charming towns on the Neckar, and its ancient market square, Marktplatz, contains one of Germany's most exquisite half-timbered buildings. It's the early 17th-century **Palmsches Haus,** its upper stories smothered with intricate timbering. The **Rathaus,** built 50 years earlier, is a modest affair by comparison.

27 Four and a half kilometers (3 miles) south of Mosbach you'll see the massive circular bulk of **Hornberg Castle** rising above the woods that drop to the riverbank. The road up to the castle leads through vineyards that have been providing excellent dry white wines for centuries. Today the castle is part hotel and restaurant (*see* Dining and Lodging, *below*) and part museum. During the 16th century it was home to the larger-than-life knight Götz von Berlichingen (1480–1562). Von Berlichingen was a remarkable fellow. When he lost his right arm fighting in a petty dynastic squabble, the Landshut War of Succession, in 1504, he had a blacksmith fashion an iron one for him. The original designs for this fearsome artificial limb are on view in the castle, as is a suit of armor that belonged to him. Scenes from his life are also represented. For most Germans, the rambunctious knight is best remembered for a remark he delivered to the Palatinate elector that was faithfully reproduced by Goethe in his play about von Berlichingen (called, simply, *Götz von Berlichingen).* Responding to a reprimand from the elector, von Berlichingen told him, more or less, to "kiss my ass" (the original German is substantially more earthy). To this day, the polite version of this insult is known as a "Götz von Berlichingen"; practice it on the Autobahn when a BMW screeches on its brakes, headlights flashing, inches from your rear bumper. ☞ *DM 2.50 adults, DM 1 children.* ⊙ *Apr.–Nov., daily 9–5.*

28 During the Peasants' War (1525), Götz von Berlichingen and his troops destroyed the fine medieval castle of **Horneck,** 5 kilometers (3 miles) upriver. It was subsequently rebuilt and stands in all its medieval glory. Once it was owned by the Teutonic Order of Knights; today it has a more mundane role as the retirement home of a German charity.

TIME OUT A few bends of the river bring you to one of the best preserved of the Neckar castles, the 15th-century **Burg Guttenberg.** Within its stout stone walls is a restaurant with fine views of the river valley. The castle is also home to Europe's leading center for the study and protection of birds of prey, and some are released on demonstration flights from the castle walls, from March through November, daily at 11 and 3.

29 30 Two spas now await the tired traveler: **Bad Rappenau** and **Bad Wimpfen.** Bad Rappenau's brine baths are said to ease not just aching limbs but asthma, rheumatism, and circulatory problems, too. It's an attractive little town, with a picturesque Rathaus (Town Hall) that was once a moated castle. However, it's Bad Wimpfen, 10 kilometers (6 miles) farther, that is of greater historic and aesthetic interest. The Romans founded it, building a fortress here and a bridge across the Neckar in the 1st century AD. By the early Middle Ages, Bad Wimpfen had become an imperial center; the 12th-century emperor Barbarossa built his largest palace here. Much of what remains of it can be visited, including the imperial living quarters with their stately pillared windows, from which the royal inhabitants enjoyed fine views of the river below. *Kaiserpl.* ☎ *07063/53151. Guided tours are given daily but must be booked in advance.*

★ After you've seen the fortress you'll want to explore the small, winding streets of the historic center, a picture-postcard jumble of Gothic and Renaissance buildings. **Klostergasse**, a stage set of a street, is the standout. If you want to see the town in more detail, follow the marked walking tour; it begins at the Rathaus and is marked by signs bearing the town arms, an eagle with a key in its beak. Highlights of the tour are two churches: the early Gothic Ritterstiftskirche (Knights' Church) of **Sts. Peter and Paul;** and the **parish church** on the market square, Marktplatz. Sts. Peter and Paul stands on a charming square, shaded by gnarled chestnut trees. The rough-hewn Romanesque facade is the oldest part of the church, left standing when the town ran out of money after rebuilding the remainder of the church in Gothic style during the 13th century. The outline of the walls of this original building are clearly visible on the floor inside. The cloisters are delightful, an example of German Gothic at its purest and most uncluttered. In the parish church, be sure to see the 13th-century stained glass; it's among the oldest in the country.

③ Motorbike fans won't want to miss the town of **Neckarsulm,** 10 kilometers (6 miles) up the valley. It's a busy little industrial center, home of the German automobile manufacturer Audi and site of the **Deutsches Zweirad Museum** (German Motorcycle Museum). It's close to the factory, where motorbikes were first manufactured in Germany. Among its 180 exhibits are the world's first mass-produced machine (the Hildebrand and Wolfmüller), a number of famous racing machines, and a rare Daimler machine, the first one made by that legendary name. The museum also has an exhibit of old bicycles, the oldest dating from 1817, and early automobiles. All are arranged over four floors in a handsome 400-year-old building that belonged to the Teutonic Order of Knights until 1806. *Urbanstr. 11.* ☛ *DM 7 adults, DM 4 children, DM 14 for a family ticket.* ☉ *Weekdays 9–noon and 1:30–5, weekends and holidays 9–5.*

㉜ It's 6 kilometers (4 miles) now to the city of **Heilbronn.** The city owes its name to a "holy well," or Heiligen Brunnen, a little fountain that bubbles up out of the ground by the church of St. Kilian; it owes its fame to the Romantic German classic *Das Käthchen von Heilbronn,* by early 19th-century writer Heinrich von Kleist. The virtuous, put-upon Käthchen was modeled by von Kleist on the daughter of Heilbronn's lord mayor, and the family home still stands on the west side of the central square, Marktplatz. Its ornate oriel, decorated with figures of four of the prophets, makes it easy to spot.

Most of the leading sights in Heilbronn are grouped in and around Marktplatz, dominated by the sturdy **Rathaus,** built in the Gothic style in 1417 and remodeled in the Renaissance. Set into its clean-lined Renaissance facade beneath the steeply eaved red roof is a magnificently
★ ornate 16th-century **clock.** It's divided into four distinct parts. The lowest is an astronomical clock, showing the day of the week, the month, and the year. Above it is the main clock; note how its hour hand is larger than the minute hand, a convention common in the 16th century. Above this there's a smaller dial that shows the phases of the sun and the moon. Then, at the topmost level, suspended from a delicate stone

surround, there's a bell, struck alternately by the two angels that stand on either side of it. Be here at noon, when the whole elaborate mechanism swings into action. As the hour strikes, an angel at the base of the clock sounds a trumpet; another turns an hour glass and counts the hours with a scepter. Simultaneously, the twin golden rams between them charge each other and lock horns while a cockerel spreads its wings and crows.

Behind the market square is Heilbronn's most famous church, the **Kilianskirche** (Church of St. Kilian), dedicated to the Irish monk who brought Christianity to the Rhineland in the Dark Ages and lies buried in Würzburg. Its lofty Gothic tower was capped in the early 16th century with a fussy, lanternlike structure that ranks as the first major Renaissance work north of the Alps. At its summit there's a soldier carrying a banner decorated with the city arms. Walk around the church to the south side (the side opposite the main entrance) to see the well that gave the city its name.

Tour 4: Stuttgart

From Heilbronn it's a 49-kilometer (30-mile) drive south on B–27 to **Stuttgart.** While the road follows along the Neckar only for a short distance, Stuttgart is right on the river (as is Tübingen, the next and final stop on this tour) and can be considered a logical extension of our tour of the Neckar Valley.

Stuttgart is a place of fairly extreme contradictions. It has been called, among other things, "Germany's biggest small town" and "the city where work is a pleasure." For centuries, Stuttgart, whose name derives from *Stutengarten,* or "stud farm," remained a pastoral backwater along the Neckar. Then the Industrial Revolution propelled the city into the machine age, after which it was leveled in World War II. Since then, Stuttgart has regained its position as one of Germany's top industrial centers.

Here, *schaffen*—"to do, make, produce"—is all. This is Germany's "can do" city, whose native sons have turned out Mercedes-Benz and Porsche cars, Bosch electrical equipment, and a host of other products exported worldwide. It is only fitting that one end of the main street, Königstrasse, should be emblazoned with a neon sign proclaiming Bosch on a high rise, and the other end shines with the Mercedes star.

Yet Stuttgart is also a city of culture and the arts, with world-class museums and a famous ballet company. Moreover, it's the domain of fine local wines; the vineyards actually approach the city center in a rim of green hills. In fact, forests, vineyards, meadows, fields, and orchards comprise more than half of the city, which is enclosed on three sides by seemingly endless woods.

An ideal introduction to the contrasts of Stuttgart is a guided city bus tour (*see* Guided Tours *in* Heidelberg and the Neckar Valley Essentials, *below*). Included is a visit to the needle-nose TV tower, high on a mountaintop above the city, affording stupendous views. Built in 1956, it was the first of its kind in the world.

On your own, any exploration of Stuttgart would start at the Hauptbahnhof (main train station) end of Königstrasse, a pedestrian shopping street, continuing on to the **Schlossplatz** (Castle or Royal Square), a huge square enclosed by reconstructed royal palaces, with elegant arcades branching off to other stately plazas. The magnificent Baroque

Neues Schloss, now occupied by the Baden-Württemberg state government offices, dominates the square.

Across the street is **Altes Schloss** (Old Castle), the former residence of the counts and dukes of Württemberg. Built as a moated castle around 1320, with wings added during the mid-15th century to turn this into a Renaissance palace, the Altes Schloss was considerably rebuilt between 1948 and 1970 to repair wartime damage. The palace now houses the **Württemberggisches Landesmuseum** (Württemberg State Museum), with imaginative exhibits tracing the development of the area from the Stone Age to modern times. The displays of medieval life are especially noteworthy. ☛ *Free.* ☺ *Tues.–Sun. 10–5, Wed. 10–7.*

Look into the neighboring **Stiftskirche** (Collegiate Church), on Schillerplatz, a late-Gothic church built in 1433–1531, before strolling through the Schlossgarten, on the other side of the Schlossplatz. If you continue in the park across Schillerstrasse, you'll come to the Park Wilhelma, home to botanical gardens and the city's renowned zoo. Here you can walk along the banks of the Neckar River.

★ For lovers of modern art and architecture the high point of a visit to Stuttgart is likely to be the **Staatsgalerie** (State Gallery), reached from the Oberer Schlossgarten by crossing Konrad-Adenauer-Strasse. The old part of the complex, dating from 1843, contains paintings from the Middle Ages through the 19th century, including works by Cranach, Holbein, Hals, Memling, Rubens, Rembrandt, Cézanne, Courbet, and Manet. Connected to the original building is the New State Gallery, designed by British architect James Stirling in 1984 as a melding of classical and modern, sometimes jarring, elements (such as chartreuse window mullions!). Considered one of the most successful Post-Modern buildings, it houses works by such 20th-century artists as Braque, Chagall, de Chirico, Dali, Kandinsky, Klee, Mondrian, and Picasso. Look for Otto Dix's *Grosstadt (Big City)* triptych, which distills the essence of 1920s Germany on canvas. *Konrad-Adenauer-Str. 30–32,* ☎ *0711/212–4050.* ☛ *Free.* ☺ *Wed. and Fri.–Sun. 10–5, Tues. and Thurs. 10–8.*

TIME OUT **Café Königsbau** (Königstr. 28, ☎ 0711/290–787) is a local institution, at once the city's most elegant and most popular café, ideally situated overlooking the Schlossplatz. Stop here for a coffee and a wedge of homemade Swabian apple cake, or a bottle of the locally brewed Dinkelacker beer.

Auto enthusiasts will want to venture somewhat out of town to visit the **Mercedes-Benz Museum,** at the oldest car factory in the world, to view the collection of historic racing and luxury cars on display, as well as pioneering engines for ships and planes. *Mercedesstr. 136, Stuttgart-Untertürkheim,* ☎ *0711/172–2578.* ☛ *Free.* ☺ *Tues.–Sun. 9–5. Closed on holidays.*

At the **Gottlieb Daimler Memorial Workshop,** where the first successful internal combustion engine was perfected in 1883, you can see the tools, blueprints, and models of early cars that helped to pave the way for the Mercedes line. *Taubenheimstr. 13, Stuttgart-Bad Cannstatt,* ☎ *0711/172–2578.* ☛ *Free.* ☺ *Tues.–Sun. 10–4.*

Perhaps only true auto aficionados will venture as far as the **Porsche Museum,** at the Porsche factory in the northern suburb of Zuffenhausen, to view a small but significant collection of legendary Porsche racing cars. Still, serious auto buffs will find the trip worthwhile. *Porschestr.*

42, Stuttgart-Zuffenhausen, ☎ 071/827–5685. ☛ Free. ⊙ Weekdays 9–4, weekends and holidays 9–5.

Tour 5: Tübingen

Following the B–27 south of Stuttgart will bring you back to the Neckar, after about 40 kilometers (25 miles), at the lovely town of Tübingen. The first sign that you're approaching this center of historic interest and charm is the little settlement of **Bebenhausen**, 3 miles outside Tübingen right at the side of the road. If you blink, you'll miss the turnoff, and that would be a shame because the **Zisterzienkloster** (Cistercian monastery) here is really worth a visit. It's rare to find an old monastery so perfectly preserved, particularly one from the late 12th century. Due to the secularization of 1806, the abbot's abode was rebuilt as a hunting **castle** for King Frederick of Württemberg. Expansion and restoration went on as the castle and monastery continued to be a royal residence into this century. Even after the monarchy was dissolved in 1918, the last Württembergs were given lifetime rights here; this came to an end in 1946 with the death of Charlotte, wife of Wilhelm II. For a few years after the war, the state senate convened here; today, both castle and monastery are open to the public, though the castle is open for guided tours only. ☛ *Zisterzienkloster: DM 2. ⊙ Tues.–Fri. 9–noon and 2–5; weekends and holidays 10–noon and 2–5. Hourly guided tours Apr.–Oct., weekends only. ☛ Castle: DM 2.50 adults, DM 2 children. Combined admission for monastery and castle: DM 4 adults, DM 3 children. Guided tours Tues.–Fri. hourly 9–4, weekends and holidays hourly 10–4.*

㉞ With its half-timbered houses, winding alleyways, hilltop location, and views overlooking the Neckar, **Tübingen** is popular with both German and foreign travelers. Dating to the 11th century, the town flourished as a trade center; in fact, Tübingen weights and measures, along with its currency, were the standard through much of the area. The town declined in importance after the 14th century, when it was taken over by the counts of Württemberg. Between the 14th and the 19th centuries, its size hardly changed as it became a university and residential town, its castle the only symbol of ruling power. Too bad, perhaps, for the merchants, but marvelous for visitors: Untouched by wartime bombings or even, it sometimes seems, the passage of time, the little town still has an authentic medieval flavor, providing for many the quintessential German experience.

This isn't to say that Tübingen has been sheltered from the world. In fact, it resonates with a youthful air. Even more than Heidelberg, Tübingen is virtually synonymous with its university, a leading center of learning since it was founded in 1477. Illustrious students of yesteryear include the astronomer Johannes Kepler and the philosopher G.W.F. Hegel. The latter studied at the Protestant theological seminary, which is still one of the cornerstones of the university's international renown in academic circles. One of Hegel's roommates was Friedrich Hölderlin, a great poet of the German Romantic movement—who went mad and died young. Tübingen's population is around 80,000, of which nearly 26,000 are students. During term time, it can be hard to find a seat in pubs and cafés; during vacations, the town sometimes seems deserted. The best way to see and appreciate Tübingen is simply to stroll around, soaking up its age-old atmosphere of quiet erudition.

★
★

The heart of Tübingen's Old City (Altstadt) is the sloping, uneven, cobblestone parallelogram of the **Marktplatz,** dominated by the ornate façade of the Renaissance **Rathaus,** bright with colorful wall paintings and a marvelous astronomical clock (1511). As is common in medieval squares, the marketplace contains a fountain—here, the **Neptune Fountain,** graced with a statue of the sea god. The Rathaus, built around 1435, was altered and expanded for another 150 years or so; its paintings are late-19th-century. The halls and reception rooms are adorned with half-timbering and wall paintings.

TIME OUT The **Gaststätte Lichtenstein,** across from the Rathaus at one corner of the marketplace (and next to the tourist office), is an atmospheric little eatery. Stop for a glass of wine and a plate of Swabian ravioli, *Maultaschen,* or *Käsespätzle* in these low-ceilinged, rustic, and cozy surroundings.

From here, it's just a short stroll to Holzmarkt and the **Stiftskirche** (Collegiate Church). This late-Gothic building is one of Tübingen's finest architectural monuments; and because of the city's peaceful history, many of its original features have lasted through the ages—the stained-glass windows, the choir stalls, the ornate baptismal font, and the elaborate stone pulpit are all originals. It's here that the dukes of Württemberg from the 15th to the 17th century are interred. ⊘ *Daily 9–5 (Nov.–Jan. 9–4).*

On and near Holzmarkt you'll also find evidence of Tübingen's role as a center of publishing (the first books were published here in 1498). Around the corner, on Münzgasse, is the former headquarters of Cotta, a leading publishing house. And just across from the church is the Heckenhauer bookstore, in a building where writer Herman Hesse lived for a few years.

From here, follow Neckargasse or Bursagasse south to the scenic bank of the Neckar, with, in season, punters to rival Oxford's (*see* Guided Tours, *below*). The riverside walk here ends at the residential house known as the **Hölderlinturm,** where the "mad poet" Friedrich Hölderlin resided with the Zimmer family for 36 years, until his death in 1843. Today the building is a museum commemorating the poet's life and work. If you don't speak German, you may want to arrange for an English tour to get the most out of the exhibits; you can also acquaint yourself with a couple of Hölderlin poems in translation to get a sense of the writer's Romantic imagery and notably "modern" style. ☎ 07071/22040. ☛ *DM 3 adults, DM 2 children. Tours weekends and holidays at 5 PM; English tours available by arrangement.* ⊘ *Tues.–Fri. 10–12 and 2–5, weekends and holidays 2–5.*

Past the Hölderlinturm is the 15th-century **Bursa,** a former student dormitory. Farther on along is the **Evangelisches Stift** (Protestant Seminary), richer perhaps in history than in immediate visual interest—from the outside it's hard to see that this place has for centuries served as a center of European intellectual thought. It was founded in 1534 partly as a political move during the Reformation; the Protestant duke of Württemberg, Ulrich, wanted facilities to train Protestant clerics so that Protestantism could retain its foothold in the region. (He would have been disappointed to know that a major Catholic seminary arrived here in 1817.) Since then, however, philosophical rather than political considerations have prevailed within these walls. Hegel, Hölderlin, and the philosopher Schelling all shared one room here during their studies: Even in a university town, this seems an unusually high concentration of brain power.

The narrow steps and cobblestones of **Burgsteige** pave one of the oldest thoroughfares in the town, and it's lined with equally aged houses. The street's name translates as "Castle Climb," which is at least honest advertising—you'll be more than a little breathless when you finally emerge before **Hohentübingen.** The castle, a replacement for 11th-century fortifications, dates from around 1600, its portal fitted out as a Roman-style triumphal arch in true Renaissance spirit. Like so many sites in southern Germany, it was a bone of contention during the Thirty Years' War, and the French blew up one of its towers in 1647. Now it serves an altogether more peaceable function, occupied not by soldiers but by several university departments, including that of classical archaeology. For tourists, a main attraction is the magnificent view over river and town.

As the university has grown, so has Tübingen expanded, spreading more modern buildings and housing developments across the hillsides around town. North of the Neckar, above the city, are two of Tübingen's favorite modern attractions: the parks and greenhouses of its **Botanische Garten** (Botanical Garden, Hartmeyerstr. 123) and the exhibition space of the **Kunsthalle.** The huge Cézanne retrospective in 1993 set all-time records for numbers of visitors. The Kunsthalle generates a special kind of "art tourism," making it nearly impossible to find lodging in Tübingen if a particularly popular show is on (watch out for Renoir in 1996). *Philosophenweg 76,* ☏ *07071/96910.* ☛ *Varies depending on the show: for Renoir, it will probably be DM 12 adults, DM 8 children.* ☉ *Tues.–Sun. 10–6 (Tues. and Fri. 10–8).*

What to See and Do with Children

The Heidelberg tourist office issues a special publication, *Heidelberg fur Kinder* ("Heidelberg for Children"), that lists activities and attractions. Pick it up free from any of the city's three tourist offices. The city has a **zoo** on the banks of the Neckar on Tiergartenstrasse. ☛ *DM 7 adults, DM 3 children, DM 4 senior citizens and students.* ☉ *Apr.–Sept., daily 9–7; Oct.–Mar., daily 9–5.*

On the Königstuhl heights above the city there's a children's park and small fairground, the **Märchenparadies,** with fairy-tale tableaux, rides, a miniature railroad, and more. ☛ *DM 4 adults, DM 3 children.* ☉ *Mid-Mar.–mid-Oct., daily 10–6 (July and Aug. 10–7).*

Children love the ride up the mountain on the funicular, too (*see* Heidelberg, *above*). Farther along the Neckar, just outside Mosbach, the reindeer are for real at the **Wildpark Schwarzach.** ☛ *DM 3 adults, DM 2 children.* ☉ *Mid-Mar.–Nov., daily 9–6.*

The **Auto and Technik Museum** at Sinsheim, 20 kilometers (12 miles) south of Neckargemünd, exhibits any- and everything having to do with machines and transportation, from cars to trains to airplanes. ☛ *DM 14 adults, DM 8 children.* ☉ *Daily 9–6.*

There is more for car lovers 32 kilometers (20 miles) east of Heilbronn on the Burgstrasse at Langenburg. The **Deutsches Automuseum** (☏ 07905/1041) has a substantial collection of veteran cars and vintage racing vehicles. ☉ *Easter–Oct., daily 8:30–noon and 1:30–6 (Sun. 1–5 off-season).*

Twenty kilometers (12 miles) south of Heilbronn, on B–27, you'll find one of southern Germany's best fun parks, the **Freizeitpark Tripsdrill,** located at Cleebronn/Tripsdill. ☛ *DM 22 adults, DM 19 children.* ☉ *Apr.–Oct., daily 9–6.*

North of Heilbronn on the same road are some intriguing caves, the **Eberstädter Höhlen.** ⊘*Daily 10–4.*

Youngsters are sure to be thrilled by the star show put on at the **Carl Zeiss Planetarium** in Stuttgart's Mittlerer Schlossgarten. Only the those over six are allowed into the regular showings; but children under the age of six get their own showing every Saturday at 2. ☛ *DM 8 adults, DM 5 children.*

Mannheim also has a **planetarium,** with a special show for children on Sundays and holidays at 3 PM. The regular program, which changes every few months and is geared to stargazers of all ages, runs other days at 3 and at other times during the week (closed Mondays). *Wilhelm-Varnholt-Allee 1,* ☎ *0621/415–692.* ☛ *DM 8 adults, DM 5 children.*

Mannheim's Museumsschiff (Museum Ship) is a restored paddle-wheel steamboat filled with information on boats and machines through the ages. *Am Museumsufer, by the Kurpfalz Bridge.* ☛ *Free.* ⊘ *Tues.–Sun. 10–5 (Wed. 10–8).*

Stuttgart's **700-foot television tower** was a technological sensation when it was built in 1954–56, a world pioneer in reinforced concrete structures. The lift ride costs DM 5 for adults, DM 3 for children. The last ride down is at 11 PM. Also popular is Stuttgart's **zoo,** the **Wihelma.**

The **Auto- und Spielzeug-Museum "Boxstop,"** in Tübingen is devoted to cars and toys—something for everyone. *Brunnenstr. 18,* ☎ *07071/929–020.* ☛ *DM 4 adults, DM 3 children, children under 10 free.* ⊘ *Apr.–Oct., Wed. and Fri.–Sun. 10–noon and 2–5; Nov.–Mar., Sun. and holidays or by arrangement.*

Off the Beaten Track

In Heidelberg, escape the crowds by crossing the Theodor Heuss Bridge to the north bank of the Neckar and climbing the heights above the river along the path called Philosophenweg.

Along the Neckar Valley road (B–27), all the small valleys—the locals call them "Klingen"—that cut north into the Odenwald are off-the-beaten-track territory. Most atmospheric of them all is the **Wolfsschlucht,** which starts below the castle at Zwingenberg. The dank, shadowy little gorge features in Carl Maria von Weber's opera *Der Freischütz.* If you see a vulture circling overhead, don't be alarmed. It's likely to be from Claus Fentzloff's unusual **aviary** at Guttenberg Castle (*see* Burg Guttenberg, *above*).

For unusual museums in Neckarland, try the **Lucky-Charm Museum** in Bad Wimpfen (Kronengässchen 2; open Fri. 4–8, weekends 11–8) and the **Bonsai** museum of miniature trees in Heidelberg (Mannheimerstr. 401; open weekdays 10–6, weekends 10–4).

In Stuttgart, architecture buffs should seek out the **Weissenhofsiedlung** (Weissenhof Colony), a minicity created for a 1927 exhibition of the "New Home." Using a zoning plan designed by Mies van der Rohe, 16 leading architects from five countries—among them Mies van der Rohe, Le Corbusier, and Walter Gropius—were invited to create residences that offered optimal living conditions at affordable prices. The still-functioning colony, which had a significant influence on the development of 20th-century housing, is situated on a hillside overlooking Friedrich-Ebert-Strasse. To get there from the city center, take Tram 10 toward Killesberg to the Kunstakadamie stop. The Stuttgart tourist office issues a brochure indicating which architects designed the various homes.

Near Heilbronn, at Bad Friedrichshall, a still-functioning **salt mine** welcomes visitors. Call 07131/959–283 if you'd like to take a tour of the works.

A classic Tübingen walk goes down from the castle to the little chapel called the **Wurmlinger Kapelle,** taking about two hours. On the way it's customary to stop off at the restaurant Schwärzlocher Hof to sample the good food and great views. The tourist office can give you a map detailing the way.

SHOPPING

Heidelberg

Heidelberg's **Hauptstrasse,** or main street, a pedestrian zone lined with shops, sights, and restaurants, stretches more than half a mile through the heart of town. Look here for the glass and crystal for which the Neckar Valley region is renowned. You can find a selection at the shop **Edm. König** (Hauptstr. 124, am Uni-Platz, ☎ 06221/20929), along with a selection of porcelain, ceramics, and handicrafts. The store **unholtz** (Hauptstr. 160, ☎ 06221/20964) carries Solingen, a famous German tableware line, maker of some of the best knives in Europe.

The region can also be a good place to find reasonably priced German antiques. Look in at **Spiess & Walther** (Friedrich-Ebert-Anlage 23a, ☎ 06221/22233) for an interesting selection. Antique hounds can also check out **B & B Antiques** (Sofienstr. 27, ☎ 06221/23003).

Heidelberg has many tempting **markets.** On Wednesday and Sunday mornings go to the central market square, Marktplatz; on Tuesday and Friday mornings, make for Friedrich-Ebert-Platz. On Sunday there's a flea market; the weekdays' offerings include produce and other edibles. There's also a flea market every other Saturday in the Heidelberg suburb of Dehner.

Heilbronn

Wine is the chief product of the Neckar region, and Heilbronn is the place to buy it. The city's internationally renowned wine festival (the Weindorf), during the second week of September, showcases more than 200 wines from the Heilbronn region alone. Outside festival time, you'll find numerous shops stocking wine along Heilbronn's central pedestrian shopping zone, and you can also buy directly from vineyards. A good, no-frills wine outlet is the **Amalienhof** (Lukas-Cranach-Weg 5, ☎ 07131/251–735). Only the vineyard's own wines are for sale—80 of them, to be precise.

Mannheim

Stores here carry some of the best in German fashions. Clothes by Jil Sander, a famous German women's designer, are stocked at the **CC-Boutique** (No. 17 Q–7 Street, ☎ 0621/25148). Or browse through the city's stylish shopping mall, the **Kurfürsten Passage,** both on P–7 Street.

Neckarzimmern

Of the numerous vineyards along the road (B–27) between Heidelberg and Heilbronn, those around **Gundelsheim** are judged to be the best, but for sheer historical worth you can't beat a bottle from the **Hornberg Castle** estate, which once stocked the table of the knight Götz von

Berlichingen. The vineyards here belong to a fine castle hotel (*see* Tour 3, *above, and* Dining and Lodging, *below*); you can also buy wine by the bottle or the case (☎ 06261/5001).

In Neckarzimmern you can get a closer look at why the Neckar Valley is famous for its glassware. The factory **Franz Kaspar,** known for its fine crystal, gives tours that demonstrate the manufacturing process; it also has an exhibition space and an outlet with a wide selection and some special offers. *Hauptstr. 11,* ☎ *06261/923–014.* ☉ *Weekdays 8–6:30, Sat. 8–2. Tours: weekdays 8–3, Sat. 8–noon.*

Stuttgart

Two of Germany's top men's fashion designers—Hugo Boss and Ulli Knecht—base themselves in Stuttgart. These and other men's labels are well represented at the exclusive men's boutique of **Holy's** (Königstr. 54, ☎ 0711/221–872).

Designer jewelry is the specialty of **Günter Krauss's** glittering shop (Kronprinzstr. 21, ☎ 0711/297–395). The design of the shop itself—walls of white Italian marble with gilded fixtures and mirrors—has won many awards.

One of the city's leading shopping streets (Calwer Strasse) is home to the glitzy arcade **Calwer Passage,** full of elegant chrome and glass. Here you'll find legion shopping opportunities, from local women's fashion (Beate Mössinger), to furniture, to a shop devoted to pipes and accessories.

Under the dome of the several-stories-high central arcade in **Breuninger,** a leading regional department-store chain, glass elevators rise and fall. They're carrying customers to floors of everything from fashion to housewares (Marktstr. 1–3, ☎ 0711/2110).

Stuttgart's central **market-hall** (entrances on Spörerstr. and on Dorotheenstr.) is also an excellent place to buy local wines and other edible regional specialties.

SPORTS AND FITNESS

Ballooning
Hot-air-balloon tours of the Neckar Valley and surrounding countryside are offered by **Balloon Tours** (☎ 06261/18477), in Mosbach.

Bowling
You can scatter the pins at Heidelberg's **Bowling Center** (Bergheimerstr. 139–151, ☎ 06221/23233) and at Stuttgart's **Bowling Zentrum** (Lautlinger Weg, ☎ 0711/780–1561).

Golf
There are two golf clubs in the vicinity of Heidelberg. **The Golfclub Heidelberg,** in the neighboring village of Lobbach-Lobenfeld (☎ 06226/40490), welcomes visitors on weekdays (but not weekends), but you must be accompanied by a member to play at the **Hohenhardter Hof Club** on weekends (Wiesloch, 20 minutes south of Heidelberg, ☎ 06222/72081). In Heilbronn you can play at the **Golfclub Heilbronn-Hohenlohe**, in the village of Friedrichsruhe (☎ 07132/179–951).

Hiking

Stuttgart has a 53-kilometer (33-mile) network of marked hiking trails in the surrounding hills; follow the signs with the city's emblem, a horse set in a yellow ring. The Tübingen tourist office has maps with routes around the town, including special historic and geologic "*Lehrpfad,*" or educational walks.

Horseback Riding

In Heidelberg there are stables at the **city zoo** (☎ 06221/480–041) and at **Pleikartsforstenhof 5** (☎ 06221/32059). Heilbronn has a riding club where you can rent horses and also take lessons, the **Reiterverein Heilbronn** (Im Sternberg 5, ☎ 07131/178–469). You can also hire horses at Stuttgart's **Schwarzbach** riding school (Handwerkstr. 39, ☎ 0711/780–2122).

Roller-Skating

Wednesday night is disco night at the roller-skating rink at **Heilbronn's Europaplatz.** It's great fun. The rink is open daily from 9 to 9.

Swimming

You'll find indoor and outdoor swimming pools in all towns and most villages along your way. Heidelberg has a pool fed by thermal water at Vangerowstrasse 4, and pools at the extensive **Tiergartenschwimm-bad** next to the zoo. Heilbronn's favorite lido, the **Freibad Neckarhalde** (☎ 07131/255–100), has a view of the river. Neckarsulm boasts an "adventure bathing" complex–complete with palm trees and whitewater river–called **AQUAtoll** (☎ 07132/2052). Swimming in the Neckar River is not advisable.

Tennis

Most towns and villages along the Neckar have local tennis clubs that accept visitors. In Heidelberg you can play at the **Tennis-Inn** (Harbig-weg 1, ☎ 06221/12106). In Heilbronn the tennis schools at Böckinger-strasse 170 (☎ 07131/46166) and Viehweide 91 (☎ 07131/34343) can arrange lessons and partners. Stuttgart is the true tennis center of the region, and the city has several clubs that welcome visitors—the largest is **Jens Weinberger's tennis and sports school** (Emerholzweg 73, ☎ 0711/808–018).

DINING AND LODGING

Dining

Heidelberg, Mannheim, and Stuttgart offer the most elegant dining in the region, though in Heidelberg you'll be dining with tradition at your table—there are few restaurants in the city that don't have decor to match the stage-set atmosphere of the town. Atmospheric restaurants in the castle hotels along the Neckar serve excellent food more often than not. In smaller towns along the valley, simple inns, dark and timbered, are the norm. Outside Heidelberg, Mannheim, and Stuttgart, prices can be low.

Specialties in the Neckar Valley are much the same as those along the Wine Road, with sausages and local wines figuring prominently. Stuttgart's more modest restaurants feature one of Germany's truly great authentic regional cuisines, based on age-old Swabian recipes; and this continues as you move South toward the Black Forest and Tübingen.

WHAT TO WEAR
Dress is casual unless otherwise noted.

RATINGS

CATEGORY	COST*
$$$$	over DM 90
$$$	DM 55–DM 90
$$	DM 35–DM 55
$	under DM 35

per person for a three-course meal including tax but not drinks

Lodging

If you plan to visit Heidelberg in summer, make reservations well in advance and expect to pay top rates. To get away from the crowds, consider staying out of town—at Neckargemünd, say—and driving or taking the bus into the city. Staying in a castle hotel can be fun. This area is second only to the Rhine for baronial-style castle hotels studding the hilltops. Most have terrific views as well as a stone-passage-way-and-four-poster-bed atmosphere. Stuttgart's hotels cater, on the one hand, to the expense-account business traveler, along with jet-setters from around the world who come here to pick up their new Mercedes or Porsche at the source, and, on the other, to German families on vacation. Thus Stuttgart has several luxury hotels as well as a wide range of family-style hotels at a relatively modest cost.

RATINGS

CATEGORY	COST*
$$$$	over DM 250
$$$	DM 180–DM 250
$$	DM 120–DM 180
$	under DM 120

Prices are for two people in a double room.

Bad Wimpfen

DINING AND LODGING

Hotel Blauer Turm. Germany's oldest sentry watchtower, Bad Wimpfen's spectacular turreted "Blue Tower," stands sentinel outside your bedroom window at this handsome old half-timbered hotel in the town center. A fine view of the Neckar River can also be enjoyed from most of the double rooms. In summer, claim a table within the leafy bower of the pergola-terrace and watch the Neckar meander by from that vantage point. There and in the smart restaurant you'll be offered a comprehensive menu that features Swabian specialties (*Spätzle,* for instance) and fresh fish from the river. ☎ *Burgviertel 5,* ☎ *07063/7884,* FAX *07063/6701. 22 rooms, most with bath. No credit cards. Restaurant closed Mon. $–$$*

Heidelberg

DINING

★ **Zur Herrenmühle.** Delicately prepared classic French cuisine is served on pewter plates adorning rough-hewn tables at this 17th-century tavern in the old town. Fish is the specialty here, and the desserts are noteworthy. In summer diners can eat in a peaceful inner courtyard. ✕ *Hauptstr. 239,* ☎ *06221/12909. Reservations advised. AE, DC, MC, V. Closed lunch and Sun. $$$*

Perkeo. Ask for a table in the atmospheric Schlosstube and, if suckling pig is on the menu, ask for that, too. You'll then be dining in the style for which this historic restaurant has been known for close to three centuries. ✕ *Hauptstr. 75,* ☎ *06221/160–613. Reservations advised. AE, DC, MC, V.* $

Schnookelooch. This picturesque and lively old tavern dates from 1407 and is inextricably linked with Heidelberg's history and its university. Every evening a piano player joins the fun. ✕ *Haspelgasse 8,* ☎ *06221/22733. Reservations advised. AE, DC, MC, V.* $

★ **Zum Roten Ochsen.** Many of the oak tables here have initials carved into them, legacy of the thousands upon thousands of former visitors to Heidelberg's most famous and time-honored old tavern. Bismarck, Mark Twain, and, many years later, John Foster Dulles, may have left their mark—they all ate here. It's been run by the Spengel family for more than a century, and they avariciously guard the rough-hewn, half-timbered atmosphere. ✕ *Hauptstr. 217,* ☎ *06221/20977. Reservations required. No credit cards. Closed Sun., holidays, and mid-Dec.–mid-Jan.* $

DINING AND LODGING

★ **Europäischer Hof–Hotel Europa.** This is the classiest and most luxurious of Heidelberg's hotels, close to just about everything in town and offering a wide range of facilities. Public rooms are sumptuously furnished, and bedrooms are spacious and tasteful. If you fancy a splurge, go for one of the suites; the best have whirlpools. ⊡ *Friedrich-Ebert-Anlage 1,* ☎ *06221/5150,* ℻ *06221/515–555 or 06221/515–556. 122 rooms, 13 suites, all with bath. Restaurant, bar, coffee shop, beauty salon. AE, DC, MC, V.* $$$$

★ **Romantik Hotel zum Ritter St. Georg.** If this is your first visit to Germany, stay here. It's the only Renaissance building in Heidelberg, and it dishes atmosphere by the barrel-load. The Red Baron would feel right at home among the exposed beams and the suit of armor in the dining room, dining on *Wild* (game) specialties such as *Hirsch* (venison) from the nearby Odenwald. Bedrooms are clean and comfortable, some traditional, some more modern. ⊡ *Hauptstr. 178,* ☎ *06221/24272,* ℻ *06221/12683. 39 rooms, 36 with bath. Restaurant. AE, DC, MC, V.* $$$$

Gutschänke Grenzhof. The Grenzhof estate existed as a simple homestead long before Heidelberg was founded. Today it's a very comfortable hotel, recently enlarged and completely renovated in German country-house style. Four more expensive maisonette suites have been added; they offer the style of a city apartment, yet they have views of rural parkland. There's also a gourmet restaurant. ⊡ *Heidelberg-Grenzhof 9,* ☎ *06202/9430,* ℻ *06202/943–100. 22 rooms, 4 maisonettes, 1 junior suite, all with bath. Restaurant, bar, beer garden, café. AE, DC, MC, V.* $$$

Gasthaus Backmulde. This traditional tavern in the heart of Heidelberg has a surprising range of items on its restaurant menu, from the delicately marinated fresh vegetables that accompany the excellent meat dishes to the imaginative soups that add modern flair to ancient recipes (a Franconian potato broth, for instance, rich with garden herbs). Guest rooms are small but comfortable. ⊡ *Schiffgasse 11,* ☎ *06221/53660. No reservations. No credit cards.* $$

★ **Hackteufel.** Once a popular student pub, the Hackteufel now has a broader clientele; friendly atmosphere and the host's good cooking are the draws. Low-slung lamps hung from dark beams cast a warm glow over the rough wood tables. If it's winter, choose a place by the handsome tile oven. And if you're tempted to stay the night, you have options: a dozen comfortable and moderately priced rooms upstairs, or a new annex that includes affordable apartments. ⊡ *Steingasse 7,*

☎ 06221/27162, ℻ 06221/165–379. *AE, DC, MC, V. Closed Dec.
23–Jan. 2.* $$

<u>LODGING</u>

Holländer Hof. The pink-and-white painted facade of this ornate 19th-
century building across from the Old Bridge stands out on the old-town
waterfront of the Neckar River. Many of its timelessly furnished rooms
overlook the busy waterway and the forested hillside above the opposite
shore. 🏠 *Neckarstaden 66,* ☎ *06221/12091,* ℻ *06221/22085. 40 rooms
and 1 suite with bath. Baby-sitting. AE, DC, MC, V.* $$$

★ **Hotel Hirschgasse.** Located across the river on the edge of town yet
only a 10-minute walk from the city center, the Hirschgasse began as
a farmhouse. Its 500-year history, which places it among the oldest buildings in the area, also includes a stint as a tavern where university students indulged their fencing duels, and a mention in Mark Twain's *A
Tramp Abroad*. Only Laura Ashley–style suites are available. The
restaurant is exceptional. 🏠 *Hirschgasse 3,* ☎ *06221/403–2160,*
℻ *06221/403–2196. 22 suites with bath. Restaurant. AE, DC, MC,
V. Closed Dec. 23–Jan. 7.* $$$

Prinzhotel. This is the elegant younger sister of the Hirschgasse, dat-
ing just to the late 19th century. It's also across the river from the old
town; fight for a room with a view of the river. A stylish restaurant,
Stars California, recently opened here. 🏠 *Neuenheimer Landstr. 5,*
☎ *06221/40320,* ℻ *06221/403–2196. 45 rooms and 3 suites, all
with bath. Restaurant, hot tub, sauna, steam room. AE, DC, MC, V.*
$$$

Heilbronn

<u>DINING</u>

★ **Café Harmonie.** Eat on the terrace in summer to enjoy the view of the
city park. Inside, the decor is traditional with a modern twist, as is the
menu. For best value, try one of the fixed-price menus. ✗ *Am Stadtgarten, Allee 28,* ☎ *07131/87954. Reservations required. Jacket and
tie. Closed Tues. and most of Aug. AE, DC, MC, V.* $$

★ **Ratskeller.** For sturdy and dependable regional specialties—try Swabian
Maultaschen, a kind of local ravioli—and as much Teutonic atmosphere
as you'll ever want, you won't go wrong in this basement restaurant
of the town hall. ✗ *Marktpl. 7,* ☎ *07131/84628. Reservations advised.
No credit cards. Closed Sun. dinner and holidays.* $$

<u>LODGING</u>

★ **Insel-Hotel.** Is it possible to sleep in the middle of the Neckar River and
yet be within walking distance of Heilbronn's old-town center? You
bet. *Insel* means "island," and that's where the luxurious Insel-Hotel
is—on a river island tethered to the city by the busy Friedrich-Ebert
Bridge. A family-run establishment, the Insel combines a personal
touch with the sleek service and facilities expected of a large chain, and
a fabulous restaurant. 🏠 *Friedrich-Ebert-Brücke,* ☎ *07131/6300,*
℻ *07131/626–060. 120 rooms with bath and 5 suites. Restaurant, bar,
café, weinstube no-smoking rooms, indoor pool, sauna, free parking.
AE, DC, MC, V.* $$$$

Hotel Zur Post. The Mangler family, who runs this sturdy hotel, offers
their guests comfort and friendly service at a very reasonable price. Personal touches include bright prints on the pastel walls and fresh flowers. The Zur Post doesn't have a restaurant, but there's no shortage of
places to eat in the neighborhood. The Manglers also run the nearby
Hotel Allee-Post; ask for rooms there if the Zur Post is full. 🏠 *Bismarckstr.
5,* ☎ *07131/627–040,* ℻ *07131/82193. 20 rooms with shower. (Hotel
Allee-Post, Titotstr. 12,* ☎ *07131/81656.) MC, V.* $–$$

Hirschhorn

DINING AND LODGING

Schlosshotel auf Burg Hirschhorn. Not so much a castle hotel as a pleasant if undistinguished modern hotel in a castle, the Hirschhorn is perched on a hilltop overlooking the medieval village and the Neckar River, 22 kilometers (14 miles) east of Heidelberg. Hallways have that rough-plaster medieval look, lest you forget you're in a castle; rooms are furnished in approved Student Prince style. The views are terrific, and the restaurant much better than average. ☎ 69434 *Hirschhorn/Neckar,* ☎ 06272/1373, FAX 06272/3267. *23 rooms and 2 suites with bath.[df] Restaurant, café. AE, MC, V. Closed Dec.–Jan.* $$$

Leimen

LODGING

Hotel Seipel. Leimen's claim to fame is as tennis star Boris Becker's hometown; otherwise, it's just a pleasant wine village 6½ kilometers (4 miles) south of Heidelberg, and as such has viable alternatives to the more expensive accommodations in the larger cities of the Neckar Valley. The Seipel is a clean, modern hotel on the edge of a sports park and woodland. The rooms are furnished in dark redwood with dove-gray drapes and upholstery. ☎ *Am Sportpark,* ☎ 06224/71089, FAX 06224/71080. *30 rooms with bath. Sauna, steam room, exercise room. AE, DC, MC, V. Closed 1st wk of Jan.* $$

Mannheim

DINING

★ **Da Gianni.** Sophisticated Italian dishes, with a distinctly nouvelle accent, are served in this classy haunt in the Quadratstadt. Chef Wolfgang Staudenmaier's sauces give the menu a Gallic-Italian flair; St. Peter fish, for instance, is served in a combination of tomatoes, potatoes, and olives. ✕ *R–7 34,* ☎ 0621/20326. *Reservations required. Jacket and tie. AE, DC, MC, V. Closed Mon. and 3 wks in July.* $$$$

★ **L'Epi d'Or.** French nouvelle cuisine and sophisticated local specialties are the hallmark of Norbert Dobler's city-center restaurant. The warm lobster salad is a classic; the saddle of lamb is a good alternative. ✕ *H–7 3,* ☎ 0621/14397. *Reservations required. Jacket and tie. AE, MC, V. Closed Sat. lunch, Sun., Mon. lunch, and 2 wks in summer (time varies).* $$$

DINING AND LODGING

Gasthof zum Ochsen. Mannheim's oldest inn is about 8 kilometers (5 miles) from the city center, in the Feudenheim district, but it's well worth the journey, particularly on clear summer days when you can eat and drink on the chestnut-tree–shaded terrace. The menu here is a mixture of French and Baden cuisines. Twelve comfortable bedrooms, furnished in fine cherry wood, are tucked away under the steep eaves. ☎ *Hauptstr. 70, Feudenheim,* ☎ 0621/799–550, FAX 0621/799–5533. *AE, DC, MC, V.* $$–$$$

Alte Munz. For old German atmosphere, local specialties, and a wide range of beers, the Alte Munz is hard to beat. Try the suckling pig if it's available. ☎ *P–7 1,* ☎ 0621/28262, FAX 0621/26555. *Reservations advised. AE, MC, V.* $$

LODGING

★ **Maritim Parkhotel.** It may be part of a chain, but the turn-of-the-century Parkhotel is the number-one choice in town, grandly offering opulent comforts. The pillared, chandelier-hung lobby sets the mood; rooms are spacious and elegant. ☎ *Friedrichspl. 2,* ☎ 0621/45071,

FAX *0621/152–424. 184 rooms and 3 suites, all with bath. Restaurant, bar, indoor pool, beauty salon, sauna, steam room, exercise room. AE, DC, MC, V. $$$$*

Hotel Löwen-Seckenheim. Light-wood furnishings and contemporary fabrics create a cheerful atmosphere in the rooms at this friendly, efficiently run hotel. Frequent buses run between Seckenheim, on the edge of the city, and the city center. A large breakfast buffet is included in the room rate. ☏ *Seckenheimer Hauptstr. 159–163,* ☎ *0621/48080,* FAX *0621/481–4154. 60 rooms with bath or shower. Restaurant, free parking. AE, MC, V. $$–$$$*

Mosbach

DINING AND LODGING

Zum Lamm. The half-timbered Lamm (Lamb) inn on Mosbach's main street is one of the town's prettiest houses. Its cozy rooms are individually furnished, with flowers filling the window boxes. The restaurant, complete with requisite exposed beams, serves local and international dishes, incorporating meat from the hotel's own butcher shop. ☏ *Hauptstr. 59,* ☎ *06261/89020,* FAX *06261/890–291. 53 rooms with bath. AE, DC, MC, V. $$*

Neckargemünd

DINING

Landgasthof Die Rainbach. This long-popular country inn just outside Neckargemünd, in the Rainbach district, changed hands recently, but the quality of its cuisine remains as good as ever, with the accent still on hearty traditional fare. If the weather's good take a table on the terrace, which commands a fine view of the river. In winter, warm up in the paneled restaurant inside with a dish of venison stew or any of the freshly prepared soups. ✕ *Rainbach 9,* ☎ *06223/2455. MC. Closed Mon. and Jan. $$*

DINING AND LODGING

Zum Röss'l. The Röss'l has been catering to Neckar Valley travelers for nearly 350 years. You'll dine in a wood-paneled restaurant or, in summer, on the delightful garden terrace. Be sure to try some of the excellent brandy that is produced in the Röss'l's own distillery. Above the restaurant are 14 small but comfortably furnished rooms (a double is around DM 100), 12 with bath. ☏ *Heidelberger Strasse 15,* ☎ *06223/2665,* FAX *06223/6859. No credit cards. $$*

LODGING

Hotel zum Ritter. Built during the 16th century, the half-timbered zum Ritter has appropriately aged exposed beams, and satisfyingly creaky passages. The hotel overlooks the Neckar, as do some of its rooms. ☏ *Neckarstr. 40,* ☎ *06223/7035,* FAX *06223/73–339. 40 rooms with bath. AE, MC, V. $$–$$$*

Neckarsulm

LODGING

Astron Hotel. Ask for a mansard room at the modern Astron—the rooms under the steep eaves are very cozy, decorated in harmonious pastel tones. Fresh flowers are a welcome touch. ☏ *Sulmstr. 2,* ☎ *07132/3880,* FAX *07132/388–113. 82 rooms, 2 suites with bath. Restaurant, bar, beauty salon, sauna. AE, DC, MC, V. $$$*

Neckarwestheim

DINING AND LODGING

Schlosshotel Liebenstein. Nestled in the hills above this Neckar River village south of Heilbronn is one of the area's most beautiful castles, Schloss Liebenstein, a Renaissance jewel whose restaurant draws diners from as far away as Stuttgart. Guest rooms have views of the surrounding forests and vineyards. Within the 3-foot-thick castle walls the peaceful hush of centuries reigns over a setting of comfort and noble elegance. ☎ *Schloss Liebenstein,* ☎ *07133/6041,* FAX *07133/6045. 24 rooms with bath or shower. Restaurant. AE, DC, MC, V. $$$$*

Neckarzimmern

DINING AND LODGING

★ **Burg Hornberg.** Midway between Heidelberg and Heilbronn stands the ancient castle where knight Götz von Berlichingen, immortalized by Goethe, spent his declining years. Your host is the present baron of the castle. The hotel's rooms are comfortable, and some have magnificent views over the hotel's own vineyards to the river. The restaurant features venison (in season) and fresh fish. ☎ *D–74865 Neckarzimmern,* ☎ *06261/92460,* FAX *06261/18864. 23 rooms with bath. Restaurant, bar, miniature golf. MC, V. Closed mid-Dec.–Feb. $$$*

Obrigheim

DINING AND LODGING

Hotel Schloss Neuburg. This centuries-old sentinel castle seems to rise above the Neckar and the Odenwald. Sensitive modernization has ensured that many original features were retained even as many essential comforts have been added. Many bedrooms have oak beams. ☎ *D–74847 Obrigheim,* ☎ *06261/7001,* FAX *06261/7747. 14 rooms with bath. Restaurant. AE, DC, MC. Closed first 3 wks in Jan. $$$$*

Schwetzingen

DINING AND LODGING

Romantik Hotel Löwe. The "Lion" has been a favorite staging post for travelers for two centuries. The attractive old house, with its steeply eaved, dormer-windowed red roof, was originally a butcher shop and wine tavern. Now it's a very comfortable hotel and an excellent restaurant, although the wine tavern is still in place, basically unchanged. The restaurant serves imaginatively prepared Palatinate specialties (the marinated beef is a must), and the famous Schwetzingen asparagus dominates the menu throughout the summer. There are 22 comfortable rooms, some with exposed beams, and each of them individually furnished. ☎ *Schlossstr. 4–6,* ☎ *06202/26066,* FAX *06202/10726. AE, DC, MC, V. $$$–$$$$*

Stuttgart

DINING

Wielandshöhe. Stuttgart's leading restaurant fits neatly into the city's sleek, businesslike image. It consists of a bright space virtually devoid of all decoration, except for bowls of flamboyant flowers that stand out against the white and gray decor. The menu is full of surprises, including breast of pigeon nestled in a tangle of tagliolini, tender duck with farmhouse red cabbage, and swordfish served with a vinaigrette sauce. The wine list is exemplary. ✕ *Alte Weinsteige 71,* ☎ *0711/640–8848. Reservations required. Jacket and tie. Closed Sun., Mon. AE, DC, MC, V. $$$$*

Zeppelin-Stüble. Hearty down-home Swabian dishes are the specialties at this cozy restaurant in the fairly buttoned-up Steigenberger-Hotel

Reality check. Call home.

—— *AT&T USADirect® and World Connect®. The fast, easy way to call most anywhere.* ——

Take out AT&T Calling Card or your local calling card.** Lift phone. Dial AT&T Access Number for country you're calling from. Connect to English-speaking operator or voice prompt. Reach the States or over 200 countries. Talk. Say goodbye. Hang up. Resume vacation.

Austria*†††.....................022-903-011	Luxembourg 0-800-0111	Turkey* 00-800-12277
Belgium* 0-800-100-10	Netherlands*................06-022-9111	United Kingdom................0500-89-0011
Czech Republic*.............00-420-00101	Norway 800-190-11	
Denmark 8001-0010	Poland†♦·.................0◇010-480-0111	
Finland 9800-100-10	Portugal† 05017-1-288	
France..................................19-0011	Romania*.....................01-800-4288	
Germany..............................0130-0010	Russia*†(Moscow)................155-5042	
Greece*..........................00-800-1311	Slovak Rep.*................00-420-00101	
Hungary*.................00◇-800-01111	Spain●........................900-99-00-11	
Ireland 1-800-550-000	Sweden 020-795-611	
Italy*.................................172-1011	Switzerland* 155-00-11	

AT&T
Your True Choice

**You can also call collect or use most U.S. local calling cards. Countries in bold face permit country-to-country calling in addition to calls to the U.S. World Connect® prices consist of USADirect® rates plus an additional charge based on the country you are calling. Collect calling available to the U.S. only. *Public phones require deposit of coin or phone card. †May not be available from every phone. †††Public phones require local coin payment during call. ♦Not available from public phones. ◇Await second dial tone. ‡Dial 010-480-0111 from major Warsaw hotels. ●Calling available to most European countries. ©1995 AT&T.

For a free wallet sized card of all AT&T Access Numbers, call: 1-800-241-5555.

All the best trips
start with **Fodor's**.

EXPLORING GUIDES

At last, the color of an art book combined with the usefulness of a complete guide.

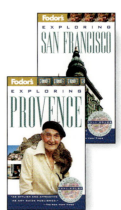

"As stylish and attractive as any guide published." —*The New York Times*

"Worth reading before, during, and after a trip." —*The Philadelphia Inquirer*

More than 30 destinations available worldwide. $19.95 each.

BERKELEY GUIDES

The budget traveler's handbook

"Berkeley's scribes put the funk back in travel."
—*Time*

"Fresh, funny, and funky as well as useful."
—*The Boston Globe*

"Well-organized, clear and very easy to read."
—*America Online*

14 destinations worldwide. Priced between $13.00 - $19.50. ($17.95 - $27.00 Canada)

AFFORDABLES

"All the maps and itinerary ideas of Fodor's established gold guides with a bonus—shortcuts to savings." —*USA Today*

"Travelers with champagne tastes and beer budgets will welcome this series from Fodor's." —*Hartfort Courant*

"It's obvious these Fodor's folk have secrets we civilians don't." —*New York Daily News*

Also available: Florida, Europe, France, London, Paris. Priced between $11.00 - $18.00 ($14.50 - $24.00 Canada)

At bookstores, or call **1-800-533-6478**

The name that means smart travel.™

Graf Zeppelin. At the top of the list are *Maultaschen*, somewhat similar to Italian ravioli, served in a delicate broth; and *Spätzle*, the tiny noodlelike dumplings that take the place of potatoes in this part of Germany. ✕ *Arnulf-Klett-Pl. 7,* ☎ *0711/20480. Reservations advised. AE, DC, MC, V. $$–$$$*

DINING AND LODGING

Am Schlossgarten. This pricey, modern eight-story glass-and-concrete hotel is set in spacious gardens in the heart of the city, a stone's throw from the Staatstheater, the state parliament, and several other landmarks. The hotel's Schlossgarten Restaurant offers a mixture of international and regional dishes. Try the consommé of fresh forest mushrooms and the turbot with leeks and lobster cream sauce. 🏠 *Schillerstr. 23,* ☎ *0711–20260,* FAX *0711/202–6888. 125 beds with bath. 2 restaurants, bar, café. AE, DC, MC, V. $$$$*

LODGING

Alter Fritz. Katrin Fritsche describes her small country mansion as a "hotel for individualists." With only 10 rooms, she is able to cater to guests' most exacting requirements with a friendly and personal touch rare in a city the size of Stuttgart. The picturesque house with its steep eaves and shuttered windows, high up on the wooded Killesberg Hill, is ideally located for visitors to the nearby trade fairground and a 15-minute bus ride from the main railway station. 🏠 *Feuerbach Weg 101,* ☎ *0711/135–650,* FAX *0711/135–6565. 10 rooms with bath or shower. Restaurant, free parking. No credit cards. $$$*

Hotel Mercure Fasanenhof. This recent addition to the Mercure chain offers the latest in comfort and service. The design is light and airy, with large windows throughout the spacious lobby, restaurant, and public rooms, and the comfortable bedrooms; everything is decorated in tasteful, pastel colors. 🏠 *Eichwiesenring 1–1,* ☎ *0711/72660,* FAX *0711/726–6444. 148 rooms with bath. Restaurant, bar, sauna, free parking. AE, DC, MC, V. $$$*

Tübingen

DINING

Waldhorn. Located in the picturesque little village of Bebenhausen, 6 kilometers (4 miles) outside Tübingen, this establishment shows how excellent Swabian restaurants can be. It's been in the same family for generations, but the present managers are the ones who trained for years to convert it into the area's best address for fine French cooking. Everything is made by hand, down to the chocolates that come with the bill, but for all its elegant furnishings and fanciness the restaurant hasn't lost its local flavor—from the warmth of the proprietors to the lunchtime menu that features traditional local specialties—with, naturally, a French twist. ✕ *Schönbuchstr. 49 (on the B–27),* ☎ *07071/61270,* FAX *07071/610–581. Reservations required. AE, DC, MC, V. Closed Mon. and Tues. $$$*

DINING AND LODGING

Hotel Am Schloss. The climb is steep from the Altstadt up to this hotel, next to the old castle that towers over the town, but the reward is lovely views from the geranium-bedecked windows of the comfortable rooms. The hotel's restaurant is known for local specialties; proprietor Herbert Rösch has written a number of books about regional cuisine in which he describes them. In warm weather you can partake of these on the small terrace overlooking the city. 🏠 *Burgsteige 18, 72070 Tübingen,* ☎ *07071/92940,* FAX *07071/929–410. 28 rooms with shower. Restaurant, free parking. AE, DC, MC, V. $$*

Hotel Hospiz. If you're not willing to hike to get back to your hotel, you'll be better off at this central Altstadt location. This little hotel was renovated in 1995; it's modern and not especially beautiful, but it provides plenty in the way of comfort, good food, convenience, and friendly service. ⌂ *Neckarhalde 2, 72070 Tübingen,* ☎ *07071/9240,* ℻ *07071/924–200. 50 rooms, most with bath or shower. Restaurant, bar, meeting room, free parking. AE, DC, MC, V. $$*

Weinheim

LODGING

Hotel Ottheinrich. Weinheim lies on the lovely Bergstrasse (Mountain Route), about 10 miles east of Mannheim and a similar distance north of Heidelberg—ideal for visitors who want to avoid the summer crush of both cities. The virtues of this privately run hotel include high standards, individuality, and charm. The rooms have stylish Italian furniture and TVs. ⌂ *Hauptstr. 126,* ☎ *06201/18070; fax 06201/180–788. 15 rooms and 9 suites with bath. Restaurant, bar. AE, DC, MC, V. $$$*

THE ARTS AND NIGHTLIFE

Information on all upcoming events in **Heidelberg** is listed in the monthly *Konzerte im Heidelberger Stern* and *Heidelberg Aktuell* (both free and available from the tourist office). The **Heilbronn** tourist office publishes a similar monthly listings magazine, *Heilbronn Today & Tomorrow;* it, too, is available free of charge. Tickets for theaters in Heidelberg are available from **Theaterkasse** (Theaterstr. 4, ☎ 06221/20519). In Heilbronn you can buy tickets from the tourist office (07131/562–270). In addition to the English-language *Stuttgart's Theatres-Museums* booklet, with detailed information on the city's theaters and museums, the **Stuttgart** tourist office issues a monthly *Monatsspiegel* (DM 2 a copy) that lists all cultural, artistic, and sporting events scheduled for that period.

The Arts

Theater and Music

Heidelberg has a thriving theater scene. The **Theater der Stadt** (Friedrichstr. 5, ☎ 06221/583–520) is the best-known theater in town; others include the **Zimmer Theater** (Hauptstr. 118, ☎ 06221/21069) and the **Theater in Augustinum** (Jasperstr. 2, ☎ 06221/3881). For information on performances at the castle during the annual Schloss-Spiele festival, call 06221/58976.

The **Zwingenberg,** above the Neckar River, also holds Schloss-Spiele festivals annually throughout the summer within its ancient walls. For program information and tickets, contact Rathaus Zwingenberg (D–69439 Zwingenberg, ☎ 06251/70030).

Heilbronn's **Stadttheater** (Berliner Pl. 1, ☎ 07131/563–001) is the leading venue in the city. In summer **classical concerts** are given in the gardens behind the Festhalle; contact the tourist office for details of performances and tickets.

Mannheim has a respectable opera company, and its theater has recently been renovated (Nationaltheater box office ☎ 0621/24844). The leading arts event in this region is the annual **Schwetzingen Festival** in May and June, which features operas and concerts by international artists in the lovely Rococo theater of Schwetzingen Palace (for information, call the tourist office: ☎ 06202/4933).

Stuttgart's internationally renowned ballet company performs regularly at the **Staatstheater** (Oberer Schlossgarten 6, ☎ 0711/221–795). The ballet alternates with opera performances by the respected State Opera; the season runs from September through June. For program details contact the Stuttgart tourist office (*see* Important Addresses and Numbers in Heidelberg and the Neckar Valley Essentials, *below*). The box office is open weekdays 9–1 and 2–5. If you'd like to see a remarkable Anglo-Saxon export, check out the **Stuttgart Musical Hall,** opened in December 1994. This is the center of an entire entertainment complex (hotels, bars, restaurants, shows) built to house the touring blockbuster musical *Miss Saigon* (rumored to be sold to capacity through 1998 or so). Call 0711/222–8246 for information and tickets.

Being a student town, **Tübingen** has an active small theater scene. Check with the tourist office for a listing of whatever happens to be going on—the more eclectic offerings are likely to be the better ones.

Nightlife

Heidelberg's nightlife is concentrated in the area around the Heiliggeistkirche (Church of the Holy Ghost), in the old town. For a fun night out, try the **Hard Rock Café** (Hauptstr. 142); it's not exactly Student Prince territory, but it's a good place for videos and burgers. For blues, jazz, and funk, try **Hookemann** (Fischmarkt 3); admission is free. Germany's oldest jazz cellar is **Cave 54** (Krämergasse 2). The **Goldener Reichsapfel** nearby (Unterestr. 35) is always crowded after 10 PM; the mood is smoky and loud. **Club 1900** (Hauptstr.) is a well-established disco. The fanciest bars, along with many trendy cafés, are along the main pedestrian street, Hauptstrasse. For most, however, nightlife in Heidelberg means a visit to one of the student taverns to drink wine and beer, lock arms, and sing. There are no better places to try than **Zum Roten Ochsen** and **Schnookelooch,** both of which have been in business for several centuries (*see* Dining and Lodging, *above*).

Heilbronn has one of the biggest and liveliest wine festivals in the Neckar Valley—the **Weindorf,** held in mid-September in the streets and squares around the city hall. But it's not all tradition in Heilbronn. The city has a colorful nightlife—for discos, try the **BOSS-Club** (Mosbacherstr. 8) or **OM** (Paulinenstr. 15).

Stuttgart's most vibrant nightlife is likely to be encountered in the numerous popular wine taverns, where just about everyone orders a *Viertelesglas,* local wine served in the typically Swabian quarter-liter glass mug with a handle. Throughout the region, between November and February, join the crowds in the *Besenwirtschaften* (broom inns), which are private inns serving the owner's new wine of the season; these are usually in nondescript houses, but you can recognize them by the broom hanging over the door. Night owls congregate at the **Schwaben-zentrum** on Eberhardstrasse, where the pubs are open until 5 AM.

HEIDELBERG AND THE NECKAR VALLEY ESSENTIALS

Arriving and Departing

By Plane

The airports nearest to the Neckar Valley are at Frankfurt and Stuttgart. From both there's fast and easy access, by car and train, to all major centers along the Neckar.

Getting Around

By Bus

Europabus 189 runs the length of the Burgenstrasse daily from May through September. There are stops at towns and villages all along the Neckar. For information, timetables, and reservations, contact **Deutsche Touring GmBH** (Am Römerhof 17, D–60486 Frankfurt/Main 90, ☎ 069/79030). Local buses run from Mannheim, Heidelberg, Heilbronn, and Stuttgart to most places along the river; post buses connect the rest.

By Car

Mannheim is a major junction of the Autobahn system, easily reached from all parts of the country. Heidelberg and Heilbronn are also served by Autobahn. A 15-minute drive on A–656 speeds you from Mannheim to Heidelberg; Heilbronn stands beside the east–west A–6 and the north–south A–81. The route followed in this chapter, the Burgenstrasse, also unromantically designated A–37, follows the north bank of the Neckar from Heidelberg to Mosbach, from which it runs down to Heilbronn as A–27. It's a busy road, and a fast one. If you need a change of pace, cross the river at Mosbach to Obrigheim and continue south on the slower B–39.

CAR RENTAL

Avis: Karlsruherstrasse 43, ☎ 06221/22215, **Heidelberg;** Salzstrasse 112, ☎ 07131/172–077, **Heilbronn;** Augartenstrasse 112–114, ☎ 0621/442–091, **Mannheim;** Katharinenstrasse 18, ☎ 0711/241–441, **Stuttgart.**

Europcar: Bergheimerstrasse 159, ☎ 06221/20845, **Heidelberg;** Neckarauerstrasse 50–52, ☎ 0621/852–055, **Mannheim;** Alexanderstrasse 42, ☎ 0711/236–4863, **Stuttgart**; Eisenbahnstr. 17, ☎ 07071/36303, **Tübingen.**

Hertz: Kurfürstenanlage 1 (in the Holiday Inn), ☎ 06221/23434, **Heidelberg;** Friedrichsring 36, ☎ 0621/22997, **Mannheim;** Leitzstrasse 51, ☎ 0711/817–233, **Stuttgart.**

By Train

Mannheim is west Germany's most important rail junction, with hourly InterCity trains from all major German cities. Nearby Heidelberg is equally easy to get to. Mannheim is also a major stop for the super-high-speed InterCity Express service, which reaches 250 kilometers (155 miles) per hour on the Mannheim–Stuttgart stretch. There are express trains to Heilbronn from Heidelberg and Stuttgart, and direct trains from Stuttgart to Tübingen. Local services link many of the smaller towns along the Neckar.

Guided Tours

Boat Tours
The **Rhein-Neckar-Fahrgastschiffahrt** (RNF) company (☎ 06221/20181) offers boat rides from Heidelberg and Mannheim along the Neckar and down the Rhine to Speyer and Worms. From Easter through October, there are regular trips on the Neckar from Stuttgart and Heilbronn. Contact the **Neckar-Personen-Schiffahrt** (☎ 0711/541–073), **Personenschiffahrt Stumpf** (☎ 07131/85430), or the tourist offices for details. The **Tübingen** tourist office organizes punting on the Neckar (Apr.–Oct.); trips leave Saturday at 4 PM from the quay by the Neckar bridge (DM 6 adults, DM 4 children).

City Tours
There are guided bus tours of **Heidelberg** at 10 and 2 daily from May through October (November through March, Saturdays only, at 2; and April, daily at 2) from the train station and Bismarckplatz. Call 06221/21341 or 06221/513–2000 for details. The tours cost DM 20 for adults and DM 15 for children.

In **Heilbronn** the tourist office offers a **"Viertel nach Sechs"** tour, meaning "quarter after six," which is just when the tour begins (that's 6 PM). The tours are given every Tuesday from early May through September; the cost is DM 7, and all tours end with a free glass of wine. On the first Wednesday in June, July, August, and September, you can take a tour in a 1927 Paris city bus. The cost of DM 21 (DM 12.50 for children) includes a welcome-aboard drink. Contact the tourist office for details (☎ 07131/562–270). Two or three times a month, except July and August, a "Heilbronn by Night" bus tour is offered. The DM 72 cost gives entry to seven wine taverns and restaurants, with drinks and snacks in each; the tour ends at a strip club. There are bus tours of **Mannheim** May–October, Monday–Saturday at 10:30. Tours leave from the Wasserturm and cost DM 18 (DM 10 for children).

The tourist office in **Stuttgart** offers daily 2½-hour sightseeing tours of the city (weekends and Mondays only November–March; cost: DM 32 for adults, DM for 25 children) as well as evening-long "Stuttgart by Night" tours every Saturday night that go to shows and nightclubs (DM 105). For details, go to the tourist board *"i-Punkt"* (☎ 0711/222–8240) in the underground Klett-Passage at the main train station.

From April to October, the **Tübingen** tourist office runs guided city tours Wed. at 10 AM, weekends and holidays at 2:30 PM; the cost is DM 5 for adults and DM 2.50 for children.

Important Addresses and Numbers

Tourist Information
For information on the entire Burgenstrasse, contact **Arbeitsgemeinschaft Burgenstrasse,** Rathaus, Marktplatz, D–74072 Heilbronn, ☎ 07131/562–271. There are local tourist information offices in the following towns and cities:

Bad Wimpfen: Verkehrsamt, Hauptstrasse 45, D–74206 Bad Wimpfen, ☎ 07063/53151.
Heidelberg: Verkehrsverein Heidelberg, Friedrich-Ebert-Anlage 2, D–69117 Heidelberg; Am Hauptbahnhof, D–69115 Heidelberg, ☎ 06221/21341.

Heilbronn: Verkehrsverein Heilbronn, Rathaus, Marktplatz, D–74072 Heilbronn, ☎ 07131/562–270.

Mannheim: Tourist-Information, Kaiserring 10/16, D–68161 Mannheim, ☎ 0621/101–011.

Mosbach: Städtisches Verkehrsamt, Rathaus, D–74821 Mosbach, ☎ 06261/82236.

Stuttgart: Verkehrsamt der Stadt Stuttgart, Tourist-Center "i-punkt," Königstr. 1a, D–70173 Stuttgart, ☎ 0711/222–8240.

Tübingen: Verkehrsverein Tübingen, An der Neckarbrücke, D—72016 Tübingen, ☎ 07071/91360.

11 Frankfurt

Because it is the air gateway to Germany—and to Europe—you'll probably at least land in Frankfurt. Many German banks are headquartered here, and the Frankfurt Börse is Germany's leading stock exchange. All this has contributed to a high rise—spiked skyline that would stun the 30 Holy Roman Emperors who were elected and crowned here. Their portraits line the banquet hall of the Römer, or city hall. Across the River Main from the heart of downtown is the residential, medieval-feeling Sachsenhausen quarter, home to many of the city's best museums.

HOME OF THE BIGGEST AIRPORT on the Continent, Frankfurt is the gateway to Germany for most air travelers. Although it ranks fifth in size among German cities (population: 650,000), it became the country's financial capital after World War II, and although larger cities such as Munich have reclaimed the physical character of their past, Frankfurt deliberately developed a New York–style skyline. You may hear the city referred to as Mainhattan, a reference to the River Main, by which it stands. Frankfurters' temperament has also been compared with that of Americans—meaning that they're aggressive and competitive yet open and hospitable.

So why come to Frankfurt? Partly because of its history, which spans more than 1,200 years. It was: one of the joint capitals of Charlemagne's empire; the city where no fewer than 30 emperors of the Holy Roman Empire were elected and crowned; the site of Gutenberg's print shop; the birthplace of Goethe, for many Germany's greatest poet; and the city where the first German parliament met.

Frankfurt's commercial clout has its historic side as well. The city was a major trading center as early as the 12th century. Its first international Autumn Fair was held in 1240; in 1330 its Spring Fair was inaugurated. Both are still going strong today. The stock exchange, one of the half-dozen most important in the world, was established in 1595. The Rothschilds opened their first bank here in 1798.

And though Frankfurt may be a city of balance sheets and share prices, it still possesses something of the glitzy panache and high living that are such conspicuous features of today's German cities. It's more than just a question of expense-account restaurants and sleek cars. There's the feeling that you are in the heart of a powerful, sophisticated, and cosmopolitan nation. There may not be much here to remind you of the Old World, but there's a great deal that explains Germany's success story.

EXPLORING

The Old Town

Numbers in the margin correspond to points of interest on the Frankfurt map.

★ **❶** Start your tour of Frankfurt at the city's historic—albeit reconstructed— heart, the ancient **Römerberg Square,** which has been the center of civic life for centuries. Taking up most of the west side of the square is the **❷** city hall, called the **Römer.** It's a modest-looking building compared with many of Germany's city halls, though it has undeniable charm. Its gabled Gothic facade with ornate balcony is widely known as the city's official emblem. Three individual patrician buildings make up the Römer. From left to right they are the Alt-Limpurg, the Zum Römer (from which the entire structure takes its name), and the Löwenstein. The mercantile-minded Frankfurt burghers used the complex not only for political and ceremonial purposes but also for trade fairs and other commercial ventures.

The most important events to take place in the Römer were the banquets held to celebrate the coronations of the Holy Roman emperors. These were mounted starting in 1562 in the glittering and aptly named

Kaisersaal (Imperial Hall), last used in 1792 to celebrate the election of the emperor Francis II, who would later be forced by Napoléon to abdicate. The most vivid description of the ceremony was written by Germany's leading poet, Goethe, in his "Dichtung und Wahrheit" ("Poetry and Truth"). It is said that Goethe, when he was 16 years old, smuggled himself into the banquet celebrating the coronation of Emperor Joseph II by posing as a waiter to get a firsthand impression of the festivities.

Today visitors can see the impressive full-length 19th-century portraits of the 52 emperors of the Holy Roman Empire that line the walls of the reconstructed banquet hall. ☎ 069/2123–4814. ☛ *DM 3 adults, DM 1 children.* ☺ *Tues.–Sun. 11–3. Closed Mon. and when official functions are taking place.*

In the center of the square stands the fine 16th-century Fountain of Justitia (Justice). At the coronation of Emperor Matthias in 1612, wine instead of water flowed from the fountain. The crush of thirsty citizens was so great, however, that they had to be restrained to prevent damage from being done to the stonework. This practice (the wine, not the crushing) has recently been revived by the city fathers, but only for special festive occasions.

TIME OUT Inside the Römer a restaurant serves local specialties and wines from the municipal vineyards in the Rheingau. Around the corner at Limpurger Gasse 2, the restaurant's shop sells the same products and is a good place to buy a bottle of Hock or Hochheimer wine.

❸ On the south side of the Römerberg is the **Nikolaikirche** (Church of St. Nicholas). It was built during the late 13th century as the court chapel for the emperors of the Holy Roman Empire. Try to time your visit to coincide with the chimes of the glockenspiel carillon, which ring out three times a day. It's a wonderful sound. *Carillon chimes daily at 9, noon, and 5.* ☺ *Nikolaikirche Mon.–Sat. 10–5.*

❹ Beside the Nikolaikirche is the **Historisches Museum** (Historical Museum), where you can see a perfect scale model of the old town, complete with every street, house, and church. There is also an astonishing display of silver, exhibits covering all aspects of the city's life from the 16th to the 20th century, and a children's museum. *Saalgasse 19.* ☛ *DM 5 adults, DM 2.50 children; Wed. free.* ☺ *Tues.–Sun. 10–5, Wed. 10–8. Children's museum 1–5.*

Behind the church, on the east side of the square, is a row of painstakingly restored half-timbered houses called the **Ostzeile,** dating from the 15th and 16th centuries. They are an excellent example of how the people of Frankfurt have begun, albeit belatedly, to take seriously the reconstruction of their historic buildings.

From the Römerberg, walk up the pedestrian street called Neue Krame. On your left you'll pass the Gothic turrets and crenellations of the **Steinernes Haus** (Stone House), originally built in 1464, destroyed in World War II, and rebuilt from 1957 to 1960 with an altered interior. Today it is the home of the Frankfurt Kunstverein (Arts Association), which regularly mounts special exhibits (☎ 069/285–339 for details). *Markt 44.* ☛ *DM 8.* ☺ *Tues.–Sat. noon–7.*

❺ Looming up on your left is the circular bulk of the **Paulskirche** (Church of St. Paul's), a handsome, mostly 18th-century building that, church or not, is more interesting for its political than its religious significance. It was here that the short-lived German parliament met for the first

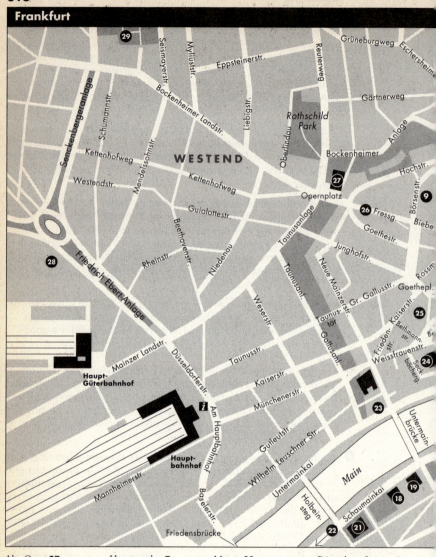

time in May 1848. The parliament was hardly a success—it was disbanded within a year, having achieved little more than offering the Prussian king the crown of Germany—but it remains a focus for the democratic aspirations of the German people. The building you see today, modeled loosely on the original, was rebuilt after the war in the expectation that it would become the home of the new German parliament. The German Book Dealers' annual Peace Prize is awarded in the hall, as is the Goethe Prize. *Paulspl.* ☉ *Daily 11–3.*

6 From Paulskirche, keep heading along the Neue Krame, which becomes Liebfrauenstrasse. Here, in more peaceful surroundings, you will come to the **Liebfrauenkirche** (Church of Our Lady), a late-Gothic church dating from the end of the 14th century. Among its few surviving features of interest are the fine tympanum relief over the south door and the ornate Rococo wood carvings. Outside, there is also a delightful Rococo fountain.

★ **7** A little farther along, Liebfrauenstrasse runs into the shopping street Zeil; turn left to reach the square called **Hauptwache,** hub of the city's transportation network. The building of the same name is a handsome 18th-century building a single story high under a steeply sloping roof. It was built as the city's guardhouse and prison; today it serves as a café. An underground shopping mall stretches below the square.

8 To the south of the square is the **Katharinenkirche** (Church of St. Katherine), the most important Protestant church in the city. What you see today is a simplified version of the second church on the site, put up after the war. It was in the original church here that the first Protestant sermon was preached in Frankfurt, in 1522. Goethe was confirmed here. Step inside to see the simple, postwar stained glass. ☉ *Daily 10–5.*

9 From Hauptwache, Schillerstrasse leads north; on the left side of the street, on Börsenplatz, is the Frankfurt **Börse** (Stock Exchange), Germany's leading stock exchange and financial powerhouse. The Börse was founded by Frankfurt merchants in 1558 to establish some order in their often chaotic dealings, but the present building dates from the 1870s. In the past, the trading on the dealers' floor was hectic. These days, computerized networks and international telephone systems have removed some of the drama, but it is still an exciting scene to watch. There is a visitors' gallery. ☎ *069/299–770.* ☛ *Free.* ☉ *Weekdays at 10, 11, and noon.*

10 Retrace your steps past the Hauptwache, and walk east along the **Zeil,** the city's largest pedestrian zone and main shopping street. It is lined with department stores selling every conceivable type of consumer goods and can get very crowded. A 15- to 20-minute walk all the way to the end of the Zeil brings you to Alfred-Brehm Platz and the entrance to the **Zoologischer Garten** (Zoological Garden). This is one of Frankfurt's chief attractions, ranking among the best zoos in Europe. Its remarkable collection includes some 5,000 animals of 600 different species, a Bears' Castle, an Exotarium (aquarium plus reptiles), and an aviary, reputedly the largest in Europe. Many of the birds can be seen in a natural setting. The zoo is an ideal place for a family outing, as it also has a restaurant and a café, along with afternoon concerts in summer. ☛ *Zoo DM 11 adults, DM 5 children.* ☉ *Apr.–Sept., daily 8–7; Oct.–Mar., daily 8–5.*

11 If you don't want to go all the way down the Zeil, turn right at the square Konstabler Wache onto Fahrgasse. Follow the signs to the **Staufenmauer,** which is one of the few surviving stretches of the old city wall. The Staufenmauer and the Saalhofkapelle (Chapel) (near the Eiserner Steg Bridge) are the two oldest parts of the medieval city in evidence today. ☞ *Free. Saalhofkapelle.* ☉ *Tues. and Thurs.–Sat. 10–5, Wed. 10–8, Sun. 10–5.*

⑫ On the nearby corner of Berlinerstrasse and Domstrasse you'll see the striking wedge-shape outline of Frankfurt's **Museum für Moderne Kunst** (Museum of Modern Art). Opened in 1991, this museum houses a spectacular collection of contemporary works by such artists as Siah Armajani, Joseph Beuys, and Andy Warhol. *Domstr. 10.* ☞ *DM 7 adults, DM 3.50 children.* ☉ *Tues., Thurs., Fri., and Sun. 10–5; Wed. 10–8; Sat. noon–7.*

TIME OUT Even if you don't have much time to spend in the museum, you can take a break from sightseeing in its bright and airy café, **Sacco and Vanzetti,** named for the celebrated anarchists of 1920s America. The prices here are low, and the quality of the coffee is very high.

⑬ Cross Berlinerstrasse at a convenient point, bear left along Braubach-strasse for a few yards, and then turn left onto Domstrasse. You are now at the church of **St. Bartholomäus** (Church of St. Bartholomew) or Kaiserdom (Imperial Cathedral), as it is more popularly known. "Cathedral" is a courtesy title; Frankfurt was never the seat of a bish-opric. This grand Gothic structure dates from 1290 and was used pri-marily for imperial coronations. It was built to replace an earlier church established by Charlemagne's son, Ludwig the Pious, on the present site of the Römerberg. The cathedral still contains many of its original magnificent Gothic carvings, including a life-size crucifixion group and a fine 15th-century altar. Its most impressive exterior fea-ture is the tall, red sandstone tower (almost 300 feet high), which was added between 1415 and 1514. Excavations in front of the main en-trance in 1953 revealed the remains of a Roman settlement and the foundations of a Carolingian imperial palace. ☞ *Free.* ☉ *Apr.–Oct., Mon. 9–12:30 and 3–6, Tues.–Sun. 8–6; Nov.–Feb., daily 9–noon and 3–5.*

From this archaeological site, walk through the pedestrian zone along-side the modern edifice of the **Schirn Kunsthalle,** a major venue for art exhibitions (*see* Sightseeing Checklists, *below*).

⑭ Continuing on will take you back to the Römerberg. From here, turn left and walk to Mainkai, the busy street that runs parallel to the tree-lined river. On your left you will see the **Rententurm,** one of the city's medieval gates, with its pinnacled towers at the base of the main spire extending out over the walls. To your right and in front is the **Eiserner Steg,** an iron footbridge that was the first suspension bridge in Europe, connecting central Frankfurt with the old district of Sachsenhausen. River trips, boat excursions, and the old steam train leave from here. (For details, *see* Guided Tours *in* Frankfurt Essentials, *below*.)

⑮ Past the Eiserner Steg is **Leonhardskirche** (St. Leonard's Church). Started in the Romanesque style and continued in the late-Gothic, it still contains two 13th-century Romanesque arches, as well as one of the few 15th-century stained-glass windows to have survived World War II and the hanging "pending vaulting" (a hanging, ornately carved piece of the ceiling vault), which was already a major Frankfurt tourist attraction during the 17th century. ☉ *Wed., Fri., and Sat. 10–noon and 3–6; Tues. and Thurs. 10–noon and 3–6:30; Sun. 9–1 and 3–6.*

★ Return to the Eisener Steg and cross the river to **Sachsenhausen.** For-merly a village separate from Frankfurt, Sachsenhausen is said to have been established by Charlemagne, who arrived here with a group of Saxon families during the 8th century and formed a settlement on the banks of the Main. It was an important bridgehead for the crusader Knights of the Teutonic Order and, in 1318, officially became part of Frankfurt. Down the bank to your left you'll catch a glimpse of the

16 15th-century **Kuhhirtenturm** (Shepherd's Tower), the only remaining part of Sachsenhausen's original fortifications. The composer Paul Hindemith lived in the tower from 1923 to 1927 while working at the Frankfurt Opera.

During the 1980s, 13 of Frankfurt's museums were built or renovated. Interesting for their architecture as well as their content, the museums have brought Frankfurt renown. Sachsenhausen, which is now largely residential, is home to no fewer than eight of these museums. They line the side of the Main, on Schaumainkai, known locally as the Museumsufer (Museum Riverbank).

17 The American architect Richard Meier designed the spacious **Museum für Kunsthandwerk** (Museum of Decorative Arts), which was opened in 1985. Here you can see a vast and stunning collection of European and Asian handicrafts, including furniture, glassware, and porcelain. *Schaumainkai 17.* ☛ *DM 5 adults, DM 2.50 children (free Wed.).* ☉ *Tues. and Thurs.–Sun. 10–5, Wed. 10–8.*

18 The extremely popular **Deutsches Architekturmuseum** (German Architectural Museum) was created by German architect Oswald Mathias Ungers. It is housed within a 19th-century villa, though the interior is entirely modern. Five floors of drawings, models, and audiovisual displays chart the progress of German architecture through the ages, along with many special exhibits. *Schaumainkai 43.* ☛ *DM 6 adults, DM 3 children (free Wed.).* ☉ *Tues. and Thurs.–Sun. 10–5, Wed. 10–8.*

Just next door, Germany's first museum devoted exclusively to the cinema, **Deutsches Filmmuseum** (German Film Museum), imaginatively
19 presents its collection of film artifacts, although the museum's own movie theater may close for budgetary reasons. *Schaumainkai 41.* ☛ *DM 5 adults, DM 2.50 children.* ☉ *Tues. and Thurs.–Sun. 10–5, Wed. 10–8.*

If you have time and energy, step away from the waterfront to explore more of the up-and-coming district of Sachsenhausen. The area has a distinctly medieval air, with narrow back alleys, quaint little inns, and quiet squares that escaped the modern developer, yet it's also full of new shops, boutiques, cafés, and bars thronging with people and activity. For Frankfurters and visitors alike, it is the place for the best nightlife—from clubs and discos to traditional taverns and restaurants, all tucked in among the half-timbered houses. The Film Museum is located at the corner of Schweizer Strasse; follow this street down
20 to **Schweizer Platz** to see the heart of Sachsenhausen.

TIME OUT   Sachsenhausen is the home of the famous *Ebbelwei* (apple-wine or cider) taverns. A green pine wreath above the entrance tells passersby that a freshly pressed—and alcoholic—apple juice is on tap. You can eat well in these small inns, too, though the menu might need some explanation. For example, *Handkas mit Musik* does not promise music at your table. The *Musik* means that the cheese, or *Kas* (from Käse), will be served with raw onions, oil, vinegar, and bread and butter. Most traditional apple-wine taverns serve this specialty without a fork, and those who ask for one give themselves away as strangers. There are about 15 of these taverns; two of the best-known are **Zum Gemalten Haus** (Schweizerstr. 67) and **Lorsbacher Tal** (Grosse Rittergasse 49).

★ ㉑ Returning to Schaumainkai and continuing east you will come to the **Städelsches Kunstinstitut und Städtische Galerie** (Städel Art Institute and Municipal Gallery). This building houses one of the most significant art collections in Germany, with fine examples of Flemish, Dutch, German, and Italian Old Masters, plus a sprinkling of French Impressionists. *Schaumainkai 63.* ☛ *DM 6 adults, DM 3 children (free Sun.).* ⊘ *Tues. and Thurs.–Sun. 10–5, Wed. 10–8.*

㉒ Finally, it's worth stopping at the **Städtische Galerie Liebieghaus** (Liebieg Municipal Museum of Sculpture). Here, in this charming 17th-century villa, is the city's internationally famous collection of classical, medieval, and Renaissance sculpture. Some pieces are exhibited in the lovely gardens surrounding the house. *Schaumainkai 71.* ☛ *DM 5 adults, DM 2.50 children.* ⊘ *Tues. and Thurs.–Sun. 10–5, Wed. 10–8.*

㉓ From here you can backtrack along the Schaumainkai to the pedestrian Holbeinsteg Bridge in front of the Städel, cross the bridge to the other side of the river, and turn left into Untermainkai. The **Jüdisches Museum** (Jewish Museum) is No. 14–15 in the former Rothschild Palais. Designed by the architect Ante von Kostelac, the museum focuses on Frankfurt's centuries-old Jewish community, the second largest in Germany after Berlin. The museum contains extensive archives of Jewish history and culture, including a library of 5,000 books, a large photographic collection, and a documentation center. *Untermainkai 14–15.* ☛ *DM 10 adults, DM 5 children (free Wed.).* ⊘ *Tues.–Sun. 10–5, Wed. 10–8.*

㉔ As you head back toward the Römer, Untermainkai becomes Mainkai; continue a short way, then turn left into the narrow Seckbächer Gasse, which will take you to the **Karmeliterkirche** (Carmelite Church and Monastery). Secularized in 1803, the church and buildings were renovated in the 1980s and now house the **Museum für Vor- und Frügeschichte** (Museum of Prehistory and Early History). At the other side of the building, the main cloister contains the largest religious fresco north of the Alps, a 16th-century representation of the birth and death of Christ by Jörg Ratgeb. The cloister also houses rotating exhibitions of modern art. *Galerie im Karmeliterkloster, Münzgasse 9.* ☛ *DM 3 adults, DM 1.50 children.* ⊘ *Tues.–Sun. 11–6. Museum für Vor-und Frühgeschichte, Karmelitergasse 1.* ☛ *DM 5 adults, DM 2.50 children (free Wed.).* ⊘ *Tues. and Thurs.–Sun. 10–5, Wed. 10–8.*

TIME OUT Pop into **Wacker's Kaffeegeschäft** (Kornmarkt, off Berliner-str.), an ancient, tiny café where you can choose a pot of coffee from 20 varieties of fresh-roasted beans. Next door, the café/restaurant **Lux** is both trendier and roomier.

★ ㉕ From here it's a short way to the **Goethehaus und Goethemuseum** (Goethe's House and Museum). Coming out of the Karmeliterkirche into Münzgasse, turn left and go to the junction of Bethmannstrasse and Berliner Strasse. Use the pedestrian walkway and cross over to the north side of Berliner Strasse, then turn left again onto Grosser Hirschgraben. Outside No. 23 there will probably be a small crowd of visitors entering and leaving. This is where Johann Wolfgang von Goethe was born in 1749. What Shakespeare is to English literature, Goethe is to German; one of his best-known works is the monumental drama *Faust.* Although the original house was destroyed by Allied bombing, it has been carefully rebuilt and restored in every detail as the young Goethe would have known it. In Goethe senior's study, look for the little window that was installed so he could keep an eye on the street outside and, in particular, on young Johann, who was well known to wander afield. The adjoining museum is closed for renovations until 1997. *Grosser Hirschgraben 23–25,* ☎ *069/282–824.* ☛ *DM 4 adults, DM 3 children.* ☉ *Apr.–Sept., Mon.–Sat. 9–6, Sun. 10–1; Oct.–Mar., Mon.–Sat. 9–4, Sun. 10–1.*

On leaving the Goethehaus turn left, and at the end of Grosser Hirschgraben bear left again and retrace your steps up Rossmarkt. Cross over to the Gutenberg Memorial and continue along the pedestrian zone to Rathenau-Platz. At the end of the square, turn left onto Grosse Bockenheimer Strasse, known locally as **Fressgasse** (Food Street) because of its many delicatessens, bakeries, and cafés. It's a gourmet shopper's paradise and one of Frankfurt's liveliest streets.

TIME OUT Stop at any of the attractive cafés or restaurants that line Fressgasse; the selection is enormous. In the summer you can sit at tables on the sidewalk and dine alfresco. If it's raining, seek out the arcade **Galerie Fressgass,** where a glass roof keeps the outdoor tables dry.

Fressgasse ends at Opernplatz and Frankfurt's reconstructed opera house, the **Alte Oper.** Wealthy Frankfurt businessmen gave generously for its original construction in the 1870s, provided they were given priority for the best seats. Kaiser Wilhelm II traveled all the way from Berlin for the gala opening in 1880. Destroyed by incendiary bombs in 1944, the opera house remained in ruins for many years while controversy raged over its reconstruction. The new building, in the classical proportions and style of the original, was finally opened in 1981 and is now a prime venue for classical concerts as well as conferences and, every now and then, an opera.

The steps of the opera house, or the Rothschild Park opposite, are a good spot from which to take in the impressive sight of Frankfurt's modern architecture. In this part of the new town you are close to the financial center (the West End), and if you look down Taunusanlage and Mainzer Landstrasse, the view both to the right and left is dominated by gleaming skyscrapers that house the headquarters of West Germany's biggest and richest banks. More than 350 international banks also have offices here, confirming Frankfurt's position as the country's financial capital. Nearest to you on the right is the 155-meter- (508-foot-) tall skyscraper housing the headquarters of the Deutsche Bank, the largest in Germany.

From here, the Taunusanlage leads south into Mainzer Landstrasse; following this route and turning left on Düsseldorferstrasse will bring you to the main train station, in Frankfurt's West End. From here, three avenues lead to the center of town: Kaiserstrasse, Münchenerstrasse, and Taunusstrasse. They are lined with fast-food joints, shops, strip clubs, cinemas, and restaurants, and at night, with neon lights flashing and rock music blaring, have a rather seedy atmosphere.

If, instead of turning left on Düsseldorferstrasse, you turn right on Friedrich-Ebert-Anlage, you'll come to the **Messe,** a vast complex of exhibition halls where some of the world's greatest trade fairs are held annually. In addition to the two major fairs in spring and fall, among the more important smaller ones are the Automobile Show in March, the Fur Fair at Easter, and the International Book Fair in early fall.

For something different, you can wander from the Alte Oper up Bockenheimer Landstrasse until you come to Siesmayerstrasse on your right; this street leads to the delightful **Palmengarten und Botanischer Garten** (Tropical Garden and Botanical Garden). The large greenhouses enclose a variety of lush tropical and subtropical flora, including 800 species of cactus, while the surrounding park offers numerous leisure facilities. During most of the year there are flower shows and exhibitions; in summer, concerts are held in an outdoor bandshell. Situated between the Palmengarten and the adjoining Grüneburgpark, the botanical gardens contain a wide assortment of wild, ornamental, and rare plants from around the world. *Entrance at Siesmayerstr. 63.* ☛ *DM 5 adults, DM 2 children.* ☉ *Apr.–Sept., daily 9–6; Oct. and Mar., daily 9–5; Nov.–Feb., daily 9–4.*

What to See and Do with Children

Your children can see birds and animals up close at the Frankfurt **Zoologischer Garten.** Of special interest is the **Exotarium,** where special climatic conditions are created, and the nocturnal section, where children can see nighttime creatures moving about. In association with the zoo is the **Natural History Museum of Senckenberg,** where exhibitions on prehistoric animals have been designed partly with children in mind. The displays will take your children back to dinosaur times and get their imaginations going (*see* Sightseeing Checklists, *below*).

For outdoor activity and a chance to run and play, Frankfurt's parks offer ample room. The **Palmengarten** has wide, open lawns landscaped with shrubs, flower borders, and trees. There is a little lake where you can rent rowboats, a play area for children, and a wading pool. Concerts take place in the music pavilion, and there is much to see in the Palm House itself (*see* Sightseeing Checklists, *below*).

Excursions on the **vintage streetcar,** the **steam train** along the river, or a **boat** will be fun and exciting for the children and provide a chance for you to sit and enjoy the scenery (*see* Guided Tours *in* Frankfurt Essentials, *below*).

Frankfurt's international airport is the busiest in mainland Europe, but it is also one of Germany's leading tourist attractions, ideal for youngsters. There's a display of old aircraft and a viewing platform above departure level A, and admission includes a ride on the "Sightseeing Train." Terminal 2, opened in 1994, also has a huge observation deck. ☛ *DM 7 adults, DM 5 children.* ☉ *9:30 AM–8 PM.*

Off the Beaten Track

The old quarter of **Höchst** is Frankfurt's most western suburb, best known today as the headquarters of the chemical concern Hoechst AG. Located on the Main River, during the Middle Ages it was a town in its own right, governed by Mainz until it was engulfed by the spread of Frankfurt. Unlike Frankfurt, however, Höchst was not devastated by wartime bombing and still possesses many of its original historic buildings. It's worth taking the time to explore the picturesque Altstadt (Old Town), with its attractive market and half-timbered houses. *Höchst can be reached via the S-1 and S-2 suburban trains from the main train station, or Konstablerwache station.*

Of special interest in the town is the factory of **Höchster Porzellan Manufaktur** (Bolongarostr. 186, ☎ 069/300–9020 or 06023/30581 to arrange for a guided tour of the works). Höchst was once a porcelain manufacturing town to rival Dresden and Vienna. Production ceased during the late 18th century but was revived by an enterprising businessman in 1965. You can also see a fine exhibit of porcelain at the **Bolongaropalast** (Bolongaro Palace), a magnificent residence facing the river. It was built during the late 18th century by an Italian snuff manufacturer. Its facade—almost the size of a football field—is nothing to sneeze at. Also on Bolongaro Strasse is the **Höchster Schloss.** Built in 1360, this castle was originally the seat and customs house of the archbishop of Mainz. Destroyed and rebuilt several times, it now houses the **local history museum.** ☛ *Free.* ⊙ *Daily 10–4.*

Of greater interest is the **Justiniuskirche,** Frankfurt's oldest building, located at the corner of Justiniusplatz and Bolongaro Strasse in Höchst. Dating from the 7th century, the church is part early Romanesque and part 15th-century Gothic. The view from the top of the hill is well worth the walk.

For the best view of Frankfurt take the lift to the viewing platform of the 1,090-foot television tower, the **Europaturm,** one of the highest towers in Europe. At the 730-foot level there's a spectacular son-et-lumière show; one floor below that is a classy restaurant, Windows. *Wilhelm-Epstein-Str. 20, Ginnheim.*

The major attraction to the southwest of the city is the **Stadtwald** (City Forest), which is threaded with lovely paths and trails and contains one of Germany's most impressive sports stadiums. Of particular interest is the Waldehrpfad—a trail leading past a series of rare trees, each identified by a small sign. The Stadtwald was the first place in Europe where trees were planted from seed (they were oaks, sown in 1398), and there are still many extremely old trees in evidence. In addition to bird sanctuaries and wild-animal enclosures, the forest also has a number of good restaurants and is a pleasant place in which to eat and linger. *Take Bus 36 from Konstablerwache to Hainer Weg.*

North of Frankfurt is the district of Seckbach. The 590-foot Lohrberg Hill is a favorite among Frankfurters, as the climb yields a fabulous view of the town and the Taunus, Spessart, and Odenwald hills. Along the way you'll also see the last remaining vineyard within Frankfurt, the Seckbach Vineyard. Take the U-4 subway to Seckbacher Landstr., then Bus 43 or 38.

Still within Frankfurt but definitely off the beaten track is scenic **Holzhausen Park.** This small park is quiet and peaceful, complete with willow trees and a little moated palace, the **Holzhausen Schlösschen.** *Take the subway to Holzhausenstr.*

The old Jewish quarter is also within Frankfurt, near Börneplatz. The **Alter Jüdischer Friedhof** (Old Jewish Cemetery) is on the east side of the square. Partly vandalized in the Nazi era, it is nearly all that remains of prewar Jewish life in Frankfurt. The cemetery can be visited by prior arrangement only. *Corner of Kurt-Schumacher-Str. and Battonstr.,* ☎ *069/561–826.*

During excavation, a **Jewish ritual bath,** or *Mikve,* was uncovered. Citizens' groups went to work to make sure that it was preserved, and it remains, incorporated into the office block and dwarfed by modern buildings. *Eckenheimer Landstr.*

Sightseeing Checklists

Historic Buildings and Sites

All of the historic buildings and sites listed below appear in the Exploring section of this chapter unless otherwise noted.

Alte Oper (Old Opera House). Built between 1873 and 1880 and destroyed during World War II, Frankfurt's old opera house has been beautifully reconstructed in the style of the original.

Bolongaropalast (Bolongaro Palace). A grand and aristocratic residence built by two Italian snuff manufacturers in the 1770s. (*See* Off the Beaten Track, *above.*)

Börneplatz. The historic center of Frankfurt's Jewish community was razed by the Nazis. (*See* Off the Beaten Track, *above.*)

Börse (Stock Exchange). This is the center of Germany's stock and money market.

Deutschordenshaus (House of the Teutonic Order). A Baroque building, it once belonged to the Knights of the Teutonic Order. It was built in 1709 above a Gothic cellar. Next door is a church that dates to 1309. *Brueckenstr. 3–7. The church can be visited by prior arrangement only* (☎ *069/609–10860*).

Eiserner Steg (Iron Bridge). A pedestrian walkway, the bridge connects the center of Frankfurt with Sachsenhausen.

Eschenheimer Turm (Eschenheimer Tower). Built during the early 15th century, this tower remains the finest example of the city's original 42 towers. *Eschenheimer Tor.*

Europaturm (Telecommunications Tower). At 332 meters (1,090 feet), this is the highest tower in Western Europe and the fourth-highest in the world. (*See* Off the Beaten Track, *above*).

Fressgasse (Food Street). The street's proper name is Grosse Bockenheimer Strasse, but Frankfurters have given it this sobriquet because of the amazing choice of delicatessens, wine merchants, cafés, and restaurants to be found here.

Goetheturm (Goethe's Tower). Located at the edge of the Stadtwald on the Sachsenhauser Berg, this is Germany's highest wood tower.

Hauptwache (Guardhouse). An attractive Baroque building, it was originally constructed as a municipal guardhouse in 1729. Today it houses a café and a tourist information office.

Höchster Schloss (Höchst Castle). This 14th-century castle, destroyed and rebuilt several times, now houses the Höchst city museum and the Hoechst AG company museum. (*See* Off the Beaten Track, *above.*)

Kuhhirtenturm (Shepherd's Tower). This is the last of nine towers, built in the 15th century, that formed part of Sachsenhausen's fortifications.

Messe (Exhibition Halls). This huge complex of buildings hosts some of the most important trade fairs in the world.

Rententurm (Renten Tower). Another of the city's fortifications, the Rententurm was built in 1456 along the Main River.

Römer (City Hall). With its gabled Gothic facade, the Römer is the traditional symbol of Frankfurt and has been the center of civic life here for 500 years.

Römerberg. This square, lovingly restored after wartime bomb damage, is the historical focal point of the city.

Sachsenhausen. The old quarter of Sachsenhausen, on the south bank of the Main River, has been sensitively preserved and continues to be very popular with residents and tourists alike.

Steinernes Haus (Stone House). This Gothic-style patrician house has also served as a trading post. Today it's an art gallery.

Zeil. This pedestrian shopping street ranks among Germany's busiest and best. (*See* Shopping, *below.*)

Churches

Dom St. Bartholomäus (Church of St. Bartholomew). Also known as the Kaiserdom (Imperial Cathedral), although it isn't really a cathedral, the church was built largely between the 13th and 15th centuries and survived the bombs of World War II with most of its original treasures intact.

Justiniuskirche (Church of St. Justinius). Situated in the old quarter of Höchst, this church dates from the days of the Carolingians and is the oldest surviving building in Frankfurt. (*See* Off the Beaten Track, *above.*)

Karmeliterkirche (Carmelite Church and Monastery). The cloisters of this former monastery contain one of the most significant religious frescoes north of the Alps; it also houses the Prehistoric Museum.

Katharinenkirche (Church of St. Catherine). This church was originally built in 1678–81, the first independent Protestant church in the Gothic style.

Leonhardskirche (St. Leonard's Church). This beautifully preserved 13th-century building with five naves has some fine old stained glass.

Liebfrauenkirche (Church of Our Lady). Dating from the 14th century, this late-Gothic church still possesses a few Rococo treasures.

Nikolaikirche (Church of St. Nicholas). The glockenspiel rings out three times a day at this small red sandstone church, which dates from the late 13th century.

Paulskirche (Church of St. Paul). Site of the first all-German parliament in 1848–49, the church is now used mainly for formal ceremonial occasions.

Saalhofkapelle (Saalhof Chapel). Near the Eiserner Stegbridge and behind the Rententurm, this small 12th-century chapel is one of the oldest buildings in the city. *Saalgasse 31.*

Museums and Galleries

Deutsches Architekturmuseum (German Architecture Museum). The museum's impressive collection of drawings, models, and audiovisual displays trace the development of German architecture.

Deutsches Filmmuseum (German Film Museum). Germany's first museum of cinematography houses an exciting collection of film artifacts.

Deutsches Postmuseum (Postal Museum). On display are the various means of transporting mail through the ages—from the mail coach to the airplane. There's also an exhibition of stamps and stamp-printing machines, as well as a reconstructed 19th-century post office. *Schaumainkai 53.* ☛ *Free.* ☺ *Tues. and Thurs.–Sun. 10–5, Wed. 10–8.*

Goethehaus und Goethemuseum (Goethe's House and Museum). The birthplace of Germany's most famous poet has been faithfully restored and is furnished with many original pieces that belonged to his family. The museum next door is currently closed for renovation.

Historisches Museum (History Museum). This fascinating museum encompasses all aspects of the city's history over the past eight centuries.

Jüdisches Museum (Jewish Museum). Housed in the former Rothschild Palais, this museum tells the story of Frankfurt's Jewish quarter.

Kaisersaal (Imperial Hall). Inside the Römer, this reconstructed banquet hall still contains a gallery of portraits of the 52 emperors of the Holy Roman Empire.

Museum für Kunsthandwerk (Museum of Applied Arts). Here more than 30,000 objects, representing European and Asian handicrafts, are exhibited in displays with changing themes.

Museum für Moderne Kunst (Museum of Modern Art). Housed in a distinctive triangular building designed by Austrian architect Hans Hollein, this collection features American Pop art and works by such German artists as Gerhard Richter and Joseph Beuys.

Museum für Völkerkunde (Ethnological Museum). The exhibits depict the lifestyles and customs of primitive societies from different parts of the world. The collection includes masks, ritual objects, and jewelry. *Schaumainkai 29.* ☛ *DM 4 adults, DM 2 children.* ⊙ *Tues. and Thurs.–Sun. 10–5, Wed. 10–8.*

Naturkundemuseum Senckenberg (Natural History Museum). Fossils, animals, plants, and geological exhibits are all displayed in an exciting, hands-on environment. The most important single exhibit is the diplodocus, imported from New York, the only complete specimen of its kind in Europe. *Senckenberganlage 25.* ☛ *DM 5 adults, DM 2 children.* ⊙ *Mon., Tues., Thurs., and Fri. 9–5; Wed. 9–8; weekends 9–6.*

Schirn Kunsthalle (Schirn Art Gallery). One of Frankfurt's most modern museums houses a good collection of 20th-century art. Located opposite the cathedral. *Am Römerberg 6a.* ☛ *DM 6–DM 9, depending on current exhibition.* ⊙ *Mon. 2–6, Tues.–Fri. 10–10, weekends 10–7.*

Städelsches Kunstinstitut and Städtische Galerie (Städel Art Institute and Municipal Gallery). One of west Germany's most important art collections, with paintings by Dürer, Vermeer, Rembrandt, Rubens, Monet, Renoir, and other great masters.

Städtische Galerie Liebieghaus (Liebieg Municipal Museum of Sculpture). The sculpture collection from different civilizations and epochs here is considered one of the most important in Europe.

Struwwelpeter-Museum. This museum contains a collection of letters, sketches, and manuscripts by Dr. Heinrich Hoffmann, physician and creator of the children's-book hero Struwwelpeter, or "Slovenly Peter," the character you see as a puppet or doll in Frankfurt's shops. *Bendergasse 1, (Römerberg).* ☛ *Free.* ⊙ *Tues. and Thurs.–Sun. 11–5, Wed. 11–8.*

Parks and Gardens

Anlagenring. When the fortification wall surrounding Frankfurt was demolished during the 19th century, the open space on both sides of the structure was turned into a park. A 3-mile ring of green now encircles the city center, north of the Main. It's an ideal circuit for joggers and fitness enthusiasts.

Nizza. On the north bank of the Main, directly opposite the museums on Schaumainkai, is this pretty promenade bordered by a wide variety of Mediterranean trees and shrubs. There are footpaths and benches, too.

Palmengarten und Botanischer Garten (Tropical Garden and Botanical Gardens). A splendid cluster of tropical and semitropical greenhouses contain a wide variety of flora, including cacti, orchids, and palms. The surrounding park has many recreational facilities. The botanical gardens feature a number of special collections, including a 2½-acre rock garden as well as rose and rhododendron gardens.

Stadtwald (City Forest). With its innumerable paths and trails, bird sanctuaries, and sports facilities, the Stadtwald is used by citizens and visitors alike for recreation and relaxation. (*See* Off the Beaten Track, *above*.)

Volkspark Niddertal. This park was the site of the 1989 *Bundes-gartenschau* (Bu'ga'schau), the annual federal garden show, which takes place in a different German city each year. The fairgrounds become a public park area after the exhibition.

Zoologischer Garten (zoo). Founded in 1858, this is one of the most important and attractive zoos in Europe, with many of the animals and birds living in a natural environment.

SHOPPING

Gift Ideas

Gifts and souvenirs are not the first things that spring to mind when one thinks of the financial capital of Germany. Like all other cities, however, Frankfurt has its shopping treasures. It is, for example, the home of the largest selection of **Meissen porcelain** outside Meissen itself, found, improbably, in the Japanese department store **Mitsukoshi** (Kaiserstr. 13, ☎ 069/293–085 or 293–086).

Porcelain from the manufacturer in the suburb of Höchst is available at the **Höchster Porzellan Manufaktur** outlet in the center of town (Berlinerstr. 60, at the Kornmarkt, ☎ 069/295–299). Here you'll find everything from figurines to dinner services, as well as a selection of glassware and silver.

La Galleria (Berlinerstr. 66, ☎ 069/281–461) has a good selection of jewelry designed and made by local craftsmen (*Goldschmeide*). There's also a range of local jewelry on sale at **Luise Schloze** (Kaiserstrasse, ☎ 069/571–769). Don't make the mistake of thinking "local" means "rustic": Jewelry-making in Germany is a highly developed and sophisticated art, as is reflected in the prices.

In Niederrad, just over the river and adjacent to Sachsenhausen, visit the stonecutter's workshop **Steinmetzbetrieb Ferdinand Stang** (Hahnstr. 18, ☎ 069/666–5990) for an amazing selection of art objects made from all types of stone.

Frankfurt may not have an abundance of fashion centers, but you'll certainly find plenty of pricey apparel here. One of the best-known designers is **Jil Sander,** whose Frankfurt outlet is on the "fashion street" Goethestrasse (Goethestr. 29, ☎ 069/283–469). A former fashion model, Sander still models her own creations in photo ads from time to time. The more affordable **Escada** sells collections made up of infinitely combinable separates and accessories (Goethestr. 31, ☎ 069/287–799).

For children, you can pick up a **Struwwelpeter** ("Slovenly Peter") puppet or doll, named after the character in the famous children's book by Frankfurt resident Heinrich Hoffmann. The **Struwwelpeter Museum** (Schirm am Römerberg, ☎ 069/281–353) has a few such dolls, as well as a range of *Struwwelpeter* children's books.

One typical Frankfurt specialty is **Apfelwein,** the famous Ebbelwei, or "apple wine," sold in most supermarkets and in the taverns in Sachsenhausen, south of the river.

If you want to stock up on "regular" local wine, stop in at the **Weinverkauf des Städtische Weingutes** in the Römer; this outlet sells wine produced in the city's own vineyards of the Rheingau. *Limpurger*

Gasse 2, ☎ *069/2123–8406.* ⊗ *Mon.–Thurs. 7:30–12:30 and 1–4, Fri. 7:30–1.*

For typical Frankfurter baked specialties, go to the renowned pastry shop **Konditorei Lochner** on the Fressgasse (Karl-Becher-Str. 10, ☎ 069/920–7320). Here you can find local delicacies such as **Bethmännchen und Brenten** (marzipan cookies) or **Frankfurter Kranz** (a sort of creamy cake). These and other sweets are also available at the café **Laumer** (Bockenheimer Landstr. 64, ☎ 069/727–912); Laumer goodies are also represented in the café in the Hauptwache.

Shopping Districts

The heart of Frankfurt's shopping district is the pedestrian street called **Zeil,** running east from Hauptwache Square. City officials claim it's the country's busiest shopping street, with an unrivaled annual turnover of more than DM 1 billion. The seven-story, metal-and-glass mall of the **Zeil Galerie** is at the beginning of the street, near the Hauptwache (Zeil 112-114, ☎ 069/9207–3414). This complex includes 56 shops and boutiques, generally ranging from low- to mid-price, as well as several types of eateries, including cafés and Japanese fare. The streets running off Zeil and the Hauptwache are home to a series of upscale fashion shops: **Goethestrasse** is the best known of Frankfurt's "quarter" for luxury shopping, with boutiques, art galleries, jewelry stores, and antiques shops.

A more upscale mall is the new **Schiller Passage,** located around the corner from the Börse (Schillerstrasse). This small, elegant shopping arcade is gradually filling with everything from shoe stores to lingerie boutiques. It centers, in the most literal sense, around the **Cafe Cult,** a restaurant, meeting point, music bar, and late-night spot for the young and beautiful. There's another ritzy mall in the **BfG building** on the corner of Willy-Brandt-Platz and Neue-Mainzer-Str.

Extending west from the Hauptwache is **Grosse Bockenheimer Strasse** (known as **Fressgasse,** or food street, to the locals). Cafés, restaurants, and, above all, food shops are the draw here. This is the place for fish—fresh or smoked—cheeses, and a wide range of local specialties, including frankfurters. Arcades such as the **Galerie Fressgasse** provide additional dining and shopping possibilities.

The multitude of stores and antiques shops across the river in **Sachsenhausen** are ever more chic. The **Metzgerei Meyer** (Schweizer Strasse 42, ☎ 069/615–010) is worth a look for its decor alone. Stark green-and-black Italian tiles and subtle spotlighting make this probably the classiest butcher shop in Germany; it looks more like a jewelry store than a place that sells sausages.

Flea Markets

Frankfurt has two weekend flea markets: on Saturday, from 9 to 2, on Schaumainkai below the Eiserner Steg, and on Sunday from 8 to 2 at the Schlachthof (slaughterhouse) on Seehoferstrasse in Sachsenhausen. Whichever you choose, get there early for the bargains. There's a wide range of goods on display, a lot of them pretty junky, but sometimes better-quality items reward the diligent browser. Shopping success or no, both markets are fun to explore and show a different shade of Frankfurt's local color.

SPORTS AND FITNESS

For information on sport clubs and organizations in Frankfurt, as well as public pools, call the city sports office (☎ 069/212–33887).

Bicycling

Opportunities in the city are limited, but get away from the downtown area and Frankfurt's parks and forests offer terrific places for recreational biking. In summer you can rent bikes at the **Goetheturm** (☎ 069/49111) on the northern edge of the Stadtwald.

Fitness Centers

Fitness Company Judokan (Zeil 109, ☎ 069/280–565) is centrally located near the Hauptwache and offers everything anyone needs to work out. There are more than 60 aerobic and gym classes, and 150 different fitness machines, from Nautilus to StairMaster. English is spoken. A day's training costs DM 25; the price includes a sauna.

Intercontinental (Wilhelm-Leuschner-Str. 43, ☎ 069/26050) overlooks the Main River, along whose banks you can jog. The hotel has an indoor pool, health club, gym, and sauna.

Hotel Gravenbruch Kempinski (Neu-Isenburg 2, ☎ 06102/5050) is about 15 minutes by car outside of Frankfurt. It's located in a 37-acre park, with tennis courts, two Olympic-size pools, and jogging paths through the woods.

Jogging

One good place to jog in Frankfurt is along the banks of the Main River. To avoid retracing your steps, you can always cross a bridge and return down the opposite side. In the center city, **Grüneberg Park** is 1 mile around, with a Trimm Dich ("get fit") exercise facility in the northeast corner. Nearby is the greenery of the **Anlagenring,** a park following the line of the old city walls around the city that is also popular with local joggers. For a vigorous forest run, take the streetcar to **Hohemark** (a 30-minute ride); a streetcar will also bring you to the **Stadtwald,** a 4,000-acre forest park south of the city where you can jog, swim, or play tennis.

Skating

Eissporthalle has two rinks, one outdoor, the other indoor. *Am Bornheimer Hang 4, Ratsweg,* ☎ *069/2123–0825. ☛ DM 10 adults, DM 8 children; skate rental: DM 6 for 3 hrs. ☺ Nov.–Feb., daily 9 AM–10:30 PM.*

Swimming

The **Rebstockbad** leisure center has an indoor pool, a pool with a wave machine and a palm-fringed beach, and an outdoor pool with giant water chutes. *August-Euler-Str. 7,* ☎ *069/708–078. ☛ 3 hours: DM 13 adults, DM 7 children. ☺ Mon. 2–10 PM, Tues. and Thurs. 9 AM–8 PM, Wed. and Fri.–Sun. 9 AM–10 PM, closed Mon.*

Another pool complex is **Titus Thermen,** with everything from "adventure pools" to squash courts. *Walter-Möller-Platz 2,* ☎ *069/958–050. ☛ 4 hours: DM 12 adults, DM 7 children.*

The **Stadionbad** has an outdoor pool, a giant water chute, a solarium, and exercise lawns. *Morfelder Landstr. 362,* ☎ *069/678–040. ☺ Mid-May–Sept.*

Also open in summer are a number of city pools, such as the **Brentanobad,** an outdoor pool surrounded by lawns and old trees, which is often crowded in summer. *Rödelheimer Parkweg,* ☎ *069/2123–9020.* ☛ *DM 5 adults, DM 3.50 children.*

Tennis

Courts are available at the **Nidda Park** sports center. Next to the **Stadionbad** (*see above*) you'll find 20 courts (cost: about DM 20 per hour, depending on the time and day of the week). Call (☎ 069/678–040) for reservations.

DINING

Dining in Frankfurt—the expense-account city par excellence—can be expensive. You'll need to make reservations well in advance, too, if you plan to eat in any of the fancier restaurants. The good news is that the range and quality of the city's restaurants are terrific. You can find everything from the most sophisticated French haute cuisine to neighborhood *Gasthofs* (beer restaurants) serving earthy local dishes.

CATEGORY	COST*
$$$$	over DM 95
$$$	DM 65–DM 95
$$	DM 45–DM 65
$	under DM 45

per person for a three-course meal, excluding drinks

$$$$ ★ **Avocado.** Huge arrangements of fresh flowers make this classy restaurant as ideal for a romantic dinner as for a business lunch. The fine bistro food with truly excellent service doesn't hurt either. Recent offerings included guinea-fowl baked in a potato coating and served in a sherry sauce. ✕ *Hochstr. 27,* ☎ *069/292–867. Reservations recommended. AE, MC, V. Closed Sun.*

$$$$ **Erno's Bistro.** Erno's is something of a Frankfurt institution. It's small and chic—*very* popular with visiting power brokers—and offers classy French cuisine. Fish dishes predominate—all the fish is flown in daily, most of it from France—with specialties varying according to what's available in the markets that day. This is one of those rare restaurants where you can sit back and let the staff—all the waiters speak English—choose your meal for you. ✕ *Liebigstr. 15,* ☎ *069/721–997. Reservations required. Jacket and tie. AE, DC, MC, V. Closed Sat., Sun., 1 wk at Easter, and mid-June–mid-July.*

$$$$ **Papillon.** Although it's part of the airport Sheraton, the Papillon has won over the country's most respected food critics—who agree that this is Germany's best airport restaurant. No whisper of a jet engine can be heard, and there's no rush or bustle in the velvety, luxurious dining room. Kitchen manager Klaus Bohler concentrates on a small but vividly imaginative daily changing menu, on which you'll find such delicacies as rolled pike perch coated in wild rice or lamb fillet served with eggplant baked in a sour-cream dough. ✕ *Sheraton Hotel, Frankfurt Airport (Terminal Mitte),* ☎ *069/697–1238. Reservations advised. Jacket and tie. AE, DC, MC, V. Closed Sat. lunch and Sun.*

$$$$ ★ **Restaurant Français.** The crystal chandeliers, tapestries on the walls, and green-and-gold surroundings of this restaurant of the incomparably luxurious Steigenberger Hotel Frankfurter Hof provide an appropriately sumptuous setting for some of the finest food in Frankfurt. The food is French (of course), traditional rather than nouvelle, and served with the sort of panache you might expect in one of the best restaurants in Paris. For a memorable gastronomic treat, try the stuffed

332

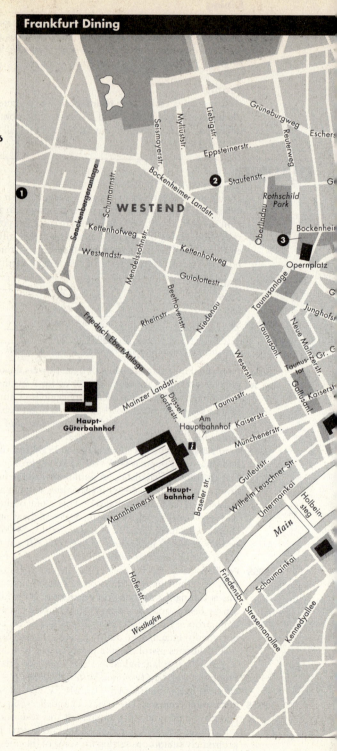

Frankfurt Dining

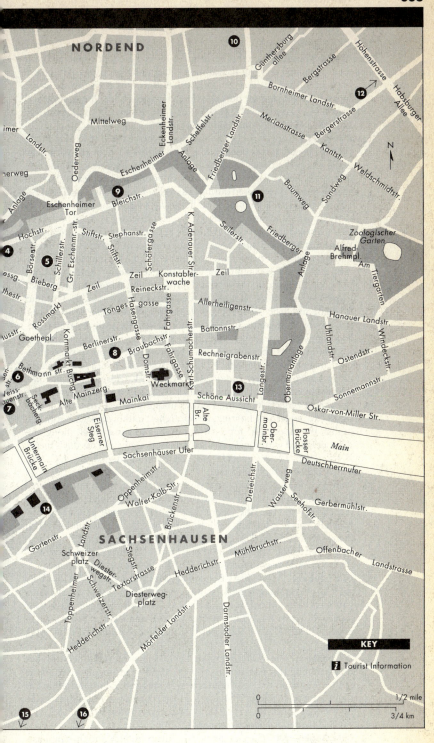

NORDEND

Mittelweg

Eckenheimer Landstr.

Scheffelstr.

Günthersburg allee

Bergstrasse

Höhenstrasse

Habsburger Allee

Bornheimer Landstr.

Merianstrasse

Bergerstrasse

imer Landstr.

Oederweg

Anlage

Friedberger Landstr.

Kantstr.

Sandweg

Weldschmidtstr.

nerweg

Eschenheimer

Anlage

Bleichstr.

Baumweg

Anlage

Eschenheimer Tor

Hochstr.

Schillerstr.

Stiftstr.

Stephanstr.

Schäfergasse

K. Adenauer Str.

Seilerstr.

Friedberger

Zoologischer Garten

Alfred-Brehmpl.

Am Tiergarten

Börserstr.

Gr. Eschenhr.-str.

Stiftstr.

Zeil

Reineckstr.

Konstabler-wache

Zeil

Bieberg

Zeil

gasse

Hasengasse

Fahrgasse

Allerheiligenstr.

Hanauer Landstr.

Uhlandstr.

Ostendstr.

Windeckstr.

Rossmarkt

Tönges

Battonnstr.

thestr.

Goethepl.

Berlinerstr.

Braubachstr.

Domstr.

Rechneigrabenstr.

Langestr.

Obermainanlage

Sonnemannstr.

Bethmann str.

Buchg.

Karl-Schumacherstr.

Fahrgasse

Weckmarkt

Schöne Aussicht

Oskar-von-Miller Str.

Alte Mainzerg.

Mainkai

Seckbacherg.

Alte Br.

Ober-mainbr.

Flosser Brücke

Main

Eiserner Steg

Sachsenhäuser Ufer

Deutschherrnufer

Untermain Brücke

Oppenheimstr.

Walter-Kolb-Str.

Dreieichstr.

Wasserweg

Seehofstr.

Gerbermühlstr.

Gartenstr.

SACHSENHAUSEN

Siegstr.

Brückenstr.

Mühlbruchstr.

Offenbacher Landstrasse

Schweizer platz

Diester-wegstr.

Textorstrasse

Hedderichstr.

Darmstädter Landstr.

Toppenheimer

Schweizerstr.

Diesterweg-platz

Mörfelder Landstr.

Hedderichstr.

0 _____ 1/2 mile

0 _____ 3/4 km

quail in truffle-butter sauce. ✕ *Am Kaiserplatz,* ☎ *069/215–865. Reservations required. Jacket and tie. AE, DC, MC, V. Closed Sun. and 4 wks in July or Aug.*

$$$ **Altes Zollhaus.** Within this beautiful, 200-year-old half-timbered house you can enjoy very good, traditional German specialties. Try one of the game dishes, or the sliced pork with mushrooms in apple-wine sauce. In summer you can eat outside while chefs grill in the huge garden. ✕ *Friedberger Landstr. 531,* ☎ *069/472–707. Reservations advised. AE, DC, MC, V. Dinner only. Closed Mon.*

$$$ **Bistrot 77.** Proprietor-chef Dominique, who learned his trade in the French Alsace, serves outstanding food in this spare bistro with plain walls and a tile floor. The accent is on fresh vegetables and fine cuts of meat, such as rosettes of lamb with young runner beans. Various special dinners are offered during the week—bouillabaisse on Tuesdays, a three-course regional meal on Thursdays—and there's always one three-course lunch for DM 48. ✕ *Ziegelhüttenweg 1–3,* ☎ *069/614– 040. Reservations advised. AE, MC, V. Closed Sat. lunch and Sun.*

$$$ **Weinhaus Brückenkeller.** Sophisticated dining in Frankfurt isn't just a
★ matter of refined French food in expense-account restaurants. This establishment offers magnificent German specialties in the sort of time-honored, arched cellar that would have brought a lump to Bismarck's throat. What's more, though the food may be unmistakably Teutonic, it's light and delicate—for example, cream of cucumber soup, or veal on tomato vinaigrette. In addition to the terrific antique-strewn surroundings and the classy food, there's a phenomenal range of wines to choose from: The cellars—don't be shy about asking to see them— hold around 85,000 bottles. ✕ *Schützenstr. 6,* ☎ *069/284–238. Reservations advised. Jacket and tie. AE, DC, MC, V. Closed lunch and Sun.*

$$ **Börsenkeller.** The dark (some would say masculine) atmosphere of this
★ restaurant reflects its favored status among workers from the nearby stock exchange. Soft lighting, heavy arches, and high-back booths establish the mood. The food is traditional and substantial, though always prepared with some style. See if venison stew is on the day's menu. ✕ *Schillerstr. 11,* ☎ *069/281–115. Reservations advised. AE, DC, MC, V. Closed Sat. dinner and Sun.*

$$ **Charlot.** The French cuisine of this very popular restaurant has acquired an Italian touch since the arrival of chef Mario, but it has survived the transition well. The Alte Oper is just across the street, so after the curtain falls you'll be fighting with the music buffs for a place in the French bistro–style dining rooms, spread over two floors. But you might also be sharing a table with Luciano Pavarotti. ✕ *Opernpl. 10,* ☎ *069/287– 007. Reservations advised. AE, DC, MC, V. Closed Sun. lunch.*

$$ **Gildestuben.** This is a lusty Bohemian beer tavern with a spacious beer garden overlooking a park. Sample such Czech dishes as *Svickova* (smoked beef and cranberry sauce with juicy dumplings). Wash your choice down with genuine Pilsener Urquell and Budvar beers. ✕ *Bleichstr. 38,* ☎ *069/283–228. Reservations not required. AE, DC, MC, V.*

$$ **Zur Müllerin.** The *Müllerin* (miller's wife) is Lieselotte Müller, who has been running this restaurant since the 1950s. Her regulars are artists and actors from the nearby theaters; expressions of appreciation for their beloved Müllerin's cooking skills decorate the restaurant walls. ✕ *Weissfrauenstr. 18, tel 069/285–182. Reservations advised. AE, DC, MC, V. Closed for lunch weekends.*

$ **Cafe GegenwART.** *Gegenwart* means "the present," and the emphasis on the second syllable means regularly changing exhibitions by local artists on the walls of this friendly, noisy café-restaurant. It's frequented by a young crowd, and in the summer diners spill out onto the pavement, where Riviera-style tables brighten up the scene. There's a French accent on the menu, too—the tomato fondue is a dream. ✕ *Berger Str. 6, ☎ 069/497–0544. No credit cards.*

$ **Pelikan.** Inexpensive but imaginative dishes from a daily changing menu are served up here on pink-lined decked tables to students and professors from the nearby university. This is one place where vegetarians are not in the minority—the Pelikan offers an unusually good selection of meatless dishes. In summer a boulevard terrace opens for business. *Jordanstr. 19, ☎ 069/701–287. No credit cards. Closed Sat. lunch and Sun., except during trade fairs.*

$ **Steinernes Haus.** An unpretentious historic inn, it was salvaged from the wreckage of World War II along with the cathedral and town hall around the corner. Traditional fare popular with locals includes *Frankfurter Rippchen* (smoked pork) and *Zigeunerhackbraten* (spicy meat loaf). ✕ *Braubachstr. 35, ☎ 069/283–491. No reservations. No credit cards.*

$ **Zum Gemalten Haus.** This is the real thing—a traditional apple-wine
★ tavern in the heart of Sachsenhausen. Its name means "At the Painted House," a reference to the frescoes that cover the walls inside and out. In summer the courtyard is the place to be; in winter you sit in the noisy tavern proper at long tables with benches. It's often crowded, so if there isn't room when you arrive, order a glass of apple wine and hang around until someone leaves. Traditional cider-tavern dishes include *Rippchen* (smoked pork), but come here for *Rinderselcher* (smoked beef). ✕ *Schweizerstr. 67, ☎ 069/614–559. No reservations. No credit cards. Closed Mon. and Tues.*

$ **Zur Eulenburg.** Take the subway or a streetcar out to Seckbacher Landstrasse, in the district of Bornheim, a mile northeast of the old town, to eat in this popular apple-wine tavern. You'd better be hungry, though: The portions would satisfy a starveling. The house speciality is home-cured roast beef with fried potatoes. ✕ *Eulengasse 46, ☎ 069/451–203. No reservations. No credit cards. Closed lunch, Mon., and Tues.*

LODGING

Businesspeople descend on Frankfurt year-round, so most hotels in the city are expensive (though many also offer significant reductions on weekends, an option worth checking out) and are frequently booked up well in advance. The majority of the larger hotels are around the main train station, close to the business district and the trade-fair center and a 15- to 20-minute walk from the old town. Lower prices and—for some, anyway—more atmosphere are found at smaller hotels and pensions in the suburbs; the efficient public transportation network makes them easy to reach. Many hotels add as much as a 50% surcharge during trade fairs (Messen), of which there are generally about 30 a year. Some dates to avoid (unless you intend to visit one of the fairs in question) are: January 27–31 (Premiere); February 24–28 (Ambiente); August 24–28 (International Autumn Fair); and the Frankfurt Book Fair, held during the second week of October. These dates may change, so it's best to confirm them with the German-American Chamber of Commerce (☎ 212/974–8830; in London, ☎ 071/734–0543) or the local tourist office..

CATEGORY	COST*
$$$$	over DM 275
$$$	DM 180–DM 275
$$	DM 120–DM 180
$	under DM 120

All prices are for two people in a double room, including tax and service.

$$$$ **Arabella Grand Hotel.** The emphasis at this recent addition to Frankfurt's list of luxury hotels is on the "grand." Everything is large-scale, from the palatial public rooms to the vast double bedrooms. The center-city location means that the views from many of the rooms are of backyards and parking lots, but pull the heavy drapes and it's a world of understated luxury. ⌂ *Konrad-Adenauer-Str. 7,* ☎ *069/29810,* FAX *069/298–1810. 367 rooms with bath, 11 suites. [df]2 restaurants, bar, pool, sauna, fitness center, beauty parlor, parking. AE, DC, MC, V.*

$$$$ ★ **Hessischer Hof.** This is the choice of many businesspeople, not just because of its location opposite the trade-fair building but for the air of class and style that pervades its handsome and imposing interior (the exterior is nondescript). The public rooms are subdued and traditional; bedrooms are elegantly chic, and many of them are furnished with antiques. The restaurant features excellent nouvelle cuisine; it also has a fine display of Sevres porcelain arranged around the walls. ⌂ *Friedrich-Ebert-Anlage 40,* ☎ *069/75400,* FAX *069/754–0924. 106 rooms and 11 suites with bath. Restaurant, 2 bars, parking. AE, DC, MC, V.*

$$$$ ★ **Hotel Gravenbruch Kempinski.** The atmosphere of the 16th-century manor house that this elegant, sophisticated hotel was built around still remains at this parkland sight, a 15-minute drive south of the downtown area. It's a combination of substantial modern luxury with Old World charm that works. All the rooms are spacious and classy and have views of the lake or the park. ⌂ *63243 Neu Isenberg,* ☎ *06102/5050,* FAX *06102/505–445. 288 rooms and 29 suites with bath. 2 restaurants, bar, indoor and outdoor pools, beauty salon, massage, sauna, tennis, convention center. AE, DC, MC, V.*

$$$$ **Parkhotel.** A member of the Forte chain, this is another businessman's favorite, conveniently located just across from the train station. The structure successfully fuses the original 19th-century red-stone building and a postwar addition. ⌂ *Wiesenhüttenpl. 28–38,* ☎ *069/26970,* FAX *069/2697884. 300 rooms with bath. 2 restaurants, bar, winestube, sauna, fitness room. AE, DC, MC, V.*

$$$$ ★ **Steigenberger Frankfurter Hof.** The combination of an old-town location, an imposing 19th-century Renaissance-style building, and full-bodied luxury makes this the leading choice for many visitors. The atmosphere throughout is one of old-fashioned, formal elegance, with burnished woods, fresh flowers, and thick-carpeted hush. The Restaurant Français (*see above*) is among the gourmet high spots of Germany; the bar is a classy late-night rendezvous. ⌂ *Am Kaiserplatz,* ☎ *069/21502,* FAX *069/215–860. 347 rooms and 10 suites with bath. 4 restaurants, 2 bars. AE, DC, MC, V.*

$$$$ ★ **An der Messe.** This little place, whose name means "at the fairgrounds," is a pleasing change from the giant hotels of the city. It's stylish, with a distinctive pink marble lobby and chicly appointed bedrooms. The staff is courteously efficient. The only drawback is the absence of a restaurant. ⌂ *Westendstr. 104,* ☎ *069/747–979,* FAX *069/748–349. 46 rooms with bath. Parking. AE, DC, MC, V.*

$$$ **Dorint Hotel.** The Frankfurt member of the Dorint chain is a modern, well-appointed hotel with all the comfort and facilities expected from

this well-run group—including a palm-fringed indoor pool. The hotel is south of the river in the Niederrad district, but there are good bus and subway connections with the city center and Sachsenhausen. ☎ *Hahnstr. 9, ☎ 069/663–060, FAX 069/6630–6600. 183 rooms (29 reserved for nonsmokers), 8 suites. Restaurant, 2 bars, indoor pool, sauna, parking. AE, DC, MC, V.*

$$$ **Liebig.** A comfortable, family-run hotel, this establishment has spacious, high-ceiling rooms and a friendly feel. Ask for a room at the back—it's much quieter. Try the Weinstube restaurant for excellent Hessen wine. ☎ *Liebigstr. 45, ☎ 069/727–551, FAX 069/727–555. 20 rooms with bath. Restaurant. AE, MC, DC, V.*

$$$ **Palmenhof.** Named for its proximity to the botanical garden, Palmengarten, this luxuriously modernized hotel occupies a renovated Art Deco *Jugendstil* (German Art Nouveau) building in Frankfurt's West End. The high-ceiling rooms have up-to-date comfort but retain the elegance of the old building. In the basement is a cozy restaurant, the Bastei, with an expensive nouvelle menu. ☎ *Bockenheimer Landstr. 89–91, ☎ 069/753–0060, FAX 069/7530–0666. 47 rooms with bath, plus 40 apartments. Restaurant, parking. AE, DC, MC, V.*

$$$ **Schwille.** Frankfurt's famous *Fressgasse* is right outside the door, although you don't have to venture too far in search of culinary attractions; the Schwille itself has an excellent café-restaurant that's so popular among the locals that it opens at six in the morning to cater to early risers. Despite the hotel's central location, its rooms are quiet. They are dark wood–toned, decorated with pleasing floral prints, but on the small side. ☎ *Grosse Bockenheimerstr. 50, ☎ 069/920–100, FAX 069/9201–0999. 51 rooms with shower or bath. Restaurant, parking. AE, DC, MC, V.*

$$ **Attache.** This simple but comfortable downtown hotel has no restaurant, but a buffet breakfast provides a hearty start to the day. Rooms are comfortably if unspectacularly furnished and have such amenities as color TV. ☎ *Kölnerstr. 10, ☎ 069/730282, FAX 069/7392194. 46 rooms with shower or bath. Bar. AE, MC, V.*

$$ **Hotel Ibis Frankfurt Friedensbrüke.** This modern hotel was recently acquired by the Ibis chain, known for providing modern comfort at affordable prices. Ask for a room overlooking the River Main and you'll have a good view and a convenient location: near the main railway station and downtown Frankfurt. ☎ *Speicherstr. 3–5, ☎ 069/273–030, FAX 069/237–024. 233 rooms with bath. Restaurant, bar, parking. AE, DC, MC, V.*

$$ **Harheimer Hof.** Modern and comfortable, this is a reasonably priced hotel packed with good facilities. It may be a few miles north of the center, in Harheim, but don't try reserving a room at the last minute. ☎ *Alt Harheim 11, ☎ 06101/4050, FAX 06101/405–411. 46 rooms with bath. Restaurant, bar, café, pool, sauna, exercise room. AE, DC, MC, V.*

$$ **Maingau.** This excellent-value hotel is within easy reach of the downtown area, close to the lively Sachsenhausen quarter and its cheery apple-wine taverns. Rooms are basic but clean and comfortable, and all have TVs. Families with children are welcome. The room rate includes a substantial breakfast buffet. ☎ *Schifferstr. 38–40, ☎ 069/617–001, FAX 069/620–790. 100 rooms with bath. Restaurant, parking. AE, MC.*

$$ **Hotel-Pension West.** For home comforts, a handy location (close to the
★ university), and good value, try this family-run pension. It's in an older building and scores high for old-fashioned appeal. The rooms are hardly luxurious, but they're more than adequate for a night or

Frankfurt Lodging

An der Messe, **4**

Arabella Grand
Hotel, **13**

Attache, **6**

Dorint Hotel, **12**

Harheimer Hof, **14**

Hessischer Hof, **5**

Hotel Gravenbruch
Kempinski, **16**

Hotel Ibis Frankfurt
Friedensbrüke, **8**

Hotel-Pension
West, **1**

Hotelschiff *Peter
Schlott*, **9**

Liebig, **2**

Maingau, **15**

Palmenhof, **3**

Parkhotel, **7**

Schwille, **10**

Steigenberger
Frankfurter Hof, **11**

Waldhotel Hensels
Felsenkeller, **17**

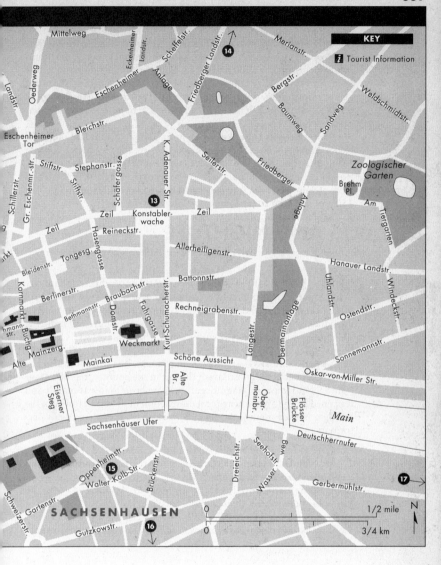

KEY

i Tourist Information

two. ⌧ *Gräfstr. 81,* ☎ *069/247–9020,* ⒡ *069/707–5309. 20 rooms with shower. AE, DC, MC, V.*

$ **Hotelschiff** *Peter Schlott.* This is Frankfurt's most unusual hotel—a riverboat moored near Höchst. Few comforts are lacking, although the rooms are unsurprisingly on the small side. Still, they offer fine views of the Main River, which laps outside the portholes. Caution is advised when guests return home after a night out in Frankfurt. ⌧ *Mainberg,* ☎ *069/315–480,* ⒡ *069/307–671. 19 rooms, half with shower. Restaurant, parking. AE, MC.*

$ **Waldhotel Hensels Felsenkeller.** Helmut Braun's traditional old hotel backs onto the woods that ring Frankfurt, yet the city center is just a 15-minute train ride away (the nearest stop is a three-minute walk). Rooms are quite basic, but there are plans to modernize them and add more amenities. ⌧ *Buchrainstr. 95,* ☎ *069/652–086,* ⒡ *069/658–379. 15 rooms, 7 with bath. Restaurant, parking. MC.*

THE ARTS AND NIGHTLIFE

The Arts

Frankfurt has the largest budget for cultural expenditure of any city in the country. Unfortunately, economic recession hit the city hard, and in 1994 it also had the highest debt of any German city. This meant introducing or raising admission fees for city museums and reducing the number of opera performances. Still, what you *can* see is likely to be first-rate. The **Städtische Bühnen**—municipal theaters, including the city's opera company—are the leading venues, but Frankfurt also has what is probably the most lavish theater in the country, the **Alte Oper** (Old Opera House), a magnificently ornate heap that was rebuilt and reopened in 1981 after near-total destruction in the war. However, the building is used mainly for classical concerts rather than opera performances.

Theater tickets can be purchased from the tourist office at Römerberg 27 and from all theaters. Alternatively, try the **Kartenvorverkauf am Liebfrauenberg** (Liebfrauenberg 52–54, ☎ 069/293–131), the ticket office in the **Hertie** department store (Zeil 90, ☎ 069/294–848), or **Kartenkiosk Sandrock** (Hauptwache Passage, ☎ 069/20115). Call for information about concerts (☎ 069/11517). Pick up a copy of the twice-monthly listings magazine *Frankfurter Wochenschau* from any tourist office.

Theater

If you speak German, you can understand the highbrow drama at the **Kammerspiele** (Hofstr. 2, ☎ 069/2123–7444) or the municipally owned **Schauspiel,** or Playhouse (Willy-Brandt-Pl., ☎ 069/2123–7444), and lighter fare at **Die Komödie** (Neue Mainzer Str. 18, ☎ 069/284–580). For a more zany theatrical experience, try **Die Schmiere** (Seckbächer Gasse 2, ☎ 069/281–066), which offers trenchant satire and also disarmingly calls itself "the worst theater in the world." Renowned for international experimental productions, including dance theater and other forms of nonverbal drama, is **Theater am Turm** (TAT) (☎ 069/154–5104 or 069/154–5110), recently moved to a new space in the Bockenheimer Depot. Another cultural center, the **Künstlerhaus Mouson Turm** (Waldschmidtstr. 4, ☎ 069/4058–9520) hosts a regular series of concerts of all kinds, as well as plays and exhibits. If you're looking for English-language productions, try either the **Frankfurt Playhouse** (Hansaallee 150, ☎ 069/151–5835) or the **English Theater**

(Kaiserstr. 52, ☎ 069/2423–1620). An international variety theater opened recently at the **Tiger Palast** (Heiligkreuzgasse 16–20, ☎ 069/289–691), with performances Tuesday–Saturday.

Concerts and Opera

The most glamorous venue for classical-music concerts is the **Alte Oper** (Old Opera) (Opernpl. ☎ 069/236–061). Even if you don't go to a performance, it's worth having a look at the ponderous and ornate lobby, an example of 19th-century classicism at its most self-confident. Under conductor Sylvain Cambreling, the **Frankfurt Opera** is making a new name for itself as a company for dramatic artistry; while the **Frankfurt Ballet,** directed by William Forsythe, is world renowned. Both perform at the **Städtische Bühnen** (Willy-Brandt-Pl., ☎ 069/236–061).

The **Festhalle** (☎ 069/75750) at the trade-fair building is the scene of many rock concerts and other large-scale spectaculars.

Nightlife

Frankfurt, for all its unabashed internationalism and sophisticated expense-account living, is unlikely to win many votes as Germany's premier after-hours town. Most of the larger hotels have bars, discos, and nightclubs. There's little to distinguish them from thousands of similar haunts the world over, but they're tried and tested. True, Frankfurt also has a red-light district, centered on the tawdry streets around the train station, though it's hardly in the same league as Hamburg's Reeperbahn.

For more genuinely local nightlife, head across the river to **Sachsenhausen,** Frankfurt's "Left Bank." It's hardly the quaint old Bohemian quarter it likes to bill itself as, but for bars, discos, clubs, and beer and wine restaurants this is about the best place to try. If you're in search of a rowdy night out, check out the **Apfelwein** (cider) taverns—they're touristy but fun. A green wreath above the door identifies them. If the area doesn't agree with you, try the ever-more-fashionable district of **Bornheim,** northeast of downtown. It has an almost equal number of bars, clubs, and the like, but the atmosphere is less forced, more authentic.

Frankfurt does have one trump card, however—**jazz.** Many German cities like to call themselves the jazz capital of the country, but Frankfurt probably has a better claim to the title than most. Fittingly, it's here, in the fall, that the German Jazz Festival is held. There are hundreds of jazz venues, from smoky back-street cafés all the way to the Old Opera House. But **Der Jazzkeller** has been the most noted venue for German jazz fans for decades (*see below*).

Bars and Nightclubs

Cooky's (Am Salzhaus 4) is one of the most popular local haunts for listening to rock music; live bands perform on Monday night. You can also dance and have a meal. It's open nightly until 4 AM. If you're seeking something altogether more soothing, try the **Casablanca Bar** (Parkhotel, Wiesenhüttenplatz 28) for piano music and a little crooning (open Mon.–Sat. 8 PM–2 AM). **Jimmy's Bar** (Friedrich-Ebert-Anlage 40), in the Hessischer Hof Hotel, is distinctly more classy—and expensive. It's a favorite with high-flying executives and other big spenders. **John's Place** (Steinweg 7) is intimate and relaxed, taking its cue from genial owner John Paris. He offers good food and a mellow atmosphere.

St. John's Inn (Grosser Hirschgraben 20) offers an English-style scene and more than 300 different whiskeys from which to choose, and the restaurant stays open until 2 AM. For a beer tour of Germany, visit the **Frankfurter Bierhaus,** where 44 different brews are served in vaulted cellars with regional tidbits (Schutzenstr. 10). The newest "in spot" is the **Cafe Cult** (Schillerstr.), in the Schillerpassage, which presents live music in the evening.

Discos

For a literally high time, take the lift to the top of the Europaturm (Messegelände), which throbs to the beat of the **Sky Fantasy** disco. Bizarre though it may seem, about the best disco in the city is at the airport. It's **Dorian Gray,** easily reached by S-bahn and located in section C, level O. It attracts a surprisingly upscale crowd and has loud music and soft lights. If it's too faddish, try the **Montgolfiere** at the nearby Steigenberger Airport Hotel. **Plastik** (Seilerstr. 34) is more obviously trendy, the sort of place where the Frankfurt beau monde flocks to see and be seen. South of the river in Sachsenhausen, try the **Evergreen** disco (Paradiesgasse 23).

Jazz

Der Frankfurter Jazzkeller (Kleine Bockenheimer Str. 18a) is the oldest jazz cellar in Germany, founded by legendary trumpeter Carlo Bohländer. It offers hot, modern, jazz, often free (although the cover charge for some performances is around DM 25). The Opera House sits above one of the city's leading jazz clubs, the **Dixie und Swing in der Alten Oper** (Opernpl.). **Jazz Kneipe** (Berlinstr. 70) is a reliable bet for swing jazz and is open until 4 AM. **Schlachthof** (Deutschherrnufer 36) is the place for Dixieland jazz, although it's scheduled to move in the near future. **Sinkkasten** (Brönnerstr. 9) features jazz, rock, pop, and African music; it's sometimes hard to get into but worth the effort for serious fans.

EXCURSIONS

Frankfurt is so centrally located in Germany that the list of possible excursions—day trips and longer treks—is nearly endless. It is a gateway to the Rhineland in the west, the Neckar Valley in the south, and Franconia in the southeast, and the ideal starting point for journeys into all of these regions. Thus, the list of excursions here is merely a selection of destinations that are not covered in other chapters. For full details of other excursions from Frankfurt, *see* Chapters 8, 9, 11, and 13.

Tour 1: Bad Homburg

Just a few miles north of Frankfurt, Bad Homburg lies at the foot of the **Taunus Hills.** The Taunus, with its rich forests, medieval castles, and photogenic towns, are regarded by many Frankfurters as their territory. On weekends you can see them enjoying "their" playground: hiking through the hills; climbing the **Grosse Feldberg;** taking the waters at a health-giving mineral spring; or just lazing in the sun. The Bad Homburg spa was first known to the Romans but was rediscovered and made famous during the 19th century. Illustrious visitors included the Prince of Wales, the son of Queen Victoria, and Tsar Nicholas II. And here, in 1841, the world's first casino was founded. Today the sights in Bad Homburg include a 17th-century castle and the picturesque Altstadt (Old Town), but perhaps the most captivating sight is the enchanting Kurpark.

Getting There

BY CAR

About 30–45 minutes of driving on the A–5 Autobahn (Frank-furt–Dortmund) will take you to Bad Homburg.

BY TRAIN AND BUS

Bad Homburg has its own station. Take the S-bahn from Frankfurt at Konstabler Wache (S-5 line). Buses and streetcars can also get you there.

Exploring

The first stop you'll want to make in Bad Homburg is at the **tourist bureau** downtown. There you'll find local maps, advice, and assistance in booking accommodations if necessary. You can also get information about and tickets to various local events. *Verkehrsamt. Louisen-str. 58, ☎ 06172/675–110. ۞ Weekdays 8:30–6, Sat. 9–1.*

The most historically noteworthy sight in the city itself is the 17th-century **Schloss.** The 172-foot **Weisser Turm** (White Tower) is all that remains of the medieval castle that once stood here. The Schloss that stands today was built between 1680 and 1685 by Friedrich II of Hesse-Homburg, and a few alterations were made during the 19th century. The state apartments are exquisitely furnished, and the Spiegelkabinett (Hall of Mirrors) is especially worth a visit. In the surrounding park, look for two venerable trees from Lebanon, now almost 150 years old. *Schlosspl.* ☛ *DM 4 adults, DM 2 children. ۞ Mar.–Oct., Tues.–Sun. 10–5; Nov.–Feb., Tues.–Sun. 10–4.*

Also within the town, and certainly its greatest attraction over the centuries, is the **Kurpark,** with its more than 31 fountains. In the park you'll find not only the popular, highly saline Elisabethenbrunnen spring but also a Siamese temple and a Russian chapel, mementos left by two distinguished guests—King Chulalongkorn of Siam and Czar Nicholas II.

Only 6½ kilometers (4 miles) from Bad Homburg, and accessible by direct bus service, is the **Saalburg Limes** fort, the best-preserved Roman fort in Germany. Built in AD 120, the fort could accommodate a cohort (500 men) and was part of the fortifications along the 342-mile-long Limes Wall. The fort has been rebuilt as the Romans originally left it, with wells, armories, parade grounds, and catapults, as well as shops, houses, baths, and temples. The fort and its museum are open daily 8–5. ☛ *DM 3 adults, DM 1.50 children.*

About a 30-minute walk from the fort is a fine open-air museum at **Hessenpark,** near Neu Anspach. The museum consists of 135 acres of rebuilt villages with houses, schools, and farms typical of the 18th and 19th centuries. A visit here yields a clear, concrete picture of the world in which the 18th- and 19th-century Hessians lived. ☛ *DM 7 adults, DM 5 children. ۞ Mar.–Oct., Tues.–Sun. 9–6.*

Just a short, convenient bus ride from Bad Homburg is the highest mountain in the Taunus, the 2,850-foot, eminently hikable **Feldberg.** From here there are easy bus connections to the towns of Königstein and Kronberg. **Königstein** is a health-resort town with the ruins of a 13th-century castle and a noteworthy **Rathaus** (Town Hall). Many painters have chosen the nearby town of **Kronberg** as their setting. This picturesque old town, with its half-timbered houses and winding streets, was the home of the Kronberger School, an important contributor to 19th-century German art. Visit the 15th-century **Johaniskirche** with its late-Gothic murals.

Dining

Most of the well-known spas in Bad Homburg have restaurants, but they tend to be very expensive. For an inexpensive and enjoyable meal, try one of the numerous Italian or Greek restaurants located throughout the city.

Sänger's Restaurant. A quintessential spa experience: fine dining at high prices. But service is friendly and the truffle risotto may make you forget the bill. ✗ *Kaiser-Friedrich-Promenade 85,* ☎ *06172/24425. Reservations advised. AE, MC. Closed Mon. and Sat. lunch, all day Sun.* *$$$*

Zum Adler. This simple restaurant serves traditional Hessian fare. It's a good break after a tour of the open-air museum at Hessenpark. ✗ *Neu Anspach* ☎ *06081/58840. AE, DC, MC, V. $$*

Dining and Lodging

Maritim Kurhaus Hotel. You have the choice here between dining in style in the hotel's elegant Park restaurant (pink table linen, fine silverware, and candlelight) with nouvelle cuisine, or more cheaply (but evenings only) in the cozy Burgerstube with traditional fare dominated by local meat dishes; the latter is worth a visit just for the collection of dolls that forms part of the rustic decor. Despite the difference in prices, both restaurants draw on the same excellently managed kitchen. The hotel stands on the edge of a spa park. The large, richly furnished rooms offer king-size beds and deep armchairs, mostly covered in pastel fabrics. ☎ *Ludwigstr.,* ☎ *06172/6600; fax 06172/660–100. 148 rooms with bath. Restaurant, 2 bars, 2 cafés. AE, DC, MC, V. $$$*

Lodging

Hartdwald Hotel. The flowers that spill from the window boxes covering the white facade of the Hartdwald have won this distinctive woodland hotel numerous local awards. These blooms are one of the many touches that make the property special. Its location couldn't be better—in the woods yet near the town center and spa park. ☎ *Philosophenweg 31,* ☎ *06172/81026 or 06172/9880,* FAX *06172/82512. 42 rooms. Restaurant, café, laundry service, parking. AE, DC, MC, V. $$$*

Hotel Molitor. Most rooms and the sun-terrace offer a fine view of Bad Homburg and the surrounding countryside; walks through the Taunus woodland start at the lodging's front door. This attractive hotel has pleasant, nicely decorated rooms. ☎ *Rotlaufweg 31,* ☎ *06172/8020,* FAX *06172/80240. Restaurant, café, laundry service, parking. AE, DC, MC, V. $$*

Haus Fischer Garni. This family-operated pension is simple and clean. It is near a park and is convenient to the old town. ☎ *Landgrafenstr. 12,* ☎ *06172/85927. 10 rooms with bath. No credit cards. $–$$*

Tour 2: Limburg

The imposing seven-spired cathedral at **Limburg** that greets you upon arrival seems to grow out of the cliff that holds it. Modern Limburg grew around its old town—a city that developed because it was at the crossroads of the Köln–Frankfurt and Hessen–Koblenz highways in the 9th century. The old town still has a number of beautiful patrician and merchant houses, evidence of the city's importance in the Middle Ages.

Getting There

BY CAR

The Frankfurt–Köln Autobahn (A–3) has two Limburg exits. Take either of them. The drive should take you less than an hour from Frankfurt.

BY TRAIN AND BUS

Limburg has its own railway station as well as regular bus service from Frankfurt, Koblenz, Wiesbaden, and Frankfurt Airport.

Exploring

Upon arriving in the center of Limburg, visit the **Verkehrsamt** (tourist office) to receive city maps, help with accommodations, if necessary, and general information. *Hospitalstr. 2, ☎ 06431/203–222. ⊘ Apr.–Oct., weekdays 8–12:30 and 1:30–6, Sat. 10–noon; Nov.–Mar., weekdays 8–12:30 and 1:30–5, closed Fri. afternoons and Sat.*

The first sight to take in is the **Dom St. Georg und Nikolaus,** the cathedral that you'll see towering above the Lahn River. Construction of the cathedral began in 1220, and evident in the building is the transition from Romanesque to Gothic style; each side presents a new perspective. Extensive restoration recently uncovered the original medieval coloring and bright frescoes from the 13th century.

Treasures from the cathedral are on display in the **Diözesanmuseum** in the Lyenschen Haus, near the cathedral. It houses ecclesiastical art treasures from the bishopric of Limburg. Be sure to see the Byzantine cross reliquary that was stolen from the palace church in Constantinople in 1204 and the Patri-Stab (Peter's Staff), set with precious stones and adorned with gold. *Domschatz und Diözesanmusem, Domstr. 12, ☞ DM 2 adults, DM 1 children. ⊘ Mid-Mar.–mid-Nov., Tues.–Sat. 10–1 and 2–5; Sun. and holidays 11–5; late Nov.–early Mar., ☎ 06431/295–233 for appointment.*

The **Schloss** adjacent to the cathedral dates from the 7th or 8th century, although the castle's current building only goes back to the 13th century. The group of residences, the chapel, and other buildings added in the 14th to 16th centuries serve as an architectural counterbalance to the cathedral. The castle is closed to visitors; it is used as a facility for conferences.

Only 6 kilometers (4 miles) from Limburg is the small town of **Runkel,** with an impressive 12th-century fortress. The fortress tower provides a panoramic view over the Taunus and the Westerwald.

About 20 kilometers (12 miles) south of Limburg is the state-recognized spa resort of **Bad Camberg,** a historic town in the western foothills of the **Hochtaunus** (Taunus highlands). This city offers numerous half-timbered houses, remains of the city's gate and fortifications, and an attractive ensemble of buildings in the center of town, including the **Hohenfeldsche Kapelle** (chapel) of 1650. They stand in striking contrast to the modern **Kurhaus** across the street.

Limburg is on one of the new driving routes called the **Deutsche Fachwerkstrassen,** or "Half-Timbered Roads," an initiative designed to make people aware of the beauty of some less-well-known villages, and to furnish an impetus to restore some decaying half-timbered houses. The "West and Central Hessia" route runs from the Frankfurt suburb of Höchst north through Limburg to Marburg and is highly recommended to anyone interested in seeing an untouristed, truly beautiful side of the country. For information, contact the Limburg tourist office.

Dining

St. Georgs-Stuben. In the Stadthalle, only a few minutes' walk from the center of Limburg, this pleasant restaurant serves local and international dishes. Try the house specialty, the St. Georgsteller, a filling pork-steak meal. ✕ *Hospitalstr. 4,* ☎ *06431/26027. No credit cards.* $$

Lodging

Romantik Hotel Zimmermann. The privately owned Zimmermann is one of the showpieces of the Romantik group, a beautifully renovated town house in the center of Lahn, but on a small, quiet side street. Rooms are individually and stylishly decorated, and those in a neighboring annex are furnished in English country-house style. The service is attentive and the breakfasts hearty. ⊡ *Blumenröderstr. 1,* ☎ *06431/4611,* ⅎⅨ *06431/41314. 30 rooms with bath or shower. Restaurant, parking. AE, DC, MC, V. Closed end of Dec. $$–$$$*

Dom Hotel. Centrally located and ideal for a brief visit to see the old town, this old established hotel offers standard comforts backed by friendly service. ⊡ *Grabenstr. 57,* ☎ *06431/24077,* ⅎⅨ *06431/6856. 48 rooms with bath or shower. Restaurant. AE, DC, MC, V. Closed end of Dec. $$–$$$*

FRANKFURT ESSENTIALS

Arriving and Departing

By Bus

More than 200 European cities—including all major former West German cities—have bus links with Frankfurt. Buses arrive and depart from the south side of the Hauptbahnhof. For information and tickets, contact **Deutsche Touring,** Am Römerhof 17, ☎ 069/79030.

By Car

Frankfurt is the meeting point of a number of major Autobahns, of which the most important are A–3, running south from Köln and then on to Würzburg, Nürnberg, and Munich; and A–5, running south from Giessen and then on to Mannheim, Heidelberg, Karlsruhe, and the Swiss-German border at Basel. A complex series of beltways surround the city. If you're driving to Frankfurt on A–5 from either north or south, exit at Nordwestkreuz and follow A–66 to the Nordend district, just north of downtown. Driving south on A–3, exit onto A–66 and follow the signs to Frankfurt-Höchst and then the Nordend district. Driving north on A–3, exit at Offenbach onto A–661 and follow the signs for Frankfurt-Stadtmitte.

By Plane

Frankfurt Airport is the biggest on the Continent, second in Europe only to London's Heathrow. There are direct flights to Frankfurt from many U.S. cities and from all major European cities. It's 10 kilometers (6 miles) southwest of the downtown area, by the Köln–Munich Autobahn.

BETWEEN THE AIRPORT AND DOWNTOWN
Getting into Frankfurt from the airport is easy. There are two S-Bahn lines (suburban trains) that run from the airport to downtown Frank-

furt. One line, S-14, goes to Hauptwache Square in the heart of Frankfurt. Trains run every 20 minutes; the trip takes about 15 minutes. The other line, S-15, goes to the Hauptbahnhof (main train station), just west of the downtown area. Trains run every 10 minutes; the trip takes 11 minutes. One-way fare for both services is DM 4.20 (DM 5.60 during rush hours). InterCity and InterCity Express (ICE) trains to and from most major West German cities also stop at the airport. There are hourly services to Köln, Hamburg, and Munich, for example. City Bus 61 also serves the airport, running between it and the Südbahnhof train station in Sachsenhausen, south of the downtown area. The trip takes about 30 minutes; the fare is DM 4.20 (DM 5.60 during rush hours). A taxi from the airport into the city center normally takes around 20 minutes; allow double that during rush hours. The fare is around DM 40. If you're picking up a rental car at the airport, getting into Frankfurt is easy: Take the main road out of the airport and follow the signs for Stadtmitte (downtown).

By Train
EuroCity and InterCity trains connect Frankfurt with all German cities and many major European cities. The new InterCity Express line links Frankfurt with Hamburg, Munich, and a number of other major German cities. All long-distance trains arrive at and depart from the Hauptbahnhof. For information, call **Deutsche Bahn** (German Railways, ☎ 069/19419) or ask at the information office in the station.

Getting Around

Boat Trips
Frankfurt is the starting point for many boat excursions, ranging from day trips on the River Main to cruises along the Rhine and Mosel as far as Trier, lasting up to three days. The **Köln-Dusseldorfer** line offers the most trips; they run from March to October and leave from the Frankfurt Mainkai am Eisernen Steg, just south of the Römer complex. For tickets and information call the Köln-Dusseldorfer agent, Malachi Faughnan (Am Eisernen Steg, ☎ 069/285–728; open 11–6). The **Fahrgastschiff Wikinger** company (☎ 069/282–886) also offers trips along the Main and excursions to the Rhine. **Deutsche Touring** (☎ 069/79030) combines boat trips with wine-tasting. At Easter and from May to October, pleasure boats of the **Primus Line** cruise the Main and Rhine rivers from Frankfurt, sailing as far as the Lorelei and back in a day. For details and reservations, contact Frankfurter Personenschiffahrt (Mainkai 36, ☎ 069/281–884).

By Bike
Theo Intra's shop (Westerbachstr. 273, ☎ 069/342–780) has a large selection of bikes, from tandems to racing models.

In summer you can rent bikes at the **Goetheturm** (Goethe Tower) at the edge of the Frankfurt Stadtwald (☎ 069/49111).

By Car
CAR RENTAL
Avis, Schmidtstr. 39, ☎ 069/730–111.

Europcar, Schlosstr. 32, ☎ 069/775–033.

Hertz, Hanauer Landstr. 106–108, ☎ 069/449–090.

By Public Transportation

Frankfurt's smooth-running, well-integrated public transportation system consists of the U-bahn (subway), S-bahn (suburban railway), and Strassenbahn (streetcars). Fares for the entire system are uniform, though they are based on a complex zone system that can be hard to figure out. A basic one-way ticket for a ride in the inner zone costs DM 2.20 (DM 2.80 during rush hours). For rides of just a stop or two, buy a *Kurzstrecke* ticket for DM 1.60. A day ticket costs DM 6 and allows unlimited travel in the inner zone for the day on which it is bought. A weekend day ticket for a small group or family of up to five persons costs DM 28. If you're caught riding without a ticket, there's a fine of DM 60. Call for information and assistance (☎ 069/269–462).

By Taxi

Fares start at DM 3.80 and increase by DM 2.15 per kilometer. There is an extra charge of 50 pfennigs per piece of baggage. You can hail taxis in the street or call them (☎ 069/250–001, 069/230–033, or 069/545–011). Note that there's an extra charge to have the driver come to the pickup point.

On Foot

Downtown Frankfurt is compact and easily explored on foot. There are fewer pedestrian-only streets in the downtown area than in some other major German cities; the most important radiate from Hauptwache Square. The Römer complex, south of Hauptwache, is also a pedestrian zone. From here you can easily cross the river on the Eisener Steg (Iron Bridge) to Sachsenhausen, where the tangle of small streets is best explored on foot.

Guided Tours

Orientation Tours

Two-and-a-half-hour bus tours that take in all the main sights with English-speaking guides are offered throughout the year. In winter (November–February), tours leave on weekends and holidays at 1 PM from outside the main tourist information office at Römerberg 27, stopping at 1:15 at the train station tourist office (opposite Track 23). In summer, tours leave from the Römer office weekdays at 1 PM and twice daily on weekends, at 10 AM and 2 PM; all of these trains leave from the train station 15 minutes later. The tour includes a visit to the Goethe Haus. The cost is DM 36 for adults and DM 18 for children. Gray Line (☎ 069/230–492) offers two-hour city tours four times a day; the price (DM 50 adults, DM 40 children) includes a typical Frankfurt snack.

Special-Interest Tours

The city transit authority (☎ 069/2132–2425) runs a brightlypainted old-time streetcar—the **Ebbelwei Express** (Cider Express)—on Saturdays, Sundays, and holidays every 40 minutes between 1:30 and 5:30. Departures are from the Ostbahnhof (east train station) and the fare—which includes a free glass of cider (or apple juice) and a pretzel—is DM 4 (DM 2 children). All the major attractions in the city are covered as the streetcar trundles along. The ride lasts just over 30 minutes. The **Historische Eisenbahn Frankfurt** (☎ 069/436–093) runs a vintage steam train along the banks of the Main River one weekend each month. The train runs from the Eisener Steg west to Frankfurt-Griesham and east to Frankfurt-Mainkur. The fare is DM 6 for adults and DM 3 for children.

Three special tours are offered by the tourist office by prior arrangement: The first covers Frankfurt's architecture (from its historic remains to its skyscrapers), the second traces the city's Jewish history, and the third follows Goethe's footsteps. The tours aren't cheap: for an English-speaking guide, the cost is DM 90–DM 100 per hour, plus tax. To book, call Mr. Weikum (☎ 069/253–253).

Walking Tours

The Frankfurt tourist office arranges walking tours on demand (☎ 069/2123–8849). Tours are tailored to suit individual requirements, and costs vary accordingly. For those who want to tour Frankfurt on foot on their own, the tourist office lends Walkman tape players equipped with a taped guided tour. The tapes cost DM 12, and a DM 50 deposit is charged for the loan of the Walkman.

Excursions

Noblesse Limousine Service (Bad Vilbel, ☎ 06101/12055), **Deutsche Touring** (Am Römerhof 17, ☎ 069/790–3268), **Gray Line** (Wiesenhüttenpl. 39, ☎ 069/230–492), and **Panorama Tours** (☎ 069/3904–0340) all offer a variety of tours into the areas immediately around Frankfurt as well as farther afield. Destinations include the Rhine Valley, with steamship cruises and wine-tasting as well as day trips to the historic towns of Heidelberg and Rothenburg-ob-der-Tauber. Additional information is available from all three organizations. A **Casino Bus** runs daily to the casino at Bad Homburg in the Taunus. It leaves every hour between 2 and 11 PM (the last bus back to Frankfurt leaves Bad Homburg at 3 AM) from the Frankfurt Hauptbahnhof (south side). The DM 9.50 fare includes entry to the casino.

Important Addresses and Numbers

Consulates
U.S. Consulate General, Siesmayerst. 21, ☎ 069/75350.
British Consulate General, Bockenheimer Landstr. 42, ☎ 069/170–0020.

Emergencies
Police: ☎ 110. **Fire:** ☎ 112. **Medical Emergencies:** ☎ 069/7950–2200 or 069/19292. **Pharmacies:** ☎ 069/11500. **Dental Emergencies:** ☎ 069/660–7271.

English-Language Bookstores
American Book Center (ABC), Jahnstr. 36, ☎ 069/552–816.
Amerika Haus (library, newspapers, cultural events), Staufenstr. 1, ☎ 069/971–4480.
British Bookshop, Börsenstr. 17, ☎ 069/280–492.

Travel Agencies
American Express International, Kaiserstr. 8, ☎ 069/210–548.
Thomas Cook, Kaiserstr. 11, ☎ 069/134–733.
D.E.R. Deutsches Reisebüro, Emil-von-Behring Str. 6, ☎ 069/9588–3650.
Hapag-Lloyd Reisebüro, Kaiserstr. 14, ☎ 069/216–2286.

Visitor Information
For advance information, write to the **Verkehrsamt Frankfurt/Main** (Kaiserstr. 52, 60329 Frankfurt, ☎ 069/2123–8800). The main tourist office is at Römerberg 27 (☎ 069/2123–8708) in the heart of the old town. It's open daily 9 AM–6 PM. A secondary information office is at the main train station (Hauptbahnhof) opposite Track 23 (☎ 069/2123–

8849). This branch is open weekdays 8 AM–9 PM, Saturday 8 AM–8 PM, and Sunday 9:30 AM–8 PM. Both offices can help you find accommodations.

Two information offices at the airport can also help with accommodations: The **FAG Flughafen-Information,** on the first floor of arrivals hall B (open daily 6:45 AM–10:15 PM) and the **DER Deutsches Reisebüro,** in arrivals hall B-6 (open daily 8 AM–9 PM).

12 The Rhineland

Vater Rhein, or *"Father Rhine,"* is *Germany's historic lifeline, and the region from Mainz to Koblenz is its heart. Its banks are crowned by magnificent castle after castle and breathtaking, vine-terraced hills that provide the livelihood for many of the villages hugging the shores. Bigger cities, too, such as Bonn, Köln, and Koblenz, thrive along the great river. Koblenz lies at the meeting of the Rhine and its most famous tributary, the Mosel, on whose banks Germany's oldest city, Trier, was established. Other cities included in the chapter are Aachen and Düsseldorf.*

THE IMPORTANCE OF THE RHINE can hardly be over-estimated. Throughout recorded history the Rhine has served as Europe's leading waterway. While by no means the longest river in Europe (the Danube is more than twice its length), it has been the main river-trade artery between the heart of the Continent and the North Sea.

The Rhine runs 1,355 kilometers (840 miles) from Lake Constance to Basel in Switzerland, then north through Germany, and then west through the Netherlands to Rotterdam. It forms a natural frontier between Germany and France for part of its length and was Europe's major highway between Basel and the Atlantic before the advent of overland transportation.

Great cities—such as Basel, Strasbourg, Mainz, Köln, and Düsseldorf—grew up along the Rhine's banks. No wonder Germans refer to their favorite river as *Vater Rhein*, or "Father Rhine," the way Americans call the Mississippi "Old Man River."

One section of the Rhine became Germany's top tourist site all of 200 years ago. Around 1790 a spearhead of adventurous travelers from various parts of Europe arrived by horse-drawn carriages to explore the sector of the river between Bingen and Koblenz, now known as the Middle Rhine Valley. Needless to say, they were all but overwhelmed by the dramatic and romantic scenery. It didn't take long for the word to spread. Other travelers followed in their coach tracks, and soon thereafter the first sightseeing cruises went into operation.

Poets, painters, and other artists were attracted by this magnet: Goethe, Germany's greatest poet, was enthralled; Heinrich Heine wrote a poem tied to the Lorelei legend that was eventually set to music and made the unofficial theme of the landmark; and William Turner captured misty Rhine sunsets on canvas. In 1834, the first-ever Baedeker guidebook described the attractions of this stretch of the river in meticulous detail. At about the same time, the railroad opened up the region to an early form of mass tourism. By the mid-19th century, the Rhine Valley was known throughout Europe; in 1878, Mark Twain's *A Tramp Abroad* spread the word to potential travelers in the United States.

Today the passage through the Rhine Valley still provides one of Europe's most memorable journeys. Ideally, the way to go is by car—up one side and down the other—with time out for a cruise. But even the train route between Wiesbaden and Koblenz offers thrilling views—the landmarks may flash by at top speed, a little like a home movie running out of control, but you still gain exposure to the essential aspects of the Rhine's beauty: hilltop castles silhouetted against the sky, ravishing river sights, and glimpses of pretty-as-a-picture wine villages.

The Mittel Rhein (Middle Rhine) could be considered an obligatory day trip out of Frankfurt—it's quite possibly Germany's number-one, not-to-be-missed excursion. But there's far more to the river as it wends its way north to Köln and Düsseldorf.

This chapter divides the Rhineland into six tours. The first two tours cover the Middle Rhine, the 129-kilometer (80-mile) stretch from Mainz (40 kilometers, or 25 miles, west of Frankfurt, the natural starting point for any visit to the Rhineland) to Koblenz. Of all the many and varied regions of the river, no other has the same array of scenery, history, architecture, and natural beauty as this magical stretch. Mention the Rhineland to most visitors, and this is the area they'll assume you mean. It is a land of steep and thickly wooded hills, of terraced vineyards rising step by step above the riverbanks, of massive hilltop castles, and tiny wine villages hugging river shores. It is also a land of legend and myth. For example, the Lorelei, a steep mountain of rock jutting out of the river, was once believed to be the home of a beautiful and bewitching maiden who lured boatmen to a watery end in the swift currents. It was the home, too, of the Nibelungen, a Burgundian race said to have lived on the riverbanks who serve as subjects for Wagner's epic opera cycle *Der Ring des Nibelungen*.

The most famous tributary of the Rhine is the Mosel, which flows into the river at Koblenz. The third tour covers its snaking passage through another great wine-producing area, with scenery almost as striking as that found along the Rhine. At its west end, almost on the French border, is Trier, once one of the greatest cities in the Roman Empire.

The fourth tour covers Bonn, a sleepy university town that unexpectedly became the capital of West Germany, and Köln (Cologne), the greatest of the Rhine cities, a vibrant and bustling metropolis with the most dramatic Gothic cathedral in the country.

The fifth tour is a side trip to Aachen, capital of Charlemagne's Holy Roman Empire during the 9th century and site of the most important Carolingian (pre-Romanesque) cathedral in Europe. Today this elegant spa town on the Belgian and Dutch borders has a quiet, civilized charm.

The sixth and final tour returns to the Rhine, to the elegant city of Düsseldorf, located 40 kilometers (25 miles) north of Köln.

If you plan to make any trip through the Rhineland, remember that this is one of Germany's major tourist areas, drawing visitors from around the world. As a result, prices here in summer are high, often substantially above those found elsewhere in the country. Make reservations, and don't expect to have the place to yourself.

In early 1995, the Rhine flooded severely, the second time in 13 months. Many establishments did all they could to pull through the first floods, leaving little or no resources for the second go-round. At press time, it was too early to know which, if any, places will have to close. To avoid disappointment and inconvenience, be sure to call ahead.

EXPLORING

Tour 1: The Mittel Rhein

Numbers in the margin correspond to points of interest on the Rhineland map.

If you're flying into Frankfurt, you'll begin your tour of the Rhine 40 kilometers (25 miles) west of the city at the point where the Main River ❶ joins the mighty Rhine, at **Wiesbaden.** It's located on the east bank of the Rhine, almost opposite the town of Mainz (*see* Chapter 10), and marks the start of the most famous stretch of the Rhine, the **Rheingau,** home of Germany's finest wines and some of its most enchanting (and crowded) wine villages.

Wiesbaden, one of the oldest cities in Germany, was founded 2,000 years ago by Roman legions attracted by its hot springs. Its elegant 19th-century face, however, is what captures one's attention today. The com-

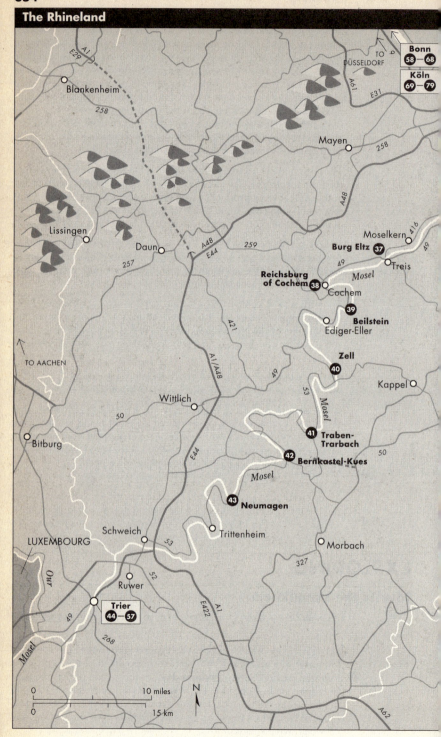

Blankenheim

A1
E29

258

TO
DÜSSELDORF

Bonn
58—**68**

Köln
69—**79**

A61
E31

Mayen

258

A48

Lissingen

257

Daun

A48
E44

259

Moselkern

416

49

Burg Eltz **37**

49

Treis

Mosel

Reichsburg
of Cochem **38**

Cochem

TO AACHEN

421

39 **Beilstein**

Ediger-Eller

Zell

40

49

Kappel

Wittlich

53

Mosel

A1/A48

50

Bitburg

E44

41 **Traben-**
Trarbach

42 **Bernkastel-Kues**

50

Mosel

43 **Neumagen**

Schweich

LUXEMBOURG

Trittenheim

Morbach

327

53

52

Our

Ruwer

Trier
44—**57**

E422

A1

Mosel

49

268

0   10 miles
0   15 km

N

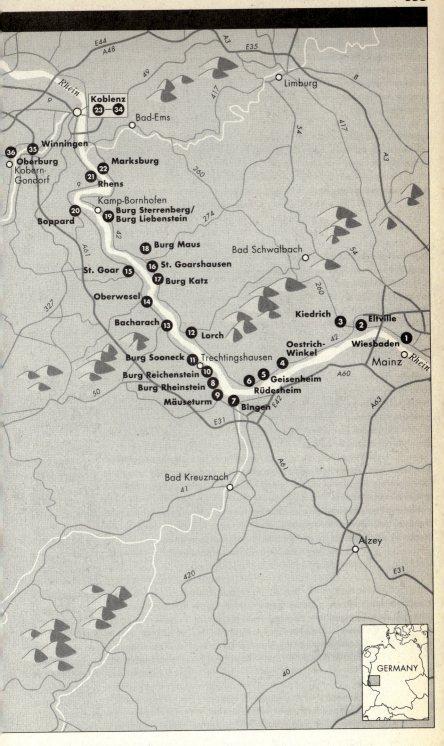

pact city gained prominence in the mid-19th century when Europe's leisure classes rediscovered the hot springs. The English, in particular, had a weakness for Wiesbaden—witness the church of **St. Augustine of Canterbury,** built between 1863 and 1865 for the city's many English visitors—but the Germans, too, were enticed.

★ By 1900, Wiesbaden was home to the largest number of millionaires of any German city, Berlin included. To get a taste of its 19th-century opulence, wander along **Wilhelmstrasse,** whose mint-condition fin-de-siècle buildings and expensive stores provide eloquent proof of the city's continuing affluence. Wiesbaden hasn't always prospered in this century, however. The outbreak of World War I in 1914 halted the social whirl, and in the war's aftermath the city was occupied by French and British troops.

The 19th-century residence of the dukes of Nassau, onetime rulers of Wiesbaden, is perhaps symbolic of Wiesbaden's fall from the social heights. Today the classical facade of the former palace houses the mundane offices of the provincial government of Hessen.

TIME OUT   Sample Wiesbaden's 19th-century charm in the wood-paneled warmth of the centrally located **Café Maldaner** (Marktstr. 34). Don't be surprised if you think you're in Vienna—the café was opened in 1859 as a Viennese coffeehouse catering to the city's Austrian visitors.

Every August, Wiesbaden hosts the Rheingau wine festival, the largest such event in Germany. The festival takes its name from the vine-covered slopes along the river between Wiesbaden and Bingen, 25 kilometers (15 miles) to the west, where the Rhine abruptly turns north. Technically, the Rheingau begins just east of Wiesbaden, at Hochheim (the town that gave its name to Hock wine), but it's the sunny, southern stretch you're about to explore that people generally think of when they hear the name Rheingau. For the most scenic route, take the river-hugging B–42.

2 The first town you'll reach on the road west is **Eltville.** It's the geographic heart of the Rheingau, though Rüdesheim, 15 kilometers (9 miles) west, enjoys greater fame. Eltville's half-timbered buildings crowd narrow streets that date from Roman times. Though the Romans imported wine to Germany, they never made it here. It was Charlemagne, so the story goes, who during the 9th century first realized that the sunny slopes of the Rheingau could be used to produce wines. Eltville's vineyards may not go that far back, but some, including **Hanach** and **Rheinberg,** have been in use since the 12th century. Today the town is best known for the production of Sekt, sparkling German wine (champagne by any other name, though the French ensured that it could not legally be called that by including a stipulation in the Treaty of Versailles in 1919). Sekt cellars rest coolly beneath the town's winding streets. Those of the **Matheus Muller Company** are several miles long and hold up to 15 million bottles. Although the cellars are not open to the public, you can amble through the courtyards of some formidable old vineyard buildings, including the white-walled, slate-roof **Eltzerhof,** one of the more beautiful. Eltville also has its own **castle,** commissioned by the archbishop of Trier in 1330. The prince-archbishop of Mainz admitted Johannes Gutenberg, father of the modern printing press, to the court in Eltville, thereby saving the inventor from financial ruin.

In Eltville the Gothic parish church of **Sts. Peter and Paul** has some fine 14th-century stained glass and ceiling frescoes; its walls are lined with the tombstones and monuments of noble families who rose to prominence on the prestige of the local wine.

3 To see one of Germany's oldest church organs, dating from around 1500, drive inland a mile or so to the village of **Kiedrich.** The west entrance to the church is richly carved.

4 The drive from Kiedrich back to the river at **Oestrich-Winkel** takes you past the largest vineyard in the Rheingau. Oestrich-Winkel is the site of the oldest stone dwelling in the country, the **Graues Haus** (Gray House). It dates from the 9th century and is now open as a very good restaurant.

5 Continue on to **Geisenheim,** a name inextricably linked with Rheingau wines at their finest. "Rhineland is wineland" is a saying in this part of the world, and, indeed, you'll see a checkerboard of terraced vineyards stretching from the Rhine's riverside villages all the way back to a protective line of forests at the base of the Taunus Mountains. Geisenheim has some of the most renowned vineyards in the area, with grapes that create wines on a par with those from the Loire Valley and Burgundy.

From the vintner's point of view, this part of Germany has the ideal conditions for the cultivation of the noble Riesling grapes: a perfect southern exposure; shelter from cold north winds; slopes with the proper pitch for drainage; soil containing slate and quartz to reflect the sun and hold heat through the night and moisture in the morning; and long sunny days from early spring until late fall. (Although the Rheingau is at approximately the same latitude as Newfoundland, you'd never know it from the weather.)

In Geisenheim, visit the 18th-century **Schloss Johannisberg,** built on the site of a 12th-century abbey and still owned by the von Metternich family. Schloss Johannisberg produces what is generally regarded as one of the very best Rheingau wines, along with a renowned Sekt. On the castle terrace you can order the elegant estate-bottled golden wine by the glass. As you savor the cool, rich, clear-as-crystal drink, you can contemplate all that makes this corner of Europe so special. Views down across the vineyards take in the river at its calmest. If you're lucky, the Rhine will be enveloped in a pastel mood worthy of a Turner painting. As you leave the castle, you can buy a bottle or two of the excellent wine at a shop just outside the walls.

6 Rüdesheim and Bingen beckon now, 8 kilometers (5 miles) west, along the banks of the Rhine. **Rüdesheim** is arguably the Rhine Valley's prettiest and most popular wine town. Set along the river's edge, it is a picturesque place of half-timbered and gabled medieval houses. Everything here is somehow related to wine or tourists or both. You can visit wine cellars to inspect great casks with elaborate and lovingly carved heads.

Angling up from the river toward the romantic Old Town is the region's most famous Weingasse (wine alley), the extraordinary Drosselgasse (Thrush Lane). This narrow, 200-yard-long cobbled lane is lined with cozy wine taverns and rustic restaurants. At night, voices raised in song and brass bands create a cacophony, shattering whatever peace the town may have known by day.

Rüdesheim can be a very plus-and-minus affair. You can love it in the morning, before the day's quota of tour buses start disgorging their passengers, and hate it at night, when it gets far too crowded for comfort. Still, all in all, it is definitely worth a visit.

Above Rüdesheim, at an elevation of 1,000 feet, stands the **Niederwald-Denkmal,** a colossal stone statue of Germania, the heroically proportioned woman who symbolizes the unification of the German Empire in 1871. Built between 1876 and 1883 on the orders of Bismarck, this giant figure came within an inch of being blown to smithereens during the dedication ceremonies. At the unveiling, held in the presence of the kaiser and Bismarck, an anarchist attempted to blow up the statue and the assembled dignitaries. However, in true comic-opera style, a rain shower put out the fuse on the bomb, and all survived.

Niederwald can be reached by car or chair lift, or you can climb to the statue's steep perch. Whichever way you choose, the ascent offers splendid views, including one of the little island in the middle of the Rhine where the Mäuseturm (Mouse Tower) is situated (*see below*). The chair-lift station to the monument is located a short walk from the Drosselgasse. It operates continually every day from late March to early November; the round-trip fare is DM 8 for adults and DM 4 for children.

Wine buffs and those who enjoy wandering through old castles won't want to miss Rüdesheim's **Schloss Brömserburg,** one of the oldest castles on the Rhine, built more than 1,000 years ago by the Knights of Rüdesheim on the site of a Roman fortress. Inside its stout walls are wine presses, drinking vessels, and collections related to viticulture from prehistoric times to the present. *Weinmuseum in der Brömserburg, Rheinstr. 2.* ☛ *DM 3 adults, DM 2 children.* ⊘ *Mid-Mar.–Oct., daily 9–6.*

❼ The town of **Bingen,** on the opposite riverbank, celebrates the festival of St. Rochus every year in mid-August. In **St. Rochus chapel,** built in 1666 in memory of Bingen's plague victims, is a portrait of Goethe, the great German writer, posing improbably as the saint. Another Bingen luminary was the 12th-century Benedictine abbess Hildegard, one of the first great women artist/scholars, who wrote on everything from the natural sciences to her religious visions; recordings of her music are also available. To get to Bingen, take the short ferry ride from the Adlerturm jetty in Rüdesheim (DM 1.40 adults, 2.50 round-trip, 75 pf children).

The number-one excursion from Bingen is the boat ride to the romantic **Castle of Burg Rheinstein.** It was Prince Friedrich von Preussen, a cousin of Emperor Wilhelm I, who acquired the original medieval castle in 1825 and transformed it into the picture-book castle you see high above the Rhine today. The prince is buried in the castle's fanciful Gothic chapel.

❽
❾ The ride to **Burg Rheinstein** takes you past one of the most famous sights on the Rhine, the **Mäuseturm** (Mouse Tower), a 13th-century edifice clinging to a rock in the river. According to legend, it was constructed by an avaricious bishop as a customs post to exact taxes from passing river traffic. The story suggests that the greedy bishop grew so unpopular that he was forced to hole up in the tower, where he was eventually devoured by mice.

Beyond the Mäuseturm there are two other medieval castles you can
❿ visit: **Burg Reichenstein,** which towers high above the picturesque wine
⓫ town of **Trechtingshausen;** and **Burg Sooneck,** which during the 12th century was the most feared stronghold in the Rhineland. Reichenstein Castle is now a luxurious hotel where you can enjoy lunch in an excellent restaurant with a sensational view. Sooneck, towering above the Rhine on a rocky outcrop, was destroyed several times during its colorful history and rebuilt in its present form in 1840 by the Prussian

king Friedrich Wilhelm IV. From the castle you can follow a path through vineyards to one of the most spectacular vantage points of the entire Rhineland: the **Siebenburgenblick** (Seven-Castle View).

Three kilometers (2 miles) north of Burg Sooneck, at the village of **Niederheimbach,** take the ferry back across the Rhine to the historic little wine town of **Lorch,** whose ancient walls mark the northernmost limit of the Rheingau. Its parish church of **St. Martin** has a Gothic high altar and 13th-century carved choir stalls.

North of Lorch there are so many attractions on both banks of the river that the only way to see them all would be to zigzag back and forth across the river by ferry. Fortunately, there are small ferries all along the Rhine between here and Koblenz.

Downstream from Lorch, on the west bank, lies busy **Bacharach,** whose long association with wine is indicated by its name, which comes from the Latin *Bacchi ara,* meaning "altar of Bacchus," the Roman god of wine. The town was a thriving center of Rhine wine trade in the Middle Ages. Something of its medieval atmosphere can still be found in the narrow streets within its 14th-century defensive walls and towers.

TIME OUT Stop by the old marketplace and look for the gold-painted sign of the **Weinhaus Altes Haus.** Wine has been served in this half-timbered tavern for four centuries. Ask for any Bacharach Riesling and you won't be disappointed. *Marktpl.*

Oberwesel, 8 kilometers (5 miles) north of Bacharach, also retains its medieval look. Sixteen of the original 21 towers that studded the town walls still stand; one does double duty as the bell tower of the 14th-century church of **St. Martin.** Towering above the town are the remains of the 1,000-year-old **Burg Schönburg,** whose massive walls, nearly 20 feet thick in places, were not strong enough to prevent its destruction by rampaging French troops in 1689. Part of the castle has been restored and today houses a comfortable hotel.

The ruins of another medieval castle, **Burg Rheinfels,** stand at the outskirts of the next stop along the road, the town of **St. Goar,** named after an early missionary who became the patron saint of Rhine boatmen and tavern keepers. The Rhine here narrows dramatically, funneling its waters into a treacherous maelstrom of fast-flowing currents and eddies. These rushing torrents are what gave rise to the legend of the Lorelei, a grim, 400-foot-high rock that protrudes from the river just outside **St. Goarshausen.** So many boats were wrecked on it that people began to credit a bewitching water nymph with golden tresses who inhabited the rock and lured sailors to watery graves using her beauty and strange songs.

These days, in season, the Lorelei's siren song can serve as a trap for tourists rather than sailors. Excursion boats leave regularly from Koblenz and Bingen on Lorelei cruises, and as these overcrowded vessels pass within sight of the famed cliffs, each and every one plays a taped version of the Lorelei song (a Heinrich Heine poem set to music), blasting the creation above the roar of the river.

You can see a statue of the Lorelei in St. Goarshausen. To get there, take the ferry from St. Goar.

If you visit this area in September, stay for the Rhein in Flammen (Rhine in Flames) festival, a pyrotechnic orgy of rockets and flares that light up St. Goar and St. Goarshausen and their surrounding vineyards.

North and south of St. Goarshausen are two castles whose 14th-century owners feuded so unrelentingly that the fortresses came to be known
⑰ as Katz (cat) and Maus (mouse). **Burg Katz,** just north of St. Goarshausen,
was built in 1371 by Count Wilhelm II von Katzenelnbogen (literally,
"cat's elbow"). It was he who dubbed the rival castle south of St. Goars-
⑱ hausen **Burg Maus.** The rivalry, however, was a serious matter. There
was constant competition between many of the castle-bound nobles
of the Rhine to establish who would extract tolls from passing river
traffic, a lucrative and vicious business. Napoléon, not one to respect
medieval traditions, put an end to the fighting in 1806 when he destroyed Burg Katz. It was later reconstructed using the original medieval
plans. Neither of the castles is open to the public.

Rivalry between neighboring castles was common even when they belonged to members of the same family. At **Kamp-Bornhofen,** 12 kilo-
⑲ meters (8 miles) north of St. Goar, are **Burg Sterrenberg** and **Burg
Liebenstein,** once owned by two brothers. When their relations dete-
riorated over a river-toll feud, they built a wall between them. Today
competing wine taverns in the castles keep the rivalry going.

Across from Kamp-Bornhofen is the mile-long promenade of elegant
⑳ **Boppard,** usually lined with excursion and pleasure boats. Luxurious
hotels, restaurants, and spa facilities are Boppard's hallmarks. There
are also wine taverns of every caliber, and substantial ruins from a 4th-
century Roman fort here. The old quarter is part of a walking tour
marked by signs from the 14th-century **Carmelite Church** on Karlmeliter-
strasse. (Inside the church, grotesque carved figures peer from the
choir stalls.) Take the chair lift up **Gedeonseck** to view this stretch of
the Rhine from on high.

㉑ At Boppard, the river swings east and then north to **Rhens,** a town that
traces its origins back some 1,300 years. A vital center of the Holy Roman
Empire, Rhens was where German kings and emperors were elected
and then presented to the people. The monumental site where the ceremonies took place, the **Königstuhl** (King's Chair), is on a hilltop just
outside Rhens, on the road to Waldesch. It was here, in 1388, that the
rift between the Holy Roman Empire and the papacy (to which the emperor was nominally subject) proved final. The six German prince-electors who nominated the emperor declared that henceforward their
decisions were final and need no longer be given papal sanction.

㉒ **Marksburg,** the final castle on this fortress-studded stretch of the
Rhine, is located on the opposite bank of the river, 500 feet above the
town of **Braubach.** Marksburg was built during the 12th century to
protect silver and lead mines in the area; so successful were its medieval
builders that the castle proved impregnable—it is the only one in the
entire Middle Rhine Valley to have survived the centuries intact. Within
its massive walls are a collection of weapons and manuscripts, a medieval botanical garden, and a restaurant.

Tour 2: Koblenz

㉓ The ancient city of **Koblenz** now looms ahead. Located at a geographic
nexus known as the **Deutsches Eck** (corner of Germany), Koblenz is
the heart of the Middle Rhine region. Rivers and mountains converge
here: The Mosel flows into the Rhine on one side, the Lahn flows in
on the other; and three mountain ridges also intersect.

Koblenz serves as the cultural, administrative, and business center of
the Middle Rhine. Its position at the confluence of two rivers bustling

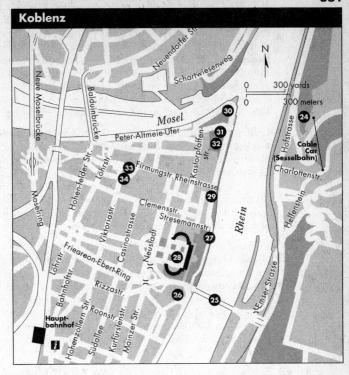

with steamers, barges, tugs, and every other kind of river boat makes
it one of the most important traffic points on the Rhine.

The heart of historic Koblenz is close to the point where the Rhine and
Mosel meet. Koblenz was founded by the Romans in AD 9. Its Roman
name, Castrum ad Confluentes (the camp at the confluence), was later
corrupted to Koblenz. It became a powerful city in the Middle Ages,
when it controlled trade on both rivers. The city suffered severe bomb
damage from air raids during the last world war (85% of its buildings
were destroyed), but extensive restoration has done much to re-create
the atmosphere of old Koblenz. English-speaking walking tours of the
old town can be arranged by the tourist office on request.

*Numbers in the margin correspond to points of interest on the Koblenz
map.*

24 Koblenz is centered on the west bank of the Rhine, but you may want
to begin your tour on the opposite side, at **Festung Ehrenbreitstein,** Europe's largest fortress. Set 400 feet above the river, it offers a commanding
view of the Old Town (the view alone justifies a visit). Take the cable
car (Sesselbahn) (DM 8 adults round-trip, DM 5 children) if the walk
is too daunting. The earliest buildings date from about 1100, but the
bulk of the fortress was constructed during the 16th century. In 1801,
Napoléon's forces partially destroyed Festung Ehrenbreitstein; the
French then occupied Koblenz for 18 years, a fact that some claim accounts for the city's Gallic joie de vivre. More concrete evidence of French
occupation can be seen in the shape of the fortress's 16th-century
Vogel Greif cannon. The French absconded with it in 1794; the Germans took it back in 1940; and the French commandeered it again in

1945. The 15-ton cannon was peaceably returned in 1984 by French President François Mitterrand. It is part of the exhibit of the history of local technologies (from wine-growing to industry) in the **County Museum** (Landesmuseum) in the fortress. *Fortress and museum:* ☛ *Free. Museum open mid-Mar.–mid-Nov., daily 9–12:30 and 1–5. Fortress open year-round. Cable car open Good Fri.–May, daily 10–5; June–Nov. 1, daily 9:30–6. Fortress may be reached by ferry (DM 1.30) from Pegelhaus (Rhine Gardens) on the Koblenz side of the Rhine.*

㉕ Begin a tour of the **Old Town** at the bridge **Pfaffendorfer** (or **Rhein) Brücke.** At its west end, between the modern blocks of the Rhein-Mosel **㉖** Halle and the Scandic Crown Hotel, is the **Weindorf,** a wine "village" constructed for a mammoth exhibition of German wine in 1925. It continues to attract tourists today, and is especially lively around carnival time. If the weather's good, sample a glass of wine in the Weindorf's leafy gardens; in summer live music spices up the scene after 7 PM and at jazz brunches on Sundays and holidays.

Running along the riverbank past the Weindorf is the 10-kilometer- **㉗** (6-mile-) long promenade of the **Rheinanlagen,** one of the longest in the Rhineland. Strolling along here toward town, you'll pass the gra- **㉘** cious **Residenzschloss,** the prince-elector's palace. It was built in 1786 by Prince-Elector Clemens Wenceslaus as an elegant replacement for the grim Ehrenbreitstein fortress. He lived here for only three years, however; in 1791 he was forced to flee to Augsburg when the French stormed the city. Today the palace is used for city offices and is closed to visitors.

㉙ Farther along, you'll come to the squat form of the **Rheinkran,** a crane built in 1611. Marks on the side of the building indicate the heights reached by floodwaters of bygone years. In the mid-19th century, a pontoon bridge consisting of a row of barges spanned the Rhine here; when ships approached, two or three barges were simply moved out of the way to let them through.

TIME OUT If the weather's good, take a seat outdoors at one of the tables by the river. Today the **Rheinkran** is a reasonably priced restaurant where you can enjoy solid German specialties while people-watching or observing the passing boats along the Rhine.

㉚ Continue along the banks to the **Deutsches Eck** at the intersection of the Rhine and Mosel, a sharply pointed piece of land jutting into the river like the prow of some early ironclad warship. This curious structure is one of the more effusive manifestations of German nationalism. In 1897 a statue of Kaiser Wilhelm I, first emperor of the newly united Germany, was erected here. This was destroyed at the end of World War II and replaced in 1953 with a ponderous altarlike monument to German unity. After German reunification, a new statue of Wilhelm was placed atop this monument in 1993, despite protest from those who felt this could be sending out some less-than-positive signals about the "new Germany." Behind it some pieces of the Berlin Wall stand as a memorial to those who died as a result of the partitioning of the country.

Standing just behind the Deutsches Eck is the spic-and-span Deutschher- **㉛** renhaus, a restored 13th-century building that now houses the new **Museum Ludwig.** Industrialist Peter Ludwig, one of Germany's leading contemporary art collectors, has founded museums in virtually every city in the Rhineland (see Cologne and Aachen tours, *below*); he's filled this museum, too, with part of his huge collection of modern art.

☞ *DM 5, children DM 3.* ⊗ *Tues., Wed., Fri., and Sat 11–5, Thurs. 11–8, Sun 11–6.*

㉜ Next to this is **St. Kastor Kirche,** a sturdy Romanesque basilica consecrated in 836. It was here in 843 that the Treaty of Verdun was signed, formalizing the division of Charlemagne's great empire and leading to the creation of Germany and France as separate states. Inside, compare the squat Romanesque columns in the nave with the intricate fan vaulting of the Gothic sections. The **St. Kastor fountain** outside the church is an intriguing piece of historical one-upmanship. It was built by the occupying French to mark the beginning of Napoléon's ultimately disastrous Russian campaign of 1812. When the Russians, having inflicted a crushing defeat on Napoléon, reached Koblenz, they added an ironic "Seen and approved" to the inscription on the fountain.

From the Deutsches Eck, the **Moselanlagen** (Mosel Promenade) leads to Koblenz's oldest restaurant, **Deutscher Kaiser,** which marks the start of the **Altstadt** (Old Town). The damage of war is evidenced in the blend of old buildings and modern store blocks on and around the central square of **Am Plan;** among the former is the lovely 16th-century building that is the **Middle Rhine Museum,** which houses the city's **㉝** art collection. On one side of the square itself is the **Liebfrauenkirche** (Church of Our Lady), which stands on Roman foundations at the Old Town's highest point. The bulk of the church is of Romanesque design, but its choir is one of the Rhineland's finest examples of 15th-century Gothic architecture, and the west front is graced with two 17th-century Baroque towers. Behind the church is the 17th-century **㉞** town hall, a former Jesuit college, and the little statue called the **Schäng-elbrunnen** (literally "scalawag fountain"), a boy who spouts water every three minutes at unwary passersby. One other highlight of this section of town is the **"Four Towers,"** restored 17th-century half-timbered houses.

Tour 3: Along the Mosel to Trier

Numbers in the margin correspond to points of interest on the Rhineland map.

While a tour along the meandering Mosel River to the historic city of Trier could be considered a regression from the Rhine, it's actually an excursion endowed with a magic and charm all its own. In fact, Trier could easily qualify as the best-kept secret when it comes to German cities. Taking the road that follows the banks of the Mosel with all its loops and turns takes three hours of driving. On the Autobahn, the distance of 125 kilometers (84 miles) between Koblenz and Trier is covered in less than an hour.

You don't have to travel far up the Mosel Valley to be reminded that wine plays every bit as important a role here as it does along the Rhine. The river's zigzag course passes between steep, terraced slopes where grapes have been grown since Roman times.

The Mosel is one of the most hauntingly beautiful river valleys on earth: turreted castles look down from its leafy perches, its hilltops are crowned with bell towers, and throughout its expanse, skinny church spires stand against the sky. For more than 160 kilometers (100 miles), the silvery Mosel River meanders past a string of storybook medieval wine villages, each more attractive than the other. The first village you'll **㉟** reach, **Winningen,** 15 kilometers (10 miles) from Koblenz, is the center of the valley's largest vineyards. Stop off to admire Germany's oldest half-timbered house in **Kirchenstrasse** (No. 1); it was built in 1320. On the slopes above Winningen's narrow medieval streets is a mile-long path reached by driving up Fährstrasse to Am Rosenhang. Once there, high above the Mosel, you'll get a bird's-eye view of the **Uhlen, Röttgen, Bruckstück, Hamm,** and **Domgarten** vineyards.

36 For an even finer view of the river and its rich valley, follow the road 8 kilometers (5 miles) to **Kobern-Gondorf,** on the north bank of the river, and turn off into the idyllic little Mühlental Valley. Here you can climb up through the steep vineyards to the remains of **Oberburg Castle,** built during the 12th century by the powerful Knights of Leyen. On the way you'll pass **St. Matthew's** a 13th-century Romanesque chapel.

★ **37** The Mosel bristles with almost as many castles as the Rhine. Among them is what many deem the most impressive in the country, **Burg Eltz.** It's located above the village of Moselkern, 15 kilometers (10 miles) from Koben-Gondorf. One way to reach the castle from Moselkern is on foot from the parking lot, a walk of about 1 hour (3 kilometers/2 miles) on a footpath through the wild valley. You can also take the small shuttle bus from the parking lot (DM 1.50 per person). Either way, it's worth the trek to see what may well be the most perfectly proportioned medieval castle in Germany. Perched on the spine of an isolated rocky outcrop, bristling with towers and pinnacles, it at first looks unreal. A closer look reveals Burg Eltz as the apotheosis of all one expects of a medieval castle: It's easily as impressive as "Mad" King Ludwig's fantasy creation, Neuschwanstein. But Burg Eltz is the real thing: an 800-year-old castle, with modifications from the 16th century. The magic continues in the interior, which is decorated with heavy Gothic furnishings. There is also an interesting collection of old weapons. The castle is depicted on the DM 500 banknote. ☛ *DM 8 adults, DM 5.50 children; price includes a guided tour.* ⊙ *Apr.–Oct., daily 9:30–5:30.*

38 Destructimon was the fate suffered by the next castle along the valley, the famous **Reichsburg** (Imperial Fortress) **of Cochem,** 15 kilometers (10 miles) from Berg Eltz. The 900-year-old castle was rebuilt during the 19th century after Louis XIV stormed it in 1689. Today it stands majestically over Cochem. ☛ *DM 5 adults, DM 2.50 children.* ⊙ *Mid-Mar.–Nov., daily 9–6; Nov.–Dec. hourly tours 11–3.*

Cochem itself is one of the most attractive towns of the Mosel Valley, with a riverside promenade to rival any along the Rhine. If you're traveling by train, just south of Cochem you'll be plunged into Germany's longest railway tunnel, the Kaiser-Wilhelm, an astonishing 4-kilometer-long (2½-mile-long) example of 19th-century engineering that saves travelers a 21-kilometer (13-mile) detour along one of the Mosel's great loops.

39 By car, follow the loop of the river fmor 8 kilometers (5 miles) past Cochem and you'll reach the little town of **Beilstein.** It has a mixture of all the picture-pretty features of a German river and wine town in this romantic area of the country. Take a look at the marketplace carved into the rocky slope.

TIME OUT At the village of **Ediger-Eller,** 10 kilometers (6 miles) from Beilstein, stop by the roadside vineyard of **Freiherr von Landenberg** (Moselstr. 60). Sample a glass of wine from the Baron's vines and visit his private viticulture museum.

40 **Zell,** 12 kilometers (8 miles) upriver, on another great loop, is a typical Mosel River town, much like Cochem. Located about midway between Koblenz and Trier, this small historic town is made up of picturesque red-roof homes and age-old fortifications falling into ruin. A scenic backdrop is provided by the vineyards that produce the famous Schwarze Katz (Black Cat) wine, which is rated one of Germany's very best whites. Stroll the town's medieval arc along the river. On your way you'll notice a small, twin-towered castle, Schloss Zell, dating from the 14th century. A restaurant here serves regional cuisine and wine from the owner's own Black Cat vineyards.

41 Straddling the Mosel 18 kilometers (11 miles) farther along is **Traben-Trarbach,** a two-town combination that serves as headquarters of the regional wine trade and offers a popular wine festival in summer. Visit the ruins of **Mont Royal** high above Traben on the east bank. This enormous fortress was built around 1687 by Louis XIV of France, only to be dismantled 10 years later under the terms of the Treaty of Rijswijk. Partially restored by the Nazis, the fortress retains some of its original forbidding mass.

42 **Bernkastel-Kues** is 22 kilometers (14 miles) away by road, but if you're in the mood for some exercise, you can reach it on foot from Traben-Trarbach in about two hours by taking the path that cuts across the tongue of land formed by the exaggerated loop of the river. The road, following the river, practically doubles back on itself as it winds leisurely along. Bernkastel, on the north bank of the river, and Kues, on the south, were officially linked early this century. **Marktplatz,** the heart of Bernkastel, meets all the requirements for the ideal small-town German market square. Most of the buildings are late-Gothic/early Renaissance, with facades covered with intricate carvings and sharp gables stabbing the sky. In the center of the square is **Michaelsbrunnen** (Michael's fountain), a graceful 17th-century work. Wine used to flow from it on special occasions in bygone years. Today, although wine flows freely in the town—especially during the local wine festival in the first week of September—only water ever comes from the fountain. There's a fortress here, too: **Burg Landshut,** a 13th-century castle glowering above the town. Visit it for some amazing views of the river either from its ramparts or from the terrace of the restaurant within its old walls, and to wander around its flower-strewn remains. In summer a bus makes the trip up to the castle every hour from the parking lot by the river.

The town's most famous wine is known as Bernkasteler Doktor. According to a story, the wine got its unusual name when it saved the life of the prince-bishop of Trier, who lay dying in the castle. After all other medicinal treatments had failed to cure him, he was offered a glass of the local wine—which miraculously put him back on his feet. Try a glass of it yourself at the castle (or buy a bottle from the vineyard bordering the street called Hinterm Graben).

The town's remaining attraction owes its existence to Cardinal Nikolaus Cusanus (Kues), a 15th-century philosopher and pioneer of German humanist thought. He founded a religious and charitable institution, complete with a vineyard, on the riverbank in Kues. The vineyard is still going strong; ask about the regular tastings in the St. Niklaus-Hospital (Cusanusstr. 2). The buildings here comprise the largest Gothic ensemble on the Mosel. Among them is the Mosel-Weinmuseum. ☛ *DM 2 adults, DM 1 children.* ⊘ *May–Oct., daily 10–5; Nov.–Apr., daily 2–5.*

From Bernkastel-Kues to Trier is a further 66 kilometers (41 miles) of twisting river road. You can also board a cruise boat from May through October that takes 4½ hours to reach Trier, with six stops along the way. (☎ 02673/1515. Cost: DM 34 one-way, DM 44 round-trip. Departs from Bernkastel-Kues 3:15, from Trier for Bernkastel-Kues at 9:15 AM; an additional boat runs Tuesday only at 10 AM.)

㊸ Endless vineyards and little river towns punctuate the snaking path of the Mosel. Among them is **Neumagen**, settled by the Romans during the 4th century. In its main square, there's a modern copy of the famous carved relief of a Roman wine ship plying a choppy-looking Mosel. If you continue on to Trier, you can see the original in the Landesmuseum.

㊹ **Trier's** (known as Treves in English) claim to fame is that it's the oldest town in Germany. It dates from 2,000 BC, when Prince Trebeta, son of an Assyrian queen, arrived here and set up residence on the banks of the Mosel; he named the place Treberis, after himself. An inscription on a historic old house on Trier's marketplace claims: *"Ante Romam Treveris stetit annis mille trecentis"* ("1,300 years before Rome stood Trier").

Eventually the legions of Julius Caesar set up camp at this strategic point of the river, and Augusta Treverorum (the town of Emperor Augustus in the land of the Treveri) was founded in 16 BC. It was described as *"urbs opulentissima"*—a most opulent city, as beautiful as any outside Rome itself.

Around AD 275 an Alemannic tribe stormed Augusta Treverorum and reduced it to rubble. But it was rebuilt in even grander style and renamed Treveris. Eventually it evolved into one of the leading cities of the empire and was promoted to *Roma Secunda,* "a second Rome" north of the Alps. As a powerful administrative capital, it was adorned with all the noble civic buildings of a major Roman settlement, as well as public baths, palaces, barracks, an amphitheater, and temples. The Roman emperors Diocletian (who made it one of the four joint capitals of the empire) and Constantine lived in Trier for years at a time.

Trier survived the collapse of Rome and became an important center of Christianity; it later became one of the most powerful archbishoprics in the Holy Roman Empire. The city thrived throughout the Renaissance and Baroque periods, taking full advantage of its location at the meeting point of major east–west and north–south trade routes, and growing fat on the commerce that passed through. It also became one of Germany's most important wine-exporting centers. A later claim to fame is the city's status as the birthplace of Karl Marx. To do justice to Trier, consider staying for at least two full days. A ticket good for all the Roman sights in Trier costs DM 9 for adults and DM 4 for children. Between May and October, there are walking tours of the city conducted by the local tourist board in English. The walking tour leaves from the gate at 2. The cost is DM 9 for adults DM 4.50 for children. The tourist office (☎ 0651/978–080) can also assist in making tour and hotel arrangements.

Numbers in the margin correspond to points of interest on the Trier map.

★ ㊺ Begin your tour at the **Porta Nigra** (the Black Gate), by the city's tourist office. This is by far the best-preserved Roman structure in Trier and one of the grandest Roman buildings in northern Europe. It's a city gate, built during the 2nd century. Its name is misleading, however: The sandstone gate is not actually black but dark gray. Those with an interest in Roman construction techniques should look for the holes left by the original iron clamps that held the entire structure together. This city gate also served as part of Trier's defenses and was proof of

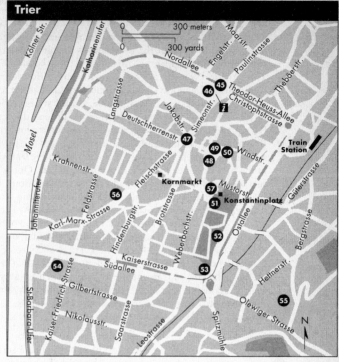

Trier

the sophistication of Roman military might and ruthlessness. Attack-
ers were often lured into the two innocent-looking arches of the Porta
Nigra only to find themselves enclosed in a courtyard—and at the mercy
of the defending forces. ☛ *DM 4 adults, DM 2 children and senior citizens.* ☾ *Apr.–Oct., daily 9–6; Nov. and Jan.–Mar., daily 9–5; Dec.,
daily 10–4.*

To the side are the remains of the Romanesque Simeonskirche, today
④⑥ the **Städtisches Museum Simeonstift.** The church was built during the
11th century by Archbishop Poppo in honor of the early medieval her-
mit Simeon, who for seven years shut himself up in the east tower of
the Porta Nigra. Collections of art and artifacts produced in Trier from
the Middle Ages to the present now commemorate Simeon's feat.
☛ *Free.* ☾ *Apr.–Oct., Tues.–Fri. 9–5, weekends 9–3; Nov.–Mar.,
Tues.–Fri. 9–5, weekends 9–1.*

Simeon also has one of Trier's main streets named after him: Simeon-
④⑦ strasse. It leads directly to **Hauptmarkt,** the main square of old Trier.
A 1,000-year-old market cross and a richly ornate 16th-century fountain stand in the square.

From Hauptmarkt, turn left (east) down Sternstrasse to see Trier's great
Dom (cathedral). Before you go in, take a look at the adjoining 13th-
④⑧ century **Liebfrauenkirche** (Church of Our Lady). It's one of the oldest
purely Gothic churches in the country. The interior is elegantly attenuated.

★ **④⑨** If you want a condensed history of Trier, visit the **Dom:** There is almost no period of the city's past that is not represented here. It stands

on the site of the Palace of Helen, mother of the emperor Constantine, who knocked the palace down in AD 330 and put up a large church in its place. The church burned down in 336 and a second, even larger one was built. Parts of the foundations of this third building can be seen in the east end of the current structure (begun in about 1035). The cathedral you see today is a weighty and sturdy edifice with small, round-headed windows, rough stonework, and asymmetrical towers, as much a fortress as a church. Inside, Gothic styles predominate—the result of remodeling in the 13th century—though there are also many Baroque tombs, altars, and confessionals. This architectural jumble of Romanesque, Gothic, and Baroque styles gives the place the air of a vast antiques shop. Make sure you visit the Gothic **Domschatzmuseum** in the treasury, site of two extraordinary objects. One is the 10th-century **Andreas Tragalter** (St. Andrews's Portable Altar), made of gold by local craftsmen. It is smaller than the Dom's main altar, but it is no lightweight. The other treasure is the **Holy Robe,** the garment supposedly worn by Christ at the time of his trial before Pontius Pilate and gambled for by Roman soldiers. The story goes that it was brought to Trier by Constantine's mother, Helen, a tireless collector of holy relics. It is so delicate and old that it is seldom displayed, but visitors in 1996 are in luck: This year is one of the rare times it is taken out from its regular abode under a faded piece of 9th-century Byzantine silk (Apr. 19–May 16). *Domschatzmuseum* ☞ *DM 1 adults, 50 pf children.* ⏰ *Apr.–Oct., Mon.–Sat. 10–noon and 2–5, Sun. 2–5; until 4 PM Nov.–Mar.*

⑤⓪ Excavations around the cathedral have unearthed a series of antiquities, most of which are housed in the **Bischöfliches Museum** (Episcopal Museum) in Windstrasse, just behind the cathedral. The exhibits include a 4th-century ceiling painting believed to have adorned the emperor Constantine's palace. *Windstr. 6–8.* ☞ *DM 2 adults, DM 1 children.* ⏰ *Mon.–Sat. 9–1 and 2–5, Sun. 1–5.*

TIME OUT There's a time-honored welcome at the **Steipe Ratskeller** in the cellars beneath the Rathaus (Town Hall), where you can tuck into the hearty local fare or just order a coffee, beer, or glass of Mosel wine. *Hauptmarkt 14.*

★ ⑤① Just south of the cathedral complex—take Konstantinstrasse—is another impressive reminder of Trier's Roman past: the **Römische Palastaula** (Roman Basilica). Today this is the major protestant church of Trier. When first built by the emperor Constantine around AD 310, it was the Imperial Throne Room of the palace. At 239 feet long, 93 feet wide, and 108 feet high, it demonstrates the astounding ambition of its Roman builders and the sophistication of their building techniques. It is one of the two largest Roman interiors in existence (the other is the Pantheon in Rome). Look up at the deeply coffered ceiling: More than any other part of the building, it conveys the opulence of the original structure. *Konstantinplatz,* ☎ *0651/978–080.* ⏰ *Apr.–Oct., weekdays 9–6, Sun. and holidays 11–6; Nov.–Mar., limited opening hrs.*

⑤② From the Palastaula, turn south. To your left, facing the grounds of the prince elector's palace, is the **Rheinisches Landesmuseum** (Rhineland Archaeological Museum), which houses the largest collection of Roman antiquities in Germany. Pride of place goes to the 3rd-century stone relief of a Roman ship transporting immense barrels of wine up the river. If you stopped off in Neumagen on the way to Trier, you probably saw the copy of it in the town square. *Weimarerallee 44.* ☞ *Free.* ⏰ *Mon. 10–4, Tues.–Fri. 9:30–4, Sat. 9:30–1, Sun. 9–1.*

53 From the museum, walk down to the ruins of the **Kaiserthermen** (imperial baths), just 200 yards away. Begun by Constantine during the 4th century, these were once the third-largest public baths in the Roman Empire, exceeded only by Diocletian's baths in Croatia and the baths of Caracalla in Rome. They covered an area 270 yards long and 164 yards wide. Today only the weed-strewn fragments of the **Calderium** (hot baths) are left, but they are enough to give a fair idea of the original splendor and size of the complex. When the Romans pulled out, the baths were turned into a fortress (one window of the huge complex served as a city gate for much of the Middle Ages), then a church, and then a fortress again. Don't confuse them with the much smaller **54** **Barbarathermen** (open same hours) which have been excavated in Südallee. ☞ *Each building: DM 4 adults, DM 2 children. Kaiserthermen open Apr.–Oct., daily 9–6; Jan.–Mar. and Nov., daily 9–5; Dec., daily 10–4. Barbarathermen open Apr.–Sept., daily 9–6; Oct.–Mar., daily 9–1 and 2–5.*

55 Just east of the Kaiserthermen are the remains of the **Amphitheater** built around AD 100, the oldest Roman building in Trier. In its heyday it seated 20,000 people. You can climb down to the cellars beneath the arena to see what's left of the machines that were used to change the scenery; in the walls are the cells where lions and other wild animals were kept before being unleashed to devour maidens and do battle with gladiators. *Olewigerstr. See Porta Nigra for hrs and admission.*

After this profusion of antiquities, you may want to shift gears and see **56** the **Karl-Marx-Haus** on Brockenstrasse, south of Kornmarkt in the Old-Town. It was here that Marx was born in 1818. Serious social historians will feel at home in the little house, which has been converted into a museum charting Marx's life and the development of socialism around the world. A signed first edition of *Das Kapital,* the tome in which Marx sought to prove the inevitable decline of capitalism, may prove a highlight for some. ☞ *DM 3 adults, DM 2 children.* ☼ *Apr.–Oct., Mon. 1–6, Tues.–Sun. 10–6; Nov.–Mar., Mon. 3–6, Tues.–Sun. 10–1 and 3–6.*

Trier is, of course, also a city of wine, and beneath its streets are cellars capable of storing nearly 8 million gallons. To get to know the wines **57** of the region, drop in for a tasting at the **Weininformation Mosel-Saar-Ruwer** (Konstantinpl. 11, ☎ 0651/73690). The city also has a wine trail, a picturesque 1½-mile walk studded with information plaques that lead to the wine-growing suburb of **Olewig.** A free map of the trail along with information on Trier's wine making is available from the tourist office.

Tour 4: Bonn and Köln

Numbers in the margin correspond to points of interest on the Rhineland map.

58 **Bonn,** the quiet university town on the Rhine, is now the interim seat of reunited Germany's federal government and parliament, but in a parliamentary vote on June 20, 1991, it lost out to Berlin as the permanent capital city of the country. In reality, Bonn will continue to share the responsibility of governing Germany with Berlin. The upper house of parliament—the **Bundesrat**—will remain in Bonn, as will nearly half the ministries and two-thirds of the civil servants. Moving the rest of the government to Berlin is expected to take 12 years and will be costly—as much as $30 billion.

The choice, in 1949, of Bonn as capital of the newly created Federal Republic was never meant to be permanent. At the time, few Germans thought the division of their country would prove anything other than temporary, and they were certain that Berlin would again become the capital before long. Popular legend now has it that Bonn, aptly described in the title of John Le Carré's spy novel *A Small Town in Germany,* was chosen as a stopgap measure to prevent such weightier contenders as Frankfurt from becoming the capital, a move that would have lessened Berlin's chances of regaining its former status.

Germans tend to deride their postwar capital for its lack of character. Some suggest that Bonn's greatest asset is its surrounding countryside: the legendary **Siebengebirge** (Seven Hills) and the **Kölner Bucht Valley.** In the capital's streets, old markets, stores, pedestrian malls, parks, and the handsome Südstadt residential area, life is unhurried and unsophisticated by the standard of larger cities. Guided tours of Bonn start from the tourist office. *Münsterstr. 20,* ☎ *0228/773–466. Tours conducted Apr.–Oct., daily at 11; May–Sept., also Sat. at 2. The 2-hr tour costs DM 18 adults, DM 9 children.*

The town center is a car-free zone. An inner-ring road circles it with parking garages on the perimeter. A convenient parking lot is just across from the railway station and within 50 yards of the tourist office.

Numbers in the margin correspond to points of interest on the Bonn map.

59 Bonn's status may be new, but its roots are ancient. The Romans settled this part of the Rhineland 2,000 years ago, calling it Castra Bonnensia. Bonn's cathedral, the **Münster,** stands where two Roman soldiers were executed in AD 253 for holding Christian beliefs. **Münsterplatz,** site of the cathedral and a short walk from the tourist office in Münsterstrasse 20, is the logical place to begin your tour. The 900-year-old cathedral is vintage late-Romanesque, with a massive octagonal main tower and a soaring spire. It was chosen by two Holy Roman emperors for their coronations (in 1314 and 1346), and was one of the Rhineland's most important ecclesiastical centers in the Middle Ages. The bronze 17th-century figure of St. Helen and the ornate Rococo pulpit are highlights of the interior. ⊙ *Daily 7–7.*

60 Facing the Münster is the grand **Kurfürstliches Schloss,** built during the 18th century by the prince electors of Köln; today it houses a university. If it's a fine day, stroll through the Hofgarten (Palace Gardens), or follow the chestnut-tree avenue called Poppelsdorfer Allee south**61** ward to another electors' palace, the smaller **Poppelsdorfer Schloss,** built in Baroque style between 1715 and 1753. The palace houses the university's botanical garden, with an impressive display of tropical plants. *Meckenheimer Allee 171.* ☛ *Free.* ⊙ *Apr.–Sept., weekdays 9–6, weekends and holidays 9–1; Oct.–Mar., weekdays 9–4.*

On your way back to the Old Town, take Meckenheimer Allee and **62** then Colmantstrasse, to see the **Rheinisches Landesmuseum** (the walk is about ¼ mile long). This large museum charts the history and culture of the Rhine Valley from Roman times to the present. The main draw is the skull of a Neanderthal man, put together from fragments found in the Neander Valley near Düsseldorf in 1856 and regarded as a vital link in the evolutionary chain. *Colmantstrasse 14–16,* ☎ *0228/72941.* ☛ *DM 4 adults, DM 2 children.* ⊙ *Tues. and Thurs. 9–5, Wed. 9–8, Fri. 9–5, weekends 10–5.*

63 At the end of Colmantstrasse, take the underpass below the railroad line and follow Thomasstrasse 300 yards to the **Alter Friedhof** (the Old Cemetery). This ornate graveyard is the resting place of many of the country's most celebrated sons and daughters. Look for the tomb of composer Robert Schumann and his wife, Clara. *Am Alten Friedhof.* ⊗ *Mar.–Aug., daily 7:15 AM–8 PM; Sept. and Feb., daily 8–8; Oct., daily 8–7; Nov.–Jan., daily 8–5.*

From the Alter Friedhof, follow Sternstrasse into the Old Town center and proceed to the **Markt** (market), where you'll find an 18th-century
64 **Rathaus** (Town Hall) that looks like a pink doll's house.

★ **65** Just north of the town hall are Bonngasse and the **Beethovenhaus.** The latter has been converted into a museum celebrating the life of the great composer. Here you'll find scores, paintings, a grand piano (his last, in fact), and an ear trumpet or two. Perhaps the most impressive exhibit is the room in which Beethoven was born—empty save for a bust of the composer. *Bonngasse 20,* ☎ *0228/635–188.* ☛ *DM 5 adults, DM 1.50 children.* ⊗ *Apr.–Sept., Mon.–Sat. 10–5, Sun. 10–1; Oct.–Mar., Mon.–Sat. 10–4, Sun. 10–1.*

A tour of Bonn would not be complete without mention of the government buildings, in a complex about a mile south of downtown. Strung
66 along the Rhine amid spacious, leafy grounds are the offices of the **Federal President,** the high-tech **Chancellery,** and the **Federal Parliament;** the '60s high rise you see contains the offices of members of parliament.

67 Recently opened near the government buildings are a trio of museums designed to bring Bonn more into the swing of things cultural. The **Kunstmuseum** is a large museum of contemporary art, and the **Bundeskunsthalle** (Art Hall of the German Federal Republic) is a space for major traveling exhibitions. *Friedrich-Ebert-Allee 2 and 4. Both museums open Tues.–Sun. 10–7.*

68 More controversial, if possibly less successful, is the **Haus der Geschichte,** a museum devoted to post–World War II German history: it displays an overwhelming amount of documentary material but avoids delving too deeply into some of the heavier issues of the period. *Adenauerstr. 250. ☯ Tues.–Sun. 9–7.*

TIME OUT On your way back to town, turn left off Adenauerallee at its intersection with Weberstrasse, cross the railway line, and make for the **Mierscheid** bar-restaurant (Weberstrasse 43), long a hangout of Bonn politicians.

Numbers in the margin correspond to points of interest on the Rhineland map.

69 **Köln** (Cologne), 27 kilometers (17 miles) north of Bonn, is the largest city on the Rhine (the fourth-largest in Germany) and one of the most interesting. Although not as old as Trier, it has been a dominant power in the Rhineland since Roman times. Known throughout the world for its scented toilet water, eau de cologne (first produced here in 1705 from an Italian formula), the city is today a major commercial, intellectual, and ecclesiastical center. The numerous trade fairs, held in the two massive convention centers on the Deutzer side of the Rhine, are a draw for many.

Köln is a vibrant, bustling city, with something of the same sparkle that makes Munich so memorable. It claims to have more bars than any other German city, and it has a host of excellent eating places. It also puts on a wild carnival every February, with three days of orgiastic revelry, bands, parades, and parties that last all night.

The tourist office (☎ 0221/221–3345), across from the cathedral, can make hotel bookings for you at a cost of DM 6. From the tourist office or your hotel you can purchase a Köln-Bonbon card for DM 26; it includes free admission to museums and a bus tour of the city (cost without the tour: DM 15). (For information about guided tours of Köln, *see* City Tours *in* Essential Information, *above.*)

Köln was first settled by the Romans in 38 BC. For nearly a century it grew slowly, in the shadow of imperial Trier, until a locally born noblewoman, Julia Agrippina, daughter of the Roman general Germanicus, married the Roman emperor Claudius. Her hometown was elevated to the rank of a Roman city and given the name Colonia Claudia Ara Agrippinensium. For the next 300 years, Colonia (hence Cologne, or Köln) flourished. Today there's evidence of the Roman city's richness in the **Römisch-Germanisches Museum,** or Roman-German Museum (*see below*). When the Romans left, Köln was ruled first by the Franks, then by the Merovingians. During the 9th century, Charlemagne, the towering figure who united the sprawling German lands (and ruled much of present-day France) and was the first Holy Roman Emperor, restored Köln's fortunes and elevated it to its preeminent role in the Rhineland. Charlemagne also appointed the first archbishop of Köln. The ecclesiastical heritage of Köln forms one of the most striking characteristics of the city, which has no fewer than 12 Romanesque churches. Its Gothic cathedral is the largest and the finest in Germany.

Köln eventually became the largest city north of the Alps, and in time evolved into a place of pilgrimage second only to Rome. In the Middle Ages it was a member of the powerful Hanseatic League, occupying a position of greater importance in European commerce than either London or Paris did.

Köln entered modern times as the number-one city of the Rhineland. Then, in World War II, bombings destroyed 90% of it. Only the cathedral remained relatively unscathed. Almost everything else had to be rebuilt more or less from the ground up, including all of the glorious Romanesque churches.

Early reconstruction was accomplished in a big rush—and it shows. Like many German cities that sprang up, mushroomlike, in the "Economic Miracle" of the 1950s, Köln is a mishmash of old and new, sometimes awkwardly juxtaposed. A good part of the former Old Town along the Hohe Strasse (old Roman High Road) was turned into one of Germany's first yet remarkably charmless pedestrian shopping malls, since emulated in so many other cities. Contrasting with its square, blocky forms are the totally re-created facades of the Old Town dwellings facing the river, which bring to mind Disneyland rather than recapturing their former dignified, venerable air. The ensemble is framed by six-lane expressways winding along the rim of the city center—barely yards from the cathedral—perfectly illustrating the problems, as well as the blessings, of postwar reconstruction.

Among the blessings is the fact that much of the Altstadt (Old Town), ringed by streets that follow the line of the medieval city walls, is closed to traffic; most major sights are within this area and are easily reached on foot. Here, too, you'll find the best shops.

Numbers in the margin correspond to points of interest on the Köln map.

★ **70** Towering over the Old Town is the extraordinary Gothic cathedral, the **Kölner Dom,** dedicated to Sts. Peter and Mary. It's comparable to the best French cathedrals; a visit here may prove a highlight of your trip to Germany. What you'll see is one of the purest expressions of the Gothic spirit in Europe. Here the desire to pay homage to God took the form of building as large and as lavish a church as possible, a tangible expression of God's kingdom on earth. Its spires soar heavenward and its immense interior is illuminated by light filtering through acres of stained glass. Spend some time admiring the outside of the building (you can walk almost all the way around it). Notice how there are practically no major horizontal lines—all the accents of the building are vertical. It may come as a disappointment to learn that the cathedral, begun in 1248, was not completed until 1880. Console yourself with the knowledge that it was still built to original plans. At 515 feet high, the two west towers of the cathedral were by far the tallest structures in the world when they were finished.

The cathedral was built to house what was believed to be the relics of the Magi, the three kings who paid homage to the infant Jesus (the trade in holy mementos was big business in the Middle Ages, and not always too scrupulous). Since Köln was by then a major commercial and political center, it was felt that a special place had to be constructed to house the relics. Anxious to surpass the great cathedrals then being built in France, the masons set to work. The size of the building was not simply an example of self-aggrandizement on the part of the people of Köln, however; it was a response to the vast numbers of pilgrims who arrived to see the relics. The ambulatory, the passage that curves

Köln (Cologne)

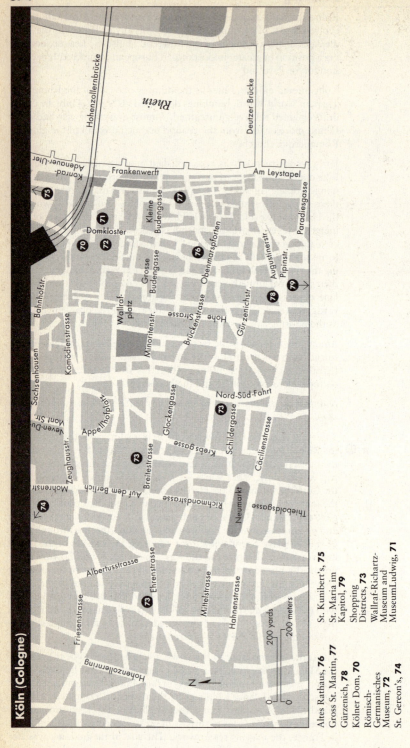

Rhein

Hohenzollernbrücke

Deutzer Brücke

Konrad-Adenauer-Ufer

Frankenwerft

Am Leystapel

Paradiesgasse

Kleine Budengasse

Domkloster

Obenmarspforten

Augustinerstr.

Pipinstr.

Bahnhofstr.

Grosse Budengasse

Wallraf-platz

Hohe Strasse

Brückenstrasse

Gürzenichstr.

Sachsenhausen

Komödienstrasse

Minoritenstrasse

Appellhofplatz

Jeven-Du Mont Str.

Glockengasse

Nord-Süd-Fahrt

Schildergasse

Cäcilienstrasse

Zeughausstr.

Mohrenstr.

Auf dem Berlich

Breitestrasse

Krebsgasse

Richmondstrasse

Neumarkt

Thieboldsgasse

Albertusstrasse

Ehrenstrasse

Mittelstrasse

Hahnenstrasse

Friesenstrasse

Hohenzollernring

200 yards

200 meters

N

Altes Rathaus, **76**
Gross St. Martin, **77**
Gürzenich, **78**
Kölner Dom, **70**
Römisch-
Germanisches
Museum, **72**
St. Gereon's, **74**

St. Kunibert's, **75**
St. Maria im
Kapitol, **79**
Shopping
Districts, **73**
Wallraf-Richartz-
Museum and
MuseumLudwig, **71**

around the back of the altar, is unusually large, allowing cathedral authorities to funnel large numbers of visitors up to the crossing (where the nave and transepts meet, and where the relics were originally displayed), around the back of the altar, and out again. Today the relics are kept just behind the altar, in the original enormous gold-and-silver **reliquary.** The other great treasure of the cathedral is the **Gero Cross,** a monumental oak crucifix dating from 971, in the last chapel on the left as you face the altar.

Other highlights are the stained-glass windows, some dating from the 13th century; the 15th-century altarpiece; and the early 14th-century high altar with its glistening white figures and intricate choir screens. There are more treasures in the **Dom Schatzkammer,** the cathedral treasury, including the silver shrine of Archbishop Engelbert, who was stabbed to death in 1225. ☞ *DM 3 adults, DM 1.50 children.* ☉ *Mon.–Sat. 9–5, Sun. 1–5.*

★ 🄐 Grouped around the cathedral is a collection of superb museums. If your priority is painting, try the **Wallraf-Richartz-Museum** and **Museum Ludwig** complex (which includes the Philharmonic concert hall). Together they form the largest art collection in the Rhineland. The Wallraf-Richartz-Museum contains pictures spanning the years 1300 to 1900, with Dutch and Flemish schools particularly well represented. Rubens, who spent his youth in Köln, has a place of honor, but there are also outstanding works by Rembrandt, Van Dyck, and Frans Hals. Other Old Masters include Tiepolo, Canaletto, and Boucher; some of the great Impressionists bring the collection into the 20th century, but it's here that the Museum Ludwig takes over. Devoted exclusively to 20th-century art, with a collection that is said to be second only to that of New York's Guggenheim, this is the flagship of the Rhineland museums donated by chocolate tycoon and mega-collector Peter Ludwig (*see* Tour 2: Koblenz and Tour 5: Aachen). The Picassos are so meritorious that a new, all-Picasso museum will be constructed for them in the next few years. *Bischofsgartenstr. 1,* ☎ *0221/221–2372 or 0221/221–3491.* ☞ *Both museums: DM 8 adults, DM 4 children.* ☉ *Tues.–Fri. 10–6, weekends 11–6.*

🄑 Opposite the cathedral is the **Römisch-Germanisches Museum,** built from 1970 to 1974 around the famous Dionysus mosaic that was uncovered at the site during the construction of an air-raid shelter in 1941. The huge mosaic, more than 100 yards square, once covered the dining-room floor of a wealthy Roman trader's villa. Its millions of tiny earthenware and glass tiles depict some of the adventures of Dionysius, the Greek god of wine and, to the Romans, the object of a widespread and sinister religious cult. The pillared 1st-century tomb of Lucius Publicius, a prominent Roman officer, some stone Roman coffins, and a series of memorial tablets are among the museum's other exhibits. Bordering the museum on the south is a restored 90-yard stretch of the old Roman harbor road. *Roncallipl. 4,* ☎ *0221/221–4438.* ☞ *DM 5 adults, DM 2.50 children.* ☉ *Tues.–Fri. 10–4, weekends 11–4.*

🄒 Back on the street, you'll have the choice of either more culture or commerce. Köln's **shopping district** begins at nearby **Wallrafplatz,** and a recommended shopping tour will take you down Hohe Strasse, Schildergasse, Neumarkt, Mittelstrasse, Hohenzollernring, Ehrenstrasse, Breite Strasse, Tunisstrasse, Minoritenstrasse, and then back to Wallrafplatz.

Six blocks west of the train station, on the site of an old Roman burial ground, stands one of the most exquisite of the city's many Romanesque churches: **St. Gereon's** (Gereonshof 4). Experts regard St. Gereon's as one of the most noteworthy medieval structures still in existence; although the postwar restorations have been carried out with more care than taste. An enormous dome rests on walls that were once clad in gold mosaics. Roman masonry still forms part of the structure, which is believed to have been built over the grave of its namesake, the 4th-century martyr and patron saint of Köln.

St. Kunibert's (Kunibertkloster 6), the most lavish of the churches from the late Romanesque period, is also on this side of the city, by the Rhine, just three blocks north of the train station. Consecrated in 1247, the church contains an unusual room, concealed under the altar, which gives access to a pre-Christian well once believed to promote fertility in women.

Now head south to the nearby **Alter Markt** and its **Altes Rathaus**, the oldest town hall in Germany (if you don't count the fact that the building was entirely rebuilt after the war). The square has a handsome assembly of buildings—the oldest dating from 1135—in a range of styles. There was a seat of local government here in Roman times, and directly below the current Rathaus are the remains of the Roman city governor's headquarters, the Praetorium. If you're here on Monday, Wednesday, or Saturday, you can join a guided tour (no charge) at 3 to go inside to see the 14th-century **Hansa Saal,** whose tall Gothic windows and barrel-vaulted wood ceiling are potent expressions of medieval civic pride. The figures of the prophets, standing on pedestals at one end, are all from the early 15th century. Ranging along the south wall are nine additional statues, the so-called *Nine Good Heroes,* carved in 1360. Charlemagne and King Arthur are among them.

Cross Unter Käster to come to the river and one of the most outstanding of Köln's 12 Romanesque churches, the **Gross St. Martin.** Rebuilt after being flattened in World War II, its massive 13th-century tower, with distinctive corner turrets and an imposing central spire, is another landmark of Köln. The church was built on the site of a Roman granary.

Gross St. Martin is the parish church of Köln's colorful old city, the **Martinsviertel,** an attractive combination of reconstructed, high-gabled medieval buildings, winding alleys, and tastefully designed modern apartments and business quarters. Head here at night—the place comes alive at sunset.

At the south end of the district, in Gürzenichstrasse, you'll find the attractive cultural center of **Gürzenich.** This Gothic structure, all but demolished in the war but carefully reconstructed, takes its name from a medieval knight (von Gürzenich), from whom the city acquired a quantity of valuable real estate in 1437. The official reception and festival hall built on the site has played a central role in the city's civic life through the centuries. At one end of the complex are the remains of the 10th-century Gothic church of **St. Alban,** left ruined after the war as a war memorial. On what's left of the church's floor, you can see a sculpture of a couple kneeling in prayer, *Mourning Parent* by Käthe Kollwitz, a fitting memorial to the ravages of war.

Directly south of the Gürzenich, across Pipinstrasse, is the Romanesque church of **St. Maria im Kapitol** (Kasinostr. 6). Built during the 11th and 12th centuries on the site of a Roman temple, St. Maria's is best known for its two beautifully carved 16-foot-high doors and its enormous crypt, the second-largest in Germany (after the one in Speyer Cathedral).

Tour 5: Aachen

It's not in the Rhineland proper, but **Aachen,** 70 kilometers (45 miles) from Köln and less than an hour away by car or train, is an essential excursion for anyone staying in Köln. At the town center, the characteristic *drei-Fenster* facades of residences, three windows wide, give way to buildings dating from the days when Charlemagne made Aix-la-Chapelle (as it was then called) one of the great centers of the Holy Roman Empire. Roman legions had pitched camp here because of the healing properties of the sulfur springs emanating from the nearby Eifel Mountains. Charlemagne's father, Pepin the Short, also settled here to enjoy the waters that gave Bad Aachen—as the town is also known— its name, and continue to attract visitors today. But it was certainly Charlemagne who was responsible for the town's architectural wealth. After his coronation in Rome in 800, he spent more and more time in Aachen, building his spectacular palace and ruling his vast empire from within its walls. One-hour walking tours depart from the tourist information office weekdays at 2, weekends at 11, April–October. English tours can be set up by prior arrangement (☎ 0241/180–2960).

★ The stunning **Dom** (cathedral), the "Chapelle" of the town's previous name, remains the single greatest storehouse of Carolingian architecture in Europe. Though it was built over the course of 1,000 years, and reflects architectural styles from the Middle Ages to the 19th-century, the commanding image is the magnificent octagonal royal chapel, rising up two arched stories to end in the cap of the dome. It was this section, the heart of the church, that Charlemagne saw completed in 800 AD. His bones now lie in the Gothic choir, surrounded by wonderful carvings of saints, interred in a golden shrine that's just one of the treasures that make the **Domschatzkammer** (cathedral treasury) perhaps the richest in Europe. Another treasure is Charlemagne's marble throne. Charlemagne had to journey all the way to Rome for his coronation, but the next 32 Holy Roman emperors were crowned here in Aachen, and each marked the occasion by presenting a lavish gift to the cathedral. In the 12th century, Barbarossa gave the great chandelier now hanging in the center of the imperial chapel; his grandson, Friedrich II, donated Charlemagne's shrine. Emperor Karl IV journeyed from Prague in the late 14th century for the sole purpose of commissioning a bust of Charlemagne for the cathedral; now on view in the treasury, this bust contains a piece of Charlemagne's skull. *Dom open daily 7–7.* ☛ *Domschatzkammer: DM 3 adults, DM 2 children and senior citizens.* ☉ *Apr.–Sept., daily 9–7; Oct.–Mar., daily 9–6. (The Schatzkammer was closed for renovation in 1995 but is scheduled to reopen in early 1996.)*

Opposite the cathedral, across Katschhof Square, is the back of the **Rathaus** (Town Hall). It was built starting in the early 14th century on the site of the Aula, or "great hall," of Charlemagne's palace. Its first major official function was the coronation banquet of Emperor Karl IV in 1349, held in the great Gothic hall you can still see today (though this was largely rebuilt after the war). On the north wall of the building are statues of 50 emperors of the Holy Roman Empire. The greatest of them all, Charlemagne, stands in bronze atop the fountain Kaiserbrunnen in the center of the square. *Rathaus.* ☛ *DM 2 adults, DM 1 children.* ☉ *Daily 10–1 and 2–5.*

To locals, Aachen is no more famous for its architecture than for its *Printen,* a kind of gingerbread. One of the best places to try this is the enchanting coffee shop called **Alte Aachener Kaffeestuben** (Buchel 18). The house was built in 1655 and has retained its original character—wood paneling, tile ovens, low ceilings and all. In addition to Printen and spice cookies called *Spekulatius,* formed in fancifully carved old wooden molds, the café serves meals.

Another old Aachen tradition that continues today is "taking the waters;" the arcaded, neoclassical **Elisenbrunnen** is south of the cathedral. Experts agree that the spa waters here—the hottest north of the Alps—are effective in helping to cure a wide range of ailments. Drinking the sulfurous water in the approved manner can be unpleasant; but as you hold your nose and gulp away you can console yourself with the thought that you're emulating the likes of Dürer, Frederick the Great, and Charlemagne. In Dürer's time, the baths were enjoyed for more than their health-giving properties, and there were regular crack-downs on the orgylike goings-on—a far cry from today's rather clinical atmosphere. You can try sitting in the spa waters at the **Kurbad** (Monheimsallee 52, ☎ 0241/180–2922; ☛ DM 16) or the **Römerbad** (Buchkremerstr. 1, ☎ 0241/180–2923; ☛ DM 11).

Like many famous German spa towns, Aachen also has its **Spielbank** (casino). It's housed in the porticoed former **Kurhaus,** on the parklike grounds fronting Monheimsallee (facing the Kurbad Quellenhof). ☎ 0241/18080. ☛ *DM 5.* ☉ *Weekdays 3 PM–2 AM, weekends until 3 AM. Jacket and tie. Bring passport for identification.*

Aachen has its modern side as well—art collector Peter Ludwig has seen to that. Opened in 1993, the **Ludwig Forum** is a space for yet another portion of Ludwig's truly enormous collection of contemporary art, as well as a venue for traveling exhibitions (Jülicher Str. 97-109). In 1994, the **Suermont-Ludwig Museum** was inaugerated. It's devoted to classical painting up to the beginning of this century (Wilhelmstr. 18). Yes, it's the same Ludwig. ☛ *Each museum: DM 6 adults, DM 3 children.*

Tour 6: Düsseldorf

The sixth and final tour returns to the Rhine, to elegant **Düsseldorf,** 40 kilometers (25 miles) north of Köln. At first glance Düsseldorf may present little of the drama of Köln, with its remarkable skyline. However, Düsseldorf is in fact unique among German cities, home to the highest concentration of top moneymakers in the country, with more than enough charm and beauty to justify including it on a Rhineland itinerary.

Düsseldorf has gained the reputation for being the richest city in Germany, with an extravagant lifestyle that long epitomized the success of the post-war "economic miracle." It is a glittering showcase for all the good things the Mark can buy. A center for the advertising industry, the city is also known as Germany's fashion capital.

Although 80% of prewar Düsseldorf was destroyed in World War II, the city has since been more or less rebuilt from the ground up—in part re-creating landmarks of long ago, restoring a medieval riverside quarter, but in the main initiating what may well be the most successful updating of a major German city.

Hard as it may be to believe today, this dynamic city at the confluence of the Rivers Rhine and Düssel started as a small fishing town. The name means "village" (*Dorf*) on the Düssel, but obviously this Dorf is a village no more. Raised expressways speed traffic past towering glass-and-steel structures; within these, glass-enclosed shopping malls showcase the fanciest outfits, furs, jewelry, and leather goods that famous designers can create and plenty of money can buy.

★ Nowhere is that more evident than on the main shopping avenue of **Königsallee,** lined with the crème de la crème of designer boutiques and stores. Known as the "Kö," this wide, double boulevard is divided by an ornamental waterway that is actually a part of the River Düssel. In the city, about 80% of the Düssel runs underground; this is one of the few places where you can see it. Rows of chestnut trees line the Kö, affording shade for a string of sidewalk cafés, and beyond the Triton Fountain at the street's north end begins a series of parks and gardens. In these patches of green one senses a joie de vivre hardly expected in a city devoted to big business and overachieving.

Head north to Corneliusplatz and walk into the lovely **Hofgarten Park,** once the garden of the Elector's Palace. Laid out in 1770 and completed 30 years later, the Hofgarten today serves as an oasis of greenery at the heart of downtown, and as a focal point for Düsseldorf culture.

In the Hofgarten is the Baroque **Schloss Jägerhof,** more a combination town house and country lodge than a castle. It houses the Goethe Museum, featuring original manuscripts, first editions, personal correspondence, and other memorabilia of one of Germany's greatest writers. *Jacobistr. 2,* ☎ *0211/899–6262.* ☛ *DM 4 adults, DM 2 children.* ☼ *Tues.–Fri. and Sun. 11–5, Sat. 1–5.*

At the garden's other end, on Heinrich-Heine-Allee, you'll find the city's opera house. Across the street, the **North Rhineland-Westphalia Art Collection** (Grabbepl. 5), removed some time ago from the Schloss Jägerhof, is now on display in a spacious new building. Here you will encounter a dazzling array of 20th-century paintings of the classical modern, including works by Bonnard, Braque, Matisse, Léger, Johns, and Pollock; there are so many by Paul Klee because the Swiss painter lived in Düsseldorf for a time and taught at the National Academy of Art. ☛ *DM 5.* ☼ *Tues.–Sun. 10–6.*

At the northern extremity of the Hofgarten, close to the Rhine, the **Kunstmuseum** (Museum of Fine Arts) features a collection of paintings by Old Masters and German Expressionists, running the gamut from Rubens, Goya, Tintoretto, and Cranach the Elder to the romantic Düsseldorf School and such modern German painters as Beckmann, Kirchner, Nolde, Macke, and Kandinsky. *Ehrenhof 5,* ☎ *0211/899–2460.* ☛ *DM 10 adults, DM 5 children.* ☼ *Tues. and Thurs.–Sun. 10–5, Wed. 10–8.*

Walk back to Corneliusplatz and the Kö, then head to the right for the restored **Altstadt** (Old Town), facing the Rhine. Narrow alleys thread their way to some 200 restaurants and taverns offering a wide range of foreign and local cuisines, all crowded into the 1-square-kilometer area between the Rhine and Heine Allee. Occasionally you can still see the *Radschläger,* young boys who demonstrate their cartwheeling abilitie, a Düsseldorf tradition, for the admiration (and tips) of visitors.

A plaque at Bolkerstrasse 53 indicates where Heinrich Heine was born in 1797, but it is at the **Heinrich Heine Institute** (Bilkerstr. 12–14) that you can find a museum and an archive of significant manuscripts of this early 19th-century poet. Part of this complex is a former residence of composer Robert Schumann. ☎ 0211/899–5571. ☛ *DM 3 adults, DM 1.50 children.* ☉ *Tues.–Sun. 2–6.*

TIME OUT Among beer buffs, Düsseldorf is famous for its Altbier, so called because of the old-fashioned brewing method still used. The mellow and malty copper-color brew is produced by eight breweries in town. The most atmospheric place to drink it is **Zum Uerige** (Bergerstr. 1). Here the beer is poured straight out of polished oak barrels and dished out by bustling waiters in long blue aprons.

The cobbled, traffic-free streets of the Old Town lead to Burgplatz, with its 13th-century **Schlosssturm** (Castle Tower), all that remains of the castle built by the de Berg family, who founded Düsseldorf. The tower also houses the **Schiffahrt Museum,** which charts 2,000 years of Rhine boatbuilding and river history. *Burgpl. 30,* ☎ *0211/899–4195.* ☛ *DM 3 adults, DM 1 children.* ☉ *Tues.–Sat. 2–6, Sun. 11–6.*

While on the Burgplatz see if you can spot the crooked spire of the Gothic **St. Lambertus Church** on nearby Stiftsplatz. The spire became distorted because unseasoned wood was used in its construction. The Vatican elevated the 14th-century brick church to a Basilica Minor (small cathedral) in 1974 in recognition of its role in church history. Built during the 13th century, with additions from 1394, St. Lambertus contains the tomb of William the Rich and a graceful late-Gothic tabernacle.

From Burgplatz or Stiftsplatz you can glimpse the Rhine, although the riverside promenade is still being landscaped following completion of the Rhine Tunnel. The tunnel means that there will be significantly less car exhaust on the riverbank when the promenade is finished.

What to See and Do with Children

There are few parts of Germany that offer more for children than the Rhineland, with its castles, legends, and easily accessible rivers. In the wooded hills above the Rhine and Mosel are several **wild animal parks.** The one near the village of **Rheinböllen** (follow the signs from Bacharach) has bears and bison, as well as the usual fallow deer. (open daily year-round). There's another well-stocked animal park just outside the Mosel wine village of **Klötten** (open mid-Mar.–Dec., daily) **Königswinter,** near Bonn, has a **crocodile and snake farm,** the only one of its kind in Germany (open daily).

You'll find **fairy-tale parks** in several parts of the Rhineland—Wiesbaden's **Taunus Wonderland** has an Indian village and a miniature Wild West railway (open daily). In Dötzheim, just outside Wiesbaden, there's a miniature **Grimm fairy-tale landscape,** with scaled-down hamlets complete with tiny houses and streets. Bonn has a young people's theater, the **Theater der Jugend** (Hermannstr. 50, ☎ 0228/463–672), and a fascinating natural-history museum, the **Museum Alexander König** (Adenauerallee 150–164, ☎ 0228/91220).

Düsseldorf's **Aqua-Zoo** (Kaiserwertherstr. 380, ☎ 0211/899–6150) in the Nordpark offers a unique exhibition of aquatic creatures in their natural habitats. Among the highlights are the tropical park with crocodiles and the penguin habitat. All tanks can be viewed from above and through glass walls. ☛ *DM 9 adults, DM 5 children.*

Köln's **zoo,** founded in 1860, is West Germany's third-oldest and one of the most interesting. Local children love it, perhaps because of its large monkey population and jungle house. *Riehlerstr. 73.* ☛ *DM 10* *adults, DM 5 children.* ☉ *Mar.–Sept., daily 9–6; Oct.–Mar., daily 9–5.*

Köln also has a **puppet theater** (Rösratherstr. 133, ☎ 02208/2408) and a **children's theater** (Bürgerzentrum Alte Feuerwache, Melchiorstr. 3, ☎ 0221/739–1073). For possibly the most popular outing of all in Köln, take your children to the **Gebrüder Grimm** (Brothers Grimm) book and toy shop on Mauritiussteinweg 110. The **Düsseldorfer Marionettentheater** (☎ 0211/328–432) is at Bolkerstrasse 7.

SHOPPING

The best souvenir of the Rheinland is **wine.** If you don't have room for a bottle or two in your carry-on luggage, settle for a related item: a couple of boxed glasses, a carved corkscrew, or a basketwork wine server. If you do want wine, bear in mind that Germany's duty-free airport shops have few bargains—buy before you get to the airport.

Aachen

Don't leave Aachen without stocking up on the traditional local gingerbread, *Aachener Printen.* Most bakeries in town offer assortments; some of the best is at the Alte Aachener Kaffeestuben, also known as the **Konditorei van den Daele** (Büchel 18, ☎ 0241/35724). The store-café is worth a visit for its atmosphere and tempting aromas, whether or not you intend to buy anything. It also ships goods.

Bacharach

Every Rhine and Mosel village has several wine shops, as well as cellars where you can sample before you buy. Many cellars offer tours with English-speaking guides. One of the best is the **Weingut Wilhelm Wasum** (Mainzerstr. 20–23, Bacharach, ☎ 06743/1234). Another reliable Bacharach cellar is the **Weingut Wolfgang Eberhard** (Borbacherstr. 6–7, ☎ 06743/1591); it's been in the same family for more than 250 years.

For wineglasses and Westerwald ceramics, seek out the **Phil Jost** shop in Bacharach (Rosenstr. 16, ☎ 06743/1224). This store is known for offering factory, rather than retail, prices on high-quality goods; it also specializes in beer mugs.

Bonn

The international comings and goings in **Bonn** keep antiques shops busy in this little town. One respected dealer is **Paul Schweitzer** (Muffendorfer Hauptstr. 37, ☎ 0228/362–659; closed Mon.). Another reliable antiques outlet is the family-run **Ehlers Antiquitäten** (Berliner Freiheit 28, ☎ 0228/676–853).

Despite its name, Bonn's **Wochenmarkt** is open not weekly but daily, filling Marktplatz with vendors of produce and various edibles. Bargain-hunters flock to the city's renowned, and huge, **flea market** (*Flohmarkt*) held on the third Saturday of each month between April and October at **Rheinaue** (Ludwig-Erhard-Str.), where you can find secondhand goods and knick-knacks of all descriptions. If you're in the Bonn area on the second weekend of September, don't miss **Pützchens Markt,** a huge country fair.

Cochem

For fine Mosel wineglasses in Cochem, as well as a selection of porcelain, head for **Liselotte Hürter** (Herrenstr. 20, ☎ 02671/3158). Herrenstrasse is lined with shops; you'll find local souvenirs at **Die Geschenkidee Heimes** (Herrenstr. 13, ☎ 02671/91122).

Düsseldorf

In **Düsseldorf,** the east side of the **Königsallee** is lined with some of Germany's trendiest boutiques, grandest jewelers, and most extravagant furriers. The most famous names in fashion, from Chanel to Louis Vuitton, are represented at the upmarket shopping arcade of **Kö Center** (Königsallee 30). Less well-known are the creations of such local designers as Ute Raasch, shown in one of the trendy fashion boutiques at the **Kö Galerie** (Königsallee 60), which also includes a Mövenpick restaurant on its luxurious two-story premises. The end of 1994 saw the opening of the **Schadow Arcade** (off Schadowplatz, at the end of the Kö), a first in this area in that it caters to normal pocketbooks, with such stores as Hennes & Mauritz and Habitat. Antiques in Düsseldorf can be found in the area around Hohe Strasse. Try the shop **Arts Decoratifs** (Hohe Strasse 28, ☎ 0211/324–553) for Art Deco furniture, tableware, and knickknacks.

Koblenz

Koblenz's main shopping streets in the old city are in the area around the market square of **Plan.** For an authentic postwar German shopping experience, venture into the American-style mall of **Löhr Center,** a modern, windowless block with some 130 shops and restaurants.

Köln

Hohe Strasse, south of the cathedral, is the main artery of a huge pedestrian shopping zone. The area's stores, including many of the main German department-store chains—Kaufhof, Hertie, and Karstadt—are rich in quantity if not always in quality, and certainly a center of city life. **Mittelstrasse** and **Hohestrasse** are best for German fashions and luxury goods. **Offermann's** (Breite Strasse 48-50, ☎ 0221/252–018) has a large selection of fine leather items and beautifully finished travel accessories.

Köln's most celebrated product is, of course, **eau de cologne.** In Glockengasse (No. 4711, of course; ☎ 0221/925—0450) you can visit the house where the 18th-century Italian chemist Giovanni-Maria Farina first concocted it. The shop has extended its selection to include other scents in addition to 4711, but the original product remains the centerpiece, available in all sizes from a purse-sized bottle to a container that holds a quart or so.

Another quintessential Köln product is **Ludwig chocolate,** which you should seek out if only in honor of all the Ludwig museums you'll encounter along your trip. You'll have no difficulty finding it in any of the delicatessens in the city center.

A flea market is held every third Saturday at the **Alter Markt** in the Old Town, and every fourth Sunday at **Nippes** (Wilhelmpl.).

Trier

For local crafts, explore the four artisans' workshops of the **Kunsthandwerkerhof,** or Artisans' Court (Simeonstiftpl. 2, ☎ 0651/42991). Here you can watch glass-blowers and -engravers, stained-glass painters, and batik artists at work.

Wiesbaden

Broad, tree-lined **Wilhelmstrasse,** with designer boutiques housed in its fin-de-siecle buildings, is one of Germany's most elegant shopping streets. At the end of June, when the **Wilhelmstrassenfest** is held, it's party time along Wilhelmstrasse—Rheingau wine and Sekt flow in abundance. Lovers of antiques will also do well in Wiesbaden, known as one of the best places in the country to find them; some of the best shops are along **Taunusstrasse.**

SPORTS AND FITNESS

Bicycling

The Mosel Valley, with its small hamlets lining the riverbanks, is an excellent area for biking. The Trier tourist office (☎ 0651/978–080) offers a free trail map. Most local train stations have bikes to rent for DM 10 a day (DM 6 if you have a valid train ticket). Listings of additional outlets for rental bikes are available from train stations.

Boating

Rowboats and canoes can be rented at most Rhine and Mosel river resorts. A list of rental outlets is included in the brochure "News," issued by the Rheinland-Pfalz tourist office (*see* Important Addresses and Numbers *in* Rhineland Essentials, *below*).

Jogging

All along the Rhine, the parks lining its banks are popular with joggers. Notable favorites are the Rheinanlagen in Koblenz or Düsseldorf's Rheinpark, in Golzheim, just north of the Altstadt.

Swimming

Even though West Germany's environmental minister swam in the Rhine in 1988 to prove that the river was no longer polluted, only the brave and/or foolhardy are likely to follow his example in either the Rhine or the Mosel. The Rhineland has a substantial number of pools, indoor and outdoor, that offer much safer swimming. Trier's **Hallenbad,** with five heated pools, and Wiesbaden's **Opelbad,** located high above the city on the Neroberg, are among the best. Köln has more than 20 outdoor pools; the one at **Müngersdorfer Stadium** (Aachenerstr.) is heated. There are also two lido-type complexes in Köln: **Deutz-Kalker Bad,** on the street of the same name, and **Kombibad Hohenberg** (Schwarzburgerstr. 91). Bonn's diplomats plunge in at the Kurfürstenbad—it's in the Bad Godesberg park.

Tennis and Squash

The **Freizeit Park** (☎ 02603/81095) in Koblenz's Industriekreisel has eight indoor tennis courts, plus a swimming pool and a sauna for postmatch relaxation. Wiesbaden's **Henkell ice stadium** (Höllerbornstr.) becomes a tennis court during the summer. The **Ferienpark Hochwald** (☎ 06589/1011) at Kell, near Trier, is one of the leading tennis complexes in Germany. In Köln, try **City Sport** (Rhöndroferstr. 10, ☎ 0221/411–092) or, for squash only, **Squashpark** (Neusserstr. 718a, ☎ 0221/740–8866). Düsseldorf's **Rhine Stadium** has 18 public courts.

DINING AND LODGING

Dining

If you come to the Rhine hoping to eat fish, you'll be disappointed: Polluted waters have destroyed all but a few of the fish that once thrived. Practically the only seafood in the region is flown in from France; prices are correspondingly high. However, there are numerous local specialties that are hearty rather than sophisticated: *Himmel und Erde,* a mixture of potatoes, onions, and apples; *Hämmchen* (pork knuckle); *Hunsrücker Festessen* (sauerkraut with potatoes, horseradish, and ham). There are many small inns and restaurants offering these and other regional dishes. At the other end of the scale, Düsseldorf, Köln, and Wiesbaden boast some of the most sophisticated restaurants in Europe, many offering delectable nouvelle cuisine. The Rhineland is wine country, and every restaurant and café offers a large selection of wines.

RATINGS

CATEGORY	COST*
$$$$	over DM 90
$$$	DM 55–DM 90
$$	DM 35–DM 55
$	under DM 35

per person for a three-course meal, including tax but not alcohol

Lodging

The most romantic places to lay your head are the old riverside inns and hotels and the castle-hotels, some of which are enormously luxurious. In the cities of the Rhineland, some of the most expensive hotels are among the finest in Europe. Modern high rises are common, as are more interesting, affordable quarters. A great many hotels close for the winter; most are also booked well in advance, especially for the wine festivals in the fall and during important trade fairs, as in Düsseldorf. Whenever possible, make reservations long before you visit.

RATINGS

CATEGORY	COST*
$$$$	over DM 250
$$$	DM 175–DM 250
$$	DM 125–DM 175
$	under DM 125

Prices are for two people in a double room, excluding service charges.

Aachen

DINING

★ **Gala.** For the most elegant dining in Aachen, reserve a table at the Gala restaurant, adjoining the casino. Dark-paneled walls and original oil paintings make the mood discreetly classy; Chef Gerhard Gartner's cooking is regional, with nouvelle and other creative touches. ✕ *Monheimsallee, 44,* ☎ *0241/153–013. Reservations required. Jacket and tie. AE, DC, MC, V. Dinner only. Closed Sun., Mon. $$$$*

La Becasse. Sophisticated French nouvelle cuisine is offered in this upscale modern restaurant, located just outside the Old Town by the Westpark. Try the distinctively light calves' liver. ✕ *Hanbrucherstr. 1,* ☎ *0241/74444. Reservations required. Jacket and tie. AE, DC, MC, V. Closed Sat. and Mon. lunch, Sun. and 3 wks in July–Aug. $$$*

Der Postwagen. This annex of the (more upmarket) **Ratskeller** is worth a stop for the building alone: an original half-timbered medieval edifice at one corner of the old Rathaus. Sitting at one of the low wooden tables, surveying the marketplace through the wavy old glass, you can dine very respectably on solid German fare. If you want to go really local, try *Unser Puttes*, a kind of blood sausage. ✕ *Am Markt,* ☎ *0241/35001. No credit cards. $$*

LODGING

★ **Steigenberger Hotel Quellenhof.** The pampered luxury at the Quellenhof is especially appealing to older guests. Built during World War I as a country home for the kaiser, it's very much one of Europe's grande dames: spacious, elegant, and formal. The rooms have high ceilings, a mix of conservative-style furniture, a walk-in baggage room, and huge, dated bathrooms that were converted from single bedrooms. For all that, they are somewhat worn, service is a little strained, and amenities are limited; cost-cutting currently characterizes aspects of Aachen's top hotel. The flower-filled Parkrestaurant, one of the best restaurants in northern Germany, serves haute cuisine in the grand manner. The hotel is near the Kurpark and the casino, and guests have direct access by lift to the thermal baths. 🖬 *Monheimsallee 52, 52062,* ☎ *0241/152–081 or 800/223–5652 for reservations in the U.S.,* FAX *0241/154–504. 160 rooms with bath. Restaurant, pool. AE, DC, MC, V. $$$$*

Krott. In the heart of the city (the traffic-free pedestrian zone), this family-run hotel offers not only convenience but also considerable comfort. It's a short walk from virtually all the major attractions. 🖬 *Wirichsbongardstr. 16, 52062,* ☎ *0241/48373,* FAX *0241/403–892. 22 rooms with bath. Restaurant, sauna. AE, DC, MC, V. $$$*

Benelux. The centrally located Benelux is one of the best deals in town. Small and family-run, it has comfortable modern rooms and a smattering of antiques in the public areas. 🖬 *Franzstr. 21, 52064,* ☎ *0241/22343,* FAX *0241/22345. 33 rooms with bath. AE, DC, MC, V. $$–$$$*

Bacharach

DINING

Hotel-Restaurant Steeger Weinstube. Less than DM 20 buys you three hearty courses at this friendly, family-run tavern-restaurant just off the Rhine tourist route. The menu changes daily, but Rhineland-style sauerbraten, homemade potato dumplings, and venison (in season) are often featured. ✕ *Blucherstr. 149, Bacharach-Steeg,* ☎ *06743/1240. AE, MC. Closed Wed. $*

DINING AND LODGING

Altkölnischer Hof. Tucked in a quiet square in medieval Bacharach, the Altkölnischer is a small, half-timbered hotel built at the turn of the century. Colorful geraniums line the small windows; rooms are simply but attractively furnished in country style; and the rustic restaurant offers typical local dishes and some excellent wines. 🖬 *Blücherstr. 2, 55422,* ☎ *06743/1339,* FAX *06743/2793. 20 rooms with bath. Restaurant. AE, V. Closed Nov.–Mar. $$*

Bernkastel-Kues

DINING AND LODGING

Zur Post. Picture-book Germany is alive and well at the appealing, early-19th-century Zur Post. Behind its colorful, flower-laden facade lurk the obligatory exposed wood beams and a dark-paneled restaurant (with more than 100 wines). Bedrooms are tastefully decorated. 🖬 *Gestade 17, 54470,* ☎ *06531/2022,* FAX *06531/2927. 42 rooms with bath. Restaurant, sauna. AE, DC, MC, V. Closed Jan. $$–$$$*

Hotel Römischer Kaiser. What better way to appreciate the views from this riverside location (on the promenade), of either the waterway or the surrounding vineyards, than from a balcony? Fortunately, all rooms here have one. The hotel's restaurant is noted for its good, reasonably priced regional wines. ⌂ *Markt. 29, 54470,* ☎ *06531/3038,* FAX *06531/7672. 35 rooms, all with bath. AE, DC, MC, V. Closed Jan.–Feb. $$*

Bingen

LODGING

Rheinhotel Starkenburger Hof. In business since the middle of the 19th century, the Starkenburger Hof, decorated throughout in warm shades of brown and gold, is the number-one choice in Bingen. It overlooks the Rhine, so don't settle for a room without a view. There's no restaurant, but a large buffet breakfast is included in the room rate. ⌂ *Am Rheinkai 1, 55411,* ☎ *06721/14341,* FAX *06721/13350. 30 rooms with bath or shower. Breakfast room. AE, DC. Closed Jan.–Feb. $$*

Bonn

DINING

Haus Daufenbach. The stark white exterior of the Daufenbach, located by the church of St. Remigius, disguises one of the most distinctive restaurants in Bonn. The mood is rustic, with simple wood furniture and antlers on the walls. Specialties include *Spanferkel* (suckling pig) and a range of imaginative salads. Wash them down with wines from the restaurant's own vineyards. ✕ *Brüdergasse 6,* ☎ *0228/637–944. Reservations advised. No credit cards. Closed Mon. and, in summer, Sun. dinner. $$*

Em Hottche. Travelers have been given sustenance at this tavern since the late 14th century, and today it offers one of the best-value lunches in town. The interior is rustic, the food stout and hearty. ✕ *Markt 4,* ☎ *0228/690–009. No reservations. AE, DC, MC, V. Closed last 2 wks in Dec. $*

LODGING

★ **Bristol.** The Bristol could be in Dallas for all the German atmosphere it has, but for modern elegance and a terrific central location, it's an established favorite. ⌂ *Prinz-Albert-Str. 2, 53115,* ☎ *0228/26980,* FAX *0228/269–8222. 120 rooms with bath. Restaurant, indoor pool, sauna, bowling. AE, DC, MC, V. $$$$*

Domicil. A group of buildings around a quiet, central courtyard has recently been converted into a hotel of great charm and comfort. The rooms are individually furnished and decorated—in styles rangingfrom fin-de-siècle romantic to Italian modern. Lots of glass gives the public rooms a friendly airiness. ⌂ *Thomas-Mann-Str. 24–26, 53111,* ☎ *0228/729–090,* FAX *0228/691–207. 42 rooms, all with bath. Restaurant, coffe shop, beauty salon, sauna. AE, DC, MC, V. Closed Dec. 25–Jan. 1. $$$$*

Sternhotel. For good value, solid comfort, and a central location in the Old Town, the family-run Stern is tops. Rooms can be small, but all are pleasantly furnished. There's no restaurant, but the bar has snacks. ⌂ *Markt 8, 53111,* ☎ *0228/72670,* FAX *0228/726–7125. 81 rooms with bath. Weekend rates. AE, DC, MC, V. $$–$$$*

Rheinland. This modest lodging has the advantage of being a short walk from the center of the Old Town. Rooms are comfortable, and although there is no restaurant, a good buffet breakfast greets the day. ⌂ *Berliner Freiheit 11, 53111,* ☎ *0228/658–096,* FAX *0228/472–844. 31 rooms with bath. AE, MC. $$*

Boppard

DINING AND LODGING

★ **Hotel Klostergut Jakobsberg.** Stay here for the amazing location on the north bank of the Rhine (the hotel's about 12 kilometers, or 8 miles, north of Boppard), the array of sports facilities, the excellent food, and the sumptuous furnishings. The hotel is in a castle (make sure you see its chapel) and has a sophisticated baronial atmosphere, due in part to an extensive collection of hunting trophies and rifles, a considerable assembly of paintings and prints, and imposing tapestries—real *Prisoner of Zenda* stuff. The hotel raises its own cattle and cultivates Japanese shiitake mushrooms, and puts both to good use in its restaurant. The veal medallions in goose-liver sauce are superb. ⌂ *56154 Boppard-Rhein*, ☎ *06742/8080*, FAX *06742/3069. 104 rooms and 7 suites with bath. Restaurant, indoor pool, sauna, golf course, tennis courts, bowling, horseback riding, squash, helipad. AE, DC, MC, V. $$$$*

Cochem

DINING AND LODGING

★ **Alte Thorschenke.** There are few more authentic or atmospheric old inns in the Rhineland than this picturesque spot in the heart of Cochem, dating from the 14th century. Creaking staircases, four-poster beds, river views, and exposed beams combine to produce an effect that's almost too good to be true. Avoid the modern annex if you want to experience the full charm of this romantic haunt. The restaurant's selection of local wines is extensive. ⌂ *Brückenstr. 3, 56812*, ☎ *02671/7059*, FAX *02671/4202. 51 rooms with bath. Restaurant. AE, DC, MC, V. Closed Jan.–mid-Mar. $$$*

★ **Weissmühle.** You'll want to stay—or eat—here as much to see the picture-book village of Endertal, just outside of Cochem, as to lay your head on the hotel's ample pillows. The place is decorated in that inimitable German gingerbread style, with carved beams and lace curtains galore. Try the trout or the spit-roasted kebabs. ⌂ *Endertal, 56812*, ☎ *02671/8955*, FAX *02671/8207. 36 rooms with shower. Restaurant, bowling. DC, MC, V. $$–$$$*

Brixiade. Despite its modern-looking facade, the Brixiade has been welcoming guests—Kaiser Wilhelm II among them—for more than 100 years. Ask for a room with a view over the town and the river. A few of the rooms also have a balcony. The restaurant offers a fixed-price menu and magnificent local wines. Dine on the terrace in summer. ⌂ *Uferstr. 13, 56182*, ☎ *02671/9810*, FAX *02671/981–100. 35 rooms with bath. Restaurant, wine bar. AE, DC, MC, V. $$*

Düsseldorf

DINING

Im Schiffchen. Although it's a bit out of the way, the fact that this is one of Germany's best restaurants makes it worth a trip. This is grande luxe, with cooking that's a fine art. The restaurant **Aalschokker,** on the ground floor, features local specialties, with the same chef but at lower prices. ✕ *Kaiserswerther Markt 9*, ☎ *0211/401–050 or 0211/401–948. Reservations required. AE, DC, MC, V. Closed Sun. and Mon., as well as lunch. $$$$*

★ **Rôtisserie.** The decor is subdued and the atmosphere hushed, but the food sparkles at this gourmet restaurant in the Steigenberger Parkhotel (*see* Lodging, *below*). Chef Alfred Schreiber serves classic French cuisine prepared with imagination and a light touch. Starters might include whipped sorrel-chervil soup and a gossamer parfait of quail with raisins and green pepper, followed by such entrées as shellfish lasagna layered with asparagus, wild mushrooms, and lobster sauce.

Some German classics are always on the menu; the restaurant's rendition of *Rote Grütze* (a red fruit compote) with vanilla sauce is especially admirable. ✕ *Corneliuspl. 1,* ☎ *0211/13810,* FAX *0211/131–679. Reservations advised. Jacket and tie. AE, DC, MC, V. $$$$*

Weinhaus Tante Anna. This charming restaurant is furnished with antiques; the cuisine presents another facet of German tradition, and shows that there's a lot more to this country's cooking than the standard platters of hearty wurst- and sauerkraut-based fare. The wine selection is particularly fine. ✕ *Andreasstr. 2,* ☎ *0211/131–163,* FAX *0211/132– 974. Reservations advised. AE, DC, MC, V. Closed lunch. $$$$*

Zum Schiffchen. Not to be confused with the luxurious Im Schiffchen (*above*), this is probably the most colorful of all the old riverside brewery taverns in the Altstadt, in business since 1628. Napoléon ate here in 1811. Today, as then, one sits at long scrubbed wooden tables and dines family style on down-to-earth fare. Beer comes straight from the barrel, including the local *Altbier*. The day's specials invariably include grilled pork chops that come to the table sizzling; eels are another good bet. ✕ *Hafenstr. 5,* ☎ *0211/132–422. Reservations required. AE, DC, MC, V. Closed Sun. and holidays. $$*

LODGING

★ **Hotel Breidenbacher Hof.** Rated among the two or three top choices in Germany, this superluxurious hotel offers understated elegance with superb, white-glove service. The location is as central as you can get. The palatial lobby is studded with 17th- and 18th-century antiques, with the theme continuing in the beautifully appointed rooms. 🏨 *Heinrich Heine Allee 36, 40213,* ☎ *0211/13030,* FAX *0211/130–3830. 132 rooms with bath. 2 restaurants, bar. AE, DC, MC, V. $$$$*

★ **Steigenberger Parkhotel.** Miraculously quiet despite its central location on the edge of the Hofgarten and at the beginning of the Königsallee, this old hotel is anything but stodgy. The soaring ceilings add to the spaciousness of the guest rooms, each individually decorated in a restrained, elegant style. The pampering continues at the breakfast buffet, served in the Rôtisserie (*see* Dining, *above*), where champagne and smoked salmon are appropriate starters for a shopping expedition on the Kö. 🏨 *Corneliuspl. 1, 40213,* ☎ *0211/13810,* FAX *0211/131–679. 160 rooms with bath. Restaurant, 2 bars, café. AE, DC, MC, V. $$$$*

Hotel Esplanade. This small modern hotel has an exceptionally quiet, leafy location still close the action. From the inviting lobby to attractive decor in the rooms, the sense here is one of intimacy. 🏨 *Fürstenpl. 17, 40215,* ☎ *0211/375–010,* FAX *0211/374–032. 80 rooms with bath. 2 restaurants, bar, pool, exercise room. AE, DC, MC, V. $$$*

Hotel Cristallo. Clearly someone took great pains with the slightly tacky but nonetheless striking decor of this well-located, midprice hotel. If you like gilt angels in the breakfast room, this is the place for you. Less subjectively judged attributes include a central location near the Kö and pleasant, eclectically furnished rooms, with comfortable sofas and color TVs even in singles. 🏨 *Schadowpl. 7,* ☎ *0211/84525,* FAX *0211/322–632. 35 rooms. AE, DC, MC, V. $$*

Koblenz

DINING

Fährhaus am Stausee. The garden terrace where you can dine on warm sunny days extends to the banks of the Mosel. The name comes from the ancient river-ferry crossing point that existed here until a bridge was built. A range of dishes, predominantly fish, fills the menu of this old, established restaurant. Rooms are available. ✕ *An der Fähre 3, Metternich,* ☎ *0261/2093. AE, DC, MC, V. $$–$$$*

Wacht am Rhein. Watch on the Rhine, as the name translates, sums it up. In summer, take a table on the outside terrace and watch the river traffic roll by; in winter, choose a window table and dine with the Rhine outside and the atmospheric warmth of the fin de siècle fittings and furnishings inside. Fish is the basis of the extensive menu. ✕ *Adenauer-Ufer 6,* ☎ *0261/15313. AE. $$*

Weinhaus Hubertus. This atmospheric old wine tavern is a great place to sample the flavors of old Koblenz. The flower-laden, half-timbered 17th-century exterior is in keeping with the rustic ambience inside. The food is ample and cooked with gusto, and the dishes are what you'd expect from a place named after the patron saint of hunting. ✕ *Florinsmarkt 6,* ☎ *0261/31177. No credit cards. Closed lunch and Tues. $–$$*

LODGING

Scandic Crown. While this may be Koblenz's best hotel in terms of modernity, it lacks charm. Except for the views of the Rhine, the uniformity of the largish rooms suggests that you're staying at a chain hotel. Bathrooms have spacious showers, but no tubs. The reception staff provides polished service, and the dining room serves French-influenced cooking. The hotel is a 10-minute walk from the Old Town and two minutes from the Weindorf (wine village). ☎ *Julius-WegelerStr. 6, 56068 Koblenz,* ☎ *0261/1360,* FAX *0261/136–1199. 159 rooms with bath. 2 restaurants, bar, sauna. AE, DC, MC, V. $$$$*

Kleiner Riesen. This is a well-run, straightforward hotel that gives value for money. Another plus is the quiet riverside location that's still within walking distance of the train station and the Old Town. There's no restaurant. ☎ *Kaiserin-Augusta-Anlagen 18, 56068,* ☎ *0261/32077,* FAX *0261/160–725. 27 rooms with bath. AE, DC, MC, V. $$$*

Köln

DINING

★ **Bado-La Poêle d'Or.** At first glance, the heavy furnishings and hushed atmosphere of the Poêle d'Or make it seem like the last place you'd find light classical cuisine in Germany. But for some years, those in the know have been claiming this as one of the finest dining establishments in Europe. Even such apparently simple dishes as onion soup win plaudits. Order salmon with lemon-ginger sauce, or goose with truffle sauce if you want to sample the full capabilities of the place. ✕ *Komödienstr. 50–52,* ☎ *0221/134–100. Reservations required. AE, DC, MC, V. Closed Sun. and Mon. lunch. $$$$*

Weinhaus im Walfisch. The black-and-white gabled facade of this 400-year-old restaurant lets you know what to expect inside—though here the local offerings are spruced up for an upmarket clientele. The menu presents fine quasi-traditional dishes with a French accent, at corresponding prices, and a wide range of wines. The restaurant is tucked away between the Heumarkt (Haymarket) and the river. ✕ *Salzgasse 13,* ☎ *0221/258–0397. Reservations advised. AE, DC, MC, V. Closed weekends and holidays. $$$*

Die Tomate. If you don't like tomatoes, stay away from this popular little restaurant. The red fruit may be seen growing at the door, and the menu may feature tomato carpaccio with tomato paste and escallop of pork as well as dishes without tomatoes, such as steak in a red-wine sauce. For dessert, try the delicious pancakes filled with apples. ✕ *Aachenerstr. 11,* ☎ *0221/257–4307. AE. Closed Sun. lunch. $$*

Gaststätte Früh am Dom. For real down-home German food, there are few places that compare with this time-honored former brewery. Bold frescoes on the vaulted ceilings establish the mood; the authentically Teutonic experience is complete with such dishes as Hämmchen. The beer garden is delightful for summer dining. ✕ *Am Hof 12–14,* ☎ *0221/258–0397. Reservations advised. No credit cards.* $$

Ratskeller. Throughout Germany, Ratskellers are usually a safe bet for traditional food at reasonable prices. Here you can eat Rheinische sauerbraten in the basement of the Altes Rathaus, or, weather permitting, the courtyard. ✕ *Rathauspl. 1,* ☎ *0221/257–6929,* FAX *0221/257–6949. AE, DC, MC, V.* $$–$$$

DINING AND LODGING

★ **Dom-Hotel.** Old-fashioned, formal, and gracious, with a stunning location right by the cathedral, the Dom offers the sort of Old World elegance and discreetly efficient service few hotels aspire to these days. The antiques-filled bedrooms, generally in Louis XV or Louis XVI style, are subdued in color, high-ceilinged, and spacious. Each room is individually furnished. Service is, for the most part, exemplary, unhurried, and personal. The view of the cathedral is something to treasure. Enjoy it from the glass-enclosed Atelier am Dom, where you can dine informally on such specialties as marinated lamb carpaccio and grated Parmesan for a light meal; or sautéed mullet on a bed of spicy tomato ragout and basil noodles. The weekend package of DM 230 per night for a double room is a bargain, including champagne on arrival and reduced museum entrance fees. ☎ *Domkloster 2A, 50667,* ☎ *0221/20240,* FAX *0221/202–4444. 126 rooms with bath. 2 restaurants, bar, café. AE, DC, MC, V.* $$$$

★ **Excelsior Hotel Ernst.** The Empire-style lobby in sumptuous royal blue, bright yellow, and gold is striking, and a similarly bold grandeur extends to the other public rooms in this 1863 hotel. Old Master paintings (including a Van Dyck) are everywhere; you'll be served breakfast in a room named after the Gobelin tapestries that hang there. Ultimately, though, it's the genuine warmth and helpfulness of the staff that make dining here a memorable experience. The restaurant Hansestube, which attracts a local business crowd with gourmet lunch specials, has a more hushed ambience in the evening, when it serves French haute cuisine with an occasional nod to the health-conscious. Mushroom lovers will want to try the veal medallions in a rich cream sauce with a huge mound of morels. The wine cellar is famous for its French Burgundies and Bordeaux. ☎ *Trankgasse 1,* ☎ *0221/2701,* FAX *0221/135–150. 160 rooms with bath, 20 suites. restaurant, bar, beauty salon, masseuse, exercise room. AE, DC, MC, V.* $$$$

Stapelhäuschen. One of the few houses along the riverbank to have survived World War II bombings, this is one of the oldest buildings in Köln. You can't beat the location, overlooking the river and right by Gross St. Martin; yet the rooms are reasonably priced, making up in age and quaintness for what they lack in luxury. The restaurant is in a slightly higher price bracket but does a respectable enough job with spruced-up versions of German specialties. ☎ *Fischmarkt 1–3,* ☎ *0221/257–7862,* FAX *0221/257–4232. AE, DC, MC, V.* $$

LODGING

Hotel im Wasserturm. What used to be Europe's tallest water tower is now an 11-story luxury hotel-in-the-round, opened at the end of 1989 after a four-year, $70 million conversion. The neoclassic look of the brick exterior was retained by order of Cologne conservationists. The ultramodern interior was the work of the French designer Andrée Putman, renowned in the United States for her work on Morgan's, in New York. ☎ *Kaygasse 2, 50676,* ☎ *0221/20080,* FAX *0221/200–8888. 47 rooms and 34 suites and maisonettes with bath. Room service, sauna. AE, DC, MC, V.* $$$$

★ **Altstadt.** Near the river in the Old Town, this is the place for charm and low rates. All the rooms are individually decorated, and the service is impeccable—both welcoming and efficient. There's no restaurant. ☎ *Salzgasse 7, 50667,* ☎ *0221/257–7851,* FAX *0221/257–7853. 28 rooms with bath. Sauna. AE, DC, MC, V. Closed Dec. 25–Jan. 1.* $$

Oestrich

DINING AND LODGING

★ **Romantik Hotel Schwan.** The Romantik chain lives up to its name with this half-timbered Renaissance building—green shutters, tubs of flowers, high gables, and sloping roofs right on the Rhine. The restaurant offers fine local specialties and an extensive wine list; wine-tasting sessions are held among the oak casks in the ancient cellars. ☎ *Rheinallee 5–7, 65375 Oestrich,* ☎ *06723/8090,* FAX *06723/7820. 45 rooms with bath. Restaurant. AE, DC, MC, V. Restaurant closed Nov.–mid-Feb.* $$$

Rüdesheim

DINING

Krone. The extensive restoration work carried out on the 450-year-old Krone Hotel included a complete renovation of its restaurant, which now ranks among the most outstanding in the region. Chef Herbert Pucher's terrines and pâtés draw regular customers from as far away as Frankfurt. His fish dishes are supreme, and the Rhine wines are the best. ✕ *Rheinuferstr. 10, Assmannshausen,* ☎ *06722/4030. Reservations advised. AE, DC, MC, V. Closed Jan. and Feb.* $$–$$$

DINING AND LODGING

Hotel Jagdschloss Niederwald. This is not so much a place to overnight as a luxury resort hotel where you might want to spend your entire vacation. It's set in the hills 5 kilometers (3 miles) out of Rüdesheim, with predictably good views over the Rhine and the Rheingau. The former hunting lodge of the dukes of Hesse, it has a lavish, baronial atmosphere. The restaurant, with panoramic views, can be magnificent. The chef, who was trained in France, transforms traditional German recipes into something more exciting. Families will appreciate the wide range of activities offered, and night owls will appreciate the late hours of the bar. ☎ *Auf dem Niederwald 1, 65383,* ☎ *06722/1004,* FAX *06722/47970. 52 rooms with bath. Restaurant, bar, indoor pool, sauna, tennis courts, health club, horseback riding. AE, DC, MC, V. Closed Jan. 1–Feb. 14.* $$$–$$$$

Rüdesheimer Hof. For a taste of Rheingau hospitality, try this typical inn. There's a terrace for summer dining, where you can enjoy excellent local specialties along with any of the many wines offered. ☎ *Geisenheimerstr. 1, 65385,* ☎ *06722/2011,* FAX *06722/48194. 42 rooms with bath. Restaurant. AE, DC, MC, V. Closed mid-Nov.–mid-Feb.* $$

Hotel und Weinhaus Felsenkeller. Located just around the corner from Drosselgasse, Hotel and Weinhaus Felsenkeller is a traditional 18th-century establishment offering modern comforts. ☎ *Oberstr. 39–41,* ☎ *06722/2094,* FAX *06722/47202. 60 rooms with shower. AE, MC, V.* $$

St. Goar/St. Goarshausen

DINING

Roter Kopf. This is a historic wine restaurant brimming with rustic Rhineland atmosphere. ✕ *Burgstr. 5, St. Goarshausen,* ☎ *06771/2698. Reservations advised. No credit cards.* $$

DINING AND LODGING

Schlosshotel auf Burg Rheinfels. Directly opposite Burg Maus, this castle-hotel breathes a regal air. Its ponderously grand interior is furnished with intricate French and Spanish antiques. Ask for a room with a view. The restaurant offers hearty regional specialties. ⌂ *Schlossberg 47, 56329 St. Goar,* ☎ *06741/8020,* FAX *06741/7652. 58 rooms with bath. Restaurant, bar, indoor and outdoor pools, miniature golf, fishing. AE, DC, MC, V. $$$*

Herrmannsmühle. This Alpine chalet-style hotel has heavy pine furnishings decorated with floral patterns. It stands just outside town by its own vineyards and offers good value at low prices, with an especially warm welcome extended by its host, Herr Herrmann. ⌂ *Forstbachstr. 46, 56346 St. Goarshausen,* ☎ *06771/7317. 10 rooms with bath. Restaurant. MC, V. Closed mid-Nov.–Feb. $*

Trier

DINING

★ **Pfeffermühle.** The stately Pfeffermühle stands alongside the Mosel, by the cable-car station. This former fisherman's home is now considered to be the best restaurant in town, and it's recently added an outdoor terrace for summer dining. The food is nouvelle French. Rabbit in sherry sauce is outstanding, as is the lobster in champagne gelée with asparagus tips. The extensive wine list features vintage Mosels. ✕ *Zurlaubener Ufer 76,* ☎ *0651/26133. Reservations required. MC, V. Closed Sun., Mon. lunch, and 2 wks in Mar. $$$*

Ratskeller zur Steipe. Buried in the vaults beneath the town hall, the Ratskeller's Teutonic mood and fare has a Russian flavor thanks to two Russian chefs. In summer you can move upstairs and eat on the terrace. ✕ *Hauptmarkt 14,* ☎ *0651/75052. Reservations advised. AE, DC, V. Closed Tues. and mid–Jan.–mid–Feb. $$*

★ **Zum Domstein.** This centrally located, bustling weinstube is built above a Roman cellar, and it takes its history seriously—keeping its wines stored within its ancient walls, as the Romans did, and serving authentic Roman dishes, as well as German fare, in the restaurant above. Many of them are the staples of today's Italian cuisine, with sauces so rich they could have contributed to the downfall of the Roman Empire. ✕ *Am Hauptmarkt 5,* ☎ *0651/74490. No reservations. DC, MC, V. Closed Dec. 25. $$*

LODGING

Hotel-Cafe Astoria. This beautifully renovated 19th-century city villa is ideally located between the Mosel River and theOld Town. Ask for a room on the first floor, as they are larger. All rooms are cozy and comfortably furnished. ⌂ *Bruchhausenstr. 4, 54290,* ☎ *0651/978–350,* FAX *0651/41121. 14 rooms with shower. Bar, café. AE, MC, V. $$*

★ **Petrisberg.** This will be the choice of anyone who values classic modern design and a location away from the downtown area. The building is unimposing externally, but inside features striking antiques and rooms with superb views overlooking vineyards, forests, and parklands, large for the price and smartly furnished in a mixture of contemporary styles. For all that, it's no more than a 10-minute walk from the Old Town. Old farm implements and an eclectic assortment of artifacts lend a homey ambience to the tiny weinstube and dining room. The owner, Herr Pantenburg, provides a warm welcome. ⌂ *Sickingerstr. 11–13, 54296,* ☎ *0651/4640,* FAX *0651/46450. 30 rooms and 3 suites with shower. Dining room, weinstube. No credit cards. $$*

Wiesbaden

DINING

★ **Die Ente vom Lehel.** The formal and elegant restaurant of the Nassauer Hof (*see below*) provides one of the most memorable dining experiences in Germany. Nouvelle cuisine is king here. Chef Hans-Peter Wodarz loves theater and tries to bring it into the restaurant through unusual presentation and service. ✕ *Kaiser-Friedrich-Pl. 3,* ☎ *0611/133–666. Reservations required. Jacket and tie. AE, DC, MC, V. Closed Sun., Mon., holidays, and 4 wks in July–Aug. $$$$*

Weihenstephan. Bavarian specialties are offered in this Alpine-style restaurant 5 kilometers (3 miles) south of the city center in suburban Biebrich. Even Bavarian beer is available, despite this being the most famous wine-producing area of the country. The mood is as hearty as the cooking. ✕ *Armenruhstr. 6,* ☎ *0611/61134. Reservations advised. AE. Closed Sat. $$*

LODGING

★ **Nassauer Hof.** Located opposite the Kurpark, the Nassauer Hof epitomizes elegance and style. Set in a turn-of-the-century building, it combines the best of Old World graciousness with German efficiency and comfort. Rooms are large and classy; the bar is a chic place for a rendezvous. ☎ *Kaiser-Friedrich-Pl. 3–4, 65183,* ☎ *0611/1330,* ⟨FAX⟩ *0611/133–632. 202 rooms and 9 suites with bath. Restaurant, bar, indoor pool, massage, sauna. AE, DC, MC, V. $$$$*

★ **Schwarzer Bock.** For period charm, few hotels beat the stylish Schwarzer Bock. The building dates from 1486, though most of what you see today is from the 19th century. The lavish public rooms are filled with antiques, flowers, and paintings; the opulent bedrooms are individually decorated in styles ranging from Baroque to modern. The thermal swimming pool will soothe away the pain of paying the bill. ☎ *Kranzpl. 12, 65183,* ☎ *0611/1550,* ⟨FAX⟩ *0611/155–111. 127 rooms and 22 suites with bath. Restaurant, bar, indoor pool, massage, sauna. AE, DC, MC, V. $$$$*

THE ARTS AND NIGHTLIFE

The Arts

Music

Aachen has a municipal orchestra that gives regular concerts in the **Kongresszentrum Eurogress,** Monheimsallee.

Bonn means Beethoven, and every three years the city hosts a **Beethoven Festival;** contact the Bonn tourist office (☎ 0228/773–466) for programs and ticket information. The Bonn **Symphony Orchestra** opens its season in grand style every September with a concert on the market square, in front of city hall. Otherwise, concerts are in the Beethovenhalle (they're free on Sunday morning). From May through October, the **Bonner Sommer** festival offers folklore, music, and street theater, much of it outdoors and most of it free. Chamber-music concerts are given regularly at the **Schumannhaus** (☎ 0228/773–6666). In May and June, free concerts are held on Sunday evening in the **Bad Godesberg Redoute.** And the **Pantheon** theater (Bundeskanzlerplatz, ☎ 0228/212521) has become a leading venue for all manner of (pop) concerts and cabaret.

Düsseldorf, once home to Mendelssohn, Schumann, and Brahms, boasts the finest concert hall in Germany after Berlin's Philharmonie: the **Tonhalle** (Ehrenhof 1, ☎ 0211/899–5540), a former planetarium on the edge of the Hofgarten. It's the home of the **Düsseldorfer Symphoniker,** which plays from September to mid-June.

In **Koblenz,** the **Rheinische Philharmonie** orchestra plays regularly in the **Rhein-Mosel-Halle** (Julius-Wegeler-Str). **Organ recitals** are frequently given in two fine churches: the **Christuskirche** and the **Florinskirche.**

Köln's Westdeutsche Rundfunk Orchestra performs regularly in the city's excellent concert hall, the **Philharmonie** (Bischofsgarten 1, ☎ 0221/2801). The smaller **Gürzenich Orchestra** also gives regular concerts in the Philharmonie, but the natural setting for its music is the restored **Gürzenich,** medieval Köln's official reception mansion. Year-round **organ recitals** in Köln's cathedral are supplemented from June to August with a summer season of organ music. Organ recitals and chamber concerts are also presented in the churches of St. Maria Himmelfahrt (Marzellenstr. 26), St. Aposteln (Neumarkt 30), and Trinitätskirche (Filzengraben 4). Call for details on all church concerts (☎ 0221/534–856).

Trier's cathedral is the magnificent setting for much of the sacred music to be heard in the city; there are **organ recital festivals** in May, June, August, and September.

Wiesbaden's Symphony Orchestra gives concerts in the **Staatstheater's Grosses Haus** and in the equally impressive **Kurhaus.** Organ recitals are given every Saturday at 11:30 in the Gothic **Marktkirche** (Marktpl.).

Theater, Dance and Opera
In **Bonn,** opera, ballet, and musicals are staged regularly at the **Oper der Stadt Bonn** (Am Böselagerhof 1, ☎ 0228/773–666), popularly known as "La Scala of the Rhineland" and led by the colorful stage director Giancarlo del Monaco. **Bonn** also hosts a famous dance festival, the **International Dance Workshop,** in July and August. Call for program details and tickets (☎ 0228/11517).

Düsseldorf's highly regarded opera company and ballet perform at **Deutsche Oper am Rhein** (Heinrich Heine Allee 16a, ☎ 0211/133–949).

Koblenz has a theatrical tradition dating back to the 18th-century rule of the Prince Elector Clemens Wenzeslaus. The gracious neoclassical theater he built in 1787 is still in regular use (☎ 0261/34629 for program details and tickets).

Köln's opera company, the **Oper der Stadt Köln,** is known for exciting classical and contemporary productions. The city's small ballet company, the **Kölner Tanzforum,** hosts an international festival, the **Internationale Sommerakademie des Tanzes,** every July. Köln's two principal theaters are the **Schauspielhaus** (Offenbachpl. 1) and the smaller **Kammerspiele** (Ubierring 45). Call (☎ 0221/221–8400) for program details and tickets for all of the above. The Schauspielhaus is also home to the 20 or so private theaters in the city: **Der Keller** (Kleingedankstr. 6, ☎ 0221/318–059) is the best-known venue for contemporary drama.

The **Hessisches Staatstheater** is based in **Wiesbaden's** fine late-19th-century theater on Christian-Zais-Strasse (opposite the Kurhaus and casino). Classical drama, opera, ballet, and musicals are presented in the **Grosses Haus** (☎ 06121/132–325); less ambitious productions are given in the **Kleines Haus** (☎ 06121/132–327). The Grosses Haus is also the scene in early summer of Wiesbaden's annual **International May Arts Festival.**

Nightlife

Nightlife in Bonn? There's the story of the visitor who asked where he could find some action in Bonn. "She's taken the night off to visit her aunt in Köln," was the reply. Things have changed since then, however—the number of bars and taverns in the Altstadt. Try a Budweiser or Pilsener Urquell in the **Lampe** (Breitestr. 35); after midnight, move on to the **Locke** (Prinz-Albertstr. 20). The **Marktschänke** (Eifelstr. 2) is popular with the dawn chorus of taxi drivers, market traders, and all-nighters. No wonder: It *opens* at 5 AM. Singles could try a bar called **Die Falle** (Belderberg 15). The **Cave Club '77** (Bertha von Süttnerpl. 25) and the **CD Nightclub** (Rheingasse 14) have music and some adult spice. The **Jazz Galerie** (Oxfordstr. 24) has live jazz and rock many nights, starting at 9 PM. The **Pinte** (Breitestr. 46) is smaller, smokier, and fun. Disco goers head for Bad-Godesburg, where the suburb's resident diplomats let their hair down at **Sky** (Bonnerstr. 48). If that's too far, settle for **La Grange,** Weselstrasse 5 (downtown). Bonn's gamblers head to nearby Bad Neuenahr, where the casino is open daily 2 PM–3 AM.

Düsseldorf nightlife is pretty much concentrated in the **Altstadt,** a landscape of pubs, discotheques, ancient restored brewery houses, and jazz clubs in the vicinity of the Marktplatz and along cobbled streets named Bolker, Kurze, Flinger, and Mühlen. These places may be crowded, but they're very atmospheric. A more sophisticated mood is set in the modern part of the city. **Bei Tony** (Lorettostr. 12) and **Front Page** (Mannesman Ufer) are fashionable upscale bars; **Sam's West** and **Checkers,** both on the Kö, are number-one discos.

Singles in **Koblenz** go to the **Tanzcafé Besselink** (opposite the main train station)—it's open until 3 AM. Disco fans favor **Studio 54** (Schulgasse 9) and the **Metro Club** in Koblenz-Hochheim (Alte Heerstr. 130). The nightclub scene is dominated by the **Klapsmühle** (Poststr. 2a) and the **Petit Fleur** (Rheinstr. 30).

Köln's nightlife is found in three distinct areas: around the **Friesenplatz** S-bahn station in **Zulpicherstrasse** and between the **Alter Markt** and **Neumarkt** in the old city. Although this is not Hamburg, virtually all tastes are catered to. Singles head for **Big Ben** (Im Klapperhof 48) and the **Intermezzo** (Unter Kaester 5). The **Moulin-Rouge Tingle-Tangle Club** (Maastrichterstr. 68) probably has the best striptease in town. This is discoland, too. **Bierdorf, Clou, Das Ding, Disco 42,** and **Zorba the Buddha** (yes, the Buddha) are all "in." For the last word in disco experience, make for the **Alter Wartesaal** in the Hauptbahnhof on Friday or Saturday night. The old waiting room has been turned into a concert hall and disco, enabling Köln's boppers to get down on ancient polished parquet and check their style in original mahogany-framed mirrors. Many streets off the Hohenzollernring and Hohenstaufenring, particularly Roonstrasse, provide a broad range of nightlife. For good classic jazz, try **Papa Joe's Biersalon** (Alter Markt 50). Two other worthwhile jazz clubs are the **Subway** (Aachnerstr. 82) and the **Stadtgarten** (Venloerstr. 40), both of which sometimes feature international musicians.

Wiesbaden's nightlife tends to center on the **casino** and **Kurhaus** complex. You'll find a mix of casino winners and losers celebrating or drowning their sorrows in the **Pavillon Bar** of the Kurhaus. Everyone else heads into nearby Frankfurt for a good time.

RHINELAND ESSENTIALS

Arriving and Departing

By Plane

The Rhineland is served by three international airports: Frankfurt, Düsseldorf, and Köln-Bonn. There are direct flights from the United States and Canada to all three, and they are all also part of a comprehensive network of air services throughout Europe. Bus and rail lines connect each airport with its respective downtown area and provide rapid access to the rest of the region.

Getting Around

By Boat

No visit to the Rhineland is complete without at least one river trip. Fortunately, there are many cruise options from which to choose (*see* Guided Tours, *below*).

By Bus

There are two Europabus routes running across the Rhineland: One originates in Britain and terminates in Munich, crossing the Rhineland between Köln and Frankfurt; the other runs between Frankfurt and Trier, stopping at the Frankfurt Airport, Wiesbaden, Mainz, Bingen, and several towns along the Mosel River. All Europabuses are comfortable and fast. For details on services and reservations, contact **Deutsche Touring** (am Römerhof 17, 60486 Frankfurt/Main, ☎ 069/790–3268). Local bus services connect most smaller towns and villages throughout the Rhineland.

By Car

The Autobahns and other highways of the Rhineland are busy, so allow plenty of time for driving. Frankfurt is 126 kilometers (79 miles) from Koblenz, 175 kilometers (110 miles) from Bonn, 190 kilometers (119 miles) from Köln, and 230 kilometers (143 miles) from Düsseldorf. The most spectacular stretch of the Rhineland is along the Middle Rhine, between Mainz and Koblenz. Highways (though not Autobahns) hug the river on each bank, and car ferries crisscross the Rhine at many points. Road conditions throughout the region are excellent.

CAR RENTAL
Avis: in **Bonn,** Adenauerallee 4–6, ☎ 0228/223–047; in **Düsseldorf,** Berliner Allee 32, ☎ 0211/329–050; in **Frankfurt,** Schmidtstr. 39, ☎ 069/730–111, in **Koblenz,** Andernacher Strasse 203, ☎ 0261/800–366; in **Köln,** Clemensstrasse 29, ☎ 0221/234–333; in **Trier,** Herzogenbuscher Strasse 31, ☎ 0651/12722.

Europcar: in **Bonn,** Potsdamer Platz 7, ☎ 0228/652–961; in **Düsseldorf,** Burgunderstrasse 40, ☎ 0211/504–7041; in **Frankfurt,** Schlossstrasse 32, ☎ 069/775–033; in **Köln,** Köln-Bonn Airport, ☎ 02203/53088.

Hertz: in **Aachen,** Juelicherstrasse 250, ☎ 0241/162–686; in **Bonn,** Adenauerallee 216, ☎ 0228/217–041; in **Düsseldorf,** Immermannstrasse 65, ☎ 0211/357–025; in **Köln,** Bismarckstr. 19-21, ☎ 0221/515–0847; in **Frankfurt,** Gutleutstrasse 87, ☎ 069/2425–2627.

Sixt-Budget: in **Düsseldorf,** Tilde-Klose-Weg 6, ☎ 0211/471–310; in **Mainz-Gonzenheim,** Im Niedergarten 24, ☎ 06131/46173; in **Trier,** Eurenerstrasse 5, ☎ 0651/820–821.

By Train

InterCity and EuroCity expresses connect all the cities and towns of the area. Hourly InterCity routes run between Düsseldorf, Köln, Bonn, and Mainz, with most services extending as far south as Munich and as far north as Hamburg. The Mainz–Bonn route runs beside the Rhine, between the river and the vine-covered heights, offering spectacular views all the way. The city transportation networks of Bonn, Köln, and Düsseldorf are linked by S-Bahn (for information contact the Verkehrsverband in Köln, ☎ 0221/547–3333).

Guided Tours

Boat Trips

Trips along the Rhine and Mosel range from a few hours to days or even a week or more in length. The major operator, with a fleet of 25 boats, is the **Köln-Düsseldorfer Deutsche Rheinschiffahrt** (Frankenwerft 15, 50667 Köln, ☎ 0221/208–8288; KD River Cruises of Europe, 2500 Westchester Ave., Purchase, NY 10577, ☎ 914/696–3600; 323 Geary St., Suite 603, San Francisco, CA 94102, ☎ 415/392–8817). It offers daily services on the Rhine, Mosel, and Main rivers from April through October, as well as a year-round program of excursions, principally along the Rhine. For the best values, check out the K-D's combined river-rail tickets, which allow you to break your river trip at any place the boats stop and continue by train. For further sailings along the Rhine, contact the Koblenz–Rüdesheim **Hebel** line in Boppard (☎ 06742/2420), which operates from March through December; for trips along the Mosel, contact **Mosel-Personenschiffahrt Bernkastel-Kues** (Goldbachstr. 52, Bernkastel-Kues, ☎ 06531/8222).

The K-D line has a weeklong "floating wine seminar" aboard the pride of its fleet, the motor-ship *Helvetia,* which makes stops at vineyards on both the Mosel and Rhine rivers on a wine-tasting route that ends in Basel, Switzerland. The K-D Rhine line also organizes three-and four-day cruises along the Mosel that stop at most of the wine villages between Koblenz and Trier.

Two shipping companies in Koblenz organize short "castle cruises" from Easter through September. Two boats, the *Undine* and the *Marksburg,* ply the Rhine between Koblenz and Boppard, passing 10 castles during the 75-minute, one-way voyage. Details and reservations are available from **Personenschiffahrt Merkelbach** (Emserstr. 87, Koblenz-Pfaffendorf, ☎ 0261/76810); and **Personenschiffahrt Josef Vomfell** (Koblenzer Str. 64, Spay/Rhein, ☎ 02628/2431). Another Koblenz operator, **Rhein und Moselschiffahrt Gerhard Collee-Holzenbein** (Rheinzollstr. 4, ☎ 0261/37744), runs day cruises as far as Rüdesheim on the Rhine and Cochem on the Mosel.

From Köln, three shipping companies operate boat tours on the Rhine: The **Köln-Düsseldorfer** line (see above) has hourly trips starting at 9:30, daily, April through September; the **Rhein-Mosel Schiffahrt** (Konrad Adenauer-Ufer, ☎ 0221/121–714) has daily departures every 45 minutes starting at 10, April through September; and the **Dampfschiffahrt Colonia** (Lintgasse 18, ☎ 0221/211–325) has daily departures every 45 minutes beginning at 10, April through October. All tours leave from the landing stages near the Hohenzollern Brücke, a short walk from the cathedral.

Bus Tours

Limousine Travel Service (Wiesenhüttenpl. 39, Frankfurt, ☎ 069/230–492) has a daily bus trip from Frankfurt along the "Riesling Route" that encompasses the vineyards of the Rhineland between Frankfurt and Rüdesheim. The tour includes a wine-tasting and a trip along the Rhine to the wine village of St. Goar. The cost is DM 105.

Bus trips into the countryside around Köln (to the Eifel Hills, the Ahr Valley, and the Westerwald) are organized by several city travel agencies. Three leading tour operators are **Globus Reisen** (Hohenzollernring 86, ☎ 0221/912–8270), **Univers-Reisen** (am Rinkenpfuhl 57, ☎ 0221/209–020), and **Küppers-Reisebüro-Etrav** (Longericher-Strasse 183, ☎ 0221/210–966).

City Tours

Bus tours of Köln leave from outside the tourist office (opposite the main entrance to the cathedral) at 10, 11, 1, 2, and 3, April through October, and at 11 and 2 November through April. The tour lasts two hours and costs DM 23 for adults and DM 8 for children; it is conducted in English and German. **"Köln by Night"** bus tours are offered Friday and Saturday during July and August. These trips leave the tourist office at 7 PM and include a tour of the city, a boat ride on the Rhine, a cold supper, and a visit to a wine tavern; the cost is DM 49. A two-hour **walking tour** of the city is also available by prior arrangement with the tourist office, as are tours of the Old Town by horse-drawn carriage (*see* Tour 5, *above*). Most central hotels offer a special tourist package, the **"Kölner Knüller,"** which includes a sightseeing tour voucher, a pass for all the city's museums, and other reductions. The package costs DM 20. **City tours** of Düsseldorf leave from Bus Quay 10, Friedrich-Ebert-Strasse (across from the Hauptbahnhof) daily at 11:15 and 2:45. The 2½-hour tour includes a visit to the top of the 700-foot-high Rhine television tower. The cost is DM 23 for adults and DM 12 for children. After May, the cost for the afternoon tour is DM 25, because the tour expands to include a boat trip on the Rhine.

Important Addresses and Numbers

Embassies

United States, Deichmanns Aue 29, 53113 Bonn, ☎ 0228/3391.
Great Britain, Friedrich-Ebert-Allee 77, 53113 Bonn, ☎ 0228/234–061.
Canada, Friedrich-Wilhelmstrasse 18, 53113 Bonn, ☎ 0228/231–061.

Travel Agencies

American Express: Burgmauer 14, 50667 **Köln,** ☎ 0221/257–7484; Kaiserstrasse 8, Postfach 100146, 60311 **Frankfurt,** ☎ 069/21051; Webergasse 8, 65183 **Wiesbaden,** ☎ 0611/39144. Heinrich-Heine-Allee 14, 40213 **Düsseldorf,** ☎ 0211/82200.

Visitor Information

The Rhineland regional tourist office, **Fremdenverkehrsverband Rheinland Pfalz** (Postfach 1420, 56014 Koblenz, ☎ 0261/31079), provides general information on the entire region. There are also local tourist information offices in the following towns and cities:

Aachen: Verkehrsverein Bad Aachen, Friedrich-Wilhelm-Platz, Postfach 2007, 52022 Aachen, ☎ 0241/180–2960.

Bernkastel-Kues: Stadt. Verkehrsbüro, Am Gestade 5, 54464 Bernkastel-Kues, ☎ 06531/4023.

Bonn: Tourist Information Cassius-Bastei, Münsterstrasse 20, 53111 Bonn, ☎ 0228/773–466.

Cochem: Verkehrsamt, Endertplatz, 56812 Cochem, ☎ 02671/3971.

Düsseldorf: Verkehrsverein, Konrad Adenauer Platz 12, 40210 Düsseldorf, ☎ 0211/172–020.

Koblenz: Fremdenverkehrsamt der Stadt Koblenz, Verkehrspavillon am Hauptbahnhof, Postfach 2080, 56020 Koblenz, ☎ 0261/31304.

Köln: Verkehrsamt der Stadt Köln, Unter Fettenhenen 19, 50667 Köln, ☎ 0221/221–3340.

Rüdesheim: Städtisches Verkehrsamt, Rheinstrasse 16, 65385 Rüdesheim, ☎ 06722/2962.

St. Goarshausen: Verkehrsamt, Bahnhofstrasse 8, 56346 St. Goarshausen, ☎ 06771/427.

Trier: Tourist Information, an der Porta Nigra, Postfach 3830, 54290 Trier, ☎ 0651/978–080.

Wiesbaden: Verkehrsbüro, Rheinstrasse 15, corner of Wilhelmstrasse, 65185 Wiesbaden, ☎ 0611/172–9780.

13 The Fairy-Tale Road

If you're in search of Cinderella, Hansel and Gretel, the Pied Piper, and Rumpelstiltskin, the Fairy-Tale Road is the place to look. One of Germany's special tourist routes, it leads through parts of Germany where the brothers Grimm lived and worked. From its start in Hanau, just east of Frankfurt, to its end in Bremen, 600 kilometers (370 miles) north, it passes dozens of picturesque towns full of half-timbered houses and guarded by castles. Hannover is the site of a magnificent Baroque park.

THE MAJORITY OF TRAVELERS who begin their Germany vacations at Frankfurt Airport head west to the Rhineland or south into the Black Forest or Bavaria. Some may find their way into the Taunus Mountains on Frankfurt's doorstep. Relatively few, however, venture north to follow a fascinating trail that leads deep into the heart of the country, not only into the land but into the German character as well.

This is the Fairy-Tale Road, or Märchenstrasse. It starts just a 20-minute rail or car journey east of Frankfurt in the town of Hanau and from there wends its way north some 600 kilometers (about 370 miles) through parts of Germany that shaped the lives and imagination of the two most famous chroniclers of German folk history and tradition, the brothers Grimm. (Note that though the route is best explored by car, many of the attractions along its meandering path can also be reached by train.)

The Fairy-Tale Road is among the most recent of Germany's special tourist routes. It doesn't have the glamour of the Romantic Road, but in its own way it is, perhaps, a route more in tune with romantics. It certainly doesn't suffer from the commercialism of the Wine Road.

Following this course from stem to stern—in other words, from Frankfurt all the way to Bremen—can make for a fairly long and tiring journey. However, you can pick up the route anywhere along its length to take in the highlights and still come remarkably close to the spirit and essence of fairy-tale Germany as recorded by these two master storytellers.

The zigzag course detailed here follows the spine of the Fairy-Tale Road and includes a number of side trips and detours to nearby destinations worthy of a visitor's attention. Fairy tales come to life in forgotten villages where black cats snooze in the windows of half-timbered houses; in ancient forests where wild boar snort at timid deer; in misty valleys where the silence of centuries is broken only by the splash of a ferryman's oar. In a way, this could be considered a dual trip, going forward geographically and at the same time back into the reaches of childhood, imagination, and German folk consciousness, to visit Old World settings steeped in legend and fantasy.

From early childhood the Grimms were enthralled by tales of enchantment, of kings and queens, of golden-haired princesses saved from disaster by stalwart princes—folk tales, myths, epics, and legends that dealt with magic and wicked witches, predatory stepmothers, along with a supporting cast of goblins and wizards.

However, the Grimms did not invent these tales, as they were in the public domain long before the brothers began collecting them. The Grimms' devotion to fairy tales could be considered merely a sideline to their main careers. Jacob was a grammarian who formulated Grimm's Law, a theory of linguistics relating Greek and Latin to German. Wilhelm was a literary scholar and critic. Together they spent most of their energies compiling a massive dictionary of the German language. But it is as the authors of *Kinder und Hausmärchen (Children's and Household Tales)*, a work that has been called the best-known book after the Bible, that they are remembered. In 1812, the Grimms introduced the world to some 200 of their favorite stories, with a cast of characters that included Cinderella, Hansel and Gretel, Little Red Riding Hood,

Rapunzel, Rumpelstiltskin, Sleeping Beauty, Snow White, and other unforgettable stars of the world of make-believe.

The Fairy-Tale Road leads through parts of Germany in which the brothers lived and gathered and situated their tales; through the states of Hesse and Lower Saxony, to follow along the Fulda and Weser rivers via a string of highways and byways that lead through a countryside as beguiling as any in Europe.

EXPLORING

Tour 1: Hanau to Hameln

Numbers in the margin correspond to points of interest on the Fairy-Tale Road map.

The Fairy-Tale Road begins in "once upon a time" fashion at a point you can reach only on foot—the brothers Grimm memorial in the Neustädter Marktplatz of **Hanau,** the town in which the brothers were born: Jacob in 1785, Wilhelm a year later. Although travelers devoted to the Grimms will want to start their pilgrimage here, they should be forewarned that Hanau has become a traffic-congested suburb of Frankfurt, with post–World War II buildings that are not particularly attractive.

The bronze memorial, erected in 1898, is a larger-than-life-size statue of the brothers, one seated, the other leaning on his chair, the two of them deep in conversation—a fitting pose for these scholars who unearthed so many medieval myths and legends, earning their reputation as the fathers of the fairy tale.

The degree to which the brothers have influenced the world's concept of fairy tales—those of *The Arabian Nights* excepted—is remarkable. But it would be a mistake to imagine them as kindly, bewhiskered old gents telling stories in their rose-clad cottage for the pleasure of village children. As already mentioned, they were serious and successful academics, with interests ranging far beyond what we may think of as children's light amusements. Their stories probe deep into the German psyche and deal with far more complex emotions than is suggested by the occasional "happily ever after" endings; witness the Stephen Sondheim–James Lapine musical *Into the Woods,* based to a large extent on the Grimm's works.

Behind the statue is the solid bulk of Hanau's 18th-century **Rathaus** (Town Hall). Every day at noon its bells play a tribute to another of the city's famous sons, the composer Paul Hindemith (1895–1963), by chiming out one of his canons. At 10 AM the carillon plays a choral composition; at 2 PM a minuet; and at 4 a piece entitled *Guten Abend* (Good Evening) rings out for the crowds hurrying across the Marktplatz to complete their shopping before returning home.

Hanau was almost completely obliterated by wartime bombing raids, and there's little of the Altstadt (Old Town) that the Grimm brothers would recognize now. Behind the Rathaus, however, is a corner that has been faithfully reconstructed. It's dominated by the **Altes Rathaus** (Old Town Hall), a handsome 16th-century Renaissance building, its two half-timbered upper stories weighted down by a steep slate roof. Today it's the home of the German goldsmiths' craft. Known as the **Deutsches Goldschmiedehaus** (German Goldsmiths' House), it contains a permanent exhibit and regular national and international displays

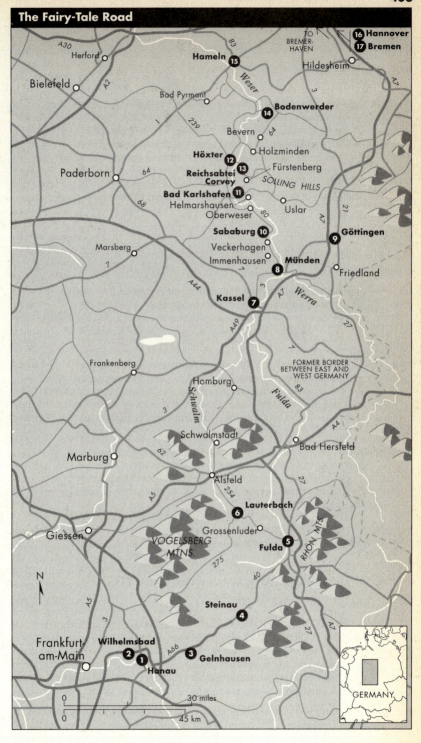

of goldsmiths' and silversmiths' crafts. *Altstädter Markt 6.* ☛ *Free.* ⏲ *Tues.–Sun. 10–noon and 2–5.*

You'll find various memorials and museums devoted to the brothers Grimm all along the Fairy-Tale Road. For the next memorial, however, you have to head in another direction—to **Schloss Philippsruhe,** a palace on the banks of the Main River in the suburb of Kesselstadt (Bus 1 or 10 will take you there in 10 minutes). Schloss Philippsruhe has much more than Grimm exhibits to offer: It's the oldest French-style Baroque palace east of the Rhine. Philippsruhe may remind you of Versailles, although its French-trained architect, Julius Ludwig Rothweil, planned it along the lines of another palace in the Paris area, the much smaller Clagny Palace. Philippsruhe—as its name, "Philipp's Rest," suggests—was built for Count Philipp Reinhard von Hanau. He didn't enjoy its riverside peace for long, however: He died less than three months after moving in. After the French builder Jacques Girard completed work on the palace, creating its very French appearance, the invading French confiscated it in 1803. Later Napoléon gave it as a present to his sister Pauline Borghese, who then put it up for sale. American forces took over Philippsruhe as a military quarters for a time in 1945, and until the postwar reconstruction of Hanau was complete it served as the town hall. Every year on the first weekend of September, the palace grounds are invaded again—this time by the people of Hanau, for a magnificent party to commemorate the rebuilding of their war-ravaged town. *Schloss Philippsruhe, Kesselstadt.* ☛ *DM 3 adults, DM 1.50 children.* ⏲ *Tues.–Sun. 11–6.*

During the early 19th century, following the withdrawal of the French from Hanau, the original formal gardens were replanned as an informal, English-style park. You'll find the contrast between formal palace and informal wooded grounds striking. As you leave or enter, pause to study the entrance gate; the 19th-century gilding, made by Parisian masters, is real gold.

TIME OUT If the weather's good, seek out a place beneath the white canvas sunshades on the palace terrace, now a café with a view overlooking the Main River that was once enjoyed by Count Philipp Reinhard. In inclement weather head for the palace's bistro, with its open fire and hot, strong coffee.

❷ Just north of Philippsruhe and a short bus ride from the center of Hanau is the city spa of **Wilhelmsbad.** It was built at the end of the 18th century by Crown Prince Wilhelm von Hessen-Kassel at the site where two peasant women, out gathering herbs, discovered mineral springs. For a few decades Wilhelmsbad rivaled Baden-Baden as Germany's premier spa and fashionable playground. Then, about 100 years ago the springs dried up, the casino closed, and Europe's wealthy and titled looked for other amusements. But this is still Grimm fairy-tale land, and Wilhelmsbad, the sleeping-beauty spa, awoke from its slumber in the '60s to become a rejuvenated resort. The fine Baroque buildings and bathhouses were restored, parkland cleared and relaid in informal English style, riding stables opened, and one of Germany's loveliest golf courses laid out where the leisure classes once hunted pheasants.

❸ Return to Hanau to rejoin the Fairy-Tale Road, following B–43 about 20 kilometers (12 miles) northeast to **Gelnhausen.** Here on an island in the sleepy little Kinzig River are the remains of a castle that might well have stimulated the imagination of the Grimm brothers in their travels in this area. Emperor Friedrich I—known as Barbarossa, or Red Beard—built the castle in this idyllic spot during the 12th century; in

1180 it was the scene of the first all-German Imperial Diet. Although located on an island, the castle was hardly designed as a defensive bastion and was accordingly sacked in the Thirty Years' War. Today only parts of the russet walls and colonnaded entrance remain. Still, stroll beneath the castle's ruined ramparts on its watery site and you'll get a tangible impression of the medieval importance of the court of Barbarossa. *Follow the signs to Burg Barbarossa.* ☎ *06051/820–054.* ☛ *DM 1 adults, 50 pf children under 14. Castle open Mar.–Oct., Tues.–Sun. 10–1 and 2–5:30; Nov.–Feb., Tues.–Sun. 10–1 and 2–4:30.*

For clear evidence of the formative influence on the brothers Grimm, you need only travel another 20 kilometers (12 miles) along the Fairy-Tale Road, to the little town of **Steinau**—full name Steinau an der Strasse (Steinau "on the road," referring to an old trade route between Frankfurt and Leipzig). Here father Grimm served as local magistrate and the Grimm brothers spent much of their childhood.

Steinau dates from the 13th century and is typical of villages in the region. Marvelously preserved half-timbered houses are set along cobblestone streets; imposing castles bristle with towers and turrets. In its woodsy surroundings one can well imagine encountering Little Red Riding Hood, Snow White, or Hansel and Gretel.

The main street is named after the brothers; the building where paterfamilias was employed is now known as the "fairy-tale house." At the top of the town stands a **castle** straight out of a Grimm fairy tale. Originally an early medieval fortress, it was rebuilt in Renaissance style between 1525 and 1558 and used by the counts of Hanau as their summer residence and later to guard the increasingly important trade route between Frankfurt and Leipzig. It's not difficult to imagine the young Grimm boys playing in the shadow of its great gray walls, perhaps venturing into the encircling dry moat.

The fine, half-timbered, turreted house where the family resided is only a few hundred yards from the castle. Officially called the **Amthaus,** it now contains the tourist office and a local history museum with a special section devoted to the Brothers Grimm. ☛ *DM 2.50 adults, DM 1.50 children.* ⊙ *Apr.–Oct., weekdays 2–5.*

There's another, larger Grimm museum in the castle itself, the **Grimm Museum im Schloss.** Climb the tower for a breathtaking view of Steinau and the countryside where the Grimm brothers once roamed. *Museum* ☛ *DM 2 adults, DM 1 children (a guided tour of the castle and museum costs DM 4 adults, DM 2 children).* ⊙ *Mar.–Oct., Tues.–Sun. 10–5; Nov.–Feb., Tues.–Sun. 10–4. Closed Jan. Tower* ☛ *DM 1 adults, 50 pf children.*

In front of the castle, in Steinau's ancient market square, Am Kumpen, is the Gothic church of **St. Catherine,** where the Grimm brothers' grandfather, Friedrich, was parson. Across the square, in the former stables of the castle, is a small puppet theater, **Die Holzkuppe,** where presentations of the Grimm fairy tales are staged. *Die Holzkuppe Marionettentheater.* ☎ *06663/245 for program details.*

In the center of the square is a **Grimm memorial fountain.** It was built only in 1985, but its timeless design blends perfectly with the background provided by Steinau's 16th-century **Rathaus** (Town Hall). The six bronze figures you see on the white stucco facade of the Rathaus represent a cross section of 16th-century Steinau's population—from the builder who helped construct the town to the mother and child who continue its traditions.

With the Rhön Mountains on your right, head north now on B–40 and leave the Fairy-Tale Road for a detour to the ancient episcopal city of **❺ Fulda,** a treasure trove of Baroque architecture. Its grandest example is the immense **bishops' palace,** on Schlossstrasse, crowning the heights of the city. The great collection of buildings began as a Renaissance palace in the early 17th century and was transformed into its present Baroque splendor a century later by Johann Dientzenhofer. Much of the palace is now used as municipal offices, but you can visit several of the former public rooms. The Fürstensaal (Princes' Hall) on the second floor provides a breathtaking display of Baroque decorative artistry, with ceiling paintings by the 18th-century Bavarian artist Melchior Steidl. Concerts are regularly held within its fabric-clad walls (contact the city tourist office in the palace for program details; ☎ 0661/102–345). The palace also has permanent displays of the faience ceramics for which Fulda was once famous, as well as some fine local glassware. *Schlossstr.* ☛ *DM 4 adults, DM 3 children.* ☉ *Sat.–Thurs. 10–6, Fri. 2–6. Guided tours, costing an extra 50 pf, are given Apr.–Oct., Sat.–Thurs. 10:30 and 2:30, Fri. at 2:30; Nov.–Mar., weekdays 2:30, weekends 10:30 and 2:30.*

Pause at the windows of the great Fürstensaal to take in the view across the palace park to the **Orangerie.** If you have time after your palace tour, stroll over for a visit. There's a pleasant café on the first floor.

Across the broad boulevard that borders the park you'll see the tall twin spires of the **Dom,** Fulda's 18th-century cathedral. The Dom was built by Dientzenhofer on the site of an 8th-century basilica, which at the time was the largest church north of the Alps. The basilica had to be big enough to accommodate the ever-growing number of pilgrims from all parts of Europe, who converged on Fulda to pray at the grave of the martyred St. Boniface, the "Apostle of the Germans." A black alabaster bas-relief depicting his death marks the martyr's grave in the crypt. The cathedral museum contains a document bearing his writing, along with several other treasures, including a fine 16th-century painting by Lucas Cranach the Elder of Christ and the adulteress (who looks very comely in her velvet Renaissance costume). *Dom Museum, Dompl.* ☛ *DM 3 adults, DM 1.50 children.* ☉ *Apr.–Oct., weekdays 10–5, Sat. 10–2, Sun. and holidays 12:30–5:30; Nov.–Mar., weekdays 10–12:30 and 1:30–4, Sat. 10–2, Sun. and holidays 12:30–4. Closed Jan.*

On one side of the cathedral you'll see one of Germany's oldest churches, the **Michaelskirche,** or Church of St. Michael, built during the 9th century along the lines of the Church of the Holy Sepulchre in Jerusalem. It has a harmony and dignity that match the majesty of the Baroque facade of the neighboring Dom.

From the Dom, head into the center of town, passing on your right the former guardhouse of the bishops' palace and on your left the 18th-century city parish church. Your goal is the Rathaus, quite possibly the finest Renaissance half-timbered town hall in this part of the country. The half-timbering, separating the arcaded first floor from the steep roof and its incongruous but charming battery of small steeples, is particularly delicate.

Kassel is the next major stop on the road north. If you're in a hurry you can reach Kassel from Fulda in less than an hour via Autobahn 7. But the Fairy-Tale Road gives Autobahns a wide berth, so if you have time, take B–254 into the Vogelsberg Mountains via Grossenluder to **❻ Lauterbach,** some 25 kilometers (15 miles) northeast of Fulda. **Lauter-**

bach, a resort town of many medieval half-timbered houses, has not just one castle but two—the Riedesel and the Eisenbach. The town is the setting of one of the Grimm's fairy tales, the one in which the Little Scalawag loses his sock. Lauterbach's other claim to fame is its garden gnomes, turned out here by the thousands and exported all over the world. These ornaments are made in all shapes and sizes, from 3 inches to 3 feet tall, by the firm of Heissner Keramik. Several shops in Lauterbach sell the gnomes if you'd like to take one home with you.

The Fairy-Tale Road continues north to **Alsfeld,** notable for its medieval town center of beautifully preserved half-timbered houses that in places lean out to almost touch one another across narrow, winding cobbled streets. Seek out Kirchplatz, a small square behind the late-Gothic Walpurgiskirche off the main square, and No. 12, whose rightward lurch seems to defy gravity. So, too, does the jewel of Alsfeld—and one of Germany's showpieces—the **Altes Rathaus** (Old Town Hall), built in 1512. Its facade, combining a stone-colonnade ground floor, half-timbered upper reaches, and dizzily steep, top-heavy slate roof punctured by two pointed towers shaped like witches' hats, would look right at home in Disneyworld. If you want to get an unobstructed view of this remarkable building (which is not open to the public) for your photo album, avoid the Marktplatz on Tuesday and Friday, when market stalls clutter the square.

From there the routing follows the little Schwalm River through a picturesque region so inextricably linked with the Grimm fairy tales that it's known as Rotkäppchenland (Little Red Riding Hood country). On a side road, **Neustadt** is the home of the 13th-century circular tower from which Rapunzel supposedly let down her golden tresses. About 10 kilometers (6 miles) north is **Schwalmstadt,** the capital of the area. If you happen to be here on one of the town's many festival days, you'll see local people decked out in the traditional folk costumes that are still treasured in these parts.

Of passing interest is the fact that some 40 kilometers (25 miles) southwest, on the Route 3 Kassel highway, is **Marburg,** where the Grimm brothers attended the university and began their folktale research.

TIME OUT At Homberg, 19 kilometers (12 miles) north of Schwalmstadt, stop at the 15th-century **Krone Inn** (☎ 05681/2407), on the market square; it's the oldest guest house in Germany. Within its half-timbered walls you can eat and drink and dream of centuries past.

❼ Some 40 kilometers (24 miles) north of Homberg you'll arrive at the ancient city of **Kassel.**

Here the brothers Grimm worked as librarians at the court of the king of Westphalia, who was Jerome Bonaparte, Napoléon's youngest brother. The Grimms continued to collect stories and legends. Many French tales were recounted to them by Dorothea Viehmann, "the Fairy-tale Lady," who lived in the neighboring village of Baunatal.

In the center of Kassel, the **Brüder Grimm Museum** occupies five rooms of the Palais Bellevue, where the brothers once lived and worked. Exhibits include furniture, memorabilia, letters, manuscripts, and editions of their books, as well as paintings, aquarelles, etchings, and drawings by Ludwig Emil Grimm, a third brother and a graphic artist of note. *Palais Bellevue, Schöne Aussicht 2.* ☞ *Free.* ☉ *Daily 10–5.* (☎ *0561/787–8002 for a guided tour.)*

Although seldom included on tourist itineraries in the past, Kassel turns out to be one of the unexpectedly delightful cities of western Germany, full of contrasts and surprises. Much of its center was destroyed in World War II, and Kassel subsequently became the first German city to construct a traffic-free pedestrian downtown. The city has an unusually spacious and airy feel, due in large part to the expansive parks and gardens along the banks of the Fulda River. Today it is a major cultural center, with a vibrant theater and an internationally known art festival, Dokumenta, held once every five years, and a Gustav Mahler festival, held every two years (both reappear on the Kassel cultural calendar in 1997).

★ Kassel's leading art gallery, the **Staatliche Kunstsammlungen** (State Art Collection), is one of Germany's best. It houses 17 Rembrandts, along with outstanding works by Rubens, Hals, Jordaens, Van Dyck, Dürer, Altdorfer, Cranach, and Baldung Grien. *Schloss Wilhelmshöhe.* ☛ *DM 3 adults, DM 1.50 children (free Sat.).* ⊘ *Tues.–Sun. 10–5.*

The art gallery is in part of the 18th-century **Wilhelmshöhe** Palace, which served as a royal residence from 1807 to 1813, when Jerome was king of Westphalia. Later it became the summer residence of the German emperor Wilhelm II. The great palace stands at the end of the 3-mile-long Wilhelmshöher Allee, an avenue that runs straight as an arrow from one side of the city to the other. Beyond the palace, the Wilhelmshöhe heights are crowned by an astonishing monument, a redstone octagon bearing a giant statue of **Hercules,** built at the beginning of the 18th century. The statue is now closed to the public after being designated a security risk, so it's no longer possible to climb inside it for the best view of Kassel. Nevertheless, from the base of the statue you have a very fine outlook over the entire city, spread out over the plain below and bisected by the straight line of the Wilhelmshöher Allee. But that's only for starters: At 2 PM on Sunday and Wednesday from mid-May through September, water gushes from a fountain beneath the Hercules statue, rushes down a series of cascades to the foot of the hill, and ends its precipitous journey on a 175-foot-high jet of water. It's a natural phenomenon, with no pumps. It takes so long to accumulate enough water that the sight can be experienced only on those two days, on holidays, and, during the summer, on the first Saturday of each month, when the cascades are also floodlit. Bus 1 runs from the city to the Wilhelmshöhe. Bus 23 climbs the heights to the octagon and the Hercules statue. A café lies a short walk from the statue, and there are several restaurants in the area.

The Wilhelmshöhe was laid out as a Baroque park, its elegant lawns separating the city from the thick woods of the Habichtswald (Hawk Forest). It comes as something of a surprise to see the turrets of a romantic medieval castle, the **Löwenburg** (Lion Fortress), breaking the harmony. There are more surprises, for this is no true medieval castle but a fanciful, stylized copy of a Scottish castle, built 70 years after the Hercules statue that towers above it. The architect was a Kassel ruler who displayed an early touch of the mania later seen in the castle-building excesses of Bavaria's eccentric Ludwig II. The Löwenburg contains a collection of medieval armor and weapons, tapestries, and furniture. ☛ *DM 4 adults, DM 2 children; includes guided tour.* ⊘ *Mar.–Oct., Tues.–Sun. 10–5; Nov.–Apr., Tues.–Sun. 10–4.*

One other museum has to be included in this tour of Kassel. It's the **Deutsches Tapeten Museum,** the world's most comprehensive museum of tapestry, with more than 600 exhibits tracing the history of the art through the centuries. *Brüder-Grimm-Pl. 5.* ☛ *DM 4 adults, DM 2 children.* ⊙ *Tues.–Sun. 10–5.*

★ ❽ Leaving Kassel, follow B–3 16 kilometers (10 miles) north to **Münden;** its official name is Hannoversch-Münden, but it is usually referred to by the contraction. This town shouldn't be missed if you're visiting the region. Back in the 18th century the German scientist and explorer Alexander von Humboldt included Münden in his short list of the world's most beautiful towns (Passau, in eastern Bavaria, was another choice). You just may agree with him when you get here.

A 650-year-old bridge crosses the Weser River to lead into this old walled settlement that appears untouched by recent history—frozen in the dim and distant past, you might think. You'll have to travel a long way through Germany to find a grouping of half-timbered houses as harmonious as those in this beautiful old town, surrounded by forests and the Fulda and Werra rivers, which join and flow as the Weser River to Bremen and the North Sea.

Take your camera with you on a stroll down Langenstrasse; No. 34 is where the famous Dr. Eisenbarth died in November 1727. The extraordinary doctor won a place for himself in German folk history as a result of his success both as a physician and as a marketplace orator; a quack who delivered what he promised! A dramatization of his life is presented in the summer in front of the medieval Rathaus. (Contact the Verkehrsbüro Naturpark Münden, ☎ 05541/75313, for details.)

❾ From Münden you'll have the choice of following the Fairy-Tale Road northward along the Weser River or making a short detour to another of the cities so closely associated with the brothers Grimm: **Göttingen,** where they served as professors and librarians at the ancient university from 1830 to 1837.

The university appears to dominate every aspect of life in Göttingen, and there's scarcely a house more than a century old that doesn't bear a plaque linking it with a famous person who once studied or taught here. In one of the towers of the city's old defense wall, Otto von Bismarck, the "Iron Chancellor" and founder of the 19th-century German Empire, pored over his books as a 17-year-old law student. It looks like a romantic student's den now (the tower is open to visitors), but Bismarck was a reluctant tenant—he was banned from living within the city center because of "riotous behavior" and his fondness for wine. The taverns where Bismarck and his cronies drank are still there, all of them associated with Göttingen luminaries. Even the defiantly 20th-century Irish Pub has established itself within the half-timbered walls of a historic old house that once belonged to an 18th-century professor.

The strong link between the students and their university city is symbolized by a statue in the central market square. There stands the **Gänseliesel,** the little Goose Girl of German folklore, carrying her geese and smiling shyly into the waters of a fountain. Above her pretty head is a charming wrought-iron *Jugendstil* (Art Nouveau) bower of entwined vines. The students of Göttingen contributed money toward the erection of the bronze statue and fountain in 1901, and they have given it a central role in a custom that has grown up around the university: Graduates who earn a doctorate traditionally give Gänseliesel a kiss of thanks. Göttingen says she's the most kissed girl in the world. There was a time, however, when the city fathers were none too pleased with this licentious boast, and in 1926 they banned the tradition. A student challenged the ban before a Berlin court but lost the case. Officially the ban still stands, although neither the city council nor the university takes any notice of it.

Directly behind the Gänseliesel is the Rathaus. It was begun during the 13th century but never completely finished. The result is the part-medieval, part-Renaissance building you see today. The bronze lion's-head knocker on the main door dates from early in the 13th century and is the oldest of its type in Germany. Step through the door, and in the lobby striking murals tell the city's story. The medieval council chamber served for centuries as the center of civic life. Within its painted walls and beneath its heavily beamed ceiling, the council met, courts sat in judgment, visiting dignitaries were officially received, receptions and festivities were held, and traveling theater groups performed.

In the streets around the town hall you'll find magnificent examples of Renaissance architecture. Many of these half-timbered, low-gabled buildings house businesses that have been there for centuries. The **Ratsapotheke** (pharmacy) across from the town hall is one; medicines have been doled out there since 1322.

A short stroll up the street on your left, Weenderstrasse, will bring you to the most appealing shop front you're likely to find in all Germany: the 16th-century Schrödersches Haus. On the way you'll pass the ancient student tavern Zum Szültenbürger. Another tavern, Zum Altdeutschen, is around the corner on Prinzenstrasse (the street is named after three English princes, sons of King George III, who lived in a house here during their studies in Göttingen from 1786 to 1791). Don't be shy about stepping into either of these taverns, or any of the others that catch your eye: The food and drink are inexpensive, and the welcome invariably warm and friendly.

Back in Weenderstrasse, take note of the Sparkasse bank building. It was once the Hotel zur Krone, where King George V of Hannover had his headquarters in June 1866 before setting off for the fateful battle of Langensalza, where he lost his kingdom to Bismarck's warrior-state of Prussia, soon to preside aggressively over the newly united Germany.

Behind Weenderstrasse, on Ritterplan, is Göttingen's only noble home, a 16th-century palace that is now the **Städtisches Museum** (City Museum). It has an instructive exhibition charting the architectural styles you'll come across in this part of Germany, as well as a valuable collection of antique toys and a reconstructed apothecary's shop. *Ritterplan 7–8.* ☛ *DM 3 adults, DM 1 children.* ☉ *Tues.–Fri. 10–5, weekends 10–1.*

Not far from the city, near Gleichen, outdoor performances of Grimm fairy tales are presented on a woodland stage at Bremke on certain summer weekends. Check with the local tourist office for dates.

To pick up the Fairy-Tale Road where it joins the scenic Weser Valley Road, return to Münden and head north on B–64. This is a beautiful drive. However, you do need your own car because there are no buses that connect Münden with Hameln and the train takes another route from the one described below. Ten kilometers (6 miles) north of Münden in the village of Veckerhagen, take a left turn to the signposted ★ ⑩ **Sababurg.** You're now on the road to Dornröschen's, or Sleeping Beauty's castle. It stands just as the Grimm fairy tale tells us it did, in the depths of the densely wooded Reinhardswald, still inhabited by deer and wild boar. Sababurg was built as a 14th-century fortress by the archbishop of Mainz to protect a nearby pilgrimage chapel. Later it was destroyed and then rebuilt as a turreted hunting lodge for the counts of Hessen. Today it is a fairly luxurious hotel. Even if you don't stay the night, a drive to the castle (it has an excellent restaurant) will be a highlight of any stay in this region.

From the castle, follow another road back to the Weser Valley riverside village of Oberweser. Turn left and take B–80 north. This is one of Germany's most haunting river roads, where the fast-flowing Weser snakes between green banks that hardly show where land ends and water begins. After about 13 kilometers (8 miles), you'll come to the Weser harbor town and spa of **Bad Karlshafen.** From its inland harbor German troops of the state of Waldeck embarked to join the English Hannoverian forces in the American War of Independence. George III, the English king who presided over the loss of the American colonies, was a Hannoverian—his grandfather, George I, spoke only German when he became king of England in 1715—and although George III sent no Hannoverian forces to America, several neighboring German states did. Flat barges took the troops down the Weser to Bremen, where they were shipped across the North Sea for the long voyage west. Many American families can trace their heritage to this small spa and the surrounding countryside.

Viewed from one of the benches overlooking the harbor, there's scarcely a building that's not in the imposing Baroque style. The grand Rathaus behind you is the best example. Bad Karlshafen stands out in solitary splendor amid its neighboring Weser Valley towns, whose half-timbered architecture has given rise to the expression "Weser Renaissance." You'll see examples of that style wherever you travel in this area, from Münden to Hameln (where it reaches a spectacular climax).

The Rathaus at **Höxter,** the next stop on the road north, is a picture-postcard-pretty example of the Weser Renaissance style, combining three half-timbered stories with a romantically crooked tower.

Across the river from Höxter lies **Reichsabtei Corvey** (the Imperial Abbey of Corvey), optimistically described by some as the "Rome of the North" and idyllically set between the wooded heights of the Solling region and the Weser. The 1,100-year history of the abbey is tightly bound up with the early development of German nationhood. It was chosen as the site of several sessions of the German Imperial Council during the 12th century, and in the 9th-century abbey church you can step into the lodge used by several Holy Roman emperors. The composer of the German national anthem, Hoffmann von Fallersleben, worked for 14 years in the abbey's vast library, where, in the 16th century, the first six volumes of the annals of the Roman historian Tacitus were discovered. ☛ *DM 4 adults, DM 2 children.* ☉ *Apr.–Oct., daily 9–6.*

Follow the Weser River north another 33 kilometers (20 miles) and you'll reach a town that plays a central role in German popular literature, **Bodenwerder,** the birthplace of the Lügenbaron ("Lying Baron") von Münchhausen. Münchhausen used to entertain friends with a pipe of rich Bremen tobacco, a glass of good wine, and stories of his exploits as a captain in wars against the Turks and the Russians. They were preposterous, unbelievable stories that one of his friends, on the run from the German authorities, had published in England. From England they found their way back to Germany, and the baron became a laughingstock—as well as a famous figure in German literary history. The imposing family home in which he grew up is now the Rathaus; one room has been turned into the **Münchhausen Museum,** crammed with mementos of the baron's adventurous life. Included is a cannonball on which the baron claimed to have ridden into orbit during the Russo-Turkish War of 1736, flying around Earth to reach the moon, or so he insisted. In front of the house you'll see a statue of Münchhausen in a scene from one of his most outlandish stories. He's riding half a horse; the other half, said Münchhausen, was chopped off by a castle portcullis, but he rode on without noticing the accident.

★ ⑮ It's back to the Grimm trail that we return now, to **Hameln** (or Hamelin, to give the city its English name), the German town of Pied Piper fame. The story of the Pied Piper of Hameln had its origins in an actual event. During the 13th century an inordinate number of young men in Hameln were being conscripted to fight in an unpopular war in Bohemia and Moravia, so that citizens became convinced that they were being spirited away by the Devil playing his flute. In later stories the Devil was changed to a gaudily attired rat catcher who rid the town of rodents by playing seductive melodies on his flute so that the rodents followed him willingly, waltzing their way right into the Weser. However, when the town defaulted on its contract with the piper and refused to pay up, the Piper settled the score by playing his merry tune to lead Hameln's children on the same route he had taken the rats. As the children reached the river, the Grimms wrote, "they disappeared forever."

This tale is included in the Grimms' other book, *German Legends*. A variation of the story appears on the plaque of a 17th-century house at 28 Osterstrasse, fixing the date of the event as June 26, 1284. In more recent times, the Pied Piper tale has been immortalized via an ultramodern sculpture group set above a reflecting pool in a pedestrian area of town. Today you'll find Hameln tied to its Pied Piper myth every bit as much, say, as the little Bavarian village of Oberammergau is dominated by its Passion Play. There are even rat-shape pastries in the windows of Hameln's bakeries. The house that bears the Pied Piper plaque—a brilliant example of Weser Renaissance—is known as the Rattenfängerhaus, the rat catcher's house, despite the fact that it was built some time after the sorry story is said to have occurred. To this day, no music is played and no revelry of any kind takes place in the street that runs beside the house, the street along which the children of Hameln are said to have followed the Piper.

The Rattenfängerhaus (now a restaurant) is one of several beautiful half-timbered houses on the central Osterstrasse. At one end is the Hochzeitshaus (Wedding House), occupied by city government offices. Every Sunday from mid-May to mid-September the story of the Pied Piper is played out at noon by actors and children of the town on the terrace in front of the building. The half-hour performance is free: Get there early to ensure a good place. The carillon of the Hochzeitshaus plays a "Pied Piper song" every day at 8:35 and 11:05, and mechanical figures enacting the story appear on the west gable of the building at 1:05, 3:35, and 5:35.

TIME OUT Just up the street is the historic old hostelry **Zur Krone** (Osterstr. 30, ☏ 05151/9070). If it's a sunny day, take a seat on the terrace in front of the hotel's half-timbered facade. If it's cool, there's a warm welcome inside. In the evening, in the middle of Old Town, the popular wood-beamed watering hole is **Die Alte Post** (Hummlstr. 23, ☏ 05151/43444), where beer flows freely and baguette sandwiches are served.

Tour 2: Hannover and Bremen

The influences that shaped the lives and work of the Grimm brothers weaken north of Hameln, but the Fairy-Tale Road continues as far as Bremen. A detour off the route, following the B-217 46 kilometers (27 miles) northeast from Hameln, is **Hannover.** It's a city of commerce and culture, Germany's major trade-fair center, and an exemplary patron of the arts, with leading museums, an opera house of international repute, and the finest Baroque park in the country. From 1714 until 1837 rulers of the House of Hannover also sat on the British throne, as kings George I–V. King George III presided over the loss of the American Revolutionary War, and reminders of that period are to be found in several Hannover museums. Today there are many more cities and towns named Hanover in the United States than in Germany—63 of them, all spelled English style (one *n*) but nonetheless mostly tracing their roots to the German mother city. It's said that the purist German is spoken in Hannover, although no objective reason for this can be found.

Bomb damage to Hannover in World War II was so devastating that a proposal to level the ruins and build a new city was seriously considered. The plan was mercifully never adopted, and Hannover arose to become, once again, a city of beauty and grace. Successive city administrations encouraged a mix of old and modern, so you'll find startling sculptural works vying for attention with stately rows of half-timbered houses (Burgstrasse, with its steel, wind-driven kinetic sculpture, is an example).

The tourist office has made things easy for the visitor by painting a red trail through the city that takes in all the major attractions. We'll follow only part of the route in our tour, beginning just south of the main railway station, at the **Opernhaus,** which ranks as one of Germany's most beautiful 19th-century classical theaters; it was built in 1845–52 as a royal opera house and is still the setting of some truly regal productions.

Cross Opernplatz and join Hannover's pedestrian precinct at Georgstrasse, pausing at the central square named Kröpcke to admire the ornate clock that has become the city's most famous meeting point. From Kröpcke, turn left onto Grosse Packhofstrasse and stay on its continuation, Seilwinderstrasse, to reach the central market square, dominated by the Gothic **Marktkirche St. Georg und St. Jacobus** (market church of Sts. George and James). It has a splendid Gothic carved altar and fine stained glass. Next to the church is Hannover's first city hall, the **Altes Rathaus,** dating from the 14th century and a notable example of Hannoverian brick architecture.

A short walk down Bohlendamm takes you to the former Hannoverian royal palace, the **Leineschloss,** standing above the River Leine and now the seat of the Lower Saxony State Parliament. Call the tourist office (☎ 0511/301–410) if you'd like to visit. On the other side of the road, facing Leinstrasse, is a smaller palace where King George V lived from 1851 to 1862. Next door is the vast bulk of the new **Rathaus,** built at the start of the century in Wilhelmine style at a time when pomp and circumstance were important ingredients of heavy German bureaucracy.

On the edge of the park that now stretches out before you are two interesting museums. The **Niedersächsisches Landesmuseum** has some priceless early art, including work by Tilman Riemenschneider, Veit Stoss,

Hans Holbein the Younger, and Lucas Cranach. The **Sprengel Museum** has one of Germany's leading collections of modern art, with important works by Max Beckmann, Max Ernst, Paul Klee, Emil Nolde, and Pablo Picasso. *Niedersächsisches Landesmuseum, Am Maschpark 5,* ☎ *0511/98075. Admission Free.* ⏰ *Tues.–Sun. 10–5, Thurs. 10–7. Sprengel Museum, Kurt-Schwitters-Platz,* ☎ *0511/168–3875.* ☛ *Free.* ⏰ *Tues., 10–10, Weds.–Sun., 10–6.*

End your city tour by relaxing now on the shores of Hannover's inland lake, the Maschsee. In summer you can swim in its warm waters or hire a sailboat.

The Strandbad café, on the edge of the lake at Karl-Thiele-Weg 28, is just the place for a reviving cup of coffee or something more substantial. For more impressive surroundings, try the restaurant in the casino on the north shore. It can be counted on for lunch, afternoon coffee, or dinner.

★ Hannover's showpiece—the gardens of the former royal summer residence at **Herrenhausen**—is outside the city center, a short ride on Tramline 5 or 16. The magnificent palace built there in the late 17th century by the Hannoverian ruler Herzog Johann Friedrich was ruined in wartime bombing and never rebuilt. But the Baroque park—unmatchable in Germany—was restored in all its formal precision, with the geometric pattern of walks, gardens, and copses framed by a placid moat. From Easter until October fountains play for a few hours daily and add their own element of Baroque grace (weekdays 11–noon and 3–4, weekends 10–noon and 3–5). An 18th-century residence at the edge of the park is now a museum, the **Fürstenhaus Herrenhausen-Museum,** affording fascinating insight into the Hannoverian court life and its links with England. ⏰ *Herrenhausen Park daily 8–4:30.* ☛ *Free. Fürstenhaus Herrenhausen-Museum, Alte Herrenhäuser Str. 14,* ☎ *0511/750–947.* ☛ *DM 3.50 adults, DM 2.50 children.* ⏰ *Tues.–Sun. 10–5.*

⓱ The great seaport of **Bremen** is on A–27 or B–6, 110 kilometers (66 miles), from Hannover. Bremen is Germany's oldest and second-largest port—only Hamburg is bigger—and it has close historical seafaring ties with North America. Together with Lübeck and Hamburg, Bremen was an early member of the Hanseatic League, and its rivalry with the larger port on the Elbe is still tangible. Though Hamburg may still claim its historical title as Germany's "door to the world," Bremen likes to boast: "But we have the key."

Forty-eight kilometers (30 miles) upriver, at **Bremerhaven,** is the country's largest and most fascinating maritime museum, the **Deutsches Schiffahrtsmuseum,** with a harbor containing seven genuine old trading ships. *Von-Renzelen-Str.,* ☎ *0471/482–070.* ☛ *DM 5 adults, DM 2.50 children.* ⏰ *Tues.–Sun. 10–6.*

Bremen is also central to the delightful fable of the Bremer Stadtmusikanten, or Bremen Town Musicians, a rooster, cat, dog, and donkey quartet that came to Bremen to seek its fortune. You'll find statues of this group in various parts of the city, the most famous being a handsome bronze of the four, one perched on the back of another, to form a pyramid of sorts. This statue stands alongside the northwest corner of the Rathaus on one of Europe's most impressive market squares, bordered by the Rathaus, the imposing 900-year-old Gothic cathedral (St. Petri Dom), a 16th-century guild hall, and a modern glass-and-steel state parliament building, with a high wall of gabled town houses as backdrop. On the square stands the famous stone statue of the knight

Roland, erected in 1400. Three times larger than life, the statue serves as Bremen's shrine, good-luck piece, and symbol of freedom and independence.

Charlemagne established a diocese here during the 9th century, and a 15th-century statue of him, together with seven princes, adorns the ancient **Rathaus**, a Gothic building that acquired a Renaissance facade during the early 17th century. The two styles combine harmoniously in the magnificent, beamed banquet hall, where painted scenes from Bremen's 1,200-year history are complemented by model galleons and sailing ships that hang from the ceiling in vivid recollection of the place such vessels have in the story of the seafaring city. In its massive vaulted cellars is further evidence of the riches accumulated by Bremen in its busiest years: barrels of fine, 17th-century Rhine wine.

Other bounty from farther afield formed the foundation of one of the city's many fascinating museums, the **Übersee Museum,** a unique collection of items tracing the histories and cultures of the many peoples with whom the Bremen traders came into contact. One section is devoted to North America. *Bahnhofspl. 13,* ☎ *0421/361–9203.* ☛ *DM 4 adults, DM 1 children.* ۞ *Tues.–Sun. 10–6.*

Don't leave Bremen without strolling down Böttcherstrasse, at one time inhabited by coopers, or barrel makers. Between 1924 and 1931, their houses were torn down and reconstructed in a style that was at once historically sensitive and modern by a Bremen coffee millionaire, Ludwig Roselius. (He was the inventor of decaffeinated coffee and held the patent for many years; Sanka was its brand name in the United States.) Many of the restored houses are used as galleries for local artists; at one end of the street is the **Roselius-Haus,** a 14th-century building and now a museum showcasing German and Dutch painting, as well as wood carving, furniture, textiles, and numerous examples of decorative arts from the 12th through the 18th century. Notice also the arch of Meissen bells at the rooftop. These chime daily at noon, 3, and 6. *Böttcherstr. 8–10,* ☎ *0421/336–5077.* ☛ *DM 8 adults, DM 4 children.* ۞ *Tues.–Sun. 11–5.*

Walk, too, through the idyllic Schnoorviertel, a jumble of houses, taverns, and shops once occupied or frequented by fishermen and tradespeople. This is Bremen's oldest district, dating back to the 15th and 16th century. Over the last decade, the area has become quite fashionable among artists and craftsmen who have restored the tiny one-up-one-down cottages to serve as galleries and workshops. Other buildings have been converted into small cafés and pubs that attract locals and visitors alike.

What to See and Do with Children

There is a fine **zoo** in Bremerhaven (open daily 8 until sunset) and a smaller one at Ziegenhagen (on the A–7 Autobahn between Göttingen and Kassel). The Ziegenhagen Zoo is part of a large theme park that includes rides, an automobile and motorbike museum, a restaurant and cafés, and picnic-grill areas. It's open March through October. There's a similar zoo and theme park just outside Steinau an der Strasse (take the Marjass road and follow the signs). A summer bob-sled run and water chute were added in 1995, vying with the "Luna-Loop" and "Steinau Express" rides for thrills. The park is open April through October, daily 9–6.

SHOPPING

Grimm-related souvenirs are to be found everywhere in this region, ranging from the cheap and vulgar to finely designed porcelain figures. Among the most popular gift ideas are bound editions of the Grimm brothers' fairy tales. The incredible tales of Baron Münchhausen make equally popular buys.

Kassel, Fulda, Göttingen, and Hameln all have attractive central pedestrian areas where it's a pleasure to shop for all manner of gift items. In Bremen bargain-hunters should head to the idyllic Schnoorvier. Bremerhaven has one of Germany's oldest established shoemakers, **Leder-Koopmann** (Georgstr. 56, ☎ 0471/302–829), where you can buy first-class footwear and all kinds of leather goods made with the kind of care that has kept the firm in business since 1898.

Germany's oldest **porcelain** factory is at Fürstenberg, high above the Weser River, halfway between Kassel and Hameln. The crowned gothic letter *F* that serves as its trademark is world-famous. You'll find Fürstenberg porcelain in shops throughout the area, and in such towns as Bad Karlshafen and Höxter. By far the most satisfying way of starting a Fürstenberg collection, or adding to it, is to make the journey up to the 18th-century castle, where production first began in 1747, and buy directly from the manufacturer. Fürstenberg and most dealers will take care of shipping arrangements and any tax refunds. *Factory and showrooms open Tues.–Sat. 9–5, Sun. 10–5.*

A good selection of **garden gnomes** featuring Grimm fairy-tale characters is available at the Heissner Shops (Schlitzerstr. 24 and Schubertstr. 14, ☎ 06641/860 for both) in Lauterbach.

If you're interested in buying **regional costumes,** such as Hessen *Trachten* dresses, try Berdux (Hirschberg 1, ☎ 06691/23029) in Schwalmstadt, just north of Alsfeld.

There are some excellent small, privately run **potteries** and **glassworks** in the area. In Bad Karlshafen you can watch the craftspeople at work in a studio in the Baroque Rathaus and buy goods directly from them. In the village of Immenhausen, just north of Kassel, you can visit a local glass foundry (the **Glashütte Süssmuth Am Bahnhof** 3, ☎ 05673/2060) and watch glassblowers create fine works that are also for sale (shop hours: weekdays 9–5, Sat. 9–1). The very finest, however, find their way into a neighboring museum (open weekdays 9–5, Sat. 9–1, Sun. 10–5), where you'll get fascinating insight into the glassblower's craft.

Steinau an der Strasse was for centuries a renowned pottery center, and in the mid-1880s, 40 potters were at work in the small town. Today there's only one, **Hans Krüger,** but he's turning out the kind of work that made Steinau so famous (Hans Krüger Kunsttöpferei, Ringstr. 52, ☎ 06663/6413).

Hannover has what it claims to be Germany's oldest flea market—certainly one of the largest and most interesting. It's held every Saturday on the banks of the River Leine (Am Hohen Ufer) from 7 to 4. The colorful sculptures by Niki de St. Phalle you'll see on the opposite bank (Am Leibnitzufer) are not for sale—they were commissioned by the city, which then had to prevent them from being added to the flea-market junk. Artistic standards prevailed, and the Niki de St. Phalle sculptures (huge maternal "Nanas") are now an indispensable part of the city landscape.

SPORTS AND FITNESS

Bicycling

Bicycles can be rented from most railway stations for DM 10 a day (DM 6 with a valid ticket) and from many tourist offices. The two Weser River excursion companies (*see* Guided Tours *in* Fairy-Tale Road Essentials, *below*) take bikes aboard their boats and recommend routes that combine riverside cycle tours and boat trips. In summer the Oberweser-Dampfschiffahrt Company offers Sunday excursions that include a guided tour of Hameln, lunch in an old tavern, a cycle trip down the Weser riverbank to Bodenwerder and a boat ride back—all for DM 55 (including bike rental). Call for details and reservations (☎ 05151/22016).

Golf

There are golf courses at Bad Orb, Bad Pyrmont, Bremen, Fulda, Göttingen, Hanau, Kassel, and Polle-Holzminden; guests are welcome at all locations. The courses at Hanau (on the former hunting grounds at Wilhelmsbad) and Kassel (high above the city on the edge of Wilhelmshöhe Park) are particularly attractive. At Schloss Schwöbber, near Hameln, golfers tee off on the extensive castle grounds (☎ 05154/9870).

Hiking

The hills and forests between Hanau and Hameln are a hiker's paradise. The valleys of the Fulda, Werra, and Weser rivers make enchanting walking country, with ancient waterside inns positioned along the way. Local tourist information offices of the area have established a hiking route from Münden in the south to Porta-Westfalica, where the Weser River breaks through the last range of north German hills and into the lower Saxony Plain. Contact **Fremdenverkehrsverband Weserbergland-Mittelweser** (D–31785 Hameln, ☎ 05151/202–517) for information.

Horseback Riding

This part of Germany is horse country, and most resorts have riding stables. There are large and well-equipped equestrian centers at Löwensen, near Bad Pyrmont (☎ 05281/10606) and Hameln (☎ 05151/3513). Stables at Otterberg, near Bremen, also have horses for rent. Katrin Graf's "Circle K ranch" at Steinau-Marborn (☎ 06663/5321) rents horses trained to be ridden western-style.

Tennis

Tennis courts are found in abundance all along the route. In Bremen the Squash-Tennis-Center (Duckwitzstr. 47, ☎ 0421/51626) is *the* place to play.

Water Sports

Great canoeing can be enjoyed on both the Fulda and Weser rivers (☎ 0561/22433 for information on Fulda River trips and canoe rental). **Busch Bootstouristik** (D–34399 Oberweser, ☎ 05574/818) rents canoes from April through October on the Fulda, Weser, and Werra and organizes trips of up to a week on all three rivers. Motorboats can be rented from **Weisse Flotte Warnecke** (☎ 05533/4864) in Bodenwerder.

DINING AND LODGING

Dining

If you are in the western area of the region, try Westphalian ham, famous for more than 2,000 years. The hams can weigh as much as 33 pounds and are considered particularly good for breakfast, when a huge slice is served on a wood board with rich, dark pumpernickel bread baked for about 20 hours. If you're keen to do as the locals do, you'll wash it down with a glass of strong, clear Steinhäger schnapps. A favorite main course is *Pfefferpothast*, a sort of heavily browned goulash with lots of pepper. The "hast" at the end of the name is from the old German word *Harst,* meaning "roasting pan." Rivers and streams filled with trout and eels are common around Hameln. Göttinger *Speckkuchen* is a heavy and filling onion tart. In Bremen, *Aalsuppe grün,* eel soup seasoned with dozens of herbs, is a must in summer.

RATINGS

CATEGORY	COST*
$$$$	over DM 90
$$$	DM 55–DM 90
$$	DM 35–DM 55
$	under DM 35

*per person for a three-course meal, including tax and excluding drinks and service charge

Lodging

Make reservations well in advance if you plan to visit during the summer. Though it's one of the less-traveled tourist routes in Germany, the main points of the Fairy-Tale Road are popular. Accommodations cover the spectrum from modern high rises to ancient and crooked half-timbered buildings.

RATINGS

CATEGORY	COST*
$$$$	over DM 250
$$$	DM 175–DM 250
$$	DM 125–DM 175
$	under DM 125

*All prices are for two people in a double room, excluding service charges.

Bad Karlshafen

DINING

Gaststätte-Hotel Weserdampfschiff. You can step right from the deck of a Weser pleasure boat into the welcoming garden of this popular hotel-tavern. Fish from the river land straight in the tavern's frying pan. There are 13 cozy rooms, most of which have river views. ✕ *Weserstr. 25, ☎ 05672/2425. Reservations not necessary. No credit cards. Closed Mon. $*

LODGING

Hessicher Hof. Located in the heart of town, the inn started as a tavern for the locals. There's still a bar, but the building has been extended and renovated, with the addition of several comfortably furnished bedrooms, all of them with showers. A few also have a small balcony. The restaurant serves good, hearty fare. Breakfast is included in the room price, or you may request half-pension. ☒ *Carlstr. 13–15, ☎ 05672/1059, FAX 05672/2515. 18 rooms with bath or shower. Restaurant, bar. AE, MC, V. $*

Bevern

DINING

★ **Schloss Bevern.** You'll dine like a baron here, within the honey-color old walls of Bevern's Renaissance castle. In the enchanting inner courtyard, a solitary dome-top, half-timbered tower stands sentinel over a 17th-century fountain. This romantic mood carries into the stylish restaurant, where you'll dine on such traditional country dishes as roast pheasant or partridge at tables with glistening silverware and finely cut glassware. ✕ *Am Schoss,* ☎ *05531/8783. Reservations essential. AE, DC, MC, V. Closed Mon., Tues. lunch. $$$*

Enzianhütte. The Weser River winds lazily below this terraced restaurant. If it's too chilly to sit outside, there's a cozy room with an open fireplace. Some traditional dishes are cooked on the grill over the fire. ✕ *Am Ochsenbrink 2,* ☎ *05535/8710. Reservations advised. AE, DC, MC. Closed Wed. $$*

Bodenwerder

LODGING

Hotel Deutsches Haus. The fine half-timbered facade of this solidly comfortable country hotel vies for attention with the nearby former home of Baron Münchhausen, now Bodenwerder's town hall. There's a lot of wood inside, too, with original beams and oak paneling adding to the rural feel of the place. The town park is outside the front door, and the Weser River is a short walk away. ☏ *Münchhausenpl. 4,* ☎ *05533/3925,* FAX *05533/4113. 40 rooms with bath or shower. Restaurant, bowling, recreation room. Closed Jan. AE, MC, V. $–$$*

Bremen

DINING

★ **Park Restaurant.** Chef Bernhard Stumpf, formerly of the renowned Restaurant Français in Frankfurt, has transformed the Park into one of the finest dining establishments in Germany. Located in the Park Hotel Bremen (*see* Lodging, *below*), it is somewhat small for a hotel restaurant, but the floor-to-ceiling windows and lacquered ceiling open up the room. Stunning in yellow, black, and cream, the dining room is decorated with shimmering crystal chandeliers, classical molding, marble urns, and Louis XVI chairs, all of which add to the sense of occasion. Chef Stumpf adds a dash of fantasy to his classic French dishes, which may include broccoli flan with autumn vegetables atop a pinenut and celery sauce, sautéed fillet of beef with ox-marrow ragout, and cottage-cheese soufflé in fig-honey sauce. ✕ *Im Bürgerpark,* ☎ *0421/34080. Reservations required. Jacket and tie. AE, DC, MC, V. $$$$*

Comturai. The vaults of Bremen's ancient Church of the Holy Spirit (Heiliggeistkirche) were secularized some time ago, becoming a beer cellar and restaurant where the cuisine is devilishly good if not exactly heavenly. Special medieval banquet menus are served to groups of more than 10, but there's often a place for a lone diner—and it's a great way to meet the locals. ✕ *Ostertorstr. 30-32,* ☎ *0421/325050. Reservations advised. AE, MC, V. $$*

★ **Grashoff's Bistro.** Locals say this is Bremen's number-one lunch-time bistro. You dine French style, at closely packed tables in a room whose walls are smothered in interesting old prints and photographs. The menu also has a French touch, with an accent on fish fresh from Bremen's market. ✕ *Contrescarpe 80,* ☎ *0421/14740. Reservations advised. DC, V. Closed Sun. and weekday evenings. $$*

★ **Ratskeller.** Said to be Germany's oldest and most renowned Ratskeller restaurant, this one specializes in solid, typical northern German fare, including the finest poultry and the freshest seafood, prepared in ingenious ways. However, it's no place for beer drinkers. Shortly after the restaurant opened in 1408, the city fathers decreed that only wine could be served there, and the ban on beer still exists. You'll dine in a cellar lined with wine casks, including an 18th-century barrel that could house a family of wine drinkers. Connoisseurs have 600 labels from which to choose. ✕ *Am Markt,* ☎ *0421/321–676. Reservations advised. AE, DC, MC, V. $$*

LODGING

★ **Park Hotel Bremen.** The service doesn't get any more gracious than at this grand hotel by a lake in the 800-acre Bürgerpark, close by the main train station. Aside from the impressive central dome, the architecture—'50s international style—is banal. What does shine is the ever-accommodating staff, who'll be glad to provide you with suitable jogging clothes for the 15-minute run to the historic center, or arrange a complimentary limousine into town if you'd rather have a ride. No one would blame you, however, if you wanted to stay put in such luxurious digs. The guest rooms differ radically in decor—Moorish, Japanese, and Italian Modern are just some of the themes (a Roman-style Pompeian suite has just been added)—and the bathrooms are lined with 12 different kinds of marble. The rooms in the wing, added in the '70s, are not as large as those in the main building. ☎ *Im Bürgerpark,* ☎ *0421/34080 or 800/223–6800 for reservations in U.S.,* FAX *0421/3408–602. 138 rooms with bath, 13 suites. 2 restaurants, bar, café, beauty salon, massage, bicycles. AE, DC, MC, V. $$$$*

Mercure Columbus. Elegantly renovated and now under French management with the Accor group, this hotel is conveniently adjacent to the train station and only a short stroll from the old-town attractions. An elegant restaurant was recently opened. The decor is modern and many of the rooms are spacious. ☎ *Bahnhofplatz 5–7,* ☎ *0421/30120,* FAX *0421/15369. 143 rooms and 5 suites. Restaurant, bar, sauna. AE, DC, MC, V. $$$–$$$$*

★ **Hotel Landhaus Louisenthal.** American visitors particularly like this family-run, half-timbered country-house hotel on the outskirts of Bremen—30% of its guests are from the United States. The 150-year-old building has Old World charm and a caring management. Bathrooms were recently renovated and are an additional touch of luxury. ☎ *Leher Heerstr. 105,* ☎ *0421/232–076,* FAX *0421/236–716. 58 rooms and 2 apartments, all with bath or shower. Restaurant, sauna. AE, DC, MC, V. $$–$$$*

Fulda

DINING

Zum Stiftskämmerer. This former episcopal treasurer's home is now a charming tavern-restaurant, its menu packed with local fare prepared with imagination and flair. A four-course menu priced at around DM 60 is an excellent value, although à la carte dishes can be ordered for as little as DM 12. Try the *Schlemmertöpfchen,* a delicious (and very filling) combination of pork, chicken breast, and venison steak. ✕ *Kämmerzeller Str. 10,* ☎ *0661/52369. Reservations advised. AE, MC, V. $–$$*

LODGING

Maritim Hotel am Schlossgarten. This is the luxurious showpiece of the Maritim chain, housed in an 18th-century Baroque building overlooking Fulda Palace Park. Chandeliers, oil paintings, and antiques maintain the historic style, which contrasts with the hotel's modern atrium. The historic atmosphere of the grand old building, however, extends to the basement foundations, where you can dine beneath centuries-old vaulted arches in the "Dianakeller" restaurant. Many rooms have fine views overlooking the Fulda Palace Park, but to be sure order one of the two suites, which have spacious terraces. ☎ *Pauluspromenade 2,* ☎ *0661/2820,* FAX *0661/78340. 110 rooms and 2 suites with bath. 2 restaurants, café, bar, indoor pool, sauna, bowling, bicycles. AE, DC, MC, V. $$$$*

★ **Romantik Hotel Goldener Karpfen.** Fulda is famous for its Baroque buildings, and this hotel is a short walk from the finest of them. The hotel, too, dates from the Baroque era but has a later facade. Inside it has been renovated to a high standard of comfort. Afternoon coffee in the comfortable, tapestry-upholstered chairs of the hotel's lounge is one of Fulda's delights, while dining in the elegant restaurant, with its crisp white linen, Persian rugs, and subdued lighting, is another. ☎ *Simpliciusbrunnen. 1,* ☎ *0661/70044,* FAX *0661/73042. 55 rooms with bath or shower. Restaurant, weinstube, sauna, exercise room. AE, DC, MC, V. $$$$*

Zum Kurfürsten. In the heart of the Old Town, this lodging is itself part of Fulda's Baroque face. But behind the venerable facade guests are assured of modern facilities. ☎ *Schlossstr. 2,* ☎ *0661/70001,* FAX *0661/77919. 50 rooms with bath. Restaurant, sauna. AE, DC, MC, V. $$*

Gelnhausen

LODGING

Romantisches Hotel Burg Mühle. *Mühle* means "mill," and this hotel was once the tithe-mill of the neighboring castle, delivering flour to the community until 1948. In the restaurant, the mill wheel churns away as you eat. Special weekend deals include two nights' accommodation and two three-course dinners for DM 195 per person. ☎ *Burgstr. 2,* ☎ *06051/82050,* FAX *06051/820–554. 34 rooms with bath. Restaurant (closed Sun. dinner), sauna, exercise room. DC, MC, V. $$–$$$*

Göttingen

DINING

Historischer Rathskeller. Here you'll dine in the vaulted underground chambers of Göttingen's 15th-century city hall, choosing from a traditional menu with the friendly assistance of chef Jens Bredenbeck. ✕ *Am Markt 9,* ☎ *0551/56433. Reservations advised. AE, DC, MC, V. $$*

★ **Zum Schwarzen Bären.** The "Black Bear" is one of Göttingen's oldest tavern-restaurants, a 16th-century half-timbered house that breathes history and hospitality. The specialty of the house is *Bärenpfanne,* a generous portion of local meats. ✕ *Kurzestr. 12,* ☎ *0551/58284. Reservations advised. AE, DC, MC, V. Closed Mon. and Sun. dinner. $*

LODGING

Gebhards Hotel. Though located just across a busy road from the train station, this hotel stands aloof and unflurried on its own grounds, a sensitively modernized 18th-century building that's something of a local landmark. Guests are mostly visitors to the university, and consequently the majority of the hotel rooms are singles. ☎ *Goethe-Allee 22–23,* ☎ *0551/49680,* FAX *0511/496–8110. 62 rooms with bath or shower. Restaurant, indoor pool, sauna, exercise room. AE, DC, MC, V. $$$$*

Hotel Beckman. The Beckman family runs this pleasant and homey hotel with friendly efficiency. The family takes particular pride in the hotel garden, a quiet and lush retreat in all seasons. The hotel is 5 kilometers (3 miles) out of town, with good bus links to downtown. *Ulrideshuser-Str. 44, Göttingen-Nikolausberg,* ☎ *0551/21055,* FAX *0551/21767. 26 rooms, 18 with bath or shower. Restaurant, café, sauna. AE, DC, MC, V. $–$$*

Hameln

DINING

★ **Rattenfängerhaus.** This is Hameln's most famous building, reputedly the place where the Pied Piper stayed during his rat-removing assignment. Rats are all over the menu, from "Rat-remover cocktail" to a "Rat-tail dessert." But don't be put off: The traditional dishes are excellent, and the restaurant is guaranteed to be rodent-free. ✗ *Osterstr. 28,* ☎ *05151/3888. Reservations advised. AE, DC, MC, V. $–$$*

LODGING

★ **Hotel zur Kröne.** If you fancy a splurge, ask for the split-level suite. With prices starting at DM 380 a night, it's an expensive but delightful luxury. The building dates from 1645 and is a half-timbered marvel. Avoid the modern annex, however; it lacks all charm. ⊡ *Osterstr. 30,* ☎ *05151/9070,* FAX *05151/907–217. 29 rooms, 5 apartments, all with bath or shower. Restaurant. AE, DC, MC, V. $$$–$$$$*

Hotel zur Börse. A long-established, family-run property in the old town, this hotel offers comfortable accommodations and friendly service. Its attractive winter garden is a pleasant retreat. ⊡ *Osterstr. 41 (entrance on Kopmanshof),* ☎ *05151/7080,* FAX *05151/25485. 34 rooms with bath or shower. Restaurant, pub. AE, DC, MC, V. Closed Dec. 25 and Jan. 1. $–$$*

Hanau

LODGING

Brüder Grimm Hotel. Located a few minutes' walk from the Brüder Grimm memorial in Hanau's central market square, the hotel that carries their name has a fairy-tale restaurant on the top floor. Accommodations are modern and comfortable. Try for the "Eckzimmer"; it's the largest and best-decorated room. ⊡ *Kurt-Blaum-Pl. 6,* ☎ *06181/3060,* FAX *06181/306–512. 80 rooms and 15 apartments with bath or shower. Restaurant, hot tub, sauna. AE, DC, MC, V. $$$*

Hannover

DINING

Grapenkieker. An ancient pot steams in the aromatic farmhouse-style kitchen of the half-timbered Grapenkieker, and the hearty hot pots it produces form the basis of the menu. Proprietors Gabriele and Karl-Heinz Wolf are locally famous for their flair in the kitchen and the warm welcome they give their guests. The restaurant is 3 miles from the city center, in the Isernhagen district, but it's well worth seeking out. ✗ *Hauptstr. 56, Isernhagen,* ☎ *05139/88068. Reservations advised. AE, DC, MC.* ☾ *Tues.–Sat. evenings only. $–$$*

LODGING

Hotel Benther Berg. This large country house hotel-cum-modern extension sits amid parkland and woods on the southern edge of Hannover, in the Ronneberg-Benthe district. Rooms are large and furnished mostly in modern dark woods and pastel shades. The restaurant attracts Hannover regulars who value its international cuisine. ⊡ *Vogelsangstr. 18, Ronneberg-Benthe,* ☎ *05108/64060,* FAX *05108/640–650.*

65 rooms, 2 suites with bath. Restaurant, café, indoor pool, sauna. AE, DC, MC, V. $$$–$$$$

Hotel Körner. The modern Körner has a traditional, almost old-fashioned feel about it, probably created by the friendly and personal service. Rooms are comfortably furnished in light veneers and pastel shades. The small courtyard and terrace are ideal for an al fresco summer breakfast. ☎ *Körnerstr. 24–25,* ☎ *0511/16360,* FAX *0511/18048. 75 rooms with bath. Restaurant, indoor pool, exercise room. AE, DC, MC, V. $$–$$$*

Höxter

DINING

★ **Schlossrestaurant Corvey.** Three kilometers (2 miles) south of the charming town of Höxter lies Corvey Abbey, whose attractions include an excellent restaurant. You can dine outside under centuries-old trees in summer and inside before a blazing hearth in winter (although the restaurant is open only on Sundays from November until Easter). The lunchtime menu is a particularly good value. ✕ *Reichsabtei Corvey,* ☎ *05271/8323. Weekend reservations advised. AE, MC. $$*

Kassel

DINING

Die Pfeffermühle. The "Peppermill" is in Kassel's Gude Hotel, but it's no conventional hotel restaurant. The menu is truly international: Indian and Russian dishes share space with traditional German fare. ✕ *Frankfurterstr. 299,* ☎ *0561/48050. Reservations advised. AE, DC, MC, V. Closed Sun. evening. $$*

Ratskeller. Here you'll eat within the embracing surroundings of cellar vaults. Owner-chef Tomislav Mravicici is Croatian, and his Balkan specialties find their way onto the predominantly German menu, which changes daily. ✕ *Obere Konigstr. 8,* ☎ *0561/15928. Reservations advised. AE, DC, MC, V. $*

LODGING

Schlosshotel Wilhelmshöhe. Set in the beautiful Baroque Wilhelmshöhe Park (5 kilometers, or 3 miles) from town, this is no ancient palace but a modern hotel with its own sports center to aid in attracting business seminars. ☎ *Schlosspark 8,* ☎ *0561/30880,* FAX *0561/308–8428. 82 rooms, 1 suite, 4 apartments with bath. Restaurant, café, bar, indoor pool, hot tub, sauna, tennis, golf, exercise room, horseback riding. AE, DC, MC, V. $$$$*

City-Hotel. This new hotel in the city center, just a few minutes from the Rathaus, is sympathetically designed to blend in with its ancient surroundings. Inside, rooms are stylishly decorated and furnished. ☎ *Wilhelmshöher Allee 38,* ☎ *0561/72810,* FAX *0561/728–1199. 65 rooms with bath. Restaurant, café, bar, indoor pool, beauty salon, sauna, therapeutic baths. Closed mid-Dec.–mid-Jan. AE, DC, MC, V. $$$*

Sababurg

LODGING

★ **Dornröschenschloss Sababurg.** A medieval fortress thought to have been the inspiration for the Grimm brothers' tale of *The Sleeping Beauty,* this is now a small luxury hotel snugly set in the castle walls and surrounded by the oaks of the Reinhardswald. Concerts and plays are held on the grounds in summer. The castle was built in 1334, but many of the palatial improvements came during the 17th and 18th centuries. However, it was not until 1960 that it became a hotel. Since that time the Koseck family has been enthusiastically welcoming visitors and showing them the magic of the area. The restaurant serves a fine haunch of venison in the autumn, but the fresh trout with a Riesling-based sauce in the spring is equally satisfying. ☎ *Hofgeismar,* ☎ *05671/8080,* FAX *05671/808–200. 18 rooms with bath. Closed mid-Jan.–mid-Feb. Restaurant. AE, DC, MC, V. $$$*

Steinau

LODGING

Weisses Ross. This may be a simple inn, but you can sleep within its gnarled walls in the knowledge that the Grimm brothers overnighted here almost 200 years ago. Rooms facing the street have views of ancient buildings but suffer a little from traffic noise. ☎ *Brüder-Grimm-str. 48, 6497,* ☎ *06663/5804. 8 rooms, most with bath. Restaurant. No credit cards. $*

Uslar

DINING AND LODGING

★ **Romantik Hotel Menzhausen.** The half-timbered exterior of this 16th-century establishment is matched by the cozy interior of its comfortable, well-appointed restaurant. The 400-year-old wine cellar harbors outstanding vintages, served with reverence at excellent prices. The hotel itself has 41 well-appointed rooms, many with antiques. Ask for one in the historic Mauerschlösschen if you're looking for the romance in Romantik. ☎ *Langestr. 12,* ☎ *05571/2051,* FAX *05571/5820. Restaurant (weekend reservations advised), indoor pool, sauna. AE, DC, MC, V. $$–$$$$*

THE ARTS AND NIGHTLIFE

The Arts

Music

Bremen has a Philharmonic orchestra of national stature. It plays regularly throughout the year at the city's concert hall; call for program details and tickets (☎ 0421/361–2615). In **Fulda,** chamber-music concerts are given regularly from September through May in the chandelier-hung splendor of the bishops' palace (☎ 0661/102–326). **Göttingen's** symphony orchestra presents about 20 concerts a year. In addition, the city has a nationally known boys' choir and an annual Handel music festival in June. Call (☎ 0551/56700) for program details and tickets for all three. **Hannover's** opera company is also nationally known, with productions staged in one of Germany's finest 19th-century classical opera houses. Call (☎ 0511/368–1711) for program details and tickets. In **Kassel,** outdoor concerts are held in Wilhelmshöhe Park on Wednesday, Saturday, and Sunday afternoons from May through September. Classical-music concerts are also given by the city's municipal orchestra in the Stadttheater. Kassel holds a Gustav Mahler festival every two years (the next one is in 1997); call (☎ 0561/10940) for program details of all concerts and tickets.

Theater

Bremen has three theaters that regularly stage classical and modern dramas, comedies, and musical comedies: the Schauspielhaus; the Concordia; and the Musiktheater. Call (☎ 0421/365–3333) for program details and tickets. In **Fulda,** one wing of the magnificent bishops' palace is now the city's main theater; call (☎ 0661/102–326) for program details and tickets. **Göttingen's** two theater companies—the 100-

year-old Deutsches Theater and the Junge Theater—are known throughout Germany; call (☎ 0551/496–911) for program details and tickets. **Hameln's** main theater, the Weserbergland Festhalle (Rathauspl., ☎ 0515/3747), has a regular program of drama, concerts, opera, and ballet from September through June. **Kassel** has no fewer than 35 theater companies. The principal venues are the Schauspielhaus, the Tif-Theater, the Stadthalle, and the Komödie. Call (☎ 0561/109–4222) for program details and tickets for all.

Nightlife

Bremen may be Germany's oldest seaport, but it can't match Hamburg for racy nightlife. Nevertheless, the streets around the central Marktplatz and in the historic Schnoor district are filled with atmospheric taverns and bars of various kinds. In **Göttingen** the ancient student taverns that crowd the downtown area are the focus of local nightlife, but for something more sophisticated try the Blue Note jazz club and disco (Wilhelmsplatz 3) or the Latin-style Caribe (Johannisstr. 33). **Kassel** is disco city. Club 21 (Friedrich-Ebert-Str. 61a) and Club 2000 (Weserstr. 15a) are two favorites. **Bremerhaven** and **Hannover** have casinos that attract gamblers from even Bremen and Hamburg. The Bremerhaven Casino (Theodor–Heuss–Platz 3) opens daily from midday, the Hannover casino (Am Maschsee) from 3 PM.

FAIRY-TALE ROAD ESSENTIALS

Arriving and Departing

By Bus
Long-distance Europabus services from Scandinavia through Germany to the Balkans call at Bremen, Kassel, and Göttingen. For information, timetables, and reservations, contact **Deutsche Touring GmbH.** (Am Römerhof 17, D–60486 Frankfurt/Main 90, ☎ 069/79030).

By Plane
Frankfurt, Hannover, and Hamburg are the closest international airports to the area. Frankfurt is less than half an hour from Hanau, the start of the route. Hamburg is less than an hour from Bremen, the end of it.

By Train
Hannover is an important railroad junction, served by InterCity and InterCity Express (ICE) trains, and on the Hamburg—Munich and Frankfurt—Berlin rail routes.

Getting Around

By Boat
From May through September two companies—**Oberweser-Dampfschiffahrt** and **Weisse Flotte Warnecke**—each with a fleet of six ships—operate daily services on the Weser River between Hameln, Bodenwerder, and Bad Karlshafen. On Monday, Wednesday, Friday, and Saturday, the Oberweser-Dampfschiffahrt boats sail as far as Münden, and on Tuesday, Thursday, Saturday, and Sunday, from Münden to Hameln. On the days when there is no service between Bad Karlshafen and Münden, a bus service ferries boat passengers between the two towns. For further information and bookings, contact **Oberweser-Dampfschiffahrt** (Inselstr. 3, D–31787 Hameln, ☎ 05151/22016) or **Weisse Flotte**

Warnecke (Hauptstr. 39, D–31787 Hameln, ☎ 05151/3975; Weser-str., Bodenwerder, ☎ 05533/4864).

By Bus
Frankfurt, Kassel, Göttingen, and Bremen all have city bus services that extend into the countryside along the Fairy-Tale Road.

By Car
Germany's Autobahn network penetrates deep into the area. Hanau, Fulda, Kassel, Göttingen, and Bremen are all served directly by Autobahns. The Fairy-Tale Road itself incorporates one of Germany's loveliest scenic drives, the Wesertalstrasse, or Weser Valley Road, from Münden in the south to Hameln in the north.

CAR RENTAL
Avis: Kirchbachstrasse 200, ☎ 0421/211–077, **Bremen;** Schmidtstrasse 39, ☎ 069/730–111, **Frankfurt;** Drehbahn 15–25, ☎ 040/341–651, **Hamburg.** Am Klagesmarkt 22, ☎ 0511/14441, Hannover.

Hertz: Neuenland Airport, ☎ 0421/555–350, **Bremen;** Gutleutstrasse 87, ☎ 069/2425–2627, **Frankfurt;** Kirchenallee 34–36, ☎ 040/280–1201, **Hamburg.** Schulenburger Landstr. 146, ☎ 0511/635–092, Hannover.

Sixt-Budget: Duckwitzstrasse 55, ☎ 0421/510–055, **Bremen;** Am Römerhof, ☎ 069/705–018, and Frankfurt Airport, ☎ 069/697–0070, **Frankfurt;** Schulenburger Landstr. 66, ☎ 0511/352–1213, **Hannover;** Leipzigerstrasse 56, ☎ 0561/54093, **Kassel.**

By Train
Fulda, Kassel, and Göttingen are served by Germany's ultramodern InterCity Express line, which reduces traveling time between Frankfurt and Hamburg to three hours and 45 minutes. All other centers and most of the smaller towns are connected by rail, supplemented by railroad buses.

Guided Tours

City Tours
Several towns on the Fairy-Tale Road offer guided tours. Fulda has a daily tour of the Old Town, starting at the Stadtschloss at 2. Göttingen shows visitors around April–October weekdays at 11 and on weekends at 2 (starting from the Old Town Hall), while Hameln has daily tours May–September Monday–Saturday at 3 and Sunday at 10, starting from the tourist office (Diesterallee 3).

By Bus
Year-round tours of the region are offered by a Hameln company, **Rattenfänger-Reisen** (Bahnhofstr. 18/20, ☎ 05151/108–484) and by Sonnental–Reise (Hesslingen 89, Hessische Oldendorf, ☎ 05152/2172). Some local authorities—Bad Karlshafen, for example—also organize bus tours. Contact individual tourist offices for details.

By Boat
The Oberweser-Dampfschiffahrt Company and Warnecke's Weisse Flotte (White Fleet) operate summer services on the Weser River between Hameln and Münden. Both companies will give you advice on how to combine a boat trip with a tour by bike, bus, or train. The Oberweser-Dampfschiffahrt Company also has a daily excursion from

Hameln to the nearby Ohrberg Park and pleasure gardens: On Sunday afternoons it offers a 2½-hour "Kaffeereise" (coffee trip) on the river. From April through October, an excursion boat makes a four-hour trip daily up the Fulda River from Kassel. It leaves the Altmarkt pier at 2 and returns at 6. The trip costs DM 18 for adults and DM 10 for children. A variety of enjoyable boat excursions leave from Bremerhaven, ranging from one-hour trips around the harbor to more ambitious cruises along the lower Saxony coast, and costing from DM 12 to DM 34. Call (☎ 0471/415–850 or 0471/477–1500) for information. There's also a daily round-trip flight from the Bremerhaven airport to the fortress-like North Sea island of Helgoland (☎ 0471/77188 for flight details).

Important Addresses and Numbers

Visitor Information

Information on the Fairy-Tale Road can be obtained from the **Deutsche Märchenstrasse** (Postfach 102660, D–34117 Kassel, ☎ 0561/707–7140). There are local tourist information offices in the following towns:

Alsfeld. Verkehrsbüro, Rittergasse 5, D–36304 Alsfeld, ☎ 06631/182–165.

Bad Pyrmont. Kur-und-Verkehrsverein, Arkaden 14, D–31812 Bad Pyrmont, ☎ 05281/4627.

Bodenwerder. Städtische Verkehrsamt, Bruckenstrasse 7, D—37619 Bodenwerder, ☎ 05533/40541.

Bremen. Verkehrsverein, Hillmannpl. 6, D–28195 Bremen, ☎ 0421/308–000.

Bremerhaven. Verkehrsamt der Seestadt Bremerhaven, van–Ronzelen-Str. 2, D–27568 Bremerhaven, ☎ 0471/946–4610.

Fulda. Städtische Verkehrsbüro Schlossstrasse 1, Fulda D–36037, ☎ 0661/102–345.

Göttingen. Fremdenverkehrsverein, Altes Rathaus, D–37073 Göttingen, ☎ 0551/54000.

Hameln. Verkehrsverein, Deisterallee (am Bürgergarten), D–31785 Hameln, ☎ 05151/202–617.

Hanau. Verkehrsbüro, Altstädter Markt 1, D–63450 Hanau, ☎ 06181/2950.

Hannover. Hannover Information, Ernst-August-Platz 2, D–30159 Hannover, ☎ 0511/301–421.

Kassel. Tourist Information, Königsplatz 53., D–34117 Kassel, ☎ 0561/34054.

Münden. Verkehrsbüro, Rathaus am Markt, D–34346 Münden, ☎ 05541/75313.

Steinau an der Strasse. Verkehrsamt Am Kumpen 1–3, D–36396 Steinau an der Strasse, ☎ 06663/5655.

14 Hamburg

The Free and Hanseatic City of Hamburg, the city's official title, is an apt description. Water—in the form of the Alster lakes and the River Elbe—is its defining feature and the secret of its success. Even before the formation of the Hanseatic League, Hamburg shipped to and from all parts of the world; this is evident in many of the city's main attractions, including the Fischmarkt, its diverse restaurants, and the red-light district (the infamous Reeperbahn).

UNTIL NOT SO VERY LONG AGO Hamburg could have been considered Germany's best-kept secret, virtually ignored by the streams of foreign visitors whose itineraries invariably included the Rhine, the Romantic Road, and Munich, but it's now neck-and-neck with Munich as Germany's second-favorite city among foreign visitors (Berlin takes first place). And yet it still has something of an image problem. Mention of the city invariably triggers thoughts of the gaudy night world of the Reeperbahn, that sleazy strip of clip joints, sex shows, and wholesale prostitution that has helped make Hamburg Europe's "sin city" supreme. But to those who know the city, the Reeperbahn's presence could be considered part and parcel of the dramatic diversity and apparently irreconcilable contradictions that make up this fascinating port.

Hamburg, or "Hammaburg," was founded in 810 by Charlemagne. For centuries it was a walled city, its gigantic outer fortifications providing a tight little world relatively impervious to outside influences. Situated at the mouth of the Elbe, one of Europe's great rivers and the 97-kilometer (60-mile) umbilical cord that ties the harbor to the North Sea, Hamburg's role as a port gained it world renown: as one of the kingpins of the Hanseatic League, that medieval mafia of north German merchant cities that dominated shipping in the Baltic and the North seas, with trading satellites set up in Bergen, Visby, Danzig, Riga, Novgorod, and other points of the compass. The city-state's official title (yes, Hamburg is both)—the Free and Hanseatic City of Hamburg—still reflects the importance of that period. The Thirty Years' War left Hamburg unscathed. Napoléon's domination of much of the Continent during the early 19th century hardly touched the city either. Indeed, it was in the 19th century that it reached the crest of its power, when the largest shipping fleets on the seas, with some of the fastest ships afloat, were based here; tentacles of shipping lanes reached to the far corners of the earth. Ties to New York, Buenos Aires, and Rio de Janeiro were stronger than those to Berlin or Frankfurt. During the four decades leading up to World War I, Hamburg became one of the world's richest cities. Its aura of wealth and power was projected right up to the outbreak of World War II, and even today it shows. Each year about 15,000 ships sail up the lower Elbe carrying more than 50 million tons of cargo—from petroleum and locomotives to grain and bananas.

What you see today is the "new" Hamburg. The Great Fire of 1842 all but obliterated the original city; a century later World War II bombing raids destroyed port facilities and leveled more than half of the city proper. The miracle is that in spite of the 1940–44 raids, Hamburg now stands as a remarkably faithful replica of that glittering prewar city, a place of enormous style, verve, and elegance with considerable architectural diversity. Of particular interest are the 14th-century houses of Deichstrasse—the oldest residential area in Hamburg—and the Kontorhausviertel (literally, "Business House Quarter"). The latter contains some unique clinker-brick buildings from the '20s. A variety of turn-of-the-century *Jugendstil* (Art Nouveau) buildings can also be found in various parts of the city. And of course, as in most German cities, high rises are much in evidence.

The comparison that Germans like to draw between Hamburg and Venice is—like all such comparisons with the *Serenissima*—somewhat exaggerated. But it is true that the city is threaded with countless canals and waterways spanned by about 1,000 bridges, more even than you'll find in Venice. Swans glide on the canals. Arcaded passageways run along the waterways. In front of the Renaissance-style Rathaus is a square that resembles the Piazza San Marco.

The distinguishing feature of downtown Hamburg is the Alster. Once an insignificant waterway, it was dammed during the 18th century to form an artificial lake. Divided at its south end, it is known as the Binnenalster (Inner Alster) and the Aussenalster (Outer Alster), the two separated by a pair of graceful bridges, the Lombard Brücke and the John F. Kennedy Brücke. The Inner Alster is lined with stately hotels, department stores, fine shops, and cafés; the Outer Alster is framed by the spacious greenery of parks and gardens against a backdrop of private mansions. From late spring into fall, sailboats and surfboards skim across the surface of the Outer Alster. White passenger steamers zip back and forth. The view from one of these vessels (or from the shore of the Outer Alster) is of the stunning skyline of six spiny spires (five churches and the Rathaus) that is Hamburg's identifying feature. It all creates one of the most distinctive and appealing downtown areas of any European city.

But what sets Hamburg apart from most other cities is the extent of greenery at its heart. Almost half of its area is devoted to either agriculture or parkland. This fondness for growing things has been a dominant treasure of Hamburg for centuries. During the 16th century anyone caught chopping down a tree was sentenced to death!

Those accustomed to the *Gemütlichkeit* (conviviality) and jolly camaraderie of Munich should be advised that Hamburg on initial exposure presents a more somber face. People here are reputed to be notoriously frugal on the one hand, generous hosts on the other, with a penchant for indulging their tastes for the most refined delicacies. In a city that vibrates with energy, the people work hard and play hard, and turn out to be friendlier than they may at first appear.

EXPLORING

Downtown Hamburg

Numbers in the margin correspond to points of interest on the Hamburg map.

1 Your tour begins at **Dammtor** train station, an elevated steel-and-glass Jugendstil structure built in 1903. Recently renovated, it is one of many Art Nouveau buildings you'll see during your stay in Hamburg. You can buy a city map at the newsstand in the station. Head out the south exit; on your right you'll see the SAS Plaza Hotel and the Congress Centrum Hamburg (CCH), a vast, modern conference-and-entertainment complex at the northeast corner of **Planten un Blomen**

2

★ **3** (Plants and Flowers) park. Planten un Blomen and the adjoining **Alter Botanischer Garten** (Old Botanical Gardens) lie within the remains of the 17th-century fortified wall that defended the city during the Thirty Years' War, the cataclysmic religious struggle that raged in Germany between 1618 and 1648. The remains of the old fortifications and moats have since been cleverly integrated into a huge, tranquil park on the edge of the city center.

The entire park area is known as **Wallringpark** and includes Planten un Blomen and the Alter Botanischer Garten, plus the Kleine and Grosse Wallanlagen parks to the south. You'll need to cover a lot of ground on foot to see everything Wallringpark has to offer, but a trip on the light railway—which crosses all four parks—will give you a taste of its many aspects. If you take the railway, aim to finish your journey at Stephansplatz.

The walking tour will take you through Planten un Blomen and the Alter Botanischer Garten. Past the Congress Centrum, bear left in a sweeping arc through the ornamental Planten un Blomen Park. This park, opened in 1935, is famous all over Germany for its well-kept plant, flower, and water gardens, and offers many places to rest and admire the flora. The Japanese Garden here is the largest of its kind in Europe and conducts traditional tea ceremonies in the summer. If you visit on a summer evening, you'll see the **Wasserballet,** an illuminated fountain "ballet" in the lake set to organ music. Make sure you get to the lake in good time for the show—it begins at 10 PM each evening during the summer (at 9 PM in September).

Follow the signs to the Alter Botanischer Garten, an equally green and open park that specializes in rare and exotic plants. Tropical and subtropical species are grown under glass in hothouses, with specialty gardens—including herbal and medicinal—clustered around the old moat. The special appeal of the **Kleine** and **Grosse Wallanlagen** parks is their well-equipped leisure facilities, including a children's playground and theater, a model-boat pond, roller- and ice-skating rinks, and outdoor chess.

When you leave, make your way to the northeast entrance to the Alter Botanischer Garten at Stephansplatz. As you head south to cross over the Esplanade, you'll pass a large gray memorial erected by Nazis to commemorate soldiers from the 76th regiment who perished in the First World War. A rare special case, it escaped the obligatory dismantling of all Nazi monuments after the Second World War because it honors pre-1933 fallen soldiers. Walk down the attractive Colonnaden to reach the **Jungfernstieg,** the most elegant boulevard in downtown Hamburg. The Jungfernstieg's wide promenade looks over one of the city's most memorable vistas—the Alster Lakes. It's these twin lakes that give downtown Hamburg its distinctive sense of openness and greenery.

Today's attractive Jungfernstieg promenade, laid out in 1665, used to be part of the muddy millrace that channeled water into the Elbe River. The two lakes meet at the 17th-century defense wall at Lombard Brücke, the first bridge visible across the water.

TIME OUT Hamburg's best-known and oldest café, the newly refurbished **Alsterpavillon** (Jungfernstieg 54), is an ideal vantage point from which to observe the constant activity on the Binnenalster (Inner Alster). It's open daily 9 AM–midnight.

In summer the boat landing below is the starting point for the *Alsterdampfer,* the flat-bottom passenger boats that teem on the lakes. Small sailboats and rowboats hired from yards on the shores of the Alster are very much a part of the summer scene. But in winter conditions can be severe enough to freeze both lakes (only 8 feet deep at their deepest point), and commuters take to their ice skates to get to work. *Alster Lake and canal tours, Jungfernstieg,* ☎ *040/341–141. 50-min lake tours leave daily every half hour 10–6 Apr.–Oct., less often the rest of the year. Fare: DM 13 adults, DM 7.50 children. A 3-hr combination lake and canal tour leaves at 9:45, 12:15, 2:45, and 5:15 and costs DM 19 adults, DM 9.50 children.*

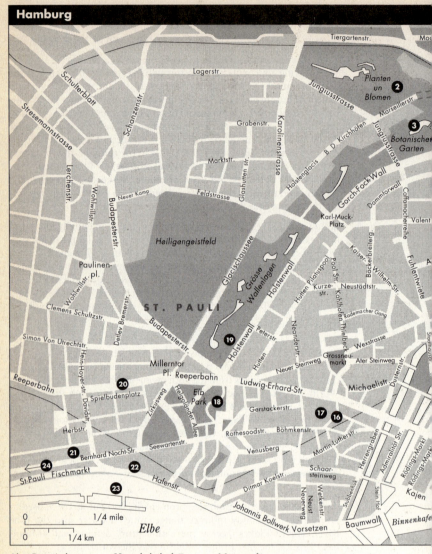

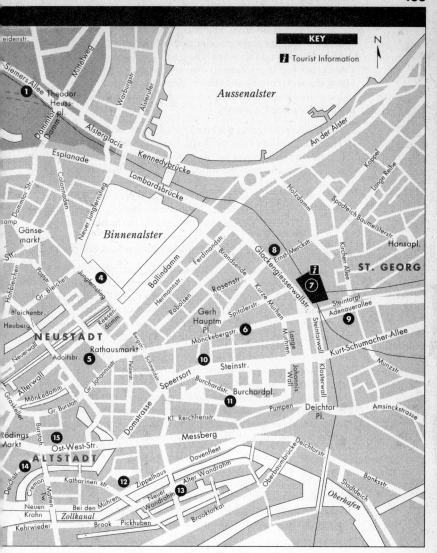

KEY

i Tourist Information

N

Aussenalster

eidenstr.

-Siemers Allee

① Theodor Heuss- Pl.

Mittelweg

Warburgstr.

Alsteruf er

An der Alster

Koppel

Lange Reihe

Dammtor Damm

Alsterglacis

Kennedybrücke

Esplanade

Colonnaden

Neuer Jungfernstieg

Lombardsbrücke

Holzdamm

Spadteich

Baumeisterstr.

Hansapl.

Dammtor Str.

camp

Gänse- markt

Binnenalster

Ferdinandstr.

Brandsende

⑧ Ernst Merckstr.

Glockengiesserwallstr.

Kirchen Allee

Baumwall

ST. GEORG

Str.

Hohebleichen

Poststr.

Gr. Bleichen

Jungfernstieg

④

Ballindamm

Hermannstr.

Raboisen

Rosenstr.

Kurze Muhren

i

⑦

Steintorpl.

Adenauerallee

⑨

Bleichenbr.

Heuberg

Reesen- damm

Gerh Hauptm Pl

Spitalerstr.

Steintorwall

Kurt-Schumacher-Allee

NEUSTADT

Neuerwall

Adolfsbr.

⑤

Gr. Johannisstr.

Rathausmarkt

Bergstr.

Mönckebergstr.

⑥

Lange Muhren

Johannis Wall

Klosterwall

Munzstr.

Alterwall

Mönkedamm

Gr. Burstah

Pelzerstr.

Schmedestr.

⑩

Speersort

Steinstr.

Burchardstr.

Burchardpl.

Amsinckstrasse

Graskeller

Gr. Burstah

Domstrasse

⑪

Pumpen

Deichtor Pl.

Rödings Markt

Burstah

⑮

Ost-West-Str.

Kl. Reichhenstr.

Messberg

Deichtorstr.

Bankstr.

ALTSTADT

⑭

Deichstr.

Cremon

Katharinen str.

⑫ Zippelhaus

Dovenfleet

Alter Wandrahm

⑬

Oberbaumbrücke

Deichtorkai

Stadtdeich

Oberhafen

Neuen Krahn

Matten Twe

Bei den Mühren

Neuer Wandrahm

Brooktorkai

Kehrwieder

Zollkanal

Brook

Pickhuben

Every Hamburger dreams of living within sight of the Alster, but only the wealthiest can afford it. Hamburg has its fair share of millionaires, some of whom are lucky enough to own one of the magnificent garden properties around the Alster's perimeter (the locals call it Millionaire's Coast). But you don't have to own one of these estates to be able to enjoy the waterfront—the Alster shoreline offers 6 kilometers (4½ miles) of tree-lined public pathways. Popular among joggers, these trails are a lovely place for a stroll.

It's hardly surprising that the area around Jungfernstieg contains some of Hamburg's most exclusive shops. Even the unpredictable nature of the northern German weather isn't enough to deter Hamburgers from pursuing a favorite pastime: window-shopping. Hidden from view behind the sedate facade of Jungfernstieg is a network of nine covered arcades that together account for almost a mile of shops offering everything from cheap souvenirs to expensive haute couture. Many of the air-conditioned passages have sprung up in the past two decades (*see* Shopping, *below*), but some existed during the 19th century: The first glass-covered arcade, called Sillem's Bazaar, was built in 1845.

★ ❺ Turn off the Jungfernstieg onto Reesendamm Street and make your way to the **Rathaus** (Town Hall). To most Hamburgers this large building is the symbolic heart of the city. As a city-state—an independent city and simultaneously one of the 16 federal states of reunited Germany—Hamburg has a city council and a state government, both of which have their administrative headquarters in the Rathaus.

Both the Rathaus and the Rathausmarkt (Town Hall Market) lie on marshy land—a fact that everyone in Hamburg was reminded of in 1962 when the entire area was severely flooded. The large square, with its surrounding arcades, was laid out after Hamburg's Great Fire of 1842. The architects set out to create an Italian-style square, drawing on St. Mark's in Venice for inspiration. The rounded glass arcade bordered by trees was added in 1982.

Building on the Nordic Renaissance–style Rathaus began in 1866 when 4,000 wooden piles were sunk into the moist soil to provide stability for its mighty bulk. It was completed in 1892, the year a cholera epidemic claimed the lives of 8,605 people in 71 days. A fountain and monument to that unhappy chapter in Hamburg's history can be found in a courtyard at the rear of the Rathaus.

No one is likely to claim that this immense building, with its 647 rooms (six more than Buckingham Palace!) and towering central clock tower, is the most graceful structure in the city, but for the sheer opulence of its interior, it's hard to beat. Although you get to see only the state rooms, the tapestries, huge staircases, glittering chandeliers, coffered ceilings, and grand portraits convey forcefully the wealth of the city during the last century and give insight into the bombastic municipal taste. The starting point for tours of the Rathaus interior is the ground-floor Rathausdiele, a vast pillared hall. *English-language tours: DM 2 adults, DM 1 children. Hourly Mon.–Thurs. 10:15–3:15, Fri.–Sun. 10:15–1:15.*

❻ Leave the Rathaus square by its east side, perhaps pausing to join other visitors to the city who are relaxing on the steps of the memorial to the poet Heinrich Heine, a real Hamburg fan. Beyond lies **Mönckebergstrasse,** a broad, bustling street of shops that ends at the Hauptbahnhof. Mönckebergstrasse is a relatively new street—it was laid out in 1908, when this part of the old town was redeveloped. Although the shops here are not quite as exclusive as those of Jungfernstieg, the department stores and shopping precincts on both sides of the street provide a wide selection of goods at more easily affordable prices. One word of warning to Saturday shoppers: Shops close at 2 PM—unless it is the first Saturday of the month, when the shops are open from 9 to 6:30. This rule applies to all of Hamburg's shopping centers and throughout most of Germany.

When you reach the end of Mönckebergstrasse, you'll meet the busy main road of Steintorwall, which was the easternmost link of the former defense wall encircling the old town during the 17th century. Rather than battling to cross against the fast-moving traffic, take the ❼ pedestrian underpass to the **Hauptbahnhof.**

The Hauptbahnhof was opened in 1906 and completely renovated in 1991. Today it caters to a heavy volume of international, national, and suburban rail traffic. Despite the fact that it was badly damaged during the Second World War and has been modernized many times over, its architectural impact remains intact. This enormous 394-foot-long cast-iron-and-glass building is accentuated by a 460-foot-wide glazed roof that is supported only by pillars at each end. The largest structure of its kind in Europe, it is remarkably spacious and light inside.

Retrace your steps and leave the Hauptbahnhof the way you entered. Turn right on Steintorwall, which continues as Glockengiesserwall, until ❽ you come to the **Kunsthalle** (Art Gallery) on the corner of Ernst-Merck-Strasse.

The Kunsthalle houses one of the most important art collections in Germany. It comprises two linked buildings: The one facing you is known as the Kunsthaus, exhibiting mainly contemporary works; adjoining it on your left is the Renaissance-style Kunsthalle, built in 1868. The entrance to both, which are known collectively as the Kunsthalle, is via the Kunsthaus building.

The Kunsthalle's 3,000 paintings, 400 sculptures, and coin and medal collection present a remarkably diverse picture of European artistic life from the 14th century to the present. Masterpieces in the gallery's possession include the oldest known representation of the murder of Thomas à Becket, the head of the English church in the 14th century. This painting, called *Thomas Altar,* was done by Meister Francke in 1424 and depicts Becket's death in Canterbury Cathedral.

One room of paintings shows works by local artists since the 16th century. There is also an outstanding collection of German Romantic paintings, including works by Runge, Friedrich, and Spitzweg. An exhibition of European art by such painters as Holbein, Rembrandt, Van Dyck, Tiepolo, and Canaletto is on display, as are examples of the late-19th-century Impressionist movement by artists ranging from Leibl and Lieberman to Manet, Monet, and Renoir. *Glockengeisserwall 1,* ☎ *040/2486–2612. ☛ DM 6 adults, DM 1 children. ☉ Tues.–Wed. and Fri.–Sun. 10–6, Thurs. 10–9.*

A quite different but equally fascinating perspective on art is offered ❾ by the nearby **Museum für Kunst und Gewerbe** (Museum of Arts and Crafts). To reach it, head in the direction from which you came and turn left on Steintordamm, crossing over the railroad tracks. The large yellow museum building is across the street, its entrance on Brockesstrasse.

The Museum für Kunst und Gewerbe was built in 1876 as a museum and school combined. Its founder, Justus Brinckmann, intended it to be a stronghold of the applied arts to counter what he saw as a decline in taste due to industrial mass production. A keen collector, Herr

Brinckmann amassed a wealth of unusual objects, including a fine collection of ceramics from all over the world. The museum houses a wide range of exhibits from a collection of 15th- to 18th-century scientific instruments (ground floor) to an Art Nouveau room setting, complete with ornaments and furniture, all either original or faithfully reproduced (first floor). *Steintorpl. 1,* ☎ *040/2486–2630.* ☛ *DM 3.* ⊙ *Tues.–Wed. and Fri.–Sun. 10–6, Thurs. 10–9.*

TIME OUT   The museum has a small restaurant called **Destille** on the first floor, offering an extensive buffet that includes salads and desserts. ⊙*Tues.–Sat. 10–4.*

⑩ Return to the city center for a visit to the **Jakobikirche** (St. James's Church), just off the Mönckebergstrasse. Turn right out of the museum, then right onto Kurt-Schumacher-Allee. Cross over Steintorwall by the subway and continue west along Steinstrasse to the Jacobikirche on your right—you'll recognize it by its needle spire.

This 13th-century church was almost completely destroyed during the Second World War. Only the furnishings, put into storage until restoration of the building was completed in 1962, survived. The interior is not to be missed—it houses such treasures as the vast Baroque organ on which J. S. Bach played in 1720 and three Gothic altars from the 15th and 16th centuries. *Steinstr.* ⊙ *Mon.–Sat. 10–5, Sun. 10–noon.*

Upon leaving the Jakobikirche, cross over Steinstrasse and head down Mohlenhofstrasse, which will bring you to Burchardplatz. This area, south of the Jakobikirche between Steinstrasse and Messberg, is known as the **Kontorhausviertel** (Office Building Quarter). Its fascination lies in a series of imaginative clinker-brick buildings designed in the New Objectivity style of 1920s civic architect Fritz Schumacher.

⑪ Of particular interest in this quarter is the **Chilehaus** at the south end of Burchardplatz, a fantastical 10-story building that at first looks like a vast landlocked ship. The Chilehaus was commissioned by businessman Henry Sloman, who traded in saltpeter from Chile. This building is the most representative example of the northern German clinker-brick architecture of the '20s.

★   Next, your tour will take you south toward the Freihafen (Free Port) to see the 19th-century warehouse city of **Speicherstadt,** with a visit
⑫ to the restored **Katherinenkirche** (St. Catherine's Church) en route. From the Messberg end of Pumpen Street, cross the busy Ost-West-Strasse by Messberg station and continue down Dovenfleet, which runs alongside the Zoll Kanal (Customs Canal). Continue until Dovenfleet turns into Bei den Mühren and you'll see the distinctive green copper spire of the Katherinenkirche.

The church (completed in 1660) is dedicated to St. Catherine, a princess of Alexandria martyred at the beginning of the 4th century. Both the exterior and the interior of the church were severely damaged during World War II, but it has since been carefully reconstructed according to the Baroque design. Almost none of the original interior furnishings escaped destruction. Only two 17th-century epitaphs (to Moller and von der Feehte) remain. *Bei den Mühren.* ⊙ *Summer, daily 9–6; winter, daily 9–4.*

Head back a short walk to the bridge you passed before, the Kornhausbrücke. Notice the sign on the bridge announcing your entrance
⑬ to the Freihafen Hamburg. The **Speicherstadt** warehouses lining the waterfront welcome you to the Free Port, one of Hamburg's most unique

areas. You'll find the Deutsches Zollmuseum (German Customs Museum) immediately to your right after crossing the bridge (*see* Museums and Galleries, *below*).

Hamburg's free-port status has existed since the 12th century, when Emperor Barbarossa, the Holy Roman Emperor Frederick I, granted the city special privileges that included freedom from customs dues on the Elbe River. The original Free Port was situated at the point where the Alster meets the Elbe near Deichstrasse, but it was moved farther south as Hamburg's trade increased during the following centuries. With Hamburg's membership in the German Empire's Customs Union in the late 1800s, major restructuring of the Free Port became necessary in order to make way for additional storage facilities. An entire residential area was torn down (including many Renaissance and Baroque buildings), and the Speicherstadt warehouses, the world's largest continuous storage space, came into being between 1885 and 1927.

The warehouses reveal yet another aspect of Hamburg's extraordinary architectural diversity. A Gothic influence is apparent here, with a rich overlay of gables, turrets, and decorative outlines. These massive rust-brown warehouses are still used today to store and process every conceivable commodity, from coffee and spices to raw silks and handwoven Oriental carpets. Although you won't be able to go into the buildings, the nonstop comings and goings you'll see as you stroll around this area will give you a good sense of a port at work.

As you leave the Free Port over the Brooksbrücke (two bridges down from the Kornhausbrücke), you'll pass through a customs control point, at which you may be required to make a customs declaration. Turn left after the bridge, where Bei den Mühren becomes Neuen Krahn. Take your second right—onto **Deichstrasse,** which runs alongside Nikolaifleet, a former course of the Alster and one of Hamburg's oldest canals.

You are now in one of the oldest residential areas of the Old Town of Hamburg, which dates from the 14th century. Many of the original houses on Deichstrasse were destroyed in the Great Fire of 1842, which broke out in No. 42 and left approximately 20,000 people homeless. The houses you see today date mostly from the 17th to the 19th century, but a few of the early dwellings escaped the ravages of the fire.

Today Deichstrasse is a protected area of great historical interest. At No. 39 Deichstrasse, for example, is the Baroque facade of a house built in 1700. And farther along, No. 27, built in 1780 as a warehouse, is the oldest of its kind in Hamburg. All the buildings in the area have been painstakingly restored—thanks largely to the efforts of public-spirited individuals. You may wish to make a small detour down one of the narrow alleys between the houses (Fleetgänge) to see the fronts of the houses facing the Nikolaifleet. After exploring this lovely area, take the Cremon Bridge at the north end of Deichstrasse. This angled pedestrian bridge spans Ost-West-Strasse.

TIME OUT There are three good basement restaurants in this area, all recommended if you are ready for a break. The **Alt Hamburger Aalspeicher** serves fresh-fish dishes; the **Alt Hamburger Bürgerhaus** specializes in traditional Hamburg fare; and the **Nikolaikeller,** an upscale old Hamburg tavern, offers the biggest herring menu in Germany. All three are on Deichstrasse and Cremon.

(15) The Cremon Bridge will take you to Hopfenmarkt Square, just a stone's throw from the ruins of the **Nikolaikirche** (St. Nicholas's Church). You won't need precise directions to find the church, with its tower. Only the tower and outside walls of the 19th-century neo-Gothic church survived World War II. Unlike most of the other war-torn churches in Hamburg, the Nikolai was not rebuilt. Instead, the tower was declared a monument to those killed and persecuted during the war.

Adjacent to the tower is a documentation center about the church. It is run by a citizens' organization that is also spearheading private efforts to partially rebuild the church and redesign the surrounding area. Beneath the former church, a wine cellar is open for browsing and wine-tasting, as well as for the purchase of wine. *Ost-West-St. by Hopfenmarkt. Information center: open Mon., Wed., and Fri. 10–6, Tues. and Thurs. 10–2. Wine cellar: open weekdays 11–6, Sat. 10–1.*

Head west on Ost-West-Strasse and cross to the other side at the Rödingsmarkt U-bahn station. Continue along Ost-West-Strasse, which turns into Ludwig-Erhard-Strasse, until you reach Krayenkamp, a side street (16) to your left that will take you to the historic **Krameramtswohnungen** (Shopkeepers-Guild Houses). The distance from the Nikolaikirche to Krayenkamp is about 1 kilometer (½ mile).

This tightly packed group of courtyard houses was built between 1620 and 1626 for the widows of members of the shopkeepers' guild. They were used as homes for the elderly after 1866, when the freedom to practice trades was granted. The half-timbered, two-story dwellings, with their unusual twisted chimneys and decorative brick facades, were restored in the 1970s and are now protected buildings.

One of the houses, marked "C," is open to the public. A visit inside the furnished setting gives one a sense of life in one of these 17th-century dwellings. Some of the houses have been converted to suit modern-day commercial purposes—you'll find a few shops and a bar-cum-restaurant in the style of Old Hamburg. *Historic House "C," Krayenkamp 10. ☛ DM 1. ☽ Tues.–Sun. 10–5.*

TIME OUT The restaurant **Krameramtsstuben** (Krayenkamp 10, ☎ 040/365–800) in the Krameramtswohnungen quarter is open daily from 10 AM to midnight.

★ (17) The Krameramtswohnungen lie in the shadow of Hamburg's best-loved and most famous landmark, **Michaeliskirche** (St. Michael's Church), on the other side of Krayenkamp Road. Michaeliskirche, or "Michel," as it is called locally, is Hamburg's principal church and northern Germany's finest Baroque ecclesiastical building. Constructed on this site from 1649 to 1661 (the tower followed in 1669), it was razed when lightning struck almost a century later. It was rebuilt between 1750 and 1786 in the decorative Nordic Baroque style but fell victim in 1906 to a terrible fire that destroyed all but the outside walls of the church. A replica was completed in 1912, but it suffered during the Second World War. By 1952, it had once again been restored.

The Michel has a distinctive 433-foot brick-and-iron tower bearing the largest tower clock in Germany, 26 feet in diameter. Just above the clock is the viewing platform (accessible by an elevator or stairs), which affords a magnificent panorama of the city, the Elbe River, and the Alster Lakes. Twice a day, at 10 AM and 9 PM (on Sundays at noon only), a watchman plays a trumpet solo from the tower platform, and during festivals an entire wind ensemble crowds onto the platform to perform. Traffic permitting, the music can be heard at street level. *Michaeliskirche:* ☉ *Apr.–Sept., daily 9–6 (Thurs. until 10); Oct.–Mar., daily 10–5 (Thurs. until 10). St. Michael's Tower:* ☉ *Apr.–Sept., Mon.–Sat. 9–6, Sun. 11:30–6; Oct.–Mar., daily 10–5. Elevator or staircase (449 steps) fee: DM 4 adults, DM 2.50 children.*

TIME OUT Just opposite the Michel is one of Hamburg's most traditional restaurants, the **Old Commercial Room.** Try one of the local specialties here, such as *Labskaus* (a traditional sailors' dish) or *Aalsuppe* (eel soup). *Englische Planke 10,* ☎ *040/366–368.* ☉ *Daily 11 AM–1 AM.*

Return to the Krayenkamp and turn right. Stay on this road for about **18** 220 yards, until you reach a park, the enormous **Bismarck-Denkmal** (Bismarck Monument) rising high above the greenery. Take the pathway leading to it, and as you climb you'll realize that part of its height is due to the sandy hill on which it stands. The colossal 111-foot granite monument, erected between 1903 and 1906, is a mounted statue of Chancellor Bismarck, the Prussian "Iron Chancellor" who was the force behind the unification of Germany. The plinth features bas-reliefs of various German tribes. Created by the sculptor Hugo Lederer, the statue calls to mind Roland, the famous warrior from the Middle Ages, and symbolizes the German Reich's protection of Hamburg's international trade.

Leave the monument by the northeast exit onto Ludwig-Erhard-Strasse. Cross it and continue straight ahead up the street called Holstenwall **19** to the **Museum für Hamburgische Geschichte** (Museum of Hamburg History).

A visit to this museum is highly recommended—it will give you an excellent overall perspective of the forces that have guided Hamburg's development throughout the centuries. The museum's vast and comprehensive collection of artifacts charts the history of Hamburg from its origins in the 9th century to the present. The Hamburg Historical Society began building the collection in 1839—three years before the Great Fire—and salvaged a number of items for display in the museum. More material was acquired in 1883 when several street blocks were torn down to make way for the expansion of the Free Port, and these provide an excellent record of life at the time.

Among the museum's many attractions are an exhibit that describes, through pictures and models, the development of the port and shipping between 1650 and 1860, and a 16th-century architectural model of Solomon's Temple measuring 11 feet square and made of five different types of wood.

Railway buffs will delight in the railway section and escape into past eras of train travel. The centerpiece of this section is a model layout of the Hamburg-to-Harburg rail link, complete with a puffing miniature steam locomotive. As a modern InterCity train is put through its paces, you may also see a 32:1 scale model of the legendary propeller-driven Reichsbahn *Zeppelin* of 1931 heading past in the opposite direction. Trains from every decade of the 20th century run strictly according to timetable on what is the largest model railway in Europe today. (Ask at the front desk for the schedule of model railway demonstrations.) *Holstenwall 24,* ☎ *040/3504–2360.* ☛ *DM 6 adults, DM 1 children.* ☉ *Tues.–Sun. 10–6.*

Of particular interest to American visitors are the museum's records of German immigrants to the United States between 1850 and 1914. The Historic Emigration Office's microfilm file lists the names of almost 6 million people who left the port of Hamburg for the promise of a better life in the New World. For a fee of DM 100 the office will comb its files and if the search is successful will issue a facsimile of the passenger list excerpt containing details of the ancestor who made the journey, with complete name, age, profession, German place of birth, the name of the ship, the date of its departure from Hamburg, and its destination in America. For a successful search the office needs as much American information about the ancestor as possible, and preparation and delivery of the facsimile can take up to eight months. The service has proved so popular that it has been moved from the museum to a special office in the harbor (Historic Emigration Office, St. Pauli Landungsbrücken, between Piers 4 and 5, ☎ 040/300–51250; open daily 9:30–5:30).

★ ⑳ Return along Holstenwall to the St. Pauli U-bahn station—you are now at the start of a long, neon-lit street stretching nearly 1 kilometer (½ mile) as far as the eye can see. This is the **Reeperbahn.** The hottest spots in town are concentrated in St. Pauli Harbor area, on the Reeperbahn and on a little side street known as the Grosse Freiheit (or Great Freedom, and that's putting it mildly!). The shows are expensive and explicit, but to walk through this area is an experience in itself, and you can soak up the atmosphere without spending anything. Indeed, compared with former times, it is quite tame. There are even two McDonald's and a Burger King on the strip. It's *not* advisable, however, to travel through this part of the city alone at the wee hours of the morning.

St. Pauli is sometimes described as a "Babel of sin," but that's not entirely fair. It offers a broad menu of entertainment in addition to the striptease and sex shows. Among its other attractions are theaters, clubs, music pubs, discos, a bowling alley, and the Panoptikum waxworks museum (located between the St. Pauli U-bahn and Davidstrasse). The Theater Schmidt on the Reeperbahn, a more recent arrival to the local scene, offers a repertoire of live music, vaudeville, chansons, and cabaret, while the St. Pauli Theater on Spielbudenplatz, a veteran of the age of velvet and plush, serves up a popular brand of lowbrow theater in Hamburger dialect.

㉑ A recent addition to the area is the **Erotic Art Museum,** with four floors of 500 original works of provocative art from 1520 to the present. This collection is presented with great taste and decorum in an attractively renovated building, so much so that it has won the respect of many who would not normally wish to view such an exhibit. *Bernhard-Nocht-Str. 69,* ☎ *040/3174757. Minimum age is 18.* ☛ *DM 15.* ☉ *Tues.–Sun. 10 AM–midnight.*

It's no understatement to say that while some of the sex clubs may be relatively tame, a good many others are pornographic in the extreme. None of them get going until about 10 PM; all will accommodate you till the early hours. Order your own drinks rather than letting the hostess do it for you, pay for them as soon as they arrive, and be sure to check the price list again before handing over the money.

★ ㉒ Saturday night finds St. Pauli pulsating with people determined to have as much fun as possible. As the bright lights begin to fade sometime around daybreak, those who are made of stern stuff continue their entertainment at the **Fischmarkt** (Fish Market).

The Altona Fischmarkt swings into action every Sunday morning at 5 in summer and two hours later in winter. It is by far the most celebrated of Hamburg's many markets and is worth getting out of bed early for. If you're coming from the Reeperbahn, make your way straight down to the water or return to the St. Pauli U-bahn station and travel one stop south to Landungsbrücken station. Turn right at the crossroads at the foot of the hill and walk beside the Elbe for about 220 yards, and you'll see the market stalls on the road to your left.

Sunday fish markets became a tradition in the 18th century, when fishermen used to sell their catch before church services began. Today freshly caught fish is only one of a compendium of wares on sale at the popular Fischmarkt in Altona. In fact, you can find almost anything—from live parrots and palm trees to armloads of flowers and bananas, valuable antiques to second-, third-, and fourth-hand junk. You'll find plenty of bars and restaurants in the area where you can breakfast on strong coffee or even raw herring, and live jazz is played in the auction hall, the Fischauktionshalle, at Sunday-morning jam sessions (Grosse Elbestrasse 9). *Fischmarkt: between Grosse Elbestr. and St. Pauli Landungsbrücken. ☉ Sun. 5–10 AM in summer and 7–10 AM in winter.*

A visit to the port is not complete without a tour of one of the most modern and efficient harbors in the world. Hamburg is Germany's largest seaport, with 33 individual docks and 500 berths lying within its 78 square kilometers (30 square miles). Short round-trips by ferry leave from the nearby landings at **Landungsbrücken.** To find the booking hall and departure point, leave the Fischmarkt and return the way you came, but instead of turning left up the hill to the U-bahn station, bear right toward the long limestone building instantly recognizable by its two towers. This is Landungsbrücken, the main passenger terminal for a whole range of ferry and barge rides, both one-way and round-trip, along the waterways in, around, and outside Hamburg. In the first-floor booking hall is the main ticket office and information desk.

There's usually a fresh breeze, so do dress warmly enough for your trip, but don't expect rolling surf and salty air, as Hamburg's port is 56 nautical miles from the North Sea. The HADAG line and other companies organize round-trips in the port lasting about one hour and taking in several docks. *Harbor tours run year-round from Piers 1–7 at Landungsbrücken. In summer they depart every half hour; in winter, whenever a boat is full. An English-language tour leaves from Pier 1 daily at 11:15 Mar.–Nov. Fare for 1-hr trip: DM 15 adults, DM 7.50 children.*

You can combine an evening trip around the harbor with a cold buffet dinner, as much beer as you can drink, and dancing on a "party ship." Book at the HADAG pavilion on Landungsbrücken (☎ 040/313–687). *Fare: DM 59. Departures late Apr.–early Dec., Sat. at 8 PM. Inquire at the information office about other special cruises.*

One trip you should try to make is to the waterside village of **Blankenese,** 14½ kilometers (9 miles) west of Hamburg. Take a ferry (14 kilometers) from Landungsbrücken to get there. You'll need plenty of energy when you arrive to tackle the 58 flights of steep and narrow lanes crisscrossing the hills and valleys of the village.

Blankenese is another of Hamburg's surprises—a city suburb with the character of a quaint fishing village. Some Germans like to compare it to the French and Italian rivieras; many consider it the most beautiful part of Hamburg. During the 14th century Blankenese was an important ferry point, but it wasn't until the late 18th and 19th centuries that it became a popular residential area.

TIME OUT   A fine view and good food await you at **Sägebiel's Fährhaus** (Blankenese Hauptstr. 107, ☎ 040/861–514), a former farmhouse where

Kaiser Wilhelm once celebrated his birthday. The fish dishes are recommended.

You have a choice of transportation back to the city—by ferry, by S-bahn, or on foot. The celebrated Elbe River walk is long—about 13 kilometers (8 miles) from Blankenese to Landungsbrücken—but it's one of Hamburg's prettiest. *Mid-Apr.–end of Aug., HADAG ferries depart from Pier 3 for Blankenese weekdays at 10:30 and 2:30, weekends at 11:30 and 3;30; they leave Blankenese weekdays at 1 and 6:30, weekends at 2 and 5:30. Ferries continue running on weekends only (at above times) through end of Sept.*

What to See and Do with Children

Harbor tours are obvious choices. Other watery options include row-boat rentals on the Stadtpark Lake (*see* Sightseeing Checklists, *below*) and surrounding canals. Hamburg's zoo, Hagenbecks Tierpark, is private and so popular that it has its own subway stop on the U–2 line (*see* Sightseeing Checklists, *below*). There are 2,500 animals, most in open-air enclosures. ☛ *DM 18 adults, DM 13 children under 14.; Dolphinarium: DM 6 adults, DM 4 children.* ☉ *Daily 9–sunset.*

Sightseeing Checklists

All sites listed below are discussed in the Exploring section, *above*, unless noted otherwise.

Historical Buildings and Sites

Alter Elbtunnel (Old Elbe Tunnel). This tunnel was built in 1907–11 to accommodate the growing traffic between St. Pauli and Steinwerder Island. Pedestrians and cars are brought down to and up from the tunnel by giant lifts. The entrance is adjacent to the Landungsbrücken. *Closed nights and Sun. U-bahn: Landungsbrücken.*

Bismarck-Denkmal (Bismarck Monument). Monument to Chancellor Bismarck, the "Iron Chancellor," who was the force behind the 19th-century unification of Germany. *U-bahn: St. Pauli.*

Chilehaus (Chile House). An unconventional office building in the heart of the Kontorhausviertel district, built in the 1920s for a businessman who traded with Chile. *U-bahn: Messberg.*

Dammtorbahnhof (Dammtor Train Station). A fine example of turn-of-the-century Jugendstil architecture.

Deichstrasse. This is the oldest residential area of the Old Town of Hamburg. *U-bahn: Rödingsmarkt.*

Hamburger Hafen (Hamburg Harbor). There's a constant bustle around the port, the largest in Germany. Choose one of the many boat excursions that leave regularly from the boat landings at Landungsbrücken. *U-bahn: Landungsbrücken.*

Hauptbahnhof (Main Train Station).

Krameramtswohnungen (Shopkeepers-Guild Houses). A tightly packed group of courtyard houses built during the late 17th century by the Merchants' Guild for the widows of its late members. *U-bahn: Rödingsmarkt.*

Rathaus (Town Hall). The late-19th-century Nordic Renaissance–style building is home to Hamburg's city council and state government. *U-bahn: Rathaus.*

Reeperbahn. This street cuts through Hamburg's lively St. Pauli entertainment quarter. *S-bahn: Reeperbahn; or U-bahn: St. Pauli.*

Speicherstadt. These imposing warehouses in the Free Port offer the world's largest continuous storage facility. *U-bahn: Baumwall, Röd-ingsmarkt, or Messberg.*

Churches
Jakobikirche (St. James's Church). This 13th-century church was re-built after severe damage during World War II, but some of its trea-sures remained intact, including a unique Baroque organ and three Gothic altars. *U-bahn: Mönckebergstr.*

Katherinenkirche (St. Catherine's Church). This restored Baroque church overlooking the harbor was dedicated to the martyred 4th-cen-tury Princess Catherine of Alexandria. *U-bahn: Messberg.*

Michaeliskirche (St. Michael's Church). This is Hamburg's most famous landmark and one of the most important late-Baroque churches in Ger-many. The viewing platform, accessible by stairs or elevator, affords a magnificent panorama of the city, encompassing the Elbe River and the Alster Lakes. *U-bahn or S-Bahn Landungsbrücken or U-bahn Rödingsmarkt.*

Nikolaikirche (St. Nicholas's Church). Only the tower and the outside walls remain of this 19th-century neo-Gothic church destroyed in World War II. *U-bahn: Rödingsmarkt or Rathaus.*

Petrikirche (St. Peter's Church). Considered the oldest church in Ham-burg, this early 12th-century building fell victim to the Great Fire of 1842 and was rebuilt shortly afterward. *U-bahn: Rathaus.*

Museums and Galleries
Erotic Art Museum. An entertaining display of sexually provocative art from 1520 to the present. *U-bahn: St. Pauli.*

Deutsches Zollmuseum (German Customs Museum). Located in an old customs building in the Free Port, this museum provides an overview of the history of German customs from antiquity to the present and gives information on the duties of the Customs Office. *Alter Wandrahm 15a-16, by the Kornhausbrücke. U-bahn: Messberg.* ☉ *Tues.–Sun. 10–5.*

Kunsthalle (Art Gallery). Hamburg's principal gallery houses one of the most important art collections in Germany, with paintings from the Middle Ages to the present. *U-bahn: Hauptbahnhof.*

Museum fur Hamburgische Geschichte (Museum of Hamburg His-tory). The museum traces the history of Hamburg from its origins in the 9th century to the present. *U-bahn: St. Pauli.*

Museum für Kunst und Gewerbe (Museum of Arts and Crafts). This interesting little museum houses a wide variety of examples of the ap-plied arts. *U-bahn: Hauptbahnhof.*

Museum für Völkerkunde (Museum of Ethnology). One of the largest museums of its kind in Germany, it has particularly good displays on Africa and South America. *Rothenbaumchausee 64. U-bahn: Haller-str.* ☉ *Tues.–Sun. 10–6.*

Oevelgönne Museumhafen (Oevelgönne Harbor Museum). The aim of this privately owned museum is to maintain and restore ships for occasional outings and public display. Most of the restored ships are seaworthy, and among the collection are steam tugs, wooden cutters, and fire-fighting ships. *Beim Anleger Neumühlen; take Bus 112 from Altona railway station.* ☉ *Weekends only 11–8. Closed Jan. and Feb.*

Open Markets
Blankenese. A lively fruit and vegetable market in the heart of this sub-urb manages to preserve the charm of a small village. *Bahnhofstr. S-bahn: Blankenese.* ☉ *Tues. 8–2, Fri. 8–6, Sat. 8–1.*

Fischmarkt (Fish Market). Fish of all shapes and sizes can be bought at this market, as can a wide range of other goods, including flowers, fruit and vegetables, antiques, and secondhand junk. For many, it's also a traditional setting for a last beer after a night on the town. *In summer, Sun. 5–10 AM; in winter, 7–10 AM. S- or U-bahn: Landungsbrücken.*

Isemarkt. This market is considered by many Hamburgers to be the city's best, with more than 300 stalls offering everything from fresh produce to clothing and toys. The stalls are set up on a strip of land beneath the elevated railway between St. Pauli and Poppenbüttel Some of the older houses on Isestrasse have particularly attractive Jugendstil facades. *Between the U-bahn stations of Hoheluftbrücke and Eppendorfer Baum. Tues. and Fri. 8:30–2.*

Parks and Gardens

Alsterpark. Lying on the northwest bank of the Alster is the 173-acre Alsterpark, a well-kept park of trees and gardens with a magnificent view of the city skyline. It is a popular destination for weekend strollers. *Harvestehuderweg.*

Hagenbecks Tierpark (Zoological Gardens). Opened in 1848, this privately owned zoo has 62 acres of landscaped gardens and parkland, with some 2,500 animals separated from the public by invisible ditches. It also has a large dolphinarium and a well-equipped children's playground. *Hagenbeckallee at Hamburg-Stellingen. ⊙ Daily 9–sunset. U-bahn: Hagenbecks Tierpark.*

Hirschpark (Deer Park). This is an attractively landscaped park with a game enclosure. Stop by the Hirschparkhaus for tea and homemade whole-grain breads at the nearby Witthüs Teestuben, a charming old thatched-roof cottage. *Main entrance: Mühlenberg. S-bahn: Blankenese.*

Stadtpark. This park, north of the city center, offers 445 acres of parkland and 19 miles of footpaths as well as recreational facilities, including open-air pools, sunbathing areas, and a planetarium. Plays are staged and rock concerts held here in the summer. *In Winterhude. U-bahn: Saarlandstr. or Borgweg.*

Wallringpark. This vast and well-kept park and garden area is just to the west of the city center and contains four parks: the ornamental Planten un Blomen flower garden; the herb and specialty gardens of the Alter Botanischer Garten; and the Kleine and Grosse Wallanlagen parks, which offer numerous leisure facilities. A miniature railway crosses all four parks. *Main entrance: Stephanspl. ⊙ Mar.–Oct., daily 7 AM–10 PM; Nov.–Feb., daily 7 AM–8 PM.*

SHOPPING

Gift Ideas

As a great port, Hamburg offers goods from all over the world. You may find it bizarre, but this is one of the best places in Europe for buying tea, for example. Smoked salmon and caviar are also terrific buys here. But for those with salt in their veins, it's the city's maritime heritage that produces some of the most typical goods. The most famous must be a *Buddelschiffe,* a ship in a bottle. There are few better places to look for one, or for a blue-and-white striped sailor's shirt, a sea captain's hat, ship models, even ship's charts, than the little shops and stalls lining the landing stages at St. Pauli Harbor. **Binikowski** (Lokstedter Weg 68, ☎ 040/462–852) is wonderful for ships in bottles. **Gäth & Peine** (Luisenweg 109, ☎ 040/213–599) is the place to look for flags from around the world. **Harry's Hamburger Hafenbasar** (Bernard-Nocht-

Str. 63), a Hamburg institution and an experience not to be missed, is the best place of all for any of these specialty goods. The city has the distinction of being home to the largest caviar mail-order business in Europe, **Seifarth and Company** (Robert-Koch-Str. 17, ☏ 040/524–0027); it offers lobsters, salmon, and exotic teas, too.

Antiques

Check out the **Antik-Center** (Klosterwall 9–21, ☏ 040/326–285) in the old market hall, close to the main train station. It features a wide variety of pieces, large and small, valuable and not so valuable, from all periods. Alternatively, take a look at the shops in the **St. Georg** district, especially those between **Lange Reihe** and **Koppel.** You'll find a mixture of genuine antiques (*Antiquitäten* in German) and junk (*Trödel*). You won't find many bargains, however. **ABC-Strasse** is another happy hunting ground for antiques lovers.

Shopping Districts

Hamburg's main shopping districts are among the most elegant on the Continent, and the city has Europe's largest area of covered shopping arcades, most of them packed with small, exclusive boutiques. The leading street is **Jungfernstieg,** just about the most upscale and expensive in the country. It's lined with classy jewelers—**Wempe, Brahmfeld & Guttruf, Hintze** are the top names—and chic clothing boutiques such as **Linette, Ursula Aust, Selbach, Windmöller,** and **Jäger & Koch.** Prices are high, but the quality is tops. The streets **Grosse Bleichen** and **Neuer Wall,** which lead off Jungfernstieg, continue the high-price-tag zone. The Grosse Bleichen also leads to three of the city's most imporant covered or indoor shopping malls. The marble-clad **Galleria** is modeled after London's Burlington Arcade. Daylight streams through the immense glass ceilings of the **Hanse Viertel,** an otherwise reddish-brown brick building. The **Kaufmannshaus,** also known as the Commercie, is one of the oldest indoor malls. The malls all connect, and energetic shoppers may want to spend several hours exploring them. The mood is busily elegant, and you'll understand why Hamburgers call it their "Quartier Satin"!

Spitalerstrasse, running from the main train station to Gerhard-Hauptmann-Platz, is a pedestrians-only shopping street that's lined with stores. Prices here are noticeably lower than those in Jungfernstieg. Parallel **Mönckebergstrasse** is also a premier shopping street and the site of the city's best-known chain department stores: Kaufhof, Karstadt, and Hertie.

Away from the downtown area in fashionable **Pöseldorf,** take a look at **Milchstrasse** and **Mittelweg.** Both are bright and classy, with small boutiques, restaurants, and cafés. The leading name is **Jill Sander** (Milchstr. 8, ☏ 040/5530–2173), the city's best-known designer of women's clothing and accessories.

Department Stores

Hamburg's most famous department store is the **Alsterhaus** (Jungfernstieg 16–20, ☏ 040/359–010). Large and elegant, it's a favorite with locals and a must for visitors. Even Prince Charles and Princess Diana stopped in here during a visit to Hamburg. Don't miss its amazing food department. Reward yourself for having braved the crowds by ordering a glass of champagne; it's a surprisingly good value. Other leading chain stores are **Kaufhof** (Mönckebergstr. 3, ☏ 040/333–070), **Karstadt** (Mönckebergstr. 16, ☏ 040/30940), and **Hertie** (Fuhlsbütterstr.

101, ☎ 040/611–330), offering much the same goods at similar prices as in branches in other cities across the country.

Food and Flea Markets

There are more than 50 markets in Hamburg each week; check with the tourist office for a full listing. The most famous is the **St. Pauli Fischmarkt.** In the heart of **Blankenese** there's a lively fruit and vegetable market. The **Isemarkt** is considered the most beautiful market in the city. (For additional information on all three, *see* Markets, *above*.)

SPORTS AND FITNESS

Bicycling

There are bike paths throughout downtown and many outlying areas. You can rent bikes from the tourist office (*see* Important Addresses and Numbers in Hamburg Essentials, *below*) for DM 2 per hour, April through September. A day's rental costs DM 10 (DM 20 for the weekend).

Golf

There are two leading clubs: **Hamburger Golf-Club Falkenstein** (In de Bargen 59, ☎ 040/812–177); and **Golf-Club auf der Wendlohe** (Oldesloerstr. 251, ☎ 040/550–5014). Visiting members of foreign clubs are welcome.

Jogging

The best places for jogging are around the Planten un Blomen and Alt Botanischer Garten parks and along the leafy promenade around the Alster. The latter is about 4 miles long.

Sailing

You can rent rowboats and sailboats on the Alster in the summer between 10 AM and 9 PM for around DM 12 an hour, plus DM 3 per additional person. For more advanced sailing, contact the **Yacht-Schule Bambauer** (Schöne Aussicht 20a, ☎ 040/220–0030).

Swimming

Don't even think about swimming in the Elbe or the Alster—they're health hazards. There are, however, pools—indoor and outdoor—throughout the city. A full listing is available from the tourist office. Two to try are **Alster Schwimmhalle** (Ifflandstr. 21) and **Blankenese** (Simrockstr. 45).

Tennis and Squash

The Hamburger Tennis Verband (Bei den Tennisplätzen 77, ☎ 040/651–2973) has full listings of the many indoor and outdoor courts in the city. Listings are also available from the tourist office. For squash, try the **Squash Center Marquardt** (Hagenbeckstr. 124a, ☎ 040/546–074). It has 17 courts, a swimming pool, a sauna, and a solarium.

DINING

The city's dining experiences range from sophisticated nouvelle cuisine in sleekly upscale restaurants to robust local specialties in simple harborside taverns. Seafood naturally figures prominently. The most celebrated dish is probably *Aalsuppe* (eel soup), a tangy concoction not entirely unlike Marseilles' famous bouillabaisse. A must in summer is

Aalsuppe grün, seasoned with dozens of herbs. Smoked eel, *Räucheraal,* is equally good. In fall, try *Bunte oder Gepflückte Finten,* a dish of green and white beans, carrots, and apples. Available anytime of year is *Küken ragout,* a concoction of sweetbreads, spring chicken, tiny veal meatballs, asparagus, clams, and fresh peas cooked in a white sauce. Other Hamburg specialties include *Stubenküken* (chicken), *Vierländer Mastente* (duck), *Birnen, Bohnen und Speck* (pears, beans, and bacon), and the sailors' favorite, *Labskaus*—a stew made from pickled meat, potatoes, and (sometimes) herring, garnished with a fried egg, sour pickles, and lots of beets.

CATEGORY	COST*
$$$$	over DM 95
$$$	DM 65–DM 95
$$	DM 45–DM 65
$	DM 25–DM 45

*per person for a three-course meal, excluding drinks

$$$$ **Landhaus Dill.** A fine fin de siècle building with views of the Elbe is home for this restaurant. It has an air of cool elegance, with crisp linen and glistening tile floors, and a high standard of cuisine. The lobster salad is still prepared at your table, and the rack of lamb comes hot from the kitchen with an aromatic thyme sauce. For dessert, try the rhubarb compote with vanilla cream. ✕ *Elbchaussee 94,* ☎ *040/390–5077. Reservations advised. Jacket and tie. AE, DC, MC, V. Closed Mon.*

$$$$ ★ **Landhaus Scherrer.** Though this establishment is only minutes from the downtown area, in Altona, its parklike setting seems worlds away from the high-rise bustle of the city. The mood is elegantly low-key—the building was originally a brewery—with wood-paneled walls and soft lighting. The food fuses sophisticated nouvelle specialties with more down-to-earth local dishes. The wine list is exceptional. ✕ *Elbchaussee 130,* ☎ *040/880–1325. Reservations advised. Jacket and tie. AE, DC, MC, V. Closed Sun.*

$$$$ ★ **L'Auberge Française.** Monsieur Lemercier, proprietor of Hamburg's most successful French restaurant, offers resolutely traditional dishes. Seafood is his specialty. Try the warm scampi salad in garlic butter or the goose liver in truffle sauce with apples. The restaurant is north of the Planten un Blomen Park. ✕ *Rutschbahn 34,* ☎ *040/410–2532. Reservations advised. Jacket and tie. AE, DC, MC, V. Closed Sun. and Dec. 20–Jan. 10.*

$$$$ ★ **Le Canard.** One of Hamburg's top restaurants, Le Canard possesses a much-coveted location overlooking the Elbe River, with enviably elegant decor and top-notch nouvelle cuisine to match. Chef Viehhauser's skills and creativity have kept the restaurant's standards high. Fish dishes predominate, but the roast lamb in thyme sauce is worth sampling. ✕ *Elbchaussee 139, tel 040/880–5057. Reservations required. Jacket and tie. AE, DC, MC, V. Closed Sun.*

$$$ ★ **Fischereihafen-Restaurant Hamburg.** For the best fish in Hamburg, dine at this big, upscale restaurant in Altona, just west of the downtown area and located right on the Elbe. The menu changes daily, according to what's available in the fish market that morning. It's a favorite with the city's beau monde. ✕ *Grosse Elbestr. 143,* ☎ *040/381–816. Reservations required. AE, DC, MC, V.*

$$$ **La Mer.** This is just about the best hotel restaurant in the city, the elegant dining room of the Hotel Prem, memorably located on the Aussenalster, a 10-minute ride from downtown. A changing host of subtle specialties are featured in this elegant restaurant, including marinated *inoki* mushrooms with imperial oysters and salmon roe, and spring venison

Hamburg Dining

KEY

i Tourist Information

EIMSBÜTTEL

NORD

ST. PAULI

Elbe

1/4 mile

1/4 km

Ahrberg, **3**

At Nali, **7**

Avocado, **16**

Fischereihafen-
Restaurant
Hamburg, **5**

Fischerhaus, **6**

Il Giardino, **12**

L'Auberge
Française, **8**

La Mer, **15**

Landhaus Dill, **1**

Landhaus Scherrer, **2**

Le Canard, **4**

Noblesse, **10**

Peter Lembcke, **14**

Ratsweinkeller, **13**

Restaurant Royal
Kopenhagen, **11**

Sagres, **9**

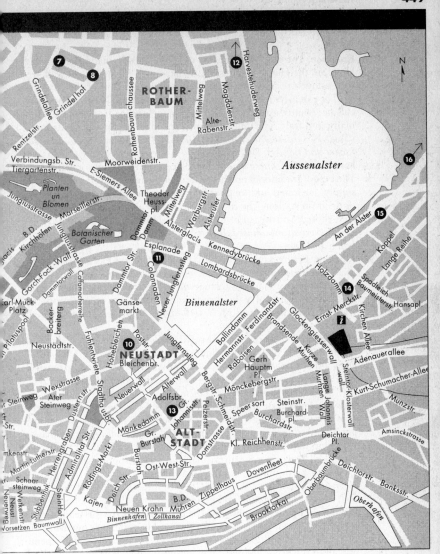

ROTHER-
BAUM

Grindelallee
Grindelhof
Rentzelstr.
Verbindungsb. Str.
Tiergartenstr.
Moorweidenstr.
E-Siemers Allee
Rothenbaum chaussee
Mittelweg
Magdalenstr.
Alte-
Rabenstr.
Harvestehuderweg

Junguusstrasse
Planten
un
Blomen
Marseillerstr.
Theodor
Heuss-
pl.
Dammtor-
Damm
Alsterglacis
Warburgstr.
Alsterufer

B.D.
Kirchhöfen
Junguusstrasse
Botanischer
Garten
Esplanade
Colonnaden
Kennedybrücke

Gorch-Fock-Wall
Dammtorwall
Dammtor Str.
Neuer Jungfernstieg
Lombardsbrücke

Aussenalster

An der Alster
Holzdamm
Koppel
Lange Reihe
Spadleich
Baumeisterstr. Hansapl.

Karl-Muck-
Platz
Pilatuspool
Backer-
breitere
Caffamacherreihe
Fuhlentwiete
Gänse-
markt
Binnenalster
Jungfernstieg
Ballindamm
Hermannstr.
Ferdinandstr.
Brandsende
Glockengiesserwall
Ernst-Merckstr.
Kirchen Allee
Adenauerallee

Neustädtstr.
Hoheblelchen
Poststr.
NEUSTADT
Bleichenbr.
Alterwall
Raboisen
Gerh
Hauptm
Pl.
Mönckebergstr.
Kurze
Muhren
Lange Johannis
Muhren Wall
Steintor-Klosterwall
Kurt-Schumacher-Allee
Munzstr.

Wexstrasse
Ater
Steinweg
Neuerwall
Adolfsbr.
Gr.
Johannsstr.
Bergstr.
Schmeidst.
Speer sort
Steinstr.
Burchard
Pl.
Burchardstr.
Amsinckstrasse

Steinweg
Düsternstr.
Stadtha usbr.
Mönkedamm
Gr.
Burstah
**ALT-
STADT**
Pelzerstr.
Domstrasse
Kl. Reichhenstr.
Deichtor
Pl.
Deichtorstr. Banksstr.

Martin-Lutherstr.
Herrengraben
Admiralital Str.
Rödings-Markt
Deich Str.
Burstah
Ost-West-Str.
Dovenfleet
Oberbaumbrücke
Oberhafen

Schaar
steinweg
Subbenhut
Steinhof
Kajen
Neuen Krahn
Mühren
Zippelhaus
Brooktorkai
Brooktorkai

Werkenstr.
Neust
Neuverweg
Vorsetzen
Baumwall
Binnenhafen
B.D.
Zollkanal

with elderberry sauce. ✕ *An der Alster 9,* ☎ *040/245–454. Reservations advised. Jacket and tie. AE, DC, MC, V. Closed Sat. and Sun. lunch.*

$$$ **Noblesse.** The elegant restaurant of Hamburg's Ramada Renaissance Hotel, in the Hanse arcades, has won awards for its cuisine and service, and it's rapidly becoming a choice eating haunt of the city center. The extensive menu combines German traditional fare and nouvelle cuisine, while the wine list includes fine selections from France, Germany, and Italy. The lunchtime menus and buffet are especially good value. ✕ *Grosse Bleichen,* ☎ *040/349–180. Reservations advised. Jacket and tie. AE, DC, MC, V.*

$$$ **Peter Lembcke.** There's no better place to eat eel soup or Labskaus.
★ The best of traditional northern German cuisine is served in this small, simply decorated and long-established restaurant, located just north of the train station. The restaurant is nearly always crowded; the service, though warm, can be uncertain. ✕ *Holzdamm 49,* ☎ *040/243–290. Reservations advised. Jacket and tie. AE, DC, MC, V. Closed Sat. lunch and Sun.*

$$ **Ahrberg.** This restaurant on the river in Blankenese has a pleasant terrace for summer dining and a cozy, wood-paneled dining room for colder days. The menu features a range of traditional German dishes and seafood specialties. Try the shrimp-and-potato soup or, in season, the fresh carp. ✕ *Strandweg 33,* ☎ *040/860–438. Reservations advised. AE, DC, MC, V. Closed Sun.*

$$ **Il Giardino.** The attractive courtyard garden here makes a delightful setting for low-key summer dining. The menu reflects a French influence, although the ambience is lively Italian. The wine list is extensive. ✕ *Ulmenstr. 17–19,* ☎ *040/470–147. Reservations advised. AE, DC, MC, V. Closed Mon. and Sun. lunch.*

$$ **Ratsweinkeller.** For atmosphere and robust local specialties, there are
★ few more compelling restaurants in Germany than this cavernous, late-19th-century haunt under the town hall. High stone and brick arches, with ship models suspended from them, and simple wood tables set the mood. You can order surprisingly fancy or no-nonsense meals. Fish specialties predominate, but there's a wide choice of other dishes, too. ✕ *Grosse-Johannisstr. 2,* ☎ *040/364–153. Reservations advised. AE, DC, MC, V. Closed Sun. and holidays.*

$$ **Restaurant Royal Kopenhagen.** The best time to go to this leading fish restaurant is on a Friday night, for the weekly buffet—as much as you can eat for DM 45 (not offered in January). Though most of the menu and all of the decor are maritime, red-meat eaters will find enough to make do here. A late-night menu is offered primarily for patrons of the nearby theater and opera house. If no table is available, try Stephans Keller downstairs (same management) for similar dishes at slightly lower prices. ✕ *Esplanade 31, at Stephanpl.,* ☎ *040/343–672. Reservations advised. AE, DC, MC, V. Closed Sun.*

$ **At Nali.** This is one of Hamburg's oldest and most popular Turkish restaurants; it has the added advantage of staying open till 1 AM, handy for those after a late-night kebab. Prices are low, service is reliable and friendly, and the menu is extensive. ✕ *Rutschbahn 11,* ☎ *040/410–3810. Reservations advised on weekends. AE, DC, MC, V.*

$ **Avocado.** The imaginative vegetarian menu at this popular, modern restaurant is an excellent value. Located in the pleasant Uhlenhorst district, close to the Aussenalster, it is Hamburg's only no-smoking restaurant. Try the salmon in Chablis. ✕ *Kanalstr. 9,* ☎ *040/220–4599. Reservations required. No credit cards. Closed Mon.*

$ **Fischerhaus.** Always busy (expect to share a table), this plainly deco-
★ rated waterfront establishment offers time-honored Hamburg fish specialties. It's hardly haute cuisine, but the standards, like the service,
are ultrareliable. This is a great place to try eel soup. ✕ *Fischmarkt
14, ☎ 040/314–053. Reservations advised. No credit cards.*

$ **Sagres.** Portuguese and Spanish restaurants are part of the city's sea-
faring tradition, and this is one of the best. The mood is busy and cheerful, the decor simple. Swordfish is an adventurous meal. Fight your way
through the Portuguese dockworkers to find a place at the bar, where
you'll probably have to wait for a table. If that doesn't work, try
Restaurant Benfica, which also specializes in Portuguese dishes, down
the street at No. 53. ✕ *Vorsetzen 46, ☎ 040/371–201. Reservations
advised on weekends. No credit cards.*

LODGING

Hamburg has a full range of hotels, from five-star, grande-dame luxury enterprises to simple pensions. The nearly year-round conference
and convention business keeps most rooms booked well in advance,
and the tariffs are high. But many of the more expensive hotels lower
weekend rates, for when all those businesspeople have gone home. The
tourist office can help with reservations if you arrive with nowhere to
stay (*see* Important Addresses and Numbers *in* Hamburg Essentials,
below); be sure to ask about the many **Happy Hamburg** special-ac-
commodation packages.

CATEGORY	COST*
$$$$	over DM 325
$$$	DM 225–DM 325
$$	DM 150–DM 225
$	under DM 150

**Prices are for two people in a double room, including tax and service
charge.*

$$$$ **Atlantic Hotel Kempinski.** There are few hotels in Germany more sumptuous than this gracious Edwardian palace facing the Aussenalster. The
mood is created with thick-carpeted, marble-inlaid panache, along
with modern touches, especially in the lighting. The lobby is positively
baronial: imposing marble pillars, leather armchairs, and a cham-
pagne-and-caviar serving snack bar. Whether the rooms are traditionally or more modernly furnished, they all are typically Hamburgian
in their understated luxury. All have a spacious sitting area with a writing desk, easy chairs, and a large bathroom, most with two washbasins,
a bathtub, and a separate shower stall. The suites are little short of palatial; Madonna, Prince, and Michael Jackson have found quarters in
the Presidential Suite. Service in the Atlantic is hushed and swift, and
the large and friendly staff will ensure that your every wish is fulfilled.
In fine weather guests can lounge in the formal outdoor courtyard, where
only the gurgling fountain disturbs the peace. The Atlantic-Restaurant
is a stunning example of Post-Modernism, with rich bird's-eye maple
details, black columns, and inlaid marble. ☎ *An der Alster 72,
☎ 040/28880, FAX 040/247–129. 243 rooms and 13 suites, all with bath.
2 restaurants, 2 bars, room service, indoor pool, beauty salon massage,
sauna, parking. AE, DC, MC, V.*

$$$$ **Hotel Abtei.** Located on a quiet, tree-lined street a mile north of the
downtown area in Harvestehude, this elegant period hotel offers understated luxury and very friendly, personal service. You can have
your breakfast in the beautiful garden and afternoon tea in the antique-
filled sitting room. In the evenings, the intimate restaurant serves care-

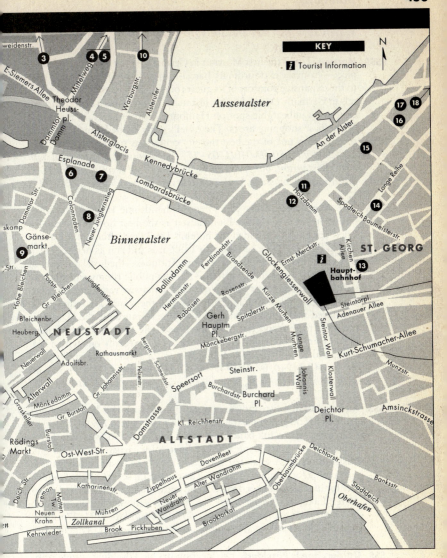

KEY

i Tourist Information

N

weidenstr.

3

4 **5**

10

Aussenalster

17 **18**

16

E.Siemers Allee

Mittelweg

Theodor
Heuss-
pl.

Warburgstr.

Alsteruler

An der Alster

Dammtor
Damm

Alsterglacis

Kennedybrücke

15

Lange Reihe

Esplanade

6 **7**

Lombardsbrücke

11

Holzdamm

Spadteich

14

Dammtor Str.

Colonnaden

8

Neuer Jungfernstieg

12

Baumeisterstr.

skamp

Binnenalster

Ferdinandstr.

Brandsende

Glockengiesserwall

Ernst Merckstr.

Kirchen
Allee

ST. GEORG

Gänse-
markt.

9

Str.

Hohe Bleichen

Poststr.

Gr. Bleichen

Jungfernstieg

Ballindamm

Hermannstr.

Raboisen

Rosenstr.

Kurze Mühren

i

**Haupt-
bahnhof**

13

Bleichenbr.

Heuberg.

NEUSTADT

Neuerwall

Alterwall

Adolfsbr.

Rathausmarkt

Bergstr.

Gr. Johannistr.

Pelzerstr.

Schmiedt.

Gerh
Hauptm
Pl.

Spitalerstr.

Mönckebergstr.

Steinstr.

Lange
Mühren

Johannis
Wall

Steintor Wall

Klosterwall

Steintorpl.
Adenauer Allee

Munzstr.

Kurt-Schumacher-Allee

Graskeller

Mönkedamm

Gr. Burstah

Burstah

Speersort

Burchardstr.

Burchard
Pl.

Deichtor
Pl.

Amsinckstrasse

Rödings
Markt

Gr. Burstah

Domstrasse

Kl. Reichhenstr.

ALTSTADT

Deich Str.

Crenon

Twi

Matten

Ost-West-Str.

Katharinenstr.

Zippelhaus

Neuer
Wandrahm

Dovenfleet

Alter Wandrahm

Oberbaumbrücke

Deichtorstr.

Stadtdeich

Banksstr.

Neuen
Krahn

Kehrwieder

Zollkanal

Mühren

Brook

Pickhuben

Brooktorkai

Oberhafen

fully prepared traditional German dishes. ⌧ *Abteistr. 14,* ☎ *040/442–905,* ⊠ *040/449–820. 11 rooms, all with bath. Restaurant. AE, DC, MC, V.*

$$$$ **Marriott.** This is the first Marriott in Germany, and it remains the showpiece—from the extraordinary barrel-roof ceiling of the reception area to the expansive comfort of its guest rooms. Unlike other Marriott hotels in Germany (Munich's, for instance), this one has a central city location, an unbeatable spot on Hamburg's Gänsemarkt, in the center of the best shopping areas. The hotel's aptly named American Place restaurant is one of the best the city center has to offer. ⌧ *ABC-Str. 52,* ☎ *040/35050,* ⊠ *040/3505–1777. 277 rooms, 10 suites, all with bath. Restaurant, bar, no-smoking rooms, room service, indoor pool, beauty salon, massage, sauna, fitness center, parking. AE, DC, MC, V.*

$$$$ **Vier Jahreszeiten.** Some claim that this handsome 19th-century town
★   house on the edge of the Binnenalster is the best hotel in Germany. Friedrich Haerlin founded the hotel in 1897, and although it was acquired by a Japanese company in 1989, it is still run as perfectly as it was under Haerlin family ownership. Antiques—the hotel has a set of near-priceless Gobelin tapestries—line the public rooms and stud the stylish bedrooms; forests of flowers stand in massive vases; rare oil paintings hang on the walls; and, of course, all the rooms are individually decorated with superb taste. Of the three restaurants, the Haerlin is the most formal and features superb nouvelle and classic specialties. If you want a room with a view of the lake, especially one with a balcony, make reservations well in advance. ⌧ *Neuer Jungfernstieg 9–14,* ☎ *040/34940,* ⊠ *040/349–4602. 148 rooms, 23 apartments, all with bath. 3 restaurants, bar, room service, beauty salon, parking. AE, DC, MC, V.*

$$$ **Aussen Alster.** Crisp and contemporary in design, this boutique hotel prides itself on giving personal attention to its guests. Rooms are compact; most have a full bathroom, and a few have a shower only. Stark white walls, white bedspreads, and light-color carpets create a bright, fresh ambience. A small bar is open in the evenings and a tiny garden is available for summer cocktails. The restaurant serves Mediterranean fare for lunch and dinner. Down at the bottom of the street is the Aussen Alster Lake, where the hotel has its own sailboat for guests' use. ⌧ *Schmilinskystr. 11,* ☎ *040/241–557,* ⊠ *040/280–3231. 27 rooms, all with bath or shower. Restaurant, bar, sauna, bicycles. AE, DC, MC, V.*

$$$ **Garden Hotels Pöseldorf.** The location in chic Pöseldorf, a mile from
★   the downtown area, may discourage those who want to be in the thick of things, but otherwise this is one of the most appealing hotels in Hamburg, offering classy and chic accommodations in three attractive city mansions. It's very much the insider's choice. There's no restaurant, but light, cold meals are served in the bar and airy winter garden. ⌧ *Magdalenenstr. 60,* ☎ *040/414–040,* ⊠ *040/414–0420. 57 rooms, 3 suites, all with bath. Bar, parking. AE, DC, MC, V.*

$$$ **Hotel Prem.** Facing the Aussen Alster, this extremely personable, quiet,
★   small hotel is Hamburg's gem. Most of its guests are repeats who have their favorite rooms; no two rooms are the same. The Adenauer Suite (West Germany's chancellor stayed here when he was in Hamburg), for example, is traditionally furnished, including an antique chaise longue and a period writing desk in a small alcove with a lake view. Room 102 across the hall has contemporary furnishings and a platform bed. Suite 2 has two modernly furnished rooms with a terrace overlooking the lake. The intimate bar is perfect for an evening drink, and the din-

ing at La Mer is superb (*see* Dining, *above*). ☎ *An der Alster 8–10,* ☎ *040/245–454,* FAX *040/280–3851. 44 rooms, 11 suites, all with bath. Restaurant, bar, sauna. AE, DC, MC, V.*

$$$ **Hotel Senator.** At this modern hotel, conveniently located two blocks from the main railway station, every room has a fresh look, with modern conveniences from hair dryers to cable TV. The largest and quietest rooms are on the fifth floor at the back of the building. Most rooms have bathrooms with a full bath; a few have only a shower. On the first floor, the reception area has a pleasant glass-enclosed terrace for breakfast as well as a bar and a lounge. ☎ *Lange Reihe 18–20,* ☎ *040/241–203,* FAX *040/280–3717. 56 rooms, all with bath. Restaurant, bar, parking. AE, DC, MC, V.*

$$ **Alameda.** Occupying the first two floors of a downtown building, the Alameda offers guests good, basic accommodations. The upstairs rooms are nicer and somewhat more spacious, but all rooms have TV, radio, and minibar. ☎ *Colonnaden 45,* ☎ *040/344–000,* FAX *040/343– 439. 18 rooms, all with shower or bath. AE, DC, MC, V.*

$$ **Baseler Hof.** It's hard to find fault with this hotel. It's centrally located near the Binnenalster and the opera house, service is friendly and efficient, rooms are neatly if functionally furnished, and prices are quite reasonable for this expensive city. The hotel caters to individuals and convention groups, so at times the lounge area, with rather formal clusters of tables and chairs, can become crowded. ☎ *Esplanade 11,* ☎ *040/359–060,* FAX *040/3590–6918. 149 rooms, all with bath. 2 restaurants, bar, room service. AE, DC, MC, V.*

$$ **Hotel-Garni Mittelweg.** With chintz curtains, flowered wallpaper, old-fashioned dressing tables, and a country-house-style dining room that, unfortunately, serves only breakfast, this hotel possesses a small-town charm that seems almost out of place in bustling, big-business Hamburg. A converted turn-of-the-century mansion in up-market Pösseldorf, it's well located on the fashionable Mittelweg, a short walk from the Aussenalster and a quick bus ride to the city center. ☎ *Mittelweg 59,* ☎ *040/414–1010,* FAX *040/4141–0120. 35 rooms, 2 apartments, all with bath or shower. No credit cards.*

$$ **Hotel-Pension am Nonnenstieg.** The owner, Frau Hodermann, is friendly and helpful and makes this unassuming little hotel homey. Extra beds for younger children can be put in rooms at no extra charge. Ask for a room with a kitchen alcove if you want to cook for yourself. There is no restaurant; only breakfast is offered. ☎ *Nonnenstieg 11,* ☎ *040/480–6490,* FAX *040/4806–4949. 30 rooms, all with bath. No credit cards.*

$$ **Ibis Hamburg Alster.** This French chain hotel may have few frills, but in this costly city it offers smart, uniformly decorated rooms at reasonable rates. Each room has a bathroom with a shower and just enough space to hang your clothes. On the ground floor the helpful, English-speaking staff are welcoming, and the lobby bar creates camaraderie among the guests. The location, across the street from the Atlantic Kempinski, is just a five-minute walk from the train station and two minutes from the Alster Lakes. ☎ *Holtzdamm 4–12,* ☎ *040/248–290,* FAX *040/2482–9999. 165 rooms. Restaurant, bar, parking. AE, DC, MC, V.*

$$ **Kronprinz.** For its down-market position (on a busy street opposite the railway station) and its moderate price, the Kronprinz is a surprisingly attractive hotel, with a whiff of five-star flair. Rooms are individually styled, modern but homey; ask for number 45, which has mahogany and red-plush decor. ☎ *Kirchenallee 46,* ☎ *040/243–258,* FAX *040/280–*

1097. *69 rooms, all with bath or shower. Restaurant, bar. AE, DC, MC, V.*

$$ **Mellingburger Schleuse.** If you want off-the-beaten-track lodgings while visiting Hamburg, this member of the Ringhotels association is the place for you. Only a 20-minute drive from the downtown area, it is idyllically located in a forest—the Alsterwanderweg hiking trail passes right by the doorstep. The hotel itself is more than 200 years old, with a thatch roof, peasant-style furnishings, and a restaurant that serves traditional northern German dishes. ⊞ *Mellingburgredder 1,* ☎ *040/602–4001,* ⨳ *040/602–7912. 40 rooms, all with bath. 2 restaurants, bar, indoor pool, fitness room, parking. AE, DC, MC.*

$$ **Nippon Hotel.** You'll be asked to remove your shoes before entering your room at the Nippon, western Germany's second exclusively Japanese hotel (the first is in Düsseldorf). There are tatami on the floor, futon mattresses on the beds, and an attentive Japanese staff. The authenticity might make things a bit *too* spartan and efficient for some, but by cutting some Western-style comforts the hotel is able to offer good value in the attractive Uhlenhorst district. The hotel has a Japanese restaurant and sushi bar. ⊞ *Hofweg 75,* ☎ *040/227–1140,* ⨳ *040/2271–1490. 41 rooms, 1 suite, all with bath or shower. AE, DC, MC, V.*

$$ **Wedina.** Rooms at this small hotel are neat and compact, with contemporary furnishings and bathrooms that have either a shower or a tub. A small bar and a restaurant area, used for breakfast only, are on the ground floor and face the veranda and small pool. The owners, who are from Switzerland, also have a small pension, Gästehaus Gurlitt, across the street with 15 simpler and slightly smaller rooms, all with shower. Both lodgings are a half block from the Aussenalster and a brisk 10-minute walk from the station. ⊞ *Gurlittstr. 23,* ☎ *040/243–011,* ⨳ *040/280–3894. 27 rooms with bath or shower. Bar, outdoor pool, sauna. AE, DC, MC, V.*

$ **Hotel-Garni Emde.** This small, friendly hotel is hard to find (the nearest S-bahn station is Hamburg-Othmarschen, on the S-I), but it's worth the trouble. Within this charming mansion set on its own lovely grounds are homey comforts and rooms that are quite luxurious for the price. ⊞ *Lüdemannstr. 1,* ☎ *040/899–7980,* ⨳ *040/8997–9820. 10 rooms, 2 suites, all with bath or shower. No credit cards.*

$ **Hotel-Pension bei der Esplanade.** Bei der Esplanade takes up the third and fourth floors of the building that houses the Alameda. The rooms are basic but quiet, clean, and comfortable. ⊞ *Colonnaden 45,* ☎ *040/342–961,* ⨳ *040/354–082. 13 rooms, some with shower. No credit cards.*

THE ARTS AND NIGHTLIFE

The Arts

The arts flourish in this elegant metropolis. The Hamburg city ballet is one of the finest in Europe—the Ballet Festival in July is a cultural high point. Full information on upcoming events is available in the magazine *Hamburger Vorschau*—pick it up in tourist offices and most hotels for DM 2.30—and the magazine *Szene Hamburg,* sold at newsstands throughout the city for DM 4.

A number of travel agencies sell tickets for plays, concerts, and the ballet. There's also a ticket office in the main tourist office in the Bieberhaus, Hachmannplatz (☎ 040/280–2848). Alternatively, try the following ticket agencies in the downtown area: **Theaterkasse im Al-**

sterhaus (Jungfernstieg 16, ☎ 040/352–664) or **Theaterkasse Central** (Gerhart-Hauptmann-Pl., ☎ 040/337–124).

Theater

The city has a full program of theater year-round, though you'll need to understand German well to get the most of the productions. Leading theaters include: **Deutsches Schauspielhaus** (Kirchenallee 39, ☎ 040/248–713), probably the most beautiful theater in the city, lavishly restored to its full 19th-century opulence in the early 1980s and now the most important venue in Hamburg for classical and modern theater; **Thalia-Theater** (Alstertor, ☎ 040/322–666), presenting a varied program of plays old and new; the newly reopened **Neue Flora Theater** (corner of Alsenstr. and Stresemannstr., ☎ 040/2707–5270), where at press time *Phantom of the Opera* continued its long run; and **Hansa Theater** (Steindamm 17, ☎ 040/241–414) Germany's oldest classical music hall. One partial solution to the language problem is to check a musical; Hamburg is by far Germany's musicals capital. **The English Theater** (Lerchenfeld 14, ☎ 040/227–7089) may provide the complete antidote: As the name suggests, all productions are in English. For alternative theater and dance productions, including groups of national and international renown, try **Kampnagel** (Jarrestr. 20-24, ☎ 040/2709–4948).

Concerts

The **Musikhalle** (Karl-Muck-Pl., ☎ 040/346–920) is Hamburg's most important concert hall; both the Hamburg Philharmonic and the Hamburg Symphony Orchestra appear regularly. Visiting orchestras from overseas are also showcased here. The **Norddeutscher Rundfunk Studio 10** (Oberstr., ☎ 040/413–2504) has regular concerts by the symphony orchestra and guest appearances by visiting musicians.

Opera and Ballet

The **Staatsoper Hamburg** (Grosse Theaterstr. 35, ☎ 040/351–721) is one of the most beautiful theaters in the country and the leading northern German venue for top-class opera and ballet. The **Operettenhaus** (Spielbudenpl. 1, ☎ 040/270–75270) puts on light opera and musicals.

Film

The **British Council Film Club** (Rothenbaumchaussee 34, ☎ 040/446–057) shows films in English.

Nightlife

The Reeperbahn

Whether you think it sordid or sexy, the Reeperbahn in the St. Pauli district is as central to the Hamburg scene as are the classy shops along Jungfernstieg. A walk down Herbertstrase (men only, no women or children permitted), just two blocks south of the Reeperbahn, can be quite an eye-opener. Here prostitutes sit displayed in windows as they await customers. Nearby on Grosse Freiheit (an appropriate name: it means Great Freedom) are a number of the better-known sex-show clubs. **Colibri** is at No. 30, **Safari** at No. 24, and **Salambo** at No. 11. They cater to the package-tour trade as much as to those on the prowl by themselves. Prices are high. If you order anything to drink, ask to see the price list first (legally, it has to be on display), and pay as soon as you're served. Don't expect much to happen here before 10 PM.

Jazz Clubs

The jazz scene in Hamburg is thriving as never before. There are more than 100 venues and few nights when you won't have a wide selection from which to choose. Among the leading clubs are **Birdland** (Gärtnerstr. 122, ☎ 040/405–277), featuring everything from traditional New Orleans sounds to avant-garde electronic noises; **Cotton Club** (Alter Steinweg 10, ☎ 040/343–878), Hamburg's oldest jazz club; and **Fabrik** (Barnerstr. 36, ☎ 040/391–079), which offers Sunday-morning *Früschoppen* (brunch) concerts at 11 (they're always packed, so get here early).

Discos

Hans-Albers-Platz and the surrounding area is the young folks' scene. **Die Insel** (Alsterufer 35, ☎ 040/410–6955), a disco and a restaurant in one, is one of the biggest night spots in Hamburg. Prices can be high, but it's always chic. Pricey, too, is **Top of the Town,** an elegant disco night spot on the 26th floor of the SAS Plaza Hotel (Marseillerstr. 2, ☎ 040/3502–3210). **Skyy** (Spielbudenpl. 16b, ☎ 040/319–1711) is tiny and plays African music. St. Pauli also has discos as well as sex clubs. **Mojo Club** (Reeperbahn 1, ☎ 040/319–1999) is a funky club-disco that plays primarily acid jazz and soul. **Grosse Freiheit 36** (Grosse Freiheit 36, ☎ 040/420–3282) has dance floors and discos spread over three stories.

EXCURSIONS

Tour 1: Ahrensburg

One of Schleswig-Holstein's major attractions is the romantic 16th-century **Schloss Ahrensburg** (Ahrensburg Castle), in the town of Ahrensburg, about 25 kilometers (16 miles) northeast of Hamburg. Ahrensburg itself is mainly a commuter town, home to about 27,000 people. The magnificent castle and nearby **Bredenbecker Teich Lake** make it worth a visit—it's an ideal day excursion.

Getting There

By Car: Take the A–1 Autobahn for 25 kilometers (15 miles), and get off at the Ahrensburg exit. Alternatively, you can take Bundestrasse B–75.

By Train: Take the S-bahn line S-4 to Ahrensburg or the U-bahn line U-1 to Ahrensburg-Ost.

Exploring

Surrounded by lush parkland on the banks of the Hunnau, Schloss Ahrensburg, a whitewashed-brick, moated Renaissance castle, stands much as it did when it was constructed at the end of the 16th century. Originally built by Count Peter Rantzau, it changed hands in 1759 and was remodeled inside by its new owner, the financier Carl Schimmelmann. The interior was again altered in the mid-19th century and recently underwent yet another renovation.

Inside are period furniture and paintings, fine porcelain, and exquisite crystal. On the grounds stands a simple 16th-century church erected at the same time as the castle, although the west tower was completed later and Baroque alterations were made in the 18th century. The church is nestled between two rows of 12 almshouses, or *Gottesbu-*

den (God's cottages). ☞ *DM 3.* ⊗ *Feb.–Oct., Tues.–Sun. 10–12:30 and 1:30–5; Nov.–Jan., Tues.–Sun. 10–12:30 and 1:30–3.*

Tour 2: Altes Land

The marshy **Altes Land** extends 30 kilometers (19 miles) west from Hamburg along the south bank of the Elbe River to the town of Stade. This traditional fruit-growing region is dotted with huge half-timbered farmhouses and crisscrossed by canals. The fertile land is a popular hiking spot, especially in spring, when the apple and cherry trees are in blossom. Some of the prettiest walks take you along the dikes running next to the Rivers Este and Lühe. Much of the territory is best covered on foot, so wear your walking shoes. You may want to bring a picnic lunch as well.

Getting There

By Car: Take B–73 west from Harburg.

By Ferry: Ferries depart from the Landungsbrücken boat landing in the St. Pauli district twice daily during the week and four times daily on the weekends from mid-April through August and only on the weekends in September. Take the ferry to Lühe. To reach Cranz take the ferry from Blankenese.

Exploring

From the dock at **Cranz,** walk south into the suburb of **Neunfelde** and visit the Baroque St. Pancras Church, with its unusual painted barrel roof. The altar inside was built in 1688, and the organ, dating from the same period, was designed by Arp Schnitger, an organ builder and local farmer.

The village of **Jork** in Lower Saxony lies some 9 kilometers (5 miles) on foot to the west of Neunfelde, just beyond the confluence of the Este and Elbe rivers. Stroll through Jork and take in the early 18th-century church and decorative farmhouses. The old windmill in nearby **Borstel** is worth a short detour.

Lühe is the ferry docking point that's closest to the town of **Stade,** but be prepared to walk about 13 kilometers (8 miles) to reach it. Stade lies on the west edge of the Altes Land on the River Schwinge and was once a member of the Hanseatic League of trading towns. Four times the size of Jork, with a population of 45,000, Stade is notable for the ruins of a rampart wall around the Altstadt (Old Town); it also contains the obligatory half-timbered houses.

HAMBURG ESSENTIALS

Arriving and Departing

By Bus

The ZOB, or **Zentral-Omnibus-Bahnhof,** Hamburg's bus station, is located right behind the Hauptbahnhof (Adenauerallee 78). For information call 040/247–575, or contact the **Deutsche Touring-Gesellschaft** (Am Römerhof 17, D-60486 Frankfurt/Main, ☎ 069/79030).

By Car

Hamburg is easier to handle by car than are many other German cities, and relatively uncongested by traffic. Incoming Autobahns connect with

Hamburg's three beltways, which then take you easily to the downtown area. Follow the signs for "Stadtmitte."

By Ferry

The Ms. Hamburg (☎ 040/383–930) carries passengers and cars three times a week for the 24-hour run between Hamburg and Harwich, England.

By Plane

Hamburg's international airport, **Fuhlsbüttel** (☎ 040/50750) is 11 kilometers (7 miles) northwest of the city. Many major U.S. airlines fly to Hamburg; there are also regular flights from Britain. There are frequent flights from all major German cities and European capitals.

BETWEEN THE AIRPORT AND DOWNTOWN

An **Airport-City-Bus** runs between the airport and Hamburg's Hauptbahnhof (main train station) daily at 20-minute intervals. Along the way, buses stop at the hotels Reichshof, Atlantic, and Hamburg-Plaza, the central bus station at Adenauerallee 78, and at the fairgrounds. Buses run from 5:40 AM to 10:30 PM. Tickets are DM 8 per person (free for children under 4). The **Airport-Express** (Bus 110) runs every 10 minutes between the airport and the Ohlsdorf U- and S-bahn stations, a 17-minute ride from the main train station. The fare is DM 3.60 for adults and DM 1.20 for children. A taxi from the airport to the downtown area will cost about DM 30. If you're picking up a rental car at the airport, follow the signs to "Stadtmitte" (downtown).

By Train

EuroCity and InterCity trains connect Hamburg with all German cities and many major European cities. Two InterCityExpress "super train" lines link Hamburg with Frankfurt and Munich, and Würzburg and Munich, respectively. There are two principal stations: the centrally located **Hauptbahnhof** and **Hamburg-Altona,** located west of the downtown area. For information, call 040/19419.

Getting Around

By Bike

Most major streets in Hamburg have paths reserved for bicyclists. From May through September, rent bikes at the tourist information office at the main train station. Prices range from DM 2 per hour to DM 20 for the entire weekend. For information, call 040/3005–1244.

By Car

CAR RENTAL

Avis, Airport, ☎ 040/5075–2314; Drehbahn 15–25, ☎ 040/341–651. **Hertz,** Airport, ☎ 040/5075–2302; Amsinckstrasse. 45, ☎ 040/230–045. **Sixt-Budget,** Airport, ☎ 040/5075–2305; Friedrich-Ebert-Damm 160a, ☎ 040/693–9393.

By Public Transportation

The HVV, Hamburg's public transportation system, includes the **U-bahn** (subway), the **S-bahn** (suburban train), and **buses.** A one-way fare starts at DM 2.30, which covers approximately four stops. DM 3.60 covers about eight stops. Tickets are available on all buses and at the automatic machines in all stations and at most bus stops. A **Tageskarte** (an all-day ticket) valid from 9 AM to 1 AM costs DM 6.90 for unlimited rides on the HVV system. If you're traveling with family or friends, a

Gruppen- od. Familienkarte (group or family ticket) is a good value; a group of up to four adults and three children can travel around for the entire day for only DM 12.20. Available from all of the Hamburg tourist offices, the **Hamburg CARD** allows free travel on all public transportation within the city, free admission to state museums, and approximately 30% discounts on most bus, train, and boat tours. For one day's use (valid starting 6 PM the previous day), the Hamburg CARD costs DM 11.80 for one adult and up to three children under the age of 12; the family card costs DM 24 for four adults and up to three children under the age of 12. The Hamburg CARD for three days (valid starting at noon the first day) costs DM 23.80 and DM 38, respectively.

Tickets are not collected as you enter or leave the platform, but if you are found without a ticket, the fine is DM 80.

In the north of Hamburg, the HVV system connects with the **A-bahn** (Alsternordbahn), a suburban train system that extends into Schleswig-Holstein.

Night buses (Nos. 600–640) serve the downtown area all night, leaving the Rathausmarkt and Hauptbahnhof every hour.

Information on the HVV system can be obtained directly from the **Hamburg Passenger Transport Board** by calling 040/322–911 (open daily 7 AM–8 PM).

By Taxi

Taxi meters start at DM 3.60, and the fare is DM 2.20 per kilometer, plus 50 pfennigs for each piece of luggage. To order a taxi, call 040/441–011, 040/686–868, or 040/611–061.

On Foot

The historic center of Hamburg can be easily explored on foot. The downtown area's Binnenalster and Jungfernstieg, many shopping streets and shopping galleries, and harbor are all close enough to make walking easy.

Guided Tours

Boat Tours

Water dominates Hamburg, and there are few better ways to get to know the city than by taking a trip around the massive harbor. During the summer excursion boats and barges leave the Landungsbrücken (piers) every half hour for one-hour tours of the harbor. During the winter departures are not as frequent, with operators usually waiting for a full boat before setting off. The boats leave from Piers 1, 2, 3, and 7, and the trips cost DM 15 for adults and DM 7.50 for children under 14. The **Störtebeker** line offers a six-course Baroque-style banquet with music during a four-hour tour of the harbor for DM 111. You must book in advance for this one (☎ 040/220–2552). For additional information on harbor tours, call 040/311–7070 or 040/314–644.

Boat trips around the Alster Lakes and through the canals leave from the Jungfernstieg in the center of the city. From April through November, they leave every half hour, less regularly in winter. The cost of the 50-minute tour is DM 13 for adults and DM 7.50 for children under 14; the complete three-hour tour costs DM 19 for adults and DM 9.50 for children.

From May through September there's a romantic, nighttime tour of the Alster Lakes leaving the Jungfernstieg every evening at 8 (the fare is DM 19, DM 9.50 for children). For information on these and other Alster tours, call 040/341–141.

Hamburg by Night
Stadtrundfahrt City Sightseeing (☎ 040/227–7595) offers "adults-only" tours of Hamburg hot spots nightly Tuesday–Saturday, from late March to early November, and on Friday and Saturday nights the rest of the year. The tours leave Kirchenallee (in front of Hauptbahnhof) at 8 and take in a cross section of the city's night spots, including St. Pauli sex bars. The DM 99 fare includes drinks along the way. If you want a taste of Hamburg's no-holds-barred nightlife but don't want to head out on your own, this is a reasonable introduction.

Orientation Tours
Sightseeing bus tours of the city, all with English-speaking guides (☎ 040/227–1060) leave from Kirchenallee by the main train station. A bus tour lasting 1¾ hours sets off at 9, 11, noon, 1, 3, and 4 daily in summer, less frequently the rest of the year, and costs DM 24 for adults, DM 12 for children. A longer tour, lasting 2½ hours, starts at 10 and 2, costing DM 30 for adults, DM 15 for children. For an additional DM 11 adults/5.50 children, both tours can be combined with a one-hour boat trip; tours are conducted at irregular times, according to season. City tours aboard the nostalgic *Hummelbahn* (converted railroad wagons pulled by a tractor) are offered daily April–October, starting at the Kirchenallee stop hourly from 10 to 5 from and at 10, noon, 2, and 4 November–March. The fare is DM 20 adults, DM 7 children for 1½ hours. On Friday and Saturday at 8 PM May–August, the *Hummerlbahn* also offers a three-hour evening tour of the city at a cost of DM 48 for adults and DM 14 for children (includes a drink). Some tours also leave from the Landungsbrücken; inquire at a tourist information office.

Walking Tours
Tours of the downtown area are organized by the **Museum für Arbeit.** They are held on weekends only May–September and are conducted in German only, May through September. Call 040/2984–2364 for information.

Important Addresses and Numbers

Consulates
U.S. Consulate General, Alsterufer 28, ☎ 040/411–710.
British Consulate General, Harvestehuder Weg 8a, ☎ 040/448–0320.

Emergencies
Police: ☎ 110. **Ambulance** and **Fire Department:** ☎ 112. **Medical Emergencies:** ☎ 040/228–022. **Dentist:** ☎ 040/468–3260 or 040/11500.

English Bookstore
Frensche (Spitalerstrasse 26e, ☎ 040/327–585) stocks books and newspapers.

Travel Agencies
American Express (Rathausmarkt 5, ☎ 040/331–141). **Hapag-Lloyd** (Verkehrspavillon Jungfernstieg, ☎ 040/3258–5640).

Visitor Information

The main branch of the tourist office is in the **Bieberhaus,** at **Hachmann-platz** (next to the main railway station, ☎ 040/3005–1244). It's open weekdays 7:30 AM–6 PM, Saturday 8 AM–3 PM. In addition to its comprehensive hotel guide, the tourist office also publishes a monthly program of events in the city, *Hamburg Vorschau,* available for DM 2.30, which details upcoming shows, plays, movies, and exhibits. The illustrated magazine *Hamburg Tips* is issued quarterly and details major seasonal events; it's free of charge.

There's also a tourist office in the **Hauptbahnhof** (the main train station; ☎ 040/300–51230); it's open daily 7 AM–11 PM. The **airport tourist office** (☎ 040/300–51240) is open daily 8 AM–11 PM. At the harbor there's an office at the **St. Pauli Landungsbrücken** (boat landings; ☎ 040/300–51200); it's open daily 9:30–5:30. There's also an office in the **Hanse Viertel** shopping mall (☎ 040/3005–1220), open weekdays 10–6:30 (Thurs. 10–8:30), Saturday 10–3 (10–6 on the first Sat. of the month).

All offices can help with accommodations, and there's a central booking office for telephone callers (☎ 040/19412). A DM 5 fee is charged for every room reserved; the cost is then deducted from your bill at the hotel.

15 Berlin

Berlin became capital of the newly unified German Empire under Bismarck in the late 1800s and hung on to that position until it was almost bombed out of existence in the struggle against Hitler and Nazism. Following the war, it was artificially partitioned and later barricaded, and the division between East and West became tangible as well as symbolic; reunification was like an impossible dream come true. Through it all, Berliners displayed a remarkable resilience, a trait they continue to need as the city works to rebuild and resume its role as Germany's capital.

BERLIN'S ROLE AS THE FOCAL POINT and touchstone of a reuniting Germany began in autumn 1989 and culminated in the historic vote on June 20, 1991, by the German parliament to make the city once again the seat of the German government. Thus ends one of the great geographic and political anomalies of the 20th century: a city split in two by a 12-foot-high concrete wall, with its larger western half an island of capitalist democracy, surrounded by an East Germany run by hard-line Communists. Built in 1961 at the height of the cold war, the Berlin Wall symbolized the separation of two sharply different political and economic systems. Ironically, though, it also became a major tourist attraction, where viewing platforms along the western side enabled visitors to see the battlefront-like no-man's-land, guarded by soldiers and peppered with deadly mines and booby traps. The wall's demolition cast it once more as a symbol: this time, though, a symbol of the change sweeping over former Iron Curtain countries. Four large chunks of the wall have been left standing as reminders of the grim past.

Berlin actually began as two cities more than 750 years ago. Museum Island, on the Spree River, was once called Cölln, while the mainland city was always known as Berlin. As early as the 1300s, Berlin prospered from its location at the crossroads of important trade routes, and it became filled with merchants and artisans of every description. After the ravages of the Thirty Years' War (1618–48), Berlin rose to power as the seat of the Brandenburg dynasty, and 200 years later when the Brandenburgian and Prussian realms united under the Hohenzollerns, Berlin was the chosen capital. The 1701 coronation of the enlightened ruler King Friedrich II—also known as Frederick the Great—set off a renaissance in the city, especially in the construction of such academic institutions as the Academy of Arts and the Academy of Sciences.

The Prussian Empire, especially under Count Bismarck in the late 19th century, proved to be the dominant force in unifying the many independent German principalities. Berlin maintained its status as the German capital throughout the German Empire (1871–1918), the post–World War I Weimar Republic (1919–33), and Hitler's Third Reich (1933–45). In the 1920s and early '30s the city also served as an important European social and cultural capital, tinged with a reputation for decadence. But during World War II, acting as the Nazi headquarters, it was bombed to smithereens—at the end of hostilities there was more rubble in Berlin than in all other German cities combined. Most of what you see there today has been built, or rebuilt, since 1945.

With the division of Germany after World War II, Berlin was also partitioned, with American, British, and French troops in the districts to the west, the Soviet Union's forces to the east. After the Potsdam Agreement in 1945, the three western zones of occupation gradually merged into one, becoming West Berlin, while the Soviet-controlled eastern zone defiantly remained separate. In 1948, in an attempt to force the Western Allies to relinquish their stake in the city, the U.S.S.R. set up a blockade cutting off all overland supply routes from the West. The Western Allies countered by mounting the Berlin Airlift, during which some 750,000 flights delivering 2 million tons of goods kept Berlin alive for most of a fateful year, until the Soviets finally lifted the blockade. As peace conferences repeatedly failed to resolve the question of Germany's division, in 1949 the Soviet Union established East Berlin as the capital of its new puppet state, the German Democratic Republic.

West Berlin was not technically part of the Federal Republic of Germany, though it was clearly tied to the East's legal and economic system. The division of the city was emphasized in 1961, when the East German government constructed the infamous Berlin Wall.

With the wall now on the junk pile of history, access to all parts of the city is taken for granted, and visitors can appreciate the qualities that mark the city as a whole. Its particular charm has always lain in its spaciousness, its trees and greenery, its racy atmosphere, and the ease of reaching the lakes and forests within its perimeter. It is a vast city, laid out on an epic scale—west Berlin alone is four times the size of Paris. Entire towns and villages are inlaid into the countryside beyond the downtown area. The really stunning parts of the prewar capital are in the eastern sector, which has grand boulevards and monumental buildings, the classical Brandenburg Gate, and the stately tree-lined avenue of Unter den Linden.

What really makes Berlin special, however, are the intangibles—the spirit and bounce of the city. Berliners come off as brash, no-nonsense types who speak German with their own piquant dialect. The bracing air, the renowned *Berliner Luft*, gets part of the credit for their high-voltage energy. But it's also attributable to the fact that residents of all ages are survivors; they have faced adversity all their lives, and have managed to do so with a mordant wit and cynical acceptance of life as it is rather than the way one hopes it might be. Crisis has been a way of life here for as long as anyone can remember. Here is life in a pressure cooker, literally and figuratively, life on the edge.

EXPLORING

Tour 1: West Berlin

Numbers in the margin correspond to points of interest on the Berlin map.

❶ Your tour of west Berlin begins on its best-known street, the **Kurfürstendamm.** Berliners (and most visitors as well) refer to it affectionately as the Ku'damm. Its 3-kilometer (2-mile) length is lined with shops, department stores, art galleries, theaters, movie houses, hotels, and some 100 restaurants, bars, clubs, and sidewalk cafés. It bustles with shoppers and strollers most of the day and fairly far into the night. Traffic can remain heavy into the wee hours of the morning.

This busy thoroughfare was first laid out during the 16th century as the path by which Elector Joachim II of Brandenburg traveled from his palace on the Spree River to his hunting lodge in the Grunewald. The Kurfürstendamm (Elector's Causeway) was developed into a major route in the late 19th century on the initiative of Chancellor Bismarck, the "Iron Chancellor," who was the force behind the original unification of Germany.

The Ku'damm is much more important today than it was to prewar Berlin. It was a busy shopping street, but by no means the city's most elegant one, being fairly far removed from the heart of the city, which was on the opposite side of the Brandenburg Gate in what became East Berlin. The Ku'damm's prewar fame was tied mainly to the rowdy bars and dance halls that studded much of its length and its side streets. Some of these were low-down dives, scenes of erotic circuses where kinky sex was the norm.

Similar clubs, along with cabarets and avant-garde theaters, were set on and along side streets of the Friedrichstrasse, in eastern Berlin. Even though Friedrichstrasse has been significantly transformed from its dreary pre-unification days and now offers a growing number of shops, restaurants, and bars, it still can't compete with the glitz and glamour of Ku'damm and the sheer number of establishments there.

Along with the rest of Berlin, the Ku'damm suffered severe wartime bombing. Almost half of its 245 late-19th-century buildings were destroyed in the 1940s, and the remaining buildings were damaged in varying degrees. What you see today (as in most of Berlin) is either restored or was constructed during the past decades. Although the street is frequently described as "glittering" and/or "sophisticated," there are those who are convinced that it has lost whatever real charm and flair it may once have possessed. But it is certainly the liveliest stretch of roadway in Berlin, east or west.

★ ❷ The Ku'damm starts at the western end of the Breitscheidplatz, a large square on which several notable landmarks stand. The ruin of the **Kaiser-Wilhelm-Gedächtniskirche** (Emperor Wilhelm Memorial Church), built between 1891 and 1895, stands as a dramatic reminder of the war's destruction. The bell tower, now known as the "hollow tooth," is all that remains of this once-imposing church that was dedicated to the emperor, Kaiser Wilhelm I. On the hour you'll hear the chimes in the tower play a melody composed by the emperor's grandson, Prince Louis Ferdinand von Hohenzollern.

A historic exhibition on the devastation of World War II inside the old tower features a religious cross constructed of nails that was recovered from the ashes of the burned-out Coventry Cathedral in England, destroyed in a German bombing raid in November 1940. *At Breitscheidpl.*, ☎ *030/218–5023.* ☛ *Free.* ✆ *Tues.–Sat. 10–5, closed holidays.*

In stark contrast to the old bell tower are the adjoining Memorial Church and Tower built in 1959–61. These ultramodern octagonal structures, with their myriad honeycomb windows, are perhaps best described by their nicknames: the lipstick and the powder box. The interior is dominated by the brilliant blue of its stained-glass windows, imported from Chartres in France. Church music and organ concerts are presented in the church regularly.

❸ Mere steps away from the new Memorial Church is the **Europa Center,** a vast shopping and business complex on the east side of the Brietscheidplatz often described as a "city within a city." This 1960s 22-story tower block—dubbed "Pepper's Manhattan" after its architect, K. H. Pepper—houses more than 100 shops, restaurants and cafés, an ice rink, two cinemas, a theater, a casino, the Verkehrsamt (tourist information center), and thermal baths at the very top. You can even find two pieces of the Berlin Wall by the Tauenzienstrasse entrance. For a spectacular view of the city, take the lift to the i-Punkt restaurant and observation platform on the top floor.

❹ Across from the entrance to the Verkehrsamt, on Budapesterstrasse, is the **Elefantentor** (Elephant Gate), which is the main entrance to Berlin's aquarium, part of the adjoining zoo complex. Before visiting the zoo, take a stroll along Tauenzienstrasse, the boulevard that runs southeast away from the corner of the Europa-Center. Tauentzienstrasse leads you straight to continental Europe's largest department store, the
❺ **Kaufhaus des Westens** (Department Store of the West; Tauenzienstr. 21), known to Berliners as KaDeWe (*see* Shopping, *below*).

KEY

i Tourist Information

Ägyptisches
Museum, **34**

Alexanderplatz, **25**

Antiken-
sammlung, **35**

Berliner Dom, **23**

Berliner Mauer, **14**

Bertolt Brecht House
and Museum, **29**

Brandenburger
Tor, **10**

Checkpoint
Charlie, **16**

Dahlem Museums, **36**

Deutsche
Staatsoper, **19**

Deutsches
Historisches
Museum, **21**

East Side Gallery, **37**

Elefantentor, **4**

Europa Center, **3**

Fischerinsel, **27**

Gendarmenmarkt, **17**

Jewish Cemetery, **31**

Kaiser-Wilhelm-
Gedächtniskirche, **2**

Kaufhaus des
Westens, **5**

Kronprinzen-
palais, **20**

Kulturforum, **13**

Kurfürstendamm, **1**

Marienkirche, **24**

Märkisches
Museum, **28**

Museum der
Verbotene Kunst, **38**

Museumsinsel, **22**

Neue Synagoge, **30**

Potsdamerplatz, **12**

Prince-Albert-
Gelände, **15**

Rathaus
Schöneberg, **32**

Reichstag, **9**

Rotes Rathaus, **26**

St. Hedwig's
Kathedrale, **18**

Schloss Bellevue, **8**

Schloss
Charlottenburg, **33**

Siegessäule, **7**

Sowjetisches
Ehrenmal, **11**

Zoologischer
Garten, **6**

Paulstr.

Lüneburgstr.

Moltkestr.

John-Foster-Dulles-Allee

Str. des 17 Juni

Tiergarten

Tiergartenstr.

Entlastungsstr.

Unter den Linden

Otto-Grotewohlstr.

Friedrichstr.

Gendarmen-markt

Schloss-pl.

Karl-Liebknecht-Str.

Rathausstr.

Stralauerstr.

Leipzigerstr.

Wallstr.

FORMER LOCATION OF BERLIN WALL

Wilhelmstr.

Friedrichstr.

Lindenstr.

Oranienstr.

Ritterstr.

Prinzenstr.

H. Heinestr.

Lützowstr.

Potsdamerstr.

Schöneberger str.

Möckernstr.

Gitschinerstr.

Urban-   str.

Baerwaldstr.

Bülowstr.

Yorckstr.

Yorckstr.

Gneisenaustr.

N

Potsdamerstr.

Hauptstr.

Monumentenstr.

Kreuzbergstr.

Victoria Park

Mehringdamm

Eberstr.

Westlangente

Kolonnenstr.

Dudenstr.

Columbiadamm

Volkspark Hasenheide

0   1/2 mile

0   3/4 km

TIME OUT Set some time aside for a coffee at **Einstein Café,** where you can select from a variety of exotic coffees. The Viennese-style coffeehouse is in a beautiful 19th-century mansion. Try its famous *apfelstrudel;* it's expensive but worth every pfennig. *Kurfürstenstr. 58, northeast of KaDeWe.*

Go into the U-bahn station near KaDeWe at Wittenbergplatz. This subway station, Berlin's first, was finished in 1913 and has recently been painstakingly restored. To reach the tour's next stop, the Zoologischer Garten, you can take the subway one stop (to the station of the same name) to the zoo's main entrance, on Hardenbergplatz, or backtrack

★ ❻ and enter at the Elefantentor. The **Zoologischer Garten** (Zoological Gardens), which opened in 1844, is the oldest zoo in Germany and is set in the southwestern corner of the 630-acre park called the **Tiergarten** (Animal Garden). Even for people who aren't zoo enthusiasts, both the park and the very modern zoo offer much of interest.

After being destroyed during World War II, the zoo was carefully redesigned to create surroundings as close to the animals' natural environment as possible. The zoo houses more than 14,000 animals belonging to 1,500 different species and has been successful in breeding rare species. Among the zoo's claims to fame are Europe's largest and most modern birdhouse, a terrarium renowned for its crocodiles, and an aquarium with more than 10,000 fish, reptiles, and amphibians. *Hardenbergpl. 8, ☎ 030/254–010. ☛ Zoo only: DM 10 adults, DM 5 children under 15. ☛ Aquarium only: DM 9 adults, DM 4.50 children. Combined tickets to zoo and aquarium: DM 15 adults, DM 7.50 children. Zoo open daily 9–6:30, 9–dusk in winter. Aquarium open daily 9–6.*

From the zoo you can set off diagonally through the Tiergarten, which during the 17th century served as the hunting grounds of the Great Elector. The park suffered severe damage from World War II bombing raids. Later, Berliners desperate for fuel during the freezing winter of 1945–46 cut down many of the remaining trees for firewood. Replanting began in 1949, and today's visitor will see a beautifully laidout park with some 23 kilometers (14 miles) of footpaths and 6½ acres of lakes and ponds.

At the center of the park you'll approach the traffic intersection known as the Grosser Stern (Big Star), so called because five roads meet here.
❼ This is the park's highest point and the site of the **Siegessäule** (Victory Column). This 227-foot-high granite, sandstone, and bronze column was originally erected in 1873 to commemorate the successful Prussian military campaigns; it was set up in front of the Reichstag, ½ mile away. The column came close to being finished off by anarchists in 1921, after the collapse of the empire. Six kilos of explosives were placed in its stairwell, and the fuse was already sizzling when the bomb was discovered. In 1938, as Hitler was having Berlin redesigned according to his megalomaniacal plans, the column was moved to its present site. A climb of 285 steps up through the column to the observation platform affords splendid views across much of Berlin. *Am Grossen Stern. ☛ DM 1.50 adults, DM 1 children under 14. ☼ Mon. 3–6, Tues.–Sun. and holidays 9–6.*

❽ Follow the Spreeweg Road from the Grosser Stern to **Schloss Bellevue** (Bellevue Palace). Built on the Spree River in 1785 for Frederick the Great's youngest brother, Prince Augustus-Ferdinand, it has served as the West German president's official residence in West Berlin from 1959 to the present but will be vacated when the federal president moves to the former German crown prince's palace on Unter den Linden in a few years. The 50-acre palace grounds have been transformed into a park with an English garden on its western edge. *Schloss Bellevue Park.* ☯ *Daily 8–dusk. Closed when the president is in residence.*

Leave the Schloss Bellevue and head east along the John-Foster-Dulles Allee, keeping the Spree River in sight on your left. You'll soon pass the **Kongresshalle** (Congress Hall), which was a feat of engineering when it was built in 1957 by Americans. Nicknamed the "pregnant oyster," the hall is now home to the World Culture House.

★ ❾ Continuing east you'll reach the **Reichstag** (Parliament Building), which was erected in the late 19th century to house the Prussian parliament and later performed a similar function for the ill-fated Weimar Republic. The Reichstag was burned to a shell under mysterious circumstances on the night of February 28, 1933, an event that provided the Nazis with a convenient pretext for outlawing all opposition parties. After rebuilding, the Reichstag was again badly damaged in 1945 in the last Allied offensive of the war. The Reichstag is once again scheduled to host the Bundestag meetings, starting in the year 2000.

Behind the Reichstag is the old line of the Berlin Wall, few traces of which now remain. It was here that visiting Western dignitaries as well as tourists stood on a wooden viewing platform to peek over the 3-foot-thick wall into the no-man's-land separating the two political halves of Berlin. At the Reichstag's northeastern corner, white wooden crosses hang on a low metal fence—grim reminders of the 80 East Germans who lost their lives while trying to escape to the West after the wall was built.

★ ❿ Just south of the Reichstag, where Strasse des 17 Juni meets Unter den Linden, is another monumental symbol of German unity and of the long division of Berlin—the mighty **Brandenburger Tor** (Brandenburg Gate). When the wall was built the Brandenburger Tor, once the pride of imperial Berlin, was left stranded in the eerie no-man's-land. When the wall came down, it was the focal point of much celebrating, for this evocative symbol of Berlin was finally returned to all the people of the newly united city. The Brandenburger Tor, the only remaining gate of an original group of 14 built by Carl Langhans in 1788–91, was designed in virile classical style, as a triumphal arch for King Frederick Wilhelm II. The quadriga, a chariot drawn by four horses and driven by the Goddess of Peace, was added in 1794. The goddess was originally naked, but puritanical protesters persuaded the city fathers to clothe her in a sheath of sheet copper. Troops paraded through the gate after successful campaigns, the last time being in 1945, when victorious Red Army troops took Berlin. The upper part of the gate, together with its chariot and Goddess of Peace, were destroyed in the war, but in 1957 the original molds were discovered in West Berlin and a new quadriga was cast in copper and presented as a gift to the people of East Berlin—a remarkable, rare instance of cold-war-era East-West cooperation.

⓫ A short distance west, along Strasse des 17 Juni—a name that commemorates the 1953 uprising of East Berlin workers that was quashed by Soviet tanks—you will reach the **Sowjetisches Ehrenmal** (Soviet Honor Monument), until 1990 a Russian enclave in the West. Built directly after the end of World War II, before power plays between opposing sides had been set in motion, it was located in the western sector. Responsibility for the monument was turned over to the German government at reunification in October 1990. Although no longer guarded by Soviet troops, it still serves as a major attraction. The semicircular monument, which shows a bronze statue of a soldier, rests on a marble plinth taken from Hitler's former Berlin headquarters, flanked by what are said to be the first two tanks to have fought their way into Berlin in 1945.

Turn south from the memorial and cross the tip of the Tiergarten to **Potsdamerplatz,** a somewhat dull-looking expanse that was once among the busiest squares in prewar Berlin. Potsdamerplatz is the point where the British, American, and Russian sectors met and was often referred to as the three-sector corner. The wall cut through the center of the square. Not far from the square, in the middle of the then no-man's-land, was a little knoll marking one of the entrances to Hitler's reinforced concrete bunker, where he spent his last days. The entire area reawakened when buses and taxis were allowed to pass through Brandenburg Gate. Cornerstones for the British and American embassies have been established here, and work on the planned reconstructed square, which will include headquarters of Sony and Mercedes, began in earnest in fall 1994.

In nearby Kemperplatz, west of Potsdamerplatz, lies the **Kulturforum** (Cultural Forum), a large square where you'll find a series of fascinating museums and galleries. Their contents will shift as state collections that were stuck on opposite sides of the wall are reunited. A new building opened in 1994, housing the **Kupferstichkabinett** (Drawings and Prints Collection) and the **Kunstbibliothek** (Art Library). The exhibitions at the Kupferstichkabinett include European woodcuts, engravings, and illustrated books from the 15th century to the present. Also on display are several pen-and-ink drawings by Dürer, 150 drawings by Rembrandt, and a photographic archive. The Kunstbibliothek contains art posters, a costume library, ornamental engravings, and a commercial art collection. *Matthäikirchpl. Kupferstichkabinett, ☎ 030/266–2002; Kunstbibliothek, ☎ 030/266–2046. ☛ Free. ☉ Tues.–Fri. 9–5, weekends 10–5.*

An additional building, slated for completion in 1996, will display paintings dating from the late Middle Ages to 1800, many of them now at the Gemäldgalerie at Dahlem (*see* Tour 3 *below*) and at the Bodemuseum on Museumsinsel (*see* Tour 2 *below*). Contact the tourist office for additional information.

The roof that resembles a great wave belongs to the **Philharmonie** (Philharmonic Hall). Built in 1963, it is home to the renowned Berlin Philharmonic Orchestra. (*see* The Arts and Nightlife, *below*). The smaller adjoining Chamber Music Hall was built in 1987. Both these buildings and the **Staatsbibliothek** (National Library; one of the largest libraries in Europe) across the street were designed by Hans Scharoun.

The Philharmonie added the **Musikinstrumenten-Museum** (Musical Instruments Museum) to its attractions in 1984. It is well worth a visit for its fascinating collection of keyboard, string, wind, and percussion instruments. *Tiergartenstr. 1, ☎ 030/254–810. ☛ DM 4 adults, DM 2 children, free Sun. and holidays. ☉ Tues.–Fri. 9–5, weekends 10–5. Guided tours Sat. at 11; presentation of the Wurlitzer organ 1st Sat. of each month at noon. Tour costs: DM 3 adults, free for children under 12.*

Opposite the Philharmonie is the **Kunstgewerbemuseum** (Museum of Decorative Arts). Inside this three-story building you'll find a display of the development of arts and crafts in Europe from the Middle Ages to the present. Among its treasures is the Welfenschatz (Welfen Treasure), a collection of 16th-century gold and silver plate from Nürnberg.

Other displays of particular interest are the ceramics and porcelains. *Matthäikirchpl.,* ☎ *030/266–2911.* ☞ *DM 4 adults, DM 2 children, free Sun. and holidays.* ☉ *Tues.–Fri. 9–5, weekends 10–5.*

Leave the museum and walk south past the mid-19th-century church of St. Matthaeus to the **Neue Nationalgalerie** (New National Gallery), a modern glass-and-steel building designed by Mies van der Rohe and built in the mid-1960s.

The gallery's collection comprises paintings, sculptures, and drawings from the 19th and 20th centuries, with an accent on works by such Impressionists as Manet, Monet, Renoir, and Pissarro. Other schools represented are German Romantics, Realists, Expressionists, Surrealists, and the Bauhaus. The gallery also has a growing collection of contemporary art from Europe and America. *Potsdamerstr. 50,* ☎ *030/2666.* ☞ *DM 4 adults, DM 2 children, free Sun. and holidays.* ☉ *Tues.–Fri. 9–5, weekends 10–5. A Tageskarte (Day Card), covers 1-day admission to all museums at Kulturforum. Cost: DM 8 adults, DM 4 children. Card is available at each museum.*

Return to Potsdamer Platz and head south along Stresemannstrasse, then east along Niederkircherstrasse, tracing the wall's former location. The old **Prussischen Landtag** (Prussian State Legislature), which now houses Berlin's House of Deputies and Senate, sits on the street's northern side. Opposite is the Martin Gropius Building, an exhibition site for various city museums and institutions. Running east along Niederkircherstrasse is one of only four still-standing sections of the

★ ⑭ infamous **Berliner Mauer** (Berlin Wall), which was erected on August 13, 1961. The other three sections are along the Schiffahrts Canal by the Invaliden Cemetery in the Mitte district, along the southern end of Bernauerstrasse, also in Mitte (a museum is planned here), and along the Spree in the Friedrichshain district (*see* Outlying Sites and Attractions, *below*).

⑮ Just south of the wall you'll find the **Prince-Albert-Gelände** (Prince Albert Grounds). Buildings here housed the headquarters of the Gestapo SS, the Main Reich Security Office, and other Nazi security organizations from 1933 until 1945. After the war the grounds were leveled. They remained so until 1987, when the remains of the buildings were excavated and an exhibit documenting their history and Nazi atrocities was opened. *Topography of Terrors, Stresemannstr. 110,* ☎ *030/2548–6703.* ☞ *Free.* ☉ *Tues.–Sun. 10–6. Tours by appointment only.*

The history of the hideous Berlin Wall can be followed in the museum

⑯ that arose at the **Checkpoint Charlie** crossing point, at Friedrichstrasse, the second cross street heading east on Niederkircherstrasse. This was the most famous crossing point between the two Berlins during the cold war; it was here that American and Soviet tanks faced each other during the tense months of the Berlin Blockade in 1948. The crossing point

★ disappeared along with the wall, but the **Haus am Checkpoint Charlie** (House at Checkpoint Charlie—The Wall Museum) is still there. The museum reviews the history of the events leading up to the construction of the wall and displays actual tools and equipment, records, and photographs documenting methods used by East Germans to cross over into the West (one of the most ingenious instruments of escape was a miniature submarine). Also displayed are paintings, drawings, and exhibits of Berlin history since the erection of the wall, and documentary films on exhibition themes are shown. *Friedrichstr. 44,*

☎ 030/251–1031. ☛ *DM 7.50 adults, DM 4.50 children.* ☉ *Daily 9* AM–*10 PM.*

TIME OUT   While trying to imagine the former Checkpoint Charlie crossing and the wall, get a window seat at **Café Adler,** which bumped right up against the wall here. The soups and salads are all tasty, and cheap. *Friedrich-str. 206.*

Tour 2: East Berlin

Much of downtown East Berlin was cleaned and restored under the East German government, the idea being that when you crossed from West Berlin you should see a modern, fresh, and above all orderly city. The lower end of the Friedrichstrasse was rebuilt, and most of the 6-square-kilometer (4-square-mile) "Berlin Mitte" district, the center of the city, got a thorough face-lift. When you wander off the beaten path, however, you will frequently find the drabness and sameness for which the socialist eastern zone was better known. Massive showcase housing and other communal projects hastily built during the '50s and '60s now show their age and shoddy construction, but newer projects are being planned on a more human scale, with greater effort to incorporate buildings into their surroundings.

For a sense of times past, enter the eastern part of Berlin at **Checkpoint Charlie.** Follow busy, shop-lined Friedrichstrasse north for six blocks to Taubenstrasse (or ride the U-bahn to Stadtmitte station) and turn ⑰ right to come to the large square called **Gendarmenmarkt,** one of Europe's finest piazzas. It's the site of the beautifully reconstructed **Schauspielhaus,** built in 1818 and east Berlin's main concert hall, and the rebuilt **Deutscher and Französischer Dome** (German—south side, undergoing restoration—and French Cathedrals). The French cathedral contains the **Hugonottenmuseum,** with exhibits charting the history and the art of the Protestant refugees from France—the Huguenots—expelled at the end of the 17th century by Louis XIV. Their energy and commercial expertise did much to help boost Berlin during the 18th century. *Gendarmenmarkt,* ☎ *030/229–1760.* ☛ *DM 2 adults, DM 1 children.* ☉ *Wed.–Sat. noon–5, Sun. 1–5.*

TIME OUT   The **Arkade Café** at the northwest corner of the square is the right spot for light snacks, a cup of coffee, or a beer. The pastries are excellent, too. *Französischstr. 25.*

⑱ Head down Französischestrasse to **St. Hedwig's Kathedrale** (St. Hedwig's Cathedral), a substantial, circular building that's similar to the Pantheon in Rome. Note the tiny street called Hinter der Katholische Kirche; it means "Behind the Catholic Church." When the cathedral was built in 1747, it was the first Catholic church built in resolutely Protestant Berlin since the Reformation during the 16th century.

⑲ Head north across Bebelplatz to reach the **Deutsche Staatsoper** (German State Opera), lavishly restored in the late '80s. A performance here can be memorable. *Unter den Linden 7.* ☎ *030/200–4315. Box office open weekdays noon–5:45.*

You are now on **Unter den Linden,** the central thoroughfare of old Berlin; its name means simply "under the linden trees." Something of its former cosmopolitan elegance is left, though these days it can hardly claim to rival the Champs Élysées. On the north side is **Humboldt University,** originally built in 1766 as a palace for the brother of Friedrich II of Prussia. It became a university in 1810, and Karl Marx and Friedrich

Engels were once among its students. Adjacent to the University is the **Neue Wache** (New Guardhouse). Constructed in 1818, it served as the Royal Prussian War Memorial until the declaration of the Weimar Republic in 1918. Badly damaged in World War II, it was restored by the East German state and rededicated in 1960 as the "Memorial for the Victims of Fascism and Militarism." In 1969, the tombs of the unknown soldier and unknown concentration-camp prisoner and an eternal flame were added. After unification it was restored to its Weimar Republic appearance and, in November 1993, inaugurated as Germany's central war memorial. Inside is an enlarged Käthe Kollwitz statue (*Mother with Dead Son*), the only contemporary addition, and the dedication: "Victims of War and Authoritarianism."

⑳ The **Kronprinzenpalais** is at the eastern end of Unter den Linden; it's the former crown prince's palace, today used as a government guest **㉑** house. Opposite it is the **Deutsches Historisches Museum** (German Historical Museum), housed in the onetime arsenal (Zeughaus). This magnificent Baroque building, constructed 1695–1730 and the oldest building on Unter den Linden, was later used as a hall of fame glorifying Prusso-German militarism. The museum's permanent exhibit provides a compendium of German history from the Middle Ages to the present. (Only a partial inventory of its objects are on display; the entire collection will be shown after a major renovation scheduled to be completed at the turn of the century). *Unter den Linden 2.* ☎ *030/215–020.* ☛ *DM 4 adults, DM 2 children.* ☉ *Thurs.–Tues. 10– 6. Tours by appointment only.*

㉒ Turn left and follow the Spree Canal and you'll come to **Museumsinsel** (Museum Island), on the site of one of Berlin's two original settlements, Cölln, dating from 1237. Today you'll find a complex of four remarkable museums here.

The **Altes Museum** (Old Museum; entrance Lustgarten) is an austere neoclassical building just north of Schlossplatz that features postwar East German art; its large etching and drawing collection, from the Old Masters to the present, is a treasure trove. The **Nationalgalerie** (National Gallery, entrance on Bodestrasse) houses an outstanding collection of 18th-, 19th-, and early 20th-century paintings and sculptures and often hosts special temporary exhibits. Works by Cézanne, Rodin, Degas, and one of Germany's most famous portrait artists, Max Liebermann, are part of the permanent exhibition.

Even if you aren't generally interested in exhibits about the ancient world, ★ make an exception for the **Pergamon Museum** (entrance on Am Kupfergraben). It is not only the standout in this complex but it is one of Europe's greatest museums. The museum's name is derived from its principal and best-loved display, the Pergamon altar, a monumental Greek temple found in what's now Turkey and dating from 180 BC. Adorning it are finely carved figures of gods locked in battle against giants. As much as anything, perhaps, this vast structure illustrates the zeal of Germany's 19th-century archaeologists, who had it shipped to Berlin piece by piece from a mountaintop. Equally impressive is the Babylonian Processional Way in the Asia Minor department.

Last in the complex is the **Bodemuseum** (entrance on Monbijoubrücke), with its superb Egyptian, Byzantine, and early Christian relics, sculpture collections, and coin gallery. The Sphinx of Hatshepsut, from around 1500 BC, is stunning, as are the Burial Cult Room and Papyrus Collection. There is also a representative collection of Italian Renaissance paintings.

For all Museumsinsel: ☎ 030/203–550. ☛ Each museum on Museum Island: DM 4 adults, DM 2 children, free Sun. and holidays. A Tageskarte (Day Card), available at each museum, covers 1-day admission to all museums. Cost: DM 8 adults, DM 4 children. All museums open Tues.–Sun. 10–6.

㉓ From the museum complex, follow the Spree Canal back to Unter den Linden and the enormous, impressive 19th-century **Berliner Dom** (Berlin Cathedral). The cathedral's impressive main nave was reopened in June 1993 after a 20-year renovation. There's an observation balcony that allows a view of the cathedral ceiling and interior. **The Märkisches Museum** (entrance on Karl-Liebknecht-Strasse) records the postwar reconstruction of the building. *Am Lustgarten. Church open Mon.–Sat. 9–6:30, Sun. and holidays 11:30–6:30. Balcony ☛ DM 3 adults, DM 1.50 children; open Mon.–Sat. 10–6, Sun. 11:30–6. Museum ☛ Free; open Wed.–Sun. 10–6.*

The colossal modern building in bronze mirrored glass opposite the cathedral is the **Palast der Republic** (Palace of the Republic), a postwar monument to socialist progress that housed East Germany's People's Chamber (parliament), along with restaurants, a theater, a bowling alley, and a disco. Since 1991, the Palast has been closed while politicians argue about whether it should be torn down or used for other purposes. The empty circular structure above the main entrance on Schlossplatz (formerly Marx-Engels-Platz) used to contain East Germany's state seal, which was found in the middle of its flag. The building at the south end of the square used to house East Germany's **Staatsrat** (Federal Senate). From the balcony of the preserved older entrance, Karl Liebknecht declared the birth of the doomed German Communist Republic on November 9, 1918.

㉔ Next, follow Karl-Liebknecht-Strasse to take a look at the 13th-century **Marienkirche** (St. Mary's Church) and its late-Gothic fresco *Der Totentanz* (*Dance of Death*). Obscured for many years, it was restored in 1950, revealing the original in all its macabre allure. Like something out of an Ingmar Bergman movie, Death dances with everyone, from peasant to king. The fresco and the tower were both 15th-century additions. *Karl-Liebknecht-Str. 8. ☉ Mon.–Thurs. 10–noon and 1–4 , weekends noon–4. Free tours Mon.–Thurs. at 1, Sun. at 11:45.*

★ ㉕ The Marienkirche borders **Alexanderplatz,** the square that formed the hub of East Berlin city life. It's a bleak sort of place, open and windswept, surrounded by grimly ugly modern buildings, with not so much as a hint of its prewar elegance—a reminder not just of the Allied bombing of Berlin but of the ruthlessness with which what remained of the old buildings was demolished by the East Germans. The square, named for Czar Alexander I, and the surrounding area will hardly be recognizable after a planned radical transformation is realized. After construction, which began in 1995 and is due to run late into the first decade of the 21st century, Berliners will have a mini-Manhattan downtown with a dozen 40-story skyscrapers.

Finding Alexanderplatz from any other part of the city is no problem; just head toward the **Fernsehturm,** the soaring TV tower, completed in 1969 and 1,198 feet high (not accidentally 710 feet higher than west Berlin's broadcasting tower, and 98 feet higher than the Eiffel Tower in Paris). The tower's observation platform offers the best view of Berlin; on a clear day you can see for 40 kilometers (24 miles). You can also enjoy a coffee break up there in the city's highest café, which rotates for your panoramic enjoyment. *Panoramastr. 1a,* ☎ *030/242–3333.* ☛ *DM 6 adults, DM 3 children.* ☉ *Daily 9 AM–midnight.*

TIME OUT If it's a cold day, escape the keen wind that almost always seems to sweep across Alexanderplatz in winter and dodge into **Café Mosaik** for one of its tasty coffee specialties. If Alexanderplatz is roasting in the sun, enjoy a glass of the Mosaik's superb natural French wines. This cozy café has a thoroughly French feel, and serves breakfast until 8 PM for late risers. *Rathausstr. 5.*

㉖ Walk across the lower end of the square past the **Rotes Rathaus** (Red City Hall), known for its redbrick design and friezes depicting the city's history. The complex of buildings next to the Rathaus has been handsomely rebuilt, centering around the remains of the twin-spire **Nikolaikirche** (St. Nicholas Church), Berlin's oldest parish church, dating from 1230. The quarter that has grown around it, the **Nikolai Quarter,** is filled with stores, cafés, and restaurants.

㉗ Wander back down Rathausstrasse—and over to the **Fischerinsel** (Fisherman's Island) area. This was the heart of Berlin 750 years ago, and today retains some of its medieval character. At Breite Strasse you'll find two of Berlin's oldest buildings: No. 35 is the **Ribbeckhaus,** the city's only surviving Renaissance structure, dating from 1624, and No. 36 is the early Baroque **Marstall,** built by Michael Matthais from 1666 to 1669.

㉘ Cross over the Gertraudenstrasse and wander up the south bank of the canal to the redbrick **Märkisches Museum,** the museum of city history. Its exhibits include a special section on the city's theatrical past and a fascinating collection of mechanical musical instruments, which are demonstrated on Sunday at 11 and Wednesday at 3. Next door to the museum live Schnutte, Maxi, and Tilo, live representations of Berlin's symbol, a bear. *Am Köllnischen Park 5,* ☎ *030/308–660.* ☛ *DM 3 adults, DM 1 children. Instrument demonstration: 2 DM.* ☉ *Tues.–Sun. 10–6.*

㉙ Take the U-2 subway from the Märkisches Museum station three stops to Stadtmitte, then change to the U-6, traveling three more stops to Oranienburger Tor. Walk north on Friedrichstrasse beyond the bend where the street turns into the Chausseestrasse to find the **Bertolt Brecht House and Museum.** The working and living quarters of Brecht and his wife, Helene Weigel, can be visited, and there's a library for Brecht scholars. The downstairs restaurant serves Viennese cuisine with recipes from Weigel. *Chausseestr. 125,* ☎ *030/282–9916. Apartment* ☛ *DM 4 adults, DM 2 children; open Tues.–Fri. 10–noon, Thurs. 10–noon and 5–7, Sat. 9:30–noon and 12:30–2. Tours every half hour. Library* ☛ *Free; open Tues.–Fri. 9–3.*

Brecht is actually buried next door, along with his wife and more than 100 other celebrated Berliners, in the **Dorotheenstädtischer Kirchhof** (Doretheer Cemetery). They include the neoclassical architects Schinkel and Schadow as well as the Berlin printer Litfass, the man who invented those stumpy cylindrical columns you'll find in Berlin and other European cities carrying advertisements and theater schedules. ☉ *Daily 8–4.*

㉚ Head back toward the center and turn left down Oranienburgerstrasse to the massive **Neue Synagoge,** which was recently restored. It's an exotic amalgam of styles, the whole faintly Middle Eastern, built between 1859 and 1866. (When its doors opened it was the largest synagogue in Europe, with 3,200 seats.) It was largely ruined on the night of November 9, 1938, the infamous Kristallnacht, when Nazi looters and soldiers rampaged across Germany, burning synagogues and smashing the few Jewish shops and homes left in the country. Further destroyed by Allied bombing in 1943, it remained untouched until restoration began under the East German regime in the mid-'80s. Today only the facade remains, and it is connected to the Centrum Judaicum, a center for Jewish Culture and learning.

The area to the northeast of the Synagogue is known as the **Scheunenviertel** (Stable Quarters) or **Judisches Viertel** (Jewish Quarter). Artisans, small businessmen, and Jews—whom the Great Elector brought into the country to improve his trade and finance situation—moved here just outside one of the city's walls during the second half of the 17th century, in addition to many of the city poor and a substantial number of military personnel (hence the stables). Early in the 18th century the city wall and the stables were moved in order to accommodate the city's growth. As industrialization intensified the quarter became poorer, and in the 1880's many East European Jews escaping pogroms settled here. By the 20th century, the quarter had a number of bars, stores, small businesses, frequented by gamblers, prostitutes (they're still here, along Oranienburgerstrasse), and poor customers from the area. Jewish religious and business life flourished here until 1933, when the Nazis conducted their first raid and made arrests. After the conference on "The Final Solution of the Jewish Question" in 1942 (in a villa in Wansee, which now houses exhibits on the conference), deportation of the city's Jews began in earnest.

TIME OUT   For coffee, cake, or an Israeli snack of eggplant and pita bread stop at the **Beth Cafe,** the first Jewish business to open in the city's former Jewish district. Beth Cafe is small and always full, so be prepared to share a table. Just around the corner from the Synagogue, the café is run by the Adass Jisroel Jewish community. *Tucholskystr. 40.*

At the end of Oranienburgerstrasse, in the Grosse Hamburgerstrasse, you'll find the quarter's old Jewish Cemetery. Destroyed by the Nazis, only a plaque and a few broken tombstones remain today. Ironically ③① and very surprisingly, Europe's largest **Jewish Cemetery** can be found just north of here, in Berlin's Weissensee district. The cemetery and tombstones are in excellent condition, a seeming impossibility, given that it was in the heart of the Third Reich. To reach the cemetery, take Tram 2, 3, 4, 13, or 23 from Hackescher Markt to Berliner Allee and head south on Herbert-Baum-Strasse. ☉ *Sun.–Thurs. 8–4, Fri. 8–1; closed on Jewish holidays.*

Tour 3: Outlying Sights and Attractions

③② After the division of the two Berlins in 1948, **Rathaus Schöneberg** (Schöneberg City Hall; at the U-4 subway stop of the same name) was home to the West Berlin Chamber of Deputies and Senate. Completed in 1914, the Rathaus has a 237-foot-high tower from which a replica of the Liberty Bell is rung each day at noon. The bell was given by the American people as a symbol of their support for the West Berliners' struggle to preserve freedom. A document bears the signatures of 17 million Americans who pledged their solidarity with the people of West Berlin. It was in the square in front of Rathaus Schöneberg that President Kennedy gave his famous "Ich bin ein Berliner" speech on June 26, 1963. *John-F.-Kennedy Pl.* ☛ *Free.* ☉ *Wed., Sun., and holidays 10–4.*

★ ㉝ The easiest way to get to **Schloss Charlottenburg** (Charlottenburg Palace) is on the U-7 line toward Rathaus Spandau. Get off at Mierendorffplatz and head south to the palace.

The Charlottenburg Palace complex can be considered the showplace of west Berlin, the most monumental reminder of imperial days in the western sector. This sumptuous palace served as a city residence for the Prussian rulers. A full day is not too much time to devote to Charlottenburg. In addition to the apartments of the Prussian nobility, there are the landscaped gardens and several excellent museums set within and just outside the grounds.

The gorgeous palace started as a modest royal summer residence in 1695, built on the orders of King Friedrich I for his wife, Queen Sophie-Charlotte. Later, during the 18th century, Friedrich the Great made a number of additions, such as the dome and several wings in the Rococo style. By 1790 the complex had evolved into the massive royal domain you see today. The palace was severely damaged during World War II but has been painstakingly restored. Many of the original furnishings and works of art survived the war and are now on display.

Behind heavy iron gates, the Court of Honor—the courtyard in front of the palace—is dominated by a fine Baroque statue, the Reiterstandbild des Grossen Kurfürsten (the equestrian statue of the Great Elector). A 156-foot-high domed tower capped by a gilded statue of Fortuna rises above the main entrance to the palace.

Inside, in the main building, the suites of Friedrich I and his wife are furnished in the prevailing style of the era. Paintings include royal portraits by Antoine Pesne, a noted court painter of the 18th century. On the first floor you can visit the Oak Gallery, the early 18th-century Palace Chapel, and the suites of Friedrich Wilhelm II and Friedrich Wilhelm III, furnished in the Biedermeier style.

Visits to the royal apartments are by guided tour only; tours leave every hour on the hour from 9 to 4. Parks and gardens can be visited for free and offer a pleasant respite from sightseeing.

A gracious staircase leads up to the sumptuous State Dining Room and the 138-foot-long Golden Gallery. West of the staircase are the rooms of Frederick the Great, in which the king's extravagant collection of works by Watteau, Chardin, and Pesne are displayed. In one glass cupboard you'll see the coronation crown, stripped of its jewels by the king, who gave the most valuable gemstones to his wife. Also in the so-called New Wing is the **Galerie der Romantik,** the National Gallery's collection of masterpieces from such 19th-century German painters as Karl Friedrich Schinkel and Caspar David Friedrich, the leading member of the German Romantic school. *Luisenpl.,* ☎ *030/320–911.* ☞ *Galerie der Romantik: DM 4 adults, DM 2 children. Guided tour: DM 4 adults, DM 2 children.* ☉ *Tues.–Fri. 9–5, weekends 10–5.*

The park behind the palace was laid out beginning in 1697 as a baroque French Garden (the only remains of it are near the palace), and was transformed into an English Garden in the early 19th century. There are several buildings in the park that deserve particular attention, including the Belvedere, a teahouse overlooking the lake and Spree River that now houses a collection of Berlin porcelain, and the Schinkel Pavilion behind the palace near the river. The pavilion, modeled on a villa in Naples where the king stayed in 1822, was built in 1824–25 by Karl Friedrich Schinkel, one of 19th-century Berlin's favorite architects. It houses paintings by Caspar David Friedrich and late-18th-century furniture.

★ ③④ Just to the south of the palace are three small, distinguished museums. The first, across from the palace, is the **Ägyptisches Museum** (Egyptian Museum, Schloss Str. 70). The building, once the east guardhouse and residence of the king's bodyguard, is now home to the famous portrait bust of the exquisite Queen Nefertiti. The 3,300-year-old Egyptian queen is the centerpiece of a collection of works that span Egypt's history since 4,000 BC and includes one of the best-preserved mummies outside Cairo.

③⑤ Opposite the Ägyptisches Museum in the former west guardhouse is the **Antikensammlung** (Antique Collection, Schloss Str. 1). The collection comprises ceramics and bronzes as well as everyday utensils from ancient Greece and Rome, and a number of Greek vases from the 6th to the 4th century BC. Also on display is a collection of Scythian gold, silverware, and jewelry found in the Mediterranean basin.

The final museum, the **Museum für Vor- und Frügeschichte** (Museum of Pre- and Early History, Spandauer Damm 22), is in the western extension of the palace opposite Klausener Platz. The museum depicts the stages of the evolution of humanity from 1,000,000 BC to the Bronze Age. *For all 3 museums, ☎ 030/320–911. Individual admission to the Ägyptisches Museum, the Antikensammlung, and the Museum für Vor- and Frühgeschichte: DM 4 adults, DM 2 children. A Tageskarte (Day Card), available at each museum, covers 1-day admission to all 3 museums. The card includes a guided tour of Schloss Charlottenburg. Cost: DM 8 adults, DM 4 children.* ☞ *Free Sun. and holidays.* ⊙ *Mon.–Thurs. 9–5, weekends 10–5.*

③⑥ Another stop on your tour of Berlin is also a cluster of museums, the **Dahlem Museums.** The best way to get there is by the U-1 subway line, ★ to Dahlem-Dorf station. The Dahlem complex includes the **Gemäldegalerie** (Painting Gallery), the **Museum fur Völkerkunde** (Ethnographic Museum), and the **Skulpturen-sammlung** (Sculpture Collection).

Begin with the **Gemäldegalerie** (entrance at Arnimallee 23–27). One of Germany's finest art galleries, it houses a broad selection of European paintings from the 13th to the 18th century. Several rooms on the first floor are reserved for paintings by German masters, among them Dürer, Cranach the Elder, and Holbein. An adjoining gallery houses the works of the Italian masters—Botticelli, Titian, Giotto, Filippo Lippi, and Raphael—and another gallery on the first floor is devoted to paintings by Dutch and Flemish masters of the 15th and 16th centuries: van Eyck, Bosch, Brueghel the Elder, and van der Weyden. Flemish and Dutch paintings from the 17th century are displayed on the floor above; it contains the world's second-largest Rembrandt collection.

The **Museum für Völkerkunde** (entrance at Lansstrasse 8) is internationally famous for its arts and artifacts from Africa, Asia, the South Seas, and the Americas: The large collection of Mayan, Aztec, and Incan ceramics and stone sculptures should not be missed. Also of interest is the display of native boats and huts from the South Seas.

The **Skulpturensammlung** (entrance at Armimallee 23–27) houses Byzantine and European sculpture from the 3rd to the 18th century. Included in its collection is Donatello's *Madonna and Child,* sculpted in 1422. *Dahlem Museums: ☎ 030/83011. Individual admission to the Gemäldegalerie, the Museum für Völkerkunde, and the Skulpturensammlung is DM 4 adults, DM 2 children. A Tageskarte (Day Card),* *available at each museum, covers 1-day admission to the entire Dahlem complex. Cost: DM 8 adults, DM 4 children. ☛ Free Sun. and holidays. ☉ Tues.–Fri. 9–5, weekends 10–5.*

Take the S-bahn from Alexanderplatz two stops to Hauptbahnhof and walk toward the Spree, to the southern end of Strasse der Pariser Kummune, to reach the **East Side Gallery,** the largest open-air gallery in the world. Between February and June of 1990, 118 artists from the world over created unique works of art on the longest—1.3-kilometer (2.1-mile)—remaining section of the Berlin Wall. One of the most well-known works, by Russian artist Dmitri Vrubel, depicts Brezhnev and Honnecker (the former East German leader) French-kissing, with the caption "My God. Help me survive this deadly love." Although the city Chamber of Deputies declared the gallery a historical monument, its future remains unclear. When reconstruction of the **Oberbaumbrücke** (Oberbaum Bridge, at the gallery's southern end) is completed in 1996, a different set of political and architectural realities may mean the gallery's end, although most likely at least a part of it will be preserved. *Mühlenstr./Oberbaumbrücke. Shop open every day in summer 10–5; rest of the year, weekends only 10–5.*

For decades a symbol of division, the Oberbaumbrücke (completed in 1896) played an important humanitarian role in the early 1970s; it was the crossing point for West Berliners when they were allowed to visit their relatives in East Berlin. The bridge reopened for pedestrian and vehicular traffic on November 9, 1994, on the fifth anniversary of the fall of the wall; work on restoring subway service to Waschauer Strasse, the subway's pre-Second World War end stop, continues. Between the Spree's bank (Gröbenufer) and Schlesische Strasse, you'll find an impressive outdoor sculpture garden.

Follow Schlesische Strasse south across the Schlesische Bridge into the (former East Berlin) Treptow district. Immediately on the right is the **Museum der Verbotene Kunst** (Museum of Forbidden Art). Situated in the former no-man's-land, the museum is housed in the last preserved watch tower of the Berlin Wall (now designated a historical monument). The tower gallery displays works from artists who were or are censored in their native countries and has a permanent exhibition called "The Inner Life of the Wall—A Journey Through the Death Strip." *Schlesischestr./Pushkinallee,* ☎ *030/229–2877.* ☛ *DM 2.* ☉ *Weekends 2–6.*

Approximately 35 kilometers (22 miles) north of Berlin is the **Sachsenhausen Memorial.** The only Nazi concentration camp near the Third Reich capital, Sachsenhausen was established in 1936. After the war the site became a Soviet internment and prison camp for German soldiers until March 1950. In 1961 the camp was made into a memorial to its more than 100,000 victims. There are a few preserved facilities and barracks, in addition to a memorial and museum. The museum's films are shown by appointment only. At press time, the three exhibits on display were "The German Past," 10 years of books against forgetting and repressing, "Jews in the Sachsenhausen Concentration Camp," and "Sachsenhausen 1945–1950." To reach Sachsenhausen, take the suburban line S-1 from Friedrichstrasse to Oranienburg, the last stop. From the station it's a 25-minute walk, or you can take a taxi. *Oranienburg, Strasse der Nationen 22,* ☎ *03301/803–719.* ☛ *Free.* ☉ *Daily 8–4:30 (including holidays). Museum closed Mon.*

Beyond the tour of monuments, museums, and other aspects relating to the wall and the divided city, no visit to Berlin would be complete

without seeing the vast world of lakes and greenery along its eastern
and western extremities. In no other city has such an expanse of uninterrupted natural surroundings been preserved. Along the city's
fringe are some 60 lakes, connected by rivers, streams, and canals, in
a verdant setting of meadows, woods, and forests. The total length of
the lakes' shorelines—if stretched out in one line—is 210 kilometers
(130 miles), longer than Germany's Baltic coastline. Excursion steamers ply the water wonderland of the Wannsee and Havel. (*See* Guided
Tours *in* Berlin Essentials, *below, for details.*)

You can tramp for hours through the green belt of the **Grunewald** (Green
Forest). On weekends in spring and fall and daily in summer Berliners come out in force, swimming, sailing their boats, tramping through
the woods, riding horseback. In winter, a downhill ski run and even a
ski jump operate on the modest slopes of the Teufelsberg Hill. You can
reach Grunewald and the Wannsee on the S-3 or S-7 suburban line from
Zoologischer Garten.

SHOPPING

Gift Ideas

Berlin is a city of alluring stores and boutiques. Despite its cosmopolitan
gloss, shop prices are generally lower than in cities like Munich and
Hamburg. Most stores offer tax-free shopping for non-European Union
citizens, so be sure to ask about it before making your purchase.

Fine porcelain is still produced at the former Royal Prussian Porcelain
Factory, now called **Königliche Porzellan Manufactur,** or KPM. You can
buy this delicate, handmade, hand-painted china at KPM's store at Kurfürstendamm 26A (☎ 030/881–1802), but it may be more fun to visit
the factory salesroom (Wegelystrasse 1, ☎ 030/310–802). It also sells
seconds at reduced prices. If you long to have the Egyptian Museum's
Queen Nefertiti on your mantelpiece at home, try the **Gipsformerei der
Staatlichen Museen Preussischer Kulturbesitz** (Sophie-Charlotte-Str.
17, ☎ 030/321–7011; open weekdays 9–4). It sells plaster casts of this
and other treasures from the city's museums.

Take home a regiment of tin figures, painted or to paint yourself, from
the **Berliner Zinnfiguren Werner Scholz** (Knesebeckstr. 88).

Antiques

On Saturdays and Sundays from 10 to 5, the colorful and lively antiques and handicrafts fair on Strasse des 17 Juni swings into action.
Don't expect to pick up many bargains—or to have the place to yourself. Not far from Wittenbergplatz is **Keithstrasse,** a street given over
to antiques stores. Eisenacherstrasse, Fuggerstrasse, Kalckreuthstrasse,
Motzstrasse, and Nollendorfstrasse—all close to Nollendorfplatz—have
many antiques stores of varying quality. Another good street for antiques is **Suarezstrasse,** between Kantstrasse and Bismarckstrasse. The
venerable auction house **Christie's** (Fasanenstr. 72, ☎ 030/881–4164)
has an outpost just off the Ku'damm.

In east Berlin, antiques are sold in numerous small shops in the Nikolai quarter. The **Berliner Antik- und Flohmarkt** (☎ 030/208–2645) offers everything from expensive antique lamps to bargain books. Many
antiques stores are under the tracks at the Friedrichstrasse station
(Mon. and Wed.–Sun. 11–6), and in the restored Husemann-Strasse.
Some private stores along the stretch of Friedrichstrasse north of the
Spree Bridge offer old books and prints. **Sotheby's** auction house (in

the Palais am Festungsgraben on Unter den Linden, ☎ 030/200–4119)
has set up shop in one of Berlin's more beautiful buildings.

Shopping Districts

The liveliest and most famous shopping area in west Berlin is the **Kurfürstendamm** and its side streets, especially between **Breitscheidplatz**
and **Olivaer Platz**. The **Europa-Center** *(☎ 030/348–0088) at Breitscheidplatz encompasses more than 100 stores, cafés, and restaurants—
this is not a place to bargain-hunt, though. Running east from
Breitscheidplatz is **Tauenzienstrasse,** another shopping street. At the
end of it is Berlin's most celebrated department store, KaDeWe. The
Uhland-Passage (170 Uhlandstr.), also relatively new, has leading
name stores as well as cafés and restaurants. The new Kempinski Plaza
(Uhlandstr. 181–183) features exclusive boutiques and a pleasant
atrium café.

For trendier clothes, try the boutiques along **Bleibtreustrasse.** One of
the more avant-garde fashion boutiques is **Durchbruch** (Schlutterstr. 54,
☎ 030/881–5568), just off Blibtreustrasse. The name means "break-
through," and the store lives up to its name by selling different designers'
outrageous styles (women's clothing only). Less trendy and much less
expensive is the shopping strip along **Wilmersdorferstrasse** (U-7 station of same name), where price-conscious Berliners do their shopping.
It's packed on weekends. This outdoor shopping mall is easily accessible via U-bahn 7 in the direction of Rathaus Spandau.

Friedrichstrasse offers the most elegnt shops in east Berlin, including
a brand new Gallerie Lafayette department store. **Unter den Linden** has
a mix of expensive boutiques, including a Meissen ceramic showroom,
and tourist souvenir shops. Around **Alexanderplatz,** more affordable
stores offer everything from clothes to electronic goods to designer pre-
fumes. A large number of clothing and specialty stores have sprung up
in and around the **Nikolai quarter**; under the communist regime, all
were supplied from the same central sources, but now they are mostly
fashionable and expensive. The thoroughly refurbished **Berliner Markt-
halle** (at the corner of Karl-Liebknecht-Str. and Rosa-Luxemburg-Str.,
☎ 030/24490) is the east's largest mall.

Department Stores

The classiest department store in Berlin is **KaDeWe** (Tauenzienstr. 21,
☎ 030/21210) the Kaufhaus des Westens (Department Store of the West,
as it's modestly known in English), at Wittenbergplatz. The biggest department store in continental Europe, the KaDeWe is a grand-scale em-
porium in modern guise. An enormous selection of goods can be found
on its six floors, but it is most renowned for its food and delicatessen
counters, restaurants, champagne bars, and beer bars covering the entire sixth floor. The KaDeWe recently acquired three additional floors,
including a rooftop winter garden. The other main department store
downtown is **Wertheim** (Ku'damm 231, ☎ 030/8800–3206). Neither
as big nor as attractive as the KaDeWe, Wertheim nonetheless offers
a large selection of fine wares.

East Berlin's former Centrum department store, at the north end of
Alexanderplatz, has been taken over by the west German **Kaufhof** department store chain (Alexanderpl., ☎ 030/24640).

Specialty Stores

MEN'S CLOTHING

Mientus (Wilmersdorferstr. 73 and Ku'damm 52, both ☎ 030/323–9077), a large, exclusive men's store, caters to expensive tastes. It offers both conventional/businesswear as well as sporty and modern looks, and carries many top designer labels. Slightly less expensive and exclusive than Mientus but still up there is **Erdmann** (in the Europa-Center facing Tauenzienstr., ☎ 030/262–7038). For elegant men's shoes, try **Budapester Schuhe** (Ku'damm 199, ☎ 030/881–1707).

WOMEN'S CLOTHING

For German designer wear, try **Bogner-Shop Zenker** (Ku'damm 45, ☎ 030/881–1000). It's not cheap, but the styling is classic. If you're looking for international labels, drop by **Kramberg** (Ku'damm 56, ☎ 030/327–9010). Next door, at **Granny's Step** (Ku'damm 56, ☎ 030/323–7660), you'll find evening wear styled along the lines of bygone times. For modern, Berlin-designed chic, check out **Filato** (Nürnbergstr. 24A, ☎ 030/218–5477). If you're feeling daring, browse through the extraordinary lingerie store **Nouvelle** (Bleibtreustr. 24, ☎ 030/881–4737). Elegant '20s intimate wear made of fine, old-fashioned materials is its specialty.

JEWELRY

Fine handcrafted jewelry can be found at **Wurzbacher** (Ku'damm 36, ☎ 030/883–3892). East Berlin's **Galerie "re"** (Friedrichstr. 58, ☎ 030/208–6870) offers good jewelry values.

SPORTS AND FITNESS

Bicycling

There are bike paths throughout the downtown area and the rest of the city. *See* Getting Around, *below, for details on renting bikes.*

Golf

Berlin's leading club is the **Golf- und Landclub Wannsee** (Stölpchen-weg, Wannsee, ☎ 030/805–5075).

Jogging

The **Tiergarten** is the best place for jogging in the downtown area. Run its length and back and you'll have covered 8 kilometers (5 miles). Joggers can also take advantage of the grounds of **Charlottenburg Castle**, 3 kilometers (2 miles) around. For longer runs, anything up to 20 miles, make for **Grunewald.**

Riding

Horses are rented out by the **Reitsportschule Onkel Toms Hütte** (Onkel-Tom-Str. 172, ☎ 030/813–2082); **Reitsportschule Pichelsberg** (Schirwindter Allee 45, ☎ 030/305–8003); and **Reitsportscule Haflinger Hof** (Feldweg 21, in Fredersdorf, close to Berlin, ☎ 033439/6371).

Sailing and Windsurfing

Boats and boards of all kinds are rented by **Albrecht Wassersport** (Kaiserdamm 95, ☎ 030/301–9555). **Windshiefs** (Havelchaussee am Wasser, ☎ 030/803–663) rents Windsurfers mid-April through mid-October.

Swimming

The **Wannsee** and **Plötzensee** both have beaches; they get crowded during summer weekends, however. There are public pools throughout the city; there's bound to be at least one near where you're staying. For full listings, ask at the tourist office. The most impressive pool is the **Olympia-Schwimmstadion** at Olympischer Platz (U-bahn: Olympia-stadion). The **Blub Padeparadis** lido (Buschkrugallee 64, ☎ 030/606–6060) has indoor and outdoor pools, a sauna garden, hot whirlpools, and a solarium (U-bahn: Grenzallee).

Tennis and Squash

There are tennis courts and squash centers throughout the city; ask your hotel to direct you to the nearest of these. **Tennis & Squash City** (Brandenburgischestr. 53, Wilmersdorf, ☎ 030/879–097) has 6 tennis courts and 11 squash courts. At **"Tennisplätze am Ku'damm"** (Cicerostr. 55A, ☎ 030/891–6630), you can step right off the Ku'damm and onto a tennis court.

DINING

Dining in Berlin can mean sophisticated nouvelle specialties in upscale restaurants with linen tablecloths and hand-painted porcelain plates, or hearty local specialties in atmospheric and inexpensive inns: The range is as vast as the city itself. Specialties include *Eisbein mit Sauerkraut,* (knuckle of pork with pickled cabbage); *Rouladen* (rolled stuffed beef); *Spanferkel* (suckling pig); *Berliner Schüsselsülze* (potted meat in aspic); *Schlachteplatte* (mixed grill); *Hackepeter* (ground beef); and *Kartoffelpuffer* (fried potato cakes). *Bockwurst* is a chubby frankfurter that's served in a variety of ways and sold in restaurants and at bockwurst stands all over the city. *Schlesisches Himmelreich* is roast goose or pork served with potato dumplings in rich gravy. *Königsberger Klopse* consists of meatballs, herring, and capers—it tastes much better than it sounds. Turkish eats are an integral part of the Berlin food scene. On almost every street you'll find snack stands selling *Döner Kepab* (grilled lamb with salad in a flat-bread pocket).

Prices in east Berlin have risen rapidly to virtually the same level as those in the western part of the city, and service has been thoroughly upgraded to match western norms. East Berlin now has some of the city's most fashionable and expensive restaurants, ranging from French and New German cuisine to such exotica as Japanese, Thai, and Indonesian a fare, and most of the restaurants featuring the national cuisine of other one-time socialist states are now gone. Wines and spirits imported from former East Bloc countries are still found in many restaurants, and can be quite good; try Hungarian, Balkan, and Bulgarian wines and, of course, Polish and Russian vodkas.

Ratings

CATEGORY	COST*
$$$$	over DM 100
$$$	DM 75–DM 100
$$	DM 50–DM 75
$	under DM 50

per person for a three-course meal, excluding drinks.

$$$$ **Bamberger Reiter.** One of the city's leading restaurants, Bamberger is
★   presided over by Tyrolean chef Franz Raneburger. He relies on fresh
market produce for his *Neue Deutsche Küche* (new German cuisine),

Berlin Dining

so the menu changes daily. Fresh flowers set off this attractive, oak-beamed restaurant. ✗ *Regensburgerstr. 7,* ☎ *030/218–4282. Reservations required. AE, DC, V. Dinner only. Closed Sun., Mon., and Jan. 1–15.*

$$$$ **Ermeler-Haus.** The Rococo grandeur of this wine restaurant reflects the ★ elegance of the restored patrician home whose upstairs rooms it occupies. The house dates from the mid-16th century and was moved to its present location in 1969. The restaurant's atmosphere is subdued and formal, the wines are imported, and the service and German cuisine are excellent. There's dancing every Saturday evening. ✗ *Märkisches Ufer 10,* ☎ *030/279–4028. Reservations advised. AE, DC, MC, V. Closed Mon.*

$$$$ **Frühsammer's Restaurant an der Rehwiese.** Here you can watch chef Peter Frühsammer at work in his open kitchen. He's ready with advice on the daily menu; salmon is always a treat. The restaurant is in the annex of a turn-of-the-century villa in the Zehlendorf district (U-bahn to Krumme Lanke and then Bus 53 to Rehweise). ✗ *Matterhornstr. 101,* ☎ *030/803–8023. Reservations required. AE, MC. Dinner only.*

$$$$ **Rockendorfs.** Only fixed-price menus, some up to nine courses, are offered in this elegant restaurant in the north of the city. Exquisitely presented on fine porcelain, the mainly nouvelle specialties are sometimes fused with classic German cuisine. The wine list—with 600 choices, one of the world's best—has the appropriate accompaniment to any menu. The furnishings are intentionally sparse. ✗ *Dusterhauptstr. 1,* ☎ *030/402–3099. Reservations required. AE, DC, MC, V. Closed Sun., Mon., 3 wks in summer, Dec. 25, and Jan. 1.*

$$$ **Alt-Luxembourg.** This popular restaurant in the Charlottenburg dis-★ trict is tastefully furnished, and attentive service enhances the intimate setting. Chef Karl Wannemacher uses only the freshest ingredients for his French-German dishes, including his a divine lobster lasagna. ✗ *Windscheidstr. 13,* ☎ *030/323–8730. Reservations required. AE, DC, V. Closed Sun. and Mon. May–Aug.; weekends Sept.–Apr.*

$$$ **Borchardt.** This is one of the most fashionable meeting places to spring ★ up in east Berlin since the wall came down. The high ceiling, columns, red plush benches, and Art Nouveau mosaic (discovered during renovations) help create the impression of a 1920s café. The restaurant serves entrées with a French accent and is well known for its luscious seafood platter (DM 58). For meat lovers, the baby lamb with a medley of vegetables is recommended. Desserts include whiskey parfait with honey sauce and strawberry parfait with rhubarb foam. Sunday brunches are particularly popular, so plan ahead. ✗ *Französischestr. 47,* ☎ *030/229–3144. Reservations advised. AE, MC, V.*

$$$ **Zur Goldenen Gans.** Regional specialties, particularly game and venison dishes prepared Thüringer Forest style, are featured in this elegant, wood-furnished restaurant. ✗ *Friedrichstr. 158–164, in the Grand Hotel,* ☎ *030/2327–3246. Reservations advised. AE, DC, MC, V.*

$$ **Alt-Nürnberg.** Step into the tavernlike interior and you could be in Füssen or Garmisch in Bavaria: The waitresses even wear dirndls. The Bavarian colors of blue and white are everywhere, and that region's culinary delights, such as *Schweinshaxe* (knuckle of pork), dominate the menu. If you prefer to eat Prussian style, order calves' liver *Berliner Art* (Berlin style). ✗ *Europa Center,* ☎ *030/261–4397. Reservations advised. AE, DC, MC, V.*

$$ **Französischer Hof.** The ceilings in this classy restaurant are high and ★ the wine list is long. International fare, with an emphasis on French dishes, is served with impeccable service. The maître d' claims that guests can find "an oasis of calm and relaxation" here, and he's right. The summer terrace offers a seat practically on the Gendarmenmarkt.

✗ *Jägerstr. 56,* ☎ *030/229–3969. Reservations advised. AE, DC, MC, V.*

$$ **März am Ufer.** This restaurant specializes in nouvelle German and Continental cuisine at its best. The creative concoctions include fresh homemade pasta with organic spinach leaves. It's near the New National Gallery, overlooking the Schöneberger Ufer. Because this is a relatively small place, ask for a table in the room away from the hustle of the bar. The marble walls and striking lighting effects may remind you of a sleek New York restaurant. ✗ *Schöneberger Ufer 65,* ☎ *030/261–3882. Reservations advised. No credit cards. Dinner only. Closed Mon. and Dec. 25–Jan. 1.*

$$ **Paris Bar.** This top-class restaurant just off the Ku'damm attracts a polyglot clientele of film stars, artists, entrepreneurs, and executives. The cuisine, including such delights as Jacques oysters and lambchops with provençal herbs, is high-powered, high-quality French. ✗ *Kantstr. 152,* ☎ *030/313–8052. Reservations advised. AE.*

$$ **Ponte Vecchio.** Delicious Tuscan-style Italian food is served here in a
★ handsome, light-wood dining room. Ask the friendly waiters for their recommendations. Like all food here, the delicate *Vitello tonnato* (veal with a tuna sauce) is excellent and simply presented. ✗ *Spielhagenstr. 3,* ☎ *030/342–1999. Reservations required. DC. Dinner only (except Sun.). Closed Tues., 4 wks in summer, and Dec. 25.*

$$ **Reinhard's.** This restaurant in the Nikolai Quarter is one of Berlin's newer popular eating establishments. Friends meet here to enjoy the carefully prepared entrées and sample spirits from the amply stocked bar, all served by friendly, bright tie–wearing waiters. The honey-glazed breast of duck, "Adlon," is one of the house specialties. If you just want to hug the bar but there's no room here, don't despair; head two doors down to Otello (under the same management), which has an accordion collection hanging from the ceiling. ✗ *Poststr. 28,* ☎ *030/242–5295. Reservations advised for dinner. AE, DC, MC, V.*

$$ **Turmstuben.** Not for the infirm or those who are afraid of heights, this restaurant tucked away below the cupola of the French Cathedral, at the north side of the beautiful Gendarmenmarkt, is reached by a long, winding staircase. Your reward at the top of the stairs is a table at one of Berlin's most original and attractive restaurants. The menu is short, but there's an impressive wine list. ✗ *Gendarmenmarkt,* ☎ *030/229–9313. Reservations required on weekends. MC, V.*

$$ **Zitadellen-Schänke.** Here you'll dine like a medieval noble, served a multicourse menu by Prussian wenches and serenaded by a minstrel group. In winter a roaring fire helps to light and warm the vaulted restaurant, which is part of Spandau's historic Zitadelle. These medieval banquets are popular, so be sure to reserve your spot at one of the heavy antique oak tables. ✗ *Am Juliusturm, Spandau,* ☎ *030/334–2106. Reservations advised. AE, DC, MC, V. Closed Mon.*

$$ **Zur Rippe.** This popular eating place in the Nikolai Quarter serves wholesome food in an intimate setting characterized by oak paneling and ceramic tiles. Specialties include the cheese platter and a herring casserole. ✗ *Poststr. 7,* ☎ *030/242–4248. AE, DC, MC, V.*

$ **Alt-Cöllner Schankstuben.** A tiny restaurant and pub are contained within
★ this charming, historic Berlin house. The section to the side of the canal on the Kleine Gertraudenstrasse, where there are tables set outside, serves as a café. The menu is relatively limited, but quality, like the service, is good. ✗ *Friederichsgracht 50,* ☎ *030/242–5972. No reservations. AE, DC, MC, V.*

$ **Arkade.** The Art Deco–style interior is a refreshing change from other
★ east Berlin restaurants, though in good weather you may choose to dine
outside. This is a convenient place to grab a snack after a performance
at the nearby Komische Oper or Konzerthaus Berlin, and it's a popular destination for ice-cream lovers on warm summer afternoons.
✕ *Französische Str. 25,* ☎ *030/2380–6153. No reservations. AE, MC.*

$ **Blockhaus Nikolskoe.** Prussian King Frederick Wilhelm III built this
Russian-style wooden lodge for his daughter Charlotte, wife of Russian tsar Nicholas I. Located south of the city in Glienecker Park, it
offers open-air riverside dining in summer. Game dishes are prominently
featured. ✕ *Nikolskoer Weg,* ☎ *030/805–2914. Reservations advised. AE, DC, MC, V. Closed Thurs.*

$ **Café Oren.** This popular vegetarian eatery is next to the Neue Syna-
gogue on Oranienburgerstrasse, not far from Friedrichstrasse. The
restaurant buzzes with loud chatter all evening, and the atmosphere
and service are welcoming and friendly. The intimate back courtyard
is a wonderful place to enjoy a cool summer evening or warm autumn
afternoon. The extensive menu offers mostly Israeli and Middle Eastern fare—including the delicious filled "Moroccan Cigars"—in addition to numerous dessert offerings. ✕ *Oranienburgerstr. 28,*
☎ *030/282–8228. Reservations advised. No credit cards.*

$ **Diyar.** In a city with close to a quarter of a million Turks, many of them
residents since the mid-1960s, Turkish food is typical, not exotic. Ergo,
what better place to try something more than a Döer Kepab street-side
than this large, spacious Turkish restaurant in Kreuzberg. It serves a
wide selection of traditional meat dishes and also has a decent amount
of vegetarian fare. In the traditional Turkish no-chair corner you can
immerse yourself even further in what some claim is the largest Turkish city after Istanbul. ✕ *Dresdnerstr. 9,* ☎ *030/615–2708. No credit
cards.*

$ **Eierscale (II).** Berlin is famous for its breakfast cafés, and this is one of
the best—and the best located, on the corner of central Rankestrasse
and the Ku'damm. It serves breakfast until 4 PM but really gets going
in the evenings, when jazz groups perform in a neighboring room. The
lunch and supper menus feature filling Berlin fare, but the Mexican-
style spareribs are especially recommended, if available. Sunday morning is *Frühschoppen* time, when live jazz accompanies the buffet
brunch; it's great fun and an opportunity to witness the highlight of a
Berliner's weekend. ✕ *Rankestrasse 1,* ☎ *030/882–5305. AE, DC, MC,
V.*

$ **Hardtke.** This is just about the most authentic old Berlin restaurant in
★ the city; it's very popular with tourists. The decor is simple, with paneled walls and wood floor. The food is similarly traditional and hearty.
It's a great place to try Eisbein. Wash it down with a large stein of beer.
✕ *Meinekestr. 27,* ☎ *030/881–9827. Reservations advised. Dress: informal. No credit cards.*

$ **Samâdhi.** This quaint restaurant just north of Savigny Platz serves a
wide variety of vegetarian Southeast Asian food. The soft lighting and
sparse interior don't exactly transport you to Asia, but you'll feel its
presence once you sample some of the delicately prepared food. One
of eight soups the restaurant offers, the Thai coconut soup with tofu
is smoothness embodied, and at DM 5 the fried banana dessert is a
bargain. ✕ *Goethestr. 6,* ☎ *030/313–1067. Reservations advised for
dinner. No credit cards.*

$ **Thürnagel.** The great food served in this vegetarian restaurant in the
Kreuzberg district makes healthful eating fun. The *seitan* (vegetable pro-
tein) in sherry sauce and the tempeh curry are good enough to convert

a seasoned carnivore. ✕ *Gneisenaustr. 57,* ☎ *030/691–4800. Reservations advised. No credit cards. Dinner only.*

$ **Zur Letzten Instanz.** Established in 1621, Berlin's oldest restaurant combines the charming atmosphere of old Berlin with a limited (but very tasty) choice of dishes. Napoléon is said to have sat alongside the tile stove in the front room, and Mikhail Gorbachev enjoyed a beer here during a visit in 1989. The emphasis here is on beer, both in the recipes and the mug. Service can be erratic, though always engagingly friendly. ✕ *Waisenstr. 14–16,* ☎ *030/242–5528. Reservations advised for both lunch and dinner. AE, DC, MC, V.*

LODGING

Berlin lost all of its grand old luxury hotels in the bombing during World War II. A few were rebuilt, but today many of the best hotels are modern, and though they lack little in service and comfort, you may find some short on atmosphere. For first-class or luxury accommodations, east Berlin is easily as good as west, for the East German government, eager for hard currency, built several elegant hotels—the Grand, Palast, and Hilton—which are up to the very best international standards and place in the very top price category. If you're seeking something more moderate, the better choice may be west Berlin, where there are large numbers of good-value pensions and small hotels, many of them in older buildings with some character. In east Berlin, however, the hostels run by the Evangelical church offer outstanding value for your money.

There are no longer any restrictions on who can stay where in east Berlin. In west Berlin, business conventions year-round and the influx of summer tourists mean that you should make reservations well in advance. If you arrive without reservations, consult hotel boards at airports and train stations that show hotels with vacancies, or go to the tourist office at Tegel Airport or at the Hauptbahnhof or Zoologischer Garten train stations. The main tourist office in the Europa-Centre can also help with reservations (*see* Important Addresses and Numbers *in* Berlin Essentials, *below*).

CATEGORY	COST*
$$$$	over DM 350
$$$	DM 270–DM 350
$$	DM 180–DM 270
$	under DM 180

for two people in a double room, including tax and service

$$$$ **Berlin Hilton.** One of Berlin's newest hotels, the Hilton overlooks the
★ historic Gendarmenmarkt and the German and French cathedrals as well as the classic *Schaupielhaus* (concert hall). It's also near Checkpoint Charlie, a location central to the entire city. All the right touches are here, from heated bathtubs to special rooms for businesswomen and travelers with disabilities. 🏨 *Mohrenstr. 30,* ☎ *030/23820,* FAX *030/2382–4269. 355 rooms with bath, 24 suites. 3 restaurants, 2 bars, cafeteria, pub, no-smoking rooms, room service, indoor pool, massage, sauna, bowling, exercise room, squash, dance club. AE, DC, MC, V.*

$$$$ **Bristol Hotel Kempinski.** Destroyed in the war, rebuilt in 1952, and ren-
★ ovated in 1980, the "Kempi" is a renowned Berlin classic. Located on the Ku'damm in the heart of the city, it has the best shopping at its doorstep and some fine boutiques of its own within. All rooms and suites are luxuriously decorated and equipped with marble bathrooms, air-conditioning, and cable TV. Children under 12 stay for free if they

Berlin Lodging

Atrium Hotel, **9**
Berlin Excelsior
Hotel, **5**
Berlin Hilton, **22**
Berlin Hilton
Krone, **23**
Berolina, **26**
Bristol Hotel
Kempinski, **6**
Charlottenhof, **20**
Econtel, **4**
Forum Hotel, **25**
Gendarm Garni
Hotel, **21**

Grand Hotel
Esplanade, **13**
Herbst, **1**
Hotel Berlin, **12**
Hotel Casino, **2**
Hotel Merkur, **19**
Hotel Müggelsee, **15**
Inter Continental
Berlin, **11**
Landhaus
Schlachtensee, **3**
Maritim Grand
Hotel, **17**

Maritim proArte
Hotel Berlin, **16**
Märkischer Hof, **18**
Radisson Plaza, **24**
Ravenna, **7**
Riehmers
Hofgarten, **14**
Schweizerhof
Inter-Continental
Berlin, **10**
Steigenberger
Berlin, **8**

share their parents' room. ☎ *Kurfürstendamm 27,* ☎ *030/884–340,* FAX *030/883–6075. 315 rooms with bath, 52 suites. 3 restaurants, bar, room service, indoor pool, beauty salon, massage, sauna, exercise room. AE, DC, MC, V.*

$$$$ **Grand Hotel Esplanade.** Opened in 1988, the Grand Hotel Esplanade exudes luxury. Uncompromisingly modern architecture, chicly styled rooms, and works of art by some of Berlin's most acclaimed artists are its outstanding visual aspects. Then there are the superb facilities and impeccable service. The enormous grand suite comes complete with sauna, whirlpool, and a grand piano for DM 2,500 per night. ☎ *Lützowufer 15,* ☎ *030/254–780,* FAX *030/265–1171. 369 rooms with bath, 33 suites. 2 restaurants, 2 bars, room service, pool, hot tub, beauty salon, massage, sauna, steam room, exercise room, library. AE, DC, MC, V.*

$$$$ **Inter Continental Berlin.** In conjunction with the recent addition of a
★ major conference center, the entire hotel was substantially improved. The rooms and suites are all of the highest standard and their decor shows exquisite taste with such refinements as luxurious carpets and elegant bathrooms. The lobby is one-quarter the size of a football field, lavishly decorated, and just the place for afternoon tea and pastries. In the evening enjoy a drink in the intimate, wood-paneled Library Bar. The newly opened L.A. Cafe serves California cuisine. ☎ *Budapesterstr. 2,* ☎ *030/26020,* FAX *030/2602–80760. 511 rooms with bath, 70 suites. 3 restaurants, 2 bars, no-smoking floor, room service, indoor pool, hot tub, sauna. AE, DC, MC, V.*

$$$$ **Maritim Grand Hotel.** East Berlin's most expensive hotel lives up to its name; opened in 1987, this establishment is grand in every sense of the word. From the moment you step into the air-conditioned atrium lobby, all is luxury. You'll wonder how this example of capitalist decadence ever fit into a socialist society. ☎ *Friedrichstr. 158–164, corner Behrenstr.,* ☎ *030/23270,* FAX *030/2327–3362. 358 rooms with bath, 36 suites. 4 restaurants, bar, café, pub, no-smoking floor, room service, pool, beauty salon, sauna, exercise room. AE, DC, MC, V.*

$$$$ **Maritim proArte Hotel Berlin.** French designer Philippe Starck (responsible for Manhattan's Paramount and Royalton hotels) took the old Metropol Hotel and transformed it into this modern, futuristic accommodation. Some space is devoted to original works by modern artists of national and international reputation. It's still a choice facility for business travelers, with a large desk, two telephones, and fax and PC connections in every room. Other luxuries—minibars, on-line movies, and bathrooms furnished with marble and black amethyst granite—will be appreciated by all. ☎ *Friedrichstr. 150–153,* ☎ *030/23875,* FAX *030/2387–4209. 403 rooms with bath, 29 suites. 3 restaurants, bar, minibars, no-smoking floors, indoor pool, beauty salon, massage, sauna, exercise room. AE, DC, MC, V.*

$$$$ **Radisson Plaza.** This is a favorite with tour groups because of its proximity to east Berlin's museums—and because it's another of the city's megafacility hotels. The recently redone lobby entrance welcomes guests into the luxury hotel; note the Haagen-Dazs ice-cream parlor, and for those needing more of a shot of home, the recently opened T.G.I. Fridays restaurant among the shops. The best rooms overlook the Spree River; those on the Alexanderplatz side can be noisy. ☎ *Karl-Liebknecht-Str. 5,* ☎ *030/23828,* FAX *030/2382–7590. 503 rooms with bath, 37 suites. 2 restaurants, bar, room service, indoor pool, massage, sauna, exercise room, travel services, car rental. AE, DC, MC, V.*

$$$$ Schweizerhof Inter-Continental Berlin. There's a rustic, alpine look about most of the rooms in this centrally located hotel; the extras, such as on-line-video and minibars, are up-to-the-minute. Ask for a room in the west wing, where rooms are larger. Standards are high throughout. The indoor pool is the largest of any Berlin hotel, and the hotel is opposite Tiergarten Park. ☎ *Budapesterstr. 21–31,* ☎ *030/26960,* FAX *030/269–6900. 430 rooms with bath, 26 suites. 2 restaurants, 2 bars, pub, minibars, room service, no-smoking floor, indoor pool, exercise room, sauna, steam room. AE, DC, MC, V.*

$$$$ Steigenberger Berlin. The Steigenberger group's exemplary Berlin hotel is centrally situated, only a few steps from the Ku'damm, but remarkably quiet. Small touches that lift the hotel above the usual run of chain establishments include a safe in every room and complimentary shoe-shine service. ☎ *Los-Angeles-Platz 1,* ☎ *030/21270,* FAX *030/212–7117. 397 rooms with bath, 11 suites. 2 restaurants, bar, 2 cafés, piano bar, pub, in-room safes, room service, no-smoking floor, indoor pool, beauty salon, massage, sauna. AE, DC, MC, V.*

$$$ Berlin Excelsior Hotel. This modern, well-run establishment five minutes away from Ku'damm is part of the Blue Band Hotels group. The comfortable rooms are furnished in dark teak and come with a minibar. The helpful front-office staff can arrange sightseeing tours and try to find hard-to-get theater and concert tickets for you. ☎ *Hardenbergerstr. 14,* ☎ *030/31550,* FAX *030/315–51002. 320 rooms with bath. 2 restaurants, bar, minibars. AE, DC, MC, V.*

$$$ Berlin Hilton Krone. Opened in 1991, the Krone is part of the Hilton Hotel complex, sharing the Hilton's excellent location on east Berlin's beautiful Gendarmenmarkt, but not its high prices. The rooms offered by the Hilton Krone are correspondingly less lavish, but they are comfortable and adequately furnished. Krone guests can use most of the Berlin Hilton facilities free of charge. ☎ *Mohrenstr. 30,* ☎ *030/2382–4212,* FAX *030/2382–4269. 148 rooms with bath.* (see *Berlin Hilton,* above). *AE, DC, MC, V.*

$$$ Forum Hotel. With its 40 stories, this hotel (owned by Inter-Continental) at the top end of Alexanderplatz competes with the nearby TV tower for the title of premier downtown landmark. As the city's largest hotel, it is understandably less personal, although a recent renovation of the public areas has made the atmosphere more welcoming. The 37th-story Panorama restaurant has good food and service, and even better views. The casino next door is the highest in Europe and is open until 3 AM. ☎ *Alexanderpl.,* ☎ *030/23890,* FAX *030/2389–4305. 943 rooms with bath, 14 suites. 3 restaurants, 2 bars, no-smoking floors, sauna, exercise room, casino. AE, DC, MC, V.*

$$$ Hotel Berlin. The hotel that bears Berlin's name is another Blue Band hotel, and has a bright and light look, furnished in enduring, understated good taste. The airy, high-ceiling lobby is an ideal location for afternoon tea or a late-night drink. The location is handy for both the Ku'damm and Unter den Linden. ☎ *Lützowpl. 17,* ☎ *030/260–50,* FAX *030/260–52716. 490 rooms with bath, 21 suites. Restaurant, piano bar, pub, beauty salon, massage, solarium, exercise room. AE, DC, MC, V.*

$$ Berolina. If being somewhat removed from the city's main tourist attractions is no deterrent, this is a pleasant hotel near Alexanderplatz. The rooms are spotless and cheerfully furnished. ☎ *Karl-Marx-Allee 31,* ☎ *030/238–13860,* FAX *030/212–3409. 380 rooms with bath, 3 suites. 2 restaurants, bar. AE, DC, MC, V.*

$$ Charlottenhof. This popular hotel-pension, ideally located on east Berlin's beautiful Gendarmenmarkt, was taken over by a large west German group in 1991. Luckily the room prices have remained moderate and the homey, friendly nature of the original establishment has been faithfully carried on. Ask for the weekend bargain rates. ☎ *Charlottenstrasse 52,* ☎ *030/238–060,* FAX *030/2380–6100. 86 rooms with bath. Restaurant, bar. AE, DC, MC, V.*

\$\$ Hotel Casino. What was once the main quarters of Imperial officers has been skillfully converted into an appealing hotel with large, comfortable rooms, all tastefully furnished and well equipped—the Prussian soldiers never had it so good! The Casino is in the Charlottenburg district. ☎ *Königen-Elisabeth-Str. 47a,* ☎ *030/303–090,* FAX *030/303–0945. 23 rooms with bath. Snack bar. AE, DC, MC, V.*

\$\$ Hotel Müggelsee. Berlin's largest and some say most beautiful lake is just beyond your balcony in this establishment, which was once a favorite among East Germany's communist leaders. The rooms are not luxurious, but they are comfortable and fairly spacious. The hotel can arrange for forest picnics and even has its own yacht for guests' use. ☎ *Am Grossen Müggelsee,* ☎ *030/658–820,* FAX *030/6588–2263. 174 rooms with bath. 4 restaurants, bar, massage, sauna, tennis court, exercise room, boating, nightclub. AE, DC, M, V.*

\$\$ Landhaus Schlachtensee. Opened in 1987, this former villa (built in
★   1905) is now a cozy bed-and-breakfast hotel. The Landhaus Schlachtensee offers personal and efficient service, well-equipped rooms, and a quiet location in the Zehlendorf district. The nearby Schlachtensee and Krumme Lanke lakes beckon you to swim, boat, or walk along their shores. ☎ *Bogotastr. 9,* ☎ *030/816–0060,* FAX *030/8160–0664. 19 rooms with bath. Breakfast room. AE, DC, MC, V.*

\$\$ Märkischer Hof. This small hotel is conveniently located off Friedrichstrasse and all of old Berlin is within easy walking distance. The rooms are fairly large, get lots of light, and have mostly new, pleasant furniture. ☎ *Linienstr. 133,* ☎ *030/282–7155,* FAX *030/282–4331. 20 rooms, most with bath. AE, MC, V.*

\$\$ Ravenna. A small, friendly hotel in the Steglitz district, Ravenna is near the Botanical Garden and Dahlem museums. All the rooms are well equipped. Suite 111B includes a large living room and kitchen for only DM 305. ☎ *Grunewaldstr. 8–9,* ☎ *030/790–910,* FAX *030/792–4412. 55 rooms with bath. Restaurant, bar. AE, DC, MC, V.*

\$\$ Riehmers Hofgarten. A few minutes' walk from the Kreuzberg Hill and the colorful district's restaurants and bars, and also near Tempelhof Airport, this small hotel has fast connections to the center of town. The late-19th-century building has high-ceiling rooms that are comfortable, with crisp linens and firm beds. ☎ *Yorckstr. 83,* ☎ *030/781–011,* FAX *030/786–6059. 21 rooms with bath. Restaurant, bar. AE, DC, MC, V.*

\$ Atrium Hotel. This little privately run hotel is located within reasonable reach of downtown. The modest rooms are comfortably furnished and clean, the staff efficient and helpful. The only drawback is that there's no restaurant. ☎ *Motzstr. 87,* ☎ *030/218–4057,* FAX *030/211–7563. 22 rooms with bath. MC.*

\$ Econtel. This family-oriented hotel is within walking distance of Char-
★   lottenburg Palace. Rooms have a homey feel, include closet safes and cable, and are spotless. A crib, bottle warmer, and kiddie toilet are available free of charge on request. The breakfast buffet offers a dazzling array of choices to fill you up for a day of sightseeing. ☎ *Sömmeringstr. 24,* ☎ *030/346–810,* FAX *030/344–7034. 205 rooms with bath. Bar, in-room safes. AE, MC, V.*

\$ Gendarm Garni Hotel. This well-run hotel is by the Gendarmenmarkt,
★   in the heart of old Berlin. All the rooms are neat and pleasantly furnished. Ask for the corner suite facing the square; the view and the large living room (for DM 225) make for one of the better deals in town.

⊞ *Charlottenstr. 60, ☎ 030/200–4180, ⅨX 030/208–2482. 25 rooms with bath, 4 suites. Bar. AE, MC, V.*

$ **Herbst.** This plain and simple bed-and-breakfast pension is in the Spandau district, where Hitler's mysterious deputy Rudolph Hess spent more than 40 years in jail. There are good connections to downtown by U-bahn. ⊞ *Moritzstr. 21, ☎ 030/333–4032, ⅨX 030/333–7365. 21 rooms with bath. AE, MC, V.*

$ **Hotel Merkur.** This small hotel is in east Berlin's central Prenzlauerberg district, within walking distance of downtown east Berlin and Museum Island. The service is friendly, and the rooms are comfortable, equipped with such extras as radio and TV. ⊞ *Torstr. 156, ☎ 030/282–8297. 16 rooms, some with bath. Minibar, in-room safes. AE, DC, MC, V.*

THE ARTS AND NIGHTLIFE

The Arts

Today's Berlin has a tough task living up to the reputation it gained from the film *Cabaret,* but if nightlife is a little toned down since the '20s and '30s, the arts still flourish. In addition to the many hotels that book seats, there are several ticket agencies, including **Ticket Counter** (in Europa-Center, ☎ 030/264–1138), **Theater-kasse Centrum** (Mienekestr. 25, ☎ 030/882–7611), and the **Hekticket** office at Alexanderplatz (☎ 030/883–6010). Most of the big stores (Hertie, Wertheim, and Karstadt, for example) also have ticket agencies. Detailed information about what's going on in Berlin can be found in *Checkpoint,* an English-language monthly cultural magazine, *Berlin Programm,* a monthly guide to Berlin arts, and the magazines *Prinz, Tip,* and *Zitty,* which appear every two weeks and provide full arts listings.

Theater

Theater in Berlin is outstanding, but performances are usually in German. The exceptions are operettas and the (nonliterary) cabarets. Of the city's impressive number of theaters, the most renowned for both their modern and classical productions are the **Schaubühne am Lehniner Platz** (Kurfürstendamm 153, ☎ 030/890–023) and the **Deutsches Theater** (Schumannstr. 13, ☎ 030/284–41225), which has an excellent studio theater next door, the **Kammerspiele** (☎ 030/284–41226). Also important are **Berliner Ensemble** (Bertolt Brecht-Pl., ☎ 030/282–3160), dedicated to Brecht and works of other international playwrights; **Friedrichstadtpalast** (Friedrichstr. 107, ☎ 030/2326–2474), a glossy showcase for revues and historic Berlin plays; **Hebbel Theater** (Stresemannstr. 29, ☎ 030/251–0144), which showcases international theater and dance troupes; **Maxim Gorki Theater** (Am Festungsgraben 2, ☎ 030/208–2783), which also has a superb studio theater; **Renaissance-Theater** (Hardenbergstr. 6, ☎ 030/312–4202); and **Volksbühne** (Rosa-Luxemburg-Pl., ☎ 030/3087–4630), known for its radical interpretations of dramas. For *Boulevard* plays (fashionable social comedies), there is the **Hansa Theater** (Alt-Moabit 48, ☎ 030/391–4460), the **Komödie** (Kurfürstendamm 206, ☎ 030/882–7893), and, at the same address, the **Theater am Kurfürstendamm** (☎ 030/882–3789).

For smaller, more alternative theaters that generally showcase different guest productions, try **Tacheles** (Oranienburgerstr. 53–56, ☎ 030/282–6185); **Theater am Halischen Ufer** (Hallesches Ufer 32, ☎ 030/251–0941); **Theater unterm Dach** (Dimitroffstr. 101,

☏ 030/4240–1086); or **Theater Zerbrochene Fenster** (Schwiebusser-str. 16, ☏ 030/694–2400).

Berlin's savage and debunking idiom is particularly suited to social and political satire, a long tradition in cabaret theaters here. The **Stachelschweine** (Europa-Centre, ☏ 030/261–4795) and **Die Wühlmäuse** (Nümbergerstr. 33, ☏ 030/213–7047) carry on that tradition with biting wit and style; east Berlin's equivalent is **Die Distel** (Friedrichstr. 101, ☏ 030/200–4704). For children's theater, try the world-famous **Grips Theater** (Althonaerstr. 22 030/391–4004), **Hans Wurst Nachfahren** (Gleditschstr. 5, ☏ 030/216–7925), or **Die Schaubude** (Greifswalder-str. 81–84, ☏ 030/423–4314), one of east Berlin's many puppet theaters. All are nominally for children but can be good entertainment for adults as well.

Opera, Musicals, and Dance

After unification Berlin decided to keep its three opera houses, all of which have their own ballet companies: the **Deutsche Oper Berlin** (Bismarckstr. 34–37, ☏ 030/343–81), one of Germany's leading opera houses, the **Deutsche Staatsoper** (Unter den Linden 7, ☏ 030/200–4762); and the **Komische Oper** (Behrenstr. 55–57, ☏ 030/229–2555). At the **Neuköllner Oper** (Karl-Marx-Str. 131–133, ☏ 030/6889–0777) you'll find showy, fun performances of long-forgotten operas and humorous musical productions. And at the **Theater des Westens** (Kantstr. 12, ☏ 030/882–2888) and the **Metropol Theater** (Friedrichstr. 101, ☏ 030/2036–4117) comic operas and musicals can be seen, such as *West Side Story, A Chorus Line,* and *Cabaret.*

Experimental and modern-dance performances are presented at **Podewill** (Klosterstr. 68–70, ☏ 030/247–496); **Tanzfabrik** (Möckernstr. 68, ☏ 030/786–5861); **Tacheles** (*see above*); **Theater am Halischen Ufer** (*see above*); and **Theater unterm Dach** (*see above*).

Concerts

Berlin is the home of one of the world's leading orchestras, the **Berliner Philharmonisches Orchester** (Berlin Philharmonic—*see below*) in addition to a number of other major symphony orchestras and orchestral ensembles. The **Berlin Festival Weeks,** held annually from August through October, combine a wide range of concerts, operas, ballet, theater, and art exhibitions. For information and reservations, write **Festspiele GmbH** (Kartenbüro, Budapesterstr. 50, 10787 Berlin).

CONCERT HALLS

Grosser Sendesaal des SFB (Haus des Rundfunks, Masurenallee 8–14, ☏ 030/303–10). Part of the Sender Freies Berlin, one of Berlin's broadcasting stations, the Grosser Sendesaal is the home of the Radio Symphonic Orchestra.

Deutschlandhalle (Messedamm 26, 030/303–81). Big rock acts and extravagant opera and musicals productions can be seen in this immense hall.

Huxley's Neue Welt (Hasenheide 108–114, ☏ 030/621–1028). A smaller, less impersonal contemporary-music venue.

Konzerthaus Berlin (in the Schauspielhaus; Gendarmenmarkt, ☏ 030/2030–92100). This beautifully restored hall is a prime venue for concerts in east Berlin.

Konzertsaal der Hochschule der Künste (Hardenbergstr 33, ☎ 030/3185–2374). The concert hall of the Academy of Fine Arts is Berlin's second biggest.

Philharmonie (Matthaikircherstr. 1, ☎ 030/261–4383). The Berlin Philharmonic is based here. The hall also houses the new Kammermusiksaal, dedicated to chamber music.

Waldbühne (Am Glockenturm, close to the Olympic Stadium, ☎ 030/305–5079). Modeled along the lines of an ancient Roman theater, this open-air site accommodates nearly 20,000 people.

Film

Berlin has about 90 movie theaters, showing about 100 movies a day. International and German movies are shown in the big theaters around the Ku'damm; the Off-Ku-damm theaters show less commercial movies. For (un-dubbed) movies in English, go to the Babylon (Dresdnerstr. 126, ☎ 030/614–6316), the Kurbel (Geisebrechtstr. 4, ☎ 030/883–5325), or the **Odeon** (Hauptstr. 116, ☎ 030/781–5667).

In February, Berlin hosts the **Internationale Filmfestspiele,** an internationally famous film festival, conferring "Golden Bear" awards on the best films, directors, and actors. Call 030/254–890 for information.

Nightlife

Berlin's nightlife has always been notorious. There are scads of places in west Berlin that revel in nighttime entertainment, and the quality ranges widely from tacky to spectacular. East Berlin's nightlife offers as much excitement and variety as that in the west—just less of it, although that's changing as new bars and clubs continue to open almost weekly.

All Berlin tour operators offer **Night Club Tours** (around DM 100, including entrance fees to up to three shows, free drinks, and, in some cases, supper). Most places in Berlin stay open late (the Western Allies abolished bar closing times to make West Berlin a western showcase, and luckily for the city's nightlife, the late hours stuck).

Clubs

Chez Nous (Marburgerstr. 14, ☎ 030/213–1810) helps Berlin live up to its reputation as the drag-show center of Germany. Empire-style plush is the backdrop for two nightly shows (reservations recommended).

You'll find three more conventional stage shows at **Dollywood** (Kurfürstenstr. 114, ☎ 030/218–8950) each night, plus a disco. **La Vie en Rose** (Europa Center, ☎ 030/323–6006) is a revue theater with spectacular light shows that also showcases international stars (book ahead). If the strip show at the **New Eden** (Ku'damm 71, ☎ 030/323–5849) doesn't grab you, maybe the dance music will (two bands nightly). The **New York Bar** (Olivaer Pl. 16, ☎ 030/883–6258) is a mellow drinking haven compared with its rowdier neighbors. You have a choice at **Zeleste** (Marburgerstr. 2, ☎ 030/211–6445): Sit back and listen to jazz or dance the night away in its disco.

Jazz Clubs

Berlin's lively music scene is dominated by jazz and rock. For jazz enthusiasts, *the* events of the year are the summer's **Jazz in the Garden** festival and the international autumn **Jazz Fest Berlin.** For information, call the **tourist information center** (☎ 030/262–6031).

Traditionally, the best **live jazz** can be found at:

Eiershale (I) (Podbielskiallee 50, ☎ 030/832−7097). A variety of jazz groups appear here at the "Egg Shell"; daily from 8:30 PM, ☛ Free.

Flöz (Nassauischestr. 37, ☎ 030/861−1000). The sizzling jazz at this club is sometimes incorporated into theater presentations.

Franz (Schönhauser Allee 36−39, ☎ 030/442−8203). This east Berlin club brings in big jazz names, and follows up the acts with hours of dancing. DM 5 after the show.

Kunstlerhaus Bethanien (Mariannenpl. 2, ☎ 030/616−9030). Jazz and "Free Music" concerts are held at this big venue.

Quasimodo (Kantstr. 12a, ☎ 030/312−8086). The most established and popular jazz venue in the city offers a great basement atmosphere and has only good seats.

Discos

Far Out (Kurfürstendamm 156). This Bhagwan-operated disco has the cleanest air in the city and one of the biggest dance floors. Thursday's no-smoking night; closed Monday.

Hafenbar (Chauseestr. 20). This is a popular east Berlin disco decorated in '50s style. Closed Wednesdays.

Metropol (Nollendorfpl. 5; Fri. and Sat. only). Berlin's largest disco, which also stages concerts, is a hot spot for younger tourists. The black dance floor upstairs is the scene of a magnificent laser light show. Its occasional gay dances are hugely popular. The DM 10 cover includes your first drink.

90 Grad (Dennewitzstr. 37). This jam-packed disco plays hip-hop, soul, and some techno and really gets going around 2 AM. The women come fashionably dressed and go right in, but the men usually have to wait outside until they get picked by the doorman.

Sophienklubb (Sophienstr. 6). A gathering spot for mostly local former East Berliners, this cramped disco always serves up a formidable music mix. Heavy on acid jazz.

Kneipen

Berlin has roughly 5,000 bars and pubs; this includes the dives, too. All come under the heading of *Kneipen*—the place around the corner where you stop in for a beer, snack, conversation, and sometimes to dance. Other than along Ku'damm, the hot places in west Berlin are around Nollendorfplatz in Schöneberg and along Oranienstrasse and Wienerstrasse in Kreuzberg. In east Berlin, most of the action is along Oranienburgerstrasse and north in Mitte and around Kollwitzplatz in Prenzlauerberg.

Bierhimmel (Oranienstr. 183). "Beer heaven" is a funky mix of kitsch and class; the "secret" back room is a red-leather-padded '50s cocktail bar that offers a venue fit for Elvis.

Café Westfall (Kollwitzstr. 64). This Kneipe was one of only a few alternative places during the communist era. Right on Kollwitzplatz, it still has an alternative feel and offers great atmosphere and food.

Ku'dorf (Joachimstaler-Str. 15). The Ku'dorf makes it easy to go from one Kneipe to another—there are 18 located under one roof here, underground, just off the Ku'damm. ⊘Monday–Saturday from 8 PM.

Leydicke (Mansteinstr. 4). This historic spot is a must for out-of-towners. The proprietors operate their own distillery and have a superb selection of wines and liqueurs.

Silberstein (Oranienburgerstr. 27). You might pass this place up at first, mistaking it for an art gallery, and you wouldn't be entirely wrong; it's that *and* one of the city's trendiest gathering places.

Sperlingsgasse (Lietzenburgerstr. 82–84). A short walk from Ku'-damm, this collection of Kneipen is smaller than its cousin Ku'dorf (13 establishments, including a pizzeria), but it has some of the best German kitsch Berlin offers. All open at 7 PM.

Wilhelm Hoeck (Wilmersdorferstr. 149). Berlin's oldest Kneipe is also its most beautiful. Its superb interior dates from 1892—all original. Frequented by a colorful cross section of the public, this is a place that's definitely worth a visit.

Zosch (Tucholskystr. 30). A mixed crowd frequents this popular Scheu-nenviertel Kneipe, which has good beer on tap and occasional concerts in its basement bar.

Zwiebelfisch (Savignypl. 7). Literally translated as the "onion fish," this Kneipe has become the meeting place of literary Bohemians of all ages. It has a good atmosphere for making new friends and having pleasant conversations.

Cafés

Cafés are popular in the evening as well as the morning. A leisurely breakfast is one of Berlin's best-loved traditions, and breakfast food is often served as late as 4 PM in cafés throughout the city. The most common menu consists of platters of cheese and cold cuts served with fresh rolls and a side order of yogurt and fresh fruit. Don't forget to order a *Milchkaffee*—a bowl of coffee and warm milk—which Berliners swear is better than café au lait.

Café Klassik (Paul-Lincke-Ufer 42). Situated in a row of cafés along the Landwehrkanal in Kreuzberg, this is the place for a mellower, quieter atmosphere, great classical music, and salads.

Orangerie (Oranienburgerstr. 32). This classic French café has soft pastel walls and a heavenly high ceiling. A few cubbyholes allow total escape from the city frenzy outside. The dessert choices leave nothing to be desired.

Schwarzes Café (Kantstr. 148). This place is popular with the city's young counterculture crowd. The downstairs is crowded and hot, but upstairs three huge rooms with beautiful plasterwork on the ceilings will tempt breakfasters to linger for hours. It's open nonstop Friday through Sunday.

Casinos

West Berlin's leading casino is in the Europa Center. It has 10 roulette tables and three blackjack tables and is open 3 PM–3 AM. East Berlin's largest casino—Europe's highest—is in the Forum Hotel.

Gay Nightlife

Berlin is unmistakably Germany's gay capital, and many visitors from other European countries also come to partake of the city's gay scene. Concentrated in Schöneberg (around Nollendorfplatz) and Kreuzberg in west Berlin, and growing in Mitte and Prenzlauerberg in east Berlin, the scene offers great diversity.

The following places are a good starting point for information. Also check out the magazine *Siegessäule* (free and available at the places listed below as well as many others around town).

Mann-O-Meter (Motzstr. 5, ☎ 030/216–8008; open Mon.–Sat. 3–11, Sat. 3–9) has extensive information about gay life, groups, and events. Talks are held in the café, which has a variety of books and magazines. **Schwuz** (Hasenheide 54, ☎ 030/694–1077) is a gay gathering spot that sponsors different events. Every Saturday starting at 11 PM there is an "open evening" for talk and dance.

KNEIPEN
Andreres Ufer (Hauptstr. 157). This hip Kneipe is frequented by a young gay and lesbian crowd. Mellow atmosphere and '50s and '60s music.
Drama (Oranienstr. 169). A straight and gay crowd mixes at this Kreuzberg-typical spot. On weekends DJs spin techno and trance music.
Hafen (Motzstr. 19). The interior and human scenery make this gay bar endlessly popular and a favorite singles place. At 4 AM people move next door to **Tom's Bar,** open until 6 AM.
New Action (Kleistr. 35). A tough leather bar that's open until 5 AM.

DISCOS
Connection (Welserstr. 24). Close to Wittenbergplatz, this disco offers heavy house music and lots of dark corners. Friday and Saturday, midnight until 6.
Metropol (*see above*).
Schwuz (*see above*).

EXCURSIONS

Tour 1: Potsdam

Exploring
Prussia's most famous king, Friedrich II—Frederick the Great—spent more time at his summer residence in Potsdam than at the official court in Berlin, and it's no wonder. Frederick was an aesthetic ruler, and he clearly fell for the sheer beauty of the sleepy township lost among the hills, meadows, and lakes of this rural corner of mighty Prussia. Frederick's father, Friedrich Wilhelm I, had established the Prussian court at Potsdam, but the royal castle didn't match the demanding tastes of his son and heir, who built a summer palace of his own amid green lawns above the Havel River. Its name, "Sanssouci," means "without a care" in French, the language he cultivated in his own private circle and within the court.

Some experts believe Frederick actually named the palace "Sans, Souci," which they translate as "with and without a care," a more apt name because its construction caused him a lot of trouble and expense and sparked furious rows with his master builder, Georg Wenzeslaus von Knobelsdorff, whom Frederick called fat and lazy. Growing increasingly restive over the expense, Frederick told von Knobelsdorff he wanted the palace to last only his lifetime, but fortunately the Prussian architect ignored him, and his creation became one of Germany's greatest tourist attractions (5 million visitors a year file through the palace and grounds).

Frederick wanted to be buried beside his hunting dogs on the terrace of his beloved Sanssouci, with no pomp and ceremony; a "philosopher's funeral" was what he decreed. His shocked nephew and successor, Friedrich Wilhelm II, ordered the body to be laid out in state and then consigned Frederick's remains to the garrison church of Potsdam. The

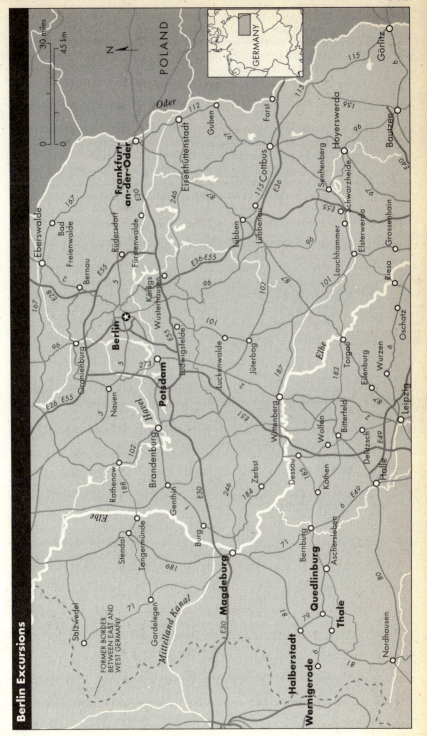

Berlin Excursions

coffin was removed to safety during World War II, after which time it went on a macabre peregrination that ended in the chapel of the Hohenzollern Castle in southern Germany. The unification of Germany in 1991 made it possible to grant Frederick his last wish. On the same day, his father's body was reinterred, marking the 250th anniversary of his death, at the so-called Peace Church on the Sanssouci grounds.

The vine-covered terraces on which **Sanssouci** stands are actually an artificial hill, rising in majestic steps from a side stream of the Havel, a few minutes' walk from the center of Potsdam. You walk through Potsdam's own **Brandenburger Tor,** a victory arch built 25 years after Sanssouci, to enter the Hohenzollern palace complex. The residence, one of Europe's most important at the time, is contained in a beautifully landscaped park, yet what you see is largely the result of a magnificent restoration job by the East Germans. Just weeks before the end of World War II, Potsdam was razed by British bombing, and the battle for Berlin finished it off. There is no charge to enter the grounds.

Executed according to Frederick's impeccable, French-influenced taste, the palace, built from 1745 to 1747, is extravagantly Rococo, with scarcely a patch of wall left unadorned. Strangely, Frederick occupied only five rooms; his bedroom, study, and circular library (beautifully paneled with cedar wood) can be visited. Five rooms were kept for guests, one exclusively reserved for the French writer and philosopher Voltaire. Johann Sebastian Bach was also a welcome visitor; he and Frederick, a competent musician, performed together in the palace music chamber, considered one of Germany's finest Rococo interiors. To the west of the palace is the **New Chambers** (1747), which housed guests of the king's family; originally it functioned as a greenhouse until it was remodeled in 1771–74. Just east of Sanssouci Palace is the **Picture Gallery** (1755–63), which still displays Frederick's collection of 17th-century Italian and Dutch paintings. It is under reconstruction and will not reopen until early 1997. *Information Center, Sanssouci:* ☎ *0331/22051. Schloss Sanssouci admission (guided tours only): DM 8 adults, DM 4 children.* ☉ *Apr.–Oct., daily 9–5, except 1st and 3rd Mon.; Feb. and Mar. daily 9–4, except 1st and 3rd Mon.; Nov.–Jan. daily 9–3, except 1st and 3rd Mon. New Chambers* ☛ *DM 5 adults, DM 3 children.* ☉ *Apr.–Oct., Tues.–Sun. 9–5; Feb. and Mar., Tues.–Sun. 9–4; Nov.–Jan., Tues.–Sun. 9–3.*

At the end of the long, straight avenue that runs through Sanssouci Park you'll see a much larger and grander palace, the **Neues Palais** (New Palace). Frederick loosened the purse strings in building this palace after the Seven Years' War (1756–63), and it's said he wanted to demonstrate to his subjects that the state coffers hadn't been depleted too severely by the long conflict. Frederick rarely stayed here, however, preferring the relative coziness of Sanssouci. Still, the Neues Palais has much of interest, including an indoor grotto hall, a Jules Verne–like extravaganza of walls and columns set with shells, coral, and other aquatic decoration. There's a fascinating collection of musical instruments that includes a 900-year-old portable organ; the Upper Gallery, which contains paintings by 17th-century Italian masters; and a bijou court theater in which performances are still given during an annual music festival held in June or July. *Neues Palais* ☛ *DM 8 adults, DM 4 children.* ☉ *Apr.–Oct., daily 9–5, except 2nd and 4th Mon.; Feb. and Mar. 9–4, except 2nd and 4th Mon.; Nov.–Jan. 9–3, except 2nd and 4th Mon.*

After Frederick died in 1786, the ambitious Sanssouci building program ground to a halt and the park fell into neglect. It was 50 years before another Prussian king, Frederick William III, restored Sanssouci's earlier glory. He engaged the great Berlin architect Karl Friedrich Schinkel to build a small palace for the crown prince. The result is the **Schloss Charlottenhof,** set in its own grounds in the southern part of Sanssouci Park. Schinkel gave it a classical, almost Roman appearance, and he let his imagination loose in the interior, too—decorating one of the rooms as a Roman tent, with its walls and ceiling draped in striped canvas. *Schloss Charlottenhof admission (guided tour only): DM 6 adults, DM 3 children.* ☉ *Mid-May–mid-Oct., daily 9–5, except every 4th Mon.*

Just north of the Schloss Charlottenhof, on the path back to Sanssouci, you'll find two other later additions to the park: Friedrich Wilhelm II's **Roman Baths** (1836) and a **Teahouse** built in 1757 in the Chinese style, which was all the rage at the time. Between the Neues Palais and Sanssouci is the **Orangerie** (completed in 1860), which, with two massive towers linked by a colonnade, evokes an Italian Renaissance palace. Today it houses 47 copies of paintings by Raphael. Elsewhere in the park, a delicious layer cake **"Mosque"** disguises pump works that operated the fountains in Sanssouci Park; the minaret concealed the chimney. The Italianate Peace Church (1845–48) houses a 12th-century Byzantine mosaic taken from an island near Venice. *Roman baths admission (additional charge for special exhibitions): DM 3 adults, DM 1.50 children.* ☉ *Mid-May–Oct., daily 9–5, except every 3rd Mon. Chinese teahouse* ☞ *DM 4 adults, DM 2 children.* ☉ *Mid-May–mid-Oct., daily 9–5. Orangerie admission (additional charge for special exhibitions): DM 4 adults, DM 2 children.* ☉ *May–Oct., daily 9–5. Mosque* ☞ *DM 2 adults, DM 1 children.* ☉ *Mid-May–mid-Oct., Wed.–Sun. 9–5; mid-Oct.–mid-May, weekends 9–4.*

TIME OUT   Halfway up the park's Drachenberg Hill, above the Orangerie, stands the curious **Drachenhaus** (Dragon House), modeled in 1770 after the Pagoda at London's Kew Gardens and named for the gargoyles ornamenting the roof corners. When built, it served as the residence of the palace vintner; it now houses a popular café.

The final addition to Sanssouci Park is equally exotic. Resembling a rambling, half-timbered country manor house, the **Schloss Cecilienhof** was built for Crown Prince Wilhelm in 1913 in a newly laid out stretch of the park bordering the Heiliger See, called the New Garden. It was here that the Allied leaders Truman, Attlee, and Stalin hammered out the fate of postwar Germany, at the 1945 Potsdam Conference. You can see the round table where they held their meetings; in fact, you can stay the night under the roof where they gathered to make history, for the Cecilienhof is today a very comfortable hotel (*see* Lodging, *below*). Also in the New Garden is the substantial two-story **Marble Palace,** completed in 1792, using gray-white Silesian marble to ornament the red brickwork. Formerly housing a military museum, it is closed for restoration until 2000. *Schloss Cecilienhof* ☞ *DM 5 adults, DM 3 children.* ☉ *May–Oct., daily 9–5, except 2nd and 4th Mon.*

Don't leave Potsdam without looking over the town itself, which still retains the imperial character lent it by the many years during which it served as royal residence and garrison quarters. The central market square, the **Alter Markt,** sums it all up: the stately, domed **Nikolaikirche** (1724), a square Baroque church with classical columns; an **Egyptian Obelisk** erected by Sanssouci architect von Knobelsdorff; and the officious facade of the former **City Hall** (1755), now the Haus Marchiwitza, with a gilded figure of Atlas atop the tower. Wander around some of the adjacent streets, particularly Wilhelm-Külz-Strasse, to admire the handsome restored burghers' houses.

Three blocks north of the Alter Markt is the **Holländisches Viertel,** built by Friedrich Wilhelm I in 1732 to induce Dutch artisans to settle in a city that needed migrant labor to support its rapid growth. (Few Dutch came, and the gabled, hip-roofed brick houses were largely used to house staff.) The Dutch government has promised to finance some of the cost of repairing the damage done by more than four decades of communist neglect.

There's a chilling reminder of the communist years a few steps away from the central shopping street, Brandenburgerstrasse. Turn down Lindenstrasse-Strasse, and at No. 54 you'll find an old Prussian guardhouse that served as a prison for victims of the East German State Security Service, the dreaded Stasi. Known then as the "Linden Hotel" among East Germans, it's now empty of its political prisoners, and you can step through the outside door and into the tiny exercise yard, overlooked by small barred windows. Tours are offered in German, but it is necessary to call ahead first; ask for Herr Werwicke at 0331/289–6803.

Dining

Am Stadttor. A five-minute walk from Sanssouci Palace and located on Potsdam's main shopping street, the Stadttor is the ideal spot for lunch. The menu isn't exactly imperial Prussian, but the dishes are filling and inexpensive. The soups are particularly wholesome, and the liver Berlin style is as good as any you'll find in the city. ✕ *Brandenburgerstrasse 1–3,* ☎ *0331/291–729. Reservations advised. No credit cards.* $

Lodging

Schloss Cecilienhof. This English country-style mansion is where Truman, Atlee, and Stalin drew up the 1945 Potsdam Agreement, and where Truman received news of the first successful atom bomb test (July 16, 1945). The hotel rooms are somewhat mundane, although comfortable and adequately equipped. The Schloss is set in its own parkland bordering a lake and is a pleasant 15-minute stroll from Sanssouci and the city center. ⊞ *Neuer Garten,* ☎ *0331/37050,* FAX *0331/292–498. 42 rooms with bath. Restaurant, room service, sauna. AE, D, MC, V.* $$

Potsdam Essentials

ARRIVING AND DEPARTING

Potsdam is virtually a suburb of Berlin, some 20 kilometers (12 miles) southwest of the city center and a half-hour journey by car or bus, or 45 minutes by S-bahn. City traffic is heavy, however, and a train journey is recommended. Perhaps the most effortless way to visit Potsdam and its attractions is to book a tour with one of the big Berlin operators (*see* Guided Tours, *below*).

By Boat. Boats leave Wannsee, landing hourly, between 10 AM and 6 PM; until 8 PM in summer.

By Bus. There is regular bus service from the bus station at the Funkturm, Messedamm 8 (U-1 U-bahn station Kaiserdamm).

By Car. From Berlin center (Strasse des 17 Juni), take the Postdamerstrasse south until it becomes Route 1 and then follow the signs to Postdam.

By Train. Take the S-bahn, either the S-3 or the S-7 line, to Potsdam Stadt (for the city and Schloss Sanssouci). Change there for the short rail trip to the Potsdam–Charlottenhof (for Schloss Charlottenhof) and Wildpark (for Neues Palais) stations. You can also take Bus 116 from Wannsee to the Bassanplatz bus station. From there you can walk down Brandenburgerstrasse to Platz der Nationen and on to the Green Gate, the main entrance to Sanssouci Park.

GUIDED TOURS

Severin & Kühn offers a whole-day tour for DM 89 (including lunch). **Berliner Bären Stadtrundfahrt** conducts an afternoon tour that includes tea in its DM 65 price. Berolina and Bus-Verkehr-Berlin also offer tours of Potsdam from Berlin. (*See* Guided Tours *in* Berlin Essentials, *below.*) The Potsdam Tourist Office also runs two tours April through October. Its three-hour tour, including Sanssouci, costs DM 35; the 1 ½-hour tour of just the city is DM 27. (*See* Visitor Information, *below.*)

VISITOR INFORMATION

The **Potsdam Tourist Office** has information on tours, attractions, and events, and also reserves hotel rooms for tourists. *Friedrich-Ebert-Str. 5, Postfach 601220, D–14467 Potsdam,* ☎ *0331/291–100.* ◷ *Apr.–Oct., weekdays 10–8, weekends 9–6; Nov.–Mar., weekdays 10–6, weekends 11–3.*

Tour 2: Magdeburg and the Elbe River Countryside

Magdeburg's great Gothic cathedral—Germany's oldest and, some say, the country's finest—is worth the trip from Berlin. Much of the city was rebuilt after the 1945 bombing in the dull utilitarian style favored by the Communists, but there are nevertheless corners of the Old Town where Magdeburg's 1,200-year history still lingers. Apart from the cathedral, the monastery church of Unsere Lieben Frauen contains much of interest. Both are a few strides from the Elbe River, where some fine walks open up through the wooded Kulturpark. The surrounding countryside, along the Elbe River between the Harz Mountains and the Brandenburg Plains, is easily explored from Magdeburg.

Exploring

If you arrive in Magdeburg by train or bus, head east from the main railway station (the bus depot is beside it) two blocks to the city center, the Alter Markt. Dominating its west side is the 17th-century **Rathaus** (City Hall), one of Magdeburg's few remaining Baroque buildings. In front of its arcaded facade is a 1966 bronze copy of Germany's oldest equestrian statue, the **Magdeburger Reiter,** completed by an unknown master around 1240. The sandstone original is now in the nearby **Kulturhistorisches Museum,** where you can also see the simple invention with which the 17th-century scientist Otto von Güricke proved the extraordinary power created by a vacuum. The device consisted of just two iron cups; von Güricke sealed them together by pumping out the air—and then attached the hollow sphere to two teams of eight cart-horses, which were urged to pull the cups apart. The vacuum proved stronger. *Otto-von-Güricke-Strasse 68–73 ,* ☎ *0391/32645* ☛ *DM 2 adults, DM 1 children.* ◷ *Tues.–Wed. and Fri.–Sun. 10–6, Thurs. 10–8.*

TIME OUT   If you're hungry after touring the museum, drop in at the **Böthelstube** on the Alter Markt. Local specialties such as *Magdeburger Lose Wurst* and *Kochklops*—a variety of sausage and dumplings—are served with an excellent beer. *Alter Markt 9,* ☎ *0391/562-0397. No credit cards.* **$**

Head down Breiter Weg (formerly Karl-Marx-Strasse, a name that was one of the first casualties of the fall of East German communism). To your left you'll see the mighty twin towers of Magdeburg's Gothic **Cathedral of Saints Maurice and Catherine** rearing up above the rooftops. Opposite the post office on Breiter Weg turn left into Domplatz, and there is the soaring west front of the cathedral before you. The awesome structure was begun in 1209, making it the oldest Gothic church in Germany; it was completed in 1520. The founder of the Holy Roman Empire, Otto I, lies buried beneath the choir, his tomb overshadowed by graceful columns of Ravenna marble. Study the representations of famous Christian martyrs on the walls of the nave; you'll find them all standing determinedly on the heads of their persecutors (that's Nero under the heel of St. Paul). A more recent memorial is Expressionist artist Ernst Barlach's sculptured group warning of the horrors of war. It was removed by the Nazis in 1933, but it's back with all its original force. *Domplatz,* ☎ *0391/32414.* ⊘ *Daily 10–5. Guided tours: Mon.–Sat. 10 and 2, Sun. 11:15 and 2.*

Just north of Domplatz and on the way back to the city center is Magdeburg's second great attraction, the Romanesque monastery church and cloisters of **Unser Lieben Frauen.** The church, built in the years 1064–1230, now serves as a concert hall and an art gallery. Gothic sculptures share space with modern East German works in sober surroundings that encourage meditation and reflection—there's also a café for more mundane requirements. *Regierungstr. 4–6 ,* ☎ *0391/541– 4722.* ⊘ *Tues.–Sun. 10–6.*

Southwest of Magdeburg is a group of historic old towns easily reached by train or car. From Magdeburg, Route 81 goes 53 kilometers (33 miles) to **Halberstadt,** the gateway to the Harz Mountain area to the south. One of the key commercial and religious centers of the Middle Ages, about 85% of Halberstadt was destroyed in April 1945. Rebuilding has left some remarkable contrasts: Half-timbered 17th-century houses stand alongside stark modern blocks. Dominating the town, the twin-towered **Cathedral** is one of the most noteworthy examples of German Gothic, completed in 1491 after 252 years of construction. Inside, note the tapestries and sculptures, the stained-glass windows, and the numerous ancient burial tombs.

TIME OUT   Just south of Halberstadt, the **Jagdschloss Spiegelberger,** a Baroque hunting lodge dating from 1782, now houses a pleasant country restaurant. In the basement is the "great wine cask," a huge wooden barrel constructed in 1594 and holding 132,760 liters (35,080 gallons) of wine.

Heading south on Route 81, look for the turnoff to the right after about 9 kilometers (5½ miles), marked for Wernigerode, which is another 14 kilometers (9 miles) along. **Wernigerode** is a colorful small city of half-timbered houses from the Middle Ages, watched over by the castle atop the nearby Agnesberg Hill. The castle was last rebuilt in 1862–85, but parts date from the 1670s and even earlier. Today the **Schloss Museum** (Castle Museum) occupies 32 of its rooms. ☎ *03943/23303.* ☛ *DM 7 adults, DM 3 children.* ⊘ *May–Oct, daily 10–6; Nov.–Apr., Tues.–Sun. 10–6.*

The 1899 vintage **Harzquerbahn,** a fascinating narrow-gauge railway line using steam power for the most part, starts from Wernigerode on its three-hour, 60-kilometer (37½-mile) run through the northern Harz Mountain area to Nordhausen. ☎ *03943/5581–0060. Wernigerode-Nordhausen trip cost: DM 16, DM 8 children under 12.*

From Wernigerode, a scenic drive winds south about 10 kilometers (6 miles) to Elbingerode, then west about 15 kilometers (9 miles) to Blankenburg. Just south of the town, a road cuts east 8 kilometers (5 miles) to **Thale**, site of the renowned **Hexentanzplatz** (Witches' Dancing Place). This rock plateau, with an elevation of 454 meters (1,475 feet), can be reached year-round by a four-minute cable-car ride from the Hubertusbrücke in Bodetal. From the top there's a splendid view out over the neighboring countryside.

Fifteen kilometers (9 miles) beyond Thale is **Quedlinburg,** known for its picturesque half-timbered houses and detailed carved wood ornamentation. Wander around the town to enjoy the medieval houses, taking special note of the two-story **Rathaus** (City Hall), completed in 1615, its ornate stone front entry dramatically punctuating the Renaissance facade. From 966 to 1802, the castle atop the **Schlossberg Hill** was the official residence of the Abbess of Quedlinburg Abbey; adjacent is the 12th-century Romanesque St. Servatius abbey church. The castle today houses a museum of local history.

Return to Berlin via Route 6 to Bernburg and then Route 71/E49 north to Magdeburg, where you can pick up the E-30 Autobahn.

Dining

Herrenkrug. This charming restaurant set in English-style gardens on the grounds of Herrenkrug Park specializes in typical German cooking with a nouvelle cuisine accent. Try the delicious liver cooked with apple rather than the Eisbein and sauerkraut. A variety of fruit with ice cream is a good way to end the meal. ✕ *Herrenkrugstr. 194, Magdeburg,* ☎ *0391/850–837. Reservations advised on weekends. AE, DC, MC, V.* $$$

Zum Alten Dessauer. Locals favor this haunt for its reliable German dishes. Here you can find juicy Schnitzel with sauerkraut and *Bratkartoffeln* (roast potatoes); for dessert, order *Rote Grütze* (red summer fruits), cooked and topped with vanilla sauce. ✕ *Breiteweg 250, Magdeburg,* ☎ *0391/543–0150. Reservations advised. MC, V.* $$

Lodging

Maritim Hotel Magdeburg. Opened in the summer of 1995, this hotel has the high standards of service that the Maritim chain is knwon for, and it's close to many of the city's attractions. The rooms are elegantly furnished and equipped with all modern conveniences. ☎ *Otto-von-Guericke-Str. 87, D–39104 Magdeburg,* ☎ *0391/59490,* FAX *0391/594–9990. 504 rooms, 11 suites, all with bath. Restaurant, bar, café, no-smoking rooms, indoor pool, sauna, exercise room, car rental. AE, MC, V.* $$$$

Herrenkrug. This Best Western hotel complex is set in the beautiful Herrenkrug park, along the Elbe River two miles from downtown, and the calm of the surrounding greenery permeates the atmosphere. The rooms, larger than average, have ample sitting areas and good-sized desks; they are modernly furnished with soft carpets and come with a safe, pants press, and hair dryer. Herrenkrug's health center fulfills the relaxation needs a tired tourist may have. ☎ *Herrenkrugstr. 194, D–39114 Magdeburg,* ☎ *0391/85080,* FAX *0391/850–8501. 159 rooms, all with bath. Restaurant, massage, sauna, whirlpool, exercise room. AE, MC, V.* $$$

Hotel International. Magdeburg's leading hotel is typically East German postwar Modern, but it has all the necessary facilities and comforts and is centrally located. Rooms are functional and uninspired in their decoration; if you're looking for space and above-average comfort, reserve a suite apartment (DM 300 or more). ⊞ *Otto-von-Güricke-Strasse 87, Magdeburg, ☎ 0391/59490. 331 rooms with bath, 9 suites. 3 restaurants, bar, café, sauna, nightclub. AE, DC, MC, V. $$$*

Magdeburg and the Elbe River Countryside Essentials

ARRIVING AND DEPARTING

By Bus. Buses leave from the Funkturm bus station in Berlin.

By Car. Magdeburg is just off the E–30 motorway, the old transit road connecting Berlin and Hannover. It's 150 kilometers (90 miles) west of Berlin, a 90-minute drive as long as the motorway is clear. (In summer and on weekends, when the E–30 gets crowded, the two-hour train ride from Berlin might be preferable.) To get to the town center follow the signs for Magdeburg-Stadtmitte.

By Train. Trains leave approximately every two hours from Bahnhof Zoo in Berlin; the trip takes about two hours.

GUIDED TOURS

There are no guided tours of Magdeburg originating in Berlin. However, the **Reisebüro** (tourist office), near the main railway station (Wilhelm-Pieck-Allee 14), offers daily two-hour bus tours of the town, leaving at 11 AM. Cost: DM 4. It also runs bus tours of the region.

Ships of the shipping line **Weisse Flotte** (☎ 0391/548–1354) embark from Magdeburg on day trips and longer cruises on the Elbe.

KD River Cruises of Europe (Frankenwerft 15, 50667 Köln, ☎ 0221/208–8288; KD River Cruises of Europe, 2500 Westchester Ave., Purchase, NY 10577, ☎ 914/696–3600; 323 Geary St., Suite 603, San Francisco, CA 94102, ☎ 415/392–8817) operates five-day luxury cruises between Magdeburg and Bad Schandau (south of Dresden), with ports of call including Wittenberg, Meissen, and Dresden.

VISITOR INFORMATION

General information about Magdeburg can also be obtained at the tourist office (Alter Markt 12, D–39104 Magdeburg, ☎ 0391/541–4794; open weekdays 10–6, Sat. 10–1).

Tour 3: Frankfurt an der Oder

Poland is so near Berlin that a day trip to the border is no problem. But where on the border? Frankfurt an der Oder is the obvious choice. Here you'll have an opportunity to observe firsthand the new European order at work.

Exploring

Ninety percent of the historic center of Frankfurt an der Oder was destroyed in May 1945, not by Allied bombing but in a devastating fire that broke out after Germany's capitulation. The fire was sparked by a confrontation between remaining units of the Nazi "Werwolf" resistance and Polish forces from across the Oder. The flames spread rapidly because the conquered city had no fire brigade. Until then, 80% of the city had survived the war undamaged. Today the strong undercurrent of anti-Polish feeling in Frankfurt an der Oder is palpable, and local police are kept busy smoothing over quarrels between the locals and Poles from across the river.

Poland virtually overlooks the center of the city, which sits in its faded Prussian glory on the banks of the Oder. The oldest building here is also the most imposing: the **City Hall,** on Marktplatz, 100 yards west of the Oder. First mentioned in official records in 1348, the building has a 17th-century Baroque facade that now looks out over the hustle and bustle of central Frankfurt. Behind the City Hall, on the banks of the Oder, you'll find another elegant, finely restored Baroque structure, the world's only museum devoted the great German writer Heinrich von Kleist (1777–1811). Kleist's birthplace in Frankfurt an der Oder was among the buildings consumed by fire in 1945, but the house containing the **Kleist Gedenk-und Forschungsstätte** does date from the year of the dramatist's birth. Kleist lived only 34 years—he shot himself in a suicide pact with his lover in Berlin—but his contribution to German literature was monumental. His works, notably the famous history play *Das Kätchen von Heilbronn* (source of one of Carl Orff's greatest compositions) and the comedy *Der Zerbrochene Krug* (premiered by Goethe in Weimar in 1808), avoid all attempts at categorization. The original manuscripts of both plays are in the museum, which traces Kleist's life and work with exemplary clarity and care. *Faberstr. 7,* ☎ *0335/23185.* ☛ *DM 3.50 adults, DM 1.50 children.* ☾ *Tues.–Fri. 10–noon and 2–4, weekends 2–5.*

Dining and Lodging

Graham's. This pension-hotel is run by a friendly staff and has a direct streetcar connection to much of the city. All the rooms will have been completely renovated, with modern bathrooms, by late fall 1995. The restaurant gives guests a choice of a rustic inn feel or a colorful café atmosphere. Both areas have the same menu, a variety of traditional German dishes and six different kinds of beer on tap. ☎ *August-Bebel-Str. 11, D–15234 Frankfurt/Oder,* ☎ *0335/433–5429,* FAX *0335/433–3991. 40 rooms, all with showers. Restaurant. AE, MC, V. $$*

Frankfurt an der Oder Essentials

ARRIVING AND DEPARTING

By Bus. There's infrequent bus service from east Berlin's Hauptbahnhof.

By Car. Frankfurt an der Oder is 90 kilometers (55 miles) east of Berlin, about an hour's drive. Head east on east Berlin's Landsberger Allee, joining the E–55 ring-Autobahn and heading south until the Frankfurt/Oder turnoff. Exit at Frankfurt-Stadtmitte.

By Train. Trains depart every two hours from east Berlin's Hauptbahnhof.

VISITOR INFORMATION

Frankfurt Tourist Information, Karl-Marx-Str. 8a, D–15230 Frankfurt/Oder, ☎ 0335/325–216.

BERLIN ESSENTIALS

More than five years after the official unification of the two Germanys, the nuts-and-bolts work of joining up the two city halves is not complete, and uncertainties abound. We have given addresses, telephone numbers, and other logistical details based on the best available information, but please understand that everything from telephone numbers to street names are still changing at a furious pace. Large state museums are being transformed as they seek to integrate their collections from east and west more fully. Inquire at the tourist information for the most up-to-date information.

Arriving and Departing

By Bus

Buses are slightly cheaper than trains; Berlin is linked by bus to 170 European cities. The main station is at the corner of Masurenallee 4–6 and Messedam. Reserve through DER (state), commercial travel agencies, or the station itself. For information, call 030/301–8028 between 9 and 5:30.

By Car

The "transit corridor" roads linking former West Germany with west Berlin are still there, but the strict restrictions that once confined foreign motorists driving through East Germany have vanished, and today you can travel through the country at will. Expressways link Berlin with the eastern German cities of Magdeburg, Leipzig, Rostock, Dresden, and Frankfurt-an-der-Oder. At press time, speed restrictions of 130 kilometers per hour (80 miles per hour) still applied, and you must carry your driver's license, car registration, and insurance documents with you. Seat belts must be worn at all times, even in the backseat.

By Plane

Airlines flying to west Berlin's **Tegel Airport** (☎ 030/410–2306) from major U.S. and European cities include United, Delta, Air France, British Airways, Lufthansa, and some charter companies. Because of increased air traffic following unification, the former military airfield at **Tempelhof** (☎ 030/691–510) is also used. East Berlin's **Schönefeld Airport** (☎ 030/60910) is about 24 kilometers (15 miles) outside the downtown area. It is used principally by Russian and Eastern European airlines, although it's been taking more and more charter traffic.

BETWEEN THE AIRPORT AND DOWNTOWN

Tegel Airport is only 6 kilometers (4 miles) from the downtown area. The No. 109 airport bus runs at 10-minute intervals between Tegel and downtown via Kurfürstendamm (downtown west Berlin), Bahnhof Zoologischer Garten, and Budapesterstrasse. The total trip takes 30 minutes; the fare is DM 3.70. Expect to pay about DM 25 for the same trip by taxi. If you rent a car at the airport, take the Stadtautobahn (there are signs) into Berlin. The Halensee exit leads to Kurfürstendamm. Tempelhof is linked directly to the city center by the U-6 subway line. From Schönefeld, a shuttle bus leaves every 10–15 minutes for the nearby S-bahn station; S-bahn trains leave every 20 minutes for the Friedrichstrasse station, downtown east Berlin, and for the Zoologischer Garten station, downtown west Berlin. Bus 171 also leaves every 10 or 15 minutes for the west Berlin Rudow subway station. A taxi ride from the airport takes about 40 minutes and will cost around DM 55. By car, follow the signs for "Stadtzentrum Berlin."

By Train

There are six major rail routes to Berlin from the western part of the country (from Hamburg, Hannover, Köln, Frankfurt, Munich, and Nürnberg), and the rail network in the east has expanded considerably, making all of eastern German more accessible. Service between Berlin and Eastern Europe has also improved significantly, resulting in shorter traveling times. Ask about reduced fares within Germany; three people or more can often travel at discounted rates. Some trains now stop at and depart from more than one of Berlin's four main train stations, but generally west- and north- originated trains arrive at Friedrichstrasse and Zoologischer Garten, and east- and south-originated trains at Hauptbahnhof and Lichtenberg. For details on rates and information, call **Deutsche Bahn Information** (☎ 030/19419) .

Getting Around

By Bike

Bicycling is popular in Berlin. While it's not recommended in the downtown area, it's ideal in outlying areas. Bike paths are generally marked by red bricks on the walkways; many stores that rent or sell bikes carry the Berlin biker's atlas to help you find the paths. Call **Fahrrad Mietzner** (Hagelbergstr. 53, ☎ 030/785−9488) for information and rental locations, or rent your bikes at most of the major hotels for approximately DM 30 for 24 hours. For bike rental in the Grunewald Forest, go to the S-bahn station Grunewald, ☎ 030/811−5829.

By Car

CAR RENTAL

Avis (Tegel Airport, ☎ 030/4101−3148; Budapesterstr. 43, Am Europa-Center, ☎ 030/261−1881; Karl-Marx-Allee 264, ☎ 030/685−2093)

Europcar (Tegel Airport, ☎ 030/4101−3354; Kurfurstenstr. 101, ☎ 030/213−1031).

Hertz (Tegel Airport, ☎ 030/4101−3315; Budapesterstr. 39, ☎ 030/261−1053).

By Public Transportation

Berlin is too large to be explored on foot. To compensate, the city has one of the most efficient public transportation systems in Europe, a smoothly integrated network of subway (U-bahn) and suburban (S-bahn) train lines, buses, trams (in east Berlin only), and even a ferry across the Wannsee Lake, making every part of the city easily accessible. Extensive all-night bus and tram service operates seven nights a weeks (indicated by the letter N next to route numbers), and the subway lines U-9 and U-12 run all night on weekends. In summer, excurion buses link the downtown with popular recreational areas.

A DM 3.70 ticket (DM 2.50 for children) covers the entire system for two hours and allows you to make an unlimited number of changes between trains, buses, and trams. Four such fares, discounted when sold together, are a good value (DM 12.50 adults, DM 8.50 children). If you are just making a short trip, buy a **Kurzstreckentarif.** It allows you to ride six bus stops or three U-bahn or S-bahn stops for DM 2.50 (DM 2.00 for children). Packs of four cost DM 8.50 for adults and DM 6.50 for children. The best deal for visitors who plan to travel around the city extensively is the **Day Card** for DM 15 (no children's discount), valid for 30 hours and good for all trains and buses. The **Group Day Card**, DM 20, offers the same benefits for two adults and up to three children. A seven-day **Tourist Pass** costs DM 40 and allows unlimited travel on all city buses and trains. Another option is the **BerlinWelcomeCard,** which costs DM 29 and entitles one adult and up to three children to three days of unlimited travel as well as free admission or reductions of up to 50% for sightseeing trips, museums, theaters, and other events and attractions. If you're caught without a ticket the fine is DM 60.

Berlin Public Transit System

U1 U-Bahn
S1 S-Bahn

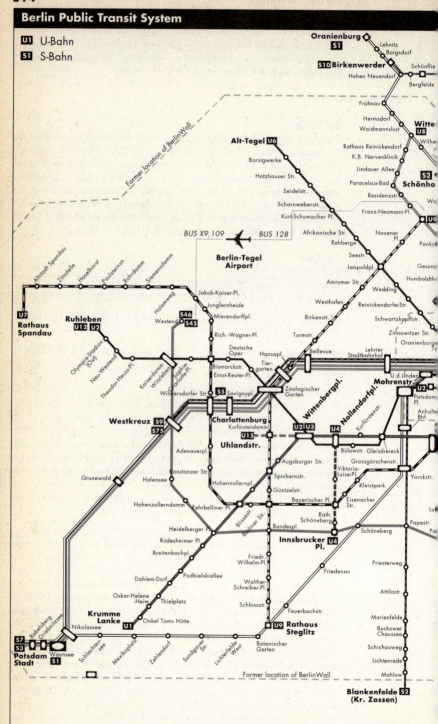

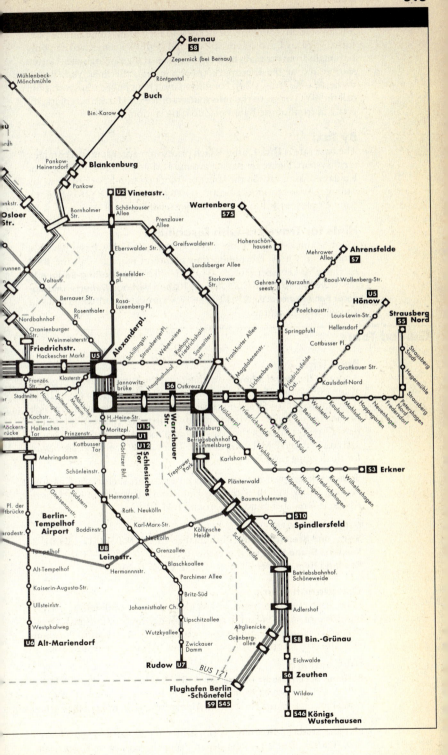

Mühlenbeck-Mönchmühle

Bernau
S8

Zepernick (bei Bernau)

Röntgental

Buch

Bln.-Karow

Pankow-Heinersdorf

Blankenburg

Pankow

Osloer Str.

Bornholmer Str.

U2 **Vinetastr.**

Schönhauser Allee

Prenzlauer Allee

Wartenberg
S75

Eberswalder Str.

Greifswalderstr.

Hohenschön-hausen

Mehrower Allee

Ahrensfelde
S7

Senefelder-pl.

Landsberger Allee

Gehren-seestr.

Marzahn

Raoul-Wallenberg-Str.

Voltastr.

Bernauer Str.

Storkower Str.

Poelchaustr.

Hönow
U5

Rosenthaler Pl.

Rosa-Luxemburg-Pl.

Louis-Lewin-Str.

Strausberg Nord
S5

Nordbahnhof

Oranienburger Str.

Hellersdorf

Springpfuhl

Cottbusser Pl

Strausberg Stadt

Friedrichstr.

Hackescher Markt

U5 **Alexanderpl.**

Schillingstr.

Strausbergerpl.

Weberwiese

Rathaus Friedrichshain

Samariter-str.

Frankfurter Allee

Grottkauer Str.

Hegermühle

Franzos. Str.

Klosterstr.

Jannowitz-brücke

Hauptbahnhof

S6 Ostkreuz

Lichtenberg

Friedrichsfelde Ost

Kaulsdorf-Nord

Strausberg

Petershagen

Fredersdorf

Stadtmitte

Hausvogteipl.

Spittelmarkt

Märkisches Museum

H.-Heine-Str.

Nöldnerpl.

Friedrichsfelde

Wuhletal

Kaulsdorf

Mahlsdorf

Hoppegarten

Neuenhagen

Birkenstein

Kochstr.

Möckern-brücke

Hallesches Tor

Prinzenstr.

Moritzpl.

U15
U1 **Schlesisches**
U12 **Tor**

Rummelsburg

Betriebsbahnhof Rummelsburg

Tierpark

Biesdorf

Elsterwerdaer Pl.

Biesdorf-Süd

Erkner

Mehringdamm

Schönleinstr.

Görlitzer Bhf.

Karlshorst

Wuhlheide

Köpenick

Friedrichshagen

Rahnsdorf

Wilhelmshagen

S3 **Erkner**

Gneisenaustr.

Südstern

Hermannpl.

Rath. Neukölln

Treptower Park

Plänterwald

Hirschgarten

Berlin-Tempelhof Airport

Boddinstr.

Karl-Marx-Str.

Köllnische Heide

Baumschulenweg

Schöneweide

Oberspree

Spindlersfeld
S10

Tempelhof

U8

Neukölln

Alt-Tempelhof

Leinestr.

Hermannstr.

Grenzallee

Blaschkoallee

Betriebsbahnhof Schöneweide

Kaiserin-Augusta-Str.

Parchimer Allee

Ullsteinstr.

Britz-Süd

Adlershof

Westphalweg

Johannisthaler Ch.

Lipschitzallee

Altglienicke

U6 **Alt-Mariendorf**

Wutzkyallee

Zwickauer Damm

Grünbergallee

S8 **Bln.-Grünau**

Eichwalde

Rudow U7

BUS 171

S6 **Zeuthen**

Flughafen Berlin -Schönefeld
S9 S45

Wildau

S46 **Königs Wusterhausen**

All regular tickets are available from vending machines at U-bahn and S-bahn stations. Punch your ticket into the red machine on the platform. The Day Cards, Tourist Pass, and BerlinWelcomeCard can only be bought from the main **BVG** ticket offices at the Zoologischer Garten station and at the Kleistpark U-bahn station (Berliner Verkehrsbetriebe, ☎ 030/752–7020). For information bout public transportation, call the BVG or go to the information office on Hardenbergplatz, directly in front of the Bahnhof Zoo train station.

By Taxi

The base rate is DM 4, after which prices vary according to a complex tariff system. Figure on paying around DM 15 for a ride the length of Ku'damm. Hail cabs in the street or from taxi stands, or order one by calling 030/9644, 030/210–202, 030/691–001, or 030/261–026. U-bahn employees will call a taxi for passengers after 8 PM

Hints for Travelers with Disabilities

Many S- and U-bahn stations have elevators, and a few buses have hydrolic lifts. Check the public transportation maps or call the **BVG** (Berliner Verkehrsbetriebe, ☎ 030/752–7020). **Servic-Ring-Berlin e.V.** (☎ 030/859–4010 or 030/9389–2410) and **Verband Geburts- und anderer Behinderter e.V.** (☎ 030/341–1797) provide information and van and wheelchair rentals.

Guided Tours

Boat Trips

A tour of the **Havel lakes** is the thing to do in summer. Trips begin at Wannsee (S-bahn: Wannsee) and at the Greenwich Promenade in Tegel (U-bahn: Tegel). You'll sail on either the whale-shaped vessel *Moby Dick* or the *Havel Queen,* a Mississippi-style boat, and cruise 27½ kilometers (17 miles) through the lakes and past forests. Tours last 4½ hours and cost between DM 15 and DM 20. There are 20 operators. *See below* for the leading ones.

Tours of downtown Berlin's **canals** take in sights such as the Charlottenburg Palace and the Congress Hall. Tours depart from Kottbusser Bridge in Kreuzberg and cost around DM 10.

TOUR OPERATORS
Stern- und Kreisschiffahrt (Pushkinallee 16-17, ☎ 030/617–3900).
Reederei Bruno Winkler (Levetzowstr. 12a, ☎ 030/391–7010).
Reederei Heinz Riedel (Planufer 78, ☎ 030/693–4646).

Orientation Tours

Four companies offer more or less identical tours (in English), covering all major sights in Berlin, as well as all-day tours to Potsdam, Dresden, and Meissen. The Berlin tours cost DM 25–45, those to Potsdam DM 50–70, and to Dresden and Meissen approximately DM 100.

TOUR OPERATORS
Berliner Bären Stadtrundfahrten (BBS, Rankestr. 35, ☎ 030/214–8790). Groups depart from the corner of Rankestrasse and Kurfürstendamm, and, in east Berlin, from Alexanderplatz, in front of the Forum Hotel.
Berolina Stadtrundfahrten (Kurfürstendamm 22, corner Meinekestr., ☎ 030/882–2091). Groups depart from the corner of Kurfürsten-

damm and Meinekestrasse, and, in east Berlin, from Karl-Liebknecht-Str., in front of the Radisson Plaza Hotel.

Bus Verkehr Berlin (BVB, Kurfürstendamm 225, ☎ 030/885–9880). Tours leave from Kurfürstendamm 225.

Severin & Kühn (Kurfürstendamm 216, ☎ 030/883–1015). Groups leave from clearly marked stops along the Kurfürstendamm and, in east Berlin, at the corner of Unter den Linden and Universitätstrasse.

Special-Interest Tours

Sightseeing tours with a cultural/historical bias are offered weekends at a cost of approximately DM 15 by **art:berlin** (Thomasiustr. 12, ☎ 030/399–4713). Tours include "Jewish History" and "Prenzlauerberg Neighborhoods" and are in German, though tour guides will provide English translation if asked. All **Berlin Walks** (Eislebener Str. 1, ☎ 030/211–6633) tours are in English. The introductory "Discover Berlin" tour takes in the major downtown sites in 2 ½ to 3 hours (10:30 daily, also at 2:30 June–Sept.). Other themed tours (Third Reich sites, Jewish life, the Wall) are shorter and run April–October. Tours depart from outside the McDonald's opposite the main entrance to the Zoologischer Garten train station and cost DM 12.50, DM 10 for people under 27, plus S-bahn transportation.

Important Addresses and Numbers

Consulates

United States (Clayallee 170, ☎ 030/819–7454); **Canada** (International Trade Center, Friedrichstr. 95, ☎ 030/261–1161). **Great Britain** (Unter den Linden 32-34, ☎ 030/201–8401), **Ireland** (Ernst–Reuter–Pl. 10, tel: 030/3480–0822).

Emergencies

Police (☎ 030/110). **Ambulance and emergency medical attention** (☎ 030/310–031). **Dentist** (☎ 030/01141). **Pharmacies** in Berlin offer late-night service on a rotation basis. Every pharmacy displays a notice indicating the location of the nearest shop with evening hours. For **emergency pharmaceutical assistance,** call 030/01141.

English Bookstores

Marga Schoeller (Knesebeckstr. 33, ☎ 030/881–1112). **Buchhandlung Kiepert** (Hardenbergstr. 4–5, ☎ 030/311–0090).

Travel Agencies

American Express Reisebüro (Uhlandstr. 173, ☎ 030/882–7575, and Friedrichstr. 172, ☎ 030/238–4102). **American Lloyd** (Kurfürstendamm 209, ☎ 030/20740).

Visitor Information

The **Verkehrsamt Berlin** (main tourist office) is in the heart of the city in the Europa-Center (☎ 030/262–6031). If you want materials on the city before your trip, write **Verkehrsamt Berlin Europa-Center** (Martin-Luther-Strasse 105, 10825 Berlin). For information on the spot, the office is open Monday–Saturday 8 AM–10:30 PM, Sunday 9–9. There are also offices at **Tegel Airport** (☎ 030/4101–3145; open daily 8 AM–11 PM) and at the train stations **Zoologischer Garten** (☎ 030/313–9063; open Mon.–Sat. 8 AM–11 PM), and **Hauptbahnhof** (☎ 030/279–5209; open daily 8–8). Berlin has an information center geared toward women, which helps with accommodations and gives information on upcoming events. Contact **Fraueninfothek Berlin** (Dircksenstr. 47, ☎ 030/282–3980; open Tuesday–Saturday 9–9, Sunday and holidays 9–3).

For information in English on all aspects of the city, pick up a copy of *Berlin Turns On,* free from any tourist office.

16 Saxony and Thuringia

This area is worth visiting for its traditional tourist sites and because it is in transition—it was bound more closely with the Soviet Union than West Germany for 45 years. Dresden's Zwinger palace complex is a cultural wonder; Leipzig, the largest eastern German city after Berlin, is an important commercial center (avoid the trade fair dates); and Weimar has many traces from its days as a cultural center in the 19th century.

MENTION OF THE FORMER GERMAN DEMOCRATIC REPUBLIC generally conjures up images of dour landscapes and grim industrial cities, even since the collapse of the communist government. It will take years before the polluted, dying forests in the south can be rejuvenated and the ancient soot-stained factories replaced. The deteriorating public housing projects of the '50s and '60s cannot be razed overnight any more than the acrid smell of brown coal smoke can be eliminated that quickly. But the small towns of eastern Germany—in the federal states of Saxony and Thuringia—will tell much more about an older Germany than the frenetic lifestyles of Frankfurt, Hamburg, Stuttgart, or Köln. The communist influence here—hard-line as it was—never penetrated as deeply as did the American impact on West Germany. East Germany clung to its German heritage, proudly preserving connections with such national heroes as Luther, Goethe, Schiller, Bach, Händel, Hungarian-born Liszt, and Wagner. And although bombing raids in World War II devastated most of its cities, the East Germans, over the years, carried out an extensive program of restoring and rebuilding their historic neighborhoods. Meissen porcelain, Frederick the Great's palace at Potsdam, the astounding collections of the Pergamon and Bode museums in Berlin, and those in the Zwinger in Dresden are now part of the total national heritage.

Traditional tourist sights aside, eastern Germany is also worth visiting precisely because it *is* in transition. In the wake of ebullient newspaper headlines and photographs of wild parties amid the rubble of the Berlin Wall, it's all too easy to simplify what's going on in the former GDR as a quest for Western-style democracy. The initiative for unification came as much from the west as it did from the east, and the former East Germans have not been altogether happy with the consequences. Though they enjoyed the highest standard of living of all the Eastern Bloc countries, a number of erstwhile East Germans still see their western compatriots as the "haves" and themselves as the "have-nots."

These people, bound politically and economically to the Soviet Union for 45 years, are still not entirely comfortable with their newly acquired freedoms and responsibilities. For most of those years, despite being communism's "Western front," the GDR was isolated from Western ideas, and many now resent having the less savory elements of Western society imposed on what was an orderly, if unexciting, way of life. Time has not stood still east of the former border, but it has taken much less of a toll than it has in the west.

The main differences for travelers are the absence of a border, not having to change currencies, and—regrettably—higher prices. But the most important change is that visitors now have complete freedom to go wherever they want, choose their own hotels, and wander off the former "transit corridors" and explore eastern Germany at will.

EXPLORING

Tour 1: Dessau to Leipzig

Numbers in the margin correspond to points of interest on the Eastern Germany map.

The southern districts of eastern Germany—Thuringia and Saxony—represent the Germany of medieval times, and as you travel these regions you'll see ample evidence of the grandeur of the past, although much has been rebuilt to replace war damages. Alas, you'll also see the ongoing (and just as devastating) damage of a modern industrial society: landscape scarred by coal pits around Leipzig, chemical pollution in the air around Bitterfeld and Wolfen north of Leipzig, and to the southeast thousands of acres of woodland destroyed by that pollution. South of Dresden, as the Elbe River leaves its broad valley, it passes through a region of dramatic narrow channels confined by stone mountains, almost like a miniature Grand Canyon. To the south, the *Erzgebirge,* or "ore mountains," form a natural boundary with Czechoslovakia.

1 Leaving Berlin, go south on the E–51, marked for Leipzig. About 120 kilometers (75 miles) from Berlin, you'll pass **Dessau,** a name known to every student of modern architecture. Here in 1925–26 the architect Walter Gropius set up his Bauhaus school of design, probably the most widespread influence on 20th-century architecture and decorative arts. Gropius's concept was to simplify design to allow mechanized construction; 316 villas in the Törten section of the city were built in the '20s using his ideas and methods. Stop to view the refurbished Bauhaus building—this was the fountainhead of ideas that have determined the appearance of such cities as New York, Chicago, and San Francisco. Still used as an architecture school, the building can be visited weekdays 10–5, and exhibits are also open weekends 10–12:30 and 2–5.

For a contrast to the no-nonsense Bauhaus architecture, look at Dessau's older buildings, including St. George's Church, built in 1712 in Dutch Baroque style, or the 18th-century late-Baroque **Schloss Mosigkau,** 9 kilometers (5½ miles) southwest of Dessau, now a museum.

Try to visit this exquisite mid-18th-century country palace in late afternoon or early evening, when the setting sun lends a warm glow to the biscuit-color facades of the three wings. Prince Leopold of Anhalt-Dessau commissioned the palace to be built for his favorite daughter, Anna Wilhelmine. She lived there alone, for she never married, and when she died she left the property to an order of nuns. They immediately tore up the formal grounds to make an English-style park, and after a post–World War II attempt to restore the original Baroque appearance, money and enthusiasm ran out. The palace itself, however, was always well maintained, and the present custodians are so concerned about its preservation that you'll be asked to put on felt slippers for your tour of its rooms. Only about one-quarter of the rooms can be visited, but they include one of Germany's very few Baroque picture galleries. Its stucco ceiling is a marvel of Rococo decoration, a swirling composition of pastel-color motifs. ☎ *0340/831–139.* ☛ *Palace: DM 5 adults, DM 2.50 children; to the palace gardens DM 1 (admission charge in both cases includes a guided tour).* ☉ *May–Sept., Tues.–Sun. 10–6; Nov.–Mar., Tues.–Fri., 10–4, weekends 11–4; Apr. and Oct. Tues.–Sun. 10–5.*

2 The E–51 Autobahn splits in two 40 kilometers (25 miles) south of Dessau: left to Leipzig, right to **Halle.** The temptation is to turn left and ignore Halle, particularly if you're in a hurry. The 1,000-year-old city, built on the salt trade, is one of eastern Germany's worst examples of communist urban planning, with a hastily built residential area whose name, Halle-Neustadt, has been shortened cynically by the locals to "Hanoi." But if you have the time, Halle is worth a visit, if only

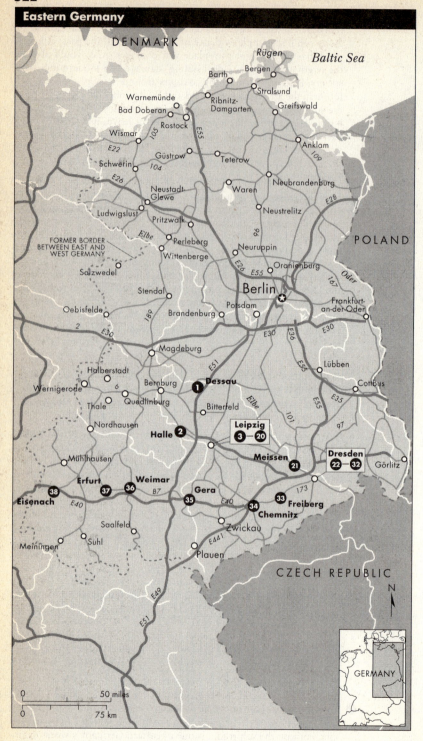

DENMARK

Rügen

Baltic Sea

Barth

Bergen

Warnemünde

Stralsund

Ribnitz-Damgarten

Bad Doberan

Greifswald

Rostock

Wismar

Anklam

Schwerin

Güstrow

Teterow

E22

Neubrandenburg

104

Waren

Neustadt-Glewe

Neustrelitz

Ludwigslust

Pritzwalk

Elbe

Perleberg

FORMER BORDER
BETWEEN EAST AND
WEST GERMANY

Wittenberge

Neuruppin

Salzwedel

Oranienburg

Berlin ✪

Oder

Stendal

POLAND

Oebisfelde

Brandenburg

Potsdam

Frankfurt-an-der-Oder

Magdeburg

Halberstadt

Lübben

Wernigerode

Bernburg

① **Dessau**

Cottbus

Thale

Quedlinburg

Bitterfeld

Elbe

Nordhausen

Halle ②

Leipzig

③—⑳

Mühlhausen

Meissen

Dresden

Erfurt

㊲

Weimar
㊱

⑳

㉒—㉜

Görlitz

Eisenach

㊳

Gera

E40

㉟

㉝ **Freiberg**

㉞ **Chemnitz**

Saalfeld

Zwickau

Meiningen

Suhl

Plauen

CZECH REPUBLIC

N

GERMANY

0   50 miles

0   75 km

to view its fine central marketplace, the **Markt,** its northern side bristling with five distinctive, sharp-steepled towers. Four of them (two connected by a catwalk bridge) belong to the late-Gothic **Marienkirche** (St. Mary's Church), completed in 1529, where Martin Luther preached and George Friedrich Händel learned to play the organ. Händel was born in Halle in 1685, and you'll find several memorials to the great composer in and around the city. The house where he was born, the **Händelhaus,** is a few steps away from the Markt. It's now a Händel museum; in the entrance hall is a display of glass harmoniums, curious musical instruments perfected by Benjamin Franklin when he was ambassador to England in the 1760s. *Grosse Nikolaistrasse 5–6,* ☎ *0345/500-900.* ☛ *DM 2 adults, DM 1 children.* ☼ *Tues., Wed., and Fri.–Sun. 9:30–5:30, Thurs. 9:30–7.*

The fifth tower on the Markt is the celebrated Roter Turm (Red Tower), built between 1418 and 1506 as an expression of the city's power and wealth; it houses a bell carillon and the local tourist office. The tower looks a bit incongruous against the backdrop of modern Halle, like an elaborate sand castle stranded by the tide. Between the Roter Turm and Marienkirche is the **Marktschlösschen,** a late-Renaissance structure that houses an interesting collection of historical musical instruments, some of which could have been played by Händel and his contemporaries. *Musikinstrumentensammlung des Händel-Hauses, Marktschlösschen, Markt 13,* ☎ *0345/202-5977.* ☛ *DM 1 adults, 50 pf children.* ☼ *Wed.–Sun. 1.30–5.30.*

On the northwest edge of the old town is a much more traditional expression of Halle's early might (which vanished with the Thirty Years' War), the **Moritzburg,** a castle built in the late 15th century by the archbishop of Magdeburg after he had claimed the city for his archdiocese. The castle is a typical late-Gothic fortress, with a sturdy round tower at each of its four corners and a dry moat. There's a cloisterlike peace in the central courtyard today, quite a contrast to the years when one army of occupation followed another with bloody regularity. In prewar years, the castle contained a leading gallery of German Expressionist paintings, which were ripped from the walls by the Nazis and condemned as "degenerate." Some of the works so disdained by the Nazis are back in place, together with some outstanding late-19th- and early 20th-century art. You'll find Rodin's famous sculpture *The Kiss* here. *Staatliche Galerie Moritzburg, Friedemann-Bach-Pl. 5,* ☎ *0345/37031.* ☛ *DM 3 adults, DM 1.50 children.* ☼ *Tues. 11–8:30, Wed.–Fri. 10–5:30, weekends 10–6.*

Some 200 yards southeast of the Moritzburg is Halle's cathedral, the **Dom,** an early Gothic church whose nave and side aisles are of equal height. The nearby former Episcopal residence, the 16th-century **Neue Residenz,** now houses a world-famous collection of fossils dug from brown coal deposits in the Geiseltal Valley near Halle. On the other side of the Saale River (cross the Schiefer bridge to get there) is another interesting museum, the **Halloren- und Salinemuseum,** which traces the history of the salt trade on which early Halle built its prosperity. The full-scale replica of a salt mine gives a depressing picture of how the miners toiled underground. *Mansfelderstr. 52,* ☎ *0345/202–5034.* ☛ *DM 1.50 adults, DM 1 children.* ☼ *Tues.–Sun. 10–5.*

❸ From just outside Halle, take the Autobahn 20 kilometers (12½ miles) to **Leipzig.** With a population of about 560,000, this is the second-largest city in eastern Germany (Berlin is the largest) and has long been a center of printing and bookselling. Astride major traderoutes, it was an important market town in the Middle Ages, and it continues to be a trading center to this day, thanks to the trade fairs that twice a year (March and September) bring together buyers from east and west.

Those familiar with music and German literature will associate Leipzig with the great composer Johann Sebastian Bach (1685–1750), who was organist and choir director at the Thomaskirche (St. Thomas's Church); with the 19th-century composer Richard Wagner, who was born here in 1813; and with German Romantic poets Goethe and Schiller, both of whom lived and worked in the area.

In 1813, the Battle of the Nations was fought on the city's outskirts, in which Prussian, Austrian, Russian, and Swedish forces stood ground against Napoléon's troops. This battle (*Völkerschlacht*) was instrumental in leading to the French general's defeat two years later at Waterloo, and thus helped to decide the national boundaries on the map of Europe for the remainder of the century.

Following the devastation of World War II, little is left of old Leipzig. Considerable restoration has been undertaken in the old city, however, and the impression is certainly that of a city with touches of Renaissance character and Jugendstil flair, although some of the newer buildings (notably the university's skyscraper tower) distort the perspective and proportions of the old city. Guided bus tours of Leipzig run daily at 10 and 1:30 (from March to mid-October, there's also a tour at 4); tours leave from the information center downtown at Sachsenplatz 1 (☎ 0341/71040).

Numbers in the margin correspond to points of interest on the Leipzig map.

4 Railroad buffs may want to start their tour of Leipzig at the **Hauptbahnhof,** the main train station (where there's also a tourist information office, opposite platform 3, open weekdays 9–5). With its 26 platforms, the station is the largest in Europe. In 1991 it was expanded to accommodate the anticipated increase in traffic resulting from reunification. But its fin-de-siècle grandness remains, particularly the staircases that lead majestically up to the platforms. As you climb them, take a look at the great arched ceilings high above you; they're unique among German railway stations.

From the station, cross the broad expanse of the Platz der Republik and you're immediately swallowed up by the jumble of streets that make up old Leipzig. To your right is a characterless square, Sachsenplatz, where you'll find Leipzig's main tourist office, Leipzig Information (Sachsenpl. 1, open weekdays 9–7, weekends 9:30–2). Continue south one block, along Katharinenstrasse, passing the "Fregehaus," No. 11, with its fine oriel and steep roof. In two minutes you'll enter Leipzig's showpiece plaza, the city's old market square, the **Markt,** only slightly smaller than St. Mark's Square in Venice. One side is occupied com-

5 pletely by the recently restored Renaissance city hall, the **Altes Rathaus,** which now houses the **Stadtgeschichtliches Museum,** where Leipzig's past is well documented. *Markt 1,* ☎ *0341/70921.* ☛ *DM 3 adults, DM 1.50 children.* ☉ *Tues.–Fri. 10–6, weekends 10–4.*

Starting from all sides of the Markt you'll find small streets that attest to Leipzig's rich trading past, and tucked in among them glass-roof arcades of surprising beauty and elegance. Invent a headache and step into the Apotheke at Hainstrasse 9, into surroundings that haven't changed for 100 years or more, redolent of powders and perfumes, home cures, and foreign spices. It's spectacularly Jugendstil, with finely etched and stained glass and rich mahogany. Or head to the anti-

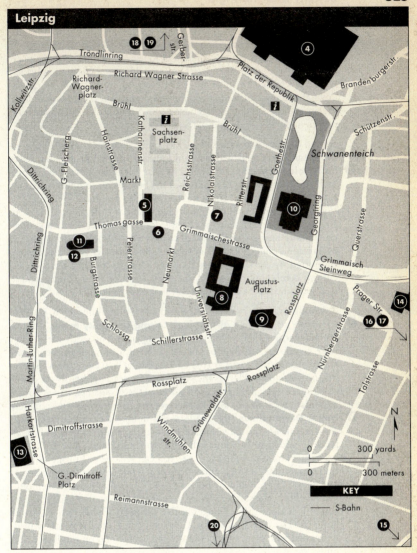

Leipzig

Altes Rathaus, **5**

Bosehaus, **12**

Botanischer Garten, **15**

Exhibition Pavilion, **16**

Gohliser Schlösschen, **18**

Grassimuseum, **14**

Hauptbahnhof, **4**

Leipzig University tower, **8**

Mädlerpassage, **6**

Museum der Bildenden Künste, **13**

Neues Gewandhaus, **9**

Nikolaikirche, **7**

Opera House, **10**

Schiller's House, **19**

Schloss Dölitz, **20**

Thomaskirche, **11**

Völkerschlachtdenkmal, **17**

6 quarian bookshops of the nearby Neumarkt Passage. Around the corner, on Grimmaischestrasse, is Leipzig's finest arcade, the **Mädlerpassage,** where the ghost of Goethe's Faust lurks in every marble corner. Here you'll find the famous Auerbachs Keller restaurant, at No. 2, where Goethe set a scene in *Faust* (*see* Dining and Lodging, *below*). A bronze group of characters from the play, sculpted in 1913, beckons you down the stone staircase to the cellar restaurant. A few yards away down the arcade is a delightful Jugendstil coffee shop called Mephisto, decorated in devilish reds and blacks.

★ **7** Behind Grimmaischestrasse is a church that stands as a symbol of German reunification. It was here, before the undistinguished facade of the **Nikolaikirche,** that thousands of East Germans demanding reform gathered every Monday in the months before the communist regime finally collapsed under the weight of popular pressure. "Wir sind das Volk" ("We are the people") was their chant as they defied official attempts to silence their demands for freedom. In the interior of the church, much more impressive than the exterior would lead you to believe, is a soaring Gothic choir and nave with an unusually patterned ceiling supported by classical pillars that end in palm-tree-like flourishes, a curious combination of styles that meld successfully. Luther is said to have preached from the ornate 16th-century pulpit.

8 Towering over the Nikolaikirche and every other building in the center of the city is the 470-foot-high **Leipzig University tower,** dubbed the "Jagged Tooth" by some of the young wags who study there. They were largely responsible for changing the official name of the university, replacing the postwar title of Karl Marx University with its original one. Augustus Platz is the vast square spread out below the tower like a space-age campus. In the shadow of the skyscraper, which houses administrative offices and lecture rooms, is the glass-and-concrete **9** **Neues Gewandhaus,** the modernistic home of the eponymous orchestra, one of Germany's greatest. (Its popular director, Kurt Masur, recently added to his duties the directorship of the New York Philharmonic Orchestra.) In the foyer you can see one of Europe's largest ceiling paintings, a staggering allegorical work devoted to the muse of music by Sighard Gilles, who employed 716 square meters to monumental effect. The statue of Beethoven that stands in the foyer won first prize for sculptor Max Klinger at the World Art Exhibition in Vienna in 1912. The acoustics of the Gewandhaus, by the way, are world-renowned, enhancing the resonance of every tone by a full two seconds.

10 Opposite the Gewandhaus, on the north side of the Augustus-Platz, is the modern, boxy **Opera House,** the first postwar theater to be built in communist East Germany.

TIME OUT You'll find several cafés lining Grimmaischestrasse, leading out of the square, but why not buy an ice cream from one of the ubiquitous stands there. The eastern Germans are in love with *Eis* and consume it year-round. The Italian-style ice cream is quite authentic.

★ **11** Continue west on Grimmaischestrasse to Thomasgasse and the **Thomaskirche,** the Gothic church where Bach was choirmaster for 27 years and where Martin Luther preached on Whit Sunday, 1539, signaling the arrival of Protestantism in Leipzig. Originally the center of a 13th-century monastery that was rebuilt during the 15th century, the tall church now stands by itself, but the names of adjacent streets recall the cloisters that once surrounded it. Bach wrote most of his cantatas for the church's famous boys' choir, the Thomasknabenchor, which was founded during the 13th century; the church continues as the choir's home as well as a center of Bach tradition. In the Middle Ages, the choir was assembled to sing at every public function—from the installation of bishops to the execution of criminals. Its ranks thinned rapidly when the boys were engaged to sing while plague victims were carted to graves outside the city walls.

Bach's 12 children and the infant Richard Wagner were baptized in the church's early 17th-century font; Karl Marx and Friedrich Engels also stood before this same font, godfathers to Karl Liebknecht, who grew up to be a revolutionary, too!

The great music Bach wrote during his Leipzig years commanded little attention in his lifetime, and when he died he was given a simple grave, without a headstone, in the city's Johannisfriedhof cemetery. It wasn't until 1894 that an effort was made to find where the great composer lay buried, and after a thorough, macabre search his coffin was removed to the cemetery church, the Johanniskirche. The church was destroyed by Allied bombs in December 1943, and Bach found his final resting place in the church he would have selected: the Thomaskirche. It's now a place of pilgrimage for music lovers the world over, and his gravestone below the high altar is never without a floral tribute. Fresh flowers also constantly decorate the statue of Bach that stands before the church. *Thomaskirchhof.* ☛ *Free.* ☉ *Daily 9–6.*

⑫ The Bach family home, the **Bosehaus,** still stands, opposite the church and is now a museum devoted to the life and work of the composer. (The exhibits are in German only; a guide to the museum in English can be purchased in the shop.) Of particular interest is the display of musical instruments dating from Bach's time. *Thomaskirchhof 16,* ☎ *0341/7866.* ☛ *DM 2 adults, DM 1 children.* ☉ *Apr.–Sept., daily 9–5; Oct.–Mar., daily 10–5.*

TIME OUT If the weather's good, sit at a table outside the **Cafe Concerto** opposite the church and take in the peace and quiet of the little square, dominated by a statue of Bach. Street musicians regularly play the man's works literally at his feet. The Jugendstil interior of the café (Thomaskirchhof 13, open daily 9–8) beckons in all weathers, with a menu of light meals, local beers and wines, and coffee.

From the Thomaskirche, follow Burgstrasse southward, past the 19th-century neo-Gothic monstrosity that now serves as Leipzig's city hall, **⑬** and you'll come to the city's most outstanding museum, the **Museum der Bildenden Künste,** an art gallery of international standard. The art collection occupies the ground floor of the former Reichsgericht, the court where the Nazis held a show trial against the Bulgarian communist Georgi Dimitroff on a trumped-up charge of masterminding a plot to burn down the Reichstag in 1933. *Georgi-Dimitroff-Pl. 1,* ☎ *0341/216–9914.* ☛ *DM 5 adults, DM 2.50 children, free on Sun.* ☉ *Tues. and Thurs.–Sun. 9–5, Wed. 1–9:30.*

⑭ Head across the Martin Luther-Ring and up the short Grimmaisch Steinweg to reach the **Grassimuseum** complex (Johannspl. 5–11), a fine example of German Art Deco, built in 1925–29 to house three important museums: the newly renovated **Museum of Arts and Crafts** (☛ DM 4 adults, DM 2 children; open Tues.–Fri. 10–6, Wed. 10–8, weekends 10–5), the **Geographical Museum** (☛ DM 5 adults, DM 2 children; open Tues.–Fri. 10–6, weekends 10–4), and the **Musical Instruments Museum** (enter from Täubchenweg 2). ☛ *DM 3 adults, 50 pf children.* ☉ *Tues.–Fri. 9–5, Sat. 10–5, Sun. 10–1.*

⑮ The **Botanischer Garten** (Botanical Gardens) is a set of splendid open-air gardens and greenhouses incorporating Germany's oldest university botanical garden, which dates from 1542. The journey to the Botaniscer Garten stop takes about 15 minutes on Tram 1. *Linnestr. 1.* ☛ *Free. Gardens open Apr.–Sept., daily 9–6; Oct.–Mar., daily 9–4. Greenhouses open Apr.–Sept., Wed. 1–6, Sun. 9-6; Oct.–Mar., Wed. 1–6, Sun. 9–4.*

⑯ Still farther out, via Streetcars 15, 20, 21, or 25, is the **Exhibition Pavilion** at Prager Strasse 210. Its main feature is a vast diorama portraying the Battle of the Nations of 1813. ☛ *DM 2 adults, DM 1 children.* ☉ *May–Sept., Wed.–Sun. 10–6; Oct.–Apr., Wed.–Sun. 9–4.*

⑰ Slightly farther on Prager Strasse is the massive **Völkerschlachtdenkmal,** a memorial in the formal park; it, too, commemorates the battle. Rising out of suburban Leipzig like some great Egyptian tomb, the somber, gray pile of granite and concrete is more than 300 feet high. Despite its ugliness, the site is well worth a visit if only to wonder at the lengths—and heights—to which the Prussians went to celebrate their military victories, and to take in the view from a windy platform near the top (provided you can climb the 500 steps to get there). The Prussians did make one concession to Napoléon in designing the monument: A stone marks the spot where he stood during the battle. ☛ *DM 3.50 adults, DM 2 children.* ☉ *May–Oct., daily 10–5; Nov.–Apr., daily 9–4.*

⑱ Outside of the center of Leipzig but reachable by public transportation (Streetcars 20 and 24, then walk left up Poetenweg, or Streetcar 6 to Menckestr.) is the delightfully Rococo **Gohliser Schlösschen** (Gohliser House), the site of frequent concerts. *Menckestr. 23,* ☎ *0341/52979.* ☉ *Mon. and Fri. 1–5, Tues., Thurs., and Sat. 9–1, Wed. 1–8.*

★ ⑲ Beyond that is **Schiller's House,** for a time the home of the German poet and dramatist Friedrich Schiller. *Menckestr. 42,* ☎ *0341/566–2170.* ☛ *DM 2 adults, DM 1 children.* ☉ *Tues., Wed., and Fri., 10–5, Thurs. 10–6, Sat. 11–5.*

⑳ **Schloss Dölitz** (Streetcar 22 or 24 walk up Helenenstrasse) contains an exhibition of *Zinnfiguren,* historical tin soldiers. *Torhaus, Schloss Dölitz, Helenstr. 24,* ☎ *0341/323–307.* ☛ *DM 2.* ☉ *Wed.–Sun. 10–5.*

Tour 2: Meissen and Dresden

Numbers in the margin correspond to points of interest on the Eastern Germany map.

㉑ Route 6 out of Leipzig will take you to **Meissen,** about 80 kilometers (50 miles) away. This romantic city on the Elbe River is known the world over for its porcelain, bearing the trademark crossed blue swords. The first European porcelain was made in this area in 1708, and in 1710 the royal porcelain manufacturer was established in Meissen, close to the local raw materials.

The story of how porcelain came to be produced in Meissen reads like a German fairy tale: Saxony ruler free-spending August the Strong (ruled 1697–1704 and 1710–1733) urged alchemists at his court to search for the secret of making gold, which he badly needed to refill a Saxon state treasury depleted by his expensive building projects and extravagant lifestyle. The alchemists failed to produce gold, but one of them, Johann Friedrich Böttger, discovered a method for making something almost as precious: fine hard-paste porcelain. Prince August consigned Böttger and a team of craftsmen to a hilltop castle outside Dresden—Albrechtsburg in Meissen—and set them to work. August hoped to keep their recipe a state secret, but within a few years fine porcelain was being produced by Böttger's method in many parts of Europe.

The porcelain works outgrew their castle workshop during the mid-19th century, and you'll find them today on the outskirts of town, at Talstrasse 9. There you can see demonstrations of pieces being prepared. In the same building, a museum displays Meissen porcelain, a collection that rivals that of the Porcelain Museum in Dresden. ☎ *0351/4680.* ☛ *Workshops (including guided tour): DM 5 adults, DM 4 children.* ☼ *Mon. 10–noon and 1–5, Tues.–Sun. 8:30–noon and 1–4.* ☛ *Museum: DM 5 adults, DM 4 children.* ☼ *Mon. 10–5, Tues.–Sun. 8:30–5.*

Meissen porcelain is to be found in one form or another all over town. A set of porcelain bells at the late-Gothic **Frauenkirche,** on the central market square, the Marktplatz, was the first of its kind anywhere when installed in 1929. The largest set of porcelain figures ever crafted can be found in another Meissen church, the **Nikolaikirche,** which also houses remains of early Gothic frescoes. Also of interest in the town center is the 1569 Old Brewery, graced by a Renaissance gable; St. Francis, now housing a city museum; and St. Martins, with its late-Gothic altar.

It's a bit of a climb up Burgstrasse and Amtsstrasse to the **Albrechtsburg castle,** where the story of Meissen porcelain really began, but the effort is worthwhile. The 15th-century Albrechtsburg is Germany's first truly residential castle, a complete break with the earlier style of fortified bastion. It fell into disuse and neglect as nearby Dresden rose to local prominence, but it's still an imposing collection of late-Gothic and Renaissance buildings. In the central courtyard, a typical Gothic *Schutzhof* protected on three sides by high rough-stone walls, is an exterior spiral staircase, **the Wendelstein,** hewn from one massive stone block in 1525, a masterpiece of early masonry. Ceilings of the halls of the castle are richly decorated, although many date only from a restoration in 1870. Adjacent to the castle is a towered early Gothic cathedral. ☛ *DM 4 adults, DM 2 children (guided tours cost an extra DM 2 per person).* ☼ *Daily 10–6; closed Jan.*

㉒ Another 20 kilometers (12 miles) southeast on Route 6 will take you to **Dresden.** Splendidly situated on a bend in the Elbe River, Dresden is a compact city that is easy to explore. In its rococo yellows and greens, it is enormously appealing, and the effect is even more overwhelming when you compare what you see today—or what Canaletto paintings reflect of a Dresden centuries earlier—with the photographs of Dresden in 1945, after a British bombing raid almost destroyed it overnight. It was one of the architectural and cultural treasures of the civilized world, and despite lack of funds and an often uncooperative communist bureaucracy, the people of Dresden succeeded in rebuilding it—an enormous tribute to their skills and dedication.

Their efforts restored at least the riverside panorama to the appearance Canaletto would have recognized, but some of the other parts of the city center look halfway between construction and demolition. In the coming years the city will look more like a building site than ever as 20 new hotels are added to provide the accommodations it so desperately needs. Don't think of visiting Dresden without reserving a hotel room well in advance.

Dresden was the capital of Saxony as early as the 15th century, although most of its architectural masterpieces date from the 18th century, when the enlightened Saxon ruler August the Strong and his son, Frederick Augustus II, brought leading Italian and Bavarian architects and designers up from the south. The predominantly Italianate influence is evident today in gloriously overblown Rococo architecture. *Streetcar tours leave from Postpl. Tues.–Sun. at 9, 11, and 1:30; bus tours, leaving from Dr.–Külz–Ring, run Tues.–Thurs. at 11 (call 0351/495–5025 for details).*

Numbers in the margin correspond to points of interest on the Dresden map.

The best introduction to Dresden is to arrive by ship (*see* Getting Around by Boat *in* Saxony and Thuringia Essentials, *below*), but for motorists or train passengers, the starting point of a Dresden tour will be the main railway station (which has adequate parking). To reach the old part of the city and its treasures you'll first have to cross a featureless expanse surrounded by postwar high rises, leading into the pedestrians-only Pragerstrasse (the tourist information office is at No. 8). Cross busy Dr.-Külz-Ring and you'll enter a far different scene, the broad **②③** **Altmarkt,** whose colonnaded beauty has managed to survive the disfiguring efforts of city planners to turn it into a huge outdoor parking lot. The church on your right, the Kreuzkirche, is an interesting combination of Baroque and Jugendstil architecture and decoration. A church stood here during the 13th century, but the present structure dates from the late 18th century. The rebuilt Rathaus is also on your right, as is the yellow-stucco, 18th-century Landhaus, which contains the Museum für Geschichte der Stadt Dresden (City Historical Museum). It was closed for extensive renovations but is now open again. ☞ DM 3 adults, DM 1.50 children. ⊙ Mon.–Thurs. and weekends 10–6; May–Sept., Wed. to 8 PM.

At the northern end of the Altmarkt, cross Wilsdruffer (or pause for a window-shopping break on this broad boulevard) into the **Neumarkt** (New Market). Despite its name, this is the historic heart of old Dresden. The ruins on your right are all that remain of Germany's greatest Protestant church after the bombing raid of February 1945. These jagged, precariously tilting walls were once the mighty Baroque **②④** **Frauenkirche,** so sturdily built that it withstood a three-day bombardment during the Seven Years' War only to fall victim to the flames that followed the World War II raid. The church is painstakingly being reconstructed with the aim of holding a reconsecration in the year 2006, the 800th anniversary of the founding of Dresden.

The large, imperial-style building looming behind the Frauenkirche is **②⑤** the famous **Albertinum,** Dresden's leading art museum. It is named after Saxony's King Albert, who between 1884 and 1887 converted a royal arsenal into a suitable setting for the treasures he and his forebears had collected. The upper story of the Albertinum, accessible from the Brühlsche Terrasse, houses the Gemäldegalerie Neue Meister (Gallery of Modern Masters), with displays of 19th- and 20th-century paintings and sculpture. Permanent exhibits include outstanding work by German masters of the 19th and 20th centuries (Caspar David Friedrich's haunting *Das Kreuz im Gebirge* is here) and French Impressionists and post-Impressionists.

Impressive as the art gallery is, it's the Grüne Gewölbe (Green Vault) that draws the most attention. Named after a green room in the palace of August the Strong, this part of the Albertinum (entered from Georg-

Dresden

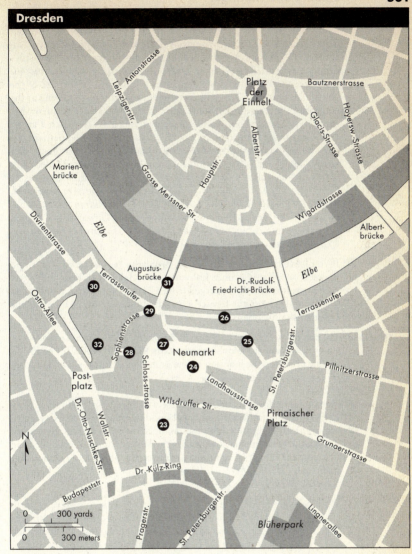

Albertinum, **25**
Altmarkt, **23**
Augustusbrücke, **31**
Brühlsche
Terrasse, **26**
Frauenkirche, **24**
Johanneum, **27**

Katholische
Hofkirche, **29**
Residenzschloss, **28**
Semperoper, **30**
Zwinger, **32**

Treu-Platz) contains an exquisite collection of unique objets d'art fashioned from gold, silver, ivory, amber, and other precious and semiprecious materials. Among the crown jewels is the world's largest "green" diamond, 41 carats in weight, and a dazzling group of tiny gem-studded figures entitled *Hofstaat zu Delhi am Geburtstag des Grossmoguls Aureng-Zeb.* The unwieldy name gives a false idea of the size of the work, dating from 1708, which represents a birthday gathering at the court of an Indian mogul; some parts of the tableau are so small that they can be admired only through a magnifying glass. Somewhat larger and less delicate is the drinking bowl of Ivan the Terrible, perhaps the most sensational of the treasures to be found in this extraordinary museum. Next door is the Skulpturensammlung (Sculpture Collection), which includes ancient Egyptian and classical works and examples by Giovanni da Bologna and Adriaen de Vries. *Albertinum, Am Neumarkt,* ☎ *0351/495–3056.* ☛ *DM 7 adults, DM 3.50 children (includes admission to the Gemäldegalerie Neue Meister, the Grünes Gewölbe, the Münzkabinett (coin collection), and the Skulpturensammlung.* ☉ *Mon.–Wed. and Fri.–Sun. 10–6.*

㉖ If you leave the Albertinum by the **Brühlsche Terrasse** exit you'll find yourself on what was once known as the "Balcony of Europe," a terrace high above the Elbe, carved from a 16th-century stretch of the city fortifications; from the terrace a breathtaking vista of the Elbe and the Dresden skyline opens up.

TIME OUT You can enjoy the view and also take a break after so much gallery-viewing by stepping into the nearby **Cafe Vis-a-Vis,** which sits handsomely in a Baroque mansion on the Brühlsche Terrasse. *Cafe Vis-a-Vis, an der Brühlsche Terrasse.*

Steps leading down from the Terrasse will bring you back to the Neumarkt and to another former royal building that now serves as a museum, the 16th-century **Johanneum,** once the regal stables. Instead of
㉗ horses, the Johanneum now houses the Verkehrsmuseum, a collection of historical vehicles, including vintage automobiles and engines. *Am Neumarkt,* ☎ *0351/495–3002.* ☛ *DM 4 adults, DM 2 children; Fri. ½ price.* ☉ *Tues.–Sun. 10–5.*

Walk behind the Johanneum and into the former stable exercise yard, enclosed by elegant Renaissance arcades and used during the 16th century as an open-air festival ground. To spare the royalty on horseback the trouble of dismounting before ascending to the upper story to watch the jousting and jollities in the yard below, a ramp was built to accommodate both two- and four-legged guests. You'll find the scene today much as it was centuries ago, complete with jousting markings in the ground. More popular even than jousting in those days was *Ringelstechen*, a risky pursuit in which riders at full gallop had to catch small rings on their lances. Horses and riders often came to grief in the narrow confines of the stable yard.

On the outside wall of the Johanneum is a remarkable example of Meissen porcelain art: a painting on Meissen tiles of a royal procession, 336 feet long. More than 100 members of the royal Saxon house of Wettin, half of them on horseback, are represented on the giant jigsaw made up of 25,000 porcelain tiles, painted in 1904–1907 based on a design by Wilhelm Walther. Follow this unusual procession to the end and
㉘ you will come to the former royal palace, the **Residenzschloss,** where restoration work is under way behind the fine Renaissance facade. Although the work is not complete, some of the finished rooms are hosting historical exhibitions. The main gate of the palace, the Georgentor,

has been restored to its original appearance, complete with an enormous statue of the fully armed Saxon Count George guarding the portal that carries his name. The palace housed August the Strong's Grünes Gewölbe before it was moved in its entirety to the Albertinum. *Sophienstr.,* ☎ *0351/495–3110.* ☞ *DM 3 adults, DM 1.50 children.* ☉ *Mon.–Wed. and Fri.–Sun. 10–6.*

㉙ Next to the Herzogschloss is the largest church in Saxony, the **Katholische Hofkirche,** also known as the Cathedral of St. Trinitas. The son of August the Strong, Frederick Augustus II (ruled 1733–1763), brought architects and builders from Italy to construct a Catholic church in a city that had been the first large center of Lutheran Protestantism. They worked away by stealth, so the story goes, and Dresden's Protestant burgers were presented with a fait accompli when the church was finally consecrated in 1754. Seventy-eight historical and biblical figures decorate the Italian High Baroque facade; inside, the treasures include a beautiful stone pulpit by the royal sculptor Balthasar Permoser and a 250-year-old church organ said to be one of the finest ever to come from the mountain workshops of the famous Silbermann family. In the cathedral's crypt are the tombs of 49 Saxon rulers and a precious vessel containing the heart of August the Strong.

㉚ Opposite the cathedral on the Theaterplatz is the restored **Semperoper** (Semper Opera house), justifiably one of Germany's best-known and most popular theaters. Richard Wagner's *Rienzi, Der fliegende Holländer,* and *Tannhäuser,* and Richard Strauss's *Salome, Elektra,* and *Der Rosenkavalier* all premiered here. The masterful Dresden architect Gottfried Semper built the opera house in 1838–1841, in Italian Renaissance style, and then saw his work razed in a fire caused by a careless candle-lighter. Semper had to flee Dresden because of his participation in a democratic uprising, so his son Manfred rebuilt the theater in the neo-Renaissance style you see today. Even Manfred Semper's version had to be rebuilt, after the devastating bombing raid of February 1945. On the 40th anniversary of that raid—February 13, 1985—the rebuilt Semperoper reopened with a performance of *Der Freischutz* by Carl Maria von Weber, another composer who did much to make Dresden a leading center of German music and culture. The demand to experience the Semper Opera again in all its glory is enormous, and tickets are difficult to obtain even in advance. If you're lucky enough to get in, however, an overwhelming experience awaits you. Even if you're no opera buff, the Semper's lavish interior—predominantly crimson, white, and gold—can't fail to impress. Marble, velvet, and brocade create an atmosphere of intimate luxury (it seats 1,323), and the uninterrupted views and flawless acoustics are renowned. You may take a tour of the opera house, but you have to book in advance for that, too (☎ 0351/440–9500).

TIME OUT Across the square, next to the Schloss, is a busy little café-bistro where you can pause on your tour for a coffee or a snack, surrounded by Dresden businesspeople taking a break from nearby offices. *Am Schloss. Schlossstr. 1.*

㉛ The impressive bridge behind the cathedral, the **Augustusbrücke,** is a rebuilt version of a historic 17th-century bridge blown up by the SS shortly before the end of World War II. The bridge was restored and renamed for Georgi Dimitroff, the Bulgarian communist accused by the Nazis of instigating the Reichstag fire; after the fall of communism the original name honoring August the Strong was reinstated.

Back on the Theaterplatz, in the center of the square directly in front of the opera house, you'll see a proud equestrian statue of King Johann, who ruled Saxony when Gottfried Semper was at work. Don't be misled by Johann's confident pose in the saddle—he was terrified of horses and never learned to ride.

The southwestern side of the square is taken up by another Gottfried Semper creation, the **Sempergalerie,** part of the largely 18th-century **Zwinger** palace complex (☎ 0351/484–0620). Built by the great architect to house parts of the art collections of the Saxon royal house, it contains the world-renowned Gemäldegalerie Alte Meister (Gallery of Old Masters). The Zwinger palace complex also contains the porcelain collection, zoological museum, and Mathematisch-Physikalischer Salon (displaying old scientific instruments).

Among the priceless paintings in the Sempergalerie collection are works by Dürer, Holbein, Jan van Eyck, Rembrandt, Rubens, van Dyck, Hals, Vermeer, Raphael (*The Sistine Madonna*), Titian, Giorgione, Veronese, Velázquez, Murillo, Canaletto, and Watteau. On the wall of the entrance archway you'll see an inscription in Russian, one of the few amusing reminders of World War II in Dresden. It reads, in rhyme: "Museum checked. No mines. Chanutin did the checking." Chanutin, presumably, was the Russian soldier responsible for checking one of Germany's greatest art galleries for anything more explosive than a Rubens nude. ☛ *DM 7 adults, DM 3.50 children.* ⊗ *Tues.–Sun. 10–6.*

The Sempergalerie forms just one side of the fabulous Zwinger, the pride of Dresden and perhaps one of the greatest examples of Baroque architecture. There are two entrances to the Zwinger; the Kronentor (Crown Gate), off Ostra-Allee, is the one through which August the Strong and his royal retinue once paraded. August hired a small army of artists and artisans to create a "pleasure ground" worthy of the Saxon court, building it on a section of the original city fortifications (the "Zwinger"). They were placed under the general direction of the architect Matthaus Daniel Pöppelmann, who was called reluctantly out of retirement to design what came to be his greatest work, started in 1707 and completed in 1728. Completely enclosing a central courtyard, filled with lawns and pools, the complex comprises six linked pavilions, one of which boasts a carillon of Meissen bells, hence its name: Glockenspielpavillon. The Zwinger is an extraordinary scene, a riot of garlands, nymphs, and other Baroque ornamentation and sculpture on the edge of an urban landscape etched in somber gray. The contrast would have been much greater if Semper had not closed in one side of the Zwinger, which was originally open to the riverbank. Stand in the center of this quiet oasis, where the city's roar is kept at bay by the palatial wings that form the outer framework of the Zwinger, and imagine the scene on summer evenings when August the Strong invited his favored guests to celebrate with him—the wedding, for instance, of his son, Prince Friedrich August, to Maria Joseph, Archduchess of Austria. The ornate carriage-style lamps shone, the fountains splashed in the shallow pools, and wide staircases beckoned to galleried walks and the romantic Nymphenbad, a coyly hidden courtyard where nude female statues are protected in alcoves from a fountain that spits unexpectedly at unwary visitors.

The Porcelain Museum, stretching from the curved gallery adjoining the Glockenspielpavillon to the long gallery on the east side, is considered one of the best of its kind in the world. The focus, naturally, is on Dresden and Meissen china, but there are also outstanding examples of Japanese, Chinese, and Korean porcelain. The Zoological Museum has a small but very interesting collection of natural history exhibits, including skeletons of wild animals that once roamed the Elbe Valley. The Mathematics and Physics Salon is packed with rare and historic scientific instruments. *Porcelain Museum ☛ DM 3 adults, DM 1.50 children. ⏲ Fri.–Wed. 10–6. Zoological Museum ☛ DM 2 adults, DM 1 children. ⏲ Tues.–Sun. 9–4. Mathematisch-Physikalischer Salon ☛ DM 3 adults, DM 1.50 children. ⏲ Fri.–Wed. 9:30–5.*

Other less central curiosities in Dresden include the **Armee-museum** (Military Museum), which covers military history predating the German Democratic Republic (Olbrichtpl. 3; ☛ DM 1.50 adults, 50 pf children; open Tues.–Sun. 9–5); the **Buch Museum** (Book Museum), which traces the history of books from the Middle Ages to the present (Marienallee 12; ☛ Free; open weekdays 9–4, guided tour Sat. at 2); and the **Deutsches Hygiene Museum** (German Museum of Health), with historical displays of medical equipment and a unique glass anatomical figure (Lingnerpl. 1; ☛ DM 4 adults, DM 2 children; open Tues.–Sat. 9–5).

Numbers in the margin correspond to points of interest on the Eastern Germany map.

From Dresden you can either take the E–40 Autobahn or, if you have
㉝ the time, the more scenic road via Freital to **Freiberg.** Once a prosperous silver-mining community, Freiberg is highlighted by two picturesque Gothic town squares, the Upper and Lower Markets. The late-Gothic cathedral, with its Golden Gate of 1230, has a richly decorated interior and a Silbermann organ dating from 1711. The 800-year-old mine that yielded riches great enough to merit the name "Reiche Zeche" (Wealthy Mine) can still be visited. *Reiche Zeche ☛ DM 15 adults, DM 10 children. ⏲ Weekdays 9:30–12:30.*

㉞ Route 173 continues on via Oederan and Flöha to **Chemnitz** (on older maps, Karl-Marx-Stadt), about 65 kilometers (41 miles) down the E–40 from Dresden. In recognition of the labor movement, East German officials renamed the city in 1953 to honor Karl Marx; in 1990 the population, now free to express a choice, overwhelmingly voted to revert to the original name. Badly damaged during World War II, Chemnitz has revived as a center of heavy industry, but it never had the architectural attractions of other cities in the area. Stop to see the rebuilt 12th-century **Red Tower** in the center of the city; the **Altes Rathaus** (Old City Hall), dating from 1496 to 1498, now incorporating a variety of styles following many reconstructions; and the 250-million-year-old petrified tree trunks, unique in Europe, alongside the city museum. Look, too, at the massive stylized head of a meditative Karl Marx, sculpted by the Soviet artist Lew Kerbel, in front of the district council building in the new city center. Behind it is the motto "Working Men of All Countries, Unite!"—in German, Russian, French, and English. At least in Chemnitz, thanks in part to the hard-fighting pro-Marx lobby, Karl Marx has resisted the post-reunification campaign to eradicate all reminders of east Germany's communist past.

㉟ Take E–40 out of Chemnitz to **Gera,** about 65 kilometers (41 miles) away. Once a princely residence and center of a thriving textile industry, the city has largely been rebuilt after the heavy damage sustained in World War II. Gera has often been compared with old Vienna, although today you have to search long and hard—and even then exercise some imagination—to discover any striking similarities between the German provincial town and the Habsburg capital. After the combined destruction of a world war and more than four decades of communist mismanagement, some ornate, albeit crumbling house facades, however, do betray Gera's rich past, although the palace in which prince-electors once held court was destroyed in the final weeks of the war and never rebuilt. The palace's 16th-century **Orangerie**, though, does still stand, in the former Küchengarten in the suburb of Untermhaus. It's an imposing semicircular Baroque pavilion, irreverently dubbed the "roast sausage" by the people of Gera, that now houses an art gallery. *Küchengartenallee 4.* ☛ *DM 3 adults, DM 2 children.* ☉ *Tues. 1–8, Wed.–Fri. 10–5, weekends 10–6.*

Gera's real claim to fame is the famous artist Otto Dix (1891–1969). The house where the satirical Expressionist painter was born is now a museum with a gallery of his work and a permanent exhibition on his life. *Otto–Dix–Haus, Mohrenplatz 4,* ☏ *03643/832–4927.* ☛ *DM 5 adults, DM 3 children (includes admission to the Orangerie).* ☉ *Tues.–Fri. 10–5, weekends 10–6.*

Don't leave Gera without checking out the central town square, the Marktplatz, its Renaissance buildings restored with rare (for eastern Germany) care. The 16th-century city hall, the Rathaus, has a vividly decorated entrance. Note the weird angles of the lower-floor windows; they follow the incline of the staircase winding up the interior of the building's picturesque 185-foot-high tower.

TIME OUT At the city hall's vaulted cellar restaurant, the **Ratskeller,** Gera's medieval past crowds in on you from all sides, with painted scenes on glass partitions and on the gnarled walls themselves. The restaurant is open daily from midmorning until midnight, so it's an ideal place for coffee, lunch, or dinner.

Nearby is the Baroque **Regierungsgebäude** (government building), incorporating pieces from an earlier 16th-century building.

㊱ Take the E–40 another 53 kilometers (33 miles) to **Weimar.** Sitting prettily on the Ilm River between the Ettersberg and Vogtland Hills, Weimar has a place in German political and cultural history out of all proportion to its size (population: 63,000), and in 1999 will become the smallest city ever to hold the title "European Cultural City," an honor awarded annually by the European Union. It's not even a particularly old city by German standards, with a civic history that started as late as 1410. But by the early 19th century it had become one of Europe's most important cultural centers, where the poets Goethe and Schiller were neighbors, Johann Sebastian Bach played the organ for his royal Saxon patrons, Carl Maria von Weber wrote some of his best music, and Liszt was director of music, presenting the first performance of *Lohengrin.* Walter Gropius founded his Staatliche Bauhaus here in 1919, and behind the classical pillars of the National Theater the German National Assembly in 1919–20 drew up the constitution of the Weimar Republic. After the collapse of the ill-fated Weimar government, Hitler chose the little city as the site for the first national congress of his new Nazi party. On the outskirts of Weimar, the Nazis built—or forced prisoners to build for them—the infamous Buchenwald concentration camp.

Weimar owes much of its greatness to the widowed Countess Anna Amalia, who went talent-hunting in the late 18th century for cultural figures to decorate the glittering court that her Saxon forebears had set up in the town. Goethe was one of her finds, and he served the countess as a counselor, advising on financial matters and town design. Schiller followed, and the two became valued visitors to the countess's home. Today their statues stand before the **National Theater,** on Theaterplatz, two blocks west of the Markt, the central market square: Goethe has a patronizing hand on the shoulder of the younger Schiller. The theater, sadly, isn't the one in which Goethe and Schiller produced some of their leading works; the Baroque building became too small to admit the increasing number of visitors to Weimar, and it was demolished in 1907 and replaced by a larger one with better technical facilities. That theater was bombed in World War II and rebuilt in its present form in 1948. It reopened with a performance of Goethe's *Faust,* which was written in Weimar.

Adjacent to the National Theater is the surprisingly modest home of Countess Anna Amalia, the **Wittumspalais.** Within this exquisite Baroque house you can see the drawing room in which her soirees were held, complete with the original cherry-wood table at which the company sat. The east wing of the house contains a small museum that is a fascinating memorial to those cultural gatherings. *For information, contact Weimar Classics Foundation, Frauentorstr. 4,* ☎ *03643/64386.* ☛ *DM 3 adults, DM 2 children.* ⊙ *Mar.–Oct., Tues.–Sun. 9–noon and 1–5; Nov.–Feb., Tues.–Sun. 9–noon and 1–4.*

★ Goethe spent 57 years in Weimar, 47 of them in the house that has since become a shrine for millions of visitors. **Goethehaus** is at the entrance of the street called Frauenplan, two blocks south of Theaterplatz. It's now a museum containing a collection of writings that illustrate not only the great man's literary might but his interest in the sciences, particularly medicine, and his administrative skills (and frustrations) as Weimar's exchequer. You'll see the desk at which Goethe stood to write (he liked to work standing up) and the modest bed in which he died. The rooms are dark and often cramped, but an almost palpable intellectual intensity seems to illuminate them. *Frauenplan 1,* ☎ *03643/545–320.* ☛ *DM 5 adults, DM 3 children.* ⊙ *Mar.–Oct., Tues.–Sun. 9–5; Nov.–Feb., Tues.–Sun. 9–4.*

Around the corner from Goethe's house, on a tree-shaded square, is Schiller's sturdy, green-shuttered home, in which he and his family spent a happy, all-too-brief three years (Schiller died there in 1805). Schiller's study was tucked up underneath the mansard roof, a cozy room dominated by his desk, where he probably completed *William Tell.* Much of the remaining furniture and the collection of books were added later, although they all date from around Schiller's time. *Schillerstr. 17,* ☎ *03643/64387.* ☛ *DM 5 adults, DM 3 children.* ⊙ *Mon. and Wed.–Sun. 9–5; Nov.–Feb., Mon. and Wed.–Sun. 9–4.*

On the nearby central town square, **Marktplatz,** you'll find another historic Weimar house, the home of the painter Lucas Cranach the Elder, who lived there during his last years, 1552–53. Its wide, imposing facade is richly decorated and bears the coat of arms of the Cranach family. It now houses a modern art gallery.

Around the corner to the left is Weimar's 16th-century castle, with its restored classical staircase, festival hall, and falcon gallery. The tower on the southwest projection dates from the Middle Ages but received its Baroque overlay circa 1730. The castle houses eastern Germany's third-largest art collection, including several works by Cranach the Elder and many early 20th-century pieces by such artists as Böcklin, Liebermann, and Beckmann. ☎ *03643/61831.* ☛ *DM 4 adults, DM 2 children.* ⊙ *June–Aug., Tues.–Sun. 10–6; Sept.–May, Wed.–Sun. 9–5.*

As in so many eastern German towns, Weimar's old town center has been reconstructed. Stop by the late-Gothic **Herderkirche,** with its large winged altar started by Lucas Cranach the Elder and finished by his son in 1555.

A short walk south, past Goethe Haus and across Wieland Platz, will take you to the cemetery where Goethe and Schiller are buried, the **Historischer Friedhof** (Historic Cemetery). Their tombs are in the vault of the classical-style chapel of the leafy cemetery, where virtually every gravestone commemorates a famous citizen of Weimar. The Goethe-Schiller vault can be visited daily 9–1 and 2–5.

On the other side of the Ilm, amid meadowlike parkland, you'll find Goethe's beloved **Gartenhaus** (Garden House), a modest country cottage where he spent many happy hours and wrote much poetry and began his masterpiece, *Iphigenie*. Goethe is said to have felt very close to nature here, and you can soak up the same rural atmosphere today on footpaths along the peaceful little river, where time seems to have stood still. ☛ *Cottage: DM 3 adults, DM 2 children.* ⊙ *Mar.–Oct., daily 9–noon and 1–5; Nov.–Feb., daily 9–noon and 1–4.*

Just across the river from the Gartenhaus is a generous German tribute to another literary giant, William Shakespeare, a 1904 statue showing him jauntily at ease on a marble plinth and looking remarkably at home in these foreign surroundings.

Just south of the city, the lovely 18th-century yellow-stuccoed **Belvedere Palace** once served as a hunting and pleasure castle; today you'll find a Baroque museum and an interesting collection of coaches and other historic vehicles inside. The formal gardens were in part laid out according to Goethe's concepts. ☎ *03643/64039.* ☛ *DM 4 adults, DM 2 children.* ⊙ *Apr.–Oct., Tues.–Sun. 10–6. Closed Nov.–Mar.*

★ In the Ettersberg Hills just north of Weimar is a blighted patch of land that contrasts cruelly with the verdant countryside that so inspired Goethe: **Buchenwald.** This was one of the most infamous Nazi concentration camps, where 65,000 men, women, and children from 35 countries met their deaths through forced labor, starvation, disease, and gruesome medical experiments. Each is commemorated today by a small stone placed on the outlines of the barracks, which have long since disappeared from the site, and by a massive memorial tower built in a style that some critics find reminiscent of the Nazi megalomania it seeks to condemn. The tower stands on the highest point of Buchenwald, approached by a broad, long flight of steps and sheltering at its base a sculpted group representing the victims of Buchenwald. ☛ *Free.* ⊙ *Tues.–Sun. 9:45–4:30. Bus tours to the site are organized by Weimar's tourist office, Weimar-Information, Markt 10,* ☎ *03643/202-173. City buses to Buchenwald leave the bus station, calling at the railway station, every 2 hrs, between 7:10 AM and 3:30 PM.*

★ ③⑦ Twenty-five kilometers (15 miles) west of Weimar (take the B-7 route, running parallel to the Autobahn) lies one of the most picturesque and best-preserved cities of Thuringia: the "flowers and towers" city of **Erfurt.** Erfurt emerged from World War II relatively unscathed, most of its innumerable towers intact (though restored during the early 1970s). Flowers? Erfurt is the center of the eastern German horticultural trade and Europe's largest producer of flower and vegetable seeds, a tradition begun by a local botanist, Christian Reichart, who pioneered seed research. The outskirts of the city are smothered in greenhouses and plantations, and one of Germany's biggest horticultural shows, the Internationale Gartenbauausstellung, takes place here every year from the end of March through September.

With its highly decorative and colorful facades, this is a fascinating city to discover on foot (though you might be tempted to climb aboard one of the old-fashioned horse-drawn open carriages that tour the old town center every Saturday and Sunday, leaving from outside the cathedral at 10 and 4). Erfurt is a photographer's delight, a city of narrow, busy ancient streets dominated by its magnificent cathedral, the 14th-century Gothic **Dom,** reached by a broad staircase from the expansive cathedral square. The Romanesque origins of the cathedral (Romanesque foundations can still be seen in the crypt) are best preserved in the choir, where you'll find glorious stained-glass windows and some of the most beautifully carved choir stalls in all Germany. They have a worldly theme, tracing the vintner's trade back through the centuries. Nearby, look for a remarkable group of freestanding figures: a man flanked by two women. The man is the 13th-century Count von Gleichen. But the two women? There are two stories: The respectable version, has it that the women are the count's wives, one of whom he married after the death of the other. The other, possibly older story claims that one of the women is the count's wife, the other his mistress, a Saracen beauty who saved his life under mysterious circumstances during a crusade. The cathedral's biggest bell, the Gloriosa, is the largest freeswinging bell in the world. Cast in 1497, it took three years to install in the tallest of the three sharply pointed towers, painstakingly lifted inch by inch with wooden wedges. No chances are taken with this two-ton treasure; the bell is rung only on special occasions, such as at Christmas and to ring in the New Year, its deep boom sounding across the entire city. *Tour: DM 2 adults, DM 1 children.* ☉ *Dom May–Oct., weekdays 9–11:30 and 12:30–5, Sat. 9–11:30 and 12:30–4:30, Sun. and public holidays 2–4; Nov.–Apr., Mon.–Sat. 10–11:30 and 12:30–4, Sun. and public holidays 2–4.*

Next to the cathedral and linked to it by a 70-step open staircase is the Gothic church of **St. Severus.** Step inside, if only to admire the extraordinary font, a masterpiece of intricately carved sandstone that reaches practically to the roof of the church.

The cathedral square is bordered by attractive old houses dating from the 16th century. Behind the predominantly neo-Gothic city hall, the **Rathaus,** you'll find Erfurt's outstanding attraction, the **Krämerbrücke** (Shopkeepers' Bridge), spanning the Gera River. You'd have to travel to Florence in Italy to find anything else like this, a Renaissance bridge incorporating shops and homes. Built in 1325 and restored in 1967–73, the bridge served for centuries as an important trading center, where goldsmiths, artisans, and merchants plied their wares. Today antiques shops fill the majority of the timber-frame houses that are incorporated into the bridge, some dating from the 16th century. The area around the bridge is criss-crossed with ancient streets lined with picturesque and often crumbling homes. The area is known as **Klein Venedig** (Little Venice), not because of any real resemblance to the lagoon city but for the recurrent flooding caused by the nearby river.

On the way back to the center of town from the Krämerbrucke, follow Gotthardstrasse and you'll pass the **St. Augustine cloisters,** where the young Martin Luther spent his formative years. Today it's a seminary. In nearby Johannesstrasse you'll find Erfurt's interesting local-history museum, housed in a late-Renaissance house, **Zum Stockfisch.** *Johannesstr. 169, ☎ 0361/562–4888. ☛ Free. ☉ Tues. and Thurs.–Sun. 10–5, Wed. 10–8 PM.*

Johannesstrasse brings you to the pedestrian-zoned **Anger,** an old street lined with restored Renaissance houses. The **Bartholomäusturm,** base of a 12th-century tower, holds a 60-bell carillon.

Just outside the center is the **Erfurt Garden and Exhibition Center.**
☞ *DM 4 adults, DM 2 children.* ⊙ *Sat.–Thurs. 10–5. Greenhouses open Tues.–Sun. 10–4.*

Slightly farther afield is **Schloss Molsdorf,** one of the most stunning Rococo castles in Thuringia, set in a lovely park in the village of Molsdorf. The complex dates from 1736 to 1745 but has been considerably renovated since. ☎ *036202/505.* ☞ *DM 3 adults, DM 1.50 children. Grounds open daily to dusk. Castle open Tues.–Sun. 10–6. Tours are given hourly.*

㊳ Eisenach, 58 kilometers (36 miles) west on either the main B-7 highway or the E–63 Autobahn (or an hour's journey by rail), is a historic city that has managed to retain its medieval atmosphere better than most cities in eastern Germany. Standing in its ancient market square, ringed by half-timbered houses, it's difficult to imagine that this town was an important center of the eastern German automobile industry, home of the now-shunned Wartburg. The solid, noisy staple of the East Germany auto trade was named after the famous castle that broods over Eisenach, high atop one of the foothills of the Thuringian Forest.

★ Begun in 1067 (and added to throughout the centuries), **Wartburg Castle** hosted the German minstrels Walter von der Vogelweide and Wolfram von Eschenbach, Martin Luther, Richard Wagner, and Goethe. Johann Sebastian Bach was born in Eisenach in 1685 and must have climbed the hill to the castle often. Legend has it that von der Vogelweide, Germany's most famous minstrel, won a celebrated song contest here, the "contest of the Minnesingers" immortalized by the Romantic writer Novalis and in Wagner's *Tannhäuser.* Luther sought shelter within its stout walls from papal proscription, and from May 1521 until March 1522 translated the New Testament from Greek into German, an act that paved the way for the Protestant Reformation. The study in which Luther worked can be visited; it's basically the same room that he used, although the walls have been scarred by souvenir-hunters who, over the centuries, scratched away the plaster and much of the wood paneling. Luther's original desk was vandalized, and the massive table before you is a later addition, though a former possession of the Luther family.

There's much else of interest in this fascinating castle, including a portrait of Luther and his wife by Cranach the Elder and a very moving sculpture, the *Kneeling Angel,* by the great 15th-century artist Tilman Riemenschneider. The 13th-century great hall is breathtaking; it's here that the minstrels are said to have sung for courtly favors. Don't leave without climbing the belvedere for a panoramic view of the distant hills of the Harz Mountains and the Thuringian Forest, and soak in the medieval atmosphere of the half-timbered, cottage-style interior courtyards of the castle. ☎ *03643/2500.* ☞ *DM 10 adults, DM 6 children (including guided tour).* ⊙ *Nov.–Mar., daily 9–3:30; Apr.–Oct., daily 8:30–4:30.*

If you're walking from the town center to the castle (be warned: the final 15-minute stretch is a stiff climb) you'll pass on the way the **Reuter-Wagner Museum,** which has the most comprehensive exhibition on Wagner's life and work outside Bayreuth. *Reuterweg 2,* ☎ *03691/203–971.* ☞ *DM 4 adults, DM 2 children.* ⊙ *Tues.–Sun. 10–5.*

Another highlight is the **Lutherhaus,** which covers the life of Luther. *Lutherplatz 8,* ☎ *03691/29830.* ☛ *DM 3 adults, 50 pf children.* ☉ *May–Sept., daily 9–5; Oct.–Apr., Mon.—Sat. 9–5, Sun. 2–5.*

The **Bachhaus** is devoted to the entire Bach family and includes a collection of historical musical instruments. *Frauenplan 21,* ☎ *03691/203–714.* ☛ *DM 5 adults, DM 2 children.* ☉ *Apr.–Sept., Mon. noon–5:45, Tues.–Sun. 9–5:45; Oct.–Mar., Mon. 1–4:45, Tues.–Sun. 9–4:45.*

At Johannesplatz 9, look for what is allegedly the narrowest house in eastern Germany, built in 1890; the width is just over 6 feet, 8 inches, the height 24½ feet, and the depth 34 feet.

Our tour of the southern part of eastern Germany ends here. You can continue west on E–40 into western Germany, which leads into Route 5 to Frankfurt-am-Main. To return to Berlin, the fastest route is east on E–40 and north on E–51. For a change of scenery, turn off E–40 onto Route 4 north to Nordhausen, where you pick up Route 81 to Magdeburg (*see* Excursions *in* Chapter 3), and from there the E–30 Autobahn back into Berlin.

What to See and Do with Children

Dresden, Leipzig, and Erfurt all have excellent zoos. In **Dresden,** the zoo is home to about 2,000 animals of some 500 species. The penguin house is particularly appealing. ☉ *Summer 8:30–6:30, winter 8:30–4:30.*

Erfurt has a fascinating aquarium, with a complete tropical reef and examples of the exotic creatures to be found within it. *Nettelbeckufer 28.* ☉ *Tues.–Sun. 9:30–noon and 2–6.*

Germany's Karl May wrote highly popular, convincing westerns without once visiting America. His birthplace, Radebeul, just outside Dresden, has Germany's leading museum devoted to the extraordinary author and his work—a must for young western fans. You'll find it in the street named after him: Karl-May-Strasse 5. ☉ *Mar.–Oct., Tues.–Sun. 9–6; Nov.–Feb., Tues.–Sun. 10–4.*

The Dresden area has two old railway lines that are still open for tourist trips. One, the Windbergbahn (timetable details, ☎ 0351/403–1602), is Germany's first mountain railway, winding up the seven-mile stretch from central Dresden to the Obergittersee Plateau. The other is a narrow-gauge railway line between Radebeul and Radeburg built between 1899 and 1930, traveled by an ancient Saxon steam train and the original wagons (call 0351/461–4100 for timetable details). In Eisenach, at Wartburg Castle, children can ride donkeys from the *Eselstation* at the start of the pathway to the castle.

Off the Beaten Track

Hellerau, on the outskirts of Dresden (adjacent to the airport), is the site of one of Europe's first experiments in "garden town" planning. It was founded in 1910 by a Dresden furniture maker who wanted to prove that artifacts of lasting beauty could be produced by workers housed in pleasant surroundings. He was helped by an enthusiastic arts lover, Wolf Dohrn, who established at Hellerau a revolutionary new school of dance theory, building Germany's first modern-style theater for the new company. The experiment foundered with Dohrn's death in a skiing accident in 1914 and the outbreak of World War I. There was a brief renaissance after the war, but the Nazis and then World War II finally obliterated Hellerau as a cultural center. The Red Army took the theater and surrounding buildings over as a military hospital and barracks after the war but gave them back to the people of Hellerau in 1992, who now plan to revive them as a pan-European cultural center.

The **Feengrotte** (Fairy Grotto) at **Saalfeld,** near Gera, is a unique underground lake, transformed into a spectacular fairyland of colored stalactites as you travel through by boat. *The Caves open mid-Jan.–mid-Nov., daily 9–5; mid-Nov.–mid-Jan., weekends only 10–5.*

SHOPPING

A post-reunification slump in exports of Meissen and Dresden porcelain means that visitors have a far wider selection than they used to. The best place to hunt for that cherished piece is in Meissen itself, either at the porcelain factory's **showrooms** (Talstrasse 9, ☎ 03521/468–0208) or at a smaller **outlet** on Meissen's market square (Am Markt 8, ☎ 03521/4680). Dresden china is made outside the city, at Freital, where there's a **showroom** and **shop** (Bachstr. 16, Freital, ☎ 0351/643–863; open weekdays 9–6). Goethe planted Germany's first ginkgo tree in Weimar, and the distinctive leaf of the tree is a favorite motif for goldsmiths and jewelry makers. You can admire the fanciful pieces at Uwe **Matthiessen's** workshop at Kupfergasse 3. Leipzig's beautiful Jugendstil shopping arcades took priority in the post-reunification renovation work in the sadly neglected city, and in such restored precincts as the Mädlerpassage you can now find boutiques as chic as any in Hamburg or Munich. There are two separate **Schatte** shops (Nos. 9 and 31) in the Mädlerpassage selling the most recent in wispy and expensive German lingerie.

SPORTS AND FITNESS

Biking
Cycling is not yet a well-developed recreation in eastern Germany, but trails will unquestionably spring up quickly with the political changes. If you're taking your own bicycle, be sure to bring essential spare parts with you. There's good cycling in Dresden along both sides of the Elbe River. Only the really fit should consider the upland Sächsische Schweiz, which is recommended for hikers and climbers.

Fishing
The Elbe River tributaries south of Magdeburg offer excellent fishing; also try the rivers and streams around Erfurt and Eisenach. Conditions should improve as the polluted waters are cleaned up.

Hiking
From Eisenach, hike into the nearby nature preserve area to the southeast.

Skiing
The region south of Erfurt, centering around Oberhof, is a popular winter-sports area, with comfortable hotels and full sports facilities.

Water Sports
There are good canoeing spots on the Gera and Saale rivers; contact the tourist offices at Gera and Halle for rental information.

Winter Sports

The upland, heavily forested Thüringer Wald is eastern Germany's second-favorite holiday destination, in summer and winter. Its center is Suhl, administrative heart of an area where every 10th town and village is a spa or mountain resort. Suhl's tourist office, Suhl Information, is at Steinweg 1, ☎ 03681/20052.

DINING AND LODGING

Dining

Many of the best restaurants are in the larger hotels. Regional specialties include *Thüringer Sauerbraten mit Klössen* (roast corned beef with dumplings), spicy *Thüringer Wurst* (sausage), *Bärenschinken* (cured ham), and *Harzer Köhlerteller mit Röstkartoffeln* (charcoal-grilled meat with roast potatoes). Seafood is plentiful in the lake areas.

CATEGORY	COST*
$$$$	over DM 60
$$$	DM 40–DM 60
$$	DM 25–DM 40
$	under DM 25

per person for a three-course meal and a beer or glass of wine

Lodging

Although the post-reunification shortage of hotels in Saxony and Thuringia is being rectified (six new hotels opened in Eisenach alone in 1994–95), comfortable, moderately priced accommodations can still be difficult to find, particularly in Leipzig and Dresden. Tourist offices are invariably sympathetic and helpful, and most have lists of private households offering bed and breakfast for as little as DM 50. If you're planning to travel during peak season, try to book in advance.

Note that during the Leipzig fair—early March and early September—all Leipzig hotels increase their prices.

CATEGORY	COST*
$$$$	over DM 250
$$$	DM 200–DM 250
$$	DM 160–DM 200
$	under DM 160

Prices are for two people in a double room.

Chemnitz

DINING AND LODGING

Adelsberger Parkhotel Hoyer. The first hotel built in Chemnitz since reunification proudly claims its position in the modern, graceful styling of the exterior and the elegant comfort of the guest rooms. The apartments under the steeply sloping eaves are particularly attractive, with cozy nooks lit by large dormer windows. The royal blue and white furnishings of the restaurant, flooded with the light from floor-to-ceiling bay windows, are a perfect accompaniment to an imaginative menu in which an international cuisine embraces some hearty Thuringian specialties. ⌂ *Wilhelm-Busch-Str. 61,* ☎ *0371/773303,* FAX *0371/773377. 22 rooms with bath, 5 apartments. Restaurant, sauna, exercise room. AE, MC, V. $$$*

LODGING

Chemnitzer Hof. You might enjoy the sense of living in another era at this city-center hotel—it's older (built in 1930, now on the national historic register), with origins in the early Bauhaus style, in which ornamentation was discarded in favor of abstract design. Inside, rooms are attractive and service friendly. ⌂ *Theaterpl. 4,* ☎ *0371/6840,* FAX *0371/62587. 98 rooms with bath, 13 apartments. 2 restaurants, bar, Bierstube, sauna, nightclub. AE, DC, MC, V. $$$$*

Hotel Mercure Kongress. This communist-era, 26-story skyscraper hotel was once uninspiring in its uniform decor, but now you'll notice a sleek Western style. Even the address is new—the hotel now stands on a renamed version of the original Karl-Marx-Strasse. For a fantastic view of the city try for a room on one of the upper floors. But book early—this is a favorite on the convention and meeting circuit. ⌂ *Brückenstr. 19,* ☎ *0371/6830,* FAX *0371/683–505. 377 rooms with bath, 9 apartments. 2 restaurants, bar, beauty salon, sauna. AE, DC, MC, V. $$*

Dresden

DINING

Kügelnhaus. A combination grill/coffee shop/restaurant/beer cellar, Kügelnhaus is extremely popular, so either get there early or reserve your table in advance. You'll find the usual hefty local dishes, but prepared with a deft touch. ✗ *Str. der Befreiung 13,* ☎ *0351/52791. Reservations advised. No credit cards. $$*

Haus Altmarkt. The choice of cuisine in this busy corner of the colonnaded Altmark is enormous—from the McDonald's that has surreptitiously wormed itself into the city landscape to the up-market Amadeus restaurant on the first floor. Between these extremes are a jolly bistrolike café and, downstairs, a vaulted restaurant with a secluded bar. The restaurant, "Zum Humpen," is the best value, with midday menu offerings of less than DM 20. In warm weather you can eat outside on a terrace and watch the marketplace bustle. ✗ *Am Altmarkt 1,* ☎ *0351/495–1212. AE, MC, V. $–$$*

DINING AND LODGING

Schloss Röhrsdorf. This beautifully restored Saxon country palace, surrounded by rolling parkland, is just a short drive from Dresden. Rooms are individually furnished, some with antiques. Old prints hang on the pastel-shaded walls, windows have heavy plush drapes, and deep-pile carpeting completes the luxury. The restaurant is of equally high standard. The hotel has its own stables and the terrain is ideal for riding. ⌂ *Hauptstr. 3, D-01809 Röhrsdorf,* ☎ *0351/285–770,* FAX *0361/2857–7263. 22 rooms with bath. Restaurant, bar, stables. $$$–$$$$*

LODGING

Hotel am Terrassenufer. Canaletto painted the same views that 20th-century guests can now enjoy from within this sleek, new, 12-story hotel on the Elbe River terrace: All rooms have panoramic views of the river and the old town, and on clear days even to the hills of the Sächsische Schweiz. The rooms are decorated in fresh pastel shades, the furniture bright cherry-wood veneers. The old city center and all major sights are a few minutes' walk away. ⌂ *Am Terrassenufer 12,* ☎ *0351/440–9500,* FAX *0351/440–9600. 190 rooms with bath, 6 suites. Restaurant, bar. AE, DC, MC, V. $$$$*

Grand Hotel Taschenbergpalais. Destroyed in wartime bombing but now rebuilt, the historic Taschenberg Palace—the work of the Zwinger architect Matthäus Daniel Pöppelmann—reopened as a magnificent hotel in early 1995. It's Dresden's premier address, a new showpiece of the Kempinski group and the last word in luxury, as befits the former residence of the Saxon crown princes. Rooms are as big as city apartments, while suites earn the adjective palatial. Business travelers are particularly well catered to, with fax/modem outlets in all rooms and a special business center, equipped with every hi-tech device and laptops. But the hotel is recommended for anyone looking for expensive pampering in the romantic heart of old Dresden. ☎ *Am Taschenberg, 01067,* ☎ *0351/478580,* 🖷 *0351/4785860. 188 rooms, 25 suites. 2 restaurants, bars, indoor pool, sauna, steam room. AE, DC, MC, V. $$$$*

Maritim Hotel Bellevue. Across the river from the Zwinger Palace, opera, and main museums, this modern hotel cleverly incorporates an old restored mansion. Rooms are luxurious and service is good, lagging only when the tour groups arrive and depart. ☎ *Grosse Meissner Str. 15, Dresden,* ☎ *0351/56–620,* 🖷 *0351/55997. 326 rooms with bath, 16 suites and apartments. 4 restaurants, bar, café, indoor pool, sauna, bowling, exercise room, jogging. AE, DC, MC, V. $$$$*

Hotels Bastei, Königstein, Lilienstein. This is three hotels in one, all part of a massive, modern complex on the Prager Strasse central shopping mall, between the main railway station and the old city center. The three communist–era hotels were taken over by the Ibis group, which lost no time in giving the drab quarters once occupied by Communist party guests the veneered, pastel-shaded, polished Ibis touch, including satellite TV. A smart restaurant was added in 1994. ☎ *Prager Str.,* ☎ *0351/485–6666,* 🖷 *0351/485–6667. 297 rooms with bath, 9 apartments. 4 restaurants, bars. AE, DC, MC, V. $$*

Hotelschiff Elbresidenz. Dresden's celebrated river panorama is right outside your cabin window on this cruise-liner hotel, moored just below the historic Augusta Bridge and a cat-walk stroll from all the major sights. The boat belongs to the KD shipping line, which operates cruises on the Elbe, and the company has proved to be as efficient in hotel management as it is in organizing its trips. The boat has spacious public lounges and a restaurant with the finest view in town. Cabins are equipped with TV, radio, and telephones. *Landungsbrücke,* ☎ *0351/459–5003,* 🖷 *0351/4595137. 90 cabins with shower. Restaurant, bar, indoor pool, sauna. AE, DC, MC, V. $$*

Eisenach

DINING

Waldschanke. This charming old restaurant is difficult to find, hidden away in a wood on the outskirts of town, but the hunt is well worth it (follow the Wartburgallee for about a mile and then watch for the signs to Prinzenteich). You'll eat lakeside in a former hunting lodge, and if you're lucky, fresh-caught fish or in-season venison will be on the menu. ✕ *Johannistal 57,* ☎ *03691/4465. Reservations advised. No credit cards. Closed Thurs. and Fri. $$*

DINING AND LODGING

Fürstenhof. The first-floor restaurant of this beautifully restored Jugendstil mansion has rapidly established itself as a premier address in all eastern Germany. You dine in princely style in a room that retains many of its 100-year-old features, including a gleaming parquet floor and floor-to-ceiling windows looking out over Eisenach. The international menu also embraces the best traditional German dishes (the marinated fillet of veal melts on the tongue). Guest rooms are large and luxurious, many of them with fine views. ☎ *Luisenstr. 11–13,* ☎ *03691/7780,* 🖷 *03691/203–682. Reservations essential. Jacket and tie. AE, DC, MC, V. $$$$*

LODGING

Auf der Wartburg. In this historic castle, where Martin Luther, Johann Sebastian Bach, and Richard Wagner were also guests, you'll get a splendid view over the town and the surrounding countryside. Rooms were redecorated and refurbished in 1993–94, and all now have private bathrooms. The standard of comfort is above average, and antiques and Oriental rugs mix with modern, moderately stylish furnishings. The hotel runs a shuttle bus service to the rail station. ☎ *Wartburg,* ☎ *03691/5111,* FAX *03691/5111. 26 rooms with bath, 4 suites. Restaurant, exercise room. AE, DC, MC, V. $$*

Glockenhof. At the base of Wartburg Castle, this former church-run hostel is now a comfortable hotel, occupying a half-timbered city mansion. The restaurant offers particularly good value, with no dish costing more than DM 25. ☎ *Grimmelgasse 4,* ☎ *03691/5216,* FAX *03691/5217. 21 rooms, most with bath. Restaurant. MC, V. $*

Erfurt

DINING

Restaurant zur Penne. This is Erfurt's oldest beer cellar, with a virtually unbroken history as such reaching back to 1515. It has eight different beers on tap and a menu bursting with hearty Thuringian fare (wild boar is a must if it's offered). In summer, a shady beer garden beckons diners to leave the shadowy but atmospheric cellar-restaurant. ✗ *Grosse Arche 3–5,* ☎ *0361/643–7469. AE, DC, MC, V. $*

Dasdie. Wolfgang Staub's Dasdie combines restaurant, bistro, bar, cabaret stage, and dance floor under one roof, so you can lunch here (for less than DM 8), return for an early supper, enjoy a show, and end the day with a dance. The food is hit-or-miss, but the place is always lively and prices are low. ✗ *Marstallstr. 12,* ☎ *0361/646–1385. AE, DC, MC, V. $*

DINING AND LODGING

Kosmos. This recent multistory intruder that looks as if it came from outer space is out of place in this town, but in it you'll be halfway between the train station and the town center. The views are splendid—ask for a room on an upper floor overlooking the old city—and the hotel is under the same efficient management that oversees the Erfurter Hof. The prices at Orbis restaurant and Galaxie café are not as far-out as the names imply. ☎ *Juri-Gagarin-Ring 126–127,* ☎ *0361/5510,* FAX *0361/551–210. 319 rooms with bath, 1 apartment. Restaurant, bar, café, sauna. AE, DC, MC, V. $$–$$$*

Gera

LODGING

Maritim Hotel Gera. Another transformed communist-era property, the Hotel Gera was turned into a luxury hotel—full of dove gray and rich burgundy shades and cherry wood veneers—by the Maritim group. The transformation is so complete that even the street on which it stands in central Gera has been renamed to remove old associations. The restaurant, "Elstertal," is well worth a visit. Book ahead around Leipzig fair time. ☎ *Heinrichstr. 30,* ☎ *0365/6930,* FAX *0365/23449. 303 rooms with bath. Restaurant, bar, café, exercise room, sauna, nightclub. AE, DC, MC, V. $$$$*

Galerie-Hotel. This small, friendly hotel near the center of town prides itself on its artistic ambience, evidence of which can be found in the modern, brightly colored furnishings and the regular exhibitions of work by Thuringian artists. Some of their work even finds its way onto the walls of the rooms, which are comfortable and well-appointed, all with satellite TV and fax outlets. The very reasonable room rate includes an extensive breakfast buffet. ☎ *Leibnitzstr. 21,* ☎ *0365/20150,* FAX *03651/201–522. 17 rooms with bath. AE, DC, V. $$*

Halle

DINING

Gildenhaus St. Nikolaus. This massive, early 19th-century colossus of a building, on the same street as the Händelhaus, served as a guildhall and a clothing-factory canteen before it opened as a restaurant. The food tends to give away its canteen past—big portions, so-so and inconsistent quality, and low prices. If you're in luck the venison stew might be at its peak. Berlin-style liver and onions can also be recommended. But the surroundings invite lingering, and it takes time to take in all its medieval-style decoration, from the stained-glass windows to the rural paraphernalia hanging on the paneled walls. In the middle of all the jumble is a mock English-style telephone booth with a phone that's about as reliable as the cuisine. ✕ *Grosse Nikolaistr. 9–11,* ☎ *0345/24700. No credit cards. $*

DINING AND LODGING

Hotel-restaurant zum Kleinen Sandberg. On a quiet side street off the main pedestrian mall, where the city prison once cast its grim shadow, stands one of Halle's prettiest medieval houses, now a small, exclusive restaurant and hotel. Behind its bright brown and white half-timbered facade is a variety of individually furnished rooms, some of them with their own whirlpool baths. The restaurant is small, divided by cross beams and an intimate bar, and serves predominantly Baden specialties—marinated meats with such regional trimmings as *Spätzle* (a variety of pasta)—with a wine list of Baden vintages. ☎ *Kleiner Sandberg 5,* ☎ *and fax 0345/770–0269. 9 rooms with bath. AE, V. $$$*

Leipzig

DINING

Apels Garten. The garden associations of this elegant little restaurant in the city center are to be found in the landscape paintings on the wall, the floral arrangements on the tables, and the fresh produce on the imaginative menu. The wild-duck soup with homemade noodles is an obligatory starter—you won't find anoter soup like it in Leipzig. ✕ *Kolonnadenstr. 2,* ☎ *0341/285–093. Closed Sun. dinner. Reservations advised. AE, DC, MC, V. $$*

★ **Auerbachs Keller.** A visit to this 1530 restaurant, which is immortalized in Goethe's *Faust,* is a must. The menu features regional dishes from Saxony, often with Faustian names. There is also a good wine list. ✕ *Mädler-Passage 2–4,* ☎ *0341/216–1040. Reservations required. Jacket and tie. AE, DC, MC, V. $$*

Zill's Tunnel. The "tunnel" refers to the barrel-ceiling, ground-floor restaurant, where foaming glasses of excellent local beer are cheerily served by a friendly staff who will also help you decipher the Old Saxon descriptions of the menu's traditional dishes. Upstairs there's a larger wine restaurant, with a welcoming open fireplace. Despite the distinction made between the two, you can drink whatever you choose on either floor: Wine buffs will single out the rare Saxon wine from a Saale Valley vineyard. Goose in a variety of forms is a staple here, and among the soups is one made with vegetables, beer, and gin—a potent mixture. ✕ *Barfussgässchen 9,* ☎ *0341/200–446. Reservations advised. No credit cards. $$*

Thüringer Hof. This fine old tavern and restaurant has been in business for centuries and its dark, paneled walls have history carved deep within the wood. The roast wild boar is served just as Leipzigers would have demanded it in ages past, and the traditional Thüringian dishes couldn't be more authentic (marinated beef, Thüringian dumplings, and red cabbage sweetened with apple, to name just one). ✕ *Burgstr. 19–23,* ☎ *0341/209–884. No credit cards. Closed Fri. and Sat. dinner. $*

LODGING

InterContinental. The city's newest and by far most luxurious hotel is imposing with its high-rise profile as well as its Japanese restaurant and garden. Rooms in this Japanese-built hotel offer every luxury, including marble-walled and floored bathrooms and full air-conditioning—and you'll be close to the main train station. ☎ *Gerberstr. 15,* ☎ *0341/9880,* ⌶ *0341/988–1229. 429 rooms with bath, 18 suites. 4 restaurants, 2 bars, coffee shop, indoor pool, massage, sauna, spa, bowling, exercise room, shops, billiards, casino, nightclub. AE, DC, MC, V. $$$$*

Maritim Hotel Astoria. Many prefer this older hotel for its grandness and solid comfort, as well as for its central location by the main train station. There's considerable traffic in the area, so you'll do best with a room on the side rather than the front. The Galerie restaurant literally puts you into an art museum for lunch or dinner. ☎ *Platz der Republik 2,* ☎ *0341/72220,* ⌶ *0341/722–4747. 309 rooms with bath. 2 restaurants, bar, café, sauna, nightclub. AE, DC, MC, V. $$$$*

Corum. The former, slightly seedy Hotel Zum Löwen was transformed in 1993 into a smart and very comfortable hotel. The change is dazzling, and unchanged, of course, is the excellent location, just across the street from Leipzig's main railway station. Rooms are still on the small side, but they lack nothing in terms of comfort and facilities and are decorated and furnished in a warm combination of cherry wood and rich blues and golds. The open-plan bar and lounge are a lively evening meeting spot. The Partout bistro serves light snacks until the early hours. ☎ *Rudolf-Breitscheid-Str. 3,* ☎ *0341/125–100,* ⌶ *0341/1251–0100. 108 rooms with bath, 14 suites. Restaurant, bar, sauna, exercise room. AE, DC, MC, V. $$$$*

Hotel Garni Silencium. This new hotel is part of the Silencium group, which guarantees its guests a peaceful night. So although it's on a busy thoroughfare, Leipzig's Silencium is quiet. The hush permeates the entire house, a beautifully converted city mansion filled with modern, comfortable rooms equipped with satellite TV and fax outlets. Though the hotel is about 3 kilometers from the city center, tram stops are nearby. It does not have a restaurant, but there is a fairly wide choice of places to eat in the immediate area. ☎ *Georg-Schumann-Str. 268, Leipzig-Möckern,* ☎ *0341/901–2990,* ⌶ *0341/901–2991. 34 rooms with bath. AE, DC, MC, V. $$$*

Zum Goldenen Adler. This traditional old Leipzig inn now offers up-to-date comfort and facilities in its handsome framework. Rooms are bright and modern, with dark woods and red upholstery predominant. The popular bistro-bar Day & Night is conveniently within the hotel, but well sound-proofed. ☎ *Portitzerstr. 10,* ☎ *0341/688–0976,* ⌶ *0341/66326. 20 rooms with bath. Brasserie. AE, MC, V. $$$*

Meissen

DINING

Burgkeller and Domkeller. After the steep climb up to the castle you'll be panting for refreshment, and two ancient taverns are waiting at the top to offer it. The first, the Burgkeller, was being renovated in 1995, and if it's still closed make for the next, the Domkeller, which is part of the same centuries-old complex of buildings that ring the lovely cathedral and its peaceful plaza. Stop on the way, though, to soak in the great view of Meissen from the terrace of the Burgkeller. The Domkeller is smaller but cozier. Both offer solid Saxon and Thuringian fare—Dresdner Sauerbraten, for instance, a delicious dish of beef marinated in a sauce enriched with currants and served with cabbage sweetened with cranberries. ✗ *Dompl. 9 and 11,* ☎ *03521/452–034. AE, DC, MC, V. $*

DINING AND LODGING

★ **Pannonia Parkhotel.** This Jugendstil villa on the banks of the Elbe, across the river from the hilltop castle, is now in the hands of an energetic and imaginative young American hotel director, Jeffrey F. Scott, who plans to make it a culinary and cultural center. The first part of his plan has been realized, with a cuisine of international flair and a dining room that makes use of such features of the old house as its original stained glass and elegantly framed doors. By 1996 it should also be the scene of regular chamber-music evenings. Although most of the luxuriously furnished and appointed rooms are in the newly built annexes, try for one in the villa—and for an unforgettable experience book the top suite (in every sense) under the eaves (around DM 400 a night). The view of the river and the castle from its two rooms and from the badminton-court-size private terrace is sensational. On weekends room rates drop by as much as half. ⊡ *Hafenstr. 27–31,* ☎ *03521/72250,* FAX *03521/722–904. 76 rooms with bath, 17 apartments, 4 suites. Restaurant, bars, sauna, exercise room. AE, DC, MC, V. $$$*

Weimar

DINING

Weisser Schwan. This historic restaurant in the center of town, right by the Goethe house (*see* Meissen and Dresden *in* Exploring, *above*), dates from 1500. Its various rooms, including the library, offer international and Thuringian specialties, particularly fish and grilled meats. ✗ *Frauenstorstr. 23,* ☎ *03643/61715. Reservations essential. Jacket and tie. AE, DC, MC, V. Closed Mon. $$$*

Hotel Thüringen. The plush elegance of the Thüringen's restaurant, complete with velvet drapes and chandeliers, makes it seem expensive, but there's a plesant surprise in store: The menu of international and regional dishes is remarkably moderately priced. An excellent Thüringer roast beef, for instance, costs less than DM 20. ✗ *Brennerstr. 42,* ☎ *03643/3675 or 03643/62900. AE, DC, MC, V. $$*

Ratskeller. This is one of the region's most authentic city hall cellar restaurants, its whitewashed, barrel-vaulted ceiling attesting to centuries of tradition. Tucked away at the side is a cozy bar where you can enjoy a preprandial drink beneath a spectacular Art Nouveau colored skylight. The delicious "Madagascar" green-pepper soup is the only exotic touch to the otherwise traditional Thuringian menu. If venison is in season try it; likewise the wild duck or wild boar in red-wine sauce. ✗ *Markt 10,* ☎ *03643/64142. Reservations advised. Closed Sun. dinner. AE, MC, V. $*

Scharfe Ecke. Thuringia's traditional Knödelare at their best here—but be patient, they're made to order and take 20 minutes. The Knödel come with just about every dish, from roast pork to venison stew, and the wait is well worth it. The ideal accompaniment for virtually anything on the menu is the locally brewed beer. ✗ *Eisfeld 2,* ☎ *03643/202–430. No credit cards. Closed Mon. $*

LODGING

Weimar Hilton. Weimar's most modern hotel combines luxury with sleek and smooth-running service. The riverside Belvedere Park that Goethe helped to plan is just across the road, and the Rococo Belvedere Palace, with its museum of ancient vehicles, is a short walk away. Weimar's center is quite a hike in the other direction, but buses are frequent. ☎ *Belvederer Allee 25,* ☎ *03643/7220,* FAX *03643/722–741. 300 rooms with bath. 2 restaurants, 4 bars, café, indoor pool, sauna, spa, bowling, exercise room. AE, DC, MC, V. $$$$*

Flamberg Hotel Elephant. The historic old "Elephant," dating from 1696, is now in the hands of the Flamberg group, which has thankfully kept the individual charm that made it one of Germany's most famous hostelries, even in communist times. Book here (well ahead) and you'll follow the choice of Goethe, Schiller, Herder, Liszt (after whom the hotel bar is named)—and Hitler—all of whom have been guests. Behind the sparkling white facade are comfortable modern rooms, thanks to renovations, but a feeling for the past is ever present. ☎ *Am Markt 19,* ☎ *03643/8020,* FAX *03643/653-10. 87 rooms with bath, 5 suites. 2 restaurants, bar, sauna, nightclub. AE, DC, MC, V. $$$$*

Christliches Hotel Amalienhof. Book far ahead to secure a room at the hotel that is rapidly becoming everyone's "inside tip." The now historic and officially protected building began life in 1826 as a church hostel, but subsequent remodelings have turned it into a comfortable, cozy, and friendly little hotel, central to all Weimar's chief attractions. Double rooms are furnished with high-class reproduction antiques, while public rooms have the real thing. ☎ *Amalienstr. 2,* ☎ *03643/5490,* FAX *03643/549–110. 22 rooms with shower. Restaurant, bar. MC, V. $$*

THE ARTS AND NIGHTLIFE

The Arts

Opera

The opera in **Dresden** has regained its international reputation since the **Semper Opera House** (Sächsische Statsoper Dresden, Theaterplatz, D–01067, Dresden), which was almost totally destroyed in World War II, reopened in 1985 following an eight-year reconstruction. Just seeing the magnificent house is worth the trip; a performance is that much better. Tickets are reasonably priced but also hard to get; they're often included in package tours. Try your luck at the evening box office (the *Abendkasse,* left of the main entrance, ☎ 0351/484–2323, 0351/484–2328, or 0351/484–2333) about a half hour before the performance; there are usually a few dozen tickets available. If you're unlucky, take one of the opera house tours offered by the Dresden Tourist Office (☎ 0351/4955–025).

Several smaller cities, notably **Chemnitz** and **Halle,** also have opera houses that turn out interesting performances, occasionally of relatively little-known or contemporary works.

Music

The Neues Gewandhaus in **Leipzig,** a controversial piece of architecture, is home to a splendid orchestra. Tickets to concerts are very difficult to obtain unless you reserve well in advance and in writing only (Gewandhaus zu Leipzig, Augustuspl. 8 Leipzig D–04109). Sometimes spare tickets are available at the box office a half hour before the evening performance. Of the music festivals in the area, the best-known are the Händel festival in **Halle** (June), the Dresden Music Festival (May and June), and the Music Days in **Leipzig** (June), as well as the International Bach Festival held every four years during September and October. **Dresden** organizes an international Dixieland festival each May.

Nightlife

Leipzig comes to life particularly during fair time, although in the past this was as much to extract hard currency from visitors as it was to entertain them. The city has one of Germany's most famous cabarets, the **Pffeffermühle** (Peppermill), with a lively bar off a courtyard opposite the Thomaskirche (Thomaskirchhof 16). On pleasant evenings the courtyard fills up with benches and tables and the scene rivals the indoor cabaret for entertainment.

Discos and nightclubs are opening up in eastern Germany with baffling speed, although the established bars and clubs of the communist era are still doing good business. Many of them are in the top hotels (*see* Dining and Lodging, *above*). In **Leipzig,** try the Astoria or Inter-Continental; in **Gera,** the Maritim Hotel; in **Erfurt,** the Erfurter Hof; and in **Weimar,** the Hilton and Elephant hotels. **Dresden**'s Hilton offers nightclubbers the choice of three bars, two taverns, and a disco.

Live jazz can be heard in Dresden most nights of the week at the **Tonne Jazz Club** (Tzschirnerpl. 3, ☎ 0351/495–1354 or 0351/496–0211). Foreign visitors are assured of a very warm welcome at this friendly, laid-back haunt. Jazz and folk music are regular features of the program at the **Club Passage** (Leutewitzer Ring 5, ☎ 0351/411–2665). Disco fans head for the **Cafe Prag** (Am Altmarkt 16–17, ☎ 0351/495–5095), where cabaret is on the program on Friday and Saturday nights. Leipzig's top discos include the **Nachtbar Tivoli** (Katharinenstr. 13, ☎ 0341/200–323) and the **Esplanade** (Richard-Wagner-Str. 10, ☎ 0341/282–330). Leipzig's lively after-dark scene includes an eye-opening "erotic show" offered by the **Aphrodite** (Bornaische Strasse 197, ☎ 0341/326-171) and an exotic café-bar, **Visavis** (Rudolf-Breitscheid-Str. 33, ☎ 0341/292-718), which has a particular welcome for "gay people, artists, birds of paradise and other aesthetes."

SAXONY AND THURINGIA ESSENTIALS

Although the two Germanys reunited in 1990, many of the old divisions between east and west are still perceptible, particularly for visitors. The east, with some shining exceptions (such as Weimar and reconstructed parts of Dresden and Leipzig) is noticeably shabbier than the west, communications are less smooth, and accommodations in all but the expensive hotels can be disappointingly basic. A continuing road-construction program still causes traffic jams, particularly on some of the Autobahns leading west; the privatization of the German railway system is proceeding slower in the east than in the west; and making telephone calls can still be a frustrating business in country districts. A hotel-building program has led to room rates that are generally higher than those in the west, with cheaper lodgings often unimproved leftovers from the days of GDR discomfort. The current problems on the lodging front, however, have given rise to a boom in private accommodations, and all tourist offices have lists of addresses of places that offer clean, adequate bed-and-breakfast accommodations at a reasonable price. The tourist offices themselves have shown the greatest improvement since German reunion, and you'll get friendly, efficient, and helpful service in even the smallest town.

We have given addresses, telephone numbers, and other logistical details based on the best available information, but remember that changes are still taking place. We strongly recommend that you contact the German National Tourist Office (*see* Chapter 1) or your travel agent for the most up-to-date information.

Arriving and Departing

By Car

Expressways connect Berlin with Dresden (the A–9) and Leipzig (A–13). Both journeys take about two hours.

By Plane

West Berlin's **Tegel Airport** (☎ 030/410–2306) is only 6 kilometers (4 miles) from downtown; east Berlin's **Schönefeld Airport** (☎ 030/691–510) lies about 24 kilometers (15 miles) outside the downtown area. **Dresden Airport** (☎ 0351/589–141) is about 10 kilometers (6 miles) north of the city. Leipzig's **Schkeuditz Airport** (☎ 0341/7240) is 12 kilometers (8 miles) northwest of the city.

By Train

International trains stop at Friedrichstrasse or Hauptbahnhof stations in former East Berlin; from there, there is direct service to Dresden, Leipzig, and most towns covered below.

Getting Around

By Boat

"White Fleets" of inland boats, including paddle sidewheelers, ply the inland lakes around Berlin and the Elbe River, starting at Meissen or Dresden, going downstream and continuing into Czechoslovakia.

KD River Cruises of Europe has two luxury cruise ships on the Elbe River. It operates a full program of cruises of up to eight days in length from mid-April until late October and from Hamburg as far as Prague. All the historic cities of Saxony and Thuringia are ports of call—including Dresden, Meissen, Wittenberg, and Dessau. For details of the cruises, contact the company in the United States (2500 Westchester Ave., Purchase, NY 10577, ☎ 914/696–3600; 323 Geary St., San Francisco, CA 94102, ☎ 415/392–8817).

By Bus

Long-distance bus services linking Frankfurt with Dresden and Leipzig were inaugurated in 1991. Within Saxony and Thuringia, most areas are accessible by bus, but service is infrequent and mainly serves to connect with rail lines. Check schedules carefully.

By Car

A fairly ambitious road-construction and -improvement program under way in eastern Germany has yet to be completeed, and you should expect traffic delays on any journey of of more than 300 kilometers (200 miles); it's advisable to calculate for delays when planning your itinerary. Rules of the road are now uniform east and west, with no official speed limit on Autobahns (but a "recommended" top speed of 130 kph/80 mph), limits of 100 kph (60 mph) on other main roads, and between 40 kph (24 mph) and 60 kph (36 mph) through built-up areas. Give way to the right on all intersections unless signs unmistakably give you precedence. The previous strict ban on drinking and driving has been relaxed somewhat to bring the east in line with the west, and the limit is now equivalent to one small beer or a glass of wine. The principal fuel companies have lost no time in establishing themselves in eastern

Germany, so you'll no longer encounter any of the problems that used to plague motorists in need of a refill.

CAR RENTAL

Cars can be rented at airports and all major hotels. Rental cars may be driven into neighboring countries, including Poland and Czechoslovakia. All the major international car-rental firms are now represented throughout eastern Germany, and rental charges correspond with those in western Germany. All major western credit cards are accepted.

Avis: Karl-Marx-Strasse 264, ☎ 030/685–2093, and Schönefeld airport, ☎ 030/6091–5710, **Berlin;** Dresden airport, ☎ 0351/589–4600, **Dresden;** Augustusplatz 5-6, ☎ 0341/214–6891, Leipzig airport, ☎ 0341/224–1804, **Leipzig.**

Hertz: Karl-Marx-Strasse 196, ☎ 030/687–2041, **Berlin;** Grosse Meissner Strasse 15 (in Maritim Hotel Bellevue), ☎ 0351/566–2840; Tiergartenstr. 94, ☎ 0351/232–8218, and Dresden Airport, 0351/589–4580, **Dresden;** Platz der Republik 2 (in Hotel Astoria), ☎ 0341/722–4701, Otto-Schill-Strasse 10 (in the Autohaus City), ☎ 0341/293954 and Leipzig Airport, ☎ 0341/4188, **Leipzig.**

InterRent-Europcar: Karl-Liebknecht-Strasse 19–21, ☎ 030/242–4403, and Schönefeld Airport, ☎ 030/678–8059, **Berlin;** Liebstädterstrasse 5, ☎ 0351/251–6263, and Dresden Airport, ☎ 0351/589–4590, **Dresden;** Wittenberger Str. 19, ☎ 0341/564–5914, and Leipzig Airport, 0341/224–1820, **Leipzig.**

Sixt-Budget: Friedrichstrasse 150–153 (Hotel Metropol), ☎ 030/242–5201, and Schönefeld Airport, ☎ 030/609–15690, **Berlin;** An der Frauenkirche 5 (Hilton Hotel), ☎ 0351/484–1696, St. Petersburger Strasse 34 (in Hotel Mercure Newa, ☎ 0351/495–6012 and Dresden Airport, ☎ 0351/589–4570, **Dresden;** Gerberstrasse 15 (Hotel Inter-Continental), ☎ 0341/799–1149, and Leipzig Airport, ☎ 0341/224–1868, Leipzig.

By Train

The German railway system, currently being privatized, is now a nationwide network, with none of the old differences between east and west. New track is still being built on some eastern routes and modernization is occurring on others, resulting in occasionally slower services. But Berlin and all east German cities are now linked (with one another and with railheads in western Germany) by InterCity, EuroCity (direct services to other European cities), and the high-speed InterCity Express trains. InterRegio services complete the express network, while slower D- and E-class trains connect smaller towns. All have first- and second-class cars; the InterCity, EuroCity, and InterCity Express have restaurant cars, the InterRegio trains have bistro-bars; and the D- and E-class trains have a trolley-bar service on longer runs. On all overnight routes, first- and second-class sleeping cars and second-class couchettes are available. To ensure that you get a berth it's essential to book in advance, either at any large travel agency or at the rail station itself.

Guided Tours

Information on travel and tours to and around eastern Germany is available from most travel agents. Most Berlin tourist offices carry brochures about travel in eastern Germany. For information about guided tours around the region, contact **Berolina Berlin-Service** (Meinekestr. 3, D–10719 Berlin, ☎ 030/882–2091) or **DER** Deutsches Reisebüro Gmbh (Augsburger Str. 27, D–12309 Berlin, ☎ 030/2199–8100).

Important Addresses and Numbers

Embassies

With the reunification of Germany, the embassies of the United States and the United Kingdom in east Berlin have been downgraded to the rank of consulates or missions. The **Canadian Embassy** in Bonn (Friedrich-Wilhelmstrasse 18, ☎ 0228/231–061) is responsible for eastern Germany. The **United States** office in east Berlin is at Neustädtische Kirchstrasse 4–5, ☎ 030/238–5174; the **United Kingdom Consulate** in east Berlin is at Unter den Linden 32–34, ☎ 030/392–9607.

Tourist Information

For tourist information about the following cities, contact:

Chemnitz: Strasse der Nationen 3, D–09008, ☎ 0371/62051.
Dessau: Rathaus, Zerbster Strasse, D–06813, ☎ 0340/214–804.
Dresden: Box 201, Pragerstrasse 10/11, D–01069, ☎ 0351/495–5025.
Eisenach: Bahnhofstrasse 3–5, D–99817, ☎ 03691/69040.
Erfurt: Bahnhofstrasse 37, D–99084, ☎ 0361/562–3436.
Freiburg: Burgstrasse 1, D–09595, ☎ 03731/23602.
Gera: Breitscheidstrasse 1, D–07545, ☎ 0365/26432
Halle: Steinweg 7, D–06110, ☎ 0345/202–4700.
Leipzig: Sachsenplatz 1, D–04109, ☎ 0341/71040.
Meissen: An der Frauenkirche 3, D–01662, ☎ 03521/454–470.
Weimar: Markt 10, D–99423, ☎ 03643/202–173.

Travel Agencies

American Express: Hotel Bellevue, Köpckestrasse, Dresden, 15, ☎ 0351/56620; Europaisches Reisebüro, Katherinenstrasse, Leipzig, ☎ 0341/79210.

17 The Baltic Coast

Between the former East—West border town of Lübeck and the Polish frontier, East Germany's vacation hot spot is now open for all to enjoy, even if many of its beach towns still seem trapped in the '30s. Miles of sandy coastline, peppered with chalk cliffs and charming little coves, have largely escaped the attention of developers. Evidence of the Hansa merchants and a wealth of architectural delights await inspection, from the well-preserved medieval town squares to the simple whitewashed seaside cottages with their roofs of reed thatch.

THE BALTIC COAST is Germany's half-forgotten eastern shoreline, as unfamiliar to most former West Germans as it is to foreigners. It's a region of white, sandy beaches (340 kilometers of them), coves, chalk cliffs, ancient ports, and fishing villages where time and custom seem to have stood still. Some of the beach resorts have been popular holiday destinations since the mid-19th century, when sunbathing and sea swimming first became fashionable. But the entire 1,130-kilometer (706-mile) weaving coastline—from the Trave River estuary, above Lübeck, to Swinemünde, at the Polish border—was plunged into isolation when the Iron Curtain came down just east of Lübeck. Although the Baltic Coast was considered the Riviera of the Eastern Bloc, and correspondingly full each summer, the communist regime did not invest in restoring or developing the resort centers of this area. On the island of Rügen, for example, the clock appears to have stopped in the 1920s and '30s; the architecture, the pace of life, even the trains—they are steam powered—are caught in a time warp.

Until 1989 Lübeck was the eastern outpost of the West. Three kilometers (2 miles) away were the watchtowers of the German Democratic Republic. Today the sense of crossing a border still prevails. Lübeck has spent the last 40 years reconstructing and restoring its Hanseatic heritage, and it is a charming town.

The new state of Mecklenburg-Vorpommern in the former East Germany, in contrast, looks very much as West Germany did in the 1950s—a depressing mixture of cheaply constructed apartment buildings and neglected buildings of the past. Forty years of communism worked at creating a workers' paradise, not a mecca for tourists. However, the new generation in former East Germany is anxious to restore what is left of the region's Hanseatic heritage and to attract tourists with new hotels and facilities. For the time being, though, the traveler here will find high prices at average hotels, inflated prices at sparkling new hotels, reasonably priced pensions of tremendously varying quality, and a short list of exceptional restaurants.

The tour threads a route through five leading Hanseatic League ports, whose medieval merchants became rich by monopolizing trade across the Baltic Sea between the 12th and 16th centuries. Much of their wealth was invested in buildings; some of the finest examples of north German Gothic and Renaissance redbrick architecture, with its tall stepped gables, are to be found here. Except for the cities of Schwerin and Rostock (the latter was former East Germany's chief port and shipbuilding center), the Baltic Coast is a rural region, but one in which the sea has long played a pivotal role. Since its development more than 800 years ago, this area has been populated largely with seafaring folk, traders, and fisherman. Despite meager attempts by the Soviets to industrialize the larger cities of the area in the 1960s and '70s, they remain uncompetitive with the West and economically depressed. Since reunification this region has embarked on intensive restoration of historic buildings and development of the tourist industry in an effort to revitalize not only the economy but pride in its Hanseatic heritage.

The route takes us east from Lübeck to Usedom Island, parallel to the coast, but slightly inland. If you see an interesting-looking road that wanders off to the north, it's likely to lead to the coast and could be worth a detour.

EXPLORING

Lübeck to Usedom Island

Numbers in the margin correspond to points of interest on the Baltic Coast map.

★ ❶ The starting point of this 525-kilometer (328-mile) tour is a historic and pretty port just west of the former East/West border. The ancient core of **Lübeck,** dating from the 12th century, is surrounded by canals fed by the Trave River and was one of the chief strongholds of the Hanseatic merchant princes who controlled trade on the Baltic. But it was the roving King Henry the Lion (Heinrich der Löwe) who established the town and, in 1173, laid the foundation stone of the redbrick Gothic cathedral.

Until recently, Lübeck was near every German's heart, but even closer to every hip pocket: The town's famous landmark, the **Holstentor** gate, appeared on the DM 50 note. The ancient gate on Holstentor Platz, built between 1464 and 1478, is flanked by two round, squat towers—solid symbols of Lübeck's prosperity as a trading center. Witnesses of Lübeck's former position as the golden queen of the Hanseatic League are found at every step in the Old Quarter. More 13th- to 15th-century buildings stand in Lübeck than in all other large northern German cities combined—a fact that in 1987 prompted UNESCO to list Lübeck's Old Quarter in its register of the world's greatest cultural and natural treasures. A short walk along Holtenstrasse brings you to one of Europe's most striking medieval market squares. Among the buildings lining the arcaded **Marktplatz,** the **Rathaus** (Town Hall), dating from 1240, is particularly noteworthy, having been subjected to several architectural face-lifts that have added Romanesque arches, Gothic windows, and a Renaissance roof. The impressive redbrick Gothic **Marienkirche,** which has the highest brick nave in the world, looms behind the Rathaus.

TIME OUT Don't miss this opportunity to sample the world-renowned Niederegger Marzipan fresh from its source, in the traditional **Cafe Niederegger,** across from the Rathaus. This firm has been producing marzipan in Lübeck since 1825; a virtual museum of marzipan, it showcases more than 300 specialties. *Breitestr. 89, ☎ 0451/530–1126.*

From the square, turn left into Breitestrasse, where you'll pass the 18th-century Baroque Buddenbrookhaus, made famous by novelist Thomas Mann's saga *Buddenbrooks.* Mann's family once lived in the house, which has recently opened as the **Heinrich and Thomas Mann Zentrum,** a museum documenting the life and works of these influential brothers. A tour and video in English are offered. *Mengstr. 4, ☎ 0451/122–4190.* ☛ *DM 4 adults, DM 2 children.* ☉ *Daily 10–5.*

Continue along Breitestrasse and turn right into Koberg. Here you will find one of the oldest and most beautiful hospitals in the world. Built during the 14th century by the town's rich merchants, the Gothic **Heiligen-Geist-Hospital** (Hospital of the Holy Ghost) is still caring for the infirm. At the other end of the old town you'll find the oldest building in Lübeck, the **Dom,** or cathedral, its foundation stone laid in 1173 by that gadabout royal Henry the Lion. The Gothic Dom, incorporating late-Romanesque and Renaissance features, was severely damaged in World War II but rebuilt from 1958 to 1977. The Dom and Marienkirche

Baltic Coast

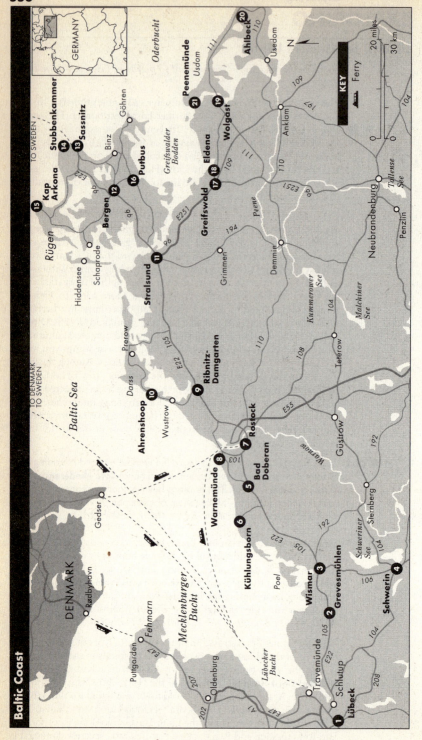

GERMANY

Oderbucht

20 Ahlbeck

Usedom

Peenemünde

Stubbenkammer

Kap Arkona

14 **13** **Sassnitz**

Göhren

21 **19** **Wolgast**

Greifswalder Bodden

Binz

Purbus **16**

12 **Bergen**

17 **18** Eldena

15

Rügen

Schaprode

Hiddensee

Greifswald

11 Stralsund

Grimmen

Anklam

Tollense See

Neubrandenburg

Penzlin

Prerow

Darss

Demmin

Peene

Kummerower See

Malchiner See

N

20 miles

30 km

KEY

Ferry

To Sweden

To Denmark
To Sweden

Baltic Sea

Wustrow

10 Ahrenshoop

9 Ribnitz-Damgarten

Rostock **7**

8 Warnemünde

Bad Doberan

5

6

Kühlungsborn

Gedser

Rødbyhavn

DENMARK

Fehmarn

Puttgarden

Oldenburg

Mecklenburger Bucht

Poel

Wismar

3 Grevesmühlen

2

Travemünde

Schlutup

1 Lübeck

Lübecker Bucht

Güstrow

Sternberg

Teterow

Warnow

Schweriner See

Schwerin **4**

Letсхвод

Baltic Sea

regularly present organ concerts, a real treat in these magnificent red-brick Gothic churches.

Leave Lübeck on Route B 105. (Don't expect a fast highway. Route 105 is a narrow two-lane road all the way to Poland, heavily traveled by slow-moving trucks.) Stop at **Grevesmühlen** to view the Gothic St. Nikolai parish church and a pretty Renaissance town hall. A couple of miles east of the town is one of the highest hills in the region, the Iserberg; from here on a clear day you can view the coastline and the island of Poel. This region has been buffeted by stiff sea storms and more: Over the centuries the armies of Sweden, Denmark, Prussia, and France fought here for control of the coast. A grim reminder of a more recent conflict can be found in nearby Tannenberg, site of a memorial cemetery for some of the 8,000 Nazi concentration camp victims who drowned when four ships that were transporting them were mistakenly attacked by Allied planes and sunk in Lübeck Bay only days before the war ended.

Back on Route 105, another 22 kilometers (14 miles) will take you to **Wismar,** a picturesque port before World War II that is now in need of restoration. It was one of the original three sea-trading towns that banded together in 1259 to combat Baltic pirates (the other two were Lübeck and Rostock). From this mutual defense pact grew the great and powerful private trading block, the Hanseatic League, which dominated the Baltic for centuries. The Thirty Years' War was particularly devastating for this region—the prewar population was halved—and the power of the Hanseatics was broken. Wismar became the victim of regular military tussles and finally fell to Sweden. The town was mortgaged to a German Mecklenburg duke in 1803 on a 100-year lease, and it was only when this expired in 1903 that Wismar legally rejoined Germany.

Despite its checkered history, the wealth originally generated by the Hanseatic merchants can still be seen in Wismar's ornate architecture, particularly in the patrician gabled houses that frame the **Marktplatz,** the main square, one of the largest and most colorful in northern Germany. The style of buildings on the square ranges from redbrick late-Gothic through Dutch Renaissance to 19th-century neoclassical. Of particular interest is the **Wasserkunst,** the ornate pumping station in Dutch Renaissance style built 1580–1602 by the Dutch master Philipp Brandin. Not only was it a work of art, it supplied the town with water until the mid-19th century.

TIME OUT The oldest building on the Marktplatz (1380) can be easily identified by its stepped gables and redbrick facade. A colorful seaman's tavern since 1878, the **Alter Schwede** has entertained guests ranging from sailors to the Swedish royal family. Traditional regional dishes are served, including the hearty potato-and-bacon casserole called *Griebenroller. Am Markt 16,* ☎ *03841/283–552.*

In 1922, filmmaker Friedrich Wilhelm Murnau used the tortuous streets of Wismar's old town in his Expressionist horror classic, *Nosferatu.*

Walk west to reach the 250-foot-high tower of the ruined **Marienkirche** church, bombed in World War II, just behind the Marktplatz and currently undergoing repairs. At noon, 3 PM, and 5 PM, listen for one of 14 hymns played on its clarion bells. Next to it stands the **Fürstenhof,** home of the former dukes of Mecklenburg, an early 16th-century Italian Renaissance structure with touches of late-Gothic. The facade is a series of fussy friezes depicting scenes from the Trojan War. Another victim of the war is adjacent to the Fürstenhof, the **Georgenkirche,** the cathedral of St. George. Today it's the biggest Gothic religious ruin in Europe.

Backtrack through the Marktplatz and along Krämerstrasse to reach the **Nikolaikirche,** a late-Gothic church with a 120-foot-high nave built from 1381 to 1487. A remnant of the town's long domination by Sweden is the additional altar built for Swedish sailors. Important architectural relics rescued from the bombed ruins of other Wismar churches are displayed here, notably the Gothic high altar from the Georgenkirche. Across the street the Dutch Renaissance **Schabbellhaus** houses a fascinating museum of local history. *Schweinsbrücke 8,* ☎ *03841/282–350.* ☛ *DM 2 adults, DM 1 children.* ⊘ *Tues., Wed., and Fri–Sun. 10–4:30, Thurs. 10–8.*

If you've got an hour to spare, wander among the jetties and quays of the port, a mix of the medieval and the modern. **To 'N Zägenkrog,** a seaman's haven decorated with shark's teeth, stuffed seagulls, and maritime gear is a picturesque pit stop along the harbor. *Ziegenmarkt 10,* ☎ *03841/282–716.*

From Wismar you can continue along Route 105 to Bad Doberan, 36 kilometers (23 miles) away. But if time permits, make a 32-kilometer detour south on the B–106 to **Schwerin,** the second-largest town in the region (Rostock is largest) and capital of the new state of Mecklenburg-Vorpommern. It's worth the side trip just to visit the giant **Schloss Schwerin** (Schwerin Palace) of the Mecklenburg royal family, located on an island on the edge of Lake Schwerin, close to the old town. The earliest palace on this site dates back to 1018. When Henry the Lion founded Schwerin in 1160 he ordered the enlargement of the existing castle. The castle you see today is a unique pastiche of historical styles, due to 800 years of fires, renovations, and additions. Surmounted by 15 turrets large and small, the palace is reminiscent of a French château, and, indeed, parts were modeled on Chambord in the Loire Valley. Its present-day neo-Renaissance aspect and many ducal staterooms date from between 1845 and1857. North of the main tower is the **Neue Lange Haus** (New Long House), built from 1553 to 1555. Surprisingly, the communist government restored and maintained the fantastic opulence of this rambling 80-room reminder of an absolutist monarchy, and used it in the 1960s and 1970s as a boarding school for the education of kindergarten teachers. Since the relocation of the regional capital to Schwerin, however, a fifth of the rooms are now used for regional government offices. Antique furniture, objets d'art, silk tapestries, and paintings are sprinkled throughout the salons (the Throne Room is particularly extravagant), but of special interest are the ornately patterned and highly burnished inlaid wooden floors and wall panels. The many tales of the good-spirited castle ghost, Petermännchen (Little Man Peter), who aids the poor and oppressed, will delight the entire family. The castle is surrounded by parkland laid out in the 18th century that contains many beautiful and rare species of trees. Sandstone replicas of the sculptures of Permoser adorn the tree-lined avenues. *Lenne*str. ☛ DM 6 adults, DM 3 children. Palace and gardens open June–Oct., Tues.–Sun. 10–6; Nov.–May, Tues.–Sun. 10–5.

TIME OUT   The King's Hall of the palace is today Schwerin's most picturesque coffee shop, **Schlosscafé,** which also makes its own ice cream. ☎

0385/525–2963. ☉ *Apr.–Oct., Tues.–Sun. 10–5:30; Nov.–Mar., 10–5:00.*

Schwerin's showpiece square, the **Alte Garten,** opposite the entrance to the palace island, was the scene of military parades during the years of communist rule. It is dominated by two buildings, the ornate neo-Renaissance state theater, 1883–86, and the Staatliche Galerie (☞ Free; open Tues.–Sun. 9–4), which houses an interesting collection of paintings by such 19th-century German artists as Max Liebermann and Lovis Corinth, plus an exhibition of Meissen porcelain. Another noteworthy sight in Schwerin's old town is the Gothic cathedral, or Dom, the oldest building (1222–48) in the city. The bronze baptismal font is from the 14th century; the altar was built in 1440. Religious scenes painted on the walls of the adjoining Marienkapelle (Chapel of Maria) date from the Middle Ages. Sweeping views of the old town and lake await those with the energy to climb the 219 steps to the top of the 320-foot-high cathedral tower. *Buschstr. Tower open Mon. 11–4, Tues.–Sat. 11–noon and 2:30–4:30, Sun. 2:30–4:30.*

The **Freilichtmuseum** (Open-air Museum) **Schwerin-Muess,** located 6 kilometers (4 miles) south of Schwerin, is a living-history museum representing traditional work and farm life in Germany. Children and history buffs will enjoy wandering through the 17 preserved buildings, which include a blacksmith's shop dating from 1736, a village school from the 19th century, a traditional fire station, a carriage house, and a barn. All buildings are precisely decorated with antiques of their era. You can watch demonstrations of the tools and traditional methods used to bake bread and work metal (*See also* What to See and Do with Children, *below*). ☎ *0385/213–011.* ☞ *DM 3 adults, DM 1.50 children.* ☉ *May–Oct., Tues.–Sun. 10–6.*

❺ Return to Wismar and pick up the B–105 again to **Bad Doberan,**
★ whose finely preserved redbrick **cloister church** is one of the finest of its kind in the region. It was built by Cistercian monks between 1294 and 1368 in the northern German Gothic style, with a central nave and transept. The main altar dates from the early 14th century and features a 45-foot-tall cross. Many of the monastic buildings have been preserved; the former corn granary has been turned into a youth center. *Klosterstr. 2,* ☎ *038203/2716.* ☞ *DM 2 adults, DM 1 children.* ☉ *May–Sept., Mon.–Sat. 9–6, Sun. noon–6; Mar., Apr., and Oct., Mon.–Sat. 9–4, Sun. noon–4; Nov.–Feb., Tues.–Fri. 9–noon and 2–4, Sat. 9–4, Sun. noon–4. Guided tours at 1, 2, and 3.*

No visit to this part of the world would be complete without a ride on
★ **Molli,** a quaint little steam train that has been chugging up and down
❻ a 10-mile-long narrow-gauge track between Bad Doberan and the nearby beach resorts of Heiligendamm and **Kühlungsborn** since 1886. The train was nicknamed after a little local dog of the same name that barked its approval every time the smoking iron horse passed by. At the start of the 40-minute journey the engine and its old wooden carriages make their way through the center of Bad Doberan's cobbled streets. *Molli* runs 13 times daily in both directions between Bad Doberan and Kühlungsborn. In the "Salonwagen" of the train you can have a cup of coffee while viewing the impressive Mecklenburg meadows and forests. ☞ *DM 8 adults, DM 4 children (there is an additional DM 3.60 if you have a bicycle). Schedule: May–Sept., 5:30 AM–8:30 PM; Oct.–Apr., 7 AM–7:45 PM.*

Horse-racing fans may be interested to know that the first race course in Europe outside Britain was established in Bad Doberan in 1822. Racing took place until the beginning of the 1950s. In 1993 the renovated track was reopened to initiate the annual international festival, **Rennwochenende** (Race Weekend), which features two days of racing during the last weekend of July.

7 From Bad Doberan, resume your journey east along the B–105 another 14 kilometers (9 miles) to **Rostock,** the biggest port and shipbuilding center of former East Germany. Founded around 1200, once-thriving Rostock suffered from the dissolution of the Hanseatic Pact in 1669, as the area was fought over and trade declined. While Hamburg, Kiel to the west, and Stettin to the east (now Poland) became leading port cities, Rostock languished until the late 1950s, when the newly formed German Democratic Republic found that it needed a sea outlet and reestablished Rostock as a major port. Since reunification, work at the port has been halved and, except for ferries coming in from Gedser (Denmark) and Trelleborg (Sweden), there is little scheduled traffic. However, there are plans to lure cruise ships and to develop the pleasure marina to attract sailing events. Even now the biggest local attraction is Hanse Sail, a week of yacht racing held in August. One of the best views of old Rostock is from the harbor (*see* Getting Around By Boat *in* The Baltic Coast Essentials, *below*).

The city suffered severe damage in the World War II bombings of the Heinkel (the Luftwaffe's bombers) and armaments factories, but much of the old town's core has been rebuilt, including large segments of the medieval town wall and the facades of the late-Gothic and Renaissance houses of the rich *Hanse* merchants. The finest examples are along the main street, the pedestrian-only **Kröpelinerstrasse,** which begins at the old western gate, the Kröpeliner Tor. About halfway down the street on your right stretches the triangular **Universitätsplatz,** commemorating the founding of Northern Europe's first university here in 1419. Rostock University's Italian Renaissance–style main building, finished in 1867, now stands on the site of the original construction. Follow Kröpelinerstrasse into the Neue Markt (town square). You'll immediately notice the architectural potpourri that is the **Rathaus** (Town Hall). Basically 13th-century Gothic with a Baroque facade, the building spouts seven slender, decorative towers, looking like candles on a peculiar birthday cake. The square is surrounded by historic gabled houses.

Head north on Langestrasse out of the square to reach the four-centuries-old **Marienkirche** (St. Mary's Church), the architectural prize of Rostock. The Gothic structure boasts a bronze baptismal font from 1290, and some interesting Baroque features, notably the oak altar (1720) and organ (1770). The unique attraction, however, is the huge astronomical clock dating from 1472; it has a calendar extending to the year 2017. At the rear of Marienkirche in Am Ziegenmarkt is Rostock's former mint, the **Münze.** The town started producing its own coins in 1361 and only relinquished this right in 1864. The Münze has a fine Renaissance arched entrance and a stone relief depicting coin makers going about their work.

Just beyond the city walls, through the Steintor, you'll come to the **Schiffahrtmuseum,** at August-Babel-Strasse 1, which traces the history of shipping on the Baltic and displays models of ships throughout the ages. ☎ 0381/492–2697. ☛ *DM 7 adults, DM 4 children Apr.–Oct., DM 5 adults, DM 3 children Nov.–Mar..* ☉ *Tues.–Sun. 9–5.*

If you have the time, you may want to visit a local curiosity. With the collapse of state communism, there were not enough buildings to house shops for the starved consumer to sort through goods brought in from the West. A ship was commandeered and moored alongside the riverbank at the Kabutzenhof, 100 yards from downtown, to become the **Port Centre**, a complex of stores, boutiques, bars, and restaurants.

8 The nearby town of **Warnemünde,** a 14-kilometer (9-mile) ride north on Route 103, is a quaint, seaside resort offering the best hotels and restaurants in the area as well as 20 kilometers of beautiful white beach. This former fishing village was annexed to Rostock in 1323 to secure safe entrance to the Hanseatic city's harbor. For years it has been a popular summer holiday destination for east German families— they're drawn by a 2-mile-long sandy beach and a giant heated salt-water pool with artificial waves as high as 4 feet, among other attractions. Children will also enjoy climbing to the top of the town landmark, a 115-foot-high **lighthouse** (1898) that on clear days offers views of the coast and Rostock Harbor. *Am Strom,* ☎ *0381/493–4963.* ☛ *DM 2 adults, DM 1 children.* ☷ *May–Sept., daily 10–6.*

Inland from the lighthouse is the area known as **Alter Strom,** once the entry into the port of Warnemünde and now the marina for yachts, bars, cozy restaurants, and specialty shops.

9 Return to Rostock and pick up Route 105, traveling east 30 kilometers (19 miles) to **Ribnitz-Damgarten.** The town is the center of the amber (in German, *Bernstein*) business, unique to the Baltic Coast. You can see a fascinating exhibition of how the precious "Baltic gold" is collected from the sea and refined to make jewelry and objets d'art in the **Bernsteinmuseum,** which adjoins the main factory. The museum has examples of amber dating back 35 to 50 million years. The biggest lump of raw amber ever harvested from the sea weighed more than 23 pounds. If it were ever cut, it could make 30 necklaces, but instead it is on exhibit in the Museum für Naturkunde in Berlin. *Im Kloster 1– 2,* ☎ *03821/2931.* ☛ *DM 4 adults, DM 1 children.* ☷ *May–Sept., daily 9:30–5; Apr. and Oct., Tues.–Sat. 9:30–4:30, Sun. 1–4:30; Nov.–Mar., Wed.–Sat. 10–4, Sun. 1–4.*

From Ribnitz, you can continue directly along Route 105 for 40 kilometers (25 miles) to the medieval port of Stralsund, the crossing point for Rügen Island, or take a circular back route (35 kilometers longer) by striking out for Wustrow on the coast and the narrow isthmus that leads to what the Germans call the half-island of **Darss.** This half-moon-shape finger of land consists of what were three separate islands that became one over centuries of shifting sand. Much of Darss has been a nature reserve since 1966, partly to protect the ancient forest of beech, holly, and juniper, but also because of its topographical uniqueness. The area contains many rare plants and provides shelter for a huge variety of sea birds. The peacefulness and seclusion of this preserve make its many paths ideal for biking and hiking. The island's best beach is "Weststrand" (west beach), a broad beach of fine white sand that is free of auto traffic and much development. Wind-sculptured trees border the beach, veterans of a long-standing battle with the forces of nature. Darss is also noted for its old fisherman's cottages with brightly painted doors and reed-thatched roofs. All new constructions are *required* to have thatched roofs in keeping with the traditional style of the island.

⑩ The village of **Ahrenshoop,** the site of an art colony that started in the late 19th century and brought together painters from across Germany and beyond, is especially picturesque,. After World War II Ahrenshoop became a mecca of sorts to artists, musicians, and writers of the GDR. Continue toward Prerow to get back to the mainland, but be sure to stop at the 17th-century seaman's church on the edge of town. The powerful simplicity of this rustic church and cemetery reflects the importance of religion in the local fishermens' lives.

★ **⑪** Follow signs to Barth to the causeway to get off the "island" and rejoin Route 105 to reach **Stralsund,** Germany's main producer of fishing boats. In 1815 the Congress of Vienna awarded the city, which had been under Swedish control, to the Prussians. Although it was rapidly industrialized, this jewel of the Baltic features a historic, rebuilt and restored city center.

Following an attack by the Lübeck fleet in 1249, a defensive wall was built around Stralsund, parts of which you'll see on your left as you come into the old town. The old market square, the **Alter Markt,** has the best local architecture, ranging from Gothic through Renaissance to Baroque. Most of the buildings were rich merchants' homes, notably the late-Gothic **Wulflamhaus,** with 17 ornate, steeply stepped gables. Stralsund's architectural masterpiece, however, is the 13th-century **Rathaus** (Town Hall), considered by many to be the finest secular example of redbrick Gothic in northern Germany. Note the coats of arms of the main towns that formed the exclusive membership of the Hanseatic League. The 13th-century Gothic **Nikolaikirche** (Church of St. Nicholas) also faces onto the square. Its treasures include a 15-foot-high crucifix from the 14th century, an astronomical clock from 1394, and a Baroque altar. Walk down the pedestrian street Ossenreyerstrasse for a glimpse of the grandiose beginnings of modern consumer culture at the turn-of-the-century department store at Ossenreyerstrasse 8–13, the site of the first in the famous Wertheim chain. Alas, fame is fleeting, and the building—with its magnificent glassed-in courtyard—is now part of the Horten chain of stores. Continue along Ossenreyerstrasse through the Apollonienmarkt to the Katherinenkloster, a former cloister, on Monchstrasse. Forty rooms of the cloister now house two museums; the famed **Meeresmuseum** with aquarium (*see* What to See and Do with Children, *below*) and the **Kulturhistorisches Museum,** exhibiting a diverse selection of artifacts from more than 10,000 years of this coastal region's history. Highlights include the toy collection and 10th-century Viking gold jewelry found on Hiddensee. ☛ *DM 4 adults, DM 1.50 children.* ☻ *Tues.–Sun. 10–5.*

Follow Monchstrasse to Neuer Markt and the monstrous **Marienkirche,** the largest of the three redbrick Gothic churches of Stralsund. With 4,000 pipes and intricate decorative figures, the magnificent 17th-century Stellwagen-Organ is a delight to see and hear (there are concerts regularly). The view of Stralsund's old city center, the surrounding coast, and Rügen Island from the church tower is well worth the 349 steps you must climb to reach the top.

★ Stralsund is also the departure point for the island of **Rügen** and its
⑫ administrative capital, **Bergen,** which is in the center of the island. (White Fleet boats will also take you from Stralsund to various towns on Rügen.) Rügen has been joined to the mainland since 1936 by a causeway that carries cars, trucks, and trains. The main road over the causeway from Stralsund (Route 96) cuts straight across the island southwest to northeast, a distance of 51 kilometers (32 miles). The route runs between the Grosser Jasmunder Bodden, a giant sea inlet, and a smaller expanse

⑬ of water—the Kleiner Jasmunder Bodden Lake—to the port of **Sassnitz,** where ferries run to Sweden. Travelers are best off at any of the island's four main vacation centers—Sassnitz, Binz, Sellin, and Göhren.

What Rügen lacks in architectural allure it makes up for in natural beauty. Its diverse and breathtaking landscapes have inspired poets and painters **⑭** for more than a century. From the chalk cliffs of the **Stubbenkammer** headland on the east coast of the island and the much photographed **Konigstuhl** rising 117 meters (351 feet) from the sea, through the blus- **⑮** tery sand dunes of **Kap Arkona** in the north, to the quiet waters and coves of the Grosser Jasmunder Bodden in the center, this is a nature lover's paradise. Kap Arkona's lighthouse marks the northernmost point in eastern Germany, and you can see the Danish island of Moen from a restored watchtower next door.

Rügen first became popular as a holiday destination with the development of the railways in the mid-19th century, and many of the grand mansions and villas on the island date from this period. Despite its continuing popularity during the communist years, little new development has taken place since the mid-1930s, leaving the entire island in a kind of time warp. For example, dances—all the rage in the 1920s and '30s—continue on Rügen with afternoon coffee dances at cafés and dinner dances at hotels. Near the city of Prora (between Binz and Sassnitz) stands another fascinating remnant of Germany's past, the ruins of an abandoned Nazi scheme to create the world's largest resort. Planned for 20,000 people, the construction was less than half-finished when it was pushed aside for more pressing matters. The East German army practiced within the complex's grounds.

A convenient place to plant yourself for a couple of days of small excursions is **Binz,** the location of the picturesque turn-of-the-century resort, Kurhaus. Take a ride on the 90-year-old miniature steam train, the Rasender Roland (Racing Roland), which runs 24½ kilometers (15 **⑯** miles) from **Putbus** to **Göhren,** at the southeast corner of the island. Trains leave hourly during the day, take 45 minutes one-way, and cost DM 10. For a splendid view in all directions, climb the cast-iron spiral staircase of the lookout tower of Jagdschloss Granitz, a hunting lodge built in 1836 by Karl Friedrich Schinkel. It stands on the highest point of East Rügen and has an excellent hunting exhibit. ☎ 038393/2263. ☛ *DM 5 adults, DM 2 children. ☉ Apr.–Oct., daily 9–6; Nov.–Mar., weekends only 10–5.*

From Sassnitz, walk into Jasmund National Park to stare in awe at the Königstuhl cliffs. Off the northwest corner of Rügen is a smaller is- ★ land, the **Hiddensee.** The undisturbed solitude of this sticklike island has attracted such vacationers as Albert Einstein, Thomas Mann, Rainer Maria Rilke, and Sigmund Freud. You will find no tennis courts, discos, ritzy tourist accommodations or even cars here. As Hiddensee is an auto-free zone, you must leave your car in Schaprode and take a ferry to this virtually undisturbed oasis whose inhabitants are fighting hard to retain its tranquility.

Retrace your route back through Rügen across the Stralsund causeway and head south along Route 96 for 32 kilometers (20 miles) to **⑰** **Greifswald,** the last in the string of Hanseatic ports on this tour. The town was a busy sea trading center in the Middle Ages but became a backwater during the 19th century, when larger ships couldn't negotiate the shallow Ryck River leading to the sea. Today's visitors have German army commander Colonel Rudolf Petershagen to thank for being able to see many of the town's original buildings. In charge of

Greifswald in early 1945, he surrendered the town to the approaching Soviet forces rather than see it destroyed. Ironically, lack of funds for restoration over the next 40 years left some historic buildings in desperate need of repair.

Stroll along Langestrasse to the Marktplatz, presided over by a medieval **Rathaus,** rebuilt in 1738–50 following a fire, modified during the 19th century and again in 1936. The square is surrounded by splendid old houses in redbrick Gothic styles. Three churches shape the silhouette of the city: the 13th-century **Dom St. Nikolai** (St. Nicholas's Cathedral) at the start of Martin-Luther-Strasse, a Gothic church from whose 300-foot-high tower one can get an impressive view; the 14th-century **Marienkirche** (St. Mary's Church), on the corner of Brüggstrasse and Friedrich-Loeffler-Strasse, the oldest surviving church in Greifswald and noted for its remarkable 60-foot-high arches and a striking four-corner tower; and the 13th-century **St. Jacob's,** later rebuilt to a three-nave design.

18 Just outside Greifswald, in what is now the suburb of **Eldena,** stand the ruins of a 12th-century Cistercian monastery made famous in a painting by Caspar David Friedrich (now at the Gallery of Romantic Painting in Berlin), who was born in Greifswald in 1774. The monastery, which led to the founding of Greifswald, was plundered by rampaging Swedish soldiers early in the Thirty Years' War and abandoned. The Gothic structure was further cannibalized by townsfolk over the next two centuries until it was made a protected national monument, a result of the publicity it gained from the celebrated Friedrich painting.

19 Still heading south, take Route 109, then Route 111 off to the left, for the quickest journey to **Wolgast** (34 kilometers, or 21 miles) and the causeway crossing to Germany's other main Baltic island, Usedom. Wolgast's chief attraction is the old town square, **Rathaus Platz,** where the pretty mid-17th-century half-timbered house known locally as the **Kaffeemühle** and a Baroque **town hall** are situated. The Kaffeemühle, far from serving coffee, is the local history museum (**Heimatmuseum**), which tells the life story of another locally born artist of the Romantic era—Philipp Otto Runge. The museum also has an exhibition detailing the development of Germany's V2 rocket during World War II, spearheaded by scientist Werner von Braun (who later developed the U.S. space program). ☎ *03836/203–041.* ☛ *DM 3 adults, DM 1.50 children.* ⊙ *May–Sept., Tues.–Fri. 9–5, weekends 9–noon; Oct.–Apr., Mon.–Thurs. 9–5, Sat. 9–noon.*

On the highest point of the old town sits the massive redbrick Gothic **St. Petri Kirche,** within whose walls one can view 24 paintings of the *Hohlbeinschen Totentanze* (Dance of Death).

20 On its seaboard side, 25-mile-long Usedom Island has almost 20 miles of sandy shoreline and a string of resorts. The best of them and the island's main town is **Ahlbeck,** which features an unusual 19th-century wooden pier with four towers. Ahlbeck's promenade is lined with turn-of-the-century villas, some of which are now small but as yet unsophisticated hotels. If you stroll along the beach to the right of Ahlbeck's pier you'll arrive at the Polish border—the easternmost corner of the island belongs to Poland. Just west of Ahlbeck is Heringsdorf, the oldest resort on the island and the place chosen by Russian playwright Maxim Gorky for a quiet sojourn in 1922. He stayed in the villa called Irmgard, now a protected monument. Much of the island is a nature preserve that provides refuge for a number of rare birds, including the giant sea eagle, which has a wingspan of up to 8 feet.

㉑ At the northern end of Usedom is **Peenemünde,** the launch site of the world's first jet rockets, the V1 and V2, developed by Germany toward the end of World War II and fired at London (*see* Wolgast, *above*). One can view these rockets as well as models of early airplanes and ships at the popular **Historischtechnisches Informationszentrum** in Peenemünde. A playground and a hands-on exhibit explaining alternative energy sources make this musuem especially good for children. There is also an exhibit about the concentration camps. ☎ *038371/20573.* ☛ *DM 6 adults, DM 4 children.* ☼ *Apr.–Oct., Tues.–Sun. 9–6; Nov.–Mar., Tues.–Sun. 10–4.*

If you are traveling by car you can leave the island by another causeway at the southwest corner, reached from the town of Usedom and emerging on the mainland at Anklam. From Anklam you can take Route 109 all the way to Berlin (162 kilometers, or 101 miles). If you are traveling on to Poland, follow Route 109 and turn left at Pasewalk into Route 104. From there it is 85 kilometers (53 miles) to the border and the Polish town of Szczecin, still called Stettin by the Germans.

What to See and Do with Children

The **Zoologischer Garten** at Rostock has one of the largest collections of exotic animals and birds in northern Germany. This zoo is particularly noted for its polar bears, some of which were bred in Rostock. *Tiergartenallee 10,* ☎ *0381/37111.* ☛ *DM 5 adults, DM 3 children.* ☼ *May–Sept., daily 10–6; Oct.–Apr., daily 10–4.*

In Stralsund, an **aquarium** of Baltic Sea life is part of the maritime museum **Meeresmuseum,** which also displays the skeleton of a giant whale, a hammerhead shark, and a 25-foot-high chunk of coral. *Katharinenberg 14–20,* ☎ *03831/295–135.* ☛ *DM 7 adults, DM 3.50 children.* ☼ *May.–Oct., daily 10–5; Nov.–Apr., Wed.–Sun. 10–5.*

Along the Warnow River 5 kilometers (3 miles) north of the center of Rostock, you'll find a **museum of shipbuilding** on board the old freighter *Frieden.* The museum is in the hold of the 10,000-ton ship, built in 1952, which also houses a youth hostel. The *Frieden* is moored to the riverbank on the right-hand side of the road. *Schiffbaumuseum. Schmarl 22, D–18106 Rostock,* ☎ *0381/716–246.* ☛ *DM 4 adults, DM 2 children.* ☼ *Tues.–Sun. 9–5.*

If the weather is too bad for outdoor swimming, children will be just as pleased to splash in the heated seawater pool at **Warnemünde.** *Meeresschwimhalle, on the Promenade next to Hotel Neptun,* ☎ *0381/777–865.* ☛ *DM 7 adults, DM 3.50 children.* ☼ *Mon. 1–8, Tues.–Fri. 10–8, Sat. 9–8, Sun. 8–8.*

A treat for children is the **Freilichtmuseums (Open-air Museums),** which provide a traditional German farm village experience, including schools, barns, and houses as well as demonstrations of crafts. The size and specialties of these museums vary, but they are worth visiting for a glimpse of the everyday German life of past centuries. The largest Freilichtmuseums in Mecklenburg-Vorpommen are in Schwerin-Muess and in Klockenhagen (on the road between Rostock and Stralsund, ☎ 03812/2775). Göhren, on Rügen Island, also has one of these experiential museums (Münchguter Museum, Strandstr. 18, D–18586 Göhren, ☎ 038308/2175). If you're venturing off the beaten path in the Mecklenburg countryside, watch for signs for Freilichtmuseums in Gross Raten (☎ 03847/2252), Woldegk (☎ 03963/333), and Tellow (☎ 039976/325).

The Baltic Coast offers two steam-powered vintage trains, the **Molli** in Bad Doberan and **Rosender Roland** in Göhren on Rügen Island (*see* Exploring, *above*). Both are guaranteed to entertain the children and provide an enjoyable tour of the beautiful Mecklenburg landscape.

The **Historischtechnisches Informationszentrum** (*see* Exploring, *above*) is a richly entertaining museum designed especially for children.

After a sea storm, head for a beach and join the locals in the perennial quest for amber stones washed up among the seaweed. Your children may also stumble upon a little pebble with a hole worn in the middle. Prevalent on this coast, they are called *Hühnergötter* (chicken gods) by the locals, who believe they bring good luck.

SHOPPING

The choice of goods, as well as the number of shops, has improved considerably in eastern Germany since 1989, but the retail industry is still very much in flux. However, antiques and bric-a-brac that have languished in cellars and attics since World War II are still surfacing, and the occasional bargain can be found. The best places to look are **Schwerin** (on and around Schmiedestrasse, Schlossstrasse and Mecklenburgstrasse) and **Rostock** (along Kröpeliner Strasse and Doberaner Platz). The Spring Markets held during April and May in **Stralsund** include a multitude of flea-market stalls. The Baltic Coast offers a few distinctive culinary and artistic specialties. Keep your eyes out for:

Bernstein (amber). These precious stones, formed from the sap of ancient conifers, are more than 35–50 million years old. You can buy amber jewelry, chess figures, and ornate jewelry boxes in the Bernsteinmuseum in **Ribnitz-Damgarten.** The jewelry, often designed with gold and silver, ranges in cost from DM 100 to DM 1,000. Fossils are often embedded in the stone—a precious find. (Hint: Only true amber floats in a glass of water stirred with 2 teaspoons of salt.)

Buddelschiffe (ships in a bottle). A symbol of the once-magnificent sailing history of this region. It looks as if building them would be easy, but it isn't, and they are quite delicate. Prices go upward of DM 120 for a small 1-liter bottle.

Echter Rostocker Doppel-Kümmel und -Korn. This Schnapps, made from various grains, is a traditional liquor of the region around Rostock. Fishermen have numbed themselves to the cold for centuries with this 40% alcoholic beverage; a 7-liter bottle costs DM 18 .

Replicas of the **Hiddensee Golden jewelry.** At the end of the 19th-century 16 pieces of 10th-century Viking jewelry were discovered (presently housed in the Kulturhistorisches Museum in Stralsund). Gold and silver replicas of their distinctive patterns are found in shops in Stralsund, on Rügen Island, and on Hiddensee Island.

Fischerteppiche (Fisherman's carpets). One square meter of these traditional carpets takes 150 hours to create, which explains why they're meant to be hung on the wall, not laid on the floor, and why they cost from DM 500 to DM 2,000. They're decorated with traditional symbols of the region, such as the griffin, pine trees, eels, sea roses, and thistles.

SPORTS AND FITNESS

Biking

The coastal region is ideal for cycling (read: flat), a fact that numerous entrepreneurs have been quick to note. Most large hotels provide bicycles for guests, and many shops rent bikes on a daily or weekly basis at modest rates. More and more train stations in this region also rent bicycles. Escorted tours are being organized by the tourist offices; contact the regional tourist office in **Rostock** for more information.

Camping

There are 150 campsites scattered along the coast. Contact the local tourist offices for a list of locations and facilities offered.

Fishing

Fishing is another rapidly expanding leisure industry. Every port along the coast now has small boats for hire, and some boatmen will lead you to the shoals. There's freshwater angling in season in the rivers and in **Schweriner See** (Lake Schwerin), but equipment may sometimes be in short supply. For information on equipment availability, contact the Rostock tourist office (☎ 0381/459−0860) for Warnemünde Harbor and the Schwerin tourist office (☎ 0385/864−509) for the Schweriner See.

Water Sports

As private enterprise revives, a wide range of water-based activities is becoming available: windsurfing, sailing, surfing (although, to be truthful, the waves here are modest), and pedal-boat riding. Equipment is available for hire at the beach resorts. If you have difficulty locating what you want, contact the local tourist offices. The best-protected area along the coast for sailing is **Grosser Jasmunder Bodden,** a huge bay on Rügen Island. Boats for the bay can be hired at **Lietzow** and **Ralswiek. Warnemünde** has an international sailing regatta in July.

Beaches

Good beaches exist all along the Baltic coast. Virtually all the sandy beaches are clean and safe, sloping gently into the water. At the height of the season (July–August), the seaside resort beaches with food services and toilets are packed. Water temperature in August rarely exceeds 20° C (65° F). The busiest are at **Bansin** (Usedom Island), **Binz** (Rügen Island), **Ostseebad Kühlungsborn,** and **Warnemünde.** More remote and quieter beaches can be found at **Timmendorf** on **Poel Island,** where the water quality is particularly good (you can drive there from Wismar or take a White Fleet boat); **Kap Arkona** (reachable on foot only); and **Hiddensee Island,** off Rügen. The prettiest coves and beaches are located at **Ahrenshoop Weststrand** on the Darss Peninsula, **Nienhagen** (near Warnemünde), and the **Grosser Jasmunder Bodden** on Rügen Island to the west of Lietzow.

Some beaches allow nude bathing; in German it's known as *Freikörperkultur* (literally, "free body culture"), FKK for short. The most popular of these bare-all beaches are at Nienhagen and Prerow (on Darss).

DINING AND LODGING

Dining

Among the local specialties to look for are *Mecklenburger Grieben-roller,* a custardy casserole of grated potatoes, eggs, herbs, and chopped bacon; *Mecklenburger Fischsuppe,* a hearty fish soup with vegetables, tomatoes, and sour cream; *Gefüllte Ente* or *Gefüllte Schweinebraten Mecklenburger Art,* baked duck or pork stuffed with breadcrumbs, apples, prunes, and raisins; and *Pannfisch,* the region's own fish patty. A delicacy that originated during the time of Sweden's influence is *Grützwurst,* an oatmeal-based liver sausage sweetened with raisins. A favorite local nightcap since the 17th century is *Eierbier* (egg beer), a concoction of egg whites, beer, ginger, cinnamon, sugar, and water stirred vigorously and served warm. It's said to soothe the stomach, and it's guaranteed to give you a sound night's sleep. In general, you will find that the menus offer fare similar to dishes served in western Germany, though you will likely find the food more simply prepared.

CATEGORY	COST*
$$$$	over DM 50
$$$	DM 40–50
$$	DM 25–40
$	under DM 25

per person for a three-course meal, excluding drinks

Lodging

Expect to pay inflated prices at recently constructed, fully equipped large hotels and the renovated high rises dating from the former regime. Because much of the new entrepreneurial spirit of the east has been directed toward the tourism industry, a potentially major player in reviving this region's sagging economy, many local, privately owned small hotels and pensions have opened up. As a rule, the staffs of these new establishments provide personalized and enthusiastic service. However, there is no industry standard just yet, so booking a pension through a tourist office amounts to picking blindly from a grab bag. Make your needs clear to the tourist office. In high season all accommodations, especially along the coast, are in great demand. If you can't book well in advance, throw yourself at the mercy of the local tourist office; it will probably be able to find you simple, inexpensive bed-and-breakfast accommodations in a private home.

CATEGORY	COST*
$$$$	over DM 250
$$$	DM 175–250
$$	DM 125–175
$	under DM 125

All prices are for a standard double room, including tax and service charge.

Bad Doberan

DINING

★ **Weisser Pavilion.** A Chinese pagodalike structure built during the 19th century in an English-style park is an exotic setting for lunch or high tea (in summer the café closes at 10 PM). But it's regional specialties that are featured here. ✕ *Am Kamp,* ☎ *038203/2326. Reservations advised. No credit cards.* $$

LODGING

★ **Romantik-Kurhotel.** Built in 1793 for a Mecklenburg duke, this historic whitewashed member of the Romantik Hotel group has been accommodating visitors for more than 200 years. Completely restored and renovated, each room exudes Old World elegance with modern comforts. The individual touches of manager Dr. Horst Metz and the friendly staff provide pleasant, personalized service in a regal setting. *Am Kamp. D–18209 Bad Doberan, ☎ 038203/3036,* FAX *038203/2126. 59 rooms, all with shower. Restaurant, café, sauna. AE, DC, MC, V. $$$–$$$$*

Greifswald

DINING

★ **Alter Speicher.** Its broad selection of delectable grilled items and its wine list have brought this comfortable steak house regional renown. To warm up your taste buds for the grilled treats, try the Kleines Ragout Fin baked with Parmesan. And to round out your meal, try one of the many tasty dessert selections. The restaurant is conveniently located on the edge of the old city center. ✗ *Rossmühlenstr. 25, ☎ 03834/2974. Reservations necessary. AE, MC. $–$$*

LODGING

Europa Hotel Greifswald. The hotel's brochure boasts of its "courage to use color," and its decoration does uniquely stand out from the standard pastel southwestern-style palette and patterns common in newly constructed hotels of this region—curtains, bedcovers, and lamp shades covered in bold stripes and flowers. Perhaps so that you will forgive the garishly bright rooms, the hotel offers modern amenities, a convenient location, a helpful staff, and an excellent restaurant. *Hans-Beimlerstr. 1–3, D–17491 Greifswald, ☎ 03834/8010,* FAX *03834/801–100. 51 rooms, all with bath. Restaurant, bar, no-smoking rooms, sauna, exercise room. AE, DC, MC, V. $$$*

Boddenhus. The exterior of this nondescript apartment-block-style building constructed in 1976 does nothing to belie what's inside: rooms with drab furnishings and plain carpets and walls. The hotel's facilities, however, are generally excellent, from the tennis courts to the sauna bar. *Karl-Liebknecht-Ring 1, D–17491 Greifswald, ☎ 03834/77241,* FAX *03834/3105. 91 rooms, most with bath, and 9 suites, all with bath. Restaurant, 2 bars, café, sauna, tennis courts. AE, DC, MC, V. $$*

★ **Hotel Maria.** Though not exactly luxurious, the facilities at this recently built hotel are clean and modern. And the friendly service is what you'd hope for from such a small, family-owned place. The hotel is right on the harbor, just a short walk from the Wiecker drawbridge; its terrace is the perfect place to linger over a drink while watching the panorama of summer sailboats. *Dorfstr. 45, D–17493 Greifswald, ☎ 03834/841–426,* FAX *03834/840–136. 10 rooms, all with bath. Restaurant. MC. $*

Kühlungsborn

DINING AND LODGING

★ **Arendsee.** The tasteful design of this new low-rise hotel blends nicely with the adjoining turn-of-the-century villas. Rooms are exceptionally well decorated in pastel colors and furnished with light, patterned easy chairs, and come with TV and minibar. Managed by the Travel Charme Hotels group, the Arendsee caters to families with young children, especially those who need connecting rooms or extra beds. The restaurant, the best in town, offers a mix of regional and international dishes. *Strasse des Friedens 30, D–18225 Kühlungsborn,*

☎ 038293/70300, ℻ 038293/70400. *60 rooms, 6 suites, all with bath. Restaurant, sauna. AE, DC, MC, V. $$–$$$*

Lübeck

DINING

★ **Wullenwever.** Culinary experts say this restaurant has set a new standard of dining sophistication for Lübeck. It is certainly one of the most attractive establishments in the town, with dark furniture, chandeliers, and oil paintings on pale pastel walls. In summer tables are set in a quiet flower-strewn courtyard. Try the homemade pasta in truffle cream, or baked pigeon with chanterelle mushrooms. ✗ *Beckergrube 71,* ☎ *0451/704–333. Reservations necessary. Jacket and tie. AE, DC, V. Closed Sun. and Mon. $$$–$$$$*

★ **Schiffergesellschaft.** Not a scent of a woman was allowed in Schiffergesellschaft from when it opened in 1535 until 1870. Today men and women alike sit in church-style pews at long 400-year-old oak tables. You'll note that at each end of the pew is a sculpted heraldic arms of a city. Ship owners had their set routes (between Lübeck and Bremen, for example), and they each had their own pew and table. A good way to begin your meal is with the *Krebs Suppe* (crab soup) made from things best not known but that will cure all ills; follow this with the *Kapitanschussel,* a kind of goulash consisting of three different meats. For dessert, try perhaps the regional specialty *Rote Grutze,* made from red berries and topped with a vanilla sauce. Dinner may be washed down with Rotspon, Lübeck's locally bottled French red wine. Make reservations for the Historiche Halle (sometimes referred to as the Langenhaus) rather than for the other rooms. ✗ *Breite Str. 2,* ☎ *0451/76776. Reservations advised. No credit cards. $$–$$$*

DINING AND LODGING

Mövenpick Hotel Lysia. The location of this ultramodern member of the Swiss-owned chain is perfect—a two-minute walk from the famous Holsten Gate and the old town, and five minutes from the main train station. If you fancy an Old World atmosphere, however, the Mövenpick is not for you. Rattan furniture, lots of brass details, and vividly colored contemporary paintings create a bright, breezy look throughout, although the built-in furniture in the guest rooms smacks of motel decor. The menu in the sprawling, too brightly lit restaurant is daunting in its variety—from such Swiss specialties as *Rösti* to venison with lingonberries and other local seasonal fare—and the chef succeeds beyond all expectations. Save room for the dizzying array of gooey ice-cream concoctions. 🏠 *Beim Holstentor, D–23554 Lübeck,* ☎ *0451/15040,* ℻ *0451/150–4111. 197 rooms, all with bath. Restaurant, bar, no-smoking rooms, room service, car rental. AE, DC, MC, V. $$$$*

★ **Jensen.** Only a stone's throw from the Holstentor and within the inner city, this long-established hotel is ideally situated for viewing all the main attractions and faces the "moat" that surrounds the old town. It's family-run and very comfortable, with modern, renovated rooms. Though not large, the rooms are big enough for adjacent twin beds and a coffee table, and come with either a shower or a bath. The popular Yachtzimmer restaurant, with exposed stone walls and an open kitchen, offers a mix of regional and international dishes. 🏠 *An der Obertrave 4, D–23552 Lübeck,* ☎ *0451/71646,* ℻ *0451/73386. 42 rooms, 2 suites, all with bath. Restaurant. AE, DC, MC, V. $$$*

LODGING

Kaiserhof. The most comfortable hotel in Lübeck consists of two early 19th-century merchant's houses linked together, tastefully renovated and retaining many of the original architectural features. It's just outside the moated old-town center—a five-minute walk from the cathedral. Although the hotel lacks a full restaurant, a marvelous breakfast (included in the room cost) is served, and there's also a cozy bar. Bedrooms vary, but all have a restful, homey ambience, and the quietest of them overlook the garden at the back. The indoor swimming pool is not only large but has sections that are similar to a whirlpool, making it quite relaxing. This family-owned and -managed hotel has yet to be computerized; guests are remembered by face and name. ⊡ *Kronsforder Allee 11–13, D–23560 Lübeck,* ☎ *0451/791–011,* ℻ *0451/795–083. 65 rooms, 6 suites, all with bath. Bar, indoor pool, sauna, exercise room. AE, DC, MC, V. $$$*

Am Strand. This small yellow hotel has been a private vacation home since its construction in the 1920s. Its guests get modest, modern comfort right on the beach promenade. ⊡ *Strasse des Friedens 16, D–18225 Lübeck,* ☎ *038293/6611. 18 rooms, all with bath. Restaurant, sauna. DC, MC, V. $$*

Altstadt. Behind the landmark old facade stands a hotel that opened in 1984. The Altstadt offers modern but not luxurious comforts. The studios, fitted with small kitchens, are a particularly good value if you plan to stay for a few days. There is no restaurant, but breakfast (included in the price) is served in the hotel. ⊡ *Fischergrube 52, D–23552 Lübeck,* ☎ *0451/72083,* ℻ *0451/73778. 20 rooms and 9 studios, some with bath. No credit cards. $*

Rostock

DINING

★ **Zur Kogge.** Looking like the cabin of some ancient sailing vessel, this old sailors' beer tavern serves mostly fish. Order the Mecklenburger Fischsuppe if it's on the menu; *Räucherfisch* (smoked fish) is also a popular choice. Starting at 8 PM, Tuesday–Saturday, live music further adds to the restaurant's authentic maritime atmosphere. ✕ *Wokrenterstr. 27,* ☎ *0381/493–4493. Reservations essential in evening. AE, DC, MC, V. $*

LODGING

Warnow. This eight-story high rise was recently treated to a badly needed renovation. Light-color, modern furnishings have replaced most of the previous clumsy mixture of styles so characteristic of vacation spots in the former East Germany. It is only a block from the Kröpeliner Gate; rooms are relatively small. Warning: More than half the rooms are singles. ⊡ *Langestr. 40, D–18055 Rostock,* ☎ *0381/45970,* ℻ *0381/459–7800. 338 rooms, 7 suites, all with bath. ∫ Restaurant, bar, beer garden, no-smoking floor, room service. AE, DC, MC, V. $$$–$$$$*

Rügen Island

DINING

Bachskiste. In business since a few months before the reunification, this restaurant serves fresh Baltic fish in an appropriately maritime atmosphere. The Fischeteller (fish plate) provides a hearty sampling of the regional fishes, garnished with potatoes or rice and veggies in a whipped wine sauce (DM 23.80). Sit on the sunny terrace overlooking the forest and enjoy the *Sekt Sorbet,* a delectable whipped mix of ice cream, champagne, and real cream. There's live music and dancing every Friday and Saturday April–October starting at 7 PM. ✕ *Waldstr. 4,* ☎ *038303/767. Reservations advised. No credit cards. $–$$*

DINING AND LODGING

★ **Cliff-Hotel Rügen.** This high-rise resort hotel complex for families and convention delegates was built in 1978 as a retreat for members of the Central Committee of the Socialist Unity party. Erich Honecker stayed here. In 1990 it became the foremost resort on the island. The rooms have been renovated in warm, if nondescript, tones of tan, but they have lots of light and views of the Baltic. There are enough distractions at this all-in-one seaside resort in Sellin to keep everyone entertained, including a 25-meter swimming pool, a bowling alley, and a small wine bar and café. At the enormous Seeterrassen dining room, meals are substantial rather than tasty. ☎ *Siedling am Wald, D–18586 Sellin–Rügen,* ☎ *038303/80,* FAX *038303/8490. 241 rooms, 6 suites, all with bath. 2 restaurants, bar, no-smoking rooms, room-service, indoor pool, beauty salon, sauna, tennis court, bowling. AE, DC, MC, V. $$$–$$$$*

★ **Nordperd.** Built in 1990, with an addition in 1994, this four-story hotel is one of the better-equipped accommodations on the island—all rooms have a TV, phone, minibar, and safe. The decor is white and bright, with cheerful patterned upholstery and curtains, though space is at a premium. Some rooms have coastal views, thanks to the hotel's location on a hill at the southeast tip of the island at the seaside resort village of Göhren. At the restaurant, which serves regional dishes, look for *Rügenwild,* a pot roast made with game. ☎ *Nordperdstr. 11, D–18586 Göhren-Rügen,* ☎ *038308/70,* FAX *038308/7160. 70 rooms, all with bath. Restaurant, bar, beer garden, sauna. AE, DC, MC, V. $$$*

★ **IFA-Ferienpark.** Perhaps the best value on the island, IFA offers reasonable prices and modern facilities, all on the beach promenade in Binz, Rügen's summer hot spot. IFA is composed of three vacation towers of the former GDR, into which 10 million marks has been invested. The resulting buildings are monochromatic—even ugly—but don't let that detract from the superb service and wide range of facilities. This hotel is extremely child-friendly; children stay at no extra cost and there is a large entertainment center called the Vitarium, with miniature golf, billiards, air hockey, and battery-operated minicars. ☎ *Strandpromenade 74, D–18609 Binz,* ☎ *038393/91101,* FAX *038393/92030. 148 rooms and 233 apartments, all with bath. 3 restaurants, bar, beauty salon, massage, sauna, exercise center, bicycles, laundry facilities, entertainment center. AE, MC, V. $$*

Rügen-Hotel Sassnitz. Many of the rooms here provide views of the busy little port of Sassnitz, where ferries to Sweden (Trelleborg) operate. Except for the coastal views, you'll find at best utilitarian comfort and an impersonal, efficient manner within these nine stories. ☎ *Seestr. 1, D–18546 Sassnitz,* ☎ *038392/32090,* FAX *038392/32175. 115 rooms, 2 suites, all with bath. Restaurant, 2 bars, café, room service. $–$$*

★ **Hotel Godewind.** Two hundred meters from the beaches of Hiddensee that have so inspired writers, this small hotel offers solid food and lodging at very reasonable prices. The apartments are a good value if you intend to stay for more than a few days. Godewind's restaurant is known on the island for its traditional regional dishes. ☎ *Süderende 53, D–18565 Vitte–Hiddensee,* ☎ *038300/235,* FAX *038300/50161. 25 rooms, most with bath. Restaurant, bar, bicycles. No credit cards. $*

Schwerin

DINING

★ **Weinhaus Uhle.** One of the most traditional and popular eating places in Schwerin, this restaurant is named after the wine merchant who opened the restaurant back in 1741. You can dine on regional specialties and international mixed grills served in a colorful, unspoiled setting, accompanied by a small band that plays nightly. ✕ *Schusterstr. 13–15,* ☎ *0385/562–956. Reservations advised. AE, MC, V. $$$*

★ **Zum Goldenen Reiter.** The classic elegance of this restaurant provides a sharp contrast to the current crop of glossy restaurant chains and mossy, old taverns. The dark-wood, candlelit rooms generate a sophisticated yet comfortable atmosphere. Head Chef Ulrich Armster serves a tender breast of duck stuffed with apples and red cabbage, a recipe lifted from an 1896 cookbook of regional specialties. For a local dessert try the Mecklenburger Semmelpudding with warm fruit and cream. ✕ *Puschkinstr. 44,* ☎ *and fax 0385/565–036. Reservations advised. AE, DC, MC, V. $$–$$$*

Ritterstube. Pleasant service and solid regional specialties characterize this remnant of the GDR era. Note the hints of "hip" mid-1970s decor in this otherwise rustic setting. House specialties include *gefüllter Nackenbraten,* green cabbage soup, and a local favorite, *Rumpsteak Mecklenburger Art,* prepared with raisins and horseradish. ✕ *Ritterstr. 3,* ☎ *0385/565–240. Reservations advised May–Sept. MC. Closed Mon. $$*

LODGING

★ **Hotel Plaza Schwerin.** This notable addition to the Best Western brigade offers first-rate service despite its aesthetically unpleasing location; it's nestled in a landscape of desolate 1950s block apartments. Designed for business types, the prices are exorbitant on weekdays, but the hotel cuts rates in half for most rooms on the weekends. ▦ *Am Grünen Tal/Hamburger Allee, D–19063 Schwerin,* ☎ *0385/34820. fax 0385/341–053. 78 rooms and 1 suite, all with bath. Restaurant, piano bar, room service, no-smoking floor, sauna. AE, DC, MC, V. $$$$*

Niederländischer Hof. The facilities at this small, comfortable, established hotel in the center of the old town are above average for the Baltic Coast. The restaurant specializes in Mecklenburg dishes. ▦ *Karl-Marx-Str. 12, D–19055 Schwerin,* ☎ *0385/555–211,* FAX *0385/550–7482. 28 rooms, half with bath. Restaurant, bar. MC. $–$$*

Strand Hotel. Built in 1910, this perfect summer getaway spot is one of the few remaining luxury resorts of communist times. It's a four-story bright-yellow hotel with bright-blue awnings on the shore of Lake Schwerin. A walk along the beach and through the Baroque palace gardens leads directly to the castle and old town. Boxy minibathrooms haphazardly added to many rooms during renovations detract from the otherwise clean, refreshing atmosphere. But at these prices—and breakfast is included—it's a steal! Book at least a month in advance, and request a lakeside room with a balcony. ▦ *Am Strand 13, D–19063 Schwerin-Zippendorf,* ☎ *0385/213–053,* FAX *0385/321–174. 26 rooms, all with bath. Restaurant, bar, café. AE, MC, V. $*

Stralsund

DINING

★ **Scheelehaus.** A high, beamed ceiling and half-timbered walls of red-brick give this centuries-old restaurant the air of a baronial hall. The 10-foot-high windows still have the original thick, bull's-eye panes. Specialties of this acclaimed restaurant include *Stralsunder Fischsuppe,* one of the best local versions of the regional dish, Gefüllte Schweinebraten, and *Kartoffelbällchen*—potato balls filled with an almond, apple, and cinnamon mixture. ✕ *Fährstr. 23,* ☎ *03831/292–987. Reservations advised. AE, MC, V. Closed Sun. and Mon. in Jan. and Feb. $$*

★ **Wulflamstuben.** The atmosphere of this relatively new restaurant perfectly suits its historic location on the ground floor of *Wulflamhaus,* a 14th-century gabled house on the old market square. Copper-plate engravings and ornate woodwork on the walls provide a regal yet pleasant setting. Steaks and fish are the specialty of the house; if you plan to visit in late spring or early summer, get the light and tasty *Maischolle* (May fish) fresh from the North Sea. The roasted duck stuffed with apples, black bread, and plums served in sweet sauce melts in your mouth. ✕ *Alter Markt 5,* ☎ *03831/291–533. Reservations necessary. AE, DC, MC, V. $$*

★ **Zur Kogge.** This dark-wood tavern has been serving sailors since 1926 and is renowned for its tasty, traditional, and atmospheric meals. House specialties include the vegetable *Hochzeit Suppe* (Wedding Soup), *Rügener Labskaus,* a fisherman's stew garnished with red beets, scrambled egg, and Matjes herring, or the *Stralsunder Fischplatte,* a sampling of fresh fish served with rice spiced with a celery-seed sauce. A reconstructed beer tavern downstairs from the restaurant has dancing on Friday and Saturday nights. ✕ *Tribseerstr. 26,* ☎ *03831/293–846,* ℻ *03831/297–686. Reservations advised. AE, MC, V. $–$$*

LODGING

★ **Hotel An den Bleichen Garni.** When friends from out of town need a place to stay, this small family-run hotel is what the locals recommend. It has tastefully decorated rooms, personalized service, and a full breakfast buffet, all at a reasonable price. Moreover, though it was built in 1993, it has a homey feel. The hotel is a 10-minute walk from the harbor and old town center. ☎ *An den Bleichen 45, D–18435 Stralsund,* ☎ *03831/390–675,* ℻ *03831/392–153. 23 rooms, all with shower. AE, MC, V. $$*

Norddeutscher Hof. It's in the old section of the city across from the St. Marien Church, but don't let the weathered facade fool you; the hotel was completely renovated a few years ago. Unfortunately, the lobby and restaurant were not as simply and tastefully redecorated as the guest rooms. Still, you get the basics at a fair price. ☎ *Neuer Markt 22, D–18439 Stralsund,* ☎ *and fax 03831/293–161. 13 rooms, all with bath. AE, DC, MC, V. $$*

Usedom Island

DINING

★ **Seebrücke.** Perched on pilings over the Baltic, the "Sea Bridge" is the historic center of Ahlbeck. The emphasis is on seafood but the menu has other choices, from *Königsberger Klops* (spicy meatballs in a thick creamy sauce) to a tender fillet of lamb. If you don't want a full meal, stop in to enjoy the building and the view over coffee and a piece of one of the delectable cakes. ✕ *Dünenstr,* ☎ *03878/8320. Reservations recommended for dinner. AE, MC, V.* ☉ *May–Sept. only. $$–$$$*

★ **Cafe Asgard.** A visit here is a step back into the 1920s, which is when this restaurant with dancing first opened its doors. You'll dine amid silk wallpaper, potted plants, crisp white napery, and fresh flowers. The specialty is *Feuertopf Göttergarten,* a spicy fondue. The Asgard is open all day, so if you stop by between meal times, settle for a homemade pastry. If you're in a foot-tapping mood, visit the Golden Twenties dance hall above the restaurant. ✕ *Strandpromenade 13, Bansin,* ☎ *038378/29488. Reservations advised. No credit cards. $$*

DINING AND LODGING

★ **Ostseehotel.** Generations of vacationing families have stayed at this snug, if slightly dated, hotel in a 19th-century villa on Ahlbeck's promenade. Rooms are airy but spartan, and most have sea views. The restaurant serves mainly hearty local pork-and-potato dishes, but the goulash soup is exceptional; also look for fresh pike-perch in season. Dances are held several times a week during the summer. ⚂ *Kurstr., D–17419 Ahlbeck,* ☎ *038378/600,* FAX *03378/60100. 42 rooms. Bar, bicycles. No credit cards. Closed Sept.–Feb. $$*

Hotel Stadt Berlin. This turn-of-the-century villa turned hotel in Heringsdorf has been accommodating summer visitors since the 1920s. Its facilities are rather well-worn and some of the furnishings threadbare and dated, but there is a friendly holiday atmosphere. The bright little restaurant serves solid but predictable local fare. During the summer there are, naturally, lively dances several times a week. ⚂ *Büllowstr. 15, D–17424 Heringsdorf,* ☎ *03878/22304,* FAX *03878/22648. 26 rooms, 1 suite, all with shower. 3 restaurants. No credit cards. $*

Warnemünde

DINING

Fischerklause. Sailors have stopped in at this restaurant's bar since the turn of the century, but it's not *that* kind of place. Locals come here, too, although they tend to go farther inside to the dining room, where they dig into some of the wide variety of seafood dishes: The smoked fish sampler served on a steering-wheel-shape lazy Susan is delicious, but the house specialty is the fish soup—best washed down with some Rostocker Kümmel Schnapps. An accordionist entertains the crowd on Friday and Saturday evenings. ✕ *Am Strom 123,* ☎ *0381/52516. Reservations necessary. AE, MC, V. $$*

Cafe 28. This candlelit bistro exudes a bohemian air, from the local artwork exhibited on its walls and the soft acoustic music playing in the background to its light, tasty, and very reasonably priced salads and pastas. It's also a fine place to stop in for a cappuccino and drink in the romantic, youthful, artsy atmosphere. ✕ *Mühlenstr. 28,* ☎ *0381/52467. No credit cards. $*

LODGING

★ **Neptun.** One of the few postwar hotels on the coast, the 19-story concrete-and-glass Neptun is an eyesore on the outside, but inside it has the redeeming qualities of a luxury hotel. Every one of the neat and tastefully decorated rooms has a sea view. ⚂ *Seestr. 19, D–18119 Warnemünde,* ☎ *0381/7770,* FAX *0381/54023. 338 rooms, 4 suites, all with bath. 3 restaurants, 2 bars, café, ice-cream stand, outdoor and indoor pools, beauty salon, sauna, spa, dance club. AE, DC, MC, V. $$$$*

Hansa Hotel. Despite its seaside location, this 1950s hotel seems a tad overpriced; it just doesn't deliver the level of luxury you'd expect. Still, it is a pleasant enough place. Many of the rooms look out to the Baltic Sea, and the dining room where the complimentary breakfast is served has a panoramic view of the beach. There is a fully staffed children's playroom, and in summer barbecues are held on the terrace. ⚂ *Parkstr. 51, D–18119 Warnemünde,* ☎ *0381/5450,* FAX *0381/545–3006. 70 rooms, 4 suites, all with bath. Bar, brasserie, no-smoking rooms. AE, DC, MC, V. $$$*

Hotel Germania. Set at the harbor entrance and only one block from the beach, the Alter Strom promenade, and some of the best restaurants in town, this small hotel's location alone makes it a good choice, and then there are the rooms; newly renovated, they are tastefully decorated in pleasing pale-blue tones and mahogany furnishings, and equipped with TV and minibar. With so many good eateries nearby you probably won't miss having a hotel restaurant, but sybarites may object to the lack of an on-site spa, sauna, pool, or fitness room. ⚂ *Am Strom 110–111, D–18119 Warnemünde,* ☎ *0381/519–850,* FAX *0381/519–8510. 18 rooms, all with shower. $$–$$$*

Stolteraa. A prime vacation spot of the former GDR, this hotel has undergone a partial modernization (new beds, TV, and minibar, and television are standard in all rooms), yet in many ways it still remains a museum of GDR-era tacky decor, from the light fixtures to the vintage 1970s wood-grain paneling. So it's the relatively low price for beachfront accommodations that makes it worth a look—as long as you remember that you get what you pay for. Here you get the beach, and seaside rooms or rooms with balconies do have stunning views; smaller rooms without views are much cheaper but also tend to be cramped and charmless. ⌕ *Strandweg 17, D–18119 Warnemünde,* ☎ *0381/54320,* FAX *0381/543–2151. 37 rooms, half with private bath. Restaurant, bar, sauna. AE, DC, MC, V. $–$$*

Wismar

DINING

★ **Alte Schwede.** Regarded as one of the most attractive, authentic taverns on the Baltic—and correspondingly busy—this eatery has a cooking staff intent on reviving Mecklenburg's traditional cuisine, which features both game and fish dishes. ✗ *Am Markt 20,* ☎ *03841/283–552. Reservations advised for dinner. AE, MC, V. $$*

Kartoffel Haus. Potato lovers come here for the potato pizza, potato crepes, potato schnapps, and the dozens more dishes and delicacies made from the humble tuber that is this restaurant's specialty and namesake (the name translates to "Potato House"). You'd never guess from the menu's unique theme and the mixed-and-matched decor that this is one link in a Germany-wide chain; this fact does explain the very reasonable prices, however. In addition to serving all things potato, Kartoffel Haus also offers a good selection of steaks. ✗ *Frische Grube 31,* ☎ *03841/200–030. Reservations advised. AE, MC. $*

Seehase. This small, no-frills fish restaurant is favored by locals as well as visitors. Ask for the rich fish-and-sour-cream soup, *Fischsoljanka.* ✗ *Altböterstr. 6,* ☎ *03841/282–134. Reservations advised. No credit cards. $*

LODGING

★ **Hotel Stadt Hamburg.** Why is this tasteful, first-class hotel, opened in 1993, less expensive than its equally luxurious neighbors? Because use of several of the facilities (i.e., health club, parking) costs extra here, so you pay only for what you actually use. Behind the hotel's historical facade is a modern, open, airy interior, with skylights and a posh lobby that would be perfectly at home in southern California. The rooms are elegantly decorated with cherry wood Art Deco–style furnishings. Downstairs, the hotel's Bierkeller, a cavernous 17th-century room with vaulted ceilings, is now a trendy nightspot adorned with avant-garde paintings, bar stools elaborately sculpted from wrought iron, and a very chic crowd. ⌕ *Am Markt 24, D–23966 Wismar,* ☎ *03841/2390,* FAX *03841/239–239. 106 rooms, all with bath. 3 restaurants, beer cellar, café, no-smoking floor, massage, sauna, exercise room. AE, DC, MC, V. $$–$$$*

THE ARTS AND NIGHTLIFE

The Arts

A resurgence of traditional *Volksfeste*—popular festivals, particularly *Fischerfeste* (fishermen's festivals) in the ports and coastal towns—is following in the wake of 1989. For a schedule of events contact the local tourist offices.

Rostock, Schwerin, and **Lübeck** have the greatest variety when it comes to entertainment, including classical music concerts. Rostock's Volkstheater (Doberanerstr. 134, ☎ 0381/492–44253) performs plays (German only) and concerts. Plays (German only) and operas are performed regularly at **Schwerin's** Mecklenburger Staatstheater (Am Alten Garten, ☎ 0385/83993). For schedules of the myriad concerts, operas, and theater in Lübeck, contact the Lübecker Musik und Kongress Zentrum, Holsteinstr. 6, 23552 Lübeck, ☎ 0451/790–400. Concerts occasionally take place at **Wismar's** Stadttheater (Philipp-Müller-str. 5, ☎ 03841/507–206). Contact the local tourist offices for the latest information on performances.

The summer season brings with it a plethora of special concerts, the highlights being the "Music in May" concerts at **Rostock** and **Stralsund; Greifwald's** Bach Week in June, including open-air concerts at the ruins of the Eldena cloister; **Schwerin** Summerfest on the Lankower See (Lake Lankower), also in June; an international brass band competition in **Rostock** in July; and a series of concerts in **Bad Doberan** in August.

Try to catch a few performances of the Schleswig-Holstein Music Festival (late June–late Aug.) in **Lübeck,** which features an orchestra of young musicians from more than 25 countries, performing in the Dom or Marienkirche. For exact dates and tickets, call 0431/567–080.

Nightlife

Rostock, Schwerin, and **Warnemünde** have the most for night owls. Nearly all the seaside resorts, right down to the smallest, have almost nightly dances during the summer months. The large hotels are the places to head for in search of fun.

In **Rostock,** the bar/café Käjahn is a stylish nightspot (Patriotischer Weg 126); the Sky Bar on the 19th floor of the Neptun Hotel in Warnemünde is your chance to sit under the stars (the roof opens up) and watch the ship lights twinkling on the sea until 4 AM. The pubs in Alter Strom, Warnemünde, are gathering places for locals and visitors alike. Discos worth trying are the Speicher (Am Strande 3), a split-level disco in **Rostock** that appeals to all ages, and the Kurhaus in **Warnemünde** (Seestr.). In **Schwerin** there's the MEXX disco next door to the sleek coffeehouse Lesecafe am Pfaffenteich (Arsenalstr. 16), which attracts a stylish young crowd. **Stralsund's** disco **Kiss Nacht** (Bartherstr. 58) offers dancing for a youthful crowd. Störtebeker Keller (Ossenreyerstr. 49) has dancing and cabaret.

THE BALTIC COAST ESSENTIALS

Arriving and Departing

By Car
Lübeck is 56 kilometers (35 miles) from Hamburg via Autobahn A1 (E–22).

By Plane
The international airport closest to the start of the tour is in Hamburg, just 45 minutes southwest of Lübeck by train or car. Berlin, with two international airports (Tegel and Schönefeld), is 280 kilometers (175 miles) south.

By Train

Lübeck is linked to the InterCity train network, with hourly connections to Hamburg, just 45 minutes away. There is also train service from Berlin to Lübeck.

Getting Around

By Boat

The **Weisse Flotte** (White Fleet) line operates a number of ferries linking the Baltic ports, as well as short harbor and coastal cruises. Boats depart from Warnemünde, Wismar, Sassnitz, and Stralsund. For information and the latest schedule, call 0381/519–860 for boats departing Warnemünde, 0381/268–116 for all other ports; or call the city's tourist office (*see below*). Harbor and coastal cruises also operate from Lübeck; contact the Lübeck tourist office for details (☎ 0451/122–8109). In addition, ferries run between Rostock, Warnemünde, Stralsund, and Sassnitz and Sweden, Denmark, and Finland.

Due to severe reductions in the fishing industry, in many of these towns former fishermen supplement their income by giving sunset tours of the harbors or shuttling between neighboring towns. This is a unique opportunity to ride on an authentic fishing ship, boost the local economy, and get a very personalized tour. Ask the tourist offices for more information.

By Bus

Local buses link the main train stations with outlying towns and villages, especially the coastal resorts. Buses operate throughout Rügen and Usedom islands.

By Car

With the exception of high summer (July and August), roads along the coast are not overcrowded. Route 105 covers much of the journey. Road surfaces in eastern Germany generally are not good, although major improvements are under way. There is a maximum speed limit of 130 kph (80 mph) on motorways in eastern Germany, and 80 kph (48 mph) on other main out-of-town roads.

CAR RENTAL

Avis: Willy-Brandt-Allee 7, ☎ 0451/72008, **Lübeck;** An Warnow Ufer 6, ☎ 0381/459–0475, **Rostock.**

Hertz: Wahlhalb Insel 1–5, ☎ 0451/71747, **Lübeck;** Röverzhagener Chausse, tel: 0381/683–065, **Rostock.**

By Train

A north–south train line links Berlin with Schwerin and Rostock. An east–west route connects Hamburg, Lübeck, and Rostock, and some trains continue through to Stralsund and Sassnitz on Rügen Island. Train service between the smaller cities of former East Germany is generally much slower than in the west due to poor track conditions. Routes between major cities, such as Leipzig, Berlin, Lübeck, and Rostock, are served by the faster, InterCity trains.

Guided Tours

Although tourist offices and museums have worked to improve the quality and amount of literature about this area in English, the availability of English-speaking tours should not be taken for granted; they must be ordered ahead of time at the local tourist office, and because most are designed for groups, there is usually a flat fee of DM 40–DM 60. Towns currently offering tours: Lübeck, Stralsund, and Rostock. For the latest schedules, contact the regional tourist office, Landesfremdenverkehrverband Mecklenburg-Vorpommern, Platz der Freundschaft 1 (☎ 0381/448–426). Guided tours of **old Lübeck** depart daily from one of Lübeck's tourist offices located on the old Markt (☎ 0451/122–8106) between mid-April and mid-October, and on weekends only from mid-October to mid-April.

Important Addresses and Numbers

Tourist Information

The principal regional tourist office for the Baltic Coast is **Ostsee Tourist,** Landesfremdenverkehrsverband, Mecklenburg-Vorpommern e.V., Platz der Freundschaft 1, 18059 Rostock, ☎ 0381/448–424.

There are local tourist information offices in the following towns and cities:

Bad Doberan: Informationszentrum, Goethestr. 1, D-18209 Bad Doberan, ☎ and FAX 038203/2154.

Greifswald: Informationsbüro, Schuhhagen 22, D-17489 Greifswald, ☎ 03834/3460.

Lübeck: Amt für Lübeck-Werbung und Tourismus, Beckergrube 95, D-23539 Lübeck, ☎ 0451/122—8109.

Rostock: Touristbüro, Schnickmannstr. 13–14, D–18055, Rostock, ☎ 0381/492–5260, FAX 0381/493–4602.

Rügen Island: Rügen Island Touristik Service, Bahnhofstr. 28b. D–18573 Altefähr, ☎ 038306/6160, FAX 038306/61666.

Schwerin: Tourist-Information, Am Markt 11, D-19055, Schwerin, ☎ 0385/560–931, FAX 0385/555–094.

Stralsund: Stadt Information, Ossenreyerstr. 1–2, D-18439 Stralsund, ☎ 03831/252–251, FAX 03831/252–2195.

Usedom Island: Fremdenverkehrverband Insel Usedom, Bäderstr. 4, D-17459, ☎ 03837/57693, FAX 03837/7694.

Wismar: Wismar Information, Stadthaus, Am Markt 11, D-23966 Wismar, ☎ and FAX 03841/282–958.

Warnemünde: Kurbetrieb Seebad Warnemünde, Weidenweg 2, Postfach 23, D–18119 Warnemünde, ☎ 0381/52456, FAX 0381/52457.

18 Portraits of Germany

GERMANY AT A GLANCE: A CHRONOLOGY

c 5000 bc Tribes settle in the Rhine and Danube valleys

c 2000–800 bc Distinctive German Bronze Age culture emerges, with settlements ranging from coastal farms to lakeside villages

c 450–50 bc Salzkammergut people, whose prosperity is based on abundant salt deposits (in the area of upper Austria), trade with Greeks and Etruscans; they spread as far as Belgium and have first contact with the Romans

9 bc–ad 9 Roman attempts to conquer the "Germans"—the tribes of the Cibri, the Franks, the Goths, and the Vandals—are only partly successful; the Rhine becomes the northeastern border of the Roman Empire (and remains so for 300 years)

212 Roman citizenship is granted to all free inhabitants of the Empire

c 400 Pressed forward by Huns from Asia, such German tribes as the Franks, the Vandals, and the Lombards migrate to Gaul (France), Spain, Italy, and North Africa, scattering the Empire's populace and eventually leading to the disintegration of central Roman authority

486 The Frankish kingdom is founded by Clovis; his court is in Paris

497 The Franks convert to Christianity

776 Charlemagne becomes king of the Franks

800 Charlemagne is declared Holy Roman Emperor; he makes Aachen capital of his realm, which stretches from the Bay of Biscay to the Adriatic and from the Mediterranean to the Baltic. Under his enlightened patronage, there is an upsurge in art and architecture—the Carolingian renaissance

843 The Treaty of Verdun divides Charlemagne's empire among his three sons: West Francia becomes France; Lotharingia becomes Lorraine (territory to be disputed by France and Germany into the 20th century); and East Francia takes on, roughly, the shape of modern Germany

911 Five powerful German dukes (of Bavaria, Lorraine, Franconia, Saxony, and Swabia) establish the first German monarchy by electing King Conrad I

962 Otto I is crowned Holy Roman Emperor by the Pope; he establishes Austria—the East Mark. The Ottonian renaissance is marked especially by the development of Romanesque architecture

1024–1125 The Salian Dynasty is characterized by a struggle between emperors and Church that leaves the empire weak and disorganized; the great Romanesque cathedrals of Speyer, Trier, Mainz, and Worms are built

1138–1254 Frederick Barbarossa leads the Hohenstaufen Dynasty; there is temporary recentralization of power, underpinned by strong trade and Church relations

1158 Munich, capital of Bavaria, is founded by Duke Henry the Lion; Henry is deposed by Emperor Barbarossa, and Munich is presented to the House of Wittelsbach, which rules it until 1918

1241 The Hanseatic League is founded to protect trade; Bremen, Hamburg, Köln, and Lübeck are early members. Agencies soon extend to London, Antwerp, Venice, and the Baltic and North seas; a complex banking and finance system results

mid-1200s The Gothic style, exemplified by the grand Köln Cathedral, flourishes

1456 Johannes Gutenberg (1397–1468) prints first book in Europe

1471 The painter Albrecht Dürer (dies 1528) is born during the Renaissance. The Dutch-born philosopher Erasmus (1466–1536), and the painters Hans Holbein the Younger (1497–1543), Lucas Cranach the Elder (1472–1553), and Albrecht Altdorfer (1480–1538) help disseminate the new view of the world. Increasing wealth among the merchant classes leads to strong patronage of the revived arts

1517 The Protestant Reformation begins in Germany when Martin Luther (1483–1546) nails his "Ninety-Five Theses" to a church door in Wittenberg, contending that the Roman Church has forfeited divine authority through the corrupt sale of indulgences. Though Luther is outlawed, his revolutionary doctrine splits the church; much of north Germany embraces Protestantism

1524–25 The (Catholic) Hapsburgs rise to power; their empire spreads throughout Europe (and as far as North Africa, the Americas, and the Philippines). In 1530, Charles V (a Hapsburg) is crowned Holy Roman Emperor; he brutally crushes the Peasants' War, one in a series of populist uprisings in Europe

1545 The Council of Trent marks the beginning of the Counter-Reformation. Through diplomacy and coercion, most Austrians, Bavarians, and Bohemians are won back to Catholicism, but the majority of Germany remains Lutheran; persecution of religious minorities grows

1618–48 Germany is the main theater for combat in the Thirty Years' War. The powerful Catholic Hapsburgs are defeated by Protestant forces, swelled by disgruntled Hapsburg subjects and the armies of King Gustav Adolphus of Sweden. The bloody conflict ends with the Peace of Westphalia (1648); Hapsburg and papal authority are severely diminished

1689 Louis XIV of France invades the Rhineland Palatinate and sacks Heidelberg. Elsewhere at the end of the 17th century, Germany consolidates its role as a center of scientific thought

1708 Johann Sebastian Bach (1685–1750) becomes court organist at Weimar and launches his career; he and Georg Friederic Händel (1685–1759) fortify the great tradition of German music. Baroque and, later, Rococo art and architecture flourish

1740–86 Reign of Frederick the Great of Prussia; his rule sees both the expansion of Prussia (it becomes the dominant military force in Germany) and the growth of Enlightenment thought

c 1790 The great age of European orchestral music is raised to new heights in the works of Joseph Haydn (1732–1809), Wolfgang Amadeus Mozart (1756–1791), and Ludwig van Beethoven (1770–1827)

early 1800's Johann Wolfgang von Goethe (1749–1832) helps initiate Romanticism. Other German Romantics include the writers Friedrich Schiller (1759–1805) and Heinrich von Kleist (1777–1811); the composers Robert Schumann (1810–1856), Hungarian-born Franz Liszt (1811–1886), Richard Wagner (1813–1883), and Johannes Brahms (1833–1897); and the painter Casper David Friedrich (1774–1840). In architecture, the severe lines of neoclassicism become popular

1806 Napoléon's armies invade Prussia; it briefly becomes part of the French Empire

1807 The Prussian prime minister Baron vom und zum Stein frees the serfs, creating a new spirit of patriotism; the Prussian army is rebuilt

1813 The Prussians defeat Napoléon at Leipzig

1815 Britain and Prussia defeat Napoléon at Waterloo. At the Congress of Vienna, the German Confederation is created as a loose union of 39 independent states, reduced from more than 300 principalities. The *Bundestag* (national assembly) is established at Frankfurt. Already powerful Prussia increases, gaining the Rhineland, Westphalia, and most of Saxony

1848 The "Year of the Revolutions" is marked by uprisings across the fragmented German Confederation; Prussia uses the opportunity for further expansion. A national parliament is elected, taking the power of the Bundestag to prepare a constitution for a united Germany

1862 Otto von Bismarck (1815–1898) becomes prime minister of Prussia; he is determined to wrest German-populated provinces from Austro-Hungarian (Hapsburg) control

1866 Austria-Hungary is defeated by the Prussians at Sadowa; Bismarck sets up the Northern German Confederation in 1867. A key figure in Bismarck's plans is Ludwig II of Bavaria (the Dream King). Ludwig—a political simpleton—lacks successors, making it easy for Prussia to seize his lands

1867 Karl Marx (1818–1883) publishes *Das Kapital*

1870–71 The Franco-Prussian War: Prussia lays siege to Paris. Victorious Prussia seizes Alsace-Lorraine but eventually withdraws from all other occupied French territories

1871 The four south German states agree to join the Northern Confederation; Wilhelm I is proclaimed first Kaiser of the united Empire

1882 Triple Alliance is forged between Germany, Austria-Hungary, and Italy. Germany's industrial revolution blossoms, enabling it to catch up with the other great powers of Europe. Germany establishes colonies in Africa and the Pacific

c 1885 Daimler and Benz pioneer the automobile

1890 Kaiser Wilhelm II (rules 1888–1918) dismisses Bismarck and begins a new, more aggressive course of foreign policy; he oversees the expansion of the Navy

1890s A new school of writers, including Rainer Maria Rilke (1875–1926), emerges. Rilke's *Sonnets to Orpheus* gives German poetry new lyricism

1905 Albert Einstein (1879–1955) announces his theory of relativity

1906 Painter Ernst Ludwig Kirchner (1880–1938) helps organize *Die Brücke,* a group of artists who along with *Der Blaue Reiter* forge the avant-garde art movement Expressionism

1907 Great Britain, Russia, and France form the Triple Entente, which, set against the Triple Alliance, divides Europe into two armed camps

1914–18 Austrian Archduke Franz-Ferdinand is assassinated in Serbia. The attempted German invasion of France sparks World War I; Italy and Russia join the Allies, and four years of pitched battle ensue. By 1918, the Central Powers are encircled and must capitulate

1918 Germany is compelled by the Versailles Treaty to give up its overseas colonies and much European territory (including Alsace-Lorraine to France) and to pay huge reparations to the Allies; the tough terms leave the new democracy (the Weimar Republic) shaky

1919 The Bauhaus school of art and design, the brainchild of Walter Gropius (1883–1969), is born. Thomas Mann (1875–1955) and Hermann Hesse (1877–1962) forge a new style of visionary intellectual writing—until quashed by Nazism

1923 Germany suffers runaway inflation. Adolf Hitler's "Beer Hall Putsch," a rightist revolt, fails; leftist revolts are frequent

1925 Hitler publishes *Mein Kampf* (*My Struggle*)

1932 The Nazi Party gains the majority in the Bundestag

1933 Hitler becomes chancellor; the Nazi "revolution" begins

1934 President Paul von Hindenburg dies; Hitler declares himself *Führer* (leader) of the Third Reich (empire). Nazification of all German social institutions begins, spreading a policy that is virulently racist and anti-Communist. Germany recovers industrial might and rearms

1936 Germany signs anti-Communist agreements with Italy and Japan, forming the Axis; Hitler reoccupies the Rhineland

1938 The *Anschluss* (annexation): Hitler occupies Austria; Germany occupies the Sudetenland in Czechoslovakia

1939–40 In August, Hitler signs a pact with the Soviet Union; in September he invades Poland; war is declared by the Allies. Over the next three years, there are Nazi invasions of Denmark, Norway, the Low Countries, France, Yugoslavia, and Greece. Alliances form between Germany and the Baltic states

1941–45 Hitler launches his anti-Communist crusade against the Soviet Union, reaching Leningrad in the north and Stalingrad and the Caucasus in the south. In 1944, the Allies land in France; their combined might brings the Axis to its knees. In addition to the millions killed in the fighting, more than 6 million Jews die in Hitler's concentration camps. Germany is again in ruins. Hitler kills himself. Berlin (and what becomes East Germany) is occupied by the Soviet Union

1945 At the Yalta Conference, France, the United States, Britain, and the Soviet Union divide Germany into four zones; each country occupies a sector of Berlin. The Potsdam Agreement expresses the determination to rebuild Germany as a democracy

1948 The Soviet Union tears up the Potsdam Agreement and attempts, by blockade, to exclude the three other Allies from their agreed zones in Berlin. Stalin is frustrated by a massive airlift of supplies to West Berlin

1949 The three Western zones are combined to form the Federal Republic of Germany; the new West German parliament elects Konrad Adenauer as chancellor (a post held until his retirement in 1963). Soviet-held East Germany becomes the Communist German Democratic Republic

1950s West Germany, aided by the financial impetus provided by the Marshall Plan, rebuilds its devastated cities and economy—the *Wirtschaftswunder* (economic miracle) gathers pace

1957　The Treaty of Rome heralds the formation of the European Economic Community (EEC); Germany is a founding member

1961　Communists build the Berlin Wall to stem the outward tide of refugees. The writers Heinrich Böll and Günter Grass emerge

1969–1974　The vigorous chancellorship of Willy Brandt pursues Ostpolitik, improving relations with Eastern Europe, the Soviet Union, and recognizing East Germany's sovereignty

mid-1980s　The powerful German Green Party emerges as the leading environmentalist voice in Europe

1989　Discontent in East Germany leads to a flood of refugees westward and to mass demonstrations; Communist power collapses across Eastern Europe; the Berlin Wall falls

1990　Political instability ushers in the year. In March the first free elections in East Germany bring a center-right government to power. The Communists, faced with corruption scandals, suffer a big defeat, but are represented in the new, democratic parliament. The World War II victors hold talks with the two German governments and the Soviet Union gives its support for reunification. Economic union takes place on July 1, with full political unity on October 3. In December, in the first democratic national German elections for 58 years, Chancellor Helmut Kohl's three-party coalition is reelected. Support for the Green Party wanes, and the Communists—renamed the Democratic Socialists—win 17 seats in the new parliament

1991　Nine months of emotional debate about the future capital of the reunited country ends on June 20, when parliamentary representatives vote in favor of quitting Bonn—seat of the West German government since 1949—and moving to Berlin, which was the capital until the end of World War II

MORE PORTRAITS

Germany is the setting for many good spy novels, including *The Odessa File*, by Frederick Forsyth; John Le Carré's *A Small Town in Germany*; Alistair MacLean's *Where Eagles Dare*; Walter Winward's *The Midas Touch*; and *The Leader and the Damned*, by Colin Forbes.

If you like to travel with a historical novel, look for Christine Bruckner's *Flight of Cranes*; Timothy Findley's *Famous Last Words*; and Fred Uhlman's *Reunion*. Also, Silvia Tennenbaum's *Yesterday's Streets* covers three generations of a wealthy German family.

Other suggested titles include Günter Grass's *The Tin Drum*; Christa Wolf's *No Place on Earth*; Thoman Mann's *Buddenbrooks*, Hermann Hesse's *Narcissus and Goldmund*, and Heinrich Böll's *The Lost Honor of Katarina Blum*. For a con-temporary study of the Germans, read *Germany and the Germans* by British author John Ardagh. Peter Schneider's *The German Comedy* deals with German life after the fall of the Berlin Wall.

For books about pre-war Berlin, pick up Vicki Baum's *Grand Hotel* or Christopher Isherwood's *Berlin Stories*. Leon Uris's *Armageddon: A Novel of Berlin* is set at the end of World War II. Contemporary novels with a Berlin setting include Len Deighton's *Berlin Game* and Peter Schneider's *The Wall Jumper*.

For a good introduction to German history, try Mary Fulbrook's *A Concise History of Germany*. For coverage of World War II and Nazism, consult William Shirer's *The Rise and Fall of the Third Reich*.

GERMAN VOCABULARY

English	German	Pronunciation

Basics

Yes/no	Ja/nein	yah/nine
Please	Bitte	**bit**-uh
Thank you (very much)	Danke (vielen Dank)	**dahn**-kuh (**fee**-lun dahnk)
Excuse me	Entschuldigen Sie	ent-**shool**-de-gen zee
I'm sorry	Es tut mir leid.	es toot meer lite
Good day	Guten Tag	**goo**-ten tahk
Good bye	Auf Wiedersehen	auf **vee**-der-zane
Mr./Mrs.	Herr/Frau	hair/frau
Miss	Fräulein	**froy**-line
Pleased to meet you.	Sehr erfreut.	zair air-**froit**
How are you?	Wie geht es Ihnen?	vee **gate** es ee-nen?
Very well, thanks.	Sehr gut, danke.	zair goot **dahn**-kuh
And you?	Und Ihnen?	oont **ee**-nen

Numbers

1 ein(s)	eint(s)		6 sechs	zex	
2 zwei	tsvai		7 sieben	zee-ben	
3 drei	dry		8 acht	ahkt	
4 vier	fear		9 neun	noyn	
5 fünf	fumph		10 zehn	tsane	

Days of the Week

Sunday	Sonntag	**zone**-tahk
Monday	Montag	**moan**-tahk
Tuesday	Dienstag	**deens**-tahk
Wednesday	Mittwoch	**mit**-voah
Thursday	Donnerstag	**doe**-ners-tahk
Friday	Freitag	**fry**-tahk
Saturday	Samstag/ Sonnabend	**zahm**-stakh/ **zonn**-a-bent

Useful Phrases

Do you speak English?	Sprechen Sie Englisch?	**shprek**-hun zee **eng**-glish?
I don't speak German.	Ich spreche kein Deutsch.	ich **shprek**-uh kine doych
Please speak slowly.	Bitte sprechen Sie langsam.	**bit**-uh **shprek**-en zee **lahng**-zahm
I am American/ British	Ich bin Amerikaner(in)/ Engländer(in)	ich bin a-mer-i-**kahn**-er(in) **eng**-glan-der(in)
My name is . . .	Ich heiße . . .	ich **hi**-suh
Yes please/No, thank you	Ja bitte/Nein danke	yah **bi**-tuh/**nine** dahng-kuh

Where are the restrooms?	Wo ist die Toilette?	vo ist dee twah-**let**-uh
Left/right	links/rechts	links/rechts
Open/closed	offen/geschlossen	O-fen/geh-**shloss**-en
Where is . . .	Wo ist . . .	vo ist
the train station?	der Bahnhof?	dare **bahn**-hof
the bus stop?	die Bushaltestelle?	dee **booss**-hahlt-uh-**shtel**-uh
the subway station?	die U-Bahn-Station?	dee oo-bahn-**staht**-sion
the airport?	der Flugplatz?	dare **floog**-plats
the post office?	die Post?	dee **post**
the bank?	die Bank?	dee **banhk**
the police station?	die Polizeistation?	dee po-lee-**tsai**-staht-sion
the American/British consulate?	das amerikanische/britische Konsulat?	dahs a-mare-i-**kahn**-ishuh/**brit**-ish-uh cone-tso-**laht**
the Hospital?	das Krankenhaus?	dahs **krahnk**-en-house
the telephone	das Telefon	dahs te-le-**fone**
I'd like to have . . .	Ich hätte gerne . . .	ich **het**-uh gairn
a room	ein Zimmer	I-nuh **tsim**-er
the key	den Schlüssel	den **shluh**-sul
a map	eine Stadtplan	I-nuh **staht**-plahn
a ticket	eine Karte	I-nuh **cart**-uh
How much is it?	Wieviel kostet das?	vee-feel **cost**-et dahs?
I am ill/sick	Ich bin krank	ich bin krahnk
I need . . .	Ich brauche . . .	ich **brow**-khuh
a doctor	einen Arzt	I-nen artst
the police	die Polizei	dee po-li-**tsai**
help	Hilfe	**hilf**-uh
Stop!	Halt!	hahlt
Fire!	Feuer!	**foy**-er
Look out/Caution!	Achtung!/Vorsicht!	**ahk**-tung/**for**-zicht

Dining Out

A bottle of . . .	eine Flasche . . .	I-nuh **flash**-uh
A cup of . . .	eine Tasse . . .	I-nuh **tahs**-uh
A glass of . . .	ein Glas . . .	ein **glahss**
Ashtray	der Aschenbecher	dare Ahsh-en-**bekh**-er
Bill/check	die Rechnung	dee **rekh**-nung
Do you have . . . ?	Haben Sie . . . ?	**hah**-ben zee
Food	Essen	**es**-en

I am a diabetic.	Ich bin Diabetiker(in)	ich bin dee-ah-**bet**-ik-er
I am on a diet.	Ich halte Diät.	ich **hahl**-tuh dee-**et**
I am a vegetarian.	Ich bin Vegetarier(in)	ich bin ve-guh-**tah**-re-er
I cannot eat . . .	Ich kann . . . nicht essen	ich kan . . . nicht es-en
I'd like to order . . .	Ich möchte . . . bestellen	ich **mohr**-shtuh buh-shtel-en . . .
Menu	die Speisekarte	dee **shpie**-zeh-car-tuh
Napkin	die Serviette	dee zair-vee-**eh**-tuh
Separate/all together	Getrennt/alles zusammen	ge-**trent/ah**-les tsu-**zah**-men

MENU GUIDE

English	German
Made to order	Auf Bestellung
Side dishes	Beilagen
Extra charge	Extraaufschlag
When available	Falls verfügbar
Entrées	Hauptspeisen
Home made	Hausgemacht
. . . (not) included	. . . (nicht) inbegriffen
Depending on the season	je nach Saison
Local specialties	Lokalspezialitäten
Set menu	Menü
Lunch menu	Mittagskarte
Desserts	Nachspeisen
. . . style	. . . nach . . . Art
. . . at your choice	. . . nach Wahl
. . . at your request	. . . nach Wunsch
Prices are . . .	Preise sind . . .
Service included	*inklusive Bedienung*
Value added tax included	*inklusive Mehrwertsteuer (Mwst.)*
Specialty of the house	Spezialität des Hauses
Soup of the day	Tagessuppe
Appetizers	Vorspeisen
Is served from . . . to . . .	Wird von . . . bis . . . serviert

Breakfast

Bread	Brot
Roll(s)	Brötchen
Butter	Butter
Eggs	Eier
Hot	heiß
Cold	kalt
Decaffeinated	koffeinfrei
Jam	Konfitüre
Milk	Milch
Orange juice	Orangensaft
Scrambled eggs	Rühreier
Bacon	Speck
Fried eggs	Spiegeleier
White bread	Weißbrot
Lemon	Zitrone
Sugar	Zucker

Appetizers

Oysters	Austern
Frog legs	Froschschenkel
Goose liver paté	Gänseleberpastete
Lobster	Hummer
Shrimp	Garnelen
Crayfish	Krebs
Salmon	Lachs
Mussels	Muscheln

Prosciutto with melon	Parmaschinken mit Melone
Mushrooms	Pilze
Smoked . . .	Räucher . . .
Ham	Schinken
Snails	Schnecken
Asparagus	Spargel

Soups

Stew	Eintopf
Semolina dumpling soup	Grießnockerlsuppe
Goulash soup	Gulaschsuppe
Chicken soup	Hühnersuppe
Potato soup	Kartoffelsuppe
Liver dumpling soup	Leberknödelsuppe
Oxtail soup	Ochsenschwanzsuppe
Tomato soup	Tomatensuppe
Onion soup	Zwiebelsuppe

Methods of Preparation

Blue (boiled in salt and vinegar)	Blau
Baked	Gebacken
Fried	Gebraten
Steamed	Gedämpft
Grilled (broiled)	Gegrillt
Boiled	Gekocht
Sauteed	In Butter geschwenkt
Breaded	Paniert
Raw	Roh

When ordering steak, the English words "rare, medium, (well) done" are used and understood in German.

Fish and Seafood

Eel	Aal
Oysters	Austern
Trout	Forelle
Flounder	Flunder
Prawns	Garnelen
Halibut	Heilbutt
Herring	Hering
Lobster	Hummer
Scallops	Jakobsmuscheln
Cod	Kabeljau
Crab	Krabbe
Crayfish	Krebs
Salmon	Lachs
Spiny lobster	Languste
Mackerel	Makrele
Mussels	Muscheln
Red sea bass	Rotbarsch
Sole	Seezunge
Squid	Tintenfisch
Tuna	Thunfisch

Meats

Mutton	Hammel
Veal	Kalb(s)
Lamb	Lamm
Beef	Rind(er)
Pork	Schwein(e)

Cuts of Meat

Example: For "Lammkeule" see "Lamm" (above) + ". . . keule" (below)

breast	. . . brust
scallopini	. . . geschnetzeltes
knuckle	. . . haxe
leg	. . . keule
liver	. . . leber
tenderloin	. . . lende
kidney	. . . niere
rib	. . . rippe
Meat patty	Frikadelle
Meat loaf	Hackbraten
Cured pork ribs	Kasseler Rippchen
Liver meatloaf	Leberkäse
Ham	Schinken
Bacon and sausage with sauerkraut	Schlachtplatte
Brawn	Sülze
Cooked beef with horseradish and cream sauce	Tafelspitz

Game and Poultry

Duck	Ente
Pheasant	Fasan
Goose	Gans
Chicken	Hähnchen (Huhn)
Hare	Hase
Deer	Hirsch
Rabbit	Kaninchen
Capon	Kapaun
Venison	Reh
Pigeon	Taube
Turkey	Truthahn
Quail	Wachtel

Vegetables

Eggplant	Aubergine
Red cabbage	Blaukraut
Cauliflower	Blumenkohl
Beans	Bohnen
green	*grüne*
white	*weiße*
Button mushrooms	Champignons
Peas	Erbsen

Cucumber	Gurke
Cabbage	Kohl
Lettuce	Kopfsalat
Leek	Lauch
Asparagus, peas and carrots	Leipziger Allerlei
Corn	Mais
Carrots	Mohrrüben
Peppers	Paprika
Chanterelle mushrooms	Pfifferlinge
Mushrooms	Pilze
Brussels sprouts	Rosenkohl
Red beets	Rote Beete
Celery	Sellerie
Asparagus (tips)	Spargel(spitzen)
Tomatoes	Tomaten
Cabbage	Weißkohl
Onions	Zwiebeln
Spring Onions	Frühlingszwiebeln

Side dishes

Potato(s)	Kartoffel(n)
fried	*Brat . . .*
boiled in their jackets	*Pell . . .*
with parsley	*Petersilien . . .*
fried	*Röst . . .*
boiled in saltwater	*Salz . . .*
mashed	*. . . brei*
dumplings	*. . . klöße (knödel)*
pancakes	*. . . puffer*
salad	*. . . salat*
Pasta	Nudeln
French fries	Pommes frites
Rice	Reis
buttered	*Butter . . .*
steamed	*gedämpfter . . .*

Condiments

Basil	Basilikum
Vinegar	Essig
Spice	Gewürz
Garlic	Knoblauch
Herbs	Kräuter
Caraway	Kümmel
Bay leaf	Lorbeer
Horseradish	Meerettich
Nutmeg	Muskatnuß
Oil	Öl
Parsley	Petersilie
Saffron	Safran
Sage	Salbei
Chives	Schnittlauch
Mustard	Senf

Artificial sweetener	Süßstoff
Cinnamon	Zimt
Sugar	Zucker
Salt	Salz

Cheese

Mild:	Allgäuer Käse, Altenburger (goat cheese), Appenzeller, Greyerzer, Hüttenkäse (cottage cheese), Kümmelkäse (with carraway seeds), Quark, Räucherkäse (smoked cheese), Sahnekäse (creamy), Tilsiter, Ziegekäse (goat cheese).
Sharp:	Handkäse, Harzer Käse, Limburger.
curd	frisch
hard	hart
mild	mild

Fruits

Apple	Apfel
Orange	Apfelsine
Apricot	Aprikose
Blueberry	Blaubeere
Blackberry	Brombeere
Strawberry	Erdbeere
Raspberry	Himbeere
Cherry	Kirsche
Grapefruit	Pampelmuse
Cranberry	Preiselbeere
Raisin	Rosine
Grape	Weintraube
Banana	Banane
Pear	Birne
Kiwi	Kiwi

Nuts

Peanuts	Erdnüsse
Hazelnuts	Haselnüsse
Coconut	Kokosnuß
Almonds	Mandeln
Chestnuts	Maronen

Desserts

. . . soufflé	. . . auflauf
. . . ice cream	. . . eis
. . . cake	. . . kuchen
Honey-almond cake	Bienenstich
Fruit cocktail	Obstsalat
Whipped cream	(Schlag)sahne
Black Forest cake	Schwarzwälder Kirschtorte

Drinks

chilled	eiskalt
with/without ice	mit/ohne Eis
with/without water	mit/ohne Wasser
straight	pur
room temperature	Zimmertemperatur
. . . brandy	. . . geist
. . . distilled liquor	. . . korn
. . . liqueur	. . . likör
. . . schnapps	. . . schnaps
Egg liquor	Eierlikör
Mulled claret	Glühwein
Caraway-flavored liquor	Kümmel
Fruit brandy	Obstler
Vermouth	Wermut

When ordering a Martini, you have to specify "gin (vodka) and vermouth", otherwise you will be given a vermouth (Martini & Rossi).

Beer and Wine

non-alcoholic	Alkoholfrei
A dark beer	Ein Dunkles
A light beer	Ein Helles
A mug (one quart)	Eine Maß
Draught	Vom Faß
Dark, bitter, high hops content	Altbier
Strong, high alcohol content	Bockbier (Doppelbock, Märzen)
Wheat beer with yeast	Hefeweizen
Light beer, strong hops aroma	Pils(ener)
Wheat beer	Weizen(bier)
Light beer and lemonade	Radlermaß
Wines	Wein
Rosé wine	Rosëwein
Red wine	Rotwein
White wine and mineral water	Schorle
Sparkling wine	Sekt
White wine	Weißwein
dry	herb
light	leicht
sweet	süß
dry	trocken
full-bodied	vollmundig

Non-alcoholic Drinks

Coffee	Kaffee
decaffeinated	*koffeinfrei*
with cream/sugar	*mit Milch/Zucker*
with artificial sweetener	*mit Sülßstoff*
black	*schwarz*
Lemonade	Limonade
orange	*Orangen . . .*
lemon	*Zitronen . . .*
Milk	Milch
Mineral water	Mineralwasser

carbonated/non-carbonated	*mit/ohne Kohlensäure*
. . . juice	. . . saft
(hot) Chocolate	(heiße) Schokolade
Tea	Tee
iced tea	*Eistee*
herb tea	*Kräutertee*
with cream/lemon	*mit Milch/Zitrone*

INDEX

Before Catching Your Flight, Catch Up With Your World.

Fueled by the global resources of CNN and available in major airports across America, CNN Airport Network provides a live source  of current domestic and international news,  sports, business, weather and lifestyle programming. Plus two daily Fodor's features for the facts you need: "Travel Fact," a useful and creative mix of travel trivia; and "What's Happening," a comprehensive round-up of upcoming events in major cities around the world.

With CNN Airport Network, you'll never be out of the loop.